The Princeton Handbook of World Poetries

PRINCETON
REFERENCE

The Princeton Handbook of World Poetries

Edited by
Roland Greene and
Stephen Cushman

Princeton University Press
Princeton and Oxford

Published by Princeton University Press,
41 William Street, Princeton, New Jersey 08540
In the United Kingdom: Princeton University Press,
6 Oxford Street, Woodstock, Oxfordshire OX20 1TW

press.princeton.edu

Library of Congress Cataloging-in-Publication Data

Names: Greene, Roland, 1957– editor. | Cushman, Stephen, 1956– editor.
Title: The Princeton handbook of world poetries / edited by Roland Greene and Stephen Cushman.
Description: Princeton : Princeton University Press, [2016] | Includes bibliographical references and index.
Identifiers: LCCN 2015044125| ISBN 9780691171524 (hardback : acid-free paper) | ISBN 9780691170510 (paperback : acid-free paper)
Subjects: LCSH: Poetry—History and criticism. | BISAC: LITERARY CRITICISM / Poetry. | LITERARY CRITICISM / Reference. | POETRY / General.
Classification: LCC PN1031 .P78 2016 | DDC 808.1—dc23
LC record available at http://lccn.loc.gov/2015044125

British Library Cataloging-in-Publication Data is available

This book has been composed in Adobe Garamond Pro

Printed on acid-free paper. ∞

Printed in the United States of America

10 9 8 7 6 5 4 3 2 1

Contents

Preface

What is "world poetry"? The term evokes at least two meanings. One suggests a rarefied canon of poetry by the few poets—for example, Homer, Sappho, Virgil, Dante, Rūmī, Ḥāfiẓ, Shakespeare, Bashō, and Neruda—whose work transcends their nations and languages. The other implies a vast, international corpus that gathers discrete canons into a network of connections and resonances: world poetry in large rather than in little. This volume both reflects and enables the latter sense of the term. Offering more than 165 entries that represent the traditions of about 100 national, regional, and diasporic poetries, *The Princeton Handbook of World Poetries* is intended for any student or reader who seeks to explore the scope and complexity of international poetry.

The entries here originate in the more extensive *Princeton Encyclopedia of Poetry and Poetics*, in which the richness of world poetry is visible alongside poetic terms and concepts as well as larger, interdisciplinary topics. The poetries of nations, regions, and languages are a traditional strength of the *Encyclopedia*; many readers have found the past editions a reliable guide to introductions to unfamiliar languages or literatures. Both the *Encyclopedia* and the *Handbook* attempt to make a distinction between poetries that are based in nations or territories and those that are based in languages, international cultures, or diasporas—no doubt sometimes an ambiguous distinction, but nonetheless one worth making. The entry on the poetry of France is discrete from entries on the various francophone poetries of Africa, Canada, or the Caribbean, while Persian poetry is best approached as a single topic with international ramifications. The entry titles "England, poetry of" and "United States, poetry of the," along with the topics they indicate, are preferable to the categories "English" or "American" poetry, with their uncertain but expansive outlines. In its coverage of the British Isles, the former entry is complemented by separate entries on Welsh, Cornish, Scottish, and Irish poetries, while the latter is cross-referenced to companion pieces on US poetries wholly or partly in other languages that can claim their own fields of study, such as French-language poetry; still other related entries, such as those on Chicana/o and Asian American poetry, are found in the *Encyclopedia*. An entry such as "German poetry" takes a linguistic rather than a national approach but is complemented by entries on Austria, Switzerland, and the Low Countries that follow geopolitical contours and discuss discrete languages within those outlines. In many cases the contributors made the final determination of what to call their entries, no doubt producing some asymmetries that reflect the differences in the fields represented here. Moreover, the reader is encouraged to consult the *Encyclopedia* for further exploration of more granular topics such as poetic movements within nations and linguistically specific forms and genres.

This *Handbook* maintains several conventions of the *Princeton Encyclopedia*. Translations are generally given within parentheses, without quotation marks if no other words appear in the parenthetical matter, but set off within quotation marks when some qualification is needed, as in the form of many etymologies: for example, arsis and thesis (Gr., "raising and lowering"). Translated titles of works generally appear in the most comprehensive articles; entries of smaller scope often give original titles without translation, although some contributors have translated titles where doing so clarifies the argument. Translated titles of books are italicized when the title refers to a published English translation: for example, the Georgian poet Shota

Rustaveli's *Vepkhis tqaosani* (*The Man in the Panther's Skin*). For poems, translated titles are given with quotation marks when the translation has been published under that title, but without quotation marks when the translated title is ad hoc.

This convention sometimes entails reproducing a nonliteral rendering that appears in a published translation, such as Boccaccio's *Trattatello in laude di Dante* as *Life of Dante*, or the Guatemalan poet Otto René Castillo's *Vámonos patria a caminar* as *Let's Go*. We believe that the value of indicating an extant translation outweighs the occasional infelicity. At the same time, it is likely we have overlooked some published translations, and many new ones will appear over the life of this book.

Dates of the lives and works of poets appear in most entries but are sometimes omitted when they are less relevant to the entry or cannot be indicated consistently. Dates of works in the age of print refer to publication unless otherwise indicated.

Articles contain two types of cross-references: those that appear within the body of an entry (indicated with asterisks or in parentheses with small capitals), and those that follow an entry, just before the bibliographies. The former are often topics that extend the issue at hand; the latter often indicate adjacent topics of broader interest to the entire entry. Of course, both kinds of cross-reference hold out the danger of infinite connection, as nearly every entry could be linked to many others. Accordingly, we have tried to apply cross-references judiciously, indicating where further reading really complements the argument of a particular entry.

The bibliographies are intended not only as lists of works cited in the entries but as guides to relevant scholarship of the distant and recent past. The bibliographies have been lightly standardized, but some entries gain from citing works of scholarship in their original iterations or languages, while many others choose to cite later editions or translations into English as a convenience for the reader.

As world poetry in its most inclusive sense becomes more frequently anthologized and the Internet brings the widest variety of poetic production within the reach of every connected reader, now more than ever there is a need for a comprehensive guide by experts to national, regional, and diasporic traditions. We hope this *Handbook* will accompany many journeys of discovery and enjoyment.

Acknowledgments

This handbook represents the work of the editorial team that produced *The Princeton Encyclopedia of Poetry and Poetics*, 4th edition: associate editors Clare Cavanagh, Jahan Ramazani, and Paul Rouzer; and assistant editors Harris Feinsod, David Marno, and Alexandra Slessarev.

We are grateful to Héctor Hoyos and Alexander Key for the expertise they contributed directly to this handbook, which will improve future editions of the *Encyclopedia*.

We gratefully acknowledge the following authors, publishers, and agents for granting us permission to use brief selections from the copyrighted material listed below. Great care has been taken to trace all the owners of copyrighted material used in this book. Any inadvertent omissions pointed out to us will be gladly acknowledged in future printings.

Arte Público Press for ten lines of "Guitarreros" by Américo Paredes, from *Between Two Worlds,* copyright © 1991 by Arte Público Press; and four lines of "Emily Dickinson" by Lucha Corpi, from *Palabras de Mediodia/Noon Words,* copyright © 1980 by Arte Público Press. Both reprinted by permission of Arte Público Press.

Gordon Brotherston for six lines of his translation of Preuss's musings on the Witoto; six lines of his translation of a traditional Quechua hymn; and twelve lines of his translation from the Nahuatl of an excerpt from *Cuauhtitlan Annals.*

The University of California Press for two lines of "Two Voices" by Khalil Gibran from *An Anthology of Modern Arabic Poetry,* edited by Hamid Algar and Mounah Khouri, copyright © 1974 by the Regents of the University of California. Reprinted by permission of the University of California Press.

Cambridge University Press for three lines of "Eulogy" by al-Mutanabbi, from *Poems of al-Mutanabbi,* translated by A. J. Arberry, copyright © 1967 by Cambridge University Press; and three lines by al-Khansa, from *Arabic Poetry: A Primer for Students,* translated by A. J. Arberry, copyright © 1965 by Cambridge University Press. Both reprinted by the permission of Cambridge University Press.

Coach House Books for four lines from *Eunoia,* by Christian Bök (Coach House Books, 2001, updated 2009).

Columbia University Press for six lines of "Tansim ka, or, Song of a Loyal Heart" from *Early Korean Literature: Selections and Introductions,* by David R. McCann, copyright © 2000 Columbia University Press; twelve lines of "Azaleas," six lines of "Winter Sky," and eighteen lines of "Grasses," each from *The Columbia Anthology of Modern Korean Poetry,* edited by David R. McCann, copyright © 2004 Columbia University Press. All reprinted by permission of the publisher.

Faber and Faber Ltd. for "Red Wheel Barrow" by William Carlos Williams, from *The Collected Poems: Volume I, 1909–1939*, copyright © 1938 by William Carlos Williams. Reprinted by permission of Faber and Faber, Ltd.

Rafael Jesús González for eleven lines of his poem "The Coin (Ars Poetica)" from *El hacedor de juegos/The Maker of Games* (San Francisco: Casa Editorial, 1977; 2nd edition, 1987), copyright © 2012 by Rafael Jesús González. Reprinted by permission of the author.

University of Hertfordshire Press for twelve lines from an untitled poem translated by Iren Kertesz-Wilkinson, published in *Romani Culture and Gypsy Identity,* edited by T. A. Acton and G. Mundy, University of Hertfordshire Press, 1997; nine lines of "O Land, I Am Your Daughter" by Bronislawa Wajs and four lines of "Roads of the Roma" by Leksa Manus, both published in *The Roads of the Roma: A PEN Anthology of Gypsy Writers,* copyright © 1998 by PEN American Center, University of Hertfordshire Press.

Houghton Mifflin Harcourt Publishing Company for eight lines of "It Is Dangerous to Read Newspapers" from *Selected Poems I, 1965–1975* by Margaret Atwood, copyright © 1976 by Margaret Atwood. Reprinted by permission of Houghton Mifflin Harcourt Publishing Company. All rights reserved.

Phoebe Larrimore Literary Agency for eight lines of "It Is Dangerous to Read Newspapers" by Margaret Atwood, used by permission of the author. Available in the following collections: In the United States, *Selected Poems I, 1965–1975,* published by Houghton Mifflin, copyright © Margaret Atwood 1976; in Canada, *Selected Poems, 1966–1984,* published by McClelland and Stewart, copyright © Margaret Atwood 1990; in the UK, *Eating Fire,* published by Virago Books, copyright © Margaret Atwood 1998.

James T. Monroe for his translation of "Envoie to a Love Poem" from *Hispano-Arabic Poetry: A Student Anthology,* published by the University of California Press, 1974.

José Montoya for six lines of his poem "El Louie."

New Directions Publishing Corporation for "In a Station of the Metro" by Ezra Pound, from *Personae,* copyright © 1926 by Ezra Pound; and "Red Wheel Barrow" by William Carlos Williams, from *The Collected Poems: Volume I, 1909–1939,* copyright © 1938 by New Directions Publishing Corp. All reprinted by permission of New Directions Publishing Corp.

Nightwood Editions for six lines of "language (in)habits" from *Forage* by Rita Wong, published by Nightwood Editions, 2007; http://www.nightwoodeditions.com.

Oxford University Press for eight lines of "It Is Dangerous to Read Newspapers" from Margaret Atwood, *The Animals in that Country,* copyright © 1969 Oxford University Press Canada. Reprinted by permission of the publisher.

Burton Raffel for his translation of a *pantun,* the traditional Malay four-line verse.

Lynne Rienner Publications for five lines of "Lazarus 1962" by Khalil Hawi from *Naked in Exile: The Threshing Floors of Hunger,* translated by Adnan Haydar and Michael Beard, © 1984. Reprinted by permission of Lynne Rienner Publications.

Maekawa Sajuro for five lines of an untitled poem from *Shokubutsusai* by Maekawa Samio, translated by Leith Morton.

Talon Books for twenty-one lines of "Naked Poems" from *Selected Poems: The Vision Tree* copyright © 1982 Phyllis Webb, Talon Books, Vancouver, B.C. Reprinted by permission of the publisher.

Alphabetical List of Entries

Africa, poetry of
Afrikaans poetry. *See* SOUTH AFRICA, POETRY OF
Akkadian poetry. *See* ASSYRIA AND BABYLONIA, POETRY OF
Al-Andalus, poetry of
Albania, poetry of
American Indian poetry. *See* INDIGENOUS AMERICAS, POETRY OF THE; INUIT POETRY; NAVAJO POETRY
American poetry. *See* UNITED STATES, POETRY OF THE
Amerind poetry. *See* INDIGENOUS AMERICAS, POETRY OF THE
Amharic poetry. *See* ETHIOPIA, POETRY OF
Arabic poetics
Arabic poetry
Arabic prosody
Araucanian poetry. *See* INDIGENOUS AMERICAS, POETRY OF THE
Argentina, poetry of
Armenian poetry and poetics
Assamese poetry
Assyria and Babylonia, poetry of
Australia, poetry of
Austria, poetry of
Aztec poetry. *See* INDIGENOUS AMERICAS, POETRY OF THE
Basque Country, poetry of the
Belarus, poetry of. *See* RUSSIA, POETRY OF
Belgium, poetry of
Bengali poetry
Bhakti poetry. *See* INDIA, POETRY OF
Bolivia, poetry of
Bosnian poetry
Brazil, poetry of
Breton poetry
Bulgaria, poetry of
Byzantine poetry
Cambodia, poetry of
Canada, poetry of
Caribbean, poetry of the
Catalan poetry
Celtic prosody
Chile, poetry of
China, modern poetry of
China, poetry of
China, popular poetry of
Chinese poetic drama
Chinese poetics
Chinese poetry in English translation
Chinese poetry in Japan
Colombia, poetry of
Cornish poetry
Croatian poetry
Cuba, poetry of. *See* CARIBBEAN, POETRY OF THE
Czech poetry
Danish poetry. *See* DENMARK, POETRY OF
Denmark, poetry of
Dutch poetry. *See* LOW COUNTRIES, POETRY OF THE
Ecuador, poetry of
Egypt, poetry of
El Salvador, poetry of
England, poetry of
Esperanto poetry
Estonia, poetry of
Ethiopia, poetry of
Finland, poetry of
Flemish poetry. *See* LOW COUNTRIES, POETRY OF THE
France, poetry of
French poetry. *See* FRANCE, POETRY OF
French prosody
Frisian poetry
Gaelic poetry. *See* IRELAND, POETRY OF; SCOTLAND, POETRY OF
Galicia, poetry of
Georgia, poetry of
Germanic prosody
German poetry
Greek poetics. *See* BYZANTINE POETRY
Greek poetry
Guaraní poetry
Guatemala, poetry of
Gujarati poetry
Gypsy poetry. *See* ROMANI POETRY
Haiti, poetry of. *See* CARIBBEAN, POETRY OF THE
Hausa poetry
Hebrew poetry
Hebrew prosody and poetics
Hindi poetry
Hispano-Arabic poetry. *See* AL-ANDALUS, POETRY OF
Hittite poetry
Hungary, poetry of
Iceland, poetry of
Inca poetry. *See* INDIGENOUS AMERICAS, POETRY OF THE
India, English poetry of
India, poetry of
Indian prosody
indigenous Americas, poetry of the
Indonesian poetry
Inuit poetry
Iran, poetry of. *See* PERSIAN POETRY
Ireland, poetry of
Italian prosody
Italy, poetry of
Japan, modern poetry of
Japan, poetry of
Japanese poetic diaries
Japanese poetics
Java, poetry of. *See* INDONESIAN POETRY
Judeo-Spanish poetry
Kannada poetry
Kashmiri poetry
Korea, poetry of
Ladino poetry. *See* JUDEO-SPANISH POETRY
Latin America, poetry of. *See* ARGENTINA, POETRY OF; BOLIVIA, POETRY OF; BRAZIL, POETRY OF; CHILE, POETRY OF; COLOMBIA, POETRY OF; ECUADOR, POETRY OF; EL SALVADOR,

Bibliographical Abbreviations

Abrams M. H. Abrams, *The Mirror and the Lamp: Romantic Theory and the Critical Tradition*, 1953
AION-SL *Annali dell'Istituto Universitario Orientale di Napoli: sezione filologico-letteraria*
AJP *American Journal of Philology*
AJS *American Journal of Semiotics*
AL *American Literature*
Allen W. S. Allen, *Accent and Rhythm*, 1973
Analecta hymnica *Analecta hymnica medii aevi*, ed. G. M. Dreves, C. Blume, and H. M. Bannister, 55 v., 1886–1922
Attridge, *Poetic Rhythm* D. Attridge, *Poetic Rhythm: An Introduction*, 1995
Attridge, *Rhythms* D. Attridge, *The Rhythms of English Poetry*, 1982
Auerbach E. Auerbach, *Mimesis: The Representation of Reality in Western Literature*, trans. W. R. Trask, 1953

Beare W. Beare, *Latin Verse and European Song*, 1957
Bec P. Bec, *La Lyrique Française au moyen âge (XIIe–XIIIe siècles): Contribution à une typologie des genres poétiques médiévaux*, 2 v., 1977–78
Benjamin W. Benjamin, "The Work of Art in the Age of Mechanical Reproduction," *Illuminations*, trans. H. Zohn, 1968
BGDSL (H) *Beiträge zur Geschichte de deutschen Sprache und Literatur (Halle)*
BGDSL (T) *Beiträge zur Geschichte de deutschen Sprache und Literatur (Tübingen)*
BHS *Bulletin of Hispanic Studies*
BJA *British Journal of Aesthetics*
Bowra C. M. Bowra, *Greek Lyric Poetry from Alcman to Simonides*, 2d ed., 1961
Bridges R. Bridges, *Milton's Prosody*, rev. ed., 1921
Brogan T.V.F. Brogan, *English Versification, 1570–1980: A Reference Guide with a Global Appendix*, 1981
Brooks C. Brooks, *The Well Wrought Urn*, 1947
Brooks and Warren C. Brooks and W. P. Warren, *Understanding Poetry*, 3d ed., 1960

Carper and Attridge T. Carper and D. Attridge, *Meter and Meaning: An Introduction to Rhythm*, 2003
CBEL *Cambridge Bibliography of English Literature*, ed. F. W. Bateson, 4 v., 1940; v. 5, *Supplement*, ed. G. Watson, 1957
CBFL *A Critical Bibliography of French Literature*, gen. ed. D. C. Cabeen and R. A. Brooks, 6 v., 1947–1994
CE *College English*
Chambers F. M. Chambers, *An Introduction to Old Provençal Versification*, 1985
Chatman S. Chatman, *A Theory of Meter*, 1965
CHCL *Cambridge History of Classical Literature*, v. 1, *Greek Literature*, ed. P. E. Easterling and B.M.W. Knox, 1985; v. 2, *Latin Literature*, ed. E. J. Kenney and W. V. Clausen, 1982
CHEL *Cambridge History of English Literature*, ed. A. W. Ward and A. R. Waller, 14 v., 1907–16
CHLC *Cambridge History of Literary Criticism*, 9 v., 1989–2005
Chomsky and Halle N. Chomsky and M. Halle, *The Sound Pattern of English*, 1968
CJ *Classical Journal*
CL *Comparative Literature*
CML *Classical and Modern Literature*
Corbett E.P.J. Corbett, *Classical Rhetoric for the Modern Student*, 3d ed., 1990
CP *Classical Philology*
CQ *Classical Quarterly*
Crane *Critics and Criticism, Ancient and Modern*, ed. R. S. Crane, 1952
CritI *Critical Inquiry*
Crusius F. Crusius, *Römische Metrik: ein Einführung*, 8th ed., rev. H. Rubenbauer, 1967
Culler J. Culler, *Structuralist Poetics: Structuralism, Linguistics, and the Study of Literature*, 1975
Cureton R. D. Cureton, *Rhythmic Phrasing in English Verse*, 1992
Curtius E. Curtius, *European Literature and the Latin Middle Ages*, trans. W. R. Trask, 1953
CW *Classical World*

DAI *Dissertation Abstracts International*
Dale A. M. Dale, *The Lyric Meters of Greek Drama*, 2d ed., 1968
DDJ *Deutsches Dante-Jahrbuch*
de Man P. de Man, *Blindness and Insight: Essays in the Rhetoric of Contemporary Criticism*, 2d ed., 1983
Derrida J. Derrida, *Of Grammatology*, trans. G. C. Spivak, 2d ed., 1998
DHI *Dictionary of the History of Ideas*, ed. P. P. Weiner, 6 v., 1968–74
Dronke P. Dronke, *Medieval Latin and the Rise of European Love Lyric*, 2d ed., 2 v., 1968

Duffell M. J. Duffell, *A New History of English Metre*, 2008

E&S *Essays and Studies of the English Association*
ELH *ELH* (formerly *English Literary History*)
Eliot, *Essays* T. S. Eliot, *Selected Essays*, rev. ed., 1950
Elwert W. T. Elwert, *Französische Metrik*, 4th ed., 1978
Elwert, *Italienische* W. T. Elwert, *Italienische Metrik*, 2d ed., 1984
Empson W. Empson, *Seven Types of Ambiguity*, 3d ed., 1953
ENLL *English Language and Linguistics*

Fabb et al. N. Fabb, D. Atridge, A. Durant, and C. MacCabe, *The Linguistics of Writing*, 1987
Faral E. Faral, *Les arts poétique du XIIe et du XIIIe siècles*, 1924
Finch and Varnes An Exaltation of Forms: Contemporary Poets Celebrate the Diversity of Their Art, ed. A. Finch and K. Varnes, 2002
Fish S. Fish, *Is There a Text in This Class? The Authority of Interpretive Communities*, 1980
Fisher *The Medieval Literature of Western Europe: A Review of Research, Mainly 1930–1960*, ed. J. H. Fisher, 1965
FMLS *Forum for Modern Language Studies*
Fontanier P. Fontanier, *Les figures du discourse*, 1977
Fowler A. Fowler, *Kinds of Literature: An Introduction to the Theory of Genres and Modes*, 1982
Frye N. Frye, *Anatomy of Criticism: Four Essays*, 1957
FS *French Studies*

Gasparov M. L. Gasparov, *Sovremennyj russkij stix: Metrika i ritmika*, 1974
Gasparov, *History* M. L. Gasparov, *A History of European Versification*, trans. G. S. Smith and M. Tarlinskaja, 1996
GRLMA *Grundriss der romanischen Literaturen des Mittelalters*, ed. H. R. Jauss and E. Köhler, 11 v., 1968–
Group μ Group μ (J. Dubois, F. Edeline, J.-M. Klinkenberg, P. Minguet, F. Pire, H. Trinon), *A General Rhetoric*, trans. P. B. Burrell and E. M. Slotkin, 1981

Halporn et al. J. W. Halporn, M. Ostwald, and T. G. Rosenmeyer, *The Meters of Greek and Latin Poetry*, 2d ed., 1980
Hardie W. R. Hardie, *Res Metrica*, 1920
HJAS *Harvard Journal of Asiatic Studies*
Hollander J. Hollander, *Vision and Resonance: Two Senses of Poetic Form*, 2d ed., 1985
Hollier *A New History of French Literature*, ed. D. Hollier, 1989
HQ *Hopkins Quarterly*
HR *Hispanic Review*
HudR *Hudson Review*

ICPhS *International Congress of Phonetic Sciences* (journal)
IJCT *International Journal of Classical Tradition*

JAAC *Journal of Aesthetics and Art Criticism*
JAC *JAC: A Journal of Rhetoric, Culture, and Politics*
JAF *Journal of American Folklore*
Jakobson R. Jakobson, *Selected Writings*, 8 v., 1962–88
Jakobson and Halle R. Jakobson and M. Halle, *Fundamentals of Language*, 1956
JAOS *Journal of American Oriental Society*
Jarman and Hughes *A Guide to Welsh Literature*, ed. A. O. H. Jarman and G. R. Hughes, 2 v., 1976–79
Jeanroy A. Jeanroy, *La Poésie lyrique des Troubadours*, 2 v., 1934
Jeanroy, *Origines* A. Jeanroy, *Les origines de la poésie lyrique en France au moyen âge*, 4th ed., 1965
JEGP *Journal of English and Germanic Philology*
JFLS *Journal of French Language Studies*
JHS *Journal of Hellenic Studies*
JL *Journal of Linguistics*
Jour. P. Society *Journal of Polynesian Society*
JPhon *Journal of Phonetics*

Kastner L. E. Kastner, *A History of French Versification*, 1903
Keil *Grammatici Latini*, ed. H. Keil, 7 v., 1855–80; v. 8, *Anecdota helvitica: Supplementum*, ed. H. Hagen, 1870
Koster W.J.W. Koster, *Traité de métrique greque suivi d'un précis de métrique latine*, 5th ed., 1966
KSJ *Keats-Shelley Journal*
KR *Kenyon Review*

L&S *Language and Speech*
Lang *Language*
Lang&S *Language and Style*
Lanham R. A. Lanham, *A Handlist of Rhetorical Terms*, 2d ed., 1991
Lausberg H. Lausberg, *Handbook of Literary Rhetoric: A Foundation for Literary Study*, trans. M. T. Bliss, A. Jansen, and D. E. Orton, 1998
Le Gentil P. Le Gentil, *La Poésie lyrique espagnole et portugaise à la fin du moyen âge*, 2 v., 1949–53
Lewis C. S. Lewis, *The Allegory of Love*, 1936
LingI *Linguistic Inquiry*
Lord A. B. Lord, *The Singer of Tales*, 2d ed., 2000
Lote G. Lote, *Histoire du vers française*, 9 v., 1940

M&H *Medievalia et Humanistica: Studies in Medieval and Renaissance Culture*

Maas P. Maas, *Greek Metre*, trans. H. Lloyd-Jones, 3d ed., 1962

Manitius M. Manitius, *Geschichte der lateinischen Literatur des Mittelalters*, 3 v., 1905–36

Mazaleyrat J. Mazaleyrat, *Éléments de métrique française*, 3d ed., 1981

Meyer W. Meyer, *Gesammelte Abhandlungen zur mittelateinischen Rhythmik*, 3 v., 1905–36

MGG *Die Musik in Geschichte und Gegenwart: Allegemeine Enzyklopaedia der Musik*, ed. F. Blume, 16 v., 1949–79

MGH *Monumenta germaniae historica*

MHRA Modern Humanities Research Association

Michaelides S. Michaelides, *The Music of Ancient Greece: An Encyclopaedia*, 1978

MidwestQ *Midwest Quarterly*

Migne, *PG* *Patrologiae cursus completus, series graeca*, ed. J. P. Migne, 161 v., 1857–66

Migne, *PL* *Patrologiae cursus completus, series latina*, ed. J. P. Migne, 221 v., 1844–64

Miner et al. E. Miner, H. Odagiri, and R. E. Morrell, *The Princeton Companion to Classical Japanese Literature*, 1986

MLN *Modern Language Notes*

MLQ *Modern Language Quarterly*

MLQ (London) *Modern Language Quarterly (London)*

MLR *Modern Language Review*

Morier H. Morier, *Dictionnaire de poétique et de rhétorique*, 5th ed., rev. and exp., 1998

Morris-Jones J. Morris-Jones, *Cerdd Dafod*, 1925, rpt. with index, 1980

MP *Modern Philology*

Murphy J. J. Murphy, *Rhetoric in the Middle Ages: A History of Rhetorical Theory from St. Augustine to the Renaissance*, 1974

N&Q *Notes & Queries*

Navarro T. Navarro, *Métrica española: Reseña histórica y descriptiva*, 6th ed., 1983

NER/BLQ *New England Review / Bread Loaf Quarterly*

New CBEL *New Cambridge Bibliography of English Literature*, ed. G. Watson and I. R. Willison, 5 v., 1969–77

New Grove *New Grove Dictionary of Music and Musicians*, ed. S. Sadie, 20 v., 1980

Nienhauser et al. W. H. Nienhauser, Jr., C. Hartman, Y. W. Ma, and S. H. West, *The Indiana Companion to Traditional Chinese Literature*, 1986

NLH *New Literary History*

NM *Neuphilologische Mitteilungen (Bulletin of the Modern Language Society)*

Norberg D. Norberg, *Introduction a l'étude de la versification latine médiévale*, 1958

Norden E. Norden, *Die antike Kunstprosa*, 9th ed., 2 v., 1983

OED *Oxford English Dictionary*

OL *Orbis Litterarum: International Review of Literary Studies*

Olson C. Olson, "Projective Verse," *Collected Prose*, ed. D. Allen and B. Friedlander, 1997

Omond T. S. Omond, *English Metrists*, 1921

P&R *Philosophy and Rhetoric*

Parry M. Parry, *The Making of Homeric Verse*, ed. A. Parry, 1971

Parry, *History* T. Parry, *A History of Welsh Literature*, trans. H. I. Bell, 1955

Patterson W. F. Patterson, *Three Centuries of French Poetic Theory: A Critical History of the Chief Arts of Poetry in France (1328–1630)*, 2 v., 1935

Pauly-Wissowa *Paulys Realencyclopädie der classischen Alterumswissenschaft*, ed. A. Pauly, G. Wissowa, W. Kroll, and K. Mittelhaus, 24 v. (A–Q), 10 v. (R–Z, Series 2), and 15 v. (Supplements), 1894–1978

PBA *Proceedings of the British Academy*

Pearsall D. Pearsall, *Old English and Middle English Poetry*, 1977

PMLA *Publications of the Modern Language Association of America*

PoT *Poetics Today*

PQ *Philological Quarterly*

PsychologR *Psychological Review*

Puttenham G. Puttenham, *The Arte of English Poesie*, ed. F. Whigham and W. A. Rebhorn, 2007

QJS *Quarterly Journal of Speech*

Raby, *Christian* F.J.E. Raby, *A History of Christian-Latin Poetry from the Beginnings to the Close of the Middle Ages*, 2d ed., 1953

Raby, *Secular* F.J.E. Raby, *A History of Secular Latin Poetry in the Middle Ages*, 2d ed., 2 v., 1957

Ransom *Selected Essays of John Crowe Ransom*, ed. T. D. Young and J. Hindle, 1984

Reallexikon I *Reallexikon der deutschen Literaturgeschichte*, 1st ed., ed. P. Merker and W. Stammler, 4 v., 1925–31

Reallexikon II *Reallexikon der deutschen Literaturgeschichte*, 2d ed., ed. W. Kohlschmidt and W. Mohr (v. 1–3), K. Kanzog and A. Masser (v. 4), 1958–84

Reallexikon III *Reallexikon der deutschen Literaturwissenschaft*, 3d ed, ed. H. Fricke, K. Frubmüller, J.-D. Müller, and K. Weimar, 3 v., 1997–2003

REL *Review of English Literature*
RES *Review of English Studies*
Richards I. A. Richards, *Principles of Literary Criticism*, 1925
RLC *Revue de littérature compareé*
RPh *Romance Philology*
RQ *Renaissance Quarterly*
RR *Romanic Review*

SAC *Studies in the Age of Chaucer*
Saintsbury, *Prose* G. Saintsbury, *A History of English Prose Rhythm*, 1912
Saintsbury, *Prosody* G. Saintsbury, *A History of English Prosody, from the Twelfth Century to the Present Day*, 2d ed., 3 v., 1961
Saisselin R. G. Saisselin, *The Rule of Reason and the Ruses of the Heart: A Philosophical Dictionary of Classical French Criticism, Critics, and Aesthetic Issues*, 1970
Sayce O. Sayce, *The Medieval German Lyric, 1150–1300: The Development of Its Themes and Forms in Their European Context*, 1982
Scherr B. P. Scherr, *Russian Poetry: Meter, Rhythm, and Rhyme*, 1986
Schipper J. M. Schipper, *Englische Metrik*, 3 v., 1881–88
Schipper, *History* J. M. Schipper, *A History of English Versification*, 1910
Schmid and Stählin W. Schmid and O. Stählin, *Geschichte der griechischen Literatur*, 7 v., 1920–48
Scott C. Scott, *French Verse-Art: A Study*, 1980
Sebeok *Style in Language*, ed. T. Sebeok, 1960
SEL *Studies in English Literature 1500–1900*
ShQ *Shakespeare Quarterly*
Sievers E. Sievers, *Altergermanische Metrik*, 1893
SIR *Studies in Romanticism*
Smith *Elizabethan Critical Essays*, ed. G. G. Smith, 2 v., 1904
Snell B. Snell, *Griechesche Metrik*, 4th ed., 1982
SP *Studies in Philology*
Spongano R. Spongano, *Nozioni ed esempi di metric italiana*, 2d ed., 1974
SR *Sewanee Review*
Stephens *The Oxford Companion to the Literature of Wales*, ed. M. Stephens, 1986

TAPA *Transactions of the American Philological Association*
Tarlinskaja M. Tarlinskaja, *English Verse: Theory and History*, 1976
Terras *Handbook of Russian Literature*, ed. V. Terras, 1985
Thieme H. P. Thieme, *Essai sur l'histoire du vers française*, 1916
Thompson J. Thompson, *The Founding of English Metre*, 2d ed., 1989
Trypanis C. A. Trypanis, *Greek Poetry from Homer to Seferis*, 1981
TPS *Transactions of the Philological Society*
TSL *Tennessee Studies in Literature*
TSLL *Texas Studies in Literature and Language*

Vickers B. Vickers, *Classical Rhetoric in English Poetry*, 2d ed., 1989
Vickers, *Defence* B. Vickers, *In Defence of Rhetoric*, 1988
VP *Victorian Poetry*
VQR *Virginia Quarterly Review*

Weinberg B. Weinberg, *A History of Literary Criticism in the Italian Renaissance*, 2 v., 1961
Wellek R. Wellek, *A History of Modern Criticism, 1750–1950*, 8 v., 1955–92
Wellek and Warren R. Wellek and A. Warren, *Theory of Literature*, 3d ed., 1956
Welsh A. Welsh, *Roots of Lyric*, 1978
West M. L. West, *Greek Metre*, 1982
WHB *Wiener Humanistische Blätter*
Wilamowitz U. von Wilamowitz-Moellendorf, *Griechesche Verkunst*, 1921
Wilkins E. H. Wilkins, *A History of Italian Literature*, rev. T. G. Bergin, 1974
Williams and Ford J.E.C. Williams and P. K. Ford, *The Irish Literary Tradition*, 1992
Wimsatt *Versification: Major Language Types*, ed. W. K. Wimsatt, 1972
Wimsatt and Beardsley W. K. Wimsatt and M. C. Beardsley, "The Concept of Meter: An Exercise in Abstraction," *PMLA* 74 (1959); rpt. in *Hateful Contraries*, W. K. Wimsatt, 1965
Wimsatt and Brooks W. K. Wimsatt and C. Brooks, *Literary Criticism: A Short History*, 1957

YFS *Yale French Studies*
YLS *Yearbook of Langland Studies*

ZCP *Zeitschrift für celtische Philologie*
ZDA *Zeitschrift für deutsches Altertum*
ZFSL *Zeitschrift für französische Sprache und Literatur*
ZRP *Zeitschrift für Romanische Philologie*
ZVS *Zeitschrift für Vergleichende Sprachforschung*

General Abbreviations

The abbreviations below are used throughout the volume to conserve space. General abbreviations may also show plural forms, e.g., "cs." for "centuries."

Af. African
Af. Am. African American
Am. American
anthol. anthology
Ar. Arabic
Assoc. Association

b. born
bibl. bibliography
Brit. British

c./cs. century
ca. *circa*, about
cf. *confer*, compare
ch. chapter
cl. classical
contemp. contemporary
crit. criticism

d. died
devel./devels. development
dict. dictionary
diss. dissertation

ed./eds. edition, editor, edited by
e.g. *exempla gratia*, for example
Eng. English
esp. especially
et al. *et alii*, and others
Eur. European

ff. following
fl. *floruit*, flourished
Fr. French

Ger. German
Gr. Greek

Heb. Hebrew
hist./hists. history

IE Indo-European
i.e. *id est*, that is
incl. including
intro./intros. introduction
Ir. Irish
iss. issue
It. Italian

jour./jours. journal

lang./langs. language
Lat. Latin
ling. linguistics, linguistic
lit./lits. literature
lit. crit. literary criticism
lit. hist. literary history

ME Middle English
med. medieval
MHG Middle High German
mod. modern
ms./mss. manuscript

NT New Testament

OE Old English
OF Old French
OHG Old High German
ON Old Norse
OT Old Testament

p./pp. page
pl. plural
Port. Portuguese
postmod. postmodern
premod. premodern
pseud. pseudonym
pub. published

r. reigned
Ren. Renaissance
rev. revised
Rev. Review
rhet./rhets. rhetoric
rpt. reprinted
Rus. Russian

ser. series
sing. singular

Sp. Spanish
spec. special
supp. supplement(ed)

temp. temporary

trad./trads. tradition
trans. translation, translated by

v. volume(s)

Contributors

This list includes all contributors credited in this volume, including some whose articles from previous editions of *The Princeton Encyclopedia of Poetry and Poetics* were updated by the editors or other contributors to the fourth edition. Those with names preceded by a dagger (†) are deceased.

Gemino H. Abad, English (emeritus), University of the Philippines
Roger M. A. Allen, Arabic Languages and Literatures (emeritus), University of Pennsylvania
Walter Andrews, Ottoman and Turkish Literature, University of Washington
†Samuel G. Armistead, Spanish (emeritus), University of California, Davis
Robert Ashmore, East Asian Languages and Cultures, University of California, Berkeley
Harry Aveling, Asian Studies, La Trobe University
Alessandro Barchiesi, Classics, Stanford University
Vincent Barletta, Iberian and Latin American Cultures, Stanford University
Henry J. Baron, English, Calvin College
Guinn Batten, English, Washington University in Saint Louis
Gary Beckman, Hittite and Mesopotamian Studies, University of Michigan
Margaret H. Beissinger, Slavic Languages and Literatures, Princeton University
Esther G. Belin, Writing, Fort Lewis College
Krzysztof Biedrzycki, Polish Literature, Jagiellonian University
Josiah Blackmore, Romance Languages and Literatures, Harvard University
C. D. Blanton, English, University of California, Berkeley
Roy C. Boland, Spanish and Latin American Studies, University of Sydney
†T.V.F. Brogan, independent scholar
Yigal Bronner, Asian Studies, Hebrew University of Jerusalem
Gordon Brotherston, Literature, Film, and Theatre Studies (emeritus), University of Essex
Enric Bou, Linguistics and Comparative Cultures, Ca'Foscari University of Venice
Matthieu Boyd, Literature, Fairleigh Dickinson University
Laurence A. Breiner, English, Boston University
Benjamin Bruch, Celtic Languages and Literature, Celtic Institute of North America
Michel Byrne, Celtic and Gaelic, University of Glasgow
Antonio Carreño, Hispanic Studies (emeritus), Brown University
†Dorothy Clotelle Clarke, Spanish and Portuguese (emerita), University of California, Berkeley
Michael C. Cohen, English, University of California, Los Angeles
Stephen Collis, English, Simon Fraser University
†Robert Cook, English, University of Iceland
Joanna Crow, School of Modern Languages, University of Bristol
Isagani R. Cruz, Literature and Philippine Languages (emeritus), De La Salle University
Michael Dash, French, Social and Cultural Analysis, New York University
Michael Davidson, Literature (emeritus), University of California, San Diego
Kathleen Davis, English, University of Rhode Island
Dirk de Geest, Literary Theory, University of Leiden
Jeroen Dewulf, German, University of California, Berkeley
Vinay Dharwadker, Languages and Cultures of Asia, University of Wisconsin–Madison
Thibaut d'Hubert, South Asian Languages and Civilizations, University of Chicago
David F. Dorsey, independent scholar
Francois Dumont, Literature, University of Laval
Sascha Ebeling, South Asian Languages and Civilizations, University of Chicago
Sveinn Yngvi Egilsson, Icelandic and Comparative Cultural Studies, University of Iceland
Robert Elsie, independent scholar
†Alan W. Entwistle, Hindi, University of Washington
Walter Farber, Near Eastern Languages and Civilizations (emeritus), University of Chicago
Ibrahim Fathy, independent scholar
Patrick K. Ford, Celtic Languages and Literatures (emeritus), Harvard University
Benjamin Foster, Near Eastern Languages and Civilizations, Yale University
†Bernard J. Fridsma, Germanic Languages (emeritus), Calvin College

Dmitry Frolov, Arabic Philology, Moscow State University
Robert Dennis Fulk, English, Indiana University
Graham Furniss, Languages and Cultures of Africa, University of London
Rene Galand, French (emeritus), Wellesley College
Leonardo García-Pabón, Romance Languages, University of Oregon
Mary Malcolm Gaylord, Romance Languages and Literatures, Harvard University
Stephen A. Geller, Bible, Jewish Theological Seminary
Edwin Gerow, Religion and Humanities (emeritus), Reed College
Robert P. Goldman, South and Southeast Asian Studies, University of California, Berkeley
Sverker Göransson, Literature, University of Gothenburg
Stathis Gourgouris, Classics, Columbia University
George G. Grabowicz, Ukrainian Literature, Harvard University
Phyllis Granoff, Religious Studies, Yale University
Erik Gray, English and Comparative Literature, Columbia University
Stephen Gray, independent scholar
Edward L. Greenstein, Bible, Bar-Ilan University
†Janet Hadda, English (emerita), University of California, Los Angeles
Charles Hallisey, Buddhist Literatures, Harvard Divinity School
Russell G. Hamilton, Portuguese, Brazilian, and Lusophone African Literatures (emeritus), Vanderbilt University
David Hargreaves, Linguistics, Western Oregon University
†Wolfhart Heinrichs, Arabic, Harvard University
James S. Helgeson, French and Francophone Studies, University of Nottingham
Benjamin A. Heller, Spanish, University of Notre Dame
Omaar Hena, English, Wake Forest University
†C. John Herington, Classics (emeritus), Yale University
H. Mack Horton, East Asian Languages and Cultures, University of California, Berkeley
Thomas John Hudak, Linguistics, Arizona State University
Wilt L. Idema, Chinese Literature (emeritus), Harvard University
Luis Miguel Isava, Language and Literature, Simón Bolívar University
Fernando Iturburu, Spanish, State University of New York, Plattsburgh
†Ivar Ivask, Modern Languages, University of Oklahoma
D.B.S. Jeyaraj, independent scholar
Ramya Chamalie Jirasinghe, independent scholar
Eleanor Johnson, English and Comparative Literature, Columbia University
Aled Llion Jones, School of Welsh, Bangor University
Ananya Jahanara Kabir, English Literature, King's College London
Andrew Kahn, Russian Literature, University of Oxford
Paul Kane, English, Vassar College
Matthew T. Kapstein, Philosophy of Religions and History of Religions, University of Chicago Divinity School
Nanor Kebranian, Late Ottoman History and Literary Studies, Columbia University
Edmund Keeley, English (emeritus), Princeton University
Jennifer Keith, English, University of North Carolina, Greensboro
William J. Kennedy, Comparative Literature, Cornell University
Dov-Ber Kerler, Jewish Studies, Indiana University
Sachin C. Ketkar, English, Maharaja Sayajirao University of Baroda
Gwen Kirkpatrick, Spanish and Portuguese, Georgetown University
Dodona Kiziria, Slavic Languages and Literatures (emeritus), Indiana University
Christopher Kleinhenz, French and Italian (emeritus), University of Wisconsin–Madison
Nisha Kommattam, South Asian Languages and Civilizations, University of Chicago
Christina Kramer, Slavic Languages and Literatures, University of Toronto
Efraín Kristal, Comparative Literature, University of California, Los Angeles
Jelle Krol, Tresoar Friesland Historical and Literary Center
Dean Krouk, Norwegian, St. Olaf College
Jill Kuhnheim, Spanish and Portuguese, University of Kansas
Leslie Kurke, Classics and Comparative Literature, University of California, Berkeley
Dov Landau, Hebrew and Comparative Literature, Bar-Ilan University
George Lang, French, University of Ottawa
Ilse Laude-Cirtautas, Russian, East European and Central Asian Studies, University of Washington
Marc D. Lauxtermann, Byzantine and Modern Greek Language and Literature, University of Oxford
John Leavitt, Anthropology, University of Montreal

Meredith Lee, German (emerita), University of California, Irvine
Young-Jun Lee, Korean Literature, Kyung Hee University
Tracy K. Lewis, Portuguese and Spanish, State University of New York, Oswego
John Lindow, Scandinavian, University of California, Berkeley
Daiva Litvinskaitė, Slavic and Baltic Languages and Literatures, University of Illinois, Chicago
Ernesto Livorni, Comparative Literature and Folklore Studies, University of Wisconsin–Madison
†D. Myrddin Lloyd, National Library of Scotland
Paul Losensky, Comparative Literature, Indiana University
Tina Lu, East Asian Languages and Literatures, Yale University
†Katharine Luomala, Anthropology, University of Hawai'i
Sverre Lyngstad, English (emeritus), New Jersey Institute of Technology
John MacInnes, School of Scottish Studies (emeritus), University of Edinburgh
Abednego M. Maphumulo, Modern and Oral Literature, University of Kwa-Zulu
Keavy Martin, English, University of Alberta
Jonathan Mayhew, Spanish and Portuguese, University of Kansas
David R. McCann, Korean Literature (emeritus), Harvard University
Robin McGrath, independent scholar
Arvind Krishna Mehrotra, independent scholar
Laurent Mignon, Turkish, University of Oxford
Ivan Mladenov, Literature, Bulgarian Academy of Sciences
Reidulf K. Molvaer, independent scholar
Leith Morton, English, Tokyo Institute of Technology
C. M. Naim, South Asian Languages and Civilizations (emeritus), University of Chicago
†James Naughton, Czech and Slovak, University of Oxford
Virgil P. Nemoianu, English and Philosophy, Catholic University of America
Jan Krogh Nielsen, Danish, University of Washington
Ranjini Obeyesekere, Anthropology (emerita), Princeton University
Mari Jose Olaziregi, Basque Studies, University of the Basque Country
Jeff Opland, Languages and Cultures of Africa, University of London
†Ants Oras, English (emeritus), University of Florida
Marta Ortiz Canseco, Philology, International University of La Rioja
Martin Orwin, Somali and Amharic, School of Oriental and African Studies, University of London
Iztok Osojnik, independent scholar
William D. Paden, French (emeritus), Northwestern University
Deven M. Patel, South Asia Studies, University of Pennsylvania
Dipti R. Pattanaik, English, Ravenshaw University
Stephen Penn, English, University of Stirling
Charles A. Perrone, Portuguese and Luso-Brazilian Culture and Literatures, University of Florida
Guillaume Peureux, French, University of California, Davis
Ineke Phaf-Rheinberger, African Literature and Culture, Humboldt University, Berlin
Marc Quaghebeur, Archives and Museum of Literature, Brussels
Jahan Ramazani, English, University of Virginia
Esperanza Ramirez-Christensen, Japanese Literature, University of Michigan
Velcheru Narayana Rao, Languages and Cultures of Asia (emeritus), University of Wisconsin–Madison
†Erica Reiner, Eastern Languages, University of Chicago
Alena Rettová, Swahili Literature and Culture, School of Oriental and African Studies, University of London
Maria G. Rewakowicz, Slavic Languages and Literatures, University of Washington
Tulku Thondup Rinpoche, Buddhayana Foundation
Hugh Roberts, English, University of California, Irvine
Françoise Robin, Tibetan Studies, Institut National des Langues et Civilisations Orientales
Armando Romero, Romance Languages and Literatures, University of Cincinnati
Sven H. Rossel, Scandinavian (emeritus), University of Vienna
Phillip Rothwell, Spanish and Portuguese, Rutgers University
Paul Rouzer, Asian Languages and Literatures, University of Minnesota
Elizabeth Sagaser, English, Colby College
Edith Sarra, East Asian Languages and Cultures, Indiana University
Haun Saussy, Comparative Literature, University of Chicago
Raymond P. Scheindlin, Medieval Hebrew Literature, Jewish Theological Seminary

Russell G. Schuh, Linguistics, University of California, Los Angeles
Jacobo Sefamí, Spanish and Portuguese, University of California, Irvine
Vered Karti Shemtov, Comparative Literature, Stanford University
Rimvydas Silbajoris, Slavic (emeritus), Ohio State University
Juris Silenieks, French (emeritus), Carnegie Mellon University
†Joseph H. Silverman, Spanish, University of California, Santa Cruz
Kirsti K. Simonsuuri, Comparative Literature, University of Helsinki
Amardeep Singh, English, Lehigh University
Guntis Šmidchens, Scandinavian Studies, University of Washington
Ivo Smits, Area Studies (Japan), Leiden University
Rupert Snell, Asian Studies, University of Texas, Austin
†Ezra Spicehandler, Hebrew Literature (emeritus), Hebrew Union College
Malynne Sternstein, Slavic Languages and Literatures, University of Chicago
Robert Sullivan, English, University of Hawai'i
†Robert Donald Thornton, English (emeritus), State University of New York, New Paltz
Francisco Tomsich, independent scholar
Humphrey Tonkin, Humanities (emeritus), University of Hartford
Chandrakant Topiwala, independent scholar
Gary Tubb, South Asian Languages and Civilizations, University of Chicago
Quang Phu Van, Vietnamese, Yale University
Valeria Varga, Central Eurasian Studies, Indiana University
Aida Vidan, Slavic Languages and Literatures, Harvard University
Robert Vilain, German, University of Bristol
Louise Viljoen, Afrikaans and Dutch, University of Stellenbosch
David A. Wacks, Spanish, University of Oregon
Roderick Watson, English (emeritus), University of Stirling
Anthony K. Webster, Anthropology, Southern Illinois University
†Uriel Weinrich, Yiddish, Columbia University
Winthrop Wetherbee, Humanities (emeritus), Cornell University
Steven F. White, Spanish and Portuguese, St. Lawrence University
Simon Wickham-Smith, Russian, East European, and Central Asian Studies, University of Washington
†John Ellis Caerwyn Williams, Welsh and Celtic, University College of Wales
†Steven Winspur, French and Italian, University of Wisconsin–Madison
†Tibor Wlassics, Italian, University of Virginia
Teri Shaffer Yamada, Asian Studies, California State University, Long Beach
Michelle Yeh, Chinese, University of California, Davis
Marc Zimmerman, Modern and Classical Languages, University of Houston
Robert Zydenbos, Institute of Indology, Ludwig Maximilian University of Munich

The Princeton Handbook of World Poetries

A

AFRICA, POETRY OF

I. English
II. French
III. Portuguese
IV. Indigenous. *See* EGYPT, POETRY OF; ETHIOPIA, POETRY OF; HAUSA POETRY; SOMALI POETRY; SWAHILI POETRY; XHOSA POETRY; ZULU POETRY.

I. English. With the end of the colonial period and the advance of literacy and higher education in Africa came a rapid efflorescence of Af. poetry written in Eng. This poetry displays the variety to be expected in so diverse a continent. Like other examples of postcolonial poetics, Af. poetry in Eng. develops out of the fusion of indigenous trads. with the literary inheritances transmitted through the colonial lang. It is responsive to local idioms, values, and hist. and at the same time remakes for Af. experience the forms and styles imported through Eng. from the Brit. Isles, America, and elsewhere. The adoption of the Eng. lang. for Af. purposes, while advantageous to writers who wish to be heard by an international audience, is fraught with political significance. Some Af. critics contend that poetry written in a historically imperialist lang. cannot be fully disassociated from colonialism's oppressive legacy.

Af. poetry written in Eng. is often seen as divided between poetry that is locally rooted and influenced by Af. oral trads. and cosmopolitan poetry, which is indebted primarily to Western literary trads. The work of Af. poets, however, complicates this distinction, since even the most cosmopolitan poets, such as the Nigerian poet Wole Soyinka, also draw on local oral trads., and even the most local, such as the Ugandan poet Okot p'Bitek (1931–82), also make use of Western literary models. In the wake of colonialism and under the influence of globalization, Af. poetry in Eng. is inextricable from Brit., Ir., Am., and other influences, even when in revolt against the West's values and cultural forms. Conversely, in the West, the descendants of enslaved Africans and economic migrants have fundamentally shaped poetry.

The first poem in the sequence "Heavensgate" (1962, rev. 1964) by Nigerian poet Christopher Okigbo (1932–67) serves as an example of the enmeshment of Af. and Western poetics in sub-Saharan Africa. The poet invokes the Igbo river goddess, near the village where he grew up: "Before you, mother Idoto / naked I stand." Reaffirming his affinity with native culture, Okigbo grounds his poem in local religion and flora (naked, he leans on the oilbean tree, sacred to Idoto, a totem for her worship). At the same time, his diction (referring to himself as "a prodigal" further in the poem) and rhet. ("Before you, mother Idoto") also recall the Christianity that missionaries imported into Igboland. The lyric is shaped by the Roman Catholicism in which Okigbo was brought up, incl. prayers to the Virgin Mary and the story of the prodigal son. The poem's final lines, which cry out to a native divinity, paradoxically echo Psalm 130 ("Out of the depths have I cried unto thee, O Lord") and Psalm 5 ("Give ear to my words, O Lord. . . . Hearken unto the voice of my cry").

Although Af. poets are indebted to religious, lyric, and other cultural forms from the West, they seldom lose their awareness of Africa's rich oral trads. A poem such as Okot p'Bitek's *Lawino* (1966) relies on Acholi songs, proverbs, repetitions, idioms, and oral address, even as it also draws on the model of the Western long poem (Okot has cited H. W. Longfellow's "Hiawatha" as a key influence). An aggrieved village woman inveighs against her husband for forsaking his local culture and being too enamored of Western ways: "Listen, Ocol, you are the son of a Chief, / Leave foolish behavior to little children." In her book-length complaint, Lawino repeatedly brandishes an Acholi proverb that warns against uprooting the pumpkin; in so doing, she emphasizes the importance of preserving the household, as well as the oral trads. that sustain it.

Between the poles marked out by Okigbo's highly literary, allusive, syntactically complex early poetry and Okot's orally based poetics of song, praise, and invective, Af. poetry has discovered a multitude of ways to mediate the oral and scribal, the local and global, the socially urgent protest and the private meditation. Indeed, as an Oxford-trained anthropologist influenced by Longfellow and the Bible, Okot cannot be reduced to simple nativism. And as a poet who absorbs drum rhythms and praise song into his later work, Okigbo—who died fighting for an independent Biafra—should not be seen as a Westernized sellout. Under the influence of intensified global communication, trade, education, and travel, younger poets work in ever-more deeply hybrid and transnational forms. The South Af. Lesego Rampolokeng (b. 1965), e.g., draws on a global array of influences, incl. rap musicians, the Af. Am. Last Poets, Jamaican dub poet Mutabaruka, and Jamaican-born Brit. reggae poet Linton Kwesi Johnson, to mount a vehement social critique of his country both before and after apartheid.

From the period of Af. decolonization, first formally achieved in anglophone Africa with Ghana's independence in 1957, to today's struggle against both external economic imperialism and the internalized colonialism of dictators and tyrants, oral and other traditional poetry has strongly influenced Af. Eng. poems. The imprint of Af. oral culture is visible in such fundamental elements as the poet's stance as defender of communal values; allusions to the hist., customs, and artifacts of the culture; and the architectonic features adapted from praise song, proverbial tale, epic, invective, and indigenous prayer. Experiments in the transmutation of traditional Af. poetic forms into Eng. vary with the culture represented.

Arising in the aftermath of modernism, much Af. Eng. poetry eschews meter and rhyme in favor of free verse, often ornamented by alliteration and assonance, although rap's influence has spawned intensely rhymed and rhythmic verse. Poems that are meant to speak to, or for, Af. communities avoid extended conceits unless they are buttressed by hard or sardonic reason or concrete imagery.

A. *West Africa.* West Africa, particularly Nigeria and Ghana, has the oldest and most influential trad. of sophisticated poetry in Eng. This lyric poetry combines audacious leaps of thought and individualized expression with social responsibility; it privileges the metaphysical, religious, and social concepts of its own society, although it also draws on concepts indigenous to Eur. cultural hist. When social protest is overt, it is usually presented with intellectual and artistic complexity rather than simplistic fervor. Exemplary Nigerian poets and their principal works include the country's oldest active poet Gabriel Okara (b. 1921; *The Fisherman's Invocation* [1978], written against the background of civil war); Christopher Okigbo (*Labyrinths* [1971], incl. the prophetic sequence "Path of Thunder"); J. P. Clark (b. 1935; *Reed in the Tide* [1965], incl. autobiographical poems; *Casualties* [1970], concerning the war between Nigeria and Biafra; *A Decade of Tongues* [1981]; *State of the Union* [1981], about Nigeria's socioeconomic and political problems in an international context); the philosopher and polemicist Chinweizu (b. ca. 1935; *Invocations and Admonitions* [1986]); the Nobel laureate Wole Soyinka (b. 1934; *Idanre* [1967], based on Yoruba mythology; *Shuttle in the Crypt* [1971]; *Mandela's Earth and Other Poems* [1988]; and a number of plays that contain poetry); Odia Ofeimun (b. 1947; *The Poet Lied* [1989], *Dreams at Work* [2000]); Niyi Osundare (b. 1947; *Village Voices* [1984], *The Eye of the Earth* [1986], *Waiting Laughters* [1990], *The Word Is an Egg* [2004]); and Tanure Ojaide (b. 1948; *Labyrinths of the Delta* [1986], *The Endless Song* [1988], *In the House of Words* [2006]).

Among Ghanaians, experiments in the trans. and adaptation of indigenous poetic forms have been common, as in the works of Kofi Awoonor (1935–2013; *Rediscovery* [1964], in which Ewe funeral dirges are brought into Eng.; *Night of My Blood* [1971], both autobiographical and political; *Ride Me, Memory* [1973], in which a Ghanaian abroad reflects on his country; *The House by the Sea* [1978]; *Guardians of the Sacred Word* [1978], a collection of Ewe poetry); Kofi Anyidoho (b. 1947; *Elegy for the Revolution* [1978], *A Harvest of Our Dreams* [1985], *Ancestral Logic and Caribbean Blues* [1992]); and Atukwei (John) Okai (b. 1941; *The Oath of the Fontomfrom* [1971], whose title poem refers to a royal drum that beats out the hist. of a society; *Lorgorligi Logarithms* [1974]; *Freedom Symphony* [2008], love poems). Closer to Western trads. of sensibility and structure are others such as Kwesi Brew (1924–2007; *The Shadows of Laughter* [1968], *African Panorama* [1981], *Return of No Return* [1995], *The Clan of the Leopard* [1996]), A. W. Kayper-Mensah (1923–80; *The Dark Wanderer* [1970]; *The Drummer in Our Time* [1975], concerning Africa's view of Europe; *Sankofa: Adinkra Poems* [1976]; *Proverb Poems* [1976]), and Frank Kobina Parkes (1932–2004; *Songs from the Wilderness* [1965]).

A notable poet of Gambia was Lenrie Peters (1932–2009; *Satellites* [1967], poems about human rights in the broadest sense; *Katchikali* [1971], which takes its name from a sacred place in Bakau, where the coast of Gambia juts into the North Atlantic; *Selected Poetry* [1981]).

Prominent poets of Sierra Leone include Syl Cheney-Coker (b. 1945; *Concerto for an Exile*

[1973]; *The Graveyard Also Has Teeth* [1980]; *The Blood in the Desert's Eyes* [1990]) and Lemuel Johnson (1940–2002; *Highlife for Caliban* [1973]; *Hand on the Navel* [1978]).

B. ***East Africa.*** East Af. poetry is dominated by two styles. One originated in Okot p'Bitek's trans. and adaptation of his own Acholi poetry. Okot (*Song of Lawino*, the lament of a rural wife over encroaching Westernization; *Song of Ocol* [1970], her husband's reply; "Song of Prisoner" [1971], a commentary on Kenyan politics; "Song of Malaya" [1971], a critique of sexual morality) was probably the most widely read poet of Africa in the later 20th c. Through long rhetorical monologues usually narrated by a victim of modernization, these poems express social commentary with lucid, graphic imagery, humorous irony, and paradoxical common sense. Another Ugandan poet who makes extensive use of Af. proverbs and folk culture is Okello Oculi (b. 1942; *Orphan* [1968], an allegorical account of Af. culture's removal from traditional values; *Malak* [1976], a narrative poem about the dictator Idi Amin's Uganda; *Kookolem* [1978], about the intersection of social and domestic oppression; *Song for the Sun in Us* [2000]).

An alternative style, more obviously indebted to West Af. poetry, uses asyndeton, subtle imagery, and erudite allusions to convey a mordant and individualized vision of mod. life. It includes a wider range of subjects, tones, and frames of reference. Preeminent poets include the Kenyan Jared Angira (b. 1947; *Juices* [1970]; *Silent Voices* [1972]; *Soft Corals* [1973]; *Cascades* [1979]; *The Years Go By* [1980]), the Ugandan Richard Ntiru (b. 1946; *Tensions* [1971]), and the South Sudanese Taban lo Liyong (b. 1939; *Meditations in Limbo* [1970]; *Frantz Fanon's Uneven Ribs* [1971]; *Another Nigger Dead* [1972]; *Ballads of Underdevelopment* [1976]; *Another Last Word* [1990]).

C. ***Southern Africa.*** Before the abolition of apartheid, Eng.-lang. South Af. poetry was most concerned with subjugation, courage, poverty, prisons, revolt, and the private griefs of public injustice. South Af. poets writing in Eng. before the 1970s were often exiles, whose works, therefore, also reflected Brit. or Am. experience—e.g., Arthur Nortje (1942–70; *Dead Roots* [1973]), Cosmo Pieterse (b. 1930; *Echo and Choruses: "Ballad of the Cells"* [1974]), and esp. Dennis Brutus (1924–2009; *Sirens, Knuckles and Boots* [1963]; *Letters to Martha and Other Poems from a South African Prison* [1968]; *Poems from Algiers* [1970]; *A Simple Lust* [1973], the collection that marked Brutus's turn from artifice toward a plain style; *China Poems* [1975]; *Stubborn Hope* [1978]; *Salutes and Censures* [1982]; *Leafdrift* [2005]). In Brutus's poetry, the speaker is often an observer combining passionate concern with reflective distance, and the imagery portrays monstrous abuse in natural and social settings of oblivious serenity. Even after the ending of apartheid, Brutus continued to write poetry that championed a more just social order than South Africa achieved as a new democracy.

The experimental adaptation of regional Af. forms to original poetry in the Eng. lang. is well represented by the work of Mazisi Kunene (1930–2006; *Zulu Poems* [1970]; *Emperor Shaka the Great: A Zulu Epic* [1979], an adaptation of a traditional epic; *Anthem of the Decades* [1981]; and *The Ancestors and the Sacred Mountain* [1982]).

Keroapetse Kgositsile (b. 1938; *Spirits Unchained* [1969]; *For Melba* [1970]; *My Name Is Afrika* [1971]; *The Present Is a Dangerous Place to Live* [1975]; *To the Bitter End* [1995]; *This Way I Salute You* [2004]) and the broadly popular Oswald Mtshali (b. 1940; *Sounds of a Cowhide Drum* [1971]; *Fireflames* [1980]) are forerunners of the dramatic change in and copious output of Af. poetry after 1970. The influence of Af. Am. musical and poetic forms, esp. jazz, rap, blues, and the renaissance of the 1960s, looking back to the Harlem Ren., is often evident. Immediacy may be reinforced by incl. phrases from South Af. langs. or Afrikaans or by directly addressing the reader as a compatriot. Major writers include poets who wrote in solidarity with the Black Consciousness movement's emphasis on the affirmation of black cultural values in the face of state-based terror and oppression, such as Mongane Serote (b. 1944; *Yakhal'Inkomo* [1972]; *Tsetlo* [1974]; *No Baby Must Weep* [1975]; *Behold Mama, Flowers* [1978]; *The Night Keeps Winking* [1982]; *Freedom Lament and Song* [1997]; *History Is the Home Address* [2004]); Sipho Sepamla (1932–2007; *Hurry Up to It!* [1975]; *The Soweto I Love* [1977]; *From Gorée to Soweto* [1988]); Mafika Pascal Gwala (b. 1946; *Jol'iinkomo* [1977]; *No More Lullabies* [1982]); James Matthews (b. 1929; *Cry Rage* [1972]; *No Time for Dreams* [1977]; *Flames and Flowers* [2000]; *Age Is a Beautiful Phase* [2008]); Daniel P. Kunene (b. 1923; *Pirates Have Become Our*

Kings [1978]; *A Seed Must Seem to Die* [1981]); and the jazz-influenced Wopko Pieter Jensma (b. 1939; *Sing for Our Execution* [1973]; *Where White Is the Colour Where Black Is the Number* [1974]; *I Must Show You My Clippings* [1977]).

Postapartheid poets in South Africa include Ingrid de Kok (b. 1951; *Familiar Ground* [1988], *Transfer* [1997], *Terrestrial Things* [2002]), Kelwyn Sole (b. 1951; *The Blood of Our Silence* [1988], *Projections in the Past Tense* [1992], *Love That Is Night* [1998], *Mirror and Water Gazing* [2001]), Gail Dendy (b. 1957; *Assault and the Moth* [1993]), Gabeba Baderoon (b. 1969; *The Dream in the Next Body* [2005], *The Museum of Ordinary Life* [2005], *A Hundred Silences* [2006]), and the performance poet Rampolokeng (*Horns for Hondo* [1990], *Rap Master Supreme—Word Bomber in the Extreme* [1997], *The Bavino Sermons* [1999]). See SOUTH AFRICA, POETRY OF.

Politics and economics have denied a wide international audience to the poetry of South Africa's anglophone neighbors. Malawian figures include David Rubadiri (b. 1930; *An African Thunderstorm* [2004]), Frank M. Chipasula (b. 1949; *Visions and Reflections* [1972]; *O Earth Wait for Me* [1984]; *Nightwatcher, Nightsong* [1986]; *Whispers in the Wings* [2001]), Jack Mapanje (b. 1944; *Of Chameleons and Gods* [1981], *Beasts of Nalunga* [2007]), and Steve Chimombo (b. 1945; *A Referendum of the Forest Creatures* [1993], *Napolo and Other Poems* [2009]).

Notable Zambian poets are Richard A. Chima (b. 1945; *The Loneliness of a Drunkard* [1973]) and Patu Simoko (b. 1951; *Africa Is Made of Clay* [1978]).

Zimbabwe has produced copious poetry reflecting both the price of liberating warfare and the consequences of victory. Preeminent poets include Samuel Chimsoro (b. 1949; *Smoke and Flames* [1978]), Musaemura Zimunya (b. 1949; *Thought Tracks* [1982], *Kingfisher, Jikinya and Other Poems* [1982], *Country Dawns and City Lights* [1985]), Mudereri Kadhani (b. 1952; *Quarantine Rhythms* [1976]), Chenjerai Hove (b. 1956; *Up in Arms* [1982], *Red Hills of Home* [1984], *Blind Moon* [2004]), and Freedom Nyamubaya (b. 1960; *On the Road Again* [1986]).

With important national and individual differences, the poetry of southern Africa still has an identifiable character. It is often premised on an intense affinity for the land and, through that, a close union between the spiritual and physical worlds. Nature is presented as a manifestation of religious forces but is also treated with a more direct, nonsymbolic sensibility than in other Af. poetry. Poet and personae are more closely identified with their community through a diction that relies on direct address to the reader as putative interlocutor, conversational apostrophe, quiet humor, anaphora, and avoidance of strident effects. Esoteric lyricism and declamation are both rare. The stresses that urban cultures impose on rural life and on personal values and identity are common themes, as well as the systemic effects of colonial and postcolonial hegemony. In form and themes, the poetry of this region adapts Eng. to provide sophisticated but unaffected articulation of traditional Af. worldviews in a context of rapid social change.

Af. poetry in Eng. displays an immense cultural and personal variety. Sometimes written in an engaged and earnest tone, frequently leavened by humor, it maintains close identification with communal values and experience while conveying personal perceptions and global influences. Inventively hybridizing Eng. poetic forms with indigenous cultural resources, Af. poetry in Eng. is true to a mod. Af. experience that straddles Western and Af. metaphysical, ethical, and aesthetic visions.

II. French. The rise of Af. poetry in Fr. cannot be understood without reference to the slave trade and the subsequent colonization of Africa, the cultural politics France and Belgium imposed during their years of occupation, and multiple forms of resistance to these conditions.

It is no accident that New World writers are usually included in studies and anthols. of Af. poetry in Fr. Both Africans and Af. Americans had to confront the same racist oppression. They accordingly made common cause and sought out each other for inspiration and readership, despite real differences. Hence, the importance of Harlem Ren. figures such as Langston Hughes and Claude McKay to the founders of Negritude, the first coherent Af. literary and intellectual movement, which can be dated to the 1930s. Of the founders of the first important literary review, *L'Étudiant Noir* (The Black Student), Aimé Césaire (1913–2008) of Martinique, Léon G. Damas (1912–78) of French Guiana, and Léopold Sédar Senghor (1906–2001) of Senegal, only the last was from Africa itself, and all three were students in Paris. This tendency toward cross-fertilization with other black lits. made Af. poetry in

Fr. intercontinental in scope. Though Césaire and Senghor and later poets repeatedly demonstrated their mastery of Fr. trad., they were drawn both to other lits. from what was then called the third world and to indigenous Af. lits. The desire to embrace and renew traditional Af. poetic practice, expressed rhetorically by the proponents of Negritude, has become increasingly important among subsequent generations, who are, however, aware of the difficulties such hybrid literary forms present.

There is no exhaustive definition for the term *Negritude*. Coined by Césaire in his 1939 *Cahier d'un retour au pays natal* (*Notebook of a Return to the Native Land*), it was, in his words, "the simple recognition of the fact that one is black, the acceptance of this fact and of our destiny as blacks, of our history and our culture." Yet there is nothing simple about this statement; its implications are manifold, and the poetry that sought to express it took many different forms, from Damas's explosive *Pigments* (1937) to Césaire's virulent defense of black culture in his *Cahier* to Senghor's lofty exaltation of Af. values beginning with his 1945 *Chants d'ombre* (*Shadow Songs*). The landmark anthol. of Negritude poetry came three years later, Senghor's *Anthologie de la nouvelle poésie nègre et malgache de langue française* (Anthology of New Black and Malagasy Poetry in the French Language, 1948), with its influential preface by Jean-Paul Sartre, "Orphée noir" ("Black Orpheus").

In Sartre's view, Negritude was but an antithesis, a second phase of reaction to white racism that, while defending the specificity of black culture, did so in view of a final synthesis, the transition to a universal (in Sartre's version, proletarian) culture with no oppressors and, ultimately, no specificity. Sartre's perspective was at odds with that of Senghor himself, who had in mind a less politicized universality, but the former set the grounds for Frantz Fanon's typology of postcolonial cultures in *Les Damnés de la terre* (*The Wretched of the Earth*, 1961), one on which most interpretations of postcolonial lit. hist. implicitly repose: a dialectical movement from a colonial period of slavish imitation of Western models to a period of revolt, exemplified by Negritude, and then a postindependence period in which Africans have taken control of their own culture, though not without outside interference.

Damas died relatively young, but Senghor and Césaire lived until the 21st c., and the canonical status of their version of Negritude has been confirmed by Senghor's weighty *Oeuvres complètes* (Complete Works, 2006) and the volumes that marked Césaire's 90th birthday in 2003. Yet, already in 1966, the anthol. by the publisher Présence Africaine, *Nouvelle somme de poésie du monde noir* (A New Survey of the Poetry of the Black World), can be seen as a more ambiguous and ambitious poetic project than those rooted in early Negritude. Foremost among the poets from that generation was Tchicaya U'Tamsi (1931–88), whose dense and difficult oeuvre combined contemp. techniques with an anguished concern for the Congo and the ravages of neocolonialism, esp. in his 1962 *Epitomé*. The number of retrospective eds. that followed his death is a mark of his influence, and it is often against the dominating figure of Tchicaya that later Af. Fr.-lang. poets are measured, not only his fellow Congolese (Brazzaville) J. B. Tati-Loutard (1938–2009, *Oeuvres poétiques* [2007]) and Sony Labou Tansi (1947–95), but, e.g. the Ivorian Jean-Marie Adiaffi (1941–99), and the Senegalese Amadou Lamine Sall (b. 1951) and Hamidou Dia (b. 1953).

Over the past three decades, Af. poetry in Fr., while still continental in scope, has become more self-consciously local, more often related to the national trads. of the individual poets. Starting with Tati-Loutard's 1976 *Anthologie de la littérature congolaise d'expression française* (Anthology of Congolese Literature in French), there began to appear critical works and collections of poetry representing the increasingly self-defining national lits. of Benin (1984), Cameroon (1982), Gabon (1978), the Ivory Coast (1983), and Togo (1980), among others. This parceling up of a subcontinent into national lits. reflects the rise of distinct national identities across Africa and inevitably points to conflicts among them. In time, *African literature* will seem as broad and as vague a concept as *European literature*, the internal differences within Africa nuancing the abstract and often racially defined concept of a single continental-wide identity.

One prominent thematic thread of contemp. Af. poetry in Fr. is the experience of exile or emigration, which has affected not only the intellectual elite that write and read poetry in Fr. but Africans of all origins from across the continent. This contemp. state of exile can readily be related back to the original diasporic displacement brought about by the slave trade, hence, the continuing relevance of Césaire's *Cahier* and the preoccupation with Af. cultural identity both at home and in the growing Af. communities around the world, in Europe but also in the Americas. It is, thus, not at all uncommon for a Congolese poet like Alain Mabanckou (b. 1966) to find inspiration not only in his homeland but in the large Af. community in Paris, and thereafter among Af.-Americans in Los Angeles. Similarly, Véronique Tadjo (b. 1955) was born in Paris but was raised in the Ivory Coast, which continues to inspire her poetry. Rare in fact is the Af. poet writing in Fr. who does not have a foothold on two continents: the Senegalese Babacar Sall (Dakar/Paris), Léopold Congo Mbemba (Brazzaville/Paris), and Amadu Elimane Kane (Senegal/Paris). This is as much the case for female as for male poets, Tanella Boni (Abidjan/Toulouse) and Clémentine Faïk-Nzuji (Kinshasa/Brussels) being additional salient cases among the former.

Many observers think that, despite the continuing hegemony of Paris as a cultural center, writing in Fr. outside France is destined to assume as important a role as writing in Eng. beyond the U.S. and Britain. Af. poetry in Fr. is arguably one of the richest sources of this *littérature-monde* (lit. of the world in Fr.). This is a less categorical claim perhaps than that made by Sartre in 1948—that Af. and Antillean poetries were the only true "revolutionary" poetries of those times. But the variety of poetic experience conveyed by Af. poets in Fr. confirms that Af. cultures can speak universally with force and authenticity (see CARIBBEAN, POETRY OF THE [French]; FRANCE, POETRY OF).

III. Portuguese. Af. poetry in Port. is often known as Lusophone Af. poetry, although some resist the term *Lusophone*, claiming it contains colonial overtones. This was arguably the first Af. poetry in a Eur. lang. to be published. Some facetious critics claim the 16th-c. Port. national bard Luís de Camões as the first Port. Af. poet, pointing to his descriptions of the continent in his literary epic *The Lusiads* (1572). The question of who qualifies as an Af. poet of Port. expression became contentious in the period immediately following the independence of the former colonies (1973–75), when the newly formed nations sought to define their own literary canons and claim historical roots that contested Port. cultural hegemony.

It is generally accepted that José da Silva Maia Ferreira (1827–81?), born in Angola and of Port. heritage, was the first poet published in Port.-speaking Africa when he released his *Espontaneidades da minha alma* (Outpourings from My Soul) in 1849. The work is probably the first collection of poems printed in the sub-Saharan region. With the independence of Angola, Mozambique, Cape Verde, Guinea-Bissau, and São Tomé e Príncipe, five increasingly diverse national poetries were born, written mainly in Port. but also, in the case of Cape Verde, Guinea-Bissau, and São Tomé, in local Port.-based creoles.

Precursors of these national poetics, such as Silva Maia Ferreira; Joaquim Cordeiro da Matta (1857–94), a black Angolan poet; and Caetano da Costa Alegre (1864–90) from the island of São Tomé, wrote verse modeled on Eur. styles and themes, though often informed by an Af. consciousness. Some wrote verse reflecting their sense of social reformism and dedication to Port. liberalism. They did not propose independence for the colonies so much as a more progressive Port. empire. Beginning in the 1930s in the Cape Verde Islands and in the 1950s in Angola and Mozambique, however, poems of cultural legitimization and growing social protest, fanned by the winds of nationalism, characterized the literary movements initiated by members of an emerging black and *mestiço* (mixed-race) intelligentsia and their Af.-born or -raised white allies.

On the largely mestiço Cape Verde Islands, a trio of poets—Jorge Barbosa (1902–71), Oswaldo Alcântara (pseud. of Baltasar Lopes da Silva, 1907–89), and Manuel Lopes (1907–2005)—founded in 1936 what became known as the *Claridade* movement, named after the group's arts and culture jour. Under the influence of Brazilian modernism and northeast regionalism, they codified the islands' Creole ethos, giving artistic expression to the prevailing Cape Verdean themes of solitude, the sea, drought, and emigration. This generation reacted to the universalism of poets such as José Lopes (1871–1962), who as well as publishing poetry in Port., wrote poems in Fr. and Eng. and defended the concept of a global Port. nation.

In the Angolan cities of Benguela and esp. Luanda, a thinly veiled nationalist poetics emerged (censorship and police repression precluded outspoken militancy) among black, mestiço, and a few white poets, some of whom would form the nucleus of the Movement of the Liberation of Angola (MPLA), founded in 1956. Poets like Agostinho Neto (1922–79), who was Angola's first president; Viriato da Cruz (1928–73); António Jacinto (1924–91);

Fernando Costa Andrade (1936–2009); and Mário António Fernandes de Oliveira (1934–89) produced poems that called for an independent Angola. Many militant poets, in Mozambique as well as Angola, were also guerrilla fighters. Others fled into exile or paid for their militancy with imprisonment.

Throughout the 1960s until the 1974 military coup that toppled the colonial government in Lisbon, much Af. poetry in Port. was produced underground. Militants distributed their poems clandestinely or published them abroad. Neto wrote surreptitiously in his prison cell in Portugal and managed to smuggle his poems out of the Aljube prison to Kinshasa, Dar es Salaam, Milan, and Belgrade, where they were published in bilingual eds. Only after independence did these poets emerge from secrecy and "return" legitimately to Angola.

In Mozambique, during the two decades before national independence, a few Europeans produced poetry that was a conscious part more of Port. lit. than of Mozambique's incipient cultural expression. Starting in the 1960s, these Euro-Mozambicans, most notably Rui Knopfli (1933–97), born and raised in the colonial city of Lourenço Marques (now Maputo), sought to represent the essence of an Afro-Eur. experience. After Mozambican independence, a debate raged within the new nation's cultural elite as to whether the work of poets like Knopfli belonged in an emerging national canon, with most considering him Port. rather than Mozambican, a position he contested. As might be expected, a poetry of Af. cultural and racial essentialism, whether by black or mixed-race Mozambicans, coincided with the rise of nationalism in the 1950s and 1960s. The mestiço poets José Craveirinha (1922–2003) and Noémia de Sousa (1926–2003) both wrote a number of memorable poems of cultural revindication. Many of the arguments used to exclude Knopfli from the Mozambican canon, most notably his absence from postindependence Mozambique, could equally well apply to de Sousa, who spent much of her life in Europe. However, few readers contest her place in the poetic canon of Mozambique.

Craveirinha, Mozambique's most celebrated writer, is considered one of the greatest Port.-lang. poets of the 20th c. In 2001, he won the Prémio Camões, the highest award granted for lifetime literary contributions to the Port. lang. Unlike many Mozambican poets of his generation, who allowed their political dogmas to dictate their aesthetic programs, Craveirinha repeatedly demonstrated how a profound lyricism could serve the political causes he supported. He was capable of exceptionally moving love poetry as well as political demands to address inequalities and social injustice.

Many of the Port. Af. poets who wrote in the years leading to independence spent some of their formative years in Lisbon. Not surprisingly, Lusophone Negritude poetry appeared there, where these poets shared ideas and influences. Most notably, Francisco José Tenreiro (1921–63), a mestiço from the island of São Tomé who lived most of his life in the Port. capital, emerged as the greatest writer of Negritude poetry in Port. Under the influence of the Harlem Ren., Afro-Cuban Negrism, and francophone poets such as Senghor and Césaire, Tenreiro wrote the poems published posthumously as *Coração em África* (My Heart in Africa, 1964).

Some Angolan writers have proclaimed that their poetry was born in the struggle for liberation, while Negritude was conceived in defeat as a Eur.-based phenomenon that had little to do with Africa. During the decade of anticolonialist wars in Angola, Mozambique, and Guinea-Bissau, poetry became increasingly combative and tendentious. Marcelino dos Santos (b. 1929), a high-ranking member of the Mozambique Liberation Movement (Frelimo), who became its vice president, was at the forefront of militant poets who wrote pamphletary verse that, during the protracted war, served as a didactic instrument as well as a goad to political mobilization. Not noted for its aestheticism, the poetry of this generation is a valuable historical document tracing the ideological concerns of the liberation movement.

In the early years after independence, a multiracial array of poets began seeking new ways to capture poetically the changed realities of their nations. In Angola, Manuel Rui (b. 1941) emerged as one of the most important poetic voices of his generation, writing the verses of the Angolan national anthem. He later concentrated on prose but always in a highly poeticized way. Similarly, Mia Couto (b. 1955) of Mozambique is a poet who became more famous for his extremely lyrical prose. His ling. innovation is so profound and celebrated that it is difficult to categorize him as anything other than a poet. Alda do Espírito Santo (1926–2010), like Rui in Angola, provided the lyrics of the national anthem of São Tomé e Príncipe and became a major literary and political presence in her nation, rising to become the speaker of São Tomé's parliament. In most of the newly independent nations, poetry and politics went hand in hand. This politicized poetry had been born of the independence struggles and continued in the early years of independence in the service of the state. However, it soon became obvious to the practitioners of poetry that the new realities of independence demanded a different kind of poetics, and the next generation of poets became less aligned with, or compromised by, the failings of the liberation movements now in power.

The imperative of new poetic discourses reflecting a changed political reality led Rui, along with fellow Angolans such as Arlindo Barbeitos (b. 1940), Rui Duarte de Carvalho (1941–2010), Jofre Rocha (b. 1941), and David Mestre (1948–97), to experiment with new styles of poetry, which followed political prescriptions less and challenged aesthetic boundaries more. Two of these poets, Duarte de Carvalho and Mestre, were born in Portugal, where Mestre died. In Mozambique, Rui Nogar (1933–93) and Luis Carlos Patraquim (b. 1953); in Cape Verde, Corsino Fortes (b. 1933), Oswaldo Osório (b. 1937), and Arménio Vieira (b. 1941); in Guinea-Bissau, Helder Proença (b. 1956); and in São Tomé, Frederico Gustavo dos Anjos (b. 1954) have all attempted, with varying degrees of success, to shift poetic boundaries away from a collective voice of protest to a more introspective interrogation of the poetic self. In Angola, Duarte de Carvalho has experimented with an integrated form of Af. oral expression and Brazilian concrete poetry, as well as repeatedly playing with the boundaries between literary genres.

Since independence, a number of poets have emerged in each of the five Port.-speaking Af. countries, inflecting the Port. lang. in ways that are often indebted to oral trads. local to their nations. At the same time, from the 1980s onward, and perhaps in response to a nascent questioning of the failure to realize the promises of independence, poetry from Port.-speaking Africa has taken a decidedly self-interrogating turn. Salient practitioners of this different type of poetics, which owes much to Af. and Eur. heritages but also to the political failures and civil strife, include the following: from Angola, Rui Augusto (b. 1958), Ana Paula Tavares (b. 1952), José Luís Mendonça (b. 1955), and Ana de Santana (b. 1960); from Mozambique, Luís Carlos Patraquim, Hélder Muteia (b. 1960), Armando Artur (b. 1962), and Eduardo White (b. 1964); and from Cape Verde, José L. Hopffer Almada (b. 1960), who organized *Mirabilis*, an anthol. of work by some 60 island poets (pub. 1991). Tavares's work has become increasingly popular and more sophisticated. Alongside Conceição Lima (b. 1961) from São Tomé, Vera Duarte (b. 1952) and Dina Salústia (b. 1941) from Cape Verde, and Odete Costa Semedo (b. 1959) from Guinea-Bissau, Tavares has demonstrated that successful and popular poetry in Port.-speaking Africa is no longer the preserve of men. Indeed, women have produced some of the most innovative poetry in the Port. lang. in recent years.

See BRAZIL, POETRY OF; PORTUGAL, POETRY OF.

■ **English.** ***Anthologies***: *West African Verse*, ed. D. Nwoga (1966); *Poems from East Africa*, ed. D. Cook et al. (1971); *The Word Is Here: Poetry from Modern Africa*, ed. K. Kgositsile (1973); *Poems of Black Africa*, ed. W. Soyinka (1975); *A World of Their Own: South African Poets of the Seventies*, ed. S. Gray (1976); *Introduction to East African Poetry*, ed. J. Kariara et al. (1977); *Zimbabwean Poetry in English*, ed. K. Z. Muchemwa (1978); *African Poetry in English*, ed. S. H. Burton et al. (1979); *Summons: Poems from Tanzania*, ed. R. S. Mabala (1980); *Somehow We Survive*, ed. S. Plumpp (1982); *The Return of the Amasi Bird*, ed. T. Couzens et al. (1982); *A New Book of African Verse*, ed. J. Reed et al. (1984); *The Heritage of African Poetry*, ed. I. Okpewho (1984); *When My Brothers Come Home: Poems from Central and Southern Africa*, ed. F. M. Chipasula (1985); *The Fate of Vultures*, ed. M. Zimunya et al. (1989); *The Heinemann Book of African Poetry in English*, ed. A. Maja-Pearce (1990); *The New African Poetry*, ed. T. Ojaide and T. M. Sallah (1999); *The Penguin Book of Modern African Poetry*, ed. G. Moore and U. Beier, 5th ed. (2007); *Bending the Bow: An Anthology of African Love Poetry*, ed. F. Chipasula (2009). ***Bibliographies***: *Bibliography of Creative African Writing*, ed. J. Janheinz et al. (1971); *Black African Literature in English*, ed. B. Lindfors (1979); *New Reader's Guide to African Literature*, ed. H. M. Zell et al., 2d ed. (1983); *Supplement to Black African Literature in English*, 1977–1982, ed. B. Lindfors (1985); *Companion to South African English Literature*, ed. D. Adey et al. (1986). ***Criticism and History***: A. Roscoe, *Mother Is Gold: A Study of West African Literature* (1971); O. R. Dathorne, *The Black Mind: A History of African Literature* (1974); K. Awoonor, *The Breast of the Earth* (1975); R. N. Egudu, *Four Modern*

West African Poets (1977); A. Roscoe, *Uhuru's Fire: African Literature East to South* (1977); G. Moore, *Twelve African Writers* (1980); K. L. Goodwin, *Understanding African Poetry: A Study of Ten Poets* (1982); J. Alvarez-Pereyre, *The Poetry of Commitment in South Africa*, trans. Clive Wake (1984); A. Z. Davies and F. Stratton, *How to Teach Poetry: An African Perspective* (1984); T. O. McLoughlin and F. R. Mhonyera, *Insights: An Introduction to the Criticism of Zimbabwean and Other Poetry* (1984); T. Olafioye, *Politics in African Poetry* (1984); U. Barnett, *A Vision of Order: A Study of Black South African Literature in English (1914–1980)* (1985); *European-Language Writing in Sub-Saharan Africa*, ed. A. S. Gérard, 2 v. (1986); R. Fraser, *West African Poetry: A Critical History* (1986); A. McClintock, "'Azikwelwa' (We Will Not Ride): Politics and Value in Black South African Poetry," *CritI* 13 (1987); E. Ngara, *Ideology and Form in African Poetry* (1990); K. A. Appiah, *In My Father's House* (1992); T. Ojaide, "New Trends in Modern African Poetry," *Research in African Literatures* 26 (1995); *Companion to African Literatures*, ed. D. Killam and R. Rowe (2000); A. Irele, *The African Imagination* (2001); J. Ramazani, *The Hybrid Muse: Postcolonial Poetry in English* (2001); R. S. Patke, *Postcolonial Poetry in English* (2006); A. A. Roscoe, *The Columbia Guide to Central African Literature in English since* 1945 (2007); S. Gikandi and E. Mwangi, *The Columbia Guide to East African Literature in English since 1945* (2007); J. Ramazani, *A Transnational Poetics* (2009); S. Egya, "Art and Outrage: A Critical Survey of Recent Nigerian Poetry in English," *Research in African Literatures* 42 (2011).

■ **French**. ***Anthologies***: *Anthologie négro-africaine*, ed. L. Kesteloot (1967); *Poètes d'Afrique et des Antilles*, ed. H. Dia (2002); *Nouvelle anthologie africaine: La poesie*, ed. J. Chevrier (2002); *Nouvelle anthologie africaine II: La poesie*, ed. J. Chevrier (2006). ***Criticism and History***: R. Cornevin, *Littératures d'Afrique noire de langue française* (1976); A. S. Gérard, *European-Writing in Sub-Saharan Africa*, 2 v. (1986); *Dictionnaire des oeuvres littérature négro-africaines de langue française*, ed. A. Kom (1983); A. Rouch and G. Clavreuil, *Littératures nationales d'écriture française* (1986); J. Chevrier, *Littérature nègre* (1999); "Que peut la poésie aujourd'hui?" spec. iss. *Africultures* 24 (2000); P. Nganang, *Manifeste d'une nouvelle littérature africaine* (2007); L. Kesteloot, *Les écrivains noirs de langue française*, 2d ed. (2010).

■ **Portuguese**. ***Anthologies***: *No reino de Caliban: Antologia panorâmica da poesia africana de expressão portuguesa*, ed. M. Ferreira, 3 v. (1975–86); *Antologia temática de poesia africana*, ed. M. de Andrade, 2 v. (1976–79); *Poems from Angola*, ed. and trans. M. Wolfers (1979); *A Horse of White Clouds*, ed. and trans. D. Burness (1989); *For Vasco: Poems from Guinea-Bissau*, trans. A.R.L. Fernandes et al. (2006). ***Bibliography***: *Bibliografia das literaturas africanas de expressão portuguesa*, ed. G. Moser and M. Ferreira (1983). ***Criticism and History***: G. Moser, *Essays in Portuguese-African Literature* (1969); R. Hamilton, *Voices from an Empire: A History of Afro-Portuguese Literature* (1975); M. Ferreira, *Literatura africana de expressão portuguesa*, 2 v. (1977); R. Hamilton, *Literatura africana, literatura necessária*, 2 v. (1981–83); *The Postcolonial Literature of Lusophone Africa*, ed. P. Chabal et al. (1996).

D. F. Dorsey, J. Ramazani (Eng.);
G. Lang (Fr.);
R. G. Hamilton, P. Rothwell (Port.)

AFRIKAANS POETRY. *See* SOUTH AFRICA, POETRY OF

AKKADIAN POETRY. *See* ASSYRIA AND BABYLONIA, POETRY OF

AL-ANDALUS, POETRY OF. Opinions are divided as to whether the Ar. poetry of the Iberian peninsula is truly distinctive within the general field of Ar. poetry. Some scholars point to the prominence of specific themes, such as nature and descriptions of flowers and gardens, as well as to the two types of strophic poem that originated in Al-Andalus, as evidence of the distinctiveness of Ar. poetry; some (Pérès, García Gómez [1946], Armistead [1980], Monroe) claim that it reflects a native Iberian trad. preserved continuously from the Roman period and reemerging later in the poetry of Spain and Portugal. Others point to the continuity of the forms, rhetorical patterns, and themes prevailing in Al-Andalus with those of the Abbasid Empire (750–1258): most poems are monorhymed, are set in quantitative meter according to certain canonical patterns, are phrased in cl. Ar., and employ the rhetorical figures associated with neoclassical Abbasid verse.

The literary dependence of Al-Andalus on Abbasid Baghdad is epitomized in the career of Abū al-Ḥassan ʿAlī ibn Nafayni (known as Ziryāb), a 9th-c. CE Iranian polymath who, arriving in Córdoba, used the prestige of his origins to set the court fashions in poetry, music, and manners in accordance with those of Baghdad. By the time of the establishment of the Umayyad caliphate of Córdoba in ca. 930 CE, the strophic *muwashshaḥ* had emerged as a distinctive local contribution to Ar. poetry, the only strophic form ever to be cultivated to any great extent by poets writing in cl. Ar. The originator of the genre is thought to be either Muḥammad Maḥmud al-Qabrī (ca. 900 CE) or Ibn ʿAbd Rabbihi (ca. 860–940 CE).

The muwashshaḥ consists of five to seven strophes, each in two parts (*ghuṣn* [pl. *aghṣān*] and *simṭ* [pl. *asmāṭ*]). The aghṣān all have the same metrical and rhyming patterns, but the rhyme sound changes from strophe to strophe; the asmāṭ are uniform in meter and in rhyme sound throughout the poem. The poem tends to begin with an opening simṭ. The final simṭ, around which the whole poem was probably composed, is the much-discussed *kharja*. The kharja is written either in vernacular Ar., in Ibero-Romance, or in some combination of the two; and it is generally believed to be a quotation from vernacular songs otherwise lost. Of great interest to Romance philologists as the earliest attestations of lyric poetry in any Ibero-Romance lang., the kharjas are thought by some to point to the existence of Iberian popular poetry predating the Muslim conquest (711 CE), supporting the theory of a continuous Iberian element in Andalusi poetry; but aside from the kharjas themselves, no such poetry is extant.

The metrics of the muwashshaḥ may also point to Romance origin. Though the poems can be scanned in conformity with the quantitative principles of Ar. poetry (*aʿrūḍ*), the metrical patterns only rarely correspond to the canonical ones, and the kharja often resists quantitative analysis altogether. The metrical principle underlying the muwashshaḥ is believed by many to be syllabic (García Gómez 1975, Monroe), though others maintain that it is quantitative, having arisen through the evolution of the *qaṣīda*. Both Hartmann and Stern pointed out that Eastern poets occasionally varied the qaṣīda's monorhyme by subdividing each of the two hemistichs with internal rhyme; the result was the pattern *bbba*, with *a* representing the constant rhyme. When a whole poem has the *bbba* pattern, each line is a miniature stanza. Thus, a subtype of the qaṣīda may have developed into an entirely new verse type. This shift may have occurred under the influence of Romance verse forms reflected in the *villancico* and the rondeau, for unlike cl. Ar. verse, the muwashshaḥ was sung, and Romance musical patterns seem to have played at least some part in shaping it. Another possible source is the stanzaic *musammaṭ* form, which is first attested to in the poetry of Abū Nuwās (d. 815 CE).

Another class of poems thought to be derived from earlier Romance models has survived in the *urjūza* poems on historical themes developed by Ibn ʿAbd Rabbihi and others; these are long poems composed of rhyming distichs in a nonclassical quantitative meter known as *rajaz*. Neither the form nor the theme was an Andalusi invention, however; they were, instead, a direct imitation of an Abbasid model, and these 9th- and 10th-c. poems do not seem to have created a lasting genre.

Though poetry is reported to have been an important feature of Andalusi culture, esp. in the Cordoban court, as it was throughout the Ar.-speaking world, little has survived from the 8th and 9th cs., and what remains is conventional in terms of theme, imagery, and verse patterns. Under the caliphate, however, Córdoba flourished as a literary center, and Andalusi poetry began to outshine even that of the East. The bulk of the poetry was courtly panegyric and lampoon in qaṣīda form, but love poetry was extremely popular, as were descriptions of wine and wine drinking, gardens, and ascetic verse. Great poets include Ibn Hānī (ca. 937–73), Ibn Darrāj al-Qasṭallī (fl. ca. 980), and al-Sharīf al-Ṭalīq (d. 1009). The latter two cultivated flower poetry, which was to become a specialty of later Andalusi poets. They employ an increasingly ornate rhetorical style (*badīʿ*) that originated in the East and is associated with the Abbasid master Abū Tammām (788–845).

The decline of the Cordoban caliphate (1009–31) and the period of the Ṭāʾifa kingdoms (1031–91) saw the greatest achievements of Andalusi poetry. Ibn Shuhayd (fl. ca. 1035) composed a body of passionate and pessimistic verse, as well as an unusual treatise on the nature of poetry in which the narrator visits and converses with the familiar spirits of dead poets. In contrast to the prevailing doctrine of poetry as a learned craft of rhetorically ornamented speech, he propounds an idea of individual poetic inspiration. The theologian and legist Ibn Ḥazm (994–1064) wrote mostly short love verses, more conventional in style, but embodying a spiritual ideal of love closely resembling that of the troubadours and worked out in detail in his prose treatise. Their younger contemporary Ibn Zaydūn (1003–71) composed a body of very individual poetry, esp. the odes arising out of his celebrated love affair with the princess Walāda bint al-Mustakfī (1001–80; also an accomplished poet) that reflect the spiritual ideals of love developed by Ibn Ḥazm. It is from this period, the late 11th c., that muwashshaḥ texts are preserved.

Under the Ṭā'ifa kings, the city states of Al-Andalus vied with each other for preeminence in the arts, esp. poetry. Seville became the city of poets par excellence, boasting the presence of the mature Ibn Zaydūn, Ibn ʿAmmār (1031–86), Ibn al-Labbana (d. 1113), and Ibn Hamdīs (ca. 1056–1133); its last Arab ruler, al-Muʿtamid Ibn ʿAbbād (1040–95), the patron of all these, was himself a gifted poet. This efflorescence of poetry was partly made possible by a policy of relative religious tolerance common at the Ṭā'ifa courts, but the Almoravids (1091–1145) introduced a fundamentalist regime that suppressed secular arts. A few great poets, trained in the earlier period, flourished, such as the nostalgic nature poet Ibn Khafāja (1058–1138), Ibn ʿAbdūn (d. 1134) of Évora, the muwashshaḥ poet Abū al-Abbas al-Amā al-Tutīlī (d. 1126), and the opaque Ibn al-Zaqqāq (1100–33); but it was also an age of anthologists. Nevertheless, the period saw the invention, probably by Ibn Bājja (early 12th c.), of the *zajal* and its full flowering in the works of Ibn Quzmān (1078–1160). These are strophic poems, similar to muwashshaḥ in that the strophes have one element whose rhyme changes from strophe to strophe and another with constant rhyme, but the lang. is colloquial Andalusi Ar., the final simṭ is not different from the rest of the poem, and there may be more than seven strophes; the asmāṭ also have only half the number of lines in the opening simṭ. The vulgar lang. of the zajal complements its theme, the bawdy, colorful life of taverns and streets, observed and turned into lit. by sophisticated poets of aristocratic origin who mock the conventions of courtly love and courtly poetry. The form was probably adapted from vulgar poetry. Apparently as a secondary devel., a type of zajal arose resembling the muwashshaḥ in everything but lang. Both types are already present in the works of Ibn Quzmān.

Under the Almohads (1145–1223), there was a revival of poetry: the great poets were al-Ruṣāfī (d. 1177); the converted Jew Abū Ishāq Ibrahīm ibn Sahl of Seville (1212–52); Ḥāzim al-Qarṭājannī (1211–85), whose work on the theory of poetry was also influential; and a famous woman poet, Ḥafsa bint al-Ḥajj al-Rakuniyya (1135–91). The most original devel., however, was the mystical poetry of Ibn ʿArabī (1165–1240), which derived its imagery from secular love poetry and its diction from the highly metaphorical style of the age. The final political phase of Al-Andalus, the Kingdom of Granada (1248–1492), produced a few important poets, incl. Ibn al-Khaṭīb (1313–74) and Ibn Zamrak (1333–93), whose poems embellish the Alhambra.

The similarity of some of the strophic patterns of Arabo-Andalusi poetry and the notions of love sung by Andalusi poets to those of the troubadours has led some to see Ar. poetry as the inspiration of the troubadours (Nykl). The exact relationship of Andalusi poetry to the troubadour lyric continues to be the subject of intense scholarly debate (Boase, Menocal 1987), as also is the problem of the zajal's influence on the Galician-Port. *cantigas*.

See ARABIC POETRY; PORTUGAL, POETRY OF; SPAIN, POETRY OF.

■ M. Hartmann, *Das arabische Strophengedicht* (1897); A. Cour, *Un poète arabe d'Andalousie: Ibn Zaïdoûn* (1920); R. Menéndez Pidal, "Poesía árabe y poesía europea," *Bulletin hispanique* 40 (1938); E. García Gómez, *Un eclipse de la poesía en Sevilla* (1945) and *Poemas arábigoandaluces*, 3d ed. (1946); A. R. Nykl, *Hispano-Arabic Poetry and Its Relations with the Old Provençal Troubadours* (1946); A. J. Arberry, *Moorish Poetry* (1953); Ibn Ḥazm, *The Ring of the Dove*, trans. A. J. Arberry (1953); H. Pérès, *La poésie andalouse en arabe classique au XIe siècle*, 2d ed. (1953); P. Le Gentil, *Le Virelai et le villancico* (1954); S. Fiore, *Über die Beziehungen zwischen der arabischen und der fruhitalienischen Lyrik* (1956); P. Le Gentil, "La Strophe zadjalesque, les khardjas et le problème des origines du lyrisme roman," *Romania* 84 (1963)—judicious review of research to 1963; W. Heinrichs, *Arabische Dichtung und Griechische Poetik* (1969); Ibn Shuhayd, *Treatise of Familiar Spirits and Demons*, ed. and trans. J. T. Monroe (1971); E. García Gómez, *Todo Ben Quzman* (1972); J. M. Solà-Solé, *Corpus de poesía mozárabe* (1973); J. T. Monroe, *Hispano-Arabic Poetry* (1974); S. M. Stern, *Hispano-Arabic Strophic Poetry* (1974); M. Frenk, *La jarchas mozárabes y los comienzos de la lírica románica* (1975); E. García Gómez, *Las jarchas de la serie árabe en su marco*, 2d ed. (1975); R. Scheindlin, *Form and Structure in the Poetry of al-Muʾtamid Ibn ʿAbbad* (1975); L. F. Compton, *Andalusian Lyrical Poetry and Old Spanish Love Songs* (1976); R. Boase, *The Origin and Meaning of Courtly Love* (1977); R. Hitchcock, *The Kharja: A Critical Bibliography* (1977); M. Frenk, *Estudios sobre lírica antigua* (1978); E. García Gómez, *El libro de las banderas de los campeones de Ibn Saʾid al Magribi*, 2d ed. (1978); S. G. Armistead, "Some Recent Developments in Kharja Scholarship," *La Corónica* 8 (1980); *GRLMA* 2.1.46–73; M. R. Menocal, "The Etymology of Old Provençal *trobar, trobador*," *RPh* 36 (1982–83); Ibn Quzmān, *El cancionero hispanoárabe*, trans. F. Corriente Córdoba (1984); M. R. Menocal, *The Arabic Role in Medieval Literary History* (1987); D. C. Clarke, "The Prosody of the Hargas," *La Corónica* 16 (1987–88); M. J. Rubiera Mata, *Poesía femenina hispanoárabe* (1989); C. Addas, "L'œuvre poétique d'Ibn ʿArabī et sa réception," *Studia Islamica* 91 (2000); A. P. Espósito, "The Monkey in the Jarcha: Tradition and Canonicity in the Early Iberian Lyric," *Journal of Medieval and Early Modern Studies* 30 (2000); T. Rosen, "The Muwashshah," *The Literature of Al-Andalus*, ed. M. R. Menocal, R. Scheindlin, and M. Sells (2000); S. G. Armistead, "Kharjas and Villancicos," and R. K. Farrin, "The 'Nūniyya' of Ibn Zaydūn: A Structural and Thematic Analysis," *Journal of Arabic Literature* 34 (2003); F. Corriente, "Again on (Partially) Romance Andalusi ʿKharajāt," *Journal of Arabic Literature* 35 (2004); H. L. Heijkoop and Otto Zwartjes, *Muwaššaḥ, Zajal, Kharja: Bibliography of Strophic Poetry and Music from Al-Andalus and Their Influence in East and West* (2004).

R. P. Scheindlin; V. Barletta

ALBANIA, POETRY OF. Albanian is an IE lang. spoken in Albania, Kosovo, and surrounding areas in the southwestern part of the Balkan Peninsula. Albania attained its independence in 1912 after five centuries as part of the Ottoman Empire.

The beginnings of written verse in Albania are strongly linked to the Catholic Church. Pjetër Budi (1566–1622), from the Mati area, trained for the priesthood at the Illyrian College of Loretto, south of Ancona in Italy, and was later bishop of Sapa and Sarda in the Zadrima region. His major publication, a catechism titled *Dottrina Christiana* (Christian Doctrine, 1618), has an appendix of 53 pages of religious poetry in Albanian, some 3,000 lines. This verse, incl. both trans. from Lat. and original Albanian poems in quatrain form, is octosyllabic, which is the standard in Albanian folk verse. Budi prefers biblical themes, eulogies, and universal motifs such as the inevitability of death. Though his rhymes are not always elegant, his verse evinces an authenticity of feeling and genuine human concern for the sufferings of a misguided world.

The Ottoman invasion and occupation of Albania, starting in the late 14th c., brought about the gradual demise of this early Catholic poetry. It was replaced by *aljamiado* verse, written in Ar. script and strongly influenced by Islamic culture. Muslim poets wrote initially in Ottoman Turkish, but by the mid-18th c., they were experimenting in Albanian as well. Among the leading literary figures of this period was Nezim Frakulla (ca. 1680–1760), from the Fier region. Nezim writes proudly that he was the first person to compose a *divan* in Albanian: "Who bade the divan speak Albanian? / Nezim has made it known, / Who bade clarity speak in Albanian? / Nezim has made it human." About 110 of his poems are preserved, all replete with vocabulary of Turkish and Persian origin.

Leaving aside the Italo-Albanian poets of southern Italy, such as Giulio Variboba (1724–88), Nicola Chetta (ca. 1740–1803), Girolamo De Rada (1814–1903), and Giuseppe Serembe (1844–1901), who all made substantial contributions to the evolution of Albanian verse, we first note a revival of verse in Albania itself in the late 19th c., during the *Rilindja* period of national renaissance. Among the leading figures of this movement for national identity and political autonomy were Pashko Vasa (1825–92) of Shkodra, whose poem *O moj Shqypni, e mjera Shqypni* (O Albania, Poor Albania), a stirring appeal for national awakening, was written in the dramatic years of the League of Prizren, 1878–80; and Naim Frashëri (1846–1900), now widely regarded as Albania's national poet. Frashëri's verse, published for the most part while he was living in Constantinople and very popular among Albanians at the time, included pastoral lyrics in the trad. of Virgil, heavily laden with the imagery of his mountain homeland; historical epics; and Bektashi religious verse.

A qualitative step forward occurred in the early decades of the 20th c., when the Albanian lang. first became widespread in education and publishing. Though the romantic nationalism of the Rilindja period was still popular, other themes were introduced, incl. love poetry, which initially caused quite a scandal. Among the leading poets of the early decades were Anton Zako Çajupi (1866–1930), who was active in Egypt; Ndre Mjeda (1866–1937) of Shkodra, whose collection *Juvenilia* (1917), influenced by the 19th-c. It. classics, included sonnets and other verse in refined meters; and Asdreni (1872–1947), from the southeastern Korça region, whose first three verse collections were well received.

The greatest figure of Albanian verse before World War II was Gjergj Fishta (1871–1940), whose 15,000-line verse epic of Albanian history, *Lahuta e Malcís* (*The Highland Lute*, 1937), caused him to be revered as the Albanian Homer. When the Communists took power in 1944, his work was swiftly repressed, and the very mention of his name was taboo for 46 years.

Two poets, entirely different from one another, may be regarded as the vanguards of modernity in Albanian lit. The messianic Migjeni (1911–38) of Shkodra turned away from the beauty of the Albanian mountains and the sacred trads. of the nation to devote his verse to the social realities of despair and ubiquitous squalor, against which he rose in defiance. His slender collection *Vargjet e Lira* (Free Verse, 1944), published posthumously, represented a literary revolution and a breath of fresh air that did away with the trads. of romantic nationalism for good. Lasgush Poradeci (1899–1987), a pantheistic poet from Pogradec on Lake Ohrid, studied the ever-changing moods of the lake to offer crystalline verse in southern Albanian folk style.

Albanian written culture and verse reached a zenith in the 1930s and early 1940s. A mod. lit. had been created, and the nation had come of age. However, it was a brief blossoming in the shadow of an apocalypse. The Stalinist takeover and purges under dictator Enver Hoxha (1908–85) caused terror in intellectual circles and snuffed out imaginative writing in the country for almost 20 years. Only Martin Camaj (1925–92), in Bavarian exile, and the unfettered poets of Kosovo were left to build on established trads.

By the early 1960s, a new generation of poets in Albania, led by Fatos Arapi (b. 1930), Dritëro Agolli (b. 1931), and Ismail Kadare (b. 1936), managed to slip elements of aesthetic finesse into their volumes of obligatory and otherwise stale partisan poetry. There was no thaw in Albanian verse during the Communist period (1944–89); but cautious openings, ever so slight, enabled some verse of quality to be published, and it immediately caught the imagination of the beleaguered public.

Ideological restrictions vanished when the Stalinist regime imploded in 1989–90, and chaos reigned in the little Balkan country for a decade. Yet, despite the harsh conditions of a free-market economy, contemp. poetry lost none of its fundamental importance in Albanian national culture. Well into the 21st c., verse collections still account for more than 50% of literary output. Albania is and remains a land of poets.

■ G. Schirò, *Storia della letteratura albanese* (1959); A. Pipa, *Albanian Literature: Social Perspectives* (1978) and *Contemporary Albanian Literature* (1991); *An Elusive Eagle Soars: Anthology of Modern Albanian Poetry*, ed. R. Elsie (1993); R. Elsie, *History of Albanian Literature* (1995) and *Studies in Modern Albanian Literature and Culture* (1996); A. Zotos, *Anthologie de la poésie albanaise* (1998); R. Elsie, *Albanian Literature: A Short History* (2005); *Songs of the Frontier Warriors, Këngë Kreshnikësh: Albanian Epic Verse* (2004) and *Lightning from the Depths: An Anthology of Albanian Poetry* (2008) ed. and trans. R. Elsie and J. Mathie-Heck.

R. Elsie

AMERICAN INDIAN POETRY. *See* INDIGENOUS AMERICAS, POETRY OF THE; INUIT POETRY; NAVAJO POETRY

AMERICAN POETRY. *See* UNITED STATES, POETRY OF THE

AMERIND POETRY. *See* INDIGENOUS AMERICAS, POETRY OF THE

AMHARIC POETRY. *See* ETHIOPIA, POETRY OF

ARABIC POETICS

I. Classical
II. Modern

I. Classical. The first Ar. works on poetics were composed at the end of the 9th and beginning of the 10th c. Four groups of scholars were in varying degrees instrumental in shaping this new literary genre: the experts on ancient poetry, the poets and critics of mod. poetry (for ancient versus mod., see below), the Qur'anic scholars, and the (Aristotelian) logicians. Earlier, the pre-Islamic poets very likely had had a professional lang. for technical features of their poetry, and there are reports about comparative evaluation of poets, but none of this amounts to an explicit *ars poetica.*

In the field of poetry, two devels. are noteworthy. First, ancient, (i.e., pre- and early Islamic) poetry became canonized as a corpus of cl. texts. This meant that ancient poetry was considered a repository of correct and authoritative speech. As such, it became the domain of the philologists, who, around the middle of the 8th c., began to collect the extant poetry into *dīwāns* and anthols.; to these they later added interlinear glosses on lexical and grammatical matters. Once the task of editing and writing commentaries had been mostly achieved, we do find one book that may be called a grammarian's poetics: the *Qawāʿidal-shiʿr* (Foundations of Poetry) ascribed to the Kufan grammarian Thaʿlab (d. 291/904—dates refer to the Muslim and the Common eras, respectively). This is a logically arranged collection of technical terms often provided with definitions and always exemplified with a number of *shawāhid* (evidentiary verses). Significantly, it starts with an enumeration of four basic types of sentences (command, prohibition, report, question) that are introduced as the "foundations of poetry," and it ends with a verse typology based on the syntactic independence or interdependence of the two hemistichs of the line in which the highest aesthetic value is accorded those lines that have two independently meaningful hemistichs. This atomistic approach to the study and evaluation of poetry prevails in most of the theoretical lit.

The second notable event that had a decisive (indeed, greater) effect on the devel. of poetics and literary theory was the rise, around the middle of the 8th c., of a new school of poetry: the *muḥdathūn* (moderns). By contrasting them with their forebears, the *qudamāʾ* (ancients), critics and theorists became aware of some of the basic dichotomies in poetry. It should be noted, however, that the model of ancient poetry was never seriously challenged, which meant that the innovations of the moderns leaned toward mannerism and relied heavily on earlier poetry. Critical discussions focused on a phenomenon called *badīʿ*—literally, "new, original, newly invented." The earliest attestations of the word suggest that it was originally used to refer to a special type of metaphor (imaginary ascriptions such as "the *claws* of death") that played an important role in the poetic technique of the moderns, who created some outrageous—and severely criticized—specimens (e.g., "the eyes of religion were cooled," meaning that the Islamic armies were victorious). However, the term soon spread to other figures of speech. The poet Ibn al-Muʿtazz (d. 296/908), who devoted the first monograph to this topic, *Kitāb al-Badīʿ* (The Book of the Novel [Style]), proposed five figures to be covered by the term—metaphors of the kind just mentioned, paronomasia, antithesis, epanalepsis (or epanadiplosis), and playful dialectics imitating theological jargon. The main goal of his book is to demonstrate that the badīʿ phenomena are not new but can be found already in ancient poetry as well as in the Qurʾan and in wisdom aphorisms; it is only their exaggerated use that is truly new.

Coming from one of the foremost poets of his time, this line of argument obviously served to legitimize the use of badīʿ. Ibn al-Muʿtazz's book became influential in several ways: (1) the discipline dealing with rhetorical figures was named "the science of badīʿ" after the title of his book; (2) the discovery of legitimizing precedent in ancient texts, esp. the Qurʾan, became commonplace, and as a result, the system of the rhetorical figures came to be considered an integral and static part of the lang.: their proliferation in later rhetorical works was thus thought to be due to closer analysis rather than new invention; (3) the emphasis on figures of speech as the central concern of literary theory originated here; and (4) the difference between poetry and prose in most respects, save the purely formal one, was considered unimportant.

The result of factor (4) in particular meant that, although works on literary theory—mostly rhetorical in outlook—continued to be produced, works on poetics proper tended to become the exception. Two of them were composed by younger contemporaries of Ibn al-Muʿtazz, one by the poet Ibn Ṭabāṭabā (d. 322/934), titled *ʿIyār al-shiʿr* (The Standard of Poetry), the other by the state scribe and logician Qudāma ibn Jaʿfar (d. after 320/932). Although Ibn Ṭabāṭabā did not use the word *badīʿ* in its technical sense, he is well aware of the predicament of the moderns, who can no longer simply utter truths, as did the ancients, but have to display their wits in a subtle treatment of well-known motifs. He is also remarkable for giving a step-by-step description of the production of a poem; this is quite rare because works on poetics usually offer theories of poetic crit. rather than *artes poeticae* in the strict sense.

This characterization is esp. true of Qudāma's poetics, which the author describes as the first book on the "science of the good and the bad in poetry" and aptly titles *Naqd al-shiʿr* (The Assaying of Poetry). His work is at the same time the first representative of the third approach to literary theory (besides the grammatical and the poetic already mentioned), namely, that of the logician in the Aristotelian trad. This characterization refers, however, less to the content than to the structure and presentation of his work: he starts with a definition ("Poetry is metrical, rhymed utterance pointing to a meaning") that yields the four constitutive elements: meter, rhyme, wording, and meaning. He then discusses first the good qualities of these elements and their combinations, followed by the bad. Although Qudāma was much quoted by later authors, his "foreign" method did not find followers.

The controversies about the mod. poets' use of badīʿ, though reflected in theory, can more accurately be gauged from works of applied crit. such as the books devoted to the controversial "rhetorical" poets Abū Tammām (d. 231/845) and al-Mutanabbī (d. 354/965). The major topics that emerge are the following: (1) The relationship between *ṭabʿ* (natural talent) and *ṣanʿa* (artful or artificial crafting). The latter term came to mean the application of badīʿ to the motif at hand. According to taste and predilection, some considered this *takalluf* (constraint, artificiality), while others pointed to the element of *taʿjīb* (causing amazement) that it imparted to well-known motifs. Given the general drift toward mannerism, this was a much sought-after effect. (2) The role of *lafẓ* (wording) versus *maʿnā* (meaning) in poetry. Already at the end of the 8th c., a consensus had been reached that poetry was to be judged by its wording, since the meaning was nothing but the material to be shaped. Some authorities are said to have given precedence to the meaning, but on closer inspection, it appears that they intended the *maʿnā al-ṣanʿa* (the special meaning created by the application of a figure of speech; this comes close to the conceit in Western mannerist poetry and thus did not undermine the priority of the wording. (3) The relationship between poetry and reality, whether *ṣidq* (truth) or *kadhib* (falsehood). In general, poetry is presumed to depict reality mimetically. Obvious "falsehoods" such as imaginary metaphors and hyperboles, therefore, tended to provoke objections on the part of the critics. Such figures became so predominant in later Abbasid poetry, however, that some theorists (Ibn Fāris, Ibn Ḥazm) posited falsehood as one of the constituent elements of poetry. (4) Regarding the question of *sariqa* (plagiarism), although this word means "theft" and originally denoted flagrant literary larceny, with the increasing tendency toward mannerism in mod. poetry, sariqa became a way of life, and the disreputable connotation of the term gave way to the more neutral one of "taking over" (an earlier motif); critics even began to talk of "good sariqas." Taking over an earlier poet's motif and improving on it, mostly by the application of badīʿ, constituted an *istiḥqāq* (better claim [to that motif]), for which the poet earned high praise.

Ar. poetics, fostered by the rise of mod. poetry, soon experienced something like arrested growth. The work of the Qurʾanic scholar and grammarian al-Rummānī (d. 384/994), *al-Nukat fī iʿjāz al-Qurʾān* (Thoughtful Remarks on the Inimitability of the Qurʾan), in which he undertook to prove this dogma on the basis of the Qurʾan's *balāgha* (eloquence), soon began to influence works on poetics and rhetorical figures. The first major compilation that resulted, the *Kitāb al-ṣināʿatayn* (Book of the Two Crafts [i.e., poetry and prose]) by Abū Hilāl al-ʿAskarī (d. 395/1004), expressly mentions proving the inimitability of the Qurʾan as its main goal and makes extensive use of al-Rummānī's work. The confluence of the two different technical terminologies, *Qurʾanic* and *poetic*, at first created a notable confusion that was only gradually eliminated, esp. by the greatest of all Ar. literary theorists, ʿAbd al-Qāhir al-Jurjānī (d. 471/1078). In his *Asrār al-balāgha* (The Mysteries of Eloquence), he tried to establish a clear and unambiguous taxonomy for the theory of imagery (simile, analogy, metaphor based on simile, metaphor based on analogy); and for the first time, he finds, designates, and describes the phenomenon of *takhyīl* (fantastic interpretation, i.e., inventing imaginary causes, effects, and proofs, often on the basis of metaphors taken literally)—which is so characteristic of later Abbasid poetry. Although not a comprehensive work on poetics, the "Mysteries" certainly is the most sustained effort to reach to the core of Ar. poetry.

Al-Jurjānī's books, the one just mentioned and his *Dalāʾil al-iʿjāz* (Signs for the Inimitability), were later reworked into parts of the scholastic *ʿilm al-balāgha* (science of eloquence) which, from the 13th c. on, dominated the teaching of rhet.—consisting of stylistics, theory of imagery, and figures of speech—in the institutions of higher learning. Poetics was thus incorporated into a discipline that served the religious purpose of demonstrating the inimitability of the Qurʾan, whence it ceased to exist in its own right.

Some theoretical and critical works were produced outside the Qurʾanic trad. One of them, *al-ʿUmda* (The Pillar), by the poet Ibn Rashīq (d. 456/1063 or later), deserves to be cited as a comprehensive handbook for poets that contains well-informed accounts of all the major topics in poetics mentioned above.

A fascinating, though not very influential, sideline of the lit. on poetics was created by Maghribi authors of the late 13th c., who, to various degrees, showed interest in "logical" poetics, i.e., the Aristotelian *Rhetoric* and *Poetics* as part of the *Organon*, a late Alexandrian trad. that was adopted into Ar. logical writings. The most sophisticated among these authors is Ḥāzim al-Qarṭājannī (d. 1285), who adopted the two central terms of logical poetics, "creation of images in the mind of the listener" (*takhyīl*) and "imitating the object of the poem by means of artful description" (*muḥākāt*), in order to identify the cornerstones of the poetic enterprise.

II. Modern. From the 13th to the 18th c., Ar. poetics tended to reflect the priorities of the audience for the lit. of the period: the intellectual elite at the various centers of political authority. Elaborating on earlier devels. in poetics, commentators and anthologizers placed primary emphasis on the formalities of rhet. and the compilation of ever-expanding lists of poetic devices and themes. It was the task of pioneers in the 19th c., such as Ḥusayn al-Marṣafī (1815–90), to revive interest in the great cl. works of poetics. However, such exercises in neoclassical revival gradually receded into the background, superseded by the increasing domination of Western literary genres and critical approaches.

From the first intimations of what has been termed *preromanticism* with poets such as Khalīl Muṭrān (1872–1949), Ar. poetry and poetics have undergone what Jabrā has termed a series of "rapid chain explosions of Eur. culture." The poetics of romanticism are reflected in works such as *Al-Ghurbāl* by Mīkhāʾīl Nuʿayma (1889–1988) and *Al-Dīwān* by two Egyptian critics, Al-ʿAqqād (1889–1964) and al-Māzinī (ca. 1889–1949). The application of Western critical approaches, predominantly Fr. and Eng., to the lit. is also evident in the writings of critics such as Ṭāhā Ḥusayn (1889–1973), Mārūn ʿAbbūd (1886–1962), and Muḥammad Mandūr (1907–65).

Following World War II and the achievement of independence by many Arab nations, lit. of "commitment" (*iltizām*) became *de rigueur* and was much reflected in critical writings. The Lebanese literary periodical *Al-ādāb*, founded by Suhayl Idrīs in Beirut in 1953, had "commitment" as its major guiding force and continues to serve as a major conduit and catalyst for trends in mod. Ar. poetics. In that role, it has since been joined by a number of other jours., most prominent among which is *Fuṣūl*, published in Cairo. More recently, growing interest in literary theory, ling., and folklore has led to significant changes in approach to the Ar. literary trad. as a whole. Numerous Western studies in semiotics, structuralism, poststructuralism, postcolonial poetics, feminist crit., and reception theory have been read by Arab critics either in the original or in the rapidly increasing library of such works in trans. The emergence of these new disciplines and approaches can be seen in the publication of critical and theoretical studies that not only reconsider the nature and precepts of the Ar. literary canon (e.g., in the realms of popular narrative and prosody) but address genres from all periods of the trad. in entirely new ways. In a number of works, the major poet-critic Adūnis (pseud. of ʿAlī Aḥmad Saʿīd Asbar, b. 1930) has devoted himself to a detailed investigation of the issue of modernity itself and the reinterpretation of the past. In his writings and those of many others, this process, at once highly controversial and stimulating, continues to have a profound effect on both the poetic trad. and on attitudes toward the adoption of various modes of interpretation.

In 1972, Adūnis was reflecting a cultural trad. of long standing in titling one of his studies *Zaman al-shiʿr* (Poetry's Time). In such a context, it may be seen as a deliberate indication of a shift in that trad. that, in 1999, the Egyptian critic Jābir ʿUsfūr (Gaber Asfour) published a work on the novel titled *Zaman al-riwāya* (The Novel's Time). The predominance of visual media in the societies of the Ar.-speaking world has indeed led to a change of balance in the markets for poetic and narrative modes of expression. There has been a concomitant rise of critical interest in the study of narratology, at the hands of scholars such as Saʿīd Yaqṭīn (Morocco), ʿUsfūr (Egypt), Yumnā al-ʿĪd (Lebanon), and Faysal Darrāj (Palestine and Syria), among many others. In the realm of poetry and poetics, a relatively new phenomenon has been a critical concentration on more popular forms of poetic expression and their modes of performance and reception.

■ **Classical:** I. Goldziher, "Alte und neue Poesie im Urtheile der arabischen Kritiker," *Abhandlungen zur arabischen Philologie* 1 (1896, rpt. 1982), ch. 2; G. E. von Grunebaum, "Arabic Literary Criticism in the 10th Century A.D.," *JAOS* 61 (1941); and "The Concept of Plagiarism in Arabic Theory," *Journal of Near Eastern Studies* 3 (1944); *A Tenth-Century Document of Arabic Literary Theory and Criticism: The Sections on Poetry of al-Bâqillânî's I ʾjâz al-Qurʾân*, ed. G. E. von Grunebaum (1950); A. Trabulsi, *La Critique poétique des Arabes jusqu'au Ve siècle de l'Hégire (XIe siècle de J.-C.)* (1955); I. Y. Krachkovsky, "Deux Chapitres inédits de l'oeuvre de Kratchkovsky sur Ibn al-Muʿtazz," *Annales de l'Institut des Études Orientales* (Algiers) 20 (1962); W. Heinrichs, *Arabische Dichtung und griechische Poetik* (1969), and "Literary Theory—the Problem of Its Efficiency," *Arabic Poetics: Theory and Development*, ed. G. E. Von Grunebaum (1973); S. A. Bonebakker, *Materials for the History of Arabic Rhetoric from the Ḥilyat al-muḥāḍara of Ḥātimī* (1975); J. E. Bencheikh, *Poétique arabe* (1975)—additional preface, 1989; V. Cantarino, *Arabic Poetics in the Golden Age* (1975)—anthol. in trans., with introductory essays often ignorant of earlier lit.; W. Heinrichs, *The Hand of the Northwind: Opinions on Metaphor and the Early Meaning of Istiʿāra in Arabic Poetics* (1977); K. Abu Deeb, *Al-Jurjānī's Theory of Poetic Imagery* (1979); G. J. van Gelder, *Beyond the Line: Classical Arabic Literary Critics on the Coherence and Unity of the Poem* (1982); A. Arazi, "Une Épître d'Ibrāhīm ben Hilāl al-Ṣābī; sur les genres littéraires," *Studies in Islamic History and Civilization in Honour of David Ayalon*, ed. M. Sharon (1986); I. ʿAbbās, *Taʾrīkh al-naqd al-adabī ʿind al-ʿarab*, rev. ed. (1993);W. Heinrichs, "*Takhyīl*: Make-Believe and Image Creation in Arabic Literary Theory," *Takhyīl: The Imaginary in Classical Arabic Poetics*, Part 1: *Texts*, ed. and trans. G. J. van Gelder and M. Hammond; Part 2: *Studies*, ed. G. J. van Gelder and M. Hammond (2008); W. Heinrichs, "Early Ornate Prose and the Rhetorization of Poetry in Arabic Literature," *Literary and Philosophical Rhetoric in the Greek, Roman, Syriac, and Arabic Worlds*, ed. F. Woerther (2009).

■ **Modern:** D. Semah, *Four Modern Egyptian Critics* (1974); Adūnis, *Al-Thābit wa-al-mutanawwil*, 3 v. (1974–79); S. al-Jayyusi, *Trends and Movements in Modern Arabic Poetics* (1977); I. J. Boullata, "Adūnis: Revolt in Modern Arabic Poetics," *Edebiyât* 2 (1977); J. Jabrā, "Modern Arabic Literature and the West," *Critical Perspectives on Modern Arabic Literature*, ed. I. J. Boullata (1980); Adūnis, *Introduction to Arabic Poetics*, trans. C. Cobham (1990); I. J. Boullata, *Trends and Issues in Contemporary Arab Thought* (1990); S. Somekh, *Genre and Language in Modern Arabic Literature* (1991); R. Snir, *Modern Arabic Literature: A Functional Dynamic Model* (2001); *Arabischen Literatur postmodern*, ed. A. Neuwirth, A. Pflitsch, B. Winckler (2004).

W. P. Heinrichs (cl.); R.M.A. Allen (mod.)

ARABIC POETRY

I. Introduction
II. Sixth to Thirteenth Centuries
III. Thirteenth to Eighteenth Centuries
IV. Nineteenth and Twentieth Centuries

I. Introduction. Until relatively recently, poetry has served as the predominant mode of literary expression among those who speak and write in Ar. Poetry was, in the traditional phrase, "*dīwān al-ʿarab*," the register of the Arabs, and poets had and continue to have a particular status in their own community. The Ar. word for poetry, *shiʿr*, is derived from the verb denoting a special kind of knowledge that was believed in the earliest times to have magical or mantic properties. While poetry has afforded poets the opportunity for personal expression, it has been more often than not a *public* phenomenon, whether addressed to the tribe of ancient times, the patron during the predominance of the caliphate and the many dynasties of the med. Islamic world, or the many political causes of the present-day Middle East.

Most hists. of Ar. poetry have adopted a dynastic approach based primarily on political and social devels., concentrating mainly on the poets, their role in society, and their themes. This approach serves to illustrate the close links between poetry and poetics on the one hand and divisions of the Islamic sciences on the other. However, while biblio. sources provide evidence of the richness of the trad. available to us, they also make clear not only that large amounts of poetry are lost to us but that much more poetry remains unpublished and unassessed within the critical canon. Further, the hist. of Ar. poetry has recently been undergoing a reevaluation, based on two interlinked phenomena. First, Ar. poetry itself has been going through a period of transformation and radical experimentation since the beginning of the 1950s: this process has led some critics to attempt a redefinition of what poetry is (or should be) and therefrom to initiate projects aimed at a reassessment of the corpus of cl. Ar. poetry. Second, critics have applied new ideas in analysis and theory—e.g., structuralism, oral-formulaic and genre theories, and metrics—to the corpus of Ar. poetry.

II. Sixth to Thirteenth Centuries

A. *The Beginnings: Oral Tradition.* What have been recorded as the beginnings of Ar. poetry are versions of a poetic corpus that is already highly developed in the late 5th c. CE. The trad. is an oral one, similar to that of the Homeric poems and Serbo-Croatian songs analyzed by Milman Parry and Albert Lord. Thus, each poem or rather the differing versions of each poem represent a single, isolated yet privileged point in a long process of devel. and transmission from poet to reciter (*rāwī*). Each poem would have been performed before an audience (perhaps accompanied by music or rhythmic beat) and transmitted through generations from one "singer of tales" to another.

B. *The Poet.* The ability to improvise was (and often still is) part of the craft of Arab poets. Many occasions would arise at which they would extemporize a poem or recite a work from memory. They were important members of the tribe, in effect propagandists, whose role was to extol the tribal virtues—bravery, loyalty, endurance, swiftness of vengeance—and to lampoon the lack of such virtues in the tribe's enemies. The various thematic "genres" used—eulogy, elegy, and satire—all concerned praise or its antithesis. The elegy (*rithā'*) provides some of the most moving examples of the poetic voice, as in the poems of al-Khansā' (d. ca. 644) for her brother, Ṣakhr, killed in tribal combat:

I was sleepless and I passed the night
  keeping vigil, as if my eyes had been
  anointed with pus,
For I had heard—and it was not news to
  rejoice me—one making a report, who
  had come repeating intelligence,
Saying, "Sakhr is dwelling there in a tomb,
  struck to the ground beside the grave,
  between certain stones."
(trans. A. J. Arberry)

The poet used the different genres to depict companionship, the benefits of tribal solidarity, the beauties of women, the qualities of animals, and the joys of wine. Part of this same environment, but from a different social perspective, were several vagabond *ṣuʿlūk* poets such as al-Shanfarā (d. ca. 525), his companion Thābit ibn Jābir (known by his nickname, Ta'abbaṭa Sharran [he who has put evil under his armpit]), and ʿUrwa ibn al-Ward (d. ca. 594). Ostracized from tribal society, they and their peers wrote stirring odes about their ability to withstand prolonged isolation, hunger, and thirst and their feelings of affinity with the wilder animals of the desert, as in this extract from the poem rhyming on the consonant "l" by al-Shanfarā:

To me now, in your default, are
  comrades a wolf untired,
A sleek leopard, and a fell hyena with
  shaggy mane.
True comrades: they ne'er let out the secret
  in trust with them,
Nor basely forsake their friend because he
  brought them bane.
(trans. R. A. Nicholson)

In contrast to this stark vision of life stands that of the courts of the Ghassanids, the tribe that served as a buffer between the Arabs and Byzantium, and the Lakhmids, who fulfilled the same function vis-à-vis Sasanid Iran from their center at al-Ḥīra (in present-day Iraq). To these courts would come not only tribal poets but professional bards like Ṭarafa ibn al-ʿAbd (d. ca. 565) and Maymūn al-Aʿshā (d. 629) in search of patronage and reward for their eulogies.

C. *The Structure of the Poem.* The process of oral transmission and the later recording of poetry in written form have not preserved the stages in the early devel. of the Ar. poem. Thus, we find examples of both the short, monothematic poem (*qiṭʿa*) and the multisectional, polythematic *qaṣīda*. Several examples of the latter came to be highly valued, esp. by the early Muslim caliphs and the ruling Arab aristocracy, which regarded these poems as a source and standard for the study and teaching of the cl. Ar. lang. Seven (and later ten) of the longer odes were gathered into what became the most famous collection of early Ar. poetry, the *Muʿallaqāt.* The *Muʿallaqa* of Imruʾ al-Qays (d. ca. 540) is the most famous poem in the collection and indeed probably in all of Ar. lit. Yet each *Muʿallaqa* manages to reflect its poet's vision of life in pre-Islamic Arabia: that of Zuhayr ibn Abī Sulmā is placed within the context of settling a tribal dispute, while the ode of Labīd (d. ca. 662), with its elaborate animal imagery and concluding aphorisms, is virtually a hymn to tribal values.

Recent analyses of some examples of the pre-Islamic qaṣīda have challenged the received view that its structure is fragmented, a view canonized in part by the conservative critical trad. of *ʿamūd al-shiʿr* (the essentials of poetry). It is now suggested that the choice and ordering of the various segments of these poems reflect the poet's desire to illustrate by conjunction and opposition the glaring contrasts in community life, making these elaborate poems a public event of almost liturgical significance. Thus, the *nasīb* (erotic prelude) of many poems will often be placed within the context of the *aṭlāl*, the section describing the poet's arrival at a deserted encampment. The opening lines of the *Muʿallaqa* of Imruʾ al-Qays are esp. famous: "Halt (you two) and let us weep for memory of a beloved and an abode / In the edge of the sand dune between ad-Dakhul and Hawmal." A transitional section describing a departure or desert journey allows the poet to give a description of his riding animal, which is often elaborate and lengthy, and provides some of the most memorable lines from this corpus of poetry. From this interweaving of segments, the poet will then turn—often by means of aphoristic sentiments—to the purpose of the poem: the bolstering of the community through praise of its virtues, criticism of contraventions of them, and sheer self-aggrandizement as a means of fostering tribal pride and solidarity.

D. ***The Advent of Islam.*** While the advent of Islam brought about radical changes in beliefs and customs in the society of the Arabian Peninsula, the poetic environment changed relatively little. Muhammad himself was not averse to poetry, as sections of *Kitāb al-aghānī* make abundantly clear. Indeed, Ḥassān ibn Thābit (d. 673) is known as "the poet of the Prophet." His contemporary, Kaʿb ibn Zuhayr, the son of the famous pre-Islamic bard Zuhayr ibn Abī Sulmā, composed a famous poem addressed to Muhammad that illustrates the continuation of the poetic trad. into the new social context; the poem is called *al-Burda* (The Cloak), since, upon hearing it, Muhammad is alleged to have placed his cloak around the poet:

> I was told that the Messenger of Allah
> threatened me (with death), but with
> the Messenger of Allah I have hope of
> finding pardon.
> Gently! mayst thou be guided by Him who
> gave thee the gift of the Koran,wherein
> are warnings and a plain setting-out (of
> the matter).
> (trans. R. A. Nicholson)

The spirit of defiance in the face of imminent danger and even death that characterizes much pre-Islamic poetry is also to be found in the odes of poets belonging to groups that broke away from the incipient Muslim community on religious grounds and fought vigorously for their conception of Islam. The poetry of the supporters of the Kharijite cause, such as al-Ṭirimmāḥ (d. ca. 723), and of the Shīʿa, such as Al-Kumayt ibn Zayd (d. 743), is esp. noteworthy in this regard. The pre-Islamic penchant for satire of rivals and enemies finds fertile ground in the tribal squabbles that continue well into the period of the Umayyads (660–750). In a series of increasingly ribald satires (gathered into a collection known as *Al-Naqāʾiḍ*), the poets Jarīr (d. 732) and Al-Farazdaq (d. ca. 730), joined among others by the Christian poet Al-Akhṭal (d. 710), followed the pattern of earlier satirical poetry in both form and imagery and adopted rhetorical strategies characteristic of verbal dueling in the Arab world.

E. ***The Emergence of New Genres.*** The oral transmission of poetry continued into the Islamic period, ensuring that the Arab poet's attachment to many of the themes and images of the desert lingered long after such environments were superseded by the emerging urban centers of the Muslim community. Thus, Dhū al-Rumma (d. 735) was often referred to as "the last of the poets" because he continued to use desert motifs in his poems a century after the advent of Islam. Inevitably, however, the gradual process of change led to the emergence of new priorities expressed in different ways. On the political level, the changes were far-reaching. During the first century or so of Islam, Muslim armies took the religion to the borders of India in the east and across North Africa to Spain in the west. The center of caliphal authority moved out of the Arabian Peninsula first to Damascus under the Umayyads and then to the newly founded city of Baghdad in 756 under the Abbasids. Under the impetus of this vast exercise in cultural assimilation, authors from different areas of the Islamic world began to adapt the traditional Ar. literary forms and to introduce new themes and genres.

Various segments of the qaṣīda gradually evolved into distinct genres. The collected works of poets composed during the first century of Islam begin to contain separate sections devoted to specific categories: hunt poems (*ṭardiyyāt*) and wine poems (*khamriyyāt*)—both of these most notably in the verse of Al-Ḥasan ibn Hāniʾ (d. ca. 810), usually known by his nickname, Abū Nuwās. His wine poetry is noted not only for its disarming lasciviousness but for how he occasionally parodies the desert imagery of the earlier poetry:

> The lovelorn wretch stopped at a (deserted) camping-ground to question it,
> and I stopped to enquire after the local tavern.
> May Allah not dry the eyes of him that wept over stones, and may He not
> ease the pain of him that yearns to a tent-peg.
>
> (trans. R. A. Nicholson)

The blind poet Bashshār ibn Burd (d. 784) displayed a similar impatience with Arabian conventions, though in his case it is linked to a desire to express pride in his own Persian ancestry. Another poet of the period, Abū al-Atāhiya (d. 828), is primarily remembered for his moral and ascetic poems (*zuhdiyyāt*).

One of the most remarkable devels. along these lines is that of the love poem (*ghazal*). Soon after the advent of Islam, two distinct trends appear in the Arabian Peninsula. The first, emerging from within the tribal poetic trad., placed the aloof and imperious beloved on a pedestal while the poet suffered the pangs of love from a distance, often leading to a love-death. This trad. is termed *ʿUdhrī* after the Banu ʿUdhra tribe, noted for having many such lovers, among whom was Jamīl (d. 701), one of the most illustrious exponents of ʿUdhrī poetry. Each of these love poets also carried the name of his beloved: Jamīl, e.g., is Jamīl Buthayna, the beloved of Buthayna; other poets of this type are Kuthayyir ʿAzza (d. 723) and, most famous of all, Majnūn Laylā. The other trad., sensual and self-centered, developed in the cities of the Ḥijāz; it is usually associated with its most famous exponent ʿUmar ibn Abī Rabīʿa (d. 719). With the gradual devel. of the genre, the two separate strands fused, as can be seen in the works of poets such as ʿAbbās ibn al-Aḥnaf (d. ca. 807) in the east and Ibn ʿAbd Rabbihi (d. 940) in Al-Andalus (as Islamic Spain was known).

F. *The Badīʿ Style: Imagery and Rhetoric*. During the caliphate of ʿUthmān (d. 644), a generally accepted version of the Qurʾan (Koran) was established in writing, a process that set in motion many intellectual currents later to have a profound effect on poetry. Scholars in Kūfa and Baṣra (both in present-day Iraq) began to prepare the materials needed for authenticating the transmission of the Qurʾan, interpreting its text, and codifying the Ar. lang. in which the sacred text proclaims itself to have been revealed. Anthols. of poetry of different genres and from particular tribes were made, a process that involved the devel. of basic critical terms for the evaluation of literary works. A philologist of Baṣra, Al-Khalīl ibn Aḥmad (d. 791), analyzed the sounds and rhythms of the earliest poetry and set down his results as a set of meters that formed part of a definition of poetry (as "rhymed and metered discourse") that was widely regarded as canonical up to the end of World War II (see ARABIC PROSODY). This philological activity was accompanied by a gradual shift away from the predominantly oral culture of pre-Islamic Arabia toward a society in which verbal art was committed to writing.

Within this environment of compilation, authentification, and analysis, there now emerges in Ar. poetry *badīʿ*, a term that literally means "innovative" but that involves a greater awareness of the potential uses of poetic imagery. The poet-caliph Ibn al-Muʿtazz (d. 908) wrote a famous analysis of the five most significant tropes (incl. simile and metaphor) entitled *Kitāb al-Badīʿ*, a work that took many of its examples from early poetry and the text of the Qurʾan. This was to be the first in an increasingly complex series of rhetorical analyses. The discussions that evolved around the subject of badīʿ were part of a dynamic period in the devel. of Islamic thought on religious, ethnic, ideological, and cultural issues. They also raised questions of literary taste and provoked fierce debate between proponents of the "new" (*muḥdathūn*) poets and the old. Much critical opprobrium was reserved for the poet Abū Tammām (d. 846), who was widely condemned for carrying the use of badīʿ to excessive lengths. At a later date, the great critic ʿAbd al-Qāhir al-Jurjānī (d. 1078) pioneered the analysis of the psychological impact of imagery on the reader and thereby accentuated the originality of many of Abū Tammām's ideas, a verdict gaining increasing credence in modern crit.

With the growth of the bureaucracy at the caliph's court and the expansion of the Islamic dominions—accompanied almost automatically by the emergence of local potentates—plentiful sources of patronage became available to reward poets who would compose occasional poems. During the heyday of cl. Ar. poetry, many such centers existed: the Umayyads and their successors in Al-Andalus; the Hamdanids in Aleppo, Syria; the Ikhshidids in Egypt; and the court in Baghdad. To all these centers poets would come in search of favor and reward. The poet who best exemplifies this patronage system is al-Mutanabbī (d. 965). He composed poems for all kinds of occasions and for a number of rulers and patrons, some of whom are eulogized and later mercilessly lampooned. Developing the use of the badīʿ style and combining a superb control of the lang. with an innate sense of the gnomic phrase, he was soon widely regarded as the greatest of the cl. Ar. poets. His *Dīwān* (collected poetry) provides us with many splendid examples of the qaṣīda as occasional poem; his examples of eulogy (*madīh*) are among the most famous contributions to a genre that was a major form of verbal art in Arab civilization:

> Whither do you intend, great prince? We
> are the herbs of the hills and you are the
> clouds;
> We are the ones time has been miserly
> towards respecting you, and the days
> cheated of your presence.
> Whether at war or peace, you aim at the
> heights, whether you tarry or hasten.
> (trans. A. J. Arberry, 1965)

A great admirer of al-Mutanabbī's poetry was Abū al-ʿAlāʾ al-Maʿarrī (d. 1057). This blind poet and philosopher began by imitating his great predecessor, but his collection of poems entitled *Luzūm mā lā yalzam* (Requirement of the Nonrequired), the title of which reflects the fact that he imposes strict formal rules on himself, combines consummate skill in the use of poetic lang. with some of the most pessimistic sentiments to be found in the entire Ar. canon:

> Would that a lad had died in the very hour
> of birth
> And never sucked, as she lay in child-
> bed, his mother's breast!
> Her babe, it says to her or ever its tongue
> can speak,
> "Nothing thou gett'st of me but sorrow and
> bitter pain."
> (trans. R. A. Nicholson)

Three poets of Al-Andalus from this period deserve particular mention: Ibn Shuhayd (d. 1035) and Ibn Ḥazm (d. 1063), both of whom contributed to crit. as well as to poetry; and Ibn Zaydūn (d. 1070), who celebrated his great love, the Umayyad Princess Wallāda, and then rued her loss to a rival at court. The Iberian Peninsula was also to contribute to Ar. poetry two strophic genres, the *muwashshaḥ* (see HEBREW PROSODY AND POETICS) and *zajal*. The origins and prosodic features of both genres are the subject of continuing and intense debate. The final strophe or refrain known as the *kharja* (envoi) was originally a popular song in Romance or a mixture of Romance and Hispano-Ar. sung by a girl about her beloved:

> My beloved is sick for love of me.
> How can he not be so?
> Do you not see that he is not allowed near
> me?
> (trans. J. T. Monroe)

This refrain provides the rhyme scheme for the other strophes in the poem that are in literary Ar. Interspersed between them are other verses with separate rhymes. In the *zajal* genre, the colloquial lang. sometimes encountered in the *kharja* of the *muwashshaḥ* is used in the body of the poem itself. With its illustrious exponent Ibn Quzmān (d. 1159), the fame of the genre spread to the East.

As the corpus of poetics and rhet. increased in scope and complexity, poetry itself tended to become more stereotyped and convention-bound, e.g., the poetry of Ibn ʿArabī (d. 1240), one of the major figures in Islamic theology; the mystical poet Ibn al-Fāriḍ (d. 1235); and Bahāʾ al-Din Zuhayr, whose death in 1258 coincides with the capture of Baghdad by the Mongols, an event generally acknowledged as signaling the end of the cl. period in Islamic culture.

III. Thirteenth to Eighteenth Centuries. The era between the 13th and early 19th cs. has often been characterized as "the period of decadence," a designation that not only reflects the distaste of subsequent critics for poetry in which a penchant for verbal virtuosity and poetic tropes prevailed but serves to conceal a general lack of research that has until recently characterized scholarly interest in this lengthy period. These six centuries have often been subdivided into two subperiods: an earlier Mamluk period (13th–16th cs.) and an Ottoman (16th–early 19th cs.). While the poetic output of the latter period still remains largely unexplored, the example of the poetry of ʿAbd al-Ghanī al-Nābulusī (d. 1731) gives an indication of the riches that further research may reveal. Meanwhile, the poetic production of the Mamluk period clearly runs counter to the "decadent" label. The so-called Burda poem (after that of Kaʿb ibn Zuhayr) composed by al-Būṣīrī (ca. 1212–96) has for centuries found a wide audience within the mystical circles of popular Islam much in evidence throughout the period; concurrently in Spain, Ḥāzim al-Qartājannī (d. 1285) was not only a major contributor to the trad. of Ar. poetics but a poet in his own right. The Iraqi poet Ṣafī al-Din al-Ḥillī (d. 1349) not only wrote his own poetry but composed a study of the muwashshaḥ and zajal. Many of these poets were adept at composing verse full of embellishments, e.g., poems in which each word begins with the same letter or each word starts with the final grapheme of the previous word. This was indeed a period of verbal artifice but also one of compilation (incl. the major Ar. dictionaries) and explication. Ibn Mālik (d. 1274) composed a poem in 1,000 verses on Ar. grammar, a text that was still in use in Egyptian religious schools at the turn of the 20th c.

The limited size of the audience for the elite lit. just outlined may account for the considerable vigor of the popular literary trad. during these centuries. This is most evident in the greatest of all narrative collections, *1001 Nights*, as well as in other popular tales that contain large amounts of poetry in a variety of styles. And, while the trad. of popular poetry is sparsely documented, some intimations of its liveliness and variety can be gauged from the (albeit bawdy) poetry to be found in the shadow plays of the Egyptian oculist Ibn Dāniyāl (d. 1311).

IV. Nineteenth and Twentieth Centuries

A. ***The Beginnings of the Modern Revival.*** The process whereby Ar. poetry enters a new phase is termed *al-nahḍa* (revival). Two principal factors are involved: what one scholar has termed "the Arab Rediscovery of Europe" on the one hand and a reexamination of the cl. trad. of Ar. poetry and poetics on the other. Esp. noteworthy figures in this revival are Rifāʿa al-Ṭahṭāwī (d. 1873) in Egypt, and Buṭrus al-Bustānī (d. 1883), Nāṣīf al-Yāzijī (d. 1871—who was particularly inspired by the poetry of al-Mutanabbī), and Aḥmad Fāris al-Shidyāq (d. 1887) in Lebanon.

B. ***Neoclassicism.*** Al-Mutanabbī was also the inspiration of one of the first major figures in the neoclassical movement, the Egyptian Maḥmūd Sāmī al-Bārūdī (d. 1904), who advocated a return to the directness and purity of cl. Ar. poetry and composed poems to illustrate his ideas. Within the chronology of its own mod. hist., every Arab country fostered neoclassical poets, e.g., the Egyptian Hāfez Ibrahim (d. 1932), the Iraqis Jamīl Ṣidqī al-Zahāwī (d. 1936) and Maʿrūf al-Ruṣāfī (d. 1945), and somewhat later, the Palestinian Ibrāhīm Ṭūqān (d. 1941). However, critical opinion is virtually unanimous in judging Aḥmad Shawqī (d. 1932) as the greatest poet of the neoclassical school. Whether in his stirring calls to the Egyptian people, his more personal descriptive verse, or his still-popular operettas, his superbly cadenced poetry seems destined to secure him a place in the pantheon of great Ar. poets. While recent devels. in Ar. poetry produced many changes, several poets continued to compose poetry in the traditional manner, esp. Muḥammad al-Jawāhirī, (d. 1997) Badawī al-Jabal (pseud. of Muḥammad Sulaymān al-Aḥmad, d. 1981), and Al-Akhṭal al-Ṣaghīr (pseud. of Bishāra al-Khūrī, d. 1968).

C. ***Romanticism.*** Signs of a reaction against the occasional nature of much neoclassical verse can be found in the works of the Lebanese poet Khalīl Muṭrān (d. 1949), although not so much in his own poetry as in his writings about poetry and particularly the intro. to his collected poems (1908). Full-blooded romanticism in Ar. poetry comes from the poets of *al-mahjar* (the émigré school), as the Arab poets of the Americas are called. While Amīn al-Riḥānī (d. 1940) was certainly much admired in the Middle East, the undisputed leader of the northern group was Khalīl Jubrān (Kahlil Gibran; d. 1931), as famous for his works in Eng. as for those in Ar.:

> Give me the flute and sing! Forget all that
> you and I have said
> Talk is but dust in the air, so tell me of
> your deeds.
> (trans. M. Khouri and H. Algar)

Far removed from their native land, Jubrān and his colleagues, among whom were Mīkhāʾīl Nuʿayma (b. 1889), Īliyyā Abū Māḍī (d. 1957), and Nasīb ʿArīḍa (d. 1946), proceeded to experiment with lang., form, and mood and, in so doing, introduced a new voice into Ar. poetry. Jubrān was also in constant touch with his fellow countrymen in South America, among whom Fawzī Maʿlūf (d. 1930) is the most significant figure.

In the Middle East, the ideals of Eng. romanticism were vigorously advocated by three Egyptian poets: al-ʿAqqād, Ibrāhīm al-Māzinī (d. 1949), and ʿAbd al-Raḥmān Shukrī (d. 1958). While all three wrote poetry, the primary function of the group was to criticize the neoclassical school in favor of a new, more individual role for the poet. The 1930s and 1940s were the heyday of romanticism in Ar. poetry. In 1932, Aḥmad Zakī abū-Shādī (d. 1955) founded the Apollo Society in Cairo, which published a magazine to which several poets, incl. Ibrāhīm Nājī (d. 1953), ʿAlī Maḥmūd Ṭāhā (d. 1949), and the Tunisian Abū al-Qāsim al-Shābbī (d. 1934) made contributions. Among other important figures in the devel. of romantic Ar. poetry are ʿUmar Abū Rīsha in Syria, Yūsuf Tījānī al-Bashīr (d. 1937) in the Sudan, and Ṣalāḥ Labakī (d. 1955) and Ilyās Abū Shabaka (d. 1947) in Lebanon. As a critic Labakī also devoted his attention to the devel. of a symbolist school of poetry, much indebted to Fr. poetic theory and associated with the Lebanese poets Yūsuf Ghuṣūb (d. 1972) and (esp.) Saʿīd ʿAql (d. 2014).

D. ***The Emergence of "New Poetry": The Role of the Poet.*** The period following World War II was one of political uncertainty, frequent changes of government, and revolution. The creation of the state of Israel in 1948 served as a major psychological catalyst in the Arab world. In the revolutionary atmosphere during the 1950s, the poetry of the late romantics, in particular symbolists such as Saʿīd ʿAql, came to be regarded as elitist, ivory-tower lit. Along with the prevalence of such causes as Palestinian rights, nationalism (whether the Pan-Arab or local variety), revolution, and communism came the rallying cry for "commitment" (*iltizām*). Not surprisingly, among the most prominent contributors to poetry of commitment have been a large group of Palestinian poets; particularly noteworthy are Maḥmūd Darwīsh (d. 2008), Fadwā Ṭūqān (d. 2003), and Samīḥ al-Qāsim (d. 2014). The other overriding topic of political poetry has been life among the poorer classes in both the cities and provinces of the Arab-world nations: the earlier poetry of Badr Shākir al-Sayyāb (d. 1964), ʿAbd al-Wahhāb al-Bayyātī (b. 1926), and Ṣalāḥ ʿAbd al-Sabūr (d. 1982) shows this concern, as do the works of Aḥmad ʿAbd al-Muʿṭī Ḥijāzī (b. 1935) and Muḥammad Miftāḥ al-Faytūrī (b. 1930). The dark visions of Khalīl Ḥāwī (d. 1982) show a more subtle kind of commitment, tinged with bitterness, as in the prescient commentary on the Arab world in the 1960s, "Lazarus 1962":

> Deepen the pit, gravedigger,
> Deepen it to bottomless depths
> beyond the sun's orbit;
> night of ashes, remnants of a star
> buried in the wheeling abyss.
> (trans. A. Haydar and M. Beard)

The most widely read poet in the contemp. Middle East in the second half of the 20th c. was undoubtedly Nizār Qabbānī (d. 1998), who earned enormous popularity for his several volumes of sensuous love poetry. During the 1950s, he also wrote poems of social protest, such as his famous "Bread, Hashish and Moonlight"; particularly following the June war of 1967, political and social issues were constant topics in his poetry. Also immensely popular was Darwīsh, who managed for over half a century to encapsulate in his exquisitely crafted poetry the experience of his own Palestinian people.

With Adūnis (pseud. of ʿAlī Aḥmad Saʿīd, b. 1930), a different kind of commitment is encountered. After editing with his colleague, the Lebanese Christian poet Yūsuf al-Khāl (d. 1987), the jour. *Shiʿr*, which has had immense influence in the devel. of a mod. poetics in the Arab world, Adūnis broke away and in 1968 founded his own jour., *Mawāqif.* He has published numerous poetry collections of startling originality:

> To a father who died, green as a cloud
> with a sail on his face, I bow.
> ("*Waṭan*" [Homeland], *Journal of Arabic Literature* 2 [1971])

Using his jour. and its coterie as a conduit for his ideas, he advocates the need for "innovation," viewing the primary purpose of poetry as the use of words in new ways.

E. ***Changes in Form.*** Strophic Ar. poetry has existed from at least the 10th c. The mod. period has also witnessed other experiments, such as blank and free verse. Also noteworthy are metrical experiments within folk poetry, particularly in Lebanon where Rashīd Nakhla (d. ca. 1940) and Michel Ṭrād (d. 1998) composed poems in strophic form and with mixed meters. In 1947, two Iraqi poets, Nāzik al-Malāʾika (d. 2007) and al-Sayyāb, initiated a break from the concept of the line as poetic unit and thus paved the way for the emergence of *shiʿr ḥurr* (free verse). In fact, al-Malāʾika's attempt to establish a new set of rules based on the single foot (*tafʿīla*) rather than the line (*bayt*) was soon discarded as poets began to experiment with both traditional and new quantitative patterns in their poetry. Other poets have pursued this trend even further by composing prose poetry (*qaṣīdat al-nathr*) in which the sheer conjunction and musicality of words contribute to the poetic moment: alliteration, assonance, and imagery are combined in the works of poets such as Jabrā Ibrāhim Jabrā (d. 1994), Muḥammad al-Māghūṭ (d. 2006), and Tawfīq Ṣāyigh (d. 1971).

The Arab poet today continues to be influenced and inspired by the great cl. trad., but the stimuli provided by his own time and world are now international and of considerable variety. While poetry continues to hold its traditionally prestigious position and to fulfill an esp. important role in times of crisis, recent cultural trends—particularly the growing prominence of visual media and their markets—have tended to afford a greater cultural priority to narrative genres. One consequence of the increasing role that such media have come to play is the enhancement of the status of more popular forms of poetry (in both standard lang. and colloquial dialects), not least through recordings of their performance modes. The public function of the Arab poet, a permanent feature of the Ar. poetic heritage, is thus being brought to a yet wider audience.

■ **General Reference Works**: C. Brockelmann, *Geschichte der Arabischen Literatur*, 2 v. (1898–1902), *Supplementbanden*, 3 v. (1937–42); A. Fischer, *Schawahid Indices* (1945); *Encyclopedia of Islam*, 2d ed. (1954–), 3d ed. (2007–); J. D. Pearson, *Index Islamicus 1906–1955* (1958), *Supplements* (1956–80); *The Fihrist of al-Nadim*, trans. B. Dodge, 2 v. (1970); M. Alwan, "A Bibliography of Modern Arabic Poetry in English Translation," *Middle East Journal* 27 (Summer 1973); F. Sezgin, *Geschichte des Arabischen Schriftums*, v. 2 (1975); *Modern Literature in the Near and Middle East 1850–1970*, ed. R. C. Ostle (1991); S. J. Altoma, *Modern Arabic Poetry in English Translation* (1993); R. Allen, *The Arabic Literary Heritage* (1998); *Encyclopedia of Arabic Literature*, 2 v., ed. J. S. Meisami and P. Starkey (1998); H. Toelle and K. Zakharia, *A la découverte de la littérature arabe* (2003); P. G. Starkey, *Modern Arabic Literature* (2006); *Histoire de la littérature arabe moderne*, ed. B. Hallaq and H. Toelle (2007).

■ **Anthologies**: *Arabic Poetry for English Readers*, ed. W. A. Clouston (1881); *Ancient Arabic Poetry*, ed. C. J. Lyall (1885); W. S. Blunt, *Seven Golden Odes of Pagan Arabia* (1903); R. A. Nicholson, *Translations of Eastern Poetry and Prose* (1922); *Modern Arabic Poetry*, ed. and trans. A. J. Arberry (1950); *The Seven Odes*, trans. A. J. Arberry (1957); *Al-Majānī al-Ḥadīthaʿan Majānī al-Ab Shaykhū*, ed. F. Afram al-Bustānī, 3 v. (1960–61); *Dīwān al-Shiʿr al-ʿArabī*, ed. Adūnis (1964–68); *Arabic Poetry* (1965) and *Poems of al-Mutanabbi* (1967), both ed. A. J. Arberry; *Anthologie de la littérature arabe contemporaine*, trans. L. Norin and E. Tarabay (1967); *An Anthology of Modern Arabic Verse*, ed. M. Badawi (1970); *Hispano-Arabic Poetry*, ed. and trans. J. T. Monroe (1974); *Mawsūʿat al-Shiʿr al-ʿArabī*, ed. K. K. Ḥāwī and M. Ṣafadī (1974–); *An Anthology of Modern Arabic Poetry*, trans. M. Khouri and H. Algar (1974); *Modern Arab Poets 1950–1975*, I. Boullata (1976); K. Ḥāwī, *Naked in Exile*, trans. A. Haydar and M. Beard (1984); *Majnun et Layla*, trans. A. Miquel and P. Kemp (1984); *Classical Arabic Poetry*, trans. C. Tuetey (1985); *Modern Arabic Poetry*, ed. S. K. Jayyusi (1987); ʿAbd. al-Wahhāb al-Bayātī, *Love, Death and Exile*, trans. B. K. Frangieh (1990); N. Kabbani, *Arabian Love Poems*, trans. B. K. Frangieh and C. Brown (1993); *Night and Horses and The Desert*, ed. R. Irwin (1999); Adonis, *A Time* *between Ashes and Roses*, trans. S. M. Toorawa (2004); S. al-Qasim, *Sadder Than Water*, trans. N. Kassis (2006); M. Darwīsh, *The Butterfly's Burden*, trans. F. Joudah (2007); Mourid Barghouti, *Midnight*, trans. R. Ashour (2008).

■ **Criticism and History**: W. Ahlwardt, *Über Poesie und Poetik der Araber* (1856); I. Goldziher, *Short History of Classical Arabic Literature* (1908), trans. J. Desomogyi (1966); R. A. Nicholson, *Literary History of the Arabs* (1914), *Studies in Islamic Poetry* (1921), *Studies in Islamic Mysticism* (1921); Ṭ. Ḥusayn, *Al-Shiʿr al-Jāhilī* (1926); H.A.R. Gibb, *Arabic Literature* (1926); U. Farrukh, *Das Bild der Frühislam in der arabischen Dichtung* (1937); N. al-Bahbītī, *Tārīkh al-Shiʿr al-ʿArabī* (1950); M. al-Nuwayhī, *Al-Shiʿr al-Jāhilī* (n.d.); R. Serjeant, *South Arabic Poetry* (1951); R. Blachère, *Histoire de la littérature arabe*, 3 v. (1952–66); G. Gomez, *Poesia arabigoandaluza* (1952); G. von Grunebaum, *Kritik und Dichtkunst* (1955); N. al-Asad, *Maṣādir al-Shiʿr al-Jāhilī* (1956); I. ʿAbbas, *Tārīkh al-Adab al-Andalusī* (1959); J. al-Rikābī, *Fi al-Adab al-Andalusī* (1960); N. al-Malāʾika, *Qaḍāyā al-shiʿr al-muʿāṣir* (1962); S. Ḍayf, *Tārīkh al-Adab al-ʿArabī*, 4 v. (1963–73); J. Kamāl al-dīn, *Al-Shiʿr al-ʿArabī al-Ḥadīth wa-rūḥ al-ʿaṣr* (1964); E. Wagner, *Abu Nuwas* (1965); M. Ullmann, *Untersuchungen zur Ragazpoesie* (1966); I. Ismāʿīl, *Al-Shiʿr al-ʿArabī al-muʿāṣir* (1967); G. Shukrī, *Shiʿrunā al-Ḥadīth* (1968); J. Vadet, *L'Esprit courtois en Orient dans les premiers siècles de l'Hégire* (1968); W. Heinrichs, *Arabische Dichtung und griechische Poetik* (1969); M. Bateson, *Structural Continuity in Poetry* (1970); M. al-Nuwayhī, *Qaḍiyyat al-shiʿr al-jadīd* (1971); R. Jacobi, *Studien zur Poetik der altarabischen Qaside* (1971); J. T. Monroe, "Oral Composition in Pre-Islamic Poetry," *Journal of Arabic Literature* 3 (1972); M. Ṣubḥi, *Dirāsāt taḥlīliyya fī al-shiʿr al-ʿArabī al-muʿāṣir* (1972); *Arabic Poetry*, ed. G. von Grunebaum (1973); J. ʿAsfūr, *Al-ṣūra al-fanniyya fī al-turāth al-naqdī wa-al-balāghī* (1974); S. Ḍayf, *Al-Taṭawwur wa-al-tajdīd fī al-shiʿr al-Umawī* (1974); A. Hamori, *On the Art of Medieval Arabic Literature* (1974); R. Scheindlin, *Form and Structure in the Poetry of Al-Muʿtamid ibn ʿAbbād* (1974); S. M. Stern, *Hispano-Arabic Strophic Poetry* (1974); M. Badawi, *A Critical Introduction to Modern Arabic Poetry* (1975); J. Bencheikh, *Poétique arabe* (1975); S. A. Bonebakker, *Materials for the History of Arabic Rhetoric from the "Hilyat al-muhādara of Hātimīi"* (1975); J. Stetkevych, "The Arabic Lyrical Phenomenon in Context," *Journal of Arabic Literature* 6 (1975); L. F. Compton, *Andalusian Lyrical Poetry and Old Spanish Love Songs* (1976); S. Moreh, *Modern Arabic Poetry 1800–1970* (1976); R. Hitchcock, *The Kharjas* (1977); S. K. Jayyusi, *Trends and Movements in Modern Arabic Poetry* (1977); K. Kheir Beik, *Le Mouvement moderniste de la poésie arabe contemporaine* (1978); M. Zwettler, *The Oral Tradition of Classical Arabic Poetry* (1978); Y. al-Yūsuf, *Al-Shiʿr al-ʿArabī al-muʿāṣir* (1980); M. Abdul-Hai, *Tradition and English and American Influence in Arabic Romantic Poetry* (1982); G. van Gelder, *Beyond the Line* (1982); *Arabic Literature to the End of the Umayyad Period*, ed. A. Beeston et al. (1983); M. Ajami, *The Neckveins of Winter* (1984); S. Stetkevych, "The Ṣuʿlūk and His Poem: A Paradigm of Passage Manqué," *JAOS* 104 (1984); Adonis, *Introduction à la poétique arabe* (1985); S. A. Sowayan, *Nabati Poetry* (1985); M. R. Menocal, *The Arabic Role in Medieval Literary History* (1988); S. Sperl, *Mannerism in Arabic Poetry* (1989); *Abbasid Belles-Letters*, ed. J. Ashtiany et al. (1990); *Religion, Learning and Science in the Abbasid Period*, ed. M.J.L. Young et al. (1990); C. Bailey, *Bedouin Poetry from Sinai and the Negev* (1991); S. P. Stetkevych, *Abū Tammām and the Poetics of the ʿAbbāsid Age* (1991); A. Hamori, *The Composition of Mutanabbi's Panegyrics to Sayf al-Dawla* (1992); *Modern Arabic Literature*, ed. M. M. Badawi (1992); M. al-Nowaihi, *The Poetry of Ibn Khafajah* (1993); J. Stetkevych, *The Zephyrs of Najd* (1993); K. Abdel-Malek, *Muhammad in the Modern Egyptian Popular Ballad* (1994); T. E. Homerin, *From Arab Poet to Muslim Saint* (1994)—on Ibn al-Fāriḍ; *Reorientations: Arabic and Persian Poetry*, ed. S. Stetkevych (1994); P. M. Kurpershoek, *Oral Poetry and Narratives from Central Arabia*, 3 v. (1994–96); D. F. Reynolds, *Heroic Poets, Poetic Heroes* (1995); *Qasida Poetry in Islamic Asia and Africa*, ed. S. Sperl and C. Shackle, 2 v. (1996); P. F. Kennedy, *The Wine Song in Classical Arabic Poetry* (1997); T. DeYoung, *Placing the Poet* (1998)—on Badr Shākir al-Sayyāb; *The Literature of Al-Andalus*, ed. M. R. Menocal et al. (2000); A. A. Bamia, *The Graying of the Raven* (2001); T. E. Homerin, *ʿUmar Ibn al-Fāriḍ, Sufi Verse, Saintly Life* (2001); S. Stetkevych, *The Poetics of Islamic Legitimacy* (2002); B. Gruendler, *Medieval Arabic Praise Poetry* (2003); H. Kilpatrick, *Making the Great Book of Songs* (2003); A. Månsson, *Passage to a New World* (2003); A. M. Sumi, *Description in Classical Arabic Poetry* (2004); *Ghazal as World Literature*, ed. T. Bauer and

A. Neuwirth, 2 v. (2005–6); M. J. al-Musawi, *Arabic Poetry* (2006); G. Schoeler, *The Oral and the Written in Early Islam*, trans. U. Vagelphol (2006); *Arabic Literature in the Post-Classical Period*, ed. R. Allen and D. S. Richards (2006); N. G. Yaqub, *Pens, Swords, and the Springs of Art* (2007); C. Holes, *Poetry and Politics in Contemporary Bedouin Society* (2009).

R.M.A. Allen

ARABIC PROSODY. Ar. versification (*al-ʿArūḍ*) is quantitative, a unique phenomenon among the Semitic langs., where accent verse systems dominate, although in the beginning the ancient Ar. verse was no different from other examples of the archaic Semitic poetry, Akkadian, Ugaritic, or biblical. Ar. poetry starts as parallelistic verse, at first even unrhymed. From the earliest examples, dating back to the 1st c. CE, it underwent a long evolution until it emerged in the middle of the 6th c. CE as a highly organized metrical system. The intermediate archaic verse forms, found by a researcher as coexisting in time, though they mark stages of devel., are the following:

(1) *Sajʿ*, often translated as "rhymed prose," but for the early oral phase, it is a verse form, based on the parallelistic technique with no concrete meter discernible, attested in the sayings of pre-Islamic *kāhins* and Bedouins, as well as in the early Meccan sūras of the Qurʾan.

(2) *Rajaz*, later incorporated in the ʿArūḍ system as one of its meters, initially it was a short verse form labeled by the Ar. scholars as "one-hemistich verse" with a rather loose structure where one can already observe the emergence of the alternative rhythm of the quantitative nature, though some of its features, such as the possibility of inner pauses within the verse line, suggest that accent still played a moderate part in creating the verse rhythm. The adaptation of its loose pattern to the strict (or can we say overstrict) ʿArūḍ rules created difficulties for Ar. scholars starting from the creator of the metrical theory, al-Khalīl ibn Aḥmad (d. 791).

Al-Khalīl noticed that the rhythmic core of Ar. prosody is the alternation of longer and shorter prosodic segments. In other words, it is based solely on quantity or temporal duration. The very notion of stress is absent from his theory. The notion of *syllable* in its cl. form is also absent, but this is not a symptom of the deficiency of the theory. Al-Khalīl invented another system of concepts for the analysis of the structure of Ar. verse, by far surpassing in that capacity the traditional Eur. notion of *syllable*, as it takes account of the fact—often neglected by Eur. scholars—that the sequence that we call *short syllable* (CV) cannot be pronounced autonomously or is not a syllable at all.

The basic notion is *ḥarf*, which can be either *sākin* (quiescent), i.e., a consonant or a long vowel, or *mutaḥarrik* (moving), i.e., a consonant followed by a short vowel. Both variants (one being structurally identical with the CV) are less than the minimum of pronunciation, as it should always begin with the "moving" ḥarf and end with the "quiescent" one. So, the minimum of Ar. speech is a two-ḥarf segment (structurally identical with a "long syllable"—CVC or CVlong).

The notion has a twofold function in the metrical structure. First, it is used as the means of the segmentation of speech into elementary prosodic units (EPU). The goal is achieved by stops at each unvocalized ḥarf; as a result, each EPU has an identical structural pattern: a number (one or more) of vocalized ḥarfs and a final unvocalized ḥarf. Second, the ḥarf is a unit of measurement of prosodic length, which can be considered a functional equivalent of the universal notion of *mora*. So, the length of EPU can be two ḥarfs (this is the minimum), three ḥarfs, four ḥarfs, and so on.

These EPU play the role of metrical syllables in the ʿArūḍ structure, the two-ḥarf unit being the short one and the three-ḥarf unit the long one. The shorter one is called *sabab* (rope or cord) and the longer one *watid* (peg); both terms go back to the image of a Bedouin tent. There is a beautiful legend about an aged shaykh teaching a youth to compose poetry. The master says that all verses are composed of two elements—*naʿam* (yes)—this is watid—and *lā* (no)—this is sabab. So, if we recite, "Naʿam lā naʿam lā lā . . . ," we get one meter, while if we recite, "Lā lā naʿam lā lā naʿam . . . ," we get another meter and so on.

The sababs and watids are the core of the alternative verse rhythm, in which the first EPU functions as *thesis* and the second as *arsis*, but the actual set of EPU postulated by ʿArūḍ is wider as it comprises four-ḥarf and five-ḥarf segments called *smaller fāṣila* and *larger fāṣila*, which can be treated as prosodic clusters made of a combination of the sababs and watids with the prosodic boundary between them eliminated.

Certain combinations of metrical syllables make ʿArūḍ feet. The theory postulates eight different types of feet, but only seven of them are real, while the eighth is a purely fictitious foot postulated by al-Khalīl to solve some theoretical difficulties he encountered. They have a uniform structure: one watid that is the arsis of the foot plus one or two sababs (or smaller fāṣila). It follows that the prosodic length of the ʿArūḍ feet is either five or seven ḥarfs (or morae). The seven foot types (presented by mnemonic word patterns taken from Ar. morphology with some modifications that go back to al-Khalīl and by numerical schemes where two stands for sabab, three for watid, and four for smaller fāṣila) are the following:

faʿūlun: 32 (trochaic foot), e.g., *kitābun, dhahabtum*
fāʿilun: 23 (iambic foot), e.g., kātibun, lam yakun
mafāʿīlun: 322 (dactylic foot-1), e.g., hunā shamsun
mufāʿalatun: 34 (dactylic foot-2), e.g., faqad dhahabū
fāʿilātun: 232 (amphibrachic foot), e.g., min kitābin
mustafʿilun: 223 (anapaestic foot-1), e.g., mustaqbalun, lam yadhhabū
mutafāʿilun: 43 (anapaestic foot-2), e.g., mutadhāhirun, wahabū lahā

It can be seen that the Ar. presentation, with the help of ḥarf/mora and EPU/metrical syllables, reveals the structural affinity of Ar. metrics with other systems of versification and gives the firm basis for typological studies.

The system of Ar. meters started to develop from three archaic rhythms, identified with three functional forms (genres) of ancient poetry that already had names in pre-Islamic vocabulary:

(1) descending, either trochaic (32) or dactylic (322/34), which was initially associated with the trad. of old Ar. singing, now extinct; this form of poetry with short (four-foot) verse lines was called *hazaj*;
(2) ascending, either iambic (23) or anapestic (223/43), which was initially associated with declamation, not singing; this—probably the oldest—form of poetry with extra-short (three-foot) lines was called *rajaz*; see above;
(3) ambivalent, ascending-descending, or amphibrachic (232), which was initially associated with the trad. of Persian singing, imported into Arabia via al-Ḥīra; this form of poetry, the most recent it seems, with short (four-foot) lines was called *ramal*.

The set of meters that constitute the classic system of ʿArūḍ was born out of the three basic rhythms with the help of the processes of elongating verse lines and of introducing strict order in the alternation of inter-watid intervals.

Al-Khalīl himself identified 15 meters, and the 16th meter was added later on. On the basis of their origin and structural affinity, they can be grouped in three metrical families.

A. ***Hazaj.*** The hazaj family comprises five meters. The rhyme schemes follow each definition:

(1) *ṭawīl* (long): An eight-foot meter of two hemistichs and the only one that does not have shorter forms. It is the main meter of *qaṣīd* poetry, almost half of which is written in this meter):

faʿūlun / mafāʿīlun / fāʿīlun / mafāʿīlun //
32 322 32 33
fāʿīlun / mafāʿīlun / fāʿīlun / mafāʿīlun
32 322 32 322

(2) *wāfir* (abundant, full): A six-foot meter that also has a rare four-foot variation, one of the four main qaṣīd meters:

mufāʿalatun / mufāʿalatun / mufāʿalatun //
34 34 34
mufāʿalatun / mufāʿalatun / mufāʿalatun
34 34 34

(3) *hazaj* (quick vibration of sound): Theoretically, a six-foot meter but used exclusively as a shorter, four-foot variation. This rare meter, rhythmically close to wāfir, is the direct heir of the archaic hazaj; see above:

mafāʿīlun / mafāʿīlun // mafāʿīlun / mafāʿīlun
322 322 322 322

(4) *mutaqārib* (contracted or drawn near each other): An eight-foot meter made only of five-ḥarf feet, which is unusual for Ar. verse—hence, its name. Its frequency is 5 to 15%, and it is one of the six most popular meters of cl. Ar. poetry. Its short six-foot

variation is much less frequent than the long one:

faʿūlun / faʿūlun / faʿūlun / faʿūlun //
32 32 32 32
faʿūlun / faʿūlun / faʿūlun / faʿūlun
32 32 32 32

(5) *muḍāriʿ* (similar): Theoretically, a four-foot meter but never used by poets. Its scheme is as follows:

mafāʿīlun / fāʿilātun // mafāʿīlun / fāʿilātun
322 232 322 232

B. ***Rajaz.*** The rajaz family comprises seven meters:

(1) *basīṭ* (outspread, unfolded): An eight-foot meter but with a shorter six-foot variation, one of the four main qaṣīd meters:

mustafʿilun / fāʿilun / mustafʿilun / fāʿilun //
223 23 223 23
mustafʿilun / fāʿilun / mustafʿilun / fāʿilun
223 23 223 23

(2) *kāmil* (complete): A six-foot meter that also has a four-foot variation, one of the four main qaṣīd meters:

mutafāʿilun / mutafāʿilun / mutafāʿilun //
43 43 43
mutafāʿilun / mutafāʿilun / mutafāʿilun
43 43 43

(3) *rajaz* (trembling sound, murmur): One of the oldest meters, rhythmically close to kāmil, used from time immemorial exclusively as a short three-foot (or even a two-foot) variation; in the theory of ʿArūḍ it is presented as a "normal" six-foot meter:

mustafʿilun / mustafʿilun / mustafʿilun //
223 223 223
mustafʿilun / mustafʿilun / mustafʿilun
223 223 223

(4) *sarīʿ* (quick): A six-foot meter that also has a short, three-foot variation. It definitely shows affinity to rajaz, and if treated according to actual prosodic practice, it becomes a specific variation of rajaz with deformation at the end of each hemistich, nothing more. In the metrical theory, though, it is presented as having at the end the anomalous prosodically incomplete foot, which, in fact, never has the ideal form (its real form can be 222 or 23 but never 223; otherwise, it would turn into rajaz):

mustafʿilun / mustafʿilun / mafʿūlātu-//
223 223 2221–
mustafʿilun / mustafʿilun / mafʿūlātu-
223 223 2221–

(5) *munsariḥ* (free, easygoing, unbound): A rare six-foot meter that also has a short, two-foot variation. In the metrical theory, it is presented as having the same anomalous foot in the middle of the hemistich, but the prosodically relevant scanning shows that it is another specific variation of rajaz with a watid shifted one step further. Both ways of scanning are shown by numerical indexes in this case:

mustafʿilun / mafʿūlātu- / mustafʿilun //
223 2221– 223 (theory)
223 2223 23 (reality)
mustafʿilun / mafʿūlātu- / mustafʿilun
223 2221– 223 (theory)
223 2223 23 (reality)

(6) *mujtaṯṯ* (cut or carved off): A very rare four-foot meter:

mustafʿilun / fāʿilātun // mustafʿilun
223 232 223
/ fāʿilātun
232

(7) *muqtaḍab* (cut or torn off): A four-foot meter that never existed in poetic practice. It is the third meter for which al-Khalīl postulated the occurrence of the same anomalous foot, which is placed in the beginning of each hemistich:

mafʿūlātu-mustafʿilun // mafʿūlātu-mustafʿilun
2221–223 2221–223
(theoretical scanning)
2223 23 2223 23
(actual prosodic scanning)

(8) One more meter can be added to this family. It is the sixteenth meter included in the system after al-Khalīl: *mutadārik*. However, the schema of this meter was never attested in poetic practice:

fāʿilun / fāʿilun / fāʿilun / fāʿilun // fāʿilun /
23 23 23 23 23
fāʿilun / fāʿilun / fāʿilun
23 23 23

The anomalous foot *mafʿūlātu-*(2221–), which is impossible as it is prosodically incomplete, is the eighth foot of the ʿArūḍ set mentioned above. It was invented by al-Khalīl to overcome a specific theoretical problem that arose in connection with meters that were heirs of the ancient rajazˁ with its loose structure. The maximum length of the ˁArūḍ foot was postulated as seven ḥarfs, and most of the meters comply with the rule; but in some schemes, we see three sababs in succession between watids, which cannot be divided between adjacent feet. So, a theoretician has an alternative: either to break the rule and postulate the existence of the super-long nine-ḥarf foot or to find another solution, as did al-Khalīl. He postulated the existence of such a foot in three meters: *muqtaḍab*, *munsarih*, *sarīˁ*, where it occupies the first, the second, and the third position in the hemistich; see above. In order to substantiate the existence of this foot, al-Khalīl had to introduce another conventional notion, that of the abnormal watid—*lātu-*, which has only one location—at the end of this very foot. It carries a significant name—*mafrūq* (disjointed) because, prosodically, it is nothing but a combination of incomplete parts of adjacent EPU. The combination was so successful that many scholars consider these conventionalities to be real and base on them their interpretation of ˁArūḍ.

C. ***Ramal.*** The *ramal* family consists of three meters:

(1) *khafīf* (light): A six-foot meter that also has a four-foot variation:

fāˁilātun / mustafˁilun / fāˁilātun // fāˁilātun /
232 223 232 232
mustafˁilun / fāˁilātun
223 232

(2) *ramal* (woven cloth; sound of raindrops): A six-foot meter that also has a four-foot variation:

fāˁilātun / fāˁilātun / fāˁilātun // fāˁilātun
232 232 232 232
/ fāˁilātun / fāˁilātun
232 232

(3) *madīd* (stretched, extended): Theoretically, an eight-foot meter but used exclusively as a shorter six-foot variation:

fāˁilātun / fāˁilun / fāˁilātun // fāˁilātun
232 23 232 232
/ fāˁilun / fāˁilātun
23 232

This classification of meters into three families is based on their rhythmical affinity, but the author of ˁArūḍ classified them differently—his famous and mysterious circles, five in number. The system of circles is, in fact, a generative device. It groups meters that can be produced from each other by the shift of the starting point one EPU forward. The generative principle can be shown in the following diagram:

. . . 322 322 322 322 322 322 322 . . .
(hazaj rhythm)
. . . 223 223 223 223 223 223 223 . . .
(rajaz rhythm)
. . . 232 232 232 232 232 232 232 . . .
(ramal rhythm)

So, the first circle is ṭawīl—madīd—basīṭ. The second circle is wāfir—kāmil. The third circle is hazaj—rajaz—ramal. The fourth circle is sarīˁ—munsariḥ—khafīf—muḍārˁ—muqtaḍab—mujtaṯṯ. The fifth circle is mutaqārib alone. Later on, *mutadārik* was added.

But the derivational device produces more schemes than are accepted by the theory. The first circle generates five schemes, and only three are recognized as meters. The fourth circle generates nine schemes, and only six are accepted. The rest are labeled as *muhmal* (neglected, unused). The mystery is that, as we have seen, some schemes that were recognized as meters of ˁArūḍ are also unused (*muḍāriˁ–muqtaḍab*), and mutadārik was included despite the fact that it was never used by Ar. poets.

The ˁArūḍ system was adopted by Heb., Persian, and Turkish poetry and has undergone serious changes in the process of adaptation to a different prosodic matter.

In the 20th c., Ar. poetry witnessed a shift away from the ˁArūḍ metrics to free verse.

■ G. W. Freytag, *Darstellung der Arabischen Verskunst* (1830); S. Guyard, "Théorie nouvelle de la métrique Arabe," *Journal Asiatique*, ser. 7, 7, 8, 10 (1877); M. Hartmann, *Metrum und Rhythmus* (1896); J. Vadet, "Contribution a l'histoire de la métrique Arabe," *Arabica* 2 (1955); G. Weil, *Grundriss und System der altarabischen Metren* (1958), and "ˁArūḍ," *Encyclopedia of Islam*, ed. H.A.R. Gibb et al., 2d ed., v. 1 (1960); S. ˁAyyād, *Mūsīqā al-Shiˁr al-ˁArabī* (1968); Ibn ˁAbd Rabbihi, *al-ˁIqd al-Farid*, v. 3 (1968); A. A. Sánchez, "K voprosu o sushchnosti sistemi arabskoy metriki," *Arabskaya Filologiya* (1968); Ibn al-Sarrāj, *al-Miˁyār fi Awzān al-Ashˁār* (1968); I. Anīs, *Mūsīqā al-Shiˁr*, 4th ed. (1972); J. Kuryłowicz, *Studies in Semitic Grammar and Metrics* (1973); K. Abū Deeb, *Fī al-Binya al-Iqāˁiyya li al-Shiˁr al-ʿArabī* (1974); E. G. Gómez, *Métrica de la moaxaja y métrica española* (1975); I. Goldziher, *Abhandlungen zur arabischen Philologie*, v. 1 (1976); J. M. Maling, "The Theory of Classical Arabic Metrics," *al-Abhāth* 26 (1977); D. Semah, "The Rhythmical Function of the *Watid* and the *Fāsila*," *Journal of Semitic Studies* 28 (1983); and "Quantity and Syllabic Parity in the Hispano-Arabic *Muwashshahāt*," *Arabica* 31 (1983); W.F.G.J. Stoetzer, *Theory and Practice in Arabic Metrics* (1989); J. Bellamy, "Arabic Verses from the First/Second Century: The Inscription of ʿEn ʿAvdat," *Journal of Semitic Studies* 35 (1990); G. Bohas and B. Paoli, *Aspects formels de la poésie arabe* (1997); D. Frolov, "The Place of *Rajaz* in the History of Arabic Verse," *Journal of Arabic Literature* 28 (1997); D. Frolov, *Classical Arabic Verse: History and Theory of ʿArūḍ* (2000); D. Frolov, "Meter," *Encyclopedia of Arabic Language and Linguistics*, ed. K. Versteegh et al., v. 3 (2007).

D. Frolov

ARAUCANIAN POETRY. *See* INDIGENOUS AMERICAS, POETRY OF THE

ARGENTINA, POETRY OF. The Argentine poetic trad. begins with a poem by a soldier on a Sp. expedition, Martín del Barco Centenera's (1535–1602) *La Argentina*, published in 1602 in Lisbon. In its style, verse form (hendecasyllabic lines with alternating consonant rhyme), and historical description of Indians, the poem echoes the Basque poet Alonso de Ercilla in *La Araucana* (1569–89), though without the same vitality, which makes del Barco's poem a less auspicious start to this national trad.

Local voices arose in the 19th c., and their styles, like many in Sp. America, featured neoclassicism and patriotic verse. "Al Paraná" by Manuel José de Lavardén (1754–1809) is a neoclassical ode published in 1801, a song of praise to the region that predates the Venezuelan Andrés Bello's more famous *Silvas americanas* (1823). The struggle toward national independence continued and extended patriotic verse, e.g., in the "Marcha patriótica" (1813) by Vicente López y Planes (1785–1856), a nationalistic hymn that would later be revised into the Argentine anthem. Another locally focused poetic style crucial to this century was gaucho poetry, and Bartolomé Hidalgo's (1788–1822) work is an early example. His *Cielitos y diálogos patrióticos* recounted events of the wars for independence and highlighted the perspective of the gauchos, or nomadic cowboys from the plains. Gaucho poetry is based on oral practice, and Hidalgo's *cielitos* are rhymed quatrains that may come from the Sp. *romance* trad. Later gaucho-style poetry was elaborated by Estanislao del Campo (1834–80) and Hilario Ascasubi (1807–75), but it is José Hernández's (1834–86) *Martín Fierro* that is widely considered to be the culmination of gauchesque lit. The first part of this long narrative poem was published in 1872 and recounts Fierro's marginalization from civilization, while the second chronicles his return (1879). Hernández employs the voice of a gaucho singer or *payador* to create the effect of improvisation for, as Ludmer has noted, in the gaucho style the lettered elite make use of the popular. Gaucho poetry offers an intriguing link between lit. and politics and highlights certain crucial tensions of the moment: between written and oral cultures and between the rural interior and urbanized center—divisions that are central to 19th-c. cultural production in Argentina.

An important figure in the national political scene, whose presence is felt in the poetry of the decade, is Juan Manuel Rosas. Elected governor of Buenos Aires in 1829, Rosas (a Federalist) later headed a dictatorial regime that lasted from 1835 to 1852. Juan Cruz Varela (1794–1839) was a poet of the opposing Unitarian Party, who composed odes to freedom of the press, commemorated key independence battles, and wrote "El veinticinco de mayo de 1838" (The 25th of May, 1838), attacking Rosas. Varela composed a long love poem, "Elvira" (1831), and odes to national heroes Juan Ramón Balcarce and Manual Belgrano; the critic Menéndez y Pelayo called him the first truly Argentine poet.

During the same period, Esteban Echeverría (1805–51) nationalized romantic poetry and prose. His *Rimas* (Rhymes, 1837) includes what would become his best-known poem, "La cautiva" (The Captive Woman), a ten-part narrative that recounts the capture of two Argentines by a group of Indians. This poem, in some ways romantic more in sentiment than in form, is an example of a Eur.-influenced aesthetic in an Am. context. It has been read in relation to the struggles for independence and other captivity narratives and creole representations of the Indian and includes references to issues such as miscegenation, gender, the role of nature, and the extension and limits of the nation in Lat. Am. Later romanticism (1852–80) is associated with the work of Carlos Guido y Spano (1827–1916), who was not known for Indian or gaucho themes but treated topics that ranged from the intimate to the heroic. He is recognized for adopting romanticism as a way of life, and some of the Parnassian elements in his poetry link him to early 20th-c. *modernismo*.

Leopoldo Lugones (1874–1938) is the Argentine most associated with modernismo and, as Kirkpatrick has observed, his work demonstrates a transformative relationship to this movement. Like other modernists, Lugones attempted to alter or refine lang. and prosody through daring rhymes, verbal skill, and a *recherché* vocabulary. In *Las montañas del oro* (The Golden Mountains, 1893), he combined a series of opposing images and linked nature and science; *Los crepúsculos del jardín* (The Garden's Twilight, 1905) featured excess and exaggeration, and all the irony and tensions of his earlier styles culminate in the parody of *Lunario sentimental* (Sentimental Moon Journey, 1909). While some qualify Lugones's work as late modernismo, others see it as part of a postmodernist reformulation and critique of that movement. In Sp. America, *posmodernismo* designates an early 20th-c. transitional period, between approximately 1905 and 1930, in which modernist characteristics expanded and shifted in poetry that largely did not participate in the avant-garde. There is some controversy about whether it exists as a separate movement or as an extension of modernismo; but in any case, it features poetry that is markedly intimate, is often situated in rural rather than urban settings, and involves perspectives regularly marginalized by the dominance of modernismo.

Associated with this early posmodernismo is Evaristo Carriego (1883–1912), whose *Misas herejes* (Heretical Masses, 1908) describes humble lives with sincerity and emotion, earning him fame as the poet of the *arrabal* or suburb (a perspective to be elaborated by Jorge Luis Borges). Baldomero Fernández Moreno (1886–1950) is known for capturing urban and rural reality in his poetry, and *Las iniciales del misal* (The Missal's Initials, 1915) relies on simple musical lyrics. Alfonsina Storni (1892–1938), the best known of this group and one of the now-canonical women poets, demonstrates in much of her poetry a feminist consciousness and anger with prescribed social roles. Her early work, *El dulce daño* (Sweet Suffering, 1918) has stylistic links to modernismo, while she moves toward the avant-garde in her later, more experimental collection *Mascarilla y trébol* (Mask and Clover, 1938).

Another Argentine response to modernismo arose in the ultraist movement of the 1920s, which advocated free verse and sought to condense poetry to its primary element—a revitalized metaphor. The movement, which emphasized aesthetics and cosmopolitanism, is associated with Borges (1899–1986) and the *Martín Fierro* magazine (1924–27), which featured the work of Borges, Guillermo de Torre, Oliverio Girondo, Norah Lange, Ricardo Molinari, and Leopoldo Marechal. These writers were also associated with the Grupo Florida, an intellectual and aristocratic assemblage concerned with aesthetic renovation, which they defined and put into action; often considered elitist, this group also exhibited some contrasting democratic, urban, and nationalistic traits. Between 1923 and 1930, Borges published three books of poetry, each of which emphasized ultraism through the use of metaphor; formally, the poems combine free verse, hendecasyllables, and the alexandrine, and many of them are concerned with a mythical space—Buenos Aires and its urban neighborhoods. Later, Borges abandoned ultraism, but he continued to write poetry throughout his life, incl. a variety of themes also present in his fiction: the search for identity, nostalgia, philosophical idealism, and Argentine folklore (e.g., he composed lyrics for tangos and *milongas*).

Leopoldo Marechal (1900–70) also participated in *Martín Fierro* in the 1920s, and his first published poetry, *Los aguiluchos* (The Eaglets, 1922) and *Días como flechas* (Days like Arrows, 1926), tends toward the avant-garde. His work deals with philosophical preoccupations, order, harmony, and lyrical interpretation of Argentine places and trads. Joining Borges and Marechal was Molinari (1898–1996), whose themes are more existential: lack, the impossibility of communication, the purity of lang. From a metaphysical perspective, he contemplates solitude, death, and time in forms such as the romance, sonnet, and ode.

Girondo (1891–1967), after Borges and Lugones, is the best known of Argentina's early 20th-c. poets, and his early work is also part of this group. *Veinte poemas para ser leídos en el tranvía* (Twenty Poems to be Read on the Streetcar, 1922), *Calcomanías* (Transfers, 1925), and *Espantapájaros* (*Scarecrows*, 1932) are all ultraist in style and, although they include some surrealist discontinuities, are more referential than most of his later works. *En la masmédula* (In the Deep Marrow, 1954) features his most radical use of lang., incl. neologisms and phonic relations between terms. Lange (1906–72) was the sole woman in the group, and her personal, dreamlike poetry had surrealist touches within fragmented yet intimate urban landscapes.

The Grupo Boedo, a leftist, socially conscious set opposed to the Florida group's aestheticism, shared a desire for something new and occasionally participated in ultraism and the avant-garde. Raúl González Tuñón (1905–74) was a poet who witnessed the city and its social life instead of producing art for art's sake. Out of *El violin del diablo* (The Devil's Violin, 1926), his first book, grew marginal figures such as the militant character Juancito Caminador (Johnny Walker). Nicolás Olivari (1900–66), also part of the Boedo group, displayed irony and sarcasm in his portraits of society in *La musa de la mala pata* (The Bad-Footed Muse, 1926); like some of his compatriots, he composed tango lyrics, notably those of *La violeta* (The Violet). Both these poets influenced Francisco Urondo (1930–76), who used his idealism and militant poetry to confront the dictatorship of the 1970s. Entering the 1930s and 1940s, previously ultraist poets turned to surrealism or neoromanticism, and the Argentine avant-garde fractured into different elements.

Essays and narrative dominated the 1920s and 1930s, but one transitional poet in this period was both part of the *Martín Fierro* group and different from it: Carlos Mastronardi (1901–76). Called an "anti-vanguard vanguardist," Mastronardi, known for translating Fr. symbolists, was a symbolist himself, whose verse engaged sensibility and landscape, drew on comparison rather than metaphor, and employed traditional musical forms rather than free verse. His poetics make him a precursor to the 1940s generation, whose poets combined avant-garde elements with symbolism and romanticism to create personal styles that bring them together eclectically as a group.

There is a tendency in mid-century Argentine letters to discuss ten-year generations, loosely affiliating poets who began to publish in the same decade and who share a literary inheritance but not a platform. Some of the 1940s poets, writing during the time that Juan Perón first came to power (1946–55), demonstrate an interest in the irrational, magical, and ritual possibilities of poetry. They tend to see the poem as a way of knowing, while at the same time questioning what it is possible to know or say. Alberto Girri (1919–91) is one of these poets, who counts Ezra Pound and T. S. Eliot among his influences. His early work, such as *Playa sola* (Lone Beach, 1946), is visionary, necromantic, imagistic, and affective. In his later work, the perspective becomes ironic and cerebral in dense, free-verse poems that explore time and space. Enrique Molina's (1910–96) work is more associated with surrealism (he translated André Breton), and in his first book, *Las cosas y el delirio* (Things and Delirium, 1941), he combines reality with hallucination, creating a sense of disintegration and of solitude as a natural experience. His long poetic novel *Una sombra donde sueña Camila O'Gorman* (A Shadow Where Camila O'Gorman Sleeps, 1973) offers its readers a dreamlike approach to a figure from Argentine hist., as well as a genre-crossing postvanguardist experiment. There is a constant tension in the poetry of Olga Orozco (1920–99): a ceaseless motif of desire and lack, a search for a fragmented god or wholeness, amid themes of distance and loss. Poetry is a ritual or an interior journey in her work, which demonstrates a notable coherence of tone, lang., and themes, from *Desde lejos* (From Afar, 1946) to the occult, metaphysical concerns of *Con esta boca en este mundo* (With This Mouth in This World, 1994). Each of these poets turned away from overt engagement with the social world in her or his work to explore other kinds of knowledge through poetry.

In the 1950s and 1960s, a number of younger poets began to publish, some continuing in the postvanguardist mode, such as Alejandra Pizarnik (1936–72), who wrote often terse, interior-focused poetry on the fringes of surrealism, while others turned to poetry as a means of social transformation. Pizarnik's work is often seen as a self-exile in lang. and away from the poetic values of her generation. She uses a dense, hypercontrolled lang. in which solitude and silence play a central role to challenge lit.'s limitations in works such as *El infierno musical* (Musical Hell, 1971). Pizarnik was an inspiration to a series of later poets, and recent readers have begun to explore the full range of her writing.

Liliana Lukin (b. 1951) acknowledges Pizarnik's writing as an inspiration to her own. Her book *Descomposición* (Decomposition, 1986) quotes from Franz Kafka (a source of intertexts favored by Pizarnik as well), whose work reminds us that reading, like writing, is a disturbing and corporeal process. Lukin uses lang. to embody absence, and in both theme and technique, this poetics becomes part of the historical recovery process after the Dirty War (the dictatorship that lasted from 1976 to 1983). Tamara Kamenszain (b. 1947) is another writer who extends Pizarnik's techniques through her concept of lang. as a trope in *Los no* (1977), in which ritualized Japanese Nō theater exemplifies the renunciation of representation, and in *La casa grande* (The Big House, 1986), a semi-surreal evocation of daily life. More recently Anahí Mallol (b. 1968) has explored the impact of Pizanik in her own work and that of others (contemps. Susana Thénon [1937–90] and Orozco, and more recent writers) whose works converse with those of Pizarnik in their intensity and struggle with the liminal zones of lang.

A contemporary of Pizarnik, Juan Gelman (1930–2014), moves through the world and makes his poetry of it, shoring up lang. against dehumanization. His early poetry (*Violín y otras cuestiones* [Violin and Other Questions], 1956) is based on local speech that links experience with imagination in primarily urban settings. Gelman was exiled from Argentina in 1975, and his later books deal with issues such as mourning, politics, and responsibility for the other, employing techniques such as syntactic and ling. alteration, idiosyncratic punctuation, intertextual references, heteronyms, and self-translations. During this time of much social and political change, Juana Bignozzi's (1937–2015) poetry joins a personal, confessional tone to social realism. Lucid and conversational, her lang. shares irony and an ethical perspective with that of Gelman; her collected works, *La ley, tu ley* (The Law, Your Law, 2000), demonstrate the scope of her expression. The work of Leónidas Lamborghini (1927–2009) grows out of a social commitment that he expresses in unadorned lang. and short lines. He highlights the construction of a poetic voice, and this, along with an attention to rhythm, unites his oeuvre. He creates a dialogue or counterpoint by rewriting earlier authors, sometimes with a parodic, ludic tone to remind his readers consistently that art is an artifice—one technique that associates him with the neobaroque.

After the dictatorship, the floodgates opened, and there was a proliferation of poetry that branched out into new areas, both stylistic and thematic. Néstor Perlongher (1949–92) was a prominent figure of the 1980s whose style is complex, focusing readers' attention on the text's surface and on lit.'s metalinguistic aspects, all elements that situate his work within the neobaroque. Perlongher describes the movement as deterritorialized (departing from the Spaniard Luis de Góngora), a postcolonial response to inherited paradigms. Although some neobaroque poets may exclude external references, Perlongher insinuates politics and hist. into his early collections (*Austria-Hungría*, 1980), in which orderly syntax and grammatical connections still predominate. In his later work, neobaroque complication reigns: *Parque Lezama* (1990) is a linguistic performance in which any normative identity is destabilized, propelling its readers to ontological questions about what speech and poetry are. Another defiant perspective of the 1980s is that of Diana Bellessi (b. 1946), who established a feminist voice (with a notably lesbian perspective in *Eroíca*, 1988) with which she recreated inherited symbols, images, and words in an often intimate tone. Her later work elaborates her ethical interests, often joining popular and high cultural registers. Bellessi's work has been taken in new directions by more recent poets such as Bárbara Belloc (b. 1968), whose *Ambición de las flores* (1997) elaborates the flower as a feminine erotic image, paradoxically loving and carnivorous.

A proliferation of jours. in mid- and late 20th-c. Argentina featured poetry: *Poesía Buenos Aires*, *A partir de cero*, and later *Literal*, *Diario de poesía*, *Ultimo reino*, and *XUL*, providing venues for local and international poetry and theoretical debate. The economic turmoil of the 1990s, which continued into the next century, heralded more social transformation and a new urban poetry featuring direct communication of experience that some critics have called hyperrealistic. Many younger poets work against alienation and give voice to disillusion through irony and references to the new social margins. Some of this poetry incorporates film, mass media, and popular culture in form and content. Through performance, poetry on the Web, and hypertextual forms, poets find new ways to seek out readers. One example of the many recent writers who challenge the status quo is Washington Cucurto (pseud. of Santiago Vega, b. 1973), whose *Cosa de negros* (Black Folks' Stuff, 2003) has developed a kind of cult following. Cucurto writes from the invisible part of his country and uses *cumbia* and other dance rhythms to express the raw experience of a peripheral world that is denigrated by the dominant culture. Like many of the poets of his generation, he uses lyric conventions to challenge these prejudices—an approach that might characterize much of the poetry of the late 1990s and the early 21st c. in Argentina.

See INDIGENOUS AMERICAS, POETRY OF THE; SPANISH AMERICA, POETRY OF.

■ **Anthologies**: *Poesía argentina del siglo XX*, ed. J. C. Ghiano (1957)—also contains hist. and crit.; *Antología lineal de la poesía argentina*, ed. C. Fernández Moreno (1968); *Antología de poesía argentina*, ed. A. del Saz (1969); *La nueva poesía argentina*, ed. N. Salvador (1969); *Antología de la poesía argentina*, ed. R. G. Aguirre (1979); *Antología de la nueva poesía argentina*, ed. H. Alvarez Castillo (1990); *Geografía lírica argentina*, ed. J. Isaacson (2003).

■ **Criticism and History**: M. Menéndez y Pelayo, *Historia de la poesía argentina* (1943); J. Ludmer, *El género gauchesco* (1988); B. Sarlo, *Una modernidad periférica* (1988); G. Kirkpatrick, *The Dissonant Legacy of Modernismo* (1989); M. González and D. Treece, *The Gathering of Voices* (1992); *Conversaciones con la poesía argentina*, ed. J. Fondebrider (1995); A. Mallol, *El poema y su doble* (2003); M. Prieto, *Breve historia de la literatura argentina* (2006); *Tres décadas de la poesía argentina 1976–2006*, ed. J. Fondebrider (2006); T. Kamenszain, *Boca de testimonio* (2007).

J. KUHNHEIM

ARMENIAN POETRY AND POETICS

- I. Pre-Christian Origins and Early Epics
- II. Ecclesiastic Poetry
- III. The Rise of Folk Songs and Armenian Classicism
- IV. The National Awakening
- V. The Rise of the Aesthetes
- VI. Poetry in Diaspora

I. Pre-Christian Origins and Early Epics. The Armenian lang., a branch of the IE ling. family, has an extensive poetic trad. originating in ancient Asia Minor and eventually spanning the globe over more than two millennia. Most historians date the emergence of the Armenians to the 6th c. BCE as a distinct ling. and cultural collective autochthonous to Anatolia in the Republic of Turkey.

Few samples of the earliest Armenian poetry remain. Two reasons account for this scarcity. First, the earliest poetry constituted a segment of the oral trad., thereby leaving no written trace. Second, the Armenians' state conversion to Christianity (ca. 314–15) precipitated the prompt effacement of the Armenian Zoroastrian and pagan pasts, incl. the narratives they inspired.

The remaining fragments, which were partially inscribed following the invention of the Armenian alphabet (ca. 406 CE), suggest rich bardic origins. Armenian historical texts indicate that the first poets were minstrels, known as *gusans*, who composed a variety of songs, ranging from eulogies for historical personages to festive wedding tunes. Pre-Christian poetry also included two categories of epics based either on legendary tales or mythologized historical themes. The legendary epic "Vahagn Vishapagagh" (Vahagn the Dragonslayer) found in the *History of the Armenians* by Movses Khorenatsi (Moses of Khoren, "Father of Armenian Historiography") constitutes the oldest surviving Armenian poem and recounts the birth of the divinity Vahagn, god of thunder. Mythologized historical epics appear during the Yervantuni dynasty (ca. 600–200 BCE) and include the popular tale *Tigran and Azhdahak*, relating the struggle between King Tigran I and the king of the Medes, Azhdahak (Astiages). It depicts the first female character to appear in an epic, Tigranuhi, Tigran's sister and Azhdahak's wife. The earliest known post-Christian epic is *Parsits Paterazm* (The Persian War), drawn from folklore and composed between the 3d and 5th cs. CE and relating the protracted struggle of the Arshakuni (Arsacid) dynasty rulers of Armenia against the Sassanid Empire.

II. Ecclesiastic Poetry. The first phase of ecclesiastic poetry commenced following the alphabet's invention by the monk Mesrop Mashtots (ca. 360–440). Though lay poetry continued to appear, verses were primarily restricted to spiritual works, which rendered biblical stories, reproduced ancient Jewish prayers and psalms, and introduced the first specimen of written Armenian lyric poetry, namely, the spiritual hymn, later known (from the 12th c. CE on) as *sharakan*. Mashtots and one of his patrons, the catholicos Sahak Partev (ca. 345–439), authored the first sharakans, which were performed on Christian feast days and holidays. In addition to Mashtots and Sahak Partev, other noteworthy sharakan writers include Moses of Khoren, renowned for his "Khorhurd metz yev skanjeli" (Great and Wondrous Mystery) sung on Christmas;

Sahak Dzoraporetsi (677–708), who wrote the first sharakans dedicated to the Cross and the Church; Stepanos Siunetsi (d. 735), who turned the canon into the liturgy by organizing hymns and arranging voices and tunes; and Sahakdukht (fl. 8th c.), Siunetsi's sister, who is the first known female Armenian poet.

In addition to sharakans, the Middle Ages also produced one of the most renowned Armenian poets, the monk Grigor Narekatsi (Gregory of Nareg, ca. 950–1003). Narekatsi is acclaimed for his monumental lyric poem *Matyan Voghbergutyan* (Book of Lamentations), known simply as *Narek*, a book of prayers consisting of 95 chapters. Its tone resembles Augustine's *Confessions* with themes of repentance and love of God, heavily imbued with simile and metaphor. After the Psalter and NT, it was the most widely circulated text of med. Armenian lit. and has remained influential.

Another influential early poet is Nerses Shnorhali (Nerses, Full of Grace, ca. 1101–1173). Shnorhali lived and wrote during a trying historical period when the displaced Armenian people were forced to relocate to Syria and Cilicia and had to struggle for autonomy from Byzantine and regional rulers. A pervasive preference for poetry had emerged that led writers and translators to render a wide variety of narratives—historical, didactic, scientific, and literary—into verse in the manner of Homer, David, Solomon, and Jeremiah, and also often converted prose texts into poetry. Shnorhali wrote in this milieu, composing in a vast array of genres. Trained as a priest and later anointed catholicos (1166), Shnorhali was committed to national and ecclesiastic concerns, exemplified in his historical epic *Voghb Yedesio* (Lament for Edessa, ca. 1145), the first of its kind in Armenian lit. The epic recounts the destruction of Edessa (1144) and the massacre of its Christian population by Emir Zangi's troops. It introduced several innovations, incl. personification and the five-syllable iambic meter, which became the standard for subsequent poets. The work helped reinforce the lament as a dominant poetic form, inspiring Grigor IV Tgha's (ca. 1133–93) *Voghb Yerusaghemi* (Lament for Jerusalem, 1189); Stepanos Orbelian's (ca. 1250–1305) *Voghb i dimats katoghikein* (Lament on Behalf of the Cathedral); and Arakel Baghishetsi's (ca. 1380–1454) *Voghb Mayrakaghakin Stampolu* (Lament for the Capital Constantinople, 1453), among others.

After Narekatsi and Shnorhali, few noteworthy names or literary devels. appear from the 13th through the 17th cs., a period of protracted political strife for the Armenians embattled by invaders and culminating in the devastating fall of the kingdom of Cilicia (1375) to Mamluk forces. The poets whose names survive from this period lived and wrote chiefly in the 13th c. Hovhannes Yerznkatsi (Pluz, ca. 1230–93) was the era's best-known scholar and philosopher. He was the first to write a secular love poem based on a folk tale about a pair of ill-fated lovers—an Armenian boy and a Muslim girl—divided by their faiths. The spirited Frik (b. ca. 1230) was popular for his bombastic poems condemning corruption and oppression in all spheres. Kostandin Yerznkatsi (ca. 1304–36) is significant for introducing extensive nature imagery and earned acclaim for his elaborate allegories.

III. The Rise of Folk Songs and Armenian Classicism. By the end of the 16th c., a new group of poets emerged consisting of Nerses Mokatsi (ca. 1575–1625), Martiros Ghrimetsi (1620–83), and Simeon Aparanetsi (ca. 1540–1614). At the time, folk songs had a great influence on poetry. Nahapet Kuchak (d. ca. 1592) was a master of the *hairen* variety, an indigenous poetic form written in four lines of couplets with a single coherent theme.

The 18th c. compensated somewhat for the immediate past's poetic stagnation. Bardic lyricism had developed in the previous century as a branch of folk songs and flourished in the 18th through the works of the two renowned bards Naghash Hovnatan (1661–1722) and Sayat-Nova (ca. 1712–95). The latter is a dominant figure in the Armenian national imagination, and his songs are still regularly performed. Bardic lyric poems were related to Perso-Arabic lit. and were sung by wandering bards who also performed non-Armenian pieces. They initially expressed historical themes but eventually evolved primarily into love songs. This period also paved the way for formal cl. pieces composed in *grabar* (cl. Armenian) such as those by Paghtasar Dpir (Grigorian, 1683–1768) and Petros Ghapantsi (d. 1784).

The 18th c. also witnessed the rise of the Mkhitarist Congregation (1717) founded by Mkhitar Sebastatsi (Mkhitar of Sivas, 1676–1749) on the island of San Lazzaro in Venice. The Mkhitarist monks were instrumental in reviving the Armenian lang. and lit. Mkhitar was their first author and wrote mainly religious poems with patriotic themes. Arsen

Bakratuni (1790–1866) and Ghevont Alishan (1820–1901) succeeded him as the two most prominent Mkhitarist poets. Bakratuni's poem *Hayk Diutzazn* (The Epic Hero Hayk) is one of the longest poems (22,332 lines) in world lit. and represents the height of Armenian classicism. It recounts the heroic exploits of the mythical Armenian forefather Hayk, deriving its influence from ancient Gr. and Lat. sources. Alishan's poems were the first to appear in mod. Armenian and initiated the romantic trad. in Armenian lit., inspiring the patriotic works of such major 19th-c. poets as Raphael Patkanian (1830–92) and Mikayel Nalpantian (1829–66). Alishan's most celebrated poems include "Voghbam Zkez Hayots Ashkharh" (I Weep for You, Armenia) and *Hushigk Hayrenyats Hayots* (Memories of the Armenian Homeland).

The 19th c. inaugurated a culturally fertile epoch, which continued into the early portion of the 20th c. Armenian poetry in particular underwent radical transformation, achieving unprecedented popularity and a central role in facilitating the Armenian national-cultural revival. Interest in the poetic trad. led folklorist Father Karekin Srvandztiantz to the major discovery and inscription in the 1870s of *Sansuntsi Davit* (David of Sassoun), part of the cycle *Sasna Tzrer* (Madmen of Sasun) and *Jojants Tun* (House of Giants). It was an epic recounted for the first time in the Middle Ages and had survived in the oral trad. of Mush, one of whose inhabitants, Krpo of Mush, had retained and retold it.

IV. The National Awakening. The second half of the 19th c. is known as the era of *Zartonk* (Awakening), which proceeded from various historical, political, and cultural antecedents: the rise of the merchant classes in Armenian global diasporic communities; the creation of Armenian printing presses; the cultural efforts of the Mkhitarist congregation; and the preoccupation of Eur.-educated intellectuals with national concerns. Four poets exemplified the spirit and poetic trends of the Zartonk generation: Mgrdich Beshigtashlian (1828–68) and Bedros Turian (1851–72), both natives of Istanbul, represented the Western Armenian dialect writing in the Ottoman Empire; and Mikayel Nalpantian (1829–66) and Raphael Patkanian (also known as Kamar Katipa, 1830–92), both from Nor Nakhichevan (Rostov-on-Don), wrote in Eastern Armenian in the South Caucasus. Beshigtashlian is renowned for his romantic lyricism, which combined naturalist imagery with nationalist motifs. His poems "Karun" ("Spring") and "Yeghpair Emk Mek . . ." (We Are Brothers . . .) highlight his delicate temperament and profound patriotism. Turian, who died prematurely from tuberculosis at the age of 21, was much beloved by his contemporaries. His poems primarily speak of unrequited love, untimely death, and patriotic struggle. His poems "Ljag" ("Little Lake"), about his imminent death, and "Trkuhin" (The Turkish Woman), about an unattainable beloved, are among his most popular works. Nalpantian was a staunch anti-imperialist activist whose poems reflect his political inclinations, esp. in "Mankutyan Orer" (Childhood Days), "Azatutyun" (Freedom), and "Mer Hayrenik" (Our Fatherland), which became the national anthem of the Republic of Armenia. Similarly, Patkanian considered his work a medium for promoting enlightenment and national consciousness through such poems as "Araxi Artasuke" ("The Tears of the Araxes") and his 1878 collection *Azat Yerger* (Free Songs).

V. The Rise of the Aesthetes. In the last decades of the 19th c., as realism gradually replaced romanticism, preference for poetry waned in favor of prose. The next wave of influential poets emerged afterward, in the first two decades of the 20th c. Taking their cues from the canon of Western lit., some of them demanded and exercised new modes of ling. refinement and aesthetic consciousness, becoming known as the Aesthetes. The outstanding names of this time include, among Western Armenians, Misak Medzarents (1886–1908), Vahan Tekeyan (1878–1945), Tanyel Varujan (1884–1915), Siamanto (Adom Yerjanian, 1878–1915); and among Eastern Armenians, Hovhannes Tumanian (1869–1923), Yeghishé Charents (Soghomonian, 1897–1937), Avetik Issahakian (1875–1957), and Vahan Terian (1885–1920).

Varujan and Charents constitute the apex of these new poetic heights and share similarly tragic fates. Varujan described his perspective as "poetic paganism," which he voiced initially with his rendition of "Vahagn." The poem appeared in his first large collection, *Tzeghin Sirde* (The Heart of the Race, 1909), which was followed by *Hetanos Yerker* (Pagan Songs, 1912), considered two of the most important books of Armenian poetry from the 20th c. On April 24, 1915, the eve of the outbreak of the Catastrophe (the genocide of Ottoman-Armenians, 1915–18), Varujan was captured by Ottoman authorities along with hundreds of his contemporaries and deported to the prison camp of Chankiri, where he was promptly executed. Charents lived across the Ottoman border, in Soviet territory. He was a staunch Communist but soon became disillusioned with the Stalinist regime, which took his life during the 1937 purges. Charents's work expresses a revolutionary spirit that responded with insight and fervor to the harrowing historicopolitical vicissitudes he observed and experienced. His best-known works in his extensive repertoire include *Tandeakan Araspel* (*Dantesque Legend*), a response to the World War I Ottoman atrocities he witnessed as a volunteer soldier; *Ambokhnerë Khelagarvatz* (The Frenzied Masses), which established him as the first major non-Russian Soviet poet; and *Girk Chanaparhi* (Book of the Road), a set of verses dedicated to major Armenian cultural figures alongside religious and love poems.

VI. Poetry in Diaspora. Following the Catastrophe and the expansion of the Armenian diaspora, poetry experienced a mixture of decline and experimentation. Surviving and emerging Ottoman-Armenian writers wrote haphazardly and consisted both of traditionalist and avant-garde wings. Among the traditionalists who conformed to the poetic ideals and methods of their predecessors were Mushegh Ishkhan (Mushegh Jerderian, 1913–90), Antranig Dzarugian (1912–90), and Vahé Vahian (Sarkis Abdalian, 1907–98). Among the avant-garde, one finds Nigoghos Sarafian (1902–72), Zahrad (pseud. of Zareh Yaldzjian, 1924–2007), Zareh Khrakhuni (pseud. of Artin Jiumbiushian, b. 1926), and Vahé Oshagan (1922–2000). Dzarugian and Sarafian have left the most indelible marks by vividly expressing their generation's orientation. Dzarugian's controversial poem, "Tught ar Yerevan" (Letter to Yerevan) targeted Soviet Armenian writers' antinationalist propagandist rhet. Sarafian paved a unique and unprecedented path with his long poem *Venseni Andare* (The Forest of Vincennes), which traces the poet's inner journey as the son of a displaced people. During the same years, Soviet Armenian poets were beset by the regime's stringent restrictions. They include Gevork Emin (1919–98), Paruyr Sevak (1924–71), and Silva Kaputikian (1919–2006).

In the wake of the 20th c., Armenian poetry is at a virtual standstill, though several promising voices in the diaspora and the Republic of Armenia remain active. Krikor Beledian (b. 1945), based in France, is author of the groundbreaking works *Yelk: Mantraner B. Shark* (Exit: Mantras B. Series) and *Deghakrutyun Kantvogh Kaghaki Me Hamar* (Diagram for a Collapsing City), which impels Armenian poetry into new uncharted realms of abstraction. Violet Grigorian (b. 1962) is a singular experimental poet whose feminist themes and provocative lang. continue to interrogate and undermine entrenched patriarchal taboos. She has published four collections of poems, incl. *Haremi Vard* (*Harem Rose*).

■ **Anthologies:** A. Issahakian, *Scent, Smile, and Sorrow: Selected Verse (1891–1957) and Jottings from Notebooks*, ed. and trans. E. B. Chrakian (1975); *Anthology of Armenian Poetry*, ed. and trans. D. Der Hovanessian and M. Margossian (1978); *Armenian Poetry, Old and New: A Bilingual Anthology*, ed. and trans. A. Tolegian (1979); K. Nahapet, *Come Sit Beside Me and Listen to Koutchag: Medieval Armenian Poems of Nahabed Kouchag*, trans. D. Der-Hovanessian (1984); *Bloody News from My Friend: Poems by Siamanto*, trans. P. Balakian and N. Yaghlian (1996); K. Nahapet, *A Hundred and One Hayrens*, trans. E. Osers (1998); *The Heritage of Armenian Literature*, ed. G. Basmajian, E. S. Franchuk, A. J. Hacikyan, and N. Ouzounian, 3 v. (2000–05); *Bosphorus Nights: The Complete Lyric Poems of Bedros Tourian*, trans. J. R. Russell (2005); *Deviation: Anthology of Contemporary Armenian Literature*, ed. V. Grigoryan and V. Ishkhanyan (2008).

■ **Collections:** *Armenian Popular Songs*, trans. G. M. Alishan (1852); V. Komitas, *Armenian Sacred and Folk Music*, trans. E. Gulbekian (1998); G. M. Alishan, *Old Armenian Songs: A Nineteenth-Century Collection*, ed. A. Nercessian (2002); *The Song of the Stork and Other Early and Ancient Armenian Songs*, trans. D. Kherdian (2004).

■ **Histories:** B. S. Hairapetian, *A History of Armenian Literature: From Ancient Times to the 19th Century* (1995); K. B. Bardakjian, *A Reference Guide to Modern Armenian Literature, 1500–1920* (2000); V. Nersessian, "Armenian," *The Oxford Guide to Literature in English Translation*, ed. P. France (2000); S. P. Cowe, "Medieval Armenian Literary and Cultural Trends," *The Armenian People from Ancient to Modern Times*, v. 1, *The Dynastic Periods*, ed. R. G. Hovanissian (2004); V. Oshagan, "Modern Armenian Literature and Intellectual History from 1700 to 1915" and R. W. Thomson, "Armenian

Literary Culture through the Eleventh Century," *The Armenian People from Ancient to Modern Times*, v. 2, *Foreign Dominion to Statehood*, ed. R. G. Hovanissian (2004); R. Panossian, *The Armenians: From Kings and Priests to Merchants and Commissars* (2006).

■ **Journals:** *Ararat: A Quarterly* (1960–); *Journal of the Society for Armenian Studies* (1984–); *Raft: Journal of Armenian Poetry and Criticism* (1984–).

■ **Translations and Criticism:** *David of Sassoun: The Armenian Folk Epic in Four Cycles*, trans. A. K. Shalian (1964); Moses of Khoren, *History of the Armenians*, trans. R. W. Thomson (1978); C. Dowsett, *Sayat'-Nova: An Eighteenth-Century Troubadour* (1997); *The Heroes of Kasht: An Armenian Epic*, ed. and trans. J. R. Russell (2000); N. Grigor, *Speaking with God from the Depths of the Heart: The Armenian Prayer Book of St. Gregory of Narek*, trans. T. J. Samuelian (2001); M. Nichanian, *Writers of Disaster*, v. 1, *The National Revolution* (2002); *Yeghishe Charents: Poet of the Revolution*, ed. M. Nichanian (2003); *Divine Liturgy of the Armenian Apostolic Orthodox Church*, trans. A. Aivazian (2005); S. A. Arak'el, *Adamgirk': The Adam Book of Arak'el of Siwnik'*, trans. M. E. Stone (2007); A. Eghiazaryan, *Daredevils of Sasun: Poetics of an Epic*, trans. S. P. Cowe (2008).

N. Kebranian

ASSAMESE POETRY. Assamese is the lang. of the state of Assam in northeast India. The earliest examples of Assamese poetry are from the 13th c. and are recreations, sometimes trans., of the great Sanskrit epics the *Mahābhārata* and the *Rāmāyaṇa* and the Sanskrit myths in the *Purāṇas*. Assam may have had its own distinctive versions of the *Purāṇas*. This would explain why Hema Saraswatī's 13th-c. *Prahlāda Caritra* (The Deeds of Prahlāda) does not conform to any existing Sanskrit text. Other early landmark texts are the 14th-c. *Rāmāyaṇa* of Mādhava Kandalī and the renderings of the *Mahābhārata* (by Kavi Ratna Sarasvatī and Rudra Kandalī). These works attest to a lively trad. of poetry inspired by the Sanskrit classics. Assam has a rich trad. of folk poetry, sung at festivals and weddings, which probably existed alongside these early literary compositions.

With the appearance of the great Vaiṣṇava leader Śaṅkaradeva (1449–1569), Assamese poetry came into its own. Śaṅkaradeva endeavored to spread the teachings of the *Bhāgavata Purāṇa*, which recounts the deeds of the god Kṛṣṇa. His literary output was considerable, incl. trans. into Assamese from the *Bhāgavata Purāṇa*, dramas (*Aṅkīya Naṭa*) on the life of Kṛṣṇa, and short hymns for private and public worship (*Kīrtana Ghoṣā* and *Bargītas*). Some of the *Bargītas* were composed by Śaṅkaradeva's disciple Mādhavadeva (1489–1596). Mādhavadeva also composed devotional and philosophical poems, *Nāma ghoṣā*, and dramas. His *Bhaktiratnāvali* is an Assamese trans. of an anthol. of verses from the *Bhāgavata Purāṇa* compiled by Viṣṇu Pūri (1485).

Roughly contemporary with Śaṅkaradeva, Pītambara Dāsa, Durgāvara, and Manakara composed poetry in a different vein. Drawing on traditional sources, their poetry described the love of the god Śiva for his wife Pārvatī, well known from the *Purāṇas*, and the marriage of the merchant Lakhindār and Behulā. Durgāvara composed the *Gīti Rāmāyaṇa*, based on the Assamese *Rāmāyaṇa* of Mādhava Kandalī. These poets wrote in the style of the oral bardic poetry of Assam, avoiding the ornate figures of speech favored by Sanskrit poets.

The disciples of Śaṅkaradeva continued to compose poems on subjects in the epics and the *Purāṇas* and to translate these Sanskrit texts into Assamese. Rāma Sarasvatī's 16th-c. *Mahābhārata* includes independent poems on the slaying of various demons. These *Vadha kāvyas* are considered a distinctive contribution of Assam to the telling of the *Mahābhārata*.

The Vaiṣṇava movement of Śaṅkaradeva gave rise to a rich biographical lit., often in verse. Daityāri Ṭhākura wrote a biography of Śaṅkaradeva and Mādhavadeva. Nīlakaṇṭha Dāsa composed a biography of Dāmodaradeva (1488–1598), a direct disciple of Śaṅkaradeva and the first schismatic. Bhadra Cāru's poem deals with the life of Ananta and his struggle with the king Gadādhara Siṃha in the 17th c. As the group split, these texts established the lineages of succession. The biographies of Śaṅkaradeva and his followers were not the only historical texts written in verse. A court astrologer, Sūrya Khaḍi Daivajña, born in the late 18th c., wrote a verse hist. of the kings of Daraṅga.

Well into the 19th c., poets continued to draw on Sanskrit sources. Ramākānta Chaudhuri (1846–89) wrote his *Abhimanyuvadha* (The Slaying of Abhimanyu, 1875) based on the story in the *Mahābhārata*. He broke with traditional verse forms and followed the Bengali poet Michael Madhusudan Dutt, whose blank verse poem on the death of the *Rāmāyaṇa* villain Rāvaṇa had caused a stir in literary circles in Calcutta. The influence of Bengal on Assamese intellectuals remained strong; and new influences, e.g., from Brit. romantic poetry, were apparent in both Bengal and Assam. The periodical *Jonākī*, which published the poems of Chandrakumar Agarwala (1867–1938) and Lakshminath Bezbarua (1868–1938), among others, was begun from Calcutta. *Jonākī* was published for only ten years. It was followed by a period of experimentation with surrealism, symbolism, and the thought of Sigmund Freud and Karl Marx. Today, this eclecticism continues; poets from diverse backgrounds continue to seek their inspiration in a variety of sources, in the diverse tribal cultures of Assam, in India's ancient Sanskritic culture, and in poetic movements elsewhere and abroad.

See INDIA, POETRY OF; RĀMĀYAṆA POETRY.

■ *Asamiya Sahityar Chaneki or Typical Selections from Assamese Literature*, ed. H. Goswami, 3 v. (1924–27); Birinchi Kumar Barua, *The History of Assamese Literature* (1964); M. Neog, *Śaṅkaradeva and His Times* (1965); M. Neog, *Asamīya Sāhityar Rūparekhā* (1981); *Medieval Indian Literature: An Anthology*, ed. K. Ayyappapaniker, 2d ed. (1997).

P. GRANOFF

ASSYRIA AND BABYLONIA, POETRY OF

I. Introduction
II. Narrative Poetry
III. Religious Poetry
IV. Didactic Poetry

I. Introduction. Assyrian and Babylonian were the two main dialects of Akkadian, a Semitic lang. Of these, Babylonian and not Assyrian was used for most of the poetry. The earliest surviving poetic texts, preserved on clay tablets written in cuneiform script, date from the end of the 3d millennium BCE. A very creative period followed in the Old Babylonian period, from ca. 1800 BCE onward. Around and after 1200, again much new poetry was composed. This material is mostly known from copies collected in royal or temple libraries in Assur, Ninive, Sultantepe, Babylon, Uruk, and Sippar in the first millennium.

Most of the texts are anonymous: as exceptions, the author of the epic poem *Erra and Ishum*, Kabti-ilani-Marduk (who claims to have written it from the gods' dictation); the author of the latest version of the *Epic of Gilgamesh*, Sîn-liqe-unninni; and the poet of the *Theodicy*, Saggil-kinam-ubbib, are known by name. Other names appearing in tablet colophons are generally those of the copying scribes, not of the poets.

With respect to genre, the corpus may summarily be divided into narrative, religious, and didactic poetry, i.e., into epics, hymns and prayers, and wisdom literature. Purely secular poetry (e.g., the humorous poems discussed below) seems to have been recorded in writing only rarely; traces of it can be found in charms to avoid scorpions, to remedy toothache, to quiet a crying baby, and so on. As part of an oral trad., the motifs and stylistic features of such poems can often be traced over long periods in ever-changing new versions. The texts themselves—often embedded in medical or magical prescriptions—resemble nursery rhymes and suggest a pattern of folk poetry made up of mostly short lines containing similes and wordplay and often concatenated repetitions, such as

Anger advances like a wild bull,
Jumps at me like a dog.
Like a lion, it is formidable in progress,
Like a wolf, it is full of fury.

Some verses whose lyricism would suggest secular love poetry mostly seem on closer reading to concern divine lovers, as in the Old Babylonian poem

The women's quarter moans, the bedchamber weeps
Wherein we were wont to celebrate the wedding;
The courtyard sighs, the loft laments
Wherein we were wont to do sweet dalliance.

In an Assyrian elegy, a woman who died in childbirth complains:

I lived with him who was my lover.
Death came creeping into my bedroom,
It drove me from my house,
It tore me from my husband,
It set my feet into a land of no return.

The most common formal characteristic of Assyro-Babylonian poetry, shared with *Sumerian and most other Semitic poetry, is syntactic parallelism, as evidenced in the examples above. It is frequently combined with chiasmus, while zeugma is rarely tolerated. A special form of enjambment, combined with chiasmus, is sometimes used to connect lines in a "Janus construction." Rhyme (more often internal than final), alliteration, onomatopoeia, anaphora, and epistrophe may be used for special effect. Rhythm is based on stress, with no strict meter; a typical line contains four measures, rarely three or five, with a caesura in the middle. The verse ending is usually trochaic, and final syllables that would make the last word a dactyl are often truncated. Acrostics and telestics in which the respective syllables spell out a name or a pious wish, as well as poems in which each line of a strophe begins with the same written sign, are also known.

II. Narrative Poetry. Babylonian epics deal with the exploits of gods or mythological beings and are, therefore, often dubbed *myths*. Many of these are already known from the Old Babylonian period, although their 1st-millennium recensions are usually more elaborate: the story of the bird Anzû, who stole the Tablet of Destinies from the supreme god Enlil and was defeated by the god Ninurta; the story of the mythical king Etana, who ascended to heaven on the back of an eagle to obtain the herb for childbearing; the story of the sage Atrahasis (Exceedingly Wise), who survived the flood brought about by the gods after they had created humankind; and the *Epic of Gilgamesh* (see below).

Of a slightly later date are the stories of wise Adapa and of Nergal and Ereshkigal, the latter telling how Nergal came to rule the netherworld together with its queen Ereshkigal. Only 1st-millennium sources are known for *Enuma Elish*, the epic of creation in which Marduk defeats the forces of chaos and creates the cosmos out of the body of the primeval monster, thereby being acknowledged as supreme god; *Erra and Ishum*, which describes the calamities that befell Babylon when the plague god Erra replaced its tutelary god Marduk; and the *Descent of Ishtar to the Netherworld*.

The 19th-c. discovery of a tablet of the *Epic of Gilgamesh* with an account of the Flood closely paralleling that in the OT triggered Western interest in this work. It deals with basic human concerns of all times—friendship and the quest for immortality and enduring fame. When Enkidu, a semisavage created by the gods to become Gilgamesh's friend and companion, dies, Gilgamesh realizes the same fate awaits him and so begins the quest that eventually leads to an encounter with the sole survivor of the Flood. There, Gilgamesh almost reaches his goal of achieving eternal life but then loses it again in a moment of inattentiveness. The epic does not end with the death of its hero, however, but as it began, with the description of the ramparts of the city of Uruk, his lasting achievement.

Some narrative poems have historical kings as heroes, e.g., a cycle about Sargon and Naram-Sin, who built the Akkadian empire in the late third millennium. An epic about the Assyrian king Tukulti-Ninurta (1243–1207 BCE) and his victory over the Babylonian king Kashtiliash reflects Assyrian political ideology, though it is actually written in the Babylonian literary dialect. Other poems are couched as autobiographies, with the king narrating his own hist. Here, the lesson to be drawn from events of the past is held up to the future ruler in a sort of *envoi* at the end, bringing the genre close to that of didactic poetry.

III. Religious Poetry. Most Babylonian hymns address gods and goddesses, but some are also in praise of cities. These poems are characterized by an elevated style and a vocabulary of rare terms, indicators of their learned origin and sophisticated audience. They are often divided into strophes that are, however, only inconsistently marked on the tablet. The *Hymn to Shamash* (the sun god and god of justice) has exactly 200 lines, divided by rulings into 100 distichs; other hymns of even greater length were addressed to Ishtar, to Marduk, and to Nabu. Some hymns, such as the 200-line "Hymn to Gula," are styled in the first person, the goddess speaking her own praise. A hymnic-epic poem from the Old Babylonian period addressed to Ishtar, the *Song of Agushaya*, blurs the boundaries of narrative and hymnic poetry.

Like hymns, prayers also address the deity with praise but stress the supplicant's misery and petition. Their poetic virtue lies in their description of mood and feeling. Their plaintive lyricism, in such phrases as "How wet with my tears is my bread!" "Man's sins are more numerous than the hairs on his head," or "What sin have I committed against my god?" reminds us of the penitential psalms. Prayers are often couched as incantations and recited during ritual ceremonies to alleviate medical conditions and other misfortunes, while prayers to the gods of divination ask for a favorable answer to the oracle query.

IV. Didactic Poetry. This group mostly comprises philosophical dialogues or monologues questioning the fairness of the fate bestowed by the gods, such as the *Theodicy*, an acrostic, and the poem of the *Righteous Sufferer*, with similarities to the biblical Book of Job. Animal fables and poetic contests in which two rivals—e.g., trees or cereals—extol their own merits and belittle those of their opponent hark back to a well-attested Sumerian genre.

Only relatively few humorous poems are known, and their relationship to didactic poetry remains under discussion. The satirical *Dialogue between Master and Servant* may belong there, while the *Tale of the Poor Man of Nippur*, having close affinities with the *Tale of the First Larrikin* of the *1001 Nights*, seems to be purely secular and has perennial appeal. The *Tale of the Illiterate Doctor*, similarly situated in the Sumerian city of Nippur, draws its humor from the ling. effects of Sumerian interspersed in the Babylonian text.

■ **Anthologies**: M.-J. Seux, *Hymnes et Prières aux Dieux de Babylonie et d'Assyrie* (1976); *Texte aus der Umwelt des Alten Testament*, ed. O. Kaiser, 3 v. and suppl. in 19 fascicles (1982–); S. Dalley, *Myths from Mesopotamia* (1989); B. Foster, *Before the Muses*, 3d ed. (2005)—contains all poems listed below, though sometimes with different titles.

■ **Editions of Individual Works**: *Babylonian Wisdom Literature*, ed. W. G. Lambert (1960)—*Dialogue between Master and Servant*, *Hymn to Shamash*, *Righteous Sufferer*, and *Theodicy*; J. Bottéro, "'Le Dialogue Pessimiste' et la Transcendence," *Revue de Théologie et de Philosophie* 99 (1966), and "Rapports sur les Conférences: Histoire et Philologie," *Annuaire: École Pratique des Hautes Études* (1966–67)—*Theodicy*; W. G. Lambert, "The Gula Hymn of Bulluṭsa-rabi," *Orientalia* n.s. 36 (1967); L. Cagni, *L'Epopea di Erra* (1969)—*Erra and Ishum*; W. G. Lambert and A. R. Millard, *Atra-ḫasīs: The Babylonian Story of the Flood* (1969)—incl. trans.; O. R. Gurney, "The Tale of the Poor Man of Nippur and Its Folktale Parallels," *Anatolian Studies* 22 (1972); P. Machinist, "The Epic of Tukulti-Ninurta I," diss. Yale Univ. (1978); E. Reiner, *Your Thwarts in Pieces, Your Mooring Rope Cut* (1985)—*Descent of Ishtar to the Netherworld*; M. E. Vogelzang, *Bin šar dadmē: Edition and Analysis of the Akkadian Anzu Poem* (1988); A. George, "Ninurta-Paqidat's Dog Bite, and Notes on Other Comic Tales," *Iraq* 55 (1993)—*Tale of the Illiterate Doctor*; B. Groneberg, *Lob der Ištar* (1997)—*Song of Agushaya*; J. G. Westenholz, *Legends of the Kings of Akkade* (1997)—*Sargon and Naram-Sin* cycle; M. Haul, *Das Etana-Epos* (2000); G. Pettinato, *Nergal ed Ereškigal* (2000); S. Izre'el, *Adapa and the South Wind* (2001); A. George, *The Babylonian Gilgamesh Epic*, 2 v. (2003); S. Maul, *Das Gilgamesch-Epos* (2005); P. Talon, *The Standard Babylonian Creation Myth* (2005)—*Enuma Elish*.

■ **Criticism and History**: J. Nougayrol, "L'Épopée Babylonienne," *Atti del convegno internazionale sul tema: La poesia epica e la sua formazione* (1970); O. R. Gurney (1972)—see above; E. Reiner (1985)—see above; W. Farber, "Magic at the Cradle: Babylonian and Assyrian Lullabies," *Anthropos* 85 (1990); N. Veldhuis, *A Cow of Sin* (1991); *Mesopotamian Poetic Language: Sumerian and Akkadian*, ed. M. Vogelzang (1996); M. L. West, "Akkadian Poetry: Metre and Performance," *Iraq* 59 (1997); F. d'Agostino, *Testi Umoristici Babilonesi e Assiri* (2000); N. Wasserman, *Style and Form in Old-Babylonian Literary Texts* (2003).

E. Reiner; W. Farber

AUSTRALIA, POETRY OF. Oral poetry among indigenous Aboriginal people in Australia is an ancient trad., reaching back as far as 40,000 years or more. It continues to this day, though much diminished as a result of colonization by the Brit., beginning in 1788. There is no one single Aboriginal trad., as there were hundreds of distinct langs., but they shared common features: the poetry was highly ritualistic and embraced a rich variety of song and narrative, incl. myths, legends, mourning poems, war poems, satires, anecdotes, and so on. Performances were usually accompanied by music, and some involved dance and even ground drawings and carvings. Early accounts of this material, starting in the 1830s and 1840s, were recorded by ethnologists, but it took another hundred years before the works of R. M. Berndt and T.G.H. Strehlow brought recognition of Aboriginal poetry as a cultural achievement to the wider world. One of the best-known Aboriginal poems is the 13-part "Song Cycle of the Moon-Bone," of the Wonguri-Mandjigai people of Arnhem Land, which opens with ceremonial preparations (in Berndt's trans.):

> The people are making a camp of branches
> in that country at Arnhem Bay:
> With the forked stick, the rail for the whole
> camp, the Mandjigai people are making
> it. . . .

Although there was Aboriginal writing in Eng. from the early colonial period, it was not until the 1960s and 70s that Aboriginal lit. in Eng. began to be widely disseminated. *We Are Going* (1964) by Oodgeroo Noonuccal (initially known as Kath Walker, 1920–93) was the first poetry collection published by an Australian Aborigine, and she was soon followed by Kevin Gilbert (1933–93) and Jack Davis (1917–2000), initiating a new phase of Aboriginal poetry. This recent trad., which has attracted considerable attention, necessarily exhibits a complex relationship to anglophone poetry in Australia generally, simultaneously being a part of it and apart from it. As is the case with other indigenous cultures within postcolonial settler nations (Canada, South Africa, New Zealand, and the U.S., among them), Aboriginal writing is a multilayered and intricate phenomenon, entailing considerations of hist., politics, lang., and identity.

Early colonial poetry also had a strong oral component. Founded as a penal colony, Australia (or New South Wales, as it was called) was populated by convicts who were predominantly poor and urban, with low rates of literacy; subsequently, folk songs, work songs, and ballads flourished alongside the nascent written lit. There are a number of vigorous anonymous ballads from this period (incl. "Van Dieman's Land" and "The Female Transport") and one significant convict poet, Francis MacNamara (or "Frank the Poet," ca. 1810–1861), whose long poem, "A Convict's Tour to Hell" (1839) is a powerful satiric dream vision in rhyming couplets ("Cook who discovered New South Wales / And he that first invented gaols / Are both tied to a fiery stake / Which stands in yonder boiling lake"). Convict verse marks the beginning of an antiauthoritarian strain in Australian culture. Australia has a strong trad. of balladry, particularly in what became known as "bush ballads," celebrating outback life and heroic deeds, incl. those of renegade bushrangers, or deploring the trials and failures that attend such hard living. Among the most accomplished and best known of these poets are Adam Lindsay Gordon (1833–70), the only Australian poet to be honored in the Poets' Corner at Westminster Abbey; A. B. ("Banjo") Patterson (1864–1941), the ever-popular author of "Waltzing Matilda" (the unofficial national anthem) and "The Man from Snowy River"; and Henry Lawson (1867–1922), who, in the pages of the popular and nationalistic jour. the *Bulletin* carried on a famous dispute with Banjo Patterson about the true nature of bush life (Lawson takes a more dour outlook, as in "Up the Country," where the speaker prefers the ease of town life by the coast, "Drinking beer and lemon-squashes, taking baths and cooling down"). It is noteworthy that much of the poetry published in the 19th c. appeared in newspapers and other periodicals, which made poetry—esp. ballads and songs—very much part of a common culture. The high-water mark for these genres was in the 1880s and 1890s, a period of intense nationalism in Australia, prior to federation (1901). But before then, there was already another trad. of "serious" verse that drew on the concerns and forms of Brit., Eur., and even Am. poetry.

The first book of poems published (privately) in Australia was by Barron Field (1786–1846), a magistrate who served in New South Wales for seven years and whose *First Fruits of Australian Poetry* appeared in 1819. His work is informed by an 18th-c. neoclassical taste, as in his wry poem, "The Kangaroo," whereby the first rhyme with "Australia" is "failure." The next significant book, *Thoughts: A Series of Sonnets* (1845), is by Charles Harpur (1813–68), an ambitious and major poet whose work inaugurates a late romantic trad., in the lyrical mode of William Wordsworth and P. B. Shelley. (The intervening quarter of a century between Field's and Harpur's books accounts for the sense of a belated romanticism that marked the devel. of Australian poetry.) In addition to loco-descriptive poems, Harpur wrote narratives, political and satirical verse, a tragedy, and several long visionary works. His most anthologized poems are "A Mid-Summer Noon in the Australian Forest" and "The Creek of the Four Graves," both of which render the Australian landscape in a new and vivid manner. Harpur was an important influence on Henry Kendall (1839–82), who extended Harpur's celebration of the landscape in a more lyrical and lush verse. Like Harpur, Kendall was eager to establish himself as a poet in Australia, but conditions were exceedingly hard financially in the new colony. Kendall did gain a reputation at the time, however, and for a long time was considered Australia's finest poet, with accolades given to "Bell-Birds," "Orara," "Beyond Kerguelen," and "To a Mountain."

Other poets of note writing in the latter half of the 19th c. include Ada Cambridge (1844–1926), whose outspokenness about gender issues was daring for the time; Victor J. Daley (1858–1905), often associated with the Celtic revival; and Bernard O'Dowd (1866–1953), a radical progressive who called for a

"Poetry Militant" and initiated a correspondence with Walt Whitman. With O'Dowd, we move into the early 20th c., which featured a number of important poets who straddled both centuries. Mary Gilmore (1865–1962), a colorful and legendary figure, probes Aboriginal subjects, the convict heritage (most notably in "Old Botany Bay"), and many social issues, often from quite radical positions. Christopher Brennan (1870–1932), a scholar of classics and philosophy who studied at the University of Berlin and later taught at Sydney University, turned to poetry after encountering the work of Stéphane Mallarmé, with whom he exchanged letters. Brennan wrote in the mode of the Fr. symbolists, composing dense, hermetic poems, frequently on magian and visionary themes. An impressive figure, he has more in common with a fin de siècle romanticism than with literary modernism. *XXI Poems: Towards the Source* (1897) and *Poems* (1913), which was conceived of as a *livre composé* (or an "architectural and premeditated book," in Mallarmé's phrase) are Brennan's major publications. A contemporary of Brennan, and in many ways his opposite, John Shaw Neilson (1872–1942) is an attractive and engaging poet whose poems are frequently set in rural Australia, where he lived and worked for many years in difficult jobs under difficult circumstances. Despite those conditions, Neilson wrote some of the finest and most delicate lyrics of any Australian poet, as evidenced in his *Collected Poems* of 1934.

Most critics consider Kenneth Slessor (1901–71) the first true modernist in Australian poetry. An early acolyte of the vitalist Norman Lindsay (1879–1969), a bohemian artist whose jour. *Vision* attracted a number of poets in the 1920s, Slessor gradually made his way toward a more experimental and mod. sensibility. A thoroughly urbanized poet, Slessor developed a hard-edged and imagistic verse that assimilated many of the modernist techniques coming out of Britain and the U.S., though never the most radical modes. Slessor's poetic output was not large, but a handful of his poems ranks among the most highly regarded in Australia, esp. the luminous elegy "Five Bells" and the war poem "Beach Burial" (Slessor was a war correspondent in the 1940s). Two other poets associated with the "Vision School" of Norman Lindsay went on to have significant careers: Robert Fitzgerald (1902–87), a discursive and meditative poet; and Douglas Stewart (1913–85), a prolific writer known for his pastoral poems and for his years as lit. ed. of the *Bulletin*. John Blight (1913–95) came to prominence as a poet of the Queensland coast, esp. with his "sea sonnets," but later, in the 1970s, changed his style to a more experimental and idiosyncratic one.

During the 1940s, in the midst of the literary ferment brought on by modernism, there was nonetheless considerable resistance to its more extravagant forms. The infamous Ern Malley hoax is the prime example. Two young (and later prominent) poets, James McAuley (1917–76) and Harold Stewart (1916–95), decided to discredit modernist pretensions by creating a fake poet, Ern Malley, whose "absurd" work they sent to the avant-garde jour. *Angry Penguins,* which then published it to acclaim in 1944. Exposure of the imposture created a sensation in the press, though "Ern Malley" continues to be regarded by many as genuine poetry of a high order of inventiveness. McAuley went on to become a major figure and write expertly crafted verse marked by fierce intelligence and emotional depth. Stewart, also productive, though more disaffected with postwar Australia, finally moved to Japan, where he devoted himself to Shin Buddhism. Like McAuley and Stewart, A. D. Hope (1907–2000) was critical of modernist excesses and quickly became known for his lashing reviews. But Hope's poetry is regarded as one of the high-water marks of Australian lit., esp. overseas. Cultivated and often epicurean, Hope was a traditionalist in verse and an ardent believer in the orphic power of poetry. Not unlike W. H. Auden, he displays a penchant for the middle style of sophisticated discursive verse but can also write with lyrical grace and distinction.

Prior to the founding of *Angry Penguins* in 1940, another movement began with a more nationalistic purpose: the Jindyworobaks. Instituted by the poet Rex Ingamells (1913–55), it looked to indigenous Aborigines for inspiration in promoting an original Australian culture, one based on appreciation for the Australian landscape and a belief in its spiritual dimension. The movement was controversial and lasted into the 1950s, attracting a number of artists and writers, most prominently the poet Roland Robinson (1912–92), who frequently incorporates Aboriginal material in his verse. Judith Wright (1915–2000) was also concerned with indigenous issues, though from a different perspective. Known as a fierce environmentalist and a stalwart activist for

Aboriginal rights, she writes passionately about Australian landscape and hist. from a deeply personal point of view. A note of despair and bitterness can sound in her work, but it is all the stronger for it. With her inaugural volume of poems, *The Moving Image* (1946), Wright moved immediately to the forefront of Australian poetry and remains one of its most revered figures. Another prolific poet of pastoral is David Campbell (1915–79), a war hero, a grazier, and a keen observer of the natural world. While many Australian poets at this time engaged thematically with the landscape, others turned to more metropolitan subjects. In Tasmania, Gwen Harwood (1920–95) created not only a series of fascinating personae in her poetry (Professors Eisenbart and Kröte) but heteronyms under whose names she published (Walter Lehmann, Francis Geyer, and Miriam Stone, among them). Renowned for her tart wit and probing intelligence, Harwood, like Elizabeth Bishop in the U.S., has increasingly become prominent in accounts of 20th-c. poetry in Australia. Vincent Buckley (1925–88), one of Harwood's early supporters, was a leading poet and an influential critic in Melbourne. His spare intellectual style could move rapidly between irony and profound emotion. Chris Wallace-Crabbe (b. 1934), also from Melbourne, quickly established himself as a leading poet of his generation and has gone on to solidify that high regard with a prolific output of verse and crit. His poems are often witty and cognitively adventurous, deploying a demotic Australian that counterpoints the sophistication of his work. More overtly sophisticated is the poetry of Peter Porter (1929–2010), an expatriate who lived in London but who maintained close ties with his homeland. Porter is regarded as a major poet in both the U.K. and Australia and is one of the most cultured and skillful of contemporary poets. Bruce Beaver (1928–2004) was influential in the devel. of more experimental poetry. Francis Webb (1925–73) extended the range of mod. Australian poetry with his intensely charged lang., reminiscent at times of Robert Lowell. Like Lowell, Webb spent time in mental asylums, dying in one at an early age, but not before creating a remarkable oeuvre that continues to influence Australian poets for its ling. facility and dynamic emotional power. Whereas Webb can appear to be a poet's poet for his level of difficulty, Bruce Dawe (b. 1930) is unusual for being a genuinely popular poet, much read in schools and widely admired for his ironic humor and colloquial manner. Another popular writer, though primarily for his fiction, is David Malouf (b. 1934), who has compiled a body of verse distinguished by its inwardness and sensitivity. Other notable poets born before World War II include the highly regarded Rosemary Dobson (1920–2012), important in the devel. of Australian women's poetry, as are Fay Zwicky (b. 1933) and Judith Rodriguez (b. 1936); Thomas Shapcott (b. 1935), who helped usher in new devels. in poetry from overseas; Peter Steele (1939–2012), a polished poet with far-ranging and deep interests; and J. S. Harry (1939–2015), an early experimental poet. By far the best-known Australian poet, nationally and internationally, is Les Murray (b. 1938). Frequently mentioned as a candidate for the Nobel Prize, Murray writes a brilliant vernacular that can be astonishing in its thematic range and ling. inventiveness. Looking back to the Jindyworobaks, Murray has woven rural and Aboriginal material together with more urban and urbane matter, creating a poetry that is at once distinctly Australian and cosmopolitan.

By the later 1960s, Australian poetry was undergoing an upheaval similar to the one in the U.S. occasioned by the "war of the anthologies" that attended Donald Allen's *The New American Poetry 1945–1960*. In Australia, the self-styled Generation of '68 or the New Australian Poetry championed an aesthetic associated with the Black Mountain, New York school, and San Francisco Ren. movements. These Australian poets comprise a lively, talented, and disparate group, a number of whom continue to be important for contemp. poetry, incl. Robert Adamson (b. 1943), a key figure in the movement and often labeled a neoromantic; John Tranter (b. 1943), an early postmodernist; Kris Hemensley (b. 1946), owner of Collected Works, an influential poetry bookshop in Melbourne; John A. Scott (b. 1948), who experimented with poetic sequences; Alan Wearne (b. 1948), author of book-length verse narratives that broke new ground; Laurie Duggan (b. 1949), who used collage techniques to good effect; Jennifer Maiden (b. 1949), one of the few women poets in the movement; and John Forbes (1950–1998), a highly gifted seriocomic poet. Out of all of them, Tranter is most active and best known, esp. for his editorship of the online jour. *Jacket*. Two poets who demurred polemically from the aesthetics of the New Australian Poetry were Robert Gray (b. 1945) and Geoffrey Lehmann (b. 1940). Gray writes a finely tuned imagistic poetry, redolent of his interest in Zen Buddhism, while Lehmann is more eclectic. Poets of note that Gray and Lehmann championed include Geoff Page (b. 1940), unusual for his formalist verse; Mark O'Connor (b. 1945); Rhyll McMaster (b. 1947); and Alan Gould (b. 1949), also a fine novelist. As the poetry wars of the 1970s and 1980s faded, other "unaligned" poets came to the fore, incl. those born in the 1940s: Jan Owen (b. 1940); Barry Hill (b. 1943), a novelist and nonfiction writer as well; Diane Fahey (b. 1945); Gary Catalano (1947–2002), an art critic; Alex Skovron (b. 1948); Martin Harrison (1949–2014); and Kate Jennings (b. 1949), an early feminist and novelist. These were followed by other prominent poets, incl. Peter Goldsworthy (b. 1951), also an essayist, novelist, and librettist; Stephen Edgar (b. 1951), a writer of unsurpassed technical facility; Dorothy Porter (1954–2008), whose lesbian detective novel in verse, *The Monkey's Mask*, was a popular sensation; Kevin Hart (b. 1954), a philosopher and theologian, whose rich meditative verse proves haunting and arresting; Peter Rose (b. 1955), a highly cultured and satiric poet; Gig Ryan (b. 1956), a minimalist and feminist; Judith Beveridge (b. 1956), a serene nature poet deeply engaged with Buddhism; Anthony Lawrence (b. 1957), an exuberant storyteller; Sarah Day (b. 1958), a writer of finely wrought lyrics; and Philip Hodgins (1959–95), whose unflinching exploration of rural life and his own terminal leukemia produced powerful poetry.

As poetry in Australia moves into the 21st c., a sense of capacious pluralism reflects the increasingly multicultural nature of the society. There has been a resurgence of Aboriginal poetry, as seen in Sam Watson (b. 1952), Tony Birch (b. 1957), Lionel Fogarty (b. 1958), Lisa Bellear (1961–2006), and Yvette Holt (b. 1971). Attention to ethnicity has always been a presence in Australia but has become more pronounced since the 1970s. Few, however, would consider themselves "ethnic" writers; indeed, the following poets are seen as mainstream: Dimitris Tsaloumas (1921–2016), Antigone Kefala (b. 1935), Ania Walwicz (b. 1951), Tom Petsinis (b. 1953), Ouyang Yu (b. 1955), Marcella Polain (b. 1958), Dipti Saravanamuttu (b. 1960), and Ali Alizadeh (b. 1976), among others. To a marked degree, poets in Australia remain open to a multitude and plurality of influences. John Kinsella (b. 1963) is an unusually prolific author whose work ranges from the highly experimental (in the Language poetry manner) to more conventional pastoral and lyrical forms. Kinsella also exemplifies an internationalist impulse that looks beyond national and nationalist borders to embrace a wide variety of poetic modes. The same could be said of John Mateer (b. 1971), of South African heritage, and Alison Croggon (b. 1962), initially from the Transvaal. There has clearly been an efflorescence of poetry in Australia in the last decades, and it is likely to be furthered by such poets as Jordie Albiston (b. 1961), Craig Sherborne (b. 1962), Brendan Ryan (b. 1963), Tracy Ryan (b. 1964), Michael Farrell (b. 1965), Peter Minter (b. 1967), Bronwyn Lea (b. 1969), Lisa Gorton (b. 1972), Judith Bishop (b. 1972), Michael Brennan (b. 1973), and Petra White (b. 1975), all of whom have published to considerable acclaim. In Australia, poetry continues to be one of the continent's most vibrant arts.

■ **Anthologies**: *Songs of Central Australia*, ed. T. Strehlow (1971); *Three Faces of Love: Traditional Aboriginal Song-Poetry*, ed. R. Berndt (1976); *Penguin Book of Modern Verse*, ed. H. Heseltine (1981); *New Oxford Book of Australian Verse*, ed. L. Murray (1986); *Inside Black Australia*, ed. K. Gilbert (1988); *Penguin Book of Modern Australian Poetry*, ed. J. Tranter and P. Mead (1991); *Australian Poetry in the Twentieth Century*, ed. R. Gray and G. Lehmann (1991); *Penguin Book of Australian Ballads*, ed. P. Butterss and E. Webby (1993); *Oxford Book of Australian Women's Verse*, ed. S. Lever (1995); *Australian Verse*, ed. J. Leonard (1998); *Landbridge*, ed. J. Kinsella (1999); *Calyx 30*, ed. M. Brennan and P. Minter (2000); *Penguin Anthology of Australian Poetry*, ed. J. Kinsella (2008); *Macquarie PEN Anthology of Australian Literature*, ed. N. Jose (2009); *Puncher & Wattmann Anthology of Australian Poetry*, ed. J. Leonard (2009).

■ **Criticism and History**: J. Wright, *Preoccupations in Australian Poetry* (1965); *Oxford History of Australian Literature*, ed. L. Kramer (1981); A. Taylor, *Reading Australian Poetry* (1987); *Penguin New Literary History of Australian Literature*, ed. L. Hergenhan (1988); P. Kane, *Australian Poetry* (1996); *Oxford Literary History of Australia*, ed. B. Bennet and J. Strauss (1998); *Cambridge Companion to Australian Literature*, ed. E. Webby (2000); M. Harrison, *Who Wants to Create Australia?* (2004); P. Mead, *Networked Language* (2008); *A Companion to Australian*

Literature since 1900, ed. N. Birns and R. McNeer (2007).

P. Kane

AUSTRIA, POETRY OF. Although the langs. of Austrian poetry—Ger. and Germanic dialects—emphasize its closeness to Ger. poetry, the geographical, historical, and political distinctiveness of Austria justify regarding Austrian poetry as a separate entity. This is largely the case throughout the hist. of Austria, whether as duchies, provinces, kingdoms, and empires under the Babenbergs (976–1246) and the Hapsburgs (1278–1918), or as a mod. republic. Nevertheless, it is difficult to speak straightforwardly of an Austrian "national" lit., since from the Middle Ages to the present regional identity has been strong.

Texts of important religious poetry from the early Middle Ages in the Danube valley survive in three ms. collections, the Wiener, the Millstätter (or Klagenfurter), and the Vorauer Handschriften (mid-to-late 12th c.). The last of these holds the first surviving poems in Ger. by a woman, Frau Ava or Ava von Melk (ca. 1060–1127), incl. *Das Leben Jesu* (ca. 1125), which shows considerable sophistication. Mariological works include the *Melker Marienlied* (ca. 1130) and the *Mariensequenz aus St. Lambrecht* (Seckau) from the later 12th c. The *St. Trudperter Hohenlied* (ca. 1160–70), based on the Song of Songs, stems from the Abbey of Admont in Steiermark.

The most celebrated secular work is the MHG *Nibelungenlied* (ca. 1200), probably by someone at the court of Wolfger von Erlau, bishop of Passau. Another secular strand was represented by the poets of *Minnesang*. The Danubian trad. flourished with Der von Kürenberg (fl. mid-12th c.), active in Upper Austria, and Dietmar von Aist (fl. ca. 1160–80), who wrote some of the first love lyrics in Ger. Kürenberg's "Swenne ich stân aleine" is the earliest example of the *Frauenlied* genre. At the same time, the satirical poet Heinrich von Melk (d. after 1150) wrote protests against love songs and a *memento mori*, *Von des tôdes gehugede*. The Minnesänger gradually developed more complex strophic forms and rhyme schemes, and the conventions of the love lyric became modified into the noble form of courtly poetry by poets such as Reinmar the Elder (d. ca. 1205), in whose verses the pain of unrequited love is sublimated into exquisite formal sophistication.

Not until the 13th c. do mss. preserve melodies for Minnesang, but by the time of Oswald von Wolkenstein (ca. 1377–1445), text and setting go hand in hand. He and the Mönch von Salzburg (late 14th c.) wrote for several voices. Many writers of the period had positions at court, incl. Walther von der Vogelweide (ca. 1170–ca. 1230), a Ger. working for Frederick I of Austria in Vienna. The patrons of Frauenlob (Heinrich von Meißen, 1280–1318), a highly original author of the eroticized *Marienleich*, the *Kreuzleich*, and the *Minneleich*, included Wenceslas II of Bohemia. Frauenlob, Walther, Neidhart (ca. 1185–1240), Oswald, and the Styrian Ulrich von Lichtenstein (1198–1275) subvert and redirect the conventions of Minnesang: in his *Vrowen dienst* (1255), e.g., Ulrich wrote perhaps the first extended autobiographical lyric.

The court of Maximilian I was an important literary center, attracting the humanist poet Conrad Celtis (1459–1508), but literary devels. in the Ren. were curtailed by the wars of the Reformation; the success of the Counter-Reformation in Austria restored the hegemony of the Catholic Church and with it Lat. as the lang. of art and learning. The outstanding Ger.-lang. poet of the late 16th c. was the Ren. humanist Christoph von Schallenberg (1561–97). His Lat. verse is formally sophisticated and religious, while the Ger. lieder are simpler and more worldly. He features in anthols. from the early 17th c., such as the *Jaufener Liederbuch*; others, such as the *Raaber Liederbuch* display the influence of Petrarch.

The influence of the It. Ren. continued into the 17th c. Verse epics such as *Die unvergnügte Proserpina* (1661) and *Der Habspurgische Ottobert* (1664) by Wolf Helmhard von Hohberg (1612–88) were inspired by Ludovico Ariosto. Like other Protestant poets, incl. his friend Catharina Regina von Greiffenberg (1633–94), Hohberg was driven into exile in Germany by the Counter-Reformation. Greiffenberg's first work, the virtuosic *Geistliche Sonnette* (1662), reflects both these political pressures and the psychological tensions of difficult family circumstances and expresses the hope that God will grant in poetry the space for her to unfold personally and spiritually. Catholic writers active in the Austrian lands included the general and statesman Raimundo Graf Montecúccoli (1609–80), author of moving sonnets, as well as members of religious orders, such as the Capuchins Laurentius von Schniflis (1633–1702) and

Procopius von Templin (1608–80), whose collection *Hertzen-Freud und Seelen-Trost* (1659) was published in Passau.

The commonplace that, between Abraham a Sancta Clara (1644–1709) and Ferdinand Raimund (1790–1836) or Franz Grillparzer (1791–1872), there is no major Austrian writer of lasting repute masks interesting devels. in poetry. Under Maria Theresa, it moved from the playfully secular *Liederbuch* (songbook) style to works with loftier ambitions. Michael Denis (1729–1800) attempted to familiarize Austria with north Ger. writing in his anthol. *Sammlung kürzerer Gedichte aus den neuern Dichtern Deutschlands* (1762–66), although his own work is more indebted to Jesuit religiosity than to the Ger. Enlightenment. F. G. Klopstock inspired the patriotic odes of Denis's pupil, Lorenz Leopold Haschka (1749–1827), author of the Austrian national anthem "Gott erhalte Franz den Kaiser!" (1797). Haschka befriended the most prominent woman author of the early 19th c., Caroline Pichler (1769–1843), who, with Joseph Franz Ratschky (1757–1810), represented a contrasting epigrammatic, satirical tone in contemp. verse. In a similar vein, Aloys Blumauer (1755–98) wrote a comic mock epic parodying Virgil, *Die Abenteuer des frommen Helden Aeneas* (1784–88). Vienna was also the center of a thriving ballad trad., similarly satirical and often anonymous, although the work of Johann David Hanner (1754–95) stands out for its acute social critique.

While Ger. romantic poetry had its imitators and defenders in Austria, Austria did not imitate Ger. romanticism. Symptomatic of much early 19th-c. lit. are tones of resignation, *Weltschmerz* (world-weariness), and self-sacrifice that reflect the lives of many authors. Some, such as Michael Enk von der Burg (1788–1843), committed suicide. The most renowned poet, Hungarian-born Nikolaus Lenau (1802–50), died in an asylum, and his work reflects a Byronic searching for meaning and justice. Nature in his poetry (*Gedichte*, 1832) carries the burden of the poet's emotions and experiences, and the lyrical voice seems attenuated and isolated. Lenau's political poetry is also significant, although that of his friend Anastasius Grün (1806–76) is more radical, with *Spaziergänge eines Wiener Poeten* (1831) and *Schutt* (1835) targeting Metternich's reactionary system and the influence of the church on the state. Similar social awareness characterizes the poetry of the otherwise conservative Ferdinand von Saar (1833–1906). The poetry, prose, and drama of Marie von Ebner-Eschenbach (1830–1916) consistently reflect her concern with the poor and the oppressed, as does her correspondence with Josephine von Knorr (1827–1908). Knorr's poetry of melancholy and transience was widely admired by contemporaries but is little known today.

As Austria turned away from Ger. romanticism, a rich trad. of writing celebrating the unique character of the Austrian regions flourished. Anthols. from all periods reflect this: in 1854, e.g., Salomon Mosenthal (1821–77) collected a representative range in his *Museum aus den deutschen Dichtungen österreichischer Lyriker und Epiker*. But Mosenthal excluded dialect poetry, another important vehicle for the expression of regional identity in the 19th c. Collections of Lower Austrian verse were published by Ignaz Franz Castelli (1781–1862) and Johann Gabriel Seidl (1804–75) in 1828 and 1844, respectively. Others include Karl Stelzhamer (1802–74, Upper Austria), author of *Lieder in obderennsscher Volksmundart* (1837); Anton von Klesheim (1812–84, Vienna); Peter Rosegger (1843–1918, Styria); and Otto Pflanzl (1865–1943, Salzburg). In the 20th c., the *Heimatkunst* (regional art) movement lent further impetus to dialect writing, inspiring Joseph Oberkofler (1889–1962, Tirol), Resl Mayr (1891–1980, Lower Austria), and Josef Weinheber (1892–1945, Vienna).

The melancholy and uncertainty of much 19th-c. Austrian poetry are perpetuated at the turn of the century, influenced by Fr. and Ger. symbolism, impressionism, decadence, and *Jugendstil* (the Ger. equivalent of the term *art nouveau*) in lit., and by devels. in psychology. In the 1890s, poetry turned from social crit. to become subjectivized, often to the point of overrefinement, nervousness, and introspection. The group known as Young Vienna cultivated nuances of feeling and subconscious drives in an effort to create a new aesthetic. The precocious Hugo von Hofmannsthal (1874–1929) was the most celebrated: his apparently effortless, expressive verse explores the semimystical power of lang. to convey truth via feeling and atmosphere, the transience of experience, and the fluidity of the boundaries of identity. Before the age of 30, Hofmannsthal ceased writing poetry almost entirely, externalizing the crisis brought about by the intrusion of consciousness between lang. and reality in the so-called Chandos Letter of 1902.

Lesser writers include Felix Dörmann (1870–1928), author of the sensuously solipsistic lyrics of *Neurotica* (1891) and *Sensationen* (1892), and Leopold von Andrian (1875–1951), who published delicate, narcissistic verse in Stefan George's *Blätter für die Kunst*. Tensions between the mannered, impressionistic *Gedichte* (1893) and the euphoric *Eherne Sonette* (1915) greeting World War I characterize the contradictory oeuvre of Richard von Schaukal (1874–1942). The Catholic writer Richard von Kralik (1852–1934) rejected subjectivist writing and turned to Germanic myth, med. mystery plays, and puppet theater to regenerate Ger. culture.

Wholly distinct from these Viennese poets, Rainer Maria Rilke (1875–1926) was among the greatest writers of Eur. modernism. From the contemplative religious lang. of *Das Stunden-Buch* (1905), via the existential and poetological reflectiveness of the *Duineser Elegien* (written 1912–22) to the celebratory enthusiasm of *Die Sonette an Orpheus* (written 1922), his poetry explores themes of death, love, and loss, mastering and imaginatively developing a huge variety of poetic forms. He interrogated the relation between his art and the world around him, moving from the neoromantic and the mystical toward the precise craft of expressing the everyday in poetry and the poet's duty to praise the world. During a period in Paris as Auguste Rodin's secretary, he learned to see and look ("Schauen," "Anschauen"), producing two books of *Neue Gedichte* (written 1902–8) that combine observation and precision with inwardness to give new definition to the concept of *Dinggedicht*.

Austrian expressionism was less politically engaged than its Ger. counterpart; it was apocalyptic and emotionally charged and formally experimental. Representatives include Oskar Kokoschka (1886–1980), whose *Die träumenden Knaben* (1908) thematizes art and dream, love and death, the inadequacy of lang. and the attraction of the exotic. His fascination with China was shared by Albert Ehrenstein (1886–1950), who, unlike many Ger. contemporaries, was never caught up by enthusiasm for the war, as *Der Mensch schreit* (1916) demonstrates. The poetry of Hans Kaltneker (1895–1919) expresses visionary intensity and an unquenchable faith in the redemptive power of love with immense ling. sensitivity. The (nondenominational) gospel of love was also propounded by Prague-born Franz Werfel (1890–1945) in his first collection, *Der Weltfreund* (1911).

The most influential Austrian expressionist was Georg Trakl (1887–1914), who, like Werfel, served on the front line. Trakl depicts a world of decay, destruction, and death. He uses lang. radically to express the ruptured universe in free rhythms, fractured syntax, and enigmatic metaphors known as *Chiffren* (ciphers), which establish a relation between the incomparable realms of the referential and the ontological. Guilt and despair are expressed in a sonorous lang. of alliteration and assonance that shows the influence of Arthur Rimbaud.

The dual monarchy of Austria-Hungary collapsed in 1918, and the succeeding republic was characterized by economic instability and political polarization. The federal government moved toward "Austro-Fascism" and Austria's annexation by Germany in 1938, while the city of Vienna remained under Social Democrat control until 1934. Contemp. sociopolitical protest was reflected in the writings of the worker-poet Alfons Petzold (1882–1923) and the muted lyricism of Theodor Kramer (1897–1958); Kramer's *Wir lagen in Wolhynien im Morast* (1931) also reflects with restrained intensity on the war. Jura Soyfer (1912–39), a powerful anti-Nazi poet, was murdered in a concentration camp. By contrast, Josef Weinheber (1892–1945) was highly conservative, claiming for the poet in *Adel und Untergang* (1934) the salvation of meaning in a meaningless world. His reputation has not recovered from associations with Nazism. He was a master of complex cl. strophic forms and the sonnet, and some of his more experimental ling. effects are recognized as precursors of postwar writing. Similarly indebted to cl. trad. was the grandiose work of the self-styled *poeta doctus* Alexander von Lernet-Holenia (1897–1976). He and Erika Mitterer (1906–2000) were also heavily influenced by Rilke. Both Rilke and the cl. trad. were important to Franz Baermann Steiner (1909–52). Forced into exile during World War II, he, like H. G. Adler (1910–88), has only recently been recognized as a major lyric talent.

The political context of Austria after 1945, in which National Socialism was interpreted as a period of occupation, meant that poetry of this period was frequently conservative, focusing on the values of *Heimat* (homeland or regional identity). Alongside Lernet-Holenia's *Germanien* (1946) and a posthumous collection by Weinheber (*Hier ist das Wort*, 1947), this trend was represented variously by the hugely popular *Heiteres Herbarium* (1950) of Karl Waggerl (1897–1973) and an *Österreichische Trilogie* (1950) by the patriotic Catholic Rudolf Henz (1897–1987). Catholic spirituality was central also to the work of the reclusive poet Christine Lavant (1915–73), whose passionate lyrics hover between poetry and prayer. Like Lavant, Christina Busta (1915–87) progressed toward a more lapidary style, gradually abandoning strict forms. By 1963, the anthol. *Frage und Formel: Gedichte einer jungen österreichischen Generation* makes overt the mod. era's ironic treatment of formal rigor and traditional themes and foregrounds a consciousness of the plasticity of poetic lang.

Excessive density, hermeticism, even a desire for "absolute metaphors" are accusations unjustly leveled at the work of the towering figure in the postwar poetic landscape, Paul Celan (1920–70), whose relationship to Austria was fatally problematized by Ger. as the lang. spoken by the perpetrators of the Holocaust. Linguistically subtle and innovative, morally uncompromising and poetologically reflexive, his works from *Mohn und Gedächtnis* (1952) to *Die Niemandsrose* (1963) and *Lichtzwang* (1970) are grounded in the belief that meaning finds itself only when it finds lang. Celan lived in Paris; his distinguished contemp. Ingeborg Bachmann (1926–73) settled in Italy. Her poetry engages critically with contemp. Austrian society's blindness to the legacy of the Nazi period using a variety of personas. Rooted in the Austrian trad. (like Celan, she drew inspiration from Hofmannsthal), her lang. is rhythmically restless and her imagery a unique blend of vivid tangibility and intense abstraction. Ilse Aichinger (b. 1921) shared Bachmann's critique of contemp. Austria (cf. *Verschenkter Rat*, 1978).

More politically direct than Celan and Bachmann, Erich Fried (1921–88) was also more formally exploratory; his use of montage and documentary materials paved the way for the explosion of experimental poetry in the 1950s that led to the formation of the Vienna Group around Friedrich Achleitner (b. 1930), Gerhard Rühm (b. 1930), Konrad Bayer (1932–64), and Oswald Wiener (b. 1935), with H. C. Artmann (1921–2000). The group acknowledged the influence of Dada, Fr. surrealism, and Ludwig Wittgenstein; and its diverse works, often in dialect or embracing concrete poetry and multimedia montage, are unified by an interest in games (*Spiel*) and the attempt to free lang. from the primacy of communication. Other avant-garde poets included Andreas Okopenko (1930–2010), exploiting the power of the grotesque and the experimental; and Ernst Jandl (1925–2000). Jandl's humorous but challenging engagement with the reader earned him popular appeal. From 1960, the liberating effects of the Vienna Group served as a springboard for a broader group of avant-garde writers, the Graz Group, which includes a broad spectrum of contemp. authors with ling. and sociopolitical interests, united by a critical stance toward the status quo in art and society. Its jour., *manuskripte*, is ed. by the poet Alfred Kolleritsch (b. 1931), whose opaque metaphors examine the content and conditions of consciousness. The Viennese poet Jutta Schutting (b. 1937) also operates in the Wittgensteinian trad., using lang. to question itself.

Avant-garde concerns continue in the work of contemp. poets Ferdinand Schmatz (b. 1953) and Raoul Schrott (b. 1964), whose verse exploits a variety of formal and typographical idiosyncrasies. Schrott is a mod.-day *poeta doctus*, whose erudition is displayed prominently within and alongside the poetry. The Austrian trad. of reflecting on the nature of lang. continues to be articulated by Peter Waterhouse (b. 1956), who brutally forces lang. to cede to a kaleidoscope of perspectives from the empirical world. After an experimental phase, the later works of Friederike Mayröcker (b. 1924) also mark a return to the real world and recognizable human emotion. This repersonalization of the lyric is reflected, too, in the elegiac poetry of Evelyn Schlag (b. 1952). Like Mayröcker and so many of her contemporaries and predecessors, in volumes such as *Brauchst du den Schlaf dieser Nacht* (2002), Schlag engages in a moving dialogue with the trad. of Austrian poetry.

■ **Anthologies**: *Lyrik aus Deutschösterreich vom Mittelalter bis zur Gegenwart*, ed. S. Hock (1919); *Die Botschaft: Neue Gedichte aus Österreich*, ed. E. A. Rheinhardt (1920); *Dichtungen in niederösterreichischer Mundart*, ed. K. Bacher et al. (1931); *Österreichische Lyrik aus neuen Jahrhunderten*, ed. W. Stratowa (1948); *Dichtung aus Österreich*, v. 2, *Lyrik*, ed. E. Thurnher (1976); *Zwischenbilanz: Eine Anthologie österreichischer Gegenwartsliteratur*, ed. W. Weiss and S. Schmid (1976); *Zeit und Ewigkeit. Tausend Jahre österr. Lyrik*, ed. J. Schondorff (1978); *Verlassener Horizont: Österreichische Lyrik aus vier Jahrzehnten*, ed. H. Huppert and R. Links (1980); *Die Wiener Moderne: Literatur, Kunst und Musik zwischen 1890 und 1910*, ed.

G. Wunberg (1981); *Austria in Poetry and History*, ed. F. Ungar (1984); *Austrian Poetry Today*, ed. M. Holton and H. Kuhner (1985); *Contemporary Austrian Poetry*, ed. B. Bjorklund (1986). ■ **Criticism and History**: A. Schmidt, *Dichtung und Dichter Österreichs im 19. und 20. Jahrhundert*, 2 v. (1964); C. Magris, *Der habsburgische Mythos in der österreichischen Literatur* (1966); *Handbook of Austrian Literature*, ed. F. Ungar (1973); *Kindlers Literaturgeschichte der Gegenwart: Die zeitgenössische Literatur Österreichs*, ed. H. Spiel (1976); *Die österreichische Literatur: Eine Dokumentation ihrer literarhistorischen Entwicklung*, ed. H. Zeman, 4 v. (1979–89); A. Best and H. Wolfschütz, *Modern Austrian Writing* (1980); *Formen der Lyrik in der österreichischen Gegenwartsliteratur*, ed. W. Schmidt-Dengler (1981); S. P. Scheichl and G. Stieg, *Österreichische Literatur des 20. Jahrhunderts* (1986); *Geschichte der Literatur in Österreich von den Anfängen bis zur Gegenwart*, ed. H. Zeman, 7 v. (1994–); *Literaturgeschichte Österreichs: von den Anfängen im Mittelalter bis zur Gegenwart*, ed. H. Zeman (1996); *A History of Austrian Literature*, ed. R. Robertson and K. Kohl (2006); A. Bushell, *Poetry in a Provisional State: The Austrian Lyric 1945–1955* (2007).

R. L. Vilain

AZTEC POETRY. *See* INDIGENOUS AMERICAS, POETRY OF THE

B

BASQUE COUNTRY, POETRY OF THE. Basque lit. bloomed late because of various sociohistorical circumstances that hindered its devel. and are tightly bound to the ups and downs suffered by Basque, or Euskara, a lang. of pre-IE origin spoken today by some 700,000 people who live on both sides of the Pyrenees, in France and in Spain. The political border that today divides the Basque Country (Euskal Herria) separates two different legislative regions. After the Sp. constitution of 1978 was approved, the Basque lang. was accepted as an official lang., together with Castilian (Sp.), in the provinces in the Sp. Basque region; however, the same is not the case in the Fr. Basque Country, where Basque does not hold the status of an official lang. The consequences of this imbalance are easy to predict: factors such as the establishment of bilingual models of teaching and the existence of grants for publications in the Basque lang. have made the literary system in the Sp. Basque Country much stronger and more dynamic than that on the French side. Within Basque lit., poetry has always been a crucial genre. The first book of any sort published in Basque was a volume of poems by Bernard Etxepare (1493?–1545); moreover, poetry has also held a position of considerable importance in Basque oral lit. Long-established genres such as improvised Basque verse singing, or *bertsolaritza*, are still very popular today.

Linguae Vasconum Primitiae (Origins of the Basque Language, 1545) by Etxepare was the first step from an oral to a written lit. It consists of 15 poems dealing with themes such as love and religion; Etxepare expresses his joy at the possibilities created by the invention of the printing press and his hope that it will help disseminate Basque lit. Etxepare had read Erasmus, and his book reveals this influence. Another foundational v., Arnaut Oihenart's *Atsotitzak eta neurtitzak* (Proverbs and Verses, 1657), is a book not only of proverbs and refrains but of love poems that follow the trad. of Petrarchism. The dominance of religious texts in this era was almost absolute; Oihenart (1592–1667) was one of the few laic Basque writers of his time.

The last decade of the 19th c. saw the emergence of a new spirit that would transform Basque lit. The dominance of devotional and didactic works began to wane, and the spectrum of literary genres widened. Indalezio Bizkarrondo or "Blintx" (1831–76) and the satiric Pierre Topet or "Etxahun" (1786–1862), e.g., were considered romantic poets.

After the Second Carlist War in 1876, the revocation of foral rights—which had ensured regional autonomy by empowering assemblies of local inhabitants—unleashed a cultural revival, *Pizkundea* (the Basque Ren., 1876–1936), the Basque equivalent of the Galician *Rexurdimento* or the Catalan *Renaixença*, in which patriotic renewal would stem from recognition of the Basque lang. The foralist movement gave way to the nationalism of Sabino Arana and from this point on, the fundamental purpose of writing in Basque would be to contribute to the creation of the Basque nation. Nationalism was to influence all Basque lit. of the first third of the 20th c. Poetry was promoted by poetic contests known as *lorejokoak* (floral games), by Basque festivals, and by the publication of songbooks containing popular folk songs. During the time of the floral games, the work of Felipe Arrese-Beitia, among others, showed anguish in the face of the potential death of the lang. In the 1930s, two poets, Xabier Lizardi and Esteban Urkiaga (Lauaxeta), explored the expressive possibilities of Basque through postsymbolist poetics. Both nationalists, they participated actively in the Pizkundea that took place during the years of the Sp. Second Republic, a time at which nationalist political and cultural activism went hand in hand. Another influential poet and translator of that time was Nicolas Ormaetxea (Orixe), whose love of cl. lit. and knowledge of Scholasticism greatly influenced his writing. *Bide Barrijak* (1931) by Lauaxeta, *Biotz begietan* (1932) by Lizardi, and *Barne muinetan* (1934) by Orixe are considered the premier poetic vs. of the pre–Sp. Civil War period.

The repression and censorship that followed the Sp. Civil War (1936–39) made it impossible to publish in Basque until 1949, when the first mod. book of poetry appeared, but it was not until the 1950s that the dialogue with modernity became more developed through the voices of two poets, Jon Mirande (1925–72) and Gabriel Aresti (1933–75). Mirande, heterodox and nihilist, was the first to transgress the religious spirit latent in Basque poetry. Echoes of his many and varied philosophical and literary readings (such as the Stoics, Friedrich Nietzsche, Oswald Spengler, E. A. Poe, and Charles Baudelaire) abound in his prose and poetry. Aresti wrote short stories and drama as well as poetry and translated such authors as Giovanni Boccaccio, T. S. Eliot, and Nazim Hikmet. His first collection of poetry was *Maldan behera* (Downhill, 1960), influenced by symbolist poetry and an Eliotian modernism. However, with *Harri eta herri* (Stone and Country, 1964), a landmark in the history of Basque lit., he moved toward a more sociopolitical poetry. Critics praised the book's modernity and innovative spirit, together with its left-wing humanism. It was followed by *Euskal harria* (Basque Stone, 1967) and *Harrizko herri hau* (This Country of Stone, 1971).

In the 1960s, political and cultural activism against the regime of Francisco Franco were closely linked, with the consequence that sociopolitical poetry found its best ally in modern Basque song, esp. in the group *Ez dok amairu*, which was formed by singers like Mikel Laboa (1934–2008) and poets like Xabier Lete (1944–2010), Joxean Arze (b. 1939), and Joxe Anjel Irigarai (b. 1942). Linked to this movement of social commitment, female poets emerged, such as Amaia Lasa (b. 1949) and Arantxa Urretabizkaia (b. 1947). Other authors took a postsymbolist stand, intending for Basque poetry to evolve toward a more concise and synthetic style (e.g., Juan Mari Lekuona, 1927–2005) or to move toward a deeper degree of introspection (e.g., Bittoriano Gandiaga, 1928–2001).

However, things changed radically after Franco's death in 1975; from then on and for the first time in hist., the Basque literary system was supported by a legal framework that allowed the establishment of bilingual education and funding for the publication of books in Basque. In 2005, a total of 1,648 books were published, 247 of which were literary works, including 37 books of poetry. In the 1970s and early 1980s, because of a proliferation of literary magazines, Basque poetry experienced its most avant-garde period. While Joseba Sarrionandia (b. 1958) reminded us that all lit. is metalit., Koldo Izagirre (b. 1953) dabbled in surrealist aesthetics. But the book that truly shook the poetry scene of the time was *Etiopia* (Ethiopia, 1978), by Bernardo Atxaga (b. 1951), the most internationally renowned Basque author. In *Etiopia*, Atxaga addresses the tedium brought about by the end of modernity and declares the impossibility of addressing poetic lang. itself. Freed from the baroque and far removed from the dramatics of his previous work, in *Poemas & Híbridos* (Poems & Hybrids, 1990) Atxaga tries to recover poetry's essence. For this purpose, he tears up the nonneutral, topical lang. that is traditionally used in the modernist poetry and mixes it with Dadaist strategies, with the primitive and the infantile, and with humor.

Contemp. Basque poetry can best be described as eclectic. Its primary characteristics include a wide diversity of poetics, the use of various narrative styles, a preference for nonaesthetic poetics rooted in the quotidian, and the emergence of women poets who reclaim other codes based on the female body. Poets such as Felipe Juaristi (b. 1957), Rikardo Arregi (b. 1958), Miren Agur Meabe (b. 1962), and Kirmen Uribe (b. 1970) seem to be influenced by the Beat poets and gritty realism. Audiences often enjoy poetic performances that combine poetry with music or other arts. What happened to the other literary genres has also happened to poetry: it has absorbed the characteristics literary critics describe as postmodern—a denial of transcendental meaning; an assertion that all lit. is metalit. in the end; a nonelitist attitude toward literary creation; the use of pastiche; a mistrust of lang.; and a hybridization of genres. That is, Basque poetry displays a tendency toward aesthetic populism and a democratizing attitude to the figure of the poet.

■ **Anthologies**: *Antología de la poesía vasca*, ed. I. Aldekoa (1993); *Etzikoak*, ed. and trans. M. Drobnic and M. Prelesnik Drozg (2006); *Montañas en la niebla*, ed. J. Kortazar (2006); *Six Basque Poets*, ed. M. J. Olaziregi (2007); *Cien años de poesía*, coord. J. Sabadell-Nieto (2007).

■ **History and Criticism:** L. Michelena, *Historia de la literatura vasca* (1960); I. Aldekoa, *Historia de la literatura vasca* (2004); *History of Basque Literature*, ed. M. J. Olaziregi (2010).

M. J. Olaziregi

BELARUS, POETRY OF.

See RUSSIA, POETRY OF

BELGIUM, POETRY OF

I. Dutch. *See* LOW COUNTRIES, POETRY OF THE.

II. French. Med. Belgian lyric poetry underwent important devels.—as much in religious as in epic, mystical, or courtly genres—in the feudal principalities that were the foundation of the country. Likewise, during the 16th and 17th cs. under the Burgundian dynasty, Chambers of Rhet. prospered whose trads. of formal invention and irony are undoubtedly similar to certain aspects of mod. poetry in Belgium. The production of original poetry, in Fr. as well as in Dutch, declined when the Netherlands, while retaining its constitution, found itself subservient to Madrid or Vienna (1585–1795).

This section concerns the production of poetry in Fr. that began after the Battle of Waterloo (1815) in the territories of the Catholic Netherlands and the Principality of Liège. The contours of a new Europe were being drawn, a Europe in which nationalist revolutions would break out, incl. the Belgian Revolution of 1830. In this setting, the concept of national lit. was affirmed, and the problem of francophone lits. was worked out; in this, the Belgian literary field was not merely a laboratory but the first great incubator, even if those interested in such questions take into account what was happening at the same time in Haiti and Switzerland. In the romantic period, freed from their imposed union with Holland, Belgian poets such as Théodore Weustenraad (1805–49), André van Hasselt (1806–74), and A.C.G. Mathieu (1804–76) used diverse forms of Fr. verse to celebrate the various industrial realizations of its modernity. As early as the 1820s, poets began to take liberties with dominant Fr. literary models, but it was not until the 1880s and 1890s that a distinctive Belgian Fr. poetry emerged, although one related to larger trends in Europe at the end of the century.

Some of these, in the Fr.-speaking world, arose in a country that hist., through its various means, had better prepared than others to break from the cl. Fr. canon. This condition brought the generation called the *Jeunes Belgique* (Young Belgium) to take over the mysteries of symbolism, the stylistic audacity of Arthur Rimbaud and the Comte de Lautréamont (both of them published in Belgium), as well as Stéphane Mallarmé's encouragement. They thus asserted a specific literary identity recognized very quickly—and first of all in other countries—without claiming it as a national possession.

Émile Verhaeren (1855–1916) with *Les Campagnes hallucinées* (The Hallucinated Countryside, 1893) and *Les Villes tentaculaires* (The Tentacular Cities, 1895); Georges Rodenbach (1855–98) with *Le Règne du silence* (The Reign of Silence, 1891); Charles van Lerberghe (1861–1907) with *La Chanson d'Ève* (The Song of Eve, 1904); Max Elskamp (1862–1931) with *Dominical* (Sunday Prayer, 1892); and the Nobel laureate Maurice Maeterlinck (1862–1949) with *Serres chaudes* (*Hot Houses*, 1899) gave to francophone as well as to world lit. works of note and influence. E.g., Antonin Artaud claimed the six *Hot Houses* in verse as an inspiration; the It. *Crepuscolari* (Twilight Poets; see ITALY, POETRY OF) would be incomprehensible without Rodenbach's stimulus, as Ger. expressionism would be without Verhaeren's poetic upheaval.

These innovators distanced themselves from their peers such as Albert Giraud (1860–1929), Iwan Gilkin (1858–1924), and Valère Gille (1867–1950) who wanted to remain faithful to Parnassianism and to the Fr. trad. These divisions, which persisted a long time, reached to the very heart of the francophone world. The ruptures of World War I and the Rus. Revolution only served to deepen them.

The flourishing of the avant-garde and a new set of exchanges with Paris followed on these beginnings. Dadaism found a special radicalism in Clément Pansaers (1885–1922), author of *Le Pan-Pan au cul du nu nègre* (Pan-Pan at the Negro Nude's Ass, 1920), who called very early for the end of the movement by its own logic. In Brussels, a surrealist movement appeared around Paul Nougé (1895–1967) as early as 1924—one that has been both compared to and differentiated from the one led by André Breton in Paris at the same time. The group's mistrust of the literary world, the clear distinction between the rules of political activity and those of writing or painting, and the very Belgian refusal to believe the evidence of lang. engendered production fundamental to the hist. of surrealism.

Of a rare quality and impertinence, as well as an exceptional rigor, this aesthetic and ethical endeavor is inscribed in the titles of the two Nougian *summas* collected by Marcel Mariën (1920–93)—*Histoire de ne pas rire* (A Story of Not Laughing, 1956) and *L'Expérience continue* (The Continuous Experience or The Experience Continues, 1966)—and in this precept: "exégètes, pour y voir clair, rayez le mot surréalisme" (exegetes, to see clearly, scratch out the word *surrealism*). Invented and shared by Marcel Lecomte (1900–66), Louis Scutenaire (1905–87), Camille Goemans (1900–60), André Souris (1899–1970), Paul Colinet (1898–1957), Irène Hamoir (1906–94), Édouard Léon Théodore Mesens (1903–71), and René Magritte

(1898–1967), this movement unfolded outside any literary milieu, in a sort of inscribed parenthesis and in a filiation or reinvention between Ger. romanticism and revolution. Entirely coherent, this strand is fundamental to those artistic approaches that exhausted all the methods of the time, incl. advertising.

This inclusivity distinguishes Belgian surrealism from the lyricism that characterizes the work of Achille Chavée (1906–69), of Hainaut, who was faithful to the precepts of Fr. surrealism, and of his follower, Fernand Dumont (1906–45), the post-Nervalian surrealist who wrote *La Région du cœur* (The Region of the Heart, 1939) and *La Dialectique du hasard au service du désir* (Dialectic of Chance in the Service of Desire, 1979). There was lyricism, too, in the work of Charles Plisnier (1896–1952), who was also actively engaged on the Left and who found the means of expressing this engagement—which the followers of Nougé rejected—in the form of the spoken choruses, such as *Odes pour retrouver les hommes* (Odes to Rediscover Men, 1935) and *Sel de la terre* (Salt of the Earth, 1936).

Close to the modernists whose postulates the surrealists violently contested (among these, Pierre Bourgeois [1898–1976], ed. of the *Journal des poètes*), Géo Norge (1898–1990), for his part, aims to plunge to the carnal heart of a *Langue verte* (green language) that he celebrates and puts to work with relish in *Les Oignons* (The Onions, 1953) and *Le Vin profond* (The Deep Wine, 1968).

This trust in the Fr. lang. and trad. likewise declined, though with entirely different connotations, in the works of Marcel Thiry (1897–1977), such as *Toi qui pâlis au nom de Vancouver* (You Who Pale at the Name *Vancouver*, 1924). Thiry expressed this lack of faith in *Le Poème et la langue* (The Poem and the Language, 1967) by opposing his vision to that of Henri Michaux (1899–1984), whose plunges into words and traits sought the instinctual, the irrational, and the irregular—in works such as *La Nuit remue* (Darkness Moves, 1935), *L'Infini turbulent* (Infinite Turbulence, 1957), and *Face à ce qui se dérobe* (Facing the Evasive, 1976). Michaux, whose first works were close to those of Goemans, nevertheless held himself at a distance from the surrealists, even if he did dedicate to Magritte one text strongly expressive of the surrealists' mode of being and of doing: *En Rêvant à partir de peintures énigmatiques* (Dreaming from Enigmatic Paintings, 1972). Furthermore, as early as 1924 in the *Transatlantic Review*, he explained how his poetics aimed to differ from that of his Belgian forefathers.

If Thiry led his reader out of the rural world, notably into the various colonies and trading posts of the planet and into industry, it was to this old harmonized world that Maurice Carême (1899–1978), whose texts such as *Mère* (Mother, 1935) and *Petites Légendes* (Little Legends, 1949) are everywhere in primary schools, preferred to return. The tormented universes of Jean de Boschère (1878–1953) are completely different in *Job le pauvre* (Job the Poor, 1923) and *Derniers poèmes de l'obscur* (Last Poems from the Darkness, 1948), whose wild lyricism is that of the aesthete and the *poète maudit*, as such is equally the case of René Verboom (1891–1955) in *La Courbe ardente* (The Burning Curve, 1922) and of Paul Desmeth (1883–1970), whose dandyism is distilled into a book much rewritten, *Simplifications* (1932).

The period after 1945 yielded a poetic scene even more divided than what had preceded it, but it broadened the already excellent diversity of the interwar years. Under the rubric of *La Belgique sauvage*, one could find the various modulations of the avant-garde, groups such as Les Lèvres nues (The Naked Lips), Phantòmas, Daily-Bul, Temps Mêlés (Mixed Times), and Le Vocatif (The Vocative). Internationally, the most prominent such venture was CoBrA (named for Copenhagen–Brussels–Amsterdam), led by Christian Dotremont (1922–79), who transformed an old house in Brussels into a center for collective innovation in both poetry and sculpture. Dedicated to finding the origin of the corporeal, this team (incl. Asger Jorn [1914–73], Karel Appel [1921–2006], and the painters known as Constant [1920–2005] and Corneille [1922–2010]), which stayed together for three years, took a break from relations with the Communist Party and displaced some key objectives of surrealism.

Next Dotremont became involved in the adventure that would lead him, via his travels to Laponia, to the invention in 1962 of logograms. On a blank sheet of paper of variable dimensions, a dancing line of China ink was traced, in the manner of the most personal of writings, which the writer-sculptor next transcribed to the underside of the page, in small penciled letters. This is how the sensory and cognitive simultaneity that haunts a major segment of Belgian poetry was attained and how the author of *De loin aussi d'ici* (From Afar as from Here, 1973) completed his research.

The years after the war also witnessed the devel. of the work of another writer-artist active from the 1920s, Michel Seuphor (1901–99), whom the publisher Rougerie strove to keep in print even as the artist's wordpaintings proliferated.

Other works, exceptions to the norm, appeared at the edges of the avant-garde. So it was with François Jacqmin (1929–92), an adolescent whom the hazards of the war took from Fr. to Eng., then from Eng. to Fr. In *Les Saisons* (The Seasons, 1979) and *Le Livre de la neige* (*The Book of the Snow*, 1990), his lucid lang. creates a relationship (to the natural world as to the self) of dissolution and absorption; he emphasizes the conjunction of mistrust and ineluctability inherent in the literary work. Jacqmin's mix of distance and sensibility is not that of Max Loreau (1928–90), the acute commentator of Dotremont and of Michaux and the high-flying philosopher of *La Genèse du phénomène* (The Origin of Phenomena, 1989), whose radical modernity tries to break lang. in order to reintroduce a lyrical celebration of the world: *Cri* (Scream, 1973), *Chants de perpétuelle venue* (Songs of Perpetual Arrival, 1977), *Florence portée aux nues* (Florence on a Pedestal, 1986).

In the next generation, the Belgian members of the Fr. group TXT, Éric Clemens (b. 1945) and Jean Pierre Verheggen (b. 1942), continued this experimentation with lang. Verheggen—author of *Le Degré zorro de l'écriture* (The Zorro Degree of Writing, 1978), *Divan le terrible* (Divan the Terrible, 1979), and *Sodome et Grammaire* (Sodom and Grammar, 2008)—infused his work with a great Rabelaisian character not unfamiliar to the emblem of Belgian letters in the 19th c., Tyl Eulenspiegel. Finally, in the surrealist circle of influence, Tom Gutt (1941–2002) produced some of the most beautiful love poems in Belgian lit.

Still, the desire to conform to Fr. models had not disappeared. It dominated Belgian poetry institutionally in the years after the war. But if this tendency—exemplified by Serge Vandercam (1924–2005), Robert Vivier (1894–1989), Jean Mogin (1921–86), Charles Bertin (1919–2003), Jean Tordeur (1920–2010), and Arthur Haulot (1913–2005)—wanted to combine the internalization of Fr. ideology (and its universality) with the celebration of humanist values destined to conjure up the ghosts of Nazi abjectness, it also led to works that opened a worldwide dialogue. Thus are the cases of Roger Bodart (1910–73) in *Le Nègre de Chicago* (The Negro from Chicago, 1958) and Fernand Verhesen (1913–2009), the smuggler of Latin Am. lits. There was also some beautiful reshuffling of trad.: Philippe Jones's (b. 1924) filtered restitution of sensory evidence; Liliane Wouters's (b. 1930) fusion with the Flemish trad.; and Henry Bauchau's (1913–2012) return to the very old rhythms of lang. in poetic works that constitute the matrix and the tension point of fiction. A unique and admirable work of this generation was Roger Goossens's (1903–54) *Magie familière* (Familiar Magic, 1956).

Likewise, but in a very different way, for the next generation: Sophie Podolski's (1953–74) *Le pays où tout est permis* (The Country Where Everything Is Allowed, 1974) was charred by the universe of repression. During this period, Claire Lejeune (1926–2008), who plunged next into the essay, destined to facilitate the social birth of the poetic, wrote *Mémoire de rien* (Memory of Nothing, 1972), a masterpiece—along with Françoise Delcarte's (1936–95) *Sables* (Sands, 1969)—of postwar women's poetry, haunted by modernity. This moment also saw William Cliff (b. 1940) charge onto the literary scene with a return to cl. verse in a narrative sequence of the blessings and misfortunes of a homosexual lifestyle (*Homo sum*, 1973); and Eugène Savitzkaya (b. 1955) in *L'Empire* (1976) and *Mongolie plaine sale* (Mongolia, Dirty Plain, 1976), who pulverizes Fr. phrases to let loose verbal hordes.

Off the beaten paths of the avant-garde and strict classicism but trusting in the strengths of poetry, various strands that evolved in the 1970s nevertheless refer to Heideggerian dogma. In *Promenoir magique* (Magical Promenade, 2009), Jean-Claude Pirotte (1939–2014) made concise Fr. the site of his renewal; in Werner Lambersy's (b. 1941) *Maîtres et maisons de thé* (Masters and Tea Houses, 1979) is a response to Asian culture. In Jacques Izoard (1936–2008), we find baroque sensuality surrounded by harsh metrics. In Christian Hubin's (b. 1941) *La Parole sans lieu* (The Word without Place, 1975), there is the dread of the rift and the threshold, while in Frans De Haes's (b. 1948) *Terrasses et Tableaux* (Terraces and Paintings, 2007), we find the pregnancy of the Bible and post-*Tel Quel* ling. work. Finally, there is the constant interrogation of the absence of the Other in Yves Namur's (b. 1952) *Le Livre des Sept Portes* (The Book of Seven Doors, 1994).

Rooted in the Walloon soil, certain poets produced works that further escaped the effects of the Francocentric literary world. In *Les Prodiges ordinaires* (The Ordinary Prodigies, 1991), André Schmitz (b. 1929) worked though contraction and attained the density of a carnal tragedy tamed, while Claude Bauwens (b. 1939) follows his white dream of return to the forgetting of oneself in *L'Avant-Mère* (The Pre-Mother, 1975) and Paul André (1941–2008) returns to the magic of a natural being-in-the-world in *C'est* (It is, 1995). Those who, like Guy Goffette (b. 1947) in *Éloge pour une cuisine de province* (Praise for a Provincial Kitchen, 1988) or Lucien Noullez (b. 1957) in *Comme un pommier* (Like an Apple Tree, 1997), left these rural shores far away from centers of cultural recognition, played, all the same, from a different score, a score that their childhoods continued to nourish deeply. This offers them a foundation that distances them from exaggerated modernism and postmodernism.

François Muir (1955–97), in *La Tentation du visage* (The Temptation of the Face, 1998), did not find these types of relative balance. Essentially published posthumously and completely iridescent, his life's work is—with Schmitz's—the most enigmatic, most consistent, and most intriguing of the last decades.

■ **Anthologies**: *Poètes français de Belgique de Verhaeren au surréalisme*, ed. R. Guiette (1948); *Lyra Belgica*, trans. C. and F. Stillman, 2 v. (1950–51); *Anthologie du surréalisme en Belgique*, ed. C. Bussy (1972); *Panorama de la poésie française de Belgique*, ed. L. Wouters and J. Antoine (1976); *La poésie francophone de Belgique*, ed. L. Wouters and A. Bosquet, 4 v. (1985–).

■ **Criticism and History**: G. Charlier and J. Hanse, *Histoire illustrée des lettres françaises de Belgique* (1958); R. Frickx and R. Burniaux, *La littérature belge d'expression française* (1980); M. Quaghebeur, *Alphabet des lettres belges de langue française* (1982); R. Frickx and R. Trousson, *Lettres françaises de Belgique, Dictionnaire des œuvres*, v. 2: *La Poésie* (1988); A.-M. Beckers, *Lire les écrivains belges*, 3 v. (1985–92); C. Berg and P. Halen, *Littératures belges de langue française* (2000); J. P. Bertrand et al., *Histoire de la littérature belge* (2003).

M. Quaghebeur

BENGALI POETRY. The Bengali lang., or Bangla, is a New Indo-Aryan speech of the northeastern part of the Indian subcontinent. The hist. of Bengali lang. and lit. closely links it to the neighboring Assamese, Oriya, and, to a lesser extent in the mod. period, to Maithili. Except for a few commentaries composed in Assam in the 16th c. CE, prose was not used in Bengali lit. before the 18th c.

The first poems in proto-Bengali were preserved in the collection of the *Caryā* songs composed by Buddhist saints in the 11th c. CE. Discovered in 1907 in Nepal, the Caryā songs were not known by later premod. Bengali authors.

Premod. Bengali poetry may be divided into short and long forms. Both forms contained lyrical aspects; performance was a central feature of their composition. The Bengali narrative verse par excellence from the 14th c. is the *payāra*. The payāra is a syllabic meter of 14 feet with a caesura after the eighth that follows a plain rhyme scheme (*aa, bb, cc* . . .). Lyrical and descriptive passages are usually composed in *tripadī*, a slightly more complex verse with two caesurae and an internal rhyme. Tripadīs are also arranged in distichs with the same rhyming pattern as the payāra. Short forms usually use tripadī and other meters borrowed from Sanskrit.

The short forms, or *pada*s, heavily drew on the subject of the love between Kṛṣṇa, the incarnation of the Hindu god Viṣṇu, and the cowherd Rādhā. Each poem is a vignette treating one episode of their relationship. Thus, the poem belongs to a wider narrative frame from which it derives its meaning and character. The main themes are love in union (*sambhoga*) and love in separation (*viraha*). The models of this lit. lie in the Sanskrit *Gītagovinda* of Jayadeva (12th c.) and the Maithili poems of Vidyāpati Ṭhākura (14th c.). Caṇḍīdāsa, who composed the *Śrīkṛṣṇakīrtana* (ca. 14th c.), is the first Bengali poet known to have used this theme. The love between Rādhā and Kṛṣṇa illustrated both the mundane ideal of courtly love and the spiritual stages of the devotee. From the 16th c. onward, with the devel. of the sect founded by Caitanya (1486–1533), a rich lit. was composed on this theme. The love between Rādhā and Kṛṣṇa became the archetype of the amatory relationship in Bengali poetry; moreover, Muslim authors also composed poetry in this vein.

Long forms are mainly represented by the *pā̃cāli* tradition. The term *pā̃cāli* refers to a mode of performance combining the declamation of a narrative poem interspersed with more lyrical parts accompanied by music and dance. The first pā̃cālis were adaptations from Sanskrit lit. The *Rāmāyaṇa* of Kṛttivāsa (ca. 15th c.) or

Mālādhara Vasu's *Śrīkṛṣṇavijaya* (The Victory of Lord Kṛṣṇa) were pā̃cālis of this kind. Some typical texts of Bengal called *maṅgalakāvyas* (propitiatory poems) narrate how a goddess imposed her worship among humans in the region. The hagiographic work entitled *Caitanyacaritāmṛta* of Kṛṣṇadāsa Kavirāja (ca. 1517–1615)—about the life and doctrine of Caitanya—pertained to some extent to the poetics of the pā̃cāli. Muslim poets such as Saiyad Sultān (fl. 1584) adapted stories of the prophets of Islam from the Persian and Ar. using the same form. Similarly, other poets like Ālāol (fl. 1651–71) who lived in Arakan, in mod. Myanmar, trans. and adapted Hindi and Persian Sufi romances into Bengali. Other important themes of pā̃cāli poetry are the stories of mythic figures like Satyapīra who belong to both Hindu and Islamic cultures in Bengal.

While premod. poetical forms continue today, Bengali poetry underwent major changes during the 18th and early 19th cs. Bhāratacandra (1712–60) was a clerk and a court poet who integrated historical themes in the pā̃cāli trad. In the early 19th c., Michael Madhusudan Dutt (1824–73), a polyglot poet and dramatist familiar with both Indian and Western cl. langs. and lits., introduced blank verse into Bengali as well as the sonnet. He composed the *Meghanādavadha kāvya* (The Slaying of Meghanada, 1861), an epic poem resorting to the poetics of Gr. tragedy but based on an episode of the Sanskrit *Rāmāyaṇa*.

The versatile author of thousands of poems and songs Rabindranath Tagore (1861–1941), known as the "universal poet" (*viśvakavi*), is a landmark of mod. Bengali poetry. He was awarded the Nobel Prize in 1913 for an Eng. version of his Bengali *Gitanjali* (Song Offerings, 1910). Tagore reshaped traditional topoi through his distinctive genius, thus illustrating the larger dynamics at work in the Bengali literary trad. between the end of the 19th and the first decades of the 20th cs. The Indian and Bangladeshi national anthems are songs composed by Tagore.

Kazi Nazrul Islam (1899–1976), the "rebel poet" (*vidrohī kavi*), was also a prolific songwriter. The themes of his poetry are variegated. He trans. Persian poems of Ḥāfiẓ (1315–89) and composed devotional works dedicated to several Hindu gods and goddesses, as well as powerful nationalist poems. As opposed to that of Tagore, Nazrul's poetry maintains a poetics of chaos and confusion from which a certain creative energy ensues.

Jibananda Das (1899–1954) is the third landmark in the hist. of mod. Bengali poetry. His poems reveal a "complexity" (*jaṭilatā*) in the poet's relation to the world. His conception of poetry as utterly shaped by individual subjectivity—a kind of hermeticism—opposed him to Tagore's universalism and prompted crit. by the followers of an ideologically committed poetry.

In the 1930s, various progressive writers shifted from Tagore's model and engaged in poetic dialogues with his oeuvre. Chief among them is Buddhadeva Bose (1908–74), who devoted several works to the interrogation of Tagore's poetry and composed poems inverting his images. Other poets such as Amiya Chakrabarti (1901–86), Sudhindranath Dutta (1901–60), and Bishnu Dey (1909–82), who did not form a homogenous group, represent different modernist attitudes of the period surrounding World War II.

The independence of India and Pakistan in 1947 marked an important turn in the hist. of Bengali poetry. Dhaka, the capital of East Pakistan, became an alternative to Calcutta as an intellectual center.

Poets of East Bengal expressed a need for a proper identity. During "the language movement" in 1952 up to the independence of Bangladesh in 1971, Bengali poetry became the privileged medium of the nationalist claims of the people of East Pakistan. A variety of voices reflecting the multiple options for the building of a Bangladeshi national identity appear in the poetry of that period. Among them, Shamsur Rahman (1929–2006) was the most influential figure. In his hymn-like poems, his voice melds with the song of freedom and independence of the people of Bangladesh. Jibananda Das's approach to poetry also had a strong influence on the prominent Bangladeshi poet Al-Mahmud (b. 1936). In West Bengal, poetry took a strong ideological turn with the growth of Marxism and the Naxalite movement. Among the noticeable poets of West Bengal of the 1970s and contemp. period are Sunil Gangopadhyay (1934–2012) and Jay Goswami (b. 1954).

See ASSAMESE POETRY; INDIA, POETRY OF; ORIYA POETRY.

■ *A Tagore Reader*, ed. A. Chakrabarti (1961); *The Thief of Love*, trans. E. C. Dimock (1963)—Bengali tales; S. Sen, *History of Bengali Literature* (1979); A. K. Banerjee, *History of Modern Bengali Literature* (1986); C. B. Seely, *A Poet Apart* (1990)—on Jibananda Das; R. Tagore, *Selected Poems*, trans. W. Radice, rev. ed. (1994);

"Bengali," *Medieval Indian Literature*, ed. K. A. Paniker, v. 1 (1997); *Voices from Bengal*, trans. and ed. M. Bandyopadhyay et al. (1997); Kṛṣṇadāsa Kavirāja, *The Caitanya Caritāmṛta*, ed. T. K. Stewart, trans. E. C. Dimock, (1999); *Fabulous Women and Peerless Pīrs*, trans. T. K. Stewart (2004); M. M. Dutt, *The Slaying of Meghanada*, trans. C. B. Seely (2004); P. K. Mitra, *The Dissent of Nazrul Islam* (2007).

T. D'HUBERT

BHAKTI POETRY. *See* INDIA, POETRY OF

BOLIVIA, POETRY OF. Hists. of Bolivian poetry have regularly struggled to incorporate the poetry created in all the langs. spoken in the nation. Besides Sp., the official lang. and lingua franca, at least three langs. are widely spoken in Bolivia: Aymara, Quechua, and Guaraní. Lit. hists. have been able to describe poetry written in Sp. since the colonial period and have sought to include the poetry written in the indigenous langs., but with limited success. The major impediment is that poetry in native langs. usually is part of an oral trad. (i.e., none of these cultures had developed advanced writing systems). Thus, hists. of Bolivian poetry usually start with those texts written in Sp. after the arrival of Francisco Pizarro and Diego de Almagro and the conquest of the Incas (1531–33). Because the major part of the territory of what today is Bolivia (then called Kollasuyo) was part of the Inca Empire, this moment in hist. is considered an origin for the production of Bolivian lit. The present article will follow this conventional route (see also INDIGENOUS AMERICAS, POETRY OF THE).

Bolivian scholars agree that, for the colonial period (1531–1825), the criteria for defining authorship should rely on location more than place of birth for attributing a text to Bolivian lit. hist. Thus Bolivian poetry of the colonial period includes both the poems written by men and women born in the region and those written by colonists of the territory of the Royal Audience of Charcas (1599), an appellate court with jurisdiction over the region that would become Bolivia. *Coplas a la muerte de Don Diego de Almagro* (Songs on the Death of Diego de Almagro, ca. 1540) is recognized as the first poem written in Bolivian territory by an anonymous Sp. poet. Not very skillfully written, this is an epic romance of the execution of Almagro perpetrated by the Pizarro family in 1538. The most important writer of the 16th c. is Diego Dávalos y Figueroa (1552–1608), an Andalusian who lived and died in the city of La Paz. Dávalos wrote a text in prose, the *Miscelánea Austral* (Austral Miscellany), and a book of poems, the *Defensa de damas* (Defense of Ladies), that were published together in Lima in 1602 and received with great admiration by the intellectuals of the Viceroyalty of Peru. Dávalos's writings are considered the best example of Petrarchism in the Sp. colonies. The life and work of Dávalos are tightly related to the intellectual life of his wife, Francisca de Briviesca y Arellano (ca. 1547–1616). She was a learned woman whose participation in her husband's production seems to have been very significant. In the *Defensa de damas*, she may be the poetess to which the poems refer, as well as the Cilena who signs one of the laudatory poems at the beginning of the book. This exquisite sonnet is the first poem published by a woman in the Viceroyalty of Peru. Moreover, the *Defensa de damas* is the first feminist poem in Bolivian—and Latin Am.—lit.

During the 16th and 17th cs., the wealth of the imperial city of Potosí, based in the exploitation of the silver in its famous mountain, attracted adventurers from the New and Old Worlds looking for quick prosperity. Potosí became an exuberant and opulent city typical of the Am. baroque, drawing numerous writers in the 17th c.

The Port. poet Henrique Garcés (ca. 1522–95), who had an important role in adapting Petrarch's poetry throughout the Viceroyalty of Peru, may have lived in Potosí while he tried to implement a process to separate silver by the use of mercury. His trans. of Petrarch's *Canzoniere* (1591) and his own poetry were so well known that Miguel de Cervantes mentioned him in a poem. The most important poet of the 17th c. to have dwelled in Potosí is Luis de Ribera (ca. 1555–1623). Born in Seville, he lived in Potosí as well as in La Plata from at least 1621 to 1623. His only book is a collection of religious poetry, *Sagradas poesías* (Sacred Poems), published in Seville in 1612. Ribera worked in a sophisticated baroque style, and despite the devotional orientation, an intense eroticism pervades many of his poems. He had a preference for biblical themes that allowed him to display erotic topics, such as the drunkenness of Lot raped by his daughters or the nakedness of Bathsheba. His poetry is considered not only one of the peaks of Bolivian and Lat. Am. colonial production, but among the best of the Sp. Golden Age. Diego

Mexía de Fernengil (ca. 1565–1634), another important figure born in Seville, resided in Potosí from 1609 to 1617. He was a friend of Ribera, with whom he shared strong religious beliefs. Mexía was a reputed translator of Ovid. In 1608, he published the first part of his *Parnaso Antártico* (Antarctic Parnassus), a trans. of Ovid's *Heroides*. While in Potosí, he probably wrote the second part of the *Parnaso Antártico*, a collection of sonnets, some of them inspired by illustrations of the life of Christ made by the Jesuit Jerónimo Nadal.

José de Antequera (1689–1731) was perhaps the finest poet of the 18th c. He was a judge of the Audience of Charcas, but he rebelled against the Sp. Crown. Sentenced to death in 1731, he wrote several sonnets while in prison, lamenting his fate and the passing of time. The "Testamento de Potosí" (Potosí's Testament, 1800), by an anonymous poet, may well be the closing text of the colonial period. This is a book of satirical poetry that anticipates the character of much 19th-c. poetry.

Bolivia began its independence movement in 1810 and became a nation in 1825. These were long years of war, and few literary texts were produced or survived the armed struggle. In the first decades of the republic, the social and political situation was not much better. Political turmoil engulfed many of the promising writers of this period. Romanticism, the dominant literary style in Sp. America, did not have large numbers of Bolivian cultivators. However, there were a few poets whose works are recognized as valuable. The outstanding poet of this period is Ricardo José Bustamante (1821–84). He studied in Paris, where he became familiar with Eur. lit.; his best-known poem is "Preludio al Mamoré" (Prelude to the Mamoré). Another important romantic poet is the blind María Josefa Mujía (1812–88), who is considered the first woman writer of the newly independent nation. Her poetry draws on her blindness to convey a dark and tragic perception of life. It is worth mentioning Manuel José Tovar (1831–69), whose poem "La creación" (The Creation), based in the biblical Genesis, is one of the jewels of Bolivian romantic poetry.

The transition to mod. poetry of the 20th c. followed two roads: one opened by the poetry of Adela Zamudio (1854–1928), inclined toward social issues; the other by Ricardo Jaimes Freyre (1866–1933), focused on the renovation of poetic lang., a phenomenon fueled by Sp. Am. *modernismo*. Zamudio's poetry is in some measure romantic, but a profound consciousness of her social situation as a woman generates a radical crit. of the hypocrisy of Bolivian patriarchal society. She is considered the most important feminist writer in Bolivian lit. In her life and works, she was a defender of childhood and women as well as a critic of Bolivian education, in the hands of the Catholic Church at the time. Her best known poem is "Nacer hombre" (To Be Born a Man), a strong crit. of men's privileges. Jaimes Freyre is considered, with Rubén Darío and Leopoldo Lugones, one of the founders of modernismo. He and Darío wrote a manifesto in 1894 that is considered the beginning of this literary movement. In 1905, Freyre wrote *Leyes de la versificación castellana* (Laws of Castilian Versification), an innovative treatise about the laws of versification in the Sp. lang. His most famous book of poetry is *Castalia bárbara* (Barbarous Castalia), a poetic recreation of some themes of Scandinavian mythology.

It has been argued that the dominant intellect of the first half of the 20th c. in Bolivia was Franz Tamayo (1879–1956). His poetry was fed by the modernist style; however, he took that style to phonetic extremes even as he used cl. Greco-Roman lit. as the foundation of his poetry. He developed a voice so distinctive that it made him the preeminent poet of Bolivia. His erudition allowed him to write poetry heavy with references to antiquity, esp. the cl. trad., as these titles may indicate: *Epigramas griegos* (Greek Epigrams), *Scopas*, and his best-known book, *La Prometheida* (The Promethiad, 1917), a meditation on the Prometheus myth.

The avant-garde movements of the first decades of the 20th c. had some late followers in Bolivia. It is worth mentioning Guillermo Viscarra Fabre (1900–80) and Julio de la Vega (1924–2010). But perhaps the most original poet with avant-garde affinities is Edmundo Camargo (1936–64). These three poets made profuse use of visual images and surrealist topics common in the period's avant-garde movements. Yolanda Bedregal (1916–99), named "Yolanda of Bolivia," was considered an official symbol of Bolivian poetry in the second half of the 20th c. The main topics of her poetry are women as the foundation of the family and God. Although love is central to her writings, it is not always viewed as an easy or pure emotion. Love in her poetry is constantly faced with emotional challenges such as hatred or abuse.

If the first half of the 20th c. was dominated by Tamayo, the second part saw two poets, both his admirers, as the major figures of Bolivian poetry: Oscar Cerruto (1912–81) and Jaime Saenz (1921–86). Cerruto's poetry continues to employ a cl. lang., but without Tamayo's considerable erudition. Impelled by a search for the "precise word" and by his admiration for Sp. Golden Age poetry, Cerruto developed an extremely unadorned poetry to express a disenchanted view of Bolivian society. Among his books, *Patria de sal cautiva* (Fatherland, Captive of Salt, 1958) and *Estrella segregada* (Outcast Star, 1975) are considered masterpieces. Saenz's alcoholism and troubling obsession with death became the source of his philosophical and poetic view of life. He experienced his life as a path to transcendental meaning, always bordering on self-destruction. His poetry is born out of this search as a mystical and demonic quest. By the use of nonsense, paradox, and oxymoron, his poetry forces lang. to the limits of signification. Books such as *Aniversario de una visión* (Anniversary of a Vision, 1960), *Recorrer esta distancia* (To Cross this Distance, 1973), and *La noche* (The Night, 1984) are extraordinary examples of a deeply eccentric Bolivian (and Lat. Am.) poetics.

The end of the 20th c. and the beginning of the 21st saw at least three important poets: Eduardo Mitre (b. 1943), Humberto Quino (b. 1950), and Blanca Wiethüchter (1947–2004). Mitre writes a celebratory poetry in a highly crafted lang. where words and objects can trade places in the seamless space of the erotic. Quino has produced a no less precise poetry but of an opposite character, by looking at himself with irony, sarcasm, and self-contempt. Wiethüchter wrote a poetry of permanent self-searching that speaks of her womanhood in terms of desire and intellectual aptitude. Her feminism can be seen in the poems of *Itaca* (Ithaca, 2000), where she uses Penelope's voice to recognize how little she needs and wants the return of Odysseus.

See GUARANÍ POETRY; SPAIN, POETRY OF; SPANISH AMERICA, POETRY OF.

■ A. Cáceres Romero, *Nueva historia de la literatura boliviana*, 3 v. (1987–95); *Cambridge History of Latin American Literature*, ed. R. González Echevarría and E. Pupo-Walker, 3 v. (1996); *Diccionario histórico de Bolivia*, ed. J. M. Barnadas, G. Calvo, and J. Ticlla, 2 v. (2002); *Hacia una historia crítica de la literatura en Bolivia*, ed. B. Wiethüchter and A. M. Paz-Soldán (2002).

L. García-Pabón

BOSNIAN POETRY. The influence of folk genres, in particular ballad and lyric songs, is characteristic of both recent and older Bosnian poetry. Traditional Bosnian poetry should be considered part of the broader South Slavic corpus, owing to a shared body of stylistic and thematic features. The first systematic study of folk poetry from this region was undertaken by Milman Parry and Albert Lord in the period 1933–35 and resulted in Lord's seminal study *The Singer of Tales* (1960). Parry and Lord devoted most of their efforts to long epics, but they also collected over 11,000 women's ballads and lyric songs. It is the shorter folk songs that have left the deepest trace on the lit. of Bosnia-Herzegovina, regardless of the author's ethnic or religious background.

Alongside a lyrical component stemming from traditional lore, in the poetry of Bosnian Muslim authors there is an esoteric-mystical dimension reflecting Islamic spirituality and drawing on poetry that reached Bosnia through the extended presence of the Ottomans in the Balkans. The older generation of authors, such as Safet-beg Bašagić (1870–1934), Musa Ćazim Ćatić (1878–1915), and Ahmed Muradbegović (1898–1972), relied heavily on patterns of folk love poetry but also introduced the refinement and sensibility of a complex multicultural environment.

The next generation of poets introduced elements of the avant-garde, which meant a departure from more traditional forms and the inclusion of the irrational, as well as a more openly erotic dimension saturated with Eastern mysticism and opulent imagery. These characteristics are particularly visible in the poetry of Hamza Humo (1895–1970). Following in this vein is the younger Skender Kulenović (1910–78), for whom poetry is both an esoteric experience and a voice of social conscience.

Several Serbian poets were active in Herzegovina for all or part of their careers, incl. the symbolist Jovan Dučić (1871–1943) and Aleksa Šantić (1868–1924), who modeled many of his works on traditional love poems. One of the greatest Croatian expressionist poets, Antun Branko Šimić (1898–1925), also spent his youth in Herzegovina before relocating to Zagreb.

Although it draws on a specifically Bosnian heritage, the poetry of Mak (Mehmedalija) Dizdar (1917–71) is stylistically highly accomplished and transcultural. His groundbreaking poem *Plivačica* (The Swimmer, 1954) is a strong statement of individuality, vitality, and formal innovation that reflects elements of surrealism but is also an overt departure from the rigid norms of social realism then prevalent. In his collection *Kameni spavač* (Stone Sleeper, 1966), he takes as his inspiration inscriptions from the *stećak* monuments (med. Bogomil tombstones) and through an ancestral poetic perspective speaks of Bosnia as a country of sorrow and resilience.

The poetry of Abdulah Sidran (b. 1944) is imbued with a sadness resulting from his perception of disharmony in the world. His poems are dialogic and often give the impression of settling accounts with life. Representatives of the younger generation, most notably Semezdin Mehmedinović (b. 1960) and Saša Skenderija (b. 1968), were deeply influenced by the wars of 1990s and often address questions of politics, identity, and everyday life in their poetry, while at the same time experimenting with hybrid genres. Among Bosnian-Herzegovinian women poets, Bisera Alikadić (b. 1939), Mubera Pašić (b. 1945), Josefina Dautbegović (1948–2008), and Ferida Duraković (b. 1957) all have written predominantly introspective, intimate poetry, while the latter two have provided memorable verses on the theme of war.

■ **Anthologies**: B. Bartók and A. Lord, *Serbo-Croatian Folk Songs* (1951); *Serbocroatian Heroic Songs*, ed. and trans. A. Lord et al. (1953–80); *Antologija bošnjačke poezije XX vijeka*, ed. E. Duraković (1995); *Scar on the Stone: Contemporary Poetry from Bosnia*, ed. C. Agee (1998); *Antologija bošnjačkih usmenih lirskonarativnih pjesama*, ed. Đ. Buturović and L. Buturović (2002).

■ **Criticism and History**: M. P. Coote, "Serbocroatian Heroic Songs," *Heroic Epic and Saga*, ed. F. J. Oinas (1978); Lord; C. Hawkesworth, *Voices in the Shadows: Women and Verbal Art in Serbia and Bosnia* (2000); A. Buturović, *Stone Speaker: Medieval Tombs, Landscape, and Bosnian Identity in the Poetry of Mak Dizdar* (2002); E. Duraković, *Bošnjačke i bosanske književne neminovnosti* (2003); A. Vidan, *Embroidered with Gold, Strung with Pearls: The Traditional Ballads of Bosnian Women* (2003).

A. Vidan

BRAZIL, POETRY OF. Colonial production of verse in Port. America included lyric, drama, and epic. Early composition comprised continuations of med. trads., popular lyrics, and courtly versions of troubadour ballads. Jesuits used dramatic verse (in Sp., Port., Lat., and Tupi) in their efforts to convert the native population to Christianity. Father José de Anchieta (1534–97) even wrote a modest New World epic in Lat. (printed in Coimbra in 1563). All attempts to write epic in Port. were penned in the shadow of Luís de Camões and *Os Lusíadas* (*The Lusiads*, 1572), his prodigious narrative of Portugal's historical achievements. The first local imitation was *Prosopopéia* (1601) by Sp.-born Bento Teixeira (1561–1600), who fled to Brazil as a young man to avoid the Inquisition. His encomiastic heroic octaves exalted the leader of the settlement of the captaincy of Pernambuco. A baroque phase begins in the mid-17th c. In the 18th c., the principal venues for poetry in large cities were academies where associates met to share work. The outstanding poet of the period was Gregório de Matos (1636–96), nicknamed Boca do Inferno (Mouth from Hell) for his biting satires that prompted authorities in Salvador, Bahia, to exile him to Angola. In a serious vein, he made devotional and amatory poetry. In his sonnets and other poems (all known through codices), Matos practiced the dominant Iberian modes of the day, characterized by conceits, formal dexterity, and imitation, both of Greco-Roman models and of the contemporaneous Sp. masters Luís de Góngora, Francisco de Quevedo, and Baltasar Gracián. While agile in the application of *conceptismo* and *cultismo*, Matos also touched on the mixed nature of Brazilian society, occasionally incorporating indigenous and even Af. elements.

A Brazilian version of arcadianism emerged in the late 18th c. in the gold-rich state of Minas Gerais. Colonial lit. had appeared with little coherence or continuity; now came forth an organized group with shared attitudes and nascent national awareness. Poets adopted pastoral pseuds. to write of bucolic ideals yet managed to constitute the beginnings of "Brazilian personal lyricism" (Coutinho). Their provincial adaptations of neoclassical poetics entailed turning away from perceived baroque excesses, a search for natural simplicity, and preference for graceful rhythmic schemes. While having studied in the Old World, they began to give voice to new feelings of belonging in the New World. As engaged citizens, they read Enlightenment authors, advocated political autonomy, and took part in the first conspiracy against the rule of Portugal (1789). The principal poets were Cláudio Manuel da Costa (1729–89), whose petrous imagery has been seen to reflect emotional attachment to the land; the Port.-born Tomás Antônio Gonzaga (1744–1810), author of the most popular collection of love poems in Port., *Marília de Dirceu* (1792); and Silva Alvarenga (1749–1814), noted for local landscapes. In Lisbon, Brazilian mulatto Domingos Caldas Barbosa (1738–1800) was elected president of the cultivated Nova Arcadia assembly but gained fame in the royal court performing his sometimes sensual songs, lyrics of which were published alongside pastoral poems. His occasional use of an Afro-Brazilian lexicon was a historical milestone.

National spirit was most evident in epic poems. *Caramuru* by José de Santa Rita Durão (1722–84) was composed of ten Camonian cantos about the Port. arrival in Bahia, and *O Uraguai* (1769) by Basílio da Gama (1741–95) narrated the Luso-Hispanic war against the Jesuit missions of southern Brazil. Efforts to relive *epopeia*—epic poetry—continued in Brazil well into the next century. Domingos José Gonçalves de Magalhães (1811–82) with his *A confederação dos tamoios* (1856) celebrated liberty in a crushing military defeat of an Indian tribe, revealing limited sensitivity toward native peoples. The poet's close ally, Manuel Araújo Porto Alegre (1806–79) tried his hand at epic in *Colombo* (1866), extolling Eur. expansionism in the figure of Columbus.

In the mid-1830s, these last two authors had formed a literary association in Paris that in essence launched Brazilian romanticism, through lyric poetry and the expository essay. The entire period was naturally marked by independence from Portugal (1822), the evolution of the only monarchy (here called an empire) in the Western hemisphere, and the pursuit of Am. forms of identity. In general, the first generation of romantics believed in a historical mission to create lit. of a national character. Led by Antônio Gonçalves Dias (1823–64), they emphasized differences from Europe and autochthonous phenomena. The multigenre movement of Indianism celebrated native peoples, places, sources, and heroism. Among Dias's "American Poems," the most recognized composition was "I-Juca Pirama" (in Tupi, "he who must die"), a classic of Indianist poetry. In this work, Dias employed varied Port. verse forms but, while he assigned narrative voice to Indian personages in some passages, never recovered an indigenous poetics per se. Dias also left an unfinished epic based on a tribal story. Perhaps the most widely known Brazilian poem of all time is his "Canção do exílio" (Song of Exile, 1843), which he wrote while studying in Portugal, where he absorbed myriad romantic influences. The strophes express the quintessential Lusitanian emotion of *saudade* (longing, homesickness) in relation to the New World homeland. With the former colony now irretrievably the focus of consciousness, the brief piece relates location—Brazil as place of desire—to the romantic emphasis on sentimentality, expressivity, and shared heritage. The poem's importance as a symbol of the country has been compared to those of the flag and the national anthem. In the second wave of romantic poetry, Manuel Antônio Álvares de Azevedo (1831–52)—a Brazilian parallel to Lord Byron, Alfred de Musset, and some Port. figures—explored intense subjectivity, bohemianism, and pessimistic introspection. In contrast, a third current during romanticism was social poetry, eminently the abolitionist works of Antônio de Castro Alves (1847–71). Influential titles were "Navio negreiro" (The Slave Ship) and "Vozes d'África" (Voice of Africa), impassioned rhetorical verse of ethical purpose known through periodical publication and public declamations. He crafted amatory, bucolic, and patriotic lyric as well. A sui generis figure of the romantic period was Joaquim de Sousa Andrade or Sousândrade (1833–1902), maker of adventurous lines that prefigure modernism, markedly in the trans-Am. neoepic *O Guesa* (London, 1888), featuring an anthological interlude titled "The Inferno of Wall Street" in its editorial revival of the 1960s.

Following the lead of France, reaction against ultraromanticism and a vogue of "realist" poetry would lead to the devel. of Parnassian poetry, a school and style based on restraint of feeling, reverence for form (particularly the sonnet), and erudition. While in Portugal this practice was relatively modest, the Brazilian applications of Parnassianism were quite extensive in size, thematic variety (from cl. mythology to historical figures of Brazil), and longevity, enduring from 1880 until the 1920s. The depth and reach of the movement are seen in a canonical trinity. Alberto de Oliveira

(1857–1937) was the most orthodox Parnassian, as seen in such titles as "Vaso grego" (Grecian urn) and his regular use of alexandrines. The scrupulous versifier Raimundo Correia (1859–1911) displayed remarkable wealth of vocabulary and expressive variety, incl. pessimism and melancholy. Crowned the Prince of Brazilian Poets (in a 1907 contest sponsored by a leading magazine), Olavo Bilac (1865–1918) cultivated, in addition to amatory themes and art for art's sake, patriotism, progress, and a work ethic. Symbolism arrived around 1890 and brought forth a major trio of poets. João da Cruz e Sousa (1861–98), son of a slave, witnessed abolition (1888), a cause he supported in print and deed. He produced poetry of pain and suffering alongside typically symbolist verse marked by musicality and spiritual concerns. A mystical poet par excellence was Alphonsus de Guimaraens (1870–1921), preoccupied with death and Catholic faith. Augusto dos Anjos (1884–1914) produced an idiosyncratic verse employing laboratorial lexicon and material philosophical concepts. His single volume, *Eu* (I, 1912), continues to be reprinted regularly. The Parnassian-symbolist phase in Brazil corresponded to *modernismo* in Spanish America, where antiromantic refinement and exaltation of form were similar but New World subject matter was more prominent.

In Port. *modernismo* refers to the complex of antitraditional and avant-garde tendencies beginning around 1920. The Brazilian movement, officially launched with the Modern Art Week of 1922 (the centenary of independence), endeavored to shake the foundations of academic writing, still stilted and Lusitanian, and to liberate poetry from the lingering constraints of obsolete Parnassianism and symbolism. The two fundamental aspects of the new creed were technical renovation of lyric, free verse above all, and attention to the national, in lang. itself (using the Brazilian vernacular) and themes (folklore, contemp. life). Rio-born Ronald de Carvalho (1893–1935) lived futurism in Paris; coedited the cutting-edge jour. *Orfeu* (1915) in Lisbon with the multifarious master of mod. Port. poetry Fernando Pessoa (1888–1935); and transported their vanguard cause to Brazil. While having Eur. links, modernismo in Brazil was driven by nationalism. In Carvalho's case such native fervor was tied, in Whitmanian fashion, to a pan-Am. spirit, evident in the neoepic sequence *Toda a América* (All the Americas, 1926). Guilherme de Almeida (1890–1969) celebrated ethnic mixture (Euro-, Afro-, Indo-) in *Raça* (Race, 1926) and essays on "nationalist sentiment." Having written in a panoply of styles, he was elected Prince of Brazilian Poets in 1958 in a poll conducted by a leading São Paulo daily. Mário de Andrade (1893–1945) exemplified an innovative approach attuned to national realities. His *Paulicéia desvairada* (*Hallucinated City*, 1922) advanced a playful musical concept of verse and probed the multicultural cosmopolis of São Paulo, while later collections contemplated the breadth of the country, incl. remote jungles. Oswald de Andrade (1890–1954) incorporated primitivism, cubism, and various conceptual currents (notably Sigmund Freud) into a clever poetic minimalism and manifestos that clamored, with abstract humor, for aggressive novelty and self-assertiveness. His title *Poesia Pau-Brasil* (1924) takes its name from brazilwood, the first natural resource for export. In a broad civilizational metaphor, the new product of poetry should aspire to reverse the unidirectional influence of the metropolis (Paris, Lisbon) over the (former) colonies. The "Manifesto antropófago" ("Cannibalist Manifesto," 1928)—the declaration of antropofagia—concerned poetry and intellectual discourse at large. Both manifestos undermined *sermo nobilis* and sought to expand the restricted literary sense of poetry. A conservative nationalist group under the banner of *verde-amarelismo* (green-yellowism) opposed "alien" influence and favored the symbol of the *anta* (tapir), an animal imagined to embody the primeval power of the land. An enduring poet of this persuasion was Cassiano Ricardo (1895–1974). In Rio de Janeiro, poets attached to the jour. *Festa* were less concerned with *brasilidade* (Brazilianness) than with mod. consciousness and spirituality. Cecília Meirelles (1901–64) wrote neosymbolist collections and a lyrical epic about the capital city itself. Poets from all provinces of Brazil came to embrace their own physical and cultural geographies, natural lang., self-veneration, and differentiation from Europe.

Modernist purposes were wholly fulfilled in the work of Manuel Bandeira (1886–1968) and Carlos Drummond de Andrade (1902–87). The former lived the transition from 19th-c. conventions to mod. flexibility, a change evident in such titles as *O ritmo dissoluto* (Dissolute rhythm, 1924) and *Libertinagem* (Libertineness, 1930). His manipulations of pointedly colloquial lang. and pursuit of popular wisdom endeared him to generations of readers. Drummond exhibited astounding range, over the decades producing *modernista* joke poems, existential reflections, social verse, philosophical meditations, gamesome ling. trials, and even erotic episodes. Among the many other modernist poets, Murilo Mendes (1901–75) composed distinguished surrealistic and metaphysical pieces, and Jorge de Lima (1895–1953) showed striking versatility, from the folk-inspired *Poemas negros* (1946) to the hermetic quasi-epic *Invenção de Orfeu* (Invention of Orpheus, 1952). The iconoclastic "heroic phase" of the modernist movement in Brazil is usually placed in the years 1922–30, while the "constructive" phase extends to at least 1945. The term *modernismo* also encompasses the later works of poets born before 1920.

Chronologically, João Cabral de Melo Neto (1920–99) coincided with the so-called Generation of '45, a mid-century cluster of neo-Parnassian poets who objected to free verse and overtly native topics, instead proposing a return to circumspect versifying and removal from quotidian affairs. A representative name in this cohort was Ledo Ivo (1924–2012). Cabral shared with them an alert regard for formal rigor and discipline, but he opposed their focus on psychic states and insistence on elevated poetic lexicon—in sum, their elitism. Cabral was concerned with tangible reality and the materiality of words rather than romantic or philosophical inspiration. He was a leading exponent of a new objectivity in postwar Lat. Am. poetry but commonly connected his lang. of objects to social facts and real-world settings, chiefly his native northeastern region. Cabral never made a concession to sentimental rhet. or confessionalism; his textual geometry and architecture always prevailed.

Brazil was a principal scene in the movement called concrete poetry, an organized international avant-garde or neovanguard of the 1950s and 1960s. The Brazilian founders were the São Paulo poets Augusto de Campos (b. 1931), Haroldo de Campos (1929–2003), and Décio Pignatari (1927–2012), who formed the Noigandres group. In the early 1950s, they produced audacious lyrical texts with vehement imagery, fragmentations, and other experimental effects. The spatial minimalism of *poesia concreta* evolved in three phases. In early years (1952–56), the prime procedures were visual—the presentation of words on the page, typography (esp. the disposition of fonts and colors), the use of empty space—along with a corresponding attention to interrupting or undermining the sentimental dimension of the poem. "Classical" or "orthodox" material arose in a second phase (1956–61) that involved ultrarational principles of composition and extensive theorization, incl. the bilingual manifesto "pilot plan for concrete poetry," built on universal and national planks, such as Stéphane Mallarmé, Ezra Pound, James Joyce, e.e. cummings, Oswald de Andrade, and Cabral. In a third stage of concretism (1962–67), open notions of invention led to several different behaviors and products, from semantic variations to word collages and abstract designs with lexical keys. Other groups theorized and practiced vanguardism, concerned with both textual innovation and sociopolitical relevance: *neoconcretismo* (ephemeral splinter of *poesia concreta*, 1959); *Tendência* (centered in Minas Gerais, 1957 and after), led by Affonso Ávila (1928–2012); *Poesia Práxis* (in São Paulo, 1962 and after), conceived by Mário Chamie (1933–2011); and *poema processo* (1967 and after), semaphoric visual poetry.

After concrete poetry per se, the paths of its principal exponents diverged. From the 1970s to the 2000s, Augusto de Campos continually created forms of lyric that crossed the generic and media borders between literary, visual, and musical arts. In the mid-1980s, his poster-poem "pós-tudo" ("Post All") ignited a landmark debate about postmodernism. No poet born in the first half of the 20th c. anywhere has better adapted to the digital age than he. Haroldo de Campos proved to be one of the most significant names of Brazilian letters since 1950, inalterably broadening the horizons of textual crit. and theory. His prose-poetry project *Galáxias* (1984) was a paragon of the Lat. Am. neobaroque, and his rethinking of mod. poetry culminated in the notion of the "postutopian poem," informed by the implications of historical transformations. A classically tinged long poem—*Finismundo, a última viagem* (The last voyage, 1990)—brought the cl. Western trad. into the age of computers. *A máquina do mundo repensada* (Rethinking the machine of the world, 2000) exquisitely interrelated Dante, Camões, Drummond, and cosmological theories. The Noigandres group also influenced Brazilian poetry with its many trans. of canonical and experimental world poetry, everything from troubadours and haiku to metaphysical poetry, Fr. symbolism, and Gertrude Stein.

In the final four decades of the 20th c. and the first decade of the 21st, Brazilian poetry was pluralistic, continually growing in diversity, thematic scope, and sociocultural reach. The poet-critic Mário Faustino (1930–62) was a skilled advocate of Poundian poetics. The widely recognized work of (José Ribamar) Ferreira Gullar (b. 1930) spanned experimentalism, committed poetry (he was the most prominent voice of the socialistic collective *Violão de rua* [Street guitar, 1962–63]), and late-modernist personal lyricism. Of recently active poets, engaging voices from different states and regions include Manoel de Barros (1916–2014), a late discovery who ponders nature and ecology; Thiago de Mello (b. 1926), a noted militant; Roberto Piva (1937–2010), transgressive, exuberant, interested in bodily mysticism; Francisco Alvim (b. 1938), known for brevity, irony, and informality; Carlos Nejar (b. 1939), with his legalistic and mythical tones; Armando Freitas Filho (b. 1940), ever sensitive to evolving modernity; Ruy Espinheira Filho (b. 1942), poet of love and memory; and Marcus Accioly (b. 1943), author of studied lyrical and epic works, incl. the vast *Latinomérica* (2001). Other long, (semi-)narrative titles of neoepic character are Gullar's *Poema sujo* (Dirty poem, 1975), *A grande fala do índio guarani* (The great speech of the Guaraní Indian, 1978) by Affonso Romano de Sant'Anna (b. 1937), *As marinhas* (Seascapes/marines, 1984) by Neide Arcanjo (b. 1940), and *Táxi ou poema de amor passageiro* (*Taxi or Poem of Love in Transit*, 1986) by Adriano Espínola (b. 1952).

In the late 1960s, 1970s, and, to a much more limited extent, beyond, a unique aspect of culture in Brazil has been the recognition of songwriters and lyricists as voices of poetry. The contemp. association of music and lit. was given impetus by Vinícius de Moraes (1913–80), salient modernist poet turned performer and foremost Bossa Nova lyricist. In the eclectic post-Bossa Nova urban popular music of the 1960s generation known as *MPB* (*Música Popular Brasileira*), two names are regularly indicated as having "literary quality": Caetano Veloso (b. 1942) and Chico Buarque (b. 1944), poet-musicians (both with complete lyrics in pub. volumes) who proved the artful complexity of song. Other poetically adept songwriters and numerous poets doubling as composers of song texts participated in this generational phenomenon. In the following decades, Arnaldo Antunes (b. 1960) rose to prominence as a rock singer and lyricist and achieved recognition as a singular visual and postconcrete poet.

In the 1970s, there was a small-press flourish of informal youth verse (dubbed *poesia marginal*), centered in Rio and São Paulo. This trend shared some traits but mostly contrasted with the rubric of "intersemiotic creation," which comprehended measured verse and nondenominational mixtures of words and sonographic elements. So-called marginal poetry cared little for nationalism or intellectual decorum, preferring casual discursivity and sociability. The concurrent constructivist tendency sought to keep technological advances and literary interrelations in sight. Beginning in the 1980s, poets turned increasingly from spontaneity, on the one hand, and visual exhibitionism, on the other, seeking instead an expressive discourse keen to the rationales of rigor and broadly based creative awareness. Contemp. practice was synthesized in the work of Paulo Leminski (1944–89) for the intensity and variety of his ideas regarding lyric. Another prematurely departed voice of distinct originality was Waly Salomão (1943–2003), whose work spanned antinormative prose poetry, song, and cosmopolitan free verse. In the 1990s and into the new millennium, a reliable taxonomy of Brazilian poetry is hindered by the multiplicity of poets and the sheer diversity of their work. With individualism dominating, ever-expanding scenes have embraced diverse and resourceful stylings by poets born in different decades. Active accomplished poets such as Salgado Maranhão (b. 1953) have already published volumes of their collected work. After Mário de Andrade, Bandeira, Meirelles, Drummond and Cabral, notable mod. and contemp. poets who have been ably rendered into Eng. (in single-author volumes) include Renata Pallotini (b. 1931), Adélia Prado (b. 1935), Astrid Cabral (b. 1936), Paulo Henriques Brito (b. 1951), and Régis Bonvicino (b. 1954). Since 1990, there have been expanded efforts to connect realms of poetry in Brazil (both its hist. and its present-day activity) with international circuits, above all within the Americas and Iberia, notably by poet-professor Horácio Costa (b. 1954). Cooperation at colloquia, writers' meetings, book fairs, and publishing houses has been complemented by articulations achieved through the boundless Internet, which has reinvigorated the past and provided previously unthinkable access to poets and readers of the present.

See INDIGENOUS AMERICAS, POETRY OF THE; PORTUGAL, POETRY OF; SPANISH AMERICA, POETRY OF.

■ **Anthologies**: *Antologia dos poetas brasileiros da fase romântica*, 2d ed. (1940); *Antologia dos poetas brasileiros da fase parnasiana*, 2d ed. (1940); *Panorama do movimento simbolista brasileiro*, ed. A. Muricy, 3 v. (1951); *Panorama da poesia brasileira*, 6 v. (1959), *Poesia do modernismo brasileiro* (1968), both ed. M. da Silva Brito; *Poesia barroca* (1967), *Poesia moderna* (1967), both ed. P. E. da Silva Ramos; *An Anthology of Brazilian Modernist Poetry*, ed. G. Pontiero (1969)—texts in Port. with annotations; *An Anthology of Twentieth-Century Brazilian Poetry*, ed. E. Bishop and E. Brasil (1972)—superb team of trans.; *26 poetas hoje*, ed. H. Buarque (1976); *Brazilian Poetry 1950–1980*, ed. E. Brasil and W. J. Smith (1983)—includes visual poetry; *Nothing the Sun Could Not Explain*, ed. N. Ascher et al. (1997)—late-century voices; *Na virada do século, poesia de invenção no Brasil*, ed. C. Daniel and F. Barbosa (2002); *Poets of Brazil*, trans. F. Williams (2004)—bilingual selection from 1500 on; *Apresentação da poesia brasileira*, 4th ed. (2009), all ed. M. Bandeira.

■ **Criticism and History**: J. Nist, *The Modernist Movement in Brazil* (1967); M. Sarmiento Barata, *Canto melhor* (1969)—intro. and anthol. of social poetry; W. Martins, *The Modernist Idea* (1970); *Poetas do modernismo*, ed. Leodegário A. Azevedo Filho, 6 v. (1972)—selections with crit. by specialists; G. Brotherston, *Latin American Poetry* (1975); *A literatura no Brasil*, ed. A. Coutinho, 5 v. (1986)—sections by scholars on poetry; G. Mendonça Telles, *Retórica do silêncio I*, 2d ed. (1989); M. González and D. Treece, *The Gathering of Voices* (1992)—sociocultural analysis; A. Bosi, *História concisa da literatura brasileira*, 2d ed. (1994)—sections on poetry and epochal styles; *The Cambridge History of Latin American Literature*, ed. R. González Echevarría and E. Pupo-Walker, v. 3 (1996)—chronological blocks since 1830s; C. Perrone, *Seven Faces* (1996); A. C. Secchin, *Poesia e desordem* (1996); A. Bueno, *Uma história da poesia brasileira* (2007)—primarily on premodernists; H. de Campos, *Novas*, ed. A. S. Bessa and O. Cisneros (2007); C. Perrone, *Brazil, Lyric and the Americas* (2010).

C. A. Perrone

BRETON POETRY. The independent state of Brittany was formally annexed to France in 1532. Breton writers have produced much Fr. poetry (see FRANCE, POETRY OF), and all educated Bretons since the med. period may be presumed to know Fr. The Breton lang., still spoken in the western half of the region (*Breizh Izel*), belongs to the Brythonic or "P-Celtic" group of Celtic langs., like Welsh and Cornish. It is derived from the speech of settlers from southwest Britain who left their homeland from the 5th to the 7th c. as the Saxons were encroaching from the east. Early Breton poetry would have had much in common with early *Welsh poetry, about which more is known. Marie de France and others indicate that med. Breton poets or bards sang of love, knightly adventures, and faery and that their compositions were the source of Marie's own form, the *lai*; but the earliest surviving Breton poetry dates from only the 14th c. It consists of fewer than 20 lines of popular verse in an indigenous metrical system whose main feature is obligatory line-internal rhyme similar to *cynghanedd lusg*: "An hegu*en* am lou*en*as / An hegar*at* an lac*at* glas" (Her smile gladdened me, / The blue-eyed love). This native prosody was predominant until the 17th c., when it was superseded by the Fr. system of syllable counting and end rhyme. Traces of it can be found in later works, and some 20th-c. poets (Arzhig, Alan Botrel) have used it deliberately.

Most of the Breton verse from the 15th to the beginning of the 19th c. consists of works of religious edification, hymns, carols, a book of hours, and the long and dreary *Mirouer de la mort* (1519). One poem stands out: *Buhez Mabden*, a powerful meditation on death printed in 1530 but probably written a century earlier. The prophetic *Dialog etre Arzur Roe d'an Bretounet ha Guynglaff* dates back to 1450. There are also numerous plays in verse. A few popular plays, such as the *Pevar Mab Emon*, are based on chivalric romances, but most derive from the Bible and saints' lives. The influence of Fr. models is evident, with a few notable exceptions, mainly mystery plays that recount the lives of Celtic saints.

New stirrings begin with the two mock-epic poems of Al Lae (close of the 18th c.), but the real impetus comes with the rise of 19th-c. romanticism. The great event is the appearance in 1839 of Théodore Hersart de la Villemarqué's *Barzaz Breiz* (Poetry of Brittany), an anthol. of supposedly ancient oral poetry, which recent scholarship has shown to be more authentic than many 19th-c. critics believed. The effect was profound. A romantic vision of the Breton past was created that stirred the imagination of many and sparked new literary enthusiasm. At the same time, François-Marie Luzel and others undertook more "scientific" collecting of

Breton folk poetry, of which there were two main kinds: *gwerzioù*, which are essentially ballads, and *sonioù*, a broader designation that extends to more lyrical verse, incl. love songs and satires. Broadside ballads in Breton also circulated. A few of the gwerzioù are demonstrably connected to med. Welsh poetry or to med. events in Brittany; some scholars claim that the gwerzioù are related to the putative Breton-lang. sources of the *lais* in OF. Songs are still an important form of Breton poetry. Mod. singer-songwriters include Glenmor, Youenn Gwernig, Gilles Servat, Jef Philippe, Louis Bodénès, Nolwenn Korbell, Denez Prigent (who composes gwerzioù of his own), and the internationally famous Alan Stivell.

After the Middle Breton literary standard lapsed in the 17th c., four main dialects emerged, associated with the regions of Léon, Trégor, Cornouaille, and Vannes. But following the lead of the grammarian Jean-François Le Gonidec (1775–1838), Breton writers again worked to establish a cultivated literary norm, largely based on the Léon dialect. The dialect of Vannes was used mostly by priests who found inspiration in their faith and in their love for their native land. Esp. popular were Msgr. Yann Vari Joubiouz's *Doue ha mem bro* (1844) and Joakim Gwilhom's imitation of Virgil's *Georgics*, *Livr el labourer* (1849). From the 1850s to the 1880s, only minor talents emerged. Living uprooted from the Breton countryside, these poets expressed in artificial diction their love of the simple life, of the homeland, and of their inheritance, which was no longer secure. This nostalgic trad. was maintained and reinvigorated in the 1890s by the rich lyricism of François Taldir-Jaffrennou and the more artistic Erwan Berthou, but the outstanding poet of their generation was Yann-Ber Kalloc'h, killed in action in 1917. His poems, written in Vannetais and published posthumously, express strong religious and patriotic convictions enhanced by rich and powerful imagery.

The 20th c. saw the vigorous growth of Breton literary periodicals, each with its coterie. Vannetais writers found expression in *Dihunamb*, ed. by the poet-peasant Loeiz Herrieu. The *Gwalarn* group, founded in 1925 under the leadership of Roparz Hémon, proved by far the most talented and creative. Maodez Glanndour and Hémon stand out from the group, although nearly all were gifted poets. Gwalarn did not survive World War II, but patriotic young writers launched new publications. Most did not last. The single exception was *Al Liamm*: under the guidance of Ronan Huon, it became the leading Breton literary jour. In their poetry, Huon and his contemporaries Youenn Olier, Per Denez, and Per Diolier, later joined by Youenn Gwernig (who also wrote in Fr. and Eng.) and Reun ar C'halan, respected the literary standards set by Gwalarn. Women have also played a significant role in the survival of Breton poetry, esp. Anjela Duval, Vefa de Bellaing, Benead, Naïg Rozmor, Tereza, and, more recently, Maï Jamin and Annaïg Renault. The jour. *Brud* (now *Brud Nevez*), founded in 1957, counted one of the best contemp. poets, Per Jakez Hélias, among its first contributors. The 1960s witnessed a strong resurgence of Breton nationalism. The *Union Démocratique Bretonne*, created in 1964, attracted several young militant poets: Paol Keineg (better known for Fr. poetry), Yann-Ber Piriou, Erwan Evenou, and Sten Kidna. Other poets have since come to the fore: Abanna, Alan Botrel, Yann-Baol an Noalleg, Koulizh Kedez, Padrig an Habask, Gwendal and Herle Denez, Tudual Huon, Bernez Tangi, to name but a few. Many were published in *Skrid* (1974–89). New jours. that regularly publish Breton poetry include *Aber*, *An Amzer*, *Al Lanv*, *HOPALA!*, and *Spered Gouez*.

Among the special interests of the 20th and 21st-cs. poets are Breton identity; issues of human rights, cultural autonomy, and lang. survival in Brittany and worldwide; other minority cultures, particularly those of other Celtic lands, an interest sometimes verging on "pan-Celticism" (beginning with the Gwalarn group, many poems have been trans. into Breton); and creative manipulation of the Breton lang. itself. The biggest challenge now facing Breton poetry is to find and maintain a knowledgeable audience outside the ranks of its practitioners.

■ **Anthologies:** *Barzaz Breiz*, ed. T. H. de la Villemarqué (1839); *Gwerziou Breiz Izel*, ed. F. M. Luzel, 2 vols. (1868–74); *Soniou Breiz Izel*, ed. F. M. Luzel and A. Le Braz, 2 vols. (1890); *Les Bardes et poètes nationaux de la Bretagne armoricaine*, ed. C. Le Mercier d'Erm (1918); *Barzhaz: kant barzhoneg berr, 1350–1953*, ed. P. Denez (1953); *Défense de cracher par terre et de parler breton*, ed. Y.-B. Piriou (1971); *Le Livre d'Or de la Bretagne*, ed. P. Durand (1975); *Anthologie de la poésie bretonne, 1880–1980*, ed. C. Le Quintrec (1980); *Du a Gwyn*, ed. D. M. Jones and M. Madeg (1982); *Barzhonegoù*, ed. *Skrid* (1986); *Writing the Wind: A Celtic Resurgence*, ed. T. R. Crowe (1997); *Anthologie de la littérature bretonne au XXème siècle/Lennegezh* *ar Brezhoneg en XXvet Kantved*, ed. F. Favereau, 3 vols. (2002–08); *The Turn of the Ermine*, ed. J. Gibson and G. Griffiths (2006).

■ **Surveys:** F. Gourvil, *Langue et Littérature bretonnes* (1952); *Istor Lennegezh Vrezhonek an Amzer-Vremañ*, ed. Abeozen [Y.F.M. Eliès] (1957); Y. Olier, *Istor hol lennegezh "Skol Walarn,"* 2 vols. (1974–75); Y. Bouëssel du Bourg and Y. Brekilien, "La littérature bretonne," *La Bretagne*, ed. Y. Brekilien (1982); J. Gohier and R. Huon, *Dictionnaire des écrivains aujourd'hui en Bretagne* (1984); *Histoire littéraire et culturelle de la Bretagne*, ed. J. Balcou and Y. Le Gallo, 3 vols. (1987); D. Laurent, *Aux sources du Barzaz-Breiz* (1989); F. Favereau, *Littérature et écrivains bretonnants depuis 1945* (1991); M.-A. Constantine, *Breton Ballads* (1996); A. Botrel, "Les chemins de la poésie en langue bretonne," *HOPALA!* 29 (2008).

■ **Prosody:** E. Ernault, *L'Ancien Vers Breton* (1912); R. Hémon, *Trois poèmes en moyen breton* (1962); F. Kervella, *Diazezoù ar sevel gwerzioù* (1965).

D. M. Lloyd; R. Galand; M. Boyd

BULGARIA, POETRY OF. Bulgarian poetry began with the adoption of an alphabet newly devised by two learned brothers of Thessaloniki, Cyril and Methodius, and with their trans. of several ecclesiastical books. The brothers devised not the Cyrillic alphabet, as is generally believed, but the Glagolitic alphabet in 855. Its complexity meant that it was quickly replaced by what we now call the Cyrillic alphabet. The Bulgarians converted to Eastern Orthodoxy in 865, under Boris I, who proclaimed it the state religion; this conversion was facilitated by the introduction of literacy in the vernacular.

The lit. in the early med. age was ecclesiastic: it focused on prayers, worship, and church rituals. Its main features fluctuate, but there is an invariant characteristic of poeticism in all eras. Cyril, Methodius, and their disciples translated a large corpus of canonical Christian texts and hymnological texts centered on the lives of the saints. These books contained mostly *troparia* (or *stikhera*) and *kontakia*, short poetical verses of two or three sentences to be sung between biblical psalmody and accepted as parts of vespers and matins. In 9th-c. Byzantium, the 12 volumes of the *Menaion* (Book of Months) were completed, containing proper offices for each day of the calendar year. From Bulgaria this ecclesiastical lit. spread to Serbia, Romania, and Russia, which helped to consolidate Slavdom in the 10th c. In accepting Christianity from Byzantium, along with its ecclesiastical and hymnological texts, Bulgaria accepted its *ars poetica* as well.

The earliest known poetic text of 9th-c. Bulgaria is the *Proglas kâm Evangelieto* (Foreword to the Tetraevangelion); it was most likely authored by Konstantine (Cyril) the Philosopher. It holds 110 verses of high artistic value, ecstatically glorifying the newly received gift the Slavs had received "from God," i.e., literacy in the vernacular. Some scholars, however, believe that this is a slightly later work, meant as a foreword to another artistic piece, *Azbouchna molitva* (Alphabet Prayer) by Konstantin Preslavski, written in 893. This work contains 40 verses with a woven alphabetical acrostic. Preslavski wrote another poetic pearl, *Ouchitelno evangelie* (Didactic Gospel), thus establishing the role of the capital city of Preslav as the birthplace of Bulgarian poetry.

Two of Cyril and Methodius's followers, Kliment and Naum, established the town of Okhrid as a second cultural center. Mss. from Preslav were written in the Cyrillic alphabet, whereas those from Okhrid were mostly written in Glagolitic. Thanks to the work in both centers, early Slavic became the written lang. of the new culture then developing alongside Byzantium. In the 9th and 10th cs., Bulgaria reached its height as a political and cultural power.

Another cultural surge occurred in 1185, when the state regained its independence from Byzantium after more than a century of subjugation. The new capital, Turnovo, became the next important cultural center. The key figure here was Patriarch Evtimii (?1325–1401), who became famous for his orthographic reform of the Bulgarian literary lang., as well as his hagiographies and eulogies (*zhitija* and *pohvalni slova*) on Bulgarian saints. His name marked the emergence of the author from med. anonymity. He also contributed to the endorsement of the hesychastic norms introduced by another outstanding leader, Teodosiy Turnovski (1300–63). Other renowned figures from the literary school of Turnovo include Kiprian (1336–1406), Grigorii Tsamblak (1330–1406), and Konstantin Kostenechki (1380–1443).

Early in the 14th c., the monasteries of Mount Athos became incubators for saving and developing Slavic letters. Parchment was gradually replaced by paper, which facilitated the spread of lit. The holy mountain with its 20 main monasteries and numerous monastic cells became a natural fortress of Slav-Byzantine culture, which was preserved and transmitted through the following centuries under Ottoman rule (1396–1878).

During this period, Bulgarian lit. withdrew into churches and monasteries. The Ottomans destroyed many churches, and only a few of the remote monasteries survived to become hidden "barrels" where national awareness fermented. The civilization of the Bulgarian Middle Ages had to be conserved and saved within the framework of an alien Islamic doctrine, as the title of Runciman's book suggests.

In the 17th c., the fashion of so-called damaskin lit. began to flourish. It represents adaptations of *slova* (eulogies) and *apocrypha* (branded as "heretical") originally composed by the 16th-c. Gr. preacher Damaskin Studit. Folklore comprising all the oral genres—tales, songs, proverbs, didactic stories, rural beliefs, calendars, and so forth—continued to develop alongside the written trad. under foreign rule.

Secular lit. of modest artistic merit, based on Rus. and later on Fr. models, appeared in the middle of the 19th c. Educated Bulgarians turned first to Russia for secular literary forms. Poetry predominated through the work of writers like Neofit Rilski (1793–1881), Dobri Chintulov (1822–86), Naiden Gerov (1823–1900), and Georgi Rakovski (1821–67), who wrote the famous poem *Gorski Putnik* (A Forest Traveler) in 1857. With the introduction of the printing press in the Ottoman Empire after 1840, new genres emerged: ballads, diaries, travel notes, pamphlets, and short stories. Around 1850, poetic works were produced mainly by teachers, resulting in *daskalska poezija* (school poetry), characterized by patriotic and didactic tendencies.

Several prominent figures who were both poets and revolutionaries spearheaded the cultural resurgence of the 19th c. Vasil Levski (1837–73) was revered by all Bulgarians as the "saint of the revolution." He was hanged by the Turks near Sofia. His life and death inspired other writers such as Hristo Botev (1848–76), who was killed in combat as he led his people against the Turks in the Balkan range. Botev composed his poems using folk motifs and colloquial idioms.

The invariant characteristic of the period's poetry was monosemanticism, in which a limited number of synonyms stand for the poetic word as such. Poets sought a word that fully exhausts its semantic value, signifying a definite meaning. This corresponded to society's sole ideal, national liberation from the Turks. For an example of monosemanticism, we might take the case of Levski; the most celebrated poem extolling his death was written by Ivan Vazov (1850–1921), who exclaimed, "Oh, heroic gallows!" Since then, this expression became a cliché for a heroic death, used to signify the death of a national hero, usually Levski.

The style of these works is most often called realistic, but the events described, witnessed by most of the authors, were so grim and shocking that it might be better termed naturalistic, even dramatic. Another stream of "quiet" poetry emerged at this time; it focused on refining the lang., finding new rhymes and inventing figures. These tales, love songs, and poems did not tell of suffering or pain.

Bulgaria was liberated in the Russo-Turkish War (1877–78). The newly emerging literary star of the time was Vazov, celebrated as the patriarch of mod. Bulgarian literature. Vazov worked across the cultural spectrum, writing poems, short stories, lyrics, dramas, and criticism.

The realistic model of lit. slowly began to crumble at this time. Authors sought to reopen a multisemantic fan behind the poetic word (polysemy as opposed to monosemanticism). Words were given an unusual set of references or paralleled by sudden rhymes that displaced their meaning: unexpected harmony was sought in distant dissonances. E.g., the word *swan* had a whole "fan of meanings," such as the poet's soul, his striving for beauty, his lover, and so forth. The leading figure in this process was Vazov's lifelong rival Pencho Slaveikov (1866–1912), a humanitarian, poet, and philosopher educated in Germany. The playwright Petko Todorov (1879–1916), the poet Peyo Yavorov (1878–1914), the critic Krustyu Krustev (1866–1919), and Slaveikov formed an aesthetic circle around the literary jour. *Misul* (Thought, 1892–1907).

Slaveikov became the first modernist in Bulgarian lit. and the first poet directly connected with international movements. He went his own way, focusing more on great aesthetic questions than on contemp. literary life. A document in the Nobel Prize Committee archive states that Slaveikov was a Nobel Prize nominee in 1912. He died before the committee meeting, however. Slaveikov inherited a rich collection of folkloric work from his father, Petko Slaveikov, and masterfully saturated his own songs with folk motifs. In the epic poems *Ralitsa*, *Boiko*, and *Kurvava pesen* (Song of Blood), he tried to place specific folk sounds within a larger Eur. frame. Slaveikov's attempt to infuse national motifs into foreign models was successfully continued by Todorov, whose refined *Idiliy* (Idylls, 1908) spoke of the deeply symbolic lang. of nature, eluding any fixed literary classifications.

The most cherished figure of the early 20th c. was Yavorov, commonly held as the greatest Bulgarian poet. Although he formally belonged to the so-called *Misul* Circle, his unique talent enabled him to create his own poetic trad. Yavorov reflected the dramatic split of his tormented soul. His personal life seemed to be performed onstage, constantly trailed by a spotlight. His suicide in 1914 seemed a logical finale to his dramatic life.

The high aesthetic criteria of the jour. *Misul* became a lyrical guidepost for many young authors from different movements. From *Misul* to the next important literary circles, *Zlatorog* (Golden Horn, 1920–43) and *Hyperion* (1922–31), the Bulgarian literary trad. remained rooted in an aesthetic romanticism, which has not ceased. Even later, when poets like Teodor Trayanov (1882–1945), Nikolai Liliev (1885–1960), Dimcho Debelyanov (1887–1916), Emanuil Popdimitrov (1855–1943), and Dimitur Boyadzhiev (1880–1911) brought symbolism into Bulgarian lit., it still occupied romantic grounds.

This is esp. true of Trayanov, who was considered Yavorov's poetic rival. Trayanov spent 20 years (1901–21) in Vienna where he studied and took a diplomatic position. In this cultural atmosphere, he absorbed the ongoing romantic trad., which remained unbroken in Ger.-speaking countries. Mod. Bulgarian crit. is divided as to who opened the door to symbolism, Yavorov or Trayanov. As the most consistent of the symbolists, Trayanov is the most likely candidate, with his poem "Novijat den" (The New Day, 1905), also published in his first collection of 1909, *Regina Mortua*. Although entirely lyrical, his work is also classically symmetrical, divided into cycles, themes, and books. The striving for wholeness that runs throughout Trayanov's verse is typically romantic. His poems resonated deeply with the mood of national resignation during the interwar period, when he wrote his *Bulgarski baladi* (Bulgarian Ballads, 1922). Though Bulgaria had won its chief battles, it lost substantial territories through poor diplomacy and the betrayal of its allies. "The Secret of the Struma" and "Death in the Plains" are his great ballads of that period.

The poetry of Popdimitrov shows the closest relationship to Trayanov. Popdimitrov revived images from the Gothic Middle Ages. Many of his poems are titled with melodious women's names ("Ema," "Iren," "Laura"). The verse of Debelyanov is romantic and elegiac but also warm and lively. It introduced new modes: drinking songs, bacchanalian songs, the confessional genre of short narrative pieces about fashionable bohemian life. Debelyanov was killed in World War I. Similar motifs were to be found in the poetry of Kiril Hristov (1875–1944), whose work is flavored with the unbridled eroticism that was his inspiration. Liliev is considered one of the finest Bulgarian lyricists. His short collections include *Ptitsi v noshta* (Birds at Night, 1918), *Lunni petna* (Moonspots, 1922), and *Stihotvoreniya* (Verse, 1931).

The Fr.-influenced symbolism of Yavorov and the Austrian symbolism of Trayanov clashed with the dominant sociorealistic tendency of Bulgarian lit. During the Communist regime, this tendency continued. But just as Trayanov is more a neoromantic than a symbolist, the "hard" realism of Bulgarian lit. is more a myth than a reality. The term *realist* became the pass, awarded by official critics, that enabled many Bulgarian literary celebrities to enter the rebuilt, low-roofed pantheon of socialist realist writing. Geo Milev (1895–1925) was an expressionist poet among the symbolists. Milev's greatest poem, "Septemvri" (September, 1924), led eventually to his incarceration and death at the hands of the regime. His poetry resumes monosemanticism on a new scale; it demonstratively rejects polysemy for the sake of synonymity, piling up many similar words for one and the same meaning.

A new generation of poets made their debuts through opposing the now old-fashioned symbolism. In his collection *Fragmenti* (Fragments, 1967), Atanas Dalchev (1904–1978) achieved a paradoxical realism based on idiosyncratic imagery. Asen Raztsvetnikov (1897–1951) composed melodious ballads with resigned overtones. Nikola Fournadzhiev's (1903–68) dark and depressive poetry in heavy rhythmic style marked a different pole. The verse of Nikola Rakitin (1886–1934) breathed a quiet and idyllic atmosphere. The poetry of Alexander Voutimski (1919–43) represented an early romantic protest against advancing totalitarianism.

The interwar period also marked the debuts of women poets who began their careers free of any dogmatism. Elisaveta Bagryana (1893–1991) is celebrated for her unrestrained personality and a worship of life, freedom, youth, and travel. Her collections include *Vechnata i svyatata* (The Eternal and the Sacred, 1927), the postwar *Ot bryag do bryag* (From Coast to Coast, 1963), *Kontrapunkti* (Counterpoints, 1972), and *Na brega na vremeto* (At the Shore of Time, 1983). Dora Gabe (1886–1983) imaginatively explored common household objects in bright, optimistic poetry. Her collections include *Zemen put* (Terrestrial Way, 1928), *Pochakai slunce* (Wait Sun, 1967), and *Sgustena tishina* (Condensed Quietude, 1973). Early in the Communist era, an attempt was made to revive a "hard" realistic method. Poets like Nikola Vaptsarov (1909–42), who was shot as a terrorist before the Communist coup, and Penyo Penev (1930–59) were used for this purpose. But resistance won in the long-term conflict. Penev lost his illusions and committed suicide. Many writers were sent to labor camps. The discord between Soviet-style socialist realism and the inventions of contemp. lit. grew rapidly. New trends, masked as experiments, permeated Bulgarian lit. Gifted writers such as Ivan Peichev (1916–76), Andrei Germanov (1932–81), Alexander Gerov (1919–97), Ivan Teofilov (b. 1931), Stefan Tsanev (b. 1936), Nikolai Kunchev (1936–2007), Boris Hristov (b. 1945), and Ivan Tsanev (b. 1941) took advantage of this relative freedom and sent a countermessage to the era's stale ideals. In the late 20th c., the poets Radoi Ralin (1923–2004), Blaga Dimitrova (1922–2003), Konstantin Pavlov (1933–2008), and Vladimir Levchev (b. 1957) became open dissidents.

Even before Communism's collapse in 1989, fresh trends of delicacy and concision could be seen in the poetry of Miriana Basheva (b. 1947), Fedya Filkova (b. 1950), and Georgi Rupchev (1957–2001). Petya Dubarova, born in 1962, was widely recognized as the most gifted younger voice; her suicide in 1979 was believed to be a tragic reaction to the brutality of society. The poetry of Ani Ilkov (b. 1957), Miglena Nikolchina (b. 1955), and Edvin Sougarev (b. 1953) can be described by terms such as expressionism, imagism, and constructivism, as long as *post-* appears before them.

Among a new wave of extremely promising authors, poets such as Georgi Gospodinov (b. 1968), Verginiya Zaharieva (b. 1959), Kristin Dimitrova (b. 1963), Elin Rahnev (b. 1968), and Mirela Ivanova (b. 1962) seek to present the complications and contradictions of the postmod. consciousness in a time of chaos, marked by destructive political events and a radical upheaval of the world picture. Their brilliantly rendered insights and linguistic games have helped to build a warmer and more generous cultural philosophy. Their books of poems have largely appeared either in Eng. or as bilingual eds. Recent names, such as Nadejda Radulova (b. 1975), Dimiter Kenarov (b. 1981), and Kamelia Spasova (b. 1982), mark new experiments, such as living in virtual reality, writing Internet poetry, reflecting on a new femininity, and more.

■ S. Runciman, *The Great Church in Captivity* (1968); *Anthology of Bulgarian Poetry*, trans. P. Tempest (1975); J. Meyendorff, *Byzantine Theology* (1987); *Clay and Star: Contemporary Bulgarian Poets*, trans. and ed. L. Sapinkopf and G. Belev (1992); *An Anthology of Bulgarian Literature*, ed. I. Mladenov and H. R. Cooper Jr. (2007); *Istoria na bulgarskata srednovekovna literature*, comp. and ed. A. Miltenova (2008).

I. Mladenov

BYZANTINE POETRY

I. Hymnography
II. Songs
III. Declamatory Poetry
IV. Epigrams
V. Religious Poetry
VI. Satirical Poetry
VII. Verse Romances and Chronicles
VIII. Didactic Poetry

The Byzantine millennium is usually divided into three periods: early Byzantine or late antique (330–ca. 600), middle Byzantine (ca. 600–1204), and late Byzantine (1204–1453). Constantinople officially became the capital of the Eastern Roman Empire (now called the Byzantine Empire) in the year 330; around 600, urban civilization and traditional power structures began to collapse, leading to the "dark age" crisis of the 7th and 8th cs. In 1204, Constantinople was conquered by the knights of the Fourth Crusade, and although it was reconquered in 1261, the Byzantine Empire had been reduced to a few territories that were gradually taken by the Ottoman Turks until the city itself fell in 1453. Although the Byzantine Empire was multilingual and produced lit. in

Gr., Lat., Coptic, Syriac, Heb., Armenian, and Slavonic, the term *Byzantine literature* stands for med. Gr. lit. Byzantine Gr. is a literary lang. harking back to the ancients (Homeric and Atticistic Gr.) and/or the Bible and the earliest Christian texts (koiné); the first experiments in the vernacular date from the 12th c. Because Byzantine lit. is imitative, it has had a bad press; but originality is a romantic concept, unknown to the Middle Ages. There are two kinds of Byzantine poetry: poetry set to music, such as hymns, acclamations, satirical songs, and folk songs; and all other forms of poetry, intended either to be declaimed in public or to be read in private. As most poetry belonging to the first category has come down to us without scores or in later musical adaptations, we are uncertain how Byzantine music, esp. in its early stages, may have sounded. As for meter, all poetry set to music and many of the unsung poems are based on rhythmical patterns regulated by the position of stress accents. Poems in prosodic meters, such as the iamb, the hexameter, or the anacreontic also survive, but these, too, obey certain rhythmical rules.

I. Hymnography. Byzantine liturgical poetry falls into three periods: the first (4th–5th c.) characterized by short hymns, the *troparia* and *stichera*; the second (5th–7th c.) by long and elaborate metrical sermons, the ***kontakia*** (clearly influenced by certain forms of Syriac hymnography); and the third (7th–9th c. and afterward) by a form of hymn-cycle called *kanon*, consisting of eight or nine odes, each set to its own music (*heirmos*). The second is the great period of Byzantine hymnography. The celebrated *Akathistos* hymn, sometimes referred to as the Byzantine *Te Deum*, dates from the 5th c. In the 6th c. lived Romanos, Byzantium's greatest religious poet. Some 85 of his kontakia have been preserved, all metrical sermons for various feasts of the Orthodox Church. Romanos, a conscientious Christian, treated his subject matter exactly as a preacher would. Occasionally, however, he gives rein to his fancy and at such times becomes grandiloquent in the style of epideictic oratorical poetry. His lang. on the whole is pure; he is rich in metaphor and imagery and often interweaves in his narrative whole passages from Holy Scripture. Andrew of Crete (around 700), initiates the third period of Byzantine liturgical poetry with his *Great Kanon*, a huge composition, in which elaboration of form results in a magnificent celebration of the Divine. Other representatives are John of Damascus, Kosmas of Maiouma, and Joseph the Hymnographer (8th–9th cs.). Though new hymns continued to be written, by the end of the 9th c., the liturgical calendar had filled up, and only few additions were made, such as a set of hymns written for the feast of the Three Hierarchs by John Mauropous (11th c.).

II. Songs. Byzantine chronicles preserve snippets of popular songs, such as the song making fun of Emperor Maurice's sexual prowess. The *Book of Ceremonies* (shortly after 963) contains the lyrics of many acclamations sung by the circus factions, unfortunately, without musical annotation. Some of the Gr. folk songs recorded in the 19th and 20th cs. by anthropologists go back to a centuries-old trad.; but in an oral trad., changes and corruptions are inevitable. There are a few texts in vernacular med. Gr. that clearly rely on an oral substratum. The most famous of these is the *Digenis Akritis* (early 12th c.?), a text of epic proportions that strings together a compilation of earlier ballads into an incoherent and disjointed narrative; the text has come down to us in various mss., the most important of which are the Escorial and the Grottaferrata versions.

III. Declamatory Poetry. Panegyrics, monodies, and ekphraseis are just a few of the genres that were intended to be declaimed either at official celebrations, at certain ceremonies, or in so-called *theatra*, literary salons where literati would present their works to each other. The two best representatives of the panegyric (epic encomium) are George Pisides (7th c.) and Theodore Prodromos (12th c.), the former writing iambic verse (called *dodecasyllable* because it consists of 12 syllables) in praise of his patron, Emperor Herakleios, and his victories over the Avars and the Persians; and the latter writing for various patrons, incl. Emperor John Komnenos and other members of the imperial family, whose military feats he celebrated in political verse (a 15-syllable verse with a caesura in the middle and an iambic rhythm). Monodies are funerary dirges declaimed at burial ceremonies: the most famous are anonymous monodies on the deaths of Leo VI (912) and Constantine VII (959), the earliest instance of political verse; other monodies mourn the loss of cities, such as the late 12th-c. dirge by Michael Choniates, in which he lamented that ancient Athens was lost forever. Among the many ekphraseis, the detailed descriptions of St. Sophia by Paul the Silentiary (6th c.) and of the Church of the Holy Apostles by Constantine the Rhodian (10th c.) deserve to be mentioned—but ekphrasis can take many forms, incl. an anonymous early 11th-c. description of a boat trip on the Bosporus or a detailed account of a day at the races by Christopher Mitylenaios (11th c.).

IV. Epigrams. Byzantine epigrams are either genuine or fictitious verse inscriptions attached to monuments or works of art or inscribed on tombs (epitaphs). There is not a single Byzantine poet without at least a few epigrams to his name. While Agathias, Paul the Silentiary, and other 6th-c. poets clung to the rules and dictates of Hellenistic epigrammatic poetry, a more Christian and less elaborate form was developed by George Pisides (7th c.), Theodore of Stoudios, and Ignatios the Deacon (both early 9th c.). However, the heyday of the Byzantine epigram spans the 10th to 12th cs.: it was then that John Geometres, Christopher Mitylenaios, John Mauropous, Nicholas Kallikles, and Theodore Prodromos flourished. The anonymous 12th-c. epigrams in the collection of Marcianus Graecus 524 are also quite exceptional. The genre of the Byzantine epigram also comprises the many book epigrams found in Byzantine mss.: epigrams written in honor of the author, the patron who commissioned the ms., or the scribe. Gnomic epigrams, of which there are many, also fall in this category: most of these pithy sayings are anonymous, but some are attributed to Kassia (9th c.), the only known female Byzantine poet.

V. Religious Poetry. Apart from hymnography, the singing of which is a communal act of devotion, there are also lyrical effusions of the soul and intimate soliloquies with God; these poems are not sung but either declaimed or read in silence. The poetry of the Church father Gregory of Nazianzus (4th c.) is a brilliant example followed by all Byzantine poets. The greatest of these are John Geometres (10th c.), Symeon the New Theologian (10th–11th c.), and John Mauropous (11th c.). Geometres' masterpiece is a long confession and prayer to the Holy Virgin, in which he tries to come to terms with his human limitations. Symeon the New Theologian was a mystic who wrote inspired poetry relating all his mystical experiences and divine revelations, such as one in which he recognizes the presence of Christ in his body. Mauropous was an intellectual reluctant to leave his books and step out into the world: when he was forced to become metropolitan of a provincial town, he wrote two poems first praying that this evil might not happen and then, when the imperial decision proved to be irreversible, asking God to teach him how to accept his fate.

VI. Satirical Poetry. Satire is ubiquitous in Byzantine poetry, in both the learned and vernacular trads. A good example of the latter are the *Ptochoprodromic Poems* (12th c.), five satires dealing with different characters who narrate their petty problems and little adventures, posing as a henpecked husband, a hungry *paterfamilias*, a poor grammarian, and a lowly and abused monk. The poems of "Poor Prodromos" are brilliant satires that describe the lives of ordinary citizens in a big city in a vernacular that serves as a vehicle of social crit. and colorful realism. Another good example of satire is the *Entertaining Tale of Quadrupeds* (14th c.), a hilarious poem about an assembly of animals who express their grudges.

VII. Verse Romances and Chronicles. In the 12th c., the ancient "novelists" Heliodorus and Achilles Tatius were imitated in a number of verse romances by Niketas Eugenianos, Theodore Prodromos, and Constantine Manasses, all of whom wrote in learned Gr. After 1204, this literary experiment was followed by verse romances in vernacular Gr., most of which also show some familiarity with Western romances of chivalry, such as the *Livistros and Rodamne*, *War of Troy*, *Achilleid*, and *Velthandros and Chrysantza*, all the works of unknown poets. Verse chronicles, too, were composed in learned and vernacular Gr.: the *Synopsis Chronike* by Manasses (12th c.), the *Chronicle of Morea* (14th c.), and the *Chronicle of the Tocco* (early 15th c.). With its emphasis on love, exploring the depths of the human soul, Manasses' chronicle might even be seen as a verse romance.

VIII. Didactic Poetry. A few names should suffice for these prose-in-verse creations on all kinds of scientific topics: Pisides' *Hexaemeron*, Leo Choirosphaktes' *Thousand-Line Theology* (early 10th c.), Niketas of Herakleia's grammatical treatises in the form of troparia and kanons (11th c.), and Manuel Philes' *On the Characteristics of Animals* (early 14th c.).

■ **Anthologies:** *Anthologia Graeca Carminum Christianorum*, ed. W. Christ and M. Paranikas

(1872); *Poeti byzantini*, ed. R. Cantarella, 2 v. (1948); *Medieval and Modern Greek Poetry*, ed. C. A. Trypanis (1951); *An Anthology of Byzantine Poetry*, ed. B. Baldwin (1985); *Three Medieval Greek Romances*, ed. G. Betts (1995); *Four Byzantine Novels*, ed. E. Jeffreys (2012).

■ **Criticism and History:** K. Krumbacher, *Geschichte der byzantinischen Litteratur*, 2d ed. (1897); H.-G. Beck, *Geschichte der byzantinischen Volksliteratur* (1971); H. Hunger, *Die hochsprachliche Profane Literatur*, 2 v. (1978); Trypanis; *Oxford Dictionary of Byzantium*, ed. A. P. Kazhdan (1991); M. D. Lauxtermann, *Byzantine Poetry from Pisides to Geometres* (2003).

M. D. Lauxtermann

C

CAMBODIA, POETRY OF. At the beginning of the Common Era, Sanskrit, the sacred lang. of India, spread along the trade routes across most of southern Asia from Afghanistan to Java. This political literary culture, referred to by Pollock as the "Sanskrit cosmopolis," shaped the aesthetics of "Cambodian" or Khmer poetry from the time of Funan, an ancient Indianized kingdom located around the Mekong Delta during the 1st c. CE.

The Khmer lang., an eastern branch of the Mon-Khmer family, which is part of the larger Austro-Asiatic lang. group, is basically monosyllabic, although words may be lengthened to an iambic disyllable by the addition of prefixes or consonants. Old Khmer (7th–12th cs.) was heavily influenced by Sanskrit throughout the Angkor period (9th–13th cs.) and by Pali, the lang. of Theravada Buddhism, from the 13th c. onward. Examples of early lit. are largely found in Sanskrit inscriptions written in verse praising the great deeds of gods and kings. The poetry of six anonymous authors can be identified as written in Sanskrit during the Angkor period.

Jacob (1991) has identified 12 different forms of meter in Cambodian poetry, with certain meters used for specific purposes. "High" vocabulary—i.e., Sanskrit or Pali borrowings—often are combined with a Khmer word as a type of reduplication in Khmer poetics. The linking of one stanza to the next through rhyme is also a feature of this poetry. Since Khmer is replete with alliterative, chiming, and rhyming words, the best poems are melodious, indicating pleasure in assonance and alliteration. Such poetry sometimes is recited to the accompaniment of a stringed instrument, reflecting the importance of its musicality. Because of this aesthetic, Jacob (1996) argues that the best representation of Khmer poetry is to be found in songs. Themes of songs and poems often touch on emotion, such as lost love or separation. Besides songs, riddles, proverbs, and didactic lit., early Khmer fictions also were written in verse. After attacks by the Siamese, the Angkor period in Cambodia came to a close around 1430. By then, many Khmer writers and books had been relocated to Siam (now Thailand). For the next five centuries, Cambodia suffered predatory attacks on its borders, along with ebbing fortunes. As in Western Europe, where Lat. lit. was largely displaced by vernacular langs. after the fall of the Roman Empire, so too would Sanskrit be displaced by the Khmer lang. during the subsequent Middle Period.

As Cambodia's fortunes declined, its lang. changed. Middle Khmer shows borrowings from Thai, Lao, and, to a lesser extent, Vietnamese. Verse, which was used for all literary texts, was written in Khmer. Because of Cambodia's troubles following the fall of Angkor, no lit. survives that can be precisely dated to the 15th or 16th cs. The earliest written extant lit. consists of the *Rāmakerti I* (Cambodian *Rāmayāṇa*), and *Cpāp'* (Codes of Conduct; 15th–16th cs.). The earliest stratum of these texts is written in *Pad kākagati* (crow's gait meter). There is a religious element to most of the verse lit. of the Middle Period. The *Rāmakerti* (*Reamker*), Cambodia's version of the *Rāmayāṇa*, was originally a Hindu text. The Cambodian version, filled with allusions to Hindu gods and geography, was influenced by Buddhism, with its hero Ram represented as Buddha. The *Cpāp'*, Buddhist moral poems that teach standards of conduct, also humorously portray details of ordinary lives. Some verses from *Cpāp'* are popularized as proverbs.

Other genres of Middle Period lit. include the *Sātrā lpaeṇ*, verse novels that tell stories of the bodhisattvas, or previous lives of the Buddha, usually portrayed as a prince, and the *jātak*, birth stories of the Buddha in verse, esp. the "ten jātak" (depicting the last ten lives of the Buddha before he entered Nirvana) and the extracanonical "50 jātak." Although originally written in Pali, versions of the 50 jatak are known only in Burma, Laos, Thailand, and Cambodia. Another Buddhist religious text of great importance is the *Trai Bhūm* (The Three Worlds), whose source is a Siamese ms. written during the reign of the king of Sukhoday.

Historically, the next genre to develop during the Middle Period is the lyric (*kaṃṇāby*). These are mss. of 18th–19th-c. court poets, whose poems express feelings of love and separation. After the fall of Angkor, the Siamese used Cambodian lit. for their own cultural purposes. After many centuries during which changes were made to the texts, the Cambodians gradually recovered much of their lit. in the

19th c. They would also adapt Thai verse forms to Cambodian-lang. poetry, such as the Thai *klong* (seven-syllable meter).

In 1863, Cambodia, along with Vietnam and Laos, became a protectorate of France. The Fr. established public schools in the new capital city of Phnom Penh, where young men were taught solely in Fr. and introduced to Fr. lit. This influence fostered Cambodian novels in prose but did not lead to the devel. of a new mod. poetry. By 1954, when King Sihanouk gained Cambodia's independence from France, Khmer writers were publishing new prose and poetry in literary magazines popular in the larger cities. In 1958, the government stipulated that the verse novel *Tum Teav*, whose authorship is contested, be included as a central text in the Khmer lit. curriculum for secondary schools. Oral versions of this tragic love story are traced to the 19th c., but it might be as old as the Middle Period. Sihanouk, who had abdicated his position as king to become head of state, was overthrown in a 1970 coup as the country gradually devolved into civil war. Poets of the early 1970s, such as Koy Sarun, dealt with the harsh realities of power. On April 17, 1975, the Khmer Rouge took control of Cambodia, emptying its capital city of inhabitants and forcing "new people" from the cities to work in gulag labor camps in remote areas of the countryside. During this period, the majority of Cambodian poets were killed or died from disease, starvation, or exhaustion. Writing was forbidden among the masses under the Khmer Rouge, but poetry reemerged after 1979, when the Vietnamese established a government in Cambodia and drove the Khmer Rouge toward the Thai border. This poetry, in traditional meter, replete with sorrow and loss, would be written by Cambodians in exile, either in refugee camps along the Thai border or in distant lands of the Cambodian diaspora. Poet U Sam Oeur, who moved to the United States, typically uses traditional meter in his poems but sometimes writes in free verse. Many of his poems describe his experience under the Khmer Rouge:

> There are no more intellectuals, no more
> professors—
> all have departed Phnom Penh, leading
> children,
> bereft, deceived to the last person,
> from coolie to king.
> ("The Fall of Culture")

Since May 1993, when elections were held in Cambodia under the supervision of the United Nations, Cambodian lit. entered an age of somewhat freer expression. Although poetry was still written in traditional verse, the use of Pali and Sanskrit to embellish it faded among the younger writers. New poetry often contains mod. themes about the environment or social conditions. Contemp. poets reflect on power and the powerless, along with the transitory quality of the natural world. Yin Luoth's poem "Crippled Soldiers" describes a common scene in Phnom Penh:

> Crippled soldiers
> walking through the market
> missing arm or leg
> hands in supplication
> everyday beg
> even without fingers
> to take the money.

The continuing influence of Buddhism in Cambodian culture, esp. its social concern for the unfortunate and injunction against greed, is also reflected in the poems of Ven. Chin Meas, whose understated symbolism gives his poetry particular poignancy. His poem "Inherited House" traces the happiness of a rural family until the death of the parents unleashes the thoughtless greed of their selfish children:

> They divided up the inherited house
> that had once given them peace
> they can never
> live together again.

Currently in Cambodia, there are very few venues for poets to present their work to the public. Poets typically subsidize the publication of 100 to 200 copies of their chapbooks, which they often give away or try to sell through the book stalls in the various markets in the cities. Phnom Penh, with the largest community of poets in the country, has the Java Café and Monument Books, which support poetry evenings. The government sponsors national literary prizes that are awarded through the National Library in Phnom Penh. The Khmer Writers Association has also sponsored poetry prizes and the publication of chapbooks. Since 1993, the Nou Hach Literary Association has held a yearly conference where prizes for poetry are awarded and then published in its annual jour., *The Nou Hach Literary Journal*, which is distributed for sale in markets. Although poetry books are not a common purchase in Cambodia, the art of poetic expression is still greatly admired by the older generation. There is a resistance to experiment with free verse, since the melodiousness of poetry—its rhyme, assonance, and alliteration—is what defines it as a genre for Cambodians. Nevertheless, younger poets are branching out to include socially critical themes in their poems and slowly experimenting with freer forms of versification.

■ J. Jacob, "Versification in Cambodian Poetry," *Cambodia's Lament: A Selection of Cambodian Poetry*, ed. and trans. G. Chigas (1991); A. Thompson, "Oh Cambodia! Poems from the Border," *NLH* 24 (1993); J. Jacob, *The Traditional Literature of Cambodia: A Preliminary Guide* (1996); *Tum Teav: A Translation and Analysis of a Cambodian Literary Classic*, ed. and trans. G. Chigas (2005); C. Meas, "The Inherited House," *Nou Hach Literary Journal* 4 (2007); S. Pollock, *The Language of the Gods in the World of Men: Sanskrit, Culture, and Power in Premodern India* (2006).

T. S. Yamada

CANADA, POETRY OF

I. English
II. French

I. English. Prior to the 20th c., Canadian poetry was strung between poles of a colonialism that sought to maintain the aesthetic and social values of the mother country and a nativism that sought to face the particular challenges of a New World exuding both promise and threat. Thus, W. D. Lighthall can, in one of the early anthols. of Canadian poetry—his 1889 *Songs of the Great Dominion*—celebrate Canada as the "Eldest daughter of the Empire" and "the Empire's completest type," while at the same moment the first generation of truly nativist poets—the so-called Confederation poets—were exploring the Canadian landscape and psyche in a lyrical nature poetry that could only have been written in the new country.

Long before this, however, the promise of the new colony sounds in what is probably the first book of poetry written in North America—Robert Hayman's (1575–1629) *Quodlibets Lately Come Over from New Britaniola, Old Newfound-Land* (1628)—in which, as governor of the colony, he advertises Newfoundland as a near-paradise, "Exempt from taxings, ill newes, Lawings, feare." The threat of the New World is given expression in Oliver Goldsmith's (1794–1861) otherwise optimistic "The Rising Village" (1825), a response to his famous great-uncle and namesake's "The Deserted Village":

> When, looking round, the lonely settler
> sees
> His home amid a wilderness of trees:
> How sinks his heart in those deep solitudes,
> Where not a voice upon his ear intrudes.

Nevertheless, one should not be given the impression that Canadian poetry before the 20th c. lacked diversity. Amid narratives of colonization and lyric bursts on nature's fickle blasts, there are poems championing the cause of the laboring classes, as in the ballads of Scottish immigrants James Anderson (1842–1923) and Alexander McLachlan (1818–96), who sounds a republican note in "Young Canada or Jack's as Good as His Master" (1874). With Pauline Johnson (1861–1913), First Nations Canadians, typically subject to their portrayal by settler poets, had their voice heard for the first time—though Johnson (her mother was English, her father Mohawk) tended to perform the archetypal noble savage for the audiences of her popular performances. Her "performance of the hybrid inheritance of Canada and the British Empire," in Gerson's words (1994), can be seen in quintessential Johnson poems such as "The Song My Paddle Sings," with its simultaneous invocations of P. B. Shelley's "Ode to the West Wind" and a solitary native paddling across prairie waters.

As mentioned above, the first generation of poets seen to embody an emergent "Canadian" poetry were the Confederation poets, who, in the decades following the 1867 Confederation, came to be seen as answering E. H. Dewart's call, in *Selections from Canadian Poets* (1864), for a national poetry as "an essential element in the formation of national character." Born in the 1860s and beginning to publish in the 1880s and early 1890s, William Wilfred Campbell (1860–1918), Charles G. D. Roberts (1860–1943), Bliss Carman (1861–1929), Archibald Lampman (1861–99), and Duncan Campbell Scott (1862–1947) were the dominant voices and driving forces in Canadian poetry for the next three or four decades. Later theories about the "Canadianness" of Canadian poetry, such as Margaret Atwood's notion of "survival" as *the* national theme, clearly required the bedrock of the Confederation poets' descriptive verse upon which to set their foundations. In this regard,

Campbell's "The Winter Lakes" (1889) can stand as a characteristic example:

Lands that loom like specters, whited
 regions of winter,
Wastes of desolate woods, deserts of water
 and shore;
A world of winter and death, within these
 regions who enter,
Lost to summer and life, go to return no
 more.

With their focus on the particularities of the Canadian landscape and climate, the heavily visual lyrics of these poets could easily give the impression that the lyric mode best characterizes Canadian poetry before World War I. However, the reality is more likely that the long narrative poem and the verse drama, as written by poets such as Charles Sangster (1822–93), Charles Heavysege (1816–76), and Isabella Valancy Crawford (1850–87), were the dominant modes, if measured in terms of their ubiquity and popular success. This trad. continues into the 20th c. in the work of E. J. Pratt (1883–1964), a poet seen either as a throwback to 19th-c. narrative verse or as the "first" modernist (so credited for his realism and use of contemp. themes).

It has sometimes been remarked that Canadian poetry skipped modernism altogether, moving directly from romanticism to postmodernism. Certainly, the "modernization" of Canadian poetry proceeded at a slow pace (if one is to take a poet like Pratt as a transitional figure); however, as early as 1914, Arthur Stringer (1874–1950) was writing in favor of the "formal emancipation" of free verse, and John Murray Gibbon (1875–1952) commented that "[r]hyme is the natural refuge of the minor poet." W.W.E. Ross (1894–1966) was writing and publishing imagist, free-verse lyrics in the *Dial* and *Poetry* in the 1920s, as was Dorothy Livesay (1909–96), before turning to her politically charged poems during the socialist 1930s and 1940s and then to later "documentary" work.

Canadian modernism had its center in Montreal, where poets A.J.M. Smith (1902–80) and F. R. Scott (1899–1985) cofounded *The McGill Fortnightly Review* in 1925. "The modern revival began in the twenties," Smith later wrote, as "Canadian poets turned against rhetoric, sought a sharper, more objective imagery, and limited themselves as far as possible to the lang. of everyday and the rhythms of speech." Scott's poetry, though modernizing in terms of "a freer diction and more elastic forms," was, nevertheless, still drawn to what were already well-established "Canadian" tropes and themes. His "Laurentian Shield" is remarkable both for its retrieval of the imagery of the proverbial Canadian "wastes" (the poem can be profitably compared to, and contrasted with, Campbell's "Winter Lakes") and for his updating of such imagery, combining it with a compressed social hist. of an industrializing Canada:

Hidden in wonder and snow, or sudden
 with summer,
This land stares at the sun in a huge silence
Endlessly repeating something we cannot
 hear.
Inarticulate, arctic,
Not written on by history, empty as paper,
It leans away from the world with songs in
 its lakes
Older than love, and lost in the miles.

The poem goes on to address the "deeper note sounding" from "the mines, / The scattered camps and the mills" as Canada's working classes enter the national dialogue (Scott was for many years associated with the country's first socialist party, the Co-operative Commonwealth Federation). However, the long-established image of the "silent" and "inarticulate" land awaiting (Eur.) inscription unquestioningly recalls the colonial roots of Canadian poetry.

The Montreal circle around Smith and Scott grew in the 1940s to include poets such as A. M. Klein (1909–72) and P. K. Page (1916–2010), as the jours. *Preview* and then *The Northern Review* became the group's main vehicles. Klein, a Ukrainian Jewish immigrant, wrote modernist-inspired lyrics on Jewish culture and hist. Page, similarly influenced by modernists such as T. S. Eliot, pursued a philosophical and introspective imagism over many decades. As Louis Dudek (1918–2001) writes in *The Making of Modern Poetry in Canada*, "By the early 1940s the development of modernism in Canada had reached the point of 'cell divisions,' showing a conflict of generations within the modern movement." Dudek himself, as both poet and ed., played an important role in this "division," as another Montreal circle formed around him to include Irving Layton (1912–2006) and Raymond Souster (1921–2012), and, for a time in the 1950s, Leonard Cohen (b. 1934) and Phyllis Webb (b. 1927). Dudek and Layton joined John Sutherland (1919–56) in editing *First Statement* (later folded, along with *Preview*, into *The Northern Review*), and then, with Souster, *Contact* magazine and press, in the 1950s. If Layton was the flamboyant, outrageous, and sensual *poète maudit* of the new grouping, Dudek was its theorist and propagandist. Dudek was influenced by the Am. modernism of Ezra Pound, as well as the editorial proselytizing of Cid Corman (and his jour. *Origin*). "Like American lit. in general," he writes in *The Making of Modern Poetry in Canada*, "Canadian poetry divides into two branches: one related through British writing to Eur. literary culture, formal and rooted in traditional sources of the imagination; the other, spontaneous and original in its sources, and relying on the direct report of local experience." Sutherland, in a similar vein, argues in *Other Canadians* that "the American example will become more and more attractive to Canadian writers; that we are approaching a period when we will have 'schools' and 'movements' whose origin will be American. And perhaps it is safe to say that such a period is the inevitable half-way house from which Canadian poetry will pass towards an identity of its own."

Two other poets who provide important bridges between mod. and postmod. Canadian poetry need to be mentioned here. Earl Birney (1904–95), who was the first significant modernist poet to be born, live, and write in western Canada (Birney was born in Calgary and lived for many years in Vancouver, where he founded the first creative writing program in the country, at the University of British Columbia), and Al Purdy (1918–2000), who was instrumental in spreading the use of vernacular, conversational (as opposed to overtly "poetic") lang. and everyday themes, influenced a generation of Canadian poets. The work of poets from British Columbia's Patrick Lane (b. 1939) to the East Coast's Milton Acorn (1923–86) and Alden Nowlan (1933–83), from "prairie poets" such as Dennis Cooley (b. 1944) and Andrew Suknaski (1942–2012) to the perennial wanderer John Newlove (1938–2003), is difficult to imagine without the vernacular trad. in part opened by Purdy's work.

In a 1955 study titled "The Poet and the Publisher," Phyllis Webb found only "two or three" presses in the country that regularly published poetry, all located in Toronto. With the 1960s and 1970s, there was an extraordinary expansion of regional presses and little magazines—in part spurred by the founding of the Canada Council for the Arts in 1957—that decidedly decentralized Canadian poetry. "Regional," Atwood noted in 1982, "has changed in recent years from a bad to a good word, in Canada at any rate." Indeed, Canadian poetry since the 1960s has seemed less a national lit. than a cluster of communities divided along regional, aesthetic, class, ethnic, and gender lines. "Canada," as Davey (1994) writes, "is a network of competing canons rather than a single canon."

Postmodernism in many ways enters Canadian poetry through Vancouver: the TISH poets—George Bowering (b. 1935), Fred Wah (b. 1939), and Daphne Marlatt (b. 1942) among them—and the 1963 Vancouver Poetry Conference, which brought leading lights from the New American poetry (Charles Olson, Robert Duncan, Robert Creeley) together to teach, read, and talk for three weeks of events. Canadian avant-gardes—in Vancouver, at least—have ever since been deeply influenced by their dialogue with similarly focused Am. poetic movements (TISH and the New American poetry, and then from the 1980s, the Kootenay School of Writing and Language poetry)—seeming to fulfill Sutherland's prophetic words cited above. Bowering, Canada's first parliamentary poet laureate, has, despite that honor, often stood more for a western Canadian sensibility and a transnational poetics that moves more north-south than east-west. Jeff Derksen (b. 1958), one of the founding members of the Kootenay School, has similarly often critiqued the centralizing formation of the nation, writing instead from a position of urban class consciousness that sees the local and global intersect in spaces formed more by late capitalism than by the nation as such.

Since the 1960s, there has been heavy traffic between Vancouver and Toronto avant-gardes, with poets such as bpNichol (1944–88) and bill bissett (b. 1939) moving between the cities. With Steve McCaffery (b. 1947) in Toronto, Nichol's experiments with the Toronto Research Group (TRG) and Four Horsemen led to many innovations in concrete and sound poetry. Such work—along with the site-specific projects of Christopher Dewdney (b. 1951)—have cast a long shadow on Toronto poetry, directly leading to the concrete and performance work of Christian Bök (b. 1966), the procedural and digital poetics of Darren Wershler (b. 1966), and—moving out from Toronto—the concrete poetry of derek beaulieu (b. 1973) and Donato Mancini (b. 1974) and sound poetry of a. rawlings (b. 1978) and Jordan Scott (b. 1978). Bök's 2001 Oulipian work *Eunoia* set the standard for, and reanimated work in, constraint-based poetics, with its five "chapters" each limited to the use of only one vowel. Chapter "A" begins:

> Awkward grammar appals a craftsman. A
> dada bard
> as daft as Tzara damns stagnant art and
> scrawls an
> alpha (a slapdash arc and a backward zag)
> that mars
> all stanzas and jams all ballads (what a
> scandal).

One could argue that "narrative" reappears in such work, in the form of the quasi-epic conventions and set pieces that structure the prose-poetry of *Eunoia*.

Feminist poetry and poetics in Canada began to find its footing in the 1980s, with notable events such as the Women and Words conference (1983) and the founding of the jour. *Tessera* (in 1984). Lesbian issues and the question of trans. often appeared (as in the case of Marlatt and Fr.-Canadian poet Nicole Brossard [b. 1943] and in the work of Erin Mouré [b. 1955]); established poets such as Webb, Marlatt, and Margaret Atwood (b. 1939) began to interact with newly emerged poets such as Sharon Thesen (b. 1946), Bronwen Wallace (1945–89), and Mouré. This trad. continues in the work of contemp. poets such as Vancouver's Meredith Quartermain (b. 1950), Torontonians Margaret Christakos (b. 1962) and Rachel Zolf (b. 1968), and Manitoba-born Sina Queyras (b. 1963).

Poets writing through an awareness of race, immigrant experience, and the diasporas of globalization often intersect with regional and avant-garde poetries in Canada. George Elliott Clarke (b. 1960) from Canada's East Coast and Wayde Compton (b. 1972) from Canada's West have both explored the hist. of black people in Canada, and Caribbean-born Dionne Brand (b. 1953) writes a similar hist. through feminist and lesbian lenses. Asian Canadian poets have tended to forge links with avant-gardes, as is the case with Roy Kiyooka (1926–94), Wah, and Roy Miki (b. 1942), all born in the prairies and moving to Vancouver to participate in the TISH movement and its aftermath. Both Wah and Miki have, as critics and university professors, influenced the work and thought of the many younger writers drawn to their politicized example. One contemp. poet mining similar territory is Rita Wong (b. 1968), whose 2007 book *Forage* explores the ground upon which race, class, and environmental degradation intersect in a recklessly globalized world:

> the gap between the crying line & electric
> speech
> is the urbanization of the mouth
> round peasant dialect vowels relocate
> off the fields into city streets
> where sound gets clipped
> like our ability to smell the wet earth.

First Nations poets, such as Marie Annharte Baker (b. 1942) and Gregory Scofield (b. 1966), update traditional themes to new urban environments. Both poets employ an urban-native vernacular and reappropriated stereotypes to question the hist. and policies of government "Indian Acts" and residential schools. The work of Jeannette Armstrong (b. 1948) and Marilyn Dumont (b. 1955) further questions notions of stable identity and literary form.

While the lyric poem, often confessional and anecdotal, has dominated Canadian poetry, Canada has also maintained a vibrant trad. around the long poem. The lyric in contemp. Canadian poetry, whether confessional or imagistic, has tended toward compressed narrative via the epiphanic anecdote. The dominance of "story" can in part be seen by how frequently Canada's best-known poets have been just as highly regarded as novelists, as in the case of Atwood and Michael Ondaatje (b. 1943). Canadian poets have also often combined fragments into long lyric sequences, with narrative present in the form of the documentary details of the life and times of the historical subject under investigation, as in Atwood's *The Journals of Susanna Moodie* (1970), Ondaatje's *The Collected Works of Billy the Kid* (1970), and Gwendolyn MacEwen's (1941–87) *The T. E. Lawrence Poems* (1982). Canadian lyric poems often combine astute observation of the external world and condensed expression of internal states with a broadly framed awareness of the social contexts the poet lives and writes through. Hist., it could be said, is the primary "story" haunting Canadian poetry, as in Atwood's "It Is Dangerous to Read Newspapers" (1968):

> While I was building neat
> castles in the sandbox,
> the hasty pits were
> filling with bulldozed corpses
>
> and as I walked to the school
> washed and combed, my feet
> stepping on the cracks in the cement
> detonated red bombs.

It is difficult to underestimate the influence Atwood and Ondaatje have had on the course of Canadian poetry, despite (or because of) their evolution into novelists. Poets such as Don McKay (b. 1942), one of the country's premier ecological poets, and Jan Zwicky (b. 1955), who investigates the philosophical underpinnings of the lyric, continue to be major practitioners of the lyric poem, as Ken Babstock (b. 1970), Karen Solie (b. 1966), and Stephanie Bolster (b. 1969) do among the younger poets.

As narrative has come to dominate the Canadian lyrical anecdote, so the contemp. Canadian long poem has moved away from narrative as such, toward serial and archival/documentary forms. Phyllis Webb's *Naked Poems* (1965), with its extended minimalism, leads the way to the contemp. long poem in Canada. Moving through a counterpointed sequence of "Suites," *Naked Poems* combines personal, social, and philosophical information into arrestingly compressed ling. spaces:

> YOUR BLOUSE
> I people
> this room
> with things, a
> chair, a lamp, a
> fly, two books by
> Marianne Moore.
>
> I have thrown my
> blouse on the floor,
>
> Was it only
> last night?

"Story" hovers here, but what the story is, the reader is never sure. Just as quickly as narrative appears, it disappears, sinking under a surface of sonic and visual detail:

> a curve / broken
> of green
> moss weed
> kelp shells pebbles
> lost orange rind
> orange crab pale
> delicates at peace
> on this sand
> tracery of last night's
> tide

Another early influence on the contemp. long poem in Canada was Robin Blaser's (1925–2009) *The Holy Forest*, the serial components of which were beginning to appear in the 1960s. Blaser, Am.-born but living in Vancouver since 1966, theorized the serial poem in his 1975 afterward to *The Collected Books of Jack Spicer*. With Blaser's work, however, we move beyond the serial or long poem to the lifelong poem, a form so elastic it comes to contain all a poet's work, coming to a conclusion only with the poet's death. Blaser's *Holy Forest*, along with Robert Kroetsch's (1927–2011) *Complete Field Notes* and Nichol's *The Martyrology* (1967–88) are three highly influential examples of such extended long forms.

More recent practitioners of the long poem tend to trouble the boundary between poem (long or otherwise) and "book," taking up the writing of a book of poetry as a research project. Anne Carson (b. 1950), Mouré, and Lisa Robertson (b. 1962) have produced some of the most innovative poetry in the country. Recalling the book-length historical projects of Atwood and Ondaatje—but minus the biographical subject and drawing on the broadly philosophical investigations and intertextuality of Blaser and Nichol's long works—these poets have rewritten cl. myths (as in Carson's 1998 *Autobiography of Red*), engaged in "transelations" with Fernando Pessoa's heteronyms (as in Mouré's 2002 *Sheep's Vigil by a Fervent Person*), and appropriated the discourse of 18th- and 19th-c. Eng. meteorologists (as in Robertson's 2001 *The Weather*). Both lyrical and formally expansive, philosophically and socially engaged, innovative and yet highly sensitive to cultural heritage on a transnational scale, the work of these poets has reached a wide international audience and is already influencing the next generation of Canadian poets.

II. French. In Fr. Canada, a genuine poetic trad. was not established until the 1830s. François-Xavier Garneau (1809–66), the first major Fr.-Canadian author, published a few poems in his youth but devoted most of his efforts to the monumental *Histoire du Canada depuis sa découverte jusqu'à nos jours* (A History of Canada from Its Discovery to the Present Time). Following Garneau, two poets, Octave Crémazie (1827–79) and Louis Fréchette (1839–1908), were known for their patriotic writing. Crémazie, whose poetry published in newspapers venerated nostalgia for France, was celebrated as a national bard, although his romantic "Promenade de trois morts" (The Promenade of the Three Dead) was met with incomprehension. Fréchette, an admirer of Crémazie and a liberal pamphleteer, honored Fr.-Canadian hist. with emphatic poems inspired by Victor Hugo. Less well known than Crémazie and Fréchette, the intimist poets Alfred Garneau (1836–1904) and Eudore Évanturel (1852–1919) are among the few 19th-c. Fr.-Canadian poets who preferred a personal register to a patriotic one.

Émile Nelligan (1879–1941) embodies the ideal of a poet dedicated to his art. Before he was permanently interned in a psychiatric hospital at the age of nineteen, he was involved in the École littéraire de Montréal (Montreal Literary School), where he was celebrated for the quality of his poetry but also criticized for his indifference toward a regionalism promoted by the religious authorities. In 1904, his poems were anthologized by Louis Dantin (1865–1945), one of the period's most accomplished critics and a poet in his own right. Some of Nelligan's poems are purely musical; others seem to foreshadow his fate. His works demonstrate a precocious assimilation of Parnassianism, symbolism, and the decadent style.

The opposition between the regionalists and those who were known as the "exotics" had a profound impact on the literary scene of the early 20th c. Celebrated by clerical critics, regionalists such as Blanche Lamontagne-Beauregard (1889–1958) sought to render the "Canadian essence." Reacting against this ideal, many poets united in 1918 under the banner of the magazine *Le Nigog* (a Native Am. word meaning "harpoon") to promote the idea of art for art's sake. Typical of the exotic poets, Marcel Dugas (1883–1947) and Paul Morin (1889–1963) lived for many years in Paris. While Dugas practiced prosaic forms of poetry, Morin was dedicated to fixed forms such as the sonnet. Their inspiration was, first and foremost, contemp. Fr. poetry.

Certain early 20th-c. poets such as Albert Lozeau (1878–1924) found themselves behind entrenched literary positions. Notably, Lozeau's first volume of rhyming poems, *L'âme solitaire* (The Solitary Soul, 1907), can be seen as a continuation of the intimist poetics of the end of the 19th c. Jean-Aubert Loranger (1896–1942), who preferred sober free-verse poetry that expressed the subject's isolation, was influenced by his readings of Fr. poets as well as by his discovery of Asian forms such as the haiku and the *outa*. As a journalist, he also published numerous tales such as "Le passeur" (The Ferryman), a parable of old age that was included in his initial collection of poems *Les atmosphères* (Atmospheres, 1920), but his poetry was not widely read until the reissue of his work in 1970. The most celebrated poet of the times, and the one who seems to surpass the age's contradictions by invoking Nelligan while addressing regionalist concerns, is Alfred DesRochers (1901–78). His collection *À l'ombre de l'Orford* (In the Shadow of Orford, 1929) includes "Hymne au vent du Nord" (A Hymn to the North Wind), a celebratory epic of the ancestors, as well as his realistic sonnets describing contemporaries: the peasants and the shantymen. Faithful to rhymed and metered verse, DesRochers remained estranged from the new lang. of free verse that became dominant during the 1930s, so much so that his work would be seen as the end of an epoch.

Hector de Saint-Denys Garneau (1912–43) experimented with an unreservedly free verse in *Regards et jeux dans l'espace* (Gazes and Games in Space, 1937), the only volume that he ever published. In a society he found to be a cultural "desert," Garneau found intellectual stimulation in the magazine *La Relève* in 1934 that pushed him to dedicate himself to writing and painting. His enthusiasm, however, would be short-lived. His jour., published in 1954, showed that, even though he continued to write poetry and to paint, his profound angst caused him to renounce publishing. After breaking off his formerly abundant correspondence with friends, Garneau was found dead near his family's manor, where he had decided to withdraw. Garneau's poems, jour., and correspondence constitute the most prominent work of a Fr.-Canadian poet since Nelligan; for both, the myth of the poet-martyr would be indissociable from their work. In retrospect, Garneau's despair seems more assumed than endured, as he describes in a famous text from his jour. titled "Le mauvais pauvre va parmi vous avec son regard en dessous" (The bad pauper going among you with his downcast gaze). A few years Garneau's senior, Alain Grandbois (1900–75) established himself in 1944 with *Les îles de la nuit* (The Islands of the Night). While these two poets are often compared, the reclusiveness of Garneau contrasts with the cosmopolitanism of Grandbois, whose travels took him as far as China. Grandbois's poetry is more eloquent than Garneau's and his style, as much as that of Fr. poets of his generation like René Char and Paul Éluard, influenced younger poets. Anne

Hébert (1916–2000), Garneau's cousin, published in 1953 *Le tombeau des rois* (The Kings' Tomb), where she explored interior impediments. This book was later published to form a diptych with her next collection of poetry, *Mystère de la parole* (Word's Mystery, 1960), which celebrated a woman's flowering consciousness witnessing the world's regeneration. The same solemn register was also present in the work of Rina Lasnier (1910–97), whose work often evoked the Christian faith, as seen in the biblically inspired *Le chant de la montée* (The Rising's Song, 1947).

During the 1930s and 1940s, a social life shattered by the economic crash dominated the work of several poets, such as Clément Marchand (1912–2013) in *Les soirs rouges* (Red Evenings, 1947). Surrealism also influenced several poetic works of the postwar era, as exemplified by Claude Gauvreau (1925–71), a signer of the *Refus global* (1948) manifesto. A poet and dramaturge, Gauvreau, along with the painter Paul-Émile Borduas, was a member and principal defender of the "automatist" group, which aimed to replace what it saw as the passivity of Fr. surrealist writing with a state of revolt. For Gauvreau, automatic writing involved accepting an unknown lang. "explorén," something he also integrated into his plays. Several years after his suicide, the publication of his *Œuvres créatices complètes* (Complete Creative Works, 1977) revealed an abundant, sustained level of production, in spite of a marginality accentuated by his mental illness. Also invoking surrealism, Roland Giguère (1929–2003) followed Gauvreau's example, albeit in a more serene fashion. His retrospective collection *L'âge de la parole* (The Word's Age, 1965) reconstituted the author's artistic journey while proclaiming the emancipation of the exploited, as typified in "La main du bourreau finit toujours par pourrir" (The Oppressor's Hand Will Eventually Rot). Giguère's poetry is full of imagery yet always straightforward, embracing both tenderness and violence, and also stresses the idea that, while it is important to map the dreamed world, it is also necessary to reveal "le pouvoir du noir" (the power of darkness).

In the 1960s, Fr.-Canadian nationalism transformed into Quebec nationalism. One of the objectives of this new nationalism was to create a distinctive Quebec lit. This project was nurtured by the publisher Éditions de l'Hexagone, founded in 1953 by a group of young Montreal poets. Resolved to make poetry more socially current, this group organized gatherings and counted on a system of subscriptions to involve potential readers in a genuine communal movement. Although many poets of this generation were devoted to Quebec's political independence, most of them insisted on the autonomy of poetry. Their writing was often labeled *la poésie du pays* (the poetry of the land), which was, above all, a quest for identity, as in Michel van Schendel's (1929–2005) *Poèmes de l'Amérique étrangère* (Poems from a Foreign America, 1958). More often than not, la poésie du pays celebrated the physical attributes of the land as the pathway to a mythical regeneration, as in Gatien Lapointe's (1931–83) *Ode au Saint-Laurent* (An Ode to the Saint-Laurent, 1963). Moreover, the theme of the land became associated with the devel. of a common lang., one capable of redefining social issues.

At the center of the Hexagone movement was Gaston Miron (1928–96), who defined himself more as its organizer than its poet. Initially, Miron published a collaborative anthol., *Deux sangs* (Two Bloods, 1953), Éditions de l'Hexagone's very first publication. Following this, he published poems in both newspapers and magazines, continually insisting on their provisional character. Miron would redraft his collection *L'homme rapaillé* (Mustered Man, 1970) many times, claiming that each version was fragmentary and incomplete. In each, early poems and political essays frame the poem's cycles in which love, the nation, and commitment are fundamental themes. A call to transform the world is coupled with the testimony of a man who ceaselessly collapses and rises in his "Marche à l'amour" (Walk to Love).

After republishing such poets as Grandbois and Giguère, Éditions de l'Hexagone allowed many young poets to write within an editorial continuity unknown by their elders. This allowed Paul-Marie Lapointe (1929–2011) to republish an anthol. of his youth, *Le vierge incendié* (The Burned Virgin), gone unnoticed when it first appeared in 1948, that became, when taken up again in *Le réel absolu* (The Absolute Real, 1971), the first steps of a literary production that never stopped exploring new directions. After the surrealist revelry of his first anthol., Lapointe coupled love with politics in long improvisations, inspired by jazz. The rest of his work was notably comprised of descriptive poems and formalist experimentations, all constituting an illustration of freedom as a "fundamental demand."

Of the same generation as Lapointe, Fernand Ouellette (b. 1930) also elaborated a varied and important body of work. Poet, essayist, and novelist, Ouellette invoked Eur. affinities (Novalis, Pierre-Jean Jouve), linking experience and transcendence by exploring sexuality (*Dans le sombre* [In the Darkness], 1967) and, in what is often cited as his best work, his father's death throes (*Les heures* [The Hours], 1987). Younger than Lapointe and Ouellette, Jacques Brault (b. 1933) also falls clearly within the framework of the poésie du pays movement in his first book, *Mémoire* (Memory, 1965), although he moved away from collective perspectives and expansive writing in his later work. In *L'en dessous l'admirable* (The Underside the Admirable, 1975) and *Moments fragiles* (Fragile Moments, 1984), the present moment constitutes the only accessible temporality; identity appears increasingly illusory but paradoxically reveals an essential, intimate life.

Paul Chamberland (b. 1939), who is associated with the socialist, separatist magazine *Parti Pris*, published in 1964 *Terre Québec* (Quebec Land), a seminal anthol. of nationalist poetry. Less embarrassed than his elders by a politicized lit., Chamberland put poetry on trial in the name of the "revolution" to be incited. A few years later, after being seduced by Am. counterculture, he invoked a new concept for the revolution. Denis Vanier (1949–2000) proved to be one of the most radical and unswerving poets of the counterculture movement at the end of the 1960s. For certain poets, countercultural references go together with nationalist demands in a quest for fraternity. Such is the case of the prolific Gilbert Langevin (1938–95), who combined the ludic and the tragic in a poetics bordering the spoken word.

Along with counterculture references, two trends influenced the poetics of the young generation of the 1970s: formalism and feminism. These two orientations came together in the work of Brossard, a leader of an avant-garde that was coming to light, most notably in the magazine *La Barre du jour*. With *Suite logique* (Logical Follow Through, 1970), Brossard opposed textual "mechanics" to literary idealism. Following this, she integrated an explicitly lesbian subject and related fiction and theory in her writing. Another avant-garde magazine founded in 1968, *Les Herbes rouges* (Red Grass), published poets such as Normand de Bellefeuille (b. 1949), Roger Des Roches (b. 1950), and François Charron (b. 1952), all of whom were initially associated with a militant formalism but who gradually diverged from the avant-garde's rhetoric. In the mid-1970s, feminism defined itself in avant-garde terms, and along with the works of Brossard, those of Madeleine Gagnon (b. 1938) and France Théoret (b. 1942) particularly influenced poetry that incorporated a critical and activist perspective.

During the 1980s, esp. with the publication of *Kaléidoscope ou Les aléas du corps grave* (Kaleidoscope or the Unforeseen Solemn Body, 1984), Michel Beaulieu (1941–85) epitomized the expansion of an intimist vein on the margins of a waning avant-garde. Beaulieu, who had experimented with several forms since his debut in the 1960s, achieved an intimist style that subtly plays with ambiguities created by enjambments. Marie Uguay (1955–81) was also attached to the inner life. Several younger poets inflected feminism with intimism, as in the work of Denise Desautels (b. 1945), or associated intimism with a spiritual quest, as in Hélène Dorion's (b. 1958) work.

With the 1980s, the pluralism of Quebec poetry continued to grow. Publishing houses such as Le Noroît and Les Écrits des Forges published a variety of work, in the trad. of L'Hexagone. The idea of a collective identity was fading, with the exception of emerging "migrant writings." Initially brought forward by Haitian Montrealers such as Anthony Phelps (b. 1928) and Serge Legagneur (b. 1937) and followed by Montrealers of It. extraction, such as Fulvio Caccia (b. 1952) and Antonio D'Alfonso (b. 1953), this movement not only extended the notion of identity in nationalist poetry but questioned the 1960s definition of the Quebec nation by exposing the cultural diversity of contemp. Quebec society. Often, this was done in a polemical fashion. Marco Micone's (b. 1945) pastiche "Speak What" (1989), e.g., displaced the perspectives of Michèle Lalonde's (b. 1937) 1960s poem "Speak White," a portrayal of Quebec based on the domination of Francophones by Anglophones. Since the 1970s, poetry has also been linked to the collective question of identity of Canadian Francophones living outside Quebec, notably the Acadians and the Franco-Ontarians. The poetry of the Acadian Serge-Patrice Thibodeau (b. 1959) is centered on wanderings, while that of the Franco-Ontarian Patrice Desbiens (b. 1948) focuses on the daily alienation of the minority condition. Furthermore, at the beginning of the 21st c., a specifically aboriginal lit. emerged, written in Fr. by such poets as Jean Sioui (b. 1948).

Although the presence of the countryside has played a role in Fr.-Canadian poetry since the 19th c., meditation on physical place has always been marginal when compared to considerations of historical destiny. By the end of the 1970s, in part inspired by Europeans such as Yves Bonnefoy and Philippe Jaccottet, many poets concentrated on place as the focus of their work. Gilles Cyr (b. 1945) with *Sol inapparent* (Inapparent Soil, 1978), Robert Melançon (b. 1947) with *Peinture aveugle* (Blind Painting, 1979), and Pierre Morency (b. 1942) with his series *Histoires naturelles du Nouveau Monde* (Natural Histories of the New World, 1989–96) emerge as the precursors of this movement. An increasing interest in the trans. of poetry, esp. from Eng., also has encouraged diversity.

See INDIGENOUS AMERICAS, POETRY OF THE; INUIT POETRY.

■ **Anthologies**: *The Book of Canadian Poetry*, ed. A.J.M. Smith (1943); J. Sutherland, *Other Canadians* (1947); *The New Oxford Book of Canadian Verse in English*, ed. M. Atwood (1982); *The New Canadian Poets*, ed. D. Lee (1985); *The New Long Poem Anthology*, ed. S. Thesen (1991); *Canadian Poetry: From the Beginnings through the First World War*, ed. C. Gerson and G. Davies (1994); *La poésie québécoise contemporaine*, ed. J. Royer (1995); *La poésie québécoise avant Nelligan*, ed. Y. Grisé (1998); *15 Canadian Poets X 3*, ed. G. Geddes (2001); *Anthologie de la littérature québécoise*, ed. G. Marcotte (2004); *Open Field: 30 Contemporary Canadian Poets*, ed. S. Queyras (2005); *La poésie québécoise des origines à nos jours*, ed. L. Mailhot and P. Nepveu (2007).

■ **Criticism and History**: G. Marcotte, *Une littérature qui se fait* (1962); L. Dudek and M. Gnarowski, *The Making of Modern Poetry in Canada* (1967); G. Marcotte, *Le temps des poètes* (1969); M. Atwood, *Survival* (1972); F. Davey, *From Here to There* (1974); P. Nepveu, *L'écologie du réel* (1988)—poetry of Quebec; C. Bayard, *The New Poetics in Canada and Quebec* (1989); R. Kroetsch, *The Lovely Treachery of Words* (1989); S. Kamboureli, *On the Edge of Genre: The Contemporary Canadian Long Poem* (1991); G. Woodcock, *George Woodcock's Introduction to Canadian Poetry* (1993); A. Brochu, *Tableau du poème* (1994)—poetry of Quebec; F. Davey, *Canadian Literary Power* (1994); C. Filteau, *Poétiques de la modernité: 1895–1948* (1994); L. Mailhot, *La littérature québécoise* (1997); P. Nepveu, *Intérieurs du Nouveau Monde* (1998); F. Dumont, *La poésie québécoise* (1999); J. Blais, *Parmi les hasards* (2001)—poetry of Quebec; P. Butling and S. Rudy, *Writing in Our Time: Canada's Radical Poetries in English, 1957–2003* (2005); M. Biron, F. Dumont, E. Nardout-Lafarge, *Histoire de la littérature québécoise* (2007).

S. Collis (Eng.); F. Dumont (Fr.)

CARIBBEAN, POETRY OF THE

- I. Dutch
- II. English
- III. French
- IV. Spanish

I. Dutch

A. ***Language***. The most outstanding character of "Dutch" Caribbean poetry is its ling. diversity. Besides poetry in Dutch, the lang. for administration since the 17th c., poetry is written in Papiamento and Papiamentu in the Leeward Islands (Aruba, Bonaire, Curaçao), whereas Eng. and creole Eng. dominate in Saba, St. Eustatius, and St. Martin, the so-called Windward Islands. Furthermore, in Suriname, the former "Dutch Guiana" on the South Am. continent, the creole lang. Sranan is the most popular, followed by indigenous langs. (Trio, Carib, Arawak), Maroon langs. (Aucan, Saramaccan), Sarnami, Javanese, Chinese, and Hindi. Poets also have a strong affinity for writing in Sp. and Eng.

Critical academic attention to poetry of the Caribbean is fairly recent and began, with a few exceptions, in the 1990s. In the essays included in a special issue of *Callaloo* (1998) and in the second volume of *A History of Literature in the Caribbean* (2001), scholars discuss the different lang. trads. separately. For references to the past, the creole langs. Sranan (Suriname), and Papiamentu (Bonaire, Curaçao) are crucial because they evolved in close relationship with the most intense times of slavery. Both langs. have an impressive record of oral and musical trads. Some written examples have emerged from the second half of the 18th c., but the real outburst came in the 20th c. and runs parallel with the process of decolonization since World War II. Suriname became an independent republic in 1975; Aruba has been an autonomous entity within the Kingdom of the Netherlands since 1986; and Curaçao and St. Martin have had the same status since the end of 2010. In contrast, Saba, St. Eustatius, and Bonaire are now completely incorporated in the Dutch administrative system.

B. *Suriname.* When Jahn published his famous anthol. *Schwarzer Orpheus* (Black Orpheus, 1954) with black poets from Africa, the Antilles, and South and North America, he included two poems from Suriname under the heading "Guyana." Jahn indicated that he had translated these poems from the Surinamese lang. (Sranan) in collaboration with A. O. Ehrhardt, a Ger. pastor who worked in Suriname. Sranan was the working lang. for *Creole Drum* (1975), a bilingual (with Eng. trans.) anthol. on creole lit. in Suriname. This ed. includes the same poem "Mama Afrika e krei fu en pikin" (Mama Africa Cries for Her Children) by Julius Koenders (1886–1957) as Jahn did, and the author is praised as the ed. of the first magazine that appeared in Sranan, *Foetoe-Boi* (Foot-Boy, 1946–56). When van Kempen reproduced Koenders's poem again in his 709-page anthol., *Spiegel van de Surinaamse poëzie* (Mirror of Surinamese Poetry, 1995), Sranan is only one of several langs. included. By then, it was no longer an exception to write in Sranan, the lang. that in colonial times was forbidden in schools. The painful process of writing poetry in this lang. is expressed by Trefossa (pseud. of Henri Franz de Ziel, 1916–75), the most outstanding Sranan poet, in a poem dedicated to Koenders from the 1950s: "one true poem is like frightening you. / one true poem is like a struggle against death."

Locally produced literary magazines such as *Tongoni* (1958–59), *Soela* (1962–64), and *Moetete* (1968–69) were catalysts for the overwhelming poetical production in Sranan as well as Dutch. Eddy Bruma (1925–2000), who founded a nationalist movement *Wie Eegie Sanie* (Our Own Things), recalled images from the past and inspired one of the best-known poets in the popular local realm, Dobru (pseud. of Robin Ravales, 1935–83), famous for his performances of the poem "Wan Bon" (One Tree) in the 1970s. February characterizes Dobru's poetry as a "linguistic tour de force" whose effect on the audience obviously was immediate. He further discusses Edgar Cairo (1948–2000), an author who moved to the Netherlands in that same period, together with a considerable part of the Surinamese population in the wake of independence. Cairo also was a performer, and February characterizes him as a "word-workman" or "word-worker," "as a cultural, historical, and literary *obja* [Obeah] man, magically transforming the life of Suriname's Creoles into a completely modern style, and reshaping their reality."

Experimental practices were much more characteristic than nationalism for Cairo as well as for other Surinamese poets living in the Netherlands. Hans Faverey, for instance, born in Paramaribo (1933–90), left an important oeuvre and was even proposed as a Dutch candidate for the Nobel Prize in Literature. For poetic experimentation, the *vijftigers*, a Dutch group of poets closely related to visual art, had prepared the reading audience for provocative metaphoric combinations. Faverey's imagination, however, also extended to memories of his native country. Jones discusses his poem "De vijver in het meer" (The Pond in the Lake), in which the Spider is visited by his son; Jones explains this metaphor of Spider as the "resourceful Anansi of Caribbean legend," judging that Faverey's Dutch has Caribbean modulations. Faverey and other poets, who receive attention in the Netherlands, do not emphasize their "Caribbeanness," as does a poet such as Astrid Roemer (b. 1947), who was at the forefront of women's liberation, ecological awareness, and the struggle against discrimination. She describes the difficulties of being published in her commemorations of Jos Knipscheer (1945–97), the owner of a courageous house for "Dutch" Caribbean authors.

Another important segment of Surinamese poetry comes from the "coolitude"—heritage. Cl. Hindi verse was introduced, and contemp. authors use this lang. together with Sarnami (a Surinamese lang. for people from Indian descent) and Dutch. This poetry also reflects on modernization, such as changing gender role patterns, intimacy and emotions, and lyrical images.

C. *Aruba, Curaçao, St. Martin.* Poets in the Netherlands Antilles mostly gather around institutions, libraries, and publishing houses in the three biggest islands of the area. In Curaçao, locally produced literary magazines promoted young talents. Agustin Bethencourt (1826–85), born in the Canary Islands, was the ed. of *Notas y Letras,* (1886–88) in Sp. He was surrounded by native Papiamentu speakers, who wrote poetry in Sp. and maintained contacts with other writers in Latin America and Spain. Joseph Sickman Corsen (1853–1911) was an exception, because he also produced poetry in his native creole lang. His poem "Atardi" (Getting Dark, 1905) is still known by most Curaçaoans today, and its melancholic, introverted tone fits perfectly within the contemp. *modernismo* sensibility on the Sp.-Am. continent.

When Chris Engels (pseud. of Luc Tournier, 1907–80)—an immigrant from the Netherlands—founded *De Stoep* (1940–51) 50 years later, writing in Sp. had become marginal, but Papiamentu writing was quite common already. It was a published lang. since *Civilizadó,* ed. by Bethencourt from 1871 to 1875, as well as thereafter the weekly *La Cruz*—since 1900—in which "Atardi" debuted. Many other publications followed, and Broek defines a prewar period of Papiamentu lit., supported by the Catholic Mission. Therefore, when *De Stoep* came out with its first issue in Dutch, a group of poets published another magazine, *Simadan* (1940), with contributions in Papiamentu. *Simadan* succeeded in bringing out only two volumes, but it became legendary for writing lit. in Papiamentu. Its initiator was Pierre Lauffer (1920–81), who even founded a musical trio, *Cancionero Papiamento*, in order to make clear in which lang. the feelings of belonging were to be found.

Existential questions were predominantly addressed in poetry written in Dutch. Some works show a strong reminiscence of the contacts with Spain and Sp. America, such as *Bekentenis in Toledo* (Confession in Toledo, 1945), in which Cola Debrot (1902–81) recalls the Sp. 17th c. Other authors who published in *De Stoep* evidence the desperate search for love and the desire to shape the colors and images of the island's landscape. Most of the local contributors were native Papiamentu speakers. Oversteegen analyzes the poem "Bezoek" (Visit, 1945), with which Tip Marugg (1923–2006) debuted, and interprets its reception as having two different levels of meaning: one for the Dutch reader and one for the Antillean, the native of Papiamentu.

Papiamentu imagination is very strong in Aletta Beaujon's (1933–2001) first work, *Gedichten aan de Baai en elders* (Poems at the Bay and Beyond, 1957), in which the sea is repeatedly placed at the center of the poetical universe. In that same year, Frank Martinus Arion (1936–2015) came out with *Stemmen uit Afrika* (Voices from Africa, 1957), an epos in which he describes the encounter of white tourists with black inhabitants of the rain forest in Africa. Arion also edited the magazine *Ruku* in the 1970s, in which black consciousness was promoted and in which he published poetry in Dutch and Papiamentu.

Poetry written in the creole lang. of Aruba, Papiamento, does not reproduce the same tension between Dutch and Papiamentu in Curaçao. *Cosecha Arubiano* (Aruban Harvest, 1983), the anthol. published by Booi and coeditors, reveals that Papiamento, Eng., Sp., and Dutch seem to coexist peacefully together without feeling specifically challenged one by the other. Generally, Papiamento is the most important medium for poetical expression. For others, living abroad, this medium becomes a relative dimension. Henry Habibe (b. 1940), the ed. of the literary magazine *Watapana* (1968–72), which published the poetry of Antillean students in the Netherlands, was highly praised for his exquisite volumes in Papiamento. However, his last poetry volume came out in Dutch. In contrast, Denis Henriquez (b. 1945), who became a well-known author of novels written in Dutch, produces poetry in Papiamento that to date has not been published.

In St. Martin, creole Eng. is even less involved in a poetical dialogue with Dutch. Wycliffe Smith (b. 1948) published a first survey of poetry in the Dutch Windward Islands, *Windward Island Verse* (1981), in Eng. Thereafter, the activities of Lasana Sekou (b. 1959), who studied in New York, have had far-reaching consequences. His publishing company, House of Nehesi, has attracted local talent and also has attracted other Caribbean writers to St. Martin. In addition, because of in part the Nigerian critic and teacher Fabian Badejo (b. 1950), who lived in St. Martin, the relationship with Africa becomes a concrete point of reference, asserted in performances, theater, and workshops, widely seen but rarely published.

D. *Traumas, Visions, Rhythms, and Sounds.* Critical work by Broek, Echteld, van Kempen, van Putte-de Windt, and Wim Rutgers repeatedly addresses the important role of literary magazines in the local settings. Poetry represents historical trauma such as slavery, the search for connections with Africa, the May 1969 rebellion in Curaçao, the December murders in Suriname in 1980, gender roles, or discrimination. The myriad of anthols., (short-lived) magazines, or self-published volumes makes it complicated to distinguish among the different "strategies and stratagems" of "Dutch" Caribbean poetry. Therefore, it might be useful to conclude with some general observations.

First, it is clear that different poetical langs. are not disappearing but are growing stronger, even though Dutch remains the condition for circulating on the literary market. Second, efforts to counter the marginalization of the creole langs. by pushing them forward as written literary langs. have succeeded since the 1940s: their rhythms and rhymes have a strong musical background, and, in this context, Caribbean poetry begins to be increasingly influential. The House of Nehesi has published volumes by Kamau Brathwaite, and his work has also been translated into Sranan in Suriname. Sekou even speaks of the Caribbean as the "universe of sound." Van Mulier, ed. of the anthol. *Nieuwe Oogst* (New Harvest, 2002), belongs to the Surinamese Writers Association in the Netherlands and has recognized this point. He has argued for more attention to musical rhythm in poetry. One of the poets in the volume, the music professor Rudy Bedacht (b. 1932), presents his composition for another melody for the national anthem, currently based on the 1876 musical composition of a Dutch teacher. The anthem, which has one Dutch and one Sranan strophe—the latter produced by Trefossa in 1959—was translated into a slightly modified Javanese version in 1998. This detail clearly reveals that the poetical sensibility in this part of America is dealing with different langs. and styles that all refer to the same native intimacy.

II. English. Speakers of Eng. begin to inhabit the Caribbean during the early 17th c., through the colonization of Barbados and then Jamaica. By the end of the 20th c., the region's anglophone poets wrote not only from former Brit. colonies large (Guyana, Jamaica, Trinidad, Barbados, St. Lucia) and small (Belize, the Bahamas, St. Vincent, Grenada, Antigua, St. Kitts, Virgin Islands, Dominica, Montserrat), but from islands that were never Brit., such as Puerto Rico and even St. Martin. In addition, many writers who regard themselves as anglophone Caribbean poets now reside for the most part in North America or the U.K. Such a list is not very helpful for identifying some common ground for all this writing beyond the accident of lang. Another frequent option, "West Indian poetry," is more explicitly grounded in the Eng.-speaking islands themselves but is commonly used more broadly. The most ingenious, and possibly most accurate, attempt at characterization associates this poetry with "the cricket-playing Caribbean."

Venturing to speak of "anglophone Caribbean poetry" turns any traditional notion of national lit. on its head. This is a body of poetry from noncontiguous territories, many of them now sovereign states, some of which once comprised a single political unit, though only fleetingly, as the short-lived Federation of the West Indies (1958–62). This is not the poetry of a nation, nor of a people, nor of a single culture, nor even, strictly speaking, of a single lang. What do we gain by having a catchall phrase for any verse written in some variant of Eng. by someone associated with the Caribbean? Even naming the region itself requires choosing among incommensurate terms: "the Caribbean," "Latin America," "the Antilles," "the West Indies." But if the difficulties of naming this body of work might suggest that it is not really viable as a single object of attention, the repeated efforts to name it seem to belie that suggestion. Indeed, throughout the Caribbean, the issues raised by the very act of naming have been central to cultural self-consciousness (and particularly to poetry) since Europe insisted these islands were "the Indies," gave the slaves ancient Roman names, and described the landscape in the vocabulary of Ren. pastoral. To propose "Caribbean poetry in English" as an object of study is to propose that regarding the poetry through such a frame or optic, rather than as sheaves of separate poems, significantly enhances our experience of the texts. For critics and poets alike, it is inherently intriguing that this body of work is problematic to name.

Thus, e.g., we might start from the common historical narrative/trajectory that these islands share. Then the qualifications must begin at once: at least two of these "islands" (Belize and Guyana) are not islands at all. But the need to make that qualification is not distracting; it sensitizes readers to different roles that topography and geography may play in shaping the local intonation of themes and images common to the experience of the region. Metaphorically speaking, many aspects of Caribbean life are instances of a broad principle, "one language, many accents." This is consistent with Antonio Benítez Rojo's (1931–2005) insight that, in the Caribbean, things are always done "in a certain kind of way." The Tobagonian poet Eric Roach (1915–74) in "Caribbean Calypso" (1965) strikingly envisions the Caribbean as a laboratory, each island a Petri dish in which initially similar cultures, once isolated, evolve quite differently under the influence of what were at first only slightly different conditions, mutations, contaminations. Caribbean writers characteristically bear in mind at once the distinctively local and its regional or international contexts.

Qualifications and variants aside, the common ground for the entire region is archipelagic geography, tropical climate, and a shared hist. Europe intrudes into Amerindian societies, and the rest follows. Emancipation brought an end to plantation slavery on different islands at different times, but in the Brit. colonies, the reach of the empire made it possible to avert the ensuing labor shortage by recruiting indentured workers from India, China, and even West Africa. After extreme economic and political changes and two world wars, Britain moved to dismantle both the plantation and the empire, creating a climate in the Caribbean for the emergence of cultural and political nationalism. Independence came for most of the Brit. Caribbean in the course of the 1960s, unexpectedly inflected by the rise of Black Power movements in the region as well as in North America and the U.K. In the sometimes disappointing aftermath of independence, the salient international pressures on the region were redefined: increasing Am. influence, globalization, and neocolonialism. Such is the grand narrative, though it played out in different terms and on different timetables from island to island.

In the anglophone case, the production of poetry from its beginnings entails decisions about three intertwined questions that have remained perennial for this body of work: Who is the audience? What is the lang. of expression (Standard English [SE] or creole)? What is the envisioned mode of expression (oral or scribal)? Throughout the colonial Caribbean, the various metropolitan langs. isolated territories from one another, while each lang. imported conventions and styles that shaped distinctive literary hists. Almost at once, a variety of creole langs. arise (new spoken langs. developing out of persistent contact between two or more other langs.), and creole becomes an influential part of the ling. experience of writers long before it emerges openly as a lang. of expression in the literary realm. Some societies respond to the emergence of a spoken creole by establishing a barrier between what are perceived as separate and unequal langs. Though the ling. hists. of the Brit. colonies vary considerably, there has been a general tendency to think in terms of a ling. continuum linking rural creole with metropolitan lang. This gives individual speakers considerable control over their self-expression, even within single sentences, and has been an important resource for the distinctive flexibility of anglophone poetry.

In the late 1790s, there appear the first transcriptions of folk songs and stories composed in an Eng.-based creole. These would have been accessible to and used by West Indians of both Af. and Eur. heritage, though it is difficult to date the actual creation of such oral materials. They are recorded in travelogues, hists., and personal jours. published mostly in London and reflect what we would now call an anthropological interest in the region, stimulated at a crucial historical moment: this is the era of the Am., Fr., and Haitian revolutions; of the abolitionist movement; and of the Brit. acquisition of Trinidad.

The first self-consciously literary poems appear somewhat earlier, from about 1750. These are fairly long narrative poems, in blank verse or couplets, written according to the conventions of contemporaneous Brit. poetry. Most of the poems of this period are published in London; while a few were printed in Jamaica or Barbados, these authors certainly aspired to reach a Brit. audience. They would also have envisioned a small but interested audience in the Caribbean, made up of planters, government officials, doctors, attorneys, and clergy. It is apparent that West Indian poets have always been aware of the challenges and opportunities entailed by addressing more than one audience at a time.

Individual poets were sporadically active during the 19th c., and it is likely that more of this work will be recovered as research into periodical publications of the era continues. Though there are intriguing exceptions, the dominant themes are predictable: nature, spirituality, moral uplift, and imperial patriotism. Issues of audience and lang. became more prominent at the end of the century with the success of "dialect poetry"—verse composed in the creole vernacular as a vehicle for comedy or social satire. Intended for newspaper publication, this poetry was written by members of the social elite for a literate readership, but the most popular practitioners reached wide audiences and published reprint collections through local printeries. Soon afterward, in 1912, the young Claude McKay (1890–1948), from a well-to-do black family in rural Jamaica, published two volumes (one in Kingston and the other in London) that are generally regarded as the collections in which poems in an anglophone creole are explicitly presented as lit.

The influence of McKay's work was seminal but delayed (perhaps because McKay almost immediately emigrated to the U.S. and never wrote in creole again).

Literary anthols. begin to appear in print in the 1920s and 1930s, but historical perspective is rare in these collections; most include only works of living authors, with few poems from before about 1900. There is one impressive exception, the first anthol. from Guyana (*Guyanese Poetry*, 1931), whose ed., Norman Cameron, unearthed work from as early as 1831. The appearance of anthols. coincides with the devel. in several territories of productive poetry groups, clubs, or salons (such as the Poetry League of Jamaica or the group associated with the *Beacon* magazine in Trinidad), and some tentative printing ventures. In the more developed colonies during this period, we can discern the crucial metamorphosis by which a scattering of writers coalesces into a lit. There is generally a new interest in local Caribbean geography and hist., and during the late 1930s and the war years, these themes mature into more overt concern with cultural and political nationalism.

From the very beginning of the century, women had taken important initiatives, and during this period, one who learned from McKay's example was Una Marson (1905–65), another Jamaican who published several collections of poetry in the 1930s and so established herself as arguably the first important modernist and the leading female voice of the time. A number of her poems experiment with the poetic resources of vernaculars, drawing on lessons learned not only from Jamaican creole but from her knowledge of Harlem Ren. poetry and its exploration of black Am. vernaculars. The greatest exponent of McKay's early mission, however, is Louise Bennett (1919–2006), a collector and performer of folk tales and songs, professionally trained in London at the Royal Academy of Dramatic Art, and the author of several collections of original poems in Jamaican creole, beginning in the 1940s. Her work, however, was not regarded as "literature" until the independence era, despite her jibe in 1944 that, though the Brit. had been trying to stabilize their lang. since the 14th c., "Five hundred years gawn an dem got / More dialect dan we!" ("Bans o' Killing," 1944).

A massive Caribbean migration to Britain occurred between the early 1950s and the restrictive immigration legislation of 1962. As in any migration, there was concern about abandoning home and losing identity, but this turned out to be something different—as Bennett phrased it, a case of "colonization in reverse." Nationalist impulses at home were complemented by the discovery, in London, of both a broader West Indian identity and a black identity. Anglophone migrants from all over the Caribbean were thrown together (Britons tended to call them all *Jamaicans*) and began to sort out not only their common traits but the distinctive differences between local island cultures—in particular (from the perspective of poets) ling. variations in the syntax, lexicon, and accent of their diverse forms of Eng. The formulation of a West Indian identity was facilitated by a number of new institutions. Most powerful in its impact was perhaps the BBC's *Caribbean Voices* program, which featured the voices of West Indian authors resident in London reading current West Indian prose and poetry for listeners in the Caribbean (a number of the early emigrants, incl. novelists Sam Selvon, George Lamming, and V. S. Naipaul, worked for the BBC and wrote their first books on its typewriters). Also significant were the Caribbean Artists Movement (which eventually migrated back to the Caribbean from England), the founding of literary jours. with regional perspective (*Bim* in Barbados [1942], *Kyk-Over-Al* in Guyana [1945], *Caribbean Quarterly* in Jamaica [1949]), and the establishment in 1948 of the University College of the West Indies (soon to become the University of the West Indies). A succeeding generation of writers, building on this thinking about West Indianness, would go on in their own work to formulate what we now call Black British identity. This pattern is repeated when the somewhat later migration to Canada leads to the emergence of yet another "colony" of anglophone Caribbean lit.

Back in the Caribbean, some of the leading poets of this period were Martin Carter (1927–97) and A. J. Seymour (1914–89) in Guyana, and Roach and Harold Telemaque (1910–82) in Trinidad. Between 1962 and 1966, Jamaica, Trinidad and Tobago, Guyana, and Barbados all became independent countries. The timing meant that the process of coming to terms with independence took place in the context of the global emergence of black consciousness. For predominantly black nations like Jamaica and Barbados, this was in the long run a positive influence. For Guyana and Trinidad, with much more diverse populations, the downside was institutionalization of political confrontation along ethnic lines. Among the positive outcomes was (on the one hand) robust growth of both recognizably Afro-Caribbean and recognizably Indo-Caribbean writing and (on the other) a growing confidence among writers about drawing on their multiple cultural trads. Everywhere writers joined in the fundamental debates about "roots"—about whether identity was to be grounded in pristine Af. or Asian heritage or in current creole realities (as in Derek Walcott's view of the archetypal Caribbean man as a "second Adam"). Discussion of the hybrid results of creolization could be framed as biological (what are your parents?), cultural (what do you do, and how do you do it?), even intellectual (what do you talk about and how?). Poets, through the content of their poems, played a vital role in those discussions, but, for the practice of poetry, the leading issues were again lang. and mode of expression.

Among the many rewarding poets of the postindependence era are Edward Baugh (b. 1936), Mervyn Morris (b. 1937), Velma Pollard (b. 1937), and Dennis Scott (1939–91) in Jamaica; Kendel Hippolyte (b. 1952), Jane King (b. 1952), and Robert Lee (b. 1949) in Saint Lucia; Ian McDonald (b. 1933) and David Dabydeen (b. 1955) in Guyana. The single most important poets of the 20th c. were Derek Walcott (b. 1930) and Kamau Brathwaite (b. 1930), both ambitious, prolific poets and highly visible figures on the Caribbean scene. Walcott began publishing in the late 1940s; his poetry has often addressed in complex ways the relation of the Caribbean to its Eur. heritage, while his verse plays have given voice to several West Indian vernaculars. Brathwaite came to prominence in the 1960s with the first volume of what became a trilogy, *The Arrivants* (1967–69), an epic poem of vast scope and resonance, which, among other innovations, set the standard for literary use of anglophone creoles.

Following the magisterial example of Brathwaite's trilogy, many poets joined the project of demonstrating that their anglophone creoles could be literary langs.; some even took the extreme view that SE could not be the lang. of their work. In some cases, the argument for creole was an argument that spoken lang. should be fundamental for poetry (an argument that echoes the likes of William Wordsworth, Chaucer, and Dante). Advocacy of spoken lang. often brought with it an advocacy of spoken *style*, of what Brathwaite called "orature": written poetry that aspired to the condition of oral poetry. This argument invoked several important values of the era: the association of oral verbal arts with the Caribbean "folk" (conceived in various ways) and with ancestral trads. in Africa, and traditional respect for the figure of the Caribbean "man of words." This, in turn, led to a new respect for performers of poetry (such as Bennett), and to the rise, esp. in Jamaica, of composers of "dub poetry" (sometimes called "reggae poetry"): poetry intended for performance that draws heavily on features of Jamaican deejay practice and is often (but not necessarily) accompanied by reggae music. Among the most compelling of these, accessible through commercial recordings, are Linton Kwesi Johnson (b. 1952), Michael Smith (1954–83), Jean "Binta" Breeze (b. 1956), and Mutabaruka (b. 1952).

From a narrowly literary perspective, the performance poets no longer dominate the Caribbean scene as they once did. A generation of younger poets has come forward, many of them not esp. interested in performance and often writing rather surprisingly in SE. In particular, women in much greater numbers (and from several generations) began publishing volumes of poetry in the 1980s; they had almost dropped out of the poetry scene during the male-dominated nationalist period. This is a body of work remarkable for diversity and audacity; it is not the exploration of "female subjects" or a narrowly defined "women's style." It addresses a variety of audiences, sometimes in creole, sometimes in SE, sometimes in both. Lorna Goodison (b. 1947) has an international reputation and a clear influence on younger writers. But there are many established figures, such as Pollard and Grace Nichols (b. 1950), while the numerous younger poets often publish locally and are best sought out in anthols.

The current poetry scene has become increasingly diverse in every respect, yet high-profile performance poets like Johnson effectively symbolize the paradox on which anglophone Caribbean poetry stands after the 20th c. Through recordings, concerts, and videos, they reach an enormous global audience, comparable to that of the reggae stars. But what they deliver is a specifically Caribbean (or in some cases Black Brit.) perspective couched in unmediated creole lang. With minimal compromise or homogenization, they do not make their lang. accessible; they successfully invite audiences to make the effort to access it. Increasingly, transnational experience and even transnational identity are marks of most Caribbean poets, yet their work seems ever more interested in the peculiarities of local speech, custom, and behavior. They preserve and celebrate what is distinctively Caribbean but project it globally.

III. French. One of the most widely accepted truths of francophone Caribbean lit., and for some readers perhaps Caribbean lit. in its entirety, is that no poetry existed before 1939. Revolutionary ideologies in the francophone Caribbean in the 1930s were constructed around myths of rupture and innovation that condemned the 19th c. as a time of unexamined imitation. This is one of the defining characteristics of the identity politics promoted in such radical jours. as *Légitime Défense*, *Tropiques*, and *La Revue Indigène*. This yearning for a violent rupture with the past led Frantz Fanon to declare, "Until 1939 the West Indian lived, thought, dreamed . . . composed poems, wrote novels exactly as a white man would have done" (*Toward the African Revolution*, 1964). Indeed, in the case of Haiti, the influential theorist of Haitian *indigenisme* Jean Price-Mars (1876–1969) dismissed his predecessors in 1928 as practicing collective "bovarysme" or "the pathological deviation [of] conceiving of ourselves as other than we are" (*So Spoke the Uncle*, 1928). More recently the promoters of *Créolité* in the Fr. Antilles blindly repeated Price-Mars's term "bovarysme collectif" to describe all the writing done in Haiti between 1804 and 1915.

Before the publication of Aimé Césaire's epic poem *Cahier d'un retour au pays natal* (*Notebook of a Return to the Native Land*, 1939) on the eve of World War II, there was good reason to believe that Fr. Caribbean poetry, at least what was produced in the Fr. colonies, was dominated by sentimental, pastoral, and, most important, apolitical evocations of nature. A local intellectual culture was never encouraged in colonies whose raison d'être was primarily commercial. Education was a fiercely guarded privilege restricted almost exclusively to the white planter elite. This drawback, combined with an inevitable sense of cultural inferiority, meant that, when it did appear, poetry was likely to offer imitative apologies for the economic status quo. For instance, Poirié de Saint-Aurèle (1795–1855), a member of the white planter class from Guadeloupe, fully deserves Fanon's dismissive description, having published a defense of plantation slavery and collections of regionalist verse (*Les Veillées francaises* [French Evenings], 1826; and *Cyprès et palmistes* [Cypresses and Palms], 1833) that defend the plantation hierarchy and display contempt for the black-slave population.

Saint-Aurèle's love for his native land and antipathy to the métropole are a product of reactionary self-interest, as he felt the way of life of the planter class increasingly threatened. This was not always the case, as regionalist verse was also inspired by the ideals of Fr. romanticism that could allow for the condemnation of racial prejudice and for a healthy interest in representing local flora and fauna. Toward the end of the century in Martinique, René Bonneville (1871–1902) published a regionalist anthol., *Fleurs des Antilles* (1900), to coincide with the Universal Exposition. In Guadeloupe, Oruno Lara (1879–1924) published much regionalist verse in his newspaper *La Guadeloupe Littéraire*. They propagated the exotic image of *les Antilles heureuses* until the outbreak of World War I. Uniform themes and unoriginal styles are the hallmark of this period of Fr. West Indian poetry, typified by such writers as Daniel Thaly (1878–1950), the titles of whose works—*Le Jardin des Tropiques* (The Garden of the Tropics, 1911), *Nostalgies françaises* (French Nostalgia, 1913)—speak for themselves. Along with this picturesque presentation of local color, there was a more ethnographic trend that insisted on a local identity. Gilbert de Chambertrand (1890–1984) and Gilbert Gratiant (1895–1985) spoke more directly to local concerns, even if in an unoriginal way. The latter experimented with poems in Creole and was even included in Léopold Sédar Senghor's 1948 *Anthologie de la nouvelle poésie nègre et malgache de langue française* (Anthology of the New Negro Poetry in French and Malagasy).

Out of this period of largely white nostalgia and mulatto mystification, there nevertheless emerged the powerful evocation of an Antillean childhood in the early verse of Saint-John Perse (1887–1975), a white Creole native of Guadeloupe. His first book of poems, *Eloges* (Praises, 1911), is as much a love song to Guadeloupe as one of loss motivated by the outlook of a displaced planter class that one finds in Saint-Aurèle. Even if the ghost of the planter patriarch haunts the pages of *Eloges*, Perse has become, as much as Césaire, a central figure in Fr. West Indian lit. The Caribbean landscape in Perse's poems is not evoked through the clichés of tropical local color as is the case with the regionalist poets. It is not so much the references to local flora and fauna as the deeply felt personal sense of a lost paradise that make these poems authentically Caribbean. The poet's plantation past becomes an Antillean *lieu de mémoire*, the poetic origin for a trad. of writing Caribbean landscape.

The dismissal of all poetry before the 1930s as Eurocentric seems particularly unjust in the case of Haiti. The themes of early Haitian poetry are drawn from the 1804 Declaration of Independence: pride in Haiti's historic defeat of Napoleon's army, the need to inspire patriotic ideals in the new nation, and the proclamation of Haiti's redemptive mission in a world where plantation slavery still thrived. From very early on, there were calls for a national lit. that would resist cl. forms and references in favor of Haitian hist. and culture. Victor Hugo's robust rhet. and militant politics were a source of inspiration at the time. One of the major exponents of this nationalist verse was Oswald Durand (1840–1906), whose *Rires et Pleurs* (Laughter and Tears, 1896) were an unflagging attempt to celebrate Haitian culture. He is remembered for his poem of unrequited love, "Choucoune" (1884), which was one of the first experiments in Creole-lang. verse. His contemp. Masillon Coicou (1867–1908) was both a military man and a poet and is best known for the tellingly named *Poésies nationales* (1892), which retold Haitian hist. and the independence struggle. At the turn of the 20th c., there was a reaction against what was seen as the excessive nationalism of the patriotic school of Haitian poets. The movement called *La Ronde* felt that, to gain international acclaim, it was necessary to avoid the trap of a narrow parochialism in poetry. Its adherents argued for a literary eclecticism and engaged cosmopolitanism in Haitian verse and felt that regionalist concerns were best left to Haiti's novelists. The works of the poets of La Ronde—Etzer Vilaire (1872–1951), Edmond Laforest (1876–1915), and Georges Sylvain (1866–1925)—were allusive, impersonal, and reminiscent of the ideals of Fr. symbolism. This poetic movement was abruptly cut short by the Am. occupation of Haiti in 1915.

Given the radical turn in Haitian poetry after 1915, Césaire's revolutionary poetics was already evident in the wake of the U.S. occupation. Well before the Negritude movement of the 1930s, the poets of the indigenist movement began to espouse the ideals of a heroic modernism that valued the poet for his or her visionary power and poetic lang. for its apocalyptic thrust. An antiestablishment iconoclasm was practiced by poets such as Emile Roumer (1903–88), Philippe Thoby-Marcelin (1904–75), and Carl Brouard (1902–65), whose work was published in *La Revue Indigène*. Brouard, in particular, could be seen as an early exponent of the values of Negritude, as he became increasingly preoccupied by Haiti's Af. past and the Vodou religion. The most outstanding figure of this time is Jacques Roumain (1907–44), who founded the Haitian Communist Party and linked the Haitian Ren. to similar movements elsewhere in the Caribbean and in North and South America. He was close to the Cuban poet Nicolás Guillén, the Chilean Pablo Neruda, and the Af. Am. Langston Hughes, who were all bound by their ties to Marxism. His fiery book of poems *Bois d'ébène* (Ebony Forest, 1945) favors the grand prophetic manner of the militant utopian rhet. of the 1940s. This epic, militant style would be continued after Roumain's death in 1944 by poets such as Jean Brierre (1909–92), René Bélance (1915–2004), and Roussan Camille (1912–61). Perhaps the most successful of the generation that followed was René Depestre (b. 1926), whose early verse *Etincelles* (Sparks, 1945) and *Gerbe de Sang* (Spray of Blood, 1946) were deeply influenced by the poetry of the Fr. Resistance, esp. that of Paul Éluard and Louis Aragon. Most of Depestre's life would be spent in exile, which would make him an early poet of what would become during the Duvalier dictatorship in the 1960s the Haitian diaspora.

Although he has been eclipsed by Césaire, the Fr. Guyanese poet Léon Gontran Damas (1912–78) was the herald of what came to be known as the Negritude movement. His book of poems *Pigments* (1937) was the first to treat the subject of an international black consciousness and to openly denounce Fr. colonialism. His poetic production was smaller than that of Césaire and his style less dependent on surrealist techniques, but his direct, spontaneous verse connected him immediately to both the Harlem Ren. and Haitian indigenisme. He pioneered the use of everyday speech in his verse, drawing on the poetic experiments with spoken Fr. by Raymond Queneau and Jacques Prévert. He found a way of creating protest poetry that could endure, manipulating pace, humor, and shock to create a number of memorable dramatic monologues. Damas is as terse and incisive as Césaire is epic and erudite.

Césaire's *Cahier d'un retour au pays natal* inaugurated the heroic modernist verse that would become the hallmark of francophone poetry in the next two decades. In the poetic masterpiece of this period of radical politics, Césaire conceives of the francophone Caribbean in terms of violent images of revolutionary decolonization. The Caribbean past was represented as a sea of running sores, a bloody, open wound with its archipelago of precarious scabs. The Caribbean people eked out a zombified, repressed existence in this putrefying world. The poet proposed a volcanic reordering of space where the tongue of volcanic flame would sweep away the old and found a new utopian order.

The championing of Césaire's apocalyptic poetics had much to do with his meeting with André Breton in 1941 as the latter was heading into exile in the United States. Breton's account of their meeting, which now forms the introduction to *Cahier*, promoted Césaire as a mystical visionary who shared with the leader of the surrealist movement the primitivist dream of an uncontaminated elsewhere beyond the reach of the nightmare imposed by Europe in the colonial past for Césaire and the Nazi present for Breton. Césaire and Breton's visits to Haiti in the coming years would help spread this apocalyptic modernism. However, there is much evidence that Césaire was at least as deeply concerned with the problems of an overly referential verse as he was with a political *prise de conscience*. His high regard for Stéphane Mallarmé, with whom he shared the view that the concrete could short-circuit the poetic, and his siding with Breton in the quarrel with Aragon as to the need for a political poetry are evidence of Césaire's passionate belief in the freedom of the poetic imagination. This is an area of ambiguity that pushes us to rethink the view that Césaire's poetry is exclusively associated with violent militancy.

When the Haitian Marxist Depestre, echoing Aragon, insisted that Caribbean poetry be accessible and nonexperimental, Césaire's response to Depestre, and by extension Aragon and the Communist Party, was indeed entitled "Réponse à Depestre poète haitien, Eléments d'un art poétique" (Response to the Haitian Poet Depestre: Elements of the Art of Poetry, 1955). By giving his reply this subtitle, Césaire invites us to see the poem as prescriptive. With unaccustomed directness, he urged Depestre not to pay heed to Aragon's call for accessible verse but to become a poetic *maroon*, after the early mod. term for escaped slaves who lived independent of colonial society. Depestre was encouraged to learn to conjugate this particular neologism—*marronner*—in the way that the 18th-c. Haitian maroon and Vaudou priest Dutty Boukman understood it. Césaire reminded Depestre that Boukman's rebellious cry incited the rebellions that became the Haitian Revolution and argued that the poetic word should strive for a similar "insane chant" as the ultimate form of marronnage. It is hard to tell whether Depestre heeded Césaire's advice. He was certainly capable of a moving and unpretentious lyricism as in *Journal d'un animal marin* (Journal of a Marine Animal, 1964), arguably the most important poetic work about exile during the Duvalier years, and more relaxed personal pieces in *Minerai noir* (Black Ore, 1957). Nevertheless, he was equally capable of inspiring, accessible verse in response to requests from the Communist Party. His Vaudou ritual poem *Un arc-en-ciel pour l'Occident chrétien* (A Rainbow for the Christian West, 1967) is structured around chants for mobilizing the Vaudou gods to wage war against U.S. imperialism. His *Poète à Cuba* (1976) shows him to be an inveterate producer of poetry for political occasions. His celebration of pagan love as the ultimate catalyst for liberating the self, however, suggests that he has not quite abandoned his early surrealist influences for the rhet. of political activism.

It could be said that Césaire straddles two aspects of literary modernism. On the one hand, he practices a heroic modernism with its notion of the poet's prophetic vision and the poem as a moment of epiphany. On the other, he also espouses a nonutopian poetics based on the values of imaginative freedom and formal experimentation. By the 1950s, however, dreams of revolutionary decolonization had begun and a monolithic racial identity had begun to yield to a poetics that no longer valued marronage and radical difference. The emergence of this new, identifiably postcolonial interest in cultural contact, hybridity, and creolization in the francophone Caribbean is as much linked to the failure of the dream of revolutionary decolonization as to the complex nature of the surrealist movement itself. We should not forget that the poetics of modernism first entered Caribbean lit. not through Césaire but through the group Légitime Défense, among whose members were the now largely forgotten writers René Menil (1907–2004) and Jules Monnerot (1909–95). Their presence has been eclipsed by that of Césaire and the Breton-sponsored idea of revolutionary poetics. However, their ideas often overlapped with members of the surrealist movement who either defected or were expelled by Breton. Here we find the origins of the post-Césairean idea of poetry in the Caribbean. While we tend to associate surrealism with the world of dreams and the unconscious, it also maintained a strong materialist interest in things, in the impossibility of creating abstract formulations from concrete reality. The inscrutable otherness of objects and the inability to systematize the concrete are crucial to the early writings of Monnerot as to such early members of the movement as Roger Caillois (1913–78) and Michel Leiris (1901–90). Subjectivity, in particular artistic subjectivity, depended on *le hasard objectif*, the inscrutable otherness of objects.

This interest in the liberating possibilities of otherness is rich in significance for Caribbean writers wrestling with colonial as well as anticolonial constructs of reality. It certainly created a suspicion of the grand ideological formulations of heroic modernism and provoked an interest in the ethnographic mapping of otherness. Some of the surrealist fellow travelers who knew each other and favored this methodology also came to the Caribbean during the 1940s. Pierre Mabille (1904–52) and later the ethnographer Alfred Métraux (1902–63) spent long periods in Haiti in the 1940s. On the invitation of Césaire, Leiris visited Martinique and Haiti in 1948. The importance of travel, the encounter with the other, and self-ethnography were all seen at this time as the supreme artistic endeavor. Global modernity had turned all places into crossroads where the unpredictable occurred. There could, therefore, be no more ancestral heartlands nor utopian elsewheres.

A prewar apocalyptic poetics now yielded to a poetry based on self-scrutiny catalyzed through interaction with the other. Poets such as Clément Magloire St. Aude (1912–71) of Haiti and Édouard Glissant (1928–2011) of Martinique became major exponents of this mode of poetic expression. The latter's 1955 *Soleil de la conscience* (Sun of Consciousness) is a perfect example of a poetic self-ethnography as the writer travels not to the native land but to Paris where he is both a stranger to and a product of that reality. The poetics of postwar modernism in the Caribbean is about not new beginnings but a postcolonial errancy that negates, as Glissant has said, "every pole and metropole." It is also not so much about self-expression as about opening poetry to the Caribbean's hemispheric horizons and ultimately to global horizons. This is the central difference between the poetics of Césaire and Glissant. The former projects island space as home, as an unambiguous foundation for the assertion of difference in the face of a deterritorializing incorporation into the transcendent values of the West. The latter replaces the Césairean romance of lost origins with an alternative poetics of location that projects island space as an open yet opaque insularity, a zone of encounter that both acquiesces in yet resists the pressures of global interaction. Consequently, Glissant's poetics was not about idealizing difference in the face of the transcendent will of the West, the reductive force of the Same. He set out, rather, to theorize a "totalizing rootedness," a coming to consciousness of the world in a particular locale. A crucial aspect of Glissant's early assertion of a totalizing vision is the density and tension of locale that underpins this relational model.

In his early book of poems *Les Indes* (1956), Glissant examines the question of place, naming, and the force of the imagination in the Indies—as much dream space as the space of historical nightmare. From the outset, Glissant saw his legacy not so much as that of a Fr. West Indian poet but as that of an Am. modernist. He felt a greater affinity with Perse and William Faulkner than with Roumain and Césaire. Breaking with the demiurgic impulse of heroic modernism, Glissant focuses on the shaping force of landscape. This time it is not the Césairean volcano but Perse's inscrutable marine world that allows Glissant to break with the *poésie de circonstance* that characterized earlier decades. The Manichean combativeness of Negritude is absent from early collections such as *Un champ d'iles* (A Field of Islands, 1953) and *La terre inquiète* (The Anxious Land, 1954). The dense poetic meditations of these early works contain the essence of Glissant's literary project, which is not about providing ideological answers but posing questions "dans la lumière trop diffuse, quand la connaissance est possible et toujours future" (in the too diffuse light when knowing is possible and always to come). Increasingly, Glissant turned from poetry to poetics, from books of poems to poetically derived theory reflecting the larger postcolonial trend in the francophone Caribbean away from poetry that no longer occupies the place it did in the mid-20th c.

Poetry may be overshadowed by prose, but it still retains its prestige because of the need for narrative to reach beyond realistic description. For instance, the novelist Daniel Maximin's *L'invention des desirades* (The Invention of Desirada, 2000) addresses both Caribbean space, as the title suggests, and the need for a verbal inventiveness made possible by poetic lang. Other Antillean writers who attempt to voice the Glissantian ideal of dream space anchored in the real are the prolific Henri Corbin (1934–2015) in works such as *Lieux d'ombre* (Shadow Places, 1991) and *Plongée au gré des deuils* (Descent into the Currents of Loss, 1999) and the densely experimental poet Monchoachi (b. 1946) in *L'Espére-geste* (The Awaited Gesture, 2003). Similar demands on poetic lang. were made by Haitian writers since the 1960s with the short-lived movement Haiti-Littéraire. René Philoctète (1932–90), Anthony Phelps (b. 1928), and Davertige (pseud. of Villard Denis, 1940–2004), among others, reacted against the militant Marxist verse of Depestre and saw the early surrealist St. Aude as their literary forebear. The dense elliptical style of George Castera (b. 1936), who returned to Haiti after the fall of Duvalier in 1986, keeps this experimental trad. alive in his prize-winning collection *Le trou du souffleur* (The Prompter's Box, 2006).

IV. Spanish. The Hispanic Caribbean is comprised primarily of Cuba, the Dominican Republic, and Puerto Rico. A strong case can be made for incl. in this cultural area the coastal zones of the Circum-Caribbean, i.e., the Gulf Coast of Mexico, the eastern coasts of the Central Am. nations, and the northern coasts of Colombia and Venezuela. However, given the paucity of major poets from these Circum-Caribbean regions, this section focuses on the three Hispanic states of the Greater Antilles. Cuba and the Dominican Republic are independent nations, while Puerto Rico is a "free associated state" of the U.S. Despite the political and economic differences among the three, a common hist. of Sp. colonialism and extractive economies (esp. the plantation), slavery, and racial and ethnic mixing has produced a certain cultural unity (Benítez Rojo).

The most notable features of the poetry of the Hispanic Caribbean are (1) a rich trad. of popular poetry in forms such as *romances*, *décimas*, and *coplas* derived from the Sp. trad., as well as forms such as the *son*, derived from the syncretic Afro-Caribbean trad.; (2) the early introduction of romanticism and modernismo (in Cuba at least) relative to the rest of Lat. Am.; (3) a rich trad. of Afro-Caribbean literary poetry; and (4) the introduction of the neobaroque strain in Lat. Am. letters.

A. *From the Conquest to the Beginning of the Independence Movements.* In contrast to Mexico and its archive of Nahuatl poetry from before and during the conquest, there are no examples of Taino poetry. The indigenous peoples of the Hispanic Caribbean were the first to encounter Sp. explorers and did not long survive that encounter. Chroniclers such as Gonzalo Fernández de Oviedo (*Historia general y natural de las Indias*, 1535) refer to Taino gatherings called *areitos*, dancing and singing rituals in which the recitation of poetry preserved a communal past. However, these poems are lost. The conquistadors were steeped in the poetic trad. of the *romances*. Many anthols. of these ballads were published in 16th-c. Spain, although the typical method of transmission was oral. Mod. Dominican versions of traditional romances—presumably extant since the early colonial period—were collected in the 20th c. by Pedro Henríquez Ureña and by Edna Garrido.

Hispaniola was the center of Eur. cultural life in the early colonial period, and some of the earliest poems in the New World were written there, often in Lat. The first example of *poesía culta* (learned poetry) in the Hispanic Caribbean is an ode written in Lat. by Bishop Alessandro Geraldini to celebrate the construction of the cathedral of Santo Domingo in 1523.

Meanwhile, 16th-c. Spain experienced a revolution in poetic form, as the It. hendecasyllable line, the *terza rima* and *ottava rima* stanza forms, the sonnet, and other models out of Petrarchism were imported to Spain by Juan Boscán and Garcilaso de la Vega. These forms—and the courtly ideals and modes of behavior they expressed—quickly became absorbed into the trad. of poesía culta and appeared in the New World. Early examples are the sonnets of the earliest known female poet of the Americas, the nun Sor Leonor de Ovando (fl. 1575).

Most critics would agree that the first major poem of the Hispanic Caribbean trad. is the *Espejo de paciencia* (Mirror of Patience, 1608), a historical epic written by the Canarian Silvestre de Balboa y Troya de Quesada (1563–1647?), a resident of Puerto Príncipe (mod.-day Camagüey), Cuba. Written in ottava rima, the epic is notable on at least two accounts. First, it is preceded by six laudatory sonnets by local dignitaries, which reflect the existence of an intellectual circle or literary academy in the area of Puerto Príncipe in the early colonial period, surprising given the political marginality of the locale. Second, the poet mixes cl. Gr. mythology with local places and flora (González Echevarría). For Cuban intellectuals, the *Espejo de paciencia* is one of the foundational texts of a transcultural national idiom, of *lo cubano* (Vitier 1958). Inasmuch as hybridity is often seen as a key aspect of the Lat. Am. baroque (*el Barroco de Indias* or "baroque of the Indies"), the *Espejo de paciencia* is viewed as one of the earliest instances.

Of the poets writing in the 17th and 18th cs. in the Hispanic Caribbean, none enjoys the stature of the Mexican nun Sor Juana Inés de la Cruz or even of the Sp. poet in colonial Peru Juan del Valle y Caviedes. Although of little significance outside their country of origin and the search for beginnings, for the 17th c. one can mention the Puerto Rican *criollo* (creole) poet Francisco de Ayerra y Santa María (1630–1708) and the Seville-born Dominican Fernando Díez de Leiva (fl. 1582), and in the 18th c., the Puerto Rican satirist Miguel Cabrera, and the Cuban poets Juan Miguel Castro Palomino (1722–88), José Rodríguez Ucres (known as Capacho, d. before 1788), and Félix Veranés, among others. It is not until the late 18th and early 19th cs. that poets of relevance for the mod. period appear, foremost among them the neoclassical Cuban poet Manuel Zequeira (1764–1846), whose "Oda a la piña" (Ode to the Pineapple, 1808) is a testimony to the growing importance of local landscape and culture.

B. *The Nineteenth Century: Romanticism, Modernismo, and the Struggle for Independence.* While romanticism in Germany and England took root at the end of the 18th c. and the beginning of the 19th, it is a somewhat later phenomenon in France, Italy, and Spain. As a general rule, it appears even later in Lat. Am., coinciding generally with the end of the wars of independence and the early postwar years but stretching across the 19th c. Yet the major Hispanic Caribbean poet of the romantic period and one of the most important romantic poets in the Sp. lang., the Cuban José María Heredia (1803–39), was a poetic innovator who had already composed many of his major poems by the mid-1820s. Like many other Lat. Am. romantics, Heredia was inspired by revolutionary politics; he spent many years in exile for his political activities and commitment to Cuban independence. Heredia's poetry breaks with the balanced tone and measured pace of his neoclassical antecedents. Like many romantics, he represents nature as an overwhelming force that awes him and puts him in contact with the divine. Nature is bound as well to the native country and embodies the desire for independence and autochthony. Other major poets of the first wave of romanticism in Cuba include Gertrudis de Avellaneda (1814–73), better known as a dramatist and novelist (esp. for the antislavery novel *Sab* [1841], 11 years earlier than Harriet Beecher Stowe's *Uncle Tom's Cabin*); the mulatto poet Gabriel de la Concepción Valdés (known as Plácido, 1809–44), author of the romance "Jicotencatl" (1838) and a number of exceptional *letrillas* (incl. "La flor de la caña" [The Flower of the Sugar Cane], 1838), and José Jacinto Milanés (1814–63), a reclusive autodidact who was also a playwright. A second wave of romantic poets in Cuba around midcentury includes Rafael María de Mendive (1821–86), leader of an important *tertulia* (salon) and teacher of José Martí; Joaquín Lorenzo Luaces (1826–67); Juan Clemente Zenea (1832–71); and Luisa Pérez de Zambrana (1837–1922). Of these, Zenea is the most noteworthy, known both for his love poetry (esp. the elegiac "Fidelia," 1860) and his patriotic verse. His involvement in the movement for Cuban independence resulted in repeated exile and, finally, execution.

The romantic movement in Puerto Rico coincides largely with this second wave of Cuban romantics. The standout is José Gautier Benítez (1851–80), who died young of tuberculosis but managed to produce many of the best-known patriotic verses of 19th-c. Puerto Rico. Having studied in Toledo, he knew Sp. poetry well, esp. that of Gustavo Adolfo Bécquer. The object of his love, however, tends to be the island; nostalgia and longing are the dominant themes of his work. Many Puerto Rican poets of the second half of the century continued in the romantic mode and, like the Cuban romantics, were similarly involved in the island's movement for independence. Lola Rodríguez de Tío (1843–1924) is notable as the first Puerto Rican woman poet with an extensive body of work and a strong believer in independence. Author of the original lyrics to "La Boriqueña" (1868), the national anthem, she cultivated the stanza form called the *copla*. Francisco Gonzalo

Marín (known as Pachín, 1863–97) ended up as a fierce militant for independence, a friend and collaborator of José Martí, after beginning his political life working for a limited autonomy from Spain. His best-known poems (from *Romances* [1892], and *En la arena* [1898]) are clearly in the patriotic mode.

One of the most interesting features of 19th-c. Hispanic Caribbean lit. is the movement toward a local, nativist poetry, emphasizing nature, country folk, the indigenous peoples who lived in the region at the time of the conquest, and popular poetic forms such as the copla and the décima. This autochthonous, *criollista* poetry played a significant role in the construction of national cultures at a time when the islands of the Hispanic Caribbean remained, with the Philippines, Spain's last colonies. In Puerto Rico, Manuel Alonso's (1822–89) book *El gíbaro* (1849) is an early representative of *cuadros de costumbres* (literary sketches of customs) mixed with creolist poetry that adopts the perspective and dialect of the poor *campesinos*, while Daniel de Rivera's (1824–58?) "Agueynaba el bravo" (Agueynaba the Brave, 1854) expressed a fervor for latter-day political independence through the representation of a historical indigenous theme. Indeed, for José Fornaris (1827–90), creator of the *siboneyista* movement in Cuba, the theme of the indigenous inhabitants was appropriate at that moment because the early inhabitants of the island felt the same love of nature and suffered under Sp. oppression as did mod. Cubans. Fornaris's 1855 *Cantos del Siboney* was one of the most popular books of poetry of the time. However, the décimas of Juan Cristóbal Nápoles Fajardo (known as El Cucalambé, 1829–62?), published in his only book of poetry, *Rumores del Hórmigo* (Sounds of Hórmigo, 1856), are the culmination of the movement, inasmuch as they seemed to give voice to country folk (the *guajiros*) and quickly became part of popular culture. In the Dominican Republic, the country's major romantic poet, José Joaquín Pérez (1845–1900), wrote in this indigenous vein in his "Fantasías indígenas" (Indigenous Fantasies, 1877), while Juan Antonio Alix (1833–1918) was a more popular poet who cultivated the décima in the country dialect of the Cibao region.

In the Caribbean, as is often the case in Lat. Am., schools of poetry that in Europe tended to follow each other in rough succession and in reaction overlapped and coexisted. Thus, in the Dominican Republic, Salomé Ureña (1850–97) followed neoclassical precepts late into the 19th c. and is known for her well-constructed civic verse, incl. the hymn to tropical nature "La llegada del invierno" (The Arrival of Winter) and the elegiac "Ruinas." Influenced by the educator and philosopher Eugenio María de Hostos, she founded the first center of higher education for women on the island.

Associated most often internationally with the name of its most vocal exponent, the Nicaraguan Rubén Darío, the literary movement *modernismo* took the Hispanic world of letters by storm at the end of the 19th c.. Cuba boasts two of the earliest *modernista* writers in Martí (1853–95) and Julián del Casal (1863–93), and the first clearly modernista work, Martí's small volume of verse titled *Ismaelillo* (1882), which preceded Darío's *Azul . . .* by six years. Active on political and literary fronts, Martí was the major catalyst of the last Cuban War of Independence from Spain (1895–98) and would likely have become the first president of the Cuban Republic if he had not been killed early in the conflict. A writer in many genres, he published two volumes of poetry in his lifetime (*Ismaelillo* and *Versos sencillos* [Simple Verses], 1892) and left several mss. of poetry at his death (*Versos libres*, *Flores del destierro*, and uncollected verse), which were published posthumously. Martí also edited magazines such as the literary *La edad de oro*, a magazine for children, and *Patria*, a magazine dedicated to Cuban independence from Spain. Like most of the major modernista poets, Martí observed the important currents of Fr. poetry (Parnassianism and symbolism, in particular) as well as the classic Sp. trad., but as he argues in the important essay "Nuestra América" (1891), he emphatically rejected servile imitation of foreign models. Thus, while he embraced the Parnassian attention to form and love of color, he yoked it to the symbolist enthusiasm for the image and suggestion, while also underscoring the social involvement of the poet and the social relevance of verse. This unique combination of elements distances his poetry from the elitist aestheticism of Darío's *Azul . . .* and *Prosas profanas*, as well as from the verse of Casal, José Asunción Silva, Manuel Gutiérrez Nájera, and the other early modernistas.

While *Ismaelillo* consecrated Martí as one of the leading voices of the new poetry, it was the *Versos sencillos* that garnered the respect and adulation of a more general public, with the apparent simplicity of its themes—nature, friendship, sincerity—and a traditional octosyllable. However, the volume only seems simple. The attention to form results at times in a complex mirroring of signifier and signified, and the book is filled with startling, multivalent images. Between the two, highly polished books that Martí published, he wrote the poems he called his *Versos libres* (Free Verse, 1882), first published posthumously in 1913. These are generally written in what he called "hirsute hendecasyllables," and like most hendecasyllabic poetry in Sp., they seem more sonorous and philosophically weighty than the shorter verse forms. One of Martí's most personal, expressionistic works, the book emphasizes above all a certain disorderly authenticity of emotion and form, heralding the works of 20th-c. poets like Neruda. Martí is clearly the most important poet and writer of the Hispanic Caribbean in the 19th c. and an influence on poets and political thinkers to the present day.

The other major modernista poet of the region is Casal, also Cuban but very different from Martí. Whereas Martí led a political life from a young age and entered into conflicts with the Sp. colonial authorities that led to prison, exile, and a peripatetic existence, Casal led a literary and sedentary city life, leaving Havana only for one brief trip to Spain. Collaborator in a number of literary and popular magazines (above all, *La Habana Elegante* and the popular *La Caricatura*), Casal published three books of poetry: *Hojas al viento* (Leaves to the Wind, 1890), *Nieve* (Snow, 1891), and *Bustos y rimas* (Busts and Rhymes, 1893). This last work was published after his early death from tuberculosis, just short of his 30th birthday. Influenced greatly by Charles Baudelaire and the Fr. Parnassians, enthralled by the paintings of Gustave Moreau that he recreated in a series of ten sonnets ("Mi museo ideal," My Ideal Museum), Casal echoes these models but transforms them into something new. Firmly within the aestheticist vein of modernismo and apparently distanced from the sociopolitical realities of his time, he has too often been contrasted with a "virile," socially engaged Martí and discounted as artificial, effete, and somehow less Cuban (by Vitier, among many others). Recently critics and younger Cuban poets have analyzed Casal through the lens of queer theory and deconstructed the Martí/Casal dichotomy (Montero, Morán), creating a much richer picture of this fine poet. Bonifacio Byrne (1861–1936) is Cuba's third modernista and author of the immensely popular patriotic poem "Mi bandera" (My Flag, 1901).

Modernismo arrived late in Puerto Rico, in part because of the Sp.-Am. War of 1898 but had strong adherents in José de Diego (1866–1918), Virgilio Dávila (1869–1943), and above all Luis Lloréns Torres (1876–1944). In tune with the patriotic, *mundonovista* strain of the later Darío, these poets adopted the stylistic innovations of the modernistas to exalt their native land (see esp. Lloréns Torres's 1913 poem "Canción de las Antillas"). In reaction to the U.S. invasion of 1898, they show a strong desire to defend what they perceive to be the essences of Puerto Ricanness. Reflecting their generally patrician roots, they cultivate a strong Hispanophilia in their work, and the theme of the *jíbaro* (country dweller supposedly of white, Hispanic ancestry) recurs. In the Dominican Republic, modernismo is also belated and dictates the style of poets such as Fabio Fiallo (1866–1942) and Enrique Henríquez (1859–1940), but the major figure at the turn of the 20th c. is Gastón Fernando Deligne (1861–1913), a psychological realist in the mode of the Sp. poet Ramón de Campoamor. His poem "Ololoi" (1907) is a stirring meditation on the conflict between liberty and the oppression of dictatorship.

C. ***The Twentieth Century and Beyond.*** While two important poets, Regino E. Boti (1878–1958) and José Manuel Poveda (1888–1926), were active in the first decades of the First Cuban Republic, these were quiet times for poetry. Boti in particular matures in his style from the modernismo of his first book, *Arabescos mentales* (Mental Arabesques, 1913), through his most coherent collection, *El mar y la montaña* (The Sea and the Mountains, 1921), to the avant-garde verses of *Kodak-Ensueño* (Kodak Daydream, 1928) and *Kindergarten* (1930). The poetic scene gained complexity during the difficult 1920s, with the introduction of the avant-garde at a time of increased political instability, economic troubles, and the ferment of student and workers' movements. The *Grupo Minorista*, incl. the painter Eduardo Abela, the future novelist Alejo Carpentier, the essayists Jorge Mañach and Juan Marinello, and the poets José Zacarías Tallet (1893–1989) and Rubén Martínez Villena (1899–1934), was primarily responsible for the introduction of the avant-garde in Cuba; a number of these figures edited the major avant-garde jour. *Revista de Avance* (1927–30). The experimental avant-garde was short lived, however, and was quickly replaced by two major trends: social poetry with early contributions from Felipe Pichardo Moya (1892–1957), Agustín Acosta (1886–1979), and Regino Pedroso (1896–1983; "Salutación fraterna al taller mecánico" [Fraternal Salutation to the Garage], 1927); and poetry inspired by the theories of Henri Bremond and exemplified most clearly by the poetry of Mariano Brull (1891–1956; *Poemas en menguante* [Waning Poems], 1928, and *Solo de rosa* [Only Rose], 1941), Eugenio Florit (1903–99; *Trópico*, 1930; and *Doble acento* [Double Accent], 1937), and Emilio Ballagas (1908–54; *Júbilo y fuga* [Joy and Flight], 1931; and *Sabor eterno* [Eternal Taste], 1939). Brull is known for his focus on sound, esp. the *jitanjáfora*, a playful use of nonsemantic sounds to achieve rhythmic effects in poetry, while Ballagas was one of the earliest practitioners of literary *afrocubanismo*.

The avant-garde is poorly represented in the Dominican Republic, although some critics (Gutiérrez) have alleged that Vigil Díaz's (1880–1961) "movement" *vedrinismo*, announced in 1912, preceded Vicente Huidobro's creationism by a few years. Lacking a true manifesto and with ultimately only two adherents, vedrinismo is responsible for the introduction of free verse into Dominican poetry, with Díaz's 1917 poem "Arabesco." The most important Dominican movement of the 1920s—Domingo Moreno Jimenes (1894–1986), Rafael Augusto Zorrilla (1892–1937), and Andrés Aveliño's (1900–74) *Postumismo*—had an ambiguous relationship with the avant-garde. Intent on creating a more mod. and more Dominican poetry (a reaction in part to the U.S. occupation of the island from 1916 to 1924), they consciously broke with what they considered an outmoded, Eurocentric national trad., cultivating free verse and opening poetic lang. to a wider register. In this rupture with trad., they were clearly avant-garde, although they programmatically rejected the *acrobacia azul* (blue acrobatics) of the more experimental "isms" (*Manifiesto postumista*), as well as the masterworks of the Western trad. Moreno Jimenes (1894–1986) was the undisputed leader of the group. His poetry is avowedly colloquial and populist, although his most moving works are profoundly personal poems that address the theme of death ("Poema de la hija reintegrada" [Poem for the Reintegrated Daughter], 1934).

In Puerto Rico, the avant-garde found early adherents in two movements. The first, *Diepalismo*, launched in 1921, was an ephemeral movement led by its only two practitioners, José I. de Diego Padró (1899–1974) and Luis Palés Matos (1898–1959), who privileged onomatopoeia as the basis for radically new verse. (The name of the group is a combination of the patronymics of the two poets.) The other avant-garde movement, of more lasting consequence, took the bombastic title of *El atalaya de los dioses* (Watchtower of the Gods) and was led from 1928 on by the gifted poet and radical nationalist Clemente Soto Vélez (1905–93). Intent on breaking with a "mummified" trad., these poets rebelled against the remnants of modernismo as well as realism and academic poetry. Like many of the other *atalayistas*, Soto Vélez was involved early on in the militant nationalist movement led by Pedro Albizu Campos and finally settled in New York. His later works, *Abrazo interno* (Internal Embrace, 1954), *Árboles* (Trees, 1955), *Caballo de palo* (Wooden Horse, 1959), and *La tierra prometida* (Promised Land, 1979), continued to engage in ling. experimentalism and to exploit the surreal images of the avant-garde.

Two other poets who came of age poetically among the avant-garde in the 1910s and 1920s deserve mention. Evaristo Ribera Chevremont (1896–1976) was not affiliated with any movement but early on was much influenced by the reigning modernista movement and the Hispanophilia of writers such as Lloréns Torres. After five years in Spain, where he was in direct contact with ultraism and Huidobro's creationism, he returned to the island as an ardent supporter of the avant-garde. He is widely credited with introducing free verse to the national poetry and, with a career spanning six decades, is one of the most prolific of Puerto Rican poets. Juan Antonio Corretjer (1908–85), a fellow member of the Atalaya group, spent five years in a U.S. prison for his work with Albizu Campos's Nationalist Party. Committed at first to the nationalist project and later to the creation of a socialist state, his poetry is a "telluric *neocriollismo*" that combines the Lat. Americanism of the late Darío with the epic ambition of Lloréns Torres (Márquez). The avant-garde is not just a historically delimited movement but a rupturalist, modernizing attitude that can recur at any moment. José María Lima (1934–2009) of the Generation of the 1960s and Joserramón Melendes (b. 1952) of the Generation of the 1970s both exemplify an experimentalist, avant-garde mode.

The Afro-Caribbean poetic movement called *negrismo*, *poesía negra*, *poesía afroantillana*, or in Cuba, *afrocubanismo* constitutes one of the most significant devels. in 20th-c. Lat. Am. poetry. Incl. poetry both about and by Afro-Caribbeans, it comes into being in the mid-1920s and culminates in the 1930s and 1940s. It is an essential part of a regionalist vein of avant-garde poetry, with analogues in Federico García Lorca's Andalusian gypsy ballads and Jorge Luis Borges's early *ultraísta* verse, and it took energy from parallel movements in the U.S. (the Harlem Ren.) and Eur. interest in the "primitive" and all things Af. Palés Matos began publishing his "black" poems in literary magazines in 1925, although they were not collected until the much later publication of his *Tuntún de pasa y grifería: Poesía afroantillana* (Tomtom of Kinky Hair and Black Things: Afro-Antillean Poetry, 1937). Like Ballagas, Ramón Guirao (1908–49), and some of the early cultivators of *afrocubanista* poetry in Cuba, Palés Matos was white and has been criticized by some as creating stereotypical images of Afro-Caribbean peoples. Nevertheless, his poetry has been immensely popular in Puerto Rico and elsewhere; rhythmic and onomatopoeic, it is esp. apt for recitation or declamation. This poetry responds to a vision of the nation as syncretic and transcultural and was daring at the time in light of the racist attitudes of many of the creole elite who saw the essence of Puerto Ricanness in the island's Hispanic—i.e., not Af.—heritage (Pedreira), when that cultural complex was experiencing the disintegrating influence of an overwhelming U.S. economic and political imperialism. Recent critics have done much to clarify Palés's historical specificity and his ludic irony and to give a balanced appreciation of his work beyond the *poesía afroantillana* (López Baralt, Ríos Avila).

In Cuba, Afro-Cuban poets (Plácido and Manzano [1797–1854], in particular) had been publishing since the romantic period, but afrocubanismo begins with the publication of Ramón Guirao's poem "Bailadora de rumba" (Rumba Dancer) in early 1928, followed soon after by Tallet's "La rumba." The next decade saw a flood of poems on Afro-Cuban themes, by both black and white poets. The most important and enduring of these was Nicolás Guillén (1902–89), whose early collections adapted the Afro-Cuban syncretic musical form of the "son" to literary language. His *Motivos de son* (Motifs from the "Son," 1930), *Sóngoro cosongo* (1931), and *West Indies, Ltd.* (1934) are clearly within the afrocubanista vein. By Guillén's second book, he is already proclaiming *mulatez* or the mixing of black and white as the essential process forming Cuban national culture, challenging the widely accepted view of national culture as rooted in the Hispanic and symbolized by the country folk or guajiros. This poetry signals the beginning of a sea change in race relations and notions of national belonging. Although afrocubanismo as a literary movement was largely over by the late 1930s, Guillén continued to publish and evolve as a poet. His poetry shows a sophisticated understanding of the trad. and possibilities of Sp. verse forms, from the Afro-Cuban *son* to the alexandrine sonnet to elegies, ballads, and all the way to the postmod. pastiche. He links this lyrical skill to an authentic concern for social justice, racial equality, and historical analysis, which first alienated him from the dictatorial Batista regime and later made him a favorite of the Cuban Revolution. His poetry, however, has enduring importance, above and beyond any political affiliation.

At this time, the Dominican Republic was suffering under the dictatorship of one of the most brutal and long-lived regimes in Lat. Am., that of Rafael Leónidas Trujillo (1930–61). Many of the major poets in the post-avant-garde period wrote some of their most important works in exile, incl. two that align with the poesía negra, Manuel del Cabral (1907–99) and Tomás Hernández Franco (1904–52). Del Cabral is one of the towering figures of 20th-c. Dominican poetry and has often been compared to the major figures of the Lat. Am. avant-garde such as César Vallejo, Neruda, Huidobro, and Guillén. His *Ocho poemas negros* (Eight Black Poems, 1935) and *Trópico negro* (1941) were signal contributions to the devel. of Dominican negrismo, although it is his book centered on the figure of the *campesino* from the Cibao region, *Compadre Mon* (1942), that has garnered the most critical attention. Del Cabral is a protean poet with a plethora of styles and subject matter, incl. the later devel. of a deep metaphysical strain (esp. in *Los huéspedes secretos* [Secret Guests], 1950) and a strong anti-imperialist stance (*La isla ofendida* [The Offended Island], 1965). Franco is known primarily for the mythical epic *Yelidá* (1942), where he insists on the superiority of racial mixing embodied in a sensual *mulata* born of a Norwegian expatriate and a Haitian woman.

In the Cuba of the latter half of the 1930s, as the afrocubanismo movement was losing momentum, a singular poet, José Lezama Lima (1910–76), transformed the poetic scene with the publication of his first poem, *Muerte de Narciso* (Death of Narcissus, 1937). Stimulated by his readings in the Sp. Golden Age poets but forging its own style, Lezama Lima's poetry baffled critics with its difficulty, its artifice, and its seeming distance from the sociopolitical realities of the time. He followed this first publication with four more books of poetry over the next four decades: *Enemigo rumor* (Enemy Rumor, 1941), *Aventuras sigilosas* (Stealthy Adventures, 1945), *La fijeza* (Fixity, 1949), and *Dador* (Giver, 1960). His final collection, *Fragmentos a su imán* (Fragments to Their Magnet), was published posthumously in 1977. Lezama Lima often takes other works of art as his starting point; his work in general is densely allusive and assimilative. Some of his best poems ("Rapsodia para el mulo" [Rhapsody for the Mule], "Pensamientos en La Habana" [Thoughts in Havana]) have much to say about Cuban national identity and the neocolonial dynamics of the time. While showing a penchant for expansive free verse, he also exploited a variety of poetic forms (the prose poem, the sonnet, the décima) over the course of his career, and although he is largely faithful to the neobaroque difficulty he first embraced in *Muerte de Narciso*, the later, posthumous poems are more luminous and personal. Lezama Lima became more known outside Cuba in the 1960s, after the publication of his monumental novel *Paradiso* (1966). In fact, there is no clear line between his poetic production and his prose, and *Paradiso* is considered by many to be the clearest exposition of the poetic system developed in his poetry and his rich body of essays. Lezama Lima's importance to Cuban and Latin Am. lit. is based in part on his own production and in part on his role as ed. of a series of influential literary jours.; the most important of these was *Orígenes* (1944–56). This jour. was the focal point for a group of writers, artists, musicians, and critics, incl. the poets Virgilio Piñera (1912–79), Cintio Vitier (1921–2009), Eliseo Diego (1920–94), Fina García Marruz (b. 1923), and Gastón Baquero (1914–97). Each of these *Origenistas* is an important figure in his or her own right. Of these, Piñera, a reluctant and confrontational member of the group, is best known as a novelist, short-story writer, and dramatist, although his important long poem *La isla en peso* (The Whole Island, 1943) bears comparison to high points of Caribbean poetry such as Césaire's *Cahier d'un retour au pays natal* and Del Cabral's *Compadre Mon* in its negative vision of an asphyxiating island life (Anderson). After Lezama Lima, Diego is perhaps the most gifted poet, deservedly well-known outside Cuba for collections such as *En la Calzada de Jesús del Monte* (On Jesús del Monte Avenue, 1949), *Por los extraños pueblos* (Through Strange Towns, 1958), *Muestrario del mundo o Libro de las maravillas de Boloña* (Showcase of the World or Book of the Wonders of Boloña, 1968), and *Los días de tu vida* (The Days of Your Life, 1977).

In the late 1950s and after the triumph of the Cuban Revolution in 1959, the Origenista poets—esp. Lezama Lima—were roundly criticized for their supposed escapism and lack of social concern. Younger poets gathered around the polemical figure of Piñera and a series of jours. that took the place of *Orígenes* as major venues for Cuban poetry and lit. crit. (*Ciclón*, *Lunes de Revolución*). The Cuban Revolution in general had a profound impact on the state of poetry. On the one hand, there was initially a widespread enthusiasm for democratization and social justice (incl. educational reform and a literacy campaign), and poetry and art in general were seen by many as tools in this collective project. On the other hand, the cultural politics of the Castro regime favored direct communication with the masses and support of the revolutionary agenda, and this support became more and more compulsory over the course of the first two decades after 1959. As a result, the group of poets known as the Generation of the 1950s, as well as younger poets that came of age in the 1960s and 1970s, shared a colloquial diction and conversational tone. Of this earlier generation, Roberto Fernández Retamar (b. 1930) stands out for his poetry (*Con las mismas manos, 1949–1962* [With These Same Hands] and *Hemos construido una alegría olvidada, 1949–1988* [We Have Built a Forgotten Joy], among many other volumes), influential essays (esp. "Calibán," 1971), and the direction of the important cultural magazine *Casa de las Américas*.

Among poets who began publishing in the 1960s, Heberto Padilla (1932–2000) and Nancy Morejón (b. 1944) have received the most critical attention. Padilla, at first an ardent supporter of the revolution whose early volume *El justo tiempo humano* (A Just Human Time, 1962) has much in common with Retamar's poetry and intellectual stance, arrived at a much more critical attitude in his 1968 *Fuera del juego* (Out of the Game), a complex, ironic collection that won an important prize that year in Cuba but catapulted Padilla into conflict with the regime. Three years later, he was detained for supposedly counterrevolutionary activities, prompting a firestorm of criticism of the Cuban government by prominent Lat. Am. and Eur. intellectuals, many of whom had previously been positive toward the revolution. Ultimately released from prison after a public self-criticism, Padilla was incessantly watched in the years that followed and allowed to leave the island for the U.S. only in 1980. In the U.S., he published two bilingual collections, *Legacies* (1982) and *A Fountain, a House of Stone* (1991), which confirmed his status as a strong poet in the conversational mode. Morejón follows in a line of important Cuban women poets such as García Marruz and Dulce María Loynaz (1902–97), but her closest model is Guillén. Of Afro-Cuban descent, Morejón began publishing after the revolution, and she has remained faithful to its ideals over the years. Author of the much anthologized poems "Mujer negra" (Black Woman) and "Amo a mi amo" (I Love My Owner), she has given women of Afro-Cuban ancestry a critical visibility they lacked in the past. Three other poets of the era 1959–80 deserve mention, although they have published the majority of their work outside the island: Severo Sarduy (1937–93), José Kozer (b. 1940), and Reinaldo Arenas (1943–90). The first two are consummate practitioners of the neobaroque mode initiated by Lezama Lima. Although known primarily as a novelist, Sarduy in his finely crafted poetry adopts the stanzaic forms and the diction of the baroque while referring to novel themes such as homosexual love or the gods of the Cuban syncretic religion, Santería. Kozer's poetry, neobaroque in its complexity, is a moving testimony to his Cuban-Jewish roots. Arenas is also primarily a novelist, but his epic poem "El central" is both daringly experimental in form and radical in its bitter denunciation of oppression.

During the 1940s in the Dominican Republic, a group emerged which shared some characteristics with the Cuban Origenistas, although lacking poets of the stature of Lezama Lima, Piñera, or Diego. This is the *Poesía sorprendida* (Surprised Poetry) group, which coalesced around the jour. of the same name, published 1943–47, and which programmatically left behind the traditional Dominican emphasis on autochthony. Openly assimilative, avowedly universalist, these poets embraced a wide range of world lit. The most important members of the group were Franklin Mieses Burgos (1907–76), Aída Cartagena Portalatín (1918–94), Freddy Gatón Arce (1920–94), Manuel Rueda (1921–99), and Antonio Fernández Spencer (1922–95), many of whom were quite prolific (esp. Gatón Arce, the most surrealist of these). Given the repressive nature of the Trujillo government, most of these poets adopted an oblique style and avoided direct criticism of Dominican society or the regime. Several other important Dominican poets active at this time did not affiliate with the sorprendida group, incl. the aforementioned del Cabral and Hernández Franco as well as Héctor Incháustegui Cabral (1912–79) and Pedro Mir (1913–2000). All these are social poets in the best sense of the term. Incháustegui Cabral's best-known collection is *Poemas de una sola angustia* (Poems of a Single Anguish, 1940), in which he took on the cause of the poor and powerless and leveled a rather direct critique at the Trujillo regime. When he was not punished for this by the dictator, he lost faith in the power of poetry to effect political change; he later became one of the few intellectuals who collaborated actively in the government. Mir, on the other hand, was consistent in his critique of Dominican elites and the Trujillo dictatorship, at the price of exile. An identification with poor workers and a spirited denunciation of U.S. imperialism is evident in most of his poetry. Recognized abroad as one of the most important voices of the Hispanic Caribbean, he gains his reputation primarily from *Hay un país en el mundo* (There Is a Country in the World, 1949) and the *Contracanto a Walt Whitman* (1952). The next few generations, the poets of the 1960s and the postwar group, were caught up in the political turmoil of that eventful decade. Their poetry is more often more political than literary. The exceptions are Alexis Gómez Rosa (b. 1950) and Cayo Claudio Espinal (b. 1955), both of whom have matured into exceptional poets unafraid of experimentation.

While Puerto Rico had no group comparable to Cuba's Orígenes or the Dominican Republic's Poesía sorprendida from the late 1930s to the 1950s, it produced two singular poets, Francisco Matos Paoli (1915–2000) and Julia de Burgos (1914–53). Matos Paoli's prolific work extends from the 1930s to the mid-1990s and shows a keen appreciation for Sp. Golden Age poets and the Generation of 1927 (esp. Jorge Guillén), along with Mallarmé and the Fr. symbolists. An ardent nationalist, he was arrested for his support of the 1950 uprising and sentenced to 30 years of prison in San Juan, although he was released in 1955 after a mental breakdown in long periods of solitary confinement. His work is characterized by its adherence to the precepts of pure poetry and its hermeticism. De Burgos launched her career in 1937 with *Poemas exactos a mí misma* (Exact Poems to Myself), followed by *Poema en veinte surcos* (Poem in Twenty Furrows, 1938) and *Canción de la vida sencilla* (Song of the Simple Life, 1939). In the early 1940s, she completed *El mar y tú* (The Sea and You), although it was not published until 1954, a year after her early death in poverty in New York from alcoholism, depression, and illness. Thoroughly nationalist, De Burgos's most famous poems (such as "Río Grande de Loíza") express a yearning for a fusion with the island landscape, esp. the waters of rivers and sea, a theme that has made her quite popular. Her later verse anticipates the alienation of the Latino immigrant in the impersonal cities of the U.S. and, in its nonconformism, prepares for the feminist poets of the 1960s and 1970s such as Rosario Ferré (1938–2016) and Olga Nolla (1938–2001), as well as the younger Vanessa Droz (b. 1952), all of whom continued to publish important collections into the late 1990s and beyond. Of the same generation as Droz, Manuel Ramos Otero (1948–90) was a complex, iconoclastic writer who deserves to be better known outside the island. Writing from an openly gay perspective, he engages the Sp. baroque trad. in expressionist meditations on death and disease (notably the AIDS epidemic) in his posthumous *Invitación al polvo* (Invitation to Dust, 1991). José Luis Vega (b. 1948), and Aurea María Sotomayor (b. 1951), also of this generation, are important critics as well as poets. Sotomayor's *Diseño del ala* (Wing Design, 2005) confirms her as a major voice in Caribbean poetry more generally.

Of the younger poets, the Cuban Generation of the 1980s has several standouts, incl. Juan Carlos Flores (b. 1962), Damaris Calderón (b. 1967), Víctor Fowler Calzada (b. 1960), and Antonio José Ponte (b. 1964), among others; several of these are also noted essayists. Reina María Rodríguez (b. 1952) and Francisco Morán (b. 1952), although older than this group, have been close fellow travelers and unifying figures. These writers have not shied away from hermetic lang., eroticism, and philosophical questions and have actively engaged an antihegemonic, less obviously political strand of the Cuban poetic trad. (Julián del Casal, Lezama Lima, and Virgilio Piñera, as opposed to Martí and Guillén). In Puerto Rico, the same generation has resistantly engaged the postmod., recognizing the failure of the dreams of independence and of socialism, while also seeing the pitfalls of neoliberalism (Martínez-Márquez and Cancel). The most important figures here are Rafael Acevedo (b. 1960), Eduardo Lalo (b. 1960), and Mayra Santos Febres (b. 1966). Lalo's postmod. cultural critiques (*Dónde* [Where], 2005), combining photography and essay, add to the interest in this multifaceted artist. The dominant voice of the Generation of the 1980s in the Dominican Republic is José Mármol (b. 1960), poet and essayist, whose training as a philosopher is apparent in prose poems that embrace both ling. and conceptual difficulty.

See AFRICA, POETRY OF; AFRICAN AMERICAN POETRY; FRANCE, POETRY OF; INDIGENOUS AMERICAS, POETRY OF THE; SPAIN, POETRY OF; SPANISH AMERICA, POETRY OF.

■ **Dutch**. *Anthologies: Schwarzer Orpheus*, ed. J. Jahn (1954); *Creole Drum*, ed. J. Voorhoeve and U. M. Lichtveld (1975); *Cosecha Arubiano*, ed. F. Booi et al. (1983); *Spiegel van de Surinaamse poezie*, ed. M. van Kempen (1995); "Special Issue: Caribbean Literature from Suriname, the Netherlands Antilles, Aruba, and the Netherlands," *Callaloo* 21 (1998); *Literatura en español en Curazao al cambio del siglo: En busca de textos desconocidos de la segunda mitad del siglo XIX y de las primeras décadas del siglo XX*, ed. L. Echteld (1999); *Nieuwe oogst*, ed. L. van Mulier (2002). ***Criticism and History***: A. G. Broek, *The Rise of a Caribbean Island's Literature* (1990); F. R. Jones, "A Leak in the Silence: The Poetry of Hans Faverey"; M. van Kempen, "Vernacular Literature in Suriname"; and I. van Putte-de Windt, "Caribbean Poetry in Papiamentu," *Callaloo* 21 (1998); A. J. Arnold, *A History of Literature in the Caribbean*, v. 2 (2001)—esp. T. Damsteegt, "East Indian Surinamese Poetry and Its Languages"; V. February, "The Surinamese Muse: Reflections on Poetry"; and J. J. Oversteegen, "Strategies and Stratagems of Some Dutch-Antillean Writers"; I. Phaf-Rheinberger, "The Crystalline Essence of 'Dutch' Caribbean Literatures," *Review* 74 (2007).

■ **English**. *Criticism and History*: R. Abrahams, *The Man-of-Words in the West Indies*

(1983); L. Brown, *West Indian Poetry* (1984); P. A. Roberts, *West Indians and Their Language* (1988); A. Benitez Rojo, *The Repeating Island: The Caribbean and the Postmodern Perspective*, trans. J. E. Maranis (1992); E. Chamberlin, *Come Back to Me My Language* (1993); *Dictionary of Caribbean English Usage*, ed. S.R.R. Allsopp (1997); L. Breiner, *An Introduction to West Indian Poetry* (1998); E. A. Williams, *Anglophone Caribbean Poetry, 1970–2001* (2002)—annotated bibl. ***Anthologies in English***: E. K. Brathwaite, *The Arrivants* (1973); *Penguin Book of Caribbean Verse in English*, ed. P. Burnett (1986).

■ **French**. M. Condé, *La Poesie Antillaise* (1977); J. M. Dash, *Literature and Ideology in Haiti* (1981); G. Gouraige, *Littérature et société en Haiti* (1987); J. M. Dash, "Engagement, Exile and Errance: Some Trends in Haitian Poetry, 1946–1986," *Callaloo* 15 (1992); *A History of Literature in the Caribbean*, v. 1, *Francophone and Hispanophone Regions*, ed. A. James Arnold (1994); M. Gallagher, "Contemporary French Caribbean Poetry: The Poetics of Reference," *Forum of Modern Language Studies* 45 (2004).

■ **Spanish**. ***Anthologies***: *Versiones dominicanas de romances españoles*, ed. E. Garrido (1946); *Antología de la poesía cubana*, ed. J. Lezama Lima, (1965); *Lecturas puertorriqueñas: Poesía*, ed. M. Arce de Vazquez, L. Gallego, L. de Arrigoitia (1968); *Poesía criollista y siboneísta*, ed. J. Orta Ruíz (1976); *La Generación de los años 50*, ed. L. Suardíaz and D. Cherición (1984); *Antología de la literatura dominicana*, ed. J. Alcántara Almánzar (1988); *Publicaciones y opiniones de La Poesía Sorprendida* (1988); *Antología de poesía puertorriqueña*, ed. R. A. Moreira (1992); *Para entendernos: inventario poético puertorriqueño: Siglos XIX y XX*, ed. E. Barradas (1992); *Antología histórica de la poesía dominicana del siglo XX, 1912–1995*, ed. F. Gutiérrez (1998); *El límite volcado: Antología de la Generación de Poetas de los Ochenta*, ed. A. Martínez-Márquez and M. R. Cancel (2000); *La casa se mueve: Antología de la nueva poesía cubana*, ed. A. Luque and J. Aguado (2000); *Poesía cubana de la colonia*, ed. S. Arias (2002); *Poesía cubana del siglo XX*, ed. J. J. Barquet and N. Codina (2002); *Puerto Rican Poetry*, ed. and trans. R. Márquez (2007). ***Criticism and History***: M. Menéndez y Pelayo, *Antología de poetas hispano-americanos*, v. 1–4 (1894); A. S. Pedreira, *Insularismo: Ensayos de interpretación puertorriqueña* (1934); C. F. Pérez, *Evolución poética dominicana* (1956); C. Vitier, *Lo cubano en la poesia* (1958); P. Henríquez Ureña, "La cultura y las letras coloniales en Santo Domingo," *Obra Critica*, ed. E. S. Speratti Piñero (1960); I. A. Schulman and M. P. González, *Martí, Darío y el modernismo* (1969); R. Friol, *Suite para Juan Francisco Manzano* (1977); J. Alcántara Almánzar, *Estudios de poesía dominicana* (1979); E. Saínz, *Silvestre De Balboa y la literatura cubana* (1982); Instituto de Literatura y Lingüística de la Academia de Ciencias de Cuba, *Diccionario de la literatura cubana* (1984); C. Vitier, *Crítica cubana* (1988); W. Luis, *Literary Bondage: Slavery in Cuban Narrative* (1990); V. Kutzinski, *Against the American Grain: Myth and History in William Carlos Williams, Jay Wright, and Nicolás Guillén* (1987); and *Sugar's Secrets: Race and the Erotics of Cuban Nationalism* (1993); R. González Echevarría, *Celestina's Brood: Continuities of the Baroque in Spanish and Latin American Literatures* (1993); O. Montero, *Erotismo y representación en Julián del Casal* (1993); *The Cambridge History of Latin American Literature*, ed. R. González Echevarría and E. Pupo-Walker, 2 v. (1996)—esp. A. Bush, "Lyric Poetry of the Eighteenth and Nineteenth Centuries," v. 1; and J. Quiroga, "Spanish American Poetry from 1922 to 1975," v. 2; B. A. Heller, *Assimilation/Generation/Resurrection: Contrapuntal Readings in the Poetry of José Lezama Lima* (1997); M. López Baralt, *El barco en la botella: La poesía de Luis Palés Matos* (1997); R. Ríos Avila, "Hacia Palés," *La raza cómica del sujeto en Puerto Rico* (2002); E. Bejel, "Poetry," *A History of Literature in the Caribbean: Hispanic and Francophone Regions*, ed. A. J. Arnold, v. 1 (2004); T. F. Anderson, *Everything in Its Place: The Life and Works of Virgilio Piñera* (2006); M. Arnedo-Gómez, *Writing Rumba: The Afrocubanista Movement in Poetry* (2006); F. Morán, *Julián Del Casal o los pliegues del deseo* (2008).

I. Phaf-Rheinberger (Dutch); L. A. Breiner (Eng.); M. Dash (Fr.); B. A. Heller (Sp.)

CATALAN POETRY. *Catalan* is the common name for the lang. spoken in Catalonia, Valencia, and the Balearic Islands. The unique hist. of the region meant that Catalan was not in continuous literary use: Occitan and Catalan were the langs. of poetry in the Middle Ages, Castilian during the phase of Sp. ascendancy, and Catalan again since romanticism, when Catalan poetry experienced a revival. The *Renaixença* (Rebirth) movement amplified the topics of romanticism and brought about an extraordinary literary period interrupted only by the dictatorship of Francisco Franco in Spain. During the years of political and cultural repression (1939–75), poetry played a prominent role in the preservation of Catalan lang. This role created a unique conflict between ideological and aesthetic objectives, resulting in an unbalanced literary trad. that promoted national survival to the detriment of artistic devel.

The Middle Ages left a rich legacy of poets and texts. *Ensenhamen*, written before 1160 in Occitan by Guerau de Cabrera (d. ca. 1160), contains a full catalog of cl. and Fr. literary topics; such long poetic narratives and brief popular songs were predominant at the time. In the 13th c., amatory and devotional songs were common among preserved texts, such as "Epístola farcida de Sant Esteve," "Plany de Maria Aujats senyors . . . ," and Escolania de Montserrat's "Virolai." When King Alfons I inherited Provença in 1166, he became a strong defender of the poetic use of Occitan, as in Raimon Vidal de Besalú's (1190–1213) *Razos de trobar*, the first poetic grammar and rhetorical treatise in any Romance lang. Thus, the first Catalan poems were written in Occitan, which influenced the subject matter, style, and versification of the genre until the 15th c. Catalan authors contributed to the troubadour trad., with spectacular poems written according to the *trobar leu* (Guillem de Berguedà, 1138–96) or *trobar ric* (Cerverí de Girona, fl. 1259–85) conventions.

In the early 13th c., Ramon Llull (1232–1315), considered the founder of Catalan literary prose, dealt with the diffusion of the Christian faith. His most notable contribution to poetry is *Libre d'Amic e Amat* (The Book of the Friend and His Beloved), a series of 365 mystical prose poems. As in France, this period generated remarkable examples of romances written in verse: works by Raimon Vidal de Besalú; *Blandín de Cornualla* and *Salut d'amor* (both anonymous); and in the 14th c., works by Guillem de Torroella (d. ca. 1348), such as the Arthurian *Faula*. This century also saw narrative poems by Pere (ca. 1336–1413) and Jaume March (ca. 1335–1410), and *Fraire de Joi e sor de Plaser*, the anonymous Catalan version of Sleeping Beauty. Francesc de la Via (ca. 1380–1445) wrote several court accounts in the style of fabliaux, such as *Llibre de Fra Bernat*, and Bernat Serradell (ca. 1375–1445) went beyond this model in *Testament d'En Bernat Serradell*.

In the 14th and 15th cs., Catalan poetry was in full bloom: liberated from their Occitan origins, new writers gained popularity by employing It. Petrarchan models. Nevertheless, the influence of Occitan poetry can still be found in authors from Majorca and northern Catalonia, whose works were collected in a Ripoll *cançoneret* after 1346. Following the example of the Tolosa poetical school, in 1393 King Joan I created the Consistori de la Gaia Ciència in Barcelona. Under the influence of this somewhat remote model, two important books were written in the late 14th c.: *Llibre de concordances* by March and *Torsimany* (incl. a rhyme dictionary) by Lluís d'Averçó (1350–1412). The It. Ren. illuminated the verse of minor poets such as Gilabert de Pròxida (d. 1405), Pere de Queralt (d. 1408), and Melcior de Gualbes (d. ca. 1400). Andreu Febrer's (1375–1444) poetry still followed troubadour models, but he was also the author of an excellent verse trans. of Dante's *Divine Comedy* into Catalan. Overcoming the durable influence of troubadour poetry, in the 15th c. two major poets started writing. Jordi de Sant Jordi (ca. 1390–1424) expressed personal sorrow while in captivity. After 1425, Ausiàs Marc (or March; 1400?–59), based in Valencia but familiar with It. models, wrote his collection of more than 100 poems. Transcending *Dolce stil nuovo* and Petrarchism, he explored the doubts surrounding love and death. Joan Roíç de Corella (ca. 1430–90) wrote poems of visual and imaginative power about sensual and divine love. He was the first to introduce into Catalan poetics the It. hendecasyllable. In the midst of civil war (1462–72), poetry became a tool for expressing ideological and political commitments. Joan Berenguer de Masdovelles (d. 1476) wrote long poems in favor of Joan II. Minor poets of the period include Bernat Hug de Rocabertí (ca. 1420–85), Pere de Torroella (d. 1475), and the politician Romeu Llull (1439–96). In prosperous Valencia, among figures such as Bernat Fenollar (1438–1516), an easygoing literary culture of satirical and humorous poems thrived. Also in Valencia, Jaume Roig (ca. 1400–78) wrote *Espill* (*The Mirror*), a prebourgeois fiction in verse with a pessimistic and rude approach to reality and traces of med. misogyny.

Although Catalan poetry was enjoying a healthy life in the early 16th c., a series of historical events related to the political misfortunes of the crown of Catalonia and Aragon subdued literary growth under a newly unified Spain. Catalonia lost two wars with Castile (1640 and 1714), and most of the nobility moved to central Spain to serve Charles V and Philip II. Also, after 1492 the main economic activity shifted from the Mediterranean to the Atlantic Basin. Because of these changes, Catalonia experienced a profound crisis, which may explain why the Ren. and its aftermath (neoclassicism, Enlightenment) were lived with less intensity. Andreu Martí Pineda (d. ca. 1566) and Valeri Fuster (d. ca. 1500) imitated bourgeois Valencian poetry from the late 15th c. Baroque writing is well represented by authors such as Joan Pujol (1532–ca. 1603), Francesc Vicenç Garcia (1578?–1623), Francesc Fontanella (1622–ca. 1682), and Josep Romaguera (1642–1723), while neoclassicism inspired the Minorcan poets Joan Ramis (1746–1819) and Antoni Febrer i Cardona (1761–1821). From the early 17th c. on, we can easily detect the influence of Golden Age and baroque Sp. writers from Garcilaso de la Vega (whose Italianate poems were first published in a famous volume of 1543 with those of his friend, the Catalan innovator Joan Boscà Almogàver [Juan Boscán, ca. 1488–1542]) to Baltasar Gracián. The lit. of the Counter-Reformation reflected rigidity and asceticism. Vicenç Garcia, also known as Rector de Vallfogona, created a "school" with imitators all the way into the 19th c. The lack of a strong elite lit. is offset by a surge in popular poetry. Some of the most outstanding poems of the time were anonymous. This trend survived until the 19th c., when popular styles were adopted by romantic authors: Pau Piferrer (1818–48), Manuel Milà i Fontanals (1818–84), and Marià Aguiló (1825–97). The myth of Count Arnau was particularly important in popular poetry and became a topic for poets in the 20th c., esp. Josep Maria de Sagarra and Joan Maragall.

During the 19th c., under the auspices of the Industrial Revolution and romanticism, poetry was employed to differentiate Catalonia from Spain. Long considered, together with the *Basque Country, Spain's industrial engine, Catalonia nevertheless carried little political weight in Sp. politics after 1714. Modernization became a means of demanding a distinct political and economic status, as evident in Catalan romantic and modernist lit. Early poetical essays such as Bonaventura Carles Aribau's (1799–1862) "A la pàtria" (To the Motherland, 1833) have long been considered the starting point of this movement, as is the first book written in Catalan, Miquel Anton Martí's (ca. 1790–1864) *Llàgrimes de viudesa* (Weeping Widowerhood, 1839). That year Rubió i Ors (1818–99), known by his pseud. Lo Gaiter de Llobregat (The Bagpiper from Llobregat), started publishing poems in *Diario de Barcelona;* they were compiled in 1841 under the same *Lo Gaiter de Llobregat*. Tomàs Aguiló (1775–1856) and Tomàs Villarroya (1812–56) followed suit in Majorca and Valencia, respectively, while Milà i Fontanals helped develop an interest in troubadour poetry from a scholarly perspective.

At first, recovery of Catalan lit. began with the Renaixença, a literary movement organized after 1859 around the *Jocs Florals* (poetic contests), competitions celebrated every first Sunday in May, which aroused new and widespread interest in Catalan lit. This movement included Josep Lluís Pons i Gallarza (1823–94), Víctor Balaguer (1824–1901), Marià Aguiló (1825–97), Teodor Llorente (1836–1911), Francesc Pelagi Briz (1839–89), Jaume Collell (1846–1932), Ramon Picó i Campamar (1848–1916), Francesc Matheu (1851–1938), Josep Anselm Clavé (1824–74), and Joaquim M. Bartrina (1850–80). Jacint Verdaguer (1845–1902), the founder of mod. Catalan literary lang., is the major literary figure of the Renaixença. His two epic poems, *Atlàntida* (1877) and *Canigó* (1885), interpreted Sp. and Catalan hist. in light of mythological and religious references in the style of the Fr. romantic poet Alphonse de Lamartine.

This cultural revival initiated a period of intense literary activity until the Sp. Civil War. Concurrent with major Eur. trends, cultural movements such as *Modernisme* (a version of flamboyant art nouveau style) and *Noucentisme* (a neoclassical revival modeled on Fr. lit.) flowered. In the 1920s and 1930s, there were strong signs of a very active avant-garde, postsymbolist modernity—a moment of splendor that was violently truncated by the onset of the Civil War (1936–39). This period was dominated by the idea of modernization, which was divided along bourgeois and proletarian lines.

At the turn of the century, we detect a second moment of this revival. Under Modernisme, Joan Maragall (1860–1911) masterfully epitomized feelings and obsessions of the time in his poems ("Oda nova a Barcelona," "Oda a Espanya," "Cant espiritual"), painting an accurate portrait of Catalan society incl. anarchism, difficult relations with Spain, and religious doubts. Santiago Rusiñol (1861–1931) wrote the first decadent prose poems in *Oracions* (1893). In Majorca, Miquel Costa i Llobera

(1854–1922) and Joan Alcover (1854–1926) wrote poetry with a more classicist penchant. The latter became inspirational for a group of young poets who wrote under Noucentisme. Josep Carner (1884–1970), Guerau de Liost (pseud. of Jaume Bofill i Mates, 1878–1933), and Josep Maria López-Picó (1886–1959) composed formalist poetry. Jours. such as *La Revista* (1915–36) were influential in the introduction of symbolism and promoted avant-gardism. Joan Salvat-Papasseit (1894–1924), Josep M. Junoy (1887–1955), and Salvador Dalí (1904–89) adapted futurism, cubism, and surrealism, respectively, with staggering results. This marks a third moment. Josep Vicenç Foix (1893–1987) combined avant-garde (*Gertrudis*, 1927) and cl. models (*Sol i de dol*, 1947). Following a postsymbolist program, Carles Riba (1893–1959), who twice translated *The Odyssey*, wrote in a severe tone (*Estances*, I [1919] and II [1930]). His *Elegies de Bierville* (1943) presents a somber account of exile. Josep Maria de Sagarra (1894–1961) and Ventura Gassol (1893–1980) were the most popular poets before World War II. Other poets drawn toward intimacy and dream include Maria Antònia Salvà (1869–1958), Josep Sebastià Pons (1886–1962), Marià Manent (1898–1988), Tomàs Garcés (1901–93), and Clementina Arderiu (1889–1976). Pere Quart (pseud. of Joan Oliver, 1899–1986) wrote satirical poetry (*Les decapitacions*, 1934), whereas personal experiences of illness and civil war appeared in the poetry of Bartomeu Rosselló-Pòrcel (1913–38) and Màrius Torres (1910–42).

Franco's regime repressed Catalonian culture. For many years, the lang. vanished from public life, with publication in it forbidden. Writers employed poetry as a means of subversion; the genre was easy to distribute illegally, and its inherent abstraction helped keep a rich cultural heritage alive. Riba and Foix presided over literary and political meetings where they inspired writers of the younger generation: Jordi Sarsanedas (1924–2006) and Joan Perucho (1920–2003). Josep Palau i Fabre (1917–2008) and Joan Brossa (1917–2008) maintained an active focus on avant-garde aesthetics. Agustí Bartra (1908–82), a minor poet who lived in exile, represented a revival of *modernista* models. When Riba died in 1959, a radical change occurred under *Realisme Històric* (Socialist Realism), as proposed in Castellet and Molas's influential anthol., *Poesia catalana segle XX*. Quart (*Vacances pagades*, 1960) and Salvador Espriu (1913–85, *La pell de brau*, 1960), created an interest in more realist approaches, particularly evident in Gabriel Ferrater (1922–72, *Les dones i els dies*, 1968). Some authors distantly related to realism are Vicent Andrés Estellés (1924–93), Marià Villangómez (1913–2002), Blai Bonet (1926–97), Josep M. Llompart (1925–93), Màrius Sampere (b. 1928), Montserrat Abelló (1918–2014), and Miquel Martí i Pol (1929–2003).

From the mid-1960s, a remarkable recovery of Catalan poetry began. The arrival of an iconoclastic generation, in dialogue with their Eur. counterparts, provoked a significant shift toward a poetry of universal interest. Characteristically, these poets worried little about the past and were overtly irreverent toward traditional topics, such as the sanctity of lang. Rather than following local literary models, they favored freedom of expression, some adopting a formalistic attitude, others vindicating obscure figures from the past. Pere Gimferrer (b. 1945, *Mirall, espai, aparicions*, 1981) is outstanding among this group, together with Feliu Formosa (b. 1934), Joan Margarit (b. 1938), Narcís Comadira (b. 1942), Francesc Parcerisas (b. 1944), Miquel Bauçà (1940–2005), and Jordi Pàmias (b. 1938). While Catalan poetry today has lost part of the aura it had during difficult times, nevertheless, poetry is very much alive, and many exceptional poets are worth mentioning: M. Mercè Marçal (1952–98), Salvador Jàfer (b. 1954), Jaume Pont (b. 1947), Josep Piera (b. 1947), Carles Torner (b. 1963), David Castillo (b. 1961), Margalida Pons (b. 1966), Jaume Subirana (b. 1963), Enric Casassas (b. 1951), Arnau Pons (b. 1965), and Lluís Solà (b. 1940).

See OCCITAN POETRY; SPAIN, POETRY OF.

■ **Anthologies**: *Anthology of Catalan Lyric Poetry*, ed. J. Triadú and J. Gili (1953); *Ocho siglos de poesía catalana: antología bilingüe*, ed. J. M. Castellet and J. Molas (1976); *Modern Catalan Poetry: An Anthology* (1979), and *Postwar Catalan Poetry* (1991), both ed. and trans. D. H. Rosenthal; *Poesia catalana del barroc*, ed. A. Rossich and P. Valsalobre (2006); *Lights off Water: XXV Catalan Poems 1978–2002*, ed. Anna Crowe (2007); "Made in Catalunya," L. Anderson, L. Reed, and P. Smith reading Catalan, http://www.llull.cat/IMAGES_2/NYSMITHREEDANDERSON.pdf).

■ **Bibliographies**: E. Bou, *Nou diccionari 62 de la literatura catalana* (2000); A. Broch, *Diccionari de la literatura catalana* (2008).

■ **Criticism and History**: M. de Riquer, A. Comas, J. Molas, *Història de la Literatura Catalana*, 11 v. (1964–88); J. Fuster, *Literatura catalana contemporània* (1972); J. Bofill i Ferro and A. Comas, *Un segle de poesia catalana* (1981); J. Marco and J. Pont, *La nova poesia catalana* (1981); A. Terry, *Sobre poesia catalana contemporània* (1985); J. Rubió i Balaguer, *Obres completes: Història de la literatura catalana* (1986); A. Terry, *Quatre poetes catalans* (1991); F. Carbó, *La poesia catalana del segle XX* (2007); LletrA: Catalan Literature Online: http://www.lletra.net/; A Rossich, *Panorama crític de la literatura catalana*, 6 v. (2009–11).

E. Bou

CELTIC PROSODY. Celtic tribes were prominent on the Eur. continent in the middle of the first millennium BCE and by the mid-3rd c. had spread into Asia Minor in the east, the Iberian peninsula in the west, and the Brit. Isles in the north. Celtic warriors sacked Rome in 380 BCE and raided the oracle at Delphi in 260 BCE; they were known as one of the four great barbarian peoples (along with Scythians, Libyans, and Persians). Our information about the nature and customs of these continental Celts comes from Gr. (and later Roman) ethnographers. Their commentaries date from around the 6th c. BCE; but from the Gr. historian Posidonius, by way of Diodorus Siculus (1st c. BCE) and the somewhat later Strabo, we discover important information about the practice of poetry. Diodorus says that the Celts had three classes of learned and privileged men: (1) βάρδοι, bards who were poets and who sang eulogies and satires accompanied by stringed instruments; (2) δρυίδαι, druids who were philosophers and theologians; and (3) μάντεις, seers (Strabo calls them ουάτεις, Lat. *vates*). Caesar too was probably drawing on the Posidonian trad. when he wrote, concerning the extensive training of the druids, that they commit to memory immense amounts of poetry and that their study may last as long as twenty years. From these and similar accounts, it is clear that poetry was a prestigious occupation among the continental Celts. But it must be emphasized that none of this poetry has survived and that, therefore, nothing is known of its prosody.

By the time Celtic tribes had migrated into the Brit. Isles, their once-common Celtic lang. had split into two principal branches: Goidelic (whence the Gaelic langs. of Ireland, Scotland, and Isle of Man) and Brittonic (whence Welsh, Breton, and Cornish [see IRELAND, POETRY OF; SCOTLAND, POETRY OF; WELSH POETRY; BRETON POETRY; CORNISH POETRY]). In these langs., and more specifically in Ir. and Welsh, we find the earliest recorded Celtic poetry, though it must be stressed that it is more properly to be regarded as Ir. poetry and Welsh poetry. We must, therefore, speak of Ir. prosody and of Welsh prosody. It is remarkable that the earliest extant vernacular manuals of prosody in Europe are Ir., dating back to the end of the 8th c. (Thurneysen [1912], 78–89; Calder).

The early Ir. and Welsh poets, like those of their forebears among the continental Celts, exercised an authoritative function in society as members of a professional class (P. Sims-Williams). The earliest Ir. poetry included both rhyming and nonrhyming verse. One type of nonrhyming verse consisted of units with two or three stressed words linked by alliteration. This type occurs in genealogical poems, poems in secular sagas, and in legal tracts. Another type of nonrhyming verse is syllabic rather than stress, e.g., a seven-syllable line with a trisyllabic cadence at the end (Breatnach). Calvert Watkins argued that the most archaic form of versification employed in Old Ir. seems to be a reflex of the IE cadenced verse form that appears in Gr., Sanskrit, and Slavic, if due allowance is made for the fact that IE prosodic patterns were determined by alternation of long and short syllables, whereas Goidelic had adopted alternation of stressed and unstressed syllables as a patterning feature. The earlier term for this nonrhyming verse is *retoiric* (Mac Cana), but the favored term now is *rosc(ad)*. While some of the earliest Ir. poetry may well continue an older system derived from IE prosody (in which case we might well call it Celtic prosody), current scholarship argues that the *roscada*, which continued to be composed well into the Old and early Middle Ir. period, are but an elevated form of literary practice and that the influence of late and med. Lat. rhetorical and poetical style on these verse forms cannot be denied (Corthals).

Lat. influence is to be seen also in the syllabic, rhymed verse that constitutes the bulk of Old and Middle Ir. poetry. Gerard Murphy argued that rhyme and regular syllable count in this poetry derived ultimately from early med. Lat. hymnic poetry. *Dán díreach*, syllabic verse with strict rules about rhyme, alliteration, and so on, characterized the poetry of the middle and early mod. periods in Ireland

and in the Gaelic-speaking parts of Scotland as well. Generic rhyme, whereby consonants were grouped in six phonetic classes, developed early, as did the marking off in the normal four-line stanzas (*rann*). The various metres of *dán díreach* demanded strict employment of consonance, assonance, dissonance, alliteration, and rhyme; rhyme might be end-line, internal between lines, or end-line with internal of the following line (*aicill* rhyme). The lang. of the poetry was learned in the bardic schools and remained unchanged throughout the period of Ir. cl. poetry, ca. 1200–1650, whether in Ireland or Gaelic Scotland. The intricacy of this poetry is almost unparalleled in Eur. poetry. The complexity of Ir. prosody is paralleled by Welsh prosody, esp. in the period of the Poets of the Princes (*Beirdd y Tywysogion*), 12th to end of the 13th c., and beyond. The following Ir. poem is in a meter called *deibhidhe*, the commonest of the syllabic meters in Ir. bardic poetry and the easiest:

> Dá mbáidhthí an dán, a dhaoine,
> Gan seanchas, gan seanlaoidhe,
> Go bráth, acht athair gach fhir,
> Rachaidh cách gan a chluinsin.
>
> (Knott 1966, 78)
>
> (If poetry were suppressed, men, so there was neither history nor old poetry, nothing would be known of any man save only the name of his father.)

The unit is the quatrain. The prosody of *dán díreach* in general involves syllabic count, generic rhyme, internal rhyme, and alliteration. A consonant alliterates either with itself or with the corresponding initial form produced by grammatical mutation; a vowel alliterates with itself or any other. In *deibhidhe*, the meter of the poem quoted, there are seven syllables in each line. Line *a* rhymes with *b*, *c* with *d*. In Ir. rhyme, the stressed vowels must be identical and the consonants of the same generic class and the same quality (i.e., broad or slender). The generic end rhyme is between words of unequal syllabic length (*dhaoine*, *seanlaoidhe*; *fhir*, *chluinsin*). There is alliteration between two words in each line, and the final word of *d* alliterates with the preceding stressed word (*chluinsin*, *cách*). There must be at least two internal rhymes between *c* and *d* (*bráth*, *cách*; *athair*, *rachaidh*). In every meter, the complete poem should end with the same word or syllable with which it began (*dúnad*, "closure").

Gaelic Scotland shared this trad. of cl. Ir. poetry. Although it was composed and sung in the courts of Scottish chieftains, it remained Ir., both linguistically and culturally (Clancy). It is virtually impossible to determine, on purely ling. or metrical grounds, whether a poem from this period (1200–1650) was composed in Ireland or Scotland or whether it belonged to the beginning or end of that period.

The earliest Welsh poetry, that of Aneirin and Taliesin in the 6th c., seems to have been accentual, although, unlike some of the early Ir. poetry, rhyme as opposed to an unrhymed cadence marked the end of the line. In that early poetry, the syllabic length of lines varies considerably (Haycock); however, the number of stresses in each line tended to produce a more or less regular number of syllables. Eventually, syllabic regularity and main rhyme (*prifodl*) characterized all meters in the *awdl*, *englyn*, and *cywydd* categories. An awdl is a poem of unregulated length, comprised of various syllabic meters; earlier *awdlau* are monorhymed. The englyn forms are stanzaic, the most common being the *englyn unodl union*, comprised of four lines with a single main rhyme. Among the later awdl meters are assymetric rhyming couplets (cywydd couplets) and, from the 14th c., a cywydd is a poem of unregulated length comprised solely of these couplets. The several varieties of these three classes made up the canonical 24 meters. As in Ireland, poets in Wales were trained in bardic schools both orally and with the use of written texts, the bardic grammars (Williams and Jones). From the beginning, intricate alliteration and internal rhyme ornamented the lines of the awdl and englyn; by the end of the 13th c., these features had evolved into the system known as *cynghanedd*. Early in the following century, cynghanedd was introduced into the cywydd, and it subsequently became an obligatory feature in every line of strict-meter verse. Dafydd ap Gwilym's cywydd address to a seagull (14th c.) is typical:

> Yr wylan deg ar lanw dioer,
> Unlliw ag eiry neu wenlloer,
> Dilwch yw dy degwch di,
> Darn fel haul, dyrnfol heli.
>
> (Fair sea gull on the certain tide, of color like snow or the bright moon, spotless is your beauty, a patch like sunlight, gauntlet of the sea.)

Each line has seven syllables; the accent in Welsh is usually on the penultimate, so each couplet rhymes a stressed monosyllable with an unstressed polysyllable. Additionally, each line must feature one of the different forms of cynghanedd. Lines 1, 2, and 4 of this citation illustrate consonantal cynghanedd, i.e., the sequence of consonants around the main stressed vowel before the caesura is exactly repeated around a different stressed vowel in the second half of the line. Lines 1 and 4 have *cynghanedd groes*; thus, in line 1, the sequence *r l n d* is echoed: yR wyLaN Dég | aR LaNw Díoer. Line 2 has *cynghanedd draws*, with unanswered consonants before the echoed sequence: úNLLiw | [ag eiry neu] wéNLLoer. Line 3 illustrates tripartite *cynghanedd sain*, where the first and second parts of the line rhyme, and the second and third demonstrate consonantal cynghanedd: dil*wch* | yw dy Dég*wch* | Dí. A further category of cynghanedd is *cynghanedd lusg*, where the unstressed penultimate syllable of the line rhymes with the syllable immediately preceding the caesura. A full discussion of cynghanedd would require many more pages.

Generally speaking, the Celtic bards, rather like the Ir. illuminators of the *Book of Kells*, chose to fill minute spaces decoratively. At their best, as in the Ir. and Welsh examples just quoted, they were capable of providing not only an intricate phonetic texture but a brilliant network of imagery that illuminated their poems in a manner that is perceptible even in trans.

Traces of one type of Welsh cynghanedd may be seen in the few bits of Breton poetry that survive from the late Middle Ages, suggesting that Brittany may have shared in a Brittonic prosodic system. The surviving late med. Cornish verse shows no signs of participating in a Brittonic or Celtic prosodic system.

With the decline of the bardic orders in the Celtic countries, new and simpler meters became increasingly popular. In part, these are the products of amateur versification; in part, they may represent the legitimization of popular and perhaps ancient song meters hitherto unrecorded; and in part, they certainly represent the adaptation of foreign meters. When the secret of generic rhyme was lost, the most appealing device for Ir. and Scottish Gaelic poets seems to have been assonance. Typical is an Ir. song composed by Geoffrey Keating (17th c.), which is in the new Ir. stressed verse known as *amhrán* and begins:

> Óm sge*o*l ar *a*rd-mhagh F*á*il ní ch*o*dlaim
> o*í*dhche.

The last stressed vowel of the five stressed syllables in the first line assonates with each of the last stressed syllables in all of the following lines of the stanza, as in the OF *laisse*. But, additionally, each of the other four stressed vowels in the first line assonates with its counterparts in all of the following lines, so that the melody of the stanza consists of a sequence of five stressed vowels (here *o-a-a-o-i*).

Scottish Gaelic song poetry begins to appear in mss. and print in the later 18th c., though its roots go back well into the Middle Ages (Gillies).

In Wales, *canu rhydd*, free-meter poetry, a poetry depending not upon syllabic regularity but rather upon rhythm and accent, had been around since the time of Aneirin but was not preserved in abundance until the 16th c. (Davies). Some of this is poetry composed in imitation of strict meters but without cynghanedd and with less attention to syllable count. The rest consists of stanzas set to existing musical airs, some of which were imported from England. However, strict-meter poetry with cynghanedd was not threatened by these popular devels., and its popularity remains strong today.

■ **General:** Parry, *History*; Williams and Ford; *Literacy in Medieval Celtic Societies*, ed. H. Pryce (1998); *The New Companion to the Literature of Wales*, ed. M. Stephens (1998).

■ **Irish:** R. Thurneysen, "Zur irischen Accent- und Verslehre," *Révue Celtique* 6 (1883–85); "Mittelirische Verslehren," *Irische Texte*, ed. W. Stokes and E. Windisch, v. 3 (1891); "Zu den mittelirischen Verslehren," *Abh. der königl. Akad. der Wiss. zu Gött., philol.-hist. Klasse* 14.2 (1912); "Über die älteste irische Dichtung," *Abh. der königl. Preussische Akad. der Wiss., philos.-hist. Klasse*, nos. 6, 10 (1914); G. Calder, *Auraicept na n-Éces, the Scholars' Primer* (1917); O. Bergin, "The Principles of Alliteration," *Eriu* 9 (1921–23); W. Meyer, "Die Verskunst der Iren in rhythmischen lateinischen Gedichten," Meyer, v. 3; E. Knott, *Irish Classical Poetry* (1957); G. Murphy, *Early Irish Metrics* (1961); C. Watkins, "Indo-European Metrics and Archaic Irish Verse," *Celtica* 6 (1963); E. Knott, *An Introduction to Irish Syllabic Poetry of the Period 1200–1600*, 2d ed. (1966); P. Mac Cana, "On the Use of the Term *Retoric*," *Celtica* 7 (1966); *Irish Bardic Poetry*, texts and trans. O. Bergin, ed. D. Greene (1970); E. Campanille, "Indogermanische Metrik und altirische Metrik," *ZCP* 37 (1979); L. Breatnach, "Poets and Poetry,"

Progress in Medieval Irish Studies (1996); J. Corthals, "Early Irish *Retoirics* and Their Late Antique Background," *Cambrian Medieval Celtic Studies* 31 (1996); P. K. Ford, *The Celtic Poets: Songs and Tales from Early Ireland and Wales* (1999); P. Sims-Williams, "Medieval Irish Literary Theory and Criticism," *CHLC*, v. 2, ed. A. Minnis and I. Johnson (2005).

■ **Scottish Gaelic:** D. Thomson, *An Introduction to Gaelic Poetry*, 2d ed. (1989); T. Clancy, "The Poetry of the Court: Praise," and W. Gillies, "Gaelic Literature in the Later Middle Ages," *The Edinburgh History of Scottish Literature*, v. 1 (2007).

■ **Welsh:** G. J. Williams and E. J. Jones, *Gramadegau'r Penceirddiaid* (1934); Jarman and Hughes, esp. E. Rowlands, "*Cynghanedd*, Metre, Prosody"; Morris-Jones; A. T. E. Matonis, "The Welsh Bardic Grammars and the Western Grammatical Tradition," *MP* 79 (1981); R. Bromwich, *Aspects of the Poetry of Dafydd ap Gwilym* (1986); T. Conran, *Welsh Verse*, 2d ed. (1986); M. Haycock, "Metrical Models for the Poems in The Book of Taliesin," *Early Welsh Poetry*, ed. B. F. Roberts (1988); C. Davies, "Early Free-Metre Poetry," and N. Lloyd, "Late Free-Metre Poetry," *A Guide to Welsh Literature*, v. 3, ed. R. G. Gruffydd (1997).

■ **Breton:** *Histoire Littéraire et Culturelle de la Bretagne*, 3 v., ed. J. Balcou and Y. Le Gallo (1987).

■ **Cornish:** R. Maber, "Celtic Prosody in Late Cornish: The *englyn* 'an lavar kôth yu lavar guîr'," *Bulletin of the Board of Celtic Studies* (1988); B. Bruch, "Cornish Verse Forms, the Evolution of Cornish Prosody," diss., Harvard University (2005); O. Padel, "Oral and Literary Culture in Medieval Cornwall," *Medieval Celtic Literature and Society*, ed. H. Fulton (2005).

P. K. Ford; A. Ll. Jones

CHILE, POETRY OF. The Sp.-lang. trad. in Chilean poetry begins with the publication of *La Araucana* (The Araucaniad) by Alonso de Ercilla (1533–94), born in Spain, who wrote about the conquest of Chile. This epic, which documents the founding of Chile, was published in three parts in 1569, 1578, and 1589; Andrés Bello called it Chile's *Aeneid*. Written in *octavas reales*, it belongs to early mod. trad. in its use of Gr. mythology, cl. references, and themes, incl. the faith and daring of the Spaniards and the heroism and sacrifice of the natives. It inspired later romantics with its vision of the noble savage and also inspired the next well-known colonial Chilean writer Pedro de Oña (1570–1643), who entered into dialogue with Ercilla with his poem *Arauco domado* (1596).

Oña's is a less idealistic portrayal of the indigenous people, written in memory of the poet's father, who was killed by Mapuches. This epic includes 19 cantos, hendecasyllabic octaves with rhyme schemes that do not follow Ercilla's octavas reales. Oña, born in Chile, received a Sp. education in Lima and has sometimes been regarded as not Chilean; it is clear in his poem that he views the country as a colony. His other notable poems include "El temblor de Lima" (The Earthquake of Lima, 1609), in which he uses a new kind of *ottava rima* and demonstrates the influence of the *culturanismo* of Sp. poets such as Luis de Góngora, and his heroic, religious poems "El Vasauro" (1635) and "El Ignacio de Cantabria" (1639).

Not much poetic production of note was recorded in the 17th and 18th cs.: there are poems of salon life, songs of praise, and popular poetry collected as part of Chilean folklore. Alegría mentions Father López, Father Oteíza, and Captain Lorenzo Mujica but categorizes them as "poets of circumstance." Popular poets wrote in *décimas*, or ten-line stanzas, and popular quatrains. *Corridos* (ballads), *payas* (poetic compositions with improvised verses), and chronicles in verse that use dramatic forms to treat human and divine themes comprise the Chilean version of the Sp. *romancero* (or ballad trad.).

Chile gained its independence in 1818, and poets of this period include Camilo Henríquez (1769–1845), a journalist who believed that poetry had a role in the moral and political education of the populace and who was recognized more for his political ideas than his poetry. Bernando Vera y Pintado (1780–1827), though born in Argentina, died in Chile and celebrated Chilean independence in his poems, one of which was transformed into the first national hymn. Mercedes Marín del Solar (1804–66) combined neoclassical and romantic styles. The Venezuelan Bello (1781–1865) and the Argentine Domingo Faustino Sarmiento (1811–88) worked and lived in Chile, and their debates (particularly about romanticism) were influential in Chilean literary conversations. José Victorino Lastarria (1817–88) wrote noteworthy essays about Chilean lit. and argued that Chile was late in developing its own lit. because of its political autocracy and backward social devel. The literary movement Generation of 1842, an answer to Lastarria, produced a national literary society that emphasized national expression, rejected Sp. romanticism, and championed renovating Chilean lit. by cultivating a progressive attitude.

Romanticism came late to Spain, and still later to Chile, and perhaps for this reason, Alegría argues, it is more distinctive there. Salvador Sanfuentes y Torres (1817–60) follows the indigenist themes of Ercilla and Oña, with *Caupolicán* (1835), a drama in verse in the romantic trad. Other important names in Chilean romanticism include Guillermo Blest Gana (1829–1904), José Antonio Soffia (1843–86), and Eusebio Lillo y Robles (1827–1910), a disciple of José Espronceda and José Zorrilla, who wrote a new Chilean national anthem.

Early 20th-c. Sp. Am. writers experienced a contradictory modernism, inheriting forms and trads. from Europe usually elaborated by elite writers, who struggled to found their own literary hist. in their poetry. This effort to develop a local perspective in Chile resulted in *Los Diez* (The Ten), a literary group dedicated to independent expression founded by Pedro Prado (1886–1952). Prado was a meditative poet who used symbolism and free verse, as well as sonnets and poetic prose, to record the local Chilean landscape and territory. Magallanes Moure (1878–1924) is another member of the group whose first book of poetry, *Facetas* (Facets, 1902), used traditional forms like the sonnet and sought modernist formal perfection in his portraits of country life. Not a member of the group but a notable early avant-garde writer of this time is Rosamel del Valle (pseud. of Moisés Filadelfio Gutiérrez Gutiérrez, 1900–65), who used long lines and a hermetic style in his sometimes visionary poetry; he published seven collections and was admired later by Vicente Huidobro. While some of these writers' styles are grounded in Sp. Am. *modernismo*, others move toward the avant-garde, which would prove to be much more fruitful and innovative than earlier poetry in Chile.

Pablo de Rokha (pseud. of Carlos Díaz Loyola, 1894–1968) is an early representative of the Chilean avant-garde. An innovator, he wrote in long lines that often lacked punctuation and chose antipoetic themes. He uses lang. as a weapon and combines many different genres: epic and lyric, popular and surrealist. He attempted to renovate poetry through excess and exaggeration, and his work is an important expression of Chilean identity. Huidobro (1893–1948), who traveled to Buenos Aires, Spain, and France, is perhaps the most recognized proponent of the post-World War II literary avant-garde. He was a modernist in his early work, but his travels led him to found a movement called *creacionismo* (creationism), complete with its own manifestos that highlighted its poetry's originality and capacity to make things happen with lang. His masterwork is the long poem *Altazor* (1931), which charts the existential and ling. crisis of its namesake.

Gabriela Mistral (pseud. of Lucila Godoy Acayaga, 1889–1957), in 1945 the first Lat. Am. to win a Nobel Prize in Literature, addressed in her poetry topics such as Chilean and Am. identity, religion, childhood, love, suffering, maternity, and rebellion. She combines a local, formal lang. with a passionate tone, often speaking as an outsider in her books: *Desolación* (Desolation, 1922), *Ternura* (Tenderness, 1924), *Tala* (Felling, 1938), and *Poema de Chile* (published posthumously in 1967). Writing during the time of multiple avant-gardes, she chose an anachronic formalism and tone; for these among other reasons, Concha argues that Mistral's work can be seen as part of an autochthonous vanguard. Mistral is recognized for her prose as well as her poetry, for her stances as an international intellectual and educator, and for her defense of human rights.

Pablo Neruda (pseud. of Ricardo Neftalí Reyes Basoalto, 1904–73) is the major figure in 20th-c. Chilean (and beyond that, Sp. Am.) poetry. In 1924, he published *Veinte poemas de amor y una canción desesperada* (*Twenty Love Poems and a Song of Despair*), his second book of poems with neoromantic roots, which remains popular today. He enters the avant-garde with his *Residencia en la tierra* (*Residence on Earth*), three volumes published in 1935–47, in which the poet uses bold metaphors and rhythmic free verse to communicate surprising experiences of the world. In *Canto general* (1950), Neruda creates a prophetic voice in a long epic poem to sing the social and political hist. of the continent, while his *Odas elementales* (*Elemental Odes*) of the 1950s are direct poems in which he draws on sometimes complex metaphors to catalog everyday objects imbued with unanticipated emotion. Like Mistral, Neruda was a renowned public figure; exiled for his political views and later a senator, he was a supporter of Salvador Allende's Popular Unity presidency, and his death coincided with the coup that brought Augusto Pinochet to power in 1973.

Neruda's work has been translated into many langs., and he is the first Chilean figure to enter the canon of world poetry; perhaps for this reason, contemporaneous poets such as Pablo de Rokha and Nicanor Parra, as well as later poets, reacted against his at times overwhelming influence.

The year 1954 is key in Chilean poetry, when Parra (b. 1914) published his *Poemas y antipoemas* (*Poems and Antipoems*) as a response to Neruda and to the conventional idea of poetry as ritual, elevated expression for elite readers. Parra forged an alternate path through poetry that used colloquial, prosaic lang., self-irony, and ludic qualities to approach everyday life. Parra's relativization of the world was reflected in new attitudes in his poetic speakers, who question and parody trad. and modernity in poems that interrogate both form and content. His ongoing struggle with convention is apparent in *Artefactos* (Artifacts, 1972), a box of picture postcard-poems that challenged the idea of the book.

Much of mid-20th c. Chilean poetry responds to these canonical figures; it splits or crosses lines of influence from the avant-garde and antipoetry (which has a decisive influence on much of the poetry that follows and is both part of the vanguards and a reaction against them). Gonzalo Rojas (1917–2011) follows Parra's lead with his vigorous social poetry, in themes that extend from the erotic to the existential and ontological. Associated with the surrealist group *La Mandrágora* (The Mandrake), Rojas sought to communicate with a broader audience. Enrique Lihn's (1929–88) work is also more closely linked to Parra's than to Neruda's. Lihn tackles definitive questions such as the meaning of life, suffering, and death and demonstrates a commitment to social reality, moving toward *poesía situada* (situated poetry), a poetics that speaks from and about the situation of the speaker and that constantly recreates itself. Closer to Neruda, perhaps, is Jorge Teillier (1935–96). He writes of Chile's southern regions in poetry of origins, childhood, nostalgia, and mythic creation; and his speaker is sometimes a visionary witness. He uses simple, direct lines and metaphor to make the region a symbolic zone. Popular poetry in this period may be seen in the work of Violeta Parra (1917–67), who was central to the Chilean New Song movement. Widely recognized as a musician, she also can be considered a popular poet.

The 1960s and 1970s include the pre-Salvador Allende generation and those who first experienced the Pinochet dictatorship following the coup of 1973. Figures of the 1960s include Waldo Rojas (b. 1944), whose work incorporates a reflexive, metapoetic intensity as he writes and rewrites his perceptions of the world. There is a continuity from his early books, such as *Príncipe de naipes* (Prince of Cards, 1966) to the later *Deber de urbanidad* (Urban Obligation, 2001), in which memory and exploration of symbolic space predominate (in the last example, the space is Paris, where Rojas moved in 1974). Jaime Quezada (b. 1942) is another member of this generation, recognized for his contemplation of daily life in an accessible style; Quezada's interest in Chilean poetry is also seen through his work as an ed. of authors such as Mistral, Neruda, and Nicanor Parra. The early idealism and political dynamism of the 1960s shifted with the political turmoil in the early 1970s. Topics such as exile, direct repression, and the climate of fear and persecution began to predominate; and for this reason, the 1970s in Chilean letters is called the dispersed or decimated generation. Some of its members are Floridor Pérez (b. 1937), who followed in the footsteps of Teillier but integrated humor and irony more characteristic of Nicanor Parra into his work. Oscar Hahn (b. 1938) uses surrealist elements and imagery in sonnets and free verse with sonorous intensity to speak of mortality, love, and alienation. Gonzalo Millán's (1947–2006) work is a constant rereading of himself. He also examines the relationship between image and text (he was a sculptor and visual artist) with complexity in poems conceived as series. His 1987 book *Virus* reflects on the function of poetry and art confronted with power. Like many members of the 1960s and 1970s generations, both Hahn and Millán spent significant time exiled from Chile.

The 1980s in Chile meant writing within the dictatorship, in a precarious and hostile situation of domination, and writers found different strategies for confronting the role of art in a repressive society. Alejandra Basualto (b. 1944) has discussed the conditions of internal exile for those who remained in the country, the lack of books coming into Chile, and the devel. of workshops to communicate at this time. A community developed among women writers, such as Eugenia Brito (b. 1950), who textualizes physical suffering and combines genres in her more recent *Extraña permanecia* (Strange Permanence, 2004); and Verónica Zondek (b. 1953), who uses her often abstract poetry to reconstruct and learn through pain and memory. Carmen Berenguer (b. 1946) has continued in the avant-garde vein with her radical, experimental, feminist work. She writes hermetic poetry that frequently deals with the situation of marginalized, oppressed, fragmented subjects both during and after the dictatorship. Elvira Hernández (b. 1951) also deals with marginal identities, expressed in ruptured syntax in books like *Santiago Waria* (1992), in which she connects the city to its indigenous past, and *La bandera de Chile* (1991), where she empties and resignifies the national emblem (some of these works circulated clandestinely before they were published in the early 1990s).

Juan Luis Martínez (1942–93) is also in the avant-garde line in his attempt to create a new kind of poetry. *La nueva novela* (1985) is a poetic object or an interartistic experiment with a new kind of literary expression that incorporates humor and textual play (he is a clear descendant of Nicanor Parra). Tomás Harris's (b. 1956) mythological and poetic voyages through the city chronicle uneven devel., while Diego Maqueira (b. 1951) combines high cultural and popular registers and alters the conventional depiction of time. Raúl Zurita (b. 1951) extends an avant-garde desire to put poetry into action and uses surrealist images, self-referentiality, and multiple voices in his poetry. He is recognized for conjoining written words with performances via sky and desert writing and photos in his texts, which form a Dantesque chronicle of Chile's suffering: *Purgatorio* (1979), *Anteparaíso* (1982), and *La vida nueva* (1993).

In the 1990s, the transition to democracy opened the doors to increased expression and new voices, many of whom have become known as the shipwrecked generation. The transition also focused attention on multiculturalism and the work of Elicura Chihuailaf (b. 1952), a Mapuche poet (see MAPUCHE POETRY) who publishes in Mapuzungun and Sp.; she became one of a number of poets who undermined the unitary vision of Chile promoted under Pinochet. In some ways, their work can be read as a response to the founding poetry of Ercilla, for they represent their own ethnic and national identity, record trads., and add their voices to political debates and land disputes (Vicuña includes Chihuailaf, Leonel Lienlaf, Jaime Luis Huenun, and Graciela Huinao in her collection). Poets of the 1990s continue the dialogue with precursors such as Lihn, Parra and *anti-poesía*, and Rokha to experiment with typography and the book (Martínez) and to acknowledge Mistral. Their diversity of topics and styles extends from globalization and mass media to love, loss, and the circumstances of late 20th-c. Chile: material excess and commoditization, visual culture, and shifting social values. One of these, Clemente Riedemann (b. 1953), offers another perspective from the south, using accessible, colloquial lang. in his ironic recording of contemp. society, esp. Chile's role at the turn of the 21st c.

The early 21st-c. poets are known as the *novísimos* (the new ones), and they return to the poets of the 1980s for inspiration. Some names associated with this group are Diego Ramírez (b. 1982), Paula Ilabaca Nuñez (b. 1979), and Héctor Hernández Montecinos (b. 1979), who chose diverse styles to question social and literary convention in work that is not limited to writing but includes music, visual elements, installation, performance, and recordings. Some recent winners of the Neruda Prize in poetry (for writers under 40) include Rafael Rubio (b. 1975), Javier Bello (b. 1972), and Malú Urriola (b. 1967).

■ **Anthologies**: *Antología de la poesía chilena contemporánea*, ed. R. E. Scarpa and H. Montes (1968); *Antología de la poesía chilena (siglos XVI al XX)*, ed. L. Cisternas de Minguez and M. Minguez Sender (1969); *Veinticinco años de poesía chilena* (1970–1995), ed. T. Calderón, L. Calderón, and T. Harris (1996); *Antología de poesía chilena nueva* (1935), ed. E. Anguita and V. Teitelboim (2001); *20 poetas mapuches contemporaneos*, ed. J. Huenún (2003); *Poesía chilena desclasificada (1973–1990)*, ed. G. Contreras and J. Concha, v. 1 (2005); *Diecinueve (poetas chilenos de los noventa)*, ed. F. Lange Valdés (2006).

■ **Criticism and History**: F. Alegría, *La poesía chilena* (1954); H. Montes and J. Orlando, *Historia y antología de la literatura chilena* (1965); J. Concha, *Poesía chilena 1907–17* (1971); "La poesía chilena actual," *Literatura chilena en el exilio* 4.1 (1977); and *Gabriela Mistral* (1987); J. A. Piña, *Conversaciones con la poesía chilena* (1990); *UL: 4 Mapuche poets*, ed. C. Vicuña (1998); F. Schopf, *Del vanguardismo a la antipoesía* (2000).

■ **Web Site**: Escritores y poetas en español, http://www.letras.s5.com.

J. KUHNHEIM

CHINA, MODERN POETRY OF. In China, there is not a single standard term for mod. poetry. Before 1949, poetry written in the contemp. vernacular and nontraditional forms was commonly called New Poetry or Vernacular Poetry. After 1949, China was divided into three political entities: the People's Republic of China on the mainland (PRC), the Republic of China on Taiwan (ROC), and Hong Kong under Brit. rule. Whereas New Poetry continued to be used in the PRC, it was gradually replaced by the term *mod. poetry* in Taiwan and Hong Kong as the result of a flourishing modernist movement.

In 1917, Hu Shi (1891–1962), then a PhD student in the U.S., published a short essay titled "A Preliminary Proposal for Literary Reform," in which he envisioned a new poetry written in the "living language" (as opposed to cl. Chinese as a "dead language") and freed from traditional forms. Although certain genres of traditional Chinese poetry, such as folk song, ballad, and *ci* (see CHINA, POPULAR POETRY OF), employ a fair share of the vernacular, the New Poetry that Hu advocated was iconoclastic in its rejection of all poetic conventions, incl. parallelism, stock imagery, allusions, and imitation of ancient masters, as well its lang. and forms.

Understandably, Hu's call for radical reform was met with crit. from conservative scholars, some of whom were his close friends. On the other hand, the poetry reform, newly dubbed Literary Revolution by Chen Duxiu (1879–1942), a mentor of Hu and then dean of humanities at Peking University, triumphed as it converged with the May Fourth movement. Born in the demonstrations against Western imperialism in 1919, the May Fourth movement was spearheaded by progressive intellectuals, some of whom were teaching at Peking University at the time. The movement critiqued all aspects of traditional Chinese culture and introduced mod. Western concepts of science, democracy, and nationalism. Within a few years, New Poetry became a standard bearer of the new "national literature" written in the "national language."

The period 1920–30 witnessed a blossoming of New Poetry. Various foreign trends—such as romanticism, symbolism, realism, Japanese *haikai*, and prose poetry—provided inspirations to a new generation of poets, many of whom had studied abroad and were avid readers and translators of foreign poetry. Poetry societies and jours. also mushroomed. Among the most influential were the Creation Society (1921), the New Crescent Society (1923), and the jour. *Les Contemporains* (1932). The Creation Society was best represented by Guo Moruo (1892–1978), who had studied in Japan and translated J. W. Goethe before he turned to proletarian lit. The New Crescent was led by Xu Zhimo (1897–1931) and Wen Yiduo (1899–1946). Xu, who had studied in the U.S. and Britain, was dubbed the Chinese Shelley in his pursuit of love, beauty, and freedom. Wen, who had studied art and lit. in the U.S., theorized the ideal poetry as a synthesis of the beauty of painting, music, and architecture. Dai Wangshu (1905–50) was the most influential poet of *Les Contemporains*; he studied in France and translated symbolist poetry into Chinese. During the 1920s and 1930s, intense debates unfolded along ideological lines, which were often simplified as art for art's sake versus art for life's sake, or pure poetry versus poetry of social conscience.

The outbreak of the Sino-Japanese War on July 7, 1937, radically changed the poetry scene. Educational and cultural institutions were destroyed or relocated, and poets were scattered across the country. As a result, mod. poetry spread to all corners of the land, from Chongqing, the temporary capital of wartime China, to Shanghai under Japanese occupation, to Kunming and Guilin in the southwest, to the northwest under the Chinese Communist Party based in Yan'an, and to Hong Kong under Brit. rule. Poets joined other writers and artists in mobilizing the masses against the Japanese invasion and promoting patriotism. Poetry was recited and performed in public, often in plain speech and lively dialogue. Whereas before the war the short lyric was the dominant mode, now long narrative poetry flourished. But not all poetry addressed the war. Modernist experiments by younger poets continued; philosophical musings on life and art reached a new height.

The year 1949 was another watershed in the hist. of mod. poetry. Under ironclad ideological control in the PRC, most poets stopped writing and focused on scholarship or trans. Even so, they did not escape persecution in the successive political campaigns throughout the 1950s and 1960s, which culminated in the Cultural Revolution (1966–76). A few weak voices from the underground were silenced. The desolate situation did not change until the late 1970s, when China under Deng Xiaoping opened its door to the free world and embarked on an ambitious program of national modernization.

On the other side of the Taiwan Strait, in contrast, a modernist movement thrived despite censorship and a cultural policy of conservatism under the Nationalist regime (KMT). Led by Ji Xian (1913–2013) and Qin Zihao (1912–63), both of whom had started writing poetry in pre-1949 China, the postwar generation of young poets in Taiwan embraced avant-garde poetry and art in the West, incl. surrealism and high modernism. The most influential poetry societies and jours. were *Modernist Poetry Quarterly* (1952) and the Modernist School (1954), the Blue Star (1954), and the Epoch (1954). They not only created experimental works of the highest caliber but interacted with young poets in Hong Kong, who shared their enthusiasm for avant-garde art and lit. In the conservative social climate in Taiwan in the 1950s and 1960s, the modernist poetry movement was often derided and attacked. However, it was unstoppable as its influence spread. As a result, *Modern Poetry* became both a standard term and an institution in Taiwan and Hong Kong.

The next challenge to mod. poetry came in the early 1970s when Taiwan suffered a series of setbacks in the international political arena: the loss of its seat to the PRC in the United Nations and the severance of diplomatic relations with Japan and the U.S. These diplomatic setbacks triggered a legitimacy crisis and an identity crisis among intellectuals and writers, who demanded a "return" to Taiwanese society and Chinese cultural roots. Mod. poetry in Taiwan took a sharp turn toward realism and nativism, with the latter paving the way for the large-scale nativist literature movement (1977–79). Many poets, both old and young, embraced an idealized rural Taiwan, expressed concern for social maladies, and even critiqued the ruling regime. Into the 1980s, as the democracy movement steadily gained momentum, mod. poetry played an important role in raising public awareness of the repressed past and the hopeful future of Taiwan.

A new page also turned in the PRC in the late 1970s and early 1980s. In the liberalizing atmosphere of post-Mao China, commonly referred to as the New Era, underground poetry burst on the scene and enjoyed phenomenal success. The immediate predecessors of underground poetry were poets who wrote during the Cultural Revolution and whose works were hand-copied and circulated among the urban youths who had been sent down to the countryside by Chairman Mao Zedong. Chinese trans. of foreign poetry also provided them with an important source of inspiration. The most influential poetry in post-Mao China was represented by *Today*, founded by a group of young poets and artists in Beijing in 1978. The new generation of poets had recently experienced the Cultural Revolution; their works expressed disillusionment with politics on the one hand and a yearning to return to the private world, romantic love, and nature on the other. The new poetry stirred up a nationwide controversy; critics who condemned its obscurity and individualism called it *Misty Poetry.* As its popularity grew, however, the negative connotations disappeared. In the latter half of the 1980s, the newcomers defined themselves against Misty Poetry, rejecting the latter's lyricism and introspection. Instead, they engaged in a broader range of experiments and developed more radical poetics.

Censorship never ceased to exist in post-Mao China. Throughout the 1980s, Deng Xiaoping authorized several political campaigns against lit. and art that were considered too liberal or "bourgeois." Misty Poetry was constantly targeted. After the violent crackdown on student demonstrations in Tiananmen Square in June 1989, several poets were arrested and imprisoned; more left China in self-imposed exile. In the 21st c., Chinese society has undergone dramatic transformations. Culturally speaking, it has become not only far more diverse but more oriented toward pop commercialism. Poetry has lost the prestige and universal appeal that it once enjoyed. Ironically, while China's economic success has made possible more poetry prizes, jours., readings, and conferences than before, poetry readership has shrunk and the impact of poetry diminished. It is also ironic that despite completely different hists., poetry in 21st-c. mainland China, Taiwan, and Hong Kong faces very similar conditions: commodification of culture, the Information Age, and new technologies. Poets tend to see themselves as poetry makers rather than "poets," and many turn to the Internet as an important venue where free, democratic, and global interactions take place.

The story of mod. Chinese poetry since 1917 is dramatic, to say the least. It arose in reaction against cl. poetry, the most ancient and respected cultural form in traditional China, and successfully established itself as a representative of mod. lit. early on. It has drawn on the rich trads. of world poetry for resources but, in doing so, has repeatedly found itself embroiled in debates that question its cultural identity. What is clear is that mod. poetry represents a new aesthetic paradigm that is simultaneously related to and clearly distinguished from cl. poetry. It has broadened the Chinese lit. trad. in lang. and form and enriched it with a wide range of subject matters and sensibilities that are unique to the mod. era.

■ **Anthologies**: *Twentieth-Century Chinese Poetry*, trans. K. Y. Hsu (1970); *Out of the Howling Storm*, ed. T. Barnstone (1993); *Anthology of Modern Chinese Poetry*, trans. M. Yeh (1994); *Frontier Taiwan*, ed. M. Yeh and N.G.D. Malmqvist (2001); *Sailing to Formosa*, ed. M. Yeh et al. (2006); *Another Kind of Nation*, ed. E. Zhang and D. Chen (2007); *Twentieth-Century Chinese Women's Poetry*, ed. J. C. Lin (2009).

■ **Criticism and History**: J. C. Lin, *Modern Chinese Poetry* (1972); M. Yeh, *Modern Chinese Poetry* (1991); M. Hockx, *A Snowy Morning: Eight Chinese Poets on the Road to Modernity* (1994); M. Van Crevel, *Language Shattered: Contemporary Chinese Poetry and Duoduo* (1996); J. H. Zhang, *The Invention of a Discourse: Women's Poetry from Contemporary China* (2004); M. Van Crevel, *Chinese Poetry in Times of Mind, Mayhem and Money* (2008).

M. Yeh

CHINA, POETRY OF. Contemp. Chinese poets have a conception of poetry much in common with the view held by their compatriots in other countries, so to use the term *Chinese poetry* may seem at first unproblematic. But before the mod. period, Chinese writers employed no single term that embraced all traditional forms of verse; they referred instead to individual genres. This article reviews major devels.; readers also should examine the detailed articles on genres.

Generally speaking, traditional Chinese poetry consists of forms of writing that employ rhyme and usually a metric defined by a set number of syllables for each line. Some verse forms also require attention to the tones of the lang., exploiting the effect of rising or falling pitch in certain prescribed patterns. Depending on the lang. register appropriate to various genres, the lang. of traditional poetry may vary from a refined cl. Chinese to a mod. or near-mod. vernacular.

The earliest surviving Chinese poems derive from religious and political rituals; some are preserved in the first significant collection, the *Shijing* (*Classic of Poetry*, also known as the *Book of Songs*), an anthol. of 305 poems composed during the Zhou dynasty (1046–256 BCE). In most cases, the *Shijing* employs four-syllable lines arranged in couplets; individual stanzas of four, six, eight, or ten lines are also typical, with the frequent employment of refrain and repetition. Though mod. readers often detect a "folk" quality in the *Shijing*, traditional commentaries stressed the ethical significance of the poems (and the poems have been read thus throughout Chinese hist.).

Originally, the term *shi* referred only to *Shijing* poems (or poems from the same era); but by the 2d c. CE, shi was also applied to contemp. verse composition, both from anonymous popular and folk sources and from educated poets (a significant group of poems with a more explicit connection to song were also termed *yuefu* or "music bureau" songs). In both early shi and yuefu, lines of five syllables became increasingly important, though four-syllable line composition continued, usually with archaic associations. Shi poets focused on couplets as the basic poetic unit, and (unlike the poets of the *Shijing*) did not usually construct shi in clear-cut stanza forms. Shi could go on indefinitely but usually lasted from four to thirty lines; long shi stretching on for a hundred lines or more do exist but are rare. Themes tended to dwell on autobiographical expression, particularly the public and political experiences of the educated male poet; ethical and spiritual self-cultivation; and the tribulations of private life. Mild erotic content was also common (if frowned on by the educated elite as "unserious"). Since the Ming dynasty (1368–1644), critics have held that traditional shi reached the pinnacle of achievement during the Tang dynasty (618–907); important devels. during this period include the increasing popularity of the seven-syllable line alongside the five-syllable line, as well as quatrain and octet forms with prescribed tonal patterns.

Shi in later ages came to be regarded as the most important form of traditional Chinese verse composition. With the advent of commercial printing in the 11th c., the publication of shi collections (often containing thousands of poems) became widespread, leading to the wholesale preservation of large collections from even minor poets. Shi composition also became common among groups outside the male Chinese elite—e.g., women poets became increasingly visible in later centuries (esp. from the 17th c. onward). Shi also commonly appeared in other contexts; it is not unusual for the author of traditional fiction to insert a shi whenever he needs to express deep emotions, portray combat on the battlefield, or evoke natural scenery. Shi also could become a sort of banal "social glue," appearing not just in literary contexts but in everyday social exchanges and daily rituals and as an inscribed ornament in practically every environment. The prestige and utility of shi resulted in its spread to other countries influenced by Chinese culture (see KOREA, POETRY OF; CHINESE POETRY IN JAPAN; VIETNAM, POETRY OF).

From the 3d to 1st cs. BCE, another form of verse evolved in south China, which achieved finalized form in the anthol. known as the *Chuci* or "Songs of Chu" (Chu being a Chinese kingdom located in the central Yangtze Valley). This form involved a more flexible meter, though couplets continued as the main structural unit. Lament was the strongest thematic strain, with erotic and religious elements also present. *Chuci*-style composition remained popular in the Han dynasty (206 BCE–220 CE) court, though it was gradually replaced by the somewhat similar but more ambitious *fu* (rhapsody). Fu were largely courtly or public in origin and became immensely popular from the end of the Han through the Tang. In style, they were rhetorical (evolving in large part from earlier trads. of political and ethical oratorical persuasion). In a broader sense, fu contributed substantially to later descriptive prose style (and, in fact, traditional theorists tended to see it as a form of prose, even though it often employed "poetic" techniques such as parallelism, couplet structures, rhyme, and tonal regulation).

After shi, the best-known genre of traditional Chinese poetry is the *ci* (song lyric), which evolved from Tang dynasty popular songs. Ci are composed to set tune patterns (*ci pai*) with rigidly prescribed line lengths, stanza divisions, and tonal requirements; in content, they originally emphasized mildly erotic themes, though by the Song dynasty, they broached typical shi topics as well. Though many ci continued to be sung, other ci pai lost their original music, resulting in a strictly spoken poetic form. The Song dynasty is held to be the acme of ci composition, but Qing dynasty (1644–1911) ci are also greatly admired.

In the past millennium, two further significant devels. emerged in traditional Chinese poetry. First, Chinese drama (which became important in the 13th c.) incorporated lyrics to set tunes that function much like the songs in Eng. ballad opera. This form of dramatic lyric became a major outlet for poetic expression both in performance and in print (see CHINESE POETIC DRAMA). Second, numerous popular narrative poetic forms appeared, many of them conveyed through oral performance by a professional storyteller class. While our knowledge of earlier centuries is spotty, from the 18th c. and later a large corpus of texts has been preserved (some produced by women); from the 20th c., we also have eds. based on recordings or oral performance.

With the arrival of the imperial powers in China in the late 19th c. and political and social pressure to use the West as the model for "modernization," traditional Chinese verse forms fell into disfavor among many progressive intellectuals and were continued mostly on the amateur level. "Serious" poetry was influenced considerably by mod. artistic movements in the West and was written in the spoken vernacular lang.; this became known generally as *xin shi* (new poetry; see CHINA, MODERN POETRY OF). Forms of free verse have been the most popular, though poets have experimented with other Western poetic forms such as the sonnet. Interestingly enough, while Chinese poets were experimenting with Westernized forms, mod. Western poets began to employ aspects of traditional Chinese poetry in their own verse experiments (see CHINESE POETRY IN ENGLISH TRANSLATION).

See CHINA, POPULAR POETRY OF; CHINESE POETICS.

■ **Criticism and History**: J.J.Y. Liu, *The Art of Chinese Poetry* (1962); B. Watson, *Early Chinese Literature* (1962); H. Frankel, *The Flowering Plum and the Palace Lady* (1976); *The Indiana Companion to Traditional Chinese Literature*, ed. W. Nienhauser (1986); M. Yeh, *Modern Chinese Poetry* (1991); W. Idema and L. Haft, *A Guide to Chinese Literature* (1997); *The Columbia History of Chinese Literature*, ed. V. Mair (2001); W. Idema and B. Grant, *The Red Brush: Writing Women of Imperial China* (2004)—includes many trans.

■ **Translations**: *Sunflower Splendor*, ed. W. Liu and I. Y. Lo (1975); *Wen Xuan*, ed. and trans. D. Knechtges, 3 v. (1982–96); *The Columbia Book of Chinese Poetry*, ed. and trans. B. Watson (1984); *The Columbia Book of Later Chinese Poetry*, ed. and trans. J. Chaves (1986); *Anthology of Modern Chinese Poetry*, ed. and trans. M. Yeh (1990); *The Red Azalea: Chinese Poetry since the Cultural Revolution*, ed. E. Morin (1990); *The Columbia Anthology of Traditional Chinese Literature*, ed. V. Mair (1994); *An Anthology* *of Chinese Literature*, ed. and trans. S. Owen (1996); *Women Writers of Traditional China*, ed. K. S. Chang and H. Saussy (1999); *Classical Chinese Literature*, ed. J. Minford and J.S.M. Lau (2002); *How to Read Chinese Poetry*, ed. Z. Cai (2007)—includes critical essays on poems.

P. Rouzer

CHINA, POPULAR POETRY OF. China has a long trad. of popular poetry. Alongside a rich and varied trad. of vernacular song, there also exists an equally rich and varied trad. of vernacular narrative verse, often of epic proportions—texts of thousands or even ten thousands of lines are no exception. And alongside this trad. of pure verse narrative, there exists an even richer trad. of prosimetric narrative. In these prosimetric narratives, composed in an alternation of prose and verse, the verse sections often are dominant. Because these verse sections were chanted or sung in performance, in contrast to the more colloquial rendition of the prose sections, the mod. Chinese designation of this body of texts is *shuochang wenxue* or "literature for telling and singing," while some Western scholars have used the Fr. term *chante-fable* (the term *shuochang wenxue* in practice also includes the many genres of vernacular verse narrative).

While to the 14th c. many forms of popular song eventually were taken up by elite writers and developed into genres of cl. poetry such as *shi*, *ci*, or *qu* (see CHINESE POETIC DRAMA), this did not happen to any of the genres of verse and prosimetric narrative. As a result, our knowledge of the early hist. of these genres is very incomplete; most of our knowledge is based on archaeological discoveries of mss. or printed texts. Texts of verse narratives or chante-fables have only been preserved in greater number from the 17th c. on, and many of them were printed in the 19th c. or later. Other texts were recorded only in the 20th c.

Verse narratives are most often composed in lines of seven-syllable verse, which are called ci or "ballad-verse" (confusingly, this ci is the same term that is also used to designate the genre of the lyric). From the 9th to the 15th c., texts written exclusively in ci are simply called *ciwen* (texts in ci). The basic rhythm of the seven-syllable line is 2-2-3, with a major caesura following the fourth syllable. Every second line rhymes. From the 15th c. on, one also encounters ten-syllable lines, which are called *zan*. These lines have a basic rhythm of 3-4-3 or of 3-3-4. Initially, the zan was used only for short descriptive passages; but their use became increasingly more common with the progression of time, and in 19th c. and later one find texts only using zan. Many prosimetric genres also rely primarily on the ci (and the zan) for their verse sections, and the element ci is often encountered as part of the name of a genre (such as *cihua* or "ballad stories," *tanci* or "string ballads," and *guci* or "drum ballads"). The earliest examples of verse or prosimetric narratives employing ci are the *bianwen* or "transformation texts" of the 9th and 10th cs., discovered at Dunhuang.

Some chante-fable genres, however, rely for their verse sections on songs whose melodies demand lines of unequal length. Whereas in some genres the author may limit himself to a single tune that is repeated as often as required in each verse section, other genres, such as the *zhugongdiao* or "all keys and modes" that flourished from the late 11th to the early 14th c., employ a bewildering variety of tunes, which are organized in suites of varying length. The zhugongdiao acquired its name from the fact that no suite could be followed by another in the same key. The musical sophistication required in the composition, performance, and appreciation of a genre like the zhugongdiao has ensured that this latter type of genre has always been in a minority.

The preserved texts may derive from oral performances, but in both premod. and mod. times such texts will have been heavily edited before they were printed. Many orally performed texts turn out, on closer observation, to be derived from written texts in some way or another. Other texts were written by performers or aficionados with performance in mind, but some texts in these genres were written primarily for reading. The highly educated women authors of tanci in the 18th and 19th cs. concerning women dressed as men outperforming men in the examinations, at court, and on the battlefield stressed that their works were intended for reading only, but even so some of these works were adapted for performance in later times. Texts from many different parts of China tend to be written in a rather uniform stylized vernacular, but some genres also systematically include the local dialect: tanci produced in Suzhou may include extensive passages in the local Wu dialect; the *muyushu* or "wooden-fish books" from Guangdong make some use of Cantonese; and the *gezaice* or "song books" from southern Fujian and Taiwan became increasingly liberal in their incorporation of Minnanese over the course of the 20th c. The local coloring of genres originating from northern China such as guci and *zidishu* or "youth books" (a genre beloved by Manchu amateurs in 18th- and 19th-c. Beijing) is less obvious because Mandarin became the basis of the mod. standard lang.

The subject matter of verse and prosimetric narrative is extremely broad. It is probably safe to say that the stories of all popular China traditional novels and plays also have been treated in shuochang wenxue. Some genres have an outspoken affinity to a certain class of subject matter. *Baojuan* or "precious scrolls" initially told pious Buddhist tales but as time went by broadened their repertoire. *Daoqing* or "Daoist sentiments" originally focused on tales of Daoist immortals and their conversions. Guci are said to have a greater affinity to tales of warfare and crime, while tanci are said to be more suitable to tales of romance and intrigue. Plots and characters were freely exchanged between the many genres. Some stories that were very popular in shuochang wenxue were rarely or never treated in fiction before the 20th c. One example is the legend of Meng Jiangnü, whose husband was drafted as a corvée laborer for the construction of the Great Wall, soon died of exhaustion, and was buried in the wall. When she came to the construction site to bring him a set of winter clothes and learned of his death, her weeping brought down the section of the wall in which he had been buried. Another example is the romance of Liang Shanbo and Zhu Yingtai. Zhu Yingtai is a girl who in male disguise leaves home and attends an academy. She falls in love with her male roommate Liang Shanbo. When she leaves, she urges him to visit her, but by the time he does so and learns she is a girl, her parents have already engaged her to the son of another family. The now-love-smitten Liang Shanbo soon dies; and when Zhu Yingtai's bridal procession passes by his grave, the grave opens up and she joins him in death, whereupon their souls turn into butterflies. While stories like these are encountered in practically all genres, other stories are more specific to a certain region or genre.

■ *Ballad of the Hidden Dragon*, trans. M. Doleželová-Velingerová and J. I. Crump (1971); *Master Tung's Western Chamber Romance*, trans. L. L. Ch'en (1976); *Tun-huang Popular Narratives*, trans. V. H. Mair (1983); V. Mair, *T'ang Transformation Texts* (1989); *The Story of Hua Guan Suo*, trans. G. O. King (1989); A. E. McLaren, *Chinese Popular Culture and Ming Chantefables* (1998); D. Overmeyer, *Precious Volumes: An Introduction to Chinese Sectarian Scriptures from the Sixteenth and Seventeenth Centuries* (1999); M. Bender, *Plum and Bamboo* (2003) on Suzhou; *Meng Jiangnü Brings Down the Great Wall* (2008), *Personal Salvation and Filial Piety* (2008), *Filial Piety and Its Divine Reward* (2009), *Heroines of Jiangyong* (2009), *Judge Bao and the Rule of Law* (2010), *The White Snake and Her Son* (2009), *The Butterfly Lovers* (2010)—all trans. W. L. Idema; W. L. Idema, "Verse and Prosimetric Narrative," *Cambridge History of Chinese Literature*, ed. K. S. Chang and S. Owen, v. 2 (2010).

W. L. Idema

CHINESE POETIC DRAMA. *Xiqu*, or "drama," literally means dramatic song, and until the advent of Western-style "spoken drama," all Chinese drama was sung by characters who belonged to role types (e.g., male lead, female lead, clown). Traditional drama encompasses hundreds of regional forms, spanning close to a millennium, from its beginnings around the year 1100 to the present. The vast majority of those forms have left no written trace. Performers rely not on *libretti* but on oral transmission and improvisation. A form as popular as Peking opera (*jingju*) has no scripts to speak of. This entry discusses the few dramatic forms that became important as written lit.: *zaju*, *xiwen* (or *nanxi*), and xiwen's much more important descendant, *chuanqi*. Even in these forms, the vast majority of scripts have been lost. Within the full panoply of Chinese performance trads., these forms—in which the page has been as important as the stage—are anomalous. A 1324 mural of a theatrical troupe that depicts the lead actress in scrupulous detail but never mentions a playwright or a play suggests that, even when it comes to zaju, our contemp. inclination to identify a playwright rather than an actor as the primary creative force might be misplaced.

No written traces of drama predate the 13th c.; however, it is clear from other sources that drama had antecedents in religious ritual and was also closely associated with other forms of poetry meant for paid performance (most particularly prosimetric lit. and *zhugongdiao* [all keys and modes]). From the earliest surviving dramatic texts, two main trads. predominate, one based on northern melodies and rhymes (zaju) and the other based on southern (xiwen). In both cases, melodies were not composed specifically for a play; instead, folk songs and popular ditties circulated as an existing repertoire.

Zaju are closely associated with the performance trads. of the great cities of the 13th c., esp. Hangzhou (then called Lin'an) and Beijing (Dadu, under the Yuan dynasty). The first playwrights whose names are known were largely men of Dadu, Guan Hanqing most famous among them. When the component songs are referred to as *qu* (songs), they relate a narrative as experienced by the individual who sings of it and are considered dramatic verse. Set to the exact same music but unconnected by plot, *sanqu* (or unconnected songs) are considered lyric poetry.

Whereas the textual integrity of *shi* or *ci* was generally respected by those who transmitted them, these early dramatic texts were clearly regarded as open to modification. We speak of the most famous of zaju, *Xixiang ji* (*The Western Wing*), as if its author were Wang Shifu, but in fact, the play appears in multiple recensions: the most important, a 17th-c. version rewritten by Jin Shengtan, and others, with layers added in the 14th and 15th cs.

Whether they are part of a play or simply a song, qu feature northern slang; a common pattern is to end with an earthy punch line delivered in colloquial northern Chinese. Like ci, qu are characterized by lines of uneven length, dictated by the melody, or *qupai*. Rather than determining the prosodic pattern as strictly as in ci, however, the melody is a signpost. This flexibility has partly to do with performance practice. When these prosodic guidelines were translated to the stage, they made for some of the unusual characteristics of zaju. Usually four acts (with a short additional act or "wedge"), each act is comprised of a single song suite—with one rhyme throughout and only a single singer. Had it not been for the use of *chengzi* (padding syllables) and a flexible understanding of rhyme (with no regard for the tone of the rhyming syllables), zaju would have involved too many prosodic strictures to allow for plot devel.

As it is, plot is secondary in zaju, and many are clearly performance pieces to highlight the skills of a single performer: consider, e.g., the scene in which Dou E is wrongfully executed in Guan Hanqing's *Dou E yuan* (*The Injustice to Dou E*). *Xixiang ji* is a formal exception, a successful romantic comedy only because it is five plays, one after the other, comprising a total of 21 acts; each of the two lovers, as well as a maidservant, takes a turn at singing.

Musically, zaju and xiwen were both governed by rules that are deeply arcane now. Melodies belonged to different modes; an act could contain melodies from a single mode, or it could include melodies from different modes, as long as these followed a prescribed pattern.

The first xiwen to circulate widely as a written text was Gao Ming's *Pipa ji* (*The Lute*), which dates from the mid-14th c. Only recently have scholars been able to collect fragments of a number of nanxi, some from the *Yongle Encyclopedia* and others from various tomb excavations. More than one character could sing within a single act; a solo could turn midstream into a duet or a trio or a chorus. From an early point, xiwen were long, 20 acts or longer and probably intended to be performed over the course of two days.

By the early decades of the Ming dynasty, zaju had become the favorite form of the imperial court. A number of scripts have survived in the imperial collections, where they were sometimes edited or even rewritten to avoid the appearance of sedition. One of the best known of early Ming dramatists was Zhu Youdun, grandson of the dynasty's founder.

Over the course of the dynasty, zaju ceased to be an important popular form of performance. What took its place was southern drama, whose great heyday was in the last decades of the Ming dynasty, a period that coincided with an explosive growth in the availability of print material. Alone of all genres of Chinese popular drama, *kunqu* (a performance style to sing chuanqi, the written plays) was essentially born in print in the 1570s, its flagship libretto *Huansha ji* (*Washing Silk*) by Liang Chenyu, who had worked closely with the musician Wei Liangfu. Many other plays in the same style began to appear immediately thereafter—and perhaps more strikingly, an entire cultural apparatus for the production and consumption of chuanqi: guidebooks to prosody, hists. of nanxi, dramatic appreciations. These long plays were probably almost always performed in excerpt. Audiences acquainted themselves with the rest of the play by reading scripts, in which prose dialogue became increasingly important.

Zaju too came under the same pressures and by the late 16th c. was increasingly tied to the world of the imprint. Xu Wei's *Sisheng yuan*

(Four Cries of the Gibbon) is four zaju dealing with the same theme, that of theatricality and identity. All the plays toy with the strictures of zaju: e.g., a monk dies midway through and is reincarnated as a woman, each the protagonist and the sole singing role in his or her respective acts. These plays were radical musically as well, mixing northern and southern melodies. After Xu Wei, numerous playwrights wrote plays that were zaju in name only: short, focusing on a single singer, but no longer adhering to the old prosodic regulations.

Much of what in recent centuries has been considered Yuan drama is filtered through a single anthol., *Yuanqu xuan* (Selection of Yuan Drama, 1611), compiled by Zang Maoxun. Comparing extant Yuan and early Ming sources with those in the anthol. reveals that Zang Maoxun had a heavy editorial hand, embellishing prose dialogue and making endings more climactic and moralistic.

Contemp. discussion of drama concerned the place of prosodic rules and of the stage. The most famous chuanqi of all, *Mudan ting* (*The Peony Pavilion*) by Tang Xianzu, originally written in the Yihuang style, was the touchstone for the 17th-c. enthusiasm for romance but almost unsingable. Both Feng Menglong and Zang Maoxun tried their hand at rewriting it according to the stricter prosodic rules advocated by another contemp. playwright, Shen Jing.

Written largely by elite men to be performed by actors, when acting was a despised profession associated with prostitution, chuanqi plays involve men and women from a range of class backgrounds, often masking their true status. Buffoons pretend to be refined scholars; refined scholars disguise themselves as poor men to avoid recognition; girls pretend to be boys—disguise is the norm, and lang. is used to dissimulate as much as reveal. This extreme heteroglossia is important at a thematic and syntactic level: since at least Song ci, one of the most important rhetorical modes of Chinese poetry is an abrupt shift in ling. register. Nowhere are sharp shifts in register more common and central than in chuanqi. The cl. trad. itself becomes the object of commentary. A single aria might include a quotation from the classics, Tang shi, Song ci, and Ming slang. Puns are common.

Chuanqi continued to be popular throughout the 17th c. and into the 18th, although fewer and fewer were written, and under the Manchus increasingly strict rules were imposed both on performance and performers. The 19th c. saw the decline of the form, which essentially was brought to an end by the Taiping Rebellion of the 1860s.

■ **Critical Studies**: W. L. Idema and S. H. West, *Chinese Theater 1100–1450, A Source Book* (1982); S. H. West, "A Study in Appropriation: Zang Maoxun's *Dou E Yuan*," *JAOS* 101 (1991); T. Lu, *Persons, Roles, and Minds* (2001); C. C. Swatek, *Peony Pavilion Onstage* (2002); *Cambridge History of Chinese Literature*, ed. K. S. Chang and S. Owen, 2 v. (2010).

■ **Translations**: *The Story of the Western Wing*, trans. W. L. Idema and S. H. West (1995); *Scenes for Mandarins*, ed. and trans. C. Birch (1995); *The Peony Pavilion*, trans. C. Birch (2002); *Select Poets and Resources: Monks, Bandits, Lovers, and Immortals: Eleven Early Chinese Plays*, ed. and trans. S. H. West (2010).

T. Lu

CHINESE POETICS. A survey of Chinese poetics must keep in view the intimate association between poetry and music in Chinese trad. The following passage from the *Shang shu* (Classic of Documents), in a section of that work that took shape during the Eastern Zhou (8th–3d c. BCE), depicting the moment when music was instituted by a command from the mythic sage-king Shun to his assistant Kui, provides one key reference point for traditional discussions of poetry:

> The divine ruler [Shun] said: "Kui! I command you to preside over music: to instruct the princes of the state, that they be upright, yet affable; tolerant, yet reverent; that they be firm, yet not cruel; and direct, yet not arrogant. The *shi* expresses aims; singing draws out the expression; the musical mode attunes the sounds, so that the eight timbres accord, none usurping another's place. Thus gods and humans are placed in harmony." Kui said, "I strike the stones, stroke the stones; the hundred beasts take up the dance."

The term *shi*, in its centrality to traditional Chinese poetic discourse, offers the nearest functional analogue to the Western category "poetry." In the above passage, *shi* means simply "lyrics," the words to a song. The statement that "the *shi* expresses aims" itself also doubles as a definition, since the graphs for "express" (*yan*) and "aim" (*zhi*) mirror the two halves of the graph shi. Shi can also designate an ancient musical repertoire overseen by musicians of the Zhou court (1046–256 BCE). This repertoire, seen as descended from the institution of music whose founding is depicted above, became central to the curriculum of traditionalist ritual and musical education. It became fixed over time, and as the old musical settings fell from memory in the Zhou's waning centuries, the remaining written text, an anthol. of 305 poems, was known as the *Shijing* (*Classic of Poetry*, also known as the *Book of Songs*). In med. and later times, the same term referred to "literati shi," i.e., poems in a range of newer verse forms, primarily in pentasyllabic or heptasyllabic lines.

For practical purposes, it is important to distinguish which of these disparate meanings applies in a given use of the term *shi*. In Chinese discussions of the fundamental nature and function of poetry, however, its explanatory power often stems precisely from the way one meaning carries resonances from one or more others. Thus, though the word in Shun's speech means "words to a song," for traditional readers the implications of this pronouncement would include its import for their own study and recitation of the *Shijing*; similarly, later critics of literati shi, even when discussing technical aspects of those later verse forms, often felt obliged to assert an underlying continuity of their activity with the *Shijing* and the sagely institution of music. Just as fully understanding a given instance of the word *shi* often meant situating the particular use in the broader context of a hist. from high antiquity to the present, skill in reading poetry (or listening to speech or song) meant skill in inferring, from the particular expression, a fullness of what the expressive act revealed, not only the poet's implicit intentions but more generally the world to which the poem responded.

Both these aspects of poetic understanding as contextualization—situating the poem in the context of the legacy of ancient music and understanding its particularity by "hearing" its layers of implication—remain prominent throughout later Chinese critical trad., as in Sima Guang's (1019–86) exegesis of the first half of Du Fu's (712–70) "Chun wang" ("Spring Prospect"):

> The capital shattered, hills and rivers remain;
> city walls in springtime: grass and trees grow thickly.
> Stirred by the season—flowers are spattered with tears;
> regretting separation—birds startle the heart.

Sima Guang comments: "The poets of antiquity are to be esteemed for the way their conceptions lie beyond the words, leaving the reader to obtain them only upon reflection; thus 'those who spoke were free from blame, and those who heard had ample means of correcting themselves.' " Here Sima Guang cites from the Mao school Great Preface to the *Shijing* the belief that the ancient shi had provided a channel for indirect expression of resentments, thus fostering social harmony. The point of the quotation is less to suggest that Du Fu was expressing a potentially dangerous resentment than to highlight and commend a latent continuity between Du Fu's poem and the ancient trad. Sima Guang next proceeds to an account of the implicit states of the poet and his world, in keeping with this idea of an ancient poetics of indirection: "To say, 'The capital shattered, hills and rivers remain' shows that there is nothing else. To say, 'city walls in springtime: grass and trees grow thickly' shows that there are no human traces. As for 'flowers' and 'birds,' in ordinary times such things are objects of delight. To see them and weep; to hear them and grieve—the sort of time this is may be known."

Though Shun's dictum states "the shi expresses aims," the scene in which this statement occurs makes clear that the motivating purpose of the institution was not to express particular aims but rather to shape the personalities of "princes of the state." Scenes in the *Analects* where Confucius (551–479 BCE) discusses the *Shi* (whose meaning, in the *Analects*, we see shifting from the musical repertoire referred to as shi toward the fully textual classic *Shi*, or *Shijing*) with his disciples show this *shi jiao* (teaching through poetry) in action. Confucius asserts that having truly studied the *Shi* should entail being competent to act autonomously as the representative of one's ruler in diplomatic exchanges (*Analects* 13.5); indeed, formal performances from the *Shi* were often required at state banquets, demanding not only a command of the repertoire but an acute sensitivity for how contextual meanings might shift with circumstances of performance.

As suggested in the *Shang shu* scene, though, the most immediate purpose of teaching through poetry lay in its shaping effect on the student's personality, instilling a delicate balance between opposed impulses: firmness is desirable but, left unchecked, might turn to cruelty; directness is desirable but, left unchecked, might lead to arrogance. Such harmonizing of opposed tendencies characterizes not only these intended effects of teaching through poetry but the personality of a sage, who is "affable, yet severe; imposing, yet not aggressive; respectful, yet at ease" (*Analects* 7.38, describing Confucius), or the legacy of sagely music itself, which is "joyful, yet not licentious; mournful, yet not grieved to the point of harm" (*Analects* 3.20).

This last comment is uttered by Confucius in response to "Guanju" (Fishhawk), the first poem in the *Shijing*. Evidence within the *Analects* suggests Confucius would have been responding not to a text but to a musical performance. For readers in ages after the musical settings to the *Shi* had been lost, those lost settings became an emblem of the distance separating them from the poems' primordial expressive and transformative power. The Song dynasty scholar Zhu Xi (1130–1200) commented that the reader of the text of "Guanju," by reflection on the poem's words, might gain an understanding of the "rightness of personality" of both the poem's central figure and the poet himself but could never capture the full "harmony of sound and breath" conveyed in the performance as Confucius had heard it. Zhu Xi continues, "[T]hough this seems regrettable, if the student will but attend to the phrases, pondering the inhering principle, so as in this way to nurture the mind, then in this way as well one may attain what is fundamental about studying the *Shi*" (*Shijing jizhuan*). The final aim of the study of the *Shijing* is to recover the efficacy of the musical legacy of the sages through alternate means.

This didactic notion of poetry as an adjunct of the transformative project of sagely music, although it exerted decisive influence over critical statements about poetry's fundamental significance throughout premod. Chinese trad., is far from encompassing the variety of poetry and song as practiced. In ritual contexts, music and song served in communicating with deceased ancestors and other unseen powers. As one human variety of the general cosmic category of *wen*, or patterning, poems were one among many sorts of wen—celestial, terrestrial, and human—that might be fraught with portent based on a dense web of latent interconnections and occult sympathies. We glimpse this element of mystery in the incantatory tone of Kui's response to Shun's charge and in his vision of music as a force to which even animals respond—Kui himself, though euhemerized in the *Shang shu* scene as a human minister, in other contexts appears as a crocodile-like figure, associated with the magical power of drumming via the use of reptile skins for drumheads.

There were always ample instances of poetry and music of ecstatic rapture, divine trance, and sensual abandon to affront traditionalist ideals of harmony and the delicate balancing of opposed impulses, filling scholars with something like the unease Plato felt about allowing poets into his ideal city. Even certain poems and sections within the *Shijing* itself, particularly the "Guo feng" (Airs of the States) sections tied to the states of Zheng and Wei, were deemed symptomatic of a loss of emotional and moral equilibrium, and the significance of their inclusion in the canon (an editorial choice attributed within the trad. to Confucius) was a fraught and productive problem for later crit. The *Chuci*, reflecting a poetics of religious ecstasy and sensual transport, along with the Western Han (206 BCE–8 CE) rise of the poetic genre of *fu*, which drew largely on both the prosody and underlying aesthetic from the Chuci trad., posed further challenges for Han and later scholars striving to accommodate these later poetic modes to the traditionalist paradigm. A typical strategy for accomplishing this involved invoking concepts such as *bian* (mutation) or *liu* (offstream), allowing these poetic modes to be seen as deviations while leaving open the possibility of viewing them as continuations of the legacy of the ancient shi by altered means, in response to larger processes of historical change.

The turn of the 3d c. saw the rise of the literati shi, along with fu and the full repertoire of genres of belletristic writing. The "Lun wen" (Discourse on Literature) of Cao Pi (186–226), first emperor of the Wei dynasty (220–65), marks a watershed both for its overt assertion that composition in these genres could be a means to cultural immortality and for its theorization of the system of affinities between particular sorts of talent and particular literary modes. Over subsequent centuries, a view emerged of poetic hist. as a repertoire of styles that could be read in terms both of divergent personalities and of distinct historical eras. Zhong Rong's (ca. 468–516) "Shi pin" (Grades of Poetry) ranked poets in the pentasyllabic shi form from its beginnings down to Zhong's own lifetime in "top," "middle," and "lower" grades, giving a précis of each poet's style and in many instances specifying its antecedents. Not surprisingly, among the most praised styles were those affiliated directly to the *Shijing*.

The intermittent inclusion during the Tang dynasty (618–907) of composition in shi and fu genres in the requirements for candidates for the prestigious *jin shi* (Presented Scholar) degree is itself unimaginable apart from the ancient conception of music and poetry as tools to mold "princes of the state" into sound administrators. The prestige of these poetic forms, along with increasingly demanding rules for tonal regulation and syntactical parallelism, created a need for instructional guides for poetic composition. The resulting body of material, largely composed of lists of prohibitions, typologies of parallel couplets, rosters of stylistic subtypes, and so on, came to be viewed as middlebrow at best, since the orthodox view of poetry as stemming organically from the poet's response to events of the world could not admit the validity of fixed rules for poetic composition.

Something of this tension between, on the one hand, the practical need for technical analysis and prescriptive methods and, on the other, reassertions of the organic connection between poetry and the broader project of cl. studies and personal transformation is reflected throughout the proliferating lit. of poetic crit. from the Song dynasty (960–1279) onward. Many of the enduring arguments reprise themes from the early hist. of shi, incl. discussions of the relation between inner emotional states and outer scene, calls for *fu gu* (restoration of antiquity), debates about the proper choice of models and about striking the proper balance in studying such models, between careful imitation and the expression of the student's own personality. Analogies to and ideas drawn from Chinese Buddhist trads. became a prominent feature of Song dynasty and later poetic crit., with the critic Yan Yu (late 12th–early 13th c.) often cited as the first to draw an explicit analogy between Zen enlightenment and poetic inspiration and Wang Shizhen (1634–1711) regarded as a highly influential late imperial exemplar.

Just as the fu had been assimilated to the traditionalist view of poetic hist. as a mutated offstream of the ancient shi, critical discourses surrounding later lyric genres incl. *ci* (song lyric) or *qu*, the diverse constellation of song forms that from the Yuan dynasty (1271–1368) onward formed the lyrical building blocks of a rich operatic lit. reflect a similar tension between genre-specific technical discussions and the impulse to link the basic expressive and transformative power of these genres back to the ancient shi and the mythology of the transformative power of music. Even seemingly remote genres such as narrative fiction and the "eight-legged essay" that was the staple of examination cultures of the Ming and Qing dynasties came to be viewed in their own ways as mutated analogues to the sagely legacy of music.

See CHINA, POETRY OF; CHINA, POPULAR POETRY OF; CHINESE POETIC DRAMA; CHINESE POETRY IN ENGLISH TRANSLATION; CHINESE POETRY IN JAPAN.

■ Liu Xie, *The Literary Mind and the Carving of Dragons*, trans. V.Y.C. Shih (1959)—trans of *Wenxin diaolong*; J.J.Y. Liu, *Chinese Theories of Literature* (1975); R. J. Lynn, "Orthodoxy and Enlightenment—Wang Shih-chen's Theory of Poetry and Its Antecedents," *The Unfolding of Neo-Confucianism*, ed. W. T. de Bary (1975); *Theories of the Arts in China*, ed. S. Bush and C. Murck (1983); S. Owen, *Chinese Poetry and Poetics: Omen of the World* (1985); *The Indiana Companion to Traditional Chinese Literature*, ed. W. Nienhauser (1986); P. Yu, *The Reading of Imagery in the Chinese Poetic Tradition* (1987); S. Van Zoeren, *Poetry and Personality: Reading, Exegesis, and Hermeneutics in Traditional China* (1991); S. Owen, *Readings in Traditional Chinese Literary Thought* (1992); H. Saussy, *The Problem of a Chinese Aesthetic* (1993); R. Ashmore, "The Banquet's Aftermath: Yan Jidao's *Ci* Poetics and the High Tradition," *T'oung Pao* 88 (2002); R. Sterckx, *The Animal and the Daemon in Early China* (2002); M. Kern, "Western Han Aesthetics and the Genesis of the *Fu*," *HJAS* 63 (2003); *Chinese Aesthetics: The Ordering of Literature, the Arts, and the Universe in the Six Dynasties*, ed. Z. Cai (2004).

R. ASHMORE

CHINESE POETRY IN ENGLISH TRANSLATION. Chinese poems began to be paraphrased in Western langs. in the 17th c. when Jesuit missionaries, seeking support for their policy of cultural accommodation, reported on the advanced literary, scientific, and philosophical state of China. Efforts at translation into Fr., Ger., and Eng. were peripheral to lit. and even to scholarship until Ezra Pound published *Cathay* (1915). This book of 14 cl. Chinese poems, rewritten from the word-for-word versions of Ernest Fenollosa and his Japanese tutors, first exhibited the characteristics of the hybrid Chinese-Eng. poetic lang.: end-stopped, stress-heavy lines, mostly monosyllabic, using coordination rather than subordination and often appearing to have left something out. See the opening lines of Pound's "Poem by the Bridge at Ten-Shin" (from Li Bai, "Gu feng 59 shou," no. 18):

> March has come to the bridge head,
> Peach flowers and apricot boughs hang over a thousand gates,
> At morning there are flowers to cut the heart,
> And evening drives them on the eastward-flowing waters.

Pound's trans. practice foregrounds the "qualities of vivid presentation" he found in Fenollosa's notes and emulates the way "Chinese poets have been content to set forth their matter without moralizing and without comment" ("Chinese Poetry, I" in *Early Writings*). As if to confirm the imagist call for "direct treatment of the thing, whether objective or subjective" and to "use absolutely no word that does not contribute to the presentation" (Pound, "Imagisme" [1913]), the 8th-c. Chinese poet here ventriloquized uses the present tense, speaks in short bursts of observation, and withholds comment on things not outwardly visible save for the (possibly idiomatic) expression of the flowers' effect on feelings. Weak personification ("March has come," "evening drives them") serves mainly to give the sentences subjects and verbs. An unobtrusive allegory (flowers driven on unidirectional currents from morning to evening) supports the elegiac tone.

Contrast the effort of Fenollosa some years earlier to render a different 8th-c. poem (Wang Wei, "Gao yuan") in Eng. verse:

> Crimson the snare of the peaches that catch the dews on the wing.
> Verdant the face of the willows that bathe in winds of the spring.
> Petals have fallen all night, but no dutiful maid is yet sweeping.
> Larks have been up with the dawn, but the guest of the mountain is sleeping.

The end-stopped sentences and the speaker's reticence are all there, but the clockwork meter and banally elaborate diction separate it from the genre of the Eng.-lang. "Chinese poem" initiated by Pound.

"The element in poetry which travels best," as Graham observed, "is of course concrete imagery": Chinese poetry came into fashion in the Eng.-speaking world just when imagery reigned supreme. Unspoken meanings, another feature of much Chinese poetry, are not the translator's problem. Most translators since Pound, those at any rate whose audience is readers of poetry, have adopted the terse plainness of *Cathay*. The 21 trans. by different hands of a single quatrain by Wang Wei, collected by Weinberger, shows the steady advance of this manner. Wai-lim Yip and Gary Snyder, poets in their own right, contend in theoretical writings and by the example of their trans. that Chinese poetry gives direct access to perception unclouded by lang., a radicalization of the theory of the ideogram: thus, their versions adapt the Eng. lang. to their purposes, shedding pronouns, tenses, prepositions and other explicative machinery. More recent translators have explored electronic means of staging Chinese poems in some form of Eng. Anthols. of Chinese poetry in trans. permit taking stock of this stream of trad.

The effortless simplicity seen in trans. Chinese poetry is not just a style but an ethos. As ethos, it becomes a mode or manner of mod. Am. poetry, for which knowledge of Chinese is not required. The poets of the Chinese canon become models, ancestors, interlocutors. James Wright addresses an 8th-c. predecessor with an echo of Charles Baudelaire ("As I Step over a Puddle at the End of Winter, I Think of an Ancient Chinese Governor," 1963). Charles Wright paraphrases Du Fu ("China Mail," 1997). Am. poetry of the 20th c. is unimaginable without the Chinese contribution. Chinese poetry since the 1980s has included this Am. poetry in a Chinese manner among its influences, a rhetorical resource separate from the models of cl. Chinese poetry.

■ A. C. Graham, *Poems of the Late T'ang* (1977); E. Weinberger, *Nineteen Ways of Looking at Wang Wei* (1987); W. Yip, *Diffusion of Distances: Dialogues between Chinese and Western Poetics* (1993); R. Kern, *Orientalism, Modernism and the American Poem* (1996); S. Yao, *Translation and the Languages of Modernism* (2002); *The New Directions Anthology of Classical Chinese Poetry*, ed. E. Weinberger (2003); E. Pound, *Poems and Translations* (2003); E. Hayot, *Chinese Dreams: Pound, Brecht, "Tel Quel"* (2004); E. Pound, *Early Writings*, ed. I. Nadel (2005); *Classical Chinese Poetry*, trans. D. Hinton (2008); E. Fenollosa and E. Pound, *The Chinese Character as a Medium for Poetry*, ed. H. Saussy et al. (2008).

H. Saussy

CHINESE POETRY IN JAPAN

I. Terminology, Genres, and Characteristics
II. History

I. Terminology, Genres, and Characteristics

A. *Terminology.* There is no consensus that "Chinese poetry in Japan" is the best way to describe poetry composed by Japanese in a script-lang. often called "Chinese." The disagreement about what to call this poetry indicates how differently these poems are viewed. One not entirely logical trad. among Western scholars uses the Japanese terms *kanshi* and *kanbun* in the sense of, respectively, poems and prose in Chinese composed by Japanese. However, since the late 19th c., these terms, often in the fused form *kanshibun* (poems and prose in Chinese) in Japan refer to any text in Chinese, usually from China; Japanese scholars commonly refer to "Japanese *kanshi*" (*Nihon kanshi*). Alternatively, kanshi from Japan have been often called "Japanese poems in Chinese" and conversely "Sino-Japanese" poetry.

Behind the terminology lurks a lang. question: namely, whether Sino-Japanese poetry is, in fact, "Chinese" or is better understood as a form of Japanese. Choice of terminology has implications for assumptions of "foreignness" of Chinese poetry in Japan. The idea that the lang. of kanshi in Japan is a form Japanese, or at the very least not the same as "Sino-Chinese," is recently gaining some ground and suggests that poems in (some form of) "Chinese" are more and more considered to be an indigenous part of the Japanese literary trad. At the same time, Sino-Japanese poetry is part of a larger East Asian body of poetry in variant forms of Chinese (China, Korea, Vietnam).

B. *Genres and Characteristics.* The poetic trad. of Sino-Japanese poetry is long and diverse, but it is important to understand that these poems are usually seen in contrast with, or even opposition to, poetry in Japanese (*waka*). Whereas some of waka's predominant features are its brevity and rather strict adherence to alternating units of five and seven syllables, its stress on ling. purity, and its inclination to limit itself to certain thematic sets (notably love and the nature imagery of the four seasons), Sino-Japanese poetry is free from most such restraints: it can be quite long (several hundreds of lines) and has total thematic freedom—a feature that most appealed to its practitioners. Grounded in a long and varied generic trad. in China, as well as Japan, Chinese poetry in Japan also knows a large variety of formats. Japanese literati of the cl. period already distinguished various literary genres: *bun* (Chinese *wen*, rhyming prose), *hitsu* (Chinese *bi*, rhymeless prose), *shi* (rhyming poem), *fu* (poetic exposition), *ku* (Chinese *ju*, couplet), etc. Rhyming or nonrhyming was perhaps an even more important distinction than poetry or prose.

Nevertheless, from the beginning, one particular form has been preferred by Japanese poets: the shi, usually of eight lines and always with equal lines of either five or seven graphs or characters. In fact, the *shi* in *kanshi* is both a generic term (a poem in Chinese, as opposed to one in Japanese) and a specific genre within the domain of Sino-Japanese poetry (i.e., rhyming poem). "Old style" shi poetry is relatively free of tonal patterns, unlike the "regulated poem" (Chinese *lüshi*, Japanese *risshi*) that became dominant in Tang period (618–907) China and later in Japan as well. Variant forms are the quatrain (Chinese *jueju*, Japanese *zekku*) and the "aligned regulated [poem]" (Chinese *pailü*, Japanese *hairitsu*; a shi of more than eight lines). The shi has a fairly standard structure in which a theme is elaborated and brought to conclusion. The shi also rhymes, which may not be as obvious as it sounds: the Sino-Japanese reading (*on*) of a graph does not lend itself easily to meaningful rhyme, and Japanese poets based their rhyme schemes on classic rhyme dictionaries. For centuries, the same held true for most poets in China.

Sino-Japanese poetry was meant to be read aloud. From at least the cl. period onward, reading, or even singing, was typically performed in *yomikudashi* (var. *kundoku*), a type of pronunciation in which clusters of words are pronounced by their *on* reading (the pronunciation that simulates to some extent Chinese pronunciation) but adjusted to Japanese grammar. This longstanding habit, which continues to this day, is one reason that some scholars feel that Sino-Japanese poetry functions as poetry in Japanese rather than in Chinese.

The composition of Sino-Japanese poetry was almost exclusively a male affair. The existence of a handful of female Sino-Japanese poets at the early cl. court or the uniquely talented Ema Saikō (1787–1861) and a few other contemp. women poets does not detract from the fact that, from the 10th c. on, women were not actively trained in writing Sino-Japanese nor encouraged to express themselves in that lang.

II. History

A. *Ancient and Classical Periods (to 1185).* By the reign of the emperor (*tennō*) Tenji (r. 661–71), the composition of poetry in Chinese seems to have been a regular activity. Not much is extant from these earliest compositions. The earliest extant anthol. of Sino-Japanese poetry is *Kaifūsō* (Patterned Sea-Grasses of a Cherished Style, 751). *Man'yōshū* (Collection for Ten Thousand Generations, mid- to late 8th c.), Japan's oldest anthol. of waka, also contains several Sino-Japanese poems. Although these early court poems in Sino-Japanese were not much alluded to by later generations, the court continued to be the important locus for the composition of Sino-Japanese poems when the capital was moved from Heijō-kyō (Nara) to Heian-kyō (Kyoto), just as Six Dynasties' (316–589) poetry from China remained a notable touchstone. Many of the poems reflect this court setting, in which congratulatory and banquet poetry formed a central genre. Important are three royal kanshi anthols.: *Ryōunshū* (Cloud Topping Collection, 814), *Bunka shūreishū* (Collection of Beauties among the Literary Flowers, 818), and *Keikokushū* (Collection for Governing the State, 827), as well as the collected poetry of Sugawara no Michizane (845–903). This was also when the Japanese discovered the works of Bai Juyi (772–846), who would remain the best-regarded Chinese poet, and became more enamored of (esp. late) Tang (618–907) poetry. An early and influential text to couple Sino-Japanese couplets (ku) to waka is *Wakan rōeishū* (Chinese and Japanese Poems to Sing, early 11th c.), which coincides with the dominance of "verse-topic poetry" (*kudaishi*): poems that were composed to set topics consisting of a line of verse. Later court poets' preference for nature and temple-visiting poetry can be gleaned from *Honchō mudaishi* (Non-Verse Topic Poems from Our Court, 1162–64?).

B. *Medieval Period (1185–1600).* With the rise of Zen institutions in Kamakura and Kyoto supported by the new shogunate and collectively known as *gozan* (the five mountains—that is, monasteries), the center of Sino-Japanese composition had by the beginning of the 14th c. shifted to monastic communities. The monasteries were also actively engaged in the printing of Chinese texts and in Chinese scholarship in general, although court scholars continued to be active as well. Unlike court poets before them, several monks visited China. In keeping with the Zen (Chinese Chan) trads. from the mainland, fostered by Chinese priests who came to Japan, such as Yishan Yining (Japanese Issan Ichinei, 1247–1317), lit. and specifically poetry played a central role in the monks' lives. Traditionally, a distinction is made between the Zen Buddhist verse (*geju*) composed by gozan poets and their thematically much freer poetry in the shi format, which shows their readings from Song (960–1279) poets. While most well-known gozan poets such as Kokan Shiren (1278–1346), Sesson Yūbai (1290–1348), Gidō Shūshin (1325–88), or Zekkai Chūshin (1336–1405) emphatically worked within their monastic institutions, the Zen monk Ikkyū Sōjun (1394–1481) operated outside them. From the 15th c., the scholarly trad. of the gozan monks gained in importance, and here the seeds were sown for the blossoming of neo-Confucian studies in early mod. Japan.

C. *Early Modern Period (1600–1868).* Although Sino-Japanese poets existed in the 17th c., notably the former warrior and recluse Ishikawa Jōzan (1583–1672) and the prolific scholar and thinker Hayashi Razan (1583–1657), not many were active. This changed dramatically after the first century of Tokugawa rule (1600–1868): during the early mod. period, Chinese studies became an integral part of literary studies in general, and poetry and prose were composed in numbers that were never equaled before or after. It was the golden age of Sino-Japanese lit. Chinese studies was a natural extension of Confucian studies and esp. the study of the thought of Zhu Xi (1130–1200). The neo-Confucian thinker Ogyū Sorai (1666–1728) and his followers, who emphasized the active composition of Sino-Japanese poetry and prose, played a pivotal role.

In 18th- and early 19th-c. Japan, the obvious centers for Sino-Japanese poets were no longer few in number. Academies (*juku*), both private and operated under the auspices of the lord (*daimyō*) of a domain (*han*), were practically everywhere, and thorough training in the classics could be had throughout the country. Scholars made a living teaching aspiring Sino-Japanese poets. Many Japanese, esp. well-educated city dwellers, both of samurai and merchant descent, were able to compose a Sino-Japanese poem, and many did. Attempts at listing major early mod. poets, therefore, fail by definition; but any list would contain Kan Chazan (1748–1827), the Zen monk Ryōkan

(1758–1831), and Ema Saikō's mentor Rai San'yō (1780–1832).

D. *Modern Period (after 1868).* The dramatic political and social changes of the mid- through late 19th c. in Japan did nothing to stem the immense outpouring of emotions and ideas in the form of Sino-Japanese poetry. This phenomenon continued even after Japanese had established itself as the new "national language" (*kokugo*), ca. 1890. A symbol of how intertwined Sino-Japanese poetry became with the hist. of Japanese lit. as a whole, Natsume Sōseki (1867–1916), perhaps Japan's most revered novelist, composed a Sino-Japanese poem nearly every day toward the end of his life.

■ **Anthologies:** *Japanese Literature in Chinese*, trans. B. Watson (1975–76); *Poems of the Five Mountains*, trans. M. Ury (1977); *Zen Poems of the Five Mountains*, trans. D. Pollack (1985); *Kanshi: The Poetry of Ishikawa Jōzan and Other Edo-period Poets*, trans. B. Watson (1990); *Great Fool: Zen Master Ryōkan*, trans. R. Abé and P. Haskel (1996); *An Anthology of Kanshi (Chinese Verse) by Japanese Poets of the Edo Period*, trans. J. N. Rabinovitch and T. R. Bradstock (1997); *Breeze through Bamboo*, trans. H. Sato (1997); *Japanese and Chinese Poems to Sing*, trans. J. T. Rimer and J. Chaves (1997); *Early Modern Literature*, ed. H. Shirane (2002); *Dance of the Butterflies: Chinese Poetry from the Japanese Court Tradition*, trans. J. N. Rabinovitch and T. R. Bradstock (2005); *Tradiional Japanese Literature*, ed. H. Shirane (2006).

■ **Criticism:** D. Keene, *World within Walls* (1976); J. Konishi, *A History of Japanese Literature*, trans. A. Catten and N. Teele (1984–91); H. C. McCullough, *Brocade by Night* (1985); R. Borgen, *Sugawara no Michizane and the Early Heian Court* (1986); D. Pollack, *The Fracture of Meaning* (1986); D. Keene, *Seeds in the Heart* (1993); I. Smits, *The Pursuit of Loneliness* (1995); A. Yiu, "In Quest of an Ending: An Examination of Sōseki's *Kanshi*," *Studies in Modern Japanese Literature*, ed. D. Washburn and A. Tansman (1997); I. Smits, "Song as Cultural History," *Monumenta Nipponica* 55 (2000); W. Denecke, "Chinese Antiquity and Court Spectacle in Early *Kanshi*," *Journal of Japanese Studies* (2004); P. Rouzer, "Early Buddhist *Kanshi*," *Monumenta Nipponica* 59 (2004); W. Denecke, "'Topic Poetry Is All Ours,'" *HJAS* 67 (2007); M. Fraleigh, "Songs of the Righteous Spirit," *HJAS* 69 (2009).

I. Smits

COLOMBIA, POETRY OF. While recent studies of Colombian poetry include the voices of pre-Columbian peoples, their legends, chants, and poems were gathered by scholars in the last 50 years. These chants belong to the U'wa, Cuna, Kogi, Mwiska, Huitoto, Guahibo, and Desana tribes, among others. Despite their ethnographic value, the oral poems of these indigenous peoples have had little effect on the formation of a Colombian poetic trad., which is based on Sp. lang. and culture.

The chronicler Juan de Castellanos (1522–1606) is considered the first Colombian poet. His monumental Ren. epic *Elegías de Varones Ilustres de Indias* (Elegies of Illustrious Men, 1589, first part), contains 113,609 hendecasyllabic verses in *octavas reales*, celebrating the heroic deeds of the Sp. conquerors in northern South America and the Caribbean. The later colonial period, from the late 16th to the 18th c., reflects the influence of Sp. baroque culture. Born in Quito, Hernando Domínguez Camargo (1606–59) is the best representative of this period. His masterpiece is *San Ignacio de Loyola, Fundador de la Compañía de Jesús: Poema Heroyco* (Saint Ignatius of Loyola, Founder of the Society of Jesus: A Heroic Poem, 1666). Domínguez Camargo brought Gongorist verse (in the vein of the Sp. poet Luis de Góngora), marked by the use of hyperbaton, elaborate metaphor, and cl. references. The nun Sor Francisca Josefa del Castillo y Guevara (1671–1742) is one of the most important writers of the colonial period. She is the author of the mystical Catholic book *Afectos espirituales* (Spiritual Feelings, 1843), which includes prose and verse, and an autobiographical *Vida* (Life, 1817). In the 18th c., the most important Colombian poet was Francisco Vélez Ladrón de Guevara (1721–81?). Mainly a poet of the viceregal court, Ladrón de Guevara wrote an elegant and crafted verse with a rococo influence, such as *Octavario a la Inmaculada Concepción* (1774).

Across Sp. America, the beginning of the 19th c. was marked by revolutionary movements against the colonial powers. In Colombia, the opposition to Sp. rule united many intellectuals and writers, incl. the poet José Fernández Madrid (1789–1830), who signed the document of Cartagena declaring independence (1811) and was persecuted and exiled by the Spaniards. His *Poesías* (1822) appeared during his exile in Cuba. He is considered a romantic liberal, the link between the neoclassical current of the 18th c. and the romantic movement of the 19th. Another important poet of this period is Luis Vargas Tejada (1802–29). A precocious intellectual, polyglot, and author of tragedies, comedies, and lyric poetry, he was consumed by the political events of his time. His neoclassical poems were published in the book *Poesías de Caro y Vargas Tejada* (1857).

Although the romantic period in Colombia lacked the resonance that it had in Europe, it represented a change in poetic attitudes and themes. Proof of this is the presence in prose and poetry of certain motifs: nature, freedom, and the faith in the individual as owner of his destiny. José Eusebio Caro (1817–53) is one of the most important Colombian poets of this period. Because of his agitated political life and early death, his poems were published only posthumously in the aforementioned volume with Vargas Tejada (1857) and *Obras escogidas* (Selected Works, 1873). Caro is considered a precursor of fin de siècle *modernismo*.

Rafael Pombo (1833–1912) is perhaps the best representative of the romantic period in Colombia. His poetry, highly passionate and obscure, includes two of the best known poems in Colombian lit. hist., "Hora de tinieblas" (Hour of Darkness) and "Noche de diciembre" (December Night). Miguel Antonio Caro (1843–1909), like Rufino José Cuervo (1844–1911), was an important philologist and grammarian. He is praised as a conservative poet who rejected the advances of Sp. Am. modernismo and looked for an ideal, almost mystical form of poetry. *Horas de amor* (Hours of Love, 1871) and *Poesías* (1896) are his most important books.

In 1886 in Bogotá, José María Rivas Groot (1863–1923) published an extensive anthol. of Colombian poets, *La Lira Nueva* (The New Lyre), seeking to indicate new directions. Thirty-three poets are included, among them Ismael Enrique Arciniegas (1865–1938), Candelario Obeso (1849–84), Carlos Arturo Torres (1867–1911), Julio Flórez (1867–1923), José Asunción Silva (1865–96), and Groot himself.

Silva is one of the leading figures of modernismo. Although his poetry is linked to the romantic period, it represents a breakthrough in Colombian poetry, unifying form, theme, and music. Silva employed an ample variety of poetic forms according to Sp. trad. as well as the resources of the Fr. symbolist movement. His books were published posthumously.

Two of the poets included in *La Lira Nueva* deserve special attention: Obeso and Flórez. Obeso is among the first Sp. Am. poets to bring Afro-Caribbean diction into Sp. For the Colombian people more than for scholars, Flórez epitomizes the honorific *poet*, despite his late romanticism and formalism.

Within modernismo, Guillermo Valencia (1873–1943) epitomizes the highly intellectual poet with a vast knowledge of forms and themes. His books include *Ritos* (Rites, 1899) and *Sus mejores poemas* (His Best Poems, 1926). Porfirio Barba Jacob (1883–1938) represents the *poète maudit*. A vagabond, drug addict, and homosexual, Barba Jacob defied Colombian society even as he published some of the better known poems of the period. His work mixed a very personal romantic tendency with modernist forms. Notable volumes are *Rosas negras* (Black Roses, 1933) and *Canciones y elegías* (Songs and Elegies, 1933). Another popular poet of this period is Luis Carlos López (1879–1950). His poetry, sarcastic and humoristic, centers on Cartagena, his native city. López's poetry departs from the main trad. in favor of colloquial and direct lang. that borders on prosaic. His books include *De mi villorio* (From My Town, 1908) and *Por el atajo* (Easy Way Out, 1920).

Best known for his novel *La Vorágine* (*The Vortex*), José Eustacio Rivera (1889–1928) is a modernist poet in the line of Parnassianism, cl. in form but not completely detached from emotion. His only book was *Tierra de promisión* (Promised Land, 1921). Contemporary with Rivera, Eduardo Castillo (1889–1938) published his books *Duelo lírico* (Lyric Grief, 1918) and *El árbol que canta* (The Singing Tree, 1927) in a symbolist aesthetic.

In 1925, the literary magazine *Los nuevos* (The New Ones) appeared in Bogotá, featuring a large group of young Colombian poets and writers. While it was not aligned with the contemporaneous avant-garde movements in Europe and Lat. Am., the jour. sought to bring a change to the literary climate of the country. León de Greiff (1895–1976) was the most important poet of this group. With a very personal voice and a practice derived from Fr. symbolism and the avant-garde, De Greiff published several important volumes, incl. *Tergiversaciones de Leo Legris, Matías Aldecoa y Gaspar* (Tergiversations on Leo Legris, Matías Aldecoa, and Gaspar, 1923) and *Libro de los signos* (Book of Signs, 1930). In contrast with de Greiff, Rafael Maya (1898–1980), another poet of Los nuevos, dedicated his life to a conservative poetics combining romanticism and modernismo in search of cl. forms.

With his book of poems *Suenan timbres* (Bells Sound, 1926), Luis Vidales (1900–90) introduced the avant-garde into the Colombian trad. The book was to resound in the years to come, esp. for the poets of the 1960s. After *Suenan timbres* Vidales changed his tone and wrote poetry of social commitment. Another poet linked to Los nuevos was Jorge Zalamea (1905–69). Known for his exemplary trans. of Saint-John Perse, his work—esp. *El sueño de las escalinatas* (Dream of the Staircases, 1964)—follows the same discursive and incantatory line, although with a political militancy.

During the 1930s, Sp. Am. poetry developed experimental works and innovative approaches based on surrealism, cubism, creationism, and other movements, both local and imported. Colombian poetry, however, took a more conservative approach, strengthening its relation with traditional Sp. poetry. The product of these ideas was a group called *Piedra y Cielo* (Stone and Sky), which took its name from a book of the Sp. poet Juan Ramón Jiménez. Aurelio Arturo (1906–74) was regularly associated with this group, although his poetry does not greatly resemble the others. In spite of his restrained style, his poetry flows with images, metaphors that illuminate the link between the human and nature (while questioning their existence), and exaltations of love. After the surge of the avant-gardes in the 1960s, Arturo had perhaps the greatest influence on other Colombian poets. He wrote few poems, collected in *Morada al Sur* (Southern Dwelling, 1975).

Eduardo Carranza (1913–85) is the most representative poet of Piedra y Cielo. While conservative and traditional, his verses manifest some traces of the Chilean poet Vicente Huidobro's creationism. The other poets of the school were Arturo Camacho Ramírez (1910–82), Jorge Rojas (1911–95), Tomás Vargas Osorio (1908–41), Darío Samper (1909–84), Gerardo Valencia (1911–94), and Carlos Martín (1914–2008).

With the poets who emerged during the 1940s and 1950s, Colombia's conservative trad. suffered a crushing blow. Although they formed no literary group, these poets have been studied as a generation under the name of the literary jour. *Mito* (Myth), published by Jorge Gaitán Durán (1934–62) in Bogotá after 1955. Gaitán Durán promoted changes in the Colombian intelligentsia, not only with respect to lit. but in the general way of thinking about the nation's problems, esp. the continuous political violence. The poetry of Álvaro Mutis (1923–2013) absorbs the freedom of the avant-garde movements without stridency or obscurity; his important books are *Los elementos del desastre* (Elements of Disaster, 1953) and *Summa de Maqroll el Gaviero* (The Summa of Maqroll el Gaviero, 1973). Fernando Charry Lara (1920–2004), another poet of the Mito generation, condenses several currents of mod. poetry to find a highly particular voice between the obscure and the transparent.

The other poets of this generational cohort are Eduardo Cote Lamus (1928–64), Héctor Rojas Herazo (1921–2002), Fernando Arbeláez (1924–95), and Rogelio Echavarría (b. 1926). Cote Lamus is a conceptual poet, with an introspective and conservative vision of existence. Arbeláez produces a sober poetry with a narrative logic and a universal vision. Rojas Herazo is an exuberant poet, with a strong voice that echoes contemp. colloquialisms. Echavarría's poetry—somber, with a strange beauty—is concentrated in the daily life of the anonymous passersby who populate big cities. His most important book is *El transeúnte* (The Transient, 1964).

Close to this group is Carlos Obregón (1929–1963). His life as well as his poetry distanced itself from the Colombian literary world because of his voluntary exile in the United States and Europe. He wrote short, reflective poems with mystical tendencies. His books are *Distancia destruida* (Destroyed Distance, 1957) and *Estuario* (Estuary, 1961).

Before the 1960s, Colombian poetry by women was scarce. Two exceptions are Maruja Vieira (b. 1922) and Dora Castellanos (b. 1924), who wrote often in traditional forms about love.

The convulsive 1960s brought drastic changes in how poets approached poetry, not only from the intellectual but from the existential point of view. The lack of a local avant-garde movement and the continuous political violence made possible the emergence of a group of poets and writers that directly challenged the order and direction of Colombian lit. This group, called *Nadaísmo* (Nothingism), was composed mainly of poets. Ostensibly having no explicit aesthetic or literary program, the group claimed its only agenda was complete freedom. The most important poets were Gonzalo Arango (1931–76), Jaime Jaramillo Escobar (b. 1932), Mario Rivero (1935–2009),

Jota Mario Arbeláez (b. 1940), Amilkar Osorio (1940–85), Eduardo Escobar (b. 1943), and Armando Romero (b. 1944).

With the slogan "we are geniuses, crazy and dangerous," Arango led the movement. Mainly a prose writer, his scarce poetry was always incendiary, colloquial, and discursive. Arango never collected his poems. A complete selection of them can be seen in the *Antología del Nadaísmo* (2009).

Although he rejected his affiliation with the nadaísta group, Rivero figured in the two main anthols. of this group and was recognized for years as a member. His poetry, colloquial and direct, looks for simplicity in the daily life of the urban dweller. Among his books are *Poemas urbanos* (Urban Poems, 1966) and *Baladas* (1980). Jaramillo Escobar's poems, obscure and transparent at the same time, deal with love, violence, and death, although with a humorous and ironic attitude. His books include *Los poemas de la ofensa* (Poems of Offense, 1968) and *Poemas de tierra caliente* (Poems of the Hot Land, 1985). Arbeláez's poetry is marked by a colloquial rhythm that borders on the prose poem. It combines witty humor with surreal metaphors and word plays, dealing with love, sex, and violence. His books include *El profeta en su casa* (Prophet in His House, 1966) and *Mi reino por este mundo* (My Kingdom in This World, 1980). Osorio cultivated a baroque poetry, learned and conceptual, in only one book, *Vana Stanza, diván selecto* (Vain Stanza: Selected Divan, 1984). Escobar's poetry, such as his first books *La invención de la uva* (The Invention of the Grape, 1966) and *Monólogos de Noé* (Monologues of Noah, 1967), is colloquial and irreverent, concerned with love and political topics. Romero's books include *El poeta de vidrio* (The Glass Poet, 1979) and *A vista del tiempo* (A View of Time, 2005).

Contemp. to the nadaístas were three poets who, cultivating a personal voice, followed the moderate character of traditional Colombian poetry. Giovanni Quessep (b. 1939) is a formalist poet who returns to symbolism for musical and verbal elements, which he will transform in incantatory and obscure poems where lyric and narrative become intertwined. José Manuel Arango (1937–2002) was a rigorous poet of brevity and musicality. His first books include *Este lugar de la noche* (This Place of Night, 1973) and *Signos* (Signs, 1978). Jaime García Maffla (b. 1944) is a philosophical and religious poet. His poems, cathedrals of lang., are obscure and liturgical.

During the 1970s, another group of poets, called by critics the *Generación sin nombre* (Generation without a Name), confronted the nadaístas. This challenge was not aesthetic or programmatic, since these poets also espoused freedom of forms and themes, colloquialism, and a questioning of conservative values. Their goal was literary-political, to reshape Colombia's literary world. The critic and poet Juan Gustavo Cobo Borda (b. 1948) was a central figure in remaking the canon, as in *La tradición de la pobreza* (The Tradition of Poverty, 1980). His poetry, however, followed the line of nadaísmo (sarcasm, humor, colloquialism) with self-confidence. María Mercedes Carranza (1945–2003) continued the trend of colloquial poetry, rejecting sentimentalism in favor of a direct, common speech. Elkin Restrepo (b. 1942) was linked to the nadaísta group at the beginning of his career, although he distanced himself early in the 1970s. His poetry, ranging from the prose poem to conventional verse, deals with urban life and a nostalgic feeling for the past. His books include *Bla, bla, bla* (1967) and *Retrato de artistas* (Portrait of Artists, 1983).

Harold Alvarado Tenorio (b. 1945) is an irreverent poet of love and Colombian society as well as a critic. Among his books are *Pensamientos de un hombre llegado el invierno* (Thoughts of a Man Come to Winter, 1972) and *Recuerda cuerpo* (Remember Body, 1983). Juan Manuel Roca (b. 1946) combines a deep lyricism and direct, almost surreal images. His themes vary from love and everyday life to social issues, without falling into politics or the colloquialisms of his time. His books include *Memoria del agua* (Memory of Water, 1973) and *Luna de ciegos* (Moon of the Blind, 1990).

Santiago Mutis (b. 1951), Ramón Cote Baraibar (b. 1963), and Orietta Lozano (b. 1956) represent a group that appeared after the turmoil of the 1960s, opening new avenues for contemp. poetry. Mutis's highly lyrical poetry, notably *Tú también eres de lluvia* (You Too Are of the Rain, 1982) and *Soñadores de pájaros* (Dreamers of Birds, 1987), often finds its imagery in paintings. Cote Baraibar is a poet of magisterial craft; his books include *Poemas para una fosa común* (Poems for a Common Grave, 1983) and *El confuso trazado de las fundaciones* (Confused Plan of the Foundations, 1991). Lozano's poetry is highly sensual and erotic, a drastic change from the cautious poetry written by most women in the Colombian trad. Her books include *Fuego secreto* (Secret Fire, 1980) and *El vampiro esperado* (Expected Vampire, 1987).

See INDIGENOUS AMERICAS, POETRY OF THE; SPAIN, POETRY OF; SPANISH AMERICA, POETRY OF.

■ C. A. Caparroso, *Dos ciclos de lirismo colombiano* (1961); R. Maya, *Los orígenes del modernismo en Colombia* (1961); A. Holguín, *Antología crítica de la poesía colombiana (1874–1974)* (1974); J. Arango Ferrer, *Horas de literatura colombiana* (1978); J. Mejía Duque, *Momentos y opciones de la poesía colombiana* (1979); A. Romero, *Las palabras están en situación* (1985); F. Charry Lara, *Poesía y poetas colombianos* (1986); H. Orjuela, *Estudios sobre la literatura indígena y colonial* (1986); *Historia de la poesía colombiana*, ed. M. M. Carranza (1991); R. Echavarría, *Quién es quién en la poesía colombiana* (1998); J. G. Cobo Borda, *Historia de la poesía colombiana* (2006).

A. ROMERO

CORNISH POETRY. The Cornish lang. was spoken in parts of Cornwall until the end of the 18th c. and was revived in the early 20th c. It belongs to the Brythonic or "P-Celtic" branch of the Celtic lang. family and is more closely related to Breton than to Welsh. While Old Cornish (9th–12th cs.) left no literary remains, several works have survived from the Middle Cornish (13th–16th cs.) and Late Cornish (17th–18th cs.) periods. Most Middle Cornish lit. consists of stanzaic verse, incl. a number of plays on religious themes that were performed in a distinctive type of open-air theater in the round known as a "playing place" or *plen-an-guary*. These plays and a closely related poem on the Passion were likely written by the canons of Glasney College in Penryn, a religious foundation dissolved in 1549. The work of Late Cornish poets is more varied, comprising a number of short poems as well as one OT play. Revived Cornish has also produced a significant body of verse lit.

The oldest surviving Middle Cornish verse is a 36-line fragment written on the back of a legal document dated 1340. This "Charter Fragment" may be an actor's part from an unknown play in which an unidentified speaker offers comic advice on marriage to a young couple. Its versification is atypical, since it uses an irregular (possibly accentual) meter and contains a number of rhymed couplets, which are otherwise quite rare in Middle Cornish. All other Middle Cornish verse is written in stanzas of four to thirteen lines, using rhyme schemes similar to those found in ME poetry. Unlike Eng., Cornish verse uses a syllabic meter with seven or, occasionally, four syllables to the line. There is no regular pattern of accentuation, and rhymes involving unstressed syllables (like *dá* : *hénna* or *bára* : *hénna*) are commonplace. The lack of a Cornish-speaking nobility during the Middle Cornish period likely prevented Cornwall from developing the complex poetic forms and ornamentation typical of med. Ireland and Wales, since there were no patrons to support a class of professional poets. As a result, Middle Cornish verse does not feature the alliteration, internal rhyme, or *cynghanedd* found in most Breton, Welsh, or Ir. poetry (see BRETON POETRY; IRELAND, POETRY OF; and WELSH POETRY).

The best-known work of Cornish lit. is the trilogy of biblical plays known as the *Ordinalia*, preserved in a ms. of the mid-15th c. The three plays are *Origo Mundi* (2,846 lines), which presents a series of episodes from the OT; *Passio Christi* (3,242 lines), which depicts Christ's life, persecution, and death; and *Resurrexio Domini* (2,646 lines), which treats Christ's resurrection and ascension and the death of Pontius Pilate. A fourth play on the subject of the Nativity may have existed but has not survived. The principal stanza type in the *Ordinalia* is a six-line verse form rhymed *aabccb* or *aabaab*, sometimes extended to *aaabcccb*. Variants in which the *b* lines have only four syllables predominate in *Resurrexio Domini*, while alternate-rhyme stanzas (*abababab* or *abab*) are common in *Origo Mundi*. The poem *Pascon Agan Arluth*, "The Passion of Our Lord," is also found in a 15th-c. ms. It covers much of the same material as *Passio Christi* and contains some verses that are also found in that play. At 2,074 lines, *Pascon Agan Arluth* is the only lengthy poem from the traditional Cornish period, and it is written almost entirely in stanzas of eight 7-syllable lines rhymed *abababab*.

Two other Middle Cornish dramas are known from 16th c. mss., the only med. plays from Great Britain that deal with saints who are not mentioned in the Bible. *Beunans Meriasek*, "The Life of St. Meriasek" (4,569 lines, dated 1504), features three largely independent storylines concerning St. Sylvester and St. Meriasek (Meriadoc). Meriasek is the patron saint of Camborne, where the play may have been performed. *Bewnans Ke*, "The Life of St. Kea"

(3,308 lines), is known from an incomplete ms. of the late 16th c. and tells the story of the patron saint of Kea parish. The second half of *Bewnans Ke* is particularly remarkable, as it comprises the only extant Arthurian material in traditional Cornish: an account largely derived from the 12th-c. *Historia Regum Britanniae* by Geoffrey of Monmouth. The versification of these two plays is substantially similar to that of the *Ordinalia*, although a new stanza form rhymed *ababcddc* with a characteristically short fifth line is prevalent in *Beunans Meriasek* and predominant in *Bewnans Ke*.

The play *Gwreans an Bys*, "The Creation of the World" (2,549 lines, dated 1611), is linguistically Late Cornish but continues the Middle Cornish literary trad., incorporating several passages from *Origo Mundi*. *Gwreans an Bys* has a more mod. feel than the Middle Cornish plays, and there is no clear evidence that it was written for performance in a plen-an-guary. Although the meter is less regular, seven-syllable lines are still the norm in *Gwreans an Bys*, and the verse forms used, while differing from those of the 16th-c. plays, are clearly derived from them. Most other Late Cornish verse dates from the late 17th and early 18th cs. and represents a sharp break from Middle Cornish practice. Late Cornish poems are comparatively short, deal with secular themes, and often use verse forms modeled on those of contemp. Eng. poetry. These works typically have an accentual rather than a syllabic meter, which may reflect a stronger Eng. influence on the stress patterns of Cornish as well as the bilingualism of the poets, many of whom were not native Cornish speakers.

The Cornish revival of the 20th and 21st cs. has also produced works of significant literary merit. Peggy Pollard's plays imitate Middle Cornish verse forms and offer a satirical reinterpretation of the Middle Cornish dramatic trad. Both N.J.A. Williams and K. J. George have also written verse dramas using stanza forms and stylistic elements found in the Middle Cornish plays. Richard Gendall's work is perhaps best known through the music of Brenda Wootton, who performed many of his songs. While many contemp. poets address themes directly related to the lang. and Cornish identity, the poetry of J.A.N. Snell and Tim Saunders treats a wide range of topics, using verse forms inspired by Eng. and Celtic sources as well as traditional Cornish lit.

■ *The Ancient Cornish Drama*, ed. and trans. E. Norris, 2 v. (1859, rpt. 1963); *The Passion: A Middle Cornish Poem* (1860–61), *Gwreans an Bys* (1864), *Beunans Meriasek* (1872)—trans. M. Harris, 1977: all ed. W. Stokes, *Transactions of the Philological Society* (1860–61, 1864); H. Jenner, "The History and Literature of the Ancient Cornish Language," *Journal of the British Archaeological Association* 33 (1877), and *Handbook of the Cornish Language* (1904); D. C. Fowler, "The Date of the Cornish *Ordinalia*," *Medieval Studies* 23 (1961); R. Longsworth, *The Cornish Ordinalia: Religion and Dramaturgy* (1967); P. B. Ellis, *The Cornish Language and Its Literature* (1974); O. J. Padel, *The Cornish Writings of the Boson Family* (1975); J. A. Bakere, *The Cornish Ordinalia: A Critical Study* (1980); T. D. Crawford, "The Composition of the Cornish *Ordinalia*" and "Stanza Forms and Social Status in *Beunans Meriasek*," *Old Cornwall* 9 (1979–85); *The Creacion of the World*, ed. and trans. P. Neuss (1983); B. Murdoch, *Cornish Literature* (1993); *The Wheel*, ed. T. Saunders (1999); *Looking at the Mermaid*, ed. A. Kent and T. Saunders (2000); *Nothing Broken*, ed. T. Saunders (2006); *Bewnans Ke*, ed. and trans. G. Thomas and N.J.A. Williams (2007); B. Bruch, "Medieval Cornish Versification: An Overview," *Keltische Forschungen* 4 (2009).

B. Bruch

CROATIAN POETRY. Owing to its firm ties with the Western world and the direct influences of Ren. humanism, Croatia developed a sophisticated lit. as early as the 15th c. The father of Croatian lit., Marko Marulić (pseud. of Marcus Marulus Spalatensis, 1450–1524) was born in Split and was a renowned Eur. humanist. In addition to philosophical and religious treatises in Lat., he wrote poetry in Croatian and is best known for his *Judita* (1501, pub. 1521) about which he explicitly stated that it is written "in Croatian verses," thus officially giving literary status to his native lang. On the matrix of the biblical story of Judith, he vividly describes in doubly rhymed dodecasyllabic lines the perils that his own nation faced before the Ottoman invasion.

Oral traditional poetry, in particular ballads and lyric songs, though widely disseminated throughout the region, left deeper traces only on the older layers of Croatian lit. This is particularly visible during the Ren. when poets in Dubrovnik and along the Dalmatian coast wove elements of Petrarchan and troubadour style with local traditional poetry to create a unique amalgam (see OCCITAN POETRY). The predominant meter is dodecasyllabic, while the thematic range tilts heavily toward love subjects, with some religious and patriotic verses. A central collection was offered by Nikša Ranjina (1494–1582), who started compiling the works of his contemporaries in 1507. Some of the most prominent names included are those of Sigismund Menčetić (1457–1527), a well-traveled writer of noble background who produced some of the period's most erotic verses, and the cleric Džore Držić (1461–1501), who wrote more restrained, sincere verses. Mavro Vetranović (1483–1576), the most prolific writer of the Dubrovnik circle, was known for his moralizing, metaphysical, and politically colored poetry.

Aside from Dubrovnik, the island of Hvar was the site of important literary activity during this period. It yielded highly respected authors such as Hanibal Lucić (ca. 1485–1553), whose Petrarchan verses are some of the best on this side of the Adriatic and whose dialogic verse narrative *Robinja* (Slave Girl, written before 1530) is the first Croatian secular play. Mikša Pelegrinović (ca. 1500–62) wrote what is likely the most popular piece of the Croatian Ren., *Jeđupka* (The Gypsy), in the vein of Florentine masquerades, with a series of related love poems. Petar Hektorović (1487–1572) is best known for his piscatorial eclogue *Ribanje i ribarsko prigovaranje* (*Fishing and Fishermen's Conversation*, 1556, pub. 1568), a philosophical meditation on the virtues of a simple life that also includes the earliest transciptions of two traditional oral songs, *bugarštice*.

The first Croatian novelistic work combining verse and prose is *Planine* (The Mountains, 1536, pub. 1569) by Petar Zoranić (1508–1569) of Zadar, which provides a patriotic vision of the Croatian Arcadia. Nikola Nalješković (ca. 1500–87) was not only a central figure in Dubrovnik literary circles but left a remarkably diverse corpus of works in terms of genre, incl. a collection of love poetry. From this younger group of Dubrovnik writers, the most renowned today is Marin Držić (1508–67), although mainly for his comedies and pastoral plays (many of them in verse) rather than for the love poetry of his youth. Dinko Ranjina (1536–1607), who like most Croatian writers of this period had close ties with Italy, published his *Pjesni razlike* (Poems of Difference, 1563) in Italy; many of them echo traditional poetry. Dominko Zlatarić (1558–1613), also of Dubrovnik, became known for his own poetry but was perhaps even more renowned for his trans. of cl. and contemp. lit.

The greatest Croatian author of the baroque period, Ivan Gundulić (1589–1638), also marked the summit of Dubrovnik's literary achievements with his reflexive poem in three cantos *Suze sina razmetnoga* (Tears of the Prodigal Son, 1621), the pastoral play *Dubravka* (1628), and the epic *Osman* (1621–38). In the first, Gundulić introduced a longer form, which became particularly popular in this period as a vehicle for pondering the question of sin and the transitory nature of human existence. His unfinished *Osman* (two of the planned 20 octosyllabic rhyming cantos were not completed) focuses on a highly pertinent issue: the precarious balance between the Eur. and Ottoman powers. Gundulić's poem, though structurally influenced by Torquato Tasso's *La Gerusalemme liberata*, does not share the It. author's reliance on events from the distant past but draws his complex narrative line from a contemp. Polish-Turkish battle.

Gundulić's contemp. Ivan Bunić (1591–1658) is a reflexive and sensual writer whose poems are akin to those of metaphysical poets and are often colored with cl. motives. Ignjat Đurđević (1675–1737) was the last great writer of the Dubrovnik Republic; his It. and Lat. poetry is characterized by tight forms and restrained subject matter, while his verses in Croatian are considerably more playful and imbued with the spirit of local traditional poetry. In the continental region, the promising literary career of Fran Krsto Frankopan (1643–71), one of the most erotic and patriotic writers of the time, was cut short by his execution at the hands of the Hapsburgs. One of the most popular Croatian books of all time, *Razgovor ugodni naroda slovinskoga* (Pleasant Conversation of the Slavic People, 1756), was written by a Franciscan monk of Dalmatia, Andrija Kačić-Miošić (1704–60), in the decasyllabic verse of folk poetry and offers a chronicle (albeit fictional) of the Slavs.

Ivan Mažuranić (1814–90), a recognized writer and the governor of Croatia during the period of national awakening, was most famous for his epic *Smrt Smail-Age Čengića* (*Smail-Aga Čengić's Death*, 1846), which describes in the style of traditional epics the Montenegrin rebellion against the Turks. He also completed Gundulić's *Osman*. Patriotic and reflexive, the poetry of Petar Preradović (1818–72) raised awareness of the importance of the national lang. at a time when Croats could not use their mother tongue for official purposes. Silvije Strahimir Kranjčević (1865–1908) was a similarly politically engaged poet whose anguish and calls for social justice were often rendered through the use of cl. motifs.

Antun Gustav Matoš (1873–1914) was a harbinger of modernism and a great practitioner of the sonnet form who shifted the focus to introspective themes and insisted on the supremacy of the aesthetic dimension. Other Croatian modernists greatly influenced by Matoš were Vladimir Vidrić (1875–1909) and Ljubo Wiesner (1885–1951), while Vladimir Nazor (1876–1949) remained faithful to Dalmatian motifs. Janko Polić Kamov (1886–1910), known as a Croatian poet-rebel, wrote expressionist verses condemning the hypocrisy of middle-class dogmas. Antun Branko Šimić (1898–1925) was a master of concision and introduced free verse to Croatian lit. Despite his early death, the expressionistic features of his only published collection had a lasting impact. Augustin Tin Ujević (1891–1955), a disciple of Matoš, likewise holds an important place for his poems of human suffering and exuberant elation. The musicality of his expression and his ling. opulence, combined with an ability to transcend the realm of the personal and convey universally recognizable mental states, make him unquestionably the most influential Croatian poet.

Miroslav Krleža (1893–1981), the greatest Croatian prose writer, also left a considerable lyric opus, much of it dealing with social themes. Ivan Goran Kovačić (1913–43) is known for his antifascist poem *Jama* (*The Pit*, 1943), while Dobriša Cesarić (1902–80) and Dragutin Tadijanović (1905–2007) have been praised for poetry that celebrates nature and the simple life but also for vignettes of everyday life rendered with seemingly effortless style. Nikola Šop (1904–1982), a Croatian poet from Bosnia, drew the attention of W. H. Auden with his Christian mystic verses and cosmic metaphors. Auden translated some of Šop's poetry into Eng. Jure Kaštelan (1919–90) and Josip Pupačić (1928–71) are both quintessential poets of the south, with the sea permeating their poems, though, in the case of Kaštelan, war also appears as a focal theme of his early period. Along with Pupačić and Kaštelan, Vesna Parun (1922–2010) marked a new postwar generation that introduced a more personal tone in a variety of subjects. Parun is particularly well known for her intimate love poetry.

Ivan Slamnig (1930–2001) gained the status of the most ironic Croatian poet and a ling. innovator whose expression bursts with neologisms, archaisms, and other wordplay. Anxiety, loneliness, and helplessness are central features in the poetry of Slavko Mihalič (1928–2007), who combines the everyday and the sublime with powerful eloquence. Antun Šoljan (1932–93), inspired by the Anglo-Am. school, in particular T. S. Eliot, wrote intellectual poetry, while Daniel Dragojevič (b. 1934) shows a philosophical orientation, often employing paradox in order to invert the world and reveal its true meaning. The lexically rich poetry of Drago Štambuk (b. 1950) employs both his native Dalmatian and cosmopolitan imagery, while that of Anka Žagar (b. 1954) plays with the notion of semantic concretization, merging stream of consciousness, syntactic distortions, and neologisms to offer one of the most engaging oeuvres in the contemp. Croatian poetic scene.

■ **Anthologies**: *Hrvatske narodne pjesme*, ed. N. Andrič et al., 10 v. (1896–1942); *Zlatna knjiga hrvatskog pjesništva od početaka do danas*, ed. V. Pavletić (1970); *Leut i truba*, ed. R. Bogišić (1971); *Antologija hrvatskog pjesništva ranog moderniteta*, ed. S. P. Novak (2004); *Utjeha kaosa*, ed. M. Mićanović (2006); *Antologija hrvatskoga pjesništva*, ed. A. Stamać (2007); *Love Lyric and Other Poems of the Croatian Renaissance: A Bilingual Anthology*, ed. and trans. J. S. Miletich (2009).

■ **Criticism and History**: J. Torbarina, *Italian Influence on the Poets of the Ragusan Republic* (1931); A. Kadić, *Contemporary Croatian Literature* (1960); R. Bogišić, *O hrvatskim starim pjesnicima* (1968); I. Slamnig, *Hrvatska versifikacija* (1981); S. P. Novak, *Povijest hrvatske književnosti* (2003).

A. Vidan

CUBA, POETRY OF. *See* CARIBBEAN, POETRY OF THE

CZECH POETRY. The first poems to appear in the Czech lands were hymns in Old Church Slavonic that date to the 9th c. The Lat. *Legenda Christiani* (Legend of a Christian), about the lives of St. Ludmila and her grandson Václav (Wenceslaus), is one of the first great poetic compositions to emerge. By the 11th c., religious poetry in Lat. had taken root, while poetry in the vernacular remained scarce.

Widely acknowledged as the first work in the vernacular, the hymn "Hospodine pomiluj ny" (Lord, Have Mercy on Us), ca. 10th or 11th c., echoes the Kyrie Eleison and impresses with its lyricism and melodic sophistication. The Czech hymn "Svatý Václave, vévodo České země" (Saint Wenceslas, Duke of the Bohemian Land), ca. 12th c., is also noteworthy. These hymns derive from 14th-c. mss. The 13th-c. prayer codex of Kunhuta, abbess of the St. George convent in Prague, contains the powerful poem known as the Ostrov Hymn, "Slovo do světa stvořenie" (The Word before the World's Creation) and the hymn "Vítaj kráľu všemohúcí" (Welcome King Omnipotent).

In the early 13th c., the Přemyslid rulers extended their domain and encountered Germanic cultural and poetic trads. The contact resulted in the courtly poetry of the *Minnesang*, which dominated Czech poetry in the late 13th c. Among long poems outstanding is the powerful *Alexandreis* or the *Alexandriad* (anonymous), composed ca. 1300 and based loosely on Gualtier de Châtillon's Lat. *Alexandriad*, though it is highly original in its treatment of the exploits and character of the warrior. Another anonymous long poem, *Dalimilova kronika* (the Dalimil Chronicle, early 14th c.) is marked by its strongly nationalistic bent. The early 14th c. sees Czech verse legends of early Christian figures such as Judas and Pontius Pilate. These were later followed by the brilliant verse legends of St. Procopius and of St. Catherine. The *Legend of St. Catherine* is outstanding for its use of the erotic lang. of courtly love poetry and its vivid portrayal of Catherine's passion during her martyrdom.

By the 14th and 15th cs.—the heyday of Czech poetry—the courtly love poetry of the Western Eur. trad. exerts a strong influence. The name of Master Zavíš stands out for the high love lyric, filled with the feudal ethos and the sense of impossible love. The almost 9,000-verse Czech version of the story of Tristan and Isolde (*Tristan a Izolde*), ca. 14th c., is based on the Ger. recension. Satirical poems about university life also emerge, such as "Svár vody s vínem" (The Dispute of Water and Wine), the exceptional "Podkoní a žák" (The Groom and the Scholar), and Czech-Lat. macaronic verses. Satires not in the "university vein" included the ca. mid-14th c. works "Satiry o řemeslnících a konšelích" (Satires on Tradesmen and Aldermen) and "Desatero kázanie božie" (The Ten Divine Commandments).

The 15th-c. Hussite revolution marked a drastic change in forms and styles. The years of Hussitism saw the rise of poems of moral edification and poetic pamphleteering. Allegorical verse was also popular, the best example being the Hussite dialogue "Hádání Prahy s Kutnou Horou" (Quarrel of Prague with Kutná Hora). Here Kutná Hora is a hag defending Catholicism, while Prague, a beautiful woman, represents the Hussite cause. The Catholics countered with the infamous "Píseň o Viklefici" (Song of the Wycliffite Woman). For the first time, Czech religious songs replaced the Lat. liturgy.

With the election of the Hussite king Jiří z Poděbrad (1420–71), humanism, influenced by It. culture, emerged as a potent force. Under the influence of Giovanni Boccaccio and others, Jiří's son Hynek z Poděbrad (ca. 1450–92) wrote erotic poems incl. "Májový sen" (May Dream, ca. 1490). Outstanding examples of Lat. verse by Czech Catholics include the *Ad sanctum Venceslaum satira* (Complaint to St. Wenceslaus, 1489) by the nobleman Bohuslav Hasištejnský z Lobkovic (ca. 1461–1510), the epicurean verses of Šimon Fagellus Villaticus (pseud. of Šimon Bouček, ca. 1473–1549), and the works of Jan Hodějovský z Hodějova (d. 1566). The most important piece to emerge from this circle is the inspired Lat. version of the Song of Songs, composed by David Crinitus z Hlaváčova (1531–86).

The defeat of the Czech Protestants after the Battle of White Mountain (1620, the culmination of the Thirty Years' War) had a decisive and detrimental effect on a literary level. The Catholic victory meant that Lat. verse returned to the fore; education and administration were conducted in Lat. The Czech literary lang. survived among determined émigrés fleeing Catholic Hapsburg rule. Most famously Jan Amos Komenský (or Comenius, 1592–1670) staunchly tried to keep literary Czech intact. From his exile in Amsterdam, Komenský had an agenda for Czech poetry: it should be unrhymed and based on quantitative—i.e., cl.—metrics. His Czech versions of the Psalms and the Song of Songs demonstrate this system's strengths. In Czech lands, Catholic poetry in Lat. enjoyed a phenomenal resurgence, esp. through the work of Bohuslav Balbín (1621–88).

Religious poetry was key during the baroque period. Brilliant poetry was written by Catholic poets such as Adam Michna z Otradovic (1600–76), composer of several collections of religious songs, and Bedřich Bridel (also known as Fridrich Bridelius, 1619–80), a Jesuit missionary and highly philosophical poet, author of the famed "Co Bůh? Člověk" (What is God? Man? 1658). Of note too is the Jesuit poet Felix Kadlinský (1613–75), who wrote a version of Friedrich von Spee's "Trutz-Nachtigal oder geistliches poetisch Lustwäldlein" (1649) on the love of Christ and of nature: courtly love poetry is reconceived as the soul longs for Christ as her groom. Catholic hymnbooks were compiled to offset the Protestant hymnbooks that had previously dominated: Václav Holan Rovenský's (1644–1718) *Capella regia musicalia* (1693) is a fine example. Secular poetry of the baroque is usually considered weak, though the work of Václav Jan Rosa (ca. 1620–89) gives examples of well-formed love lyrics. Outstanding among the period's satirical poems is Václav František Kocmánek's (1607–79) "Lamentatio Rusticana" (Lament of the Countrymen, 1644).

By the mid-18th c., religious prose had risen to dominance, though Catholic spiritual verse proved to be a stable force in lyrical poetry. Other verses on topics from sheep farming to gingerbread making also emerged during this time, along with folk songs and popular melodies. These last would exert a great influence over Czech poets of the "Revival" period.

The *Národní obrození* or Czech National Revival dates to the 1770s and 1780s. At the end of the 18th c., the Czech lands underwent dramatic changes, incl. the introduction of a new religious tolerance and the end of the feudal system under Hapsburg ruler Josef II. The ed. of the verse anthol. *Básně v řeči vázané* (Poems in Metrical Verse, 1785, some of which he composed himself), Václav Thám (1765–1816) is widely considered the father of mod. Czech poetry. The collection included imitations of anacreontic verse alongside adaptations of Czech baroque poetry. The ode and the mock heroic/epic came to prominence, along with a shift, under the influence of Josef Dobrovský (1753–1829), to accentual meters. Antonín Jaroslav Puchmayer (1769–1820) also set out to develop a specifically Czech poetic style at this crucial juncture. Among his anthols. are the five-volume *Sebrání básní a zpěvů* (Collection of Poems and Songs, 1795), and *Nové básně* (New Poems, 1798). His own work includes animal fables (another newly popular genre), "Óda na Jana Žižku z Trocnova (Ode to Jan Žižka, 1802), and "Na jazyk český" (Ode to the Czech Language, 1816). Another giant of the revival, Josef Jungmann (1773–1847) did not write much verse but contributed innovations in sonnet form and a narrative poem. In 1818, Pavel Josef Šafařík (1795–1861) and František Palacký (1798–1876) wrote the groundbreaking *Počátkové českého básnictví obzvláště prozódie* (Elements of Czech Versification, especially Prosody), which once again promoted cl. (quantitative) meters over accentual ones.

The Slovak poet Jan Kollár (1793–1852), who wrote in Czech, composed the best of the early romantic works, *Slávy dcera* (Daughter of Slavia) in 1824; in this sonnet sequence, the love of the poetic "I" for a maiden becomes an allegory for his bond with his native land. Another romantic poet followed James Macpherson's lead in creating an ancient pedigree for his native trad. Václav Hanka (1791–1861) forged two mss. written in quasi-med. Czech: the *Rukopis královédvorský* (Dvůr Králové Ms., 1817) and the *Rukopis zelenohorský* (Zelená Hora Ms., 1817), great poetic works in their own right.

The greatest of the Czech romantics, Karel Hynek Mácha (1810–36), gained notoriety for the scandalous publication of his seminal work *Máj* (May, 1836). Mácha revolutionized prosody in Czech with this narrative poem by using iambs, a form to which Czech is particularly unsuited. The poem describes the love of a bandit, Vilém, for Jarmila, a young woman who has been seduced by his father. Karel Havlíček Borovský (1821–56) is remembered for his acerbic wit and the satirical poem "Křest sv. Vladimíra" (The Christening of St. Vladimir, 1876), which bucks all regnant institutions and ideologies.

A new generation of Czech writers came to prominence in 1848. Deeply influenced by Mácha, they gathered around the jour. they named *Máj* in his honor. These poets included Jan Neruda (1834–91), the leading member of this group (whose name was later taken as a pseud. by Pablo Neruda); Vítězslav Hálek (1835–74); and Karolina Světlá (1830–99). Another important poet, Karel Jaromír Erben (1811–70), reached his apogee in the balladic collection *Kytice z pověstí národních* (Bouquet of National Legends, 1853).

In the late 19th c., writers split into two factions. The poets who congregated around the jour. *Lumír*, such as Jaroslav Vrchlický (1853–1912), espoused cosmopolitanism in Czech letters, while those who wrote for the jour. *Ruch* were known as the national poets; the dominant figure was Svatopulk Čech (1846–1908). These writers were intent on preserving specifically Czech, or Slavophile, trads.

By the end of the century, the work of poets Otokar Březina and Petr Bezruč marked a turn to symbolism. Březina's (1868–1929) use of free rhythms influenced poetry in the 20th c. and beyond. The Silesian poet Bezruč (1867–1958) created a mod. prophetic persona in his *Slezské písně* (Silesian Songs, 1909) and fashioned poems about the oppression of Czechs under Ger., Polish, and native aristocratic powers. Realism was represented by the poet Josef Svatopluk Machar (1864–1942), who exposed social injustice in his poetry, e.g., the oppression of women in "Zde by měly kvést růže" (Here Should Roses Bloom, 1894). Decadent poets, allied with the jour. *Moderní revue*, included Karel Hlaváček (1874–98), whose poetry follows the typical decadent aesthetics of eroticism and decay; and Jiří Karásek ze Lvovic (1871–1951), whose collections *Sexus necans* (1897) and *Sodoma* (1895) abound in allusions to sadomasochism and necrophilia.

The installation of the First Republic (1918) marked a revolution in Czech lit. Cubism, futurism, and civilism emerged as prominent movements in poetry and the arts. Leftism dominated the new schools, and Czech poetry generally found a key influence in Karel Čapek's (1890–1938) groundbreaking trans. of mod. Fr. verse, The poetist movement, influenced by Dadaism and futurism, called for a poetry that would merge all arts and mod. life together in a playful, populist manner. Poetism had its great theorist in the multitalented Karel Teige (1900–51) and was cultivated by poets such as Vítězslav Nezval (1900–58), Jaroslav Seifert (1901–86), and Konstantin Biebl (1898–1951).

Nezval later passed through a surrealist phase only to turn subsequently to a more socialist realist poetry. Seifert left the Communist Party in the 1930s and abandoned his experimental poetry in favor of a lyrical intimacy. He survived most of his poetist brethren and won the Nobel Prize in Literature in 1984. The poets František Halas (1901–49) and Vladimír Holan (1905–80) also emerge in the interwar period. Halas's highly religious poetry explores mysticism and notions of time. Holan is best known for his postwar works; during communist rule, he went into self-imposed home exile.

The postwar communist regime imposed severe restrictions on writers; socialist realism became the official literary doctrine. Only long after Stalin's death in 1953 did the censorship relax; esp. after 1964, writers were granted greater freedom of expression. The jour. *Květen* (May) published the sui generis poetry of the poet and immunologist Miroslav Holub (1923–98), among others, and long-banned poets began to publish once more. The late 1960s also witnessed a return to extraordinary poetic forms: experimental and surrealist modes were embraced by Emanuel Frynta (1923–75), Josef Hiršal (1920–2003), Ladislav Novák (1925–99), and Vratislav Effenberger (1923–86).

After the Warsaw Pact invasion of 1968, many writers emigrated, while others wrote for the *samizdat* (self-publication) press, "for the drawer," or had their mss. published abroad. By the 1980s, a new generation of poets began to rebel against the so-called normalization. Their work is aggressive and at times purposefully controversial. In samizdat and even in official publishing houses, younger poets like Jáchym Topol (b. 1962), whose collection *Miluju tě k zbláznění* (I Love You to Insanity, 1991) caused an uproar with its intentional vulgarity; Sylva Fischerová (b. 1963); and Zuzana Brabcová (1959–2015) dominated the "subversive" scene.

The fall of Communism in 1989 marked a radical change in Czech lit. Works by many illegal, oppressed, and exiled authors working under the communist regime were published for the first time, and the authors themselves were rehabilitated. The most celebrated poets of recent years include Petr Kabeš (1941–2005), whose poetry draws on *skaz*, direct speech, and colloquialisms; and Petr Borkovec (b. 1970), who combines prosodic virtuosity with precise observations documenting this most recent period of upheaval in Czech culture. He enjoys popularity with readers and critics alike and has earned an international reputation.

■ J. Goll, *Anthologie české lyriky* (1872); *České květy: výbor naší lyriky*, ed. K. Adamec et al. (1890); *Česká poesie* XIX věku (1897–99); *Bělohorské motivy: jubilejní anthologie z české poesie*, ed. J. V. Frič and J. Werstadt (1920); *Modern Czech Poetry*, ed. and trans. P. Selver (1920); *An Anthology of Czechoslovak Poetry*, ed. C. A. Manning, A. V. Čapek, A. B. Koukol (1929); *Anthologie de la poésie tchèque*, ed. H Jelínek (1930); *Lyrika českého obrození (1750–1850)*, ed. V. Jirát (1940); J. Vilikovský, *Staročeská lyrika* (1940); *The Soul of a Century: A Collection of Czech Poetry in English*, ed. R. A.

Ginsburg (1942); *Počátky novočeského básnictví: Počátky novočeského básnictví*, ed. K. Polák (1946); J. Mukařovský, *Kapitoly z české poetiky* (1948); B. Václavek, *Od umení k tvorbe: studie z prítomné ceské poesie* (1949); *Nová česká poesie: výbor z veršů XX. století*, ed. F. Buriánek et al. (1955); J. Jíša, *Česká poesie dvacátých let a básníci sovětského Ruska* (1956); *A Book of Czech Verse*, ed. A. French (1958); *A Handful of Linden Leaves: An Anthology of Czech Poetry*, ed. J. Janu (1960); A. M. Píša, *Stopami poezie: studie a podobizny* (1962); *Versované skladby doby husitské*, ed. F. Svejkovský (1963); F. X. Šalda, *O poezii Uspoř*, ed. M. Petříček and B. Svozil (1970); *Three Czech Poets: Vítězslav Nezval, Antonín Bartusek, Josef Hanzlík*, trans. E. Osers and G. Theiner (1971); *Anthology of Czech Poetry*, ed. A. French (1973); *The Pipe: Recent Czech Concrete Poetry*, ed. and trans. J. Valoch and bpNichol (1973); *Česká poezie 17. a 18. století*, ed. Z. Tichá (1974); *Pohledy: poezie*, ed. J. Balík et al. (1974); *Tisíc let české poezie*, ed. J. Hrabák (1974); V. Kolář, *Mladé zápasy: studie o mladé poezii* (1981); *Vzkazy: výbor ze současné české poezie*, ed. J. Badoučková (1976); R. Jakobson, *Poetry of Grammar and Grammar of Poetry*, ed. S. Rudy (1981); A.M.K. Píša, *Vývoji české lyriky: studie a recenze* (1982); *Zbav mě mé tesknosti*, ed. M. Kopecký, Lat. trans. R. Mertlík (1983); M. Kubínová, *Proměny ceské poezie dvacátých let* (1984); *Rytířské srdce majíce: česká rytířská epika 14. století*, ed. E. Petrů et al. (1984); Z. Pešat, *Dialogy s poezií* (1985); *The Poet's Lamp: A Czech Anthology*, ed. and trans. A. French (1986); *The New Czech Poetry*, ed. J Cejka et al. (1988); Z. Hrubý, *Na strepech volnosti: almanach české poezie* (1989); M. Červenka, *Slovník básnických knih: díla české poezie od obrození do roku 1945* (1990); *Na strepech volnosti: almanach umlčene české poezie*, ed. J. Horec (1991); M. Červenka, *Styl a význam: studie o básnících* (1991); *Vrh kostek: česká experimentální poezie*, ed. J. Hirsal, B. Grögerová, Z. Barborka (1993); J. Trávníček, *Poezie poslední možnosti* (1996); *Prague 1900: Poetry and Ecstasy*, ed. E. Becker et al. (1999); *Six Czech Poets*, ed. and trans. A. Büchler (2007); *Up the Devil's Back: A Bilingual Anthology of 20th-Century Czech Poetry*, ed. B. Volková and C. Cloutier (2008).

M. Sternstein

D

DANISH POETRY. *See* DENMARK, POETRY OF

DENMARK, POETRY OF. Rune inscriptions prove the existence of a lost heroic poetry in Denmark, known only from Saxo Grammaticus's Lat. prose and hexameter rendering in *Gesta Danorum* (ca. 1200). *Bjarkamál* (The Lay of Bjarke)—whose heroes also appear in the OE poems *Widsith* and *Beowulf*—and the so-called Lay of Ingjald celebrate courage and loyalty, reflecting an aristocratic ethos that epitomizes the ideals of the Viking age.

During the Middle Ages (1100–1500), Danish poetry follows the Eur. models of courtly and sacred poetry. In the five lyric poems to the Virgin Mary attributed to Per Räff Lille (ca. 1450–1500), troubadour influences blend with imagery from the biblical Song of Songs. The anonymous *Den danske Rimkrønike* (The Danish Rhymed Chronicle), a hist. of the Danish kings, is an important work in *Knittelvers*. The dominant genre of the Middle Ages, however, is the folk ballad, which reached Denmark from France in the early 12th c. In the 16th c., poetry in the vernacular was still med. in spirit and form, notably subject to a growing Ger. influence in the wake of the Lutheran Reformation.

In the 17th c., as the Ren. reached Denmark, efforts were made to create a Danish national poetry on cl. models. Anders Arrebo (1587–1637) produced a religious epic, *Hexaëmeron* (ca. 1622, pub. 1661), describing the six days of Creation. Based on Guillaume de Salluste du Bartas's *La Sepmaine*, it is composed partly in twice-rhymed hexameter, partly in alexandrines. The artificiality of the poem's cl.-mythological diction is offset by descriptive details from Scandinavian nature and folk life. Following Martin Opitz's *Das Buch der Deutschen Poeterey* (The Book of German Poetics, 1624), Hans Mikkelsen Ravn (1610–63) in 1649 published a manual of prosody with illustrations, making available to future poets a varied formal repertoire. Anders Bording (1619–77) is noted for his anacreontic verse, but he also single-handedly published a rhymed monthly newspaper, *Den Danske Mercurius* (The Danish Mercury, 1666–77), composed in stately alexandrines. Thomas Kingo (1634–1703), a much greater poet, was able to exploit fully the new formal variety. His principal achievement is his two volumes of church hymns, still sung today, *Aandelige Siunge-Koor* (Spiritual Choirs, 1674–81). With their thematic counterpoints, sensuous imagery, and often high-strung metaphors, Kingo's hymns are unmistakably baroque in style, the highlights being his Easter hymns.

In the early 18th c., Fr. neoclassicism entered Danish lit., mainly because of the activity of the Dano-Norwegian Ludvig Holberg (1684–1754). Best known for his bourgeois prose comedies, Holberg in his verse mock epic *Peder Paars* (1719–20) showed himself to be a brilliant satirist. The rationalism of Holberg, and of the period, is counterbalanced, however, by a sentimental undercurrent, represented by Ambrosius Stub (1705–58) and Hans Adolf Brorson (1694–1764). Stub practiced a wide variety of genres, from religious lyrics to drinking songs. His concise, graceful form and light, melodious rhythms are influenced by the It. operatic aria, and his delicately picturesque style reveals rococo features. Brorson, a religious Pietist, also composed hymns in complex meters derived from the elegant rococo aria, with its dialogue and echo effects.

Danish neoclassicism was continued by a group of Norwegian authors living in Copenhagen, members of *Det norske Selskab* (The Norwegian Society), while Johannes Ewald (1743–81), a preromantic deeply influenced by the Ger. poet F. G. Klopstock, championed the claims of subjectivity. Ewald's mythological dramas on ON themes are largely forgotten, but his pietistically inspired lyric verse is very much alive. He excelled in the religious ode, exemplified by *Rungsteds Lyksaligheder* (The Joys of Rungsted, 1773), where nature description is a vehicle for the glorification of God. The only noteworthy poet of the last 20 years of the century was Jens Baggesen (1764–1826), a mercurial spirit who alternated between cl. and romantic sensibility in accordance with the tenor of his personal experience.

Adam Oehlenschläger (1779–1850) achieved the breakthrough of romanticism in Danish poetry; his first collection, *Digte* (Poems, 1803), was inspired by the aesthetics of the Jena school of Friedrich Schelling, A. W. Schlegel, and K.W.F Schlegel as mediated by the Copenhagen lectures of Henrich Steffens (1802). These poems signified a fierce rejection of the rationalist spirit of the 18th c., together with a rediscovery of Nordic hist. and mythology and a glorification of the creative genius who alone is capable of a unified view of nature and hist. Oehlenschläger increased his range in *Poetiske Skrifter* (Poetic Writings, 1805), which contained prose and poetry, narrative cycles, drama, lyric, and ballads and romances in varying meters. After 1806, Oehlenschläger's subjectivism is tempered by the growing influence of J. W. Goethe's and Friedrich Schiller's objective poetry and the Heidelberg romantic school, reorienting his work—as well as Danish lit. generally—toward national and patriotic themes. *Nordiske Digte* (Nordic Poems, 1807) included several dramas based on ON figures and themes. The narrative cycle *Helge* (1814), with its impressive array of metrical forms and styles marking subtle shifts of moods, rises to Sophoclean heights in the concluding dramatic episode. Prompted by Oehlenschläger's publication of *Digte* (1803), A. W. Schack von Staffeldt (1769–1826) published his own collection titled *Digte* (1804), and later *Nye Digte* (New Poems, 1808). Staffeldt's poetry, with its emphasis on the poet's longing to bridge the separation between this world and a divine, Platonic world of Ideas, received little attention during his lifetime but is now considered an important contribution to Danish romanticism. The work of another romantic, N.F.S. Grundtvig (1783–1872) was more national in inspiration. Grundtvig, while more a cultural leader than a poet, created an enduring literary monument in his hymns. With their union of humanism and Christianity and their pervasive imagery taken from the Danish landscape and Nordic mythology, they represent a unique poetic achievement.

Around 1830, Danish poetry moved toward greater realism and psychological diversity, its focus shifting from an idealized past to a more complex present. Johan Ludvig Heiberg (1791–1860), the theorist of *romantisme*, as this movement has been called, managed to shuttle elegantly between actuality and the dream world in his romantic plays. Christian Winther (1796–1876) blended lyric and narrative elements in the idyll, as in *Træsnitt* (Woodcuts, 1828). Winther's formal virtuosity is demonstrated in the romance *Hjortens Flugt* (The Flight of the Hart, 1855), set in med. times and employing a modified Nibelungenstrophe. The cycle of love poems *Til Een* (To Someone, 1843, 1849), in which eros is worshipped as a divine force, is notable for its poignant lyricism. The brief lyrics of the Heinrich Heine–inspired *Erotiske Situationer* (Erotic Situations, 1838) by Emil Aarestrup (1806–56), with their picturesque detail, psychological complexity, and emotional dissonance, express a distinctly mod. sensibility—sophisticated and sensual—and represent a high point in Danish love poetry. While the early work of Frederik Paludan-Müller (1809–76) is fraught with aestheticism, *Adam Homo* (1841–48), a three-volume novel in verse, embodies a rigorous ethical philosophy. Through its portrait of a gifted, opportunistic antihero who pays for worldly success with the loss of his soul, the book presents a satirical picture of contemp. Danish culture.

After naturalism was introduced by the critic Georg Brandes (1842–1927) around 1870, writers turned their attention to political, social, and sexual problems—fitter subjects for prose than poetry. Yet Brandes was important to both Jens Peter Jacobsen (1847–85) and Holger Drachmann (1846–1908), each with a distinctive profile as a poet. The sparse but first-rate lyrical production of Jacobsen, known chiefly as a novelist, was published posthumously as *Digte og Udkast* (Poems and Sketches) in 1886. Unique are his "arabesques," capriciously winding free-verse monologues—the first modernist poetry in Denmark—whose intellectual probing is veiled in colorful ornamental lang. and evocative moods. The youthful *Digte* (1872) of Drachmann more directly echoed the radical ideas of Brandes, as in the poem "Engelske Socialister" (English Socialists). But soon Drachmann abandoned ideology for personal lyricism. In *Sange ved Havet* (Songs by the Sea, 1877), his best collection, the sea is perceived as an image of his own protean spirit. With *Sangenes Bog* (Book of Songs, 1889) radicalism reappeared, though now tempered by an awareness of age and mutability that lends a poignant existential resonance to the texts. Through his free rhythms and melodiousness, formal inventiveness, and unprecedented range of moods and attitudes, Drachmann renewed the style of romantic verse and made an extraordinary impact on subsequent Danish poetry.

Both Drachmann and Jacobsen, as well as Charles Baudelaire and Paul Verlaine, influenced the neoromantic movement of the 1890s in Danish poetry, which rejected naturalism in favor of an aesthetic demand for beauty and a mystically colored religiosity. Its program was formulated in *Taarnet* (The Tower, 1893–94), ed. by Johannes Jørgensen (1866–1956), who with *Stemninger* (Moods, 1892) had introduced the dreams and visions of symbolism into Danish poetry. Jørgensen's later poetry is marked by his 1896 conversion to Catholicism. After 1900, he further refined his condensed mode of expression, employing simple meters and rhythms to express a fervent religiosity. A more consistent follower of Fr. symbolism, as both a metaphysical and an aesthetic theory, was Sophus Claussen (1865–1931). This outlook is evident in his erotic poetry, where the surface sexual theme masks an underlying ontology, one of irreducible opposites. Claussen was deeply concerned with the nature of the creative process and with the poet's role. In his last major collection, *Heroica* (1925), a highlight of Danish poetry, art and beauty are invoked as the only means of spiritual survival in a materialistic world. Notable is the poem "Atomernes Oprør" (Revolt of the Atoms), a dystopian fantasy in which Claussen shows himself to be the last great master of the hexameter in Danish poetry. Other major neoromantics were Viggo Stuckenberg (1863–1905), Helge Rode (1870–1937), and Ludvig Holstein (1864–1943). While Stuckenberg's melancholy meditations on love's tragedy are executed with an exquisite sense of style, Rode's ethereal poems verge on the ecstatic. The best of Holstein's unadorned lyrics derive from his pantheistic vision of the unity of the human being and nature.

Danish poetry of the 20th c. encompasses diverse currents and styles, determined partly by international vogues, partly by sociopolitical events. The period before World War I replaced the introverted neoromanticism of the 1890s with realism. A Jutland regional lit. emerged, dominated by Jeppe Aakjær (1866–1930). The central poet of the period, and one of Denmark's greatest writers, was the Nobel Prize winner Johannes V. Jensen (1873–1950). His first collection, *Digte* (Poems, 1906), a milestone in mod. Danish poetry, centers on a conflict between longing and a zest for life, alternating with *Weltschmerz*. Characteristic are a number of prose poems in which Jensen voices his worship of 20th-c. technology, together with a yearning for distant places and periods rendered in timeless, mythic images. After 1920, he used more traditional meters as well as alliterative ON forms. Jensen's poetry constitutes a unique blend of precise observation, philosophical reflection, and romantic vision. His innovative poetic diction, with its incongruous mixture of crass realism and refined sensuousness, bold visionary imagery and muted lyricism, has been enormously influential.

During and after World War I, a generation of poets emerged who, inspired by Jensen and by expressionism in painting and in Ger. poetry, endeavored to create new forms of beauty. Most sensational was Emil Bønnelycke (1893–1953), whose exuberant zest for life and glorification of technology were expressed in hymnlike prose poems, but Tom Kristensen (1893–1974) was artistically more accomplished. In *Fribytterdrømme* (Buccaneer Dreams, 1920), Kristensen conveyed the restless spirit and explosive primitivism of the Jazz Age in an orgiastic display of color and sound. In the poem "Reklameskibet" (The Show Boat, 1923), Otto Gelsted (1888–1968) charged expressionist art with pandering to commercialism and neglecting fundamental human concerns from a Marxist point of view.

The poetry of Nis Petersen (1897–1943) and Paul la Cour (1902–56), the dominant figures of the 1930s, is also informed by humanist concerns. Petersen's anguished verse voices concern for the predicament of Western culture. La Cour, whose sensibility was formed by Claussen and mod. Fr. poets, stressed the redemptive nature of poetry. His *Fragmenter af en Dagbog* (Fragments of a Diary, 1948), which mingles philosophy, poetic theory, and verse, profoundly influenced the poets who came to maturity during the war. The surrealist Jens August Schade (1903–78) defined his attitude to the times by espousing a Lawrencian primitivism. His *Hjertebogen* (The Heart Book, 1930) contains sexually explicit love poems, along with nature impressions transformed by erotic feeling and a cosmic imagination.

Under the pressure of war and Nazi occupation, the 1940s instilled new vigor and urgency into Danish poetry. Two distinct responses to the brutality and destructiveness of World War II were evident: an activation of political consciousness, on the one hand, and an intensive quest for a meaningful, often metaphysical worldview, on the other. Inspirational was the work of Gustaf Munch-Petersen (1912–38), a literary existentialist who foreshadowed postwar modernism; through his death in Spain fighting Fascism, he became the prototype of the committed writer. Possessed by a vision of total union between conscious and subconscious, dream and reality, and stimulated by the imagism and surrealism of the Swedish and Finland-Swedish modernists, Munch-Petersen created a remarkable poetry that expressed a personal myth of self-making and self-liberation. Another paradigmatic poet was Morten Nielsen (1922–44), whose hard, weighty, unfinished verse oscillates between an existentialist affirmation of self and renunciation and death. Closely related to these two figures was Erik Knudsen (1922–2007), who, torn between beauty and politics, increasingly used poetry as the vehicle for a Marxist critique of society.

The central poets of the 1940s, following la Cour, saw poetry as a means of personal and cultural redemption. Striving for a form that would mirror their perception of a fragmented reality, they shaped a richly symbolic style inspired by T. S. Eliot and R. M. Rilke. The absence of a shared cultural and spiritual heritage, together with messianic longings, was most convincingly expressed by a group of poets whose original forum was the jour. *Heretica* (1948–53). Ole Sarvig (1921–81) and Ole Wivel (1921–2004) both embodied the pattern of rebirth after cultural catastrophe in their poetry, utilizing essentially Christian symbolism. Thorkild Bjørnvig (1918–2004) saw poetry itself as a liberating force. In his first, Rilke-inspired collection, *Stjærnen bag Gavlen* (The Star behind the Gable, 1947), eros is the predominant theme, treated with classic discipline in stanzas of great musicality and substance. In the 1970s, Bjørnvig changed the focus of his poetry to deal with ecological issues.

Others pursued different paths, unaffected by ideology or metaphysical probing. Tove Ditlevsen (1918–76) followed trad. and wrote rhymed verse in a neoromantic style. Piet Hein (1905–96) in his 20 volumes of *Gruk* (*Grooks*, 1940–63) combined scientific insights with a skillful, epigrammatic play of words and ideas. And Frank Jæger (1926–77), an elusive successor to Schade, noted for his verbal wizardry, cultivated the idyll, though in a broken form with an ominous undertone.

During the 1960s, an extroverted poetic experimentalism emerged, directed both against the materialism of the mod. welfare state and against prevailing ivory-tower literary attitudes. This change was largely due to Klaus Rifbjerg (1931–2015), the most versatile Danish postwar writer. Rifbjerg's verse registers the chaotic plenitude of experience in technological society by means of a fractured syntax and a vast, often technical-scientific vocabulary. Rifbjerg's two early collections *Konfrontation* (1960), with its photographically precise observations of the mod., technical world, and *Camouflage* (1961), which draws on cinematic montage and free association in a surrealist search for origins and a liberated self, profoundly affected Danish modernism. The themes of Rifbjerg's many subsequent collections of poetry are diverse and include everyday life, politics, and mythology.

A continuation of the introspective approach of the 1940s is evident in the poetry of Jørgen Sonne (1925–2015), which is marked by intellectual complexity and formal rigor, and Jørgen Gustava Brandt (1929–2006), who used myths and religious symbols to express a longing for epiphany.

In the mid-1960s, a tendency emerged toward ling. experimentation and concretism, the use of words as building blocks possessing intrinsic value, without reference to any other reality. This structuralist approach is present in *Romerske Bassiner* (Roman Pools, 1963) by the Marxist poet Ivan Malinowski (1926–1989). In the esoteric, systemic texts of Per Højholt (1928–2004), a major figure in Danish poetic modernism, lang. is transformed into intellectually challenging signs and closed symbols. Characteristic for Højholt's experimental and often humorous approach are *Poetens hoved* (The Poet's Head, 1963), *Turbo* (1968) and the 12 volumes of his *Praksis* (Practice, 1977–96) series. In his similarly untraditional and experimental poetry, the very productive Peter Laugesen (b. 1942) uses a genre-defying and self-reflective poetic lang. inspired by Beat poetry, surrealism, and Zen Buddhism to expose and confront the ideological lang. of power and society. Wordplay and verbal ambiguity also characterize the popular, witty, and thought-provoking verse of Benny Andersen (b. 1929). Klaus Høeck (b. 1938) uses systematic compositional principles inspired by mathematics, ling., and other forms in his often monumental poetry collections, as in *Hjem* (Home, 1985), where lang. is recast into complex structures in an attempt to illustrate the poet's striving to define God. Poul Borum (1934–96) connected visual perception with existential reflection. The poetry of Henrik Nordbrandt (b. 1945) often displays a sense of melancholia expressed in paradoxical metaphorical descriptions of an existential interplay between presence and absence.

Inger Christensen (1935–2009) used complex systems and principles to shape her poetry. An important work in Danish modernism, *det* (*it*, 1969), incorporates terms from the work of the linguist Viggo Brøndal and is structured according to mathematical systems. In *Alfabet* (*Alphabet*, 1981), the alphabet and the Fibonacci sequence (1-2-3-5-8-13-etc.) are used to create a compositional structure. A classic in Danish lit., *Sommerfugledalen—et requiem* (*Butterfly Valley: A Requiem*, 1991) combines a received poetic structure, the sonnet sequence, with mod. and existential themes: life, death, memory, lang.

Following the political and social changes of the late 1960s and early 1970s, Danish poetry became more realistic. The poems of Vita Andersen (b. 1942) revolve around childhood experiences and the workplace, and the collections of Marianne Larsen (b. 1951) analyze sexual repression, class struggle, and imperialism from a feminist perspective.

By the end of the 1970s, a new poetry, frequently referred to as *body modernism*, began to emerge, building on the ling. experiments of the 1960s but with a focus on the body, city life, and a sense of alienation. F. P. Jac (1955–2008) created a unique poetic lang., breaking up grammatical categories and constructing new words and expressions. Jac's *Misfat* (1980) is typical for the period with its insistence on erotic and bodily ecstasy as a liberating force and its fascination with the nightlife of the city, themes that also characterize the poetry, both desperate and ecstatic, of Michael Strunge (1958–86). City life is also the preferred environment in *City Slang* (1981) by Søren Ulrik Thomsen (b. 1956). In *Hjemfalden* (Reverted, 1991) and *Det skabtes vaklen* (The Wavering of Creation, 1996), Thomsen reflects on death, loneliness, and aging, using intricate poetic lines. The poetry of Pia Tafdrup (b. 1952) combines the erotic with images of nature in rhythmic, sensuous lang. *Dronningeporten* (*Queen's Gate*, 1999) interweaves images of water in nature (sea, river, rain) with an inner emotional landscape.

Danish poetry of the 1990s incorporated ling. and postmod. awareness with an interest in everyday life. In *Mellem tænderne* (Between the Teeth, 1992), Kirsten Hammann (b. 1965) dismissively describes the body in playful, ironic, and colloquial lang. Pia Juul (b. 1962) experiments with the poetic voice, creating a fragmented, dialogical poetry that mirrors everyday spoken lang. in *sagde jeg, siger jeg* (I said, I say, 1999). The emotionally charged poetry of Naja Marie Aidt (b. 1963) is centered on everyday life. The complex, hermetic poetry of Simon Grotrian (b. 1961), inspired by surrealism, concretism, and baroque poetry, combines striking poetic images with religious elements.

A multidimensional mix of poetic styles, genres, topics, and influences characterizes the poetry of young Danish poets after 2000. Ursula Andkjær Olsen (b. 1970) plays with lang. by breaking up and reassembling colloquial phrases and dead metaphors in a combination of styles, commenting on daily life, ideology, politics, commercials, and other topics. Similarly multifaceted and unconventional, in style and content, is *kingsize* (2006) by Mette Moestrup (b. 1969).

■ **Anthologies and Primary Texts**: *Oxford Book of Scandinavian Verse*, ed. E. W. Gosse and W. A. Craigie (1925); *The Jutland Wind*, ed. R. P. Keigwin (1944); *In Denmark I Was Born*, ed. R. P. Keigwin, 2d ed. (1950); *Twentieth-Century Scandinavian Poetry*, ed. M. S. Allwood (1950); *Modern Danish Poems*, ed. K. K. Mogensen, 2d ed. (1951); *Danske lyriske digte*, ed. M. Brøndsted and M. Paludan (1953); *A Harvest of Song*, ed. S. D. Rodholm (1953); *Den danske Lyrik 1800–1870*, ed. F.J.B. Jansen, 2 v. (1961); P. Hein, with J. Arup, *Grooks* (1966–78); *Danish Ballads and Folk Songs*, ed. E. Dal (1967); *A Book of Danish Ballads*, ed. A. Olrik (1968); *A Second Book of Danish Verse*, ed. C. W. Stork (1968); *Anthology of Danish Literature*, ed. F.J.B. Jansen and P. M. Mitchell (1971); *A Book of Danish Verse*, ed. O. Friis (1976); *Contemporary Danish Poetry*, ed. L. Jensen et al. (1977); F. Paludan-Müller, *Adam Homo*, trans. S. I. Klass (1980); *Seventeen Danish Poets*, ed. N. Ingwersen (1981); *Scandinavian Ballads*, ed. S. H. Rossel (1982); *Digte fra 1990'erne*, ed. N. Lyngsø (2000); *Danske forfatterskaber*, ed. S. Mose, P. Nyord, O. Ravn, 4 v. (2005–6); I. Christensen, *Alphabet*, trans. S. Nied (2001); P. Tafdrup, *Queen's Gate*, trans. D. McDuff (2001); I. Christensen, *Butterfly Valley: A Requiem*, trans. S. Nied (2004), and *it*, trans. S. Nied (2006).

■ **Criticism and History**: A. Olrik, *The Heroic Legends of Denmark* (1919); C. S. Petersen and V. Andersen, *Illustreret dansk Litteraturhistorie*, 4 v. (1924–34); H. G. Topsøe-Jensen, *Scandinavian Literature from Brandes to Our Own Day* (1929); E. Bredsdorff et al., *Introduction to Scandinavian Literature* (1951); P. M. Mitchell, *A Bibliographical Guide to Danish Literature* (1951); J. Claudi, *Contemporary Danish Authors* (1952); F.J.B. Jansen, "Romantisme européen et romantisme scandinave," *L'Âge* *d'Or* (1953); *Danske metrikere*, ed. A. Arnoltz et al., 2 v. (1953–54); S. M. Kristensen, *Dansk litteratur 1918–1952*, 7th ed. (1965); and *Den dobbelte Eros* (1966)—on Danish romanticism; F.J.B. Jansen, *Danmarks Digtekunst*, 2d ed., 3 v. (1969); *Modernismen i dansk litteratur*, ed. J. Vosmar, 2d ed. (1969); S. H. Larsen, *Systemdigtningen* (1971); P. M. Mitchel, *History of Danish Literature*, 2d ed. (1971); *Nordens litteratur*, ed. M. Brøndsted, 2 v. (1972); *Opgøret med modernismen*, ed. T. Brostrøm (1974); *Dansk litteraturhistorie*, ed. P. H. Traustedt, 2d ed., 6 v. (1976–77); P. Borum, *Danish Literature* (1979); S. H. Rossel, *History of Scandinavian Literature 1870–1980* (1982); *Digtning fra 80'erne til 90'erne*, ed. A.-M. Mai (1993); P. Stein Larsen, *Digtets krystal* (1997); and *Modernistiske outsidere* (1998); *Danske digtere i det 20. århundrede*, ed. A.-M. Mai, 4th ed., 3 v. (2000); E. Skyum-Nielsen, *Engle i sneen* (2000); *Læsninger i dansk litteratur*, ed. P. Schmidt et al., 2d ed., 5 v. (2001); J. Rosiek, *Andre spor* (2003); E. Skyum-Nielsen, *Dansk litteraturhistorie, 1978–2003* (2004); *Dansk litteraturs historie*, ed. K. P. Mortensen and M. Schack, 5 v. (2006–9).

S. Lyngstad; S. H. Rossel; J. K. Nielsen

DUTCH POETRY. *See* low countries, poetry of the

E

ECUADOR, POETRY OF. The hist. of Ecuadorian poetry has been divided into common Lat. Am. periods: pre-Hispanic, colonial, 19th c., and contemp. But it also has been divided in accordance with international literary movements—baroque, neoclassical, romantic, modernist, postmodernist, realist, and so forth. While pre-Hispanic poetry remains to be reconstructed to enter the Ecuadorian canon and the making of a list of nationally recognized poets has largely depended on literary critics' predilections and their relations to power, it is commonly accepted that the Jesuits Jacinto de Evia (b. 1629) and Juan Bautista Aguirre (1725–86), whose work shows the influence of Sp. poets of their times such as Luis de Góngora and Francisco de Quevedo, are the first poets of Ecuador. Aguirre's poetry is baroque and satirical and reflects the political dilemmas of the period, namely, the dominance of regionalism and the conflict between Ecuadorians from the coast and those from the Andean highland. During the 19th c., José Joaquín de Olmedo (1780–1847) wrote the epic poem "La victoria de Junín: Canto a Bolívar," and his poetic contributions have been widely celebrated in literary anthols. (Franco, Anderson Imbert and Florit).

Dolores Veintimilla de Galindo (1829–57), the only 19th-c. female poet to be studied in Ecuador at present, combines in her work a romantic style with a questioning of the limits imposed on women during the independence period. Her poem *Quejas* (Complaints), usually cited as a testimony of personal suffering and the social misunderstanding of women, also foretells the poet's suicide. Luis Cordero (1833–1912), a former president of Ecuador (1892–95), wrote epigrammatic and satirical poems in Quechua and in Sp. (Echeverría, Mera, Molestina).

At the beginning of the 20th c., the young poet Medardo Angel Silva (1898–1919) embraced in his life and work the transition between late romanticism and *modernismo*. He played the piano, read several langs., and wrote poetry and urban chronicles in a local newspaper. He also disdained money, fame, and power, displaying a belated, decadent Baudelairean style as a *flâneur* in Guayaquil. His hidden Af.-Ecuadorian ancestry and his early, tragic death are topics of gossip as well as scholarship (Benavides).

Equally important is the contribution of the avant-garde Hugo Mayo (1897–1988). Mayo's style was mainly abstract, hermetic, and humorous; and he was one of the most influential figures of the 20th c., providing new ling. and imaginative avenues to be rediscovered by later poets.

During the first half of the 20th c., Ecuadorean and international scholars agree, the work of Alfredo Gangotena (1904–44), Jorge Carrera (1902–78), and Gonzalo Escudero (1903–72) represents the most challenging poetry of Ecuador. Partly because of their family influences and economic positions, these three poets were in constant literary exchange with other poets around the world, and much of their work was translated into Fr., Eng., and Ger. Their poetry is mainly personal, metaphysical, and religious. But social issues also emerge in their works and remind us of their shared convictions about justice and freedom. César Dávila (1919–67) followed the steps of his three predecessors but embraced a more fantastic and abstract lang. in his work. His preference for obscuring the meaning of his poems became more relevant to poets such as Efraín Jara (b. 1926); Oswaldo Calisto Rivera (1979–2000, also known as Cachivache); and others who promote an obscure, bookish, and pedantic style as fundamental literary values of the late 20th c. Dávila also wrote short stories and, to the surprise of many, a long poem titled *Boletín y Elegía de las Mitas* to protest the inhumane conditions endured by Indians since the Sp. conquest. His tragic end occurred in Caracas, and his poetry immediately became *razón de culto* for young readers.

Jorge Enrique Adoum (1926–2009) and Hugo Salazar Tamariz (1923–99) were friends and contemporaries of Dávila. Their poetry is clearly marked by Marxist political convictions and, thus, by socialist realism and the style of the Rus. poet Vladimir Mayakovsky. The volumes of their collected poems, recently released in Ecuador, provide examples of social concerns and give us a clear idea of hegemonic literary discourses in the context of the cold war.

During the last half of the 20th c., Ecuadorian poetry matured and slowly became more international and ambitious. Hence, it reflects varied personal views shaped by global and national events, as well as inevitable literary influences from Europe and the U.S., while presenting a wide range of contemp. styles, voices, and themes. Ecuadorian poetry from the second half of the 20th c. includes the work of Carlos E. Jaramillo (b. 1932), David Ledesma (1934–61), Fernando Cazón (b. 1931), and other members of the *Grupo Madrugada* (Group of the Dawn) and the *Generación Huracanada* (Wrecked Generation) of the late 1950s and 1960s. The poets of these groups were united in revolt against governmental violence, repression, and social injustice, both domestic and worldwide. During the 1970s, the decade of the last Ecuadorian military dictatorship, Hipólito Alvarado (b. 1934), Agustín Vulgarín (1938–86), Euler Granda (b. 1935), Antonio Preciado (b. 1941), Humberto Vinueza (b. 1942), Julio Pazos (b. 1944), Sonia Manzano (b. 1947), Fernando Nieto (b. 1947), Javier Ponce (b. 1948), and Hernán Zúñiga (b. 1950, best known as a painter) were actively involved in developing and experimenting with new forms of poetry. The voice of the poor, represented through the use of urban colloquial lang. such as that of Guayaquil, was a special concern of the group *Sicoseo*, with Nieto as its mentor and leading figure.

The poetry of two members of Sicoseo—Fernando Balseca (b. 1959) and Jorge Martillo (b. 1957)—as well as that of Maritza Cino (b. 1957), Edwin Madrid (b. 1961), Eduardo Morán (b. 1957), Roy Sigüenza (b. 1958), and Diego Velasco (b. 1958) belongs to the 1980s. These poets were highly influenced by Ecuadorian predecessors but also by their times: the return of democracy to Ecuador, the end of national and international communist aspirations, and the impact of postmod. culture.

Among the dozens of new poets whose work has appeared in recent years are Siomara España (b. 1976), Luis Alberto Bravo (b. 1979), Augusto Rodríguez (b. 1979), Alex Tupiza (b. 1979), Víctor Vimos (b. 1985), Ana Minga (b. 1983), and Dina Bellrham (1984–2011). They have been actively involved in public literary events and exchanges with poets from other countries and are the most innovative voices of their groups (*Buseta de papel, Reverso*), making extensive use of blog writing and integration of poetry with the visual arts (Iturburu and Levitin).

See INDIGENOUS AMERICAS, POETRY OF THE; SPANISH AMERICA, POETRY OF.

■ V. E. Molestina, *Lira Ecuatoriana* (1866); J. A. Echeverría, *Nueva lira ecuatoriana* (1879); J. L. Mera, *Ojeada histórico-crítica sobre la poesía ecuatoriana* (1893); E. Anderson Imbert and E. Florit, *Literatura hispanoamericana* (1970); O. H. Benavides, *The Politics of Sentiment: Imagining and Remembering Guayaquil* (1970); J. Franco, *An Introduction to Spanish-American Literature* (1975); *Tapestry of the Sun: An Anthology of Ecuadorian Poetry*, ed. F. Iturburu and A. Levitin (2009).

F. ITURBURU

EGYPT, POETRY OF

I. The Old Kingdom (ca. 2750–2260 BCE)
II. The Middle Kingdom (ca. 2134–1782 BCE)
III. The New Kingdom (ca. 1570–1070 BCE)
IV. The Coptic Period (284–640 CE)
V. Poetry in Arabic (640–present)

Poetry in Egypt passed through epochal changes in langs.: the ancient Egyptian, the Coptic, and the Ar. Whatever continuity there may be has less to do with any constant poetic heritage than with the common history and psychology of the Egyptian people.

The ancient Egyptian era is subdivided into three periods.

I. The Old Kingdom (ca. 2750–2260 BCE). We can suppose that, in addition to the poetry written in heightened lang. by educated scribes, there existed a less sophisticated "poetry," which was simple and humble, represented in the singing of the working people in accompaniment to their work.

The poetry in elevated langs. can hold place beside the achievements of the Egyptians in the artistic and technical spheres. They took pleasure in giving artistic shape to their songs, tales, and a world of contemplation extending beyond the quotidian routine and religion (Erman).

All that scribes wrote falls into short lines of equal length. Knowing nothing about their sound, we can regard them as verse, but their meter remains unknown. It is generally supposed, however, that there are verses esp. characterized by the free rhythm. In the early 1970s, Assmann argued that it was necessary to view Egyptian lit. (esp. poetry) not only as an instrument for the systematizations of religious or social rules but also as autonomous cultural discourse. Lichtheim (1973) based her literary classification on three categories: free prose; poetry (esp. characterized by the use of parallelism or a mixed genre she calls "systematically structured speech"); and orational style. Egyptian literary texts were not read silently by individuals but were recited on special occasions.

Of the old poetry, little survived. What remains is only formulas and religious hymns (songs of praise, chorales, carols, psalms). They are spirited and suggestive. The pyramid texts contain a collection of ancient formulas concerned with the destiny of the blessed dead kings, hymns, and banquet songs glorifying the deceased (Hassan).

During the fifth dynasty (2750–2625 BCE), the autobiography acquired its characteristics: a self-portrait in words mingling the real and the ideal, and emphatically eulogistic. The instructions in wisdom are a major literary genre created in the Old Kingdom (Lichtheim 1973).

II. The Middle Kingdom (ca. 2134–1782 BCE). Egypt's cl. age introduced extensive literary works in a variety of genres with accomplished command of forms. In the composition known as *The Eloquent Peasant*, rich in metaphors and other poetic imagery, the art of fine speaking was made to serve the defense of justice. Hymns to the gods are a close relation to the biblical psalms, and hymns to the kings were expressed in emotionally charged poems. *The Story of Sinuhe*, the crown jewel of Middle Kingdom lit., employs three styles: prose, poetry, and oration. The narration is interspersed with three poems, each being an example of a genre. Other genres include coffin texts and didactic writing. The so-called coffin texts were written in the intermediate period between the Old and Middle Kingdoms. Coffins of nonroyal well-to-do persons were inscribed with spells designed to protect the dead against the perils of the netherworld. Didactic lit. (wisdom and the genre of instruction) was not just the guidelines of a father to his son but the contemplation of profound problems of the human condition.

The theme of national distress or even human torment was only a literary topos that required no basis in society ("The Complaints of Khakheperr-Sonb"). The author addresses his complaints to his heart, and poetic elaboration uses overstatements.

In the "Satire of the Trades," a father instructs his son in the duties and rewards of the scribal profession, ridiculing the other trades. The composition is in the orational style.

III. The New Kingdom (ca. 1570–1070 BCE). One characteristic of ancient Egyptian poetry in general is the integrating of elements from different genres such as teachings, laments, eulogies, and oral compositions. But the epic form appears for the first time in the Kadesh Battle inscriptions of Ramses II in the long section known as the *Poem*. Hymns to the gods are another genre in which the New Kingdom went beyond the Middle, depicting new trends of religiosity: the god of all who is accessible to the pious individual. A large number of hymns are addressed to the sun god. A qualitative change, the doctrine of the sole god worked out by Amonhotep IV, Akhenaten's monotheistic teachings, followed.

The Book of the Dead is the continuation of the coffin texts. Instead of being inscribed on coffins, the spells are now written on papyrus scrolls, grouped into chapters and accompanied by vignettes (Lichtheim 1976).

Although lyric poetry was well developed in the Middle Kingdom, love lyrics seem to be a creation of the New Kingdom. Love poems are rich in elaborate puns, metaphors, and rare words. Calling them *love poems*, rather than *love songs*, emphasizes their literary origin. The lovers referred to each other as brothers and sisters. The poems have conceptual accessibility and a pithiness of lang.

IV. The Coptic Period (ca. 284–640 CE). In the earliest stage of Christianity, poetry and religion were rather coextensive, but at a later stage, poetry separated itself to some extent from religion. Drama also separated itself from liturgy. The relation between religion and poetry, however, was closest in the lyric. The lyric expressed the individual's sense of awe, wonder, or guilt in the presence of the sacred. Mystic poets used erotic metaphors to express their epiphanies.

The Coptic lang. and literary trad. use familiar, simple, and direct expressions inspired by the Bible. The influence of the NT can be found not only in the ideas but also in symbols and diction.

V. Poetry in Arabic (640–present). In 640 CE, the forces of Islam conquered Egypt, and some Arab tribes settled in Egypt. Their poets produced mainly vainglorious poems in meter and rhyme, part of the collective trad. However, Egyptian poetry developed historically under political and social conditions different from those in many Arab countries, and it changed in isolation. Egypt attracted many Arab poets in pursuit of rewards and settlement. Many remarkable Arab poets visited Egypt, among whom were Jamil Buthayna (d. 701) and Kuthayyir ʿAzza (ca. 660–723), two poets of platonic love; and Abū Nuwās (756–814) and Abū Tammām (788–845). Under the reign of the Tulunids (868–905), Egypt had many poets, e.g., al-Kassem ben Yehia Almaryamy (d. 928) and al-Hussain Ibn Abel-Salam (d. 871). The great poet al-Bohtory (b. ca. 821) praised Ahmed Ibn Tulun and his successor. After ending his relation with his patron Saif al-Dawlah in 951, the great Ar. poet al-Mutanabbī (915–65) came to Cairo and lavishly praised the ruler Kafur. When the latter did not respond to the poet's political ambitions, al-Mutanabbī fled at night and cruelly satirized him.

In later centuries, Ibn Maṭrouh (1196–1251), Bahā al-dīn Zuhayr (1186–1258), Ibn Nubatah al Misri (1287–1366) and Ṣafī al-Din al-Ḥillī (d. 1349) made Cairo an important cultural center.

The poetic genre that had dominated poetry was eulogy, which was initially meant to depict the ideal image of the perfect man. Soon the panegyric lost much of its credibility, and the genre became imitative, repetitious, and tedious.

After the caliphate disintegrated, small regions were governed by many minor rulers, many of whom did not speak Ar. and had no interest in poetry. Over long periods, poetry stagnated; artificial embellishments and wordplay took the place of serious concerns. This kind of poetry was contemporaneous with enduring experiments in Sufi and religious poetry, a prominent representative of which was Ibn al-Fāriḍ (ca. 1181–1235). His mystical poetry was characterized by its rich imagery of symbolic wine and love. Al-Būṣīrī (ca. 1212–96) wrote the "Qaṣīdat al-Burdah" (Mantle Ode), a luminous ode in praise of the Prophet.

Bahā' al-Dīn Zuhayr, born in Mecca, spent most of his life in Egypt. He was a favorite of the Ayyubid ruler al-Malek al-Ṣaleh. His poems were lucid, simple, and very close to spoken lang.

Egyptian cultural life was roused from its lethargy by Napoleon's expedition of 1798, with little immediate effect on poetry. Mohamed Ali's cultural innovations were in the sphere of education. Egyptian students were sent to study in France; the Bulaq printing press was founded; and Enlightenment books were ordered to be trans. leading to an important trans. movement and a shift in readership, which was confined earlier to the traditional Islamic scholars (Starkey). A major role in the devel. of the literary revival was played by the press.

A great part of Ar. poetry had declined from the fall of Baghdad in 1258 to the Fr. occupation of Egypt in 1798. Mahmoud Sami al-Barudi (1835–1904) tried to restore the style, spirit, and trads. of the great Ar. poets. This was possible only through the availability of eds. of their collections of poems by the printing press. The Eur. concept of neoclassicism, however, does not apply to al-Barudi and his successors, Ahmad Shawqī (1869–1932) and Hāfez Ibrāhīm (1871–1932). Al-Barudi wrote mainly in the manner of pre-Islamic poets about love, war, and desert life in a tribal heroic society. At his best, he was a conscious innovator with an ability to express vividly his subjective experiences through traditional idioms.

After al-Barudi, it is possible to speak of a school that included Shawqī, Hāfez, Ismail Sabri (1854–1923), Ali al-Jarem (1881–1949), and others, although it was a school without theoretical foundations. The trad. considered the poet as the spokesman of his nation, the enlargement of his tribe, which was a function long lost (Badawi). Shawqī, the poet laureate, initially composed panegyrical poems on official occasions. The Brit. authorities exiled him; he went to Spain, where he reflected his deep nostalgia for Egypt. After his return, he expressed the popular attitude toward national and social subjects and refused to be the mouthpiece of the court. During this period, he wrote most of his poetic dramas. He used the idioms and imagery of traditional Ar. poetry to address contemp. social, cultural, and political concerns. The critic Taha Hussain described him and comparable poets as mere revivalists, but in 1927 he was called the Prince of Poets by fellow Arab poets.

A great Lebanese poet, Khalīl Muṭrān (1872–1949), who settled in Egypt, was one of the first Arab romantic poets to create new themes and imagery, in addition to his full mastery of conventional poetic diction. In Egypt, he had many admirers, among them many prominent romantic poets such as Ibrāhīm Nājī (1898–1953), ʿAlī Maḥmūd Ṭāhā (1901–49), and Saleh Jawdat (1912–76), who all joined the Apollo group founded by Aḥmad Zakī abu-Shādī (1892–1955) in 1932. The group included members writing in different styles, but all worked for "lofty poetical ideals," as the group stated in its manifesto. Abu-Shādī was not considered a great poet, but he was a versatile experimenter with *muwashshaḥ* forms (a postclassical form of Ar. poetry arranged in stanzas) and Eng. free verse and sonnets, but with no followers.

The movement called *al-Dīwān* (The Register) appeared at the turn of the 20th c. in opposition to Shawqī and Hāfez. It aspired to be a new direction that endeavored to establish a genuine Egyptian lit. under the influence and guidance of Western literary romantic ideas. This trend was defended by Mahmoud Abbas al-ʿAqqād (1889–1964), Abdel-Raḥmān Shukrī (1886–1958), and Ibrāhīm Abdel-Kader al-Māzinī (1889–1949). Their so-called revolution tried to find the appropriate form to express the Egyptian national spirit, but it did not lead to new forms: the Ar. literary trad. dominated the poetry of this movement.

After World War II, there were attempts to formulate new forms of poetic discourse to express new national and popular requirements. Sometimes, these attempts were under the banner of what was called "commitment," i.e., commitment to revolutionary subjects of independence and social justice, whose prominent contributors were the leftist poets Kamal Abdel-Halim (1926–2004) and Abdel-Rahman al-Sharqawi (1920–87). A leading figure in that movement was Fouad Haddad (1927–85), who wrote in colloquial Ar. Those poets published in leftist magazines, e.g., *Almalayeen* (Millions) and *Al Kateb* (The Writer), as well as in other cultural reviews of daily newspapers. The movement for what was called *modern poetry* was wider than the commitment in themes, incl. quotidian and existential experiences. It included among many poets Ṣalāḥ ʿAbd al-Sabūr (1931–81), Ahmad Ȧ. Hijazy (b. 1935), and Muḥammad Miftāḥ al-Faytūrī (b. 1936?). ʿAbd al-Sabūr wrote dramatic pieces on the theme of cosmic distress. Hijazy was the poet of the Arab revolution, though his views radically changed later. What was known as mod. poetry in Egypt was mainly based on the single foot (*taf'ela*) rather than the complete meter (*baḥr*) and on a variety of rhymes.

The generation that followed in the 1960s included Amal Dunqul (1940–83), Mohamad Afifi Matar (1935–2010), and Mohamad Ibrahim Abu-Sinna (b. 1937), who were of different orientations. Dunqul was popular for his poems against the official politics. Abu-Sinna is known for his revolutionary romantic verses. Afifi Matar was known for his significant contribution to experimental poetry and his influence on the next generation of poets.

The 1970s were the years of the defeat of the Arab national project after the war with Israel and the occupation of Arab territories in 1967. Two groups of poets issued collective manifestos in Egypt: *Iḍā'a 77* (Illumination) and *Aswāt* (Voices). These groups were similar in experimental orientation and their rejection of the traditional canon. They set themselves apart from the poets of the 1950s and 1960s and opposed the status quo. Among the Idā'a group were Helmy Salem (b. 1951), Hassan Tilib (b. 1944), Rifʿat Sallam (b. 1951), Mahmoud Nasim (b. 1955) and Sha'ban Youssef (b. 1955). The Aswāt group included Abdul-Mon'im Ramadan (b. 1951), Ahmad Taha (b. 1948), Ȧbdul Maqsud Ȧbdul-Karim (b. 1956), Mohamed Eid Ibrahim (b. 1955), and Mohamed Sulaiman (b. 1946), who also experimented with prose poems in the 1990s. Their poetry abandoned ideology and nationalism, focusing on personal and relative truth. Other Egyptian poets, such as Mohamed Salih (1940–2009), Fathy Abdulla (b. 1957), Fatma Qandil (b. 1958), and Ali Mansour (b. 1956), did not belong to either of the two groups but became prominent for their prose poems (Mehrez). Since the 1990s, the poetry scene has been characterized by the predominance of the prose poem.

■ M. Lichtheim, *Ancient Egyptian Literature*, v. 1: *The Old and Middle Kingdoms* (1973), foreword by A. Loprieno (2006); M. Badawi, *A Critical Introduction to Modern Arabic Poetry* (1975); S. Mureh, *Modern Arabic Poetry, 1800–1970* (1976)—devel. of its forms and themes; J. Brugman, *An Introduction to the History of Modern Arabic Literature in Egypt* (1984); S. Mehrez, "Experimentation and the Institution, The Case of Idâ'a 77 and Aswât," *Alif* 11 (1991); A. Erman, *Ancient Egyptian Poetry and Prose*, trans. A. Blackman (1995); S. Hassan, *Encyclopedia of Ancient Egypt*, v. 17 and 18: *Ancient Egyptian Literature* (2000)—in Ar.; J. Assmann, *The Mind of Egypt: History and Meaning in the Time of the Pharaohs*, trans. A. Jenkins (2002); S. Deif, *History of Arabic Literature*, v. 7: *Epoch of States and Emirates, Egypt* (2003)—in Ar.; R. Allen, "The Post-classical Period: Parameters and Preliminaries," *Cambridge History of Arabic Literature: Arabic Literature in the Post-Classical Period*, ed. R. Allen and D. S. Richards (2006); M. Lichtheim, *Ancient Egyptian Literature*, v. 2: *The New Kingdom*, 2d. ed., foreword by H. Fischer-Elfert (2006); P. Starkey, *Modern Arabic Literature* (2006).

I. Fathy

EL SALVADOR, POETRY OF. According to the Sp. scholar Marcelino Menéndez y Pelayo, no country as small as El Salvador should be able to lay claim to so many fine poets. The hist. of Salvadoran poetry is characterized by two salient features: individuals who shine like beacons among their contemporaries and the tragic nexus between lit. and politics.

The Salvadoran poetic trad. dates to before 1524, when Pedro de Alvarado conquered the pre-Columbian kingdom of Cuscatlán. Its principal inhabitants, the Pipiles, spoke Nahuatl, an Aztec lang. Although no record remains of Nahuatl lit., echoes of its sung poetry have survived in oral trads. Oswaldo Escobar Velado (1919–61) and Salarrué (pseud. of Salvador Salazar Arrué, 1899–1979) employed features of Nahuatl poetry, incl. formulaic repetitions, parallelisms, a fondness for diminutives, a profusion of metaphors, and creation myths.

Some poetry of note was produced during the colonial era, mainly by Sp. administrators or clerics. The colonial poet Juan de Mestanza (b. 1534) lord mayor of Sonsonate between 1585 and 1589, was praised by Miguel de Cervantes for his witty sonnets. A national lit. arose during the Salvadoran struggle for independence (1811–59). The first national poet, Miguel Alvarez Castro (1795–1856), wrote neoclassical patriotic verses, such as "A la muerte del Coronel Pierzon" (Upon the Death of Colonel Pierzon, 1827).

Romanticism prevailed from mid-century to the first decade of the 20th. Significant poets in this mode were Juan J. Cañas (1826–1918), who composed the national anthem, and Antonia Galindo (1858–93), the first major woman poet. Two talented romantics whose careers were cut short by suicide were José Calixto Mixco (1880–1901) and Armando Rodríguez Portillo (1880–1915). The multifaceted work of Vicente Acosta (1867–1908) reflects a shift from romanticism to the novel aesthetic of *modernismo*.

The high priest of Salvadoran modernismo was Francisco Gavidia (1864–1955), a pioneer in the application of Fr. forms to Sp. poetry. In such poems as "Stella," "La ofrenda del bramán" (The Brahman's Offering), "Sóteer o tierra de preseas" (The Savior or Land of Precious Things), and "La defensa de Pan" (In Defense of Pan), Gavidia addressed national themes in many forms, incl. *romances* (ballads) and *redondillas* (Sp. quatrains). The next poetic movement in El Salvador was *costumbrismo* (lit. of customs and manners), represented by Alfredo Espino (1900–28). Espino's posthumous collection, *Jícaras tristes* (Gourds of Sadness, 1930), celebrated El Salvador's natural wonders and indigenous heritage.

La Matanza (the Great Slaughter) in 1932 of more than 30,000 peasants ushered in six decades of turmoil until the brutal civil war between 1980 and 1992. During this time, writing became a medium for evading or confronting political horror. Claudia Lars (pseud. of Carmen Brannon, 1899–1974) became known as "the divine Claudia" for her mastery of cl. meters to treat spiritual, mystical, and erotic themes. Meanwhile, some poets strove to preserve truth and beauty from the contamination of politics, among them Vicente Rosales y Rosales (1894–1980), Serafín Quiteño (1899–1952), and Hugo Lindo (1917–85). Raúl Contreras (1896–1973) wrote a series of haunting sonnets under the pseud. Lydia Nogales.

During these decades, a constellation of women poets cultivated cl. forms (particularly the sonnet) and a lyrical idiom to explore a gamut of themes. Noteworthy names include Alice Lardé (1896–1983), María Loucel (1899–1957), Lilian Serpas (1905–85), Berta Funes Peraza (1911–98), Matilde Elena López (1922–2010), and Mercedes Durand (1933–99). Hypnotic images and surrealism were the hallmarks of Emma Posada (1912–97). Lydia Valiente's (1900–76) book *Raíces amargas* (Bitter Roots, 1952) employed choral verse in a proletarian voice to denounce injustice.

Defiance and rebellion motivated successive poetic generations, the first of which included Pedro Geoffroy Rivas (1908–79) and Antonio Gamero (1917–74). Escobar Velado's *10 sonetos para mil y más obreros* (10 Sonnets for a Thousand Workers and More, 1950) inspired the Committed Generation, represented by Italo López Vallecillos (1932–86), Tirso Canales (b. 1930), and Manlio Argueta (b. 1935), who in turn influenced "the poetry of combat and resistance" by José María Cuéllar (1942–80) and Miguel Huezo Mixco (b. 1954). Marxist fervor infuses the work of guerrilla-poet Roque Dalton (1935–75), a master of collage who blended verse with songs, letters, reportage, and historical chronicles. Claribel Alegría (b. 1924), a Salvadoran-Nicaraguan, combined revolutionary commitment with aesthetic refinement in such collections as *Sobrevivo* (I Survive, 1978) and *La mujer del río Sumpul* (The Woman of the Sumpul River, 1987). Alegría also excels at poetry of sensuous lyricism, incl. love poems for her deceased husband and translator Bud Flakoll (*Thresholds/Umbrales*, 1996).

Among the poets straddling the civil war are Roberto Armijo (1937–97), Roberto Cea (b. 1939), and Alfonso Kijadurías (or Alfonso Quijada Urias, b. 1940). Undoubtedly, the most talented nonpartisan poet is David Escobar Galindo (b. 1943). From his first collection, *Las manos en el fuego* (Hands in the Fire, 1967), to his most recent, *El poema de David* (David's Poem, 2007), he displays mastery of versification.

Since the civil war, Salvadoran poets at home and among the diaspora in North America, Australia, and Europe, incl. Ricardo Lindo (b. 1947), Javier Alas (b. 1964), Álvaro Darío Lara (b. 1966), and Luis Alvarenga (b. 1969), have eschewed partisan ideologies to probe the paradoxes of identity and existence. Liberated women poets, incl. Claudia Herodier (b. 1950), Silvia Elena Regalado (b. 1961), Brenda Gallegos (b. 1972), and Claudia Meyer (b. 1980), explore sex and desire in a range of registers, from the controlled passion of Carmen González Huguet (b. 1958) to the graphic eroticism of Dina Posada (b. 1946) in "Plegaria al orgasmo" (Prayer to Orgasm, 1996). In conclusion, as anthols. by Poumier (2002) and Amaya (2010) attest, poets of different generations, genders, and styles continue to build upon El Salvador's vibrant literary trad.

See INDIGENOUS AMERICAS, POETRY OF THE; SPANISH AMERICA, POETRY OF.

■ *La margarita emocionante*, ed. H. Castellanos Moya (1979); L. Gallegos Valdés, *Panorama de la literatura salvadoreña* (1981); *Poesía de El Salvador*, ed. M. Argueta (1983); *Indice antológico de la poesía salvadoreña*, ed. D. Escobar Galindo (1988); *Piedras en el huracán*, ed. J. Alas (1993); *Alba de otro milenio*, ed. R. Lindo (2000); R. C. Boland, "A Short History of the Literature of El Salvador," *Antípodas* 18.19 (2002); *Poésie Salvadorienne du XX Siècle*, ed. M. Poumier (2002); *Una madrugada del siglo XXI*, ed. V. Amaya (2010).

R. C. Boland

ENGLAND, POETRY OF

I. Old English, 650–1066
II. Middle English, 1066–1500
III. The Renaissance, 1500–1660
IV. The Restoration and the Eighteenth Century, 1660–1789
V. The Romantic Period, 1789–1830
VI. The Victorian Period, 1830–1900
VII. Modernism to the Present, from 1901

I. Old English, 650–1066. When Lat. literary culture took hold in early med. England, one surprising result was a flourishing of vernacular verse in a wealth of genres, from sophisticated riddles and emotionally intense lyrics, to long biblical narratives and epics such as *Beowulf*. Although writing occurred almost exclusively in monastic scriptoria where Lat. predominated, OE poetry developed alongside Anglo-Lat. lit. Nearly all OE poems survive as copies in four codices dating from the late 10th or early 11th c.: the Exeter Book, the Vercelli Book, the *Beowulf* or Nowell Codex, and the Junius ms. It is, therefore, extremely difficult to establish dates of composition or to track changing metrical patterns. Nonetheless, we know that OE poetry was composed at least from the late 7th through the 11th c. In his *Ecclesiastical History of the English People* (completed 731 CE), Bede (673–736) describes a body of written vernacular biblical verse, which he attributes to the miracle of an illiterate lay worker named Cædmon (fl. 657–79) whose divinely inspired songs were transcribed by the brothers at Whitby. The illustrated Junius ms., clearly the work of multiple authors, contains the long biblical verse narratives *Genesis*, *Exodus*, *Daniel*, and *Christ and Satan*, although its hist. is obscure. A few OE poems, such as "The Battle of Brunanburh," "The Battle of Maldon," and "Durham," can be securely dated to the late 10th and 11th cs. because they refer to contemp. events.

OE poetry's stress-based, alliterative verse was cultivated from traditional, probably oral, forms in the context of Lat. versification and Saxon poetry written on the continent (see GERMANIC PROSODY). This verse bears affinities to accentual verse, which is organized by count of stresses rather than syllables, but its emphasis is on patterns of alliterating stresses that bind half lines across a caesura; the total number of stressed syllables in a line can vary, although syllabic count, a feature of Romance prosodies, may have been a consideration for some OE poets. Literary interchange, particularly with Carolingian courts and with Rome, was rich and complex. Some Anglo-Saxon authors knew an array of cl. and early med. *Latin poetry, incl. Virgil's *Aeneid*, and Lat. meter was among the topics taught at Canterbury in the 7th c. by Archbishop Theodore and Abbot Hadrian, both from the Gr.-speaking Mediterranean.

This confluence of langs. and poetic conventions generated a robust verse suitable for lyric, martial, or religious poetry. Kennings and other metaphoric compounds (such as *hran-rad*, "whale-road," for "sea" and *ban-hus*, "bone-house," for "body"), litotes, strings of appositional modifiers, and a heroic, aristocratic tenor feature prominently. OE poets experimented with rhyme, and occasionally with stanzaic form and macaronic verse. Poets who composed in OE probably also composed Anglo-Lat. poetry, which shares some characteristics with OE poetry. A good deal of alliterative, rhythmic OE prose survives, and the line between prose and poetry is sometimes unclear.

OE poets experimented with first-person voice, using it to realize emotional intensity and to sustain unity, often with self-conscious reference to poetic composition. The speakers of lyrics such as "The Wanderer," "The Seafarer," "The Riming Poem," and "The Order of the World" meditate poignantly on the transience of worldly joy, offering poetic imagination and their own experience as a bridge to wisdom and theological understanding. The poet Cynewulf, whose dates are uncertain, muses on his own artistry and on salvation as he disperses the letters of his name, encoded in runes, across each of the lyric epilogues to "Fates of the Apostles," *Christ II*, *Elene*, and *Juliana*. The speaker of *Widsith* (far-traveler) seems the voice of poetry itself, cataloguing his successes as a court poet for kings whose historical existence far exceeds a single lifespan. Objects often speak, particularly in riddles, which share qualities with both lyric and gnomic poetry. In Riddle 26, the first-person voice speaks of itself as both a living animal and an ornamented gospel book made from the animal's skin, and vaunts its salvific qualities. In "The Dream of the Rood," the first dream vision in Eng., the rood describes itself as a living tree and a jeweled cross and commands the dreamer to compose its story. OE poetry maintains strong ties to material culture, and some objects, such as the Alfred Jewel, also bear first-person inscriptions. Most notably, a runic poem corresponding to a portion of "The Dream of the Rood" is carved into the stone shaft of the 8th-c. Northumbrian Ruthwell Cross. First-person lyric also punctuates long historical poems such as *Beowulf*, particularly at points of transition, where it links narrative segments and distant times.

In many poems of different genres, this dramatic voice turns dialogic. In the saints' lives *Andreas, Juliana, Guthlac A*, and *Elene*, and in the epic *Christ and Satan*, rhetorically heightened episodes—such as Andrew's probing interrogation of Christ, Juliana's and Guthlac's verbal duels with demons, Elene's interchange with the Jewish priest Judas, and the fallen Satan's dialogue with his inferiors—anchor the narrative structures and dramatize didactic lessons. Different in tone but no less dramatic are the *Advent Lyrics* (also known as *Christ I*), a series of apostrophes inspired by the Advent antiphons and addressed mainly to God, Christ, or Mary, with the exception of *Lyric VII*'s cagey dialogue between Joseph and Mary regarding her pregnancy.

Many OE poems are considered trans., although their inventive reworkings of sources attest to a process that brought extensive study, bold interpretation, and poetic imagination to bear on even the most sacred texts. The epic *Genesis*, a portion of which translates an Old Saxon poem, begins with the apocryphal fall of the angels and includes an unusual version of the temptation. Hagiographical poems such as *Andreas* (on the Apostle Andrew's conversion of the cannibal Mermedonians), *Juliana* (an early Christian virgin-martyr tale), and *Elene* (a version of St. Helen's discovery of the true cross) work freely with multiple Lat. versions, adapting them to the heroic style characteristic of OE poetry. Although most trans. are biblical or hagiographical, the Exeter Book, a diverse anthol. of poetry, contains three trans. from *Physiologus* ("The Panther," "The Whale," and "The Partridge") and "The Phoenix," which translates and then interprets the "De Ave Phoenice" attributed to Lactantius.

All long narrative OE poems except *Beowulf* are biblical or hagiographical. What these poems have in common, however, is historiography. Anglo-Saxon authors, beginning with Bede, worked assiduously to weave northern Eur. hist. into the strands of universal hist., dominated by biblical Heb. genealogy and the ascendance of the Roman Empire. Despite its many fantastical elements, *Beowulf* is deeply grounded in hist.: it documents the military and territorial campaigns of the Danes, Swedes, and Geats; it describes Grendel as "kin of Cain," thus incorporating its narrative into the sweep of biblical hist.; and it features ancestors who also appear in genealogies of the *Anglo-Saxon Chronicle* and other historiographical texts. Together with more localized martial poems such as "The Battle of Maldon" and native saints' lives like the *Guthlac* poems, this epic stakes a claim for Eng. in literary hist.

II. Middle English, 1066–1500. The later Eng. Middle Ages bear witness to an intense period of literary experimentation. Almost all of this experimentation is in poetry; nonrhythmic prose is not a coherent medium (with cultural prestige, genres, and so on) in literary Eng. composition until after the invention of the printing press in about 1450. The experimental impulse originates from a fundamental ling. change: in the aftermath of the Norman Conquest (1066), which roughly divides the two phases of the Middle Ages in England, Norman poetic practices collide with OE practices to produce the first flowering of ME poetry, incl. *The Owl and the Nightingale* (late 12th c.). It deploys debate conventions that appear in both OE and Fr. but also uses a continental octosyllabic line and mixes courtly Fr. vocabulary into its largely Eng. lexicon. The synergy between Fr. and insular lang. and literary convention yields new literary forms from the 12th through the 14th c. These new forms arise both in narrative and lyric poetry and in both religious and secular contexts, though one upshot of the experimental energy of the period is that both of these oppositions—narrative versus lyric, religious versus secular—are examined and reinvented by the end of the Middle Ages, particularly in the large-scale narrative fictions of the major poets of Edwardian, Ricardian, and Lancastrian England.

In the first phase of ME narrative poetry, the literary landscape is dominated by biblical paraphrase, hagiography, and homily. Incl. *Genesis and Exodus* (1250), the *South English Legendary* (late 13th c.), the *Gospel of Nicodemus* (1325), the *Poema morale* (ca. 1170), and the *Ormulum* (ca. 1200), these religious narratives announce their primary cultural purpose as didactic, though many (the *Ormulum* in particular) have a clear and sustained interest in lang., rhythm, and the aesthetic field in which didacticism is produced.

Early lyrical poetry, too, is often religious in theme. Many early religious lyrics are structured as apostrophes to the Virgin Mary, while others are prayers to Jesus. As in OE poetry, some of the most interesting religious lyrics are dialogic, for instance containing an exchange between Mary and Jesus. There is no single unifying or typically "Eng." lyrical form for religious verse in the period; instead, a wide variety of Fr. and Lat. verse forms and meters are adapted to the exigencies of Eng. stress patterns. Line lengths and rhyme schemes in lyric poetry are variable, as are the lengths of stanzas and the prosodic patterns within lines.

Contemporaneous with biblical narratives and devotional poetry, more secular poetic works appear in early ME as well. Early secular lyrics are deeply indebted to Fr. and Norman amatory lyric forms; again, as poets adapt these forms to ME, a great deal of formal innovation results. These early experiments with lyrical form, meter, and syntax prove a crucial resource for later makers of large-scale fictional narrative, who interpolate short lyrical passages into their larger works.

Extensive, nonbiblical narrative poetry has often been categorized either as fact-based historical chronicle or as fictional romance, though recent scholarship suggests that the boundary demarcating "fact-based" hist. from "fictional" romance may have been far blurrier in the Middle Ages than it seems to mod. readers, since many of the "romance" narratives clearly understand themselves as historical, pertaining either to Brit. prehist. (Lawman/Layamon's *Brut*, ca. 1205; *King Horn*, ca. 1225; *Havelock the Dane*, ca. 1280), Lat. prehist. (the Alexander romances *Alisaunder*, *Alexander and Dindimus*, and *Wars of Alexander*; and the Trojan hists. *Gest Historiale of the Destruction of Troy*, ca. 1350–1400, and the *Seege of Troye*, ca. 1300–25), or, more rarely, Fr. hist. Toward the 14th and 15th cs., the Arthurian romances flourish, incl. the alliterative *Morte Arthure*, the ballad *Legend of King Arthur*, and the justly famous *Sir Gawain and the Green Knight*, which synthesizes insular and Fr. verse forms (alliteration with rhyme; long verses with stanzaic organization), narrative and lyrical formal strategies (large-scale chronological story told through an intricately versified stanzaic form), and historical and fantastic material (Trojan backstory and supernatural contemp. events). Largely through its formal complexity, *Gawain* constitutes what many scholars see as the pinnacle of romance invention in ME.

Another reason for the critical accolades to *Sir Gawain and the Green Knight*, however, is its larger context, both in the ms. in which it appears (Cotton Nero A.x) and the literary movement to which it bears witness, the Alliterative Revival. The Cotton Nero ms. contains *Gawain* and three other poems: *Cleanness*, *Patience*, and *Pearl*, all of which seem to have been composed by the *Gawain* poet. *Patience* is a dramatic and animated paraphrase of the book of Jonah, and it thus represents a late and unusually artful instance of biblical paraphrase narrative. *Cleanness* ranges more widely in its plot, covering stories of the Flood, the destruction of Sodom, and Belshazzar's feast. In *Pearl,* courtly lang. blends with theological content to create an elegant meditation on the nature of loss: the dreamer-poet mourns the loss of his "precious pearl," a daughter who has died in infancy. The poem's elaborate artistry and profound rendering of human emotion find no parallel in ME poetry. Though *Pearl* is unique in having end rhyme, alliterative patterning, and stanzaic structure, the rest of the Cotton Nero poems are also formally intricate, written in an alliterative meter, which is the staple meter of all those poems that have come to be loosely denominated as the Alliterative Revival. The generic multiplicity and stylistic variation of Cotton Nero A.x suggest that its poet was very much part of his or her cultural moment: the corpus of works composed in this late phase of ME lit. by the major authors is likewise characterized both by synthesis and revision of extant and authoritative literary forms and genres.

Of late med. writers, William Langland (ca. 1330–1400) is the first and arguably the most influential. Of the over 50 surviving copies of his *Piers Plowman* (written ca. 1360–87), there are three authorial versions, A, B, and C. These three revisions, though unquestionably motivated in part by aesthetic concerns, are likely also responses to the sociopolitical and theological controversies that wracked England in the middle and late 14th c., incl. the culmination and end of King Edward III's tumultuous reign and the increasing theological threat posed by the reform-minded Wycliffites and Lollards. Responding to these sociopolitical pressures, in each of Langland's revisions the poem changes its theological shape and political tenor, though, in all cases, it is rubricated into a *visio,* which recounts the dreaming narrator's vision of the social ills of 14th-c. England, and a *vita,* which recounts his pilgrimage to Truth. Langland's poem is notoriously slippery of genre, encompassing not only dream vision and pilgrimage narrative but consolation, autobiography, personification allegory, debate, philosophy, trial drama, and apocalypse. Moreover, its episodic construction and its three distinct versions make the basic plot of the poem very difficult to tease out, though this resistance to interpretation may have been what made the poem wildly successful and influential in its own time, by inspiring readers to engage actively with the strangeness and complexity of its ideation and its self-conscious positioning both as a literary work and a sociopolitical and theological treatise.

Whether Geoffrey Chaucer (ca. 1345–1400) read Langland's marvelously complex poem remains an open issue, although the thematic and formal consonances in their major works (both tell pilgrimage narratives; both are interested in the interplay between allegory and autobiography; both work with the Boethian *consolatio* genre; both stitch together a series of shorter vignettes into a more expansive fictional narrative; both are profoundly interested in the social fabric of 14th-c. England) make it seem likely that Chaucer was at least somewhat influenced by *Piers Plowman,* particularly later in his career. The precise chronology of Chaucer's poetry is unknown, although it is usually divided into an earlier "French" period (influenced by Jean de Meun, Guillaume de Machaut, and Jean Froissart) and a later "Italian" period (influenced by Dante and Boccaccio). Many of Chaucer's early works are either trans. (*Roman de la Rose*) or dream-vision narratives that work within and reinvent the conventions of the debate genre, while also being written for particular occasions (*Book of the Duchess* commemorates the death of Blanche of Lancaster; *Parliament of Fowls* is a Valentine's Day poem). By the mid-1380s, Chaucer's poetry took a significant turn. He translated Boethius's *De Consolatione philosophiae* into prose, and spent much of the rest of his life revisiting its themes in his poetry. Based on Giovanni Boccaccio's *Il Filostrato,* Chaucer's *Troilus and Criseyde,* for instance, sets a star-crossed love affair against the historical events of the Trojan War as a pre-Christian test case for Boethian philosophy. In particular, in this poem, Chaucer stages the inevitable tragedy of the Trojan War as an occasion for meditating on the Boethian notions of fate versus free will, the nature of fortune, and the emptiness of worldly desire.

Having completed his antiquarian and philosophical romance, Chaucer turned his energies toward the contemp. reality of late med. England as his primary subject matter: by the late 1380s, he was working on the unfinished collection of ten extant fragments that are now known as the *Canterbury Tales.* The "General Prologue" that opens the poem describes the 29 characters on a pilgrimage to Canterbury both as occupational types (e.g., a lawyer, a parson, a wife) and as unique individuals. Throughout the *Tales*, to fulfill the terms of a tale-telling contest, each pilgrim tells a prologue and then a tale to the rest of the pilgrims. Chaucer likely derived his inspiration for this narrative invention from Boccaccio's *Decameron* (see ITALY, POETRY OF) and, in all likelihood, from the Ar. frame tale (see ARABIC POETRY). In the *Canterbury Tales*, however, Chaucer experiments with the templates he inherits. First, he devises a dynamic interplay between the prologue and the tale, which complicates each speaker's character and his or her place in the larger social world. Second, he develops distinct and socially situated voices for all his pilgrims; in doing so, he engages with and undercuts the genre of estates' satire, which depicts the world as comprised of only three basic social groups, clergy, warriors, and workers. Third, each pilgrim tells a tale that fits into and often reinvents an available literary genre: romances, fabliaux, fables, sermons, saints' lives, allegories, tragedies, and exempla all appear in the *Tales*. In its use of dialectic structure to devise characters who are at once types and individuals, in its exploding of social ideology, and in its relentless will to integrate a polyphony of different literary modes, voices, and genres into a single, unified, and remarkably realistic composition, the *Canterbury Tales* remains one of the most innovative compositions of the Middle Ages in any lang.

Where Langland's career was influenced by Edwardian politics and Chaucer's by Ricardian, John Gower's (ca. 1330–1408) poetic career straddles the late Ricardian and early Lancastrian positions, and his poetry reflects that historical positioning—indeed, his magnum opus the ME *Confessio amantis* (written ca. 1386–90) has two prologues, one written in dedication to Richard II, the other to Henry IV. After the prologue follow eight books, each of which comprises a series of moral tales organized around the central theme of sin and right behavior. Seven sections draw from penitential manuals in the period; the outlier responds to the emerging vernacular *Fürstenspiegel* genre, also known as *mirror for princes*. This genre (which also includes Chaucer's "Tale of Melibee" in the *Canterbury Tales*, as well as certain passages from *Piers Plowman*) seems to gain power in the literary imagination of the late Ricardian and early Lancastrian periods, perhaps in response to the political turmoil of the period, as Richard II is forcibly deposed and Henry IV comes to power. Couching what could be incendiary political content carefully in literary form, Gower enfolds his gargantuan compilation of didactic exempla into a tidy fictive frame, adapted from the dream-vision narratives of Boethius, Jean de Meun, and Alan of Lille, in which a lover (Amans, later revealed to be Gower himself) seeks amatory counsel from a beneficent teacher (the Confessor). Perhaps because of the political bent of his writings or the overtly moralizing thrust of his composition and certainly because of Chaucer's famous dedication of his *Troilus* to "moral Gower," Gower was absorbed into lit. hist. as a "moral" writer, more concerned with didacticism than pleasure or entertainment.

The two most significant poets of the 15th c. are John Lydgate (ca. 1370–1449) and Thomas Hoccleve (ca. 1370–1430), both of whom read Chaucer extensively, and at least Hoccleve likely also read Langland and Gower. Lydgate is esp. well known for his aureate diction, his assembly of extensive works of hist., and his interest in the mirror-for-princes genre. Over the course of his long poetic career, however, he composed in nearly every important med. genre and, thus, represents a synthesis and culmination of ME poetic hist. Like Lydgate, Hoccleve experiments with a variety of poetic genres and modes, ranging from religious lyric to autobiography, from political poems to a voluminous mirror for princes. But Hoccleve also picks up from his Ricardian and Lancastrian forebears an ironic fluency and self-mocking tone, which make him seem startlingly "mod." and his works a bridge between the Middle Ages and the early poetry of the Ren.

III. The Renaissance, 1500–1660. When William Caxton opened England's first printing press in Westminster in 1476, he not only disseminated a standard early mod. Eng. but also helped establish Eng. as a literary lang. Caxton printed Eng. poetry—Gower, Lydgate, and Chaucer—for the first time. He also published trans. of cl. and continental poetry, making available various literary models for future generations. As the 16th c. unfolded, printing and literacy increased, and Eng. education was transformed by humanism—"the new learning" imported from continental Europe with its cornerstone disciplines of rhet. and eloquence. Particularly in the second half of the century, inventive, well-made poetry was useful and often esteemed; it elevated the lang. and thereby England itself, as well as the poet's own status. The Reformation also thrust poetic lang. into the forefront of culture. Distrustful of the ecclesiastical hierarchies of the established church, Protestants sought truth in scripture itself (trans. now into the vernacular) and embraced devotional verse as a pathway to God.

Usually considered England's first Ren. poet, John Skelton (ca. 1460–1529) was on the cusp of this new momentum. Learned and versatile, Skelton tutored the young Prince Henry (later Henry VIII) in the court of Henry VII, and he wrote occasional poetry celebrating the reign of the Tudors. Most of his poems, however, exhibit an independent mind, by turns reflective, playful, and satiric. He draws on ME forms and conventions, esp. alliteration, but develops his own contemp. voice, particularly when he writes in the style later dubbed *Skeltonics*—short, rhyme-rich lines featuring colloquial diction and rhythms. Skelton's major poems include *The Bouge of Court* (1499), an allegorical dream vision warning of court corruption; "Speak, Parrot," "Colin Clout," and "Why Come Ye Not to Court?" (written ca. 1522), fierce satires lambasting the powerful Cardinal Thomas Wolsey; and *Philip Sparrow* (written ca. 1509), an exaggerated elegy for a young girl's pet, replete with liturgical allusion and structure, spiritual instruction, social satire, erotic suggestion, everyday emotion, and reflections on cl. and Eng. poetry.

Thomas Wyatt (1503–42) is widely considered the first great Eng. poet of the Ren. Rigorously educated in the humanist trad. and a diplomat for Henry VIII, Wyatt was well prepared to represent the complexities of the Tudor court, particularly the intermeshing of political and personal desires. Wyatt's verse letters and satires warn of court corruption, and his dozens of poems about love recount and enact disillusionment, incl. his much-anthologized rhyme-royal masterpiece "They Flee from Me" (ms. ca. 1530s); his lyrics for musical accompaniment, such as "My Lute, Awake" (ms. ca. 1530s); and the sonnets he adapts from Petrarch's *Canzoniere*, such as "Whoso list to hunt" (ms. ca. 1526–27) based on *Canzoniere* 190 "Una candida cerva." Wyatt's Petrarchan sonnets are the first known sonnets in Eng. excepting Chaucer's trans. of *Canzoniere* 132 in *Troilus and Criseyde*. Wyatt also translated the seven penitential psalms, introducing *terza rima* to Eng. and representing David as a prototype of the reformed Protestant seeking his own intimate connection to God.

Wyatt's poems were not printed during his lifetime but circulated in ms., the expected mode of publication for the courtly elite through the 16th c. Such mss. often found their way into print after an author's death and sometimes before. In 1549, Wyatt's penitential psalms appeared in print, and eight years later, 97 of his secular poems were published by an enterprising printer, Richard Tottel, in a popular collection of poems titled *Songes and Sonettes* and later known as *Tottel's Miscellany*.

Tottel's collection also featured the poetry of Henry Howard, the Earl of Surrey (1517–47), a fact noted prominently on the title page. Highborn, polished, and ambitious, Surrey was still famous a dozen years after he had lost his head to an aging, suspicious Henry VIII. Surrey adapted sonnets from the *Canzoniere* into Eng. as his friend Wyatt also did, but Surrey is credited with inventing the Eng. sonnet (later called the Shakespearean sonnet), by organizing the 14 lines into three quatrains and a couplet (*ababcdcdefefgg*) instead of the It. sonnet's octave (*abbaabba*) and sestet (rhyming in several ways, incl. *cdcdcd* or *cdecde*). Surrey also developed blank verse in Eng. for the first time, translating books 2 and 4 of Virgil's *Aeneid* into lines of unrhymed iambic pentameter.

Another popular book in the second half of the 16th c. was *A Mirror for Magistrates* (1559), a collection of poems by various authors recounting the downfall of princes and other powerful figures in Eng. hist. With various additions and deletions, the collection was reprinted eight times between 1559 and the end of the century and has engaged students of early mod. political culture since then. Poetically, it is not generally distinctive, but there are exceptions, incl. the chilling "Induction" and "Complaint of Henry, Duke of Buckingham" by Thomas Sackville (1536–1608).

Queen Elizabeth I began her long reign in 1558. Exceptionally intelligent, fluent in several ancient and mod. langs., and educated by leading humanists of the day, Elizabeth I wrote her own famous speeches, volumes of official and personal correspondence, and a handful of poems. She understood the theatrical nature of monarchy and the myriad ways political and poetic lang. inform each other, and she expected her courtiers to understand these subtleties as well. She also undersood the capacity of poetry (in a popular play or in love poems circulating at court) to engage, instruct, unite, or distract people. Moreover, her reinstatement of "the reformed religion," Anglican Protestantism, fostered the translating into Eng. of biblical verse, as well as the composing of original devotional poetry.

In 1560, having returned to England from exile during Mary's reign, Anne Lock (1530–after 1590) published the first known sonnet sequence in Eng., *A Meditation of a Penitent Sinner* (1560), appended to a trans. of four sermons by John Calvin. The sequence includes five prefatory sonnets followed by 21 sonnets dilating on a passage in Psalm 51. From a family of moderate means and personally acquainted with the Scottish Calvinist John Knox, Lock received an excellent education for a woman of the period. While many intellectual leaders of the later 16th c. advocated literacy in women, few encouraged them to study rhet., the lifeblood of humanism and poetics.

Isabella Whitney (fl. 1567–73), a servant through at least part of her life, was thus unusual in her publishing of a love complaint (ca. 1567) and a collection of poems and prose, *A Sweet Nosgay, or Pleasant Posye* (1573). The latter is based on Hugh Plat's anthol. *The Flowers of Philosophy* (1572) but evidences Whitney's female experience, colloquial voice, and sense of purpose. In some poems, such as "The Will and Testament," an elegy for the London her impoverishment required her to leave, we find her appropriating conventional male genres with wit and self-assurance.

George Turberville (1544–97), Barnabe Googe (1540–94), and George Gascoigne (1534–77) also wrote compendiums of verse and prose in the 1560s and 1570s. All favored a mostly straightforward plain style. The numerous engaging poems in Gascoigne's *A Hundred Sundry Flowers* (1573) include "Gascoigne's Lullaby," in which the poet offers subtle wisdom in direct speech, blending melancholy and humor, self-mockery and self-acceptance.

Known to later times as "the poet's poet," Edmund Spenser (1552–99) appeared in the late 1570s with a very different poetic sensibility. Spenser embraced Eng. on every level—semantic, syntactic, etymological, and musical. He reveled in abstract metrical and aural patterns while simultaneously immersing readers in a unique lexicon, one that included OE terms, Chaucerian words, ornate phrases, and original coinages in which spelling itself was a medium of expression, able to make a pun, recall an etymology, or sound a chord. Spenser launched his career with *The Shepheardes Calender* (1579), a collection of 12 eclogues, one for each month, in various forms and meters, some monologues, some dialogues. Published with fine woodcut illustrations and scholarly notes like those accompanying cl. lit., the printed text insisted on its own importance. Furthermore, by making his debut in the pastoral mode as Virgil had done with his *Eclogues*, Spenser placed himself in the most august literary canon, and he put the Eng. lang. in the prestigious company of Lat. and Gr. as one of the world's great literary langs. He continued these associations in "Astrophel" (1595), a pastoral elegy for his friend and fellow poet Philip Sidney based on Virgil's fifth eclogue. In 1595, Spenser also published his *Amoretti,* an elaborate Petrarchan sonnet sequence, and in the same volume, his *Epithalamion,* a wedding-day gift for his bride.

Spenser's greatest work is *The Faerie Queene,* an allegorical epic that aims to "fashion a gentleman or noble person in vertuous and gentle discipline," as Spenser explains in a letter to Walter Ralegh, arguing that "delight" and "doctrine by ensample" are better teachers than "good discipline . . . sermoned at large" and "doctrine . . . by rule." Elizabeth I is the Faerie Queene, he explains, who "in a dream of vision" has inspired Arthur (not yet king) to find her. Arthur possesses Aristotle's 12 moral virtues, and each of 12 books of the epic will follow the adventures of a knight representing one of these virtues. Spenser ultimately wrote six books of 12 cantos each, and two cantos of a seventh book. These last two cantos, later known as the "Mutability Cantos," recount the goddess Mutability's attempt to reign over all other forces and her compelling but unsuccessful trial in Nature's court. *Faerie Queene* books 1–3 were published in 1590, books 1–6 with the "Mutability Cantos" in 1596. Cl. allusion abounds in the *Faerie Queene*, but Eng. hist. and legend are also pervasive. In many obvious ways, the epic celebrates Elizabeth I and Tudor rule, but it is also a complexly satiric, richly suggestive text, full of surprises and contradictions. Spenser created a new stanza for his masterpiece, nine iambic lines—eight pentameter, the ninth hexameter—rhyming *ababbcbcc*. The Spenserian stanza feels like an expansion and intensification of rhyme royal and makes the *Faerie Queene* all the more suspenseful, thought-provoking, musical, and even mesmerizing.

Born the same year as Spenser, Walter Ralegh (1552–1618) was an ambitious courtier and explorer as well as a poet. Although Ralegh perfected that meshing of poetic and political rhet. so valued by Elizabeth I, particularly in "The Ocean to Cynthia," his long poem of praise for the queen who (for a while) raised him to great status, he is better known for his cynical and world-weary lyric poems recounting human vanity and the futility of life, e.g. "On the Life of Man," "The Lie," "Nature that washed her hands in milk," and "Even such is time." A more playful poem is "The Nymph's Reply to the Shepherd," a shrewd response to Christopher Marlowe's seductive "The Passionate Shepherd to His Love." Ralegh's poems circulated in ms. and also appeared in various miscellanies of the late 16th and early 17th cs., most notably the popular *The Phoenix Nest* (1593).

In Thomas Hoby's 1561 trans. of Baldassare Castiglione's *Il Cortegiano* (*The Courtier*), the premier handbook for Ren. courtiers, Castiglione advises courtiers "to practice in all things a certain *sprezzatura* [nonchalance], so as to conceal all art and make whatever is done or said appear to be without effort and almost without any thought about it." It is this quality exactly that describes the poetry and prose—and indeed, the person—of Philip Sidney (1554–86). Born to enormous power and privilege, Sidney was politically ambitious as well as a champion of the Eng. lang. and a great patron of fellow poets. His own poetry and prose circulated in ms. in the 1570s and 1580s, entertaining and inspiring an elite circle of readers, incl. his younger sister, Mary Sidney Herbert, Countess of Pembroke, who soon became a poet in her own right. Sidney dedicated to Mary the *Old Arcadia* (also known as *The Countess of Pembroke's Arcadia*), a prose romance bejeweled with 78 lyric poems, incl. the beautiful double sestina "Ye Goteherd Gods." In 1579, Sidney circulated his rhetorically dashing *Defence of Poesy* (1595; also called *An Apology for Poetry*) in which he refutes charges against poetry (and lit. in general) with sparkling logic, learning, and wit.

Sidney's most influential work is his sequence of sonnets and songs *Astrophil and Stella*, consisting of 108 mostly Petrarchan sonnets and 11 songs in various forms. Astrophil (lover of stars) woos and muses on Stella (star), representing ever-changing states of mind and a sophisticated literary self-consciousness. Petrarch's *Canzoniere* is the prototype for Sidney's sequence, but Astrophil's passion takes place in the present-day Elizabethan court, and Stella is well aware that she is being pursued. Astrophil's voice is youthful, energetic, ironic, playful, defiant, self-mocking—and ultimately dejected. *Astrophil and Stella* caused a stir when it appeared in print in 1591 after Sidney's premature death, prompting the publication of numerous sonnet sequences during that last decade of the century, incl. Samuel Daniel's *Delia* (1592), Michael Drayton's *Idea's Mirror* (1594), and Spenser's aforementioned *Amoretti* (1595).

It was most likely within this decade as well that William Shakespeare (1564–1616) wrote most or all of the sonnets that would be published in 1609, probably surreptitiously, under the title *Shakespeare's Sonnets*. This text is not only the most innovative and psychologically complex of all the sonnet sequences but also arguably one of the greatest collections of lyric poems in Eng. Developing further the Eng. sonnet first established by Surrey, Shakespeare represents the mind in many moods and patterns of thought. His sonnets do not sound like imitations of other sonnets but instead seem driven by lived—and living—experience. Vulnerability, anxiety, longing, rejection, confidence, disgust, worldliness, anger, regret, hope, jealousy, and depression are all palpable at various points in the sequence. In many of the poems, the speaker tries to meet his most profound challenge, confronting the ravages of time and the facts of mortality; as he says succinctly in sonnet 64, "Ruin has taught me thus to ruminate, / That time will come and take my love away." These confrontations are esp. moving because Shakespeare's speaker does not seek conventional consolations nor defer to religious views. He is not dismissively cynical but unrelentingly analytical and self-scrutinizing. His sonnets revise and explore themselves before our eyes, and repeatedly they implicate us, the readers of the future, for the beloved can only live on in the poem's lines "as long as men can breathe, and eyes can see."

Shakespeare's sonnets are also unconventional because the poet-lover addresses not a lady but a beloved young man (in sonnets 1–126), and when he does address a lady (in sonnets 127–52), we learn quickly that she is neither ideal nor unattainable; to the contrary, she and the poet-lover are sexual partners. With pleas, praise, questions, accusations, confessions, and hard-won yet unresolved insight, the speaker represents the crises of intimacy and identity provoked by these relationships.

The sonnet sequence was not the only popular genre of the 1590s. Also popular were long narrative poems based on erotic tales in cl. (usually Ovidian) mythology, called *epyllia* by 19th-c. scholars. The best of these are Shakespeare's *Venus and Adonis* (1593) and *The Rape of Lucrece* (1594), and Christopher Marlowe's unfinished *Hero and Leander* (1598). *Venus* (99 stanzas of *ababcc* iambic pentameter) and *Hero* (409 heroic couplets) are masterpieces of lush, seductive storytelling, dazzling rhet., erotic tension, and comedic use of syntax, meter, and rhyme. *Lucrece*, 265 stanzas of rhyme royal, is all these things but in a darker key.

Mary Sidney Herbert, Countess of Pembroke (1561–1621), was the most accomplished female writer of the 16th c. She translated Petrarch's *Trionfo della Morte* (*Triumph of Death*) into Eng. terza rima and Robert Garnier's *Antonius, A Tragœdie* (1592) into Eng. blank verse. *Antonius* probably influenced Elizabeth Cary, Lady Faulkland (1585–1639) in her writing of the closet drama, *The Tragedy of Mariam* (1613), the first original blank-verse play by an Englishwoman. Pembroke's greatest achievement was her completion of a trans. of the Psalms begun by her brother Philip Sidney, who had translated 43 of the psalms by the time of his death. Pembroke translated the remaining 107 psalms, incl. the 22 poems that make up Psalm 119. She was meticulous in her consultation of sources in Eng., Fr., and Lat., but she artfully cast the psalms into varying Eng. forms and meters and wove into the poems her own sensibility and arguably female perspective. Her psalms, thus, convey both deference and boldness, scholarship and innovation. Particularly interesting are the two original dedicatory poems that survive with one ms. copy of the sequence. In "Even now that care," the more formal of the two, Pembroke addresses Queen Elizabeth. In "To the Angell Spirit of the most excellent Sir Philip Sidney," she addresses her late brother's spirit—at least, she begins to, but images of his death interrupt her, and she finds herself conjuring not Philip's spirit but her own memory. She struggles to resume her dedication, succeeds somewhat, but again is distracted by grief and self-doubt. Throughout the poem, Pembroke's anguished longing flares up as she strives to maintain the dedication's lofty diction and apparent purpose. The result is a compelling poetic voice. Although not published until the 19th c., the Sidney Psalter circulated widely in its own time. John Donne, among many poets influenced by the text, praised the siblings' collaboration in his poem, "Upon the Translation of the Psalms by Sir Philip Sidney, and The Countess of Pembroke" (1621). Other important poets influenced by the psalter include Aemilia Lanyer, George Herbert, Henry Vaughan, and John Milton.

Among the poets Pembroke invited into her circle of patronage was Daniel (1562–1619), who addressed his sonnet sequence *Delia* (1592) to Pembroke herself. Daniel also wrote *A Defence of Ryme* (1603) in which he celebrates the Eng. lang. and the poetic forms it generates, not only praising the sensual pleasures of lang. but associating these pleasures with reason, judgment, and memory. Daniel's essay is an answer to the somber tract *Observations in the Arte of English Poesie* (1602) by a young and temporarily didactic Thomas Campion (1567–1620), who, at that point in his career, advocated writing Eng. poetry in "numbers"—quantitative meter, as in Lat. Happily for readers and listeners, Campion did not spend much more time in theoretical arguments. He wrote instead some of the most beautiful unrhyming and rhyming Eng. lyrics in his age, many of which he set to music.

In the rapidly growing city of London in the last decades of the 16th c., the art and business of theater took root and flourished. Each week, thousands of Londoners (up to 15,000 by one estimate) visited worlds beyond their own, witnessed human character and conflict on a grand scale, and listened to thousands of lines of poetry. Some plays were written in prose, but predominantly, they were written in iambic pentameter, usually in blank verse. Able to represent a person thinking or speaking in a fairly natural yet elevated way, iambic pentameter developed in lyric, narrative, and dramatic genres at once.

In 1587, the tempestuous university wit Marlowe (1564–93) transfixed audiences with the blank verse of his two-part tragedy *Tamburlaine the Great*. In the next few years, until his death in a tavern brawl at age 29, Marlowe confirmed his place as the Elizabethans' most exciting dramatist with a series of highly successful plays: *Doctor Faustus* (written ca. 1588), *The Jew of Malta* (written 1589), and *Edward II* (written ca. 1593). Marlowe's protagonists compelled audiences with their self-aggrandizing speeches replete with Latinate polysyllabic words and sweeping metaphors, all in thundering end-stopped iambic pentameter. Marlowe was the star poet-playwright when Shakespeare arrived on the scene in the late 1580s or early 1590s. The rivalry that ensued benefited both dramatists and, of course, their audiences. At Marlowe's death, Shakespeare had written seven plays. He would write almost 30 more.

In the early plays, Shakespeare's lines are frequently end-stopped like Marlowe's. Unlike Marlowe's, Shakespeare's lines also sometimes rhyme, particularly when love-struck characters strive to woo—in *Love's Labour's Lost* (written 1594–95), *A Midsummer Night's Dream* (written 1595–96), *As You Like It* (written 1599–1600), and *Much Ado About Nothing* (written 1598–99), e.g. In *Romeo and Juliet* (written 1594–95), the star-crossed lovers create a sonnet when they first speak with each other (1.5.93–106). Dialogue in later plays rarely rhymes, but magic spells, riddles, and chants surely do (witness *Macbeth* [written 1605–6], or *The Tempest* [written 1611]), and rhyming songs can be found in nearly every play, from lullabies to drinking songs to country ballads at sheep-shearing festivals.

As his career progressed, Shakespeare explored with increasing nuance the expressive possibilities of blank verse, esp. enjambment. The result is a poetry that highlights the stops and starts of troubled thought, the momentum of suspicion, ambition, or anger, the questions and obsessions of grief or love, and subtle degrees of understanding, cooperation, curiosity, tension, or antagonism between characters. Esp. in later plays—*King Lear* (written 1606), *Antony and Cleopatra* (written 1606–7), *The Tempest*, *The Winter's Tale* (written 1611–12), and others, Shakespeare's enjambments are as powerful as John Milton's will be in *Paradise Lost*.

In his plays as in his sonnets, Shakespeare demonstrates fluency in the diction, idioms, and rhetorical styles heard in many venues of the day, from street to court, village to university, craftsman's shop to merchant's office—and with these, a heightened perception of political, social, and esp. interpersonal contexts for lang. This fluency and perception yield a wide range of complex, credible characters and perpetual metaphoric richness.

In the late 1590s, the brilliant and irascible Ben Jonson (1572–1637) established himself as a superb writer of satiric comedy with *Every Man in his Humour* (written 1598) and *Every Man out of his Humour* (written 1599). His numerous plays include the masterpieces *Volpone* (written 1605–6), *Epicoene or the Silent Woman* (written 1609–10), *The Alchemist* (written 1610), and *Bartholomew Fair* (written 1614). Jonson constructed his plays according to cl. rules for drama, but they are as urban and contemp. as can be in lang., plot, and reference.

Until the Puritans closed the theaters in 1642, many playwrights succeeded in entertaining London audiences with rousing and sometimes innovative dramatic verse, incl. John Webster (ca. 1578–1625), John Fletcher (1579–1625), Thomas Middleton (1580–1627), Philip Massinger (1583–1649), and Francis Beaumont (1584–1616). However, no plays engaged and influenced poetry as much as Shakespeare's did, and no playwrights beyond Shakespeare, Jonson, and, to a lesser extent, Marlowe achieved greatness as narrative or lyric poets.

As a conventional period of literary study, the 17th c. begins in 1603, the year of Queen Elizabeth I's death and King James I's accession, and runs to the Restoration in 1660, though anthols. and academic courses often follow Milton's career through the writing and publication of *Paradise Lost*, which closes this signal episode in Eng. lit. hist. James I was an advocate not only of plays but of masques—lavish, symbolic court theatricals in which the nobility themselves performed. Jonson tried his hand at this genre early on in the new reign and triumphed so thoroughly that he quickly became the court's premier writer of masques, a position he held for more than two decades. With their seductive musical verse, nuanced allegory, and carefully calibrated timing and proportions, Jonson's masques established a new standard in the genre.

As a lyric poet, Jonson modeled himself on his beloved Gr. and Roman poets, favoring their genres of epigram and satire and alluding to them frequently. His poems evoke ease and polish whether reflecting on personal struggles or making social overtures. In elegies for his children, "On My First Son" (1616) and "On My First Daughter" (1616), he is earnest and vulnerable. In his epigrams, he is ironic and amused. We hear an affable, epicurean, and intermittently self-effacing voice in "Inviting a Friend to Supper" (1616) and a polished witty tone in his flattering poems to patrons, most notably his famous country house poem "To Penshurst" (1616). In 1616, Jonson published grandly his own collected works in folio ed., making sure as Spenser always had that the importance of his work was evident in its very presentation. Seven years later, Jonson wrote a tribute to the contemporary he envied and admired most.

"To the Memory of My Beloved, Master William Shakespeare, and What He Hath Left Us" appeared in the First Folio of Shakespeare's plays (1623). Aptly, he addresses Shakespeare as "Soul of the age!" and asserts, "He was not of an age, but for all time!"

John Donne (1572–1631), considered by many to be one of England's greatest poets, was born the same year as Jonson and, like Jonson, was prolific, ambitious, and often keenly satirical. Both poets were fluent in colloquial and dramatic speech. However, where Jonson's voice is measured and cultivated, Donne's is passionate, argumentative, and immediate: "For God's sake hold your tongue, and let me love!" the speaker begins in one poem; "Busy old fool, unruly Sun!" in another. Donne foregrounds colloquial diction and syntax, enjambment, exclamations, imperatives, and references to the speaker's immediate surroundings. His unexpected metaphors yoke specific and abstract phenomena in contemp. science, travel and exploration, recent political and social events, and everyday objects and happenings. Critiquing the presence of these conceits and arguments in love poetry, John Dryden accused Donne of "affecting the *metaphysics*." The term stuck, but not in the pejorative sense Dryden had intended. In some poems, Donne's speaker swaggers and brags about sexual conquests; in some, he unleashes all his rhetorical cleverness to seduce a desired other. In many other *Songs and Sonnets*, his speaker attests to loving one woman profoundly and rejects the conventional dichotomies of body and soul to represent the completeness of that love. "Nothing else is," he argues in "The Sun Rising."

For practical as well as philosophical reasons, Donne converted to Anglicanism as a young man. He saw no benefit in dying for Catholicism as his uncles and brother had done. He was not eager to be an Anglican priest, but after years of struggling to support a large family (ten children at the final count) and believing, as he writes in one of his famous sermons, that "No man is an Island, entire of it self," he responded to King James I's urging that he take orders. Donne rose quickly in the church, becoming Dr. Donne, dean of St. Paul's Cathedral, in his early forties and writing sermons of arresting eloquence and imagination. He also wrote some of England's greatest religious poetry, incl. the famous *Holy Sonnets* (1633). Petrarchan instead of Eng. in form, the octave-sestet structure of these poems dovetails with Donne's dramatic sentences: dependent clauses build in intensity; then at line nine, there is a shift to a simpler lexicon and syntax.

Although religious verse was the most conventionally acceptable kind of poetry for women to write, Aemilia Lanyer's (1569–1645) *Salve Deus Rex Judaeorum* (1611), a retelling of Christ's passion in stately rhyme royal with a protofeminist agenda, was anything but conventional. Appended to *Salve Deus* was "Description of Cookeham," a country house poem published before (and possibly written before) Jonson's "To Penshurst." In heroic couplets, Lanyer honors and mourns the house in which she spent her formative years under the guardianship of a noble family.

While the middle-class Lanyer dared enter the realm of patriarchal theology, the aristocratic Lady Mary Wroth (ca. 1587–1651) braved the male-dominated sphere of secular lit., particularly the genres popularized by her uncle Philip Sidney. Wroth wrote both the first pastoral romance and the first secular sonnet sequence to be published by a woman: *The Countess of Montgomery's Urania* (1621), an epic-length romance incl. more than 50 poems; and *Pamphilia to Amphilanthus* (1621), a Petrarchan lyric sequence of 103 sonnets and songs. Wroth also composed the unfinished but already epic-length pastoral romance *Love's Victory*, a sequel to *Urania*.

At his death, George Herbert (1593–1633) left to a friend the fate of his unknown collection of sacred poems *The Temple*. The volume appeared in print soon after and became so popular it was reprinted at least seven times before the end of the century. To dazzling and often haunting effect, Herbert juxtaposes ideas, events, and imagery in unexpected ways; he is as metaphysical as Donne. However, where Donne exhibits a rhetorician's persuasive intensity, Herbert gives us a storyteller's quiet magnetism, using original stanza forms, enjambment, shifting verb tenses, and other techniques to involve our attention. And while Donne speaks to and about God in urgent, sometimes violent lang., Herbert's addressing of God evokes the trust between a child and a loving parent. At the same time, Herbert conveys a profound awareness of the paradoxes involved in his project, incl. the central fact that the very medium of his relationship to God, poetry, could be merely "pretense" and "fine invention." Among Herbert's most admired poems are "The Pulley," "The Collar," "Love III," and the technopaegnion "Easter Wings." A few of the many poets who emulated Herbert did so with skill and independence enough to forge distinctive voices of their own, particularly Henry Vaughan (1621–95), Richard Crashaw (ca. 1613–49), and Thomas Traherne (1637–74).

In contrast to Herbert, Cavalier poets were libertines who admired the bawdy classicism and elegant metrical verse of Jonson and, of course, were influenced by the sexual frankness of Donne's *Songs and Sonnets*. In general, they supported the institutions of King Charles I and the Anglican Church; some even fought for the king in the Civil War and fled the country during Oliver Cromwell's government. Among the best-known Cavaliers are those followers of Jonson known as the Tribe of Ben (also called Sons of Ben), incl. Robert Herrick (1591–1674), Thomas Carew (1595–1640), and John Suckling (1609–42).

Herrick was the foremost member of the tribe and wrote two spirited tributes to the elder poet. Though an Anglican preacher and author of *Noble Numbers*, a collection of sacred verse, Herrick was a secular poet above all. His *Hesperides*, the volume of poems published with *Noble Numbers* in 1648, includes some of the most joyful poetry of the century or any century—fine-tuned, playful, erotic poems often in iambic trimeter or tetrameter about the small wonders and sensual pleasures of country life, friendship, and love. The flip side of Herrick's focus on beauty and pleasure is his keen awareness of mortality, and he makes this awareness plain in numerous poems, particularly his much-anthologized "To the Virgins, to Make Much of Time" ("Gather ye rosebuds while ye may").

Katherine Philips (1632–64) was the most accomplished and admired female poet of her generation. In her poems for close female friends—e.g., "Friendship's Mystery, To my Dearest *Lucasia*," and "To Mrs. M.A. at Parting"—she argues in elegant metaphors that friendship between women is greater than military conquest, political power, or other measures of success in a patriarchal world. In "A Married State" she warns women about the unending the burdens that follow "love's levity." She is also known for the explicitly political "Upon the Double Murder of King Charles" and the intensely personal elegies for her infant son Hector, in which she struggles to reconcile hard facts with conventional consolation. Philips circulated her work but seems to have agreed with other intellectual women of her day, incl. her close friend, the brilliant letter writer Dorothy Osborne (1627–95), that it was unseemly for a woman to display her feelings and opinions publicly. Most likely the 1664 volume of Philips's poems was published without her knowledge.

Milton (1608–74) is universally considered one of England's greatest poets. His far-reaching imagination, tremendous ambition, profoundly sensitive ear for the music and rhythms of lang. (with echoes of Spenser and Shakespeare, yet his own synthesis and subsuming of these), and deeply considered knowledge of the Western world, particularly of biblical hist. and ancient langs. and lits., are evident already in "On the Morning of Christ's Nativity," written when Milton was 21. Other early work includes "On Shakespeare" (1632), published in the second folio, and "L'Allegro" and "Il Penseroso," companion poems in iambic tetrameter couplets addressed to Mirth and Melancholy, respectively, that reenact contrasting states of mind and ways of being. *Comus, a masque performed at Ludlow Castle in 1634*, anticipates major themes of *Paradise Lost*, incl. seduction. In "Lycidas," a pastoral elegy published in a 1637 volume of commemorative verses on his classmate and fellow poet Edward King, Milton questions the meaning and possibilities of life, death, poetry, pleasure, faith, fame, and authority of all kinds—literary, religious, and political. These are questions and anxieties he confronts in all his work, but always anew, with added complexity, self-consciousness, or vision. Milton makes every form he uses his own. In his sonnets, enjambment and nimble syntax sometimes double the power of words and lines, and sentences of multiple dependent clauses and interweaving rhymes draw the reader to an intense experience of thought.

Through the Civil War and Interregnum, Milton turned from poetry to political writing and action, publishing radical, influential arguments for freedom of the press, divorce, and republican government. In the first decade of the Restoration, having endured one severe loss after another (the death of both his first and second wives and an infant daughter, the loss of his eyesight, and the failure of his hopes for the revolution and republic), he wrote his first and greatest epic poem *Paradise Lost*. His purpose was no less than to "justify the ways of God to men," and his attempt yields a hybrid of cl. epic, Christian prophecy, and recent Brit.

revolutionary hist. Since it was first printed in ten books in 1667 and then in its final form of 12 books in 1674, the epic has not failed to engage, provoke, inspire, anger, vex, and dazzle its readers. *Paradise Lost* gives us a Satan who says, "the mind is its own place, / And in itself can make a hell of heaven, / A heaven of hell"; a God who resembles at times King Charles I and at times Cromwell; an Adam and Eve who love each other more humanly than any god could have imagined; vivid scenes of hell, heaven, paradise, and chaos; suspenseful, persuasive dialogue, and soliloquies that expose the contradictory inner travails of the mind. In his invocations to books 1, 3, 7, and 9, Milton reflects on the project with varying degrees of confidence, ambition, humility, and doubt.

The poetic career of Milton's friend Andrew Marvell (1621–78) spanned the Civil War, Interregnum, and first two decades of the restored monarchy. Like Milton, Marvell was a worldly, multilingual scholar, poet, and statesman deeply involved in the political complexities of his day. Unlike Milton, Marvell exuded flexibility and ironic detachment in both his life and work. His sophisticated rhyming couplets, often in iambic tetrameter, contrast strikingly with Milton's late style of boldly enjambed blank verse. During the Protectorate, Milton served as Cromwell's secretary for foreign tongues and Marvell as Milton's assistant. When the Protectorate crumbled, Marvell not only evaded reprisal but became a member of Parliament and probably facilitated Milton's release from prison in 1660. Marvell's political poems—incl. commendatory verses on both Cromwell and Charles II—are polished and canny, imparting irony only to those who are looking for it. His pastoral poems—"The Garden," the group of "mower" poems, and many more—simultaneously embrace and interrogate the idea of pastoral. Marvell's love poems are frequently grouped with Donne's and described as metaphysical, a particularly apt description of Marvell's "The Definition of Love" and his tour de force, "To His Coy Mistress." In this widely anthologized poem, Marvell's speaker concludes: "though we cannot make our sun / Stand still, yet we will make him run."

IV. The Restoration and the Eighteenth Century, 1660–1789. The variety of topics and tones achieved in Restoration and 18th-c. poetry reminds us of the now-lost status of poetry in society: not only was it considered the most important genre for treating weighty matters—political, social, or religious—but it could touch the smallest events of daily life. To teach and be taught are desires that animate much Restoration and 18th-c. poetry. Many poems teach their readers how to live morally, where such instruction is often inseparable from 18th-c. readers' growing preoccupation with the search for happiness. Such guidance is heard in Samuel Johnson's (1709–1784) counsel to "raise for Good the supplicating Voice, / But leave to Heav'n the Measure and the Choice" (*The Vanity of Human Wishes*, 351–52 [1749]). The expanding presence of poetry coincides with a time in which poets and readers came from a wider range of social and educational backgrounds than ever before in Eng. lit. While many writers and readers knew poetry by exchanging it in ms., the availability of relatively inexpensive print materials, incl. broadsides, chapbooks, and periodicals, significantly increased poetry's accessibility to new readers eager for its pleasures and wisdom.

With Janus-faced vision, Restoration and 18th-c. writers transformed poetic practices and criteria. On the one hand, many poets attended to cl. models, as did their immediate predecessors in the Ren., and through trans. made the classics available to readers untrained in Lat. or Gr. Trans., however, was often an exercise of modernization, where the poet "imitated" the old text to make it new, renovating it to the concerns, tastes, and langs. of the present. Restoration and 18th-c. poets changed the landscape of poetry in Eng. by their experiments not only with the classics but with kinds (e.g., the georgic) and modes (e.g., satire). At the beginning of the period, the traditional hierarchy of kinds tied poetic achievement to difficulty: thus, an excellent pastoral, nearer the bottom of the hierarchy, could never equal an excellent epic, at the top. An easy crit. of this era's poetry is that it produced no great epic, yet this judgment resuscitates the hierarchy of poetic kinds that many poets worked to dismantle. Many of the cultural functions of epic were supplanted by the works of John Dryden (1631–1700) and Alexander Pope (1688–1744), who translated into Eng. Virgil and Homer, respectively. Numerous writers in this era revised the functions of epic by developing the range of mock epics, satire, and the encyclopedic quality of the long descriptive poem in blank verse. With various genres and modes often used and modified by a single poet, this period saw the proliferation of hybrids and new kinds of poems that cumulatively reorganized and redefined poetic voice and values. The wit of Dryden's *Absalom and Achitophel* (1681) lies as much in its verbal inventiveness as in its mixture of biblical prophecy, satire, and hist. to create didactic political allegory. The revisions of the lyric by John Wilmot, the Earl of Rochester (1647–80), turned this "lower" kind into a scathing critique of power relations, desire, and hypocrisy. Anne Finch (1661–1720) blended pastoral, "retirement" poetry, autobiography, and religious confession in "The Petition for an Absolute Retreat" (1713). Among the new generic achievements was the congregational hymn, associated esp. with Charles Wesley (1707–88). Variations on the hymn and other religious verse are among the major accomplishments of Christopher Smart (1722–71; *Jubilate Agno* [written ca. 1758–63] and *A Song to David* [1763]) and William Cowper (1731–1800) in the *Olney Hymns* (1779).

Restoration and 18th-c. poets' experiments with the lyric often mix private matters with public ones. In the Restoration, the song is the dominant kind of lyric poem and partakes of a social setting (even if on an intimate scale) in its framework of a musical performance. Similarly, the era's revisions of the ode, originally an elevated form of the lyric intended for public occasions, rapidly expanded this kind to treat a range of more personal topics and experiences far from its traditional uses. Anne Finch's ode "The Spleen" (1701) addresses this condition, known today as depression, to pursue its "still varying" and "perplexing form." Never abandoned in the Restoration and earlier 18th c., the sonnet reemerged as an important shape for the lyric in the second half of the century. But by this time, poets were using the brevity of the form to focus less on the qualities of Petrarchan love and more on the speaker's sensitive perceptions of the landscape. In the last decades of the 18th c., Anna Seward (1742–1809) and Charlotte Smith (1749–1806) would develop the sonnet to treat a new range of topics, such as Smith's meditations on the speaker's suffering in contexts that replace Petrarchan frames with material exigencies.

Such changes in poetic kinds combined with other forces to further the inclusiveness of poetry. One of the era's most transformative values is its fascination with occasions. Tuned to large and small events, occasional poetry articulates affairs of state (e.g., Dryden's *Annus Mirabilis*, 1667) or affairs of the day (e.g., John Winstanley's "To the Revd. Mr— on his Drinking Sea-Water," 1751). Poetry's role in affairs of state did not deter women writers from engaging in the same, as seen in Anna Letitia Barbauld's (1743–1825) "Corsica" (1773). Critiques of gender norms and patriarchy invoked poetry's role as a vehicle of political and social intervention (e.g., Mary Collier's *The Woman's Labour* [1739]). Concern with social and political issues informed the extraordinary satires of this era. Even an incomplete roll call reminds us of the heterogeneity in topic and tone of these works: Rochester's "Upon Nothing" (1679), Aphra Behn's "The Disappointment" (1680), Dryden's "MacFlecknoe" (1682), Jonathan Swift's "Verses on the Death of Dr. Swift" (1739), Pope's *Dunciad* (final version, 1743), Lady Mary Wortley Montagu's *Six Town Eclogues* (printed in part 1716, in full 1747), Mary Leapor's "Man the Monarch" (1751), and Charles Churchill's *Night* (1761).

Writers changed the practice and values of poetry by experimenting with kinds as well as with the couplet and blank verse. Couplets could continue for short or long verse paragraphs, conveying complex arguments where structures within the couplet enabled amplification, example, antithesis, and parallelism. With couplets, writers could achieve the clarity, formality, and lapidary compression that suited the poet's public voice and role in affairs of state. Just as effectively, couplets evoked the cadences of conversation or jaunty humor that made poetry and daily life inseparable for those who could write or read it. In his extraordinary dexterity with the couplet, Pope reveals the invisible sylphs: "Transparent forms, too fine for mortal sight, / Their fluid bodies half dissolv'd in light" (*The Rape of the Lock* 2.59–62 [1714]). In "Eloisa to Abelard" (printed in different versions 1712–17), his couplets express the force of Eloisa's desperate command to Abelard: "Come, if thou dar'st, all charming as thou art! / Oppose thy self to heav'n; dispute my heart; / Come, with one glance of those deluding eyes, / Blot out each bright Idea of the skies" (281–84).

Blank verse offered a flexible form different from the couplet but also allowed for any number and size of verse paragraphs. James Thomson's (1700–48) expansive blank verse and richly descriptive diction in *The Seasons* (first printed in its entirety in 1730) demonstrated that the seriousness and beauty of the form was not confined to Milton's achievement in his major poems. In *The Task* (1785), Cowper's blank verse is as various as the kinds and modes from which he borrows. He layers the tones of stately pronouncement, compassion, satiric attack, and prophetic warning in this description of urban poverty: "'Tis the cruel gripe / That lean hard-handed poverty inflicts, / The hope of better things, the chance to win, / The wish to shine, the thirst to be amused, / That at the sound of Winter's hoary wing, / Unpeople all our counties, of such herds / Of flutt'ring, loit'ring, cringing, begging, loose / And wanton vagrants, as make London, vast / And boundless as it is, a crowded coop" (3.826–34).

Elastic forms and genres for varied subjects complemented the era's changing aesthetic values. The verse epistle is an important case where genre and relation—the letter—are also an aesthetic value that was for the first time fully developed in Eng. by poets in this era. Unrestricted by "high" or "low" subject matter, the verse epistle values sociable exchange, but it esp. explores how the "private" can be read by the "public" to assert the relations between these domains (e.g., "Epistle to Dr. Arbuthnot," 1735). The epistolary poet expects, or imagines, that the reader can write back, and although such a sense of conversation and participation is often elite, it epitomizes how so many poems were written and read as social actions. The verse epistle's compelling paradox of privacy and exposure was one of several means used by Restoration and 18th-c. writers to shape an aesthetics of intimacy that was also social.

Aesthetic values such as wit, the sublime, the imagination, taste, and sensibility drove shifts in the topics, forms, and langs. of poetry. Empiricism opened worlds of sensory perceptions with widely divergent literary results, from the philosophical and sexual libertinism of the Restoration to the cult of sensibility associated esp. with the middle and end of the 18th c. The lang. of the senses draws much into its orbit in the era's poems of natural description. In Finch's "A Nocturnal Reverie" (1713), the senses work with animating imagination to describe the moment "When in some River, overhung with Green, / The waving Moon and trembling Leaves are seen" (9–10). Thomson's *The Seasons* explores the processes of nature that include the human and divine but could not have been so expressed without empirical attention to detail: "Th' uncurling Floods, diffus'd / In glassy Breadth, seem thro' delusive Lapse / Forgetful of their Course. 'Tis Silence all, / And pleasing Expectation" (*Spring*, 159–62). In "Elegy Written in a Country Churchyard" (1750) by Thomas Gray (1716–71), the fading of "the glimmering landscape on the sight" turns the speaker toward the air, which "a solemn stillness holds," and the sounds of twilight "where the beetle wheels his droning flight" (5, 6, 7). As poets looked at and listened to the world around them, they also saw and heard themselves: a heightened self-consciousness about perception and creative processes gives the faculty of imagination supreme power in Mark Akenside's (1721–70) *The Pleasures of Imagination* (1744), Joseph Warton's (1722–1800) *The Enthusiast: Or, the Lover of Nature* (1744), and Thomas Warton's (1728–90) *The Pleasures of Melancholy* (1747). *Imagination* shifts from its earlier sense (the common human capacity for image making) to a rarified individual talent; and *genius*, long understood as something one could have or participate in, becomes a term limited to and originating in the rare artist-figure. The increasing attention to taste, often seen as an attempt to instate another form of cultural and social hierarchy on literary value in the growing print culture, likewise turned the hierarchy of poetic kinds into an inward scale where tasteful aesthetic judgment defined new poetic values.

The cult of sensibility, with its pendulum of self-absorption and social consciousness, privileged an individual's perceptions and feelings that could also extend to sympathy with the sufferings of those oppressed by patriarchy, poverty, or slavery (e.g., George Crabbe's [1754–1832] *The Village*, 1783, and Cowper's "The Negro's Complaint," 1789). Sensibility privileged intensity of feeling as an index of aesthetic merit—in poet and reader—and as a moral good. Readers looked anew at oral poetry, esp. the ballad. A fascination with "untutored" poets who possessed "natural" genius extended the langs. of and criteria for poetry. Thomas Percy's (1729–1811) *Reliques of Ancient English Poetry* (1765) heightened the interest in indigenous trads. and langs. (whether real or imagined, as in James Macpherson's [1736–96] *The Works of Ossian*, 1765, and Thomas Chatterton's [1752–70] Rowley poems, posthumously collected in 1777) and prepared for a growing appreciation of dialect poetry, incl. that of Robert Burns (1759–96).

V. The Romantic Period, 1789–1830. The romantic period in Eng. poetry is traditionally considered to date from 1789, the beginning of the Fr. Revolution.

While the poetry of William Blake (1757–1827) had a modest impact when first published, Blake is now regarded as one of the most original Eng. poets and a major figure in the romantic movement. His early *Songs of Innocence and of Experience* (1794) foreshadowed the interest in simple lang., as well as the fascination with the imaginative world of childhood, that would later characterize the work of William Wordsworth (1770–1850) and S. T. Coleridge (1772–1834). Blake's prophetic poems, meanwhile, incl. *The Marriage of Heaven and Hell* (1790), *The Four Zoas* (1797), and *Milton* (1804), display in extreme form the political radicalism and the visionary imagination that typify much romantic writing. The form of these later poems is also significant: written predominantly in long, unrhymed lines that resist regular meter, they anticipate the innovations of Walt Whitman.

Nearly as radical as Blake's work, and more directly influential, was Wordsworth and Coleridge's *Lyrical Ballads* (1798), probably the most important single volume of poetry of the romantic period. Its protagonists are rustic, often marginalized figures—vagrants, madwomen, a mentally retarded child—but they are not sentimentalized and are always treated as individuals. The poems are written, for the most part, in deliberately simple lang., avoiding the elaborate diction of much 18th-c. poetry. Wordsworth, who wrote the great majority of the volume, defended these choices in his famous Preface to the 2d ed. (1800). Perhaps the chief claim of the preface, however, is that the true importance of any situation (and of any poem) is wholly subjective, deriving from the feeling it engenders in the perceiver; poetry, then, ultimately reflects not the world but the self. This notion is exemplified by the poem commonly known as "Tintern Abbey," the last in the 1798 *Lyrical Ballads*, in which Wordsworth's speaker surveys a landscape, not to reveal its inherent or universal significance, but to explore its personal meanings and associations.

Most of Wordsworth's greatest poetic accomplishments are concentrated in the years immediately after *Lyrical Ballads*, yet they cover a wide variety of genres. His "Ode: Intimations of Immortality" (1804), like "Tintern Abbey," regrets the loss of youthful immediacy and seeks recompense in a greater sense of human sympathy. Wordsworth's masterpiece, *The Prelude*, was largely complete by 1805, though not published until after his death (1850). A blank-verse autobiographical epic, *The Prelude* traces the growth of the poet's mind and sensibility, exploring how his "love of nature" led to a "love of mankind." Although it follows a roughly chronological organization, the poem focuses not on what would usually be considered major life events but on what Wordsworth calls "spots of time"—moments of sudden, often fearful perception, which are not fully understood at the time and which for that very reason continue to haunt and shape the poet's imagination. Beginning in 1802, Wordsworth also began composing sonnets, a form that had been revived toward the end of the 18th c. Wordsworth's sonnets, which in their mingling of public and personal concerns harken back to those of Milton, contributed to the popularity of the form through the rest of the 19th c.

Wordsworth developed many of his theories and practices in collaboration with Coleridge. The latter's poetic output was relatively small, but his three vivid and often psychologically harrowing supernatural poems—*The Rime of the Ancient Mariner* (1798), "Kubla Khan" (1816), and "Christabel" (1816)—have bewitched generations of readers. "Christabel" also reintroduced into Eng. poetry (outside the ballad) the widespread use of accentual verse. But Coleridge's most important contribution to Eng. poetic hist. was his devel., in such pieces as "The Eolian Harp" (1795) and "Frost at Midnight" (1798), of the conversation poem—short, blank-verse lyrics characterized by their colloquial style, which prefigure the dramatic monologues of the Victorians.

The next generation of romantic poets appealed to their readers' emotions even more directly than Wordsworth and Coleridge had, while at the same time exhibiting a keener sense of irony and skepticism. Felicia Hemans (1793–1835), for instance, won tremendous popularity with her early poems of passion and patriotism, but her most important work, *Records of Woman* (1828), mingles these themes with a more critical view of the trials faced by women throughout hist. Lord Byron (1788–1824), meanwhile, first achieved fame with the publication of *Childe Harold's Pilgrimage* (1812), the eponymous hero of which is brooding and passionate, yet at the same time world-weary and cynical. This figure of the so-called Byronic hero, who was quickly identified with the poet himself, reappears under various names in a series of Orientalist romances (*The Giaour*, 1813; *The Corsair*, 1814) that won Byron adulation throughout Europe. But Byron's greatest work by far was his last, the sprawling comic picaresque *Don Juan* (1819–24), left unfinished at his death. Irreverent (even blasphemous) and sentimental at once, *Don Juan* set new standards both for satire and for narrative in Eng. poetry.

Byron's friend P. B. Shelley (1792–1822) was, with Blake, the most radical and politically engaged of the romantic poets, although his poetry, like Blake's, tends toward metaphysical abstraction, even in such an explicitly topical work as the populist *Mask of Anarchy* (1832). Much of Shelley's best poetry (incl. the *Mask*) went unpublished in his lifetime, as did his brilliant critical treatise *A Defence of Poetry* (1840), which defines the act of poetic composition as a noble but ultimately futile attempt to recapture an original moment of fleeting inspiration. The same theme, of the idealistic pursuit of evanescent beauty, informs Shelley's finest lyric poems, incl. "Hymn to Intellectual Beauty" (1817) and "To a Skylark" (1820), as well as his great allegorical narratives, such as "Alastor" (1816). Shelley's full powers are on display in "Adonais" (1821), his elegy for John Keats, which while eschewing religious consolation (Shelley being a self-proclaimed atheist) expresses a deep faith in the ability of the human imagination to transcend all things, incl. death.

Keats (1795–1821), the latest born as well as the shortest lived of the major Eng. romantics, developed with astonishing rapidity over the course of his brief career. The lushly sensuous lyrics of his first volume of poems (1817) and his extended cl. reverie *Endymion* (1818) display enormous promise, often self-consciously: many of Keats's early sonnets, such as "On First Looking into Chapman's Homer" (1817), candidly describe his eager poetic ambition. That promise found fulfillment in the handful of masterpieces Keats went on to compose before tuberculosis rendered him too weak to write, most of which were published in his final volume of verse (1820). These include two romances, "Lamia" and "The Eve of St. Agnes," both rich in brilliant description, which explore the troubled interaction between the world as we know it and the immortal world of dreams; and *Hyperion*, a powerful epic fragment in Miltonic style. The most enduring works of Keats's final period are his great odes—incl. "Ode to Psyche," "Ode on a Grecian Urn," "Ode to a Nightingale," and "To Autumn"—which in controlled yet richly textured lang. explore the pains and challenges of mortal life and the ability of art to redeem or overcome them. Although he died in relative obscurity, Keats gained a devoted following, which has increased ever since, through the sheer beauty of his poetry; and his unstinting commitment to (in his words) "a life of sensations rather than of thoughts" has earned him a place beside Wordsworth as an archetype of the romantic poet.

VI. The Victorian Period, 1830–1900. By the time Queen Victoria came to the throne in 1837, almost all the major romantic poets had either died or ceased writing their best poetry. The traditional division of 19th-c. Eng. poetry into "romantic" and "Victorian" (Victoria reigned until 1901) is therefore sensible, although the new generation of poets that began publishing in the 1830s remained deeply influenced by their immediate predecessors. One significant difference lay in their avoidance of the directly personal, confessional style of poetry popularized by Byron and Shelley—a reticence reflected in the early work of Alfred, Lord Tennyson (1809–92), who went on to become poet laureate and a dominant figure of the period. The finest poems of his first two volumes (1830, 1833), incl. "Mariana" and "The Lady of Shalott," focus, like many romantic poems, on an isolated, introverted consciousness, but that consciousness is explicitly not the poet's own. This preference for displaced self-consciousness led Tennyson shortly afterward to develop (at the same time as Robert Browning, but independently) the classic Victorian form of the dramatic monologue; his paired monologues "Ulysses" and "Tithonus" are exemplary of the genre.

Tennyson's greatest work was *In Memoriam* (1850), his hauntingly beautiful book-length elegy for his friend Arthur Hallam. In contrast to the earlier lyrics, *In Memoriam* is avowedly a deeply personal poem. Yet its widespread appeal—it was a best seller and quickly made Tennyson a household name—derives from its extraordinary ability to connect private grief to issues of major public concern, incl., most notably, the contemp. struggle between traditional religious faith and mod. scientific discoveries. Tennyson's later achievements include *Maud* (1855), a sensational narrative in the spasmodic mode conveyed entirely through lyrics, and *Idylls of the King* (1859–85), a 12-book, blank-verse epic recounting the rise and (more successfully) decline of King Arthur's Camelot.

Robert Browning (1812–89) is often paired with Tennyson as the representative Victorian poet, but his reputation came late because of the frequent obscurity of his poetry. Browning's reputation today rests almost entirely on his dramatic monologues, of which he is the acknowledged master. His early monologues ("My Last Duchess," 1842; "The Bishop Orders His Tomb," 1845) tend to feature vivid, often grotesque speakers who reveal more about themselves than they intend and frequently undermine their own purpose in speaking. The irony is gentler in the mature monologues of his two most important collections, *Men and Women* (1855) and *Dramatis Personae* (1864), which include such psychologically nuanced portraits as "Andrea del Sarto" and "Rabbi Ben Ezra." Browning's experiments with the dramatic monologue culminate in his most ambitious work, the epic-length *The Ring and the Book* (1868–69), in which the story of an obscure 17th-c. murder case is retold from nine viewpoints. In its characterization of the speakers and protagonists, the poem, which finally won Browning his overdue recognition, reaches a Shakespearean pitch of complexity and profundity.

When Elizabeth Barrett Browning (1806–61) married Robert Browning in 1846, her reputation far exceeded his, and it grew even greater with the publication of her *Sonnets from the Portuguese* (1850), which was written during their courtship. *Sonnets from the Portuguese* (the title is deliberately misleading: the poems are not trans.) is the first amatory sonnet sequence in Eng. since the Ren. and represents a brilliant contribution to, and revision of, the genre. Just as impressive is Browning's experimental verse novel about a professional woman writer, *Aurora Leigh* (1856). Alongside these longer works, Browning produced lyric poems on a wide range of social and political issues, incl. child labor, the It. struggle for independence, and most movingly abolition ("The Runaway Slave at Pilgrim's Point"). Her poetry was a major source of inspiration for a younger generation of women, incl. Christina Rossetti, Augusta Webster, and, in the U.S., Emily Dickinson.

Religious faith and its mod. vicissitudes form a recurrent concern of mid-Victorian poetry. Much of Matthew Arnold's (1822–88) best poetry, such as "The Scholar-Gipsy," laments the aimlessness of mod. life, esp. the loss of a simple, reliable religious faith (notably in "Stanzas from the Grande Chartreuse" and "Dover Beach"). Arnold's friend A. H. Clough (1819–61) also wrote extensively about a rapidly secularizing world—although his most accomplished poem, the urbane epistolary romance *Amours de Voyage* (1855), is in a very different vein. Christina Rossetti (1830–94), by contrast, maintained a devout Anglo-Catholic faith, which is reflected in her large body of typically brief, breathtakingly understated religious lyrics. Her best-known and most original poem, however, *Goblin Market* (1862), though it has religious overtones, differs sharply from the majority of her work. Cast as a children's fairy tale, yet filled with surprisingly graphic violence and sexuality, it remains one of the era's most fascinating works. Similarly devout but of a very different texture are the poems of the Jesuit G. M. Hopkins (1844–89), which, when finally published in 1918, had a profound impact on modernist poetics. Hopkins's highly original experiments with what he called *sprung rhythm*, together with his heavy use of alliteration, neologism, and knotty syntax, lend his poems of religious praise and occasional religious despair (the so-called terrible sonnets) extraordinary force and conviction.

Some Victorian poetry aimed at realism, incl. E. B. Browning's *Aurora Leigh* and George Meredith's (1828–1909) *Modern Love* (1862), a subversive sonnet sequence (the "sonnets" have 16 lines) detailing the breakdown of a marriage. But realism was mostly ceded to the increasingly dominant genre of the novel, while poetry moved in an opposite direction. Dante Gabriel Rossetti (1828–82), for instance, the brother of Christina and one of the founders of the Pre-Raphaelite Brotherhood of painters, extended the often ornate, medievalizing style of his painting to his poetry as well; his sonnet sequence *The House of Life* (1881) contrasts with Meredith's in its heavy use of allegory. William Morris (1834–96), another member of the Pre-Raphaelite circle, wrote primarily on legendary themes, recounting stories from the Arthurian trad. and, more unusually, from Norse sagas. Perhaps the most significant poet of this group was the spectacularly talented A. C. Swinburne (1837–1909), whose celebrations of pagan sensuality were partly inspired by the work of the Fr. poet Charles Baudelaire (see FRANCE, POETRY OF), but whose style of fluid verbal and imagistic profusion is all his own.

Influenced by these precedents, as well as by the theories of Walter Pater, poets of the aesthetic movement of the 1880s and 1890s (incl. Oscar Wilde, Ernest Dowson, Michael Field, and the young William Butler Yeats) turned away from the moral and social concerns of much mid-Victorian verse to concentrate on the cultivation of beauty for its own sake. The most enduring work from the end of the century, however, is A. E. Housman's (1859–1936) *A Shropshire Lad* (1896), a collection of deceptively simple, deeply melancholic lyrics of pastoral nostalgia. A similarly melancholy pessimism, though more ironic, marks the poetry of Thomas Hardy (1840–1928), who is usually classed (and who classed himself) as a Victorian poet, even though the majority of his poems were written in the 20th c. Hardy's verse is characterized by idiosyncratic vocabulary and often contorted syntax reminiscent of Robert Browning. His finest work, a series of elegies for his late wife titled *Poems of 1912–13*, looks back even more to *In Memoriam*—but, crucially, without the ultimately consolatory faith and resolution displayed by Tennyson's poem 60 years earlier. The fracturing of faith and form, which had been foreshadowed by Tennyson and which grew more pronounced across the Victorian period, prepared the way for the major poetic devels. of the 20th c.

VII. Modernism to the Present, from 1901. From Hardy's pessimistic belated romanticism to the aestheticism (tinged with Ir. cultural nationalism) of the early Yeats (1865–1939), the voices of the early 20th c. remained rooted in 19th-c. styles and concerns, accommodating changing historical circumstances in contradictory ways. Rudyard Kipling (1865–1936) projected an expansive view of Eng. imperial culture, while others reconsidered the domestic fate of received forms. Robert Bridges (1844–1930) explored the syllabic resources of traditional prosodies and introduced sprung rhythm through the posthumous publication of Hopkins. Anthologized between 1911 and 1922, Georgian poets included such popular figures as Walter de la Mare (1873–1956) and John Masefield (1878–1967), as well as D. H. Lawrence (1885–1930). Georgian anthols. also introduced a generation of writers best known for increasingly bitter depictions of World War I (1914–18). Moving from Rupert Brooke's (1887–1915) patriotic sonnets and Edward Thomas's (1878–1917) ambivalent bucolics to the pointed ironies of Siegfried Sassoon (1886–1967) and Wilfred Owen (1893–1918), war poetry progressively deployed the resources of 19th-c. lyricism to call its underlying values into question, systematically turning experience against inherited notions of beauty.

Gathering force before the war and consolidating an ambitious aesthetic program after it, modernism assailed such values comprehensively, introducing new forms and subjects, often challenging conventional distinctions between verse and prose. Fusing the influence of Fr. symbolism after Baudelaire and Gustave Flaubert with the iconoclasm of later avant-gardes such as F. T. Marinetti's It. futurism, early modernists such as T. E. Hulme (1883–1917) and F. S. Flint (1885–1960) rejected expressive rhetorical modes in favor of a spare free verse predicated on the image. Codified in the manifestos and prosodic experiments of the Am. Ezra Pound (1885–1972), early modernism absorbed the influence of historically distant forms (such as the Occitan *trobar clus* and the Chinese ideogram) and registered shifts under way in other arts, from painting and sculpture to architecture and music. The Poundian avant-garde (captured in Wyndham Lewis's jour. *Blast* [1914]) traded insular frames of reference for the expatriate's cosmopolitan London, attuned to multiple trads. and langs. and populated by artists from Ireland, North America, and Europe, working in every medium. Before memorializing his departure from London with *Hugh Selwyn Mauberley* (1920) and embarking on *The Cantos*, Pound consolidated extensive networks of literary magazines significantly dedicated to new poetry. The open forms most identified with a modernist style have never been uncontroversial, often associated with Am. rather than Brit. idioms, but may nonetheless be found in figures as various as Edith Sitwell (1887–1964) and Mina Loy (1882–1966).

Pound also impressed his influence on the work of Yeats and of contemporaries such as James Joyce (1882–1941) and T. S. Eliot (1888–1965). High modernism of the early interwar years aspired to more monumental forms, culminating in the publication (in Paris) of Joyce's *Ulysses* (1922). Poetically, the period is galvanized by the austere turn of Yeats's most anthologized work, driven to explicitly political and philosophical themes from *The Wild Swans at Coole* (1919) to *The Tower* (1928). The pressures of Ir. politics and the emergent Free State pervade "Easter, 1916" and "Meditations in Time of Civil War" (1923) while "Leda and the Swan" (1928) and "The Second Coming" (1920) link social turbulence to the esoteric historical views propounded in *A Vision* (1925) and adduced as artistic models in "Among School Children" (1926) and "Sailing to Byzantium" (1927). Uniting private mythology with an insistently public and prophetic voice, the stark verse of Yeats's late serial epitaphs such as "Under Ben Bulben" (1939) and "The Circus Animals' Desertion" (1939) projects an oracular shadow over later Eng. and Ir. poets alike.

It was Eliot, however, who most decisively shaped the period's aesthetic as poet, critic, and later ed. at Faber and Faber, still England's premier poetic imprint. *Prufrock and Other Observations* (1917) decomposed the form of the dramatic monologue in a fragmented arrangement of densely orchestrated figures and rhythms, stylistically derived from Stéphane Mallarmé, Jules Laforgue, and Eng. metaphysical poetry but set against the mundane scenes of the mod. city. This effect was heightened in "Gerontion" (1920), which maintained the monologue's shape but abandoned any single identifiable voice, while other poems from *Ara Vos Prec* (1919) explored the satiric possibilities of stricter forms, inspired by Théophile Gautier's quatrains. Eliot's resonant musical conception of free verse, designed not to displace meter and rhyme but rather to restore their harmonic variety and intensity, sought to create an impersonal classicism capable of rendering the "simultaneous existence" and "simultaneous order" of "the whole of the literature of Europe from Homer," as he writes in "Tradition and the Individual Talent" (1919). For Eliot, "poets in our civilization, as it exists at present, must be *difficult*. . . . The poet must become more and more comprehensive, more allusive, more indirect, in order to force, to dislocate if necessary, lang. into his meaning" ("The Metaphysical Poets," 1921). *The Waste Land* (1922) enacted this argument poetically. Compressed to 434 lines by Pound's severe editing, Eliot's masterpiece discarded unities of narrative and voice, compiling allusive fragments of other texts into an intricate depiction of London and interwar Europe. Setting refrains from Dante, Baudelaire, and Richard Wagner alongside an array of mythic elements and demotic passages, the poem paradoxically shored fragments against ruins, juxtaposing haunting signs of cultural sterility with a rich archive of elusive critical meanings, buttressed by Eliot's own (often ironic) annotations. Eliot's Anglican conversion is reflected in *Ash Wednesday* (1930) and in the looser meditative tone of *Four Quartets* (1936–42), concerned with theological problems of time and hist. and, in "Little Gidding" (1942), with the searing experience of the second war.

The 1930s witnessed ambivalent reactions to modernism's recondite styles, most notably in the work of W. H. Auden (1907–73) and the poets around him: Cecil Day-Lewis (1904–72), Stephen Spender (1909–95), and Louis MacNeice (1907–63). Radicalized to varying degrees by the influence of Karl Marx and Sigmund Freud and by the decade's political and economic crises, Auden's generation balanced traditional forms against contemp. subject matter. The terse lyricism of Auden's (usually untitled) early poems and the political urgency of longer works such as *The Orators* (1932) gave way to more resigned tones by the decade's end. MacNeice's *Autumn Journal* (1939) and Auden's *Another Time* (1940) record the turn of the Spanish Civil War and the more general Eur. collapse before an ascendant Fascism. Auden's emigration to the United States prompted a series of more meditative volumes, often preoccupied with religious and philosophical matters: *New Year Letter* (1941), *For the Time Being* (1945), *The Age of Anxiety* (1947). Elsewhere, the 1930s saw the devel. of modernist tendencies in other directions. Hugh MacDiarmid (pseud. of Christopher Grieve, 1892–1978), the leading voice of the Scottish renaissance, adapted collage forms into Scots with *A Drunk Man Looks at the Thistle* (1926) and mingled nationalist and communist programs through *In Memoriam James Joyce* (1955). David Jones (1895–1974) probed Welsh lang. and culture to explore the memory of war with *In Parenthesis* (1937) and Catholic liturgy in *The Anathémata* (1952).

With Yeats's death, Eliot's increasing reticence, and Auden's departure, mid-century poetry lost its guiding authorities. The light verse of John Betjeman (1906–84) and exuberant neoromanticism of Dylan Thomas (1914–53) gathered popular followings but never defined durable trajectories, while singular figures such as R. S. Thomas (1913–2000) in Wales and Norman MacCaig (1910–1996) and W. S. Graham (1918–1986) in Scotland received less popular attention. The definition of a recognizable postwar style instead fell to the Movement, comprising the poets grouped around Philip Larkin (1922–84) in anthols.

of the 1950s, incl. Donald Davie (1922–95), Kingsley Amis (1922–95), Elizabeth Jennings (1926–2001), and Thom Gunn (1929–2004). Explicitly rejecting both modernist obscurantism and neoromanticism in favor of accessible plain speech, the Movement sought to restore insular trads. (championing Hardy, e.g.). The wry postimperial sensibility of the Movement lyric as perfected by Larkin uses insistently regular stanzas and meters to measure the ironic distance between a rich cultural heritage and the diminished realities of postwar social life. Poems such as "Church Going" (1954) and "The Whitsun Weddings" (1958) adopt a detached but elegiac attitude toward increasingly anachronistic rituals, while later pieces like "High Windows" (1967) exploit and preserve a tension between apparently degraded everyday speech and scattered moments of vision that it fails to eclipse.

Resistance to the Movement's perceived gentility, polemically intimated in *The New Poetry* (1962, 1966), catalyzed more expansive styles in succeeding generations, often receptive to both traditional and modernist formal practices. Ted Hughes (1930–98) developed a distinctively bardic voice, grounded in the immediacy of an often ruthless nature. Volumes from *The Hawk in the Rain* (1957) to *Crow* (1970) use animals to conjure scenes of primal violence and transformation, while later sequences concentrate on the slower rhythms of rural life at the fringe of mod. devel. Hughes's extremity is perhaps matched only by that of Sylvia Plath (1932–63), whose posthumous *Ariel* (1965) fuses confessional and naturalist elements with nightmarish visions of 20th-c. hist. Jon Silkin (1930–97) and Charles Tomlinson (1927–2015) have suffused a deep awareness of Eng. lit. hist. with the influence of other cultural and poetic trads. Roy Fisher (b. 1930) has adapted collage techniques to an ongoing excavation of his native Birmingham. The densely textured lang. of Geoffrey Hill (1932–2016), developed in *King Log* (1968) and *Mercian Hymns* (1971), turns Eliotic difficulty to the work of historical meditation and recovery, mixed in later volumes with implacable strains of religious and political prophecy. Tony Harrison (b. 1937) has infused the precision of modernist classicism with an unsparing political urgency, anchored in the perspective of working-class Leeds.

The Brit. Poetry Revival of the late 1960s and early 1970s saw the resurgence of more distinctly experimental strains, resistant to mainstream conventions and enabled by the proliferation of loosely affiliated networks of small presses. With the appearance of his late masterpiece *Briggflatts* (1966), the spare but sonorous musicality of Northumbrian modernist Basil Bunting (1900–85) inspired an eclectic array of younger poets, as did a host of postwar Am. and Eur. avant-gardes. Though short-lived, the revival left behind vibrant artistic scenes in northern England, in London, and in Scotland, with Edwin Morgan (1920–2010) and Ian Hamilton Finlay (1925–2006). In the work of figures from Tom Raworth (b. 1938) and Allen Fisher (b. 1944) to Maggie O'Sullivan (b. 1951), it also systematically integrated other arts and media. Elsewhere, the intensely wrought manner of J. H. Prynne (b. 1936) has fostered a range of more academic and self-consciously critical styles, garnering international interest even when resisted by the Brit. mainstream. The same synthesis of formal and conceptual rigor marks the work of younger figures from Veronica Forrest-Thomson (1947–75) to Denise Riley (b. 1948).

More general notice has gathered to poets emerging from Northern Ireland, from John Montague (b. 1929) to the group originally centered in Belfast, incl. Michael Longley (b. 1939), Derek Mahon (b. 1941), and Seamus Heaney (1939–2013), perhaps the most widely read Eng.-lang. poet of the era. Like Yeats, Heaney has synthesized and reworked Eng. and Ir. trads. alike, crafting a lyricism that simultaneously imbibes and seeks to transcend place and historical circumstance. More recently, the intricate verbal dexterity of Paul Muldoon (b. 1951), elusive syntax of Medbh McGuckian (b. 1950), and adventurous long lines of Ciaran Carson (b. 1948) have united an expansive sense of postmodern play with an often fraught sense of Ir. hist.

Recent laureates Andrew Motion (b. 1952) and Carol Ann Duffy (b. 1955) have emphasized accessibility in mainstream poetic culture, respectively recovering elements of the Movement's legacy and developing an inclusive dramatic populism alert to larger social issues. Often sustained by an expanding economy of prizes and writing programs, the New Generation of the 1990s includes Simon Armitage (b. 1963), Lavinia Greenlaw (b. 1962), Kathleen Jamie (b. 1962), and Glyn Maxwell (b. 1962), among numerous others. Furthermore, the poetic culture of the late 20th and early 21st cs. has expanded to new sites and incorporated accents from beyond the Brit. archipelago, ranging from the dub rhythms of Linton Kwesi Johnson (b. 1952) to the diasporic hists. underlying the work of David Dabydeen (b. 1955) and Grace Nichols (b. 1950).

See CARIBBEAN, POETRY OF THE; CORNISH POETRY; IRELAND, POETRY OF; LATIN POETRY; SCOTLAND, POETRY OF; WELSH POETRY.

■ **General**: T. Warton, *History of English Poetry* (1774–81); S. Johnson, *Lives of the English Poets* (1781); Brooks; S. Fish, *Surprised by Sin: The Reader in "Paradise Lost"* (1967); B. H. Smith, *Poetic Closure* (1968); H. Bloom, *The Anxiety of Influence* (1973); R. L. Colie, *The Resources of Kind* (1973); P. H. Fry, *The Poet's Calling in the English Ode* (1980); Attridge, *Rhythms*; J. A. Winn, *Unsuspected Eloquence: A History of the Relations between Poetry and Music* (1981); C. Ricks, *The Force of Poetry* (1984); Hollander; H. Vendler, *Voices and Visions* (1987); J. Hollander, *Melodious Guile* (1988); H. Vendler, *The Music of What Happens* (1988); C. Ricks, *Essays in Appreciation* (1996); S. Stewart, *Poetry and the Fate of the Senses* (2002); T. Eagleton, *How to Read a Poem* (2007); *The Oxford Handbook of the Elegy*, ed. K. A. Weisman (2010). ***Digital Resources***: Early English Books Online, http://eebo.chadwyck.com/home; Eighteenth-Century Collections Online, http://gale.cengage.co.uk/product-highlights/history/eighteenth-century-collections-online.aspx; Orlando: Women's Writing in the British Isles from the Beginnings to the Present, http://library.mcmaster.ca/articles/orlando-womens-writing-british-isles-from-beginning-present; Perdita Manuscripts: Women Writers, 1500–1700, http://www.amdigital.co.uk/Collections/Perdita.aspx; Literature Online, http://lion.chadwyck.com; Representative Poetry Online, http://rpo.library.utoronto.ca.

■ **Old English.** ***Anthologies***: *Anglo-Saxon Poetic Records*, ed. G. Krapp and E. Dobbie, 6 v. (1931–53); *An Anthology of Old English Poetry*, trans. C. W. Kennedy (1960); *Poems of Wisdom and Learning in Old English*, ed. and trans. T. A. Shippey (1976); *The Old English Riddles of the Exeter Book*, ed. C. Williamson (1977); *A Choice of Anglo-Saxon Verse*, ed. and trans. R. Hamer (1981); *Anglo-Saxon Poetry*, trans. S.A.J. Bradley (1982); *Old English Minor Heroic Poems*, ed. J. Hill (1983); *The Earliest English Poems*, trans. M. Alexander (1991); *The Old English Elegies*, ed. A. L. Klinck (1992); *Sixty-Five Anglo-Saxon Riddles*, ed. and trans. L. J. Rodrigues (1998); *Old and Middle English*, ed. E. Treharne (2000); *Eight Old English Poems*, ed. J. C. Pope, rev. R. D. Fulk (2001); *The Word Exchange: Anglo-Saxon Poems in Translation*, ed. G. Delanty and M. Matto (2010). ***Criticism and History***: *Essential Articles for the Study of Old English Poetry*, ed. J. B. Bessinger and S. J. Kahrl (1968); S. B. Greenfield, *The Interpretation of Old English Poems* (1972); F. C. Robinson, *Beowulf and the Appositive Style* (1985); S. B. Greenfield and D. G. Calder, *A New Critical History of Old English Literature* (1986); N. Howe, *Migration and Mythmaking in Anglo-Saxon England* (1989); G. R. Overing, *Language, Sign, and Gender in Beowulf* (1990); K. O'Brien O'Keeffe, *Visible Song* (1990); *Old English Shorter Poems: Basic Readings*, ed. K. O'Brien O'Keeffe (1994); *Beowulf: Basic Readings*, ed. P. S. Baker (1995); *Cynewulf: Basic Readings*, ed. R. E. Bjork (1996); *Beowulf: A Verse Translation*, ed. D. Donoghue, trans. S. Heaney (2002); *The Poems of MS Junius 11*, ed. R. M. Liuzza (2002); T. A. Bredehoft, *Early English Metre* (2005); E. M. Tyler, *Old English Poetics: The Aesthetics of the Familiar* (2006); J. D. Niles, *Old English Heroic Poems and the Social Life of Texts* (2007); R. R. Trilling, *The Aesthetics of Nostalgia* (2009). ***Digital Resources***: Labyrinth: Resources for Medieval Studies, http://www8.georgetown.edu/departments/medieval/labyrinth/; Internet Medieval Sourcebook, http://www.fordham.edu/halsall/sbook.html; *The Electronic Exeter Anthology of Old English Poetry: An Edition of Exeter, Dean and Chapter MS 3501* (DVD-ROM), ed. B. J. Muir (2006); *Dictionary of Old English: A to G online*, http://tapor.library.utoronto.ca/doe/; *The Electronic Beowulf*, ed. Kevin Kiernan, http://www.uky.edu/~kiernan/eBeowulf/guide.htm.; Old English Newsletter Bibliography Database, http://www.oenewsletter.org/OENDB/index.php; *Norton Anthology of English Literature: Middle Ages*, http://www.wwnorton.com/college/english/nael/middleages/topic_4/welcome.htm.

■ **Middle English.** ***Anthologies***: *Secular Lyrics of the Fourteenth and Fifteenth Centuries*, ed. R. H. Robbins, 2d ed. (1955); *Historical Poems of the Fourteenth and Fifteenth Centuries*, ed. R. H. Robbins (1959); *Early Middle English Verse and Prose*, ed. J.A.W. Bennett and G. V. Smithers (1968); A. C. Spearing, *Readings in Medieval Poetry* (1987); *Alliterative Poetry of the Later Middle Ages*, ed. T. Turville-Petre (1989); *A Book of Middle English*, ed. T. Turville-Petre and J. A. Burrow (1996). ***Criticism and History***: P. Dronke, *The Medieval Lyric* (1968);

J. A. Burrow, *Ricardian Poetry* (1974); *Middle English Alliterative Poetry and Its Literary Background*, ed. D. A. Lawton (1982); A. C. Spearing, *Medieval to Renaissance in English Poetry* (1984); J.A.W. Bennett and D. Gray, *Middle English Literature* (1986); *Medieval Literary Theory and Criticism, c. 1100–c. 1375,* ed. A. J. Minnis and A. B. Scott (1988); P. Zumthor, *Toward a Medieval Poetics*, trans. P. Bennett (1992); *Medieval Lyric: Genres in Historical Context*, ed. W. Paden (2000); C. Chism, *Alliterative Revivals* (2002); *The Cambridge History of Medieval English Literature*, ed. D. Wallace (2002). ***Chaucer***: C. Muscatine, *Chaucer and the French Tradition* (1957); D. W. Robertson Jr., *A Preface to Chaucer* (1962); B. F. Huppé, *A Reading of the "Canterbury Tales"* (1964); E. T. Donaldson, *Speaking of Chaucer* (1970); P. M. Kean, *Chaucer and the Making of English Poetry* (1972); J. Mann, *Chaucer and Medieval Estates Satire* (1973); D. R. Howard, *The Idea of the "Canterbury Tales"* (1976); V. A. Kolve, *Chaucer and the Imagery of Narrative* (1984); C. Dinshaw, *Chaucer's Sexual Poetics* (1989); P. Strohm, *Social Chaucer* (1989); J. Fleming, *Classical Imitation and Interpretation in Chaucer's "Troilus"* (1990); H. Marshall Leicester, *The Disenchanted Self* (1990); L. Patterson, *Chaucer and the Subject of History* (1991); S. Lerer, *Chaucer and His Readers* (1993); D. Wallace, *Chaucerian Polity* (1997); C. Cannon, *The Making of Chaucer's English* (1998); K. L. Lynch, *Chaucer's Philosophical Visions* (2000); M. Miller, *Philosophical Chaucer* (2004); L. Scanlon, *Narrative, Authority, and Power* (2004). ***Fifteenth-Century Poets***: A. Renoir, *The Poetry of John Lydgate* (1967); D. Lawton, "Dullness and the Fifteenth Century," *ELH* 54 (1987); D. Pearsall, "Hoccleve's *Regement of Princes*: The Poetics of Royal Self-Representation," *Speculum* 69 (1994); P. Strohm, *England's Empty Throne* (1998); E. Knapp, *The Bureaucratic Muse* (2001); J. Simpson, *The Oxford English Literary History*, v. 2, *Reform and Cultural Revolution, 1350–1547* (2002); M. Nolan, *John Lydgate and the Making of Public Culture* (2005). ***Gawain-/Pearl Poet***: M. Borroff, *Sir Gawain and the Green Knight* (1962); J. A. Burrow, *A Reading of "Sir Gawain and the Green Knight"* (1965); L. D. Benson, *Art and Tradition in "Sir Gawain and the Green Knight"* (1965); L. M. Clopper, "Pearl and the Consolation of Scripture," *Viator* 23 (1992); A. Putter, *An Introduction to the Gawain-Poet* (1996); *A Companion to the Gawain-Poet*, ed. D. Brewer and J. Gibson (1997); M. Borroff, *Traditions and Renewals* (2003). ***Gower***: R. Peck, *Kingship and Common Profit in Gower's "Confessio amantis"* (1987); R. F. Yeager, *John Gower's Poetic* (1990); J. Simpson, *Sciences and the Self in Medieval Poetry* (1995); D. Aers, *Faith, Ethics and Church* (2000); L. Staley, "Gower, Richard II, Henry of Derby, and the Business of Making Culture," *Speculum* 75 (2000); D. Watt, *Amoral Gower: Language, Sex, and Politics* (2003); P. Nicholson, *Love and Ethics in Gower's "Confessio amantis"* (2005). ***Piers Plowman***: M. Bloomfield, *"Piers Plowman" as a 14th-C. Apocalypse* (1962); K. Kerby-Fulton, *Reformist Apocalypticism and "Piers Plowman"* (1990); S. Justice, *Writing and Rebellion: England in 1381* (1996); E. Steiner, *Documentary Culture and the Making of Medieval English Literature* (2003); N. Zeeman, *"Piers Plowman" and the Medieval Discourse of Desire* (2006).

■ **Renaissance.** ***Anthologies***: *English Poetry of the Seventeenth Century*, ed. G. Parfitt (1992); *English Poetry of the Sixteenth Century*, ed. G. Waller (1993); *The Penguin Book of Renaissance Verse*, ed. D. Norbrook and H. Woudhuysen (1993); *Women Poets of the Renaissance*, ed. M. Wynne-Davies (1999); *Early Modern Women Poets*, ed. J. Stevenson and P. Davidson (2001); *Poetry and Revolution: An Anthology of British and Irish Verse, 1625–1660,* ed. P. Davidson (2001); *Sixteenth-Century Poetry*, ed. G. Braden (2005); *Seventeenth-Century British Poetry, 1603–1660,* ed. J. Rumrich and G. Chaplin (2005); *Metaphysical Poetry*, ed. C. Ricks and C. Burrow (2006); *The New Oxford Book of Seventeenth-Century Verse*, ed. A. Fowler (2008); *New Oxford Book of Sixteenth-Century Verse*, ed. E. Jones (2009); *Elizabeth I and Her Age*, ed. S. Felch and D. Stump (2009); *Women Writers in Renaissance England: An Annotated Anthology*, ed. R. Martin (2010); *The Broadview Anthology of British Literature: v. 2: The Renaissance and the Early Seventeenth Century*, ed. J. Black et al., 2d ed. (2010). ***Criticism and History***: S. Greenblatt, *Renaissance Self-Fashioning* (1980); J. Guillory, *Poetic Authority* (1982); *Re-membering Milton: Essays on the Texts and Traditions*, ed. M. Ferguson and M. Nyquist (1988); *The Spenser Encyclopedia*, ed. A. C. Hamilton (1990); A. R. Jones, *The Currency of Eros: Women's Love Lyric in Europe, 1540–1620* (1990); *The Cambridge Companion to English Poetry, Donne to Marvell*, ed. T. Corns (1993); A. Marotti, *Manuscript, Print, and the English Renaissance Lyric* (1995); D. K. Shuger, *Habits of Thought in the English*

Renaissance: Religion, Politics and the Dominant Culture (1997); *Worldmaking Spenser: Explorations in the Early Modern Age*, ed. P. Cheney and L. Silberman (1999); A. Hadfield, *The English Renaissance, 1500–1620* (2000); *A Companion to Early Modern Women's Writing*, ed. A. Pacheco (2002); *A Companion to English Renaissance Literature and Culture*, ed. M. Hattaway (2002); D. Norbrook, *Poetry and Politics in the English Renaissance* (2002); *Reading Early Modern Women*, ed. H. Ostovich and E. Sauer (2002); *Renaissance Poetry and Its Formal Engagements*, ed. M. Rasmussen (2002); R. Smith, *Sonnets and the English Woman Writer, 1560–1621* (2005); *Early Modern Poetry: A Critical Companion*, ed. P. Cheney, A. Hadfield, G. Sullivan (2006); J. Griffiths, *John Skelton and Poetic Authority* (2006); *John Donne's Poetry*, ed. D. Dickson (2007); A. Nicolson, *Quarrel with the King: The Story of an English Family on the High Road to Civil War* (2008); *Aemilia Lanyer: Gender, Genre, and the Canon*, ed. M. Grossman (2009); *The Cambridge Companion to Early Modern Women's Writing*, ed. L. Knoppers (2009); H. Dubrow, *The Challenges of Orpheus: Lyric Poetry and Early Modern England* (2011). ***Digital Resources***: Voice of the Shuttle: Renaissance and Seventeenth Century, http://vos.ucsb.edu/browse.asp?id=2749; *Luminarium: Renaissance and Seventeenth Century*, http://www.luminarium.org; Mr. William Shakespeare and the Internet, http://shakespeare.palomar.edu/; CERES Cambridge English Renaissance Electronic Service, http://www.english.cam.ac.uk/ceres/; *Norton Anthology of English Literature—16th Century and Early 17th Century*, http://www.wwnorton.com/college/english/nael/welcome.htm; CRRS Centre for Reformation and Renaissance Studies, http://crrs.ca/; The Folger Shakespeare Library, http://www.folger.edu/; The English Renaissance in Context (ERIC), http://sceti.library.upenn.edu/sceti/furness/eric/index.cfm; Representative Poetry Online, http://rpo.library.utoronto.ca/display/index.cfm; John Milton—The Milton-L Home Page, https://facultystaff.richmond.edu/~creamer/milton/; The Milton Reading Room, http://www.dartmouth.edu/~milton/reading_room/contents/index.shtml; Christ's College Cambridge—400th Anniversary Celebration of Milton, http://www.christs.cam.ac.uk/milton400/index.htm; The Edmund Spenser Homepage, http://www.english.cam.ac.uk/spenser/; The Sidney Homepage, http://www.english.cam.ac.uk/sidney/index.htm.

■ **Restoration and the Eighteenth Century.** ***Anthologies***: *Kissing the Rod: An Anthology of Seventeenth-Century Women's Verse*, ed. G. Greer et al. (1989); *Eighteenth-Century Women Poets*, ed. R. Lonsdale (1989); *Amazing Grace: An Anthology of Poems about Slavery, 1660–1810*, ed. J. G. Basker (2002); *Poetry from 1660 to 1780: Civil War, Restoration, Revolution*, ed. D. Wu and R. DeMaria (2002); *Eighteenth-Century English Labouring Class Poets*, ed. J. Goodridge et al., 3 v. (2003); *The Poetry of Slavery: An Anglo-American Anthology, 1764–1865*, ed. M. Wood (2003); *Eighteenth-Century Poetry*, ed. D. Fairer and D. Gerrard (2004); *British Women Poets of the Long Eighteenth Century*, ed. P. R. Backscheider and C. Ingrassia (2009); *Restoration Literature*, ed. P. Hammond (2009); *The New Oxford Book of Eighteenth-Century Verse*, ed. R. Lonsdale (2009). ***Criticism and History***: E. Rothstein, *Restoration and Eighteenth-Century Poetry, 1660–1780* (1981); J. itter, *Literary Loneliness in Mid-Eighteenth-Century England* (1982); D. B. Morris, *Alexander Pope: The Genius of Sense* (1984); A. Williams, *Prophetic Strain: The Greater Lyric in the Eighteenth Century* (1984); M. A. Doody, *The Daring Muse: Augustan Poetry Reconsidered* (1985); C. Gerrard, *The Patriot Opposition to Walpole* (1994); B. Parker, *The Triumph of Augustan Poetics* (1998); S. Kaul, *Poems of Nation, Anthems of Empire* (2000); W. J. Christmas, *The Lab'ring Muses* (2001); D. H. Griffin, *Patriotism and Poetry in Eighteenth-Century Britain* (2002); D. Fairer, *English Poetry of the Eighteenth Century* (2003); P. R. Backscheider, *Eighteenth-Century Women Poets and Their Poetry* (2005); P. Hammond, *The Making of Restoration Poetry* (2006); W. Overton, *The Eighteenth-Century British Verse Epistle* (2007); P. M. Spacks, *Reading Eighteenth-Century Poetry* (2009); J. Sitter, *The Cambridge Introduction to Eighteenth-Century Poetry* (2011). ***Digital Resources***: Eighteenth-Century Resources, http://ethnicity.rutgers.edu/~jlynch/18th/index.html; *18thConnect*, http://www.18thconnect.org; Literary Resources on the Net, http://ethnicity.rutgers.edu/~jlynch/Lit; Voice of the Shuttle, http://vos.ucsb.edu.

■ **Romantic Period**. ***Anthologies***: *New Oxford Book of Romantic Period Verse*, ed. J. McGann (1993); *English Romantic Writers*, ed. D. Perkins (1995); *British Literature, 1780–1830*, ed. A. Mellor and R. Matlak (1996); *British Women Poets of the Romantic Era*, ed. P. Feldman (1997); *Romantic Women Poets*, ed.

A. Ashfield (1998); *Longman Anthology of British Literature: The Romantics and Their Contemporaries,* ed. S. Wolfson and P. Manning (1999); *New Penguin Book of Romantic Poetry,* ed. J. and J. Wordsworth (2001); *Romanticism,* ed. D. Wu (2006); *Romantic Poetry,* ed. M. O'Neill and C. Mahoney (2008). ***Criticism and History***: Abrams; H. Bloom, *The Visionary Company* (1961); G. Hartman, *Wordsworth's Poetry, 1787–1814* (1964); M. H. Abrams, *Natural Supernaturalism* (1971); K. Kroeber, *Romantic Landscape Vision* (1975); M. Jacobus, *Tradition and Experiment in Wordsworth's Lyrical Ballads* (1976); A. Mellor, *English Romantic Irony* (1980); J. McGann, *The Romantic Ideology* (1983); H. Vendler, *The Odes of John Keats* (1983); S. Curran, *Poetic Form and British Romanticism* (1986); M. Levinson, *Wordsworth's Great Period Poems* (1986), *Keats's Life of Allegory* (1988); J. Watson, *English Poetry of the Romantic Period, 1789–1830* (1992); K. Kroeber, *Ecological Literary Criticism* (1994); J. J. McGann, *The Poetics of Sensibility* (1996); M. O'Neill, *Romanticism and the Self-Conscious Poem* (1997); S. Wolfson, *Formal Charges* (1997); J. Chandler, *England in 1819* (1998); S. Wolfson, *Borderlines: The Shiftings of Gender in British Romanticism* (2006); *Cambridge Companion to British Romantic Poetry,* ed. J. Chandler and M. McClane (2008); D. Gigante, *Life: Organic Form and Romanticism* (2009).

■ **Victorian Period.** ***Anthologies***: *Victorian Poetry and Poetics,* ed. W. Houghton and G. R. Stange (1968); *New Oxford Book of Victorian Verse,* ed. C. Ricks (1987); *Victorian Women Poets,* ed. A. Leighton and M. Reynolds (1995); *Nineteenth-Century Women Poets,* ed. I. Armstrong and J. Bristow (1996); *Penguin Book of Victorian Verse,* ed. D. Karlin (1997); *Broadview Anthology of Victorian Poetry and Poetic Theory,* ed. T. Collins and V. J. Rundle (1999); *The Victorians,* ed. V. Cunningham (2000); *Victorian Poetry,* ed. F. O'Gorman (2004); *Decadent Poetry,* ed. L. Rodensky (2007); *Victorian Women Poets,* ed. V. Blain (2009). ***Criticism and History***: E.D.H. Johnson, *The Alien Vision of Victorian Poetry* (1952); R. Langbaum, *The Poetry of Experience* (1957)—dramatic monologue; C. Ricks, *Tennyson* (1972); D. Mermin, *The Audience in the Poem* (1983); H. F. Tucker, *Tennyson and the Doom of Romanticism* (1988); E. Griffiths, *The Printed Voice of Victorian Poetry* (1989); A. Leighton, *Victorian Women Poets* (1992); I. Armstrong, *Victorian Poetry* (1993); Y. Prins, *Victorian Sappho* (1999); M. Reynolds, *The Realms of Verse, 1830–1870* (2001); B. Richards, *English Poetry of the Victorian Period, 1830–1890* (2001); *Companion to Victorian Poetry,* ed. R. Cronin, A. Chapman, A. Harrison (2002); R. Cronin, *Romantic Victorians* (2002); *The Fin-de-Siècle Poem,* ed. J. Bristow (2005); H. F. Tucker, *Epic: Britain's Heroic Muse* (2008); L. K. Hughes, *Cambridge Introduction to Victorian Poetry* (2010); V. Cunningham, *Victorian Poetry Now* (2011). ***Digital Resources***: Nineteenth-century Scholarship Online, http://www.nines.org/; Romantic Circles, http://www.rc.umd.edu/; William Blake Archive, http://www.blakearchive.org/blake/; British Women Romantic Poets, http://digital.lib.ucdavis.edu/projects/bwrp/; Poetess Archive, http://unixgen.muohio.edu/~poetess/; Rossetti Archive, http://www.rossettiarchive.org/; Morris Online, http://morrisedition.lib.uiowa.edu/; Swinburne Project, http://swinburnearchive.indiana.edu/swinburne/www/swinburne/.

■ **Modernism to the Present.** ***Anthologies***: *Georgian Poetry,* ed. E. Marsh (1911–22); *Des Imagistes* (1914) and *Catholic Anthology* (1915), both ed. E. Pound; *Some Imagist Poets* (1915); *New Signatures* (1932), *New Country* (1933), and *Faber Book of Modern Verse* (1936), all ed. M. Roberts; *Oxford Book of Modern Verse,* ed. W. B. Yeats (1936); *The New Apocalypse,* ed. J. F. Hendry (1939); *New Verse,* ed. G. Grigson (1942); *Faber Book of 20th-Century Verse,* ed. J. Heath-Stubbs and D. Wright (1953); *Poetry of the 1950s,* ed. D. J. Enright (1955); *New Lines,* ed. R. Conquest (1956); *The New Poetry* (1962), ed. A. Alvarez, rev. ed. (1966); *Children of Albion,* ed. M. Horovitz (1968); *British Poetry since 1945,* ed. E. Lucie-Smith (1970); *Oxford Book of Twentieth-Century English Verse,* ed. P. Larkin (1973); *Oxford Book of Contemporary Verse,* ed. D. J. Enright (1980); *Penguin Book of Contemporary British Poetry,* ed. B. Morrison and A. Motion (1982); *A Various Art,* ed. A. Crozier and T. Longville (1987); *The New British Poetry,* ed. G. Allnutt et al. (1988); *Conductors of Chaos,* ed. I. Sinclair (1996); *Penguin Book of First World War Poetry* [1979], ed. J. Silkin, rev. ed. (1996); *Out of Everywhere,* ed. M. O'Sullivan (1996); *Penguin Book of Poetry from Britain and Ireland since 1945,* ed. S. Armitage and R. Crawford (1998); *Harvill Book of Twentieth-Century Poetry in English,* ed. M. Schmidt (1999); *Other: British and Irish Poetry since 1970,* ed. R. Caddel and P. Quartermain (1999); *Bloodaxe Book of 20th Century Poetry from Britain and Ireland,* ed. E. Longley

(2001); *Anthology of Twentieth-Century British and Irish Poetry*, ed. K. Tuma (2001); *Norton Anthology of Modern and Contemporary Poetry*, ed. J. Ramazani, R. Ellmann, R. O'Clair (2003); *New British Poetry*, ed. D. Paterson and C. Simic (2004). ***Criticism and History***: A. Symons, *The Symbolist Movement in Literature* (1899), rev. ed. (1919); I. A. Richards, *Science and Poetry* (1926); F. R. Leavis, *New Bearings in English Poetry* (1932); C. Brooks, *Modern Poetry and the Tradition* (1939); Eliot, *Essays*; D. Davie, *Purity of Diction in English Verse* (1952); and *Articulate Energy* (1955); H. Kenner, *The Pound Era* (1971); D. Davie, *Thomas Hardy and British Poetry* (1972); S. Hynes, *The Auden Generation* (1975); D. Perkins, *A History of Modern Poetry*, 2 v. (1976, 1987); B. Morrison, *The Movement* (1980); V. Cunningham, *British Writers of the Thirties* (1988); D. Davie, *Under Briggflatts: A History of Poetry in Great Britain, 1960–1988* (1989); N. Corcoran, *English and Irish Poetry since 1940* (1993); A. Duncan, *The Failure of Conservatism in Modern British Poetry* (2003); R. Stevenson, *The Last of England?* (2004); P. Middleton, *Distant Reading* (2005); P. Barry, *Poetry Wars* (2006); S. Broom, *Contemporary British and Irish Poetry* (2006); J. Ramazani, *A Transnational Poetics* (2009). ***Digital Resources***: The First World War Poetry Digital Archive, http://www.oucs.ox.ac.uk/ww1lit/; The Modernist Journals Project, http://dl.lib.brown.edu/mjp/.

K. Davis (OE); E. Johnson (ME);
E. H. Sagaser (Ren.); J. Keith
(Restoration and 18th C.);
E. Gray (Romantic and Victorian);
C. D. Blanton (Mod. to Present)

ESPERANTO POETRY began with the booklet *International Language Esperanto*, published in Warsaw in 1887 by Lazar Ludvik (Markovich) Zamenhof (1859–1917) under the pseud. Dr. Esperanto (one who hopes). The booklet included three poems—one trans. and two original—to demonstrate that this proposed second lang. for international use was no lifeless project but a potential living lang. Zamenhof also produced numerous Esperanto trans., incl. *Hamlet* (1894) and the entire OT. The earliest Esperanto magazines published poetry, early poets drawing on their native trads. to establish poetic norms for Esperanto. Numerous periodicals now publish trans. and original Esperanto poetry. Esperanto lit. runs to several thousand volumes, and the Esperanto lang. is used or understood by several million speakers in the world. Esperanto is a planned, Eur.-based language with simplified grammar and pronunciation but a large vocabulary of fresh and interesting word forms and grammatical combinations unknown in Eur. langs., e.g., Eugen Michalski's poetic coinage *chielenas* (goes upward to the sky), in which *-as* denotes the present tense, *-n* direction toward, and *-e* the adverbial ending, while *chiel-* is the root associated with sky or heaven, *chielo*. Thus, *chiele* = in the sky; *chielen* = toward in-the-sky; and *chielenas* = is toward in-the-sky.

Serious projects for universal langs. began in the 17th c. with George Dalgarno (1661) and John Wilkins (1668) and engaged the attention of René Descartes, G. W. Leibniz, and Isaac Newton. Apart from Esperanto, only Volapük (1880) and Ido ("offspring"; 1908), a modification of Esperanto, developed any significant following, now dissipated. By 1900, Esperanto had spread beyond Poland, Russia, and Germany to Western Europe. Collections of poems appeared, incl. three by the Czech Stanislav Schulhof (1864–1919) and the polished and musical *Tra l'silento* (Through the Silence, 1912) of Edmond Privat (1889–1962). Antoni Grabowski (1857–1921), friend of Zamenhof and skilled linguist, published an international anthol., *El parnaso de popoloj* (From the People's Parnassus, 1913), and a brilliant trans. of the *Pan Tadeusz* of Mickiewicz (1918). His audacious ling. experiments prepared for the flowering of Esperanto poetry. The Hungarians Kálmán Kalocsay (1891–1976), in *Mondo kaj koro* (World and Heart, 1921), and Gyula Baghy (1891–1967), in *Preter la vivo* (Beyond Life, 1922), led the way. They founded the influential magazine and publishing company *Literatura Mondo* (Literary World) in 1922.

Zamenhof's interest in Esperanto lit. aimed to create an Esperanto literary and cultural trad., to expand and test the lang. by stretching it to its limits, and to demonstrate that it was as capable of expression as any ethnic lang. Unlike some other projects for an international lang. (none of which withstood the test of time), Esperanto did not spring fully armed from its creator's head. Zamenhof's 1887 booklet contained only the basis of Esperanto; others expanded its lexicon and discovered latent syntactic and morphological possibilities. Kalocsay, in numerous trans. and original poetry (esp. *Strechita kordo* [Tightened String], 1931), sought diversity: his work includes lyrics, free verse, and strict verse forms. The Rus.

Eugen Michalski (1897–1937) wrote introspective poems of startling imagery and ling. experiment. While Privat and Kalocsay demonstrated Esperanto's affinities with the Eur. trad., Michalski sought originality. But Stalinism claimed Michalski's life and silenced the talented Nikolai Hohlov (1891–1953). Kalocsay dominated the interwar years as mentor, ed., and publisher. Kalocsay and Gaston Waringhien's *Parnasa gvidlibro* (Guidebook to Parnassus, 1932) with its *Arto poetika* and glossary of literary terms and neologisms helped establish an Esperanto trad.; in 1952, *Kvaropo* (Quartet) extended this trad. This work, by four Brit. poets incl. William Auld (1924–2006), began a new era. Auld's *La infana raso* (The Child Race, 1956), a modernist poem of great variety and technical virtuosity, is widely regarded as the most impressive achievement of Esperanto poetry to date, though rivaled by the epic breadth of *Poemo de Utnoa* (Utnoa's Poem, 1993) by the Catalan Abel Montagut (b. 1953). Poets of Auld's generation include the Icelander Baldur Ragnarsson (b. 1930), whose collected works *La Lingvo Serena* (The Serene Language, 2007) established him as the leading poetic voice of the day. Other major contributors to Esperanto poetry in the latter years of the 20th c. include the Brit. scholar Marjorie Boulton (b. 1924), the Czech Eli Urbanová (1922–2012), the Japanese Miyamoto Masao (1913–89), the Brazilians Geraldo Mattos (1931–2014) and Roberto Passos Nogueira (b. 1949), the South African Edwin de Kock (b. 1930), and the Rus.-Israeli Michael Gishpling (b. 1924).

The poetic trad. has been enriched by numbers of East Asian poets, among them Ueyama Masao (1910–1988) of Japan and Armand Su (1936–1990) and Mao Zifu (b. 1963; *Kantoj de Anteo* [Songs of Anteo], 2006) of China, representative of a long history of Esperanto in China and Japan, where the lang. was associated with anarchist and left-wing causes and with efforts at romanization. The task of codifying and establishing this poetic trad. has fallen in part on a succession of writers on the ling., prosodic, and cultural issues involved in writing Esperanto poetry, among them Auld, Ragnarsson, and Gaston Waringhien (1901–91) of France, who also wrote exquisitely crafted poetry under the pseud. Georges Maura.

In the Esperanto poetic trad., trans. and original work are closely linked. Trans. incl. many of Shakespeare's plays (some by Kalocsay and Auld), his *Sonnets* (trans. Auld), Luís de Camões's *Lusiads*, Dante's *Divine Comedy*, the *Kalevala*, the Qur'an, and works by J. W. Goethe, Charles Baudelaire, Sophocles, Antônio de Castro Alves, Federico García Lorca, ʿUmar Khayyām, Rabindranath Tagore, and many others. Anthols. of national lits. (Eng., Scottish, It., Catalan, Chinese, Estonian, Swedish, Australian, Hungarian, and others) are frequently published, with trans. of poetry.

With its concision and suitability for ling. experiment, Esperanto poetry has developed faster than the novel or drama, though in recent years many original novels have appeared. Esperanto's lexicon has expanded: Zamenhof's initial vocabulary comprised fewer than 1000 roots, from which perhaps 10,000 words could be formed. The largest contemp. dicts. now contain 20 times that number. The lexicon remains largely Eur., but Esperanto grammar and syntax resemble isolating langs., like Chinese, and agglutinative langs., like Swahili and Japanese. The future of Esperanto poetry is promising. Poets such as Zifu and Montagut, Mauro Nervi (b. 1959) of Italy, Krys Ungar (b. 1954) of Britain, Jorge Camacho (b. 1966) of Spain, and Gonçalo Neves (b. 1964) of Brazil live in an era of increased scholarly attention to Esperanto. Esperanto appears to have established itself as a ling. and cultural community with its own critical norms and standards.

■ W. Auld, *The Development of Poetic Language in Esperanto* (1976), and *Enkonduko en la originalan literaturon de Esperanto* (1979); P. Ullman, "Schizoschematic Rhyme in Esperanto," *Papers on Language and Literature* 16 (1980); *Esperanta antologio*, ed. W. Auld (1984); H. Tonkin, "One Hundred Years of Esperanto: A Survey," *Language Problems and Language Planning* 11 (1987); D. Richardson, *Esperanto: Learning and Using the International Language* (1988)—learning the lang.; P. Janton, *Esperanto: Language, Literature, and Community* (1993)—lang., lit., and community; H. Tonkin, "The Role of Literary Language in Esperanto," *Planned Languages,* ed. K. Schubert; J. Pleadin, *Ordeno de verda plumo* (2006)—encyclopedia; H. Tonkin, "Recent Studies in Esperanto and Interlinguistics," *Language Problems and Language Planning* 31 (2006); G. Sutton, *Concise Encyclopedia of the Original Literature of Esperanto* (2008).

H. Tonkin

ESTONIA, POETRY OF. The Estonian lang., like Finnish, has the word accent on the first syllable, is highly inflected, and tends toward polysyllabism. Its relatively small number of initial consonants favors alliteration, which, however, is unobtrusive because of the unemphatic articulation. Oral folk poetry, recorded in hundreds of thousands of texts, features an octosyllabic, trochaic meter that is shared with the other Balto-Finnic peoples. Alliteration within lines and semantic parallelism between lines are characteristic:

Igav on olla iluta,
hale olla laulemata,
kole käo kukkumata,
raske rõõmuta elada!

(Boring to be without beauty,
sad to be without song,
terrible without a bird's twitter,
hard to live without happiness!)

Written poetry and metrical trads. began with trans. Lutheran hymns; Reiner Brockmann (1609–47) also wrote dedicatory verses in Estonian. The first known example of a poem written by a native Estonian is "Lament about the Destruction of Tartu" (1708) by Käsu Hans. Serfdom and Baltic-Ger. social, economic, and political domination harnessed the intellectual life of the Estonians until the early 19th c. Poets of the Estonian national renaissance drew inspiration from folklore, cl. antiquity, and Finnish and Ger. romantic and preromantic poetry. The first notable poet, the short-lived Kristjan Jaak Peterson (1801–22), wrote inspired Pindarics. F. R. Kreutzwald's epic *Kalevipoeg* (1857–61), based on runic folk ballads and meter, owed much to Elias Lönnrot's Finnish *Kalevala*. The powerful patriotic lyrics of Lydia Koidula (1843–86) developed the romantic *lied* genre. A more intimate poetry emerged later in the century, exemplified in the profoundly personal, tragic symbolism of seemingly simple lyrics by Juhan Liiv (1864–1913). Symbolism in its Western form, intellectually searching, emphasizing individualized, sophisticated style, appears in the verse of the *Noor-Eesti* (Young Estonia) group; its leader Gustav Suits (1883–1956) was torn between high flights of emotion and bitter, satirical skepticism. The quiet, introspective mysticism of Ernst Enno (1875–1934) and the sensitive island landscapes of Villem Grünthal-Ridala (1885–1942) added new wealth of lang., imagery, and versification to a rapidly expanding lit.

Toward the end of the World War I, shortly before the Estonian declaration of independence in 1918, a new group, named after a mythological bird, *Siuru*, inaugurated an era of lyrical exuberance and extreme individualism in both form and content. Its leaders, Marie Under (1883–1980) and Henrik Visnapuu (1889–1951), later abandoned subjectivism for strenuous thought, universal themes, and firmly crystallized form. Under, the greatest master of lyrical intensity, passed through psychological and metaphysical crises culminating in a poetry of extraordinary translucency and human insight, expanded by the eclectic but keenly picturesque aestheticism of Johannes Semper (1892–1970). The deeply rooted native tendency toward symbolism reasserted itself in a disciplined new form among the *Arbujad* (Magicians) group, including Uku Masing (1909–85), Bernard Kangro (1910–94), Heiti Talvik (1904–47), and Betti Alver (1906–89). Keenly aware of the great trad. of Eur. poetry and thought, these poets sought "to enclose in slim stanzas the blind rage of the elements" (Talvik, "Dies irae," part 12 [1934]), imposing the finality of perfect expression on the emotional turbulence of a world heading toward chaos.

After World War II, during Stalinist rule in Estonia, socialist realism was compulsory. Only those who left Estonia could write freely; among them were Under, Kangro, and Suits, succeeded by Kalju Lepik (1920–99), the surrealist Ilmar Laaban (1921–2000), the lyrical dialect poet Raimond Kolk (1924–92), and Ivar Grünthal (1924–96). Ivar Ivask (1927–92), ed. of *Books Abroad*, wrote *Baltic Elegies* in Eng., concluding the rich, tragic hist. of Estonian poetry in exile.

In Soviet Estonia, the Stalinist poetry of Juhan Smuul (1922–71) demonstrated professionally crafted eloquence. Other pre-Soviet poets were persecuted: Talvik died in a Siberian labor camp, his gravesite unknown. Alver refused to cooperate with the Soviets, earning the label of "formalist," which barred publications until the 1960s; she was a moral compass for emerging poets. Debora Vaarandi (1916–2007) broke from her earlier Stalinist praise poetry in 1957, reviving lyrical attention to "simple things." Alver and other Arbujad expelled from the Writers Union in the 1940s were rehabilitated; among them was August Sang (1914–69), whose humane, self-deprecating poetry signaled a "new beginning."

After Stalinism, a revival of poetry was spearheaded by Jaan Kross (1920–2007), writing in an Aesopian style, and by Artur Alliksaar's (1923–66) surrealist-absurdist wordplay. From 1959 to 1961, Ain Kaalep (b. 1926), notable for creating Estonian equivalents of cl. Gr. and Lat. meters, precipitated a public debate over free verse; the poetry of Kross and of Ellen Niit (1928–2016) was also accused of displaying "decadent tendencies." The mid-1960s witnessed existential despair and the mysticism of nature, followed by a return to formal verse, irony, and surrealism in the 1970s. Hando Runnel (b. 1938) confronted the imminent destruction of the Estonian nation through Sovietization. Jaan Kaplinski's (b. 1941) austere, epiphanic free verse opened windows to Buddhism and ecological harmony. Viivi Luik's (b. 1946) mystical nature poetry shifted in the 1970s to express muted rage bordering on despair. The polyphonic lyricism of Paul-Eerik Rummo (b. 1942), the ironical personae employed by actor Jüri Üdi (Juhan Viiding, 1948–95), and the masterfully crafted, reserved love poetry of Doris Kareva (b. 1958) still hold their power. New works by these authors who emerged during the Soviet "thaw" are major cultural events today. In the Soviet period, an explicit distance between poet and lyric first person protected authors from accusations of disloyalty if their works contained subversive ideas; Kaplinski's intensely personal poems reconnected author and works. Poetry's status as semisacred ritual dissolved with the end of censorship in the late 1980s, and metaphorical lang. of tragic intonations gave way to antipoetry or metapoetry, with the occasional comic twist.

Under the Soviets, Runnel's and Rummo's censored poetry circulated in ms.; a more radical underground poetry appeared in the mid-1980s, when Matti Mogući (pseud. of Priidu Beier, b. 1957), produced three volumes of obscene and offensive poems, among them the ironic "Hymn to the KGB." In the 1990s, Sven Kivisildnik's (b. 1963) "politically incorrect" parodies desacralized Rummo and other prophets of the Soviet period. Pronouncing himself a "national poet," he wrote aggressive, sarcastic, and innovative haiku that rails against the market economy and commercialism. The mercilessly honest fs (pseud. of Indrek Mesikapp, b. 1971) continues trads. of social crit., but he is above ground, a recipient of national poetry awards.

In recent decades, a new generation has stretched the limits of physical form, publishing in virtual hypertext, on beer-bottle labels, and even in a deck of playing cards doubling as an anthol. of new poetry. Valdur Mikita's (b. 1970) ironic poems force a reader to interpret pictograms. Poetry has merged with song in punk, rap, slam, and improvised *regilaul* performances; some argue that performers such as Tõnu Trubetsky (b. 1963) belong to pop culture, not poetry. Poets today play with a mixture of langs. and orthographies, melding together high and low style, folk poetry and mod. slang. *Ethnofuturism*, a fluid term invented by Karl Martin Sinijärv (b. 1971), embraces a new current that joins archaic, uniquely Estonian form or content with futuristic content or form. Kauksi Ülle's (b. 1962) poems in Võro, the lang. or dialect of southern Estonia, are emblematic. On the other hand, Margus Konnula (b. 1974) in *Tarczan* (1998) presents the mass-culture, cosmopolitan Tarzan in the national, archaic form of the 19th-c. epic *Kalevipoeg*; neither hero nor form offers a satisfactory frame for Estonian poets gazing into their lit.'s future. The future foundations, however, are clearly intertextual. Hasso Krull's (b. 1964) "Meter and Demeter: An Epic" (2004) experiences in 100 stanzas the destruction of the world by deluge and the creation of the world that follows or precedes, in the myths of many nations and epochs. Its untranslatable medium contains multiple allusions to Estonian literary trad., from *regilaul* to Kaplinski, connected by rhythms, sounds, and grammatical concepts available only in the Estonian lang., at times merging future, present, and past tense:

kui lõpeb vihm
siis on lõppenud kõik
nii lõppenud et ainult vesi on
alguses ikka veel olemas

(When the rain ends
then all has/will have ended
so ended that only water is/will be
remaining in the beginning)

■ **Anthologies**: *An Anthology of Modern Estonian Poetry*, ed. W. K. Matthews (1953); *Kalevipoeg*, ed. J. Kurman (1982); *Contemporary East European Poetry*, ed. E. George (1985); *Ilomaile*, ed. J. Kurrik (1985); *Sõnarine*, ed. K. Muru, 4 v. (1989–95); *Varjatud ilus haigus*, ed. K. Pruul (2000); *Windship with Oars of Light*, ed. D. Kareva (2001), and *Six Estonian Poets in Translations of Ants Oras* (2002); *Anthology of Estonian Traditional Music*, ed. H. Tampere et al. (2003)—field recordings of folk songs with

Eng. trans.; *A Sharp Cut*, ed. H. Krull (2005), http://www.estlit.ee/public/A_Sharp_Cut.pdf. ■ **Criticism and History**: W. F. Kirby, *The Hero of Esthonia*, 2 v. (1895)—on *Kalevipoeg*; W. K. Matthews, "The Estonian Sonnet," *Slavonic and East European Review* 25 (1946–47); E. Nirk, *Estonian Literature* (1987); E. Annus et al., *Eesti kirjanduslugu* (2001); I. Tart, *Eestikeelne luuleraamat 1638–2000* (2002)—statistical poetic analysis of 4,887 books by 933 authors; M. Väljataga, "Vee uputuste vahel," *Eesti Express* (Feb. 9, 2004); A. Annist, *Friedrich Reinhold Kreutzwaldi Kalevipoeg* (2005); *Estonian Literary Magazine*, http://elm.einst.ee; *Looming*—annual poetry surveys in March issue; Estonian Literature Centre, http://www.estlit.ee.

A. Oras; I. Ivask; G. Šmidchens

ETHIOPIA, POETRY OF

I. Folk Poetry
II. Church-Inspired Poetry
III. Modern Poetry

Ethiopian poetry can be divided into three groups: traditional folk songs and poetry; church-inspired poetry; and mod. poetry. After Ethiopia became officially Christian in the early 4th c., it established educational institutions that standardized rules for poetic creation and influenced both traditional and mod. poetry.

I. Folk Poetry. Folk poetry is found in all of Ethiopia's approximately 80 cultural groups and langs., although most of what exists in print is in the national lang., Amharic, and the northern lang. Tigrinnya. Professional singer-poets (*azmarî*) are admired for their ability to compose songs on the spur of the moment, commenting on day-to-day matters. Ballads are rare; short, pithy poems are more common and popular. The most common kinds of folk poetry are the following:

(a) love songs, often expressing nostalgia for a desired girl or woman, such as a lament written by a local governor when he received news that his wife had taken a lover;
(b) dirges, mostly performed in standardized form by professional wailing women, although specific poems about the dead person are often composed by members of the bereaved family;
(c) songs celebrating important historical events. These are plentiful in so-called royal chronicles, which have been written since the 13th c.;
(d) imperial praise songs; sometimes also songs mocking an unpopular emperor, e.g., Téwodros II;
(e) martial songs (*shillela* and *fukkera*), which are performed either by warriors or by hired minstrels and which consist of boasts about heroic deeds;
(f) litigation in poetic form. There was a time when plaintiff and defendant conducted their own cases in court in poetic form, and the one who impressed and pleased the listeners most won the case, irrespective of right or wrong;
(g) occasional verse by professional singers, who compose songs and also sing and play an instrument (mostly the one-stringed violin, *krar*). They often improvise and comment on a situation as it occurs, in some cases composing songs on behalf of competing groups, e.g., of two men who both want the same woman; but political messages may also be passed on in this way, often in cryptic form. The cryptic form in such contexts is usually a vulgarized application of what is called the "wax and gold" (*sem-inna-werq*) method of writing poetry developed in ecclesiastical institutions of learning (see below), based on puns and double meanings. Ambiguity has served the need for secrecy often associated with political power in Ethiopia, where too-open expressions of opinions and sentiments could be risky.

II. Church-Inspired Poetry. *Qiné*, or church-inspired poetry, is both religious and secular, distinguished by form rather than content. It is primarily written in Geez (old Ethiopic) and Amharic. Such poems are named after their forms (depending on the number of syllables in a line and the number of lines in the poem). The originator of this poetic form is commonly believed to be St. Yaréd, who lived in the holy city of Aksum in the 6th c.; but some of the religious poetry beloved in Ethiopia is ascribed to St. Efrem of Edessa, who lived in the 4th c. and translated into Geez. Qiné was further developed in the Amhara culture from the 16th c. or somewhat earlier. Prominent qiné poets include Yohannis Geblawî (15th c.), Tewaney (16th c.), and Kifle-Yohannis (17th c.).

Before Western models of mod. education became common in Ethiopia (primarily during the reign of Emperor Haile Selassie, 1930–74), most Ethiopians who sought an education went to religious institutions called "church" or "priest schools" or to monastic schools for higher learning, where they could learn to appreciate and create qiné. A prominent feature of this poetry is the use of "wax and gold." Its basis is the Monophysite conception of Christ professed by the Ethiopian national church. In this belief, Christ was God and man, but his manhood was only a shell that hid his real, divine essence. The poetry framed on this model is not only ambiguous but also contains a superficial meaning (the wax) that "hides" the genuine message (the gold). The rules of this poetry are complicated and take years to master. Main centers for teaching this type of poetry are found in the provinces of Gojjam (at Gonj, Weshira, and Méch'a), Begémdir (at Ch'ereqa in Dawint, and in the town of Gonder), Wello (at Tabor in Sayint), and Lasta (at Abdîqom in Wadla). The main forms of qiné have names according to how many syllables there are in a line (e.g., Gubaé Qana, 4+4; Ze-Amlakîyyé, 4+4+4; Wazéma, 6+4+4+3+3; Meweddis, 9+4+5+3+3, etc.; there are 13 main forms). There are two different main styles of qiné, taught in the schools of Gonj and Wadla, respectively.

Religious poetry is found, e.g., in parts of the *Diggwa*, which contains songs for Lent, ascribed to St. Yaréd; *Zimmaré*, sung after Mass; *Mewasît*, which are prayers for the dead; *Qiddasé*, sung during Mass but containing also the Hourly Prayers, the Horologium (*satat/seatat*); *Selamta*, songs of praise to God and homage to saints. There is no congregational singing in this church, and the songs/hymns are mostly performed by church-educated but unordained persons known as *debtera*; but there are also occasions (mainly on public religious holidays) when priests perform songs accompanied by drums and sistra, and the rhythm is beaten with prayer-staffs, while the priests dance on the pattern of OT Levites.

St. Yaréd is believed to have both composed hymns and set them to music. The Ethiopian church is conservative and has preserved old songs with little innovation in its liturgies or anaphoras (of which the church has 14); but new poetry is constantly being made in other contexts. Here the secular use of the poetic styles developed in monastic institutions is marked. A well-known name among church-trained people who used the "wax and gold" model both for serious poetry and in other contexts was *Aleqa* (scholar) Gebre-Hanna Gebre-Mariyam, who was in the service of several emperors in the 19th c. Many of Ethiopia's foremost mod. poets have also been exposed to this kind of poetry and use it (sometimes somewhat freely) in their modernized poetry.

III. Modern Poetry. Ethiopia was only marginally influenced by the colonial movement and, thus, has kept much more of its traditional culture than the rest of Africa. Mod. Ethiopian poetry has received significant influences from outside, esp. the West and mostly from poetry written in Eng. but also to some extent Fr. and It. However, even the most Westernized poets have retained strong traditional elements, not least as this was passed on by church institutions. Among the foremost mod. poets is Kebbede Mikaél (1914–98), whose first foreign lang. was Fr. and who did not attend Ethiopian church schools. He wrote nationalistic poems (and may be regarded as a forerunner of Negritude poetry) in opposition to the It. invasion and occupation of Ethiopia (1935–41). Mengistu Lemma (1928–88) was educated in both church and mod. schools and became an advocate of the socialist revolution of 1974. He has more humor in his poems than is common in Ethiopian writers. One of the foremost mod. poets, more experimental and more influenced by foreign models than those mentioned above, was S'eggayé (Tseggaye) Gebre-Medhin (1936–2006). Because he coined new Amharic words based on old Ethiopic as well as Eng. roots or ideas, his poetry is often considered difficult but of a high artistic order. Debbebe Seyfu (1950–2000), often inspired by visions of a more prosperous Ethiopia, also often played on words in keeping with the "wax and gold" device. A poet of a lighter kind was Afeqerq Yohannîs (1927–80), whose poems were much read and sung by Ethiopia's most popular singers. Almost all poets, and writers generally, in Ethiopia are men, but a few women authors are coming up, incl. the pioneer Siniddu Gebru (1916–2009), though she published only one book of poetry.

Poetry is popular in Ethiopia, and many try their hands at it, often in praise of the ruler or prevailing ideologies. Western churches have put down roots in Ethiopia and introduced congregational singing. The quality often shows more enthusiasm than talent, but dedicated and capable poets are not lacking, even with limited opportunities to express rebellious ideas. Ethiopian poetry is usually idealistic, expressing hope for the country and encouraging fellow Ethiopians to promote the best interests of their native land. Poets of note in more recent years include Aseffa Gebre-Mariyam Tesemma (b. 1935), the author of the national anthem, and Aberra Lemma (b. 1953).

■ E. Littmann, *Die altamharischen Kaiserlieder* (1914); Hiruy Welde-Sillasé, *Mis'hafe qiné* (1926), and *Iné-nna wedajocché* (1935); Mahteme-Sillasé Welde-Mesqel, *Amarinnya qiné* (1955); M. Kamil, *Amharische Kaiserlieder* (1957); Haddis Alemayyehu, *Fiqr iske meqabir* (1965); Habte-Mariyam Werqineh, *T'intawî ye-Îtyopiya timhirt* (1970); R. K. Molvaer, *Tradition and Change in Ethiopia: Social and Cultural Life as Reflected in Amharic Fictional Literature ca. 1930–1974* (1980); Mengistu Lemma, *Yegi'iz qinéyat, yenne t'ibeb qirs* (1987); Gebre-Igziabiher Elyas and R. K. Molvaer, *Prowess, Piety and Politics: The Chronicle of Abeto Iyasu and Empress Zewditu of Ethiopia (1909–1930)* (1994); R. K. Molvaer, *Socialization and Social Control in Ethiopia* (1995); "About the Abortive Coup Attempt in Addis Abeba from 5 Tahsas to 8 Tahsas 1953 (14–17 December 1960)," *Northeast African Studies* 3 (1996); *Black Lions: The Creative Lives of Modern Ethiopia's Literary Giants and Pioneers* (1997); and "Siniddu Gebru: Pioneer Woman Writer, Feminist, Patriot, Educator, and Politician," *Northeast African Studies* 4 (1997); Ayele Bekerie, *Ethiopic: An African Writing System: Its History and Principles* (1997); R. K. Molvaer, "The Achievement of Emperor Téwodros II of Ethiopia (1855–1868): From an Unpublished Manuscript by *Aleqa* Tekle-Îyesus ('*Aleqa* Tekle') of Gojjam," *Northeast African Studies* 3 (1998); "Afewerq Yohannis and Debbebe Seyfu: Notes on Ethiopian Writers of the Late Twentieth Century," *Northeast African Studies* 6 (1999); and "Some Ethiopian Historical Poems," *Aethiopica* 9 (2006).

R. K. Molvaer

F

FINLAND, POETRY OF

I. The Beginnings
II. The Rise of Finnish Poetic Language
III. The Modern Period

Finnish poetry has developed over a long hist., though the oldest extant texts written in Finnish date only from the early 19th c. and though some of its classics were initially written in Swedish. It presents a complex hist. of cultural and literary influences, but thematically and taken as a whole, it shows a remarkably unified inspiration from early oral trad. to contemp. modernism. The Finnish lang. belongs to the non-IE, Finno-Ugrian group of langs. like Hungarian and Estonian. Finnish poetry has developed at the periphery of the IE family of langs. but has had close cultural contacts with the major movements of Eur. civilization.

I. The Beginnings. A rich treasury of traditional oral songs and tales, representing both the lyric and the epic genres, is extant, incl. about 1,270,000 lines and 85,000 variants of the poetry composed in the so-called Kalevala meter (trochaic tetrameter in its simplest form). These works are traditionally that of anonymous singers, men and women, but some of the principal singers are known by name, such as Arhippa Perttunen and Ontrei Malinen, both of whom were important sources for Elias Lönnrot's compilations, the epic *Kalevala* (1835, 1849), and the *Kanteletar*, a collection of lyrics and short narrative poems (1840–41). Finnish folk poetry consists of elements dating from different periods and deriving from various cultural strata. There is evidence of the existence of a vital oral poetry before the Swedish cultural and political expansion during the 12th c. that brought Christianity via Sweden to Finland. Finno-Ugric mythology, based on animistic and shamanistic religion, is an intrinsic part of the early cosmogonic poems, magic songs, and ritual incantations of this trad. Med. Christianity introduced new elements to Finnish folk poetry. Ballads, legends, and laments expressed both religious and secular themes, and poems sung at weddings or at burials reflected their function for the life of the community. In an exquisite cycle about the birth of Christ, a Finnish maiden, Marjatta, a variant of the Virgin Mary, becomes pregnant by eating cranberries (Finnish *marja*). The religious basis of these poems, which were composed by individual singers according to their poetic skill, derives from a fusion of native rituals, Catholic, and Gr. Orthodox beliefs.

While oral poetry survived in the agrarian parts mostly of eastern Finland, its importance decreased as other attempts were made to forge the Finnish lang. into a literary medium. Most important of these is Mikael Agricola's (1510?–57) trans. of the NT (1548), a decisive ling. landmark, as well as one of the first literary monuments of the Protestant era. At the end of the 17th c., Lat. and Swedish-lang. poems were composed, but the verse remained conventional and derivative, with the exception of a few names such as Juhana Cajanus (1655–81) and Jakob Frese (1691–1729). It was not until the rediscovery of the oral trads. in the 18th c., inaugurated by the study of Finnish folk poetry such as Henrik Gabriel Porthan's (1739–1804) *De poesi fennica* (1766–78), that Finnish-lang. poetry began to emerge from obscurity. The realization that the Finnish people had created poetry worthy of comparison with the *Iliad* and the *Odyssey* had an enormous impact in Finland. The lines by Arhippa Perttunen illustrate the proud self-assertion of a native poet:

> My own finding are my words
> my own snatching from the road.
>
> (*Finnish Folk Poetry*, trans. K. Bosley)

II. The Rise of Finnish Poetic Language. While Swedish-lang. poetry of Eur. orientation dominated literary production in Finland, examples of early Finnish-lang. poetry belong to the didactic and exhortatory trad. of the Enlightenment. The termination of Swedish rule in 1809 brought about an altogether new situation. A few Swedish-lang. poets, such as Frans Michael Franzén (1772–1847), whose poetry expressed a strong preromantic conception of nature and of humanity as divine creation, were also influential in the devel. of Finnish poetry. As the Napoleonic wars resulted in a redistribution of the northern territories of Europe, Finland fell under Rus. rule as a virtually autonomous

Grand Duchy in 1809. This situation compelled the Finns, incl. the Swedish Finns, to turn their philosophical and literary attention to questions of Finnish national identity. It was an original moment in Finnish lit. hist. Helsinki became the center of Finnish cultural and literary life. The university was moved there from Turku in 1827, the Finnish Literary Society was founded in 1831, and the newspaper *Helsingfors Tidningar* (Helsinki News) began to appear in 1829. J. L. Runeberg (1804–77) became the foremost Swedish-lang. poet of that time with his *Dikter* (Poems, 1830). Combining a deep feeling for simple country folk with expert knowledge of both cl. lit. and Finnish oral trad., Runeberg renewed lyrical lang. with his mastery of technique. His epic poems in hexameters, e.g., the *Elgskyttarne* (Elkhunters, 1832), a narrative about love and hunting, demonstrate how cl. style can be effectively used to describe humble country life. His romanticism, both lyrical and patriotic, may be seen as an important precursor of the Finnish-lang. poetry that emerged in the 1860s.

Runeberg, the philosopher and writer J. V. Snellman (1806–81), Lönnrot (1802–84), and the writer and poet Zachris Topelius (1818–98) all shaped the Finnish national consciousness and cultural identity, but the conditions were not yet ripe for the production of Finnish poetry of merit. Lönnrot showed some genuine poetic talent in assembling the epic *Kalevala* by introducing lyric material into the narratives, adding songs, and replacing missing lines according to his vision. But the preeminent figure at the time was Aleksis Kivi (pseud. of Alexis Stenvall, 1834–72), primarily a playwright and novelist whose poetic achievement was not fully recognized until the 20th c. Kivi's contemporaries considered his poetry unfinished: it was more daring and personal than anything written at the time. Many of his poems were lyrical narratives that broke away from rhyming verse and used free rhythms, creating an intensity familiar from the folk lyric. From the mod. perspective, Kivi is recognized as one of the greatest Finnish poets.

After Kivi, there were no major poets until the end of the 19th c., though Kaarlo Kramsu (1855–95) and J. H. Erkko (1849–1906) played important roles in forging Finnish poetic lang. that could effectively express new social and historical themes. Industrialization, educational reforms, and new scientific thought were reflected in the work of Finnish novelists and dramatists, who explored the forms of Eur. realism in the 1880s. Swedish-lang. poetry was mainly represented by J. J. Wecksell (1838–1907) and Karl August Tavaststjerna (1860–98), who reflects the new sense of alienation felt by the Swedish-speaking writers.

National neoromanticism was the term coined by the poet Eino Leino (1878–1926) to characterize certain currents in Finnish lit. and in the fine arts influenced by Eur. symbolism. It combined enthusiasm, determination, and outstanding talent in all fields: the composer Jean Sibelius, the painter Akseli Gallen-Kallela, and the architect Eliel Saarinen were all representatives of Young Finland. A prolific poet, Leino developed an innovative technique that radically changed the Finnish poetic idiom. Leino put the stamp of originality on everything he wrote. While drawing on traditional sources such as myth and folk poetry for themes and motifs, he was fully versed in Eur. and Scandinavian lit., and translated Dante, Pierre Corneille, Jean Racine, J. W. Goethe, and Friedrich Schiller. His *Helkavirsiä* (Whitsongs, 1903, 1916) recreate the most ancient folk trads. in narrative lyrics of visionary character having a symbolic resonance that transcends the national sphere. Leino's lyrical lang. is supple and resourceful: in "Nocturne" (from *Talvi-yö* [Winter Night], 1905), the melodious lines evoke the infinite in a clearly defined space:

> The corncrake's song rings in my ears,
> above the rye a full moon sails; . . .
>
> (trans. K. Bosley)

The inner dynamics of Leino's poetry spring from a fruitful tension between an ultraindividualistic, egocentric, amoral hero and a prophet-seer who could capture and articulate the complex spirit of his epoch.

Several of his contemporaries added other elements to the vigorously developing Finnish poetic lang. Leino's companion L. Onerva (1882–1972) provided a free spirit to explorations of femininity in sensual lyric verse, while Otto Manninen (1872–1950) and V. A. Koskenniemi (1885–1962) wrote in the Eur. classic mode. Manninen, a virtuoso poet, wrote clear, concise verse on symbolist themes and translated Homer, Gr. tragedy, and Molière. Koskenniemi expressed his pessimistic philosophy in tightly controlled verse inspired by ancient poetry. With Finland's independence in 1917, poetry reconfirmed its central role in the expression of both individual and social sentiments. And by 1920, Finnish poetic lang. had attained a variety and depth that guaranteed it a worthy place among Eur. lits.

III. The Modern Period. While Leino has a strikingly mod. timbre at times, modernism appeared in Finnish poetry only after World War I. This was in the unique work of the Finnish modernists writing in Swedish, such as Edith Södergran (1892–1923) and Elmer Diktonius (1896–1961). Literary modernism coincided with antipositivism in philosophy and was a reaction against 19th-c. empiricism and realism. In the 1920s, Eur. movements such as futurism, cubism, constructivism, expressionism, and surrealism arrived in Finnish art and poetry almost simultaneously. Denying the ability of art to describe reality, the new poets increasingly turned away from mimetic art, even as they rejected the past and everything connected with it. This was first seen in lang. experiments, e.g., in *Jääpeili* (Ice Mirror, 1928) by Aaro Hellaakoski (1893–1952), in the poetry of Katri Vala (1901–44), in the prose of Olavi Paavolainen (1903–64), and in the early work of P. Mustapää (1899–1973). The new generation that brought modernism to Finland formed a group called the Firebearers, publishing albums and a jour. of that name, *Tulenkantajat*. The Firebearers issued a manifesto in 1928, declaring the sacredness of art and life in tones reminiscent of the writings of the Finland-Swedish modernists, but with an even greater fervor and passion. Vala and Uuno Kailas (1901–33) expressed these ideals, and by this time, all important literary movements had arrived in Finnish poetry. Another literary group, *Kiila* (The Wedge), devoted itself to radical socialism after 1936. Arvo Turtiainen (1904–80) and the novelist Elvi Sinervo (1912–86) were among its most important members, many of whom were imprisoned during World War II. The nation, divided by the Civil War (1918–19) following Finnish independence, unified again for the effort of the Winter War, but the schism was not closed until the postwar era, as is described by Väinö Linna (1920–92) in his epic trilogy *Täällä Pohjantähden alla* (Here under the North Star, 1959–62).

In the 1950s, poetic modernism in Finland turned antitraditionalist, dissociating itself from ordinary lang. While drawing inspiration from East and West, America and the Far East, its lang. became more hermetic. Paavo Haavikko (1931–2008), Eeva-Liisa Manner (1921–95), Helvi Juvonen (1919–59), and Marja-Liisa Vartio (1924–66) were among the most important poets, followed by other original talents such as Mirkka Rekola (1931–2014), Tyyne Saastamoinen (1924–1998), Lassi Nummi (1928–2012), and Pentti Holappa (b. 1927). Pentti Saarikoski (1937–83), whose first collection, *Runoja* (Poems), appeared in 1958, is not tied to any movement or decade. Saarikoski, a maverick genius and iconoclast, was one of the most learned of mod. Finnish poets, as well as a translator of Homer, Euripides, James Joyce, and others. With his *Mitä tapahtuu todella?* (What Is Going On, Really?, 1962) Finnish poetic lang. was taken to a new level where everything had to start from point zero in order to go on: the split word, the word mobile, the collage, and the explicit rejection of poetic structure all conveyed a sense of both freedom and despair. Saarikoski's work culminated in a long, free-floating philosophical poem *Hämärän tanssit* (*The Dances of the Obscure*, 1983), written during the period when the poet lived in Sweden. It expresses the poet's yearning for beauty and the unification of all living things.

Rekola, Haavikko, and Manner, in their different ways, have been regarded as the leading Finnish modernists. Haavikko uses compelling rhythmic sequences and incantations to express, through a series of negatives, abstractions, and ironies, his skepticism about the relationship of lang. to the external world. It is an original vision, and in 1984, Haavikko received the Neustadt Prize for his achievement. Rekola, who was a candidate for the Neustadt Prize in 2000, studies lang. and perception in a universal trad. Manner has explored the conflict between magical order and logical disorder, as she calls it, and has brought to Finnish poetry, since her breakthrough collection *Tämä matka* (This Journey, 1956) a mythical dimension, a lang. suggestive of another reality.

Finnish poetry in recent times and since Finland's entry in the European Union in 1994 shows an unprecedented diversity; all directions seem possible. As the motto of the Firebearers once indicated, Finnish poetry has become receptive to world literary currents. Among the poets writing in contemp. Finland are Sirkka Turkka (b. 1939), Kari Aronpuro (b. 1940), Pentti Saaritsa (b. 1941), Kirsti Simonsuuri (b. 1945), Caj Westerberg (b. 1946), and Arja Tiainen (b. 1947). Saaritsa, Westerberg, and Simonsuuri are also major translators of world poetry into Finnish. The new generation is represented by Olli Heikkonen (b. 1965),

Sanna Karlström (b. 1975), Teemu Manninen (b. 1977), Katariina Vuorinen (b. 1976), and numerous other poets born in the 1980s, and there is a new intellectual current in Finnish lit. Both poetry and prose continue occupying an important place in contemp. cultural life. Finnish-Swedish modernists like Bo Carpelan (1926–2011) and Solveig von Schoulz (1907–95) have carried on the earlier modernist trad. while adding new elements. In the present day, one is justified in speaking of Finnish poetry as including all verse written by Finns, whether in Swedish or in Finnish, and whether in or outside Finland.

See SWEDEN, POETRY OF

■ **Anthologies and Translations:** *Moderne Finnische Lyrik*, ed. and trans. M. P. Hein (1962); *Suomen kirjallisuuden antologia I–VIII*, ed. K. Laitinen and M. Suurpää (1963–75); P. Haavikko, *Selected Poems*, trans. A. Hollo (1974); *Finnish Folk Poetry: Epic*, ed. and trans. M. Kuusi et al., trans. K. Bosley (1977); E. Leino, *Whitsongs*, trans. K. Bosley (1978); *Snow in May*, ed. R. Dauenhauer and P. Binham (1978); *Territorial Song: Finnish Poetry and Prose*, trans. H. Lomas (1981); P. Saarikoski, *Selected Poems*, trans. A. Hollo (1983); *Salt of Pleasure: 20th-Century Finnish Poetry*, ed. and trans. A. Jarvenpa and K. B. Vähämäki (1983); E. Södergran, *Complete Poems*, trans. D. McDuff (1983); P. Saarikoski, *Love and Solitude*, trans. S. Katchadourian (1985); *Modern finlandssvensk Lyrik*, ed. C. Andersson and B. Carpelan (1986); B. Carpelan, *Room without Walls: Selected Poems*, trans. A. Born (1987); P. Saarikoski, *Dances of the Obscure*, trans. M. Cole and K. Kimball (1987); *Ice around Our Lips:. Finland-Swedish Poetry*, ed. and trans. D. McDuff (1989); *The Kalevala*, trans. K. Bosley (1989); *Poésie et prose de Finlande*, ed. M. Bargum (1989); *Enchanting Beasts: An Anthology of Modern Women Poets in Finland*, ed. and trans. K. Simonsuuri (1990); *Contemporary Finnish Poetry*, ed. and trans. H. Lomas (1991).

■ **Criticism and History:** E. Enäjärvi-Haavio, "On the Performance of Finnish Folk Runes," *Folkliv* (1951); J. Ahokas, *History of Finnish Literature* (1974); *Modern Nordic Plays: Finland*, ed. E. J. Friis (1974); T. Wretö, *Johan Ludvig Runeberg* (1980); *The Two Literatures of Finland*, spec. iss. of *World Literature Today* 54 (1980); M. Kuusi and L. Honko, *Sejd och Saga* (1983); T. Warburton, *Åttio år finlandssvensk litteratur* (1984); G. Schoolfield, *Edith Södergran* (1984); K. Simonsuuri, "The Lyrical Space: the Poetry of Paavo Haavikko," *World Literature Today* 58 (1984); *Europe: Littérature de Finlande* (June–July 1985); K. Laitinen, *Literature of Finland: An Outline* (1985); P. Leino, *Language and Metre: Metrics and the Metrical System of Finland*, trans. A. Chesterman (1986); K. Laitinen, *Finlands Litteratur* (1988); *A History of Finnish Literature*, ed. G. C. Schoolfield (1998); "Finnish and Finland-Swedish," *The Oxford Guide to Literature in English Translation*, ed. P. France (2000).

K. K. Simonsuuri

FLEMISH POETRY. *See* LOW COUNTRIES, POETRY OF THE

FRANCE, POETRY OF

I. Medieval to Early Modern
II. Early Modern to 20th Century

I. Medieval to Early Modern. To assume that *poetry* is a self-evident term, that it denotes, in Charles Baudelaire's expression, "rhythm and rhyme," or that it has inhabited since antiquity three well-defined categories—epic, dramatic, lyric—is to overestimate the transparency of these terms. Such categories are useful (e.g., scholars routinely speak about "lyric" and "epic" poetry in the Middle Ages) but even when they are applicable, these terms are unstable in meaning. The word *poète* (poet), e.g., comes into use in the 13th-c. *Roman de la Rose*, where it means "Latin poet" or "poet whom one glosses." In the 14th c., it comes to be used of vernacular poets, often with the primary sense of "allegorist." The words *poésie* or occasionally, as in the early 15th-c. poetic theorist Jacques Legrand, *poetrie* (in the etymological sense of "making" and even "feigning") also appear in the 14th c., although vernacular treatises of versification will not become *arts poétiques* until the middle of the 16th c. Indeed, *poésie* is not an esp. common term for vernacular verse in Fr. until the early mod. period.

While the earliest texts in Fr. date from the 9th c., there is almost nothing written in prose before the early 13th c. that would commonly be called "literary." In the Middle Ages, writing in verse is assimilated both to rhet. (part of the trivium of arts) and to music (part of the quadrivium of mathematical disciplines). Eustache Deschamps (ca. 1346–1407) commemorated ca. 1377 the great 14th-c. poet and composer Guillaume de Machaut in these terms: "the death of Machaut, the noble Rhetorician." In a treatise on versification, *L'Art de dictier* (1392), Deschamps defined verse as a kind of "natural music." The distinction between *verse* and *prose* was operative in the med. period. The It. scholar Brunetto Latini distinguished between these two "manners of speaking" in his 13th-c. *Li Livres dou Tresor* (ca. 1264), and the distinction had already given rise to much debate in the early 13th c.: verse had come to be seen as inherently mendacious, and many verse narrative works were translated into prose. The term *seconde rhétorique* (second rhetoric) to distinguish verse from prose, common in the 15th c., appears first in Occitan, in the *Leys d'amors* (1356) often attributed to Guilhem Molinier, probably under the influence of the verse-prose distinction found in Brunetto. Yet "rhythm and rhyme" do not always make "poetry" in the early periods. E.g., after Aristotle's *Poetics* had been rediscovered and disseminated in the Lat. West in the 16th c., much effort was expended to determine which kinds of verse qualified for the title of *poetry* by virtue of being mimetic, i.e., of following Aristotle's idea that poetry required the imitation of reality.

The tripartite division of poetic genres that mod. readers often assume to be of cl. origin—epic, dramatic, lyric—owes more to the 19th c. (esp. G.W.F. Hegel's *Aesthetics*) than to antiquity. The triad does not appear in this form in Aristotle or Horace, in the Middle Ages or the early mod. period (though Antonio Minturno [ca. 1500–74] makes what seems a similar distinction in his *De poeta* of 1559). The word *lyrique* (lyric), often applied to a large part of the med. poetic corpus, does not appear in Fr. until the early 15th c. (as a calque for the Lat. *lyrica*, in a discussion of Horace). It denotes "lyric" poetry in the vernacular only from the 1490s and remains rare enough in the mid-16th c. for the young Joachim du Bellay to be mocked in print for using it as late as 1550. The mod. sense of lyric as personal verse becomes current in the 18th c. Similarly, *épopée* (epic) and *roman* (romance)—the latter being the more common term until the late Ren.—are not clearly distinguished either in the Middle Ages or the 16th c. (the prominent humanist poet Pierre de Ronsard called Homer's *Iliad* a "roman"). Although verse theater in Fr. certainly existed from very early times, the term *dramatic* seems to have appeared in the late 14th c. to denote verse compositions in which the several persons represented were clearly distinguished from an authorial persona. Thus, the problem of classification is a stubborn one. Familiar terminology may be useful but cannot be taken for granted.

A. ***The Middle Ages.*** A salient distinction in med. and Ren. poetics is between poetry written in rhyming couplets (*rime plate*) and that written in other schemes. The former tends to appear in longer narrative (e.g., romance) or narrative-didactic poetry (e.g., the *Roman de la Rose*) and in theater, while the latter in poetry on other topics, e.g., in amatory poetry. This distinction is not airtight: many stanzaic forms are lengthy and contain narrative and indeed "dramatic" elements (e.g., the dialogue poems, or *joc-partits*, of which there are a number of examples in Occitan and in early Fr. poetry). Moreover, *chansons de geste* are not generally written in rime plate but instead in assonant or monorhyme stanzas. Short, fixed forms are also interspersed into longer narrative works in rime plate and even with prose, notably from the 14th-c. Guillaume de Machaut (ca. 1300–77) but also in the anonymous, probably 13th-c. prosimetrum *Aucassin et Nicolette*.

The verse produced between ca. 1100 and 1470 in what is now France was written in two dialect groups, broadly speaking: OF, spoken in northern France (the *langue d'oïl*), and Occitan (what used to be called Provençal, the *langue d'oc*). A greater proportion of the narrative poetry we possess is in northern Fr. dialects, although there is a considerable corpus in both langs.

We have several hagiographic narrative poems in OF from before the turn of the millennium: the "Séquence de Sainte Eulalie," probably written at the end of the 9th c., about 50 years after the Strasburg Oaths of 842 (the first recorded text in OF and OHG), and the 10th-c. *Vie de Saint Léger*, in octosyllables. Another early saint's life is the 11th-c. *Vie de Saint Alexis*, in assonant decasyllables. Later important saints' lives include an account of St. Mary the Egyptian by the late 13th-c. poet Rutebeuf, in octosyllabic couplets.

The chansons de geste or "songs of great deeds" are patriotic accounts of aristocratic and royal valor, incl. in later cases stories of the crusades. The *Chanson de Roland* (early 12th c.), preserved in a ms. in the Bodleian Library in Oxford, recounts an episode in Charlemagne's war against the Moors in Spain. This is the earliest remaining long narrative poem in Fr. The form of the *Chanson de Roland* is a series of assonant stanzas or *laisses* of unequal length, imbricating the material from one to the next. While this version, apparently not widely disseminated, survives only in the Oxford ms., the story was adapted in the 12th c. in rhyming verse. Other chansons de geste include the royal cycle, the cycles of Guillaume d'Orange and Doon de Mayence, and two cycles narrating the exploits of the crusades.

At most, two extant chansons de geste (the Oxford *Roland* and the *Chanson de Guillaume*) predate the earliest romances we possess. Most of the production of chansons de geste is contemporaneous with that of verse romance, although it continues for longer, verse romance giving way to prose romance before chansons de geste become unrhymed. Romance differs from chanson de geste in subject matter: chanson de geste is generally concerned with the matter of France, romance with the matter of Britain—in particular the stories of the Arthurian court, the Round Table, and the Grail—and the matter of Rome, consisting of adaptations of Lat. lit. such as Virgil's *Aeneid*. The trad. of verse historiography, e.g., the 12th-c. Wace, a court poet to the Eng. Henry II, or Gaimar's account of the battle of Hastings, which is the earliest surviving text in octosyllabic rhyming couplets, is important to the devel. of verse romance, where octosyllabic rime plate comes to predominate, although other verse forms occasionally appear, such as the 12-syllable line of the *Roman d'Alexandre*, from which the alexandrine gets its name. Chrétien de Troyes's five verse romances of the later 12th c., incl. *Lancelot*, *Erec et Enide*, and the unfinished but much continued *Li Contes del Graal*, are sophisticated examples of the "romance" genre, voluminously imitated in other Eur. langs., notably Ger., in both verse and prose. The form of the romance gave birth to perhaps the most influential long narrative poem in med. Fr.: the *Roman de la Rose*, the work of Guillaume de Lorris (ca. 1205–40) and Jean de Meun (ca. 1240–1305). Guillaume's 4,056-line version, written ca. 1230, inspired a continuation more than four times longer. Guillaume's poem is an allegory in which a young man of 20 enters a mysterious walled garden and falls in love with a rose he espies while looking into the fountain of Narcissus. Jean de Meun's continuation (ca. 1270–80) marshals a number of personified philosophical and ethical concepts (e.g., Dangier, Faulx Semblant) in a poem of initiation and encyclopedic knowledge liberally spiced with misogyny. The *Rose* was enormously popular; Chaucer translated part of it into Eng. The *Rose* informs much of the allegorical practice of the 14th and 15th cs., and the poem was widely read as late as the 16th c. (an adaptation, often attributed to the Ren. poet Clément Marot, was published in 1526). The long *dits amoureux* of Guillaume de Machaut, often interspersed with short lyric pieces set to music of his own composition—e.g., his *Remède de Fortune* and *Voir dit*—breathe the same Ovidian atmosphere as the *Rose*, a poem that they imitate, transform, and critique.

Smaller-scale narrative forms include, in addition to saints' lives, e.g., the shorter narrative lays attributed to a 12th-c. Anglo-Norman poet who identifies herself as "Marie" from "France" (and whom the trad. has styled Marie de France [ca. 1135–1200]) as well as numerous fabliaux (short, often bawdy stories of the sort that inspired Boccaccio's *Decameron* and Chaucer's *Canterbury Tales*). The humor and irony of the fabliau blossoms in *Le Roman de Renart*, a long satirical animal epic written in several parts or "branches," probably by several poets of the 12th and 13th cs.

Short poems, often in stanzaic, sometimes heterometric fixed forms, not usually written in rhyming couplets, are conventionally considered "lyric" forms. Many of these were sung, or at least written in forms with musical conventions such as the later med. rondeau and ballade. The Occitan trad. is the earlier one, its influence waning after the Albigensian crusades of the early 13th c. *Occitan poetry, long somewhat neglected by Fr. scholars constructing a homogeneous national trad., despite its centrality to the devel. of OF "lyric," has been claimed by It. and Catalan scholars for their own literary hists. (see Burgwinkle et al.). Dante and Petrarch admired and imitated the poetry of, e.g., the 12th-c. troubadour Arnaut Daniel.

No doubt the corpus of Occitan poetry is one of the most sophisticated, influential, and intellectually ambitious poetic trads. in Eur. lit. hist. Occitan poets are troubadours or "finders" of both words and music: the production of troubadour poetry seems to have spanned the social classes from the most elevated aristocrats to indigent traveling musicians. Many of the aspects of lyric poetry that contemp. readers might take, mistakenly, as mod.—self-reference and metatextual play, the blurring of the borders between the fiction of love and the artifice of poetry, the trenchant analysis of the circulation of desire—are already present in the earliest troubadour lyrics. The works of Guilhem IX, Duke of Aquitaine, such as his "Farai un vers de dreyt nien" (I will make a poem from entirely nothing; ca. 1100), have appealed to postromantic readers, who see there a reflection of their own concerns or a premonition of Stéphane Mallarmé's poetics of negation and ling. self-containment. The terrifying, cruel distance of the object of desire, the *domna*, reduced to a ling. sign or *senhal*, has inspired the psychoanalyst Jacques Lacan and, through him, readers with psychological and philosophical interests. The knotty verse of Marcabru (associated with what is called the *trobar clus* or closed style), has particularly spoken to recent readers (see the ed. [2000] by Simon Gaunt, Ruth Harvey, and Linda Paterson), although the more accessible *trobar leu*, e.g., the poetry of Bernart de Ventadorn, is also much read. Jaufré Rudel, who sang of the *amor de lonh*, or "love from afar," is perhaps the best known of the troubadours today. There is also a considerable body of troubadour lyric written by (or attributed to) women, known as *trobaritz*, of whom the 12th-c. Comtessa de Dia is now perhaps most read. Unfortunately, a great number of the names of the trobaritz have disappeared. Still, ms. culture stressed the production of a poetic persona whose life was supposedly reflected in the poetry and tended to situate troubadours and trobaritz in a brief biographical fiction called a *vida*.

Many of the early lyric songs in the langue d'oïl, OF, are anonymous *chansons de toile, reverdies, chansons d'aube*, or *pastourelles*, dating from the 12th and 13th cs. The *trouvères*, counterparts in northern France to the troubadours, took up many of the techniques and themes of troubadour poetry; these include the 13th-c. King of Navarre, Thibaut de Champagne (1201–53), a direct descendant of Guilhem IX and the great-grandson of Eleanor of Aquitaine, who wrote in Fr. (and was quoted by Dante). As was the case for the troubadours, many of the trouvères were aristocratic, although 13th-c. poets such as Rutebeuf, Gilbert de Berneville, and Adam de la Halle were commoners; the last two are associated with the flowering of Fr. poetry in the northern city of Arras, whereas Rutebeuf was Parisian.

It was esp. in the north of France that the musical trad. of med. poetry would develop in notable ways. With the refinements in mensural notation and consequently in polyphony in the 13th and 14th cs., such forms as the polytextual motet—a type of layered song counterposing several poetic texts—flourished. Adam de la Halle (ca. 1250–1306) cultivated the genre of the motet, which came to a very high level of sophistication in the works of the 14th-c. Guillaume de Machaut. Such songs, fusing Christian and cl. topoi, demand a complex process of reception. Since the texts, sung simultaneously, are not easily intelligible, interpretation depends as much on written texts (Machaut took great care in the presentation of his mss.) as on performance and requires, in particular, accounting for the text of the fragment of plainchant on which they were constructed. E.g., one of Machaut's motets, built on a fragment of chant, the "tenor," recounting David's grief on the death of Absalom (the text is *ego moriar pro te*, "I will/would die for you"), collates two Fr. texts derived from the Ovidian myth of Narcissus and Echo. Fourteenth-c. poets also worked in the fixed forms that would be developed by late med. writers, the *virelai* and particularly the rondeau and the ballade; these were cultivated by Machaut and his contemporaries and particularly by the poets of following generations who, unlike Machaut, were not generally composers, e.g., Deschamps, Christine de Pizan (1363–1430), Alain Chartier (ca. 1385–1433), and in particular Charles d'Orléans (1394–1465), who wrote hundreds of rondeaux and ballades, both in Fr. and, during a 25-year period of captivity in England, in Eng.

For mod. readers, perhaps the best known of all late med. poets is François Villon (1431–after 1463), a young Parisian with a colorful, much romanticized life. Villon, of whose biography we know little for certain, is the author of several extended works in autobiographical guise, incl. a *Testament*, detailing the mock legacy of a poor poet and interspersing refined examples of the ballade and the rondeau. Villon, who was once condemned to death and composed a quatrain for the occasion of his hanging later adapted by François Rabelais (fl. early 16th c.), disappears without a trace after 1463. Collections of his poems are among the first printed poetry collections of late 15th-c. France; Clément Marot published an ed. of his poetry in 1533. Villon's *Lais* (*Legacy*, composed 1456) and *Grand testament* (composed 1461) are important laboratories for the devel. of a highly stylized first-person voice, the precursor for many later writers and for the romantic *poète maudit* (cursed poet). It would be a mistake to assume that the type of mock-testament that Villon composes is an entirely new devel.; the genre has important 13th-c. antecedents in Jean Bodel, Baude Fastoul, and Rutebeuf.

The 15th c. saw important devels. in verse drama, both religious (e.g., the lengthy *Mystère de la Passion*, ca. 1425, or an even longer mid-century passion play attributed to Arnoul Greban) and secular, most notably the anonymous *Farce de Maître Pierre Pathelin* (1465), which Rabelais knew and which is still performed. Devels. in theater built on a lively native Fr. trad. of mystery plays and other varieties of med. drama, the latter exemplified already in the 13th c. by Adam de la Halle's plays *Jeu de Robin et Marion*, written in Italy for Charles I of Naples, and his *Jeu de la Feuillée*.

B. ***Sixteenth and Seventeenth Centuries.*** Although the 16th c. is one of the richest periods in the hist. of Fr. poetry, the 17th c. is often considered an era of relative decline, at least in nondramatic poetry. There is some truth to this received notion, even if it is also informed by ideologies of literary taste inherited from that century.

The historiography of Fr. lyric poetry in the 16th c. has long cited Joachim du Bellay's *La deffence et illustration de la langue françoyse* (1549), an aggressive plea for the foundation of a new national poetry worthy of the cl. past, as a reference point. Du Bellay's treatise, along with Pierre de Ronsard's *Odes* (1550), has rather too neatly divided the century into two halves. Many earlier commentators took du Bellay's dismissal of most of the poetic production in Fr. before his time at face value, when du Bellay's treatise, a polemical response to Thomas Sébillet's erudite *Art poétique françoys* of 1548, clearly aims to establish his poetry and that of his contemporaries as the foundation of a new Fr. trad. Although the period of poetic production falling roughly between 1549 and 1585 is one of the most impressive in the entire hist. of Fr. poetry, critical work on 16th-c. Fr. poetry in the last century has demonstrated the richness of the reign of François I (1515–47), and indeed the extent to which the poets of the Pléiade build on humanist ideas already firmly in place early in the 16th c., and in some cases in the 15th c. as well. Both the pre-Pléiade poets and their poetic descendants imported It. forms (such as the sonnet, brought into Fr. by Marot and Mellin de Saint-Gelais in the 1530s and made Fr. by the Pléiade in the 1550s), and philosophical currents such as Ficianian Neoplatonism that had already attracted the attention of Fr. readers by the end of the 15th c.

The *Grands Rhétoriqueurs* stand at an awkward juncture in Fr. poetic hist., on the (arbitrary) border between "late medieval" and "Renaissance" poetics. The poets of the *Grande Rhétorique*, attached to the courts of Burgundy and France, develop a particularly complex poetics, playing on the possibilities of late med. allegory in intricate ways and developing verse forms and rhyme schemes of unparalleled complexity in the Fr. trad. A volume of "arts of second rhetoric" compiled by E. Langlois in 1902 is a useful primary source for the study of 15th-c. verse. The Grands Rhétoriqueurs, manipulating traditional fixed forms such as the rondeau and ballade, reworked these in ways that distanced them from their musical conventions. The rondeau, e.g., was reimagined in ways that made it difficult, even impossible, for the text to be set to music in the conventional way (Villon's "Mort, j'appelle de ta rigueur," from the *Testament*, is a good early example). In this, poetic practice reflects compositional practice among late 15th- and early 16th-c. composers such as Josquin des Prez (ca. 1450–1521).

The innovations of Grands Rhétoriqueurs such as Jean Meschinot, Jean Molinet, Guillaume Cretin, Jean Marot, and Jean Lemaire de Belges, poets long disparaged in the critical trad., certainly underlie many of the devels. in verse in the era of François I, most notably the work of Clément Marot (ca. 1496–1544), whose father, Jean, was also a court poet. Early poems by the young Marot show his mastery of the word games of the Grande Rhétorique, evincing as well his ability to play on the exigencies of poets obliged to curry favor with aristocratic patrons. Marot's collection *L'Adolescence clémentine* (1532) and its 1534 continuation are collectively a summa of late med. poetic forms. Marot later abandoned the fixed forms of the Middle Ages for more classically inspired ones, in particular the epigram. He is also responsible for some of the early trans. of Petrarch's poetry into Fr. A strong supporter of religious reform who spent a number of years in exile for his beliefs, Marot is the author of still-popular trans. of the Heb. Psalms, a crowning achievement of his career. Nonetheless, it would be too simple to reduce Marot's poetics entirely to his religious faith. He translated, e.g., bawdy epigrams by Martial around the same time as the Psalms, and such an alternation of the worldly and the sacred represents the period. Marot's poetry is an important influence on the philosophically minded Maurice Scève (ca. 1511–64), the author of the first Petrarchan love sequence in France and the winner of a contest for the composition of *blasons* of the human body organized by Marot in 1536. The works of Scève's Lyonnese contemporaries Pernette du Guillet and Louise Labé are infused with Petrarchan lang. as well as topoi derived from Ficinian Neoplatonism. Neoplatonic ideas about music and poetry underlie much of lyric production after 1549, as in the works of the mathematician and poet Jacques Peletier du Mans (1517–82). The treatises of Scève's friend and disciple Pontus de Tyard (1521–1605) influenced the founding by Jean-Antoine de Baïf and Thibault de Courville in 1570 of a royal Academy of Poetry and Music, which was intended to resurrect the "effects of music" described in mythological stories like those of Orpheus and Amphion in the interest of promoting harmony within the kingdom.

Ronsard (1524–85) and du Bellay (ca. 1522–60) were the preeminent Fr. poets of their generation, and indeed, much of the poetry not only of the 16th but of the 17th c. should be read in relationship to Pléiade aesthetics and its rejection by 17th-c. theorists. Certainly, the body of Fr. poetry produced in the period of Ronsard's dominance is now among the most highly prized in the entire Fr. trad. More than any other poet, Ronsard naturalized the sonnet in Fr. in a number of important collections beginning with his *Amours* (1552), published with a musical supplement in 1552 and reissued in 1553 with an innovative, erudite commentary by Marc-Antoine Muret. Ronsard's contemp. du Bellay also published a number of significant sonnet collections, incl. *L'Olive* (1549), *Les Regrets* (1558), and *Les Antiquitez de Rome* (1558). Ronsard experimented with other, more metaphysically ambitious lyric works, incl. the *Odes* (1550) and *Hymnes* (1556), whereas du Bellay cultivated an intimate, "low" style and a melancholic meditation on the impermanence of things and the venal political ambitions of his contemporaries, one much inflected by Ovidian topoi. The poets of Ronsard's generation were much influenced by the distinguished humanist Jean Dorat, teacher of Ronsard and Baïf, who wrote principally in Lat. Other important members of the group initially called the *Brigade* and later the Pléiade included Pontus, Peletier, Étienne Jodelle, and Remy Belleau.

Of the generation following Ronsard, Philippe Desportes (1546–1606) and Agrippa d'Aubigné (1552–1630) are probably the most noted writers of lyric verse. The former inspired François de Malherbe's (1555–1628) call for the reform of Fr. versification often cited as the birth of neoclassicism in poetry. (In one of his most famous lines, Nicolas Boileau later praised Malherbe for bringing order to the alleged disorder of Pléiade poetics: "enfin Malherbe vint" [Finally Malherbe arrived].) Trad. has tended to situate 17th-c. poetic production between Malherbe's castigation of Pléiade and post-Pléiade verse and Boileau's orderly ideal of a balanced poetry whose regular cadences please and instruct the reader. Indeed, Boileau suggested, in his 1674 *Art poétique*, that little of note had happened in Fr. verse between Malherbe's reform in the opening years of the 17th c. and his own time. Of course, this is far from true: a number of worthy poets fit awkwardly into what has often been seen as the period's predominantly classicizing aesthetics: Théophile de Viau, Marc-Antoine Girard de Saint-Amant, Tristan l'Hermite, and Vincent Voiture are "lyric" poets whose posthumous reputations, although respectable, have suffered from ideological accounts of the Grand Siècle and its cl. rigor. In the 1630s and 1640s, Vincent Voiture resurrected late med. forms such as the rondeau in an effort to bring back the "elegant banter" (Boileau's expression) of Clément Marot's court poetry, while Viau had earlier been tried for "libertine" tendencies, in relation to the affair of the *Parnasse des poètes satyriques* (1622).

Both the 16th and 17th cs. saw the continued flourishing of devotional poetry, a genre that often overlaps with the other lyric forms already discussed. The religious poems of Queen Marguerite de Navarre, e.g., the *Miroir de l'ame pecheresse* (1531), condemned initially by the Sorbonne and later translated into Eng. by Elizabeth I, are early 16th-c. examples. Jean de Sponde (1557–95) is no doubt the preeminent late 16th-c. religious poet. There are also a number of collections of Christianized love poetry by poets like Ronsard, intended to be sung by the devout, often to popular tunes. The 17th c. continues the trad. of devotional verse, notably in Jean de La Ceppède's *Théorèmes* (1613, 1621) or Claude Hopil's *Les douces extases de l'âme spirituelle* (1627). Contemplative religious poetry appears throughout the 17th c.; a significant late 17th-c. example of the genre is Racine's *Cantiques spirituels* (1694).

New forms of narrative poetry also appeared during these centuries. Du Bellay had called for the writing of "long poems," new Fr. "Iliads" based on the native mythical-historiographical trads. On a royal commission, Ronsard composed four books of an unfinished epic, *La Franciade* (1572), based on the story of Francus, a traditional account, attested as early as the 7th c., of the Trojan origins of the Fr. monarchy. But it is perhaps in the trad. of all-encompassing "scientific" poetry, a form with precedents in the encyclopedic tenor of such med. long poems as the *Roman de la Rose*, that we see the most original devels. Such poems as Scève's *Microcosme* (1562), a 3,003-line account of human knowledge and the fall of humankind, and Guillaume de Salluste du Bartas's (1544–90) much longer and more influential *La Sepmaine: ou, Creation du monde* (1578) and *Seconde Sepmaine* (1584) are important in this vein, as is the somewhat more peculiar *La Galliade, ou de la révolution des arts et sciences* (1578, expanded 1582) by Guy Le Fevre de la Boderie, which claims that France is the wellspring of worldly knowledge. D'Aubigné's seven-book *Les Tragiques*, an immensely powerful account of the religious wars from a Protestant standpoint, begun by d'Aubigné in the 1570s but published anonymously only in 1616, is probably the most significant of the early mod. narrative long poems. Later in the 17th c., there are a number of epics on national themes, e.g., in the context of the conflict with Spain (such as works by Antoine Godeau and Georges de Scudéry), none of which seems to have gained much favor among readers then or now. Mock epic has several instances at mid-century, in particular Paul Scarron's parody of the *Aeneid* entitled *Virgile travesti* (1648–52). For all this, the great master of 17th-c. narrative poetry, working on a much smaller scale, is probably Jean de La Fontaine (1621–95), whose *Fables* show a prodigious variety of verse styles. La Fontaine became, with the prose writers François de La Rochefoucauld and Jean de La Bruyère, a preeminent commentator on the social mores of Louis XIV's France. The rise of the cl. trad. of Fr. theater, culminating in the triumvirate of Corneille, Racine, and Jean-Baptiste Poquelin (i.e., Molière), is a central aspect of the devel. of Fr. verse in the 17th c., with important predecessors in such 16th-c. dramatists as Théodore de Beza, whose *Abraham sacrifiant* of 1550 is often called the first tragedy in Fr., and Robert Garnier, whose best known play is no doubt *Les Juives* (1583). Sixteenth-c. theater often intercalates lyric forms in imitation of the ancient choral odes separating the scenes of Gr. dramas. The regulation of verse conventions, in particular after the foundation of the Fr. Academy in 1635, means that the hist. of Fr. versification is inseparable from debates concerning the decorum of drama.

II. Early Modern to Twentieth Century.

A. ***Eighteenth Century.*** Considered by many of his contemporaries the greatest poet of the c., François-Marie Arouet, known as Voltaire (1694–1778), is best known in poetry for his verse tragedy *Zaïre* (1732), but he tried his hand at many genres and forms. His epic *La Henriade* praises the ascension of Henri IV, who brought an end to the religious wars in France. He also wrote philosophical poems, which suited his antilyrical nature, in addition to satires and occasional verses celebrating such luminaries as Isaac Newton's Fr. translator, Mme. de Châtelet. Although verse was overshadowed during the Enlightenment by prose works (e.g., Voltaire's volumes on hist., his philosophical tale *Candide*, or Denis Diderot's monumental *Encyclopedia*), a few writers became famous for their poetic meditations on nature and landscapes. Jean-François de Saint-Lambert's *Les Saisons* (1769) explores both the sensorial richness of the months' cycle and the underlying harmony of the universe. Jacques Delille tested his verse in well-known trans. of Virgil's *Georgics* and John Milton's *Paradise Lost* and then proposed his own vision of natural beauty in *Les Jardins ou L'Art d'embellir les paysages* (1782). Other poets, such as Jean-Baptiste Rousseau or Jean-Baptiste Gresset, had already made names for themselves by openly opposing the Encyclopedists or by imitating classicist writers such as Boileau.

Once the century had ended and the Fr. Revolution had overturned both political and cultural orthodoxies, one victim of the Reign of Terror gained posthumous fame both as a martyr to tyranny and as the epitome of a poet's resistance to cold rationalism. André Chénier (1762–94) was condemned to the guillotine because, in newspaper articles, he had criticized the execution of Louis XVI. Although few of his poems had been published before his death, a footnote in François-René de Chateaubriand's *Génie du christianisme* (1802) helped turn Chénier into a legend. The note recounts that, on standing next to the guillotine, the poet had moved his hand to his forehead and said, "To die! I had something there in my mind!" Not only did this help turn the poet into a hero for counterrevolutionary Royalists in the 1820s, but it led a generation of romantic poets such as Alfred de Vigny (1797–1863) to align themselves with the legend of a misunderstood poetic genius and conflate the pathos of tragedy with a putative inner voice of poetry. *Les Iambes,* which Chénier wrote while he was imprisoned, is a skillfully crafted work of satire that uses Gr. and Lat. models that the author had read in the original. His *Hymnes* and *Odes* follow the model of occasional verse from the 18th c. but are often infused with passionate appeals for justice—as in his defense of Charlotte Corday, who had assassinated Marat, or in his most famous ode "La Jeune captive," which was inspired by a young woman Chénier met in prison. The woman's appeal to have her life spared, and the poet's reflection in the last two stanzas on his verse rendition of her appeal, became a model for the heart-cries that the romantics would emulate and develop.

B. ***Romanticism.*** Jean-Jacques Rousseau's final book, *Les Rêveries du promeneur solitaire* (*Reveries of a Solitary Walker,* 1782), set the tone for Fr. poetry in the first half of the 19th c. According to this prose account of walks taken by the author in the countryside around Paris and of others taken earlier when he lived near Geneva, Rousseau (1712–78) found refuge from his critics by making forays into nature. Such occasions restored the natural calm that he craved and led him to balance the movements of nature with his own search for happiness. Following his lead, the romantic poets Alphonse de Lamartine (1790–1869) and Victor Hugo (1802–85) would turn into verse the sort of meditations on loss, self-isolation, and nature's restorative power that Rousseau developed in his last book. A second group of writers, most notably Aloysius Bertrand (1807–41) and Charles Baudelaire (1821–67), refined the formal links forged by Rousseau between the rhythms of poetic prose and the cadence of walking by developing the new medium of prose poetry.

Despite its brevity, Lamartine's *Méditations poétiques et religieuses* (1820) immediately earned its author praise for the simplicity of its evocations of past happiness and the smooth-flowing reveries that his verse sustained. In "Le Lac," the poet laments the inevitable passage of time, echoed in a lake's lapping waves, and asks the rocks and vegetation on the shore to attest to the moment of passion that he shared there, months earlier, while rowing his beloved who has since died. "L'Isolement" and "Le Vallon" imply in their descriptions of meadows and valleys an ascent toward the Christian paradise, with death proclaimed as a joyous release. Less religious but just as poignant in their depictions of the instability of human attachments are Marceline Desbordes-Valmore's *Poésies* (1830) and *Les Pleurs* (1833). The direct evocations of hardship (e.g., the illness and death of a child, abandonment by a lover) and subtle reversals of anticipated meanings near the ends of her poems are prime illustrations of poetry's power to surprise.

Hugo placed surprise at the heart of his romantic aesthetic, writing in *Les Contemplations* (1856) that, when reading lyric verse, "Il faut que, par instants, on frissonne, et qu'on voie / Tout à coup, sombre, grave et terrible au passant, / Un vers fauve sortir de l'ombre en rugissant!" (We must, at some moments, shudder when we see / All of a sudden, the dark, somber and terrifying movement / Of a wild verse emerge from the darkness roaring!). Having published in 1822 a first volume of verse that reworked legends of folklore (*Les Odes et poésies diverses*), Hugo set a new course with his second book, *Les Orientales* (1829). In it, he depicted distant lands while working out a broad variety of verse forms that detached lyric from the dominant alexandrine line that Chénier and Lamartine had used. Embracing exoticism was not a novelty, since Montesquieu had made the subject popular almost a century earlier with his *Lettres persanes* and exiled writers such as Chateaubriand had placed their prose dramas in distant countries (the latter's *René* and *Atala* are set in Amerindian territories around the Mississippi). Hugo too would undergo the rigors of exile in 1851 when he fled France to protest Napoleon III's reign, spending 19 years on the island of Guernsey. Yet by tying Hugo's poetry to a setting in Muslim North Africa and Spain, *Les Orientales* set in motion an appropriation of other cultures, epochs, and langs. that would become a hallmark of romanticism and make its poetry a fundamentally composite genre.

In the shorter preface to *Les Orientales,* Hugo compared the new literary movement to a med. town whose irregular streets, winding between buildings of all types, and teeming citizenry, living amid disorder and change, represented the ferment of life. Instead of imitating Gr. and Roman subjects (as Chénier and earlier poets had done), Hugo challenged his contemporaries to engage readers with outbursts of energy and passion drawn not only from remote places (Egypt, Constantinople, or the Danube basin) but from different epochs (biblical times, the Middle Ages, or contemp. events). Alfred de Vigny rose to the challenge, evoking in such poems as "La Maison du berger" and "L'Esprit pur" the joy of being transported beyond the mod. world of railways and riches to seats of lasting power—nature's gradual changes or the realm of spiritual serenity. Another poet who defined poetry as a spiritual quest was Gérard de Nerval (1808–55). His two-volume *Voyage en Orient* chronicles his travels to North Africa, while his trans. of J. W. Goethe's *Faust* led him to discover Ger. mythology. In his collection of sonnets *Les Chimères* (1854), he excelled in transposing personal grief into psychological studies of heroes from ancient, Christian, or Eng. myths. Théophile Gautier (1811–72) lived for a period in Spain, and while there composed *España* (1845), which began the transpositions of paintings and sculptures that would exemplify his cult of beauty in *Emaux et camées* (1852).

Romanticism's complex appropriation of other worlds and the creation of composite verses that collated the diversity of France's colonial empire in Africa, the Caribbean, and the Pacific gained impetus from several writers who had first-hand knowledge of lands beyond Europe. Charles-Marie Leconte de Lisle's *Poèmes barbares* (1872) draws on Hindu myths, tropical vegetation, and animals common to the Asian and Af. continents, as well as elements gleaned from the first 18 years of his life on a sugar plantation in Réunion, an island in the Indian Ocean. Like J.-M. de Heredia, who left his native Cuba in 1850 at age eight, Leconte de Lisle (1818–94) wrote finely crafted poems based on myths of different civilizations, and both poets began by publishing discrete poems in an anthol. entitled *Le Parnasse contemporain* in 1866. Along with François Coppée and other poets published in the collection, both authors adopted the name *Parnassiens* and developed the doctrine of art for art's sake first proposed by Gautier in 1836. According to Gautier, poetry could attain greatness only by abandoning any claim to moral pronouncements or the analysis of sentiment and by instead transposing into words the richness of color and composition exemplified in the plastic arts. Another poet of foreign birth, the Uruguay-born Isidore Ducasse (1846–70), published under the pseud. Comte de Lautréamont a long prose poem in six cantos, *Les Chants de Maldoror* (1869). It recounts in graphic detail the struggle between God and a romantic hero (whose name in the book's title illustrates romanticism's privileging of liminal moments between night and day: *mal d'aurore*). The publisher decided that, given the work's seeming immorality, it was better to distribute it outside France, which meant that it was little read until Remy de Gourmont praised its formal beauty in 1891. The composite genre of poetry in prose had been tried earlier by Aloysius Bertrand in his posthumous *Gaspard de la nuit* (1842). Most of its short texts are either portraits of artisans or detailed descriptions of landscapes, so that the work in its entirety is reminiscent of paintings by Johannes Vermeer and other Dutch artists. While acknowledging Bertrand, in the preface to *Le Spleen de Paris* (1869), Baudelaire pushed the hybrid genre in a new direction and linked the fluid rhythms of poetic prose to surprises and ecstatic moments found by a man walking through Paris. Giving his book the subtitle *Petits poèmes en prose*, Baudelaire also coined the term *prose poems*.

Widely considered the most important poet of the 19th c. and the writer responsible for placing poetry at the vanguard of artistic experimentation and ethical questioning, at least up until the surrealists of the 1930s, Baudelaire led a life marked by debt, illness, and a difficult stepfather. His early publications were reviews of the annual Parisian Salons, in which painters such as Eugène Delacroix exhibited their work. The first Fr. translator of E. A. Poe and an admirer of Gautier, he reoriented romanticism with his masterpiece *Les Fleurs du mal*, which was censored two months after its publication in 1857 for causing an outrage to morality. Baudelaire maintained that the judgment betrayed a misreading of his book since the poems' depictions of sadism, prostitution, and other addictions do not glorify evil but unmask the hypocrisy of his day. The first and longest section in the book, "Spleen et Idéal," also demonstrates what prevents human beings from achieving a romantic fusion with Beauty or Nature. First there is resignation to despair and then comes the numbing effect occasioned by merely satisfying our appetites, instead of embracing life's unpredictability and its fragile richness. The two poles of human experience—ecstasy or the enslavement to false value—are evoked in the transporting rhythms and promised happiness of "L'Invitation au voyage" and in the claustrophobic melancholy of the fourth "Spleen" poem that begins "Quand le ciel bas et lourd pèse comme un couvercle . . ."

(When the low and heavy sky weighs like a lid). Although famous for his poetry, Baudelaire had to write prose articles and reports to pay his creditors. His death at age 46 came two years before the appearance of his complete volume of prose poems.

Hugo outlived almost all the preceding writers, and he kept in touch with devels. in the romantic movement, from Lamartine's introspective questionings to Baudelaire's experimental fusions of verse and ethics, prose and poetry. Hugo's own verse, however, followed its own trajectory. During his exile in Guernsey, he completed not only his novels *Les Misérables* and *L'Homme qui rit* but also satirical verses against Napoleon III, *Les Châtiments*, and some of his best-known poems. These appeared in the elegiac *Contemplations* (1856) and his epic recounting of humankind's rise to spirituality, *La Légende des siècles*, the three volumes of which were published in 1859, 1877, and 1883. The pantheistic beliefs that Hugo came to espouse during his exile were further developed in poems that appeared posthumously in *Dieu* and *La Fin de Satan*. When he died in 1885, Hugo was celebrated as a national hero, for his return to France in 1870 had coincided with the abdication of Napoleon III and a humiliating defeat of the Fr. army by Prussia. His body lay in state at the Arc de Triomphe, but he had insisted before his death that his corpse be laid in a pauper's coffin. The procession taking the coffin on its workhouse hearse took six hours to move through the crowd and reach the Pantheon, where Hugo was then buried alongside France's greatest.

C. ***Symbolism.*** Stéphane Mallarmé (1842–98) wrote in his essay "Crise de vers" (1886, 1896) that Hugo's death was the turning point for Fr. poetry, since the fixed verse patterns that Hugo and the romantics had perfected had died with him. Mallarmé's disciple Paul Valéry (1871–1945) would later characterize the contrast between Hugo and Mallarmé by an elliptical formula: "Hugo: how to say everything in verse. Mallarmé: how to say nothing except what is verse." Not only does this motto point to a radical change, underscored by Mallarmé, in the sorts of things that poems should say—not information, facts, or what the latter termed "l'universel reportage"—but it indicates a break in the way that a poem actually says anything. Versification was altered but so too was what it served. Both of these changes reverberated throughout the loosely associated group of poets known as the symbolists.

To start with versification, the freeing of verse had begun 20 years earlier. After Paul Verlaine's *Poèmes saturniens* appeared in 1866, more poems eschewed the standard alexandrine line and used lines of ten, eight, four, seven or five syllables. The last two cases were important since an uneven number of syllables meant that verses were no longer divisible into symmetrical halves, which allowed poems where the rhythms often ran from one uneven verse line into another. Verlaine (1844–96) developed this technique in his books *Fêtes galantes* (1869) and *Romances sans paroles* (1874), and the use of uneven syllabic lines became a credo in his poem "Art poétique," which called for allying poetry with music, while loosening semantic exactitude through combinations of sounds. Arthur Rimbaud (1854–91), who accompanied Verlaine during extended stays in Belgium and England, freed the alexandrine further from its stock rhythms by using run-on lines and surprising pauses at the beginnings or ends of the lines. His poem "A la musique" (written in 1870) goes beyond Verlaine since, in all his verses, Rimbaud blended innovative rhythms with ironic twists of meaning. So, when readers reach the end of "Le Bateau ivre" or "Les Effarés," they are shocked to find that what they assumed to be either the subject or the tone of the poem is upturned. Rimbaud's extremely short poetic career, from age 16 to 18, encompassed intense spells of creativity in which he not only produced experimental verses but pushed the prose poem to new heights—in *Une saison en enfer* (*A Season in Hell*, 1873) and *Illuminations*, which was published after his death.

Common to Verlaine's moody evocations of landscapes and solitude and to Rimbaud's complex staging of sentiments is the belief that a poem's force lies not in its mode of representation (or its ability to describe everyday scenes and emotions) but in the innovative effects that the poem produces for its readers. This lies at the heart of not only the symbolists' fascination with music but their emphasis on suggesting multiple meanings in the same poem, so that the text's patternings outdo in richness the events or thoughts that led to its composition. Jule Laforgue's parodies of romantic melancholy in *Les Complaintes* (1885) give a comic tone to this self-reflexivity, while Jean Moréas (1856–1910), who wrote a symbolist manifesto in 1886, evokes the power of fleeting illusions in his collection *Les Syrtes* (1884). It was, however, Mallarmé's poetry that exemplified a poem's ability to stand as a self-sufficient object whose sounds and senses echo each other indefinitely. Although he published relatively few verses, some prose poems, and influential essays, his reunions every Tuesday with fellow poets helped establish him as the unofficial leader of symbolism. His one collection of poems, *Poésies*, appeared in 1899, a year after his death, and contained "L'Après-midi d'un faune" (initially written for a staged performance to be accompanied with a score by Claude Debussy) along with sonnets that illustrated his goal of "painting not the thing but the effect that it creates."

Paul Valéry gave theoretical support to the symbolists' belief that a poem could create new experiences. Setting aside poetry in 1892, he devoted the next 20 years to writing down his reflections on mathematics, philosophy, and lang. in essays such as "Une soirée avec Monsieur Teste" and in notebooks that he would work on each morning after rising at 5:00. Covering a wide range of topics, the notebooks scrutinize the symbolic transformations, or what Valéry called a calculus, that give words their power. Rather than reflect preexistent ideas or thoughts, words for Valéry are integers in pragmatic calculations whose utterances are meant to change the world, thus anticipating by 40 years Ludwig Wittgenstein's writings on lang.-games and J. L. Austin's notion of performatives. Valéry also recognized that poetry has more potential for transforming the meanings of utterances than any other use of written symbols. If we consider his poem of 1891 "Narcisse parle" (which the poet would revise later in his career, in order to perfect its sonic transformations), we find the Gr. mythological hero voicing his last thoughts before suicide:

> Farewell, lost reflection on the sealed up
> waters,
> Narcissus . . . this very name is a tender
> fragrance
> To the delicate heart. Sprinkle for the
> shades of the departed
> This empty grave with petals from the funereal rose.

Not only do these lines take up aspects of the tragic search for self that Mallarmé had explored in his poem "Hérodiade" (1887), but they fuse a "name," a "fragrance," and a "heart" into one symbolic evocation by which the name *becomes* the fragrance, which in turn exchanges its "delicate" nature for the "tender" one associated with the heart. The fusion is helped by the phonetic properties of the name "Narcisse" that lends its sounds *n* (*nom*, name), *ar* (*parfum*, fragrance), and *ss* (*suave*, delicate) to the words following it. It is also helped semantically by the devel. of the flower code ("fragrance," "petals," "rose"), which is both a metaphor for transient beauty and the context for the literal meaning of the common name "Narcissus." The aural properties of this particular word, in conjunction with its verbal associations, consequently turn it into the very name for the sadness-in-perfection that the poem unfolds. Valéry later took up writing verse long enough to publish his most famous collection, *Charmes*, in 1922. "Le Cimetière marin," one of its longer poems, is considered by many to be an illustration of Valéry's definition of poetic "charms"—"a prolonged hesitation [perceived by the reader] between [a verse's] sound and sense."

Another symbolist who pushed the boundaries of thought by creating a new poetic form was Victor Segalen (1878–1919). His collection *Stèles* (1914), written while the poet worked as a doctor in China, was based in part on two long journeys he made on foot and on horseback to the center of the country. Each stele offers lapidary pronouncements about different paths to joy. Paul Claudel (1868–1955) in his finely crafted prose poems *Connaissance de l'Est* (1914) drew inspiration from walking around Chinese cities. His later verse and dramatic works would use symbolist evocations of feeling as a path to Christian spirituality. Satirical poets had already put the performative power of poetry to new uses during the final decades of the 19th c. Meeting at the Chat Noir cabaret in Paris (1885–96), such *fumiste* writers as Alphonse Allais would perform spectacles overturning romantic or cl. works. Their biting humor and riffs on advertising and popular songs prepared the way for Dadaist performances a quarter-century later.

D. *Avant-Gardes of the Twentieth Century.* By 1912, Paris had become the cultural capital of Europe, attracting innovators in all branches of the arts. Important collaborations ensued between artists working in different media. Painters from abroad, such as Pablo Picasso, would join experimenters such as Sergei Diaghilev and his Rus. ballet troupe to produce works that set new aesthetic standards. The poet Guillaume Apollinaire (1880–1918) wrote program notes for Diaghilev's ballet *Parade* as well as the first essays explaining cubist painting to the general public.

Poetry played a key role in the devel. of these avant-garde aesthetics. In 1908, the young writer Jules Romains (1885–1972) published a book-length poem in two parts called *La Vie unanime* that called for a new form of lit., unanimism. Written in verses of varying syllabic counts grouped into regular stanzas, the book demonstrates how individual consciousness can be absorbed by the various rhythms of life around it—animal, chemical, electrical, machine or human. The massed comings and goings of city crowds inspired many of Romains's pages. F. T. Marinetti's "Futurist Manifesto," published in Paris a year later, cut poetry free from old myths such as idealizing statuesque beauty. It proposed instead that a new cult be formed around speed and the dynamism of machines. Blaise Cendrars's 1913 poem "Prose du Transsibérien et de la petite Jehanne de France" is an account written in free verse of a train journey across Russia, and it evokes the giddiness of hurtling through time and space that futurists valued. Nevertheless, there is a tension in the poem between nostalgia for the past and the dynamism of fast travel.

The writer who best captured the exhilaration of the new horizons made possible by mass communication, the telegraph, and travel was Apollinaire. His book *Alcools* (1913) opens with the declaration "A la fin tu es las de ce monde ancien" and goes on to praise the poetry of advertisements, catalogs, and posters. After enlisting in the Fr. army in World War I, Apollinaire would write part of his most innovative volume, *Calligrammes* (1918), while serving at the front. Printed on army paper, the third part of the book was distributed to fellow soldiers, and it contains some poems lamenting lost comrades and turning the soldiers' routine and squalid conditions into beautiful testimonials. The visual form of some calligrammes, scattering words and letters across the page, allowed Apollinaire to embed his verses within line drawings of a heart, a fountain, or a rifle. Mallarmé's philosophical poem *Un coup de dés* (*A Throw of the Dice*, 1897) had been the first work to exploit the entire space of a page, allowing readers to scan words in multiple directions, but Apollinaire's war poems and Pierre Reverdy's book *Les Ardoises du toit* (*Roof Slates*, 1918) used new typographical arrangements to evoke simple situations that resonate through a web of strong emotions.

As the reality of the Great War's slaughter and futility became known, some artists used poetry's performative force to attack the basis of everyday lang. that for them had been contaminated by politicians' speeches and jingoistic nationalism. In April 1916, a group of performers began an entertainment review, the Cabaret Voltaire, in a Zurich café. Their rallying cry was "Dada," which they defined not as an aesthetic movement but as a systematic destruction of meaning. The Dada manifestos were not published but proclaimed in public alongside performance poems—sound events juxtaposing phonemes from different langs. and recited by different performers. Paris became a center of Dada creativity once Tristan Tzara came there in 1920 to join writers of an experimental review called *Littérature*. Two of the writers, André Breton (1896–1966) and Philippe Soupault (1897–1990), had developed a technique of collaboratively transcribing dreams, which they called automatic writing. Others such as Robert Desnos (1900–45), Paul Éluard (1895–1952), and Louis Aragon (1897–1982) published poems in which sounds or typographical shapes were reinvented. These innovations precipitated calls for a new lyricism that would directly express the unconscious while being a collaborative endeavor, since artistic "genius," according to these writers, was illusory. Their rallying call appeared in 1924 under the title *Surrealist Manifesto*, which borrowed its name from a term that Apollinaire had used earlier to describe artists' refusal to slavishly copy traditional forms.

Combining the iconoclastic force of Dada (esp. in their public denunciations of idealist art) with a new cult of feminine beauty, the surrealists wrote novels, essays, and poems that gave voice to nascent desire. Love lyrics such as Éluard's "L'Amoureuse" in *Capitale de la douleur* (1926) show that refusals of conventional logic (the poem begins "She is standing on my eyelids") can allow rhetorical figures to represent the all-encompassing power of passion. Fraught by internal struggles, surrealism lost many of its members by the mid-1930s, after expelling Aragon for putting Communism before art or attacking rival groups such as the review *Le Grand Jeu*. The latter's cofounder, René Daumal, had set the foundations for a poetry of change and a rejection of self-identity in his *Contre-ciel* (1936). Although some surrealist poems such as Éluard's "Liberté" became famous statements of resistance during the Nazi occupation of France, by 1945 the movement had ceased being a mirror for important innovations in poetry.

E. *Strands of Post–World War II Poetry.* No one movement or set of aesthetic principles characterizes the broad diversity of poems published since 1950. Yet common strands in these works emerge once we examine three types of action that mod. poetry accomplishes in its efforts to change the world—political action, transformation of a person's interactions with the material world, and the forging of new connections with other forms of expression.

Poetry's power to disrupt not only political *doxa* but facile uses of lang. is brilliantly illustrated by René Char's wartime fragments collected in *Feuillets d'Hypnos* (1946) and by his finely crafted books *La Parole en archipel* (1962) and *Aromates chasseurs* (1975). However, it was outside France that one poem gained fame as a rallying cry for justice, not only in the Caribbean of which it speaks, but across the francophone world. Aimé Césaire's *Cahier d'un retour au pays natal* (*Notebook of a Return to the Native Land*, 1939) is part narrative and part invective against the inequalities imposed by Caribbean plantation economies and colonialism. Its 174 stanzas in free verse are tightly organized around recurring phrases that rise in a concluding crescendo that calls on the black population of Martinique (and other islands) to shake off its collective shame and fight for self-determination. The first text to make use of the term *négritude*, Césaire's poem inspired many writers in and beyond France to blend poetry and political commitment. The Guadeloupean writer Édouard Glissant (1928–2011) connected the hist. of Caribbean slavery to early epochs in the trade and uses of salt throughout his long poem *Le Sel noir* (1960). Modeled on the renewed epic form of Saint-John Perse's *Amers* (1957), with its long stanzas of free verse and complex forms of address, Glissant scans lost civilizations of Carthage, Rome, and Celtic Brittany as well as Africa. He also turns Perse's chronicles of individual quests (most notably in *Anabase*, 1924) into a song of peoples on the move. Léopold Sédar Senghor developed Césaire's concept of négritude in his fusion of West African trads. and politically inspiring lyrics (*Ethiopiques*, 1956), while Raymond LeBlanc's *Cri de terre* (1972) unearths the violent suppression of Acadian culture in the coastal landscape of New Brunswick, Canada. Michèle Lalonde's poster-poem "Speak White" (1970) allies the call for Quebecois' self-respect to that of black pride. More recently, Herménégilde Chiasson and Robert Dickson have crafted poetic monuments to the anxieties of Fr.-speaking cultures in the anglophone Canadian Maritimes and Ontario.

A second strand of political poetry developed in the wake of Francis Ponge's (1899–1988) method of implying a materialist theory of happiness through meditations on objects and nature. The intricate prose poems of his *Le parti pris des choses* (1942) underscore modes of living that are in harmony with the rhythms of nonhuman organisms. "Notes pour un coquillage" argues that lang. should be used not as a mirror for ideas but as a tool for improving our lives with others, and this lesson was not lost on writers who turned to poetry in order to reinvigorate lang. and reconnect speakers with the material world. Eugène Guillevic (1907–97) developed his own minimalist forms of lyric that celebrate natural forces and the lessons they embody. Yves Bonnefoy (1923–2016), France's most famous poet of the second half of the 20th c., has written essays and poems in which a search for presence is the overarching goal; poets such as Philippe Jaccottet (b. 1925) have continued in this vein. André du Bouchet (1924–2001) wrote experimental poems in which the careful placement of a few words in unique typographical arrangements across entire pages is part of a conjoined exploration of lang.'s potential and of life rhythms connecting a walker to the hills he traverses. The poems of Jacques Dupin, André Frénaud, or Jacques Réda are less experimental than du Bouchet's, yet they continue to fathom the human body's relation to space, as does the work of Jacqueline Risset and James Sacré. Bernard Noël has developed a highly original form of philosophical poetry that proposes the singularity of bodily sensation as a counterweight to idealist illusions. In Noël's book *La Chute des temps* (1983), perceptions are transposed as events that allow us to escape the hold of clock time, grounding poetry in an awareness of living that is close to the self-sufficient joys described by Baudelaire.

A final group of writers has reinvented poetry's ties to other art forms. Beginning with Henri Michaux (1899–1984), the shared mechanics of writing and drawing have become central to poems that exploit typographical invention. Concrete poets Pierre Garnier (b. 1928) and Jean-Pierre Faye (b. 1925) moved beyond Apollinaire's shoehorning of spoken verses into calligrams and proposed new types of visual syntax. Pierre-Albert Jourdain (1924–91) and Michel Deguy (b. 1930) managed, in different ways, to draw innovative effects from varying their poems' visual shape. Emmanuel Hocquard (b. 1940) has experimented with poems written in a tabular form (in *Théorie des tables*) or with poetry and photography. Members of the Oulipo group refuse the assumption that lyric verse expresses an individual's emotions and invented numerical patterns for syllabic and linear arrangement that place mathematical properties, rather than sentiment, at the heart of a poem. For instance, Jacques Roubaud's collection of verses ϵ (1967) is structured around moves in the Japanese game Go. Michelle Grangaud's *Geste: narrations* (1991) is composed of three-line stanzas (with lines of five, five, and eleven syllables), each of which recounts a circumstance that may be combined with other stanzas to produce an indeterminate number of narratives. By bringing into question the opposition between narrative and lyric, Oulipo writers and others such as Pierre Alféri and Dominique Fourcade might be said to have brought Fr. poetry full circle, since their work recalls the formal experiments of Occitan and early Fr. writers who blended elements of the two forms.

See CANADA, POETRY OF; CARIBBEAN, POETRY OF THE.

■ **Anthologies, Manifestos, and Translations**: *Anthologie de la nouvelle poésie nègre et malgache*, ed. L. S. Senghor (1942); *Modern French Verse*, ed. P. Mansell Jones (1957); *Anthologie de la poésie française du XVIème siècle*, ed. F. Gray (1962); *Anthology of Modern French Poetry*, ed. C. A. Hackett (1967); A. Breton, *Manifestoes of Surrealism*, trans. R. Seaver and H. R. Lane (1969); *La Poésie française des origines à nos jours: Anthologie*, ed. C. Bonnefoy (1975); *Modern French Poetry: A Bilingual Anthology*, ed. P. Terry and S. Gavronsky (1975); *Anthologie des grands rhétoriqueurs*, ed. P. Zumthor (1978); T. Tzara, *Sept manifestes Dada, Lampisteries* (1978); *L'Anthologie arbitraire d'une nouvelle poésie, 1960–82: Trente poètes*, ed. H. Deluy (1983); *The Random House Book of Twentieth-Century French Poetry*, ed. P. Auster (1984); *The Defiant Muse: French Feminist Poets from the Middle Ages to the Present*, ed. D. C. Stanton (1986); *Anthologie de la poésie du XVIIe siècle*, ed. J.-P. Chauveau (1987); *Anthologie de la poésie lyrique française des XIIe et XIIIe siècles*, ed. J. Dufournet (1989); *La Poésie acadienne, 1948–1988*, ed. G. Leblanc and C. Beausoleil (1992); *Poèmes de femmes des origines à nos jours*, ed. R. Deforges (1993); "La Poésie contemporaine en France," *Littéréalité*, ed. S. Villani (1994); *Anthology of First World War French Poetry*, ed. I. Higgins (1996); *Les Poètes du Chat Noir*, ed. A. Velter (1996); *Anthologie de la poésie française*, ed. J.-P. Chauveau, G. Gros, D. Ménager (v. 1), M. Bercot, M. Collot, C. Seth (v. 2) (2000); *Anthologie de la poésie française du XX siècle*, ed. M. Décaudin (2000); *Anthologie de la poésie française du XVIe siècle*, ed. J. Céard and L.-G. Tin (2005); *Futurist Manifestos*, ed. U. Apollonio (2009).

■ **Criticism and History**: T. de Banville, *Petit traité de poésie française* (1935); J. Paulhan, *Clef de la poésie* (1944); S. Bernard, *Le Poème en prose de Baudelaire jusqu'à nos jours* (1959); R. Lalou, *Histoire de la poésie française* (1963); M. Sanouillet, *Dada à Paris* (1965); G. E. Clancier, *De Chénier à Baudelaire* (1970); *Essais de sémiotique poétique*, ed. J. A. Greimas (1972); G. Brereton, *An Introduction to the French Poets* (1973); *The Appreciation of Modern French Poetry: 1850–1950*, ed. P. Broome and G. Chesters (1976); M. Riffaterre, *Semiotics of Poetry* (1978); J.-M. Gleize, *Poésie et figuration* (1983); *The Prose Poem in France: Theory and Practice*, ed. M. A. Caws and H. Riffaterre (1983); M. Riffaterre, *Text Production*, trans. T. Lyons (1983); M. Bishop, *Contemporary French Women Poets* (1984–85); W. Calin, *In Defense of French Poetry: An Essay in Revaluation* (1987); R. Chambers, *Meaning and Meaningfulness* (1987); R. R. Hubert, *Surrealism and the Book* (1988); M. Collot, *La Poésie moderne et la structure d'horizon* (1989); J. Chénieux-Gendron, *Surrealism* (1990); C. Prendergast, *Nineteenth-Century French Poetry: Introductions to Close Readings* (1990); *The Ladder of High Design: Structure and Interpretation of the French Lyric Sequence*, ed. D. Fenoaltea and D. L. Rubin (1991); *Poetry in France: Metamorphoses of a Muse*, ed. K. Aspley and P. France (1992); "Mallarmè, Theorist of Our Times," ed. S. Winspur, *Dalhousie French Studies* 25 (1993)—spec. iss.; *Understanding French Poetry: Essays for a New Millennium*, ed. S. Metzidakis (1994); P. D. Cate and M. Shaw, *The Spirit of Montmartre: Cabarets, Humor, and the Avant-Garde, 1875–1905* (1995); A. Gendre, *Evolution du sonnet français* (1996); *La Poésie française du Moyen Age jusqu'à nos jours*, ed. M. Jarrety (1997);

C. Scott, *The Poetics of French Verse* (1998); E. S. Burt, *Poetry's Appeal: Nineteenth-Century French Lyric and the Political Space* (1999); S. Gaunt and S. Kay, *The Troubadours: An Introduction* (1999); J.-J. Thomas and S. Winspur, *Poeticized Language: The Foundations of Contemporary French Poetry* (1999); *Poétiques de la Renaissance: Le modèle italien, le monde franco-bourguignon et leur héritage en France au XVIème siècle*, ed. P. Galand-Hallyn and F. Hallyn (2001); F. Rigolot, *Poésie et Renaissance* (2002); M. Shaw, *The Cambridge Introduction to French Poetry* (2003); *A Short History of French Literature*, ed. S. Kay, T. Cave, M. Bowie (2003); G. W. Fetzer, *Palimpsests of the Real in Recent French Poetry* (2004); J. Acquisito, *French Symbolist Poetry and the Idea of Music* (2006); C. Chi-ah Lyu, *A Sun within a Sun: The Power and Elegance of Poetry* (2006); *Sens et présence du sujet poétique: La poésie de la France et du monde francophone depuis 1980*, ed. M. Brophy and M. Gallagher (2006); J. Petterson, *Poetry Proscribed: Twentieth-Century (Re)Visions of the Trials of Poetry in France* (2008); "Uncanny Poetry/ Méconnaissance de la poésie," ed. C. Wall-Romana, *L'Esprit Créateur* 49.2 (2009)—spec. iss.; *Cambridge History of French Literature*, ed. W. Burgwinkle, N. Hammond, E. Wilson (2011); A. Armstrong and S. Kay, *Knowing Poetry: Verse in Medieval France from the "Rose" to the "Rhétoriqueurs"* (2011).

J. S. Helgeson (med. to early mod.);
S. Winspur (early mod. to 20th c.)

FRENCH POETRY. *See* france, poetry of

FRENCH PROSODY. Metrically, Fr. poetry is syllabic, based on a fixed number of syllables in each line that need not have the same duration or pitch contour. Rhythm is based on word order, sound devices (alliteration, assonance, sound symbolism, etc.), modulations of vowel pitch (such as oratorical, affective, emotional, emphatic, logical, distinctive, contrastive, social, and local accents), and the quantity or duration of the syllables, all these in relation to the metrical foundation of the verse line. In most Fr. poems, rhythmic factors are not periodic (i.e., a pattern does not occur at least twice in the same order); the syllable count and the stanza are metrically determinant. This means, as Louis Du Gardin argued in *Les Premières Addresses du Chemin du Parnasse* (1620), that a Fr. verse line cannot be metrical by itself but only in relation to another line. The perception of the poem as such depends on context ("equivalences contextuelles"; Cornulier 1982, 1995). Therefore, sentences in prose texts such as "Parce que c'estoit luy, parce que c'estoit moy" (Because it was he, because it was I; Michel de Montaigne, *Essais*) or "Et qui vit sans tabac, n'est pas digne de vivre" (Whoever lives without tobacco does not deserve to live; Molière, *Dom Juan*), despite their perceptible 6 + 6 rhythm, should not be considered as verse lines (*vers blanc*).

From the 16th to the 19th c., certain poets (e.g., Jean-Antoine de Baïf) and theorists (e.g., Marin Mersenne) tried to promote a form of Fr. poetry (i.e., the *vers mesurés à l'antique*) based on differences in syllabic duration. They failed because this system was too complicated and too unlike the established one. The syllabic foundation of the Fr. verse line strongly prevailed over Latinate prosody: syllabation characterized the prosody of "classical poetry" until the mid-19th c., even though, to the 18th c. at least, Fr. speakers probably differentiated heavy or long from light or short vowels.

This syllabic system is derived from med. Roman poetries. Poets of the Middle Ages produced different types of metrical combinations for which they drew on cl. Lat. prosody, Lat. prose, and a type of Lat. prosody that disregarded the position of accents or included the same number of words on each verse line (Norberg). The *Cantilène de Sainte Eulalie* (ca. 878), for instance, is a mixture of varying couplets (lines of 10 to 13 syllables; some couplets have one meter, others two) and of two langs. (Lat. and *langue d'oïl*), and the *Vie de Saint Léger* (1040) is made up of iambic couplets whose final assonances make them sound like a combination of two distinct metrical systems. It is likely that the syllabic system prevailed in Fr. on account of its convenience for composition and reception.

Although the notion of accent in the Fr. lang. is strongly controversial and covers different meanings of the word, some scholars since Scoppa have argued that the syllabic foundation of the verse lines, and of the 6 + 6 alexandrine in particular, should be complemented by a fixed or varying number of accents. Since meters reflect speech to some degree, the hemistichs that constitute the verse line must contain emphasized or tonic syllables. In fact, these emphasized syllables owe their existence not to metrics but to the rhythms of speech: because the last vowel pronounced in a word group is usually emphasized in Fr., the last masculine vowel of any metrical pattern is necessarily emphasized. There is, in a word, no metrical stress. The strict cl. superimposition of syntax and meaning on the metrical pattern is not mandatory; it simply helps the reader or listener feel the rhythm:

Mais elle était du monde où les plus belles
choses
Ont le pire destin,
Et rose elle a vécu ce que vivent les roses,
L'espace d'un matin.

(François de Malherbe,
"Consolation à M. du Périer")

(But she was of the world where the most
beautiful things
Have the worst fate;
And being a rose, she lived what roses live,
The space of a single morning.)

From the mid-16th c. to about 1830, poets tended to place words that could potentially receive stress at the end of a given metrical pattern. This allowed them consistently to avoid filling the last position of the pattern with a determiner, a pronoun that comes before its noun, a one-syllable preposition, a countable *e*, a word crossing over between the hemistichs, etc. (Cornulier 1982, 1995; Gouvard).

As illustrated in the above example from Malherbe, Fr. poetry has two types of verse lines. The shorter *vers simples* (lines 2 and 4) have from one to eight syllables. The longer *vers complexes* (lines 1 and 3) contain nine (5 + 4, 4 + 5), ten (4 + 6, 6 + 4, 5 + 5), eleven (5 + 6, 6 + 5), or twelve syllables (6 + 6) and are divided in two hemistichs. In cl. poetry, the caesura clearly marks the frontier between the hemistichs; this metrical mark weakens under the attacks of poets from 1850 onward. Cornulier (1982) formulated a nonmetrical principle applied to Fr. prosody, known as *la loi des huit syllabes,* or the eight-syllable law: we are unable to sense the periodicity of acoustic signals of more than eight phonetic events. In Fr., identification of the exact number of syllables in a line is limited to eight. This cognitive limit explains why lines longer than eight syllables have to be divided. Nevertheless, there are some eight-syllable lines that contain a caesura (in the Middle Ages) as well as nine-syllable lines that do not (in Pierre de Ronsard).

The unstable *e* is one the most noticeable properties of Fr. poetry (Réda). It tends to differentiate poetry and spoken lang. Some parts of southern France aside, it has not been pronounced since the mid-16th c. (as in the word *samedi,* which yields "sam'di" [samdi] in spoken lang., instead of "samedi" [samEdi] in poetic diction), but it is articulated in Fr. poetry not followed by a vowel, an aspirated consonant *'h*, or a line break:

L'alcyon, quand l'océan gronde,
1 23 4 5 67 8
Craint que les vents ne troublent l'onde
1 2 3 4 5 6 7 8
Où se berce son doux sommeil.
1 2 3 4 5 6 7 8

(Victor Hugo, "Le poète dans
les révolutions")

(The Halcyon, when the ocean roars,
Fears the winds ruffle the waters
Where his sweet sleep rocks.)

By contrast, the *e* is elided before a vowel and before the nonaspirated consonant *h*:

Jeun(e) homm(e), ainsi le sort nous presse.
(Young man, thus is destiny pressing us)

At the end of the feminine verse line, the nonaspirated consonant *h* is not counted, as in the following examples from Charles Baudelaire:

Rien n'égale en longueur les boiteuses journées.
1 2 3 4 5 6 7 8 9 10 11 12

("Spleen")

(Nothing is as long as the limping days)

and:

C'est le Diable qui tient les fils qui nous
1 2 3 4 5 6 7 8 9 10
remuent!
11 12

("Au lecteur")

(The Devil pulls the strings that move us!)

There is some dispute about the function of rhyme in Fr. poetry. Some scholars, like Aquien, think it is a prosodic unit the function of which is to indicate the end of the verse line. Cornulier (1981, 2005) objects to these suggestions: if the second occurrence (the echo) may signal the end of a verse line, the first (the call) cannot. Furthermore, since this poetry is based on the repetition of a fixed number of syllables from one line to the next, the second occurrence of a stanza enables the perception of meter(s). Finally, if the last syllable of a group of words is necessarily emphasized, its repetition through rhyme has no metrical function (this is why Ronsard, Joachim du Bellay, and others could write nonrhymed poems). Rhyme, or the identity of the last counted vowel of two or more verse lines, should thus be seen as a rhetorical ornament. Nevertheless, the rhyme scheme has a metrical function since it guarantees the periodicity of stanzas:

Mignonne, allons voir si la rose	a	fem.
Qui ce matin avoit desclose	a	fem.
Sa robe de pourpre au Soleil,	b	masc.
A point perdu ceste vesprée	c	fem.
Les plis de sa robe pourprée,	c	fem.
Et son teint au vostre pareil.	b	masc.
Las! voyez comme en peu d'espace,	a	fem.
Mignonne, elle a dessus la place	a	fem.
Las! las ses beautez laissé cheoir!	b	masc.
Ô vrayment marastre Nature,	c	fem.
Puis qu'une telle fleur ne dure	c	fem.
Que du matin jusques au soir!	b	masc.
Donc, si vous me croyez, mignonne,	a	fem.
Tandis que vostre âge fleuronne	a	fem.
En sa plus verte nouveauté,	b	masc.
Cueillez, cueillez vostre jeunesse:	c	fem.
Comme à ceste fleur la vieillesse	c	fem.
Fera ternir vostre beauté.	b	masc.

Ronsard, *Odes*

(Darling, let's see if the rose
that unfolded this morning
its purple robe in the sun,
has not lost tonight
the folds of its purple dress,
And its complexion, that is like yours.

Alas! see as in such a little space,
darling, on the ground,
Alas! Alas! It dropped its beauty.
Oh, really cruel mother Nature,
since such a flower lasts
from the morning through the night.

Then, if you believe me, darling:
while your age blossoms,
in its most green novelty,
pick, pick your youth.
As for this flower, old age
Will tarnish your beauty.)

The rhyme scheme (*aabccb*) and the order of feminine and masculine rhymes of the first stanza are reiterated in the following stanzas, but the graphemes included in the rhymes change from one stanza to the other. To the degree that it becomes a periodic pattern, rhyme is metrically determinant. The description of cl. stanzas by Cornulier (1995) and Aroui (2000) is probably the most relevant. Cornulier shows that there are pure simple stanzas (*aa*) (*abab*) and (*aabccb*), mixed cl. stanzas (combination of pure simple stanzas), and inverted cl. stanzas (*abba*) and (*aabcbc*).

Since the end of the 18th c. and esp. since Hugo's preface to *Cromwell* (1827), many poets have tried to regenerate Fr. prosody, arguing that the cl. metrical foundation is not musical enough and hinders the successful implementation of rhythmic poetry. They have proposed to dissociate syntax from metrics, shifted the alexandrine caesura (e.g., from 6+6 to 8+4 or 4+8), and eventually broken the metrical foundation of the verse line (Gouvard), as in Arthur Rimbaud's "Qu'est-ce pour nous mon cœur . . ." (What does it matter to us, my heart . . .):

Tout à la guerre, à la + vengeance, à la terreur,
Mon esprit! Tournons dans + la morsure : Ah! passez,
Républiques de ce + monde! Des empereurs,
Des régiments, des co + lons, des peuples, assez!

(All to war, to vengeance, to terror,
my Soul! Let us turn in the wound: Ah! disappear,
republics of this world! Of emperors,
Regiments, colonists, peoples, enough!)

There is no easy or permanent scansion for these lines. Rimbaud wished to destroy the alexandrine and cl. prosody with it. There is no perceptible periodicity. These lines are the culmination of what Murphy (1985) calls "déversification": between 1850 and 1870, poets gradually renewed syllabism. This led to the emergence of *vers libre* (free verse), which, as Roubaud has shown, has always been conceived in reference to the alexandrine. So deeply rooted in Fr. culture is syllabic poetry that its prosody remains the fundamental rhythmical basis even for contemp. poets.

The eight-syllable law and its consequences, or the binary foundation of cl. stanzas, suggest that a cognitive approach would be fruitful for future study of the origins and history of Fr. versification.

■ A. Scoppa, *Vrais Principes de la versification, développés par un examen comparatif entre la langue italienne et la langue française* (1811–14); W. F. Patterson, *Three Centuries of Poetic Theory* (1935); Lote; Norberg; J. Roubaud, *La Vieillesse d'Alexandre: Essai sur quelques états récents du vers français* (1978); C. Scott, *French Verse-Art* (1980); B. de Cornulier, "La rime n'est pas une marque de fin vers," *Poétique* 46 (1981); and *Théorie du vers: Rimbaud, Verlaine, Mallarmé* (1982); H. Meschonnic, *Critique du rythme: Anthropologie historique du langage* (1982); C. Scott, *Vers Libre: The Emergence of Free Verse in France 1886–1914* (1990); J. Bourassa, *Rythme et sens: Des processus rythmiques en poésie contemporaine* (1993); B. de Cornulier, *Art poëtique* (1995); C. Gérard, "The Structure and Development of French Prosodic Representations," *L&S* 41 (1998); R. Pensom, *Accent and Metre in French* (1998); J.-L. Aroui, "Nouvelles considérations sur les strophes," *Degrés* 104 (2000); J.-M. Gouvard, *Critique du vers* (2000); *Le Vers français*, ed. M. Murat (2000); *Le Sens et la mesure: De la pragmatique à la métrique*, ed. J.-L. Aroui (2003); R. Pensom, "La poésie moderne française a-t-elle une métrique?," *Poésie* 103 (2003); S. Murphy, *Stratégies de Rimbaud* (2004); J. Réda, *L'Adoption du système métrique: Poèmes (1999–2003)* (2004); M. Aquien, *Le Renouvellement des formes poétiques au XIXe siècle* (2005); B. de Cornulier, "Rime et contre-rime en traditions orale et littéraire," *Poétique de la rime*, ed. J. Dangel and M. Murat (2005); C. Scott, "*État présent*: French Verse Analysis," *FS* 60 (2006); G. Peureux, *La Fabrique du vers* (2009); T. M. Rainsford, "Dividing Lines: The Changing Syntax and Prosody of the Mid-Line Break in Medieval French Octosyllabic Verse," *TPS* 109 (2011).

G. Peureux

FRISIAN POETRY. Frisian, the nearest continental relative of Eng., was once the speech of an independent and extensive maritime nation along the North Sea coast but is today the lang. of a minority people living partly in the Netherlands and partly in Germany. It exists in three forms: East and North Frisian, spoken in Germany; and West Frisian, spoken in the Netherlands. Only West Frisian, which now has legal status both in the schools and in the public life of Netherlands Friesland (or Fryslân, its official name, in the Frisian lang.), has developed into a full-fledged literary lang. and *Kultursprache*.

As is the case with other Germanic peoples, lit. among the Frisians began with the songs of bards celebrating the great deeds of kings and heroes, though none of those early epics has survived. What has survived is a valuable body of Frisian law, the earliest dating from the 11th c., in a distinctive form marked by such literary devices as alliteration and parallelism and often genuinely poetic in thought and feeling.

When, in about the year 1500, Friesland came under foreign control, Frisian lost its position as the lang. of law and public life, and Frisian lit. sank to a low level. No great poetic figure appeared on the scene until Gysbert Japicx (1603–66), an eminent Ren. poet who with his *Rymlerije* (Poetry), published posthumously in 1668, reestablished Frisian as a literary and cultural lang. The 18th c. saw the rise of many followers and imitators of Japicx; however, no outstanding poetic figure came to the fore. In the 19th c., Eeltsje Halbertsma (1797–1858) dominated the scene; much of his work is folk poetry inspired by Ger. romanticism. Another outstanding figure is Harmen Sytstra (1817–62), a romantic inspired by his country's heroic past, whose work reveals a desire to restore the old Germanic verse forms. The latter half of the 19th c. produced many folk poets, the most popular of whom were Waling Dykstra (1821–1914) and Tsjibbe Gearts van der Meulen (1824–1906). Piter Jelles Troelstra (1860–1930), with themes centering on love, nature, and the fatherland, ushered in a second romantic period.

The 20th c. ushered in a new spirit to Frisian poetry, perhaps most evident in the work of Simke Kloosterman (1876–1938), whose poetic art is both individualistic and aristocratic. In her poems, she gives intense utterance to the longings and disillusionments of love. Rixt (pseud. of Hendrika A. van Dorssen, 1887–1979) also wrote verse characterized by emotional intensity. A first-rate poet at the beginning of the century was Obe Postma (1868–1963), whose verse has vigor, penetration, and philosophical insight. Much of it is poetry of reminiscence; still more is a paean to life and the good earth. Postma was the first to use free verse in Frisian and to use it well.

The new spirit came to full expression and brought about a literary renaissance in the Young Frisian movement, launched in 1915 and led by the daring young nationalist Douwe

Kalma (1896–1953). A talented poet and critic, Kalma sharply denounced the mediocrity and provincialism of 19th-c. Frisian letters. With him and his movement, Friesland began to have an independent voice in Eur. culture. Kalma's genius appears at its freshest in his classic *Kening Aldgillis* (King Aldgillis, 1920), a historical play in blank verse. Kalma's lyric poetry is technically skillful but often nebulous in content. His work—like that of his school—suffers from aestheticism and a poetic jargon laden with neologisms and archaisms.

Among the poets of merit who had their start in the Young Frisian school are R. P. Sybesma (1894–1975), an excellent sonneteer, and D. H. Kiestra (1899–1970), a poet of the soil with a vigorous talent. For decades, the most popular poet was Fedde Schurer (1898–1968), a versatile artist who preferred national and religious themes. His early poems show the influence of Young Frisian aestheticism; those written after 1946 are more direct, unadorned, and mod. In 1946, he helped launch *De Tsjerne* (The Churn), the literary periodical with which most of the important names in Frisian letters were associated until 1968.

Around 1935, some of the younger poets, such as J. D. de Jong (1912–96), Ype Poortinga (1910–85), and G. N. Visser (1910–2001), showed signs of breaking away from the Young Frisian movement, both in spirit and in poetic diction. Douwe A. Tamminga (1909–2002) created his own poetic idiom, based largely on the lang. of the people that he transfigured and sublimated into pure art.

Since World War II, more than 600 books of poetry have been published in Friesland, half of which appeared since the 1990s because of easier ways of getting poetry into print. Postwar disillusionment and existential despair informed much of the poetry of the late 1940s and 1950s, when biting satire and experimental forms openly declared all trads. meaningless. Among the mod. voices were Anne Wadman (1919–97) and Jan Wybenga (1917–94), who led the way in experimental poetry. An experimentalist group led by Hessel Miedema (b. 1929), Steven de Jong (b. 1935), and Jelle de Jong (b. 1933) started its own jour., *Quatrebras* (1954–68). Miedema's *De greate wrakseling* (The Great Wrestle, 1963) in particular clearly demonstrated a refusal to be restricted by conventional thought or form. Sjoerd Spanninga (pseud. of Jan Dykstra, 1906–85) introduced exotic imagery from foreign cultures, esp. Asian, through a wide variety of forms. The verse of Marten Sikkema (pseud. of G. A. Gezelle Meerburg, 1918–2005), Freark Dam (1924–2002), and Klaes Dykstra (1924–97) was more traditional. Other older poets continued to write: Tamminga's *In Memoriam* (1968), written after his son's untimely death, is a masterpiece of profound thought and feeling cast in disciplined but fluid form. Tiny Mulder (1921–2010) is another distinguished poet who frequently effects a remarkable fusion of significant form and content and evinces a penetrating vision that affirms life without evading its horrors and sorrows. A similar life-affirming attitude can also be discerned in the poems by Tsjits Peanstra (pseud. of Tsjits Jonkman-Nauta, 1924–2014), Berber van der Geest (b. 1938), Baukje Wytsma (b. 1946), Eppie Dam (b. 1953), and Margryt Poortstra (b. 1953). Deeply personal, erotic poetry was written by Ella Wassenaer (pseud. of Lipkje Post-Beuckens, 1908–83). A reactionary response toward earlier generations and movements can be found in the work of Tjitte Piebenga (1935–2007) and Trinus Riemersma (1938–2011), whereas a mock-serious tackling of Frisian reality pervades poems by Jan J. Bylsma (b. 1931) and R. R. vander Leest (b. 1933).

In 1967, in order to present poetry to the public at large, the idea of Dial-a-Poem was launched by F. S. Sixma van Heemstra (1916–99). This Frisian initiative, known as *Operaesje Fers*, was soon picked up all over the world. The group of poets who developed this idea included Josse de Haan (b. 1941), whose poems show affinities with surrealism; Meindert Bylsma (b. 1941), whose work reflects a certain playfulness; and Daniel Daen (pseud. of Willem Abma, b. 1942), who has been not only prolific but consistently impressive in his ability to fuse the concrete and abstract.

From the 1970s until the 1990s, two jours. dominated the Frisian literary scene: *Trotwaer* (Sidewalk, 1969–2002) and *Hjir* (Here, 1972–2008). Whereas the first initially contained many contributions by a group of young intellectuals—de Haan and Riemersma among them—who had joined hands to start a nonprofit publishing house, the second depended mainly on work written by young teachers, such as Sybe Krol (1946–1990), Piter Boersma (b. 1947), Jelle Kaspersma (b. 1948), and Jacobus Quiryn Smink (b. 1954). One of this group, Tsjêbbe Hettinga (1949–2013), gained international renown. His compact poetic idiom throbs with the longing to travel to mythical shores. Hettinga knew how to perform; his sonorous recitations attracted large crowds. Hettinga's brother Eeltsje Hettinga (b. 1955) also wrote enticing poems and initiated poetic productions, e.g. *Gjin grinzen, de reis* (No Borders, the Voyage, 2004). Following the example of Tsjêbbe Hettinga, the most recent generation of poets—such as Anne Feddema (b. 1961), Elmar Kuiper (b. 1969), Nyk de Vries (b. 1971), Tsead Bruinja (b. 1974), and Arjan Hut (b. 1976)—are in the recitation of their poems as much performers as they are poets. With poets such as Harmen Wind (1945–2010), Wilco Berga (b. 1947), Jabik Veenbaas (b. 1959), and Albertina Soepboer (b. 1969), they write both in Dutch and in Frisian, unlike the older generations who were solely committed to the Frisian lang. However, Frisian identity continues to be a recurring topic, as in the work of Bartle Laverman (b. 1948), Cornelis van der Wal (b. 1956), and Abe de Vries (b. 1965). The 21st-c. successor to *Trotwaer* is the bilingual (Frisian and Dutch) periodical *De Moanne* (The Month/The Moon), while the monolingual *Ensafh* (Etcetera) has succeeded *Hjir*.

■ **Anthologies**: *It sjongende Fryslân*, ed. D. Kalma (1917); *De nije moarn*, ed. D. Kalma (1922); *Fiifentweintich Fryske dichters*, ed. F. Schurer (1942); *Frieslands dichters*, ed. A. Wadman (1949)—poetry since 1880, Dutch trans.; *Friesische Gedichte aus West-, Ost- und Nordfriesland*, ed. Y. Poortinga et al. (1973)—Ger. trans.; *Country Fair: Poems from Friesland since 1945*, trans. R. Jellema (1985); *The Sound That Remains: A Historical Collection of Frisian Poetry*, trans. R. Jellema (1990); *Frisian Literature Today*, ed. B. Oldenhof (1993); *Hinter Damm und Deich: Die friesische Landschaft wie sie die Dichter sehen*, ed. M. Brückmann et al. (1997)—poems in East, North, and West Frisian, Ger. trans.; T. Hettinga, *Strange Shores/ Frjemde kusten*, trans. J. Brockway (1999); *Gysbert Japix: Een keuze uit zijn werk*, ed. P. Breuker (2003)—Dutch trans.; *Droom in blauwe regenjas: Een keuze uit de nieuwe Friese poëzie sinds 1990*, ed. T. Bruinja and H. J. Hilarides (2004)—Dutch trans.; *Gjin grinzen, de reis/ Geen grenzen, de reis/No Borders, the Voyage*, ed. E. Hettinga (2004)—Dutch and Eng. trans.; O. Postma, *What the Poet Must Know*, trans. A. Paul (2004); *Het goud op de weg: De Friese poëzie sinds 1880*, ed. A. de Vries (2008)—Dutch trans.; *Spiegel van de Friese Poëzie van de zeventiende eeuw tot heden*, ed. P. Boorsma et al., 3d rev. ed. (2008)—Dutch trans.

■ **Criticism and History**: E. H. Harris, *Literature in Friesland* (1956); J. Piebenga, *Koarte skiednis fen de Fryske skriftekennisse*, 2d ed. (1957)—hist., http://www.sirkwy.nl/xmlboeken.html&bid=9&part=2; J. Smit, *De Fryske literatuer 1945–1967* (1968); K. Dykstra, *Lyts hânboek fan de Fryske literature*, 2d ed. (1997)—survey of Frisian lit. from beginnings to 1990s, http://www.sirkwy.nl/xmlboeken.html&bid=76; T. J. Steenmeijer-Wielenga, *A Garden Full of Song: Frisian Literature in Text and Image*, trans. S. Warmerdam (1999); *Handbuch des Friesischen/Handbook of Frisian Studies*, ed. H. H. Munske et al. (2001); *Zolang de wind van de wolken waait: Geschiedenis van de Friese literatuur*, ed. T. Oppewal et al. (2006); *Asega is het dingtijd? De hoogtepunten van de Oudfriese tekstoverlevering*, ed. O. Vries (2007).

■ **Web Sites**: Tresoar: Fries Historich en Letterkundig Centrum, http://www.tresoar.nl; Sirkwy: Fryske literatuerside, http://www.sirkwy.nl.

B. J. Fridsma; H. J. Baron; J. Krol

G

GAELIC POETRY. *See* IRELAND, POETRY OF; SCOTLAND, POETRY OF

GALICIA, POETRY OF. Spreading from the pilgrimage center of Santiago de Compostela throughout Galicia and northern Portugal, Galician-Port. *cantigas* were among the earliest lyric forms in the Iberian peninsula. Most of the secular cantigas are preserved in the *Cancioneiro* (Songbook) *da Ajuda* (mid-14th c.), *Cancioneiro da Vaticana* (end of 15th c.), and the *Cancioneiro Colocci-Brancuti* (now *Cancioneiro da Biblioteca Nacional de Lisboa*, 16th c.). King Alfonso X *el Sábio* (The Wise) was responsible for the religious *Cantigas de Santa María* (13th c.). Galician poets from 1200–1350, the period of greatest achievement, include Martín Codax, Afonso Eanes de Cotón, Bernal de Bonaval, Joan (García) de Guilhade, Joan Airas, Pai Gomes Chariño, Airas Nunes, Pero García, and Pedro Amigo de Sevilla. The Galician-Port. school, although following Occitan models (see OCCITAN POETRY), is best exemplified by the apparently native *cantiga de amigo*, a song of melancholy nostalgia by a maiden for her absent lover.

After the death of Portugal's King Diniz (1325), the old lyric declined; from 1400, Castilian began to replace Galician as the lang. of poetry in the peninsula. The bilingual *Cancioneiro de Baena* (1445) still has a few Galician poems by Macias "o namorado" (fl. 1360–90), the Arcediano de Toro (fl. 1379–90), and Alfonso Álvarez de Villasandino (1340?–ca. 1428). Until the 18th c., little written Galician poetry had been preserved. Diego A. Cernadas de Castro (1698–1777), "el cura de Fruime," wrote bilingual occasional verse and with Manuel Freire Castrillón (1751–1820) marks the gradual rebirth of Galician lit.

Romanticism brought more interest in Galicia's past and its ancient lit., folklore, and other indigenous features. Among others, Antolín Faraldo (1823–53) defended Galician autonomy and, with Aurelio Aguirre (1833–58), the Galician Espronceda, promoted literary regionalism. Francisco Añón y Paz (1812–78), "el Patriarca," is remembered for his patriotic odes and humorous compositions. Alberto Camino (1821–61), author of sentimental and elegiac verse, is a forerunner of the *Rexurdimento* (Renaissance) led by Rosalía de Castro (1837–85). The rebirth was signaled by the Floral Games of La Coruña in 1861, the winning poems of which were published in the *Album de caridad* (1862). In 1863, Castro published *Cantares gallegos* (Galician Songs), the first book written in Galician in the mod. period. In 1880, Castro's *Follas novas* (New Leaves) appeared. Castro also wrote in Castilian, but her social concerns are most obvious in Galician. Moreover, her themes include some of the earliest feminist statements in Galicia, if not on the peninsula. Two of her important contemporaries were Eduardo Pondal y Abente (1835–1917), who wrote *Queixumes dos pinos* (Complaints of the Pines), and Manuel Curros Enríquez (1851–1908), forced to emigrate to Cuba after writing anticlerical verse. There he wrote the nostalgic *Aires da miña terra* (Airs of My Land, 1880). Valentín Lamas Carvajal (1849–1906) sang elegiacally of the peasant life in works such as *Espiñas, follas e frores* (Thorns, Leaves and Flowers, 1875). Other poets of the later 19th c. are José Pérez Ballesteros (1883–1918), known for the three-volume *Cancionero popular gallego* (1885–1912); Manuel Leiras Pulpeiro (1854–1912); and Manuel Lugrís Freire (1863–1940).

Among contemp. poets, the lang. has become more sophisticated. Troubadour trads., *saudade*, and Galician nationalism are still present, while numerous foreign poetic movements have also been influential. The foremost poets of the early 20th c. are Antonio Noriega Varela (1869–1947), Ramón Cabanillas (1876–1959), Victoriano Taibo (1885–1966), and Gonzalo López Abente (1878–1963). Noriegas's ruralism is close to that of the previous generation, but Cabanillas and López Abente reflect Sp.-Am. *modernismo*. Taibo's peasant themes express his social commitment. The best poet of the avant-garde in Galician was the sailor Manoel Antonio (1900–30), who collaborated with the artist Álvaro Cebreiro in the iconoclastic manifesto *Mais Al* (Beyond, 1922). During his lifetime, he published *De catro a catro* (Four to Four, 1928); posthumously, the nearly complete works have appeared, showing him to be a true disciple of creationism in the manner of Vicente Huidobro and Gerardo Diego. Luis Amado Carballo (1901–27) wrote a more pantheistic, vanguard poetry. Ricardo Carballo Calero (1910–90), Florentino Delgado Gurriará (1903–86), Xulio Sigüenza (1900–65), and Eugenio Montes (1900–82) also wrote avant-garde verse before the Sp. Civil War. In the same period, there was Aquilino Iglesia Alvariño (1909–61), and above all, Luis Pimentel (1895–1958). Fermín Bouza Brey (1901–73), one of the best-known Galician writers of the postwar period, also employed elements of med. poetry in the so-called New Troubadourism; in the same vein was Álvaro Cunqueiro (1911–81). In the 1940s and 1950s, Luz Pozo Garza (b. 1922), María do Carme Kruckenberg (1926–2015), and Pura Vázquez (1918–2006) were, among others, the best-known poets, with a wide range of lyrical motives. The Galician landscape is present in the extensive works of Uxío Novoneyra (1930–99). His native mountains of Caurel were presented in a cosmogonic vision of himself. He is present in María Mariño's (1918–67) and Bernardino Graña's (b. 1932) poetry.

Since 1976, Galician poetry has undergone rapid change. The proliferation of texts and critical studies led to the identification of a Golden Age of poetry. Some, such as X. L. Méndez Ferrín (b. 1938), have followed Celso Emilio Ferreiro (1914–79) and Lorenzo Varela's (1917–78) social poetry, while others have maintained Antonio's avant-garde orientation, adding a tendency toward intimism (Claudio Rodríguez Fer, b. 1956), and biographical content (Antonio Tovar, 1911–84).

The last decades of the 20th c. saw the emergence of three poetic groups, each associated with a major metropolitan area—Vigo; A Coruña; and the spiritual and cultural center of Galicia, Santiago de Compostela—and each characterized by generational and poetic conditions. Already well established by the 1980s, the Vigo group of Víctor Vaqueiro (b. 1948) and Alfonso Pexegueiro (b. 1948) witnessed the emergence of Xavier Rodríguez Baxeiras (b. 1945) and, later, incorporated poets such as X. M. Álvarez Cáccamo (b. 1954) and Manuel Vilanova (b. 1944), who had previously written in Castilian. Also linked to the Vigo group are the younger poets of the Rompente group. The A Coruña group, Nebulosa Poética (Nebulous Poetics), brings together a diverse stock of poets, some more representative of the group's philosophy than others. The cultural magazine *Dorna*, supported by a student group from the Universidad de Santiago de Compostela, provided a forum for mature and young voices alike: Luisa Castro (b. 1966), Ramiro Fonte (1957–2008), Luis Gónzalez Tosar (b. 1952), and Ana Romaní (b. 1962). Linked to the Cravo Fondo group are Xesús Rábade (b. 1949), Helena Villar (b. 1940), and Xulio and Xesús Valcárcel (b. 1953 and 1955, respectively). Darío Xohán Cabana's (b. 1952) excellent trans. of Dante and Petrarch were already regarded highly by the 1970s and 1980s. Cabana explores in sonnet form personal experience and the call of his homeland. And despite his meager output in Galician, José Ángel Valente (1929–2000) left a notable mark on its lyric with *Cantigas de Alén*.

Later poetic currents followed a more culturalist approach, incorporating elements of the Port., Eng., and Am. trads., as well as those associated with mod. and postmod. aesthetics. Characteristic of such a poetics are varied musical, visual, and philosophical references and the desire to establish a new, cultured discourse capable of voicing idiomatic and formal experimentation. New conceptualizations of space, metrical form, rhythm, and imagery accompany the assimilation and transcendence of a cl. past. Arcadio López Casanova (b. 1942) is an innovative and foundational figure in this vein. In *Mesteres*, physical and spiritual exile is embodied in a solemn soliloquy that recalls the tragic, polyphonic chorus of antiquity, as it evokes the land and men of Galicia. Also worthy of mention is the vast oeuvre of Méndez Ferrín and, no less so, the innovative work of Vilanova, whose collection *E direivos eu do mister das cobras* could be considered a Galician "happening."

The 1990s ushered in a new wave of perspectives (feminist, ecological, antimilitarist), questioned earlier modes of expression, and reread myth and trad. from a parodic, often subversive, standpoint. The written word's capacity to represent alienation and otherness is explored by María Xosé Queizán (b. 1939). Romaní projects the self onto a vast seascape through the Homeric characters Odysseus and Penelope. Chus Pato (b. 1955) prefers to transgress conventional syntax; Marta Dacosta (b. 1966) fuses landscape and biography; and Helena de Carlos (b. 1964) is firmly anchored in a rigorous, cl. style. The poetry of Isolda Santiago (b. 1960), Yolanda Castaño (b. 1977), and Olga Novo (b. 1975) ranges from sensorial experience and preciosity to primeval, telluric, tribal eroticism.

Antón R. Reixa (b. 1957) weaves colloquial, popular discourse with advertising; Xavier Santiago is drawn to the audiovisual experience of urban environments. Rafa Vilar (b. 1968) is known for his minimalist style; Martín Vega (b. 1975) for his meticulously refined, cosmopolitan style; and Xosé M. Millán Otero (b. 1964) for his seminal conception of the word. Rodríguez and Seara's anthol. (1997) draws together many of these poets who accompany a selection of their work with insightful, critical self-analysis. Still relevant is the creative voice of López Casanova, who, in *Liturgia do corpo* (Liturgy of the Body, 1983), presents a lyrical anthem of self-immersion in response to the inevitability of death. In the epic work of Manuel María (1929–2004), the voice revels before a humanized nature; and the vigor of Méndez Ferrín, in *Estirpe* (Origin, 1994), restructures origins, ethnicity, hist., and land.

Among the most critically acclaimed voices is that of Rodríguez Baxeiras, who received the leading prize for Galician poetry for *Beira norte* (North Border, 1997), a symbolic journey homeward, toward the interiority of the lyrical voice. The books of Fonte, cofounder of the poetic collective Cravo Fondo and an active participant in *Dorna*, fuse personal, intimate experience with plurality and acceptance. Miguel Anxo Fernán Vello's (b. 1958) celebratory, erotic discourse, and Pilar Pallarés's (b. 1957) life-affirming poetics have been equally successful among critics. Manuel Forcadela's (b. 1958) works pay homage to and parody the early works of Román Raña (b. 1960), Paulino Vázquez (b. 1962), and Anxo Quintela (b. 1960). Rodríguez Fer combines critical essay writing with poetic, phonic, graphic, and above all, erotic experimentation. Among the poets exiled in Argentina who contributed significantly to Galician lyric are Varela, Eduardo Blanco Amor (1897–1979), and Luis Seoane (1910–79).

Several collectives have given impetus to poetic production: Brais Pinto (1950s), Rompente, Alén, and De amor e desamor. Galician jours.—*Nordés*, *Cen Augas*, *Dorna*, *Escrita*, *A nosa terra*, *Nó*—have provided space for both the established writers and the new. Luciano Rodríguez's anthol. *Desde a palabra, doce voces* (From the Word, Twelve Voices, 1985) gathers the most representative poetry of the early 1980s. Losada's (1990) and López-Barxas and Molina's (1991) anthols. assemble, with a few notable exceptions, a similar selection.

See BASQUE COUNTRY, POETRY OF THE; CATALAN POETRY; PORTUGAL, POETRY OF; SPAIN, POETRY OF.

■ **Anthologies**: *Cancionero popular gallego* (1886), ed. J. Pérez Ballesteros, 2 v. (1942); Alfonso X, el Sábio, *Cantigas de amor, de escarño e de louvor*, ed. R. Carballo Calero and C. García Rodríguez (1983); *Antología de la poesía gallega contemporánea*, ed. C. A. Molina (1984); *Desde a palabra, doce voces*, ed. L. Rodríguez Gómez (1986); *Festa da palabra*, ed. K. N. March (1989)—contemp. Galician women poets; *Poesía gallega de hoy. Antología*, ed. B. Losada (1990); R. de Castro, *Poems*, ed. and trans. A. M. Aldaz et al. (1991); *Fin de un milenio. Antología de la poesía gallega íntima*, ed. F. López-Barxas and C. A. Molina (1991); *Para sair do século. Nova proposta poética*, ed. L. Rodríguez Góez and T. Seara (1997).

■ **Criticism and History**: A. Cruceiro Freijomil, *Diccionario bio-bibliográfico de escritores*, 3 v. (1951–54); J. L. Varela, *Poesía y restauración cultural de Galicia en el siglo XIX* (1958); R. Carballo Calero, *Historia da literatura galega contemporánea* (1981); L. Méndez Ferrín, *De Pondal a Novoneyra* (1984); C. Davis, *Rosalía de Castro e o seu tempo* (1987); C. Rodríguez Fer, *A literatura galega durante a guerra civil (1936–39)* (1994); A. Tarrío, *Literatura galega* (1994); R. Raña, *A noite nas palabras* (1996); D. Vilavedra, *Historia da literatura galega* (1999).

A. Carreño

GEORGIA, POETRY OF. A written Georgian lit. starts with the beginning of the Christian era (4th c.). The earliest poetic forms are psalms and hymns, initially trans. from Gr. Over the next four or five centuries, Georgian monks, priests, and biblical scholars created an impressive body of ecclesiastical poetry. Ioane-Zosime (10th c.) was a tireless liturgical scholar, writer, translator, and poet, and the likely author of the hymn "Kebai da dibeai kartulisa enisai" (Praise and Glory to the Georgian Language), which suggests that Christ, in his Second Coming, will address the faithful in Georgian. Gradually, spiritual songs acquired more secular coloring, evolving into lyric poems. From the early med. period to the beginning of the 20th c., poetry persists as the predominant mode of literary expression.

In the 11th and 12th cs., narrative poems emerged as the major genre of Georgian poetry. It reached its peak in the 12th c., under Queen Tamar (1184–1213). Among the distinguished poets of her court were Chkhrukhadze, Ioane Shavteli, and Shota Rustaveli; the last is acknowledged as the greatest master of Georgian poetic art. His epic poem *Vepkhis tqaosani* (*The Man in the Panther's Skin*) recounts the adventures of a young prince who aids his friend in search of his beloved, captured by devils. The poem's exceptional richness of vocabulary, powerful images, exquisite alliterations, and complex rhyming are unsurpassed in Georgian poetry.

Rustaveli's poem became a paradigm for poets of the following four centuries, which mark a low point in the devel. of Georgian poetry. The themes and plots of *The Man in the Panther's Skin* are imitated in lyric and narrative poems alike. In the 16th and 17th cs., several Georgian kings distinguished themselves as poets. King Teimuraz I (1588–1662) translated Persian love poems, giving them a distinctly Georgian flavor. He also wrote an epic poem *Tsameba ketevan dedoplisa* (The Martyrdom of Queen Ketevan) dedicated to his mother, Queen Ketevan, who had been held hostage in Persia and was later tortured to death for refusing to renounce her Christian faith. King Archil II (1647–1713) wrote several didactic poems that contemplated the destiny of his country, religion, morals, and the art of poetry. Another writer of royal birth was Vakhtang VI (1675–1737), a poet, translator, and literary commentator. His refined allegorical love poems are tinged with mystical longing.

A far more radical innovator was David Guramishvili (1705–92), a Georgian nobleman who became an officer in the Rus. army. Although his major work, *Davitiani* (The Story of David), is written in traditional metrics, in his shorter lyrics he introduces a great variety of metrical forms and rhyming patterns inspired by folk poetry. *Davitiani* consists of several short narrative poems in which the author both expresses his religious and political thoughts and recounts his tumultuous and eventful life.

Bessarion Gabashvili (1740–91), better known as Besiki, was the next notable figure, a court poet of King Heraclius II. Love is the major theme of his remarkably elegant and sonorous lyrics. He also composed satirical poems aimed at his adversaries at the court.

In the early 19th c., Georgia was annexed by Russia, and Georgian nobility and intellectuals became acquainted with the literary trads. of Russia and Western Europe. Georgian poetry of the following decades displays romantic influences. The movement is best represented by Alexandre Chavchavadze (1786–1846), Grigol Orbeliani (1804–83), and Nikoloz Baratashvili (1817–45). Chavchavadze and Orbeliani express their pride in the Georgian heroic past or meditate on the country's lost glory. Other poems, marked with vibrant sensuality, praise the earthly joys of love, friendship, and feasting. However, Baratashvili is the epitome of Georgian romanticism. In his best-known poem, "Merani" (The Steed), Baratashvili's poetic persona is a passionate rebel challenging his destiny. In his only narrative poem, *Bedi kartlisa* (The Fate of Georgia), he contemplates the consequences of the last devastating battle of King Heraclius II against the Persian invaders. Baratashvili significantly reformed Georgian versification, introducing new metrical forms and integrating contemp. spoken lang.

The second half of the 19th c. is marked by increased dissatisfaction with oppressive Rus. policies. The most prominent figure of this generation was Ilia Chavchavadze (1837–1907). An outspoken critic of the policy of Russification and an advocate of an independent Georgian state, he wrote lyrical as well as narrative poems of patriotic appeal. His friend and contemporary Akaki Tsereteli (1840–1915) enjoyed far greater popularity among the general public, because of the clarity of his images, simplicity, and sonority of his lang. Many of his love poems have become popular songs. Vazha Pshavela (pseud. of Luka Razikashvili, 1861–1915) wrote poems in the vernacular of his native Pshavi, a mountainous region in Georgia. The tragic clash between the society's moral code and ethical concerns of an individual is the major theme of his narrative poems.

The first decade of the 20th c. witnessed a new surge of Western influence in a proliferation of poetic schools that assimilated simultaneously symbolist, futurist, and decadent forms and ideas. In 1916, a group of poets including Titsian Tabidze (1895–1937), Paolo Iashvili (1894–1937), and Giorgy Leonidze (1899–1966) raised the banner of the symbolist movement in Georgian poetry. These poets experimented boldly with vocabulary and versification and adjusted Western genres to the traditional forms of Georgian poetry. Georgian futurist poets—Nikoloz Shengelaia (1903–43), Simon Chikovani (1903–66), Shalva Alkhasishvili (1899–1980), and others—strained the potentialities of lang. to the breaking point, reflecting the same preoccupations as their

Eur. and Rus. counterparts. Galaktion Tabidze (1891–1959), who did not belong to any literary group, is considered the most brilliant poet of the century. An acute sense of loneliness, mourning for loss, and at times a Baudelairean ennui and nostalgia find poignant expression in his fluid and sonorous verses.

After the socialist revolution of 1917, Georgia enjoyed a brief period of independence (1918–21), but in February 1921, the Red Army installed a Bolshevik government. A variety of poetic groups flourished through the 1920s. But the censorship's ever-tightening control resulted in the creative barrenness of the following two decades, as Georgian poets were required to extol the political and ideological superiority and economic achievements of the Soviet state. Several outstanding poets, incl. Tabidze and Iashvili, fell victim to the political purges of the late 1930s.

By the late 1950s, a new generation of poets emerged: Ana Kaladadze (1924–2008), Mukhran Machavariani (1929–2010), Otar Chiladze (1933–2009), Shota Nishnianidze (1929–99), and others. Taking advantage of the relatively liberal political atmosphere, they expressed their sentiments with remarkable vigor, imagination, and technical artistry. From the late 1960s, Lia Sturua (b. 1939), Besik Kharanauli (b. 1939), and many others embraced *vers libre*. In subsequent decades, Manana Chitishvili (b. 1954), Tsira Barbakadze (b. 1965), Giorgi Lobzhanidze (b. 1974), Rati Amaglobeli (b. 1977), and others introduced new rhythms and styles. Kote Qubaneishvili (b. 1953) became the standard-bearer of the postmodernist generation whose flamboyant poetic vocabulary broke many literary taboos.

■ S. Rustaveli, *The Man in the Panther's Skin*, trans. M. S. Wardrop (1912); C. Beridze, "Georgian Poetry," *Asiatic Review* 17 (1930–31); R. P. Blake, "Georgian Secular Literature: Epic, Romance and Lyric (1110–1800)," *Harvard Studies and Notes on Philosophy and Literature* 15 (1933); J. Karst, *Littérature géorgienne chrétienne* (1934); *History of Georgian Literature*, ed. A. Baramidze, 6 v. (1962–78)—in Georgian; *Georgishe poesie aus acht Jahrhunderten*, ed. A. Endler (1971); *L'avangardia a Tiflis*, ed. L. Magarotto (1982); *The Literature and Art of Soviet Georgia*, ed. S. Dangulov (1987); D. Rayfield, *The Literature of Georgia: A History* (1994); *An Anthology of Georgian Folk Poetry*, ed. K. J. Tuite (1994); H. I. Aronson and D. Kiziria, *Georgian Language and Culture* (1999).

D. Kiziria

GERMANIC PROSODY. The earliest poetry recorded in Germanic langs. takes the form of alliterative verse (AV), in which stress, syllable weight, and the matching of syllable onsets (i.e., alliteration) all play structural roles. Although all the Germanic langs. eventually abandoned AV during the Middle Ages and adopted poetic forms characterized by rhyme and alternating stress at equal intervals on the basis of Lat., Occitan, and OF models, the alliterative form appears to have been the only variety in use before Christian missionaries introduced writing on parchment and Lat. poetic types. The Roman historian Tacitus (*Germania*, ca. 98 CE) describes oral poetry (or songs, *carmina*) as the only form of historical lore among the early Germanic peoples, and presumably the form was AV, though this cannot be proved. Neither can AV be proved in connection with any of the references to songs performed by early Germanic people (often to the accompaniment of a lyre or harp) to be found in Gr. and Lat. sources of the 2d to the 6th c., incl. works of Procopius, Jordanes, and Venantius Fortunatus.

The form is usually assumed to have originated relatively late in Germanic prehist., since varieties of it are found in several early Germanic langs., which also offer evidence of a shared poetic trad. in the form of many items of chiefly or exclusively poetic vocabulary, e.g., OHG *balo*, Old Saxon *balu*, OE *bealu*, and Old Icelandic *bǫl*, all meaning "misfortune." The AV form cannot antedate the Common Germanic shift of accent to most nonprefixal initial syllables, since both alliteration and the metrical form depend on stress placement. This accent shift appears to have been a relatively late prehistoric devel. The earliest AV attested takes the form of brief runic inscriptions, beginning with the Norwegian Tune Stone of about 400 CE. The earliest datable examples in ms. are also mostly brief, coming from England. These include the nine-line "Hymn" of Cædmon (ca. 670, first found in mss. of the 8th c.), the five-line "Death Song" of Bede (735, found in 9th-c. mss.), and the two-line "Proverb from Winfrid's Time" (757–86). In addition, the 818-line "Guthlac A," in a ms. of the 10th c., purports (plausibly) to have been composed within a life span of the saint's death in 714. Several other Anglo-Saxon poems show archaic ling. and formal features resembling those encountered in "Guthlac A," but there is no reliable basis for dating them very precisely.

Quite small is the surviving corpus of AV in OHG, fewer than 250 lines all told, amounting to two poetic fragments of the 9th c., *Hildebrandslied* (a heroic lay) and *Muspilli* (a sermon on the Last Judgment), plus a number of shorter poems (see GERMAN POETRY). In Old Saxon are preserved the 9th-c. *Heliand* (a life of Christ) in nearly 6,000 lines and the 337-line *Genesis*; another 600 or so lines of the latter are preserved in an OE trans. A comparatively large corpus of early Germanic AV comes from England (see ENGLAND, POETRY OF). Among the more than 30,000 lines of verse in OE, all the longer poems but *Beowulf* are based on Lat. sources, while the shorter lyrics (such as "The Wanderer" and "The Wife's Lament"), heroic compositions (such as "Waldere" and "The Fight at Finnsburg"), and wisdom poetry (such as "Precepts" and "Maxims I") tend to be more original compositions. The estimable corpus of surviving AV in ME is more diverse, incl. romances (such as *Sir Gawain and the Green Knight* and *The Alliterative Morte Arthure*), historical works (such as the *Destruction of Troy* and *The Wars of Alexander*) and works of religious and/or social commentary (such as *Wynnere and Wastoure* and *Piers Plowman*). Also sizable is the body of extant Old Icelandic AV (see NORSE POETRY), which differs from West Germanic AV in that its form is stanzaic. Of the various eddic meters, which are preserved in about 7,100 long lines, the commonest is *fornyrðislag*, which is also the meter that most closely resembles West Germanic AV. The *dróttkvætt* meter of most skaldic verse (a corpus of nearly 6,000 strophes, mostly of eight lines each) resembles fornyrðislag with the addition of a trochaic cadence, with certain alliterative and syntactic adjustments.

In the earliest poetry in ms., the alliterative long line comprises two verses, an *on-verse* and an *off-verse*, linked by alliteration. An example from the OHG *Hildebrandslied* will illustrate:

x Px x P pxx Px
Mit gēru scal man geba infāhan.
(With a spear should one receive gifts.)

The alliterating words *gēru* and *geba* receive the greatest degree of stress, both being nouns. Syllables bearing a lesser degree of stress (*man* and *-fā-*, a pronoun and a verb root, respectively) are not required to alliterate; in fact, no stressed syllable after the first may alliterate in the off-verse. The remaining syllables are unstressed and alliterate only by coincidence. A vowel may alliterate with any other vowel, but each of the clusters *sp*, *st*, and *sk* (*sc*) alliterates only with itself.

Under the most widely accepted analysis of the form, that of Eduard Sievers, a typical verse comprises four metrical positions. Each position may be filled by one of three metrical entities: (1) a lift, which is usually a heavy, stressed syllable (represented by *P* in the scansion above), (2) a half-lift, which is a syllable of lesser stress, either heavy or light, or (3) a drop, which is paradigmatically one or more unstressed syllables (represented by *x* or *xx*, etc.). A stressed light syllable (represented by *p* above) may combine with another syllable to serve as a lift, a substitution known as resolution; *geba* in the off-verse above, with a light initial syllable, is an example. In combination with the principle of four positions to the verse, restrictions on the placement of half-lifts ensure that the metrical pattern will conform to one of five types. In addition, there are restrictions on the number of syllables that may appear in a drop, the count being more circumscribed in the coda of the verse, which, as in other IE verse forms, is more rigidly structured than the verse onset.

Alternative analyses have been proposed. Heusler (1925–29, 1941) argued that a verse comprises two isochronous measures that may be scanned using musical notation. In 4/4 time, a lift corresponds to a half note and a drop to a quarter or eighth note. Pope refined this analysis, filling the rests allowed by Heusler with notes on a lyre (though this explanation for rests will not serve for Scandinavian verse, which appears not to have been performed to the accompaniment of a musical instrument). Although isochronous theories are still discussed in some Ger.-lang. scholarship, they no longer play any prominent role in anglophone lit., in part because they are not easily reconcilable with the prevailing analysis of Sievers (despite the efforts of Pope). In particular, they ignore the requirement of four metrical positions to the verse that is fundamental to Sievers's analysis. More compatible with Sieversian approaches is the word-foot theory of Russom, according to which verses comprise feet whose contours correspond to the prosodic patterns encountered in the words of the lang. Allowable verse types are then determined by restrictions on the ways feet may be combined. Alternative analyses continue to be proposed because of the relative abstractness and complexity of Sieversian metrics, particularly because of the typological peculiarity of this approach, since quantity and stress (lexical and clausal) both play indispensable roles in the scansion. By contrast, the prosodies of related langs. are based either on syllable quantity alone (as in Gr. and Sanskrit, where the pitch accent is of no account in verse construction, and in Lat., where the stress accent plays no role) or on accent and/or syllable count alone (as in most mod. Eur. langs., in disregard of syllable quantity). Despite its unusual nature, however, and the questions it raises about performance and how the audience could have perceived the metrical template, the analysis of Sievers is verifiable as accurate in ways that the alternative analyses are not.

The prosodic contours allowed by the Sieversian framework dictate that the syntax of AV should differ from that of prose. Words of intermediate stress (or *particles*), such as finite verbs, pronouns, and demonstrative adverbs, are treated as stressed or unstressed in accordance with their position within the clause, as observed by Kuhn. They tend to be grouped before or immediately after the first lift, where they are unstressed; if they appear later in the clause, they bear ictus. Two successive verses in *Muspilli* illustrate the principle: der inan uarsenkan scal: / pidiu scal er in deru uuicsteti (who shall let him fall: / therefore he shall on the battlefield). Here "scal" (shall) is stressed at the end of the clause in the first verse and unstressed in the first drop of the second verse. The regularity is observed with much greater fidelity in OE and in native Old Icelandic compositions in fornyrðislag than in Old Saxon and OHG; indeed, it is violated in the verses from *Hildebrandslied* cited above. It is probably no accident that in OE and Old Icelandic poetry, the use of particles is minimized: in these trads., unlike in Old Saxon and OHG, elimination of unstressed function words, esp. pronouns and articles, was plainly regarded as a stylistic virtue, with the result that Sievers's four-position principle is more plainly discernible in the verse structure.

Although a variety of AV forms arose in Scandinavia, primarily because of the thoroughgoing reduction of unstressed syllables in North Germanic, the older forms persisted nearly unchanged, at least in Iceland, until their demise (or fundamental modification) in the 14th c. The Sieversian patterns are as plain in poetry of the 10th c. as of the 14th. By contrast, even before the Norman Conquest, the form of OE AV was evolving: in some poetry of the late 10th c. and later, the four-position principle at the heart of Sievers's analysis is partly obscured, because of the increased use of particles, and most metrists agree that ME AV does not conform to this pattern at all. In form, some ME AV is less reminiscent of OE poetry than of the alliterative prose style adopted by the homilist Ælfric, ca. 1000 CE, though a genetic connection is dubitable because of the rarity of poetic vocabulary in Ælfric's works. In some other ME works descended from the OE alliterative trad., esp. Lawman's (Layamon) *Brut* (ca. 1200), even alliteration is not essential, as it may be replaced by rhyme. On the continent, where the structure of AV was looser, the appeal of Lat. forms was felt earlier: already ca. 868 (i.e., not long after the composition of the *Heliand*) the monk Otfrid in Alsace composed his *Evangelienbuch*, a gospel harmony in rhymed couplets. By the MHG period, even alliteration had been discarded, and all that remained of the original alliterative form was the mid-line caesura.

■ Sievers; A. Heusler, *Deutsche Versgeschichte*, 3 v. (1925–29); H. Kuhn, "Zur Wortstellung und -betonung im Altgermanischen," *BGDSL (H)* 57 (1933); A. Heusler, *Die altgermanische Dichtung*, 2d ed. (1941); J. C. Pope, *The Rhythm of "Beowulf,"* rev. ed. (1966); W. Hoffmann, *Altdeutsche Metrik* (1967); J. Kuryłowicz, *Die sprachlichen Grundlagen der altgermanischen Metrik* (1970); J. K. Bostock, "Appendix on OS and OHG Metre," *Handbook of Old High German Literature*, 2d ed. (1976); D. Hofmann, *Die Versstrukturen der altsächsischen Stabreimgedichte Heliand und Genesis*, 2 v. (1991); G. Russom, *"Beowulf" and Old Germanic Metre* (1998); K. E. Gade, "History of Old Norse Metrics," *The Nordic Languages*, ed. O. Bandle et al., v. 1 (2002); S. Suzuki, *The Metre of Old Saxon Poetry* (2004); J. Terasawa, *Old English Metre* (2011).

R. D. Fulk

GERMAN POETRY

I. Medieval
II. Early Modern
III. Seventeenth Century
IV. Eighteenth and Early Nineteenth Centuries
V. Nineteenth Century
VI. Twentieth Century

I. Medieval. The written record of Ger. poetry begins in the early 9th c. Charlemagne's biographer Einhard attests to the emperor's interest in preserving pre-Christian poetry (*barbara et antiquissima carmina*), but no collection of vernacular poetry predating the conversion of the Germanic tribes to Christianity has survived. The written remnants of this oral culture are few. Singular in its prominence is the *Hildebrandslied* (*The Lay of Hildebrand*), a 68-line fragment in OHG in irregular alliterative long-line verse (*Germanic prosody) recorded around 830. Also rooted in pagan oral trad. are the two *Merseburger Zaubersprüche* (Merseburg magical charms).

With the consolidation of political power under the Carolingian dynasty (752–911), monasteries became the principal site of literary activity. Almost all extant vernacular texts served religious ends, incl. the *Wessobrunner Gebet* (Wessobrunn Prayer, ca. 814); *Muspilli*, a late-9th-c. fragment employing eschatological visions to promote a godly life; and the Old Saxon (Low Ger.) *Heliand* (The Savior, ca. 830), a gospel harmony in traditional alliterative verse. Theologically learned and a key document within OHG poetics, Otfrid of Weissenburg's *Evangelienbuch* (Gospel Book, ca. 863–71) demonstrated that end rhyme, an innovation derived from Lat. hymns, could effectively replace alliteration as the binding structure in a modified heroic long line. Rhyme is also used in the *Ludwigslied* (Song of Ludwig, ca. 882), a poem celebrating King Louis III of France as a Christian warrior-king, and in the short *Petruslied* (Song of Peter, ca. 900), the oldest known Ger. hymn, a strophic text with neumes, or musical notation, which probably served as a processional song.

While some vernacular poetry certainly persisted during Carolingian rule and later under the Ottonian and Salian emperors, textual evidence is scarce. Lat. prevailed, memorably in the dramas and verse of the abbess Hrotsvit of Gandersheim (ca. 935–973). A substantial 11th-c. collection of Lat. lyric poetry, *Cambridge Song* includes among its many poems of Ger. origin two macaronic poems in OHG and Lat. Several Lat. verse narratives suggest vernacular ties, incl. a heroic epic loosely based on Germanic tribal hist. (*Waltharius*, 9th–10th c.), the first med. beast epic *Ecbasis captivi* (Flight of the Prisoner, ca. 1045), and the romance epic (*Ruodlieb*, mid-11th c.). Only in the mid-11th c. did written Ger. texts begin to reappear, initially with a religious purpose. Prominent examples include the *Ezzolied* (*Ezzo's Song*, ca. 1064), a salvation hist.; the *Annolied* (*The Song of Anno*, ca. 1080), a hagiographic poem in praise of Archbishop Anno of Cologne that is also a world chronicle; and poems and a life of Jesus by the Lower Austrian recluse Ava (ca. 1060–1127), the earliest preserved works of a Ger.-speaking woman writing in the vernacular. Mystics such as Hildegard of Bingen (1098–1179) continued to have their visions and songs recorded in Lat.

In the 11th c., powerful ducal and episcopal courts increasingly supplemented monasteries as sites of active literary interest. The Ger. lang. was changing as well. The transition from the dialects of OHG to MHG is generally dated from 1050. Verse narratives drawing on Fr. sources like Lamprecht's *Alexanderlied* (Song of Alexander, ca. 1150) and Konrad's *Rolandslied* (Song of Roland, ca. 1170) and adventure tales such as *König Rother* (*King Rother*, ca. 1150) and *Herzog Ernst (The Legend of Duke Ernst*, ca. 1180) registered new ling. and cultural confidence. Pointing to the future, in his *Eneit* (Aeneid, 1174–89) Heinrich von Veldeke (ca. 1150–1210) adapted the OF *Roman d'Eneas* in a polished MHG greatly admired by his contemporaries.

The courtly epic was one of two poetic genres that flourished in the decades that followed, a 50-year period, 1170–1220, that defines the high point of MHG lit. The writers were typically aristocrats bound in service to a greater noble and writing under his patronage. Texts were performed orally, providing entertainment and instruction through an idealized fusion of Christian and chivalric principles. Poets found particular inspiration in Fr. texts (notably Chrétien de Troyes) and the Arthurian romances and Anglo-Celtic materials transmitted through them. Three poets stand out. The first, Hartmann von Aue (ca. 1160–65–after 1210), wrote two Arthurian epics (*Erec*, ca. 1180; *Iwein*, ca. 1200), a verse tract about *minne* or courtly love (known as *Die Klage* [The Dispute] or *Das Büchlein* [The Little Book], ca. 1180–85), an atonement legend (*Gregorius*, ca. 1188), and an exemplary tale of self-restraint and compassion (*Der arme Heinrich* [*Poor Heinrich*], ca. 1195). Wolfram von Eschenbach (ca. 1170–1220), arguably the greatest of the three, is remembered principally for his *Parzival* (ca. 1210), a monumental work of some 25,000 lines in which the eponymous hero on an idiosyncratic quest finds the inner nobility and mature religious understanding essential to true knighthood. The third is Gottfried von Strassburg

(d. ca. 1210), whose incomplete *Tristan* (ca. 1210) celebrates the endurance of love beyond all trial and suffering.

For one additional work of distinction, however, there is no known author. The violently tragic narrative of the *Nibelungenlied* (ca. 1200) reaches back to events and characters associated with the Germanic migrations of the 5th and 6th cs. and preserved in oral trad. Although set in the contemp. world of courtly culture, a heroic ethos motivates the action and leads to the final bloodbath. Unlike the courtly epics in rhymed tetrameter couplets, the *Nibelungenlied* features some 2,300 four-line stanzas in the distinctive *Nibelungenstrophe*.

Like the writers of courtly epics, the writers of courtly love poetry, the second major MHG genre, were primarily of knightly origin, composing and performing their works with musical accompaniment within aristocratic circles. A significant selection of their poetry, known collectively as *Minnesang*, remains, although little of their music has been preserved. Early examples are localized in Upper Austria/Bavaria, 1140–70, where relatively simple poems employed the Nibelungenstrophe and featured indirect exchanges between male and female voices and other native forms. After 1170, *Occitan poetry mediated by troubadours and *trouvères* prompted more complex content based on courtly love conventions and formally sophisticated stanza structures. The Minnesang poet typically placed himself in service to a high-born lady of exceptional beauty and virtue, unattainable despite his musical wooing and display of virtuosity. Major poets among the some 150 whose works have been preserved include Friedrich von Hausen (d. 1190), Heinrich von Morungen (d. 1222), Reinmar the Elder (d. ca. 1205), and three poets also known for their courtly epics: Wolfram, master of the subgenre known as *tagelied* (dawn song, *alba*) in which lovers must part at daybreak; Heinrich von Veldeke; and Hartmann von Aue. The greatest is Walther von der Vogelweide (ca. 1170–1230), a professional poet who reinterpreted courtly trads. and expanded Minnesang to praiseworthy women of lower social standing. Walther also provided his patrons with encomiastic tributes and offered social-critical judgments in shrewd single- and multistanza poems (*Spruchdichtung*), a flexible didactic genre of growing importance in the 13th c. He is the first important political poet in Ger.

Courtly love poetry had a long life. Poets sustained and modified its conventions for several centuries. Esp. in later decades, but already in the poems attributed to Neidhart (ca. 1185–1240), more patently sexualized encounters with villagers led to greater realism and also to parody and a trad. of bawdy satire. The images of courtly love were adapted to religious use by the visionary mystic Mechthild of Magdeburg (ca. 1207–1282). Minnesang is the first Ger.-lang. poetry to be preserved in elaborate ms. collections; the most important is the *Grosse Heidelberger Liederhandschrift* (Great Heidelberg Songbook, ca. 1300), also known as the Codex Manesse. Somewhat earlier, some 52 MHG stanzas were recorded in the Codex Buranus (ca. 1230), a compilation largely of Lat. Goliardic verse best known as the textual source for Carl Orff's 1937 cantata *Carmina Burana*.

The 13th c. saw an expansion of didactic poetry. Spruchdichtung was used for tributes; laments; and religious, moral, and political commentary. The most prominent practitioner was the widely admired Heinrich von Meissen, known as Frauenlob (Praise of Our Lady, ca. 1250–1318). The prolific and witty poet known as Der Stricker (The Weaver, ca. 1190–1250) spanned many genres, incl. fables, romances, and short poems. Like a growing number of poets, he was not of knightly origin. Indeed, the world of chivalric valor was becoming increasingly anachronistic. In his satirical narrative *Meier Helmbrecht* (Farmer Helmbrecht, ca. 1268), Wernher der Gartenaere (mid- to late 13th c.) addressed the general social decay. Others settled for adventure and entertainment, writing romances, farcical tales, and continuations of popular epic material. Influential didactic works of the 13th and 14th cs. include Freidank's gnomic *Bescheidenheit* (Sagacity, ca. 1215–30), Hugo von Trimberg's (b. ca. 1230) moral sermon *Der Renner* (The Runner, 1300), and Heinrich der Teichner's (ca. 1310–1378) scolding *Reimreden* (Rhymed Speeches, 1350). The multistrophic *leich* also flourished in the 13th and 14th cs., a virtuoso form employed in musical performance for large-scale themes, both religious and secular.

A growing body of vernacular religious poetry, largely trans. from Lat., served as popular paraliturgical aids: processional songs, pilgrimage hymns, Marian hymns and prayers, confessional poems and sequences. Several well-known hymns of anonymous provenance, incl. the 12th-c. "Christ, der ist erstanden" (Christ, he is risen; later expanded) and the 14th-c. Lat.-Ger. Christmas hymn "In dulci jubilo," remain in active use.

A belated and final example of the great med. poets of aristocratic origin, the Tyrolean Oswald von Wolkenstein (1377–1445), successfully recapitulated the major genres of MHG poetry. He also experimented with polyphonic structures, esp. in two-voiced love songs. But like so much written before 1450, Oswald's work was soon forgotten. A sustained recovery of MHG poetry would begin in the 18th c.

II. Early Modern. In the transition from late med. to early mod. society, the new urban centers and their interests came to dominate literary activity. Didactic poetry was retooled for the urban setting. Writing for a clerical and courtly audience, Heinrich Wittenwiler (ca. 1395–1426) had used a peasant wedding and ensuing conflict to depict a world of grotesque madness in his verse satire *Der Ring* (ca. 1410). In contrast, the Basel humanist Sebastian Brant (1457–1521) populated his *Narrenschiff* (*The Ship of Fools*, 1494) with fools from all social strata. The work achieved unprecedented renown, its verse couplets and woodcuts illustrating human folly (many by the young Albrecht Dürer) reprinted and trans., incl. a Lat. version that made it a Eur.-wide success. Amid a general proliferation of narrative verse in rhymed couplets, the Low Ger. animal fable *Reinke de Vos* (*Reynard the Fox*, 1498) proved esp. popular.

Secular and religious songs also flourished, many compiled in hand-copied mss. and after 1520 in print. Forms ranged from simple strophic songs (later idealized as folk songs, although largely of urban middle-class origin) to the complex stanza structures codified by the Meistersingers, artisan poets who organized instructional schools to pass on their poetic and musical craft. The most famous was the Nürnberg shoemaker Hans Sachs (1494–1576). In *Meistersang*, religious topics dominated. In popular song, sociability was at the fore, even in the laments about the vicissitudes of love, in ballads narrating remarkable events, and in evocations of the solitary life of the journeyman.

A final major devel. in the transition to the new urban culture was the growth after 1400 of humanistic studies. In prosperous cities in the southwest of Germany, an educated elite promoted renewed attention to the ancients and to the poetics of a polished Lat. The new learning imported from Italy also found advocates in progressive courts and bishoprics and, less quickly, selected universities (Heidelberg, Erfurt, Tübingen, Wittenberg, Ingolstadt). The humanist vision would link learned culture across Europe and decisively affect the devel. of Ger. poetry in the 17th c. In the 16th c., however, urbane Neo-Lat. poetry, with its metrical and ling. virtuosity, remained a separate sphere from vernacular verse. The leading Ger. humanist Conrad Celtis (1459–1508), known for his erotic *Amores* (Loves, 1502), recovered forgotten Lat. texts from the Ger. past (incl. the dramas of Hrotsvit of Gandersheim). Celtis was crowned *poeta laureatus* (poet laureate) by Emperor Friedrich III in 1487, the first Ger. to receive the honor.

The finest and most influential poet of the 16th c. was Martin Luther (1483–1546). In his Bible trans. (1522, 1534), Luther affirmed the vernacular and contributed to the gradual standardization of New High Ger. in his attempt to reach a transregional audience. His vividly powerful hymns, many using familiar melodies from religious and secular sources, include "Ein feste burg ist unser Gott" ("A Mighty Fortress Is Our God," 1528) and the Christmas hymn "Vom Himmel hoch da komm ich her" ("From Heaven Above," 1533). His activity led to a radical increase in literacy and set off a wave of song production.

Among the poets who responded with enthusiasm to the reform movement unfolding around Luther, the scrappy humanist Ulrich von Hutten (1488–1523) trumpeted his allegiance in his Ger. poem "Ain new Lied" (A New Song, 1521). A staunch defender, Hans Sachs greeted Luther as "Die Wittembergisch Nachtigall" ("The Wittenberg Nightingale," 1523) in an allegory first written as a Meistersang but then refigured for popular distribution in *Knittelvers*, a simple rhymed form that served as the common verse throughout the 16th c., later becoming directly associated with Sachs and his tone of homespun good humor.

The Reformation and the conflicts that it unleashed provided subject matter for Ger. poetry for the next 100 years. Invectives flew off the presses. Internal strife among the reformers and counterattacks from Catholic intellectuals accompanied the violence and confusion of the late 16th c. Economic and social crises led to an increase in penitential poetry and expressions of a more individualized piety among Lutheran hymn writers, incl. women who also wrote hymns and devotional poetry. Verse narratives continued to enjoy wide popularity, esp. those with a satirical purpose.

III. Seventeenth Century. What decidedly altered Ger. poetry in the 17th c. was the question of how the cultural practices of the learned elite who were writing a polished and erudite Lat. might be realized also in Ger. On the example of Ital., Fr., and Dutch poets who demonstrated that a learned vernacular literature was possible, the new standard was set by Martin Opitz (1597–1639) in his handbook *Buch von der Deutschen Poeterey* (Book of German Poetics, 1624). The reforms that Opitz introduced privileged alternating meters, pure rhymes, mastery of grammar and rhet., and a general literacy in the cl. and Neo-Lat. trads. He insisted on the coincidence of word accent and metric stress. If he was subsequently faulted for his overly prescriptive pronouncements, Opitz's larger vision of how the Ger. lang. might become an apt vehicle for learned culture unquestionably prevailed.

In the new Ger. poetry, eloquence and polish were highly prized but also wit and conceptual invention. Two of the most common genres emphasized the order and constraint of lang.: the epigram and the sonnet. But Ren. poetics and the It. example legitimated a range of options, some defined by formal features and others by content. Occasional verse and poetry with a didactic purpose flourished in all genres. Emblem books, starting with Andrea Alciato's Lat. collection published in 1531 in Augsburg, made ideas and visual materials from the Ren. and classics widely available. After 1617, societies dedicated to the cultivation of the Ger. lang. (*Sprachgesellschaften*) served as intellectual and social networks in selected principalities and urban centers.

Yet Germany itself was split by confessional allegiances and divided into some 300 territories and principalities. In the absence of a single cultural center, regionalism prevailed. The Thirty Years' War (1618–48) devastated both the countryside and the cities, introducing financial chaos, famine, and widespread suffering. Unsurprisingly, poetry also displayed regional and confessional differences. While the widely used term *baroque* usefully signals Ger. poetry's common cause with numerous Eur. vernacular lits., it should not obscure the diversity of texts written between 1600 and 1700.

Major poets after Opitz include Paul Fleming (1609–40), initially a Neo-Lat. love poet, who wrote elegant Ger. verse on Ren. models. The greatest poet of the 17th c., the Silesian Andreas Gryphius (1616–64), wrote rhetorically powerful sonnets, largely on somber themes capturing the traumas of the age and the transitory nature of human experience. The Silesian courtier Friedrich Logau (1604–55) mastered the epigram. Attentive to pastoral themes as well as acoustic effects, the Nürnberg poets, incl. Georg Philipp Harsdörffer (1607–58) and Johann Klaj (1616–56), promoted dactylic verse, as did Philipp von Zesen (1619–89), and they developed a more mannerist style. The Breslau patrician Christian Hofmann von Hofmannswaldau (1617–79) proved a virtuoso master, intellectual, highly sensual, and ironic. His gallant verse, together with the works of his fellow Silesian Daniel Caspar von Lohenstein (1635–83), embodied the excesses of baroque poetry in the eyes of 18th-c. neoclassicists. A simpler, more personal tone was created by Johann Christian Günther (1695–1723), esp. in his love poetry.

Almost all 17th-c. poets wrote religious as well as secular poetry. The Jesuit Friedrich Spee (1591–1635) wrote mystical poetry blending pastoral and Petrarchan elements in his *Trutz-Nachtigall* (Defiant Nightingale, 1649). Johannes Scheffler (1624–77), who took the name of Angelus Silesius when he converted to Catholicism, collected his intellectually paradoxical epigrams and sonnets in his *Cherubinischer Wandersmann* (*The Cherubinic Wanderer*, 1675). The learned Lutheran mystic Catharina Regina von Greiffenberg (1633–94) wrote sonnets and songs marked by metaphorical inventiveness and evident delight in the natural world. The Lutheran pastor Paul Gerhardt (1607–76), the most significant hymnist since Luther, achieved a tone of simple devotion and clarity. Many of his hymns are still sung today, incl. his free trans. of "Salve caput cruentatum" as "O Haupt voll Blut und Wunden" ("O Sacred Head now wounded"), the anchoring chorale in J. S. Bach's *St. Matthew Passion*.

Participation in the literary culture of 17th-c. Germany required education. Its formal institutions were closed to women, and only a few women were afforded the luxury of private tutoring enjoyed by Greiffenberg or Sibylle Schwarz (1621–38), daughter of a Greifswald patrician. Religious experience, however, increasingly legitimated the individual voice, and both men and women responded. The devotional hymns and poems by the Schleswig-Holstein dissenter Anna Ovena

Hoyers (1584–1655) lacked metrical regularity and other signs of Opitz's reforms, but she was capable of an assertive verse in defense of her sectarian commitments. At the end of the 17th c., the introspection and emotionality of Pietist worship impelled Gottfried Arnold (1666–1714), Gerhard Tersteegen (1697–1769), Count Nikolaus Ludwig von Zinzendorf (1700–60), and some 100 new poets to song.

IV. Eighteenth and Early Nineteenth Centuries. The 18th c. witnessed broad social and intellectual changes incl. the postwar economic recovery of urban centers, the growing cultural influence of middle-class professionals, and the expansion of the book trade. Scientific wonder combined with a vital interest in perception to modify the lang. of theology and bring new visual energy to poetry. The Swiss scientist Albrecht von Haller (1708–77) probed central issues of moral philosophy in his verse treatises and celebrated the sublimity of *Die Alpen* (*The Alps*, 1729). The Hamburg patrician Barthold Heinrich Brockes (1680–1747) published nine volumes of his *Irdisches Vergnügen in Gott* (Earthly Delight in God, 1721–48) in which his physicotheological poetry proclaimed evidence of divine providence in every aspect of the natural order. The call of the Frenchman Nicolas Boileau and others for a renewed commitment to the classics was answered as poets polished the vernacular in trans. and adaptations from Lat. and Fr. In his *Versuch einer critischen Dichtkunst* (Attempt at a Critical Poetics, 1730), the Leipzig professor Johann Christoph Gottsched (1700–66) defined neoclassical norms in a Ger. context and struggled to give order to the abundance of poetic forms. The poetic values of gallant verse found middle-class adaptation in the polished social songs of Friedrich von Hagedorn (1708–54) and in the playfully erotic anacreontic poetry of Johann Wilhelm Ludwig Gleim (1719–1803) and many others. Christian Fürchtegott Gellert (1715–69) gave didacticism new poetic grace in his *Fabeln und Erzählungen* (Fables and Tales, 1746), the best seller of the century. In his verse narratives, Christoph Martin Wieland (1733–1813) combined a cultivated, elegant wit with urbane sensuality and accelerated the devel. of a transregional readership for Ger. poetry in his jour. *Der Teutsche Merkur* (The German Mercury, 1773).

Women were increasingly among the readers of poetry and, if more slowly, among its writers. Anna Luise Karsch (1722–91), a self-taught poet of humble origins and a voracious reader, was the most famous woman poet of the era, celebrated for her "native genius." After 1740, Eng. poetry joined Fr. and It. as models for emulation. John Milton's *Paradise Lost* became the focus of heated debates on the limits of the creative imagination. The new and the marvelous gained footing within a poetological discourse previously constrained by rationalist principles.

At midcentury, F. G. Klopstock (1724–1803) revealed the eruptive power of poetic lang. in the opening cantos of *Der Messias* (*The Messiah*, 1748–73), his epic of Christ's passion and triumph. In his bid to create the great Ger. epic, Klopstock introduced the hexameter line and intensified syntax and diction. His imaginative breadth and affective rhet. offended those committed to neoclassical reforms but attracted readers putting the text to devotional use and writers eager to enhance Ger.'s expressive capacity. His *Oden* (Odes, 1771) became the basis for enthusiastic and even brash critical pronouncements, the most important by J. G. Herder (1744–1803), and accelerated discussion about original genius and the sublime. Klopstock eschewed rhyme and the simple alternating rhythms that dominated 18th-c. poetry and instead wrote odes and elegies in adapted cl. meters, in original meters of his own definition, and in free rhythms legitimated by the example of Pindar and the Psalms. He demonstrated how Ger. might serve as a vehicle for the depths of sentiment as well as hymnic sublimity, stimulating a vast poetry of sensibility (*Empfindsamkeit*) with its trope of heartfelt emotion.

On Klopstock's example, Herder proclaimed the ode and, with it, all lyric poetry, the highest of the literary genres. For Herder, true poetry resided in the premod. era, with Homer, the Hebrew Psalms, the songs of Germanic bards, Ossian, and similar works valued as songs of the people (*Volkslieder*). In his estimation, Klopstock came the closest of any mod. writer to recovering their lost immediacy and enthusiasm. Klopstock became the idol of many younger poets, incl. those in Göttingen who formed a fellowship around his example (the *Hainbund*), and who featured his poetry in a new transregional *Musenalmanach*. Such poetry almanacs became the principal vehicle for the distribution of poetry in the next decades. Ludwig Christoph Heinrich Hölty (1748–76), the strongest lyric talent in the group, followed Klopstock's example by employing cl. meters in his odes. Johann Heinrich Voss (1751–1826) later distinguished himself for his idylls and his hexameter trans. of Homer. Friedrich Stolberg (1753–1835) and his brother Christian (1748–1821) enthusiastically echoed Klopstock's patriotic poetry. On the fringes of the Göttingen circle, Gottfried August Bürger (1747–94) made his name on the basis of his ballads and love poems.

J. W. Goethe (1749–1832) is not only the single most important heir to these midcentury transformations of Ger. poetry but a major participant in them. His specific attentiveness to Klopstock is evident in the remarkable free-rhythm poems written between 1772 and 1774, in which he probed the construction of poetic enthusiasm and emotional immediacy, incl. "Wandrers Sturmlied" ("The Wanderer's Storm Song"), "Ganymed," and "An Schwager Kronos" ("To the Postilion Chronos"). But unlike his peers, Goethe moved with decisive energy to create a poetry apart from and, indeed, well beyond the 18th-c. example. A dramatist, novelist, scientist, and court administrator in Weimar, as well as a poet, Goethe constantly experimented in terms of genre, voice, and form, absorbing and reworking all that he appreciated from the most colloquial style to the highest hymnic verse and making most of what he wrote seem utterly effortless. What he created frequently became the genre's new paradigm, as, e.g., his recreation of the Lat. love elegy in mod. setting in the elegiac distichs of the *Römische Elegien* (*Roman Elegies*, 1795) or the classic epic in the hexameters of *Hermann und Dorothea* (1797) with its response to the dislocations of the Fr. Revolution. Unlike Klopstock, Goethe remained appreciative of rhyme, although not wedded to its use. The relationships of love, desire, and creativity and the continuity and coherence of the natural world, with its analogues in human experience, became his greatest themes, to which he returned again and again. In *Faust* (1808, 1832) Goethe programmatically recapitulated much of the Eur. poetic trad. from Gr. trimeter, through folk song, Minnesang, Knittelvers, to Sp. trochees, Fr. alexandrines, Eng. blank verse, and It. *ottava rima* and *terza rima*. In his middle years, he turned to Persia and the Near East, engaging the poetry of Ḥāfiẓ (d. 1389) in a substantial lyric cycle, the *West-östlicher Divan* (*West-Eastern Divan*, 1819). He later wrote a smaller cycle evoking Chinese poetry, *Chinesisch-Deutsche Jahres- und Tageszeiten* (Chinese-German Seasons of the Year and Day, 1827), and he actively promoted his notion of world lit., envisioning dynamic exchange among literary cultures large and small with salutary political influence. With Goethe, Ger. poetry decisively achieved full Eur. stature.

No single poet has had as major an impact on Ger. poetry as Goethe. Consequently, it can be easily forgotten that, in the 1780s, Bürger, Hölty, Voss, even the early Friedrich Schiller (1759–1805) were better known as poets. Goethe was celebrated primarily as a novelist and dramatist in his first decades of writing. In the 19th c., he came to dominate Ger. letters and, in particular, Ger. poetry.

Schiller, primarily a dramatist and theorist, published poetry in the 1780s that seemed unlikely to compel broad interest; much was rhetorically cumbersome, sober, and overtly philosophical. But his lament at the loss of Gr. antiquity with its divinity-filled world in "Die Götter Griechenlands" ("The Gods of Greece," 1788) proved electrifying in its indictment of contemp. society for its mechanistic notions of nature and impoverished abstractions; and his hymnic "An die Freude" ("An Ode to Joy," 1785) sparked utopian dreams. (Ludwig van Beethoven's setting in his Ninth Symphony serves as the new Eur. anthem.) In partnership with Goethe after 1794, Schiller used his poems and essays to articulate an agenda for the renewal of Ger. culture that has become known as Weimar Classicism. "Das Ideal und das Leben" ("The Ideal and the Actual Life," 1795) can stand for multiple poems proclaiming the mediating function of aesthetic experience between the material and the ideal. In "Der Spaziergang" ("The Walk," 1795), an elegy in cl. distichs in which landscape poetry is recast for philosophical purposes, Schiller provides a cultural-historical meditation on human devel. from the blissful constraints of primitive experience through mod. alienation to the recovery of harmony at the heights of poetic consciousness. Both were published in *Die Horen* (The Hours), his high-minded but short-lived periodical, where he also published his theory of naïve and sentimental poetry and other aesthetic treatises.

Schiller and Goethe collaborated on a collection of ballads that appeared in Schiller's *Musenalmanach* in 1797. The mod. ballad rightly claims its generic roots in med. and early mod. oral trad. In its 18th-c. revival, Bürger's "Lenore" (1773) and Goethe's "Der König in Thule" ("The King of Thule," 1774) and "Erlkönig" ("The Elf

King," 1782) consciously evoked earlier stylistic gestures and supernatural strains. The ballads of 1797, incl. Goethe's "Die Braut von Korinth" ("The Bride of Corinth") and "Der Zauberlehrling" ("The Sorcerer's Apprentice") and Schiller's "Die Kraniche des Ibykus" ("The Cranes of Ibykus"), are more intellectually self-conscious. The ballad, and its variant the "Romanze" with generic links to Sp. and other Romance models, would prove to be a favored vehicle of the romantic poets, who emphasized its affinities with the folk song.

In his laments about the mod. age, its alienation and fragmentation, its deadening materialism and rationalism, Schiller inspired an entire generation of romantic poets. Their core narrative of a primal unity once experienced in nature, in childhood, in ancient Greece, the Middle Ages, and other cultural-historical moments given Edenic status, but now lost in the present, found endless variation in the expression of crisis and the quest for renewal and restoration. Aesthetic experience, the imagination, and, above all, poetry itself became potential agents of redemption.

The single most compelling representation of the poet's plight in the present moment, intensified by acute knowledge of the richness of what has been lost appears in the works of Friedrich Hölderlin (1770–1843). The lost ideal is figured in images of plentitude, in a personalized and benevolent natural world vibrant with divinity, in the cultural-historical ideal of cl. Greece, and in idyllic images of childhood, home, and loving embrace. Hölderlin assigned heroic stature to the poet, who most urgently and painfully bears the knowledge of the mod. day's impoverishment. The poet is also the purveyor of hope as he creates a remnant in poetic speech of what once was and anticipates what might yet be. Like that of many romantics, Hölderlin's vision of hist. was deeply rooted in Christian eschatological structures, an appropriation evident in his great elegy "Brod und Wein" ("Bread and Wine," 1800–01) and the late hymns such as "Patmos" (1802–03). The verbal power of his poetry is based on a richly inflected lang. indebted to Klopstock's example and his own intensive study of Gr. poetry, esp. Pindar and Sophocles; on intentional musicality; on the use of cl. forms; and on tautly structured lines with resonant symbolic metaphors. Although 70 of Hölderlin's poems were published before his confinement in 1806 due to recurring mental illness, which lasted until his death, they were scattered and largely unknown. Appreciation for his great elegies and hymns and later fragments was made possible by the rediscovery of his works in the early 20th c.

Like Hölderlin, Friedrich von Hardenberg (1772–1801), who published as Novalis, transformed existing religious discourse to shape a syncretistic vision with a Christian core. Reversing the spatial trajectory of key Enlightenment terms, the quest in Novalis's single most important piece, "Hymnen an die Nacht" ("Hymns to the Night," 1800), a six-part prose poem with lyric inserts, leads downward into the darkness of earthly despair and eroticized longing. Out of individualized anguish arises the emotionalized certainty that death marks the recovery of wholeness in the final mystical union with Christ as beloved. The poem was published in the *Athenaeum*, the principal organ of the romantic writers in Jena who sought to revolutionize philosophy and lit. by freeing them from rationalist and classicist constraints, and more boldly, to transform the human spirit.

Within the Jena circle, August Wilhelm Schlegel (1767–1845), in particular, worked to expand Ger. poetic forms by promoting Romance models. The Petrarchan sonnet became the signature genre of the romantic movement, produced in staggering quantity, and a lightning rod for attacks on its new poetic directions.

In Heidelberg, the second principal site of romantic activity, an enthusiasm for recovery of the Ger. past also had immediate impact on poetry. Achim von Arnim (1781–1831) and Clemens Brentano (1778–1842) gathered more than 700 poems from printed and oral sources and edited these "songs of the people" to make them compelling for mod. readers, to publish the landmark anthol. *Des Knaben Wunderhorn* (The Youth's Magic Horn, 3 v., 1805–08). Herder had provided a precedent in 1778–79 with his successful two-volume collection of folk poetry drawn from international sources. But it is the Ger.-speaking world that is monumentalized in these "old German songs," the collection's subtitle. The simple strophic song, with its accessible diction, generally naïve tone, suggestion of orality, abundant rhyme, and thematic preoccupation with ordinary people and nature, became in the next decades a vehicle by which multiple poets sought to create a new Ger. poetry.

There was a precedent. In a large body of poetry that is mostly forgotten today, Ludwig

Tieck (1773–1853) had scripted new formulas and metaphors for romantic verse devoid of cl. forms and mythology and inserted examples into his early narrative works. Brentano readily absorbed the new lang., but he also strained the simplicity of the folk-poetry model in his musically evocative verse, where his virtuosity was enhanced by the legacy of baroque and med. poetry. In repeating laments of estrangement and loss, he attested to the inadequacy of romantic aesthetic solutions to human existential need. After returning to his Roman Catholic faith in 1817, Brentano readdressed much of his creative effort to religious purposes. Joseph von Eichendorff (1788–1857) also adapted the forms and ambience of folk song in his ostensibly artless but carefully crafted poetry. His poems convey a pervasive longing for something beyond reach and definition and feature beautiful, ominous enticements from the imaginative depths, often explicitly erotic, that promise consolation and release. The answer Eichendorff endorsed in his poetry lay elsewhere, heavenward and in the future, located for him by his firm Catholic faith. But he never ceased evoking the attraction of the earthly enchantments whose power he repeatedly sought both to awaken and to constrain in his highly musical poetry.

Tieck, Arnim, Brentano, and Eichendorff all embedded their poems and songs in their novels (as did Goethe in *Wilhelm Meisters Lehrjahre* [*Wilhelm Meister's Apprenticeship*, 1795]). Single collected volumes of poetry were still relatively rare. The most enduring legacy for this large body of romantic poetry is musical; Beethoven, Franz Schubert, Robert Schumann, Johannes Brahms, Hugo Wolf, Gustav Mahler, Richard Strauss, and many lesser composers have guaranteed its international fame as the Ger. *lied.* Some poets, such as the epigonal romantic Wilhelm Müller (1794–1827), author of the cycles *Die schöne Müllerin* (*The Beautiful Maid of the Mill*, 1821) and *Die Winterreise* (*Winter Journey*, 1824), are known primarily through the musical settings of their works.

V. Nineteenth Century. In response to the events of the Fr. Revolution, Klopstock wrote a substantial number of poems celebrating its promise and later condemning its excesses. The Napoleonic invasion and the Wars of Liberation (1805–15) again led to excited poetic responses. Ernst Moritz Arndt (1769–1860), Friedrich de la Motte-Fouqué (1777–1843), and Theodor Körner (1791–1813) joined in the poetic call to arms. Unlikely forms such as Friedrich Rückert's (1788–1866) *Geharnischte Sonette* (Armored Sonnets, 1814) were also fielded in the fight for "folk and fatherland." The ballads and earnest folk songs of Ludwig Uhland (1787–1862) served political ends in gentler more conservative ways. Rückert later turned his attention as a scholar to irenic purposes, finding refuge in the rich poetic world of Persia and the Near East. Near Eastern forms, prominently the *ghazal*, were popularized by him and August von Platen (1796–1835).

After 1815, most poets were keenly aware that not only a political era had passed but a poetic one; they were uncertain about the future and the status of poetic lang. An heir to the legacy of romantic tropes and forms and a master in his demonstration of the artifice as well as the seductive attraction of the world constructed from them, Heinrich Heine (1797–1856) used irony and self-deprecating humor to define dissonance and disillusionment as the 19th-c. poet's plight. His early collection *Das Buch der Lieder* (*The Book of Songs*, 1827) provides multiple variants on the theme of unrequited love, incl. the well-known "Loreley" and the rhythmically agile two-part cycle *Die Nordsee* (*The North Sea*, 1825–26). His verse satires *Atta Troll* (1843, rev. 1847) and *Deutschland. Ein Wintermärchen* (*Germany: A Winter's Tale*, 1844) written after emigration to Paris in 1831, where he lived out his life as a journalist and writer in political exile, mark his critical hostility to the political verse of his contemporaries as well as to the philistine culture of bourgeois Ger. society. In the freshest components of his *Neue Gedichte* (*New Poems*, 1844), *Romanzero* (1851), and later poems, Heine delivered sharp political and social commentary, grappled with his Jewish identity, and registered the suffering of debilitating illness that confined him to bed in his final eight years.

August Heinrich Hoffmann von Fallersleben (1798–1874), Ferdinand Freiligrath (1810–76), Georg Herwegh (1817–75), and others writing in the 1840s, the so-called *Vormärz* of optimism that preceded the failed revolution of 1848, produced rousing, occasionally bombastic songs to promote the liberal vision of Germany unity and radical reform. Many were set to familiar tunes, such as Hoffmann von Fallersleben's "Deutschland, Deutschland über alles" (1841), which became the national anthem, 1922–45 (the third stanza serves as the current national anthem of the Federal Republic of Germany).

After 1849, bitterness and silence largely replaced their boisterous verse.

Most poetry of the mid-19th c. registered Germany as a political and cultural backwater. In this period of resignation and restraint, the so-called *Biedermeier* era, poets turned inward, socially and psychologically. The carefully ordered life and the cultivation of the home-grown idyll were accompanied by pronounced strains of melancholy, psychological frailty, and unsettling premonitions of unseen menace. Poets typically had a narrow range and used their art in varying ways to flee lives they experienced as deficient and distasteful. Platen polished his sonnets, odes, and imported verse forms, seeking an aesthetic refuge from life's muddle and guilt. Nikolaus Lenau (pseud. of Franz Nikolaus Niembsch, 1802–50), first built a reputation on evocations of the Hungarian landscape of his childhood and then made melancholy and despair the thematic core of his culturally pessimistic work. The best poets, such as Eduard Mörike (1804–75), demonstrated new ways to express elusive sensations, fleeting perceptions, and fragile moments of aesthetic pleasure. Mörike stands out for his exceptional facility in a range of inherited genres and verse forms, from cl. meters and sonnets to folk song, and for the evocative lyricism of his verse. Whether probing the unconscious or evoking the biological world of her beloved Westphalia in precise realist diction or grappling with received religious lang. to express faltering conviction, the lyric poetry and ballads of Annette von Droste-Hülshoff (1797–1848) reveal an interest in interiority, the instability of human identity, and the ambivalence of perception. Anchored and constrained by class and gender, the aristocratic Droste-Hülshoff repeatedly staged a surrendering to imaginative depths with varying consequences: fright, guilt, unresolved longing, and resignation or relief on return to the familiar but rarely any alteration in the external world of her poetic protagonists.

Even though the second half of the 19th c. has been widely considered hostile to poetry, epigonal poets such as the immensely popular and now forgotten Emanuel Geibel (1815–84) prospered. Poets remained largely unresponsive to industrialization, urbanization, secularization, and other large-scale social changes. Lyric poetry was confirmed as a refuge, domestic and psychological, from all that was shifting in the public sphere. Exceptions such as the Swiss realist Gottfried Keller (1819–90) struggled to find appropriate poetic voice. The period 1840–1914 witnessed an enormous growth in poetic anthols., which were deemed supremely fit for moral improvement, educational purposes, and social entertainment.

VI. Twentieth Century. The notion that poetry, and more broadly art and beauty itself, must proclaim a timeless realm apart from public and political life was embraced not only by middle-class readers but also by fin de siècle artists who otherwise rejected bourgeois notions of artistic consumption. They radicalized the claim: only apart from all things external and contingent can true art flourish. Mörike's "Auf eine Lampe" ("To a Lamp," 1846) and the Swiss Conrad Ferdinand Meyer's (1825–98) "Der römische Brunnen" ("The Roman Fountain," 1882) had prefigured the interest in self-sufficient artifacts and symbolic lang. transcending ephemeral experience. Stefan George (1868–1933) embodied aesthetic modernism in its most elitist expression. From 1890 onward, he carefully printed his poems in stylized orthography in limited eds. on fine paper as repositories of a poetic beauty otherwise lost to what he saw as a debased and vulgar civilization. Poetry served a sacred function in a sectarian cult with strong homoerotic attachment and messianic zeal. His collections include *Das Jahr der Seele* (The Year of the Soul, 1897) with its refined symbolic landscapes, and *Der siebente Ring* (The Seventh Ring, 1907) with its dreams of civilization renewed. Among the younger writers attracted to the aestheticist vision was the Viennese prodigy Hugo von Hofmannsthal (1874–1929), who wrote exquisite and surprisingly mature poetry while still of school age. In the ten years of his poetic production after 1890, Hofmannsthal evoked a world of impression in which the formal perfection of the poem served as the sole site of stability in a transient phenomenal world. Later, Hofmannsthal rejected this aestheticist vision—and with it, lyric poetry—on ethical grounds, turning to drama, opera, and other forms.

Rainer Maria Rilke (1875–1926), who began in Prague as a prolific but unexceptional poet, ended his career acclaimed as the major lyric voice of the early 20th c. A search for meaning distinguished each phase of Rilke's devel. and repeatedly altered his stylistic choices. His poems trace a general path from subjectivity and emotionalism in *Das Stunden-Buch* (*The*

Book of Hours, 1905) via *Das Buch der Bilder* (*The Book of Images*, 1902, 1906) to a focus on external objects, particularly works of aesthetic value, in *Neue Gedichte* (*New Poems*, 2 v., pub. 1907–08). His *Dinggedichte* implicitly underscore how alienated he believed mod. humans to be from the integrity and intensity of the phenomenal world. In the *Duineser Elegien* (*Duino Elegies*, 1923), a ten-poem cycle in free-rhythm verse, and the two-part cycle *Sonette an Orpheus* (*Sonnets to Orpheus*, 1923), works that are generally considered Rilke's greatest achievement, solutions for the human plight are proclaimed in the creative and transforming word, an aesthetic redemption that turns the visible world into an inner invisible one, bestowing purpose in the face of transience.

The creative energy that surged through the Ger.-speaking world after 1890 did not run its poetic course with George, Hofmannsthal, and Rilke. There was scarcely a poet of note who did not share a fundamental antipathy toward the perceived self-satisfactions of bourgeois society, with its sentimental heroic trappings, growing bureaucracy, philistine if prosperous tastes, and enforced propriety. Some marked their distance through fanciful ling. play, like Christian Morgenstern (1871–1914), best known for his humorous *Galgenlieder* (*Gallows Songs*, 1905). Others fashioned their lives as well as their poetry around imaginary identities and exotic alternatives to Wilhelmine society, such as the unconventional feminist Else Lasker-Schüler (1869–1945), whose protective disguises and ling. creativity could not, in the end, ward off forced exile as a Jew.

After 1910, a poetic explosion signaled the arrival of new, determinedly disruptive voices. Expressionism was edgy and assertive; it broke decisively with the cadences of aestheticism and the cult of the beautiful. Jakob van Hoddis's (1884–1942) disjunctive images ordered in simple rhymed stanzas in "Weltende" ("End of the World," 1911) became a model for multiple poetic collages, half-real, half-surreal. Apocalyptic anticipation marked the work of Georg Heym (1887–1912), and ling. experiments honed lang. to maximize intensity in the futurist poetry of August Stramm (1864–1915). Ernst Stadler (1881–1914) filled long irregular lines with vitalistic assertions. Expressionist poetry burned brightly and quickly. By the end of World War I, it yielded center stage to drama, where calls for a new man and a new community continued to be sounded. *Menschheitsdämmerung* (*Dawn of Humanity*, 1920), its signature anthol., was assembled retrospectively by Kurt Pinthus (1886–1975).

The Salzburg medical orderly Georg Trakl (1887–1914), who died from a drug overdose after the battle of Grodek, wrote purposefully hermetic poetry. Trakl employed resonant lang. with self-consciously repetitive and derivative images (often from the poetic repertoire of Hölderlin and the romantics), reassembled like fragments in associative structures. He obsessively filled his symbolic landscapes with signs of decline, disintegration, and guilt only partially clarified.

In terms of cynicism, Gottfried Benn (1886–1956), a physician, surpassed the provocations of his contemporaries in his early collections beginning with *Morgue* (1912). Benn later insisted on a stern and individualized cerebralism, denying the mod. human any consolation in nature or sentiment, religious community or social program of salvation (his public, if short-lived, affiliation with National Socialism notwithstanding). In his *Statische Gedichte* (Static Poems, 1948) largely written between 1935 and 1945, the poetic word in abstracted form is considered the sole authentic bulwark against nihilism and pure of the deceits of cultural hist. His late poems and his theory of absolute poetry in *Probleme der Lyrik* (Problems of Lyric, 1951) proved esp. attractive to young writers in postwar Germany, where he replaced Rilke as a poetic example.

But in the era of the Weimar Republic, other alternatives to Benn's stern modernism existed. The most radical was the short-lived culture of Dada, created in 1916 by avant-garde artists in Zurich, the center of political and intellectual exile. Under Hugo Ball, the Cabaret Voltaire offered soirées pillorying established culture. Poetry performances included sound experiments (from phonetic patterning to pure noise), repudiation of ling. sequencing (play with simultaneity and with stasis), and montage. Dada with a more political edge followed in Berlin in 1918 and other Eur. cities.

In other ways, poetry became more public. Cabarets and revues brought poetry onto the stage in the form of chansons and songs. Joachim Ringelnatz (pseud. of Hans Bötticher, 1883–1934), poet and cabaret performing artist, added humor to the scene, as did Erich Kästner (1899–1974). Kurt Tucholsky (1890–1935) wrote satirical poems with pointed political purpose.

The most important poet to arise out of this milieu was Bertolt Brecht (1898–1956). In his early collection *Hauspostille* (*Devotions for the Home*, 1927), Brecht deftly subverted a range of bourgeois pieties, incl. religious sentiment and idealizations of landscape and love. Under the banner of *Gebrauchslyrik* (useful lyric), he developed a verse free of psychological excess, public in its reporting, and often polemical in its instructional intent. Brecht typically set his understated speech in simple rhymed stanzas, largely devoid of metaphor but enriched by colloquial phrases, biblical lang. and hymns, and citations of well-known poems. Many of his social-critical songs and ballads were inserted into his plays. Substantial collections include the *Svendborger Gedichte* (*Svendborg Poems*, 1939), written in Danish exile after he fled Nazi Germany in 1933, and the laconic *Buckower Elegien* (*Buckow Elegies*, 1953) written after his 1948 return to East Berlin. Brecht's impact on poets both East and West in the second half of the 20th c. was singular.

With the founding of the German Democratic Republic (GDR) and the Federal Republic of Germany (FRG) in 1949, two separate political cultures laid claim to the poetic past. The GDR proclaimed itself heir to all things progressive within Ger. lit., celebrating in particular the legacy of Weimar Classicism, Heine and the Young Germans, and the realistic-critical lit. of the Weimar Republic. Johannes R. Becher (1891–1958), who began as an expressionist poet, emerged as the embodiment of orthodox GDR verbal culture, embracing the forms and diction of traditional poetry to promote a new socialist society. He wrote the national anthem and became the minister of culture in 1954. Less orthodox but astute and inventive to the end, Brecht was the undisputed literary star and a major example for the next generation of GDR poets, incl. the laconic skeptic Günter Kunert (b. 1929) and the anti-establishment songwriter and performer Wolf Biermann (b. 1936). Modernism was suspect. Nature poets Peter Huchel (1903–81) and Johannes Bobrowski (1917–65) reinvigorated their genre as well as the landscapes they evoked with a sharpened focus on human activity and hist. In the 1960s, a younger, energetic generation of poets born in the 1930s altered the ongoing debate about poetry's function within socialist society by pressing the question of subjectivity and the expression of individual experience. The new poets wrote poetry that proved more critical, experimental, and personal than the conservative GDR cultural authorities desired. Within a decade, political realities led to censorship, harassment, and mounting disillusionment with the East German state and, after 1970, multiple relocations to the West. The forced expatriation of Biermann in 1976 proved a watershed. In the end Huchel, Kunert, and, from the 1930s generation, Reiner Kunze (b. 1933), Bernd Jentzsch (b. 1940), Sarah Kirsch (1935–2013), and Kurt Bartsch (1937–2010) left. Volker Braun (b. 1939), Heinz Czechowski (1935–2009), Rainer Kirsch (1934–2015), and Karl Mickel (1935–2000) remained. The 1980s saw growing disengagement. Younger poetic voices, uneasy within inherited ling. and political boundaries, placed a renewed emphasis on formal experimentation that would continue after the collapse of the GDR in 1989.

After the formation of the FRG in 1949, it was Benn who first dominated poetic discussion. His emphasis on form above content, on hist.'s emptiness, and on words stripped of ideology attracted younger writers seeking refuge from the trauma of the war years. Similarly, nature poetry seemed to offer a refuge, evoking a world of tangible plants and animals. Here also was continuity with the past. Among the authors associated with the example of Oskar Loerke (1884–1941) and the prewar jour. *Kolonne* (Convoy, 1929–32), the mythopoetic Wilhelm Lehmann (1882–1968) and Catholic Elisabeth Langgässer (1899–1950) evoked a natural world largely apart from human activity. Günter Eich (1907–72) proved more overtly political; Eich developed a terse, minimalist style that secured his postwar reputation. Writing in a lang. uncontaminated by National Socialism became a priority. *Gruppe 47* (Group 47), a gathering of authors committed to renewing democratic lit. first convened by Hans Werner Richter (1908–93) in 1947, established a general modernism and encouraged critical opposition to the political restoration.

The most important new poetic voices came from outside the FRG. Austrian-born Ingeborg Bachmann (1926–73) asserted the need to reclaim poetic lang. in the present setting of disillusionment with bold metaphors and a desire for utopian dreaming coupled with fundamental unease about the present. Nobel laureate of 1966 Nelly Sachs (1891–1970) wrote more directly from her Swedish exile, where she survived the war, straining to say the unspeakable not only about the Shoah but about personal suffering. Romanian-born Paul Antschel, who changed his name to Celan (1920–70), witnessed to the past in a lang. that he experienced as both essential and suspect. The son of Ger.-speaking Jews who died in the Holocaust, Celan moved after the war to Paris and became a Fr. citizen. His early and best-known poem "Todesfuge" ("Death Fugue") in *Mohn und Gedächtnis* (Poppy and Memory, 1952) evoked the death camps in a musical counterpoint atypical in its fluidity and accessibility. Later works, such as the collections *Sprachgitter* (*Speech-Grille*, 1959), *Atemwende* (*Breathturn*, 1967), and *Fadensonnen* (*Threadsuns*, 1968), testified to growing despair and silence communicated in a lang. that had become fragmented, compounded, and parched. An accomplished translator of the Fr. symbolists as well as contemp. poets, the polyglot Celan estranged lang. to the limits of comprehension while underscoring the urgency of dialogue.

Lang. was also the immediate concern of poets reviving the international avant-garde trads. of ling. experimentation. They privileged phonetic, graphic, and morphological elements in order to liberate lang. from grammatical convention. Eugen Gomringer's (b. 1925) concrete poetry isolated verbal materials in visual settings. Helmut Heissenbüttel (1921–96) inventoried words, writing "texts" rather than poems; Jürgen Becker's (b. 1932) "texts" also ignored traditional genre boundaries. In Austria, the *Wiener Gruppe* (Vienna Group) initiated bohemian events. H. C. Artmann (1921–2000) exploited dialect, and Friederike Mayröcker (b. 1924) experimented widely, incl. with montage. Ernst Jandl (1925–2000) evidenced humor as well as self-irony in performance and in his collections of sound poetry.

By the mid-1960s, ever more politically potent poetry was appearing. Already in the mid-1950s Hans Magnus Enzensberger (b. 1929) had faced the emerging social and political reality of postwar Germany more resolutely than most of his contemporaries. Versatile and ironic, he provoked and prodded in his richly allusive verse. Brecht's influence was increasingly evident. Günter Grass (1927–2015), Peter Rühmkorf (1929–2008), and Biermann, performing and publishing in the West, mobilized political sentiment in print and in concert. Erich Fried (1921–88), living in Great Britain, wrote outspoken political poetry, incl. *Warngedichte* (Poems of Warning, 1964) and *und Vietnam und* (and Vietnam and, 1966).

In counterpoint, the new subjectivity of the 1970s focused on everyday needs and personal experience. Rolf Dieter Brinkmann (1940–75), emerging from the counterculture, used seemingly banal moments to capture "snapshots" of everyday reality. Sarah Kirsch had long reflected on nature and love; her collection *Katzenleben* (*Catlives*, 1984), published after her 1977 departure from the GDR, marked a personal coming to terms with the writers' life within political and social constraints. The women's movement and the question of female subjectivity led both writers and critics to new appreciation of forgotten poets such as Karoline von Gunderrode (1780–1806) and to recognition of common themes of identity, exile, and loss in the poetry of Jewish women writers such as Lasker-Schüler, Sachs, Gertrud Kolmar (1894–1943), Rose Ausländer (1901–88), Mascha Kaléko (1907–75), Hilde Domin (1912–2006), and Ilse Aichinger (b. 1921).

Others shifted gears. Karl Krolow (1915–1999), known for modernist poems such as *Fremde Körper* (*Foreign Bodies*, 1959), grew more laconic and elegiac. In the 1980s, a general disillusionment characterized the work of many older and still-productive poets, who approached the future with apocalyptic visions and dire warnings. In contrast, younger poets writing in the 1980s and 1990s evidenced wider stylistic modes, a revival of hermetic poetic gestures, more explicit citations of the larger poetic trad., and a return to overt demonstrations of formal virtuosity. Technology often replaced nature as an imagery source. Thomas Kling (1957–2005) experimented with typography and orthography, fractured syntax, and intertextual citations. Former East German Uwe Kolbe (b. 1957) combined radical subjectivity with ling. play.

In the 21st c., Ger. poetry continues to prosper, despite repeated assertions about its decline. Durs Grünbein (b. 1962) can be seen as representative of a great many poets working with questions of postunification culture who seek to keep alive the recent past and yet reclaim the larger Ger. poetic trad. The number of new poets continues to increase in a highly educated society, where their work is supported by a well-established system of jours., publishing houses, prizes, academies, civic grants, and media.

See AUSTRIA, POETRY OF; FRISIAN POETRY; GERMANIC PROSODY; SWITZERLAND, POETRY OF.

■ **Anthologies.** *German*: *Epochen der deutschen Lyrik*, ed. W. Killy, 10 v. (1969–77); *Seventeen*

Modern German Poets, ed. S. Prawer (1971); *Lyrik des Barock*, ed. M. Szyrocki, 2 v. (1971); *Spätmittelalter, Humanismus, Reformation*, ed. H. Heger, 2 v. (1975–78); *Deutsche Dichterinnen vom 16. Jahrhundert bis zur Gegenwart*, ed. G. Brinker-Gabler (1978); *Lyrik-Katalog Bundesrepublik*, ed. J. Hans, U. Herms, R. Thenior (1978); *Lyrik für Leser: Deutsche Gedichte der siebziger Jahre*, ed. V. Hage (1980); *Modern deutsche Naturlyrik*, ed. E. Marsch (1980); *German Poetry*, ed. M. Swales (1987); *Deutsche Gedichte von 1900 bis zur Gegenwart*, ed. F. Pratz, 2d ed. (1987); *Frühe deutsche Literatur und lateinische Literatur in Deutschland 800–1150*, ed. W. Haug and B. K. Vollmann (1991); *Deutsche Lyrik des frühen und hohen Mittelalters*, ed. I. Kasten (1995); *Humanistische Lyrik des 16. Jahrhunderts*, ed. W. Kühlmann, R. Seidel, and H. Wiegand (1997); *Deutsche Lyrik des späten Mittelalters*, ed. B. Wachinger (2006); *Reclams grosses Buch der deutschen Gedichte*, ed. H. Detering (2007); *In welcher Sprache träumen Sie? Österreichische Lyrik des Exils und des Widerstands*, ed. M. Herz-Kestranek and K. Kaiser, D. Strigl (2007). ***English***: *The Penguin Book of German Verse*, ed. L. Forster, rev. ed. (1959); *Anthology of German Poetry from Hölderlin to Rilke*, ed. A. Flores (1960); *The German Lyric of the Baroque in English Translation*, ed. and trans. G. Schoolfield (1961); *Modern German Poetry 1910–1960*, ed. M. Hamburger and C. Middleton (1962); *Twentieth-Century German Verse*, ed. P. Bridgwater (1963); *Anthology of German Poetry through the 19th Century*, ed. A. Gode and F. Ungar (1964); *The Penguin Book of Lieder*, ed. and trans. S. Prawer (1964); *An Anthology of Concrete Poetry*, ed. E. Williams (1967); *Medieval German Lyric Verse in English Translation*, ed. and trans. J. Thomas (1968); *German and Italian Lyrics of the Middle Ages*, ed. and trans. F. Goldin (1973); *East German Poetry*, ed. M. Hamburger (1973); *Twenty-five German Poets*, ed. and trans. W. Kaufmann (1975); *German Poetry, 1910–1975*, trans. M. Hamburger (1977); *German Poetry from 1750 to 1900*, ed. R. Browning (1984); *Austrian Poetry Today*, ed. and trans. M. Holton and H. Kuhner (1985); *Contemporary Austrian Poetry*, ed. and trans. B. Bjorklund (1986); *The Defiant Muse: German Feminist Poems from the Middle Ages to the Present*, ed. S. Cocalis (1986); *Evidence of Fire: An Anthology of Twentieth-Century German Poetry*, ed. R. Ives (1988); *German Lieder*, ed. P. Miller (1990); *Menschheitsdämmerung/Dawn of Humanity*, ed. K. Pinthus, trans. J. M. Ratych, R. Ley, R. C. Conard (1994); *The Cambridge Songs*, ed. and trans. J. Ziolkowski (1994); *German Epic Poetry*, ed. F. Gentry and J. Walter, trans. F. Ryder and J. Walter (1995); *German Poetry in Transition, 1945–1990*, ed. and trans. C. Melin (1999); *Sovereignty and Salvation in the Vernacular, 1050–1150*, ed. and trans. J. Schultz (2000); *After Every War: Twentieth-Century Women Poets*, ed. and trans. E. Boland (2004); *The Faber Book of Twentieth-Century German Poems*, ed. M. Hofmann (2005).

■ **Criticism and History.** ***German***: *Geschichte der politischen Lyrik in Deutschland*, ed. W. Hinderer (1978); *Die deutsche Lyrik, 1945–75*, ed. K. Weissenberger (1981); *Gedichte und Interpretationen*, ed. V. Meid et al., 7 v. (v. 1–6, 1982; v. 7, 1997); *Geschichte der deutschen Lyrik vom Mittelalter bis zur Gegenwart*, ed. W. Hinderer (1983); G. Schulz, *Die deutsche Literatur zwischen Französischer Revolution und Restauration*, 2 v. (1983, 1989); B. Sorg, *Das lyrische Ich* (1984); H.-G. Kemper, *Deutsche Lyrik der frühen Neuzeit*, 6 v. (1987–2002); G. Kaiser, *Augenblicke deutscher Lyrik* (1987); *Deutsche Lyrik nach 1945*, ed. D. Breuer (1988); *Gedichte und Interpretationen: Deutsche Balladen*, ed. G. Grimm (1988); W. Haubrichs, *Die Anfänge: Versuche volkssprachiger Schriftlichkeit im frühen Mittelalter* (1988); G. Kaiser, *Geschichte der deutschen Lyrik von Goethe bis Heine*, 3 v. (1988); *Frauen dichten anders*, ed. M. Reich-Ranicki (1998); *1400 Deutsche Gedichte und ihre Interpretationen*, ed. M. Reich-Ranicki, 12 v. (2002); F.-J. Holznagel et al., *Geschichte der deutschen Lyrik* (2004); H. Korte, *Deutschsprachige Lyrik seit 1945*, 2d rev. ed. (2004); H. Hiebel, *Das Spektrum der modernen Poesie*, 2 v. (2005); B. Böschenstein, *Von Morgen nach Abend* (2006); R. Klüger, *Gemalte Fensterscheiben* (2007). ***English***: P. Demetz, *Postwar German Literature* (1970); R. M. Browning, *German Baroque Poetry, 1618–1723* (1971); G. Gillespie, *German Baroque Poetry* (1971); A. De Capua, *German Baroque Poetry* (1973); E. Blackall, *The Emergence of German as a Literary Language*, 2d ed. (1978); R. Browning, *German Poetry in the Age of the Enlightenment* (1978); Sayce; *German Baroque Literature*, ed. G. Hoffmeister (1983); S. Jaeger, *The Origins of Courtliness* (1985); P. Demetz, *After the Fires: Recent Writing in the Germanies, Austria and Switzerland* (1986); M. Hamburger, *After the Second Flood* (1986); *German Poetry through 1915*, ed. H. Bloom (1987); B. Peucker, *Lyric Descent in the German Romantic Tradition* (1987); J. Rolleston, *Narratives of Ecstasy* (1987); *Modern German Poetry*, ed.

H. Bloom (1989); K. Leeder, *Breaking Boundaries: A New Generation of Poets in the GDR* (1996); D. Wellbery, *The Specular Moment* (1996); M. Gibbs and S. Johnson, *Medieval German Literature* (1997); W. Haug, *Vernacular Literary Theory in the Middle Ages* (1997); M. Lee, *Displacing Authority* (1999); *Landmarks in German Poetry*, ed. P. Hutchinson (2000); R. Owen, *The Poet's Role: Lyric Responses to German Unification by Poets from the G.D.R.* (2001); I. Stoehr, *German Literature of the Twentieth Century* (2001); C. Edwards, *The Beginnings of German Literature* (2002); *Literature of the Sturm und Drang*, ed. D. Hill (2003); A. Classen, *Late-Medieval German Women's Poetry* (2004); *Early Germanic Literature and Culture*, ed. B. Murdoch and M. Read (2004); *German Literature of the Early Middle Ages*, ed. B. Murdoch (2004); *The Literature of German Romanticism*, ed. D. Mahoney (2004); *A New History of German Literature*, ed. D. Wellbery (2004); *German Literature of the Eighteenth Century*, ed. B. Becker-Cantarino (2005); *German Literature of the Nineteenth Century, 1832–1899*, ed. C. Koelb and E. Downing (2005); *The Literature of Weimar Classicism*, ed. S. Richter (2005); *German Literature of the High Middle Ages*, ed. W. Hasty (2006); *Early Modern German Literature 1350–1700*, ed. M. Reinhart (2007); B. Bennett, "Histrionic Nationality: Implications of the Verse in *Faust*," *Goethe Yearbook* 17 (2010).

M. LEE

GREEK POETICS. *See* BYZANTINE POETRY

GREEK POETRY

I. Classical
II. Medieval. *See* BYZANTINE POETRY.
III. Modern

I. Classical

A. ***The Preliterate Period (ca. 2000–750 BCE).*** The earliest Gr. verses preserved in writing date from the 8th c. BCE, and poetry has continued to be composed in Gr. from that time until the present day. But mod. research indicates that the Gr. poetic trad. is, in fact, far older than the introduction of writing. The nature of the word groups of which the Homeric epics are largely composed, as well as the content of those epics, imply a preexisting oral trad. of dactylic heroic poetry extending back into the Bronze Age civilization of the Mycenaeans, which came to an end about 1100 BCE. The aeolic meters that are widely used in extant Gr. poetry, notably by Sappho and Alcaeus, presuppose an even more ancient oral trad. of song, for they show clear affinities with the meters of the Indian Vedas; their ultimate origins may, therefore, date back as far as about 2000 BCE. It is also now generally recognized that Gr. poetry emerged from and participated in an ancient Near Eastern and Eastern Mediterranean cultural koiné. These links with the music, poetry, and culture of the ancient Near East are strongest perhaps in the preliterate and earlier archaic periods, but various kinds of cultural interaction almost certainly continued to influence Gr. verse throughout its hist.

The introduction of an alphabet specifically adapted to the recording of Gr., which took place not later than the mid-8th c. BCE, was no doubt the most important single event in the hist. of Gr. poetry. Gr. (and Eur.) lit. begins here, at the point where the songs could be fixed in permanent form and transmitted to posterity. Yet for many centuries after, Gr. poetry continued to bear the deep imprint of ancient oral trad., incl. two of its most distinctive characteristics: (1) its mythological and heroic content and (2) its long dependence on oral performance as the means of reaching its public.

Ancient Gr. poetry in nearly all genres worked within a frame of reference provided by the traditional gods and the heroes of the Bronze Age. That mythic-legendary world afforded the poets both their basic story patterns and their paradigms of conduct. Heroic epic, many forms of choral lyric, and tragedy directly represented characters and incidents drawn from that world; epinikion and monodic lyric constantly evoked it as a standard against which the human condition might be measured.

For more than three centuries after the introduction of writing, Gr. poetry continued as before to be enacted orally, often with the accompaniment of music or dancing or both, before audiences as small as dinner parties and as large as the vast crowds at religious festivals—Plato (*Ion* 535d) mentions audiences of 20,000 for performances of epic at such festivals. Thus, Gr. poetry of the archaic and high cl. eras combined features that may at first sight seem contradictory. It had the elaboration, finish, and durability that belong to book poetry as opposed to oral poetry, yet insofar as its intended public was concerned, it remained an oral and often even visual and quasi-dramatic entertainment.

To this inheritance from the preliterate trad. may also be attributed certain other characteristics of archaic and high cl. Gr. poetry: its richness in aural effects (the immense variety and musicality of its quantitative meters, for instance, are unmatched in any Eur. poetry); the prominent part it played in the cultural life of the society as a whole; and the wide range of its human appeal, particularly in its most popular genres, epic and drama.

In dealing with ancient Gr. poetry, it must always be borne in mind that we have less than 5% of all that was originally produced—the tiny proportion that has made it through the processes of selection, reperformance, and preservation spanning the more than 2,500 years since the invention of the Gr. alphabet. This means that our story necessarily tracks and depends on the Greeks' own processes of canon formation, which probably had their start already in the education system of 5th-c. Athens, continued in the work of the Hellenistic scholars in the 3d and 2d cs. BCE, and finally depended on whether Gr. texts made the crucial transition from papyrus (the writing material of the ancient world) to longer-lasting vellum in the 4th c. CE. Over the last 150 years, however, substantial ancient papyrus finds preserved in Egypt have significantly enhanced and diversified our knowledge of Gr. poetry, both supplementing our corpora of canonical poets and offering us vivid glimpses of the kaleidoscopic range and variety of Gr. verse beyond the cl. canon.

B. *The Earlier Archaic Period (ca. 750–600 BCE).* Thanks (it seems) to the introduction of writing, a great number of poems dating from this period were known to the later Greeks. With the exception of the major poems attributed to Homer and Hesiod, however, most of this work survives only in quotations, summaries, and allusions (and now, to some extent, in fragmentary papyrus finds), but these are enough to permit a sketch map, at least, of a complex literary landscape. All the major nondramatic genres of subsequent cl. poetry are already in existence, but they tend to be associated with particular regions. Of these, four stand out: Ionia, Lesbos, Sparta, and Boeotia.

The Ionic-speaking region embraced the central part of the west coast of Asia Minor and the islands that stretch from there toward Greece proper. Here, the most important and longest-lasting of all Gr. and Lat. verse forms—the dactylic hexameter (– ⏖ | – ⏖ | – ⏖| – ⏖| – ⏖| – –)—seems to have achieved its definitive form. The "formulas" of which the hexameters of Homer are largely composed show elements of several Gr. dialects, but the predominant and apparently latest stratum is Ionic. It is generally inferred that the trad. of hexameter composition, after passing through the bards of one or two other dialectal regions, culminated in Ionia; and, in fact, the oldest Gr. trads. concerning Homer place him in Chios or Smyrna, cities that belong to this region. Ionia, then, was the probable birthplace of the two great epics that later Greece, and later Europe, perceived as the fountainhead of their lit., the *Iliad* and the *Odyssey*. Since the 18th c., a debate has raged over the genesis, authorship, unity, and dates of completion of these poems (see the fourth section of the bibl., esp. the intro. to Parry). But one certainty at least remains: from the earliest period, they stood as models of the poetic art, above all for the satisfying unity of their plots and for their brilliant technique of characterization through speeches.

Also from Ionia during this period come the first examples of iambic and elegiac poetry. In both these genres, the poems were relatively short monologues, predominantly concerned with war, political and personal invective, and love; but the elegiac tended more than iambic to include a gnomic element, i.e., meditation and advice on various aspects of the human condition. Metrically speaking, *iambic* by the ancient Gr. definition embraced poems composed in the iambic trimeter (a three-metron or, in mod. parlance, six-foot iambic line: ⏓ – ⏑ – | ⏓ – ⏑ – | ⏓ – ⏑ –) and in the trochaic tetrameter catalectic (– ⏑ – ⏓ | – ⏑ – ⏓ | – ⏑ – ⏑ | – ⏑ –). The first of these was to have a rich afterlife in cl. (and to some extent later Eur.) lit. as the standard verse form for dialogue in drama. Elegiac poetry was composed in elegiac distiches—a dactylic hexameter followed by a dactylic pentameter, so-called (–⏖ – ⏖ – | – ⏑⏑ – ⏑⏑ –); this meter also was to become an enormously important medium, not least in the epigrams of the *Greek Anthology*.

The most famous and, so far as the Greeks were in a position to know, the first composer in both genres was Archilochus, of the Ionic island Paros (fl. 648 BCE). Some Gr. authors actually put his poetry on a level with that of Homer, in its very different way; the intensity and metrical perfection of his surviving fragments seem to confirm that judgment. Archilochus was also the earliest known composer of a third variety of "iambic" poetry as anciently defined, the epode, which consisted of alternating long and short lines predominantly in iambic or dactylic meters; this was a superb instrument for invective from Archilochus to the Roman Horace. Several other iambic and elegiac poets flourished in 7th-c. Ionia, esp. Semonides, Callinus, and Mimnermus. The only distinguished elegiac poet working on the Gr. mainland during this period was Tyrtaeus (fl. ca. 640 BCE), whose martial and political poems, composed in Sparta, survive in several extensive fragments.

The poetry of the Ionian region in all its genres is remarkable for the clarity of its expression and metrical form (the repeated line and the repeated couplet are the only options available) and for a rather sophisticated realism. For lyricism during this period, one must turn elsewhere. Gr. lyric (or melic) poetry by the ancient definition was poetry sung to instrumental accompaniment. In practice, it fell into two broad categories: choral lyric, which was normally a dance as well as a song and might be composed in an almost infinite variety of meters and stanza forms, and solo lyric (sometimes misleadingly called *personal lyric*), composed for accompanied singing only, in a more limited though still extensive range of meters, and falling into short stanzas, most often quatrains. Both kinds of lyric emerge from the mists of preliteracy during this period, primarily in two centers, Aeolic-speaking Lesbos and Doric-speaking Sparta.

From the late 8th into the early 6th c., a series of choral and solo lyric poets is recorded on the isle of Lesbos. Most of them, such as Terpander and Arion, are now scarcely more than sonorous names, but Sappho and Alcaeus, who both flourished ca. 600 BCE, have left many fragments of solo lyric poetry. Both composed in approximately the same range of aeolic lyric meters (two of the most famous aeolic stanza forms, the sapphic and the alcaic, are named after them), and in the same soft and musical Aeolic brogue, but, in content and tone, they are vastly unlike each other. For the power and beauty of her songs of love and loss, Sappho has no peer in Gr. lit. Alcaeus's songs on the turbulent politics of the island, his hymns to the gods, and, above all, his drinking songs, crisply and forcefully composed, were to prove of great influence on later Eur. lyric.

Seventh-c. Sparta was famed for the competitions in choral lyric at its great religious festivals, but the only one of its poets about whom anything significant is known is Alcman (second half of the 7th c.). From his numerous and in some cases quite substantial fragments, it can be deduced that his choral lyrics already embodied the most striking characteristics of the choral lyric genre as it was later known. The long polymetric stanzas of his First Partheneion, e.g., its extensively narrated examples from myth or saga, its gnomic passages in which the singers reflect on the universal meaning of their tale, can still find parallels in Pindar and Bacchylides a couple of centuries later.

In central Greece, Boeotia in this period saw the composition of a great number of poems; only three survive complete—the *Theogony*, the *Works and Days*, and the *Shield of Herakles*—but a fourth, the *Ehoiai* or *Catalogue of Women*, can now be restored to a considerable extent from papyrus fragments. Both the lost and the surviving poems of the Boeotian corpus were generally ascribed in ancient times to the great Hesiod, who seems to have flourished ca. 700 BCE, but most mod. critics deny the authenticity of the *Shield* and several that of the *Ehoiai*. In any case, all are composed in a medium that is virtually indistinguishable from that of the Homeric epics: the meter is the same, almost the same formulary is employed, and the same mixture of dialects is evident. But there the resemblance ends. The Hesiodic works show nothing of the architectonic skill of Homer or of his genius for realizing character through speech. They are essentially episodic codifications of ancient lore. The *Theogony* presents the origin and hist. of the Greek gods, organizing the material by generations; the *Ehoiai* followed the hist. of the heroic families by clans and, within clans, by generations; the *Works and Days* is a manual of the art of living, proceeding from ethical and political considerations to practical instruction in farming, navigation, and the rules of daily conduct. But this essentially catalogic principle of composition does not mean that Hesiod lacks art. Largely through the characteristically archaic techniques of ring composition and significant repetition, he succeeds in making his topics and episodes cohere within themselves and between each other. In addition, it is sometimes claimed that Hesiod represents the first self-conscious authorial "I" in Eur. lit.: thus, in the proem to the *Theogony* and in a couple of metapoetic passages in the *Works and Days*, he builds up an impressive persona of "Hesiod." But this claim to innovation over Homer is largely a mirage of historical preservation. It seems likely that ancient bards in performance particularized themselves and their songs in *prooimia* or proems adapted to a local audience. While we have lost these prooimia for Homeric epic, we have them preserved for Hesiod; hence, the apparent difference of the lofty, seemingly anonymous third-person narration of Homeric epic vs. the self-revelatory intimacy and immediacy of the Hesiodic persona. Though debate still rages on this point within mod. scholarship, it seems likely that "Hesiod" and his foolish brother "Perses" (the addressee of the *Works and Days*) are fictive personae adapted to the needs of the didactic genre.

Much other hexameter poetry was composed in various regions of Greece during this period; the hexameter, in fact, seems early on to have become a kind of poetic koiné. Particularly important in its time was the Epic Cycle, a catena of medium-length epics by various hands that covered the entire Troy saga. Other epics since lost are known to have told of the legendary hist. of Corinth, the story of the Argonauts, and the house of Oedipus. Other extant examples of early hexameter poetry are certain poems in the heterogeneous collection that has come down to us under the title of the *Homeric Hymns*: at least Hymns II (to Demeter), III (to Apollo), and V (to Aphrodite) probably belong to this period. It is a remarkable fact that by about 600 BCE all the major nondramatic genres of Gr. poetry were already in existence: heroic epic, iambic, elegiac, solo and choral lyric, and, at least in some sense, didactic (for Hesiodic poetry, though far wider in scope than the didactic poetry of later antiquity, was certainly its inspiration).

C. *The Later Archaic Period (ca. 600–480 BCE).* The diversity of later archaic Gr. poetry was great, but three general trends may be distinguished: the major poetic genres become less tied to specific regions of Greece (or more "Panhellenic"), and lyric poetry in particular shows a growing sophistication, metrically as well as intellectually. Also in this period, real, historically verifiable authors and poets first emerge into the full light of hist., since, in many cases, the earlier authors' names seem to be fictions standing for the poetic trads. and genres they are said to have invented or in which they were thought to excel. Composition in epic hexameters continued in many parts of Greece; some poems of the Epic Cycle and of the Hesiodic corpus, as well as several of the Homeric hymns, probably belong to the earlier part of this period. The most significant discernible devel. is the gradual disintegration of the system of formulas characteristic of the older epics. By the late 6th c., the first tentative signs of a "literary" or "secondary" epic may perhaps be made out in the work of Panyassis of Halicarnassus, an uncle or cousin of the historian Herodotus.

An outstanding exponent of both elegiac and iambic poetry was the statesman Solon (fl. 594 BCE), the earliest recorded Athenian poet. The quite substantial fragments of his work are partly gnomic or personal in content—in this, conforming to Ionian precedent—but the majority addresses political principles and issues connected with Solon's famous reforms of the Athenian economy and constitution. Across the Aegean, Hipponax of Ephesus (fl. 540 BCE) culminated the Ionian trad. of iambic invective and lampoon. His favorite meter was one that now appears for the first time, the *scazon* or limping iambic trimeter (⏓ – ⏑ – | ⏓ – ⏑ – | ⏓ – – –). The last of the major archaic elegists, Theognis of Megara (second half of the 6th c.?), is represented by a large number of poems, predominantly gnomic in character, in the 1,300-line anthol. of elegiacs that somehow survived the Middle Ages and now goes under the title of *Theognidea*, the only corpus of archaic elegiac poetry to be preserved through continuous ms. transmission. Finally, the elegiac, iambic, and hexameter fragments of Xenophanes of Colophon (ca. 570–478 BCE) open a new dimension in poetry, the philosophic and scientific; his penetrating physical and ethnographic observations and his crit. of Gr. anthropomorphic religion are expressed in lively and elegant verse. The two other poet-philosophers who followed him, Parmenides and Empedocles, belong rather to the hist. of philosophy than to that of poetry.

In lyric poetry, there were spectacular devels. Papyrus discoveries of the 1970s and 1980s have greatly enriched our knowledge of Stesichorus of Himera in Sicily, who seems to have flourished in the first half of the 6th c. They fully confirm the ancient trads. that he composed songs very much in the epic manner, and even approaching the epic scale, and also that he adopted or perhaps invented the practice of composing choral lyric by triads (strophe, metrically responding antistrophe, nonresponding epode), which is the most striking formal characteristic of subsequent Gr. choral lyric. Ibycus of Rhegium in southern Italy (fl. ca. 535 BCE) and Simonides of the Aegean isle of Ceos (556–468) each left superb fragments of lyric. Simonides, in particular, seems to have been a great innovative master, turning his hand to many different varieties of choral lyric, incl. the epinikion (which he may have originated) and the short epigram in elegiac distiches, a form that had an immense literary future before it.

Anacreon of Teos in Ionia (ca. 575–490) brought solo lyric poetry to heights of wit and technical polish that were matched in cl. times perhaps only by the Roman poets Catullus and Horace. His many brilliant fragments sing mostly of love and wine but also occasionally flare with trenchant abuse or touch on more somber themes of old age and death. Metrically, he was not a great innovator, but he seems to have been the first poet to make extensive use of the catchy rhythm ◡ ◡ – ◡ – ◡ – –, later called the anacreontic after him. (This meter plays a great part in the extant collection of light verse that seems to have been continuously composed in imitation of Anacreon through the Roman and Byzantine periods; this collection, which goes under the title *Anacreontea*, had great popularity and influence in 16th- to 18th-c. Europe.)

The most momentous poetic devel. in this period was the introduction of poetic drama. Officially sponsored performances of tragedy at the Great Dionysia festival in Athens are first attested in ca. 534 BCE and of comedy in 486 BCE. The ultimate origins of both genres and their hists. down to the time of the great Persian invasion of Greece in 480–79 BCE are still problematic for want of adequate evidence; the archaeological evidence and (often contradictory) ancient accounts of the origins of drama are collected in Csapo and Slater. Our extant examples of tragedy and comedy date only from the ensuing period. In antiquity, Athens proudly claimed the invention of both tragedy and comedy, but this claim was not uncontested. In fact, abundant ancient evidence suggests that many different Gr. cities may have been developing different forms of choral drama more or less simultaneously in the 6th c. BCE. Thus, Herodotus (5.67) mentions "tragic choruses" performed in honor of a cult hero in 6th-c. Sicyon in the Peloponnese, while we have reports of early comic performances in Megara, in the Gr. city of Syracuse on Sicily, and of early satyr plays in Phleius (also in the Peloponnese). It is, moreover, noteworthy that, even in Athens, almost a third of the poets whose names are preserved as practicing tragic playwrights in the 5th c. are non-Athenian. The fact that we have extant dramas from Athens alone—that Athens essentially wins this ancient contest—may have more to do with political, economic, and military factors discussed below than with issues of literary or aesthetic quality. But once developed, the arts of tragedy, comedy, and satyr play were elaborated by the Athenians with great energy and success, so that drama (along with painted pottery) became one of Athens's great export commodities. Ancient evidence suggests that, already by the last two decades of the 5th c., Attic tragedy was being performed in southern Italy (and probably many other places in the Gr. world), while the 4th c. witnessed an explosion in the building of monumental stone theaters throughout the Gr. cities of the Mediterranean that scholars have connected with the expanding performance horizons of Attic drama.

D. ***The High Classical Period (ca. 480–400 BCE).*** After the Persian Wars, Athenian power and dominance reached their peak. The years between 479 and Athens's defeat by Sparta in 404 saw the creation of a naval empire in the eastern Mediterranean, the exaction of "tribute" from the allied Gr. cities of the empire, the Periclean democracy, the erection of the great buildings and sculptures on the Acropolis—and the composition of all the surviving masterpieces of Attic tragedy. Elsewhere in Greece, choral lyric continued to be practiced with great success. Our firsthand knowledge of the tragic art depends almost exclusively on the extant plays of the three most famous Attic tragedians, Aeschylus (525–456), Sophocles (496–406), and Euripides (ca. 480–406); the earliest surviving example, Aeschylus's *Persians*, was produced in 472. On the strictly *dramatic* aspects of the art, much is to be found elsewhere (see Lesky, Goldhill). Viewed in the context of Gr. poetry, tragedy is remarkable for the manner in which it appropriated and combined so many existing poetic genres. In tragic tone, in characterization through speech, and to some extent even in plot construction, the tragedians picked up and developed precedents in Homeric epic (as Aristotle implies throughout the *Poetics*, e.g., 1449b17: "anybody who can tell a good tragedy from a bad one can do the same with epics"). In metrics, they owed less to the epic than to iambic, solo lyric, and choral lyric. They added little to the existing repertoire of Gr. meters but combining freely metrical elements that had previously been confined to separate genres. The result, esp. in the choral odes and the arias of tragedy, is a poetry of unprecedented richness and variety in tone, tempo, and rhythm. Fifth-c. Attic tragedy is, thus, both a synthesis of all the earlier modes of Gr. poetry and the starting point of Eur. drama.

Probably an art of such power and wide popular appeal was bound, in time, to overshadow the traditional genres of Gr. poetry, and by the end of the 5th c., this process had taken place. Elegiac and solo lyric continued to be practiced until the last few decades but only falteringly. Choral lyric alone was still able to reach great heights, but even that genre faded out of hist. with the death of Pindar of Thebes (ca. 522–443). The most famous of all the choral lyricists, Pindar was master of a great range of song types for a variety of occasions. When the Hellenistic scholars came to edit his complete poems, they grouped them under the headings of *hymns*, *paeans*, *dithyrambs*, *partheneia* (songs for girl choruses), *hyporchemes* (dance poems), *encomia, threnoi* (death laments), and *epinikia* (victory odes); the titles may not in every case have reflected Pindar's intent, but they give a vivid notion of the diapason of Gr. choral lyric. Of all these, only the *Epinikia*, praising the victors at the four great athletic festivals, have survived intact through direct ms. transmission. Varying in length from one to thirteen triads, these odes concentrate not so much on the transient details of the athletic success as on its significance in the divine and human cosmos: the human victory is measured against mythological precedents the evocation of which—sometimes continuously, sometimes only in brief glimpses of dazzling vividness—may occupy much of the ode.

Pindaric poetry is not easy reading. It may well have been more readily comprehensible in its original performance, when it was *heard* and its message was reinforced by music and choral dancing; its allusiveness, the intricacy of its word placing and metrics, and the never-failing originality and precision of its diction keep a reader in constant tension. But it is poetry of unsurpassed metaphorical richness, intensity, and visionary power. Far more accessible is the choral lyric of Bacchylides of Ceos, many of whose songs—mostly epinikion odes and dithyrambs—have been discovered on papyri in mod. times. Bacchylides was a younger contemporary of Pindar, all of whose datable poems fall within the period 485–452. Clarity and grace mark his poetry; his meters are simple and tuneful, his mythical narratives interestingly chosen, visually evocative, and delicately ambiguous.

The first extant Gr. comedy is Aristophanes' *Acharnians*, produced in Athens in 425. Since antiquity, it has been customary to divide the hist. of the Attic comic art into three phases: Old, Middle, and New. Old Comedy extended from the institution of the comic contests at the Great Dionysia in 486 until the opening decades of the 4th c., but most of our knowledge of it depends on Aristophanes' 11 surviving plays. Of all the poetry created by the Greeks, Old Comedy has the widest metrical and stylistic range and allows by far the freest play of fantasy. Its basic dialect is the local vernacular—colloquial Attic speech in all its vigor and explicitness, sexual and scatological. Further, the extant Aristophanic comedies display an extraordinary aptitude for the parody of every other poetic genre, not least of tragedy. But Old Comedy's single most extraordinary feature was its total freedom to create characters and situations. In most Gr. poetry up to that time, the basic narratives and characters were drawn from the ancient myths and sagas. The majority of Old Comic plots, however, seem to have been free fictions, some of them blossoming into poetic fantasies that might embrace Hades (as in Aristophanes' *Frogs*) or the entire universe (as in his *Birds*).

The last two or three decades of this period saw a revolutionary movement in Gr. music and poetry that is known to us primarily from allusions in Old Comedy, from a partially preserved lyric text, *The Persians*, by Timotheus of Miletus (fl. ca. 450–360), and from some of the songs in Euripides' late plays (as well as references to it by Plato, Aristotle, and later writers on music). This seems to have been mainly a musical revolution, provoked by the increasing professionalization of musicians—esp. pipe or aulos players—that resulted from the enormous, expanding popularity of tragedy and choral dithyramb throughout the Gr. world. Professional musicians were interested in developing a freer, more virtuoso style to showcase their skills. The references to this New Music outside of Timotheus and Euripides tend to be disapproving but are clearly tendentious and ideologically driven, an elite reaction to the rise to prominence of lower-class professional musicians. In relation to poetry, the most remarkable technical features of the New Music were its abandonment of the triadic arrangement of responding stanzas that had characterized all earlier lyric verse and the opening of a split between the words and the melody of a lyric. For the first time, the evidence suggests, one syllable, instead of being set to one note, might be extended over several notes, as in the melisma of mod. song. These and other innovations in the instrumentation and performance of poetry effectively created a permanent break with the trad. of archaic and high cl. lyric poetry that had flourished since at least the early 7th c. In terms of preservation and posterity, these New Musical experiments were ultimately undone by a hostile conservative trad. Thus, although there is evidence that the songs of Timotheus continued to be learned and performed throughout the Gr. world for six centuries (until the 3d c. CE), they failed to make the crucial transition to vellum in the late antique period and so are almost entirely lost to us. For the Greeks (and so necessarily for us), the "lyric age" ended in 450 BCE, with Pindar and Bacchylides, the last of the canonical "lyric nine."

E. ***The Fourth Century BCE.*** From the perspective of what the Greeks canonized and preserved, the outstanding event in Gr. lit. of this period is the triumph of prose. Prose as a literary medium had developed rather slowly in the outer regions of the Gr. world from the mid-6th c. BCE onward. In Athens, it did not establish itself until the second half of the 5th c.; only in the 4th c.—and above all in the works of Isocrates, Plato, Xenophon, and Aristotle—did it acquire an unchallengeable position as the medium for the exploration of the deepest human concerns, philosophical, psychological, and political. Accordingly, the poet was gradually forced from his supreme role as universal teacher into the role of, at most, entertainer. The most flourishing variety of Gr. poetry in the 4th c. was comedy. Aristophanes' last surviving play, the *Ploutos* or *Wealth* (388), is often taken to mark the transition from Old to Middle Comedy. Certainly, the relative tameness of its central comic fantasy, its drastic reduction of the chorus's role, and its almost total elimination of any lyric element all seem to have been characteristics of Middle Comedy, which is conventionally dated ca. 380–320. New Comedy (ca. 320–250) is much more accessible to us, thanks to extensive papyrus discoveries. Most of these are plays by the most famous of the New Comic poets, Menander (ca. 342–291). The New Comic plots continue the trad. of Old Comedy in that they are fictional and set in contemp. Greece, but the fictions are now much more realistic, closer to mod. romantic comedy or situation comedy. Within this frame, Menander crafts exquisite plots and creates a long series of delicately shaded character studies. The predominant meter of his comedies is the iambic trimeter. Lyric now has no place in the fabric of the comedies, although they are divided into acts (regularly, it seems, five) by pauses in the scripts marked *Khorou*—"[song] of a chorus"—apparently songs unrelated to the dramatic action and probably not composed by the playwright. This last traceable phase of Gr. poetic drama, through the Lat. adaptations by Plautus and Terence, was to provide the formal model for both the tragedy and comedy of Ren. Europe: the five-act play in iambic verse.

Noncomic poetry apparently continued robustly throughout the 4th c., but the preserved remnants are pitifully meager. Tragedies continued to be produced in large numbers at the Great Dionysia in Athens, though, perhaps significantly, canonization of the three great 5th-c. tragedians was already taking place through reperformance of their plays alongside new compositions. The New Music movement in lyric poetry (see above) had apparently run its course by the middle of the century. The epic and elegiac poems by Antimachus of Colophon (fl. ca. 400) had their admirers in later antiquity. But at least to the Greeks' own perception (what they considered worth canonizing and preserving), the great era of Gr. poetry (dramatic and nondramatic) that had sustained itself continuously from the preliterate period had come to an end. The stage was clear for a new kind of poetry.

F. ***The Hellenistic Age (ca. 300–21 BCE).*** In Athens, New Comedy—the last survivor of any of the publicly performed cl. genres—continued in full vigor during the earlier part of this period. Elsewhere, the circumstances and character of Gr. poetry changed radically. The conquests of Alexander the Great (d. 323) had extended the power, and with it the lang., of the Greeks into the Near and Middle East, a shift soon followed by a shift in the focuses of literary activity. The newly founded Gr. metropolises, above all Egyptian Alexandria, attracted talent of every kind from wherever Gr. was spoken. But the new poetic culture that arose in those vast cities, with their diverse mixture of Gr.-speaking immigrants and native populations, was necessarily a culture of the book; its audience was no longer the citizen in the marketplace. The result was a learned poetry of exquisite technical finish and literary allusiveness—a poetry, for the first time in this story, analogous to that of Virgil, John Milton, or T. S. Eliot. At the same time, however, the Hellenistic poets were very conscious of the need to validate the new kind of poetry by ensuring the *appearance* of continuity with the older Gr. poetic trad. Many of the archaic genres were now revived in form, if transfigured in scope and tone. The most versatile of the Hellenistic poets, Callimachus (active in Alexandria ca. 280–245), offers a good example of the process. His *Hymns* deliberately recall the Homeric hymns of archaic Greece. Yet these Callimachean counterparts are not so much acts of piety as masterpieces of delicate wit and fantasy; and more than one of them incorporates a literary evocation of the festival at which it was to be *imagined* as delivered. Similar imitations and transpositions are to be found in Callimachus's *Iambi*, where Hipponax is an acknowledged model, and in his *Aetia*, where he invokes the precedents of Mimnermus and Hesiod.

In this general revival of the archaic genres, it was impossible that Homer should be neglected, but he now elicited very diverse literary responses. To Callimachus and many other Hellenistic poets, notably Theocritus, the vast scale and heroic temper of Homeric epic were no longer achievable or even desirable, for these men aimed above all at brevity, polish, and realism. They devised their own brand of narrative poetry, the brief epic, adopting (with refinements) the Homeric medium, the hexameter, but limiting the scale to a few hundred lines. Within this space, there could be no question of retelling a heroic saga; rather, the poet would illuminate a single heroic episode, bringing out its full color and detail. Examples of this form are Callimachus's fragmentary *Hekale*, Theocritus's *Idyll* 13 on Herakles and Hylas, and, at a later date, Moschus's *Europa*. A number of Hellenistic poets, however, did compose large-scale epics, though the only one that survives is the *Argonautica* of Apollonius Rhodius, a younger contemporary of Callimachus. In its versification, its lang., and its similes, this poem abundantly testifies to Apollonius's long study of Homer, yet in content and tone it is utterly un-Homeric. Apollonius's passive and hesitant hero, Jason, belongs rather to our world than to the world of Achilles and Odysseus, and the depiction in book 3 of Medea's love for him is a breakthrough in the psychological depiction of passion, at least in the epic context.

Hesiod was the alleged model for the many didactic poems composed in the Hellenistic period, though the wide human scope of Hesiodic poetry tended to be reduced simply to the versification of this technology or that. The most notable surviving example is Aratus's *Phainomena*, on astronomy and meteorology. The only altogether new genre created by the Hellenistic poets (or, if not created, adapted from subliterary songs and mummings of an earlier period) was pastoral poetry. The earliest known examples are the work of Theocritus, who was approximately a contemporary of Callimachus and Apollonius. The collection of his poems that has reached us under the title of *Idylls* consists of relatively short pieces, mostly in hexameters, but only a minority of them are pastorals, and one of Theocritus's most brilliant dialogue poems, *Idyll* 15, is set in the multicultural hubbub of Alexandria itself. Both the nonpastoral and the pastoral poems display the Callimachean preference for brevity and precise detail, but, in his control of verbal music, Theocritus may be thought to surpass even Callimachus.

The great creative impetus of Hellenistic poetry was limited to the first half of the 3d c. BCE. Thereafter, very little new ground was broken. The various genres that were then reestablished or created continued to be practiced, but the surviving examples are of little poetic significance.

G. ***The Roman Imperial Period.*** With the battle of Actium in 31 BCE, Rome's empire over the Mediterranean and Near East was decisively established. Paradoxically, it was the Roman poets who henceforth most successfully exploited the legacy of Hellenistic Gr. poetry; the three great poems of Virgil himself, for instance, would be inconceivable but for the precedents of Hellenistic pastoral, didactic, and epic. Though a great many poems were composed in Gr. under the empire, none matches the work of the major Roman poets in intrinsic interest or influence on subsequent Eur. poetry. Thus, the trad. of ancient Gr. poetry, while competently perpetuated during this period, was gradually losing its momentum. Two slow but steady devels., one ling. and the other social, were finally to bring that trad. to an end: a change in the pronunciation of Gr., whereby quantity is replaced by stress, and the triumph of the Christian imagination over the pagan. From about the beginning of the Christian era, the distinction in colloquial Gr. speech between long and short vowel quantities began to disappear, and the musical pitch accent that had prevailed since archaic times began to be replaced by a tonic stress accent similar to that of mod. Gr. or Eng. Literary Gr. poetry responded only very slowly to these changes, but by the 6th c. CE, the characteristic Byzantine versification was well established, its guiding principle no longer syllable quantity but recurrent stress accent. In this fashion, Gr. poetry gradually lost the superb metrical system that, in the hands of Pindar, the Attic tragedians, and Theocritus, had generated such an incomparable wealth and variety of verbal music. Simultaneously, Gr. poetry was also being gradually distanced from pagan mythology—from the rich intellectual and imaginative resource that had provided it with its themes since the preliterate era. As a consequence of these two devels., Gr. poetry was no more the same art. No absolute date can be set to that final transformation, and exceptions to the general trend can always be found: for instance, scholars continued to compose verses in quantitative Gr. meters down through the Middle Ages and Ren. But, effectively, the change had taken place by the end of the 6th c. CE.

Most of the Gr. poetry that survives from the Roman imperial period falls under one of three genres: didactic, epic, and epigram. Tragedy and comedy were no longer composed, and the few known examples of lyric poetry are not very striking either in substance or metric. The didactic poets followed closely in the steps of their Hellenistic predecessors, composing versified textbooks of varying interest and merit on such subjects as geography and fishing. Epic both mythological and panegyric (i.e., celebrating the exploits of some political figure) was very widely composed. Much the most interesting example is the *Dionysiaca* composed by Nonnus of Panopolis in Egypt in the early 5th c. This story of the triumphant career of Dionysus, in 48 books (matching the total number of books in the *Iliad* and the *Odyssey*), is the last major Gr. poem in hexameters.

Alone among the Gr. genres, the epigram never fell out of fashion. This kind of brief, finely worked, and pointed poem, somewhat comparable in finish and compactness to the haiku or the heroic couplet, most often took the form of one to four elegiac distichs. The earliest examples are inscriptions (*epigrammata*) on gravestones or votive objects of the archaic period. During the 5th c. BCE, the form was increasingly adapted to literary purposes, and the range of its content was extended beyond the funereal and dedicatory to many other human concerns—above all, love, humor, and wine. The great surviving corpus of epigrams, the *Greek Anthology*, put together for the most part by the 10th c. CE, is one of the most moving and impressive of all the monuments of ancient Gr. poetry. Within it are found epigrams by most of the famous poets, and philosophers too, composed over a span of approximately 14 centuries.

II. Medieval. *See* BYZANTINE POETRY.

III. Modern. As Greece's modernity is dated along with national independence (1828), any discussion about lit. in the expansive terrain of the post-Byzantine period necessarily concerns poetic instances of vernacular expression and is specifically tied to the multifarious uses of the Gr. lang. The institution of mod. Gr. lit. cannot be separated from the problem of the "proper" Gr. literary lang., and it can just as easily be said that the very hist. of mod. Gr. lit. (esp. poetry) ultimately decides the thorny issue identified as "the language question." This polemic involves advocates of the formal idiom (*katharevousa*—a constructed form with archaic resonance that literally means "pure") against advocates of the quotidian spoken idiom (*dēmotikē*—demotic), a fierce battle that began in mid-19th c. and ended, in favor of the second, with 1930s modernism, even though katharevousa remained the official state lang. until 1976. But the overarching problematic of mod. Gr. poetry also involves an array of other lang. uses, from local dialects to diasporic idioms, which enable the coincidence of numerous ling. registers, much to the benefit of poetic creativity. This gives Gr. poets an extraordinary expressive range, often impossible to render in trans.

Between the fall of Constantinople to the Ottomans (1453) and the Greek War of Independence (1821–28), literate poetry flourished mainly in Gr. lands under Venetian influence, esp. Crete. What was later named the Cretan Renaissance is standard reference to the production of poetic romances that draw a great deal on It. models but have a distinctive character. The exemplary poet of the Cretan Ren. is Vitsentzos Kornaros (1553–1613), whose genre-defining epic romance *Erotokritos*—a poem of 10,000 rhyming 15-syllable iambic verses in the Cretan dialect—narrates the chivalrous love of Erotokritos for the princess Aretousa and their union after long and arduous adventures of deception and intrigue. The most recognized antecedent is the Frankish romance *Paris et Vienne* (1487), with additional influences traceable to Ludovico Ariosto and the Cretan folk-song trad., but Kornaros forges a poetic idiom, whose innovation, within the parameters of the Gr. lang., is broadly recognized, thanks to Gr. modernist interpretations.

In the rest of the Gr. world under Ottoman rule, poetry flourishes in the folk-song form. From the painstaking collection of folk songs by folklorist Nikolaos Politis (1852–1921), we now recognize the heyday of this anonymous popular poetic form to be the 18th c., when a vast range of improvised love songs, songs of travel, lullabies, and dirges comprise poetic material of profound beauty and innovation, arguably superior to any poetry in Gr. since the close of the 9th c. In terms of both form and poetic lang., the Gr. folk song proved remarkably influential, even in the most experimental of romantic and modernist expressions.

The inaugural modernity of Gr. poetry belongs to Dionysios Solomos (1798–1857). Although Solomos was established as national poet laureate because the first two stanzas of his "Hymn to Liberty" (1823—one of few poems completed and pub. in his lifetime) became the Gr. national anthem, he is nonetheless characterized by inimitable experimentalism in both lang. and form, having introduced into Gr. a number of Western metrical forms (sestina, *ottava rima*, *terza rima*) that freed Gr. poetry from the compulsion toward the 15-syllable verse. As a member of the Ionian aristocracy (the Ionian islands were never under Ottoman rule), Solomos was bilingual and certainly more adept in It. than Gr. Because of his struggle with the Gr. lang., he wrote in dēmotikē, itself a groundbreaking gesture in the devel. of mod. Gr. poetry. He was influenced philosophically by G.W.F. Hegel and Ger. romanticism and, in literary terms, by cl. It. and his sparse knowledge of the Gr. folk-song trad. His Gr. poetic oeuvre is comprised of an extraordinary series of fragments and voluminous marginal notes in It., the ensemble constituting an as yet unmatched experiment in poetic modernity. Solomos's idiosyncratically inventive way of creating composite words in several ling. registers makes trans. exceedingly difficult. The pinnacle of Solomos's achievements is *The Free Besieged*, a long unfinished poem drafted between 1833 and 1847 in several versions that include rhymed 15-syllable and free verse, single-verse fragments, interspersed prose, and a theoretical preamble—all experimenting with lyric, epic, and dramatic styles in order to capture the atmosphere of the heroic resistance and exodus of Messolonghi (1826) during the Greek War of Independence. Messolonghi, as the site of Lord Byron's demise, also inspired Solomos to a series of odes and fragments in Byronic style.

The other groundbreaking poet of this era, Andreas Kalvos (1792–1869), was also Ionian, and he, too, wrote his first texts (tragedies and dramatic monologues) in It. Later in life, he also wrote prose texts in Eng., having spent a good part of his life in England as a country squire. His only poetic output in Gr. is a book of *Odes and Lyrics* (1826), which was rejected by the Gr. intelligentsia of his day but granted him instant recognition in Fr. trans. Kalvos, too, is characterized by an idiosyncratic poetics that combines archaic and demotic metrics and ling. registers to produce an unusual manner, simultaneously stern and sentimental, intellectual and lyric, pagan and traditionally romantic. Kalvos's influence is traced explicitly in various modernist and contemp. experiments (notably the prosody movement of the 1990s), but his poetic legacy continues to produce vehement disputes. Both Solomos and Kalvos (like C. P. Cavafy later) wrote outside the national territory and in idiomatic Gr., prompting George Seferis to claim in 1936 that the inauguration of contemp. Gr. poetics belonged to "our three great deceased poets who did not know Greek."

In the aftermath of national independence, canonical Gr. romanticism flourishes in Athens, at the heart of national-cultural and intellectual life. The founder of the romantic school of Athens was Alexandros Soutsos (1803–63), a fervent admirer of Victor Hugo and Byron, whose exuberant romantic and patriotic writings, however, do not capture the spirit of their models. Though he was terse and vigorous as a satirist, Soutsos exercised a stultifying influence on Gr. poetry. Most representatives of this school were bound to an exaggerated romanticism, using a stilted formal idiom (katharevousa) for painstakingly patriotic poetry. Achilleas Paraschos (1838–95) is the leading figure in the last period of the school. His contemporaries were all overshadowed by his reputation, in spite of the greater sincerity and more delicate technique of many of their works. Some of them have come to be appreciated in recent years—Demetrios Paparrhegopoulos (1843–73) as a refined lyricist, Alexandros Vyzantios (1841–98) as sharp-witted satirist, and Georgios Vizyenos (1849–96) as the most important 19th-c. innovator of the short-story form.

About 1880, a young group of poets, influenced by the virulent crit. of Emmanuel Roidis (1836–1904), a brilliant novelist and public intellectual, formed the New School of Athens. They aspired to become the Gr. Parnassians, masters of a restrained and objective art. The central figure was Kostis Palamas (1859–1943), a man of wide learning whose works blended not only the ancient and mod. Gr. trads. but the social and spiritual convulsions of the late 19th and early 20th cs. *The Dodecalogue of the Gypsy* (1907) is perhaps his crowning achievement. Its hero, the Gypsy musician, a symbol of freedom and art, gradually deepens into the patriot, the Greek, and finally the Hellene—citizen and teacher of the world. This powerful epic-lyric, together with *The King's Flute* (1910), a historical epic, and *Life Immovable* (1904), the most important of his lyric collections, solidified an enormous influence both on contemporaries of the school and their immediate successors. The poets of this generation should be credited for introducing symbolism and free verse into Gr. poetry, much to the benefit of their 20th-c. counterparts.

Yet arguably the greatest poet of the mod. Gr. trad. remained untouched by Palamas's influence. C. P. Cavafy (1863–1933) was an Alexandrian by both birth and sensibility. His inimitable achievement was the creation of a mythical world of diasporic Hellenism characterized by irony, eroticism, and a tragic vision that celebrates those who gracefully deviate from the norm or singularly embody what is fleeting and irreproducible or face disaster with honest self-awareness. Cavafy's mythographic universe parallels those fashioned by eminent contemporaries (W. B. Yeats, Ezra Pound, T. S. Eliot) and has thus gained him a place in the pantheon of modernist poetry worldwide. Cavafy wrote both historical and lyric poetry with equally erotic sensibility and, more than any other Gr. poet, he can be said to embody a pagan spirit, unperturbed by the social and cultural institutions of his day. He remained uninterested in publishing and preferred to distribute his poetry in folios he variously assembled on his own, following no chronological order. He is, thus, quintessentially modernist in disregarding both the commercial sphere and the establishment of a legacy.

Cavafy exercised no influence on his contemporaries, although his influence on subsequent generations to this day is unsurpassed. The most significant of early 20th-c. poets succeeded in distinguishing themselves from the dominance of Palamas's poetics. Kostas Varnalis (1884–1974) rivals Palamas as a socially conscious poet, the first to bear a strong political voice and the inaugural figure in the long trad. of 20th-c. leftist poetics. Less directly influential but more poetically significant is Kostas Karyotakis (1896–1928). A complex man of great talent and fragile sensibility, Karyotakis wrote lyric and satirical poems with equal skill: witness *Elegies and Satires* (1927). His unfortunate liaison with the lyric poet Maria Polydouri (1902–30), his rejection of bourgeois patriotic propriety, and his subsequent suicide were later recognized to reflect a poetic sensibility of unusual daring, reversing belief that he epitomized the Gr. malaise of post-Asia Minor Catastrophe (1922). Counterposed to Karyotakis's sensibility is Angelos Sikelianos (1884–1952). Powerfully elegiac, Sikelianos construes Gr. nature and hist. in both Apollonian light and Dionysian mystery. With a rich diction and avowedly Delphic spirit, the natural landscape, the human form, and abstract thought are all brought into clear-cut relief in exceedingly singular lyrical form. Additionally, Nikos Kazantzakis (1885–1957), renowned as a novelist, deserves mention for the most conceptually daring work of his time: a formidable 33,333-line mod. sequel to the *Odyssey* (1938), written in Cretan dialect and radical (bordering on artificial) dēmotikē, in which the Odyssean hero, haunted by Nietzschean nihilism, searches for existential salvation in an incessant journey through various modes of thought.

The modernist movement, known as the Generation of the 1930s, having reconfigured the terms of the entire mod. Gr. poetic trad., still exercises a catalytic influence. Accordingly, it produced two Nobel Prize winners, George Seferis (1963) and Odysseus Elytis (1979), and the Lenin Prize recipient Yiannis Ritsos (1977); all three poets saw their work set to music by the composer Mikis Theodorakis in a gesture that brought the sensibility of Gr. modernism to a broad public. Seferis (1900–71) ushers a style, method, and vision in conversation with Eliot and Paul Valéry, by casting the mod. predicament in a Gr. literary landscape that encompasses ancient epic and tragic poetics, the Cretan Ren., and the entire demotic trad. in order to produce a new mythical lang. in dramatic free verse, rich in nuance while spare in decoration, which poeticizes a Gr. psyche in the midst of a ruined past to be overcome. This poetic project enhanced with carefully timed publications of literary essays, over a 30-year period, which sealed Seferis's unparalleled hegemonic influence on Gr. letters. Similarly committed to the project of Gr. modernism but in an entirely different style, Elytis (1911–96) wielded his influence more by virtue of a lyrical technique that crafts a personal mythology in celebration of the natural-material features of the Gr. imagination. Initially following a surrealist juxtaposition of disparate images in flamboyant lyricism, Elytis's gravity is measured by the intricate poetics of *Axion Esti* (1960), an extended secular hymn that draws on Gr. Orthodox liturgy, 19th-c. demotic trad., dramatic prose, and historical material from World War II to sculpt and praise the spiritual dimension of the Gr. psyche in the world of the senses.

Gr. surrealism in this generation (in direct association with its Fr. strains) is exemplified by Andreas Embeirikos (1901–75), who was also the first Gr. psychoanalyst and who wrote in exceedingly ornate lang., occasionally adopting archaisms with unabashed relish; and Nikos Engonopoulos (1910–85), who was also the most radical and yet most representative painter of his generation. Initially of this group, Nikos Gatsos (1911–92), who published only one poetry book in his lifetime, the sumptuous *Amorgos* (1943), is nonetheless considered one of the most influential figures of this generation because of his production of several hundred song lyrics, written with remarkable skill, imagination, and grace (and set to music by many Gr. composers, notably Manos Hatzidakis) that singlehandedly raised the genre to a high art form. Certainly worth mentioning here is Giorgos Sarantaris (1908–41), whose hapless death brought to an unjust end the work of the most important philosopher-poet in 20th-c. Greece.

The magnitude of this generation is sealed by Ritsos (1909–90), who, along with Cavafy and Seferis, is the most influential Gr. poet worldwide. An inordinately prolific poet, Ritsos excelled in several forms: traditional folk metrics (*Epitaphios*, 1936), long-form dramatic verse (*Moonlight Sonata*, 1956), and short, sparse object-oriented poems (*Gestures*, 1972), as well as a variety of theatrical and prose pieces. What unites these concerns is an overt political voice, for which Ritsos was exiled and interned in concentration camps for most of his life as an avowed communist. Ritsos favors tragic landscapes, where the old gods no longer survive, while dispossessed humans, wounded and still threatened by the civilization they inhabit in ruined cities and arid plains, envision alternate universes in material household details, dreamlike encounters, and new myths.

Ritsos's figure permeates the post-Civil War generation of leftist poets, who wrote in conditions of persecution what was named the *poetry of defeat*: poetry of profound irony and self-critique against the backdrop of the bleakest landscape, where glimpses of real friendship provide the only possible resistance. This reticent poetry of extreme talent, sensitivity, and responsibility is exemplified by Manolis Anagnostakis (1925–2005), Aris Alexandrou (1928–78), Tasos Leivaditis (1922–88), and Titos Patrikios (b. 1928). Also writing in this period, Miltos Sahtouris (1919–2005), Nikos Karouzos (1926–90), and Eleni Vakalo (1921–2001) are three major poets who work in a postsurrealist mode but cannot be categorized. Sahtouris paints nightmare dreamscapes of a world that appears to have survived the destruction of humanity, often with characteristic humor. Karouzos favors a highly personal idiom, sometimes cryptically invoking a pre-Socratic sense of the universe. Vakalo, also the premier art critic of her time, engages in a self-conscious poetry of the object, which implicates a beautifully open-ended, if stark, poetic persona.

The generation following, known as the Generation of the 1970s, wrote out of the experience of the Gr. Junta years (1967–74) and in the atmosphere of global youth culture, in the aftermath of an internationalist antiestablishment poetics that spans the range from Beat poetry to rock-music aesthetics. This uncategorizable poetry incorporated a generally irreverent attitude toward bourgeois consumerist complacency by exploiting the full riches of colloquial speech, incl. imported terms and commercial monikers, and calling into question all orthodox beliefs and established positions, incl. gender roles and dogmatic political commitments. The tendency was to elucidate a bereft and absurd world in a lang. as contemporary as the drifting scene it depicted. Of the great number of poets in this generation, who emerged (often to submerge again in silence or long absence), it is worth noting, not as representative but by virtue of singular achievement and uniqueness, Dimitris Kalokyris (b. 1948), whose additional inordinate talents as storyteller, artist, art designer, pioneering publisher, and translator of Jorge Luis Borges are encapsulated in a poetry of magical effect; Maria Laina (b. 1947), who perfected a subtle, laconic, yet pulsating lyricism; and Dionysis Kapsalis (b. 1952), whose theoretical learning, studious contemplation of even minor traditional elements, and unequaled skill in the rhythmic use of the Gr. lang. (evident in his trans. of Emily Dickinson and Shakespeare's sonnets) pioneered a contemp. return to metrics.

The proliferation of poetic writing worldwide, aided by electronic media even if in the context of poetry's increasing irrelevance to popular art, renders all assessment of contemp. poetic production in Greece difficult. Yet there is no doubt that, of all literary forms, poetry has wielded the most decisive force in mod. Gr. culture. This gravity cannot be outmaneuvered. In the end, the future of Gr. literary expression will be waged on the permutations of continuing to fashion Gr. poetic lang., in whatever form this is to be actualized.

See LATIN POETRY.

■ **Classical**. ***Anthologies***: *Greek Lyric Poetry*, ed. D. Campbell (1982)—Gr. text and commentary; *Penguin Book of Greek Verse*, ed. C. A. Trypanis, 3d ed. (1988); *Hellenistic Poetry* (1990) and *Archaic Greek Poetry* (1992), both ed. and trans. B. Fowler; *Greek Lyric Poetry*, ed. G. Hutchinson (2001)—Gr. text and commentary. ***Bibliographies***: *L'Année Philologique: Bibliographie critique et analytique de l'antiquité gréco-latine* 1–(1927–), http://www.annee-philologique.com/aph/. ***Criticism and History***: D. L. Page, *Sappho and Alcaeus* (1955); A. E. Harvey, "The Classification of Greek Lyric Poetry," *CQ* n.s. 5 (1955); W. B. Stanford, *The Sound of Greek* (1967); Parry; F. Cairns, *Generic Composition in Greek and Roman Poetry* (1972); K. J. Dover, *Aristophanic Comedy* (1972); M. L. West, "Greek Poetry 2000–700 BCE," *CQ* 23 (1973); and *Studies in Greek Elegy and Iambus* (1974); H. F. Fränkel, *Early Greek Poetry and Philosophy*, trans. M. Hadas and J. Willis (1975); W. G. Arnott, "Introduction," *Menander*, v. 1 (1979)—comedy; R. Janko, *Homer, Hesiod, and the Hymns* (1982); T. G. Rosenmeyer, *The Art of Aeschylus* (1982); A. P. Burnett, *Three Archaic Poets* (1983); M. Griffith, "Personality in Hesiod," *Classical Antiquity* 2 (1983); A. Lesky, *Greek Tragic Poetry*, trans. M. Dillon (1983); A. P. Burnett, *The Art of Bacchylides* (1985); T. Figueira and G. Nagy, *Theognis of Megara* (1985); J. Herington, *Poetry into Drama* (1985); E. L. Bowie, "Early Greek Elegy, Symposium and Public Festival," *JHS* 106 (1986); E. Bundy, *Studia Pindarica*, 2d ed. (1986); S. Goldhill, *Reading Greek Tragedy* (1986); G. F. Else, *Plato and Aristotle on Poetry* (1987); M. W. Edwards, *Homer* (1987); H. White, *Studies in Late Greek Epic Poetry* (1987); B. Gentili, *Poetry and Its Public in Ancient Greece*, trans. A. T. Cole (1988); G. O. Hutchinson, *Hellenistic Poetry* (1988); R. Lamberton, *Hesiod* (1988); R. Hamilton, *The Architecture of Hesiodic Poetry* (1989); R. P. Martin, *The Language of Heroes* (1989)—*Iliad*; A. W. Pickard-Cambridge, *The Dramatic Festivals of Athens*, 2d ed. (1989); G. Nagy, "Hesiod and the Poetics of Pan-Hellenism," *Greek Mythology and Poetics* (1990); S. Goldhill, *The Poet's Voice* (1991); L. Kurke, *The Traffic in Praise* (1991)—Pindar and choral lyric; J. Redfield, *Nature and Culture in the "Iliad,"* 2d ed. (1994); A. Cameron, *Callimachus and His Critics* (1995); E. Csapo and W. J. Slater, *The Context of Ancient Drama* (1995); P. DuBois, *Sappho Is Burning* (1995); D. Konstan, *Greek Comedy and Ideology* (1995); M. Detienne, *The Masters of Truth in Archaic Greece*, trans. J. Lloyd (1996); R. Hunter, *Theocritus and the Archaeology of Greek Poetry* (1996); G. Nagy, *Poetry as Performance* (1996); F. I. Zeitlin, *Playing the Other* (1996); E. Bakker, *Poetry in Speech* (1997)—Homer; E. Stehle, *Performance and Gender in Ancient Greece* (1997); M. L. West, *The East Face of Helicon* (1997); A. Carson, *Eros the Bittersweet*, 2d ed. (1998); K. Gutzwiller, *Poetic Garlands* (1998)—Hellenistic epigrams; D. Selden, "Alibis," *Classical Antiquity* 17 (1998); A. Carson, *Economy of the Unlost* (1999); G. Nagy, *Best of the Achaeans*, 2d ed. (1999); S. Stephens, *Seeing Double* (2003)—Hellenistic poetry in Egyptian context; E. Csapo, "The Politics of the New Music," *Music and the Muses*, ed. P. Murray and P. Wilson (2004); C. A. Faraone, *The Stanzaic Architecture of Early Greek Elegy* (2008); D. J. Mastronarde, *The Art of Euripides* (2010). ***General Histories***: *CHCL*, v. 1; A. Lesky, *History of Greek Literature*, 2d ed. (1996). ***Primary Texts***: Bibliotheca Teubneriana series (1888–)—crit.

texts without trans.; Loeb Classical Library series (1912–)—texts, with facing trans., of all the major poets, incl. D. A. Campbell, *Greek Lyric* 5 v. (1982–93); D. E. Gerber, *Greek Elegiac Poetry*; and *Greek Iambic Poetry* (both 1999); *Callimachus*, ed. R. Pfeiffer, 2 v. (1949); *Theocritus*, ed. A.S.F. Gow, 2 v. (1950); D. L. Page, *Poetae Melici Graeci* (1962); M. L. West, *Iambi et Elegi Graeci ante Alexandrum cantati*, 2d ed. (1989–92); Oxford Classical Texts series (1980–)—good critical texts without trans. ***Prosody***: Wilamowitz; Dale; Halporn et al; Snell; West.

■ **Modern.** ***Anthologies***: *Anthologia 1708–1933*, ed. E. N. Apostolidis (n.d.); *Modern Greek Poems*, trans. T. Stephanidis and G. Katsimbalis (1926); *Eklogai apo ta tragoudia tou Hellenikou Laou*, ed. N. Politis, 3d ed. (1932); *Modern Greek Poetry*, trans. K. Friar (1973); *Voices of Modern Greece*, trans. E. Keeley and P. Sherrard (1981); *Greek Poetry: New Voices*, ed. D. Connolly (1999); *A Century of Greek Poetry 1900–2000*, ed. P. Bien et al. (2004); *The Greek Poets: Homer to the Present*, ed. P. Constantine et al. (2009). ***Criticism and History***: P. Sherrard, *The Marble Threshing Floor* (1956); G. Seferis, *On the Greek Style: Selected Essays in Poetry and Hellenism*, trans. R. Warner and T. D. Frangopoulos (1966); M. Vitti, *Storia della letteratura Neogreca* (1971); C. T. Dimaras, *A History of Modern Greek Literature*, trans. M. Gianos (1972); L. Politis, *A History of Modern Greek Literature*, trans. R. Liddell, 2d ed. (1975); A. Karantones, *Eisagoge ste neoteri poiese*, 4th ed. (1976); R. Beaton, *Folk Poetry of Modern Greece* (1980); Z. Lorenzatos, *The Lost Center* (1980); E. Keeley, *Modern Greek Poetry: Voice and Myth* (1983); D. Tziovas, *The Nationism of the Demoticists* (1986); G. Jusdanis, *The Poetics of Cavafy* (1987); V. Lambropoulos, *Literature as National Institution* (1988); D. Ricks, *The Shade of Homer* (1989); S. Gourgouris, *Dream Nation* (1996); D. Dimiroulis, *O poiētēs ōs ethnos* (1997); K. Van Dyck, *Kassandra and the Censors* (1998); D. Holton, *Literature and Society in Renaissance Crete* (2006).

C. J. Herington, L. Kurke (Cl.);
E. Keeley, S. Gourgouris (Mod.)

GUARANÍ POETRY. Though spoken in neighboring countries, Guaraní is present primarily in Paraguay, where, unique among Amerindian langs., it is the majority tongue of a nonindigenous and mestizo population of several million.

Of the considerable lit. in Guaraní, poetry is the dominant genre and the one that most exhibits Paraguay's historical spectrum from indigenous to nonindigenous. As sacred indigenous song of *ñe'ẽ* (word/soul), poetry has been present from the beginning, explaining and celebrating a vast cosmology that flows from the moment when Ñamandu Ru Ete (True Father Ñamandu) set life in motion by forming in himself the foundation of the word. Paralleling this trad., a corpus of *campesino* oral verse also developed in the colonial period, expressed often in the Guaraní-Sp. blend known as *jopara*, with a frequent focus on Christian religious themes.

Unfortunately, much remains unknown about this orature, and it was not accompanied by a significant written counterpart until after the catastrophic War of the Triple Alliance (1864–70), when Guaraní assumed greater importance as an emblem of nationalism. The decades between 1870 and the Chaco War against Bolivia (1932–35) saw themes of nature, love, war, and poverty woven into verse by Narciso R. Colmán, Manuel Ortiz Guerrero, Emiliano Fernández, and others. Following Paraguay's victory in the Chaco War, Guaraní's role in lit. expanded. Poets of the mid-20th c., among them Darío Gómez Serrato, Pedro Encina Ramos, Epifanio Méndez Fleitas, and Teodoro Mongelós, elaborated their predecessors' themes while adding distinctive experiments with rhyme, phrasing, and lineation.

The hardships of the Alfredo Stroessner dictatorship (1954–89) and the post-Stroessner period have seen considerable efforts to define a Guaraní poetics rooted in campesino life and Paraguay's diverse heritage. Protagonists in this effort have included Gumersindo Ayala Aquino, Félix de Guarania, Juan Maidana, Carlos Martínez Gamba, Lino Trinidad Sanabria, and Rudi Torga, all of whom use the Guaraní lang. as a conduit to express Paraguay's authentic *teko* (character).

What role Paraguay's indigenous heritage plays in this teko continues to be debated. The anthropological writings of Kurt Unkel Nimuendaju and León Cadogan concerning, respectively, the concepts of *Yvy Marae'y* (the Land without Evil) and *ayvu rapyta* (the basis of lang.) have encouraged much discussion. Whereas writers such as Encina Ramos used Eur.-inspired prosody to romanticize Guaraní mythology, recent poets like Susy Delgado, Ramón Silva, and Zenón Bogado Rolón have sought a deeper synthesis. They and others, incl. Miguelángel Meza, Feliciano Acosta, and Mario Rubén Álvarez, continue to explore the singular capacity of Guaraní to express Paraguay's particular confluence of cultures.

See INDIGENOUS AMERICAS, POETRY OF THE.

■ T. Méndez-Faith, *Breve diccionario de la literatura paraguaya* (1996); *Poesía paraguaya de ayer y de hoy: tomo II, guaraní-español*, ed. T. Méndez-Faith (1997); *Antología de las mejores poesías en guaraní*, ed. R. Torga (1998); F. Acosta, *Ñe'ẽporãhaipyre guaraní, literatura guaraní* (2000); *Forjadores del Paraguay: Diccionario biográfico* (2000); *Antología de la poesía culta y popular en guaraní*, ed. R. Bareiro Saguier and C. Villagra Marsal (2007); *Literatura oral y popular del Paraguay*, ed. S. Delgado and F. Acosta (2008); Portal Guaraní, http://www.portalguarani.com/autores.

T. K. Lewis

GUATEMALA, POETRY OF

I. The Precolonial Period to the Nineteenth Century
II. The Mainstream Tradition (1920s–2010)
III. New Women's and Indigenous Poetry in Guatemala

I. The Precolonial Period to the Nineteenth Century. Poetry in Guatemala has served as a vehicle of emergent national expression, with the marked limitation that a great part of Guatemala's population has been made up of non-Sp.-speaking Indian peoples whose writings have disappeared. Even the *Popol Vuh*, the most important work in the Quiché lang. and a veritable storehouse of images that constantly re-emerged in the poetry of the 20th c., was written after the arrival of the conquistador Pedro de Alvarado. The *Rabinal Achí*, a dramatic work involving dance and poetry, is thought to date from the 15th c. The administrative seat of Spain's Central Am. colonial rule, Guatemala dominated regional discourse for over 400 years, generating a canon of lit. based on Eur. models and centered on prose. From the 16th to the 19th c., poetic production took forms such as the *villancico*, the *sainete*, the *jácara*, the *tonada*, and the *cantata*, with poets such as Rafael Antonio Castellanos (ca. 1725–91) and Manuel José de Quirós (ca. 1765–90) writing music as well as verse.

In the 18th c., Rafael Landívar (1731–93) wrote his *Rusticatio mexicana* (1782) in Lat.; and in the early 19th, the Sp.-born Pepita Garcia Granados (1781–1845) broke religious and sexual taboos with her scandalous, salacious verse, while José Batres Montúfar (1809–44), influenced by Eur. romanticism, wrote verse of satire, irony, wit, and political commentary. However, while the Nicaraguan modernist Rubén Darío drew on Fr. symbolism as opposed to the Sp. trad., to provoke a virtual revolution involving an aesthetically driven poetry, called *modernismo*, in much of Latin America and extending back to Spain, Guatemala's most important *modernistas*, Enrique Gómez Carrillo (1873–1927) and Rafael Arévalo Martínez (1884–1975), as well as most later Guatemalan writers, were better known for their prose than for their poetry.

II. The Mainstream Tradition (1920s–2010). The *vanguardismo* movement, Latin America's response to Eur. and U.S. avant-garde trends, saw the emergence of the first two Guatemalan poets of international stature, Miguel Ángel Asturias (1899–1974) and Luis Cardoza y Aragón (1901–92), both of whom began their careers as students living in Paris, studying pre-Columbian culture and absorbing the fashionable literary trends in the city's émigré community during the post-World War I period. The two writers shared an interest in primitivism, surrealism, and other avant-garde movements, as well as in Indian themes (*indigenismo*) that they related to such political themes as Central Am. unionism and democratic reforms. While Cardoza was perhaps Guatemala's greatest poet, bringing surrealism to bear on Lat. Am. themes, he is better known for his memoirs and his essays on Guatemalan hist. and culture, as well as on the Mexican mural movement, esp. during his long period of exile in Mexico after the 1954 military coup in his native country. Asturias, a Nobel Prize laureate mainly known for his novels, became the most famous of the *vanguardistas*. While most of his poetry is forgotten, his work often figures in discussions of the representation of Mayan life and culture in contemp. Guatemalan lit.

The 1930s saw a growing emphasis on indigenismo in the work of *Grupo Tepeus* and other writers. The key figure was novelist Mario Monteforte Toledo (1911–2003), but the leading poets were Alfredo Balsells Rivera (1904–40) and Oscar Mirón Álvarez (1910–38), who frequently wrote on life in Guatemala City under the dictatorship of Jorge Ubico (1931–44).

The October Revolution of 1944 led to Juan José Arévalo's reform government (1945–51) and a new poetry alive to the moment. Inspired by Pablo Neruda's most militant poetry, Enrique Juárez Toledo (1910–99), Raúl Leiva (1916–74), and Otto Raúl González (1921–2007) formed *Grupo Acento* (Focus Group). Some years later, several group members joined *Saker-ti,* a literary-cultural group comprised mainly of young students and cultural workers, which sought to create a "democratic, nationalist and realist art" just as Jacobo Árbenz came to power (1951). Saker-ti included the poets Miguel Ángel Vazquez (1922–2010), Julio Fausto Aguilera (b. 1929), Melvin René Barahona (1931–65), Augusto Monterroso (1921–2003), and Carlos Illescas (1918–98), while the group's leading ideologue was the left-wing activist and polemicist Huberto Alvarado (1927–74). But the U.S.-supported coup of 1954 led to the silence or exile of many of the writers, some of whom pursued their work in Mexico and elsewhere.

With the 1954 coup, *La Generación Comprometida* (the Committed Generation) emerged in the 1960s as a new group of writers who questioned both U.S. imperialism and the political consensus represented by the October Revolution. Repudiating Asturias for accepting an ambassadorship in France, the group adopted his motto "the poet is a form of moral behavior" in their argument for poetry in the name of armed struggle. Otto René Castillo (1934–67) became the leader of the group, and his poem "Intelectuales apolíticos" (Apolitical Intellectuals) served as their poetic manifesto. Castillo's poetry, framed by simple metrical forms and emotionally direct lang., is more lyrical and metaphorical than epic and historical. In this, he typified his generation's reaction against the grand Nerudian model of political poetry, and the group's turn to a conversational tone popular in the early years of the Cuban Revolution. Castillo's book *Vámonos patria a caminar* (*Let's Go!,* 1965) contains themes of love and commitment, injustice and tragedy, revolutionary hope and death—incl. the premonition of his own end (he was executed by the military in 1967)—as part of the process leading to social transformation.

Meanwhile, poets such as Edwin Cifuentes (b. 1926), Arturo Palencia (1931–81), and Marco Antonio Flores (1937–2013) explored themes of alienation, conquest, subjugation, and rebellion. Gradually disillusioned with the Left in the late 1960s, Flores turned from poetry to the acidic, disenchanted prose fiction represented by his novel *Los compañeros* (*Comrades,* 1976). However, three poets of La Generación Comprometida—Luis Alfredo Arango (1936–2001), Francisco Morales Santos (b. 1940), and Roberto Obregón (b. 1946)—joined three older writers—Antonio Brañas (1920–98), Fausto Aguilera, and José Luis Villatoro (1932–98)—and one younger woman writer, Delia Quiñónez (b. 1946), to form the group *El Nuevo Signo* (The New Sign) in 1968.

The Nuevo Signo poets explored the crisis of conscience in the face of militarized society, lending their poetry a testimonial and denunciatory function. They sought to identify alternatives to continued military rule and explored the lang. and themes of the rural Guatemalan experience. Several members of the group came from poor, rural backgrounds and tended to focus on peasant themes. But Nuevo Signo's poetry was also a response to previous indigenist discourse in Guatemala. In place of Asturias's "lyric exaltation" of Indian and pre-Columbian myth and Castillo's celebration of Mayan roots, the Nuevo Signo writers strove for a more sober treatment of Indian realities.

Obregón began to publish in his teens, when he went to study in Moscow. In 1970, working with the guerrillas, he was "disappeared" by a Salvadoran army patrol. His surviving poetry exhibits a flair for dramatic and extreme metaphors centered on blood and fire, death and rebirth. Most of the Nuevo Signo writers tried to avoid partisan poetry, however, electing instead to explore the broader forces operating in Guatemalan society, with Arango emerging as the crucial master poet of his generation and Morales as the group's leading spokesperson. Nuevo Signo poets also sought to explore complex states of subjectivity while observing the 1960s idea that the personal is political.

Headed by Manuel José Arce (1935–85) and Carlos Zipfel (1937–2013) and joined by Margarita Carrera (b. 1929), Luz Méndez de la Vega (1919–2012), and others, *Grupo Moira* represented cosmopolitan, modernizing concerns defined by their interest in existentialist, psychological, and aesthetic themes. Arce and Zipfel were major lyric poets in the intimist mode. Before his death in 1985, Arce produced a remarkable body of political poetry. Meanwhile, Carrera and Méndez cultivated Freudian and feminist perspectives that opened the way to a serious body of women's poetry.

Two literary groups—*La Galera* (The Galley) and *Grupo Literario Editorial RIN-78*—emerged in the wake of the 1976 earthquake and continued military rule. Incl. writers such as Luis Eduardo Rivera (b. 1949), Roberto Monzón (1948–92), Otoniel Martínez (b. 1953), and Aida Toledo (b. 1952) and heralded by Enrique Noriega Jr.'s (b. 1949) *¡Oh banalidad!* (1975), La Galera rejected the lit. of political denunciation and national transformation, expressing disillusionment with life in the nation and the lit. expressing it and valorizing poetry, aesthetics, and bohemianism.

Under Efrain Ríos Montt's dictatorship, several writers of varying political tendencies joined together in a kind of literary popular front to maintain a culture of writing and publishing activities in a period of retrenchment. Taking on the name of Grupo Literario Editorial RIN-78, the project included poets associated with Nuevo Signo and the new feminist poetry, as well as younger writers. The term RIN came from a Japanese ideogram standing for unity, toleration, and diversity. Thus, the group did not attempt to articulate any particular political ideology but rather outlined goals that were "cultural and promotional." In a short period, they produced 36 books, incl. 15 of poetry.

After the failed military coup against the reformist government of Marco Vinicio Cerezo in 1987, a new group emerged playfully calling itself *La Rial Academia* (i.e., not the Royal [Real] but the Laughable Academy) and dedicating itself to attacking RIN-78's neutrality. While several of its members wrote about poetry, René Leiva (b. 1947) was one of the few to publish volumes of verse.

III. New Women's and Indigenous Poetry in Guatemala. There are some antecedents for women's poetry in 20th-c. Guatemalan lit. hist. Luz Valle (1896–1971), Magdelena Spinola (1886–1975), Romelia Alarcón de Folgar (1900–70), and Alaide Foppa (1914–80) were prominent women writers who sought to rise above the quietistic "feminine as opposed to feminist" mode of the upper-class *poetisa* model prevalent in Central America. Antimilitary resistance emerging among Guatemalan women poets of the 1970s would change that identification dramatically. A well-known feminist, Foppa became a political force in life and poetry after her children were disappeared and until she herself was disappeared in 1980. The youngest member of Nuevo Signo and the only woman among its founders, Quiñónez went to the forefront of an emerging movement of Guatemalan women's poetry. Ana Maria Rodas's (b. 1937) militant *Poemas de la izquierda erótica* (Poems of the Erotic Left, 1973) rebuked the *machismo* of the male revolutionary Left. More recently, several women poets—incl. Carmen Matute (b. 1944), Isabel de los Ángeles Ruano (b. 1945), and Toledo—showed their ability to write a richly layered, imagistic, and subjectivist poetry, often expressing eroticism, deep psychic disturbance, and metaphysical explorations while registering a political, specifically feminist agenda.

The most significant new devel. of the 1980s was, however, the appearance of a Mayan testimonial poetry practiced by men and women alike, incl. Nobel Peace Prize winner Rigoberta Menchú (b. 1959). The first mod. indigenous voice was the Nuevo Signo member Luis de Lión (1940–84), an only partially ladinized Indian, who was disappeared by the military. After him came one of the initial members of RIN-78, Enrique Luis Sam Colop (1955–2011).

These three writers drafted their poems in Sp., offered as "translations" from the Quiché, in an invented indigenous tonality expressing the pain and resistance of their people. Similarly, Humberto Ak'abal (b. 1952) emerged in the 1990s as the first fully celebrated indigenous poet. In his work, the indigenous question is one not of radical separatism but of the creation of conditions for mutual recognition and respect. His poems draw upon Quiché trads. to reshape ling. and poetic norms in relation to dimensions of indigenous culture, emphasizing city versus country, the struggle against communal destruction, and the capacity of modernity and globalization to deepen rather than dilute indigenous cultural devel. Ak'abal includes elements of shamanism and magic in his texts, but he also employs ladino poetic trads. and tropes, enmeshing them with indigenous images.

In these indigenous writers and the new women poets, incl. many appearing in the 21st c., we see fresh beginnings for poetry in Guatemala's future. In the midst of globalization and local power struggles, poets shift their focus from national identity to more panindigenous and universal themes, linking Guatemala to the larger world, but never losing sight of their own local issues.

See INDIGENOUS AMERICAS, POETRY OF THE; SPANISH AMERICA, POETRY OF.

■ *Poesía revolucionaria guatemalteca*, ed. M. L. Rodríguez Mojón (1971); F. Albizúrez Palma and C. Barrios y Barrios, *Historia de la literatura guatemalteca*, 3 v. (1981–87); R. Armijo, "Introducción," *Poesía contemporánea de Centro América*, ed. R. Armijo and R. Paredes (1983); A. Chase, "Prólogo," *Las armas de la luz: Antología de la poesía contemporánea de la América Central*, ed. A. Chase (1985); D. Vela, *Literatura guatemalteca* (1985); *Ixok amar·go: poesía de mujeres centroamericanas por la paz. Central American Women's Poetry for Peace*, ed. Z. Anglesey (1987); *Exodus: An Anthology of Guatemalan Poets*, ed. A. Saavedra (1988); D. Liano, "Studio introduttivo," *Poeti di Guatemala: 1954–86*, ed. D. Liano, trans. A. D'Agostino (1988); J. Beverley and M. Zimmerman, *Literature and Politics in the Central American Revolutions* (1990); *Nueva poesía guatemalteca*, ed. F. Morales Santos (1990); M. Zimmerman, *Literature and Resistance in Guatemala: Textual Modes and Cultural Politics from El Señor Presidente to Rigoberta Menchú* (1995); *Voices from the Silence: Guatemalan Literature of Resistance*, ed. M. Zimmerman (1998).

■ **Web Sites**: B. Mateos, *Palabra virtual: voz y video en la poesía iberoamericana*, http://www.palabravirtual.com—sections on Guatemala; *Poesía guatemalteca*, http://www.poesiaguatemalteca.com/.

M. Zimmerman

GUJARATI POETRY. For many years, Narsinh Mehta (15th c.) was the first known poet in the hist. of Gujarati lit., but after dozens of mss. of old Gujarati lit. were recovered from the protected Jain scriptoria at Jesalmer, the record of Gujarati poetic hist. was extended to the 11th c. CE. This new literary era was called the pre-Narsinh or Rāsā period and included many Jain and a few non-Jain texts. Among them, Jain texts such as Jinpadmasūri's *Sirithulibhadda Fāgu* (ca. 1334) and Rahshekhar's *Nemināth Fāgu* (ca. 1344) and non-Jain texts such as the anonymous *Vasant Vilās* (1452) stand out for their creative fervor. The med. Gujarati lit. that followed is divided into the Bhakti, Akhyān, and Vairagya periods. The sweet feminine melancholy of Mīrābāī, the master narratives of Premanand Bhatt (1649–1714), the exotic storytelling of Sāmal Bhatt (1718–65), the philosophical sarcasm of Akho, and the devotional eroticism of Dayārām enriched the med. canvas. The transcendental vision of med. Gujarati poetry was conveyed with native lyricism in varied oral and singable verse forms.

Under Brit. rule, new technological advances and educational policies and, in particular, the imported model of Eng. romantic poetry brought the med. Gujarati era to an end. The literary period that followed continued until shortly after the departure of Brit. rule in 1947. This era is divided into three parts: the Reformist (1850–85), Pandit (1885–1915), and Gandhi (1915–45) periods.

Dalpatrām (1820–98) and Narmad (1833–86) emerged as the most significant poets of the Reformist period; the former was a conservative, and the latter was a radical reformer. Uneducated in Eng., Dalpatrām was influenced by Vraj poetics and was a master of prosody. His poetry was distinguished by wit and satire. Narmad, the first pioneer of the mod. era, adopted the Eng. romantic model and dealt with personal topics such as love and nature. In spite of his enthusiasm and quest for beauty, his verse is often considered inexpert.

The Pandit period was characterized by a discriminatory attitude toward Eng. values. Poets of this period chose instead to assimilate the Sanskrit and Persian trads. Narsinhrao Divetiā (1859–1937) continued in the romantic model, but other poets soon complicated this conservatism. The sculpturelike structure of Kavi Kānt's (1867–1923) *Khandkavya*, the verseless outburst of Nānālal's (1877–1946) platonic idealism, the pensive juvenile world of love and separation built by Kalāpi (1874–1900), and the robust poetic lang. of run-on verses inscribed by B. K. Thākore (1869–1952) were remarkable landmarks of the Pandit period of Gujarati poetry.

As Mohandas K. Gandhi entered the Indian political scene, the new themes of truth and nonviolence pervaded all spheres of life. While combating Brit. rule, Gandhi confronted the cardinal issues of untouchability, village reforms, and the unequal distribution of wealth. He aimed at simplicity and compassion and ultimately aspired to forge a universal brotherhood. The Gujarati poetry in this period appropriated the Gandhian vision. Two major poets, Sundaram (1908–91) and Umāshankar Joshi (1911–88), made experimental and often eclectic poetry in this vein. Their poetry railed against political and social inequality, calling for a humane and compassionate approach toward the downtrodden and the exploited. Meanwhile, the Bengali poet Rabindranath Tagore's (1861–1941) aesthetic theories were at work during this period.

Umāshankar Joshi, recipient of the prestigious Jnānpith Award, lived in three successive literary periods (the premodernist, modernist, and postmodernist periods). His poem "Chhinnabhinna Chhun," one of the seven components of his influential long poem *Saptapadi*, became the harbinger of the modernist period. Suresh Joshi (1921–86), who discarded much of the idealism of the Gandhian period; Rājendra Shāh (1913–2010), another Jnānpith Award winner; and Niranjan Bhagat (b. 1926), a premodernist poet of urban inclination, provided the springboard for a new period of international poetry. Poetry of this era was concerned with pathos and the meaninglessness of contemp. life, private idiosyncrasy, repressed psyche, the subconscious, the inwardness of individual experience, the dislocation of logic, and the use of associative lang. Lābhshankar Thākar (1935–2016), with his dissociation of sensibility, and Sitanshu Yashaschandra (b. 1941), with his surreal verve and apolitical tone, confidently carry on this trad.

In the latest phase of postmodernity, Gujarati poets explore new themes, such as Dalitism and feminism, in traditional forms such as *ghazals* and songs. Meanwhile, Gujarati poetry continues to look toward new gravity and grandeur.

See BENGALI POETRY; INDIA, POETRY OF; SANSKRIT POETICS; SANSKRIT POETRY.

■ N. Bhagat, "Experiments in Modern Gujarati Poetry," *Indian Literature* 21 (1978); R. Joshi, "Recent Trends in Gujarati Literature," *Indian Literature* 27 (1984); *Modern Gujarati Poetry*, trans. S. Ramanathan and R. Kothari (1998).

C. TOPIWALA

GYPSY POETRY. *See* ROMANI POETRY

H

HAITI, POETRY OF. *See* CARIBBEAN, POETRY OF THE

HAUSA POETRY. In the Hausa lang. as spoken in Nigeria, Niger, and parts of Ghana, the single term *waka* is applied to two closely related trads., song and written poetry (verse). Popular song and courtly praise singing are oral, professional, and instrumentally accompanied, typically with interaction between lead singer(s) and chorus. Poetry, on the other hand, is chanted without accompaniment, and reward for performance is not usually sought. Poems are composed in roman or in *ajami* (Ar.) script and often circulate in ms. or in printed form. Both song and poetry can be scanned according to patterns of heavy and light syllables. Song follows traditional patterns (Greenberg) or parallels instrumental accompaniment. Poetry usually has scansions corresponding to those of cl. Ar. meters. In song, the words of the lead singer are interrupted by the refrains or repetition of the *amshi* (chorus); this may occasion variation in the length of "verses" between choruses. Commonly, poetry is in couplets displaying syllable end rhyme or in five-line stanzas with end rhyme in the final line, supplemented by internal rhyme in the first four lines. It has been claimed that, in some cases, tonal rhyme can accompany syllable rhyme.

Of the 16 cl. Ar. meters, nine are found in Hausa poetry (in descending order of frequency), *kaamil, mutadaarik, mutaqaarib, rajaz, basiiṭ, waafir, khafiif, ramal,* and *ṭawiil.* Claims for other meters require liberal interpretation of the cl. Ar. form. There is some controversy over whether the traditional Ar. method of analysis is appropriate to Hausa, even for meters of Ar. provenance (Galadanci, Schuh). Since at least the latter part of the 20th c., there has been cross-fertilization between song and poetry, with poets adopting meters that originated in song (Muhammad 1979).

Mod. poetry in roman script (starting in 1903) developed from the trad. of Islamic religious verse in ajami of the 19th c. Since at least the time of the Islamic *jihaad* (holy war) of Shehu Usman dan Fodio (1804), the propagation of the faith has involved the writing of Hausa poetry that circulated both in ms. form and through the performances of religious mendicants, often blind. Such poetry fell broadly into the categories of theology, praise of the Prophet, biography of the Prophet and his companions, admonition and exhortation, religious obligations, law, and astrology. While strictly religious poetry continues to be written, the 20th c. saw a great broadening in themes, which now cover such diverse subjects as Western education, hygiene, the evils of drink, filial piety, and many topical subjects such as the population census and the introduction of new currency. Poetry writing along with song has been an important part of the political process with the approach of Nigerian independence (1960); the Civil War (1967–70); the rise of political parties in northern Nigeria during the civilian political eras of the 1960s, 1980s, and 2000s; and the creation of new states in the 1980s and 1990s. To a considerable extent, Hausa poetry retains, as its most prominent characteristics, didacticism and a concern for social issues inherited from Islamic trad. Personal lyrical expression has traditionally been restricted to the category of *madahu* (praise of the Prophet), where the lang. of deep personal devotion, longing, and desire was both legitimate and appropriate. More recently, however, love poetry, which had in the past been private, entered the public arena through the publication of the anthol. *Dausayin Soyayya.*

Mod. Hausa poetry has been published regularly in the newspaper *Gaskiya Ta Fi Kwabo* (founded 1939), and prominent poets such as Akilu Aliyu, Mudi Sipikin, Na'ibi Wali, Salihu Kwantagora, and others have reached a wider audience in broadcasts over radio stations in northern Nigeria. Poetry-writing circles have been formed and have access to radio. While the majority of poets have been men, women such as Hauwa Gwaram and Alhajiya 'Yar Shehu have written on contemp. social and religious issues, following in the footsteps of the poet and translator Nana Asma'u, daughter of Shehu Usman dan Fodio, leader of the jihaad of 1804, and scholar in her own right (Boyd and Mack).

Song has been available on recordings since the 1950s and is a mainstay of radio programming and, more recently, television. The popular music of northern Nigeria is that of singers in traditional soloist and chorus ensembles, such as Mamman Shata and Musa Dan Kwairo (succeeded by his sons), and soloists accompanying themselves on stringed instruments, such as Dan Maraya Jos and Haruna Oji. A more recent devel., thanks to the burgeoning film and video industry, is film music, often in imitation of Indian film music but with Hausa metrical forms.

■ **Anthologies**: *Wakokin Mu'azu Hadejia* (Poems of Mu'azu Hadejia, 1955); N. Sulaimanu, et al., *Wakokin Hausa* (Poems in Hausa, 1957); *Wakokin Sa'adu Zungur* (Poems of Sa'adu Zungur, 1966); *Tsofaffin Wakoki da Sababbin Wakoki* (Old and New Poems of Mudi Sipikin, 1971); *Wakokin Hikima* (Poems of Wisdom, 1975); A. Aliyu, *Fasaha Akiliya* (The Skill of Akilu, 1976); *Zababbun Wakokin Da da na Yanzu* (Selected Poems of Yesterday and Today), ed. D. Abdulkadir (1979); B. Sa'id, *Dausayin Soyayya* (The Mellowness of Mutual Love, 1982); *The Collected Works of Nana Asma'u*, ed. J. Boyd and B. B. Mack (1997).

■ **Criticism and History**: J. H. Greenberg, "Hausa Verse Prosody," *JAOS* 69 (1949); D. W. Arnott, "The Song of the Rains," *African Language Studies* 9 (1969); M.K.M. Galadanci, "The Poetic Marriage between Arabic and Hausa," *Harsunan Nijeriya* 5 (1975); M. Hiskett, *A History of Hausa Islamic Verse* (1975); D. Muhammad, "Interaction Between the Oral and the Literate Traditions of Hausa Poetry," *Harsunan Nijeriya* 9 (1979) and "Tonal Rhyme: A Preliminary Study," *African Language Studies* 17 (1980); G. L. Furniss, *Poetry, Prose and Popular Culture in Hausa* (1996); R. G. Schuh, "Metrics of Hausa and Arabic poetry," *New Dimensions in African Linguistics and Languages*, ed. P.F.A. Kotey (1999).

G. Furniss; R. G. Schuh

HEBREW POETRY

I. Introduction
II. Biblical and Medieval
III. Modern

I. Introduction. Heb. lit. spans three millennia and ranks among the world's oldest. Heb. poetry began to appear at least by the 11th c. BCE and flourishes in contemp. Israel. Whatever gaps disrupted this virtually continuous literary flow should be attributed more to the loss of linking texts than to a diminution of creativity. Heb. poets may not always have been aware of their entire literary heritage, but most often they did have both a diachronic and synchronic knowledge of much of it.

In every age, the Heb. Bible has constituted the foundation and principal component of that heritage, a major source for literary forms, symbols, rhetorical tropes, syntactic structures, and vocabulary. There has been, however, no uniformity in metrical systems: these have varied from age to age and, following the biblical period, were usually adapted from those employed in the area where the Heb. poet happened to reside. In the Persian period (5th–4th cs. BCE), Aramaic began to replace Heb. as the vernacular in Palestine, continuing as the spoken lang. long into the Byzantine period (4th–7th cs. CE), while Gr. prevailed in the Mediterranean diaspora. With the rise of Islam in the 7th c., Ar. became the lingua franca for Jews of the Middle East, North Africa, and Spain. In Christian Europe, the various IE langs. were adopted. From the Middle Ages until the early 20th c., Yiddish was the vernacular used by the majority of Eur. Jewry as the centers of Jewish population shifted to Central and Eastern Europe. The interplay of these non-Hebraic langs. and lits. with Heb., the literary lang. of the Jews, broadened and altered Heb. poetry, affecting its syntax, vocabulary, themes, and genres.

The scope and variety of these phenomena make it as difficult to formulate a single comprehensive definition of Heb. poetry as it is to formulate one for world poetry. Still, the definition of poetry proposed by Barbara Herrnstein Smith is sufficient to accommodate the entire gamut of Heb. poetry: "As soon as we perceive that a verbal sequence has a sustained rhythm, that it is formally structured according to a continuously operating principle of organization . . . we are in the presence of poetry and we respond to it accordingly, expecting certain effects from it and not others" (*Poetic Closure*, 1968).

II. Biblical and Medieval

A. ***Biblical Poetry (1100 BCE–150 BCE).*** The Heb. Bible (or OT) is an assemblage of sacred texts composed over a span of about a thousand years. The earliest mss.—primarily the Dead Sea Scrolls—date only from the 2d–1st c. BCE, but ling. and historical considerations provide a basis for ascribing the composition of most of the included texts to earlier centuries. The relative date and general period of most texts can be determined with some assurance, but the date of many poems and even of books remains controversial. Close to a third of the Heb. Bible is poetry. Many scholars believe the most salient feature of biblical poetry, like the Semitic, and esp. Ugaritic (13th-c. North Canaanite), poetry that preceded it, is *parallelismus membrorum* (Lowth) or parallelism. There also appears to be a quasi-metrical feature in this poetry, in that the lines forming most couplets and the occasional triplet are of similar length (Herder). Efforts to define the prosodic component more precisely are, however, unconvincing, usually involving manipulations of the received text to suit a particular theory. And no early Heb. poem maintains a consistent line length throughout.

No poetics of Heb. poetry was transmitted in ancient times. The earliest attempts to describe biblical prosody were performed by some of the church fathers, who tended to compare contemp. Gr. and Lat. forms, and more extensive treatments by Jewish scholars began only in the Middle Ages (Cooper, Kugel 1979, Berlin 1991, Harris). Recent decades have seen several substantial efforts to describe biblical poetry (e.g., O'Connor, Alter, Berlin 1985, Watson, Pardee, Alonso Schökel).

Defining the basic components of biblical Heb. poetry depends on how one views the matter of meter. Phonological meter in the strict sense, although proposed in one way or another since Sievers (1901; see, e.g., Stuart), cannot be established. Counting major words or word accents as one beat each, or counting syllables with or without attention to phonemic accent, does not yield convincing results (Pardee, Vance). O'Connor has suggested instead a meter founded on syntactic constraints—only so many words, so many constituents, so many clauses within a line. The wide flexibility of the poetic line in the Bible leads Hrushovski to conceive of free rhythms ("rhythm[s] based on a cluster of changing principles") for biblical verse (cf. Dobbs-Allsopp 2009). Nevertheless, taken by itself, no prosodic or purely syntactic meter can be used to characterize a single line of biblical text as poetic. For that reason, most students of biblical poetry define the basic unit of verse as a two-part line (comprised of cola, hemistichs, or versets) or simply a couplet (of two lines). The poetic line is usually composed of two cola—sometimes three or four—that are parallel to each other.

While most descriptions of biblical parallelism up through the mid-20th c. focus on a reiteration of semantic sense and/or sentence structure, more recent accounts, influenced by Roman Jakobson's seminal work, highlight repetitions of ling. features in all areas of lang. Hrushovski summarizes the possibilities: "It may be a parallelism of semantic, syntactic, prosodic, morphological, or sound elements, or of a combination of such elements." Observing that there is more often repetition of sound within the line than between lines, Greenstein (1986–87) downplays the phonological element. He also separates out semantic content, which is context-dependent and unquantifiable, from the other, properly formal components and points to three primary features of biblical parallelism: first and foremost, relative balance of line length; second, a repetition of syntactic structure, on either the surface or underlying (deep) level, from line to line; and third, a distribution of conventionally associated words or phrases between the lines of the couplet. These can be a paradigmatically related set of words paired in the poetic trad. For example, *rosh-qodqod* (head, pate); *yayin-dam 'anavim* (wine, blood of grapes); *shama'-bin* (hear, discern) or a syntagmatically related set of words, known in biblical studies (Melamed) as the breakup of a stereotyped phrase (e.g., "Balaam son of Beor" split into "Balaam"—"son of Beor"). All parallel lines have at least one, and ordinarily more than one, of these three features.

Some of the repetitive patterns that constitute parallelism occur in biblical prose, esp. in legal formulations. However, this does not mean that the boundary between prose and poetry in the Bible is indistinct. For one thing, although an umistakably poetic couplet may be embedded within a distinctly prose context (e.g., Gen. 7:11b), in a full poem, the parallelisms occur in an uninterrupted series of couplets, triplets, and an occasional single line. For another, in addition to the properties of parallelism, biblical poetry is typically characterized by a number of optional tropes, incl. but not limited to syntactic deletion in the second line with lengthening of a nondeleted constituent as "compensation" to maintain the balance of line length (Geller); variations in word order (e.g., chiasmus); alliteration, assonance, and rhyme; figuration; distinctively poetic diction (e.g., *tehom* [sea, subterranean ocean]; *mahats* [smite]); ambiguity or double entendre; paronomasia; terseness or concision of expression—and more specifically, parataxis and nonuse of the relative pronoun (*'asher*), the direct-object marker (*'et*), and the definite article (*ha-*)—and other archaic ling. features (Robertson).

Moreover, in early biblical poetry, and in many later poems as well, there is a different, more archaic verbal system. In the earlier system, the present and future, or foreground, are expressed by the prefixed form *yiqtol* (old West Semitic *yaqtulu*), while the past, or background, is expressed by the suffixed form *qatal* (old West Semitic *qatala*). This system contrasts with that of biblical prose, in which the past is conveyed by *way-yiqtol* in clause-initial position and *qatal* in noninitial position, and the future by *we-qatal* clause-initially or *yiqtol* noninitially (Niccacci). Last but not least, biblical poetry is composed largely of verbal clauses with little embedding, while biblical prose tends to have nominal chains and embedded clauses. As Polak has shown, there is a direct correlation between the syntactic simplicity of poetic lines in the Bible and the oral character of Heb. verse. Be that as it may, if we bear all these criteria in mind, it is difficult not to recognize a biblical Heb. poem, or even a couplet, when we see one.

Consider this short song, which is quoted with an introduction in a prose narrative context (Num. 21:17–18):

> ʿalí beʾér / ʿenú-láh
> beʾér ḥaparúha sarím
> karúha nedibé haʿám
> bimḥoqéq / bemishʿanotám
>
> (Arise, O well! / Sing to it!
> The well the princes have dug,
> [The well] the people's leaders have excavated,
> With their staffs, / with their walking-sticks.)

The poem is constructed of four couplets in parallelism. The first and last are either brief couplets or lines featuring internal parallelism. The middle two lines, longer than the first two but balanced between themselves, are a couplet, two roughly synonymous relative clauses with "well" as their head, each formed of the same syntactic pattern, except that the head ("well") is deleted in the second line. Note that the subject noun-phrase in the second line is longer than that in the first line, compensating for the quasi-metrical weight that is lost as a result of the deletion. The last line (or couplet) comprises two fairly synonymous adverbial complements, which are structurally as well as lexically (the anaphoric preposition *bi*) repetitive. There is sound repetition in the first couplet between the first and last syllables. There is word repetition (*beʾér*) from the first couplet to the second. In the second couplet, the first line displays assonance between the first two words (*b-r* followed by *p-r*), while the verb in the second line echoes and rhymes with the verb in the first line. Archaic features include the omission of the definite article (*ha-*) in all but the third line (*haʿam*) and of the relative pronoun in both lines of the middle couplet. Each couplet is syntactically dependent on the preceding one, but from a purely semantic perspective, the second line of each couplet adds little to the sense. The entire song boils down to a single sentence—*Arise, O well that the princes have dug with their walking sticks!* It is typical of biblical poetry, however, to advance the message in steps, adding a point or a nuance here, burnishing or refining an image there. In this poem, parataxis governs the whole; there are no connectives. In later biblical poetry, parataxis decreases and variety and flexibility increase, but the essential features remain the same.

In ancient Semitic poetry preceding the Heb. Bible, such as the strongly cognate verse from Ugarit (see above), poetry serves as a narrative mode, as in an epic as well as a lyric mode, as in hymns and prayers. Biblical poetry is characteristically nonnarrative. In biblical poetry, events are not recounted but dramatized (Lichtenstein). Moreover, poetry of any length in the Bible is always discourse—it is spoken by a named or implied speaker (Greenstein 2000). When the speaker expresses thoughts and feelings, it may be lyric (Dobbs-Allsopp 2006, Linafelt). When the speaker gives instructions or advice, it may be gnomic. The poetic discourse may take the form of hymns or songs embedded in narratives (e.g., the Song at the Sea in Exod. 15, the Song of Deborah in Judg. 5, the prayer of Jonah in Jon. 2) or collected in the book of Psalms; or of prophetic oracles, mostly assembled in the books of the prophets; or of epigrams, as in the book of Proverbs. The elegies of the book of Lamentations and the rhapsodies of the Song of Songs are in poetry. The contrasting functions of prose for narrative and poetry for discourse are well exemplified by the book of Job, whose narrative framework is prose and whose lengthy speeches are in poetry. There is a tendency toward parallelism, the hallmark of biblical poetry, in discourse within prose narrative as well.

Imagery and metaphor, though not invariably present in biblical poetry, are prominent in many genres and poems. Some metaphors, such as the wicked as a predator and the needy as vulnerable sheep, are the biblical poet's stock in trade. Most often, a particular figuration will not be employed for more than one instance at a time. Even in Psalm 23, the image of God as shepherd gives way to that of host, spreading out a table for the speaker in view of his adversaries. In the poetry of some of the prophets, Job, and other texts, however, an image or metaphor may pervade a large stretch of verse (e.g., Isa. 5:1–4) or even several chapters (for Jeremiah, see Jindo).

B. *Extracanonical Works* (i.e., works not included in the Heb. biblical canon). The book of Sirach (the sole apocryphal work, a substantial part of which is preserved in the Heb. original) and the Dead Sea Scrolls discovered in 1947–48 indicate that poetic activity did not cease after the canonization of the Heb. Bible in the 2d c. BCE. Most scholars ascribe the apocryphal works to the 2d or 1st c. BCE, and their poetry is akin to that found in the wisdom lit. The author of Sirach at times displays a remarkable fluency and originality, as when he describes the High Priest's entry into the Holy of Holies on Yom Kippur:

How glorious (he was) when he emerged
from the Sanctuary
And stepped out from inside the curtain;
Like a star shining through thick clouds,
Like a full moon on feast days,
Like the sun combing the King's palace,
Like a rainbow seen in the cloud,
Like a lily by a flowing stream,
Like a flower of Lebanon on a summer's day
Like the fire of frankincense upon the
offering.

(50:5–9)

C. *The Mishnaic and Talmudic Period (ca. 100 BCE–500 CE).* The lit. that has survived from the Mishnaic-Talmudic era is primarily legal or homiletic, but it contains several occasional poems celebrating important events in life: births, circumcisions, marriages, and epitaphs. These were preserved not for their aesthetic quality but because they honored important scholars. Stylistically, they mark a break with the biblical trad. Instead of parallelism, many use a four-colon line. The poems are not laced with biblical quotations, their vocabulary is a mixture of biblical and postbiblical words, and their syntax is late Heb.

D. *The Byzantine Period (500–800). Piyyut* (derived from Gr. *poiētēs*) or synagogue hymnography is distinctive in both its volume and its focus from biblical psalmody and poetry. This type of poetry was produced since the late Roman period in Jewish communities and congregations where poetry was allowed to embellish Jewish liturgy. Such compositions were preferably written for the Sabbath and festivals when statutory prayers were supposed to have a link with the theme of the day. The majority of Jewish liturgical poems (*piyyutim*) for the Sabbath relates to biblical topics or addresses ways of exegesis with regard to biblical themes, whereas festival compositions extensively deal with the aspects of the holiday involved. Since the early 20th c., tens of thousands of piyyutim have been re-collected from the Genizah mss., deciphered, reconstructed, and edited in critical eds., with important results in particular for our knowledge of Byzantine-Jewish and Babylonian-Jewish liturgy and hymnology. By virtue of these textual studies, names and works of long-forgotten synagogue poets (*paytanim*) in different temporal and regional settings have been added to the corpus, leading to great progress in the knowledge about distinct piyyutic genres and forms. We would not have known otherwise about the significance and growth of the early *qinot* (threnodies), *selihot* (penitential hymns), *'avodot* (compositions for the Day of Atonement), *qedushta'ot* or *yozrot* (multipart hymns for the Sabbath and festival morning services); nor would we have been acquainted with the names of great hymnists who have been crucial for the trad. of Piyyut.

Piyyut as a phenomenon in Jewish culture and lit. deserves further investigation concerning its interactivity with surrounding cultures and religions. Themes and motifs are not exclusively versified recounts of rabbinic-midrashic materials but also draw on other noncanonical and nonrabbinic sources or can be considered as intrinsically paytanic. Piyyut lang. is a fascinating combination of biblical, rabbinic, and "jargonic-piyyutic" grammar and vocabulary, at times mixed with elements from Aramaic and Gr.

Yose ben Yose (4th c.) is the first *paytan* whose name is known. He heads a line of major composers who wrote in Palestine between the

6th c. until after the Muslim conquest of Jerusalem in 636 CE, the most famous among them being Yannai (6th c.), Simeon bar Megas (6th c.), Yehudah (6th c.), Eleazar birabbi Qillir (7th c.), Yohanan ha-Kohen (7th c.), and Joseph ben Nisan (7th c.). During the 5th and 6th cs., the various piyyut forms became standardized and were usually inserted into key sections of the synagogue liturgy. These hymnists introduced consistent strophic and rhyme schemes; they also favored other intricate poetic structures and employed a rich variety of prosodic devices and lexical patterns. There can be little question that the cantor-poets were widely regarded as the mouthpiece of their communities. The med. *Chronicle* of Ahima'ats (1017–60) proves to be particularly informative in this regard, since it preserves an account of the Palestinian *hazzan* Ahima'ats who, during his visit to southern Italy, was invited to recite in synagogue the poems of other hymnists, incl. the poem of a locally rejected paytan called Silano. By adapting some of Silano's verses accusing the Karaites of heresy and favoring the Rabbanites, Ahima'ats succeeded in regaining the confidence of the Jerusalem rabbis, and he eventually rehabilitated Silano's piyyutim in his hometown. The story affords us some idea of the socioreligious context in which the cantor-poets functioned.

E. *Muslim Spain (900–1100).* The ling. studies of Heb. in the Islamic East in the hands of Saadia Gaon (882–942), Dunash Ibn Labrat (920–90), and others—some of them migrated from Iraq to Spain—stimulated the Jews of Muslim Spain to engage in a renaissance of Heb. lang. and lit. Andalusian-Jewish poets combined the role of poet and philologist and earned a living by their work by the patronage of Jewish aristocratic courtiers, who employed them for the sake of their status and position. The most famous example is Hasday Ibn Shaprut (ca. 915–975), the Jewish counselor of Caliph Abdarahman III of Córdoba, who maintained a coterie of Jewish poets at his court. These composers were aware of contemp. tastes as well as of the Jewish poetic trad., inducing them to emphasize a greater purity of Heb. in the biblical sense. Grammatical correctness was appreciated and a biblicist style was applied. However, they were also eager to invent new ways of composing in Heb. in close familiarity with the themes and techniques of Ar. poetry and poetics. Ar. influence is particularly felt in the description of themes such as love, wine, and nature in secular verse and in the use of metrical schemes that became standardized in both secular and liturgical poetry. But it was not only the new metrical forms that were borrowed from the Arabs: Heb. poets adopted the rules of composition fixed by the Arab rhetoricians, their rhyme patterns, and various other themes. They also favored the local Sp. version of the popular "girdle" poems or *muwashshaḥāt.* The last couplets of these compositions were often written in either Ar. or Sp., mostly derived from popular lyrics. These parting lines are very instructive for the comprehension of some of the surviving Ar. or Romance vernacular. Only when they wrote piyyutim or synagogue hymns did they sometimes adhere to traditional models. More often than not, they employed the Arab structures and techniques even in the religious domain. In terms of their Heb. diction, they eschewed the cavalier way by which the paytanim constructed words and phrases, considering these to be barbarisms. If the Arab rhetoricians had insisted that the lang. of the Qur'an was the epitome of good writing, their Heb. counterparts adhered to the biblical models, though on rare occasions they allowed themselves to draw their vocabulary from Talmudic sources. Because Heb. and Ar. are both Semitic langs., they infused Heb. words at times with Ar. connotations.

One of the most common genres was the Ar. ode or *qaṣīda*, which soon became the vehicle for occasional verse written to celebrate an important event or to praise a patron. The Heb. imitations of such poems would begin in a purely lyrical vein, describing the beauties of nature, a drinking party, or a meeting of friends or would develop a philosophical meditation; the poet would then shift into a laudatory mode praising a patron or colleague. A prolific poet was Samuel the Prince, Samuel Ibn Nagrela ha-Nagid (993–1056), who attained the powerful position of chief vizier of Granada and head of the Muslim army of the Berber king Habbus. Because of his military career, he wrote a great deal of secular poetry on the battlefield, a phenomenon never repeated by any other med. Heb. poet. He was followed by Solomon Ibn Gabirol (ca. 1021–55) from Malaga, a philosopher and poetic genius. His secular poetry includes amatory poems of much beauty, while his religious works give expression to his Neoplatonic ideas. In his lyric-cosmological composition *Keter Malkhut*

(Kingly Crown, ca. 1041), he contrasts the glory of God the Creator with the tragic shortcomings of the human. Moses Ibn Ezra (1055–1135) was noted for his deep familiarity with Ar. poetry. Ibn Ezra is the leading theoretician of the Andalusian-Heb. school of poetry. His *Sefer ha-'Iyyunim we-ha-Diyyunim* (Book of Discussion and Commemoration, ca. 1135) is a valuable source for the study of aesthetic principles of Heb. secular poetry based on Ar. poetics. The standards of purity listed by Ibn Ezra were, in fact, valid for both liturgical and secular verse. A protégé of Ibn Ezra and the most renowned of all Andalusian-Heb. poets was Jehudah Halevi (ca. 1074–1141), born in the Christian north of Spain and also acclaimed as the author of a widely read philosophical treatise entitled the *Kuzari* (ca. 1140). His poem "Tsiyyon ha-lo tish'ali" (Zion, will you not ask; 1120–40), a song of love and longing for the land of Israel, was widely known and inspired many imitators. At the end of his life, Halevi indeed traveled to the crusader's kingdom of Palestine, reached Jerusalem, and died under unknown circumstances. The Andalusian school of Heb. poetry, of which Halevi undoubtedly is the most illustrious example, had a continuing influence on the trends emerging in Heb. secular poetry of Christian Spain.

F. ***Italian.*** The It. Jewish community was established in Roman times. Although it was small in numbers, it was highly cultured and, until the 19th c., made important contributions to the corpus of Heb. poetry. The first It. poet known to us is Silano of Venosa (9th c.), who wrote piyyutim in the style of the Palestinian school that had dominated It. Heb. poetry until the 12th c. Among Italy's leading paytanim were Shephatiah ben Amittai (d. 886) and Amittai ben Shephatiah (9th c.) of the Ahima'ats family and Meshullam ben Qalonymos (10th c.).

Between the 12th and 15th cs. the influence of Sp.-Heb. poetry—its syllabic meters, subject matter, and structures—prevailed, but vernacular It. forms were gradually introduced, esp. the sonnet in the 14th c. and *terza rima* in the 15th. The leading poets of this period were Benjamin ben Abraham degli Mansi (13th c.) and the renowned Immanuel of Rome (see below).

The final period begins at the close of the 15th c. and ends at the opening of the 20th. At first, we feel the impact of the Sp. Jewish exiles who reached Italy after 1492. Religious poetry is now dominated by the Kabbalah or Jewish theosophy. Secular poetry, on the other hand, reflected the increasing contact with It. culture. More It. poetic forms are introduced: the *ottava*, the *canzone*, the *canzonetta*, the madrigal, and blank verse (*versi sciolti*). Heb. poetic drama appears in the 17th c., to be followed by many such works in the 18th and 19th cs. Ar. quantitative meter is soon modified by the elimination of the distinction between short and long syllables so that the lines began to resemble the It. *endecasillabo* (Pagis 1976). The 17th-c. poet Nathan Jedidiah of Orvieto even made an attempt to write poems in accentual meter, but the hendecasyllabic line prevailed.

Four poets stand out: Immanuel of Rome (ca. 1261–1332), Jacob and Immanuel Francis (16th c.), and Moses Hayyim Luzzatto (1707–46). Immanuel of Rome was undoubtedly the greatest of the Italians. His *Mahberot Immanuel* (Immanuel's Compositions) is a collection of *maqamot* containing 28 sections, the last of which, *ha-tophet we-ha-Eden* (Hell and Paradise), was inspired by Dante's *Divine Comedy*. Immanuel first introduced the sonnet into Heb. poetry. His supple verse reflects the culture of the Ren.; his bawdy verses are a rarity in Heb. letters. Immanuel composed a rhetorical work in which he described the new forms in It. verse and insisted that the *acutezza* (*agudeza* or wit) of the poem's diction and subject matter must be primary. By this term, he meant the use of surprise, either formally (oxymoron) or conceptually (paradox), by strange and complex metaphors or uncommon conceits. In this, he was faithful to the baroque school then current in Italy and Spain. Jacob and Immanuel Frances of Mantua wrote polemic satires against the supporters of Shabtai Zevi (17th c.), the mystical Messiah.

Luzzatto composed poems and allegorical closet dramas similar to the It. works of his day. His first play, *Migdal 'Oz* (Tower of Strength, 1737), was modeled after Giovanni Battista Guarini's *Il pastor fido*. Luzzatto combined an awareness of 18th-c. science with a deep Kabbalistic faith. His achievement lies on the border between a late Ren. and a mod. worldview.

The Heb. poetry produced by premod. Ashkenazi Jewry was almost entirely religious, influenced by the Palestinian and It. schools. It consisted of liturgical hymns and dirges commemorating the massacres during the Crusades. A particular genre of martyrological poetry was the *'aqedah*, which celebrated the sacrifice of Isaac as a symbol of the martyrdom of Jews.

Ephraim of Bonn (12th c.) has a fine example of this genre (discussed by Shalom Spiegel, *The Last Trial*), *Unetaneh toqef* (10th c.), a prayer attributed to the martyr Amnon of Mayence, which still holds a prominent place in the Yom Kippur liturgy.

By the 16th c., the center of Ashkenazi Jewry had moved from Germany to Eastern Europe. The Jews in the Polish-Lithuanian kingdom expressed their piety by the meticulous observation of the *halakhah* (Jewish Law) and by the study of religious texts. They inhabited a cultural milieu that infrequently resorted to the arts—not even to the composition of religious hymns.

III. Modern

A. ***The European Period (1782–1918).*** At the end of the 18th c., a new kind of Heb. poetry emerged in Central Europe. This poetry was part of the Jewish Enlightenment, or *Haskalah*, a term derived from the Heb. word for intellect. From the Middle Ages until the 1780s, Heb. had been used primarily for religious texts, with the exception of works by the aforementioned It.-Jewish poets. The Jewish Enlightenment, in contrast, promoted the use of Heb. for educational, scientific, philosophical, and aesthetic works. The poems of the Haskalah, thus, came to be viewed as an alternative to the religious Heb. canon.

The Haskalah movement began in Germany with influential figures such as the philosopher Moses Mendelssohn (1729–86) and the Ger. Jewish Hebraist, educator, and poet Naphtali Hirz Wessely (1725–1805). Wessely published the manifesto of the movement, *Divre Shalom ve-Emet* (Words of Peace and Truth, 1782). Other important figures of the early movement were Isaac Eichel (1756–1804), a student of Immanuel Kant, and Baruch Lindau (1759–1849). Together they founded the first club of Enlightenment poets and thinkers, known as the *Maskilim* (Enlighteners or Proponents of Enlightenment); the club published the first Heb. periodical, *Ha'me'asef* (The Gatherer), a collection of mostly didactic Heb. poetry by contemp. writers.

The Haskalah soon spread to Jewish communities in Vienna and Prague and expanded eastward from there to the region of Galicia in Eastern Europe. By the middle of the 1820s, the movement had reached Russia. In all these places, the Maskilim advocated a rationalist intellectual Heb. discourse espousing universal and humanistic values, a strong commitment to Jewish society, and a wish to reform its traditional structures. They promoted openness to the ideas of the local Western culture; however, when it came to poetic form, they strictly followed the syllabic meters of the It. Heb. poets of the previous century. The Maskilim poets developed a new style of writing, a collage of biblical Heb. phrases called *melitsah*. This style was described by the poet and thinker Shlomo Levisohn (1789–1821) in his 1816 book *Melitsat Yeshurun* (The Eloquence of Yeshurun).

While literary historians generally agree about the role of the Haskalah in the devel. of the new poetry, some date the emergence of mod. Heb. poetry only to the middle of the 19th c., while others place it as late as the end of the century. However, there is no doubt that the 1850s and 1860s saw rapid growth in the community of readers and in the publication of Jewish poems, poetry books, and periodicals such as *Ha'magid* (The Preacher), *Ha'carmel* (The Carmel), and *Ha'melitz* (The Advisor). A new Heb. lit. crit. also arose. In terms of style, the didactic epos of the Haskalah was replaced in prose with the new Heb. novel and in poetry with the modern long poem.

In the mid-19th c., Heb. poetry grew to include a wider scope of themes and genres. Talented new poets soon established themselves as major Heb. writers, among them Micha Joseph Levenson (also known as Michal, 1828–52) and the most renowned poet of the Haskalah, Judah Leib Gordon (1830–92). Gordon's long poems were mostly on biblical themes. Some of his writings, however, included strong social and political messages, referring, e.g., to the condition of women in religious Judaism in *Kutzo Shel Yod* (The Point on Top of the Yod, 1878); criticizing religious dogmatism; or calling on the Jewish people to emancipate themselves (while also questioning their ability to do so), as in his poem "Hakitza Ami" (Awake My People, 1863).

Another strand of mod. Heb. poetry emerged with the pre-Zionist national movement, *Hibbat Zion*, in Eastern Europe, which brought about a wave of sentimental Heb. poems addressing or describing the national homeland. Poets writing about and to Zion included Mordecai Zevi Manne (1859–86), Naphtali Herz Imber (1856–1909), and Menahem Mendel Dolitzki (1856–1931).

In Italy, meanwhile, a few poets continued to write in Heb. Rachel Luzzatto Morpurgo

(1790–1860), for instance, wrote mostly sonnets on religious, mystical, and secular themes. The work of the It. poet, philosopher, and biblical commentator Samuel David Luzzatto (also known as Shadal, 1800–65) reached Jewish communities beyond Italy and influenced the devel. of Jewish nationalism in lit. Mod. Heb. poets such as Hayyim Nachman Bialik were influenced also by the earlier work of Moses Hayyim Luzzatto (also known as Ramchal), a major It. Jewish writer who was considered by some to be the first mod. Heb. poet, predating even the works of the Haskalah poets. However, by the second half of the 19th c., Heb. poetry in Italy had declined, and Eastern Europe became its main center. Additionally, in the 19th c., a number of non-Eur. Jews composed Heb. verse. The Baghdadi-born Palestinian poet Avraham Barukh Mani (1854–82), e.g., wrote poetry in the It. Heb. style.

A major shift in Heb. poetry and in Jewish hist. took place around 1881–82, following the pogroms in Russia. These years mark the beginning of what Harshav has called the Modern Jewish Revolution, when ideas that had developed in relatively small circles for many years were rapidly adopted by millions of Jews. It was in this period that Hayyim Nachman Bialik (1873–1934) published his first poems. Bialik's poetry combined accentual-syllabic meters from Rus. poetry with the rich sounds of the Ashkenazi pronunciation of Heb. In his poems, Heb. was not restricted to the vocabulary and syntax of the Bible but drew on the entire spectrum of Heb. lit. Bialik wrote about longing for Zion and life in the diaspora, about love, the struggle with faith, the pogroms, and much more.

Bialik's contribution to Heb. lit. included not only poetry but major essays on lang. and lit. He was an influential ed. and publisher in Russia, Berlin, and, later, Tel Aviv. Though his production was relatively small, the quality and importance of his work, along with the prophetic tone of some of his poems, earned him the title of the Heb. poet laureate. Many historiographies of Heb. poetry consider him the father of mod. Heb. poetry.

Bialik's contemp. Saul Tchernikhovsky (1875–1943) also furthered the devel. of an accentual-syllabic Heb. poetry and greatly enriched Heb. lit. with sonnets, idylls, and other poetic forms. His trans. from ancient Gr., Akkadian, and Finnish, and his original poetic work in Heb., introduced his readers to Eur. myths, ideas, and verse forms. Bialik and Tchernikhovsky as well as other poets of the Heb. revival juxtaposed historical and national themes with a growing focus on the individual. Some of these poets were influenced by Eur. romanticisms and introduced to Heb. lit. elaborate descriptions of nature, thus expanding the vocabulary of the lang. to include names of flora and fauna. In this way, the Heb. poetry of this period contributed significantly to the revival of Heb. as a spoken lang.

Tchernikhovsky and Bialik were followed by major writers such as Jacob Fichman (1881–1958), Yehuda Karni (1884–1949), Zalman Shneor (1887–1959), and Jacob Steinberg (1887–1947).

B. ***Europe, 1918–48.*** The school of Bialik dominated Heb. poetry until the 1930s. By then, younger Heb. poets, many of whom had arrived in Israel following World War I and the Rus. Revolution, had begun to rebel against the older poets' linear and symmetrical forms, as well as their traditional sources and themes. Once used almost exclusively for rabbinical writings, Heb. had now become a full-fledged spoken lang., and the new poetry was tempered by the vernacular. It also reflected the Socialist-Zionist ideology of the pioneer culture, which was far less traditionally "Jewish" in theme and was permeated by the new Mediterranean landscape.

The most prominent "pioneer" poets were Nathan Alterman (1910–70) and Abraham Shlonsky (1900–73). Both were influenced by the Rus. revolutionary poets Alexander Blok, Vladimir Mayakovsky, and Sergei Esenin and by expressionism. In their work, the ennui of the disintegrating urban Eur. culture, the destruction wrought by war, and the impending Holocaust vied with enthusiasm for the daring novelty of the reborn homeland, its bright but uncompromising colors, its sand dunes, and its sea. Another pioneer poet, Rachel Bluwstein Sela (1890–1931), wrote lyrical short poems in a clean and precise lang. that was influenced by the Rus. poet Anna Akhmatova and Rus. acmeism. Rus. influence also made its way into Heb. poetry in Palestine through the works of the communist poet Alexander Penn (1906–72), who translated poems by Mayakovsky to Heb., and by Leah Goldberg (1911–70), a scholar, writer, and trans. (see RUSSIA, POETRY OF).

The uprooted poets of this generation wandered through the capitals of Europe, absorbing the cultures of their temporary homes. They were exposed not only to Rus. poetics but to Ger. expressionism, Fr. symbolism, the existentialism of R. M. Rilke, Freudian and Jungian views of the arts, and much more. Many of these poets translated poems and plays from It., Fr., Rus., and Eng. into Heb. Shlonsky and Goldberg wrote poems and plays for both adults and children; Alterman published a highly influential political and satirical newspaper column in verse called *Hatur Hashvi* (The Seventh Column). Thus, in a relatively short period, these poets created a large canon of native Heb. *Eretz Israeli* poetry.

Another major figure in the devel. of Heb. poetry in Eretz Israel was the poet and activist Uri Zvi Greenberg (1894–1981). Greenberg broke away from Socialist-Zionist ideology to create a new poetic style with a messianic tone. For him, the "return" to the land was a return to God's historic covenant, a rejection of what he perceived as the "false" morality of the gentiles, and a dedication to the miracle of divine providence. Greenberg's style is often extravagantly Whitmanian. He eschews foreign verse forms, preferring the cadences of the biblical peroration and Jewish liturgical verse (piyyutim). His vocabulary is sometimes drawn from Kabbalistic texts.

Jonathan Ratosh (1908–81) and the Canaanite movement represented still another ideological direction in Heb. poetry. This movement tried to create a strong connection among land, lang., and poetry by reviving Canaanite sounds and the Canaanite pantheon. A very different connection between the land and poetic style can be found in the work of Esther Raab (1894–1981), Israel's first native-born woman poet, who was also the first to describe the landscape of Israel without the ambivalence of the immigrant poets.

While Heb. poetry of the early 1920s is characterized by modernist and experimental styles and by its break from the rhythms and meters of the Ashkenazi pronunciation of Heb., much of the poetry written in the late 1920s, 1930s and even 1940s—esp. by poets from the Shlonsky-Alterman-Goldberg school—represented a return to constrained poetic expressions, to postsymbolism, and to the prosodic forms of the now established Eretz Israeli pronunciation.

While some poets from the 1920s onward wrote in free verse, most were considered minor voices at the time. E.g., in 1923 in Vienna, David Vogel (1891–1944) published a collection of modernist lyric poems in free meter titled *Lifnei Sha'ar ha-Afel* (In Front of the Dark Gate). In Palestine, Avraham Ben-Yitzhak (1883–1950) experimented with a mod. form of biblical parallelism in "Bod'dim Omrim" (Loners Say, 1918) and in "Ashrei Hazor'im v'lo Yiktzoru" (Happy Are They Who Sow, 1930). Avot Yeshurun (1904–92) challenged readers with enigmatic, idiosyncratic, and complex poems and forms. Contrary to the ruling conventions of his time, he wrote in a lang. that openly reflected the multilingualism of both the immigrant writer and the land by including Yiddish and Ar. sounds and words. These poets were at the margins of the canon when their works were published; but the poets and critics of the next generation moved them to the center, as part of their revolt against Alterman, Shlonsky, and Goldberg.

C. *Israeli Poets (1948–2010).* With Israel's War of Independence in 1948, a new generation of Heb. poets arose. These were either native Israeli poets or products of the Heb. school system that the Zionists had established in Eastern Europe, who arrived in Palestine as young pioneers before the outbreak of World War II. For them, Heb. was a vibrant spoken lang., and Israel's landscape was the landscape of their youth, if not their infancy. While most no longer drew from the traditional religious world of Eastern Europe, the Bible and the Prayer Book (*Sidur*) continued to serve them as major sources, and biblical phrases, allusions, forms, and myths continued to occupy much of their poetry.

The older writers of the Israeli generation who began as junior members of the Shlonsky-Alterman school, such as Haim Guri (b. 1923), remained committed to the Socialist-Zionist ideology. Following the War of Independence and the mass immigration to Israel, however, many discovered that there were no simple solutions to the problems of their new society. Once independence was attained, individualism, which had been suppressed during the struggle, broke loose, and subjectivism became the rule.

In this era, poets such as Yehuda Amichai (1924–2000), Amir Gilboa (1917–84), and Abba Kovner (1918–87) abandoned the strict metrical and stanzaic patterns to which the Shlonsky-Alterman generation had adhered. Amichai chose his metaphors from quotidian experience—a newspaper headline, the terms of a contract, a cliché—as well as from traditional Jewish texts, to which he often gave an ironic twist. His poetry evoked a tension between the sacred and profane experiences of the mod. poet as a Jew, an Israeli, a Jerusalemite, and a human being.

By the 1950s, literary influences on Heb. poetry had become less Ger. or Rus., and more Anglo-Am. The poets known as the Statehood Generation, such as Amichai, Nathan Zach (b. 1930), Moshe Dor (1932–2016), David Avidan (1934–95), and Dahlia Ravikovitch (1936–2005), rebelled against the poetic style of Shlonsky and Alterman. Zach attacked what he termed the monotonous rhythms of Alterman and called for a new poetry in which line and stanza were freed from traditional rules. He also called for a new poetic diction characterized by semantic significance rather than mechanical regularity. He believed that poems should be not neatly rounded to a close but fluid and open-ended. Figurative lang. should be used sparingly: i.e., the poet should avoid manifestly poetic diction and syntax and draw upon everyday speech, incl. slang. Zach also attacked "objective" or "ideological" poetry: the artist, he believed, should concentrate on the subjective, existential experience of a complex mod. world. While not all the poets of the Statehood Generation followed Zach's views, most of them saw their work as an attempt to focus on the concrete, on the "here and now." In some of the poems of Avidan, e.g., the focus on the "now" meant constant questioning of the boundaries of the poetic lang. and form and bringing into poetry some of the sounds and patterns of the media and technology of a rapidly changing world. Toward the end of the 1960s, Avidan's poetry became even more concrete in an objectivistic and even pseudo-Talmudic manner.

Ravikovitch, a feminist poet whose sophisticated naïf poems have been widely acclaimed, focused on concrete and subjective experiences but in a rich lang. that drew from the many historical layers of Heb. Her collection *Ahavat Tapu'ach Hazahav* (The Love of the Orange, 1959) is lush with musical patterns. It is one of the most influential poetry collections of the later 1950s and the beginning of the 1960s, together with Zach's *Shirim Shonim* (Different Poems, 1960), Amichai's *Shirim 1948–1962* (Poems), and Avidan's *Masheu Bishvil Misheu* (Something for Somebody, 1964).

In the 1960s, the poets Meir Wieseltier (b. 1941), Yair Horvitz (1941–88), and Yona Wallach (1944–85) created the Tel Aviv Circle and published some of the major works in mod. Heb. poetry. Wallach shocked Israeli readers with her daring expressions of sexuality and the decidedly Jungian bent of her poetry.

With the Lebanese War of the 1980s, Heb. poets reverted to more directly political poetry. In the wake of the war, several volumes of protest poetry appeared in which Zach and Ravikovitch, once the apostles of subjectivism, and younger poets such as Yitzhak Laor (b. 1948) participated. For Ravikovitch, this meant protesting against oppression and suffering through intimate situations and the experiences of women and children. Political poetry, from both the Right and the Left, held sway until the 21st c. (see e.g., the work of Aharon Shabtai [b. 1939]).

Heb. poetry of the later 20th and early 21st cs. has been enriched by the interplay among multicultural Israeli voices. The works reflect the varied origins of both immigrants and their children and of different social and ethnic groups: the religious world of Zelda Mishkovsky (1914–84); the middle Eur. roots of Zach, Amichai, and Dan Pagis (1929–86); the Rus. Polish milieu from which sprang Kovner and Gilboa; the Anglo-Am. influences on T. Carmi (1925–94), Gabriel Preil (1911–93), who lived in New York, and Simon Halkin (1898–1987); the Mediterranean world of Mordecai Geldman (b. 1946); the Maghrebian world of Erez Biton (b. 1942); and the Arab-Jewish roots of Ronny Someck (b. 1951), Amira Hess (b. 1956), Haviva Pedaya (b. 1956), and Almog Behar (b. 1978).

Periodicals and jours. had been major venues for mod. Heb. poetry from its beginning, but the end of the 20th and beginning of the 21st cs. demonstrated a sudden growth in new jours. and a slight change in their role and format. It is difficult to predict which of the current directions in Heb. poetry will have a lasting influence, but the jour. appears to reflect a need for literary spaces that accommodate a diverse range of social, ethnic, and political affiliations, as well as the search for new poetic styles. Some of the jours. embodying these sentiments include *Ha'Kivun Mizrach* (To the East), a jour. focusing on Mizrahi and Arab-Jewish issues and questions of identity; *Mashiv Haru'ach* (Make the Wind Blow), a jour. devoted primarily to religious Heb. poetry; *Mita'am: A Review of Literature and Radical Thought*, ed. by Laor; *Emda* (Position), ed. by Ran Yagil, which calls for a return to modernist poetic values and to a new kind of poetic (but not social) elitism; *Maayan* (Spring), a forum for poetry in Israel and beyond; and the renewed format of *Achshav* (Now), a jour. that was instrumental in the devel. of Israeli poetry for many years and now appears in a new format. In 2005, a small group of poets and writers became associated with a new literary jour. titled *Ho!* Poets in *Ho!* strive to restore formal rhythms and rhymes to Heb. poetry and to create a poetry that is not specifically Israeli but more "cosmopolitan."

See AL-ANDALUS, POETRY OF; HEBREW PROSODY AND POETICS; JUDEO-SPANISH POETRY; YIDDISH POETRY.

■ **I. Biblical**: R. Lowth, *Lectures on the Sacred Poetry of the Hebrews*, trans. G. Gregory (1787); J. G. Herder, *The Spirit of Hebrew Poetry* [1783], trans. J. Marsh (1833); E. Sievers, *Metrische Studien I–II* (1901–7); G. B. Gray, *The Forms of Hebrew Poetry* (1915); T. H. Robinson, *The Poetry of the Old Testament* (1947); E. Z. Melamed, "Break-up of Stereotyped Phrases as an Artistic Device in Biblical Poetry," *Studies in the Bible*, ed. C. Rabin (1961); S. Gevirtz, *Patterns in the Early Poetry of Israel* (1963); R. Jakobson, "Grammatical Parallelism and Its Russian Facet," *Language* 42 (1966); B. Hrushovski, "Prosody, Hebrew," *Encyclopedia Judaica* (1971); D. A. Robertson, *Linguistic Evidence in Dating Early Hebrew Poetry* (1972); A. M. Cooper, *Biblical Poetics* (1976); D. K. Stuart, *Studies in Early Hebrew Meter* (1976); S. A. Geller, *Parallelism in Early Biblical Poetry* (1979); J. L. Kugel, "Some Medieval and Renaissance Hebrew Writings on the Poetry of the Bible," *Studies in Medieval Jewish History and Literature*, ed. I. Twersky (1979); and *The Idea of Biblical Poetry* (1981); E. L. Greenstein, "How Does Parallelism Mean?" *A Sense of Text* (1983); M. H. Lichtenstein, "Biblical Poetry," *Back to the Sources*, ed. B. W. Holtz (1984); R. Alter, *The Art of Biblical Poetry* (1985); A. Berlin, *The Dynamics of Biblical Parallelism* (1985); W.G.E. Watson, *Classical Hebrew Poetry* (1986); E. L. Greenstein, "Aspects of Biblical Poetry," *Jewish Book Annual* 44 (1986–87); L. Alonso Schökel, *A Manual of Hebrew Poetics*, trans. L. Alonso Schökel and A. Graffy (1988); D. Pardee, *Ugaritic and Hebrew Poetic Parallelism* (1988); A. Niccacci, *The Syntax of the Verb in Classical Hebrew*, trans. W.G.E. Watson (1990); A. Berlin, *Biblical Poetry through Medieval Jewish Eyes* (1991); S. E. Gillingham, *The Poems and Psalms of the Hebrew Bible* (1994); M. O'Connor, *Hebrew Verse Structure*, 2d ed. (1997); F. H. Polak, "The Oral and the Written: Syntax, Stylistics, and the Development of Biblical Prose Narrative," *Journal of the Ancient Near Eastern Society* 26 (1998); E. L. Greenstein, "Direct Discourse and Parallelism," *Studies in Bible and Exegesis* 5 (2000—in Heb.); D. R. Vance, *The Question of Meter in Biblical Hebrew Poetry* (2001); R. A. Harris, *Discerning Parallelism* (2004); F. W. Dobbs-Allsopp, "The Psalms and Lyric Verse," *The Evolution of Rationality*, ed. F. L. Shults (2006); T. Linafelt, "Lyrical Theology: The Song of Songs and the Advantage of Poetry," *Toward a Theology of Eros*, ed. V. Burrus (2006); F. W. Dobbs-Allsopp, "Poetry, Hebrew," *New Interpreter's Dictionary of the Bible*, v. 4 (2009); J. Y. Jindo, *Biblical Metaphor Reconsidered* (2010).

■ **II. Medieval**. ***Anthologies and Editions, in English***: *A Treasury of Jewish Poetry*, ed. N. and M. Ausubel (1957); *An Anthology of Modern Hebrew Poetry*, ed. S. Y. Pnueli and A. Ukhmani (1966); *The Penguin Book of Hebrew Verse*, and trans. T. Carmi (1981); *Wine, Women, and Death*, ed. R. P. Scheindlin (1986); R. Loewe, *Ibn Gabirol* (1989); *The Gazelle*, ed. R. P. Scheindlin (1991); A. Schippers, *Spanish Hebrew Poetry and the Arabic Literary Tradition* (1994); *The Modern Hebrew Poem Itself*, ed. S. Burnshaw, T. Carmi, E. Spicehandler (2003); D. Bregman, *The Golden Way*, trans. A. Brener (2006); *The Dream of the Poem*, ed. and trans. P. Cole (2007). ***In Hebrew***: *Diwan of Yehudah ha-Levi*, ed. H. Brody, 2 v. (1894–1930); J. Schirmann, *Hebrew Poetry in Spain and Provence*, 4 v. (1954–56); *New Hebrew Poems from the Genizah*, ed. J. Schirmann (1965); *Israel Levin Jubilee Volume*, ed. R. Tsur and T. Rosen (1994); *Eretz Israel and Its Poetry, Studies in Piyyutim from the Cairo Geniza*, ed. M. Zulay (1995); *Jewish Palestinian Aramaic Poetry from Late Antiquity*, ed. J. Yahalom and M. Sokoloff (1999); *Tahkemoni or Tales of Heman the Ezrahite*, ed. J. Yahalom and N. Katsumata (2010). ***Criticism and History, in English***: S. M. Stern, *Hispano-Arabic Strophic Poetry* (1974); R. Brann, *The Compunctious Poet* (1990); Á. Sáenz-Badillos, *A History of the Hebrew Language* (1993); R. Drori, *Models and Contacts* (2000); *The Literature of Al-Andalus*, ed. M. R. Menocal, R. P. Scheindlin, M. Sells (2000); J. Tobi, *Proximity and Distance: Medieval Hebrew and Arabic Poetry* (2004). ***In Hebrew***: E. Fleischer, *Hebrew Liturgical Poetry in the Middle Ages* (1975); D. Pagis, *Change and Tradition in Secular Poetry: Spain and Italy*

(1976); J. Schirmann, *Studies in the History of Hebrew Poetry and Drama* (1979); T. Rosen-Moked, *The Hebrew Girdle Poem (Muwashshah) in the Middle Ages* (1985); J. Yahalom, *Poetic Language in the Early Piyyut* (1985); D. Pagis, *Hebrew Poetry of the Middle Ages and the Renaissance* (1991), and *Poetry Aptly Explained* (1993); J. Schirmann and E. Fleischer, *The History of Hebrew Poetry in Muslim Spain* (1996); J. Schirmann and E. Fleischer, *The History of Hebrew Poetry in Christian Spain and Southern France* (1997); J. Yahalom, *Poetry and Society in Jewish Galiliee of Late Antiquity* (1999); J. Yahalom, "Poet-Performer in the Synagogue of the Byzantine Period," *Continuity and Renewal*, ed. L. I. Levine (2004); M. Rand, *Introduction to the Grammar of Hebrew Poetry in Byzantine Palestine* (2006). ***Byzantine Period and Muslim Spain***: I. Davidson, *Thesaurus of Mediaeval Hebrew Poetry* (1924); J. Schirmann, "The Research on Spanish-Hebrew Poetry 1919–1939," *Sedarim* (1942); *J. Schirmann's Bibliography of Studies of Mediaeval Hebrew Poetry 1948–1978: Accumulative Index*, ed. E. Adler et al. (1989); *Ma'agarim Online Historical Dictionary*, http://hebrew-treasures.huji.ac.il (in Heb.); Piyyut Project of the Institute for the Research of Hebrew Poetry.

■ **III. Modern**. ***Anthologies, in English***: *Modern Hebrew Poetry*, ed. and trans. R. F. Mintz (1966); "Israel," *Modern Poetry in Translation*, ed. R. Friend (1974); *Modern Hebrew Literature*, ed. R. Alter (1975); *Fourteen Israeli Poets*, ed. D. Silk (1976); *Contemporary Israeli Literature*, ed. E. Anderson (1977); *Modern Hebrew Poetry*, ed. and trans. B. Frank (1980); *Modern Hebrew Poetry*, ed., A. Mintz (1982); *Israeli Poetry*, ed. W. Bargad and S. F. Chyet (1986); *Modern Hebrew Literature in English Translation*, ed. L. I. Yudkin (1987); *No Rattling of Sabers*, ed. E. Raizen (1996); *Found in Translation*, ed. E. Friend (2007); *Poets on the Edge*, ed. T. Keller (2008). ***In Hebrew***: *Sifruthenu ha-Yafah*, ed. J. Lichtenbaum, 2 v. (1962)—mod. *Shirah Tse'irah*, ed. B. Yaoz and Y. Kest (1980). ***Bibliographies, in English***: Y. Goell, *Bibliography of Modern Hebrew Literature in English Translation* (1968)—7,500 items from 1880–1965; *Bibliography of Modern Hebrew Literature in Translation* (1975)—700 items since 1917; I. Goldberg and A. Zipin, *Bibliography of Modern Hebrew Literature in Translation* (1979–)—series providing current bibl. and extensive retroactive coverage. ***In Hebrew***: *Shishim ve-shisha Meshorerim*, ed. Z. Stavi (1996); *Shira Chadasha*, ed. M. Izakson and A. Kosman (1997); *Shirat Ha'tchiya Ha'ivrit*, ed. B. Harshav (2000); *Lanetsach Anagnech*, ed. M. Shaket (2003); *Ve-karati Lecach Ahava*, ed. M. Dor (2008). ***Criticism and History, in English***: D. Goldstein and B. Hrushovski, "On Free Rhythms in Modern Poetry," Sebeok; S. Halkin, *Modern Hebrew Literature*, 2d ed. (1970); E. Spicehandler, "Hebrew Literature, Modern," *Encyclopaedia Judaica* (1971–92); I. Zinberg, *A History of Jewish Literature*, ed. and trans. B. Martin, 12 v. (1972–78); E. Silberschlag, *From Renaissance to Renaissance*, 2 v. (1973–77); C. Kronfeld, *On the Margins of Modernism* (1996); D. Jacobson, *Does David Still Play before You?* (1997); R. Kartun-Blum, *Profane Scriptures* (1999); M. Gluzman, *The Politics of Canonicity* (2002); D. Miron, *The Prophetic Mode in Modern Hebrew Poetry* (2009). ***In Hebrew***: J. Klausner, *Historiyah Shel-ha-Sifrut ha-Ivrit ha-Hadashah*, 6 v. (1930–50)—F. Lachover, *Toldot ha-sifrut ha-Ivrit ha-Hadashah*, 4 v. (1936–48)—mod.; A. Ben-Or, *Toldot ha-Sifrut ha-Ivrit be-Dorenu*, 2 v. (1954–55)—D. Miron, *Arba' Panim ba-Sifrut ha-Ivrit Bat Yamenu* (1962)—contemp.; A. M. Habermann, *Toledoth Hapiyyut Vehashir* (1970).

E. Spicehandler (intro., extracanonical, It., mod.); E. L. Greenstein (bib.); W. van Bekkum (med.); V. K. Shemtov (mod.)

HEBREW PROSODY AND POETICS

I. Biblical
II. Medieval
III. Modern

I. Biblical

A. ***Prosody.*** Approximately one-third of the Heb. Bible (to which discussion is here confined) in many eds. is presented in a format that suggests that the content is to be viewed as verse. In fact, all talk of "verse" or "poetry" in the Bible is the result of mod. scholarly hypothesis, so that no discussion of biblical prosody can be entirely descriptive. No trad. about the nature of biblical prosody has survived for the received Masoretic text. To be sure, a number of passages termed "song" (*shirah*)—like the "Songs" of Miriam (Exod. 15), of Moses (Deut. 32), of Deborah (Judg. 5), and of David (2 Sam. 22), as well as a few Dead Sea texts—are so arranged as to suggest an effort at indicating verse. The special system of punctuation in the so-called poetic books (Psalms, Proverbs, and Job) as well as the format of their text in some biblical mss., incl. the Aleppo Codex (the earliest nearly complete form of the Masoretic text), may point in a similar direction; but we have no explicit statement of underlying prosodic principles. Early references by authors such as Josephus and the church fathers to cl. meters like hexameters and pentameters in the Bible are simply apologetic in nature, designed to appropriate for the Bible the heritage of the cl. Gr. trad., comprehensible to the Hellenistic audience and intended to elicit its respect.

Biblical study in the 18th and 19th cs. also attempted to force passages considered "poetic" into approximations of cl. meters. But by the late 19th c. and despite the efforts of no less a metrist than Eduard Sievers, it was generally recognized that prospects for exact scansions were chimerical, not least because of uncertainties in regard to key aspects of ancient Heb. pronunciation. A loose working hypothesis was reached that, without claiming to be an adequate statement of biblical prosody, still allowed prosodic considerations to play a role in practical exegesis.

An essential empirical fact is the general symmetry in clause length displayed in most passages that, on other grounds, might reasonably be termed "poetic." In books like Job or Psalms, most clauses consist of from two to six words, the majority having from three to five. (By contrast, in books like Genesis or Judges, mainly narrative in content, clause length seems to be random.) It is reasonable to suppose that passages with such symmetry form an expectation in the reader's mind that, after a certain number of words, a caesura or line break will occur. The specific phonetic, and therefore prosodic, aspect is the silence, real or potential, awaited at the limit of expectation, which usually corresponds to clause closure. The unit so delimited is the line (in other common terminologies, colon, stichos, hemistich, verset). So firm is the perceptual base that long clauses tend to be analyzed as two enjambed lines: "wa'ani nasakti malki / ál ṣiyyon har qodši"(For I have anointed my king / On Zion, my holy mountain [Ps. 2:6]).

Within lines, a meter might potentially be either isosyllabic or accentual. Syllabic analysis has been attempted several times, esp. for some early verse (Freedman, Stuart). But even recourse to a reconstructed ancient pronunciation cannot remove the many examples of syllabic asymmetry between lines. For this reason and many others, it is better to speak of rhythm rather than meter in discussing biblical prosody. The consensus has long been that the rhythmical basis for biblical prosody lies in the stresses of speech (the Ley-Sievers system). Heb. is a lang. with a strong stress accent that is phonemic (e.g., *qáma*, "she arose," vs. *qamá*, "rising" [participle]). The system may be summarized as follows: lines contain from two to six stresses, the great majority having three to five. Each metrical unit, or foot, receives a single stress, although long terms, usually of five or more syllables, may have two stresses. By "metrical unit" is meant in most cases what is commonly presented as a "word" in the Masoretic graphemic system.

The overall system has rightly been termed "semantic-syntactic-accentual" (Hrushovski). The essential device for linking verses or sense units together within the system is parallelism of the couplet (in other terminologies, bicolon, distich, stichos). The great majority of couplets can be represented as 3:3, 2:2 (often doubled to 2:2::2:2, sometimes best analyzed as 4:4), and 3:2 (often analyzable as 5), where the numbers refer to words or stresses. Also present are slightly asymmetrical couplets like 2:3 or 4:3, etc. Extreme asymmetries like 4:2 or 2:4 are likely to be "regularized" by emendation *metri causa*, but the asymmetry may have been obscured in sung or chanted performance. A unit of three lines, the triplet (tricolon, tristich) is also common, as well as the quatrain. Larger units like strophes are frequently discernible in context. Biblical verse rarely employs a single meter throughout a poem, although 3:3 is so common as to appear dominant. Alternations of 3:3 and 2:2 seem to occur esp. in early poems. Scansion of a given passage, therefore, often depends on one's assessment of the soundness of the text, interpretation of the meaning, and willingness to view certain elements as "extrametrical." E.g., Isa. 1:1–2:

> Hear O-heavens/And give-ear, O-earth,
> For-YHWH has-spoken:
> Sons I-have-reared and-raised,
> But-they have-rebelled against-me!

may be scanned in several ways: as 2:2:2 + 3:3; or, if "For-YHWH has-spoken" is viewed as extrametrical, as 2:2 + 3:3; or, if one joins the monosyllabic preposition in the final line to its verb ("have-rebelled-against-me"), as 2:2 + 3:2. Such a loose system will never satisfy purists, who can point to passages in supposed "prose" that also scan quite regularly. Some have despaired of uncovering *any* biblical rhythm, and some have denied the very possibility of its existence. But since there are rhythmic symmetries accompanied usually by parallelism and a host of devices often associated with verse in other prosodies—alliteration, assonance, rhyme (all common if random in biblical verse), archaisms, and tropes—it has seemed to most scholars satisfactory as a general or working hypothesis to speak of biblical rhythm, if not meter, and prosody.

Parallelism is commonly included in discussions of biblical prosody because of the constitutive role it clearly plays in the rhythm of biblical verse. Most scholars include both grammatical and semantic aspects in parallelism. Aside from sporadic examples of earlier awareness, the concept and term of parallelism were introduced by Bishop Robert Lowth in the mid.-18th c. Lowth recognized two aspects of *parallelismus membrorum*: "constructive" (i.e., grammatical) or parallelism of form; and semantic or parallelism of meaning. He isolated three categories: "synonymous," "antithetic," and (a catchall) "synthetic." Despite the fact that the last category in particular was unclear, Lowth's classification remained basically unchanged until refined by G. B. Gray in the early 20th c. It is now generally recognized that the term "synthetic parallelism" has no real meaning.

The basic unit of parallelistic verse is the couplet, with its A and B lines (a triplet adds a C line, a quatrain a D line). Parallelism between individual members of the lines may be complete—a situation commonly represented by the schema *abc/a'b'c'* (each letter stands for a stressed metrical unit, those in the B line being marked with a prime)—but it is frequently partial or incomplete. The most common type involves ellipsis, or "gapping," of an A-line term in the B line, in the deep structure of which it is, however, still present or "understood" (O'Connor). Apparently from a desire to maintain general syllabic symmetry, the approximate number of syllables in the gapped term may be "compensated" for by an expanded or longer B line parallel ("ballast variant"). A typical schema is *abc/b'c'2*.

Semantic correspondence between parallel terms extends from actual identity via repetition to varying degrees of synonymity and antonymity, to relationships that may be labeled complementary (*eat/drink*), merism (*heaven/earth*), whole-part or part-whole (*Pharaoh and his hosts/his chief officers*), metaphorical (*the wicked/chaff*), and epithetic (*God/the Holy One of Israel*), among others. Some parallel pairs, e.g., silver/gold or heaven/earth, are so common as to become virtual formulas. Such A- and B-line "word pairs" may stem from oral composition, but in most biblical verse represent merely a form of poetic diction. It is now known that word pairs and many other features of parallelism go back at least as far as the Ugaritic texts of the 13th c. BCE and form part of the extensive Canaanite heritage of biblical verse. Among the most striking parallel patterns is "climactic parallelism," which may be represented by the schema *abc/abd*, in which the first two words of the A line are repeated, but the last term is gapped and replaced at the end of the B line by another term. E.g., Ps. 92:10: "For-behold your-enemies, O Lord, // For-behold your-enemies shall-perish!"

Little work has been done on the hist. of biblical parallelism, although it is possible to discern a difference between an earlier, stricter form in which parallelism is mainly between individual constituents of the couplet and a later, looser form in which whole lines, or even couplets, are merely general semantic equivalents of other lines and couplets, as in Ps. 23:3–6. In general, parallelism allows almost endless variation without obscuring its basic contours. Roman Jakobson, who viewed parallelism as the basic device of all poetry, said that it activates all levels of lang.

B. *Poetics.* The Bible contains no explicit statements about poetics in regard to the nature of either poetry or poetic composition. However, an implicit poetics may be inferred from the complaint of the prophet Ezekiel that people consider him a mere "maker of parables" (Ezek. 21:5), a singer of "love songs, sweetly sung and skillfully played" (Ezek. 33:32). "Parables" (Heb. *mashal*, the meaning of which extends from "proverb" to larger literary compositions of several types) and secular song were the province of Wisdom in Israel, as was elsewhere in the ancient Near East the trad. of science, intellect, and conscious literary art. Although the "wise" probably claimed some type of inspiration for their productions, their art was viewed predominantly as an expression of human skill. Prophets, on the other hand, although employing the forms of poetic expression cultivated by the "wise," were believed to be mere "mouths," passive transmitters of divine messages. To view their oracles as "art" violated their prophetic function, even though, as Fisch has observed, their message achieved its effect partly via the literary artifice employed. Implicit in the conflict between prophecy and poetry is a poetics of tension between aesthetics and religion that has had a profound influence on Western culture. Meir Sternberg has explored similar tensions in the poetics of biblical narrative. Related to this is the Bible's remarkably free use of genre. Although form critics long ago isolated most of the genres used by biblical authors and related them to their analogues in the ancient Near East, analysis often shows that the traditional forms have been "sprung" or "undermined" (Fisch) by introducing an element of tension, esp. in hymns, where myth is combined with hist. in a manner unattested elsewhere in the ancient world. F. M. Cross has explored the historicizing of myth in Heb. texts. E.g., a key myth found in many places in the Heb. Bible centered on a cosmic battle between the deity and a sea monster (representing Chaos), followed by creation and, as a capstone, the erection of the divine palace, the shrine. These traditional elements are applied in a cl. biblical hymn, the "Song of the Sea" (Exod. 15), to the formative events of the "creation" of Israel—the exodus from Egypt and conquest of Canaan. However, the old mythical motifs of the theme are radically redefined, so that the cosmic foe, the sea, becomes the natural agent of the destruction of Pharaoh and his army, while the conquest is described in quasi-mythic terms as the establishment of a shrine on the hills of Canaan. The ambiguity that arises from the indeterminacy of hist. and myth results in that tension that gives the poem, as so much of biblical poetry, its transcendent dimension.

II. Medieval. Med. Heb. poetry comprises two distinct branches of verse, each governed by its own characteristic poetics and systems of versification. Generically speaking, these branches are *piyyut* (Gr. *poiēsis*, liturgical poetry) and nonliturgical or secular poetry. The poetic styles and verse forms developed by each branch varied widely according to epoch, historical school, and geographic center.

A. *Prosody.* Until the High Middle Ages, liturgical poetry predominated in Heb. writing to the complete exclusion of the secular. Piyyut emerged in Palestine (probably in the 4th c.) as a popular supplement to the increasingly standardized and fixed (prose) prayer. Additionally, complex poetic cycles (*yotser* and *qedushta*) whose themes were related to the weekly recitation of scripture were incorporated into the synagogue service. The genres of piyyut were thus determined by specific liturgical contexts, and piyyut texts were always intended for public recitation. The rules pertaining to form (most *piyyutim* were strophic), structure, and rhyme were also closely tied to the liturgical function of the poem. Idiosyncratic and complex rhymes (initial, internal, and terminal) are characteristic of early piyyut, but end rhyme eventually became the prevalent form. Acrostics based on the 22-letter Heb. alphabet or the poet's name constituted an important formal feature of nearly all piyyut.

Over the course of its long evolution, piyyut came to employ four distinct systems of versification. In its earlier phases, it was composed in two verse forms similar to those found in the Heb. Bible, one based on an equivalent number of words in parallel versets, the other an accentual system based on three to five word stresses per line. Later, in a postclassical devel. (Spain, 10th c.), syllabic meters, which make no distinction in vowel length but fix the number of syllables per line (six to eight syllables per verset or line is common), were used extensively. Finally, the quantitative meters associated with secular poetry (see below) were employed sporadically in strophic liturgical verse after the 10th c.

Secular Heb. poetry emerged in Muslim Spain in the 10th c. as a subcultural adaptation of *Ar. poetry. Two main verse forms were cultivated. The predominant type, written in the cl. mold of Ar. courtly poetry, forms one continuous sequence of lines, ranging from an epigrammatic couplet to a formal ode (*qaṣīda*) of more than 50 lines. Regardless of length, this type of composition is governed by a single meter and end rhyme that are carried through every line of verse without variation. Rhyme words ending in a vowel include the consonant preceding the vowel (CV); for words ending in consonants, the rhyme must encompass the preceding vowel and antepenultimate consonant (CVC). (See AL-ANDALUS, POETRY OF.)

The second type of secular composition was strophic in form and closely connected to musical performance. The *muwashshaḥ*, as it was known in Ar. (Heb. *shir ezor*, "girdle poem"), was usually devoted to the genre of love poetry or, in a secondary devel., to panegyric. Conservative Ar. literati tended to regard the muwashshaḥ with disdain because it did not meet the strict prosodic requirements of cl. Ar. poetry. Jewish courtly circles, however, enthusiastically accepted it (11th c.), possibly on account of the prevalence of similar strophic forms in the pre-Andalusian piyyut. The muwashshaḥ employed the quantitative meters used in the cl. monorhyming poem but did so in a highly irregular fashion: i.e., the meter of the first part of a strophe often differed from that of the second part of the strophe. Additionally, the muwashshaḥ used quantitative meters in nonstandard patterns. Tonic elements may also have come into play, though this is a matter of dispute. Muwashshaḥāt also differed from poems of the cl. type in allowing great flexibility in the use of rhyme. One rhyme of the muwashshaḥ (that of the first part of the strophe) varies from strophe to strophe; a second rhyme (that of the last part of each strophe) remains fixed throughout the poem (e.g., *aaabb*, *cccbb*, *dddbb*). In addition to its appealing rhyme schemes and often complex metrical patterns, a striking feature of the muwashshaḥ is its *kharja* (exit) or envoi. Heb. muwashshaḥāt frequently conclude with romance or colloquial Ar. kharjas (in Heb. script), usually in the form of a quotation from a popular Old Sp. or Hispano-Ar. love song.

The quantitative meters employed in both types of secular composition, as well as in some liturgical poetry, were created by means of an artificial system that transposed the distinctive prosodic patterns of Ar. into Heb. In Ar., as in cl. Gr., quantitative meters are based upon the distinction between long and short syllables. It is the pattern of long and short syllables that creates the different meters. A line of verse (Ar. *bayt*; Heb. *bayit*, "house") was typically composed of metrically equivalent versets made up of from two to four metrical feet (*čamudim*). Since cl. Ar. preserved the phonological values of long and short vowels to a greater degree than biblical Heb., the system required that certain liberties be taken with Heb. grammar and phonology. Twelve of the 16 basic cl. Ar. meters were reproduced in simplified form; with variants (lengthened or shortened metrical feet), the number of Heb. quantitative meters amounted to approximately 60. This Ar.-style quantitative prosody subsequently attained a normative status in various Near Eastern, Eur., and Mediterranean communities. It was still popular in Italy in the Ren., when Heb. poetry came under the influence of It. There, It. verse forms and poetic styles were assimilated into Heb.; eventually, quantitative metrics was exchanged for purely syllabic schemes akin to those employed in It.

B. *Poetics.* Secular poetry, which represented a fusion of Ar. form and style with biblical Heb. diction and imagery, was conventional in content and stylized in form. Its modes of expression and choice of themes were generally lyrical and descriptive (love and wine poetry as well as panegyric are well represented genres), and its purpose was to entertain and persuade. Manneristic virtuosity and rhetorical ornamentation were highly prized in secular verse, but, at least among the better poets, the importance attached to conventionality, rhetorical technique, and florid style did not preclude the expression of intense feeling, particularly in poems of a personal and occasional nature.

Piyyut, by contrast, was conceived as an ennobling poetry given over to the communal passion to draw closer to God. Until the 9th c., piyyut tended to be esoteric and elusive; it was suffused with arcane references to Talmudic texts and rabbinic interpretation of scripture and consciously lacking in metaphor and simile. After the 10th c., when liturgical poets of the Mediterranean lands were frequently engaged in the production of the prestigious secular verse, the prosody and style of secular poetry cross-fertilized piyyut. The old type of piyyut continued to be composed alongside newer, more intelligible piyyutim. The poets of Muslim Spain led the way, using many of the forms and genres of the postcl. Iraqi piyyut and creating some new ones of their own (notably the *rĕshut*, a short poetic meditation on the theme of the prose prayer), but they abandoned the eclectic and inventive lang. of early and cl. piyyut for the biblical purism they propagated in secular verse. Similarly, they revamped the austere poetics of the earlier piyyut trad., replacing it with the ornamental and decorative approach of their secular poetry. For most of the High and later Middle Ages, then, piyyut and secular poetry coexisted in "creative dissonance."

III. Modern

A. *Prosody.* Heb. prosody has not stagnated over the past 200 years. On the contrary, it has passed through stages of quick devel. and has changed to some extent at each of the major centers of Heb. poetry. From the beginning of the Ren., Heb. poetry—centered in Italy after the Jews were expelled from Spain—began to assimilate Eur. poetic styles and conventions. Immanuel of Rome (ca. 1261–1332), a contemporary of Dante, used the It. sonnet form for lines written in Gr. meters. However, the natural accents of the Heb. lang. made it difficult to assimilate quantitative meter. Apparently, the pronunciation of long and short vowels in Heb. had been forgotten during the Middle Ages. The accepted substitution for the difference in length between parts of the foot, the *t'nua* (vowel) and the *yated* (one long and one short syllable), served Heb. poetry in Italy until the beginning of the 20th c. Hence, for 600 years (until 1900), the accepted meter of the Heb. sonnet was a hendecasyllabic line with a stress on the penultimate syllable (Landau).

The harbinger of mod. Heb. prosody was N. H. Weizel (1725–1805) in his *Shirey Tiferet* (1785–1805 [Songs of Glory]). Weizel sensed the strangeness of the meter used for Heb. poetry in Spain and also the difficulty of assimilating Gr. meter. In his desire to write a Heb. epic in a form similar to the Gr. hexameter, he devised a line of 13 syllables with a strong caesura and penultimate stress. He used couplets separated by unrhymed lines and at times the envelope rhyme scheme, *abba*. This system remained in effect until the Hibat Zion period (1881–97), though with variations.

During the Hibat Zion period, meter began losing its independence, and poetics increased its influence on prosody. In addition to the lyrical-didactic fusion that appeared during the Enlightenment, rhythm was introduced in questions and answers as composed by Abraham Ber Gotlover: "Why are you weeping, my People, and why are you crying out?" ("Nes Ziona," in Karton-Blum). This is even more apparent in Judah Leib Gordon: "What are we, you may ask; what is our life? / A People are we, like the Peoples around us?" (*Eder Adonai* [The Flock of God] in Karton-Blum). The dialogue, the quotations, the succession of ideas or feelings came to occupy a strong position and determined the nature of the meter and rhythm. Prosody was set aside and played a decreasing role in poetry, while the rhythm of the content took its place. The stress on the content intensified the persona of the artist and highlighted the new positive approach to what is holy to Israel and to the Zionist feelings expressed in the poetry (Karton-Blum).

After Weizel, all the common stanza forms of Eur. lit. appeared in Heb. poetry (Shpan). But today Weizel's meter seems something artificial, for it does not distinguish between naturally accented syllables and those whose accent is weak. The blurring of the tonic differences renders this meter as monotonous as the Heb.-Ar. meter of the Middle Ages. Only during the period of Hayyim Nachman Bialik (1873–1934) was a way found to absorb Gr. meter into Heb. poetry: accented syllables were treated as long, while unaccented syllables (or ones with a secondary accent) were treated as short.

During Bialik's generation, the dominant Ashkenazi vocalization of Heb. affected the poetry. This system stresses the penultimate vowel and pronounces certain vowels and consonants differently from the Sephardic pronunciation. For example, the vowel *o* is pronounced *oy*, and the consonant *th* is pronounced *s*. The tonic meter merged well with Ashkenazi pronunciation. One esp. notes the flexibility of the amphibrach, well loved by Bialik (Benshalom). Use of the Sephardic pronunciation accepted in Israel today did not become widespread until the following generation (Shavit).

Saul Tchernikhovsky (1875–1943) trans. Gr. epic poetry into Heb. and thereby created the Heb. dactylic hexameter, in which trochees take the place of spondees (Shpan). The following generation (Jacob Kahan [1881–1967] and Jacob Fichman [1881–1958]) preserved the traditional rhythms; only Uri Zvi Greenberg (1895–1981) and Abraham Shlonsky (1900–73) completely broke with the earlier framework. Greenberg abandoned regular meter and rhyme to create an extended rhythm, which was the only means, he felt, to create a poem with the pathos necessary to express this generation's pain (Hrushovski). Shlonsky, on the other hand, disregarded meter altogether. After an extended struggle, Greenberg and Shlonsky succeeded in exchanging the Ashkenazi vocalization with the Sephardic pronunciation and began a new era in Heb. poetics and prosody. Jonathan Ratosh's (1908–81) poems are distinguished by a virtuoso rhythm built on repetition of sounds, words, and sentences that flow at a dizzying, intoxicating tempo. It is interesting that Nathan Alterman (1910–70), who is an extreme modernist with regard to lang., reverted to regular meter, esp. the anapest, and to regular rhyme (though a certain estrangement is expressed in his use of assonance), but he found few disciples.

In contrast to Alterman, Nathan Zach (b. 1930) gave up all the forms of harmony, even the standard harmony of the stanza (the length of the lines, rhyming, assonance, etc.). Zach even criticized Bialik's rhythms as schematic and boring. Though he dealt at great length with the problems of prosody, it seems that poems whose content had a dramatic flair affected his changes in prosody. In consequence of this trend, traditional prosody lost most of its effect on Heb. poetry. In contrast, Martin Buber, in his essay "On Culture" (*Pnei Adam*, [The Face of Man]), established the rule of rotation in culture. He maintains that when a culture declines to its low point or becomes most distant from its original sources, a striving toward rising higher develops and a desire to return to its sources. Something like this occurred also to the prosody and poetics of Heb. Apparently in line with this conception, at the height of Shlonsky's rebellion in prosody, there were already in Heb. lit. restrained artists such as Shin Shalom (1905–90) and Leah Goldberg (1911–70) who refrained from utilizing strangeness in their lang.; indeed, they returned to rhyming and meters within their poetic stanzas and even composed sonnets. Sonnets can be found even by the ironic and bitter Yehuda Amichai (1924–2000). Since the 1980s, restrained modernism has played a dominant role in the prosody of Heb. poetry (rendering it meterless, rhymeless, and structureless).

In an insightful study, Aharon Mirsky revealed that the structure of the Heb. lang. creates a rhythm that can serve as an alternative to punctuation. This characteristic of the Heb. lang. has been exploited by end-of-the-century poets in order to create a mod. rhythm that is both moderate and pleasant to the ear and that relies on daily speech rhythms. This is how Zelda constructed her poems, basing them on the rhythm of speech and on functional rhythm (Bar-Yosef).

B. *Poetics.* The poetics of mod. Heb. has also been dynamic, changing from period to period in accord with its prosody. Moses Hayyim Luzzatto (1707–46) viewed lit. as "the creation of something good and pleasant," thus equating the artist with the aesthete. His conceptions of figurative lang. were derived from cl. rhet. His explanations were based on the Bible, and they concur with the approach that views the arts as decorative. Shlomo Levisohn (1789–1821) regarded the Bible as an example of the poetics of the sublime. The trans. of the Bible into Ger. and the preparation of the "Commentary" during Moses Mendelssohn's period (1729–86) created a poetics that also served the new poetry. Such poetry attempted to educate the Jewish nation and, therefore, had to be expressed in Heb., for it alone was understood by all Jewish people. At first, the poetry was composed in the lang. of the Bible, but this archaic diction reminded one more of ancient landscapes than of the current world. Words integrally linked in a poem proved to mean something else when taken out of context and thus distanced the poem from real life; the rhet. (*melitsa*) remained meaningless to most of its readers.

It was Bialik who created the synthesis of the lang. of the Bible, the sages, and the Middle Ages; he even created new words. His symbols are rich and romantic. His lang. is not built on completely figurative elements taken from ancient sources: his sources are familiar to us, yet they do not stand out in his poetry. Greenberg created symbols, such as "Sinai," "Jerusalem," "Massada," "light," "yearning," and "sublime," which refer to national myths (Kurzweil). Shlonsky rebelled against the poetic conventions of Bialik's period. He opposed usage of biblical similes; he drew his imagery from his current surroundings. He created metaphors and similes open to variable interpretation, such as "breasts of the night" and "night like the altar stone." Yet despite his estrangement from Bialik's style, there are those who speak of "Shlonsky in Bialik's bonds" (Hagorni).

The world wars, the Holocaust, and existentialism stimulated—though relatively late—the appearance of an expressionist poetics in mod. Heb. poetry. In this mode, the sentence, the word, and even sense are broken, incomplete. Following Shlonsky and Greenberg, Amir Gilboa (1917–84) and others use ambiguity for effect: at times a word is linked to what precedes it as well as what follows, as, e.g., "Also in the city on sidewalks you will run from them." The expression "you will run" (a single word in Heb.) is linked to "sidewalks" as well as "from them" (Barzel). For the same reasons noted above, bathos is dominant in recent Heb. poetry, as in the poetry of Amichai who writes, "The memory of my father is wrapped in white paper / Like slices of bread for the working day."

The poetry of the Holocaust, its symbols and metaphors, returned to Heb. poetry its exaltedness and pathos, esp. with regard to death, and thus Itamar Yaoz-Kest wrote in his Bergen-Belsen poems: "It seems that we were thrown into a fiery flame / Yet meanwhile we reflected on life and death" (in Österreich). Avner Treinin used allusions even to the stories of Joseph in his poem "The Striped Coat of the Man in the Camp": "And his brothers did not envy him / his striped coat / in which they, too, were dressed / when lowered from the [railroad] lines." The atmosphere in this poem is melancholy and elegiac, with no sarcastic attitude toward the terrors of the Holocaust.

Toward the close of the 20th c., the canon of Heb. poetry accepted even poems with a religious undertone such as those by Yosef Zvi Rimon, Aharon Mirsky, Zelda, Yaoz-Kest, and others. It seems that Heb. poetry continues to stream in two channels. On the one hand, we find leftist poetry with what remains of mod. rebellious poetics and prosody accompanied by a distancing from the lang. and culture of national sources. On the other hand, we find the minor conservative channel of poetics with restrained modernism that preserves the traditional character. The poets Yaoz-Kest, Mirsky, Zelda, Tuvia Ribner, Dan Pagis, Shlomo Zamir, Shalom Ratzabi, and others stand out in this trend.

See HEBREW POETRY, YIDDISH POETRY.

■ **Biblical:** R. Lowth, Lecture 19, *De sacra poesi Hebraeorum*, trans. G. Gregory (1753), "Preliminary Diss.," *Isaiah* (1778); E. Sievers, *Metrische Studien* (1901–7); G. B. Gray, *The Forms of Hebrew Poetry* (1915, rpt. 1972 with essential "Prolegomenon" [with bibl.] by D. N. Freedman); T. H. Robinson, "Basic Principles of Hebrew Poetic Form," *Festschrift Alfred Bertholet*, ed. W. Baumgartner et al. (1950); P. B. Yoder, "Biblical Hebrew [Versification]," in Wimsatt; B. Hrushovski (in bibl. to section II below); F. M. Cross, *Canaanite Myth and Hebrew Epic* (1973); F. M. Cross and D. N. Freedman, *Studies in Ancient Yahwistic Poetry* (1975); D. Stuart, *Studies in Early Hebrew Meter* (1976); S. Geller, *Parallelism in Early Biblical Poetry* (1979), part 1 and appendix B; D. N. Freedman, *Pottery, Poetry, and Prophecy* (1980); M. O'Connor, *Hebrew Verse Structure* (1980); J. Kugel, *The Idea of Biblical Poetry* (1981), incl. survey of theories in section 7.2; W. Watson, *Cl. Heb. Poetry* (1984); R. Alter, *The Art of Biblical Poetry* (1985); A. Berlin, *The Dynamics of Biblical Parallelism* (1985); *The Hebrew Bible in Literary Criticism*, ed. A. Preminger and E. Greenstein (1986); M. Sternberg, *The Poetry of Biblical Narrative* (1985); H. Fisch, *Poetry with a Purpose* (1988); L. Schoekel, *A Manual of Hebrew Poetics* (1988); W. Watson, *Traditional Techniques in Classical Hebrew Verse* (1994); J. P. Fokkelman, *Major Poems of the Hebrew Bible*, 3 v. (1998–2003); *Poetry of the Hebrew Bible*, ed. D. Orton (2000); D. Vance, *The Question of Meter in Biblical Hebrew Poetry* (2001).

■ **Medieval:** B. Hrushovski, "*Ha-shitot ha-ra'shiyot shel heḥaruz ha-'ivri min ha-piyyut' ad yameinu*," *Hasifrut* 2 (1970–71); and "Prosody, Heb.," *Encyclopaedia Judaica* 13 (1971–72), 1203–24; E. Fleischer, *Shirat ha-qodesh ha-'ivrit bi-ymei ha-beinayim* (Hebrew Liturgical Poetry in the Middle Ages, 1975); D. Pagis, *Ḥiddush u-masoret be-shirat ha-ḥol ha-'ivrit bi-ymei ha-beinayim* (Change and Tradition in Secular Poetry: Spain and Italy, 1976); R. Brann, *The Compunctious Poet* (1990); Joseph Tobi, *Proximity and Distance* (2004).

■ **Modern:** B. Z. Benshalom, *Mishkalav shel Bialik* (Bialik's meters, 1942); B. Kurzweil, *Sifrutenu Hahadasha Hemshekh o Mahapekha* (Our new literature—Continuation or revolution, 1959); S. Shpan, *Masot Umehkarim* (Essays and Studies, 1964); M. M. Buber, *Pnei Adam* (The Face of Man, 1965); N. Zakh, *Zeman Veritmus Etzel Bergson Uvashira Hamodernit* (Time and Rhythm in Modern Poetry, 1966); R. Karton-Blum, *Ha- Shirah ha-'ivrit bi-tekufat Hibat Tsiyon* (Hebrew Poetry during the Hibat Zion period, 1969); D. Landau, *Hayesodot Haritmiyim shel Hashira* (The Rhythmic Elements of Poetry, 1970); and "Hitpathut Hasonneta Basifrut Haivrit" (Development of the Sonnet in Hebrew Literature), diss., Univ. Bar-Ilan, Israel (1972); B. Hrushovski, *Ritmus Harakhavut* (The Rhythm of Extensity, 1978); U. Shavit, *Hamahapekha Haritmit* (The Rhythmic Revolution, 1983); H. Barzel, *Amir Gilbo'a* (1984); A. Hagorni, *Shlonski Be'avotot Byalik* (Shlonsky in Bialik's bonds, 1985); R. Tsur, *On Metaphoring* (1987); Ch. Bar-Yosef, *Al Shirat Zelda* (On the poetry of Zelda, 1988); D. Landau, *Iduna shel Sheaga* (The Refinements of Roars, 1990)—on lyric poetry; R. Tsur, *Toward a Theory of Cognitive Poetics* (1992), and *Rhythm, Structure and Performance* (1998); A. Mirsky, *Signon Ivri* (Hebrew Style, 1999).

S. A. Geller (biblical); R. Brann (medieval); D. Landau (modern)

HINDI POETRY. The heritage of Hindi lit. is a palimpsest inscribed with a range of dialects and with multiple sensibilities. Though the contemp. poetry mostly reflects a standardized mod. lang. and articulates ideas parallel to those of many mod. lits., it also contains deep resonances of its premod. legacy. An outline of Hindi poetry must, therefore, survey a period of several centuries, from the time that Hindi and other northern Indian langs. first emerged as distinct forms of regional speech from earlier Sanskrit-derived langs. such as Prakrit and Apabhraṃśha.

One of the greatest strengths of premod. culture—its often oral medium—is also one of the greatest impediments to our knowledge of its early circumstances. The ebullient genres of ballads of the seasons, marriage songs, versified saws and aphorisms, bardic panegyrics, devotional hymns and prayers, and many other such phenomena typical of Indian culture certainly predate any written record of their existence. Only in recent times has this oral trad. begun to fade, eclipsed by the easy seductions of the mod. media.

Following these dimly perceived early genres of Hindi verse that left little written record of their existence, the most powerful catalyst to the trad. was a flowering of devotional religion, or *Bhakti*, in northern India in the 15th and 16th cs. This period saw the emergence of a newly "emotional" style of devotionalism in which human relationships served as paradigms for the love of God; though primarily Hindu in orientation, it shared many general characteristics with parallel trads. of ecstatic Sufism. The image of Viṣṇu (Vishnu) as a compassionate deity, esp. in his incarnations as Kṛṣṇa (Krishna) and as Rāma, was a compelling focus, and the loci of the earthly lives of these deities, earlier recorded in the sacred geographies of Sanskrit lit., were transformed from textual abstractions into palpable centers of devotional worship and pilgrimage.

Descriptions of the sports of the heroic and sublimely beautiful Kṛṣṇa in the bucolic setting of Braj, Kṛṣṇa's "earthly paradise" on the banks of the river Yamuna to the south of mod. Delhi, had long featured in such Sanskrit texts as the *Purāṇas* (esp. 4th–9th cs. CE). In the 12th c., Jayadeva's sensuous Sanskrit poem *Gītagovinda* added Kṛṣṇa's consort Rādhā to the picture. The love of Rādhā and Kṛṣṇa became a favorite theme for generations of "poet-saints" in successive centuries, with figures such as Sūrdās (early to mid-16th c.) achieving fame for the beauty of their compositions and the incisiveness of their devotional vision. Their poems were mostly written in Braj Bhasha, the dialect of Hindi that was and is spoken in the Braj region, sometimes assumed (ahistorically) to be Kṛṣṇa's own lang. With the exception of some exegetical commentaries, most composition was in rhymed verse, and many genres were intended for singing. The poetry was typically eulogistic, sweetly celebratory, and ecstatic in tone: and though the Braj poets inherited aesthetic codes and literary tropes from the Sanskrit trad., they showed enormous creativity in their evocations of Kṛṣṇa as the divine lover who was simultaneously the supreme deity—God himself. Certain themes became firm favorites: the pranks of Kṛṣṇa the child-god; the sensuality of his persona as a voluptuous youth; the appeal of his seductive flute; his moonlit "round-dance" with the *gopīs*; his secluded assignations with Rādhā; and in thematic counterpoint, his status as a savior who bestows grace on his devotees.

The most popular genre consisted of individual songs, *bhajans*, which were disseminated by performance, eventually to be written down and compiled in anthols. The sacred content of the songs made ms. copying an act of piety that brought its own rewards; written and oral recensions would often develop side by side. For all the prestige of the great poets, matters of authorship counted for little, and many a poet's corpus grew steadily over the centuries. Textual ascription can sometimes be validated on the basis of whatever mss. have survived the rigors of climate, the appetites of insects, and the indifference of custodians. For most devotees of such poetry, however, authenticity depends on spiritual potency rather than dry historiography.

The asocial mores of Kṛṣṇa-as-lover were complemented by the impeccable moral rectitude of Rāma, hero of the epic *Rāmāyaṇa*. Told in many langs. over at least two millennia, this narrative found its vernacular exemplar in the *Rāmcaritmānas*, a magisterial poem by the brahmin Tulsīdās (1532–1623) begun in 1574. Tulsī's epic was written in Awadhi, the dialect spoken around Rāma's capital of Ayodhya toward the eastern end of the Hindi area; but in his choice of both lang. and poetic form, Tulsī was also following the precedent of such Sufi poets as Manjhan (fl. mid-16th c.) and Jāyasī (b. ca. 1494) whose allegorical Awadhi romances *Madhumālatī* and *Padmāvat* (respectively) had pioneered this epic format some decades earlier. This formal connection between genres whose communities have become differentiated—if not mutually alienated—in more recent times reminds us that a rich symbiosis existed between various different religious paths in premod. India. Today's misplaced association of Tulsīdās with an intolerant Hindu chauvinism is belied by the wit, subtlety, and sublime perceptiveness of his poetic voice.

Another strand in the fabric of premod. poetry is of similarly devotional character but has a different coloration. Throughout the late med. period, a loose grouping of poets known as the *sants*, typically from the lower strata of society (as opposed to the mostly high-born Kṛṣṇa and Rāma poets), chose a more uncomfortable, abstract, and hard-hitting rhet. for their religious songs and verse. The best-known figure in this trad. is the weaver Kabīr, born in the mid-15th c. Kabīr's poetic vision perceives God as transcending all form, whether anthropomorphic or otherwise; the poet roundly excoriates priesthood, ritual, scriptures, and all the trappings of organized religion, instead advocating a personal search for the divine within the human soul. Kabīr's *bānī* or sacred utterances are recorded in three main recensions with little material held in common between them. One of the three is the *Gurū Granth Sāhib* of the Sikh faith that was founded by another *sant* poet, Kabīr's contemp. Gurū Nānak (1469–1539), who wrote in Punjabi (see PUNJABI POETRY).

Religion was not the only theme in premod. poetry. With the enrichment of courtly culture during the Mughal period, poets enjoying the patronage of local kingdoms began to compose highly sophisticated verse with a more worldly flavor and a more self-consciously literary orientation. The subject of their brilliantly ornate verse was often poetry itself, and in their elaboration of tropes, they drew on two complementary aspects of Indian literary trad. First, their rhetorical typologies embroidered the age-old poetics of Sanskrit lit.; and second, the well-established figures of Kṛṣṇa and Rādhā became the perfect hero and heroine to model these elegant tropes. Braj Bhasha continued to serve as the dialect of choice for poetic composition, regardless of the native tongue of the individual poet. This new mode of poetry, written for (and sometimes by) the regional kings of northern India, came to be called *rīti*—a "stylist" mode, an embodiment of literary style; but the borders between this and devotional verse were always porous, with traffic flowing continuously between the complementary genres.

The 19th c. saw deep-seated changes in Indian society as Eng.-lang. culture made its presence felt with increasing strength. Interregional communications improved, the printing press arrived, a middle-class disposition developed, the small minority of Indians literate in Eng. grew steadily; and as the century progressed, a Victorian ethos penetrated deep into the consciousness of many writers. Lit. came to be seen as a medium through which social change might be effected; and as though to distance this new consciousness from the old tropes of rīti and devotional poetry, writers began to switch dialects, forsaking the sweetly lyrical associations of Braj Bhasha for a more utilitarian idiom in Khari Boli, the dialect from the Delhi region that already served as a lingua franca across the Hindi-speaking north. Poetry found a new rival in the rapid devel. of prose genres, often inspired by new models in Western fiction and polemics and expressed in the nascent media of Hindi newspapers and jours. The spirit of the age was represented in the person of the polymath Bharatendu Harishchandra of Banaras (1850–85), who maintained the old Braj idiom in his verse while leading a generation of writers in the new style of Khari Boli prose.

Unsurprisingly, new poetic conventions in Khari Boli took some time to find their feet, and the early accomplishments were to have little enduring appeal for Hindi readers; few poets from the opening years of the 20th c. are enjoyed today. But a confident new style was not long in coming, with poets such as Suryakant Tripathi "Nirala" (1896–1961) and Mahadevi Verma (1907–87) writing Khari Boli verse of great power and personality. The headstrong, eccentric Nirala strode the literary stage in moods of anger, sadness, and deeply humanist compassion, while the lyrical laments of Mahadevi reminded readers of the passionate outpourings of a 16th-c. forebear, the Rajasthani princess Mīrābāī, whose Kṛṣṇa songs are among the most enduring voices from any period of Hindi poetry. The romanticist idiom of Mahadevi and other like-minded poets writing in the 1920s was dubbed *Chāyāvād* (Shadowism); but like many a derogatory sobriquet, the name stuck, becoming a neutral title for this loosely affiliated group of poets. A more populist style was that of Harivansh Rai Bachchan (1907–2003), a teacher of Eng. lit. at Allahabad University; his romantic, Khayyām-and-Fitzgerald-inspired *Madhuśālā* (The House of Wine), won him a huge following at *kavi sammelans* or poetic symposia, which have always been successful in projecting Hindi poetry well beyond the small cliques of intellectual literati.

Following Chāyāvād, several schools of poetry rose and set. *Pragativād* enshrined a progressivist agenda, and the subsequent *Prayogvād* was experimentalist in character: such labels and themes show the Hindi poets' engagement with Western literary trends. But rather than pursuing the ephemeral fashions of modernist idiom, we may rather mention a single voice, one that defines the mid-20th c. more than any other. S. H. Vatsyayan (1911–87) was a champion of the so-called *Nayī Kavitā* or New Poetry, and perhaps its finest exponent also. His pseud. Agyeya (also transliterated Ajneya, and meaning "the unknowable"), alludes to the secret smuggling of his early nationalistic writing from a British jail cell during the independence struggle. Agyeya was both a novelist and a poet. Like many of the other poets featured in the volumes of verse compiled under his editorship, he wrote in a style that combines the sonorous grandeur of the cl. Sanskritic heritage with the variously gritty, sweet, and forceful vernacular idiom of contemp. Hindi speech. This combination is seen in its fullest glory in his long poem *Asādhya Vīṇā* (The Unmastered Veena, alluding to the most cl. of India's lutes), a long and deeply emotive poem written in 1961. Rich with description and allusion, this poem functions as a summation of the Hindi poetic trad. thus far, ranging from the humanist concerns of today, through the romanticism of earlier decades, back to the diction and musical phrasing of the premod. poets; echoing through all these modalities is an apprehension of the broader Indian trad., rooted in its cl. past and flowering in the creative energy of a forward-looking present.

Contemp. Hindi poetry has many moods, registers, and styles—from the popular lyrics of cinema (themselves rooted in traditional genres of music and poetry) to the intellectually rigorous verse of such poets as Muktibodh (pseud. of Gajanan Madhav, 1917–64), Raghuvir Sahay (1929–90), and Kunwar Narain (b. 1927). The parallel trad. of Urdu verse is also accessible to speakers of Hindi, esp. when performed at recitals where distinctions of script (Devanagari for Hindi, Persian for Urdu) melt away. The old devotional poetry of Braj and Awadhi may no longer be popular with mainstream writers, but its echoes still resound, and it has never been relinquished by the Hindi-speaking public. Thus, inscriptions from every layer of Hindi's poetic palimpsest remain visible to the readers of today, inspiring many to wield pens of their own.

See INDIA, POETRY OF; RĀMĀYAṆA POETRY; SANSKRIT POETICS; SANSKRIT POETRY; URDU POETRY.

■ Ajneya, *Nīlāmbarī* (1981)—Eng. trans.; K. Schomer, *Mahadevi Varma and the Chayavad Age of Modern Hindi Poetry* (1983); R. S. McGregor, *Hindi Literature from Its Beginnings to the Nineteenth Century* (1984); *Songs of the Saints of India*, trans. J. S. Hawley and M. Juergensmeyer (1988); D. Rubin, *The Return of Sarasvati: Translations of the Poems of Prasad, Nirala, Pant and Mahadevi* (1993); Manjhan, *Madhumālatī: An Indian Sufi Romance*, trans. A. Behl and S. Weightman (2000); *New Poetry in Hindi: Nayi Kavita, an Anthology*, ed. and trans. L. Rosenstein (2003); K. Narain, *No Other World: Selected Poems*, trans. A. Narain (2008).

R. SNELL

HISPANO-ARABIC POETRY. *See* AL-ANDALUS, POETRY OF

HITTITE POETRY. The great bulk of the lit. recovered from Hattusa (Boğazköy/Boğazkale, located about 62 miles northeast of Ankara), capital of the Hittites from the 17th to the early 12th c. BCE, was written in prose. A metrical analysis of those texts definitely composed in bound lang., such as the mythological compositions known as "Songs," is difficult because of a number of technical characteristics of the script in which they are written: as a syllabary, cuneiform is unable to render precisely the phonology of an IE lang. such as Hittite, since it cannot express consonant clusters adequately, esp. at the beginning or end of words. Furthermore, the Hittite scribes often used ideograms for many common lexemes, thus concealing their phonological shape from the uninitiated reader. Finally, breaks between lines of poetry are quite often not indicated either by line breaks or by punctuation, which was not a feature of cuneiform texts in any event.

The earliest scrap of Hittite poetry we possess, a soldier's lament, is included in an historical text composed in the 16th c. BCE:

Nesas waspus[1] Nesas waspus[2] // tiya-mu[3] tiya[4]
nu-mu annasmas[1] katta arnut[2] // tiya-mu[3] tiya[4]
nu-mu uwasmas[1] katta arnut[2] // tiya-mu[3] tiya[4]

(Clothes of Nesa, clothes of Nesa—
approach me, approach!
Bring me to my mother—approach me,
approach!
Bring me to my *uwa*—approach me,
approach!)

The basic principle underlying this Hittite versification is phrasal stress, namely, regular lines of four stresses each, falling into two cola. The rules governing the presence or absence of stress (on, e.g., enclitics, noun phrases, and adverbs)—whose details still remain somewhat obscure to mod. scholars—have been shown to be applicable in Hittite prose as well. Therefore, this type of poetry is a native Anatolian ling. phenomenon and not, as had been suggested previously, the result of trans. into Hittite of poems originally composed in the Hurrian or Akkadian langs. It seems that assonance, alliteration, rhyme, and synonymous parallelism also played some role in Hittite poetry, but none of these techniques was structural to its practice.

Many of the incantations and short hymns featured in Hittite ritual and cult employ at least some elements of poetic lang., but it is the "Songs" adapted from Hurrian-lang. forerunners that best illustrate Hittite poetry. These include the constituents of the Kumarbi Cycle: the "Song of Emergence" (often referred to today as "Kingship in Heaven"), the "Song of Hedammu," the "Song of Ullikummi," the "Song of Silver," the "Song of the Protective Deity," as well as the "Song of the Sea" and the Hurro-Hittite bilingual "Song of Release."

Despite the seeming aberrance of the final line, this quatrain from the "Song of Ullikummi" provides a good impression of the style of Hittite epic poetry:

Kumarbis^{1}-za hattatar^{2} // istanzani^{3} piran
daskizzi^{4}
nu idalun^{1} siwattan^{2} // huwappan^{3}
sallanuskizzi^{4}
nu-za Tarhuni^{1} menahhanda^{2} // idalawatar^{3}
sanhiskizzi^{4}
nu Tarhuni^{1} // tarpanallin^{2} sallanuskizzi^{3}

([The god] Kumarbi takes wisdom into his
mind.
He rears a bad day as Evil.
He seeks evil for the Storm-god.
He rears a rival for the Storm-god.)

See SUMERIAN POETRY.

■ H. Th. Bossert, "Gedicht und Reim im vorgriechischen Mittelmeergebiet," *Geistige Arbeit* 5 (1938); H. G. Güterbock, "The Song of Ullikummi," *Journal of Cuneiform Studies* 5 (1951); I. McNeill, "The Metre of the Hittite Epic," *Anatolian Studies* 13 (1963); S.P.B. Durnford, "Some Evidence for Syntactic Stress in Hittite," *Anatolian Studies* 21 (1971); H. Eichner, "Probleme von Vers und Metrum in epichorischer Dichtung Altkleinasiens," *Hundert Jahre Kleinasiatische Kommission*, ed. G. Dobesch and G. Rehrenböck (1993); O. Carruba, "Poesia e metrica in Anatolia prima dei Greci," *Studia classica Iohanni Tarditi oblata*, ed. L. Belloni et al. (1995); O. Carruba, "Hethitische und anatolische Dichtung," *Intellectual Life of the Ancient Near East*, ed. J. Prosecky (1998); H. A. Hoffner, *Hittite Myths*, 2d ed. (1998); H. C. Melchert, "Poetic Meter and Phrasal Stress in Hittite," *Mír Curad*, ed. J. Jasanoff et al. (1998); R. Francia, "'Montagne grandi (e) piccole, (sapete) perchè sono venuto?' (in margine a due recitativi di Iriya, CTH 400–401)," *Orientalia* 73 (2004); G. Beckman, "Hittite and Hurrian Epic," *A Companion to Ancient Epic*, ed. J. M. Foley (2005); G. Beckman, "Hittite Literature," *From an Antique Land*, ed. C. S. Ehrlich (2008).

G. BECKMAN

HUNGARY, POETRY OF. The origins of Hungarian poetry can be traced back to the oral trad. of tribes that settled in the Carpathian basin around the 9th c., although there is no record of these primarily shamanistic songs and their afterlife is part of Hungarian folklore, not lit. The trad. of pagan bards was, after the establishment of a Christian Hungarian state at the end of the 10th c., slowly absorbed by entertainers of the Middle Ages. The first literary record can be dated from the end of the 12th c. (a funeral sermon) and the first instance of lyric poetry, *The Lament of Mary*, from the second half of the 13th c. This lament, like most early Hungarian poetry, is based on Lat. models; however, it is not a trans. in the mod. sense of the word but a re-creation, a poetically powerful rendering of Mary's loss, using both rhyme and alliteration. Chronicles from the 11th to the 14th c. frequently recorded ancient legends ("The Legend of the Miracle Stag," "The Legend of Álmos") that became part of the poetical trad. and formed the basis for later retellings, most notably by the 19th-c. poets Mihály Vörösmarty (1800–55) and János Arany (1817–82).

The early poetry of Hungary was predominantly Lat., and the first significant Hungarian poet, Janus Pannonius (pseud. of János Csezmiczei, 1434–72) wrote exclusively in Lat. His poetry is steeped in Ren. humanism; after completing his education in the cultural centers of Italy, he became bishop in the southern city of Pécs. The poetry of Pannonius follows cl. antiquity in its form (epigrams and elegies were favored) and the humanist rhet. of 15th-c. Lat. in its lang. but stays connected to Hungarian topography and experiences. His accomplishment was to bring Ren. humanism to Hungary and to leave the first body of work to bear the mark of an independent poetic voice.

The Reformation saw the first partial, and later complete, trans. of the Bible (the work of Gáspár Károli [1529?–91], pub. 1590), which instantly enriched the poetic trad. of Hungary. A notable example of this influence can be seen in the Psalm trans. of Albert Szenci Molnár (1574–1639). Other important figures of this period include the writer and publisher Gáspár Heltai (ca. 1490–1574), the Bible translator János Sylvester (ca. 1504–1551), and Péter Bornemissza (1535–84). An important evolving poetic genre of the period is the song, often accompanied by music, with Sebestyén Tinódi Lantos (1510?–56) as its most important contributor. The main theme of his collected songs (*Cronica*, 1554) is the struggle against Turkish rule, thus establishing a strand in Hungarian lit. concerned with the country's independence and the fate of its inhabitants. Another important new genre emerging at the end of the 16th c. is that of versified narratives, best exemplified by Péter Ilosvay-Selymes's *The Story of the Remarkable Miklós Tholdi's Extraordinary and Brave Deeds*, and with the work of Albert Gergei, whose *The Story of Prince Argirus and a Fairy Virgin* is based on the It. *bella istoria*. This secular narrative poetry is devoid of didactic elements and, through its concise style and colorful descriptions, marks a significant moment in the devel. of Hungarian lit.

Although not the first to write lyric poetry in Hungarian, Bálint Balassi (1554–94) is the first outstanding lyricist of the Hungarian lang. His oeuvre consists of martial poetry (he was active in politics and warfare against the Turks; "In Praise of the Outposts"), love songs ("When He Met Julia, He Greeted Her Thus"), and religious poetry ("He Prays to God"); and his innovations include a new verse form (the Balassi stanza) and the conscious composition of complete sets of poems, with cycles arranged into tightly structured eds. With Balassi, Hungarian poetry reaches maturity in both lang. and form, and his poetry can be compared to accomplishments in other Eur. langs. in the 16th c. He inspired a group of followers, notably János Rimay (1569–1631), a mannerist poet who exemplifies the transition from the late Ren. to the baroque.

The major poet of the baroque era is Count Miklós Zrínyi (1620–64); his 15-canto epic *The Siege of Szigetvár* follows the epic ideals exemplified by Virgil and the It. Torquato Tasso but adapts them into a uniquely Hungarian version, with the heroic battle of his great-grandfather against the army of the Ottoman Empire as its subject. Zrínyi himself became an accomplished general in the fight against the Turks and a leading political figure of his time; although poetry was not his primary concern, he was conscious of the importance of a literary legacy and published his epic, along with his love poems, in 1651. *The Siege of Szigetvár* is built around cl. norms but also uses the rhyming and compositional patterns of earlier Hungarian narrative poetry. The epic form remains an important element in 17th-c. Hungarian poetry; besides Zrínyi, the most important contributor is István Gyöngyösi (1629–1704), whose pseudoepics focus on current events and are characterized by both rich baroque lang. and a political purpose.

Popular poetry of the 17th c. is mostly political in its nature, as Hungary's quest for independence remained a major concern. Anti-Turkish and anti-Hapsburg sentiments are at the core of the so-called *kuruc* poems, a collection of popular songs from the decades between 1670 and 1710, the time of the freedom fights that ended with the armed struggle led by Count Ferenc Rákóczy II (1676–1735). As often happens in Hungarian hist., the efforts for independence ended in heroic defeat; this further strengthened the important thematic trad. of defeat and loss in the poetry of Hungary. Mod. philology has proved many of the kuruc songs to be the fabrications of Kálmán Thaly (1839–1909), not unlike James Macpherson's *Ossian*; but, as a cultural idiom, it is part of Hungarian lit.

The intellectual hist. of 18th-c. Hungary followed major Eur. trends. By the century's end, Enlightenment ideals were increasingly accepted, culminating in the movement of the Hungarian Jacobins, heavily influenced by the Fr. Revolution. As the official langs. of the country were still Ger. and Lat., the establishment of the Hungarian vernacular became a goal of the progressive intelligentsia, effectively uniting political and literary goals. The most important representatives of this movement were Ferenc Kazinczy (1759–1831) and János Batsányi (1763–1805), both of whom made invaluable contributions toward establishing an independent Hungarian literary community, with proper institutional support.

The most important lyric poet after Balassi is Mihály Csokonai Vitéz (1773–1805); despite many hardships and a brief life, he was able to produce remarkable poetry that is characterized by strong musical qualities, a rococo playfulness, and great symbolic power ("To the Echo of Tihany," "To Hope"). His love poetry (addressed to Julianna Vajda, whom he called *Lilla*) is among the best ever written in Hungarian. Csokonai was a great innovator, who used his knowledge of Eur. artistic and philosophical trends of his time to enrich the poetic trad. of his native tongue. An admirer of Jean-Jacques Rousseau, Csokonai appears at the end of the Hungarian Enlightenment. The other important poet at the turn of the 18th and 19th cs. is Dániel Berzsenyi (1776–1836), a reclusive nobleman who became the greatest master of cl. verse forms in Hungarian, successfully transplanting the most difficult Gr. and Lat. metrics into a Hungarian poetic idiom ("The Approaching Winter"). Berzsenyi is not a pure classicist, however; his poetry demonstrates preromantic tendencies, and his influence can be felt well into the 20th c.

The Reform Age, as the first half of the 19th c. is commonly called in Hungarian intellectual hist., was focused on the political progress championed by the liberal nobility. The literary achievements are grouped under the label of romanticism, and this period is arguably the golden age of Hungarian poetry, with a wealth of canonized masterpieces. Ferenc Kölcsey (1790–1838), a critic, poet, and leading literary figure, became the author of the national anthem; his poetry is marked by both classicism and romanticism ("Vanitatum Vanitas," "Huszt"). The poetic oeuvre of Vörösmarty is probably closest in its qualities to Eur. romanticism, both in voice and scope. He began with epic poetry; his *The Flight of Zalán* (1825), a heroic epic written in hexameter, made his reputation in literary circles, although it is less often read than his later lyric and philosophical poetry ("Appeal," "Thoughts in the Library," "On Mankind"). His late masterpiece "The Ancient Gypsy" is one of the greatest expressions of the desperation following the failure of the 1848–49 War of Independence. The poet forever associated with this war and the preceding revolution of 1848 and one of the best-known poets both in and outside Hungary is Sándor Petőfi (1823–49). Petőfi was the first true Hungarian literary celebrity and the first national poet who tried to earn his living as a writer. His life and death at the battle of Segesvár are part of the nation's cultural memory. Petőfi's poetry is influenced by folk poetry; he transformed the short song into an expression of his poetic persona, while also creating longer, narrative poetry, incl. the remarkable "John the Valiant" and "The Hammer of the Village." His love poems are classics of the genre ("At the End of September"), and the most important political poem in the Hungarian trad. is his "National Song," written and performed on the outbreak of the 1848 revolution. A counterpoint to Petőfi's short life and popular oeuvre is that of his friend Arany, who created the greatest examples of the ballad in Hungarian ("Bards of Wales," "The Two Pages of Szondi"), and wrote superb epic poetry (*Toldi Trilogy*). His late poetry ("Autumn Bouquet") shows great emotional and lyrical maturity and successfully redefines the cliché of the young romantic poet. Arany is known for his intellectual integrity, and his impact on the devel. of the Hungarian poetic lang. cannot be overestimated.

The second half of the 19th c. sees the disillusionment after the failed War of Independence slowly diminish, as economic progress transforms the Austro-Hungarian Empire into a mod., developing state. János Vajda (1827–97), a major, if uneven, poet, is known for his philosophical pessimism; while József Kiss (1843–1921) became the first Hungarian poet with a Jewish background and an interest in representing the urban experience. The century's turn saw an unprecedented rise in the numbers of literary publications and marks the start of the golden age of mod. Hungarian lit., which centers around the writers associated with the literary review *Nyugat* (The West), published between 1908 and 1941. The goal of *Nyugat* was to introduce the achievements of Eur. lit. through trans. and to create a platform for the progressive elite of Hungarian lit. Like many in his generation, Endre Ady (1877–1919) was heavily influenced by Fr. symbolism; his poetry is considered the starting point for the mod. age in Hungarian lit. His unique style is easily recognizable; his main themes are the backwardness of his country ("At the Gare de l'est," "Upward Thrown Stone"), and his love for Léda ("Beautiful Farewell Message"), along with religious poetry. Ady provokes both controversy and admiration, and his legacy has undergone several changes, but his influence on his contemporaries is undeniable. Árpád Tóth (1886–1928) is best described as a melancholy symbolist, whose basic mood is one of sad longing; part of his poetic oeuvre, as is typical for the *Nyugat* generation, is trans. from Eng., Fr. and Ger. Gyula Juhász's (1883–1937) lifelong battle with depression left a mark on his musical, art nouveau-influenced poetry; besides the Anna cycle (chronicling his unfulfilled love), he is known for his landscape poetry depicting the river Tisza around the southern town of Szeged. The two greatest poets belonging to the first generation of *Nyugat* are Mihály Babits (1883–1941) and Dezső Kosztolányi (1885–1936). Babits, who translated Dante's *Divine Comedy*, was a true *poeta doctus* whose erudition influenced the themes and style of his poetry. He spoke out against World War I in "Before Easter," and his late masterpieces "The Book of Jonah" and "Jonah's Prayer" foreshadow the looming catastrophe of Europe in a beautiful biblical voice. Kosztolányi has a different poetic persona; his early "Laments of a Poor Little Child" show the influences of modernist trends such as impressionism and expressionism, while his late poetry is focused on death and the great questions of life, in part following stoic sentiments. Kosztolányi's writing is always crafted with great attention to the poetic medium, his beloved Hungarian lang.

The most important poetic genius of the interwar period is Attila József (1905–37), a tormented man with a difficult upbringing who suffered from psychosis: his genuine, sincere poetry is a towering achievement. He wrote in many forms, with a keen sense of composition, while experimenting with varied poetic sensibilities. Some of his poetry is politically charged, as he sought to give voice to the working poor; more important, though, his poetry can be characterized as an honest exploration of the depths of torment, sometimes presented in a seemingly simple and straightforward manner ("With a Pure Heart," "Ode," "For My Birthday," "By the Danube"). He took his own life at the age of 32, leaving a poetic heritage that has never been surpassed.

The international avant-garde (futurism and expressionism) is the main influence on the poetry of Lajos Kassák (1887–1967), who chiefly employed free verse. His style changed during his lifetime, but his political activism was always tied to a search for progressive forms of literary expression ("The Horse Dies, the Birds Fly Away"). Kassák was also a painter, typographer, and graphic artist, with an interest in the visual qualities of poetry, and promoted early avant-garde art forms through the jours. he edited.

A member of the second generation of the *Nyugat*, the poet Lőrinc Szabó (1900–57) chronicled the evolution of his own self and the hist. of his relationships. Szabó became a master of the sonnet, which he arranged into book-length cycles, besides being a prolific translator. The fate of Miklós Radnóti (1909–44) was marked by his heritage: as a baptized Jew, he fell prey to the discriminatory Jewish laws introduced in the 1930s and died in a forced-labor camp, leaving behind the most significant Hungarian Holocaust poetry ("Forced March," "Razglednica"). He was a classically oriented poet, who used cl. forms as a refuge against the ever-growing horrors of Nazi Europe. Another representative of this generation, Gyula Illyés (1902–83), wrote mostly in free verse, under the influence of Fr. surrealism and expressionism, and later became part of the populist writers' movement. He was well regarded by the socialist government of the postwar period, though he struggled to maintain his independence. Sándor Weöres (1913–89), the creator of nursery rhymes that are known to almost all Hungarians, is a poet of immense erudition and great talent, who has an unparalleled ability to evoke musical qualities in his complex, universal poetry influenced by both Eastern philosophies and Western mysticism. A very different kind of poet, János Pilinszky (1921–81), used a reduced, bare lang. to comunicate the anxieties of a moral being in the 20th c., always struggling with questions of faith. He belonged to a group of poets gathered around *Újhold* (New Moon), the short-lived but significant postwar literary magazine; it also included the poet Ágnes Nemes Nagy (1922–91).

The great survivor of 20th-c. Hungarian poetry is György Faludy (1910–2006), who was acquainted with József yet lived into the 21st c. His poetic persona can be described as a vagabond, traveling and experiencing life to the fullest. He spent a considerable part of his life in exile (after being imprisoned by the communist regime) but returned in 1988, before the political changes. Among his best known work is his trans. of François Villon, first published in 1934.

An important part of Hungarian culture comes from Transylvania, now part of Romania, where the greatest number of Hungarians live outside Hungary. Domokos Szilágyi (1938–76) should be mentioned as a poet from this region whose ling. and formal invention is noteworthy, while András Ferenc Kovács (b. 1959) is a living Transylvanian poet who reinterprets (through palimpsest and pastiche) the greater heritage of Eur. poetry with considerable poetic force.

A humorous tone, political engagement, and confessional themes dominate the poetry of György Petri (1943–2000), who was part of the antiestablishment of the 1970s and 1980s. The leading female poet of the contemp. era is Zsuzsa Rakovszky (b. 1950), a careful examiner of the fragility and insecurity of human experience. A prolific, though uneven, contemp. poet well known for his philosophical yet playful poetry, Dezső Tandori (b. 1938) is associated with the renewal of the poetic idiom in the 1970s. Two notable contemp. poets are János Térey (b. 1970), who experiments with longer verse narratives, and Dániel Varró (b. 1976), whose sense of rhyme and poetic tone is displayed in his playful and often intertextual poetry.

Since 1989, Hungary has undergone many transformations, and Hungarian poets are trying to find their role and tone in a world marked by new and powerful modes of communication, a new evolving social structure, and changes in the consumption of lit. Because of its relative ling. isolation, Hungarian poetry is still not widely known in the outside world, although new anthols. have been published and recent trans. may bring new audiences to its hidden gems.

See SLOVAKIA, POETRY OF.

■ **Anthologies:** *Magyar Poetry* (1908), *Modern Magyar Lyrics* (1926)—both trans. and ed. W. N. Loew; *The Magyar Muse*, ed. and trans. W. Kirkconnell (1933); *Magyar versek könyve*, ed. J. Horváth (1942); *A Little Treasury of Hungarian Verse*, ed. and trans. W. Kirkconnell (1947); *Hungarian Poetry*, ed. E. Kunz (1955); *Hét évszázad magyar versei*, ed. I. Király et al., 4 v. (1978–79); *Old Hungarian Literary Reader*, ed. T. Klaniczay (1985); *The Face of Creation: Contemporary Hungarian Poetry*, ed. and trans. J. Kessler (1988); *In Quest of the "Miracle Stag,"* ed. A. Makkai (1996); *The Colonnade of Teeth: Modern Hungarian Poetry*, ed. G. Gomori and G. Szirtes (1997); *Magyar nőköltők a XVI. századtól a XIX. századig*, ed. M.S. Sárdi (1999).

■ **Bibliographies:** *Bibliography of Hungarian Literature*, ed. S. Kozocsa (1959); A. Tezla, *An Introductory Bibliography to the Study of Hungarian Literature* (1964)—annotated; and *Hungarian Authors: A Bibliographical Handbook* (1970).

■ **Criticism and History:** F. Toldy, *A magyar költészet története* (1867); G. Király, *Magyar ősköltészet* (1921); J. Horváth, *A magyar irodalmi népiesség Faluditól Petőfiig* (1927), and *A magyar irodalmi műveltség kezdetei* (1931); A. Schöpflin, *A magyar irodalom története a XX. században* (1937); T. Kardos, *Középkori kultúra, középkori költészet* (1941); J. Horváth, *A magyar vers* (1948); J. Waldapfel, *A magyar irodalom a felvilágosodás korában* (1954); T. Kardos, *A magyarorszagi humanizmus kora* (1955); A. Szerb, *Magyar irodalomtörténet* (1958); *A magyar irodalom története,* ed. M. Szabolcsi, 4 v. (1966); P. Rákos, *Rhythm and Metre in Hungarian Verse* (1966); J. Horváth, *Rendszeres magyar verstan* (1969)—systematic Hungarian poetics; A. Karátson, *Le symbolisme en Hongrie* (1969); A. Kerek, *Hungarian Metrics* (1971); *L'Irréconciliable: Petőfi, poète et révolutionnaire*, ed. S. Lukácsy (1973); M. Szegedy-Maszák, *Vilagkép és stílus* (1980); *Pages choisies de la litterature hongroise des origines au millieu du XVIIIe siècle*, ed. T. Klaniczay (1981); *Vándorének*, ed. M. Béládi (1981)—Hungarian poets in Western Europe and overseas; *A History of Hungarian Literature*, ed. T. Klaniczay (1982); B. Pomogáts, *A nyugati magyar irodalom története* (1982); L. Czigány, *The Oxford History of Hungarian Literature* (1984); *A nyugati magyar irodalom 1945 után*, ed. M. Béládi et al. (1986). E. Kulcsár Szabó, *A magyar irodalom története 1945–1991* (1993); M. Szegedy-Maszák, *Literary Canons: National and International* (2001); G. Szirtes, *An Island of Sound: Hungarian Poetry and Fiction before and beyond the Iron Curtain* (2004); *A magyar irodalom történetei*, ed. M. Szegedy-Maszák et al. (2007); L. C. Szabó, *A magyar költészet századai* (2008).

V. Varga

I

ICELAND, POETRY OF. (For information on Icelandic poetry before 1550, see NORSE POETRY.) Considering the difficult living and cultural conditions in Iceland after its literary peak in the 12th to 14th cs., and esp. the period from 1600 to 1800, with its severe cold, epidemics, famines, volcanic eruptions, and oppressive political conditions under Danish rule, it is remarkable that there was any Icelandic poetry at all at this time. Poetry's success was facilitated by a fairly high rate of literacy as well as an almost universal custom of composing, memorizing, and reciting verse.

Whether oral or literary, secular or religious, popular or learned, poetry was to remain the principal genre of Icelandic lit. for centuries after the Reformation in 1550, only giving way to works of prose in the late 19th and early 20th cs. One notable feature is Icelandic poets' use of alliteration, a poetical device common to many Germanic literary trads. in the Middle Ages but surviving into the mod. period only in Iceland. Traditional alliteration was not seriously challenged until Icelandic modernists started advocating and practicing free verse around the middle of the 20th c., and it is still used sporadically in mod. Icelandic poetry and lyrics.

The introduction of paper in the 16th c. had a greater impact on Icelandic poetry than two other phenomena from the same period, the introduction of Danish Lutheranism and printing (which was monopolized by the Church until 1772). Paper made it economically feasible for farmers and priests all over the country to copy mss., and through these copies, as well as extensive memorization, secular lit. was disseminated. The kenning-based, alliterative and rhymed narrative poetry known as *rímur* held sway over other kinds of secular poetry from the 14th to the 19th cs., whereas Lutheran psalms came to prominence in religious poetry during the Reformation; their impact proved enduring.

Bishop Guðbrandur Þorláksson (ca. 1541–1627) laid the foundations for the reformed lit. of the country by publishing and commissioning psalms and other religious poetry. His *Vísnabók* (Book of Poems) of 1612 bears witness to the strength of the poetic trad. in Iceland. Whereas in countries such as Denmark and Germany clerical writings shaped the lang., in Iceland the Church had to rise to the level of the vernacular. Earlier trans. of Lutheran hymns into Icelandic had failed miserably in this respect. Bishop Guðbrandur thus enlisted the service of the best poets he knew for this volume, such as the Reverend Einar Sigurðsson (1538–1626), among whose poems is a tender lullaby on the birth of Jesus, "Kvæði af stallinum Kristí" (Poem on Christ's Cradle) in the popular dance meter *vikivaki*. His son, the Reverend Ólafur Einarsson (1573–1659), also a notable poet, contributed a gloomy complaint on the times to *Vísnabók*. In a rare instance of poetic genius passing from parents to children through three generations, Ólafur's son, the Reverend Stefán Ólafsson (ca. 1619–88), became one of the leading poets of the 17th c. He wrote, as did his father, complaints on laborers and Icelandic sloth, as well as love lyrics and poems about the pleasures of tobacco, drink, and horses.

A poet who wrote little in this light, worldly vein was the Reverend Hallgrímur Pétursson (1614–74), indubitably the major poet of the 17th c. in Iceland. He did not, like Stefán Ólafsson, mock the common people, but he was not shy about attacking the ruling classes. After commenting on Pilate's error in consenting to Jesus's death in his 50-poem cycle *Passíusálmar* (*Hymns of the Passion*, 1666), Hallgrímur adds, "God grant that those in power over us avoid such monstrous offenses" (hymn 28). As a religious work, the *Passíusálmar* is unsurpassed in Icelandic lit. and a baroque tour de force, full of striking imagery. An excellent shorter hymn, "Um dauðans óvissan tíma" (On the Uncertain Hour of Death), is still sung at funerals, a good example of the role that poetry of a high order has played in Icelandic life. Hallgrímur also wrote three rímur cycles and other secular poems, such as "Aldarháttur" (Way of the World), contrasting the degenerate present with the glorious period of the past Icelandic Commonwealth.

Two figures stand out in 18th-c. Icelandic poetry. Jón Þorláksson (1744–1819) wrote several popular short poems, incl. one on a dead mouse in church ("Um dauða mús í kirkju"), and long trans. of Alexander Pope's *Essay on Man*, John Milton's *Paradise Lost*, and F. G.

Klopstock's *Messias*, the latter two in *fornyrðislag*. Eggert Ólafsson (1726–68) was a child of the Enlightenment who, having studied natural hist. in Copenhagen and made a survey of Iceland, preached the beauty and usefulness of Icelandic nature in poems such as "Íslandssæla" (Iceland's Riches) and the long georgic "Búnaðarbálkur" (Farming Poem).

This positive attitude toward Icelandic nature, along with a yearning for independence, became an important feature of Icelandic romanticism, whose major poet is Jónas Hallgrímsson (1807–45). Apart from his lyrical descriptions of nature, which tend toward the pastoral but also include sublime elements, as in "Ísland"—which begins "Iceland, frost-silvered isle! Our beautiful, bountiful mother!"—he is remembered for his poems on the pain of lost love and for his mastery of many poetic forms, incl. (for the first time in Iceland) the sonnet and *terza rima*. The other great romantic poet is Bjarni Thorarensen (1786–1841), who portrayed nature in similes and personifications and tended to glorify winter rather than summer, esp. in his poem "Veturinn" (Winter). He also raised a traditional Icelandic genre, the memorial poem, to a new height. Quite different from these Copenhagen-educated men is the poor folk poet and wood-carver Hjálmar Jónsson (1796–1875), known as Bólu-Hjálmar. His large body of verse includes personal invective, rímur, bitter complaints about poverty, and poems about death.

One of the greatest poets of the later 19th c. is Matthías Jochumsson (1835–1920), a free-thinking parson and newspaper ed. who wrote inspired lyrics, hymns, and memorial poems and also made masterful trans. of four of Shakespeare's tragedies. Around the turn of the century, Einar Benediktsson (1864–1940) was a powerful figure who, as a kind of latter-day Eggert Ólafsson, sought to improve Iceland by forming international corporations to mine gold and harness water power. He used lang. as he used wealth, to gain power, and his nature poems, like "Útsær" (Ocean), are rich with the imagery of opposing elements in nature and his view of the pantheistic force uniting all things.

As the 20th c. wore on, Icelandic poetry was pulled in two opposite directions, toward social engagement or a kind of realism on the one hand and introspective lyricism or modernism on the other. A number of poets took sides in this respect, but some swung between the opposing poles throughout their careers. Steinn Steinarr (1908–58) came to the rapidly modernizing town of Reykjavík as a poor youth in the late 1920s, and in his first collection (1934), he produced poems of social protest, sympathizing with hungry workers who "don't understand / their own relationship / to their enemies." This same poem, "Veruleiki" (Reality), in free verse, goes beyond skepticism of the social order, however, to speak of the illusory nature of existence itself. This note of doubt, alienation, and nihilism later became predominant in Steinn's finely pruned, paradoxical poems, the longest and most highly regarded of which is the poetic cycle *Tíminn og vatnið* (Time and the Water, 1948), an enigmatic and symbolic meditation probably meant to be sensed rather than comprehended.

Many poets followed the example of the modernists of the 1950s—the so-called *Atómskáld* (Atom Poets) such as Sigfús Daðason (1928–96)—and tried to break with trad., experimenting with various poetic practices of modernism. Others tried to merge the mod. with the traditional in order to benefit from both. Hannes Pétursson (b. 1931) has produced sensitive and meticulously crafted lyrics on a variety of subjects incl. Icelandic folklore, historically charged Eur. locations (the prison camp at Dachau, the Strasburg cathedral), and cl. figures like Odysseus. He writes on such themes as the emptiness of lang. and humankind's separation from nature. His poetical cycle *Heimkynni við sjó* (Living by the Sea, 1980) marks a return to nature and a new awareness of surroundings and oneself, rendered through arresting images and metaphors. More often, however, the city shows itself to be the natural habitat of the mod. poet, as witnessed by the urbane and imaginative poetry of Kristján Karlsson (1922–2014) and Sigurður Pálsson (b. 1948). But Gyrðir Elíasson (b. 1961) has also proved that a fresh look at nature is still possible in postmod. times, tinged though it may be with romantic sympathies and otherworldly broodings.

Women were instrumental in transmitting and developing folk poetry through the centuries, but few became prominent as poets in their own right until the 20th c. Unnur Benediktsdóttir Bjarklind (1881–1946), who published under the pseud. Hulda, revived and developed such rhapsodic folk-poetry genres as *þulur* (sing. *þula*) and also became one of the main proponents of symbolism (or neoromanticism) in Iceland. Another breakthrough in women's poetry came with the first volumes of the poems of Vilborg Dagbjartsdóttir (b. 1930), published in the 1960s. Since then, many Icelandic women have made their name as poets, with work ranging from the sensual lyricism of Nína Björk Árnadóttir (1941–2000) to the clear-eyed and socially engaged poetry of Ingibjörg Haraldsdóttir (b. 1942) to the poetical playfulness of Steinunn Sigurðardóttir (b. 1950).

■ **Bibliographies:** P. Mitchell and K. Ober, *Bibliography of Modern Icelandic Literature in Translation*, 3 v. (1975–97)—trans. of works since the Reformation to the late 20th c.

■ **Criticism and History:** *A History of Icelandic Literature*, ed. D. Neijmann (2006); *Íslensk bókmenntasaga*, ed. V. Ólason, H. Guðmundsson, and G. A. Thorsson, 5 v. (1993–2006); M. Eggertsdóttir, *Barokkmeistarinn* (2005)—Hallgrímur Pétursson and baroque poetry; S. Y. Egilsson, *Arfur og umbylting* (1999)—Jónas Hallgrímsson and Icelandic romanticism; E. Þorvaldsson, *Atómskáldin* (1980)—modernism in Iceland; Þ. Þorsteinsson, *Ljóðhús* (2007)—on Sigfús Daðason.

■ **Primary Texts:** *Bishop Guðbrand's "Vísnabók" 1612*, ed. S. Nordal (1937)—facsimile with Eng. intro.; *Hymns of the Passion by Hallgrímur Pétursson*, trans. A. C. Gook (1966); *Íslenzkt ljóðasafn*, ed. K. Karlsson, 6 v. (1974–78)—comprehensive anthol. of Icelandic poetry; *Bard of Iceland: Jónas Hallgrímsson, Poet and Scientist*, ed. and trans. D. Ringler (2002); *Stúlka: Ljóð eftir íslenskar konur*, ed. H. Kress, 2d ed. (2001)—an anthol. of poetry by Icelandic women; *The Postwar Poetry of Iceland*, trans. S. A. Magnússon (1982); *Brushstrokes of Blue: The Young Poets of Iceland*, ed. P. Valsson, trans. D. McDuff (1994).

R. Cook; S. Y. Egilsson

INCA POETRY. *See* indigenous americas, poetry of the

INDIA, ENGLISH POETRY OF. Two figures dominate 19th-c. Indian poetry in Eng.: Henry Louis Vivian Derozio (1809–31), a Eurasian of Port. descent, and Toru Dutt (1856–77). There could have been a third, Michael Madhusudan Dutt (1824–73, no relation to Toru); but after publishing one book, he more or less gave up writing in Eng. in favor of his native Bengali, becoming the first great mod. poet in that lang.

"Born, and educated in India, and at the age of eighteen he ventures to present himself as a candidate for poetic fame," Derozio wrote in the preface to *Poems* (1827), his first book. It bore the impress of its times: the Scottish Enlightenment, the poetry of Lord Byron and P. B. Shelley, and the Gr. war of independence all found their way into it. The new lit. that marks its beginning with Derozio has since had many unsatisfactory names: Indo-Eng., India-Eng., Indian Eng., Indo-Anglian, and even Anglo-Indian. In "The Harp of India," the famous opening sonnet of *Poems*, the poet sang of India before there was an India to sing of or sing to: "Thy music once was sweet—who hears it now?" Later, often decades later, others in the Indian langs. picked up the nationalist theme. An irony of Brit. colonialism was that, as it expanded, it also, through education, spread the Eng. lang. among Indians, which, in the argumentative Indian mind, planted the seed of freedom not only from colonial rule but from religious and social orthodoxies. Derozio taught at the Hindu College in Calcutta, where his radical ideas greatly influenced his students, some of whom were among the earliest Indian poets and prose writers in Eng.

Derozio died at 22, of cholera. Toru Dutt was 21 when she died of tuberculosis; her only book to be published during her lifetime was a volume of trans. of Fr. poetry. The poets in Dutt's *A Sheaf Gleaned in French Fields* (1876) include Victor Hugo, Alphonse de Lamartine, Gérard de Nerval, Charles Baudelaire, and Charles-Marie Leconte de Lisle. Dutt clearly was a poet of wide literary tastes and, as a translator, handled a variety of verse forms with ease, unafraid to use the spoken idiom when required. All this is evident in her own poems as well. "Sita," "Baugmaree," and "Our Casuarina Tree," which appeared in the posthumous volume *Ancient Ballads and Legends of Hindustan* (1882), are among the finest lyrics in Indian poetry. As A. Chaudhuri pointed out, in "Baugmaree," which is the name of the Calcutta suburb where the Dutt family had its country house, the poet adapts the sonnet in ways that It., Eng., and the other Western Eur. poetries had not seen.

During the last decades of the 19th c. and in the first half of the 20th, much poetry was written that is now forgotten but not entirely forgettable. Fredoon Kabraji's (1897–1986) self-deprecating title *A Minor Georgian's Swan Song* (1938) is representative—but he is a better poet than the title suggests. The postindependence poets—Nissim Ezekiel (1924–2004), Jayanta Mahapatra (b. 1928), A. K. Ramanujan (1929–93), Arun Kolatkar (1931–2004), Kamala Das (1934–2009), Keki N. Daruwalla (b. 1937), Dom Moraes (1938–2004), Dilip Chitre (1938–2009), Eunice de Souza (b. 1940), Adil Jussawalla (b. 1940), Arvind Krishna Mehrotra (b. 1947), Agha Shahid Ali (1949–2001), Manohar Shetty (b. 1953), Imtiaz Dharker (b. 1954)—had little to do with the 150-year-old trad. of Indian poetry in Eng. In the absence of critical eds. or even anthols., most of this poetry was unavailable to them anyway. Like the 19th-c. poets, they had to start afresh, assembling their trad. however they could. They fashioned it from what they found at hand (the *Bhakti* poets) and farther afield (G. G. Belli, Robert Browning, W. B. Yeats, André Breton, T. S. Eliot, Ezra Pound, W. C. Williams, Robert Lowell).

"My backward place is where I am," Ezekiel, the preeminent Indian poet in Eng. after independence, wrote in "Background, Casually" (1976), both describing his location and stating its centrality to his poetics. His low-key, plain style marked a clear shift away from poets like Sarojini Naidu (1879–1949), whom Mahatma Gandhi called the nightingale of India, and Sri Aurobindo (1872–1950), who had preceded Ezekiel. Ezekiel called his first book *A Time to Change* (1952). Staying clear of Indian myths and legends, he is also the first poet to write about the Indian city, in his case Bombay, a "Barbaric city, sick with slums, / Deprived of seasons, blessed with rains," as he called it in "A Morning Walk" (1959).

Kolatkar, Chitre, Mahapatra, and Ramanujan, like M. M. Dutt, wrote in Eng. as well as in their native tongues (Kolatkar and Chitre in Marathi, Mahapatra in Oriya, Ramanujan in Kannada). Das, under the pseud. Madhavikutty, was a renowned writer of short fiction in Malayalam, a fact largely unknown to her Eng. readers. Ramanujan, Kolatkar, Chitre, and Mehrotra also translated from the Indian langs. (Tamil Sangam poetry, Prakrit love poetry, the Bhakti poets Nammalvar, Tukaram, and Kabīr). Their trans. mirrored their Eng. poems, just as their Eng. poems mirrored their trans. Poets also ran publishing cooperatives (Clearing House, Newground, Praxis) and edited magazines (*Poetry India*, *Chandrabhāgā*) and anthols. The canon of Indian poetry in Eng. has been shaped not by Indian scholars but by the poets.

Ramanujan wrote a poetry of self-revealing masks. Even his inventive stanza shapes were another mask in his poetic wardrobe, behind which the falling, plunging self was terrifyingly visible. Ramanujan's reputation as a poet, at least in the United States, where he taught at the University of Chicago, has been eclipsed by his reputation as a folklorist, essayist, and trans., as the inventor of Tamil poetry for contemp. times.

The most remarkable Indian poet of the 20th c. was Kolatkar, who created two independent, major bodies of work in two langs., Eng. and Marathi. *Jejuri* (1976), a sequence of 31 poems about a visit to a temple town of the same name in Maharashtra, established his international reputation. He published three more volumes, two of which appeared in the year he died and the third posthumously. He was an elusive figure who had a horror of mainstream publishers. At the heart of his work lies a moral vision, the basis of which is the things of this world, precisely, rapturously observed: "A sawed off sunbeam comes to rest / gently against the driver's right temple" ("The Bus," 1976).

The postindependence poets and their 19th-c. predecessors may seem to have little in common, but the parallels of cosmopolitanism, bilingualism, and trans. are too striking to be missed.

See ASSAMESE POETRY; BENGALI POETRY; GUJARATI POETRY; HINDI POETRY; INDIA, POETRY OF; KANNADA POETRY; KASHMIRI POETRY; MALAYALAM POETRY; MARATHI POETRY; NEPALI AND PAHARI POETRY; NEWAR POETRY; ORIYA POETRY; PUNJABI POETRY; RĀMĀYAṆA POETRY; SANSKRIT POETICS; SANSKRIT POETRY; TAMIL POETRY AND POETICS; TELUGU POETRY; URDU POETRY.

■ *Ten Twentieth-Century Indian Poets*, ed. R. Parthasarathy (1976); N. Ezekiel, *Collected Poems* (1989); *The Oxford India Anthology of Twelve Modern Indian Poets*, ed. A. K. Mehrotra (1992); B. King, *Modern Indian Poetry in English*, rev. ed. (2001); J. Ramazani, "Metaphor and Postcoloniality: A. K. Ramanujan's Poetry," *The Hybrid Muse* (2001); A. Chaudhuri, "A State of Commerce," *The Telegraph* (April 7, 2002); *A History of Indian Literature in English*, ed. A. K. Mehrotra (2003); *Early Indian Poetry in English*, ed. E. de Souza (2005); B. King, *Three Indian Poets*, rev. ed. (2005); *The Bloodaxe Book of Contemporary Indian Poets*, ed. J. Thayil (2008); A. K. Mehrotra, "The Emperor Has No Clothes," *Partial Recall* (2011).

A. K. MEHROTRA

INDIA, POETRY OF

I. Ancient Period (ca. 1200 BCE–1200 CE)
II. Middle Period (ca. 1200–1800 CE)
III. Modern Period (since ca. 1800)

The term *Indian poetry* commonly refers to an immense and diverse body of poetry produced on the Indian subcontinent and by authors of subcontinental origin, since about 1200 BCE. Also known as South Asia, this region is now divided into seven nations (incl. India, Pakistan, Bangladesh, Nepal, and Sri Lanka) and is as large and varied as western Europe. Indian poetry does not belong to a unified, monolingual trad. but rather is a constellation of interacting trads. in about 25 major lit. langs., many of which are used widely for everyday communication in South Asia in mod. times.

The subcontinental langs. have preserved their poetic trads. in oral as well as written forms, using a dozen different script systems of indigenous and foreign origin. The langs. belong to four families: Indo-Aryan, Dravidian, Austro-Asiatic, and Sino-Tibetan. Of these, the Indo-Aryan and Dravidian langs. have been predominant as literary media and, since about 1000 CE, they have been strongly associated with specific geographical regions within the subcontinent. At the same time, langs. from abroad, such as Persian (between the 13th and 19th cs.) and Eng. (since the late 18th c.), have periodically come into widespread use, greatly complicating Indian ling., regional, national, and cultural identities, as well as conceptions of poetry, genre, and aesthetics.

This article surveys the general patterns and transformations in poetry of the subcontinent as a well-defined multilingual area over time. It focuses on the most important poetic practices and innovations of each historical period and on changes in poetics and in historical and cultural circumstances. The broad historical divisions here are the ancient period (ca. 1200 BCE–1200 CE), which includes the early epic period (ca. 600 BCE–400 CE) and the cl. Sanskrit period (ca. 400–1200 CE); the middle period common to many langs. (ca. 1200–1800); and the mod. period (ca. 1800 to the present). For details of particular Indian poetic trads., consult the entries by lang.

I. Ancient Period (ca. 1200 BCE–1200 CE)

A. *Conceptions of Poetry.* For about 2,500 years, Indian theorists and literati have frequently used the word *kāvya* for poetry to distinguish it from other kinds of verbal composition. In its earliest and narrowest meaning (ca. 600 BCE), kāvya characterizes the poetry of the *Rāmāyaṇa*, which is epic in scope, narrative in structure, and lyrical in effect, with relatively straightforward syntax and diction. In a second, wider meaning (ca. 200 CE onward), kāvya signifies composition in verse or prose, designed to give its audience an experience of *rasa*, the aesthetically fashioned representation of emotions.

In its widest sense (popular ca. 700–1200 CE), kāvya designates the full range of imaginative composition, in verse (*padya*), prose (*gadya*), and mixtures of the two (*miṣra*', *campu*). It includes drama and performance texts, which often are multilingual in the cl. period, with different characters speaking in different langs. or social and regional dialects for verisimilitude. Kāvya in this sense further includes prose narrative, both "fictional" (*kathā*) and "nonfictional" (*ākhyāyikā*), covering what we now call myth, legend, short story, novella, novel, moral tale, fable, biography, and history. Kāvya in the latter part of the ancient period thus coincides with the meaning of lit. itself (*sāhitya*), although the term still does not cover the "total order of words" (*vānmaya*) in a given lang. Within this framework, Indian theorists distinguish between *dṛṣya kāvya*, poetry that has to be "seen" to be properly understood (dramatic poetry and performance), and *śravya kāvya*, poetry that needs only to be "heard" to be grasped fully (epic, lyric, prose).

B. *Early Epic.* The period during which the major epics, the *Rāmāyaṇa* and the *Mahābhārata*, were probably composed (ca. 600 BCE–400 CE) constitutes an essential backdrop for later Indian poetry. Society at this time is almost entirely Hindu, with the institutions of caste, endogamy, and Vedic ritual already in place, along with the proscriptions against pollution. The two epics represent a world in which Hinduism as a polytheistic way of life was divided mainly between followers of the major gods Viṣṇu and Śiva and in which the subcontinent is organized politically into small and large republics ruled by dynasties of kings. Works belonging to this period are composed, preserved, and transmitted orally, using elaborate techniques of memorization and verification; indigenous script systems and writing (with a stylus, on prepared bark or palm leaf) become available only around the 2d c. BCE. In this setting, the *Rāmāyaṇa* and the *Mahābhārata* appear as heroic sagas in verse that draw on bardic materials and conventions, folklore, romance, and hist., with many themes resonating strongly with the Troy cycle of stories and Gr. and Roman myths, and hence pointing to shared IE sources.

Vālmīki, the original author of the *Rāmāyaṇa*, is recognized as the "first *kavi*" or ur-poet, and the poem itself is the "original kāvya," standing at the head of the subcontinent's lit. trads. Vālmīki defines the *śloka* as the ideal vehicle for poetic emotion as well as verse narrative, and his virtuoso handling of this unrhymed metrical verse form (resembling a closed couplet, divided by caesuras into quarters) becomes an enduring model for subsequent craftsmanship in narrative, dramatic, and lyric verse. The *Rāmāyaṇa* and the *Mahābhārata* together define some of the overarching subjects of Indian poetry: *dharma* (law, duty, obligation), justice, war, love, and the irrevocability of vows, curses, and promises. Most important, they become reservoirs of stories from which poets of all subsequent generations draw. At the level of technique, they invent framed narratives, in which smaller stories are nested inside larger tales, and the outermost frame gathers them all into a cohesive poetic structure. Emboxed narratives find their way from the epics into the Buddhist *Jataka* tales (4th c. BCE) and the Hindu *Panchatantra* fables (2d c. CE), and ultimately into Somadeva's *Kathasaritsagara* (11th c. CE); from these widely circulated texts, the device then migrates to Persian, Ar., the Romance langs., and Eng., influencing the poets of the *1001 Nights* as well as Boccaccio and Chaucer.

C. *Classical Sanskrit.* By the cl. period (ca. 400–1200 CE), Indian society had become more varied; besides numerous caste divisions (*jatis*), it included many new ethnic communities with distinctive ways of life. The primeval forests had been cleared; the Indo-Gangetic plains and the Deccan Plateau were well populated; networks of roads connected market towns, pilgrimage centers, ports, and royal capitals, signifying a shift toward urban culture, travel, and prosperity. Politically, republics had given way to imperial formations covering large portions of the subcontinent. Hinduism was still the predominant religion, but it now emphasized large public temples, pilgrimage sites, and domestic rituals and flourished alongside Buddhism and Jainism as alternative worldviews.

In verse, cl. Sanskrit poetry centered around three primary classes of texts. (1) The category of *mahākāvya* and *dirgha-kāvya*, poems in "major forms" divided into *sargas* (cantos, chapters, sections), which devised large-scale structures for the saga of a royal clan, the heroic battle poem, and the courtly epic (written to order for a patron), among other subgenres. (2) The category of *laghukāvya* and *khanda-kāvya*, which consisted of short and medium-length poems, poetic segments, and fragments and extracts from longer works. It included the *subhāṣita*, a beautifully crafted verse that could stand on its own, as well as the poetic sequence, a thematic arrangement of separate verses or passages. (3) The category of *kośa* or edited anthology brought together short poems, either by a single author or by many hands, often arranged by form and theme. In later centuries, the cl. mahākāvya and dirgha-kāvya (rather than the *Rāmāyaṇa* and the *Mahābhārata*) became the practical models for epics and long poems in the mod. Indian mother tongues; the subhāṣita served as the norm for brevity, elegance, and lyricism; and the kośa, secular and inclusive, defined the ideal anthol. of poetry.

In addition, cl. Sanskrit expanded the concept of kāvya to include prose works as well as drama. The *ākhyāyikā* (the short or extended "true story") provided new frameworks for biographical and historical writing, whereas the kathā, a short tale that retells a received narrative or narrates an invented fiction, showcased fantastic events as well as verisimilar representations of human characters (both individuated figures and stock types), together with social and psychological realism. The *nataka* or poetic play in several acts (a variety of dṛṣya kāvya) created the model of multilingual drama in a mixture of prose and verse, with the former utilized for dialogue and the latter for emotional intensity, foregrounding, and allusion. While ancient Gr. drama is distinguished by its invention of tragedy and Aristophanic comedy, the distinction of cl. Sanskrit drama lies in its invention on stage of the heroic romance, the farce, and esp. the romantic comedy (as in Kālidāsa's [4th c. CE] *Śakuntalam*).

As a distinctive style, kāvya in its cl. phase sought to create a verbal texture pleasing to both the ear and the mind and became an aesthetic model for the later Indo-Aryan and Dravidian langs. It involved not only rasa but extensive figuration and embellishment (*alaṃkāra*), the use of indirect suggestion (*dhvani*) over and above connotation and denotation to convey meaning, a display of learning in the arts and sciences, an intricate syntax and an enormous vocabulary, and a wide variety of complicated meters and verse forms. Thematically and formally, esp. in the category of short or fragmentary poems, cl. kāvya opened up a fresh range of generic possibilities for subsequent Indian poetry, from descriptions of the seasons, confessional poetry, epigrams, and erotic poetry to hymns and prayers, philosophical reflections, didactic poetry, and even short dramatic monologues. The richness of cl. kāvya style revolved around concrete imagery, precise representation, nuanced emotion, refinement of sensibility, and memorability.

Passing through a number of well-defined phases (in Sanskrit, from Vedic to epic to cl.; in cl. Tamil, from *caṇkam* to epic to devotional), Indian poetry of the ancient period came to constitute a massive, multiform body of verbal composition. In the middle and mod. periods, this body became a repository of commonplaces for poets and audiences to tap and a canon to which they could respond, as they created fresh configurations of lang., theme, aesthetics, religious belief, social thought, and politics.

II. Middle Period (ca. 1200–1800 CE)

A. *Historical and Cultural Changes.* The middle period begins and ends at different times for langs. and regions of the subcontinent; but most poetic trads. undergo vital transitions in the late 12th and late 18th cs., so its common historical span may be specified as 1200–1800. In the largest internal change marking the end of the cl. and the beginning of the middle period, Sanskrit ceases to be the primary medium of literary composition, giving way to writing in about 15 mother tongues. Similar to the transition from Lat. to the vernaculars in Europe around the same time, this ling. and literary shift is accompanied by a selective but concerted devaluation of the ancient Indian past and particularly by the rise of new chauvinisms centered around the geographical domains of the various mother tongues.

This cultural transformation coincides with several other historical changes. By about 1200, gradual Muslim conquest, migration, and settlement on the subcontinent had led to Muslim imperial rule, which lasted for six centuries. Indian society was more mixed and fragmented, being characterized by a foreign ruling elite, new immigrant and settler communities from central and western Asia, and segregation among different races, religions, and langs. By the 13th c., Islam was the religion of power, Buddhism had migrated out of the Indian mainland, and Hinduism had been altered by the emergence of *Bhakti.* Islam brought its own divisions: the Sunni, Shi'a, and Sufi religious communities, as well as the Ar., Persian, and Turkish ling. communities (each with its own literary trads.). Moreover, by the 13th c., the technology of writing with reed pen and ink on paper had arrived on the subcontinent, drastically altering the material existence and possibilities of lit. Under such circumstances, the change of verbal medium, from half a dozen ancient literary langs. dominated by Sanskrit to about 15 regional mother tongues and two or three foreign langs., engendered far-reaching changes in the very conception of poetry and its functions.

B. *Bhakti Poetry.* The most prominent literary, religious, and social movement of the middle period is Bhakti ("devotion" to a god, often classified as theism), which began in the far south (the Tamil region) after the 6th c. and spread with surprising success over the subcontinent by the 16th c. Despite ling. diversity and local and regional variations, Bhakti poetry has common features across a dozen major langs. The movement involves several thousand poets, called *bhaktas* and *sants*, as well as many disparate "communities" or "paths" (*sampradayas, panthas*) focused variously on Viṣṇu and his avatars, Śiva, Devi (the universal goddess), or an undifferentiated godhead.

In Bhakti poetry, which strongly parallels Christian mystical poetry in late med. and early mod. Europe, a poet expresses his or her intensely personal devotion to a particular god, goddess, or godhead. True poetry in this trad. must be spontaneous, urgent, personal, and "divinely inspired" and should be composed in the more natural mother tongue than in an artificial lang. like Sanskrit. Bhakti poets and poems, therefore, tend to be more immediate, colloquial, autobiographical, confessional, and dramatic than many of their cl. counterparts, swerving away from impersonal kāvya on a significant scale. Most Bhakti poetry is composed in short or minor forms of local or regional origin (not borrowed from Sanskrit), and it is usually metrical and uses verse forms with end rhyme (rare in the cl. langs.). Many poems in the trad. are addressed to fellow worshippers; others are addressed to a god or to the poet's audience and, hence, are unlike Western lyrics. Short Bhakti poems are set to music and sung, often in a congregation; and they are also used frequently in such performance arts as dance, dance-drama, and folk theater.

Bhakti alters the historical evolution of poetry on the subcontinent on several fronts. It is the first comprehensive movement in the new regional lits. emerging at the end of the cl. period, and it shapes their characteristic *topoi* and themes, forms and genres. Socially and politically, many bhaktas and sants are radicals who substantially modify or even reject the Hinduism and priestly culture of the ancient period; some belong to very low or "untouchable" castes, and they participate fully in the movement's outspoken "counterculture." In religious, theological, and philosophical terms, Bhakti defines a major alternative to ritualized "salvation" in ancient Hinduism, and it provides the central impetus for Sikhism, a new religion that arose in the 16th c. Notable formal innovations in short Bhakti poems include an opening refrain, which becomes prominent in musical performance; and a concluding signature line that explicitly identifies its author, in marked contrast to the impersonality of the subhāṣita and of laghukāvya in cl. Sanskrit.

III. Modern Period (since ca. 1800)

A. *Colonization and Modernity*. For large parts of the subcontinent, the mod. period of hist. begins with Brit. rule in the mid-18th c., whereas literary modernity appears only in the 19th. Many material, ideological, and practical factors contribute directly and indirectly to this large-scale transition from a "traditional" to a "modern" society: the military success of a foreign power on the subcontinent; the establishment of a rationalized system of administration (in contrast to the disarray of late Mughal administration in the 18th c.); the introduction of journalism, newspapers, and periodicals, as well as of a comprehensive postal system; the formation of a full-fledged, multilingual print culture; the emergence of a public sphere that allowed rational debate on issues of common concern (in spite of colonial censorship); the popularity of civic associations and literary societies, modeled on Eur. institutions; Brit. and Eur. critiques of traditional Indian culture; and esp. the availability of Western-style education in schools, colleges, and universities.

In the later 19th c., Indian poets began encountering Anglo-Am. literary works and reading Eng. trans. of Gr., Roman, and mod. Eur. lits. Many of them subsequently began to imitate their Western predecessors and contemporaries, significantly changing the formal, thematic, and generic complexion of the lits. in indigenous langs. The Westernization of India under Brit. rule also went one step further: it created the poet who wanted to write poetry of the Anglo-Am. kind directly in the Eng. lang. But the modernity of Indian writing after about 1800 does not consist solely in its Westernization, and Indian writers did not become mod. merely by imitating Euro-Am. writers. In most Indian mother tongues, the 18th and 19th cs. were largely periods of very complex, creative interaction among local, regional, subcontinental, and international trads., leading as much to reactionary traditionalism and reactive nationalism as to stimulating cultural syncretism.

The overall effect of colonization on Indian poetry was thus multifaceted and far-reaching: the encounter with Eur. cultures drove Indian writers to experiment with poetry markedly different from anything the Indian trads. themselves had invented; it went hand in hand with a renewed interest in their own trads. of the ancient and middle periods; and it introduced yet another foreign literary lang., Eng., into the Indian Babel. These effects have continued from the early 19th c. to the present, and the grafting of Western "influences" onto "indigenous" sensibilities has resulted in a hybrid lit. that has broken away sharply from many of the patterns in Indian poetry of the preceding three millennia. *Ādhunik kāvita* (mod. poetry) swerves away in complicated ways from *prācīn kāvya* (ancient or old poetry), whether that of cl. Sanskrit or of the Bhakti movement, and pushes kāvya and kavitā across new frontiers.

B. *Modern Poetic Genres*. The shift away from the poetry and poetics of the middle period was signaled by a concerted change in poetic forms, themes, conventions, images, metrical frames, and structural principles, as well as by radical changes in the conception of who the poet (kavi) is, what his or her functions are, and how his or her audience is constituted. Moreover, the transformed situation of Indian poets in the 19th and early 20th cs. generated new attitudes, concerns, tones, and voices: they explored enjambed lines, Elizabethan blank verse,

Eng. epic conventions, Miltonic similes, and romantic lyrics; experimented with specific Eur. and non-Indian verse forms grafted onto Sanskrit-based prosody; and elaborated themes related to nation, identity, and social, religious, and political change. This multifarious transition led to writing that, when placed beside earlier Indian poetry, strikes a remarkably cosmopolitan, mod. note; but its novelty, whether in the indigenous langs. or in Eng., does not result simply from a rejection of the Indian past.

The varieties of creative synthesis in mod. Indian poetry are evident in the new genres that appeared in the 19th and 20th cs. Among them are the long philosophical or speculative poem, epic in size and scope and envisioning a new worldview (e.g., Aurobindo Ghose's [1872–1950] *Savitri* in Eng., G. M. Muktibodh's [1917–64] *Andhere men* in Hindi); the nationalist epic, retelling an ancient Hindu myth or story, esp. from the *Rāmāyaṇa* or the *Mahābhārata* (e.g., Michael Madhusudan Dutt's [1824–73] *Meghanādvadha* in Bengali, Jaishankar Prasad's [1889–1937] *Kāmāyanī* in Hindi); the long sequence of short poems, whether religious, philosophical, satiric, or personal in theme, modeled on the Western poetic sequence as well as on premod. Indian sequences (e.g., Rabindranath Tagore's [1861–1941] *Gitanjali* in Bengali; Subramania Bharati's [1882–1921] "prose poems" in Tamil; Rajagopal Parthasarathy's [b. 1934] *Rough Passage* in Eng.); the short metrical lyric in a mod. rhymed stanza form, sometimes set to music, as well as the modernized lyric based on premod. Indian and foreign verse forms (e.g., Faiz Ahmed's [1911–84] *ghazals*, *nazms*, and *gits* in Urdu; B. S. Mardhekar's [1909–56] and Vinda Karandikar's [1918–2010] *abhangas* in Marathi; Buddhadev Bose's [1908–74] sonnets in Bengali); and the "free-verse" poem, varying in length from a few lines to several hundred and ranging in theme from autobiographical and confessional to mythological, political, and historical (e.g., the love poems of P. S. Rege [1910–78] in Marathi; the political poems of Dhoomil [1936–75], Shrikant Verma [1931–86], and Raghuvir Sahay [1929–90] in Hindi; the bilingual poetry of A. K. Ramanujan [1929–93] in Eng. and Kannada and of Arun Kolatkar [1932–2004] in Eng. and Marathi; and protest poetry, Dalit poetry, and contemp. feminist and women's poetry in most langs.).

In the course of these devels., the tensions between modernity and trad., Indianness and Westernization, have played a shaping role. Like many of their 19th-c. predecessors, 20th- and 21st-c. Indian poets reject certain aspects of their past but at the same time make use of it, achieving a modernity in which Westernization and Indianness stand in a constant and constantly productive conflict. As a result, mod. Indian writers, critics, and common readers now refer to all varieties of poetry as *kāvya*; in its broadest usage around the millennial moment, kāvya, thus, embraces a vast quantity of diverse poetry in about 25 major langs. produced over some 3,000 years.

See ASSAMESE POETRY; BENGALI POETRY; GUJARATI POETRY; HINDI POETRY; INDIA, ENGLISH POETRY OF; KANNADA POETRY; KASHMIRI POETRY; MALAYALAM POETRY; MARATHI POETRY; NEPALI AND PAHARI POETRY; NEWAR POETRY; ORIYA POETRY; PUNJABI POETRY; RĀMĀYAṆA POETRY; SANSKRIT POETICS; SANSKRIT POETRY; TAMIL POETRY AND POETICS; TELUGU POETRY; URDU POETRY.

■ A. B. Keith, *A History of Sanskrit Literature* (1928); *An Anthology of Sanskrit Court Poetry*, trans. D.H.H. Ingalls (1965); *The Mahābhārata*, trans. C. V. Narasimhan (1965)—handy abridgement; A. K. Ramanujan, *Speaking of Śiva* (1973); *The Mahābhārata*, trans. J.A.B. van Buitenen, 3 v. (1973–80); E. C. Dimock et al., *The Literatures of India* (1974)—compact intro.; E. Zelliot, "The Medieval *Bhakti* Movement in History," *Hinduism*, ed. B. L. Smith (1976)—a balanced subject guide; D. Kopf, *The Brahmo Samaj and the Shaping of the Modern Indian Mind* (1979)—historical and cultural contexts; *Hymns for the Drowning*, trans. A. K. Ramanujan (1981); S. Lienhard, *A History of Classical Poetry* (1984); *The Rāmāyaṇa of Vālmiki*, trans. R. Goldman et al., 5 v. (1984–2005); *The Bhagavad-Gitā*, trans. B. S. Miller (1986); *Poems of Love and War*, trans. A. K. Ramanujan (1986)—from cl. Tamil; *Songs of the Saints of India*, ed. and trans. J. S. Hawley and M. Juergensmeyer (1988); S. K. Das, *A History of Indian Literature*, 3 v. (1991–2005)—incomplete but informative; *The Oxford Anthology of Modern Indian Poetry*, ed. V. Dharwadker and A. K. Ramanujan (1994)—selections from 15 langs.; A. K. Ramanujan, *Collected Essays* (1999); *Kabir: The Weaver's Songs*, trans. V. Dharwadker (2003); *Literary Cultures in History: Reconstructions from South Asia*, ed. S. Pollock (2003)—best crit. overview of major Indian lits.; S. Pollock, *The Language of the Gods in the World of Men* (2006)—excellent, comprehensive.

V. DHARWADKER

INDIAN PROSODY

I. Classical Languages: Sanskrit, Prakrit, and Tamil
II. The Modern Vernaculars

I. Classical Languages: Sanskrit, Prakrit, and Tamil. Indian metrics is one of the world's most complex prosodic trads. Though perhaps best treated historically, it must in an article such as this be surveyed formally. Indian meters fall into three main types: (a) those that fix the quantity of each syllable (*varṇavṛtta*), (b) those that fix the total quantity of each line (*mātrāvṛtta*), and (c) those that appear to mix the two types (*śloka*). Like the metrics of Gr. and Lat., Indian versification is based on a prosodic distinction between *heavy* and *light* syllables. A heavy syllable contains a long vowel or a short vowel followed by two or more consonants. A light syllable contains a short vowel followed by at most one consonant. The distinction of vowel quantity is inherent in the phonology of Sanskrit and the other Indian langs.

A. *Fixed-syllable Meters.* The elegant meters of cl. Sanskrit poetry are of this type. The general formula calls for four usually identical feet (*pāda*), which in practice may vary from eight to 21 or more syllables each. *Mandākrāntā* (the meter of Kālidāsa's *Meghadhūta*) may be taken as an example. Each of its four 17-syllable feet realizes the following pattern: G G G G L L L L G / G L G G L G x (G = *guru*, or heavy syllable; L = *laghu*, or light syllable; x = a syllable of variable quantity; "/" marks the *yati*, or caesura). Less common meters may vary identical first and third feet with identical second and fourth feet or may have four different feet, but the principle remains the same: the quantity of each syllable is predictable and the sequence or pattern is fixed. In recitation, a chanting intonation is usually employed, modeled on the quantitative sequence of the line. Though some common recitative patterns are noticeable, each reciter may also cultivate a personal style. The names of the meters generally scan in the meter and often suggest appropriate associations: *mandākrāntā*, ([a lady] slowly approaching).

B. *Fixed-Line or Moric Meters.* Here the quantity of the total line is fixed by considering a laghu worth one "measure" (*mātrā*; cf. Lat. *mora*) and a guru two. Free variation of syllables within the line is, however, restricted by several conventions, which demonstrate the influence of a regular beat—indicating that these meters were probably sung. It is forbidden, for instance, that the beat fall on the second half of a guru syllable. If we assume one beat every four mātrās (three, five, and six are also possible), this convention will, in effect, articulate the line into groups (*gaṇa*) of four mātrās each, which have only the shapes G G, G L L, L G L, L L G, or L L L L, each signaled by an initial beat. The *āryā*, which probably originated in popular, non-Sanskritic milieux and remained the meter of choice for cl. Prakrit poetry, may serve as a typical example: it is composed of two lines, the first of which must contain 30 mātrā, the second 27. The simple tetramoric pattern (above) is, however, complicated (and syncopated) by adding to seven of these gaṇa an eighth of two mātrās (for a total, in the first line, of 30), and, further, in the second line, by reducing the sixth gaṇa to a single laghu (i.e., 27). Convention also restricts the kinds of gaṇa that do, in fact, occur in given loci in the verse; e.g., in the āryā, L G L is possible only for the second and fourth gaṇa. The meters of the songs of the *Gītagovinda* (13th c.) and those employed in middle Indic devotional poetry and in the mod. north Indian langs. are generally of the moric type, which is subject to extreme variation. Beginning with the *Gītagovinda*, end rhyme is frequently associated with moric meter, and later vernacular poetry is regularly rhymed. Alliteration, though not unknown in earlier poetry, also becomes an increasingly prominent feature of moric verse. As may be surmised, the correlation of moric meter with song is in the mod. period even more marked.

The meters of the Dravidian langs. of the south (Tamil, Telugu, Kannada, Malayalam) are based on a somewhat more complicated scansion (in certain circumstances, treating as light even a syllable containing a long vowel); but during the long course of coexistence and mutual contact, there has been a give and take of both theory and practice with the Sanskritic north. The oldest Dravidian (viz., Tamil) meters greatly resemble the moric meters of the Prakrits, employ alliteration with great effect, and are definitely rhythmical (cf. again the *Gītagovinda*). On the other hand, they often feature initial rhyme, based on the first interior consonant of the line—virtually unknown in the north. Lines most commonly consist of four feet (*cīr*) comprising two or three syllables (*acai*). The earliest treatise on prosody in the Dravidian langs. is the *Ceyyuḷiyal* chapter of the

Tamil *Tolkāppiyam* (3d to 5th cs. BCE). The cl. meters prevailed until the end of the 1st millennium CE, when folk meters were popularized by devotional poets.

C. ***Śloka.*** The most common Sanskrit meter is partly fixed, partly free. Śloka (praise) is both a type and a species, deriving in its special epic and later form (after 500 BCE) from the meters found in the oldest extant Indic text, the *Rig Veda* (ca. 1500–1000 BCE). The cl. śloka is like type (a) in that it is composed of four feet, each of which must have eight syllables; but it is like (b) in that its line appears to fall into two four-syllable halves, the first of which is quantitatively quite free (though x L L x does not normally occur), the second of which is obligatorily L G G x in odd feet and in even feet L G L x. A "trochaic" cadence, thus, alternates with an "iambic." Many variations on this pattern are, however, found. The older Vedic meters (*chandas*) are composed generally of feet with 8, 11, or 12 syllables. Of the eight-syllable meters, some have three feet (*gāyatrī*), some four (*anuṣṭubh*). This latter is evidently the ancestor of the cl. śloka, but it lacks, along with the other Vedic meters, the contrast between even and odd feet. Its usual shape is x G x G /L G L x. The 11-syllable meters (*triṣṭubh*) generally have the same attack and the same cadence but add a middle sequence of L L G (/). The *jagatī* adds a syllable to the triṣṭubh but is otherwise like it. Like the anuṣṭubh, the triṣṭubh and jagatī have descendants in the cl. metrics—the family of 11-syllable meters called *upajāti*, and 12-syllable meters such as the popular *vaṁśastha* and *drutavilambita*. The style of śloka recitation is more or less uniform over all of India, testifying to its antiquity. The Vedic meters have been deformed by the superimposition of later prosodic features, such as the obligatory *sandhi* (ling. junctures) of the cl. lang. and are only dimly perceptible in the (otherwise) beautiful ritual chanting of the Vedic priest, itself the likely precursor of cl. Indian music.

The śloka is not "poetic" in the usual Western sense, however. Though it is metrical, it is functionally the equivalent of Western prose in that it is the mode of choice for an entire range of literate composition, from epic (*Mahābhārata, Rāmāyaṇa*) and fable (*Kathāsaritsāgara*) to grammar (*Vākyapadīya*) and astronomy (*Sūryasiddhānta*)—doubtless reflecting the importance of memorization in Indian religious and cultural trad.

The study of prosody is very old in India, being counted as one of the six "ancillaries of the Veda" (*vedāṅga*). A *sūtra* attributed to Piṅgala, portions of which may be as old as 600 BCE (the rest as late as 500 CE), describes about 160 meters, but surprisingly not the śloka that we know. In the late cl. period (after 900 CE), an elaborate technical lit. (*chandaḥśāstra*) grew up, based on Piṅgala, wherein were defined the various meters in actual use and, with mathematical completeness, many meters merely possible. Associations with moods, time of day, and colors were sometimes also made, testifying to an effort to integrate metrics into the larger domain of aesthetics.

II. The Modern Vernaculars. Throughout the med. and early mod. periods, the end-stopped rhyming couplet was the preferred medium of expression for poets in the New Indo-Aryan langs. (Hindi, Punjabi, Gujarati, Marathi, Bengali, Assamese, and Oriya). As in cl. Sanskrit, lines are usually divided by caesurae into two, three, or four feet (*pāda* or *caraṇ*). The most popular verse form for the vast number of devotional lyrics produced in this period is the *pad*, a stanza of from four to eight lines (but often extended to several more), all having the same metrical structure and frequently the same rhyme. Often the lyric begins with a shorter line that in performance serves as a refrain. Alliteration is prevalent throughout the med. period; among the poets of Rajasthan, it becomes obligatory.

On the whole, Hindi poets favored moric meters, esp. those with a tetramoric pattern. It appears that the poets normally had a specific rhythmic cycle (*tāla*) in mind when they chose the meter. Often this was a cycle of 16 beats divided into four equal sections, the common time of Indian music. The majority of lyrics have 16 morae in the first foot of each line and from 10 to 16 in the second.

The *dohā* is a rhyming couplet commonly used for aphorisms, as well as for longer narrative and didactic poetry. The first foot of each line has 13 morae and the second 11. In the case of Kabīr and other *sant* poets, it is called *sākhī*, and in the *ādigranth* of the Sikhs, it is termed *salok* (from Sanskrit *śloka*, of which it was the vernacular equivalent). The basic unit of the narrative poems composed in the Avadhī dialect of Hindi (notably the Sufi romances and the *Rāmcaritmānas* of Tulsīdās) was a stanza of from five to eight distichs in the 16-moric *caupāī* meter followed by a dohā.

Hindi poets also used syllabic meters, the most common being two types of quatrains called *savaiyā* and *ghanākṣarī.* The former has lines of 22–26 syllables with a trisyllabic rhythm and a medial caesura; the ghanākṣarī line has three feet of eight syllables and a fourth of seven or eight. The tetrasyllabic rhythm of the latter prevailed in other vernaculars, which used mainly syllabic meters. The most common meter in Eastern India (Bengali, Assamese, and Oriya) was the *payār*, a rhyming couplet used for both lyric and narrative poetry. Here, each line has 14 syllables divided 8 + 6 but subdivisible into a 4 + 4 + 4 + 2 structure. Another popular couplet form was the *tripadī*, of which each line has two feet of equal length, often with end rhyme, followed by a third that is slightly longer, e.g., 6 + 6 + 8 or 8 + 8 + 10.

Similar to the payār are the *abhaṅga* and the *ovī*, the most popular forms used by Marathi poets. The shorter type of abhaṅga is composed of rhyming octosyllabic sections; the longer abhaṅga has lines of four feet (6 + 6 + 6 + 4 syllables) with the second and third rhyming. The ovī is considered a folk meter from which the abhaṅga derived. Its first three feet are of equal length and have end rhyme, while the fourth is slightly shorter and rhymeless.

These are the most common types of meter. The theorists describe many more, of which several are adaptations of Sanskrit meters or permutations of the basic vernacular ones, but the more recondite meters are usually confined to the work of scholastic court poets. Poetry in Urdu stayed within the Perso-Ar. trad., using principally the *ghazal* and *masnavī* forms.

Med. and mod. Tamil poets retained their purely indigenous meters; those who composed in the other Dravidian langs. (Kannada, Telugu, Malayalam) more readily assimilated the meters and vocabulary of Sanskrit. Kannada and Telugu poetry, of which the earliest examples emerged about a thousand years ago, used meters derived from Sanskrit as well as Dravidian meters that are found earlier in Tamil, adapting some of them to the Sanskrit method of scansion. Though Telugu poets were stricter in observing metrical rules, they modified the Sanskrit meters more than their Kannada counterparts and also accepted enjambment. Many of the meters used in Malayalam bear Sanskrit names but are freer than Sanskrit in their syllabic structure.

A form of prose poem in Kannada is found in the short *vacana* (utterances) of Basavaṇṇa (12th c.) and subsequent Vīraśaiva poets of Karnataka. Comparable, though more regular, are the *vākh* of the Kashmiri female saint Lalla (or Lal Ded; early 14th c.): these are quatrains of approximately seven syllables and four stresses in each line with occasional rhyme. In the 19th c., familiarity with Eng. poetry encouraged Bengali poets, and later those writing in other langs., to experiment with blank verse and enjambment. Rabindranath Tagore, besides writing blank and free verse, maintained the moric trad. but simplified the rules for measuring quantity by giving all open syllables the value of one mora and all closed syllables two.

See ASSAMESE POETRY; BENGALI POETRY; GREEK POETRY; GUJARATI POETRY; HINDI POETRY; INDIA, POETRY OF; KANNADA POETRY; MALAYALAM POETRY; MARATHI POETRY; ORIYA POETRY; PUNJABI POETRY; TAMIL POETRY AND POETICS; TELUGU POETRY.

■ E. W. Hopkins, *The Great Epic of India* (1901), esp. ch. 4; E. V. Arnold, *Vedic Metre* (1905)—the standard authority; A. B. Keith, *A History of Sanskrit Literature* (1920), esp. ch. 20, sections 3–4; H. Weller, "Beiträge zur Metrik der Veda," *Zeitschrift für Indologie und Iranistik* 12 (1922); J. Hermann, "Über die älteste indischer Metriker und ihr Werk," *Indian Linguistics* 3 (1933); H. D. Velankar, "Apabhraṁśa Metres," *Journal of the University of Bombay (Arts)* 131 (1933), 137 (1936); and "Chandaḥ kośa," *Journal of the University of Bombay (Arts)* 131 (1933)—rpt. as Appendix 2 to his *Kavidarpaṇa* (1960); A. C. Chettair, *Advanced Studies in Tamil Poetry* (1943); H. N. Randle, "Sanskrit and Greek Metres," *Journal of Oriental Research* 17 (1947); H. D. Velankar, "Prosodical Practices of Sanskrit Poets," *Journal of the Bombay Branch of the Royal Asiatic Society* n.s. 24–25 (1948–49); H. Weller, "Metrica," *Beiträge zur indischen Philologie und Altertumskunde* (1951); V. Raghavan, "Sanskrit and Prakrit Metres," *Journal of the Madras University* 23 (1952–53); L. Renou, *L'Inde Classique*, v. 2 (1953), App. 2, and "Sur la Structure du Kavya," *Journal Asiatique* 247 (1959); M. Sinha, *The Historical Development of Medieval Hindi Prosody* (1964); A. K. Warder, *Pali Metre* (1967); A. D. Mukherji, "Lyric Metres in Jayadeva's Gitagovinda," *Journal of the Asiatic Society of Bengal* (1967, pub. 1969); H. Jacobi, *Kleine Schriften* (1970); P. Kiparsky, "Metrics and Morphophonemics in the *Rigveda*," *Contributions to Generative Phonology*, ed. M. K. Brame (1972); D. Matthews and C. Shackle,

"Note on Prosody and Metre," *An Anthology of Classical Urdu Love Lyrics*, ed. D. Matthews and C. Shackle (1972); *Indian Literature*, ed. A. Poddar (1972); N. Sen, *Early Eastern New Indo-Aryan Versification* (1973); Allen; G. Nagy, *Comparative Studies in Greek and Indic Metre* (1974); S. Pollock, *Aspects of Versification in Sanskrit Lyric Poetry* (1977); S. Subrahmanyan, *The Commonness in the Metre of the Dravidian Languages* (1977); J. F. Vigorita, "The Trochaic Gayatri," *ZVS* 93 (1979); C. E. Fairbanks, "The Development of Hindi Oral Narrative Meter," *DAI* 42 (1982); S. Lienhard, *A History of Classical Poetry: Sanskrit–Pali–Prakrit*, ed. J. Gonda (1984); E. Gerow, "Jayadeva's Poetics and the Classical Style," *JAOS* 109.4 (1989)—spec. iss.; J. S. Klein, *On Verbal Accentuation in the Rigveda* (1992); W. P. Lehmann, "Poetic Principles in the South Asian Literary Tradition: Interrelatedness of Grammar, Prosody, and Other Elements of Language," *College Literature* 23.1 (1996); M. Witzel, "Sarama and the Panis: Origins of Prosimetric Exchange in Archaic India," *Prosimetrum: Crosscultural Perspectives on Narrative in Prose and Verse*, ed. J. Harris and K. Reichl (1997); U. Niklas, "A Short Introduction to Tamil Prosody, Part I," *Kolam* 3 (1999); A. Sharma, "Of Śūdras, Sūtas, and Ślokas: Why is the Mahābhārata Preeminently in the Anuṣṭubh Metre?" *Indo-Iranian Journal* 43 (2000); A. S. Deo, "The Metrical Organization of Classical Sanskrit Verse," *JL* 43 (2007); A. Mahoney, "The Feet of Greek and Sanskrit Verse," *Greek and Latin from an Indo-European Perspective*, ed. C. George et al. (2007).

E. Gerow (cl. langs.); A. W. Entwistle (mod. vernaculars)

INDIGENOUS AMERICAS, POETRY OF THE

I. Amazonia
II. Tahuantinsuyu
III. Anahuac
IV. Turtle Island

Knowing what may or may not constitute the roots of poetry and poetics indigenous to America involves factors specific to the continent. The first issues from its sheer size and shape, esp. in the midriff tropical zone. Extending northwest from Brazil, the Am. tropics cover one fifth of the globe, an ancient, unbroken, and culturally rich landmass found on no other continent. Then, from Alaska to Tierra del Fuego, confidently identified langs. and even lang. families are myriad, some written long before Rome could impose its alphabet. In Mesoamerica (roughly the tropics north of the isthmus and self-defining as *Anahuac*), stone inscriptions written in the visible lang. known as *tlacuilolli* in Nahuatl—a script that may represent sound while depending on the phonetics of no particular speech—date back more than two millennia and find elaborate expression in scrolls, maps, and screen-fold books of native paper and deerskin (known as the *codices*). Before and after the Classic Period (3d to 10th c. ce), the related story of lowland Maya hieroglyphs is similar. Their speech-specific phonetics were transcribed into the Roman alphabet after the invasion, in the *Chilam Balam* books of Chumayel and other Yucatecan towns, notable for their poetic wordplay with philosophical paradoxes and puns emanating from understandings of time both long resident and Eur.

Once arrived, the Eur. invaders are notorious for having burned whole libraries of books in Mesoamerica. On the Pacific Rim, the same fate was accorded in the Andes to libraries of Inca texts written in the knotted cord script known in Quechua as the *quipu*. It is now slowly becoming apparent (Julien, Brokaw) that the quipu recorded in Quechua—besides statistical information pertinent to the pastoral economy and subjects of the Inca Tahuantinsuyu and their calendar—kingship drama, chronicles, and liturgy, notably the hymns in praise of the supreme Inca, sun king and shepherd/llama herder. In 18th-c. Europe, these served as a source for the *Encyclopédie* (notably in its entry on script) and inspired the royal performances at Versailles known as *Indes galantes* that were enhanced by Jean-Philippe Rameau's music and Jean-François Marmontel's prose.

Besides cultural geography, ling. diversity, and written precedent, most telling of all these given factors in America are the recent revisions of the archaeological underpinnings on which lit. hist. and geography ultimately rely. Most salient is the case of Amazonia now recognized as the site of the continent's oldest ceramics (Neves), while the clarification of texts inscribed at Chavin de Huantar, the metropolis on the uppermost Amazon that served as portal to the Pacific Ocean, confirmed them as an enduring ideological premise (Burger, Salomon 2004). In the isthmus that joins South America to Anahuac east to west, pointers to ancient travel routes in fresh eds. of classic texts such as the Toltec lament (*Popol Vuh*, 6065–67;

Cantares mexicanos, folio 26v) are corroborated in the 1570 *Relaciones geográficas* of Cholula and Tepeaca and by archaeology at San Agustín (Colombia), Subtiaba (Nicaragua), and Yojoa (Honduras). Similar attention has been paid to the northwest continuations of Mesoamerica (Neurath), long distorted by U.S. discourse on its Southwest, esp. when it touches the open wound of Turtle Island's Ghost Dance. Chosen in 1825 by the Iroquois historian David Cusick to refer to America north of Mexico, *Turtle Island* has long been the term used by the Algonkian peoples to refer to the widespread territory of their langs.

In this predicament, a useful way to proceed is to rely wherever possible on native authority and start by acknowledging a category of classic texts that weld political hists. onto the world ages of Am. genesis, whose conception and scope make them poetry in the fullest sense. At the same time, we need not relinquish that wondered sense of a New World that animated thinkers in the late 16th c., before the fetters of Eur. ideology and social control (let alone mapping) had tightened. Of these, Michel de Montaigne merits close attention, for the pair of Am. *Essais* that effectively chart the continent, profoundly unsettling the authority of the Bible and the Greco-Roman classics. "Des cannibales" (1580) acknowledges the lowland rainforest of America as a prime source of poetry. "Des coches" (1588) does the same for the Inca and the Aztec empires along the continent's Pacific Rim, Montaigne having read in the meantime Francisco López de Gómara's *Historia general de las Indias* (1552).

With Montaigne and native validation in mind, we proceed, then, by discussing in turn four first sources of New World poetry: Amazonia, Tahuantinsuyu, Anahuac, and Turtle Island, each in its way an indispensable precedent for poetry composed in indigenous speech and in imported Port., Sp., and Eng. A corresponding range of poems trans. and in the original is available in Alcina Franch, Péret 1969, Rothenberg 1972, and Dorn and Brotherston, while Tomlinson provides wide overall contextualization. For drama in verse, see Meneses.

I. Amazonia. As the allies of the Fr. who ensured them victory over the Tupiniquin and the Port., the Tupinamba of Brazil (or France Antarctique) were invited to Henry II's court at Rouen in 1550, where they reenacted their triumph in a rainforest setting, singing songs of victory in their lang. A precedent for Montaigne, the event effectively belonged to the Americanist royal court trad. furthered at Versailles in the Indes galantes performances, which lauded Louis the Sun King in terms borrowed from Inca liturgy. Direct contact with the Tupinamba at Rouen under Charles IX and acquaintance with someone who had lived in their territory provided Montaigne with the two examples of native poetry that he included in "Des cannibales."

In the genre of the taunt (*carbet*), Montaigne's first cannibal poem fuses standard Eur. fear of naked savages who terrify enemy captives by threatening to eat them with the core drama of the Christian Eucharist and actual instances of anthropophagy among the Europeans of Montaigne's day. For their part, as members of the Tupi-Guaraní lang. family and culture, the Tupinamba authors of the taunt explicitly draw on notions of transubstantiation and eschatology widespread in extensive poetic texts composed in Tupi terms and in the Tupi tongue. In them, a principal reference is the *yvy tenonde* (land without ill), an obtainable earthly paradise that has for centuries inspired pilgrimage along the length of the Amazon. Fleeing Eur. invaders in 1549, a group of coastal Tupi are reported to have traveled up to Chachapoyas, the ancient Andean city of circular ruins. After missionary beginnings, these texts have come to constitute an enduring focus for anthropology in Brazil, in the work of Egon Schaden, Curt Nimuendajú, and more recently Eduardo Viveiros (Sá). They are usefully complemented in Eng. by Whitehead's ed. of the autobiographical *Warhaftige Historia* (1557) by Hans Staden, who, when captive, heard Tupi taunts firsthand, in the flesh as it were.

In his essay, besides the taunt, Montaigne dwells on a Tupi poem he called anacreontic, which asks a snake to allow the speaker to copy the exquisite designs on its skin, in a girdle he would give to his lover. Reviled in biblical teaching, the snake here is honored in an interspecies dialogue characteristic of Amazonian poetics. It plays on the idea of the snake's pride in its speckled hue, paying keen attention to visual design in the serpentine labyrinths likewise found on the continent's oldest known ceramics. In Marajó, the island at the river's mouth, these reached extremes of sophistication.

The Tupi trad., which includes Guaraní, the first lang. of Paraguay, for centuries served as the lingua franca or *Lingua Geral* of lowland South

America. In the 20th c., it was enriched by no less than two trans. (by Eduardo Saguler in 1951 and Dacunda Díaz in 1996) of José Hernández's *Martín Fierro*, the great gaucho epic of the Argentinean pampa, being ethnically the despised mother tongue of the eponymous hero; more recently, it has come to play a role in the cultural politics of MercoSur. The poetics of this trad. delights in exploring how word concepts are born in the first place and inhere in trains of thought. These are superbly exemplified in the classic work *Ayvu rapyta* of the Mbya Guaraní, a title that means something like the source of human lang.; through intense cogitation, it establishes the rain forest itself as the mid-earth from whose trees lang. flows.

The concentration on dream and the flow of thought, the dreaming of the world into existence seen as a precondition for deed and creation, may be held to typify Amazonian genesis and characterize work of Umasin Panlon and other authors of FOIRN (Federação das Organizações Indígenas do Rio Negro). Musings on these beginnings by the Witoto gathered by Preuss begin thus:

> a phantasma, naino, nothing else
> the father touched the image of the
>   phantasm
> touch a secret, nothing else
> the father Nainu-ema, who-has-the-phan-
>   tasm, held it by a dream
> to himself
> thought hard about it

Rothenberg translated Preuss's text to great effect in *Technicians of the Sacred*, a foundational work of ethnopoetics.

Studies and anthols. of Tupi-Guaraní poetry and poetics (Cadogan 1959, Bareiro Saguier) have abounded since Montaigne's pioneer commentary, and the trad. has been indispensable to the growth of Brazilian lit. Poems and songs in Lingua Geral were collected in the late 19th c. by João Barbosa Rodrigues, when they could still be heard in the markets and festivals in the lower Amazon. He gave the result of his labors under the hybrid title *Poranduba amazonense*, an abundant anthol. of texts that reserves a special place for the Amazonian midwife. We learn of the greenstone *muiraquitã*, the charm typically carved in the form of early vertebrates like the frog or the fish and bestowed on the father of the female rather than the male child; the lean new moon and the full moon mirrored in the lake that yields the muiraquitã; moons as measures of time, sidereal (27.32 nights) when black-faced incestuous male and synodic (29.54 nights) when female lying in her hammock; and the armadillo (*tatu*), whose dance leads to safety deep in the forest.

In their ed. of Joaquim de Sousândrade's substantial epic *O Guesa* (1888), Augusto and Haroldo de Campos have drawn out the significance of these precedents for the remarkable sequence of cantos known as Tatuturema, the armadillo dance-song that celebrates local understandings of genesis. In the complex societies characteristic of Manaus and the confluence of the Amazon with the Rio Negro, Lingua Geral also preserved the legends and the night music generated by the "devil" Jurupari (Medeiros).

Jurupari, himself a recalcitrant product of the midwife cult and the focus of a major epic, affirms his gender and his origins by tracing them to the Milky Way and a gestation period said to last ten (sidereal) moons rather than the usual nine (synodic). He does this when literally orchestrating his federation. He bestows on each of its 11+3 wind instruments, seen and played exclusively by males, word-poem definitions, each belonging to a distinct lang. or dialect of multilingual Manaus, overall Arawak to the east and Tucano to the west. Jurupari appears as the lure in the *Travels on the Amazon and Rio Negro* of Charles Darwin's contemp. A. F. Wallace (ch. 17) and, after him, in Oscar Wilde's *The Picture of Dorian Gray* (ch. 11).

The Mbya Guaraní *Ayvu rapyta* epitomizes lowland South America as a poetics of dreaming the world into being that is simultaneously cosmogony, a genesis poetic in dealing with primordial origins (Cadogan 1959). In the Carib trad., it is matched as such by *Watunna* of the Soto and by the Makunaima corpus of their Pemon neighbors. Recalled in poetically dense Adeni (a kind of script within speech) and ritually recited at the annual harvest festival of its name, *Watunna* (Civrieux) recounts the felling of the great tree whose branches and roots conjoined sky and earth and whose petrified stump is the Marahuaca massif, the Soto homeland in Venezuela. The felling precipitates a great flood and reveals Marahuaca to be a watershed common via the (hydrographically improbable) Casiquiare canal to both the Amazon and the Orinoco.

The felled tree also initiates the saga of agriculture, the first seedlings being brought from

Roraima, a petrified tree stump to the northeast and a botanical El Dorado fondly recalled in Pemon dream songs. While people work in the fields learning to plant from the birds, the known loners tapir and jaguar engage in a wry dialogue that opposes the former's slow wits with the keen senses of the latter in the wild forests of the night (William Blake's bright-burning tiger began life as a jaguar from Surinam). The climax of the whole planting saga comes when Huioo, the great water snake, seeing all the birds flying resplendent above, leaps up in the air to join them, crying "I want my feather crown." There could hardly be a clearer pointer to the multiple meanings embodied in the hybrid bird-reptile figure revered throughout the continent and seminal in Mesoamerican genesis as the plumed serpent Quetzalcoatl.

Gathered by Theodor Koch-Grünberg, the Pemon texts deal with these and cognate motifs, like love for an evanescent fish bride, a fearsome father-in-law figure, and the trickster evident elsewhere in Carib lit. that came to inspire Mário de Andrade's epochal novel *Macunaíma* (1928).

In Surinam, the story of the Trio culture hero Pereperewa lends Carib creation a particular resonance at the moment when he is taken by his fish bride to meet her alligator father, who proves to be a creature of many simultaneous identities (Rivière). Reflected in the dark waters of the river, his red cayman eyes produce terror, as does his size as he rises to reveal the load he carries on his back like a canoe, a word synonymous with *alligator*. Surviving the encounter, Pereperewa learns the advantages of cultivation, in food he is able to take back to his people: peanuts, chili peppers, squash, and the Amazonian staple manioc.

Archaeology is now corroborating the deeper reverberations of the Pereperewa story, fine example of Carib poetry that it is, in a cultural coherence that runs for millennia along the entire length of the Amazon. Toward the headwaters in the west, in the ancient city of Chavin, an obelisk carved about three millennia ago to represent two caimans and named after the Peruvian who excavated the city in the 1920s, Julio Tello, identifies the achievements of Amazonian agriculture as the "gifts of the caiman," specifying exactly the same examples as the Trio do today, far away toward the mouth of the Amazon.

If Tupi-Guaraní and Carib texts indicate the ancient and rich relationship between lowland South America and the Andes, so too do those of a third major Amazonian group, the Bororo-Gé, with whom Claude Lévi-Strauss in the 1930s began the work that culminated in the four volumes of *Mythologiques* (1964–71), the Bororo being the author of his primary myth. In their own *Enciclopédia* (1962–76), the Bororo highlight the dual role of the jaguar, founding father both terrestrial as the occupant of the last of the 7 caves and celestial as the first of the 11 constellations to rise over the eastern horizon. Implicit throughout their culture and songs and quite explicit in their painted jaguar skins (*adugo biri*), the significance of the Bororo pair of prime numbers 7 and 11 can, in its turn, be traced back to stonework at Chavin. There, to either hand in the great circular court, pairs of jaguars with such night-sky identification process toward the exit.

In the Muisca kingdoms that are now Colombia (Krickeberg), lowland precedent is celebrated in the corpus of greenstones directly reminiscent of the muiraquitã. One such from Sopó, adorned with the customary midwife motifs of frog and fish, is illustrated in Alexander von Humboldt's great work *Vues des cordillères et monuments des peuples indigènes de l'Amérique* (1810, plate 44), where it merits a commentary as substantial as that he accords to the Mexica Sunstone (plate 23). This logs the Guesa's indiction at 15 years (when the annual difference between sun and moon amounts to 15 nights and the difference between synodic and sidereal cycles of the moon amounts to 15 moons). Drawing on accounts of Muisca belief recorded by Pedro Simón and others, Humboldt's commentary on this greenstone directly inspired the first attempts in independent Lat. Am. at the cl. Eur. epic genre, not only *O Guesa* but Andrés Bello's *Silvas americanas* (1823).

Within the larger Chibcha category, in lang. the Muisca are kindred of the Kogi of northern Colombia, the Cuna of Panama, and the Talamanca of Costa Rica. Kogi songs and legends are notable for naming the 11 constellations that match those of the Bororo and Desana in Amazonia and for monitoring the now ever-higher snow line in their mountains. A prime focus for the Cuna is the declaration by Nele de Kantule of the isthmian republic in 1925 within but independent of Panama.

Extensive and often recorded as verse or incantation in its own local script, Cuna lit. hinges on the *ikala* or "way," a mode proper to curing, initiation, the rhythms of the moon

(*Ni*), childbirth (*Mu*), supporting the dead on the journey into the afterlife (*Serkan*), therapy, cosmogony (*Pap*), and political hist. that, in being inseparable from *myth*, is necessarily poetic. Performed over the course of a night once every moon, women sitting in a middle circle with men on three sides of the room, the most comprehensive is the *Tatkan ikala*, which stretches from beginnings of the world to the present. It falls into four parts: cosmic comings into being; epic deeds of culture heroes (*Neles*); migrations and foundings of villages; and the invasion from Europe and its current consequences (Kramer).

Echoes of Amazonia are constant: the first forefather's two wives, one brown/black, the other white; the felling of the great tree of life, *Palu uala*, and the consequent flood; lunar incest instigated by the brother who advances on his sister's hammock in the dead of night, she being able to stain his face black, the whole being explicitly referred to the female synodic moon and the quicker male sidereal moon; and successive catastrophes inflicted on the world (flood, darkness, storm, warfare) that elaborate the world-age genesis story.

Diagnostic of the Chibcha territory common to the Muisca and the Cuna are creatures and objects formed of gold, the man named El Dorado celebrated in Muisca myth and goldwork and known as Organ in the ikala, and the specifically Cuna *Olopatte*, the golden platter on which early heroes arrive on earth. Also, explicit in the *Pap ikala*, though rare in world-age genesis in South America, is the epic that follows the course of the inner planets (Mercury and Venus), which appear to pass through the underworld in moving from the western sunset to the eastern dawn.

II. Tahuantinsuyu. In Quechua, the lang. of the Inca empire, *Tahuantinsuyu* means four districts. Montaigne finds poetry in its road system and sheer social organization: the causeway that ran "straight, even and fine" from Quito to Cuzco and the well-stocked palatial inns (*tambos*) along the way. Returning in conclusion to his title and theme ("Des coches"), he admires the blind courage of those who tried unsuccessfully to save Atahuallpa, in his litter, from Francisco Pizarro, in a tragedy that, unknown to Montaigne, entered the cycle of Quechua kingship drama (Lara 1957, 1969).

The early 17th-c. Quechua text known as the *Huarochirí Manuscript* (1991) makes clear the antiquity of the Tahuantinsuyu concept, tracing its beginnings to the deeds of Huarochirí's own culture hero Pariacaca. Commemorated by a stairway that joins Apurimac and the headwaters of the Amazon to Rimac (Lima) on the Pacific coast, Pariacaca starts life as a glorious snow-covered mountain on Huarochirí's horizon. With cosmic force, Pariacaca tames both the rainforest Antisuyu and the coastal Condesuyu, the latter supplying his demand for spondylus or thorny redshell oyster. Brought fresh to the highlands from the equatorial seas of Ecuador, spondylus had value as shell adornment and as shellfish delectable to eat. The bivalve spondylus (*mullo*) stands most tellingly as the initial glyph on the Tello obelisk at Chavin, and its mouth-womb is a motif in coastal ceramics, notably among the Moche, 1–500 CE.

Through his son, Pariacaca sets up the first Tahuantinsuyu dynasty, which passing through Ayacucho and other centers, eventually becomes Inca in Cuzco. Archaeologically, the fourfold Tahuantinsuyu emblem—the open Andean cross—is to be seen on the Tello obelisk, opposing Antisuyu caiman to Condesuyu spondylus, with Chinchasuyu extending to the north and Collasuyu to the south. Unambiguous and unmistakable, this open-cross emblem is also found in the isthmus, suggesting widespread recognition north and west of Chinchasuyu, to the very threshold of Anahuac.

As evidence of idolatry gathered by the mestizo priest Francisco de Ávila (who provided a brief Sp. trans. of the earlier chapters), the *Huarochirí* text leaves little doubt about the power of pagan belief in world-age genesis expressed through worship of *huacas* (phenomena, natural and constructed, of imposing size and significance), in cults centered typically on mountains like Pariacaca, the stairway over its shoulder that links Amazonian Apurimac with Rimac and canals on the continental watershed engineered to reverse the water flow in favor of Antisuyu and Amazonia. The narrative begins with the initial pair of destructions of the world through flood and solar eclipse; before each, a llama, through its finer senses, warns its duller human masters of approaching catastrophe, and each is tied to a period of five days. Though the biblical parallel is acknowledged in the flood, in the Andes, people are saved not by Noah but a mountain they flee toward. The eclipse provokes the uprising of pastoral creatures like the llama who foresaw it, a rebellion that results from the breaking of the interspecies contract that enables pastoralism in the first place. Christian ideology was seen to have broken this contract by privileging human over other life.

Thereafter, attention focuses on Pariacaca himself as main actor in the world-age genesis. Raining down volcanic fire, he destroys the primeval cannibal Caruincho, along with Caruincho's consort, and sets up Huaca guardians toward both Amazonia (Antisuyu) and the ocean (Condesuyu), thereby explicitly establishing the beginnings of Tahuantinsuyu. He then punishes the neighboring Colli for failing to respect fundamental laws of hospitality, sending them winds of hurricane force, evidence being found in eroded rocks of human shape. Like the first pair of catastrophes of flood and eclipse, this pair of events—rain of fire and hurricane—too is tied to periods of five days each, a score in all.

A first concern in the *Huarochirí* text is Pariacaca's precedence over the main god in the Inca system, Viracocha. In Quechua, Viracocha is the focus of extensive liturgy, most concisely the hymns or prayers of the Zithuwa ritual (Rowe 1953) that accords him the epithets *earth-maker, lightning, guardian of crops,* and *herder of humans and llamas alike*.

A work contemp. with the *Huarochirí* narrative, Guamán Poma's (ca. 1535–1616) *El primer nueva corónica y buen gobierno* (ca. 1615; see Murra and Adorno), registers the very geography of the Inca Tahuantinsuyu in terms of the music, dance, and song characteristic of each quarter and the metropolitan center, Cuzco. Intercalated with page-framed images, this alphabetic text in Quechua and Sp. notes its immediate source as quipu records. In its own version of world-age genesis, people of each successive world age are distinguished by such features as clothing, houses, and style of prayer. Poma's work reveres the pastoral llama, who at the *raymi* solstice festival literally gives the keynote for the Inca emperor to begin the songs and music proper to Cuzco at the center of the four *suyu*.

El Inca Garcilaso de le Vega (1539–1616) gives a privileged version of this heritage in his Comentarios reales (1609), also contemp. with the *Huarochirí* narrative and Poma's *Corónica*. Garcilaso confirms the literary functions of the quipu in recording poetry and chronicle, as well as counts of llama herds and people. He includes a hymn collected by Blas Valera (1545–97) in a trilingual version—Quechua, Sp., and Eng.—as well as a love poem, measures of his taste as courtly scion of the imperial Inca. The two Quechua poems quoted by Garcilaso had the egregious distinction of being chosen by J. G. Herder as "voices of the people in song" (*Stimmen der Völker in Liedern*), songs of wild Am. people at that ("die Wilden"). Persuasive as Herder's sense of *Stimmen* may be, his venture into Inca hymnology exemplarily signals a mismatch between beginnings of Eur. romantic need and this branch of Am. poetics with its courtly pastoral underpinnings:

> Viracocha, you say
> may the sun be, may the night be
> in peace, in safety
> sun, shine on and illume
> the Incas, the people, the servants
> whom you have shepherded

The kingship verse drama *Apu Ollanta* (1735) exerted such strong appeal in colonial times that Spain outlawed performances of it after Tupac Amaru II's uprising of 1780, which foreshadowed independence. Deriving from the Quechua *haraui* (elegiac song; cf. *haravek*, the term for poet) and integrated early into *Spanish prosody, the verse form known as the *yaraví* enjoyed great appeal during this period, thanks initially to the martyr poet Mariano Melgar (1790–1815), while Wallparamachi and his guerrilla fighters sang in Quechua to further their struggle. Extremely sensitive accounts of similar forms in context, like the *huayno* and the *jailli*, are found in the novels and essays of José María Arguedas (1911–69), the anthropologist-poet who compiled the landmark collection *Canto Kechwa* (1938). The resilient huayno conjoins native and mestizo and respects distinctive styles in Huamanga, Apurimac, and elsewhere (Rowe 1996). Some idea of the powerful political charge these trads. acquired during the Sendero Luminoso (Shining Path) era can be had from the well-titled volume *Sangre de los cerros* (1987) by the Montoya brothers. Their broader aesthetic potential is patent in the work of Odi Gonzales (b. 1962) and the trilingual (Quechua, Sp., Eng.), New York-based Fredy Amilcar Roncalla (b. 1953), among others. At the turn of the century (1905), Alencastre, a landowner from Cuzco (see Warak'a 1999), had been preceded at the other end of the social scale by *Tarmap pacha huaray*, an anthol. of Quechua poems from Tarma got together by self-professed pariahs ("unos parias").

Expatriate for much of his life in Paris, the poet César Vallejo (1892–1938) repeatedly acknowledged a debt to his Andean birthplace, from the exquisitely figured gold panels of the Cuzco Coricancha (*Nostalgias imperiales*, 1918) and the wave-and-step motifs of the coastal architecture (*Escalas melografiadas*, 1923) to the drama of Inca power (*La piedra cansada*, 1938), based on a legend told in Poma's chronicle.

Poetry in Ecuador is known in Quichua, a version of the Inca Quechua that, dating back to Atahuallpa's Quito, has its own Amazon approaches (Harrison). As for Bolivia, the superbly documented study of indigenous lits. in the Andes by Arnold and Dios Yapita has made it possible for the first time in Eng. to appreciate the immense wealth and complexity of the entire region's poetry and poetics. This is strikingly so with regard to the Aymara and Collasuyu precedent for Inca and Quechua practice, within the pastoral economy and ideology characteristic of the Andes, starting with Cuzco's appropriation of Tiahuanaco herds. The authors are able to show how much is owed in Andean song and drama to the Aymara, from the quipu numeracy of tethering and the weft and warp of the textile text to principles of origin and rulership.

Diagonally opposite Chinchasuyu and its extension into Colombia and the isthmus, Collasuyu has its heart in Lake Titicaca and the pastoral wealth of the Aymara in Bolivia (Lara 1947) and finds its southern frontier in what is now Chile. On the other side of this Tahuantinsuyu frontier stand the fiercely resistant Mapuche, who, having held off the Inca, did the same when the Spaniards arrived, to be commemorated in Alonso de Ercilla's epic *La Araucana* (1569–89).

Known as *Ftah Mapu* in their lang. (Mapudungun), Mapuche territory concentrates in the landscape of the southern cordillera (Pire Mahuida) around Lacar and the lakeland passage between Chile and Argentina, which functions likewise as the setting for world-age genesis far more ancient than those nation states. In this case, refuge from the flood is sought in Mount Threng Threng and the fossil-rich strata of Trompul, bones of the fish to which protohumans reverted. *Foro-lil* (bonestone), these fossils kilometers above sea level correspond to nocturnal shades who emerge to haunt as snake, bird, and vampire, with finwings and beady eyes that stare back through time (it was here that such fossils were shown to Darwin during his voyage on the *Beagle*). The floodwater threshed up by the snake Kai-Kai in the mountain lakes finds parallels along the ocean coast in terrifying tidal waves and tsunami known as *tripalafken*. After the catastrophes of the world ages, the Mapuche community clusters around the emblematic tree of the Pacific coastal forests as the face carved in the east-facing Rehue and defers to the insight and curing power of the Machi shaman (most often a woman).

Reflecting the cultural resilience and political wisdom that has enabled them still to defend at least some small part of their territory, the poetry of the Mapuche, reborn in 1966 in the work of Sebastián Queupul (b. 1936), stands out on the continental map. *Ül* (Song) is the title of a 1998 collection of four poets: Leonel Lienlaf (b. 1969), Elicura Chihuailaf (b. 1952), Jaime Luis Huenún (b. 1967), and Graciela Huinao (b. 1956), whose work privileges their native tongue (Vicuña).

Previously recognized and translated into Sp. by the Chilean poet Raúl Zurita (1989), Lienlaf contrives to recover the sensibility that brings together for the Mapuche, in their lang., world-age genesis, military struggle initially against the sword and the Christian cross, and then "pacification" by machine gun on both sides of the Andes. Enduring over "a hundred generations" and threaded into the Rehue and the Machi chant, time is marked in tree growth by *rupamum* (footsteps). This is the time of ancient trans-Andean memories, recorded just after World War I by Kössler-Ilg, that extend from world-age genesis to the late 19th-c. resistance led by Calfucurá.

Chihuailaf is notable for choosing to translate into Mapudungun the fellow Chilean poet Pablo Neruda (1904–73) in *Ti kom vl* (1995). The poems and volumes of Neruda's that Chihuailaf selects, and the way he plays Mapudungun against Sp., brilliantly begin to recover for Chile exactly the imaginative possibilities that Neruda came to dream of during and after his Am. epic *Canto general* (1950). Translated as "Todos los cantos," the title poem breathes local life and hist. into the elegiac image of the trees and stones of Arauco that closes the first canto of Neruda's epic, peopling and enlivening them in ways unsuspected half a century ago.

III. Anahuac. Known as *Anahuac* between the seas, Atlantic to the north and Pacific to the south, and as *Amoxtlan* (the "land of books" in Nahuatl), Mesoamerica has long held a special position in the geography of the continent.

Montaigne's encounter with it is striking, since, as proof of its high civilization, in his second Am. essay he actually cites the cosmic poem of world-age genesis: "They believed the state of the world to be divided into five ages, as in the life of five succeeding Suns, whereof four had already ended their course or time." Montaigne had translated his text from Gómara's Sp., who, in turn, had drawn on Motolinía (pseud. of Fray Toribio de Benavente, 1482–1568), an early extirpator of idolatry in Cholula, deeply familiar with the Nahuatl lang. inherited by the Mexica or Aztecs.

The extant version of this cosmic poem closest to the Nahuatl trad. of the Aztecs and their predecessors is found in the *Cuauhtitlan Annals* (ca. 1570; Bierhorst 1992) and begins:

Y ynin ce tonatiuh onmanca yn itzinecan
4 atl yn itonal
mitoa atonatiuh
yc ipan in ye yquac
yn mochih yn atocoac.
Yn anenenztihuac
yn tlaca michtihuac

Y ynic ome tonatiuh onmanca
4 ocelotl yn tonal catca
motenehua ocelotonatiuh
ypan mochiuh
tlapachiuh yn ylhuicatl

(The first sun to be founded
has the Sign Four Water,
it is called Water Sun.
Then it happened
that water carried everything away
everything vanished
people changed into fish.

The second sun to be founded
has the Sign Four Jaguar
it is called Jaguar Sun.
Then it happened
that the sky broke down)

The Nahuatl text goes on to tell how, since the sun no longer followed its course, night came and, in the dark, people were torn to pieces by jaguars plunging from the sky; this was the time of the giants. In the third sun, called 4 Rain, fire and volcanic ash (*tezontli*) rained down, and rocks boiled and twisted up; in the fourth, 4 Wind, wind carried everything away, and people changed into monkeys. Having of its own accord started to move (a pun on *ollin*, which also denotes both rubber and earthquake), the current fifth sun, 4 Ollin, will end in earthquake and hunger.

Anticipating Western geology and evolutionary theory by several centuries, the cataclysms and metamorphoses of Anahuac genesis take us back to tlacuilolli, the visual lang. of Mesoamerica from which the Nahuatl had been transcribed. Of the several examples of this world-age story that exist on paper and in stone in tlacuilolli, easily the most monumental is the Aztec or Mexica Sunstone or *Piedra de los soles*, the inscribed basalt disk that before the invasion proclaimed the world-age story in Tenochtitlan's Templo Mayor. In chronological terms, the sunstone locates the 5,200 or so years of our current fifth world age, named Nauh (4) Ollin, as a fifth (in the thumb-fingers proportion 1:4) of the precessional year that, in turn, forms a core unit of the many millions of years of genesis inscribed in Maya hieroglyphs and reflected in tlacuilolli.

The recovery of the sunstone in 1790 from under a corner of Mexico City's nearby cathedral enabled Humboldt to publish an image of it with an extensive commentary in his *Vues des cordillères*. Ideologically, the event fomented the independence cause. In poetics, susceptible to decipherment in many pages of alphabetic prose yet succinct and synchronic in its circular form, a map of simultaneity, the sunstone has come to be acknowledged as a superb poem in the visual lang. tlacuilolli. In early 20th-c. Europe, it became the prompt for the first of Guillaume Apollinaire's "concrete" *Calligrammes*, "Lettre-Océan."

In Anahuac, the fullest alphabetic account of this cosmic saga can be found in the *Popol Vuh*, the "Bible of America" written in the mid-16th c., in their lang., by the Maya Quiché of Guatemala. A narrative in paired verses, this text starts from the very beginnings of time and falls into two parts. These hinge on the creation of humankind from maize, a motif developed, e.g., in Classic Period hieroglyphic texts at Palenque that correlate the event with the start of the Olmec and Maya Era just less than 5,200 years ago. In the ingenious way that the text itself offers clues about how they connect and interweave, the main phases of part 1 can be seen to correspond to the sunstone, notably the metamorphoses into fish in the flood of the first age and into monkeys (elder brothers of the Hero Twins) in the hurricane of the fourth; these events are recounted in Nahuatl in the *Cuauhtitlan*

Annals and *Leyenda de los soles*. Esp. vivid and also reflected in Maya art are the domestic revolt in the eclipse in the second age, the Twins' childhood taming of bird-reptile monsters in the volcanic landscape of the third age, and their epic descent to the underworld Xibalba that prepares for the maize creation.

The line of tlacuilolli texts to which the sunstone account belongs begins in the east with the world-age *Map of Coixtlahuaca*, the town that controlled the east-west tribute road taken by the Mexica in the reign of Moctezuma I (1440–69).

At the first level, the *Coixtlahuaca* text is overtly a map of four places subject to that city, which, again in the simultaneity characteristic of tlacuilolli, may be read both as town toponyms and as emblems of the world ages. Mictlan (southeast) and Teotlillan (northeast) recall flood and eclipse, while Nexapa (southwest) and Tepexic (northwest) recall rain of fire and hurricane. While this is the pattern inherited in the sunstone, the Mexica make one critical change. For Coixtlahuaca, the fish-tail caiman seen rising from volcanic ash in Nexapa (curiously reminiscent of the life form inscribed on Chavin's obelisk) reappears above in Tepexic, endowed with Quetzalcoatl feathers, atop a twin peak baring tooth and claw. For Tenochtitlan, the two caimans encircle the disk with imperial might, fish tails above, arms and heads (crowned by the septentrion) below. Moreover, their form invokes the metamorphic Xiuhcoanahual, the ophidian familiar that, for the Mexica, configures world-age genesis and the gyres of time counted out on the literal scales of the sunstone caiman.

The sunstone likewise reworks the central chapter of *Codex Borgia* of Cholula, whose chronicles tell of the road east toward the isthmus and beyond, to Popayan and South America. Like the affine screen-folds *Cospi* and *Vaticanus B*, *Codex Borgia* opens with an eight-page chapter based on human gestation, the 9x29 nights of the *tonalpoualli*, which simultaneously may be read as the succession of suns and in space as a map of Anahuac between north and south seas, dazzling tlacuilolli prospects of tropical America seen from south (east to right) and north (east to left). Read from top to bottom, the 10 + 8 pages of *Borgia* 's central chapter focus rather on Mesoamerica's other main time cycle, the year of 18 Feasts each of 20 days, beginning with the summer solstice, and involve a turn at midwinter from the end of one side of the screen-fold text to the start of the other. In the switch from recto to verso, the text even contrives visually to register the winter solstice as the passage through the underworld followed by the inner planets and the hero twins of the *Popol Vuh*. The codex pages configure a supremely elegant time map of tropical America.

The highland Maya *Popol Vuh* of the Quiché coincides with and interestingly differs on doctrinal points of diet from the genesis account of the neighboring Cakchiquels, on the shores of Lake Atitlan. This focus is also that of the Quiché dance drama *Rabinal Achí*. Like *Ollanta* and other Inca kingship propaganda and like an abundance of missionary plays in Quechua, Tupi, Nahuatl, and other langs. whose roots are deeply pre-Cortesian, this highland Maya work explores the boundaries between verse and theater, as Tedlock expertly shows in his ed. (2003).

The lowland Maya version of world-age genesis, transcribed in part into the alphabet from hieroglyphic stanzas (Alvarez), is found in the *Chilam Balam* books of the towns of Yucatan (Barrera Vásquez and Rendón). The *Book of Chumayel* excels in its witty play with biblical notions of time, the successive invasions of the peninsula in which the Christians come third, and the riddles of Zuyua that are invitations to brilliant conceptual insight formally derived from political tests of candidates for official position in the Katun calendar system.

In the dense polyphonic epic that issues into the current world age and Era, the hieroglyphic antecedent (Dresden Codex) has recently been shown to resolve the long-standing debate about correlating its inaugural date (4 Ahau 8 Cumku) with the Roman calendar (Julian day 584.283 in the year 3114 BCE).

Reflecting on the consequences of Eur. arrival, the *Book of Chumayel* draws on the hieroglyph-based prophecy chronicles of the Katun and Tun calendar cycles. (As *Cuceb*, the latter are meticulously edited in Bierhorst's *Four Masterworks*.) One such prophecy chronicle begins thus:

> [T]he true God, the true Dios, came, but
> this was the origin too of affliction for us.
> The origin of tax, of our giving *them* alms,
> of trial through the grabbing of petty cacao
> money, of trial by blowgun, stomping the
> people, violent removal, forced debt created
> by false testimony, petty litigation, harass-
> ment, violent removal . . .

Such incredulous pain echoes that expressed in Nahuatl in the *Tlatelolco Annals* (1528) and indeed exemplifies a whole mode of postinvasion composition (León-Portilla 1964a).

Because of its scale and ambition in presenting world-age genesis in sharply poetic terms, the *Huarochirí Manuscript* has been referred to as the *Popol Vuh* of the Andes. Apt, the comparison requires that we acknowledge the level of theoretical understanding that, during the second world-age eclipse, may equate the pastoral llamas who rebelled in the Andes with their nearest domesticated equivalents in Mesoamerica, dogs and turkeys.

As the provenance of screen-fold books, notably *Codex Borgia*, Cholula was known as the Rome of New Spain. Guardian of cults stemming from the Olmec, this pyramid city was a major precedent for the Mexica, as they make clear in postinvasion codices like *Telleriano Remensis* and in the Nahuatl of their "Twenty Sacred Hymns."

Looking for evidence of idolatry, the Franciscan missionary Bernardino de Sahagún (ca. 1499–1590), whose 12-book *Florentine Codex* (completed 1577) grew from the four, dense tlacuilolli chapters of the *Tepepulco Manuscript*, found these hymns so devilish and difficult that he refrained from trying to translate them from Nahuatl. He left the originals to an appendix to book 2, while book 6 deals with the challenges posed by Nahuatl poetics. Their huge poetic power was acknowledged by D. G. Brinton in the title he gave to his Eng. trans. *Rig Veda Americanus*, a key volume in his Philadelphia Library of Aboriginal American Literature series (1882–90). An important way of facing the difficulty posed by the hymns has proved to be recognizing their dependence on the rich poetic capacity of tlacuilolli. The hymn to the rain god Tlaloc, e.g., relies on a multiple pun involving the semantics of the XX Signs, their respective numbers in the series as Snake lightning (V), Jaguar thunder (XIV), and Rain (XIX), and the sheer phenomenon of storm. The arithmetic (V + XIV = XIX) is clearly legible in the hypnotic image of Tlaloc seen on the penultimate page of a book from Teotlillan (*Codex Laud* 45), where this rainmaker is revered as *ocelocoatl*, the Jaguar-Snake of the Nahuatl hymn, and can be seen roaring thunder from under his elaborate Jaguar headdress, while holding the Snake scepter of lightning.

A similar case is the celebration of Itzpapalotl, the Obsidian Butterfly (hymn 4), whose name in tlacuilolli when read as a calendrical date comprises numbers belonging to the set of 9 Night Powers (*Yoalitecutin*) and the 13 Fliers (*Quecholli*). Central to these 13 as number 7, the butterfly's metamorphic body conjoins the vitreous edge that, like obsidian, is sharp but brittle with the beauty of the wing that, lacking the vertebrate strength of the other 6+6 fliers, is easily damaged. Relying on the fact that Hermes (Mercury) goes around the sun 22 times every seven years, Itzpapalotl's hermetic teachings underlie the considerable corpus of Chichimec lit. in which, abused and seeking vengeance, she leads the Chichimec archers south into the tropics from Chicomoztoc, their desert fastness that translates as "Seven Caves." As the eponymous *Mariposa de obsidiana* (in Garibay's trans., 1958), Itzpapalotl also prompted one of the most powerful poems in Octavio Paz's (1914–98) *Águila o sol* (1950).

In order to function practically, the Mexica tribute system relied on a multilevel arithmogram that correlates the districts in the quarters west, south, east, and north of Tenochtitlan with the tonalpoualli nights of human gestation, synodic and sidereal moons, and the days of the year. The tribute due from each district is listed in the tlacuilolli *Matrícula de tributos*, to which *Codex Mendoza* adds a map (a quincunx oriented to west). The analogies to Cuzco's Tahuantinsuyu are strong, and, in each case, songs served as tribute items of value that characterized cultural geography. Demanding the performance of a song in the lang. and style of a region was a right of conquest in Cuzco and Tenochtitlan alike, which links further back again to the Tupi carbet.

In the imperial court of Tenochtitlan, this practice helped form the collection of poems known as *Cantares mexicanos*. Copious, this Nahuatl work encompasses poems both ancient, like a Toltec lament that also appears in the *Popol Vuh*, and mod., like those that parody Christian liturgy. Revealing overall the immense richness inherent in the Nahuatl term for poetry itself (*xochi-cuicatl*, "flower-song"), it draws on well-recognized modes proper to mourning ("orphan"), planting ("green"), and war ("enemy").

After the invasion, analogous encodings of precious knowledge in concept and number continue to inform the shamanic rhet. of ritual cure, as in the Maya *Ritual of the Bacabs* (Arzápalo) and the Nahuatl *Tratado* of 1629.

The range and power of native poetry in contemp. Mexico are evidenced in the first volume of Carlos Montemayor's *Escritores indígenas actuales* (1992). A strength of this volume is to show the survival of poetic speech in the three main lang. families of Mexico, Otomanguan, Maya, and Nahuatl. In Otomi, Thaayrohyadi Bermúdez appeals to that people (and their Purépecha neighbors) who have lived longest along its banks for the life and health of the river Lerma, threatened as it increasingly is by attitudes and policies rooted in the exploitative ideology of the invasion begun by Christopher Columbus. Its concentration on the idea of water, primal and unpolluted, curiously echoes what is known of the celebrated poet-king of Texcoco, Nezahualcoyotl (1402–72), named in the *Cantares mexicanos*, whose first compositions are recorded in Otomi.

We have seen the bridging role of the isthmus between Meso- and South America corroborated from the east in the Andean cross emblem *chakana* found in the ceramic codex of Yojoa in the ambit of the Maya metropolis Copan (Honduras), while from the west, Nahuatl lies at the root of the names *Guatemala*, *Cuzcatlan* (El Salvador), and *Nicaragua*. A theater piece focused on the tall tales of the widely traveled *pochteca* (trader and tax collector) published in Brinton's library as *The Gueguënce: A Comedy-Ballet in the Nahuatl-Spanish Dialect of Nicaragua* (1883) reveals wit sustained by the intense cultural traffic to and fro along the isthmus. For its part, the ceramic codex of Yojoa in the Ulua homeland of the Lenca juxtaposes motifs that include the Olmec caiman whose maw is a cave, the dancing armadillo of the Amazonian midwives, the literal runner bean of coastal Peruvian ceramics, the jaguar defending the night with tooth bared and claw unsheathed, the monkey *pochteca*, the rebellious turkey of the eclipse, the craftsman whose deep inspiration flows vertebrally from a fishy forebear, and well-dressed Maya dignitaries of the nearby metropolis Copan, also in Honduras.

In mod. times, the isthmus spirit can be seen to suffuse the remarkable line of Nicaraguan poets Rubén Darío (1867–1916), Pablo Antonio Cuadra (1912–2002), and Ernesto Cardenal (b. 1925), who have all recognized native America as a chief source. The poems in Cardenal's *Homenaje a los indios americanos* (1970) work directly from native texts from the entire continent. Before him, Cuadra had found a manifold reference for his poetry in the *doble yo* (double I) concept, a human head that is shielded by and beneath a back and head that belong to a powerful beast. This motif is seen alike in Amazonian stone sculpture, in San Agustín at the headwaters of the Magdalena in Colombia, in the isthmus and, most magnificently, in the statues of Maya potentates. As for Darío, the *modernista* founder of Sp. Am. poetry, he spoke for his work and the movement as a whole when, in the "Palabras liminares" to *Prosas profanas* (1896), he wrote that, if poetry was to be found in "nuestra América," then it would be in the old things, in the legendary Indian, the refined and sensual Inca, the lowland and highland Maya cities of Palenque and Utatlan, and the great Moctezuma's golden throne. The Otomanguan family is also represented by Zapotec, in Victor de la Cruz's (b. 1948) *Guchachi' Reza*, supported by artist Francisco Toledo, which has included trans. of Bertolt Brecht's poetry. For its part, like that of Rigoberta Menchú (b. 1959), the work of the contemp. Maya Quiché poet Humberto Ak'abal (b. 1952) defends the Maya world in his native lang. and in Sp. as living perception.

IV. Turtle Island. A century and a half after Montaigne, Anahuac's northern continuity with parts of America now occupied by the U.S. and Canada inspired Lorenzo Boturini (1702–1753), a student of Giambattista Vico, to write *Idea de una nueva historia de la América septentrional* (1746). The base of mod. codices scholarship, this "new idea" relies heavily on the royal library built up by Nezahualcoyotl (Lee) in Texcoco, on the east bank of the highland lake, which Boturini cataloged and tried to reassemble. Texcoco is the focus of the *Romances de los Señores de la Nueva España*, an extensive anthol. of Nahuatl poetry that complements the *Cantares mexicanos* of Tenochtitlan on the west bank, being similarly based on both ancient memory and current tribute practice (Garibay 1964–68).

In documenting their origins in Texcoco, Nezahualcoyotl and his ancestors celebrated the Chichimec saga that had first brought them south across the tropical line from the 7th c. on, led by the obsidian butterfly Itzpapalotl from their homeland Chicomoztoc (Seven Caves). Visually, the most brilliant version of this saga is to be found in *Codex Borgia*, where the butterfly is seen about to emerge from her cocoon under seven caves marked by the stars of the septentrion, on a path that leads east, north, and west before plunging south. For its part, at Tepexic the Coixtlahuaca map establishes the hermetic nature of her teachings, literally, by correlating in Seven Caves the cycles of the moon and the planet Mercury (Hermes), in the synodic formula that approximates the nights of four moons with the 116 of the planet, and the sidereal formula that does the same for three moons and 88 nights of the planet.

Exactly this hermetic logic pervades corresponding sagas of crossing the tropical line told by those who live north of it, northwest of Mesoamerica. The exemplary case is that of the Zuni, who as neighbors have the Keres-speaking Pueblo to the east and the Hopi (in speech, kin to the Nahua) to the west. Culturally, the coherence of this landscape has long been embodied in the quincunx of mountains seen in Pueblo murals, which later gave shape to the sand or dry paintings of the Navajo, and their corresponding chants or ways (Wyman). The novel *Ceremony* (1976) by the Laguna Pueblo Leslie Marmon Silko (b. 1948) focuses on Tsepina, the turquoise mountain closest to home, later called Tsodzil by the Navajo, where it generates power both poetic and therapeutic. The same power imbues the verse in her *Storyteller* (1981).

In their genesis, the Zuni emerge through rooms that are world ages, upward, as in the architecture of multistory Pueblo houses. They then migrate to find their location on the Continental Divide, between the headwaters of the Rio Grande (southeast) and those of the Colorado River (southwest). Recalled in ceremonies over the year and in corresponding iconography in underground *kiva* temples, the story falls into episodes and culminates in the arrival of Sp. invaders from Mexico, who were successfully resisted, and then of the U.S. in the last years of the 19th c. When the U.S. was still invading, a particularly sensitive account of this trad. was given by Frank Cushing, who learned the Zuni lang. and went to live among them. A century later, Tedlock published versions performed in his presence in *Finding the Center*, a magnificent work that adjusts typography to the needs of ethnopoetics.

Identified at dawn by the macaw feather he wears in his hair as he rises before the sun heliacally, the Zuni hero Nepayatamu by night is honored at the kiva shrine of the Milky Way Newekwe. From the four sides of Newekwe and after four moons, he hails his planet's return, sheltering the metamorphic butterfly in his flute. He shares these hermetic characteristics with counterparts among the Pueblo to the east like the "Sun youth" in Boas's *Keresan Texts* and among the much-visited Hopi, where the butterfly is enshrined at Awatobi and where, journeying back and forth across the tropical line, it is inseparable from genesis and the birth of maize. Throughout this territory, in the hermetic butterfly complex, there are specific and striking echoes of the poetry and visual art of Anahuac, particularly the major cities of Teotihuacan and Cholula.

In the story they tell of themselves as invaders of the Pueblo in *Diné Bahane'* (Zolbrod), the Navajo make many of these connections plain. The case of the Apache is comparable, and as Athapaskan relatives, they defended together a last frontier that stretched from Mexico and Apacheria to the Black Hills of Dakota.

The debt to the Anahuac codices, esp. their quatrefoil and quincunx maps, is patent in the sand or dry paintings laid out on the hogan floor to complement the therapeutic chants of the Navajo ways over as many as nine nights. Mutually enriching each other as they do in tlacuilolli fashion as visual and verbal lang., the dry paintings and the chants may fairly be regarded as literary bedrock among the Navajo, a celebrated example being the *Kledzhe Hatal* (*Night Chant*, last of Bierhorst's four masterworks). Moreover, this is a living trad., from which poets who write in Navajo, like Luci Tapahonso (b. 1953), may draw strength.

In defining territory, the Navajo paintings serve as an excellent guide to cultural hist. Toward the Great Plains that stretch northeast beyond the mountains, we see and hear the buffalo. Shot steadily after 1864 from transcontinental trains so as to starve still-resistant Indians to death, the buffalo embodies time and life itself on the plains. According to the Sioux Winter Counts by High Hawk and Brown Hat (Mallery), it is Buffalo Woman who brings the first gifts to the peoples of the plains, the tobacco peace pipe, maize of four colors and in all its preparations, the tipi circle, and their respective songs, which become a main ingredient in the dazzling visions of Black Elk.

Belief in the return of the buffalo to the plains was fundamental to the Ghost Dance of 1890, coincident with the Wounded Knee massacre. To remain undaunted in the face of ever more violent white assault, tribes from Mexico to Canada and from California to Oklahoma gave each other their songs, ascribing to them the value they had had as tribute items among the Aztecs and the Inca. The trance sought in the songs brought back, too, the ghosts of many thousands of the fallen. On those grounds, Bierhorst (1985) has argued strongly for detecting a similar dimension in the *Cantares mexicanos*.

"We shall live again," a main refrain in the songs heard by such poets as Gary Snyder (b. 1930) and echoed repeatedly in subsequent U.S. mass movements, implies concern with beginnings, notably among the Arapaho and Cheyenne, a principal contingent in the dance (Mooney 1896). The tongue of both is Algonkian, called the "language of America" by Roger Williams in 1643, which stretches east across the continent to include those who first encountered the Eng. in Massachusetts, in Manhattan, and with Powhatan. Algonkian genesis is typified in the song to the turtle (Bruchac), which, floating in the cosmic ocean, has borne the weight of the earth itself since "the beginning of human existence."

Adherence to this "floating island" version of Am. genesis became paramount among the Algonkian-speaking Ojibwa, midway between west and east around the frontier lakes that feed the uppermost Mississippi (a focus mapped in Lévi-Strauss's *Mythologiques*). Before Europeans arrived, these beliefs sustained the Midewiwin, a shamanic society where initiation demanded knowledge of sacred songs whose syllables and stanzas correspond to designs inscribed on birch-bark scrolls (Dewdney). This Mide writing seemed dangerous enough to Anglican missionaries to warrant suppression and Christian replacements, likewise on birch bark but printed alphabetically. Through his Ojibwa wife, Schoolcraft gained privileged insight into this trad. (see also Carr).

Among much else, texts in Mide script graphically chart the chants of genesis, the trance journey through zenith and nadir (in which in shamanic time nights are years, as they can be in the Winter Counts, as indeed they actually are near the pole), and the power of Manito. Widely shared Algonkian belief in the trance journey much strengthened the uprisings led by the Ottawa Pontiac in 1761 and by his Shawnee successor Tecumseh. Depicted in the scrolls, one of the five most powerful Manitos is the turtle who sustains the earth. Represented ubiquitously in the artwork of Turtle Island, this creature inaugurates the epic of the Lenape (Delaware), of which Constantine Samuel Rafinesque provided a version in Mide script entitled *Walum Olum* (1836; later included in Brinton's Philadelphia library). The importance of these precedents today are made clear in the example of Gerald Vizenor (b. 1934), the Ojibwa novelist who began his career by compiling an anthol. of poetry in his lang.

In northern Appalachia, these beliefs were incorporated into the Iroquoian genesis, which is why, in his *Sketches of Ancient History of the Six Nations* (1825), the Iroquois historian Cusick referred to the whole of America north of Mexico as Turtle Island, distinguishing it from lands farther south with their early knowledge of maize and of humankind's simian forebears (this before Darwin). Belief among the Canadian Iroquois in the turtle that created the island which became the first earth was noted by the Jesuit Joseph-François Lafitau (1681–1746) in 1724. The turtle that can burrow to the very heart of the earth is invoked in the curing chants written by the Cherokee (Iroquoian neighbors in Appalachia) in their Sequoya syllabary (Mooney 1992). The syllabary texts draw likewise on shared Iroquoian reverence for maize as one of the three sisters who are the "three graces" in their common agricultural hist., maize, beans, and squash. Graphic antecedents may be found in the mound culture ceramics at Cahokia.

The syllabary texts also respect the power of mound-builder forebears in southern Appalachia who, according to the chants, still live inside the Cherokee mounds, as a hidden resource in defense. Thereby they establish effective links, often in precise detail, with cultural norms current over a thousand years ago, detected today also among the Yuchi and the Musgokee and their neighbors.

Apart from impinging on the initial framing of the U.S. constitution, the Five (later Six) Nations of the Iroquois left a magnificent record of themselves in their *Ritual of Condolence*, another of Bierhorst's four masterworks. The rhet. relied on what Lafitau called the council style of the Iroquois; its chronology was extensive, and, in it, nights could count for years.

Farther west, connections can be made with Iroquoian speakers beyond the Mississippi, such as the Caddo and the Pawnee, whose Hako ceremony entered western poetics in 1900, having been recorded on the ethnologist Alice Fletcher's (1838–1923) phonograph.

At the turn on the 20th c., H. W. Longfellow's "Hiawatha" (1855) was massively propagated throughout the U.S. school system and was the most read and performed poem of its day. Founder of the Iroquois League of Nations, its eponymous hero lives a life heavily reliant on Algonkian legend, as critics never tire of noting. What tends to be less noticed is the imaginative precision of Mide song symbols in the Eng.-lang. poem and Turtle Island perspectives that had been shared in any case by both Algonkian and Iroquois. Perhaps yet more consequentially, "Hiawatha" proved to be a major factor in Carl Jung's hypothesis of the collective unconscious and his break with Sigmund Freud.

See GUARANÍ POETRY, INUIT POETRY, MAPUCHE POETRY, NAVAJO POETRY.

■ H. R. Schoolcraft, *Historical and Statistical Information Respecting the History, Condition and Prospects of the Indian Tribes of the United States* (1851–57); H. Hale, *The Iroquois Book of Rites* (1883); *The Lenape and Their Legends* (1884); *Ancient Nahuatl Poetry* (1887); and *Rig Veda Americanus: Sacred Songs of the Ancient Mexicans* (1890), all ed. and trans. D. G. Brinton; G. Mallery, *Picture-Writing of the American Indians* (1893); J. Mooney, *The Ghost-Dance Religion and the Sioux Outbreak of 1890* (1896); A. C. Fletcher, *Indian Story and Song from North America* (1900); K. T. Preuss, *Die Religion und Mythologie der Uitoto* (1921); M. Austin, *The American Rhythm* (1923); R. Harcourt and M. d'Harcourt, *La musique des Incas et ses survivances* (1925); F. Boas, *Keresan Texts* (1928); W. Krickeberg, *Märchen der Azteken und Inkaperuaner, Maya und Musica* (1928); J. M. Arguedas, *Canto Keshwa* (1938); A. M. Garibay, *Poesía indígena de la Altiplanicie* (1940); J. Lara, *Poesía popular quechua* (1947); A. G. Day, *The Sky Clears: Poetry of the American Indians* (1951); N. M. Holmer, *The Complete Mu-Igala in Picture-Writing: A Native Record of a Cuna Indian Medicine Song* (1953); J. H. Rowe, "Eleven Inca Prayers from the Zithuwa Ritual," *Kroeber Anthropological Society Papers* 8–9 (1953); B. Kössler-Ilg, *Indianermärchen aus den Kordilleren* (1956); *El libro de los cantares de Dzitbalche*, ed. A. Barrera Vásquez (1956); J. M. Arguedas, *The Singing Mountaineers: Song and Tales of the Quechua* (1957), and *Floresta literaria de la América indígena* (1957); J. Alcina Franch, *Floresta literaria de la Améica indígena* (1957); J. Lara, *Tragedia del fin de Atawallpa* (1957); A. M. Garibay, *Veinte himnos sacros de los nahuas* (1958); *Ayvu rapyta*, ed. L. Cadogan (1959); *Anthologie des mythes, legends et contes populaires d'Amérique*, ed. B. Péret (1960); M. A. Asturias, *Poesía precolombina* (1960); K. A. Nowotny, *Tlacuilolli: Die mexikanischen Bilderhandschriften, Stil und Inhalt* (1961); A. Barrera Vásquez and S. Rendón, *El libro de los Libros de Chilam Balam* (1963); N. M. Holmer, *Dos cantos shamanísticos de los indios cunas* (1963); A. M. Garibay, *Poesía náhuatl* (1964–68); M. León-Portilla, *Las literaturas precolombinas de México* (1964a), and *El reverso de la conquista: Relaciones aztecas, mayas e incas* (1964b); *La literatura de los Guaraníes*, ed. L. Cadogan (1965); J. Lara, *La literatura de los quechuas* (1969); P. Rivière, *Marriage among the Trio* (1969); M. de Civrieux, *Watunna: An Orinoco Creation Cycle*, trans. D. Guss (1970); F. W. Kramer, *Literature among the Cuna Indians* (1970); M. Edmonson, *The Book of Counsel: The Popol Vuh of the Quiché Maya of Guatemala* (1971); G. Reichel-Dolmatoff, *Amazonian Cosmos: The Sexual and Religious Symbolism of the Tukano Indians* (1971); J. Rothenberg, *Shaking the Pumpkin: Traditional Poetry of the Indian North Americas* (1972); D. Tedlock, *Finding the Center: Narrative Poetry of the Zuni Indians* (1972); E. Cardenal, *Homage to the American Indians*, trans. M. Altschul and C. Altschul (1973); M. C. Alvarez, *Textos coloniales del Libro de Chilam Balam de Chumayel y textos glíficos del Códice de Dresde* (1974); J. Bierhorst, *Four Masterworks of American Indian Literature: Quetzalcoatl, The Ritual of Condolence, Cuceb, The Night Chant* (1974); S. Dewdney, *The Sacred Scrolls of the Southern Ojibway* (1975); G. Brotherston, *Image of the New World: The American Continent Portrayed in Native Texts* (1979); R. Bareiro Saguier, *Literatura guaraní del Paraguay* (1980); G. Poma, *El primer nueva corónica y buen gobierno*, ed. J. V. Murra and R. Adorno (1980); "*In Vain I Tried to Tell*": *Essays in Native American Ethnopoetics*, ed. D. H. Hymes (1981); G. Vizenor, *Summer in the Spring: Ojibwa Lyric Poems and Tribal Stories* (1981); P. G. Roe, *The Cosmic Zygote: Cosmology in the Amazon Basin* (1982); T. Meneses, *Teatro quechua colonial* (1983); *Songs from This Earth on Turtle's Back*, ed. J. Bruchac (1983); L. C. Wyman, *Southwest Indian Dry Painting* (1983); *Treatise of Ruiz de Alarcón* [1629], ed. J. R. Andrews and R. Hassig (1984); *Diné Bahané: The Navajo Creation Story* (1984), trans. P. Zolbrod; J. Bierhorst, *Cantares mexicanos: Songs of the Aztecs* (1985); *Technicians of the Sacred*, ed. J. Rothenberg, 2d ed. (1985); M. León-Portilla, *Coloquios y doctrina Cristiana: Los diálogos de 1524* (1986); R. Arzápalo Marín, *El ritual de los bacabes* (1987); R. E. Montoya and L. Montoya, *La sangre de los cerros* (1987); J. Sherzer and A. C. Woodbury, *Native American Discourse: Poetics *and Rhetoric* (1987); R. Harrison, *Signs, Songs and Memory in the Andes: Translating the Quechua Language and Culture* (1989); F. Salomon, *The Huarochirí Narrative: A Testament of Ancient and Colonial Andean Religion*, trans. F. Salomon and G. L. Urioste (1991); J. Bierhorst, *History and Mythology of the Aztecs: The Codex Chimalpopoca* (1992); G. Brotherston, *The Book of the Fourth World: Reading the Native Americas through Their Literature* (1992); R. L. Burger, *Chavin and the Origins of Andean Civilization* (1992); J. Mooney, *History, Myths and Sacred Formulas of the Cherokee* (1992); H. Carr, *Inventing the American Primitive: Politics, Gender and the Representation of Native American Literary Tradition* (1996); W. Rowe, *Ensayos arguedianos* (1996); D. Bahr, L. Paul, V. Joseph, *Ants and Orioles: Showing the Art of Pima Poetry* (1997); G. Brotherston, *Painted Books from Mexico* (1997); E. Chiauilaf, *Ti kom ül: Todos los cantos* (1998); C. Vicuña, *Ül: Four Mapuche Poets* (1998); *The Sun Unwound: Original Texts from Occupied America*, trans. E. Dorn and G. Brotherston (1999); K. Warak'a, *Taki Parwa/22 Poemas*, trans. O. Gonzáles (1999); C. Julien, *Reading Inca History* (2000); J. de Sousândrade, *O Guesa* [1888], ed. A. de Campos and H. de Campos (2002); S. Medeiros, *Makunaíma e Jurupari: Cosmogonias ameríndias* (2002); M. León Portilla, *Códices: Los antiguos libros del Nuevo Mundo* (2003); *Rabinal Achi: A Mayan Drama of War and Sacrifice*, ed. and trans. D. Tedlock (2003); D. Arnold and J. de Dios Yapita, "The Nature of Indigenous Literatures in the Andes," *Literary Cultures of Latin America*, ed. M. J. Valdés and D. Kadir (2004); L. Sá, *Rain Forest Literatures: Amazonian Texts and Latin American Culture* (2004); F. Salomon, *The Cord Keepers* (2004); G. Brotherston, *Feather Crown* (2006); E. G. Neves, *Arqueologia da Amazônia* (2006); G. Tomlinson, *The Singing of the New World: Indigenous Voice in the Era of European Contact* (2007); J. Lee, *The Allure of Nezahualcoyotl: Pre-Hispanic History, Religion, and Nahua Poetics* (2008); J. Neurath, *Por los caminos del maíz: Mito y ritual en la periferia septentrional de Mesoamérica* (2008); H. Staden, *Warhaftige Historia* [1557], ed. N. Whitehead (2008); G. Brokaw, *A History of the Khipu* (2010).

G. Brotherston

INDONESIAN POETRY is written in Bahasa Indonesia, the national lang. of the Republic of Indonesia and a distinct dialect of Malay. There are approximately 740 different langs. spoken across the archipelago; although most of these have had extensive oral poetic trads., only eight have longstanding written lits.—Javanese, Balinese, Sundanese, Malay, Minangkabau, Batak, Macassarese and Buginese (McGlynn). A "mod. Indonesian poetry" is the product of sociopolitical and educational changes that gathered momentum from the beginning of the 20th c. Indonesia became a unitary state in 1945; the Indonesian lang. was defined as separate from Malay in 1928 during the emerging nationalist movement and has developed its own lit., most commonly written by young, well-educated, urbanized men and relying on the market distribution of printed books and literary magazines.

Mod. Indonesian poetry is conventionally considered to have begun in 1922 with the publication of *Andalas Nusa Harapan* (Sumatra, Island of Hope) by the Sumatran-born poet Muhammad Yamin (1903–62). The poems collected in this brief anthol. combine the traditional four-line couplets of the indigenous *pantun* with the longer sonnet form characteristic of the Dutch Neo-romantic movement of 1880 that the emerging Indonesian poets had studied in school. Driven by powerful emotions (real or imagined), this first generation of Indonesian poets contemplated the beauty of nature from a careful distance and were commonly left in a condition of profound melancholy connected to a nostalgia for previous states of emotional comfort. Such longing (*rindu*) found its origins variously in memories of one's parents, childhood, home village, local scenery, cl. monuments, and religious certainty. Yamin's "Sedih" (Sorrow, 1934) is typical of this poetry. The sonnet opens with an evocation of the Barisan Mountain ranges of Central Sumatra and of a distant village that seems to be calling the wanderer home. Alone and uncared for, he sadly remembers his father, now deceased, lying in a grave covered with a basil plant and a single frangipani. The form and lang. are reasonably mod.; the concluding images are common pantun images: the frangipani is found in cemeteries, and the word for "basil" (*selasih*) rhymes with "love" (*kasih*).

The outstanding poet of the 1920s to 1930s was Amir Hamzah (1911–46). A prince deeply steeped in traditional Malay lit., Hamzah imbued these romantic conventions with deeply felt grief arising from his own failed relationships. In his youthful poetry, *Buah Rindu* (Fruits of Melancholy, not pub. until 1941), the relationships were with his mother, his home in

East Sumatra, and the woman with whom he had fallen in love only to lose her in her unwilling marriage to another. In his mature verse, *Nyanyi Sunyi* (Songs of Loneliness, pub. earlier, 1937), Hamzah channeled his frustration into an angry, empty search for an absent God. While other poets of this period—Rustam Effendi (1903–79), Sanusi Pane (1905–68), and Sutan Takdir Alisjahbana (1908–94)—were struggling to find more contemp., though still elegant, forms of Indonesian, Hamzah is sometimes considered "the last Malay poet" because of his use of a vast cl. vocabulary, trad. quatrains, and familiar patterns of imagery.

Indonesia was occupied by Japanese military forces from 1942 to 1945 and fought for its independence from the Dutch from 1945 to 1949. Such circumstances obviously made beauty and melancholy into more difficult topics. A complete change in form, subject matter, and emotional content was brought about in a short period by the bohemian poet Chairil Anwar (1922–49). Writing under the influence of Eur., particularly Dutch, poetry of the 1930s, Anwar used free verse to describe feelings of alienation and desolation (*sepi*) experienced in dark, tightly confined, urban settings. Anwar's influence was powerful and can be discerned in the work of his close peers Asrul Sani (1926–2004) and Rivai Apin (1927–95). The name of Sitor Situmorang (1924–2014) is particularly worthy of note: Sitor intensively explored themes of place and love over five decades.

A middle position was achieved with the emergence of a New Generation of poets in the 1950s. Relatively free of Eur. models and confident in their use of Indonesian, they turned to regional themes. Ajip Rosidi (b. 1938) dealt in depth with the society, as well as the folk and Islamic spirituality, of West Java; he was also a strong proponent of writing in Sundanese. W. S. Rendra (1935–2009) was both a major poet and dramatist; his work focused on the lives of "the ordinary people" of Central Java. He also wrote personal love poems and more widely based works drawing on a Catholicism colored by pantheism. In the poem "Litani Domba Kudus" (Litany for the Holy Lamb, 1955), Christ is a white flower, an ivory dove, a king dwelling among paupers, and a golden deer. "Sebuah Dunia Yang Marah" (An Angry World, 1960) concludes:

> God always weeps and understands.
> Is always stabbed. Always betrayed.

In these poems, God is most to be found in "the enemies of the police": soldiers, prostitutes, the unemployed and beggars ("Masmur Mawar" [Rose Psalm], 1959).

Free literary expression was increasingly suppressed under the later regime of Sukarno (president from 1945 to 1967). As the nation moved increasingly to the Left, major themes became "heroism," "social destiny," "great principles," and "praise of the fatherland and the masses, and historical optimism" (Mohamad). These same themes continued to be prominent in the early work of the Generation of 1966, under the second Indonesian president Suharto (president from 1967 to 1998), only to be almost completely dropped in a second wave of personal poetry that developed after 1968. The one outstanding exception was Taufiq Ismail (b. 1937), who was able to carry his political concerns into a humorous and wide-ranging social analysis of the problems of the Suharto era.

Three major directions can be discerned in this newer work. The first was the gentle lyricism of Sapardi Djoko Damono (b. 1940), esp. as found in his anthol. *dukaMu abadi* (the Eternal Sorrow of God, 1969). Sapardi developed a carefully contrastive pattern of imagery, describing the human pilgrimage between life and death in terms of the natural progression of day to night.

A second direction was the emergence of a strong female voice for the first time. Particularly important was the work of Toeti Heraty (b. 1933). Sapardi searched for a God whom he doubts exists; in *Sajak-sajak 33* (33 Poems, 1971), Toeti sought an equally impossible object—a love in which she could participate as an equal and not as an object. The rituals of status, role-playing, and emotional control are analyzed in her poetry as the tools by which open and honest relationships are avoided.

The third direction was the move toward "concrete absurdist" poetry, esp. at the hands of Sutardji Calzoum Bachri (b. 1942). Sutardji's poetry emphasized sound at the expense of meaning and claimed to be returning poetry to the realm of the preliterate spell. His major topics were the violence of sexual relations, the pain of everyday existence, and the awesome arbitrariness of the divine. Perhaps his most intriguing poem is "Q," composed of the Ar. letters "alif," "lam," "mim" (known in the Qur'an as "the mysterious letters"), and a series of exclamation marks. The letters may stand for "Allah" and "Muhammad."

The mid-1980s mark a further turning point in the devel. of mod. Indonesian poetry. The poets who emerged during this decade had been born after independence, wrote naturally in Indonesian, and had been formed by Indonesian lit. Their work moved in two different directions. Some were caught up in the worldwide Islamic Revival, bringing an affirmative Muslim orthodoxy to the center of Indonesian poetry, contrary to the "mod." secularism or doubt that had prevailed throughout the rest of the century. Among the New Sufis were Emha Ainun Nadjib (b. 1953), Ahmadun Yosi Herfanda (b. 1956), and Acep Zamzam Noor (b. 1960). Others, such as Sitok Srengenge (b. 1965) and Dorothea Rosa Herliany (b. 1963), remained defiantly concerned with the complexities of their own emotions and the repressive environment of the late Suharto era. Herliany rejected the uncertainty about relationships that characterized Toeti Heraty's poetry and in *Kill the Radio* demanded dominance rather than equality.

The decade after the Reformation movement of 1998 has seen all these writers continue to grow in depth and subtlety. New writers have, of course, continued to appear, including a significant number of women writers, esp. Rieke Diah Pitaloka (b. 1974), Shinta Febriany (b. 1979), and Putu Vivi Lestari (b. 1981). Indonesian lit. has also begun to move into cyberspace. Together, the writers of the 1980s and their new peers are described as the Generation of 2000, a reference not to their set place in Indonesian writing but to their future promise.

■ **Anthologies and Translations**: *Pujangga Baru* (1962); *Gema Tanah Air* (1948); *Angkatan 66* (1968), all ed. H. B. Jassin; *Anthology of Modern Indonesian Poetry,* ed. B. Raffel (1970); *Complete Poetry and Prose of Chairil Anwar*, ed. and trans. B. Raffel (1970); *Ballads and Blues: Selected Poems of W. S. Rendra*, ed. and trans. B. Raffel and H. Aveling; *Contemporary Indonesian Poetry* (1975), *Arjuna in Meditation* (1976), *Secrets Need Words* (2001), all ed. and trans. H. Aveling; *Angkatan 2000 dalam Sastra Indonesia*, ed. K. L. Rampan (2000); D. R. Herliany, *Kill the Radio* (2001), *Saint Rosa* (2006), both trans. H. Aveling.

■ **Criticism and History**: H. B. Jassin, *Chairil Anwar* (1954), and *Amir Hamzah* (1962); A. Teeuw, *Modern Indonesian Literature*, 2 v. (1967, 1979); B. Raffel, *The Development of Modern Indonesian Poetry* (1967); G. Mohamad, "Njanji Sunji Kedua," *Horison* (April 1969); H. Aveling, *A Thematic History of Indonesian Poetry: 1920 to 1974* (1974); M. H. Salleh, *Tradition and Change in Contemporary Malay-Indonesian Poetry* (1977); *Indonesian Heritage*, ed. J. McGlynn (1998); *Cyber Graffiti*, ed. S. Situmorang (2004).

H. Aveling

INUIT POETRY

I. Traditional Song and Poetry
II. Contemporary Song and Poetry

The Inuit (pl. form; sing. Inuk), formerly called *Eskimos*—a term considered offensive by many Inuit—live along some 5,000 miles of Arctic coastline, so comments about any one aspect of their culture are generalizations. As noted by both anthropologists and Inuit political organizations, however, the Inuit have a strong ling. and cultural connection across the circumpolar world. The Inuit lang. belongs to the Eskimo side of the Eskimo-Aleut family, and it has two branches: Inuit—known as *Kalaallisut* in Greenland; *Inuktitut*, *Inuinnaqtun*, or *Inuvialuktun* in Canada; and *Iñupiaq* in Alaska—and *Yup'ik*, spoken in several varieties in Alaska and Siberia. Traditional Inuit poetry is generally performed, rather than written and read, and it is often accompanied by drum, choral background, or dance. While the contemp. corpus includes verse written in the Western trad., Inuit poetry continues to be a highly musical production, with an emphasis on performance and the sung and spoken word.

I. Traditional Song and Poetry. Traditional Inuit poetry takes a variety of forms and was often composed to be performed in the *qaggiq* (communal celebration house). As Lowenstein points out, many of the songs reflect on the process of song-making, often via comparison to a task such as hunting or to material objects or crafts. This practice of metaphor illustrates both the skill required to create songs that would be subject to public evaluation and the extent of their value or usefulness to the community. Inuit poetry was ceremonial, possessing powers to make changes in the physical world, but it was also commonplace, a part of everyday life.

The Inuit songs known best to outsiders were recorded in the early 20th c. by the anthropologist Diamond Jenness and by the Greenlandic poet and scholar Knud Rasmussen. Rasmussen's trans., in particular, have been widely disseminated and republished, though they have often been stripped of important contextual information in the process. Rasmussen attempted to organize Inuit poetry into the following four categories: charms, hunting songs, songs of mood, and songs of derision. More recently, Emile Imaruittuq, an elder from Igloolik, described the following three categories of songs:

A. *Pisiit* (pl. form; sing. *pisiq*), or personal songs. Although the term *pisiit* is now often used to refer to hymns, the more traditional pisiit tell stories and express the singer's feelings and often make use of the *ajaajaa* (refrain). This category would encompass Rasmussen's songs of mood and hunting songs. According to Imaruittuq, pisiit can also be called *qilaujjarusiit*, which indicates that they are performed with a drum dance. In terms of content, the lyrics are often highly metaphorical, and they may contain a lesson for the listeners. Imaruittuq notes that while pisiit could be performed by someone other than the owner or composer, credit was always given before the singing. A song whose lyrics have been altered by successive singers is called an *ikiaqtagaq* (split song). In the western (Copper Inuit) region, Jenness noted a variety of drum song called *aton* but was unable to distinguish it from the pisiq.

B. *Iviutiit* (pl. form; sing. *iviutiq*), or songs used to ridicule or embarrass people, often as part of a duel. Called "songs of derision" by Rasmussen, these song duels have a judicial function in that each singer is allowed to voice complaints against the other in public, and each is given an opportunity to respond. They may provide a cheerful, loving correction or a vicious assault on a reputation. The song duel varies greatly from one area to another, occasionally involving boxing, and is usually also considered entertainment. Iviutiit make use of comical euphemisms, often explicit in content.

C. *Sakausiit* (pl. form; sing. *sakausiq*), or songs used by *angakkuit* (shamans). Rasmussen called these charms or magic songs and recorded several examples. The Igloolik shaman Avva, for instance, knew songs that could be used to stop bleeding, to make heavy things light, to call spirit helpers, or to attract game. These powerful tools were guarded by their owners (though Rasmussen succeeded in trading for some of them). The use of obscure or archaic diction—the highly metaphoric lang. of the angakkuit—frequently makes the sakausiit incomprehensible even to native speakers.

II. Contemporary Song and Poetry. As soon as Christian missionary projects and whalers brought written texts to the Arctic, Inuit began using syllabic and alphabetic orthographies to write their langs. The technology of writing, however, was more often employed pragmatically and rhetorically in the composition of letters, diaries, and political documents, rather than in the creation of books of poetry. As the Church became a dominant force in the Arctic, the performance of pisiit, iviutiit, and sakausiit fell out of favor, even as many elders continued to compose and sing songs. The older song texts, meanwhile, have been extensively collected, translated, and republished by eds. such as Jerome Rothenberg, James Houston, Guy-Marie Rousselière, Charles Hoffman, Edward Field, John Robert Colombo, Edmund Carpenter, and Tom Lowenstein. McCall and others have pointed out, however, that the publishing process, while well intentioned, has tended to strip songs of the context that gives them meaning—esp. in cases where the identity of the composers has been omitted. In this form, they appear more like lyric poems than an accurate representation of Inuit poetry.

As McGrath observes, there is not a large body of Inuit poetry well known outside the Inuit homeland, but within Inuit communities, the trad. is flourishing. Inuit poetry is rarely published in chapbooks or in collections, but some writers, such as Greenland's Aqqaluk Lynge or Labrador's Philip Igloliorti, have published books of verse. More commonly, Inuit poetry can be found in smaller, community-based publications or online. McGrath has argued that the four genres identified by Rasmussen can also be applied to the contemp. corpus. The mood poems, she observes, are now written about mod. life in the communities and are often worked into photographs, drawings, or prints so that illustration and text are indivisible. Magic chants and incantations are no longer evident, but Christian hymns, trans. or adapted from Eng. and Danish or composed originally in Inuit lang., are widely promulgated. The hymns of Rasmus Berthelsen are known throughout Greenland, while in Canada, Armand Tagoona was a well-known composer of Christian songs. Hunting continues to be a major theme in Inuit poetry, but rather than being memorial or personal, hunting poems now tend to express a longing by young, urban writers for the old way of life. Many of these works also carry an environmentalist message, reflecting larger concerns in the North about the impacts of resource devel. and climate change. In mod. Inuit poetry, the song duels and derisive poems generally do not exist in their traditional form, having been banned by Christian missionaries, but certain elements have survived. The question-answer sequence and the repeated use of the interrogative are features of contemp. Inuit political poetry, though the respondent is as likely to be a garbage can or an alien from Mars as a snowy owl or an offended husband.

The devel. of the epic is a major innovation in mod. Inuit poetry; Frederik Nielsen's trilogy on Qitdlaussuaq traces the 18th-c. Inuit migration from Canada to Greenland; Alootook Ipellie's long poem "The Strangers" describes the Inuit occupation of the Arctic from ancient times and examines the consequences of Eur. contact; Villads Villadsen's Christian epic *Nalusuunerup Taarnerani* (In Heathen Darkness) describes the death of the last Norseman in Greenland and the eventual conversion and baptism of Aattaaritaa the exorcist. The politically inspired poems are sometimes purely didactic but are more frequently satiric and ironic.

Even in the 21st c., written Inuit poetry does not entirely represent the contemp. Inuit poetic corpus. Indeed, the most vibrant Inuit poetry continues to be sung and performed rather than confined to the page. Despite the interventions of the Church and of the schools, the somewhat isolating activities of reading and writing are not esp. popular in many Inuit communities; instead, the works of musical performers such as Charlie Adams, Charlie Ningiuk, Henoch Townley, Tumassi Quitsaq, Laina Tullaugak, Leena Evic, Susan Aglukark, Elisapi Isaac, Lucie Idlout, Tumivut, and Beatrice Deer are recognized throughout the Arctic; and the lyrics of their songs constitute a poetic trad. that is constantly being revised, referenced, and reperformed by other Inuit artists—rather like the traditional ikiaqtagaq or adapted song. This is not to say that Inuit poets are traditional; rather, they braid their song trads. with other musical and poetic influences. As documented by Inuit circumpolar music blogger Stéphane Cloutier, the extensive music scene in Kalaallit Nunaat (Greenland) features many hip-hop artists. Increasingly, even Inuit writers do not seem to be relying on print publication to disseminate their work, as spoken-word artists like Mosha Folger and Taqralik Partridge are already acquiring a significant following through the use of online media sites. These younger artists expand on a range of themes related to contemp. Inuit life and identity, and, notably, many of them continue to compose in their own lang. This ling. persistence ensures that the audience of contemp. Inuit poetry is primarily Inuit, unlike the Eng.-lang. poetry of other contemp. indigenous trads., which is more readily accessible to mainstream readers.

See CANADA, POETRY OF; INDIGENOUS AMERICAS, POETRY OF THE.

■ **Anthologies and Primary Texts**: H. Rink, *Tales and Traditions of the Eskimo*, trans. R. Brown, 2 v. (1875); W. Thalbitzer, "Old Fashioned Songs," *Phonetical Study of the Eskimo Language* (1904); H. Roberts and D. Jenness, *Songs of the Copper Eskimos* (1925); K. Rasmussen, *Report of the Fifth Thule Expedition*, 1921–24, v. 7–9 (1930–32); *Anerca*, ed. E. Carpenter (1959); *I Breathe a New Song*, ed. R. Lewis (1971); *Eskimo Poems from Canada and Greenland*, ed. T. Lowenstein (1973); *Kalaallit Taallaataat Nutaat INUIT Ny Gronlandsk Lyrik*, ed. K. Norregaard (1980); *Paper Stays Put*, ed. R. Gedalof (1980); *Poems of the Inuit*, ed. J. R. Colombo (1981); C. Berthelsen, *Gronlandsk Litteratur* (1983); "Alaska Native Writers, Storytellers and Orators," spec. iss. of *Alaska Quarterly Review* 4.3–4 (1986); *Northern Voices*, ed. P. Petrone (1988); M. Aupilaarjuk, E. Imaruittuq, et al., "Pisiit, Songs," *Perspectives on Traditional Law*, ed. J. Ooste, F. Laugrand, W. Rasing (2000); *Words of the Real People*, ed. A. Fienup-Riordan and L. Kaplan (2007).

■ **Criticism and History**: S. Frederiksen, "Henrik Lund, A National Poet of Greenland," *American Philosophical Society* 96 (1952); and "Stylistic Forms in Greenland Eskimo Literature," *Meddelser om Gronland* 136 (1954); E. Carpenter, "Eskimo Poetry: Word Magic," *Explorations* 4 (1955); H. Lynge, "The Art and Poetry of Greenland," *Greenland Past and Present*, ed. K. Hertling et al. (1971); R. Wiebe, "Songs of the Canadian Eskimo," *Canadian Literature* 52 (1972); R. McGrath, *Canadian Inuit Literature* (1984); R. Pedersen, "Greenlandic Written Literature," *Handbook of North American Indians*, ed. D. Damas, v. 5 (1984); C. Berthelsen, "Greenlandic Literature: Its Traditions, Changes, and Trends," *Arctic Anthropology* 23 (1986); R. Hulan, *Northern Experience and the Myths of Canadian Culture* (2002);

S. McCall, "I Can Only Sing This Song to Someone Who Understands It," *Essays on Canadian Writing* 83 (2004); *Uqalurait: An Oral History of Nunavut*, ed. J. Bennett and S. Rowley (2004); D. Serkoak, A. Meekitjuk-Hanson, P. Irniq, "Inuit Music," *Nunavut Handbook*, ed. M. Dewar (2004); S. Cloutier, "Inuit Circumpolar Music" (2010), http://pisiit.blogspot.com/; K. Martin, "Is an Inuit Literary History Possible?" *American Indian Culture and Research Journal* 34 (2010); L. J. Dorais, *The Language of the Inuit* (2010).

R. McGrath; K. Martin

IRAN, POETRY OF. *See* persian poetry

IRELAND, POETRY OF

I. Irish: Sixth to Nineteenth Centuries
II. English: Eighteenth Century and the Celtic Revival
III. After Yeats (Irish and English)

I. Irish: Sixth to Nineteenth Centuries. As the oldest vernacular lit. north of the Alps, Ir. poetry, according to the Old Ir. *Auraicept na n-Éces* (*Primer of the Poets*), consisted of "what was best then of every language . . . what was widest and finest was cut into Irish" (Ó Cathasaigh). Although the country was never colonized by Rome, the native Ir. nevertheless adapted an alphabet from some knowledge of Lat., perhaps as early as the 2d c. ce, called *ogam*, inscribed on upright stones. Oral Ir. lit. is believed to long precede the 5th-c. arrival of the literate Lat. culture of such missionaries as Patrick; but in the oldest existing tablets and vellum (from the 6th and 7th cs., respectively), the vernacular tongue, often expressed in verse, already coexists with ecclesiastical texts in Lat. By the 8th c., missionaries from Ireland reversed the direction of literary exchange, carrying back to Europe instruction in cl. learning as they founded monasteries in Scotland and on the continent. With the displacement of their Druidic religion by Christianity in the 5th c., Ir. poets who composed orally (*filid*, sing. *fili*) maintained their identity as scholars and poets, even as their verse now shared the meters of church and legal texts (Ó Cathasaigh).

The earliest Ir. verse, which had originated in the same IE system as did Sanskrit and Gr. verse (see celtic prosody; also Watkins), was gradually incorporated into complex rhyming syllabic meters. Scholars once thought that this change occurred under the influence of late Lat. verse, but more recent scholarship argues, to the contrary, that the versification of early Ir. poetry influenced med. Lat. verse. In Ireland, the most famous collection of poems in this style by the Ir. Latinists is *Hisperica Famina* (Western Orations; 7th c.). This Hisperic or rhyming style was subsequently employed in the OE "Rhyming Poem." As Christianity became established in Ireland in the 6th c., the roles of the native filid coexisted with those of monastic clerics and jurists in a system of aristocratic patronage, but it was to the scholars of the monasteries that this task largely fell. Clerics in the Ir. monasteries who copied, for preservation and dissemination, sacred texts also compiled the pre-Christian lit. of Ireland, incl. tales of destructions, cattle raids, and wooings (Ó Cathasaigh). At this time, the poems being composed by the Ir. filid, patronized to promote the claims to property and power of his king (MacCana, Caball and Hollo), consisted typically of encomiastic genealogies and hists., but they also included more fanciful narratives, incl. the voyage saga (*echtrae*). From the 6th to the 12th c., verse is introduced into what is predominantly prose (Ni Mhaonaigh) in what is called prosimetrum. E.g., in the voyage tales to the Otherworld (*immrama*) and in *Buile Shuibne* (Sweeney's Frenzy, the tale of an exiled king who achieves enlightenment in the wilderness), poetic passages give emphasis to already heightened emotion. Predominantly alliterative and unrhymed (*retoiric*), the poetry of this period also included rhyming syllabic forms (*nua-chrotha*, "new forms"). The use of *roscad*, a form of obscure verse, was restricted to esoteric contexts.

Lyrics from med. Ir. scribes also survive, much of it in the margins of Lat. mss., escaping not just the task at hand but also the traditionalism of the filid. Early Ir. nature poetry at its best can be seen in the 9th or 10th c. Writing during a period of Viking raids on Ireland, the poet describes the reddened bracken, "its shape hidden; / The wild goose has raised his familiar cry" (MacCana, trans. G. Murphy).

Bardic or cl. Ir. poetry is usually dated from 1200–1600, a period in which the turmoil of the Norman invasion was exacerbated by the displacement of the native monasteries with continental institutions. The important role of the poet in sustaining the social order was reinforced under a new confederation of learned families, contributing to the standardization of poetic forms in the aristocratic families of Scotland as well as Ireland. In families that came to include assimilating Anglo-Norman Catholics, poetry was the hereditary vocation of professional poets. The once separate functions of the learned filid and the nonliterate bard now merged in the figure of the poet whose verse is both composed and performed orally, the latter accompanied by harp, even though a written record often would follow (Wong). *Dán díreach* (strict verse) is the generic name for the syllabic meters that were to be the hallmark of Ir. poetry in religious verse as well as court poetry until the 17th c. Virtuosity and artifice, learned lang. and ornateness were prized, contributing to the distinctive styles of the lore of places (*dindshenchas*, mod. spelling *dinnseanchas*) and the narrative or *laoithe* poems concerning roving warriors (*fiana*) known as *fianaigheacht*. They included ballads, a "vibrant and earthy manifestation of popular Gaelic culture" (Caball and Hollo), and they retained their popularity in high as well as low culture (see James Joyce's *Finnegans Wake*). Less elaborate forms were employed, however, as early as the 12th c. in love poems termed *dánta grádha*, which were once believed to have been composed contemporaneously with the *amour courtois* of Fr. trad., arriving in Ireland with Norman settlers. The trad. in Ir. now seems more likely to have been a "non-professional stream of Gaelic literary culture coterminous with the professional," what Caball and Hollo call an "amalgam of traditions" in which the earliest datable poem was composed by the Anglo-Norman Gerald fitz Maurice (1357–98). It was a "cosmopolitan combination of Gaelic, English and broader Eur. literary cultures," according to Caball and Hollo, to which aristocratic women as well as men contributed. Adapting to Ir. such forms as the echo poem (echoing the beginning and ending of quatrains), poems written by both sexes explore more personal subjects such as the impact of sectarian difference in relationships, and they came to include poems of male friendship (see Piaras Feiritéar [ca. 1600–53]).

After the military defeat of the Ir. chieftains at Kinsale in 1601 and the flight of the earls in 1607 to the courts and armies of Catholic Europe, for some decades Ir.-lang. writers often wrote from the courts, monasteries, and battlegrounds of Europe, preserving and expanding the filid trad., incl. the ongoing chronicling of Ir. hist. since antiquity. But with the Cromwellian settlements of 1652–54, the defeat of James II in 1690, and the ensuing Penal Laws, the economic structure that had supported the privileged status and function of the poet crumbled. Thus, much of the poetry of the 17th and 18th cs. is overtly political, a poetry of defiance, of mourning for the old order and contempt for the new. Aogán Ó Rathaille (ca. 1670–1729) and his contemporary Dáibhí Ó Bruadair (ca. 1625–98) inherited the residual role of the fili that in their own lifetime was abruptly withdrawn. Ó Bruadair, reduced to agricultural labor, in a trans. by the 20th-c. poet Michael Hartnett ruefully remembers the pen he once wielded: "From guiding the run of the clay-blade my knuckles all swollen are / And the spadeshaft hath deadened my fingers" (cited in Wong). By the 18th c., the poet Eoghan Rua Ó Súilleabháin (ca. 1748–84) makes a colorful poetic persona of his life as a *spailpín* (itinerant laborer) in Munster. Reflecting the massive social and political upheaval of the 17th c., the form and content of postbardic poetry remains ornate, but increasingly, like the folk poetry of the period, it is colloquial in diction and tone and is composed in accentual rather than syllabic verse. It is also adapted to the purposes of satire. If Jonathan Swift, a Dublin contemporary of Ó Rathaille's, was notorious for Eng.-lang. love poems that convert feminine allure into sexual threat, Brian Merriman (1750–1805) in a mischievous poem titled *The Midnight Court* written in Ir. in 1780 (but drawing on the Eur. trad. of the court of love) offered such an explicit and exuberant sexual empowerment of women, led by the goddess Aoibheall, that it would be censored in Eng. trans. well into the 20th c.

Already by the beginning of the 18th c., there is a different use of the pre-Christian myth of "Ireland" as the goddess Sovereignty or *Ériu,* the possession of whom legitimates Ir. kinship. Now personified as captive to a foreigner, she appeals to the poet in dream visions to win her freedom. The vision, or *aisling*, poem, derived from Jacobite trads., would culminate in the 18th c. with such poems as "The Churchyard of Creagán" by Art Mac Cumhaigh (ca. 1738–73) and "Gile na Gile," ("Brightness Most Bright") by Ó Rathaille in which "our mild, bright, delicate, loving, fresh-lipped girl" falls prey to "that black, horned, foreign, hate-crested crew" (Kinsella 1981). There is a decline of literacy in the Ir. lang., such that, by the 19th c., Eng. was rapidly becoming the vernacular lang. of Ireland, a process accelerated by the famine of the 1840s and the massive emigration that followed. In the poetry and in the life of the blind poet and musician Antaine Raiftearaí (1779–1835) may be seen the merging of literary style with folk music and ballad but also the invention of a new trad.: the sorrowful last survivor of a noble past. It was once presumed by scholars that Gaelic culture had sunk to that of an impoverished and oppressed peasantry. Poets were, it is true, reduced to employment as hedge-school masters, minstrels, or (as in Ó Bruadair's example) agricultural laborers, and certainly poetry moved closer to the people and the oral trad., even employing song meter (*amhrán*). But Denvir questions the widespread notion that the Ir.-lang. poet had become, as in James Macpherson's enormously popular reclamation for Scots (and Brit.) heritage of the Fenian warrior-poet Ossian, merely a moribund relic of a dying culture. "Celticism," which, in the late 18th-c. idiom of romanticism, promoted the stereotype of the bard as a living relic, belies the lively exchanges across ling. borders in the everyday life and the lit. of Ireland at that time as well as the ongoing vitality of the filid heritage, both in the poems and ballads being written and in the oral contributions by storytellers (*seanchaí*).

An example of the interfusion of the two may be witnessed in a major example of the bardic lament of the 18th c. as it was influenced by the oral keening trad. of women. Eibhlín Dubh Ní Chonaill's (c. 1743–c. 1800) celebrated *Lament for Art O'Leary* was occasioned by the murder of her husband, who resisted compliance with the Penal Laws. It survived through oral performances into the 20th c. The success of such poetry in the trad. of the filid was facilitated by devices that include the repetition of the beginning in the ending lines and *conchlann*, the repetition of the last word of a stanza to initiate the stanza that follows (devices still employed by such 21st-c. poets as John Montague and Paul Muldoon). If in the 18th and 19th cs. the forms of high culture enter into popular usage, anonymous folk poetry written in the 17th and 18th cs. was itself sometimes composed mainly in accentual meters in forms that were technically sophisticated. "Roísín Dubh" ("Dark Rose") extends the aisling trad., but there are also homelier love poems of the time such as "Remember that Night," in which the speaker urges her beloved to "come some night soon / when my people sleep." She promises, on that night, to "put my arms round you / and tell you my story" (Kinsella 1981). Such continuity with the cultural wealth of the past was enabled in the 19th c. by a scribal culture in the Ir. lang. that was given new life by such Eng. institutions in Ireland as the Ordnance Survey, to which local poets contributed. It also, however, as Denvir notes, meant that the poetry largely sought "Gaelic and Catholic triumphalism" rather than the republicanism of the largely Eng.-speaking United Irishmen.

II. English: Eighteenth Century and the Celtic Revival. The devel. in Ireland of a literate, middle-class, and urban Eng. lang. culture, Catholic as well as Protestant, early in the 18th c. supported a growing publishing industry. Jonathan Swift (1667–1745) ambivalently acknowledged the vitality of ongoing Ir.-lang. social mores in poems such as "The Description of an *Irish-Feast* " (1720), and he translated at least one song by the blind Ir. harper Turlough Carolan (ca. 1670–1738). Swift, if less hostile than Edmund Spenser (1552–99), who wrote *The Faerie Queene* from the rebellion and plantation of Munster, enlarges a trad. where alienation was often the defining experience for the nonnative, expatriate, or Anglo-Irish poet. For Swift's contemporary Mary Barber (ca. 1685–1755), the troubles of Ireland are a metaphor for the straitened domestic circumstances of women. Indeed, political sovereignty in Ireland, in the bardic past underwritten by the sexual union of the native leader to "Sovereignty," making fecund the soil, becomes an ironic dream.

While the Gaelic Revival at the end of the 19th c. would celebrate a demotic trad. "racy of the soil" (Denis Florence MacCarthy, 1817–82), a more complicated picture is already available at the end of the 18th c. in a poem, written by an Irishman living in England, that at once celebrates and mourns a struggling rural culture: "The Deserted Village" by Oliver Goldsmith (1728–74). A half century later, the Great Famine, in which at least half a million Ir. people died and hundreds of thousands emigrated on less favorable terms than did Goldsmith, would devastate Ir. culture on all levels. While such poets as Jeremiah Joseph Callanan (1795–1829) would collect from Ir. speakers the fairy tales circulating in a still-populous countryside that would soon be deserted, by 1850 the Famine had produced a veritable subgenre of rural lit. in such notable works as the 1849 "The Year of Sorrow" by Aubrey de Vere (1814–1902); "The

Famine Year" by the mother of Oscar Wilde, Jane Elgee Wilde (Speranza, ca. 1821–96); and a decade later the publication of *Laurence Bloomfield in Ireland*, one of the major long poems in Eng. of the century, by William Allingham (1824–89).

Before the Famine, Ireland produced poets whose work parallels that of the Eng. romantic period: Mary Tighe (1772–1810), whose *Psyche* influenced John Keats; and two members of the United Irishmen, William Drennan (1754–1820) and James Orr (1770–1816). The most celebrated Ir. poet of the period was Thomas Moore (1779–1852), a close friend of Lord Byron's but also of Robert Emmet's, the executed leader of the 1803 uprising. Moore in his 1807 elegy for Emmet, "Oh! Breathe Not His Name," established the tone and theme of the Ir. political elegy, praising self-sacrifice as an act of national renewal. Moore's unabashedly sentimental lyrics set to music, *Irish Melodies*, stoked an ongoing enthusiasm for ballads, incl. nationalist ballads revived from 1798. The continuing frequency of anonymous or pseudonymous publication in 19th-c. Ireland, contrary to what we might expect, may have proved poetically enabling for poets such as James Clarence Mangan (1803–49), who, under other names and in voices shaped by different langs., forged a distinctively "non-English" voice out of estrangement from his own speech, incl. in his revivals of the Ir. aisling in his version of the anonymous "Roísín Dubh" ("Dark Rose") and "Kathleen Ny-Houlahan." If for Mangan and Young Ireland the personal lyric of Eng. romanticism had become a mask that questioned "authenticity," such masks become ostentatious in the prose of Oscar Wilde (1854–1900). In Wilde's own Ir. ballad, however, "The Ballad of Reading Gaol," the anger is undisguised. Samuel Ferguson (1810–86), who wrote "Dialogue between the Heart and Head of an Irish Protestant," would provide W. B. Yeats (1865–1939) with another poetic counter to the stereotype of the ardent, heartfelt, and bardic Celt.

Yeats, Ireland's most celebrated poet, collected rural folk tales even as he promoted the poetry, and the nationalist politics, of Young Ireland. At the same time, in his own, early poems, he cast these Ir. themes in relation to those of the Eng. romantic poets he admired, P. B. Shelley and William Blake. Yeats sought to enlarge the scope of Celticism—in his poems but also in the Ir. nation—by promoting two other commitments to which he would devote his life. The first was to the occult, which culminated with *A Vision* (1925, rev. 1937), an ambitious recasting into the "gyres" of temporal change his lifelong investigation of historical patterns first cast in such notions as the mask, the phases of the moon, and the construction of individual identity within larger structures of fate. Its influence may be seen in "The Second Coming" with its concluding lines "And what rough beast, its hour come round at last, / Slouches towards Bethlehem to be born?" The second, more personal commitment was to the militant nationalist Maud Gonne (1866–1953), famous for her courage and her beauty, who, in refusing his repeated proposals of marriage, forced Yeats to make of "mere words" a model for the mod. love poem in Eng. As Yeats came to find aesthetically and intellectually crippling both Fenian nationalism and the Gaelic League with which he had allied his early literary interests, he developed a style that he hoped would seem "a moment's thought" ("Adam's Curse"), a poetry "as cold / And passionate as the dawn" ("The Fisherman"). Such art in its "arrogance" returned to the Protestant and Ascendancy heritage of Swift's savage indignation, even as Yeats assumed, as poet, the mask of "the wise and simple" figure of the "folk" in "The Fisherman." "All those things whereof / Man makes a superhuman, / Mirror-resembling dream" ("The Tower") Yeats claimed for the Ir. poet, even in the face of a world war larger than Ireland's "Troubles," for "All things fall and are built again / And those that build them again are gay" ("Lapis Lazuli").

III. After Yeats (Irish and English). The event that gave Yeats the title of perhaps the best-known elegy of the 20th c., "Easter, 1916"—with its refrain "All changed, changed utterly: / A terrible beauty is born"—ended early the life of Patrick Pearse (1879–1916), the poet who gave to the Ir. lang. revival, as O'Leary writes, "a personal, and recognizably modern, voice." Pearse was best known for his overtly patriotic "Míse Eire." The Ir.-lang. trad. gathered new strength by the middle of the 20th c. in poems that responded to contemp. life in Ireland, and beyond, as in Máirtín Ó Direáin's (1910–88) "All This and the Hydrogen Bomb Too." Máire Mhac an tSaoi (b. 1922), celebrated for producing a poetic subject subversive of narrow attitudes toward women and sexuality in Ir. lang. culture, is followed by one female successor, Biddy Jenkinson (b. 1949), who has said that the Ir.-lang. poet should be a "trouble-maker." Nuala Ní Dhomhnaill (b. 1952), the most celebrated Ir.-lang. poet of her generation, puts the "language issue" (in a poem so titled, in Eng.) into "the lap, perhaps, / of some Pharaoh's daughter" ("Ceist na Teangan") while in "Dubh" (Black), she writes powerfully of ethnic violence in mod. Europe while echoing the figure of the Roisín Dubh (see Mangan). Ní Dhomhnaill—with Michael Davitt (1950–2005), Gabriel Rosenstock (b. 1949), and Cathal Ó Searcaigh (b. 1956)—emerged in the generation of Ir.-lang. poets influenced at University College Cork by Seán Ó Riordáin (1916–77) and Sean Ó Tuama (1926–2006). Michael Hartnett (1941–99), already a distinguished writer of poetry in Eng., at mid-career published critically acclaimed collections in Ir.

Samuel Beckett (1906–89), was—like many 20th-c. Ir. poets—influenced by the Irishman best known for his prose and his facility with langs., James Joyce (1882–1941). Perhaps following their examples in prose, and in personal mobility, more than their poetry, their successors, sharing a cosmopolitan skepticism of cultural nationalism and an awareness of how insularity may look from elsewhere, include Denis Devlin (1908–59), Pearse Hutchinson (1927–2012), and a few modernist contemporaries, such as Trevor Joyce (b. 1947), but also, and more vitally, such recent Ir. poets as Harry Clifton (b. 1952), Peter Sirr (b. 1960), Vona Groarke (b. 1964), Conor O'Callaghan (b. 1968), Justin Quinn (b. 1968), Catriona O'Reilly (b. 1973), David Wheatley (b. 1970), Sinead Morrissey (b. 1972), and Leontia Flynn (b. 1974).

Of the distinguished poets writing immediately after Yeats (one of whom was Padraic Fallon [1905–74]), it was the native Dubliner Austin Clarke (1896–1974) who brought Joyce's polyvocal playfulness and criticism of sexual hypocrisy into his poetry, even as he drew authoritatively on prosodic devices from the Ir. and, in poems such as "Aisling" and "The Straying Student," Gaelic themes. Another satirist of an Ireland isolated from Europe by neutrality in the war and culturally restricted by Catholicism at home was a poet who grew up in rural Monaghan, Patrick Kavanagh (1904–67), best known for the scathing rural realism of *The Great Hunger* but late in life a celebrant, like Clarke, of sexual love and bodily realities in "Canal Bank Walk" and "The Hospital." From the North, Louis MacNeice (1907–63), who made his reputation as a chronicler, in verse and in radio drama, of wartime and postwar London, wrote with equal deftness of the languid satisfactions of the Eng. suburbs and his own aversion and devotion to an Ireland of "dolled up Virgins / and your ignorant dead" ("Valediction"). He is particularly remembered for his ambitious and emotionally nuanced *Autumn Journal*, which follows into its private, fragile places the waxing and waning of love during the months, in London, when the rumblings of war cast in new light the day to day. MacNeice wrote memorable lyrics, precise in diction, elegant but informal in voice, and almost always tonally dark—such as "Snow," "Meeting Point," "Sunday Morning," and "The Sunlight on the Garden"—that particularly influenced the poets of the North of the next generation. A Protestant contemporary who stayed in Ulster, John Hewitt (1907–1987) was another source of influence in the North.

On both sides of the Ir. border poets emerged in the postwar decades who, by the early 1970s, had received such international acclaim that a second 20th-c. revival in Ireland was proclaimed in the Am. popular press, one that has been too restrictively called the Ulster Ren. In the South, the writers included John Montague, born in America in 1929 and raised in the North, and the author of the major historical narrative of the Ir. Troubles, *The Rough Field*, a sequence that is modernist and even postmodernist in its juxtaposition of past and present, of historical voices and artifacts, family lore, and personal lyric. Richard Murphy (b. 1927), who has written with frankness and stark beauty about the natural world and sexuality and about relationships with men as well as women, has evoked his own haunting by the land, sea, and cultural life of the west of Ireland. The leading Ir. poet of his generation, Thomas Kinsella (b. 1928), has made the Dublin of his ancestors a topos as memorable as Joyce's, where what he calls "established personal places" may "receive our lives' heat" and, in so doing, "adapt in their mass, like stone" ("Personal Places"). At the same time, he has been, after Yeats, the poet in Ireland who has combined with a personal, and sometimes angry, voice—cadenced so naturally, often in free verse, that its rhetorical power and even eloquence follows an innate urgency—with an effort to imagine sweeping, transhistorical patterns of recurrence, repossession, and renewal that give purpose to the most intimate and sometimes brutal acts of kinship and conquest. A translator and scholar of Ir.-lang. poetry (incl.

a major trans. of *The Tain*), adopting for his own themes the early Ir. *Book of Invasions*, Kinsella has resourcefully exploited what he has called the "gapped and polyglot" trad. of Ir. poetry. The strength of poetry south of the border, and its international reach, may be witnessed in such successors as Brendan Kennelly (b. 1936), Eamon Grennan (b. 1941), Paul Durcan (b. 1944), and Dennis O'Driscoll (1954–2012).

Site of Ambush, a formally achieved and historically precise rendering of an ambush in the Ir. War for Independence, was published in 1975 by a young (and polyglot) scholar of the Eng. Ren., Eiléan Ní Chuilleanáin (b. 1942). She writes with equal poise and power of the quiet heroism of women's lives, sometimes in traditional roles of mourning and in preserving and renewing the past, as in "The Architectural Metaphor," which reminds us that, however "out of reach" might be the help we seek, we may see, through metaphor, where we dwell with fresh vision, "the world not dead after all." In the first Ir. revival, there were, of course, women poets, incl. Katharine Tynan (1861–1931) and Dora Sigerson Shorter (1866–1918); they were followed by mid-century by the example of Mhac an tSaoi and Blanaid Salkeld (1880–1959). The arrival of Ní Chuilleanáin and of Eavan Boland (b. 1944), the latter assuming the role of spokesperson for what she calls, in the subtitle of her 1995 *Object Lessons*, "the life of the woman and the poet in our time," ushered in a new perspective on Ir. trads. Boland's version of Pearse's "Míse Eire" is, e.g., an ironic overturning of the aisling convention. Boland in particular has inspired Paula Meehan (b. 1955), even as Meehan also has developed an inimitable idiom by drawing on trads. from Am. poetry, Buddhism, and proletarian North Dublin. Of that same generation of distinguished Ir. women poets is Moya Cannon (b. 1956) and the Ger.-born Eva Bourke (b. 1946). Medbh McGuckian (b. 1950), a Catholic poet from the North, praised for poems that seem postmod. in shifting rapidly between abstraction and intimate, sensual particularity, evokes political threat—with an increasing attunement in later volumes to republican hist. as it enters into male bodiliness—but always with a sense of the possibility that lang. may itself alter ("radicalize") the very root of the speaking tongue or metric foot or native culture, offering "a seed-fund, a pendulum / pressing out the diasporic snow" ("Dream-Language of Fergus").

Seamus Heaney (1939–2013), a Nobel laureate and the best-known Ir. poet of the current age, was part of the Belfast scene in the early 1970s that encouraged McGuckian and fellow students at Queens University, Paul Muldoon (b. 1951) and Ciaran Carson (b. 1948). Heaney, from his first poems, made palpable and universal the rituals of daily life on a Derry Catholic farmstead. Yet he also writes movingly of sorrow in such communities, whether the deaths are political or personal, as in "Clearances:" "A soul ramifying and forever / Silent, beyond silence listened for." Of Heaney's own generation, which included the *Honest Ulsterman* founder James Simmons (1933–2001), and a little later Tom Paulin (b. 1949), two other poets have enjoyed distinguished careers and international reputations. Derek Mahon (b. 1941) combined the forms of high Yeatsian rhet. with a voice that undercut its own stance, calling "poetry" a "dying art / An eddy of semantic scruple" ("Rage for Order"), driven by a postapocalyptic vision in which in "a lost hub-cap is conceived" whatever "ideal society" will "replace our own" ("After Nerval"). Michael Longley (b. 1939) is a keen observer of a quieter, more humane nature in such poems as "Madame Butterfly," yet his "Ceasefire" is perhaps the poem most often quoted on the Troubles and the hopes that followed the event that gave the 1994 poem its title.

Muldoon, while he has approached the Troubles more obliquely than these Northern predecessors, has developed dazzling, dizzying rhyme schemes (as in the 150-page sestina "Yarrow"). His formal ingeniousness, combined with liberties taken with the sonnet and with Yeats's *ottava rima* (and with bodies that are, like his own previous themes and even phrases, subject to disfigurement), has driven Muldoon's inimitable and arresting explorations of love and abjection in a time of violence, a hist. that he does not limit geopolitically to the North of Ireland. As much a poet of the cold war (and later the Am. wars in the Islamic world) as of the Troubles that he knew close up in rural Armagh, Muldoon's "voice" is thrice removed and yet intimate and invasive when the imprisoned hunger strikers speak (as mushrooms) in "Gathering Mushrooms": "lie down with us now and wrap / yourself in the soiled grey blanket of Irish rain." Carson, who learned Ir. in his Belfast home, has made a dual career as a prolific producer of musical and verbal arts that cross the boundaries among poetry, prose, song, trans., and even ethnography, suggesting new possibilities for imagining trads. in both langs., Ir. and Eng., as they spar with and spur one another. As he writes in "Hamlet," in passing the time at the local pub, hist. itself comes alive, proposing new endings to tragic episodes, because conversation *is* itself time, so the past, hedged by words that "blossom" in creative, oral exchange, "flits incessantly into the present."

■ **Anthologies in English and Translations from Gaelic**: *The Love Songs of Connacht* and *The Religious Songs of Connacht*, ed. and trans. D. Hyde (1893, 1906); *Bards of the Gael and Gall*, ed. and trans. G. Sigerson (1897); *Selections from Ancient Irish Poetry*, ed. and trans. K. Meyer (1911); *An Anthology of Irish Verse*, ed. P. Colum (1922); *Love's Bitter-Sweet*, ed. and trans. R. Flower (1925); K. A. Jackson, *Studies in Early Celtic Nature Poetry* (1935); *1000 Years of Irish Poetry*, ed. K. Hoagland (1947); *A Celtic Miscellany*, ed. and trans. K. A. Jackson (1951); *Irish Poets of the Nineteenth Century*, ed. G. Taylor (1951); *Early Irish Lyrics*, ed. and trans. G. Murphy (1956); *Kings, Lords and Commons*, ed. and trans. F. O'Connor (1959); *Love Poems of the Irish*, ed. and trans. S. Lucy (1967); *The Penguin Book of Irish Verse*, ed. B. Kennelly (1970); *The Book of Irish Verse*, ed. J. Montague (1974); *An Duanaire, 1600–1900: Poems of the Dispossessed*, ed. and trans. T. Kinsella and S. O'Tuama (1981); *Early Irish Verse*, ed. and tran. R. Lehmann (1982); *Poets of Munster*, ed. S. Dunne (1985); *The Bright Wave*, ed. D. Bolger (1986); *The New Oxford Book of Irish Verse*, ed. T. Kinsella (1986); *Contemporary Irish Poetry*, ed. A. Bradley (1988); *Contemporary Irish Poetry*, ed. P. Fallon and D. Mahon (1990); *Field Day Anthology of Irish Writing*, ed. S. Deane, 3 v. (1991); *Modern Irish Poetry*, ed. P. Crotty (1995); *Wake Forest Anthology of Irish Women's Poetry, 1967–2000*, ed. P. O'Brien (1999); *Writing Irish*, ed. J. Myers Jr. (1999); *Field Day Anthology of Irish Literature: Vols. IV–V: Irish Women's Writing and Traditions*, ed. A. Bourke et al. (2002); *In the Chair: Interviews with Poets from the North of Ireland*, ed. J. Brown (2002); *The New Irish Poets*, ed. S. Guinness (2004); *Irish Literature, 1750–1900*, ed. J. Wright (2008); *Anthology of Modern Irish Poetry*, ed. W. Davis (2010); *The Penguin Book of Irish Verse*, ed. P. Crotty (2010).

■ **Bibliographies**: R. I. Best, *A Bibliography of Irish Philology and of Printed Irish Literature* (1913); K.G.W. Cross and R.T.A. Dunlop, *A Bibliography of Yeats Criticism, 1887–1965* (1971); R. Bromwich, *Medieval Celtic Literature: A Select Bibliography* (1974); M. Lapidge and R. Sharpe, *A Bibliography of Celtic-Latin Literature, 400–1200* (1985); K.P.S. Jochum, *W. B. Yeats: A Classified Bibliography of Criticism* (1990).

■ **Criticism and History**: E. O'Reilly, *A Chronological Account of Nearly Four Hundred Irish Writers* (1820); E. A. Boyd, *Ireland's Literary Renaissance* (1916); D. Corkery, *The Hidden Ireland* (1924); A. De Blacam, *Gaelic Literature Surveyed* (1929); R. Flower, *The Irish Tradition* (1947); M. Dillon, *Early Irish Literature* (1948); E. Knott, *Irish Syllabic Poetry, 1200–1600* (1957); C. Watkins, "Indo-European Metrics and Archaic Irish Verse," *Celtica* 6 (1963); C. Donahue, "Medieval Celtic Literature," Fisher; *Early Irish Poetry*, ed. J. Carney (1965); P. L. Henry, *The Early English and Celtic Lyric* (1966); P. Power, *A Literary History of Ireland* (1969); O. Bergin, *Irish Bardic Poetry* (1970); H. Bloom, *Yeats* (1970); J. E. Stoll, *The Great Deluge: A Yeats Bibliography* (1971); T. Brown, *Northern Voices: Poets from Ulster* (1975); *Two Decades of Irish Writing*, ed. D. Dunn (1975); R. Finneran, *Anglo-Irish Literature: A Review of Research* (1976); D. Perkins, *A History of Modern Poetry*, 2 v. (1976, 1987); S. O'Neill, "Gaelic Literature," *Dictionary of Irish Literature*, ed. R. Hogan et al. (1979); G. J. Watson, *Irish Identity and the Literary Revival* (1979); R. Welch, *Irish Poetry from Moore to Yeats* (1980); T. Kinsella and S. Ó Tuama, *An Duanaire: Poems of the Dispossessed, 1600–1900* (1981); *Ireland: A Social and Cultural History, 1922–79*, ed. T. Brown (1981); A. N. Jeffares, *Anglo-Irish Literature* (1982); *The Pleasures of Gaelic Poetry*, ed. S. MacReammoin (1982); S. Deane, *Celtic Revivals* (1985), and *A Short History of Irish Literature* (1986); R. Garratt, *Modern Irish Poetry* (1986); D. Johnston, *Irish Poetry after Joyce* (1986); E. Longley, *Poetry in the Wars* (1986); P. L. Marcus, *Yeats and the Beginning of the Irish Renaissance*, 2d ed. (1987); *Tradition and Influence in Anglo-Irish Poetry*, ed. T. Brown and N. Grene (1989); P. MacCana, "Introduction: Early and Middle Irish Literature (c. 600–1600)," *Field Day Anthology of Irish Writing*, ed. S. Deane, v. 1 (1991); *The Chosen Ground*, ed. N. Corcoran (1992); *Improprieties*, ed. C. Wills (1993); E. Boland, *Object Lessons: The Life of the Woman and the Poet in Our Time* (1995); D. Kiberd, *Inventing Ireland* (1995); T. Kinsella, *The Dual Tradition* (1995); *Modernism and Ireland*, ed. P. Coughlan and A. Davis (1995); S. Ó Tuama, *Repossessions* (1995); P. Haberstroh, *Women Creating Women* (1996); B. Howard, *The Pressed Melodeon* (1996); S. Deane, *Strange Country* (1997); S. Matthews, *Irish Poetry* (1997); P. McDonald, *Mistaken Identities* (1997); G. Schirmer, *Out of What Began* (1998); A. Fogarty, "'The Influence of Absences': Eavan Boland and the Silenced History of Irish Women's Poetry," *Colby Quarterly* 35 (1999); E. Grennan, *Facing the Music* (1999); *Poets of Modern Ireland*, ed. N. Corcoran (1999); F. Brearton, *The Great War in Irish Poetry* (2000); J. Goodby, *Irish Poetry since 1950* (2000); D. Kiberd, *Irish Classics* (2000); D. O'Driscoll, *Troubled Thoughts, Majestic Dreams* (2001); N. Vance, *Irish Literature after 1800* (2002); *Cambridge Companion to Contemporary Irish Poetry*, ed. M. Campbell (2003); A. Gillis, *Irish Poetry of the 1930s* (2005); H. Clark, *The Ulster Renaissance* (2006); *Cambridge History of Irish Literature*, ed. M. Kelleher and P. O'Leary (2006)—esp. essays by T. Ó Cathasaigh, M. Ní Mhaonaigh, M. Caball, K. Hollo, A. Fogarty, N. Buttimer, M. Campbell, G. Denvir, D. Wong, P. O'Leary, L. de Paor, D. Johnston, G. Batten, and B. Nic Dhiarmada; *A Companion to Irish Literature*, ed. J. Wright, 2 v. (2010).

G. Batten

ITALIAN PROSODY

I. Introduction
II. Meter
III. Rhyme
IV. Poetic Forms

I. Introduction. At its beginnings in the 13th c., It. poetry imitated many of the themes and forms of Occitan and OF poetry (see occitan poetry; france, poetry of). Med. Lat. rhythmical verse also exerted a strong formal influence on many of the nascent vernacular lyrical modes in Italy. In addition to his preeminence as Italy's leading poet, Dante (1265–1321) was the first among many well-known theoreticians of prosody. In the *Vita nuova* (ch. 25), Dante expresses his views on the hist. of poetic composition in the Eur. vernaculars and argues that, on the model of their Gr. and Lat. predecessors, It. poets should be allowed to use rhetorical figures. He also recognizes not only the seriousness of lit. but his own role as an inventive artist and his place in the literary trad.

Dante's literary career essentially retraces the trajectory of lyric poetry in 13th-c. Italy, from the Sicilian school through the *Dolce stil nuovo*; thus, his remarks on and practice of versification are of particular importance for the It. poetic trad. In his unfinished treatise, *De vulgari eloquentia* (*On Vernacular Eloquence*, ca. 1304), Dante situates poetic praxis within a more theoretical discussion of the nature of poetic lang., esp. the search among the various It. dialects for a sufficiently noble literary lang., one that would be, in his terms, "illustrious, cardinal, courtly, and curial" (1.17.1). Such a lang. would be the proper medium for refined lyric poetry in the "high" or "tragic" style on one of the three noble themes: prowess in arms, love, and moral virtue (2.2.7). From the "question of language," Dante passes to an extended discussion of metrical forms (2.3.1–3), particularly the construction of the *canzone*: the grammatical structure of the verse period, the qualities of words, varying line lengths, the *aab* structure of the canzone stanza, and the particular nature of rhyme words and rhyming devices. While intending to treat this last point in the (unwritten) fourth book of the treatise, Dante discusses the ordering of the canzone through placement of rhymes and discourages certain practices: excessive use of the same rhyme, equivocal rhymes, and rhymes with harsh sounds. Not extant—if they were ever written—are sections on the *ballata* and sonnet, both of which belong to the "middle" style. Nevertheless, Dante's codification of It. prosody served as a touchstone for centuries of both praxis and crit.

II. Meter. It. metrics is based both on number of syllables and on the position of the primary accent in the line, the latter being the determining factor in meter. Syllables are counted only up to the last accent; if any follow it, they are ignored. Hence, the hendecasyllable (*endecasillabo*), the most excellent of meters according to Dante and the one most appropriate for subjects in the high style, is not necessarily determined by the presence of 11 syllables, as its name implies, but rather by the placement of the primary accent on the tenth syllable and a secondary stress on either the fourth or sixth syllable. While a "normal" hendecasyllable (*endecasillabo piano*) adheres to the 11-syllable model, it may have as few as 10 syllables (*endecasillabo tronco*) or as many as 12 or 13 (*endecasillabo sdrucciolo* or *bisdrucciolo*). Contiguous vowels must often be elided for a verse to scan, via either synaloepha or synaeresis. At other times, such vowels must be pronounced separately, via dialoepha (across a word boundary) or diaeresis (within a word).

After the hendecasyllable, the seven-syllable line (*settenario*) is the next most popular It. meter, with the principal stress always on the sixth syllable, as in "Il Cinque Maggio" by Alessandro Manzoni (1785–1873). Dante notes that verses with an odd number of syllables (3, 5, 7, 11) are generally to be preferred; thus, we find verses in all periods of It. lit. with five syllables (*quinario*: major stress on the fourth), as, e.g., in "La pioggia nel pineto" by Gabriele D'Annunzio (1863–1938). Although in early It. poetry the *trisillabo* (major accent on the second syllable) is generally found only as a rhyming component (internal rhyme: *rimalmezzo*) of a longer verse, it sometimes appears as a separate verse. The trisillabo, however, occurs with some frequency in mod. poets, as in D'Annunzio's "La pioggia nel pineto" (14–15), where he combines a quinario with a trisillabo. Dante holds the nine-syllable line (*novenario*: major accent on the eighth syllable) in contempt for giving "the impression of being three lines of three syllables" (*De vulgari eloquentia* 2.5.6; trans. Haller), but it has been used by Gabriello Chiabrera (1552–1638), Francesco Redi (1626–98), Giosuè Carducci (1835–1907), Giovanni Pascoli (1855–1912), and D'Annunzio.

Dante considers lines with an even number of syllables decidedly less noble (2.5.7), perhaps because the regularity of the stress pattern led to a monotonous cadence. Nevertheless, there are numerous examples of octosyllabic verse (*ottonario*, accent on the seventh syllable), esp. in poems of popular inspiration; similarly, we have examples of six-syllable verses (*senario*, accent on the fifth syllable) and four-syllable verses (*quadrisillabo*, accent on third).

Many early narrative poems were written in stanzas composed of 14-syllable lines, *alessandrini*, which imitate OF verses; these are essentially double heptasyllables (*doppi settenari*, accents on the sixth and thirteenth syllables) with a caesura after the first settenario. They were also called *versi martelliani*, after Pier Jacopo Martelli (1661–1727), who composed tragedies in this meter based on the model of Pierre Corneille and Jean Racine, and were used subsequently by Carlo Goldoni (1707–93) and Giuseppe Giacosa (1847–1906) in their comedies and by Carducci in his *Rime nuove*. Decasyllables (*decasillabi*, accent on tenth syllable) also were first modeled on OF meters; these enjoyed a certain popularity in the 19th c. with Manzoni, Giovanni Berchet (1783–1851), Giuseppe Giusti (1809–50), and Pascoli.

Both in the Ren. and in the 19th c., we find examples of the imitation of cl. meters. The first conscious attempts were made by Leon Battista Alberti (1404–72) and Leonardo Dati (1360–1425), who composed It. hexameters for the poetry contest—the *certame coronario*—of 1441. Ludovico Ariosto (1474–1533) tried his hand at reproducing the Lat. iambic trimeter in hendecasyllables. In the 16th and 17th cs., Claudio Tolomei (1492–1555) and Chiabrera attempted to resolve the conflict between the Lat. quantitative and the It. accentual systems. Carducci also experimented with "barbarian" poetry (*metrica barbara*)—for such it would have appeared and sounded to the ancients—based on accentual imitations of cl. meters, e.g. Virgilian hexameters and Catullian elegiac distichs. In his *Odi barbare*, Carducci is esp. indebted to Horace.

III. Rhyme. Rhymes in It. are exact. Rhyme sounds are identical from the major stress to the end of the word: *amóre* / *dolóre*; *compí* / *sentí*; *cántano* / *piántano*. Eye rhymes (*rime all'occhio*), which are apparently but not actually identical, are infrequent (*pálmi* / *sálmi* / *almí*; Dante, *Inferno* 31.65, 67, 69). Examples of composite rhymes (*rime composte*) may be found in early poetry (*chiome* / *oh me*; *Inferno* 28.121, 123) and esp. in the poetry of Guittone d'Arezzo (ca. 1225–93) and his followers. Other unusual sorts of rhyme found among the early lyrics include equivocal rhyme (*traductio*, where the word is the same but has a different meaning), derivative rhyme (*replicatio*, where the rhyme words have the same root), and rich rhyme (*rima cara*, *ricca*, where an uncommon word form is used).

In the early lyrics, there is a phenomenon known as Sicilian rhyme (*rima siciliana*), which refers to words that in the dialect of the Sicilian poets would have rhymed because of the identity of the vowels *e* and *i*, and *o* and *u*. Thus, *diri* (= *dire*) and *taciri* (= *tacere*), as well as *tuttu* (= *tutto*) and *muttu* (= *motto*), rhyme in Sicilian, but not in It. When the Sicilian lyrics were copied into mss. by late 13th-c. Tuscan scribes, these forms were "Tuscanized," i.e., regularized orthographically, and thus emerged rhymes such as *ride* / *vede* (Sicilian *ridi* / *vidi*) and *ascoso* / *incluso* (Sicilian *ascusu* / *inclusu*).

Generally speaking, most med. It. poetry is rhymed, although we do find occasional examples of assonance or consonance, as e.g., in the *Laudes creaturarum* of St. Francis of Assisi (1182–1226), and some examples of *versi sciolti*, poems with unrhymed lines, the first example of which is the anonymous 13th-c. poem "Il mare amoroso." This It. variety of blank verse was reintroduced in the Ren., first by Giangiorgio Trissino (1478–1550) in his epic *L'Italia liberata dai Goti*.

IV. Poetic Forms. For Dante, the canzone represents the height of artistic perfection. It developed in Italy under the direct influence of the Occitan *canso*, the OF *chanson*, and the German *Minnesang*. Canzoni generally have several strophes composed mainly of endecasillabi and settenari, all of which follow the same structure (a one-stanza canzone is called a *cobbola*). Canzoni composed entirely of shorter meters are called by the diminutive *canzonette*; these were esp. privileged in the 17th and 18th cs. by Chiabrera, Carlo Innocenzo Frugoni (1692–1768), Pietro Metastasio (1698–1782), and Giuseppe Parini (1729–99).

The essential division of the canzone strophe is bipartite, the first part being termed the *fronte* and the second the *sirma*. The fronte usually divides into two (sometimes three) equal parts called "feet" (*piedi*); the sirma sometimes divides into two equal parts called *volte* or *giri*. The passage from fronte to sirma, which marks the change from one musical pattern to another, is generally known as the *diesis*. Some canzoni conclude with a *commiato* (*envoi*), a short stanza generally having the same pattern as the sirma (or a part of it), in which the poet sometimes addresses his composition and instructs it where it should go, with whom it should speak, what it should say, and so on.

These rules were followed rigidly until the 17th c., when the rise of the *canzone libera* signaled the abandonment of prosodic uniformity among strophes. Poets were thus presented with two possibilities: following the older, traditional forms or the newer, freer models. While some poets adhered in part to the earlier modes (Vittorio Alfieri [1749–1803], Vincenzo Monti [1754–1828], Ugo Foscolo [1778–1827], Manzoni, Carducci), most followed the newer forms, perhaps best exemplified by Giacomo Leopardi (1798–1837) in his *Canti*.

Other important forms include the ballata, which arose in the mid-13th c. as a song to accompany a dance and has essentially the same form as the canzone, except that the ballata begins with a refrain, the *ritornello* or *ripresa*, which in performance was repeated after each stanza and the last rhyme(s) of which recurs at the end of each stanza. The ballata was very popular in the Middle Ages and Ren. and found illustrious practitioners in Dante, Petrarch (1304–74), Lorenzo de' Medici (1449–92), Angelo Poliziano ([Politian] 1454–94), and Pietro Bembo (1470–1547). It was revived briefly in the late 19th c. by Carducci, Pascoli, and D'Annunzio. The *lauda* adopted the metrical form of the secular ballata under the guidance of its first great practitioner, Jacopone da Todi (1236?–1306), but its very popular use for religious subjects did not extend past the 15th c. In imitation of the Occitan troubadour Arnaut Daniel (fl. 1180–95), Dante introduced the sestina; later practitioners include Petrarch, Michelangelo (1475–1564), Carducci, D'Annunzio, and Giuseppe Ungaretti. The 14th c. saw the advent of other lyrical modes, esp. the madrigal and *caccia*. In the 16th and 17th cs., the madrigal became the preferred form to be set to music, e.g., by Giovanni Palestrina (ca. 1525–94) and Claudio Monteverdi (1567–1643); the caccia disappears after the 16th c.

The sonnet, arguably the single most important creation of It. prosody, was apparently invented in the second quarter of the 13th c. by Giacomo da Lentini (fl. first half of 13th c.), a notary at the court of Frederick II in Sicily. Although perhaps formed by the reduction of two *strambotti*, it more likely developed in imitation of the strophe of the canzone. In early It. lit., the rhyme schemes of the quatrains and tercets are more flexible than later. The sonnet was also used as the vehicle for verse epistles in the *tenzone*, an exchange of sonnets in which a topic or question was proposed for discussion to one or more poets. (Generally, as the tenzone developed, it became the rule that the response would have the same rhymes and metrical scheme as the initial sonnet, hence the phrase "rispondere per le rime," to reply by the rhymes.) Under the influence of Petrarch, perhaps its most important practitioner, and Petrarchism, the sonnet sequence spread throughout Europe. It. poets who have cultivated the sonnet include Michelangelo, Torquato Tasso (1544–95), Alfieri, Foscolo, Carducci, and D'Annunzio, although its popularity in It. has steadily diminished since the 17th c.

In narrative poetry, *ottava rima*, used first by Giovanni Boccaccio (1313–75) for his verse narratives (*Teseida, Filostrato, Ninfale fiesolano*), became the staple for both the epic and the popular *cantare*, which had for its subject matter cl. and med. myths and legends, as well as contemp. political events and humorous tales. Following Boccaccio's lead, the great epic poets of the Ren. used ottava rima for their chivalric poems (Matteo Maria Boiardo [1441–94], *Orlando innamorato*; Ariosto, *Orlando furioso*; and Tasso, *Gerusalemme liberata*), as did other poets such as Luigi Pulci (1432–84, *Morgante*), Politian (*Stanze per la giostra*), Giambattista Marino (1569–1625, *Adone*), and Alessandro Tassoni (1565–1635, *La secchia rapita*).

Allegory, didactic poetry, and the dream vision generally were composed in *terza rima*, following the great model of Dante's *Divine Comedy*. Thus, Boccaccio used terza rima in the *Amorosa Visione*, Petrarch in the *Trionfi*, and Fazio degli Uberti (ca. 1307–70) in the *Dittamondo*. In later centuries, terza rima, often in the form of the *capitolo*, was incorporated by poets for a variety of compositions: satires (Ariosto, Francesco Berni [?1497–1535], Alfieri, Leopardi), historical fictions (Niccolò Machiavelli [1469–1527]), eclogues (de' Medici), amorous elegies (Ariosto, Foscolo, Carducci), and political allegories (Monti).

The rules of It. prosody were essentially fixed for subsequent poets in the first two centuries of It. lit., because of the examples of Dante, Petrarch, and Boccaccio and the work of early compilers of metrical treatises such as Francesco da Barberino (1264–1348; *Documenti d'Amore* [1306–13]), Antonio da Tempo (ca. 1275–1336; *Summa artis rithimici vulgaris dictaminis* [1332]), and Gidino da Sommacampagna (fl. late 14th c.; *Trattato dei ritmi volgari* [1381–84]). To be sure, metrical innovation has always taken place, particularly in the 20th c. with literary movements such as futurism and hermeticism. Nevertheless, while prosodic forms are no longer followed strictly, poets still imitate, albeit unconsciously, the cadences of traditional verse.

See ITALY, POETRY OF.

■ G. da Sommacampagna, *Trattato dei ritmi volgari*, ed. G.B.C. Giuliari (1870); P. E. Guarnerio, *Manuale di versificazione italiana* (1893); F. Flamini, *Notizia storica dei versi e metri italiani* (1919); R. Murari, *Ritmica e metrica razionale italiana* (1927); V. Pernicone, "Storia e svolgimento della metrica," *Problemi ed orientamenti critici di lingua e di letteratura italiana*, ed. A. Momigliano, v. 2 (1948); M. Pazzaglia, *Il verso e l'arte della canzone nel "De vulgari eloquentia"* (1967); A. B. Giamatti, "Italian," in Wimsatt; *La metrica*, ed. R. Cremante and M. Pazzaglia (1972); D. S. Avalle, *Sintassi e prosodia nella lirica italiana delle origini* (1973); F. Caliri, *Ritmica e metrica* (1973); Spongano; M. Fubini, *Metrica e poesia*, 3d ed. (1975); *Literary Criticism of Dante Alighieri*, ed. and trans. R. S. Haller (1977); Antonio da Tempo, *Summa artis rithimici vulgaris dictaminis*, ed. R. Andrews (1977); L. Castelnuovo, *La metrica italiana* (1979); D. Alighieri, *Opere minori*, ed. P. V. Mengaldo (1979); M. Shapiro, *Hieroglyph of Time: The Petrarchan Sestina* (1981); Brogan—bibl. to 1981, supp. in *Verseform* (1988); F. P. Memmo, *Dizionario di metrica italiana* (1983); Elwert, *Italienische*; A. Menichetti, *Metrica italiana* (1993); S. Orlando, *Manuale di metrica italiana* (1994).

C. Kleinhenz

ITALY, POETRY OF

I. Duecento: The 1200s
II. Trecento: The 1300s
III. Quattrocento: The 1400s
IV. Cinquecento: The 1500s
V. Seicento: The 1600s
VI. Settecento: The 1700s
VII. Ottocento: The 1800s
VIII. Novecento: The 1900s

I. Duecento: The 1200s. The Middle Ages, from the fall of the Roman Empire to the 1300s, was long regarded as merely an epoch of barbarism. Mod. historiography, however, has rediscovered the period from Charlemagne to the birth of the Romance vernacular lits. as a time of fervent incubation, a preparation for the cultural rebirth of the 13th and 14th cs. During this period, the autonomous existence of the Neo-Lat. langs. became evident. The first documents of It. lang. and lit.—from the doubtful *Indovinello veronese* (Veronese Riddle, 9th c.) and the *Ritmo laurenziano* (Laurentian Verse, ca. 1150) to St. Francis's "Hymn," Jacopone's poems, and the Sicilian and Tuscan love lyrics—should be examined in the light of three conditioning facts: (1) the political conformation of the It. Peninsula—the constant tension between temporal and ecclesiastical power and its result, the Guelph-Ghibelline wars; (2) the influence of Fr. and Occitan literary models—the Fr. lang. precedes It. by a century or more, the delay usually being attributed to a tenacious survival of Lat., though it also reflects the absence of a central power, hence a slower evolution of feudal structures in the peninsula; and (3) the widespread religious revival beginning around the year 1000 and its vast influence throughout the 1300s.

Directly related to the latter is the religious order founded by Francis of Assisi (1182–1226), who is also the first It. poet worthy of note. His "Cantico delle creature" (Song of the Creatures, also known as the *Laudes creaturarum*), a thanksgiving hymn by and for the creature to the Creator, reflects a spirit of humility and simple faith, as well as a newfound wonder at the beauty of the creation and an implicit refusal to see earthly life as a mere valley of tears. The primitive diction should not mislead the reader: Francis is a conscious inventor of poetry. This can be seen in the careful structure of the hymn, in the purposeful ambivalence of word choice, and in the celebrated adjectival series that define each "member" of the grace-giving choir.

The genre of the *lauda*, enriched by the example of med. Lat. liturgical lit., became high poetry in the hands of Jacopone da Todi (1236?–1306), an attorney spiritually reborn after the tragic death of his wife. Jacopone vigorously opposed the power plays of Pope Boniface VIII (Dante's archenemy) and was excommunicated and imprisoned by him; a number of the approximately 100 extant laude by Jacopone are against the simony of the Church (e.g., "O Papa Bonifazio"). Jacopone's best poetry is inspired by his feeling of isolation in his mystical passion, and his masterpiece, the "Donna del Paradiso" (Lament of Mary), presents Christ's passion as seen through the eyes of his mother. Here Jacopone reaches lyric heights never before attained in It. poetry.

The first matrix of It. literary trad. is the Sicilian school. Centered at the court of Frederick II (1194–1250), the group devolved from the Occitan troubadour trad., superimposing the rituals of feudal bondage and court protocol onto a concept of love, its only topic, in which the perfect submission by the lover corresponds to the heavenly perfection of the lady. The school had great cultural importance, and its major exponent, the notary Giacomo da Lentini (fl. first half of 13th c.), probably invented the sonnet. Mentioned by Dante as the foremost poet of the Magna Curia, Giacomo was a faithful adapter of the troubadours' and *trouvères'* schemata of *fin'amors*. Other members of the Sicilian school were Giacomino Pugliese (fl. 1325–50), Rinaldo d'Aquino (?1227–81), and Pier delle Vigne (ca. 1190–1249?).

The emperor Frederick, himself a poet, had vainly attempted to unify his Ger. and It. domains against violent ecclesiastical opposition. During his reign arose the Ghibelline (imperial) and Guelph (papal) factions, antagonists for over a century in It. politics. After the battle of Benevento (1266), which marked the end of the Hohenstaufen dynasty, the practice of poetry survived but was transplanted to Tuscany in central Italy. Its first noteworthy heir, Guittone d'Arezzo (ca. 1225–93), a Guelph exiled from his homeland, renewed and enriched the earlier lyric trad. by extending its topics to ethical and social concerns. As an extension of the *trobar clus*, Guittone's hermetic poems sound cold and artistically stifling. His technically complex style attracted imitators, such as Chiaro Davanzati (d. 1304) and the abstruse Monte Andrea (fl. 2d half 13th c.). Guittone's poetic corpus is both a bridge and a hurdle to be overcome between the Sicilians and the first great flowering of It. lyric, the school of the Sweet New Style, the *Dolce stil nuovo*.

The very existence of such a "school," posited only by a vague reference in Dante's *Purgatorio*, is unsure. Certain, however, is a common conception of love as "dictator" (inspirer and despot). The Bolognese judge Guido Guinizzelli (ca. 1240–76), praised by Dante as the father of the style *dolce* (sweet, not bitterly harsh, as in Guittone) and *nuovo* (original), left a celebrated summary of the new amorous *ars poetica* in his *canzone* "Al cor gentil": true nobility comes not from lineage but from virtue; love is a positive force: through the lady, admired from afar, the lover with a "noble heart" attains spiritual perfection. Guido's corpus (about 20 extant texts) shows a youthful vitality, also present in Dante's *Vita nuova*. Among the numerous adepts of the Sweet New Style are Lapo Gianni (d. after 1328), Gianni Alfani (fl. late 13th–early 14th cs.), Dino Frescobaldi (1221–1316), and the prolific Cino da Pistoia (ca. 1270–1336), usually viewed as a link between Dante and Petrarch. The maturity of the school is represented by Guido Cavalcanti (ca. 1255–1300), Dante's "*primo amico*" (first friend), whom legend depicts as a haughty loner, an image probably inspired by his poems (52 extant), his ars poetica, and theory of love, captured in the complex canzone "Donna me prega." Cavalcanti's interest in the mechanics of feelings, esp. the anguish of love, gives him a "morbid and mournful" air, as he observes the torment of his own soul. In his concept of love, the sight of a "real" woman stimulates the lover to form an idea of beauty that pervades his soul and, in turn, prods him to strive vainly toward the "original."

Parallel to the *stil nuovo*, a trad. of jocose (or bourgeois) poetry developed. The "Contrasto" by Cielo d'Alcamo (ca. 1200–50) is a highly artistic, lively amorous dialogue between a cynical minstrel and a clever young woman. The Sicilian court poets' recurrent topics (praise, submission) and artful ling. koiné are the ironic subtext to this still-enjoyable little masterpiece. Parody of stil nuovo themes results in shrill outbursts in Cecco Angiolieri (1260–1313?), the skilled Sienese sonneteer (over 100 extant poems), whose themes include wild quarrels with his lady (Becchina, who is no lady), tavern brawls, the sorry state of his purse, and the stinginess of his parents. Cecco is no It. Villon, as he has been called. His texts are meant for recital in the inn or square; the punch lines are ideally completed by guffaws from the guzzlers. A gentler realism inspires the sonnets of Folgóre, poet of San Gimignano (ca. 1265–before 1332), reflecting the chivalric ceremonies of polite society. The frank pursuit of pleasure here is tempered by a code of behavior based on good taste.

II. Trecento: The 1300s. In retrospect, the first hundred years of It. lit. appear as preparation for Dante's poetry. This perception, philologically speaking, is quite correct. Aesthetically, however, a veritable chasm separates Duecento poetry from the *Divine Comedy*. For valid parallels, one must turn to the fine arts and Giotto (ca. 1267–1337) or to philosophy and Thomas Aquinas (1225–74).

Little is known of Dante Alighieri's life. Born in 1265 in Florence into a Guelph-leaning family of lesser nobility, he studied rhet. with Brunetto Latini (ca. 1220–94). Lasting influences on his youth included his friendship with Cavalcanti; his discovery of his own talent for poetry; and, esp., his love for a Beatrice Portinari, wife of the banker Simone dei Bardi. Remaining devoted to Beatrice in her life and after her death, Dante recounts their lopsided love story in the *Vita nuova* (*New Life*); in his *magnum opus*, written to honor this young woman who died at 25, Beatrice is present from beginning to end. Dante never mentions his wife Gemma and their children (two sons, Jacopo [1289–1348] and Pietro [1300–64], wrote commentaries on their father's work). After 1295, documents attest to Dante's participation in the civic life of his city; in 1300, he became one of six *priori* (cabinet members) in a Florence torn between the two factions of the Guelph party: Blacks, subservient to Rome, and Whites, anti-imperial but resistant to papal hegemony. Dante sided with the latter. In 1301, he was sent by his party, then in power, as ambassador to Pope Boniface VIII, who promptly detained him, while the Blacks, with Fr. and papal help, seized power in Florence. Dante, sentenced in absentia to be burned at the stake, never again set foot in his city. In exile over 19 years, he hoped at first to deserve recall on the strength of his learning: he produced works on ling. (*De vulgari eloquentia* [*On Vernacular Eloquence*], in Lat., incomplete), philosophy (*Convivio* [*The Banquet*], unfinished), and political science (*Monarchia*). Scholars date the composition of the *Divine Comedy* from 1307 to the year of Dante's death in Ravenna, 1321.

The *Vita nuova* (1292–93) is a collection of poems connected by prose passages relating a tenuous love story from the meeting between Dante and Beatrice, both aged nine, to her death in 1290 and beyond. It is a story made up of abstract emotions, the most daring "real" event being Beatrice's one-time reciprocation of Dante's greeting. Neither autobiography nor total fiction, the *Vita nuova* is rather a typology of youthful love, pervaded by a quasi-religious, mystical solemnity and by an oneiric vagueness of detail. Dante's *Rime* comprise the poems excluded from the *Vita nuova* and those written after 1293, incl. the *canzoni* of his maturity and exile; closest to the inspiration of the *Comedy* is the poem "Tre donne" ("Three Women").

The 14,233 verses of the *Comedy* (for Dante, *comedy* and *tragedy* refer to both content and style) took 15 years to compose. In addition to the glorification of Beatrice and the exile's wish to show his worth, the purpose of the poem is expressed in Dante's letter to Can Grande (*Epistle* 13, of debated attribution) as the messianic mission "to lead the living out of a state of misery into a state of bliss." The poet achieved his literary purpose of fashioning with words a world that in its miraculous credibility vies with God's own creation. We must remember that the *Comedy* is a fiction, the work of a poet and master storyteller, not of the Holy Spirit. This obvious truth sets a limit to symbolic interpretation, even though the med. practice of allegory is ever-present in the text. What distinguishes

Dante's from earlier otherworldly journeys is that his predecessors are *all* allegory; we read Dante after seven centuries for what we find beyond his didactic purposes. Allegory is a premise of the *narratio*, flexible and often ambiguous: it is part of the polyvalence present in all enduring poetry. While Beatrice and Virgil may be, respectively, "theology" and "reason," we believe and love them primarily because Dante "forgot," more often than not, their roles as abstractions.

The *Comedy* is the fictive, visionary account of a redemptive journey through hell and purgatory to paradise and God, by a pilgrim, Dante Alighieri, who is guided first by Virgil, later by Beatrice, and finally by St. Bernard. Hell holds the souls of the damned, distributed into nine "circles" set up according to Aristotle's categories of sin (incontinence, violence, fraud [heresy was unknown to the Greek]). Purgatory is segmented into the seven deadly sins of Christian dogma (with Ante-Purgatory and Earthly Paradise bringing the number of divisions to nine). Paradise comprises the nine heavens of Ptolemy's geocentric universe, from the seven planetary spheres to the fixed stars, the *Primum Mobile*, and the Empyrean, abode of all the souls happy in the sight of God. The recurrence of the number three and its multiples, as well as other divisions in the edifice, such as the 100 *canti* or the strophic scheme of three lines of eleven syllables each—*terza rima*—or the canto and episode parallelisms and contrasts at corresponding "locations" in the three *cantiche* are important for Dantean exegesis.

Of the three canticles (34 + 33 + 33 canti), *Inferno* is the most dramatic and suspenseful. Memorable characters and events dominate several canti: Francesca's story of love and death, Farinata's "war memoirs," Chancellor Pier delle Vigne's suicide, Ulysses' last voyage, the prison "cannibalism" of Count Ugolino of Pisa. *Purgatorio* is the realm of elegy, subdued sadness, and hopeful yearning: it is the most "earthly" cantica, with feelings of brotherly affection. *Paradiso* is the triumph of Beatrice, who is both symbol and real woman. Among the blessed, absolute equality is the rule: no character should emerge. The sequence of heavens is transformed into a transcendental fireworks display of growing intensity. Humanity is never absent from the rarefied mysticism signaling God's presence. And the great saints appear in person to test, prod, warn, and guide the pilgrim toward fulfillment. God, thanks to Dante's magnificent intuition, is depicted here not as the bearded elder of Judeo-Christian iconography but as a blinding point of light immeasurably both far and near. In *Paradiso*, Dante gives evidence of his most sublime, mature genius.

Dante's robust spirituality, unshaken religious convictions, and firm belief in the continuity of social structures were rooted in the apparent stability of the "old" world, the thick Ages in the Middle. The *curriculum vitae* of Francesco Petrarca (Petrarch, 1304–74) coincides with a historical moment of accelerated change and crumbling certainties. Petrarch appears much closer to us than does Dante: closer than the generation or two that actually separate these two quasi-contemporaries. The mod. instability of Petrarch's psychic makeup is manifest in his vast correspondence, in his treatises (e.g., on "solitude," on the "remedies against Fortune"), and esp. in his Lat. *Secretum* (*Confessions*), which is a microscopic analysis of that nameless something that forever anguished his soul. Born in Arezzo of a Florentine bourgeois family in exile, Petrarch was brought up in southern France. He studied jurisprudence at Montpellier and Bologna. On April 6, 1327, his destiny was redirected when he met, in Avignon, Laura, the unidentified woman whom he loved in life and in death (she died of the plague in 1348) and whom he immortalized in his poetry. Petrarch is the forefather of humanism, the revival of Greco-Roman culture that would dominate the next century. His work in Lat. is immense, esp. his epic in hexameters, *Africa*, which procured him the title and crown of poet laureate conferred by the Senate of Rome on April 8, 1341. The uncontested arbiter of Eur. lit., Petrarch lived the latter half of his life mainly in Italy.

Petrarch expected enduring fame from his Lat. work; immeasurably superior are his modestly titled (with affected scorn) *Rerum vulgarium fragmenta* (freely rendered, "Italian bits and pieces") or *Canzoniere*. In spite of his expressed desire to burn the collection, he kept revising and perfecting the ms. to his dying day. The 366 poems (317 sonnets, plus 29 canzoni, nine sestinas, seven *ballate*, and four madrigals) record the earthly (not at all merely spiritual) passion inspired by Laura, even after her "flight to heaven." Petrarch is the last great representative of the troubadour trad. (afterward there will be epigones and Petrarchism). Some critics have doubted the very existence of Laura, assuming her to be a composite of the poetic trad. While the "love story" behind the stylized abstractions is clearly an unrequited love, the human passion of the poet, with its ebb and flow over the years, its brief joys and long despair, its cries and silences, and its phases of resignation and rebellion, recreates the anonymous Beloved, body and soul. Although Petrarch veils and stylizes his earthly model, the living warmth of his words makes the reader mentally recreate Laura. There is no direct description of her in the *Canzoniere*, yet we never lose sight of her.

There is something artful if not artificial in this process—the something that made De Sanctis remark that, while Dante was more poet than artist, Petrarch was more artist than poet. Nevertheless, readers have always privileged the poems written about Laura and the self-analytic pauses. Set aside the opening and closing pieces as well as the few nondirectly Laura poems, and what remains engraved in memory are the dreamy evocation of the fateful day (2); the old pilgrim (16) on his way to Rome; a *solo e pensoso* walk across the fields (35); the tired prayer of the penitent (62); a lovely shape made of transparencies (90 and the famous 126); the *cameretta* (little room) of the poet (234); and, in the death of Laura, the inexorable march of days and years (272), the useless return of spring (310), and the sad song of a nightingale telling us that "nothing here below delights—and lasts" (311). A certain repetitiveness has been observed in the *Canzoniere*; but, in fact, the work was meant to be sampled in small doses, rather than by continued perusal. A monochrome uniformity is genuine in Petrarch's only other It. verse work, the later *Trionfi*. Heavily allegorical, unfinished and unrefined, these series of Dantesque *terzine* sing the "triumphs" of Love, Chastity, Death, Fame, Time, and Eternity.

Among the minor *Trecento* poets are the late *stilnovista* Fazio degli Uberti (ca. 1305–67) from Pisa; the courtly poet Antonio Beccari (1315–before 1374) from Ferrara; the prolific Florentine popularizer of vernacular lit., Antonio Pucci (ca. 1310–88); and the fine author of ballads Franco Sacchetti (ca. 1330–1400). The third component of the great Trecento triumvirate, Giovanni Boccaccio (1313–75), father of mod. storytelling, was an uninspired but evidently inspiring versifier—e.g., Chaucer's vast and undervalued debt to Boccaccio's *Filostrato* (1336?), the romance of Troilus in octaves and *Teseida* (1341?), an epic, the Palamon and Arcite story. Boccaccio's own "Vita nuova" (*Commedia delle ninfe*, 1341) and allegorical vision in *terzine* (*Amorosa visione*, 1343?) influenced in turn Petrarch's *Trionfi*. There are more than 100 lyric compositions also attributed to Boccaccio, counting the ballads from the frame of the *Decameron*.

III. Quattrocento: The 1400s. The sudden blossoming of vernacular lit. in the 14th c. carried in it the seeds of decadence or rather of exhausted retrenchment during the first half of the next century. Petrarch and Boccaccio (and protohumanist Dante) were indeed the fountainhead of the cultural movement called *humanism*, essentially an enthusiastic revival of Lat. lit. (as opposed and "superior" to It. lit.). The trend, initially a passion for cl. learning and a rediscovery of many major texts of Lat. and Gr. antiquity, by degrees became a belief in the panacea of cl. education, capable of "freeing" humankind. The main creative tenet of this new classicism was *imitatio*, theorized by Petrarch and the basis for the later Petrarchism. The new blooming of Lat. lit. highlights such well-known humanists as Giovanni Pico della Mirandola (1463–94), Lorenzo Valla (1406–57), Coluccio Salutati (1331–1406), Giovanni Pontano (1426–1503), and Marsilio Ficino (1433–99). Far from being slavish imitators, the humanists in fact ended by "dethroning the ancients from their exalted position" (Guarino, in Bondanella) by reexamining under the microscope of philology the old texts and by historicizing classicism. Humanism was nothing short of a discovery of hist. in the mod. sense of the word.

Poetry in It. continued to be produced, marginally as it were, often in its "lower" species as imitations of popular song. The Venetian patrician Leonardo Giustiniani (1338–1446) became a sort of bestseller on account of his talent for reproducing the sonorities and easy grace of the *canzonette* sung by gondoliers on the *laguna*. The same taste for the simple diction of popular genres inspired the Florentine Luigi Pulci (1432–84), but with a different result. Pulci is a "humorist" in the true sense of the word: for him, life was a "harmonious mixture of sweet and bitter and a thousand flavors." Not merely a parody of the solemnities of the Fr. *chansons de geste*, Pulci's mock-heroic "epos" *Morgante* is the amusing product of a whimsical comic genius. Its rough model is enriched by characters alive on the page—in spite of their irrational capriciousness. In addition to the usual types, Pulci introduced Morgante, the giant, inspirer of Rabelais; the ribald monster Margutte who dies of immoderate laughter at a gross practical joke; and the amusing "logician" fiend Astaroth, spokesman for Pulci's religious doubts and occult leanings.

Matteo Maria Boiardo (1441–94) made reference in a serious vein to the same material. Pulci's attitude toward the Carolingian sources had reflected popular Tuscan city-bred tastes; Boiardo brought to them the conservative provincial atmosphere of northern courtly life. The incomplete *Orlando innamorato* (Roland in Love) injects Arthurian elements into the chivalric material: all-conquering love now presides over the knights' and ladies' adventures. The poem is a whirlwind of disparate episodes, unified, if at all, by overwhelming passion and vigorous action. The idiom, of strong regional flavor, hindered wide diffusion of the original; up to the 19th c. *Orlando* was read in Tuscanized versions done by Francesco Berni and others.

Florence, transformed from Dante's *comune* into a *signoria* under the Medicis, reacquired its cultural centrality during the second half of the century. Pulci's lord protector, Lorenzo de' Medici (1449–92, known as Il Magnifico), was himself a versatile poet. Critical appraisals of Lorenzo's poetry range from enthusiastic endorsement of his artful masquerades to viewing his output as the pastime of a statesman, the amusement of a dilettante. In truth, he was simply one of the many skillful literati of his court. His principal merit, other than his all-important patronage, lies in his vigorous defense of literary It.: Lorenzo contributed in a decisive way to the final prevalence of the Tuscan-Florentine trad. and the decline of literary writing in Lat.

Still, it may well be that Lorenzo's most enduring achievement was the discovery of the poetic talent of Politian (Poliziano), pseud. of Agnolo Ambrogini (1454–94) from Montepulciano (hence the name). Politian became a leading humanist, rediscovering and editing ancient texts. Apart from his poetry in Lat. and Gr., Politian wrote canzoni and other lyric poems. In his masterwork, the unfinished *Stanze* (Strophes, in *ottave*), he retells allegorically the meeting between Giuliano de' Medici, a youth devoted to pleasure and adventure, and the nymph of unearthly beauty Simonetta (Vespucci). The airy lightness of the *Stanze* is a poetic miracle, every octave a mixture of reminiscences, references, and reminders (Homer, Horace, Virgil, Dante, Petrarch, and many others), but the result appears perfectly natural. Moments of noble melancholy accent the pellucid text, mementos of the fragility and transience of all earthly things. Politian is the first poet of mod. times whose subject is poetry; a poet's poet, he saw lit. as the essence of life.

Composed during the last two decades of the century, the *Arcadia* of Jacopo Sannazaro (1458?–1530), a mixture of prose tales and pastoral songs, has enjoyed great fortune over the years, cyclically renewed and, in a way, enduring into our own times of recurrent ecological lamentation. "Antimetropolitan" yearnings (anachronistic already at inception) for a nonexistent rural simplicity, together with the immemorial myth of a lost Golden Age, inspire this early environmental manifesto.

IV. Cinquecento: The 1500s. The *Rinascimento*, the It. Ren., is the age of artistic and literary splendor between the age of humanism and the advent of baroque. Its poetic practice is pervaded by the heritage of the Trecento, esp. Petrarch (Dante was considered a "primitive" by this age of refinement), filtered through the classicism that prevailed in the 15th c. The Rinascimento is the age of Petrarchism, an age of not only servile imitation of the themes and style of the *Canzoniere*, not only the fashionable organization of one's poetic output into an ideal love story, but an adherence to the Platonic ideal of love and to the ling. ideal of purity, harmony, and elegance of expression, which later deteriorated into mere technical virtuosity. The patron saints of the Eur. 1500s were Petrarch and Plato; however, Aristotle's *Poetics* was also rediscovered and deeply, at times obsessively, studied—and in part misconstrued. The tenet of imitatio became paramount. Literary genres were rigidly codified, just as social behavior came to be governed by a code—its great documents are Baldassare Castiglione's *Il Cortegiano* (*The Courtier*, 1528) and Niccolò Machiavelli's *Il Principe* (*The Prince*, 1532). At the threshold of this great age stands the historically important but poetically insignificant Cardinal Pietro Bembo (1470–1547), friend of Lorenzo and Politian. Bembo, as codifier of Petrarchism and Platonism, is the embodiment of the Ren. His *Rime* (Poems) are little more than textbook examples to illustrate his theories, but his treatise, *Prose della volgar lingua* (Writing in the Vernacular, 1525), became something of a bible for the literati of the century. This inclusive codification of literary taste and ling. choice had a decisive influence on the diction of authors from Ludovico Ariosto to Torquato Tasso.

The essence of the Rinascimento is best revealed in the epic romance *Orlando furioso* (The Frenzy of Roland), whose author, one of the most likeable figures in the annals of It. lit., is Ludovico Ariosto (1474–1533). Ariosto's minor work illustrates the frustrations of a harried existence. His lyric poetry was inspired by his lifelong devotion to Alessandra Benucci, whom he married secretly so as not to forfeit ecclesiastical benefits. The seven *Satire* recount his travels and reflections. The last years of life were devoted to the definitive revision of his epic poem (pub. in 1532 in 46 canti). *Orlando*, 30 years in the making, pools the experience of the minor work, the warmth and immediacy of the love poetry, the detached and smiling wisdom of the *Satire*, and the character sketching of his theatrical pieces. The external occasion for the poem was Boiardo's unfinished *Orlando innamorato*: the *Furioso* completes the story, closely following its sources in the Carolingian epic cycle and the Celtic Arthurian legends in narrative detail but renewing the material with poetic license. This master storyteller holds hundreds of threads in hand at once and unerringly weaves them into an immense coherent tapestry. The great movers of the threefold plot are Ariosto's passions: first, love conceived as an earthy emotion, frankly sensual; second, the forms of knightly behavior and of court ritual; third, an insatiable appetite for adventure. Voltaire noted that Ariosto is always "superior" to his material: he tells his story "jokingly"—taking seriously and yet mocking his inventions: hence, the frequent authorial intrusions (comments, tongue-in-cheek explanations, ironic misdirection); hence, the fable-like and dreamy atmosphere around Ariosto's knights and ladies. Painstaking realism of detail fuses with an oneiric vagueness of context. The description of Atlante's castle and the invention of the lunar travels of Astolfo are emblematic of this attitude.

The form of the *Orlando furioso* is nothing short of prodigious. The octaves of narrative poetry—woody and lagging in Boccaccio's youthful poems, prosily stammering in Pulci's *Morgante*, loosely dressing Boiardo's laborious inventions—coincide here, for the first time in It. poetry, with the "breathing" of author and reader. Ariosto lives in his octave, in the six (the alternately rhymed verses) plus two (the clinching couplet) pattern of his strophe, each one a microcosm, in its perfectly controlled and yet wondrously airy architecture, of the entire magnificent construction.

Ariosto's Petrarchan love lyrics are undistinguished products of the age, similar to myriad contemp. songbooks. Little talent emerges from the crowd of the *Cinquecento petrarchisti*. Monsignor Giovanni della Casa (1503–56), remembered for his *Galateo* (Book of Manners), shows a nostalgia for robust emotions and monumental imagery. Two women poets introduce a welcome variation in a field dominated by the stylized male psychology of emotions: Vittoria Colonna (1492–1547), of aristocratic family and patroness of artists, authored a conventional songbook; Gaspara Stampa (1523–54), probably of low social standing, occasionally allows life to show through her imitative verse. Even more creatively, the feverish and disordered rhythms of a passionate existence seem to influence her songs, which are suggestive of entries in a love diary.

Intimations of the incipient baroque taste have been detected in Luigi Tansillo (1510–68). His too-easy sonorities, abuse of color, predilection for horrid landscapes, and colloquial touch seem, indeed, to point toward Giambattista Marino. But more noteworthy than the lyric output of the age and its vast and forgotten epic feats (the best are Giangiorgio Trissino's *L'Italia liberata dai Goti* [Italy Freed from the Goths], Luigi Alamanni's *Avarchide*, and Bernardo Tasso's *Amadigi*) is its humorous or light verse. Two cultivators of this genre had vast influence throughout the following century. Francesco Berni (1498–1535), Tuscan refurbisher of Boiardo's epic, is the wellhead of the *bernesco* poem, still jokingly cultivated in Italy—a buffoonery of "sitcom" heavy on puns. Written in an irresistibly funny It. modeled on Lat. (or a Lat. bastardized by It.), the mock-heroic epic *Baldus* by Merlin Cocai (pseud. of the rebellious Benedictine monk Teofilo Folengo, 1491–1544) extends Pulci's *Morgante* by recounting the farcical adventures of Baldus, a descendant of Rinaldo.

The last great poetic voice of the Ren., Torquato Tasso (1544–95), is the spiritual forerunner of baroque poetics. Most likely inheriting a psychic disorder, he became distraught by the mental effort required to produce his masterwork, the epic *Gerusalemme liberata* (*Jerusalem Delivered*, 1581). Episodes of irrational behavior at the court of Ferrara and aimless excursions across the peninsula eventually led to Tasso's confinement for seven years in the dungeon asylum of Sant'Anna. Pirated eds. of his poem, attacks from pedantic critics, and obsessive religious doubts exacerbated his illness; he died in Rome. His minor work alone would be sufficient to give him a high rank among the Petrarchans and epic poets of his century. His nearly 2,000 lyrics (*Rime*) are a workshop in which the poet perfected techniques and experimented with sentimental situations; these are interspersed with lyrics of admirable invention and masterful execution, esp. his madrigals, a genre congenial to Tasso's evanescent moods. The Petrarchan model here appears at one remove, filtered through the Petrarchans of the early 1500s—Bembo, della Casa—as indeed Petrarch will be read through Tasso by the next generation of poets, Marino and his school. The chivalric poem *Rinaldo* (12 canti of ottave) betrays the adolescent's hand as well as features that will later govern the inspiration of his epic. Already here, the war chronicle of the sources is constantly squeezed out by courtly love. Tasso first favored the idyll, and his pastoral play *Aminta* is rightly spoken of in the same breath with his lyric output: its theatrical pretext gives way to the emotional situations and flights of pathos in the *Rime*.

Whether *La Gerusalemme liberata* is the first full poetic manifestation of the incipient baroque age (some critics hold that the very terms *baroque* and *Marinism* are misnomers for "Tassism" and "Tassomania") or, inversely, the last bloom of the "sane" Rinascimento is an academic question; and interestingly, it parallels the great 17th-c. controversy (which engaged Galileo Galilei) on the relative worth of the two great narrative poems of the preceding age, those of Ariosto and Tasso. Tasso's epic, its pretext the last phase of the First Crusade, has a cast composed of both lifeless historical characters and fictive personae of the poet himself, each endowed with throbbing life. To Ariosto's objectivity, detachment, and irony, Tasso opposes his subjectivity, participation, and sentimentality. All the great passionate characters of the oft-abandoned plot are facets of Tasso's psychic makeup, exhibiting the excesses and morbidity that landed their creator in Sant'Anna. The *Gerusalemme* is, in this sense, a truly autobiographical epos. Long traverses through Aristotle's poetics and the theory of the epic preceded and accompanied the feverish composition, but the rules reaffirmed were soon discarded by Tasso's more powerful sentimental inspiration. The Crusade cedes place to the multiple, strangely disturbed love stories of the variously and wrongly assorted couples. The whole is immersed in an overheated atmosphere of gratuitous heroism, white and black magic, cliffhangers cum heavenly intervention, duels to the death, and battle scenes of vast confusion. In the *Orlando furioso*, the good-natured "colloquial" voice of Ludovico the Amiable constantly tended to overdub the narrator, while in the *Gerusalemme*, Torquato's falsetto breaks through, fitfully as it were, to lend his creations a hundred diverse intonations of emotional disorder.

Tasso's *ottava*, ordered into obsessive parallelisms and chiastic contrasts, offers an ineffable musicality and a psychomimetic finesse never before heard. It is masterfully torn by the high drama of enjambments. Indeed, Tasso addresses his poem to a new audience of a new age and sensibility, that of the Counter-Reformation, an age of earthshaking upheavals. This critical view allows us to reevaluate Tasso's reworking of *Gerusalemme conquistata* (Jerusalem Recovered), a text of vaster and more solemn architecture, characterized by a baroque heaviness of pace and expression and universally judged a complete failure until the late 20th c. The characteristics of *Gerusalemme conquistata* are in evidence in Tasso's late poem *Il mondo creato*, a ponderous account of the Creation similar in flavor to an overripe fruit.

V. Seicento: the 1600s. The 17th c., a Golden Age in the Spain of Luis de Góngora and Miguel de Cervantes, in the France of Jean Racine and Jean de La Fontaine, and in the England of the metaphysical poets, was long considered to have been an age of decadence in Italy. Its dominant Tassesque aesthetics certainly revealed the exhaustion of a long-mined vein, an exasperation of the drive for outward perfection yearned for by the Ren. The age frittered away its heritage in an obsessive search for originality and "marvels." Foreign (Sp.) and papal domination in the peninsula, the newborn religious dogmatism imposed by the Counter-Reformation, the general lowering of ethical standards owing perhaps to the riches from the New World, and the universal instability of ideas in this age of scientific revolution have all been indicated as causes for the alleged poetic aridity of the age. The baroque age in Italy adopted the ars poetica of the late Ren., developing Tasso's theories and example toward a concept of poetry as a nonrational activity, and it endorsed a view of literary production and appreciation based on taste and feeling.

Giambattista Marino (1569–1625), a Neapolitan, became the high priest of the new school of writing usually called Marinism (also *Seicentismo*, conceptism, and *manierismo*). He was the theorizer and the most prolific practitioner of the poetics of *meraviglia* (of astonishment—at all costs), a style in search of the arduous and the complex. A genre loved by Marino and the *marinisti* was poetry on art (e.g., his collection *Galleria*), a species of poetry feeding on itself (his *Lira*, [Lyrics]) and pillaging all preexistent lit.—as does Marino's masterpiece the *Adone* (Adonis), in almost every one of its 40,000 verses. The poem is truly a miracle of words growing on words and never managing to cover the void under them.

Among Marino's contemporaries, two poets sought independence from the master: Gabriello Chiabrera (1552–1638), whose anacreontic songs are another "reading" of Tasso, and Alessandro Tassoni (1565–1635), remembered for his mock-heroic *Secchia rapita* (The Ravished Pail, 1622). The most notable recovery of late-20th-c. crit. is the poetry of the philosopher Tommaso Campanella (1568–1639), whose work closely parallels the metaphysical songs of John Donne, George Herbert, and Richard Crashaw. This Calabrese monk suffered a monstrous fate, 30 years in prison (several years in the flooded underground dungeon of St. Elmo with hands and feet chained) for heresy and rebellion. Campanella's poems, owing to their forbidding complexity of concepts and diction, were judged by their rare readers almost devoid of interest. But today these canzoni, esp. the beautiful "Hymn to the Sun," composed in the depth of St. Elmo, strike us as the "missing link" in It. baroque poetry. In his translucent verses, the chained poet attains the lyrical height for which Marino always strove but rarely reached.

VI. Settecento: The 1700s. The latter half of the 1600s produced a general decadence in poetry. The antibaroque backlash came as a call to "return to nature," to observe the limits of good taste and common sense, and to renew imitatio and the cult of the classics. The adepts of this neoclassical revival congregated in the Academy of Arcadia (a loose association of literati, self-defined "shepherds"), founded in 1690 by Queen Christina of Sweden, then in exile in Rome. Arcadia promoted pastoral poetry, sobriety of lang., and faithfulness to trad., discarding the whole Marinist century to hark back to Sannazaro's Cinquecento. However, this school also became in turn the matrix of mediocre versifiers of derivative bucolic idylls. An intermittently genuine poetic voice is heard in the tenuous lyrics of the great libretto dramatist Metastasio (pseud. of Pietro Trapassi, 1698–1782), poet-in-residence for most of his life at the Hapsburg court in Vienna. His many melodramas (e.g., *Didone abbandonata, Olimpiade, Demoofonte*, and *Demetrio*) are deservedly famous. In his *Canzonette* (Songs), Metastasio introduced a facile sentimentalism and an evanescent lyricism that he, unlike his predecessors, couched in down-to-earth lang.

René Descartes's rationalism influenced practically all intellectual trends in 18th-c. Italy. The influence of the Fr. Encyclopedists—Voltaire, Montesquieu, and Denis Diderot—on the one hand and of the Ossian craze, with the nocturnal and sepulchral fashion it brought with it, on the other, became paramount. The first civic poet of Italy, the Lombard Giuseppe Parini (1729–99), represents the sober awakening of the age leading to the Fr. Revolution. A seriousness of ethical purpose and a sense of mission in his social crit. distinguish this Catholic priest, ed., and schoolteacher. Parini is remembered for his long and unfinished poem of bitter social comment, *Il giorno*, depicting one day in the life of a "giovin signore," a young man about town. The satire, ferociously allusive and resentful, and seldom attenuated by the smile of superior comprehension, seems at times shot through by a secret nostalgia for the world of fashion and elegance. Parini is the first in the hist. of It. poetry to have obtained from the "short" hendecasyllable effects vying with those of the flexible cl. hexameter.

The essence of pure poetry—as opposed to the practically ambitious *engagé* verse of Parini—is represented by the domineering figure of the preromantic playwright Vittorio Alfieri (1749–1803), scion of an old aristocratic family from Italy's Piedmont region. The first fruit of his illumination, the tragedy *Cleopatra*, was followed by a feverishly fertile decade of dramatic production (1776–86): 18 more tragedies, dramatic verse in dialogue form. The Alfierian hero, a pure revolutionary, acts out the abstract libertarian rebellion of the poet's soul, scornful of any pragmatic effort at real social progress. Alfieri's stay in Tuscany afforded him time to refine his Piedmontese, Frenchified ling. and cultural background. In Paris in 1789, he was at first wildly enthusiastic about, then bitterly disappointed in, the Fr. Revolution.

In 1792, he escaped the Terror to spend his last years in Florence writing six comedies, his violent anti-Fr. *Il misogallo* (The Francophobe), and his celebrated *Vita* (Memoirs), with its relentlessly, almost breathlessly drawn portrait of the poet-hero.

Alfieri represents the *Sturm und Drang* of It. poetry. His collection of lyrics (*Rime*) amounts to a spiritual autobiography of a soul tormented by dreams of immensity. The idealized and idolized figure of the poet, alone, in haughty solitude, looms large. The Petrarchan subtext of these poems signifies a return to the source; it is the manifestation of a genuine "elective affinity" rather than the obligatory imitation of an earlier century. However, the greatest lyric poetry of this "lion of Asti" is to be found in his tragedies, texts of a lyrical essentiality, of an elliptic diction, a barebones structure, and an unrelenting pace. By critical consensus, Alfieri's most acclaimed tragic pieces, *Saul* (1882) and *Mirra* (Myrrha, 1887), are staged poems on the sublime.

VII. Ottocento: The 1800s. The Arcadian trend had sown the seeds of a rebirth of taste for cl. ideals of beauty. In Italy, these preromantic stirrings coincide with a short period of neoclassical predominance in art (Antonio Canova) and lit. concurrent with the Napoleonic age. The two movements, Arcadism of the late 1700s and neoclassicism of the early 1800s, shared an attention to form, an aesthetics based on the renewed concept of the sublime, a taste for the genuine and primordial, and a purism in the medium of art. Ippolito Pindemonte (1735–1828), remembered for his *Poesie campestri* (Rustic Verses), and Vincenzo Monti (1754–1828) were the most coherent adepts of the new trend.

The poetic genius of the imperial *intermezzo* was Ugo Foscolo (1778–1827). His poetry fuses the classicist's love for perfection of form with the heritage of Parini and Alfieri and with Eur. romanticism. Born of a Gr. mother on the Ionian island of Zante, Foscolo was, so to speak, a congenital classicist in his psychic makeup. His tempestuous age provided the background for a truly romantic curriculum of wars and turbulent loves. In 1802, he published *Ultime lettere di Jacopo Ortis* (Last Letters of Jacopo Ortis), an epistolary novel of love and suicide inspired by J. W. Goethe's *Werther*. Foscolo's 12 sonnets (among them the masterpieces "Alla Musa," "A Zacinto," "Alla sera," and "In morte del fratello Giovanni") and his two major odes (1800–03) are perfect expressions of the cl. ideal implanted in a romantic soul. His principal claim to posthumous glory should have been the three-part hymn *Le Grazie* (The Graces), a vast corpus of fragments composed over the course of 20 years. The immaterial lightness of diction and verse can only increase our regret at the structural sketchiness of the magnificent torso. Though 20th-c. exegesis, with its bias for the fragmentary, has rediscovered this great mass of poetic wreckage, attempts at a coherent reconstruction have not been wholly convincing. The entire experience of the poet's "life in art" is the true theme of the poem.

Foscolo remains best known for his "Dei sepolcri" (On Tombs, 1806), written in 295 blank verses. The theme, occasioned by the Napoleonic decree prohibiting burial within urban limits, is left behind, replaced by a poetic meditation on life and death, on the immemorial rites of burial, on fame surviving the tomb, and on the great men of the past and their sepulchers. The evocation of the nocturnal cemetery, the "triumph" in the Petrarchan sense of posthumous glory over death, the celebration of memory as a cenotaph to greatness, the motif of tears and consolation—all are close to the central topics of romanticism. In his "Sepolcri," Foscolo emerges as the "father of Italian romanticism."

The new mode of conceiving the human condition given by romanticism, with its components of Enlightenment rationalism and Restoration historicism, with its taste for the unsophisticated and primordial, and with its repertory of lugubrious themes came of age in Italy in the 1820s. It. romantics, who first gathered around the Florentine periodical *Conciliatore* (1818–19), distinguished themselves from their fellows in Germany and England by their concern with the social and ethical role of lit. The Risorgimento (It. national "Resurgence," a movement that would result in 1860 in the birth of a unified mod. Italy) was an important factor, mainly through the educative influence of such protagonists as the patriot Giuseppe Mazzini (1805–72), the publicist Vincenzo Gioberti (1801–52), and the literary historian Francesco De Sanctis (1817–83).

The great models—Friedrich Schiller, Lord Byron, François-René de Chateaubriand, and Walter Scott—had only limited direct influence on literary works. The most conventional It. romantic poet, Giovanni Berchet

(1783–1851), left a thin collection of songs and ballads, which is a veritable index of the items dear to Eur. romanticism. Berchet's theoretical *Lettera semiseria* (Semiserious Letter) had a lasting impact on the reception of romantic ideology. A more interesting figure is Niccolò Tommaseo (1802–74), the blind lexicographer and Dante scholar and author of lyric poetry of "cosmic nostalgia" and a prophetic tone. The bitterness of a bleak existence inspired the Tuscan Giuseppe Giusti (1809–50), who wrote poetry marked by sarcasm and despair. Alessandro Manzoni (1785–1873) is best known for his great novel *I promessi sposi* (*The Betrothed*); his verses are marginal products, but his five "Hymns" (1812–22), of deep religious inspiration, his commemorative poems, and the choral passages from his plays *Carmagnola* (1820) and *Adelchi* (1822) show the great novelist's precise diction as well as the characteristic undercurrent of *I promessi sposi*: compassion for the humble, the disinherited, and the marginal.

The realistic penchant of the romantic movement in Italy, its bias for the popular and immediate, favored the flowering of dialect poetry. The traits of dialectal speech included a down-to-earth tone, a direct documenting of life, and a built-in smile owing to the use of dialectal variation as a vehicle of low humor. The two greatest It. dialect poets show a taste for the "slice of life," for a ready plebeian wit, and for the antiliterary spirit congenital to the realistic facet of romanticism. Carlo Porta (1775–1821) derived some of his inspiration from the decidedly nonpoetic contacts through his clerk's window in the Milan tax offices. His masterworks are versified *novelle*: the "disasters" of a semiderelict (the "Giovannin Bongee" stories), the "lamentations" of a poor street fiddler (bow-legged "Marchionn"), and the tale of a streetwalker ("Ninetta del Verzee"). Porta's laughter never becomes a sneer; behind his smile, one often senses the sadness of the wise. The encounter with Porta freed Giuseppe Gioacchino Belli (1791–1863) from his failed attempts at It. verse and opened up the dialect of the Roman plebs as inspiration. A minor cleric, Belli left behind about 2,000 sonnets (pub. in the 1880s) inspired by a violent anticlericalism, irreverent and often obscene. He too is a poet of metropolitan low-class life—vagrants and beggars, monks and spies, flunkeys and whores—with an infusion of prelates.

The greatest poet of mod. Italy, Giacomo Leopardi (1798–1837) was born to an impoverished aristocratic family in Recanati. The poet's professed revulsion for his backward hometown and his disciplined upbringing (esp. the conservatism of his father) have been made much of in critical attempts to trace the roots of his cosmic pessimism. Young Giacomo spent his adolescence in obsessive studies, amassing an astonishing amount of writing: verses, plays, and learned (though all compilative) essays and treatises, almost blinding himself in the process. Though merely the products of a pedantic youth, the early works have been shown to contain the germ of Leopardi's later and most persistent *leitmotif*: the attraction to illusions and delusions, the heroic striving toward an abstract glory marking one's passage on earth (for Leopardi, humankind's only existence). These motifs are recurrent in the immense notebook collection, the *Zibaldone* (1815–32). The clash of nature and reason, the dominant theme of the Enlightenment, was at first given by young Leopardi a Rousseauian solution (benign nature vs. the ills brought on by human reason), but the contrary prevails in his later work: hostile nature, a "stepmother" for humankind, undermines all human endeavors. The romantic elements influencing Leopardi's system underwent a characteristic transformation: the denial of the poet's social role (and the belief in pure poetry, anticipating the "decadent" poetics to come), a materialistic worldview, a refusal of almost all nonlyric content, and a bias for the "pathetic" based on "immediacy" of feeling.

The concepts of "infinity" and "remembrance" are the cornerstones of Leopardi's best verse and are strongly present in his poetry until 1821, when the poet "escaped" from Recanati. "Rimembranze" (Recollections) and "Appressamento della morte" (Nearness of Death), written at age 18, experiment with fashionably lugubrious topics; a number of *engagé* compositions and poetic meditations show Leopardi's search for his poetic voice. He discovers it in the idyll "La Vita solitaria" (Life of Solitude) and esp. "La Sera del dì di festa" (Sunday Night). The tension is maintained through the whole (short) poem in the admirable "Alla luna" ("To the Moon"); however, "L'Infinito" ("The Infinite"), a poem of a mere 15 lines written before the poet's flight from his family, is universally recognized as his masterwork—it is, with Dante's "Tanto gentile," the most renowned It. lyric. Its contents are of a lightness and evanescence that elude paraphrase. Its last line with its sign of *cupio dissolvi* (the "sweetness of shipwreck") ties Leopardi to such key texts of mod. poetry as Arthur Rimbaud's "Le Bateau ivre" and Stéphane Mallarmé's "Brise marine."

The years 1822–28, a period of uneasy independence interrupted by desperate returns to Recanati, mark an intermission in Leopardi's poetry. He fitfully produced the *Operette morali* (Little Moral Exercises, 1824), pensive and ironic dialogues on ontological questions, in this pause, a gathering of strength before his second creative period (ca. 1828–30), an economically forced return to Recanati for 16 months of ennui. The cosmic meditation of "Canto notturno" (Nocturne of a Nomadic Shepherd in Asia) is "one of the supreme mod. songs of existential anguish" (Perella, in Bondanella). "A Silvia" (written in Pisa, "perhaps the most poignant elegy in the Italian language"), "Le Ricordanze" (Memories), and "Il Sabato del villaggio" (Saturday in the Village) are the most characteristically Leopardian texts in his collection of *Canti* (1831), with their tone of thoughtful melancholy and disconsolate contemplation of the nullity of all things under the empty heavens. The elegy "La Quiete dopo la tempesta" (The Calm after the Storm) looks for happiness in death.

Leopardi lived to see his *Canti* published in a definitive ed. in 1836. Their themes have a common denominator: the loss of dreams—of youth, of happiness, of heroic existence—a loss restated with calm despair in the cruel light of cold and godless reality. The meter is a kind of early free verse: discarding the strophic models of the past, Leopardi relied on a loose rhythm, now expanded freely, now suddenly restrained. While the incisive "A se stesso" (To Himself) is a pitiless spiritual self-portrait, the poet facing his bleak universe and murmuring his final renunciation, the late elegies "Amore e morte" (Love and Death) and "Tramonto della luna" (Moon Setting), as well as his last poem, "La ginestra" (The Desert Flower), seem to be not only the conclusion of an experience but a hint at another incipient search for new directions.

The reaction to the excesses of romanticism, such as the lachrymose sentimentalism of the Prati-Aleardi school, took place in Italy under a double flag, realism and classicism. On the one hand, the call for a return to the sanity of everyday life as the master theme of literary mimesis was spread by a largely Lombard group of poets known as *Scapigliati* (the unkempt ones)—a movement parallel to the Fr. *Bohème*. The salient figures of the movement, the Boito brothers, Camillo (1836–1914) and Arrigo (1842–1918, also remembered for his librettos); Emilio Praga (1839–75); and Carlo Dossi (1849–1910) professed an ars poetica based on the "slice of life." For the most part, they produced "little proses in verse," unwittingly turning upside down Charles Baudelaire's ambition of *petits poèmes en prose*.

The classicists' reaction, on the other hand, to the romantic mania for originality had at first a rather ineffectual leader in Giacomo Zanella (1820–88), who revived the minor neoclassical trad. of Monti and Pindemonte, a trend largely exhausted by mid-century. The heritage of classicism in Alfieri and Foscolo, and even in the young "civic" Leopardi, was pressed into the service of antiromanticism by Giosuè Carducci (1835–1907), a poet of vast authority who was the uncontested focal point of It. fin de siècle poetry. Carducci attempted to confer dignity and discipline on a field that, by his maturity, had lost or refused both. Carducci, chair of It. at Bologna, was "the last great *literatus*" Italy had. His professed ideal of a "sane, virile, strong-willed" lit. has lost most of its appeal in mod. times; his reclaiming for the poet the immemorial function of *vates* has an archaic flavor. His lyric production in traditional form appeared in the collections *Levia gravia* (Light and Heavy, 1861–71), *Giambi ed epodi* (Iambs and Epodes, 1867–69), and *Rime nuove* (New Verses, 1861–87). Carducci believed in the possibility of transplanting Greco-Lat. metrics into It. versification; while probably overrated as a prosodic experiment, it makes an interesting *curiosum* out of his most discussed volume, *Odi barbare* (Barbaric Odes, 1877–89).

VIII. Novecento: The 1900s. Currents as diverse as positivism and decadence, the *Voce* and the *Ronda* groups, the Twilight poets and the futurists, hermeticism and neorealism not only coexist but in retrospect appear to be interdependent elements of the same whole. Two monumental figures, Gabriele D'Annunzio and Giovanni Pascoli, preface and condition contemp. poetry; neither strictly belongs to a "school," but each recapitulates and anticipates several.

Carducci today appears firmly rooted in the century of Leopardi and Manzoni, while the poetry of Giovanni Pascoli (1855–1912), his successor at Bologna, stretches far into our own. Some of his best-known pieces from *Poemetti* (1897) and *Canti di Castelvecchio* (1903) most surely have been swept away by the tears shed over them (e.g., "Cavallina storna" [The Dappled-Gray Pony], memorized by generations of schoolchildren). But his thin first collection, *Myricae* (1891), remains the cornerstone of mod. It. poetry. The title "Tamarisks" hints at the "lowly shrubs" of the fourth eclogue, but this "last descendant of Virgil" is not merely a poet of simple rustic scenes, as his themes seem to suggest. His quaint syntax and vocabulary, invasive onomatopoeia, dialect and Lat. words, and exotic and technical terms, e.g., signal the complexity underlying his deceptively simple landscapes. Pascoli's interest never fixes on the positive spectacle of human labor in the fields; his rural tableaux radiate a mysterious feeling, an almost religious stupor. A pattern in Pascoli's constructions may be discerned: a rural view is sketched out by broad brush strokes, then filtered and "undefined" through some optical disturbance: haze, mist, fog. A minimal sign of life appears, slowed at once almost to a standstill. The cadence remains "the beating of his own heart" (Garofalo, in Bondanella)—though with the constant sinking feeling of skipped beats. At last, a tiny acoustic element is added to the landscape—the chirping of a bird, the rustle of leaves, a snatch of faraway singing. That is all, but the whole remains miraculously suspenseful, suggestive not of something "else" but of itself. Even the most allegorical-seeming texts of Pascoli—e.g., his best *poemetti*, "Il vischio" (Mistletoe) and "Digitale purpurea" (Foxglove)—suggest, rather than a meaning, an abstract horror, a visionary experience of evil. The tragedy of Pascoli's life, the unsolved murder of his father in 1867, fixed his poetic age at 12: there is a sense of bewildered wonder in front of an uncomprehended world, the urge to escape, the need for refuge—a need he soon identified with poetry. In the poet's psyche, the unknown assassin assumes the features of humankind, driven on by the eternal enigma of evil. In an 1897 essay, "Il fanciullino" (The Child), Pascoli shaped this very concept into an ars poetica.

If Pascoli's "life in art" had few events, D'Annunzio (1863–1938) construed his life as a work of art. A cross between Friedrich Nietzsche's "superman" and J.-K. Huysmans's Des Esseintes (*À rebours*, 1884), he was the last vates of It. lit. "More a rhetorician than poet" (Sapegno), a "dilettante di sensazioni" (Croce), D'Annunzio titled his mature collection *Laudi* (1903–4). Composed of three parts, *Maia*, *Electra*, and *Alcyone*, it is a *laus vitae*, a celebration of life, in which he seems intoxicated by his own exultation. His extraordinary imitative skill fills his writing with disparate echoes: some from the Fr. and Eng. Parnassians and Pre-Raphaelites, some deliberate impersonations of stil nuovo and OF masters. This mimetic bent reflects D'Annunzio's principal characteristic, the musicality of his verse. The best of D'Annunzio is often his most extreme: poems in which the thematic pretext is at its baroque flimsiest and the text a polyphony, as in "La pioggia nel pineto" (Rain on the Pine Trees).

In a 1910 article ("Poets on the Wane," in De Bernardi) Borgese defined as *crepuscolari* a group of young poets whose cult of quotidian themes and slipshod expression seemed to signal the end of a great lyric trad. The term took root without its negative connotation and denotes a tone shared by most verse published in the decade preceding World War I. Not a formal school, Waning Poetry was as much a derivation from as a reaction to Pascoli's mystic rusticism and D'Annunzio's pompous alexandrinism. *Poesie scrittie col lapis* (Poems Written with a Pencil) by Marino Moretti, *Armonie in grigio et in silenzio* (Harmonies in Gray and Silence) by Corrado Govoni, *Piccolo libro inutile* (Useless Booklet) by Sergio Corazzini—the very titles of these slim volumes announce deliberate colorlessness and monotony, everyday emotions about banal objects. The most versatile member of the group was Corrado Govoni (1884–1965), who later became a futurist. Dying at 20, a consumptive Sergio Corazzini (1886–1907) declined the title of poet for that of a "weeping child" who "knows nothing but how to die." Two poets of the first rank are customarily included here: Aldo Palazzeschi (1885–1974) exceeds all labeling and warrants treatment apart; Guido Gozzano (1883–1916) survived tuberculosis long enough to see the success of his *Colloqui* (1911). Gozzano's mild irony blends with his mild yearning.

Historically, "crepuscularism" and futurism rise from the same impulse, the need to escape D'Annunzio's dominance and Pascoli's classicism. Futurism burst on the scene with the 1909 manifesto of F. T. Marinetti (1887–1944). Marinetti trumpeted activism at all costs, adventure and aggression, speed and the triumph of the machine, destruction of the past, war as the "hygiene" of hist., and scorn for women and sentiment. The very scope of its ludicrous claims killed the school; after its disintegration (1915), however, futurism was adopted by National Socialism, Marinetti becoming a sort of poet laureate of the regime. Still, Marinetti's poetics had a vast and, on the whole, salutary influence. His main thesis—simultaneity of impression and expression (hence, fusion of object and image)—influenced Guillaume Apollinaire's calligrammes, Dada, cubism, and Vladimir Mayakovsky. In Italy, futurism's best adherents soon developed in different directions, turning against its ontological claims (Gian Pietro Lucini, Ardengo Soffici [1879–1964]) or deriving from its libertarian impulse a ludic concept of poetry (Govoni, Palazzeschi).

Gian Pietro Lucini (1867–1914), between his early Parnassian sonnets and his late antifuturist stance, published his theory of free verse in Marinetti's review ("Poesia," 1908) and then his *Revolverate* (Gunshots, 1909). Resistance to time attests to the greatness of Palazzeschi, a much appreciated novelist. The production of his "poetic" decade (1905–15) differs from the humorless declamation of mainline futurists. Its wit and charm are seen in his celebrated phonomimetic "Fontana malata" (Ailing Fountain). His "L'incendiario" (The Arsonist) records the urge to break with trad.—without the obsessive need for activism or ling. anarchy.

A flourishing literary culture in the years preceding World War I gave rise to a number of periodicals, many of them Florentine. The most influential, *La voce* (1908–13), was directed by Giuseppe Prezzolini (1882–1982), who gathered together a heterogeneous group of collaborators. *La voce* became associated with nearly all the trends in vogue during its run. It offered a first forum to the best-known autochthonous poetic movement in 20th-c. Italy, later called *hermeticism*. The forefather of this novel trobar clus, Dino Campana (1885–1932), came to notice after the "school" had gained notoriety with Giuseppe Ungaretti and Eugenio Montale. Campana is often compared to Rimbaud and Georg Trakl for his aimless wanderings over the world, interrupted only by his stays in mental asylums (he was permanently committed in 1918), and for his poetics of total faith in the magic of the word. The *Canti orfici* (1914) refer to Orpheus: here poetry is a descent into hell and a religion for initiates.

Two other influential poets who matured in the *La voce* context produced poetry in a vein related to Campana's. The existential adventure of Clemente Rébora (1885–1957), not less erratic than Campana's, took place all *within*, as a lifelong struggle with his own soul and a periodically despairing search for superior truth. Rébora's only inspiration is his need to find the all-encompassing word. His aptly titled *Frammenti lirici* (1913) and *Canti anonimi* (1922) record in their daring analogies, in Rébora's characteristic "*imagine tesa*" (taut imagery), a "sort of transcendental autobiography" of powerful originality (Contini). Camillo Sbárbaro (1888–1967) sang the "monotonous recurrence of indifferent life," withdrawing from the bustle into his private drama, in *Resine* (Amberdrops, 1911) and *Pianissimo* (1914).

The review *La ronda* (1919–23) welcomed the voices of reaction to the cult of originality in prewar poetry. Its founder, Vincenzo Cardarelli (1887–1959), advocated a return to the classics (esp. Leopardi and Manzoni), i.e., to syntax, logic, and immediate comprehension. The progress of hermetic poetry, supported by parallel trends abroad among the Fr. and also in T. S. Eliot and Ezra Pound, proved irresistible. Its principal exponents are less typical of its program than its lesser adepts (Salvatore Quasimodo [1901–68], Alphonso Gatto [1909–76], Mario Luzi [1914–2005], Leonard Sinisgalli [1908–81], Vittorio Sereni [1913–83]). All share the quasi-mystical concept of "poetry as life," as a magic formula capable of revealing, under the semblances of this phenomenal world, "universal reality" (Manacorda).

Giuseppe Ungaretti (1888–1970) will be long appreciated for his prosodic innovation, based on the lesson of Rimbaud's *Illuminations* and Mallarmé's *Un coup de dés* (*A Throw of the Dice*). Fragmenting the *vers libre* of his futurist beginnings, Ungaretti eliminated punctuation and transformed poetic diction into a series of fragments lit up by intermittent floodlights. His first book of verse, *Allegria* (1916; repub. in 1923 with a preface by Benito Mussolini) remains the overture to a new phase of It. poetry. The title of his collected poems, *Vita d'un uomo* (A Man's Life), points to his dominant theme, the sublimation of his experiences, though these, esp. in the verse of the 1930s and 1940s, at times remain untranslated into poetry.

Eugenio Montale (1896–1981) may well be perceived as the true heir to Pascoli. His poetry is Pascolian in its resignedly hopeless scrutiny of the "ontological mystery," its vague desire for an escape route from the *male di vivere* (both "pain of life" and "evil of living"), for a "broken seam / in the net that constrains us." Pascolian, too, is Montale's characteristic of transforming emotion into landscape. Pascolian is, in his epoch-making *Ossi di seppia* (*Cuttlefish Bones*, 1925), Montale's metaphysical and baroque mythmaking, soberly desolate as it is. Much has been made of the political texts by antifascist Montale (from *Occasioni*, 1939, to *Satura*, 1971), endlessly deciphered by immense and often too-hermetic exegesis.

Variously related to hermeticism are four poets: Umberto Saba (1883–1957), Cesare Pavese (1908–50), Sandro Penna (1906–77), and Pier Paolo Pasolini (1922–75). Saba was in a sense prehermetic; his *Canzoniere* (*Songbook*) "reads as a 19th-century work" (Debenedetti). His simplicity and trite diction prompted critics to see in him an authentically popular poet. It slowed recognition and led Saba to publish a chronicle (1948) effectually advertising his own songbook. A typical motif is animal life related to human behavior. Pavese offered a model of antihermetic poetry in his realistic and matter-of-fact *poesie-racconto* (story-poems) in *Lavorare stanca* (*Hard Labor*, 1936), but the project failed both in this role and as a matrix of poetry.

"Hermetic" in a special sense ("coding" for this gay poet was a must), Penna's only topic is love, *dolce pena*, "cross and delight," "strange joy" (the last two are titles of collections). This "vigorous outsider" was also an *ermetico* in his refusal of easy legacies, in his ironclad rule of conciseness, and in his stenographic imagery. His best poems, always centered on his beloved *ragazzi*, are prodigies of a balanced moment suspended in timelessness. Everything is burned off in the white heat of the poet's dogged hammering at the "right word." Pasolini, the filmmaker whose 1957 *Le ceneri di Gramsci* (Gramsci's Ashes) is widely acknowledged as one of the most important collections of poetry published in the postwar period, had a different and more tragic purity of voice. Paroxysms of paradox interrupt his song. The popular brand of Marxism he professed never overcame his bourgeois values. Pasolini took idiosyncrasy for ideology: the pangs of libido appear in some of his purposely controversial and perhaps less enduring pieces as the stirrings of hist.

Around the critic Luciano Anceschi (1911–95) and his influential periodical *Il Verri* sprang into being the self-styled Gruppo 63 (so called from its founding meeting at Palermo in 1963). Three poets associated with it are likely to mark the last decades of the 20th c. with their names: Antonio Porta (1935–89), Andrea Zanzotto (1921–2011), and Edoardo Sanguineti (1930–2010). In their verse, the ling. revolution begun by Pascoli comes full circle; his weakening of the tie between signifier and signified reaches the final stage of divorce. The movement has been compared in its sound and fury to futurism; however, the poetry initially born out of and later in some cases opposed to Gruppo 63 is distinguished by a theoretical rigor unknown to Marinetti et al. Porta was first brought to critical notice by the collective volume *I novissimi* (1961). His poems reveal a strongly individual voice and have an eerie capacity to suggest, behind a deliberately gray diction, vast threatening conspiracies by unknown objects and persons. Porta went beyond his *novissimi* origins and alliances. Some critics distinguish his poetry as the first real novelty after hermeticism.

Zanzotto "joined" the group after the fact, as it were. His early collections—*Dietro il paesaggio* (Behind the Landscape, 1951), *Elegia* (1954), *Vocativo* (1957), and *IX Ecloghe* (1962)—are characterized by traditional form (Zanzotto even wrote Petrarchan sonnets, the only 20th-c. poet to do so outside of parody). Zanzotto's arcane Arcadia suggests spectral visitations, séances of literary ghost-evoking. Lang. acts here as a trance-inducing drug. New revolutionary techniques appear with *La beltà* (Beauty, 1968) and subsequent collections of ever-increasing textual complexity.

An original member of the Palermo group, Sanguineti had anticipated in his *Laborintus* (1956) its ideological and technical characteristics. A shocked Pavese refused to consider seriously Sanguineti's early samples, and Zanzotto later called them the "record of a nervous breakdown." Sense in *Laborintus* is replaced by obsessive paronomasia. Sanguineti's collected poems, *Segnalibro* (Bookmark, 1982), and esp. his *Novissimum Testamentum* (1986), rank him with the best of contemp. Eur. poets.

Among the poets active in the second half of the 20th c., Franco Fortini (1917–94) and Paolo Volponi (1924–94), *engagé* writers of the older generation, deserve more than a summary listing, as well as Luciano Erba (1922–2010), Maria Luisa Spaziani (1924–2014), Giovanni Raboni (1932–2004), Dario Bellezza (1944–96), and Fabio Doplicher (1938–2003). Curiously, while the dialects of the peninsula had seemed doomed by 20th-c. mass education and media diffusion, poetry in dialect shows no sign of decadence. Among its practitioners, heirs to Meli, Porta, and Belli, were the first-rate poets Virgilio Giotti (1885–1957) and Giacomo Noventa (1898–1960). A generation of younger poets is gathered in the anthol. ed. by Giancarlo Pontiggia and Enzo Di Mauro, *La parola innamorata* (The Enamored Word, 1978): Maurizio Cucchi (b. 1945), Giuseppe Conte (b. 1945), Milo De Angelis (b. 1951), Valerio Magrelli (b. 1957), and Cesare Viviani (b. 1947).

See ITALIAN PROSODY.

■ **Criticism; History, Specialized; Primary Texts**: E. Underhill, *Jacopone da Todi, Poet and Mystic* (1919); E. Garin, *Il Rinascimento italiano* (1941); F. Flora, *La poesia ermetica* (1947); C. Calcaterra, *Il Barocco in Arcadia* (1950); A. Momigliano, *Saggio sull' "Orlando Furioso"* (1952); A. Bobbio, *Parini* (1954); A. Galletti, *Il Novecento* (1954); *Marino e marinisti: opere scelte*, ed. G. Getto, 2 v. (1954); *Lirici del Settecento*, ed. B. Maier (1960); *Poeti del Duecento*, ed. G. Contini, 2 v. (1960); A. Viscardi, *Storia della letteratura italiana dalle origini al Rinascimento* (1960); E. H. Wilkins, *The Life of Petrarch* (1961); *Leopardi's Canti*, trans. J. H. Whitfield (1962); G. Santangelo, *Il secentismo* (1962); M. Bishop, *Petrarch and His World* (1963); J. V. Mirollo, *The Poet of the Marvelous: Giambattista Marino* (1963); G. Petronio, *Il Romanticismo* (1963); A. Del Monte, *Le origini* (1964); B. Maier, *Il Neoclassicismo* (1964); G. Singh, *Leopardi and the Theory of Poetry* (1964); J. H. Whitfield, *Giacomo Leopardi* (1964); T. G. Bergin, *Dante* (1965); C. P. Brand, *Torquato Tasso . . . and His Contribution to English Literature* (1965); *Complete Poems and Selected Letters of Michelangelo*, trans. C. Gilbert (1965); G. Pozzi, *La poesia italiana del Novecento* (1965); *Dante's Lyric Poetry*, ed. K. Foster and P. Boyde (1967); M. Fubini, *Ritratto dell'Alfieri* (1967); G. Getto, *L'interpretazione del Tasso* (1967); G. Contini, *Letteratura dell'Italia unita, 1861–1968* (1968); G. Manacorda, *Storia della letteratura italiana contemporanea* (1968); P. Nardi, *La Scapigliatura* (1968); W. Binni, *Saggi alfieriani* (1969); P. Dronke, *The Medieval Lyric* (1969); T. G. Bergin, *Petrarch* (1970); *Tasso's "Jerusalem Delivered,"* trans. J. Tusiani (1970); *Enciclopedia dantesca*, ed. U. Bosco, 5 v. (1970–78); A. Vallone, *Dante* (1971); L. Anceschi, *Le poetiche del Novecento in Italia* (1973); M. Marti, *Storia dello stil nuovo* (1973); C. P. Brand, *Ludovico Ariosto: A Preface to the "Orlando Furioso"* (1974); G. Debenedetti, *Poesia italiana del Novecento* (1974); R. Griffin, *Ludovico Ariosto* (1974); *Francis Petrarch Six Centuries Later: A Symposium*, ed. A. Scaglione (1975); M. Fubini, "Arcadia e Illuminismo," *Dal Muratori al Baretti* (1975); A. Seroni, *Il decadentismo* (1975); *Ariosto's "Orlando Furioso,"* trans. B. Reynolds (1975–77); *Petrarch's Lyric Poems*, trans. R. M. Durling (1976); U. Bosco, *Petrarca* (1977); G. Getto, *Carducci e Pascoli* (1977); M. Fubini, *Ugo Foscolo* (1978); *Il Novecento*, ed. G. Grana, 10 v. (1980); *The New Italian Poetry: 1945 to the Present*, ed. and trans. L. R. Smith (1981)—bilingual anthol.; T. Barolini, *Dante's Poets* (1984); K. Foster, *Petrarch* (1984); U. Foscolo, *Poesie e carmi*, ed. F. Pagliai et al. (1985); C. Kleinhenz, *The Early Italian Sonnet* (1986); A. R. Ascoli, *Ariosto's Bitter Harmony* (1987); P. Hainsworth, *Petrarch the Poet* (1988); *New Italian Poets*, ed. D. Gioia and M. Palma (1991); *Shearsmen of Sorts: Italian Poetry 1975–1993*, ed. L. Ballerini (1992); S. Sturm-Maddox, *Petrarch's Laurels* (1992); Dante, *Vita Nuova, Rime*, ed. D. De Robertis and G. Contini (1995); Petrarch, *The Canzoniere*, trans. M. Musa (1996); *Come leggere la poesia italiana del Novecento*, ed. S. Carrai and F. Zambon (1997); L. Pulci, *Morgante*, trans. J. Tusiani (1998); *Gruppo 63: l'antologia*, ed. N. Balestrini and A. Giuliani (2002); G. Pascoli, *Poesie*, ed. M. Pazzaglia (2002); M. Arcangeli, *La Scapigliatura poetica Milanese e la poesia italiana fra Otto e Novecento* (2003); *Gruppo 63: critica e teoria*, ed. R. Barilli and A. Guglielmi (2003); *La poesia italiana del Novecento*, ed. M. Bazzocchi and F. Curi (2003); N. Merola, *Poesia italiana moderna: da Parini a D'Annunzio* (2004); *Dopo la lirica: poeti italiani 1960–2000*, ed. E. Testa (2005); A. Manzoni, *Le poesie*, ed. V. Marucci (2005); *La poesia italiana del secondo Novecento*, ed. N. Merola (2006); S. Zatti, *The Quest for Epic: From Ariosto to Tasso*, trans. S. Hill (2006); *Twentieth-Century Italian Poetry*, ed. E. Ó Ceallacháin (2007); G. Leopardi, *Canti*, trans. J. G. Nichols (2008); *An Anthology of Modern Italian Poetry in English Translation*, ed. and trans. N. Condini (2009).

■ **History, General**: A. Momigliano, *Storia della letteratura italiana* (1936); F. Flora, *Storia della letteratura italiana*, 4 v. (1940–41); N. Sapegno, *Compendio di storia della letteratura italiana*, 3 v. (1954); J. H. Whitfield, *A Short History of Italian Literature* (1960); F. De Sanctis, *History of Italian Literature* (1870), trans. J. Redfern (1968); *Storia della letteratura italiana*, ed. E. Cecchi and N. Sapegno, v. 8–9

(1969); *I classici italiani nella storia della critica*, ed. W. Binni, 3 v. (1971–77); *Dizionario critico della letteratura italiana*, ed. V. Branca (1973); Wilkins; *Orientamenti culturali: La Letteratura italiana: I maggiori, I–II; I minori, I–IV; Le correnti, I–II; I contemporanei, I–VI* (1975–); *Letteratura italiana, profilo storico*, ed. I. De Bernardi et al., 3 v. (1980); M. Puppo, *Manuale critico bibliografico per lo studio della letteratura italiana* (1985); B. Croce, *Essays on Literature and Literary Criticism* (1972), ed. and trans. M. E. Moss (1990); *Storia della civiltà letteraria italiana*, ed. G. Bárberi Squarotti, F. Bruni, and U. Dotti (1990–96); *Storia della letteratura italiana*, ed. E. Malato (1995–); *Dictionary of Italian Literature*, ed. P. and J. C. Bondanella, rev. ed. (1996); *Storia generale della letteratura italiana*, ed. N. Borsellino and W. Pedullà (1999); *Medieval Italy: An Encyclopedia*, ed. C. Kleinhenz et al., 2 v. (2004); *Encyclopedia of Italian Literary Studies*, ed. G. Marrone et al., 2 v. (2007); *Seventeenth-Century Italian Poets and Dramatists*, ed. A. N. Mancini and G. P. Pierce (2008).

T. Wlassics; C. Kleinhenz; E. Livorni

J

JAPAN, MODERN POETRY OF

I. Tanka
II. Haiku
III. Free Verse

While many mod. Japanese poets adapted traditional forms such as *tanka* and haiku in directions compatible with mod. concerns and interests, others cultivated mod. verse forms influenced by the West. The following traces the devel. of mod. tanka, mod. haiku, and mod. free verse.

I. Tanka. Mod. tanka began with an explosion of polemic stimulated by the introduction of new literary forms and ideas that accompanied the opening of Japan to the world in the mid-19th c. A tanka is simply a different name for the *waka*, a term dating back to the beginning of the genre, meaning a short poem written in a fixed pattern of 5-7-5-7-7 syllables, with various conventions relating to subject, vocabulary, and so on. In the closing years of the 19th c., both terms were used simultaneously to refer to the same verse genre, but the word *tanka* was preferred by poets who considered themselves reformers. Old-style tanka known as *kyūha-waka* had been dominated by the Outadokoro (Palace School) poets who were associated with courtier families and with the imperial family itself, which had authorized the establishment of the office of Palace Poetry in 1871. Opposed to the hidebound, moribund mode of expression favored by these poets, such young iconoclastic writers as Ochiai Naobumi (1861–1903), his pupil Yosano Tekkan (1873–1935), and Masaoka Shiki (1867–1902), better known as a haiku reformer but who also took up the banner of tanka renewal, wrote several critical essays arguing for tanka as high lit. open to the new intellectual currents from the West, rather than an exercise in trad. Tekkan's "Bōkoku no On" (Sounds Ruinous to the Country, 1895) and Shiki's "Utayomini atauru Sho" (Letters to a Tanka Poet, 1898) are typical of the attacks launched by reformers in their attempts to revivify tanka composition. A number of the reformers advocated the explicit linking of tanka to *shintaishi* (new-style verse), the new free-verse form imported from the West, esp. Tekkan who called for tanka to be renamed *tanshi* (short poems). In their efforts to dissolve the barriers hitherto existing between traditional modes of poetry like tanka and the new free verse modeled on Western poetry, several of the reformist poets also composed free verse and prose to stake their claims for tanka as art. The first fruits of this new style of tanka came from poets associated with the *Myōjō* (Morning Star) magazine, above all from the brush of Yosano Akiko (1878–1942), the wife of Tekkan. Akiko's first tanka collection *Midaregami* (*Tangled Hair*, 1901) shocked the traditional tanka world with its daring, sensual poems openly celebrating female sexuality and its use of diction and imagery never seen before in tanka.

By 1910, literary naturalism had become all the rage in Japan and tanka poets moved variously to embrace a plainer, more naturalistic style of expression. By this time the leadership role in tanka composition had passed from poets associated with *Myōjō* to poets associated with the *Araragi* (Japanese Yew Tree) magazine. The most important poet of the period was Ishikawa Takuboku (1886–1912), who was originally linked to *Myōjō*. Takuboku's first tanka collection, *Ichiaku no Suna* (A Handful of Sand), was published in 1910 and focused in clear, limpid verse on the poet's sensibility: his existential loneliness and spiritual malaise. The following tanka by Takuboku, first published in 1909, is typical of his poetry:

Jinjō no odoke naramu ya	Not just a common buffoon
Naifu mochi shinu mane o suru	Knife in hand, faking suicide
Sono kao sono kao	That face that face

Takuboku popularized the fashion for writing tanka as a three-line verse (earlier it had been written in a single unbroken line), and his intensely personal angst amid the new, mighty metropolis of Tokyo captured legions of readers.

The leading poet of the Araragi coterie was Saitō Mokichi (1882–1953) who emerged as one of the greatest tanka poets of the 20th c. Trained as a psychiatrist, Saitō was originally attracted to modernist modes of writing imported from the West, although he eventually rejected modernist poetics in favor of a more traditional aesthetic. The greatest modernist poet of the prewar period was Maekawa Samio (1903–90), who originally came to attention because of his "proletarian" tanka, written in a free meter, that extolled left-wing activism. In 1930, Samio turned his back on his proletarian comrades with the publication of his first volume of tanka, *Shokubutsusai* (Botanical Revels). This collection of 574 tanka was imbued with the modernist poetics of writers like Jean Cocteau. Samio openly embraced Fr. surrealist techniques, as the following dislocatory verse from this volume demonstrates:

Toko no ma ni	In the alcove
Matsurarete aru	Placed on a pedestal
Waga kubi o	My head.
Utsutsu naraneba	Because this is not real
Naite miteishi	In tears I stared at it.

In 1926, the famous tanka poet Shaku Chōkū (better known as Orikuchi Shinobu, 1887–1953) had declared the tanka was well on the way to extinction. Samio's riposte in the form of modernist verse was itself criticized in Matsumura Eiichi's 1934 article titled "Tanka Sanbunka" (Prosifying Tanka), which took Samio as well as other poets like Mokichi to task for using foreign vocabulary in their verse. What actually brought tanka to the brink of extinction was World War II. The mass of xenophobic prowar tanka penned by Samio and Mokichi, and just about everybody else, led to a disastrous drop in artistic standards and provoked revulsion on the part of postwar poets against the tanka genre itself and its long association with Japanese trad. The first substantial attack on tanka appeared in May 1946. The critic Usui Yoshimi (1905–87), in an article titled "Tanka e no Ketsubetsu" (Farewell to Tanka), criticized tanka poets for their unquestioning support of the war and for the awful verse produced as a result. The philosopher Kuwabara Takeo (1904–88) followed up a like-minded attack on haiku with an article in January 1947, titled "Tanka no Unmei" (The Fate of Tanka), that argued the tanka form itself was unable to express the mod. world or the mod. spirit. Other attacks on tanka swiftly followed. This storm of crit. led to a loss of confidence among tanka poets esp. younger poets only beginning to come to notice. Established poets like Kondō Yoshimi (1913–2006) and Miya Shūji (1912–86) led the counterattack and revived tanka by composing verse simultaneously celebrating and criticizing the U.S. occupation, which lasted until the end of 1951. Poets such as these also attempted to document the war in their tanka, realistically and graphically expressing the emotions of the Japanese people.

Tsukamoto Kunio (1922–2005) was the leading avant-garde tanka poet in the immediate postwar period. Such tanka had been suppressed during wartime because of its connections to Western art and lit. Tsukamato sought to reestablish the literary credentials of tanka in the face of attacks on the genre itself by emphasizing the literary and artistic qualities of the genre. By the 1960s and 1970s, tanka had been restored to legitimacy as a literary art but the genre did not regain the prestige and influence that it had wielded before and during the war. Poets like Terayama Shūji (1935–83), who was also active as a free-verse poet and dramatist, wrote innovative and fresh tanka that in its use of free meter and subject seemed appropriate to the new age. Women tanka poets also occupied a larger part of the poetry scene than before. Baba Akiko (b. 1928) became a powerful presence from this period onward not only for the cl. elegance of her verse that hearkened back to the waka trad. but for her tanka crit. and scholarship. Tawara Machi (b. 1962) created a sensation with her debut volume *Sarada Kinenbi* (Salad Anniversary, 1987), which sold over a million copies and became the most successful tanka collection of the mod. era. Composed in simple colloquial diction, this collection told of the love affair of the young woman narrator, breaking completely with the more ornate style of older tanka still favored occasionally by mod. poets. A flood of similar collections followed, most of which imitated Machi's style. The 100-year debate over whether to compose tanka in colloquial rather than cl. lang. seemed by the 21st c. to have been won in favor of the former, with the success of Machi and her followers. But many amateur tanka poets prefer to cleave to older models of tanka; and as cl. waka are still widely read and also taught in schools, there seems little possibility that the cl. style will disappear altogether. In that respect, tanka still retains a sense of continuity with cl. waka poetry, linking the poetry of the present with the literary legacy of a past over a millennium in length.

II. Haiku. By the mid-19th c., haiku was trapped in a cultural discourse that saw the genre as something more than lit.; indeed, some schools of traditional haiku argued that haiku was not lit. at all but a unique expression of the Japanese spirit, something akin to religion. Such schools saw great haiku masters like Matsuo Bashō (1644–94) as spiritual gurus rather than excellent poets. On the other hand, haiku was composed by a host of ordinary people as a pastime or hobby expressing their personal feelings or simply documenting the events in their lives. This led to a crisis of legitimacy about whether haiku could actually be described as a serious literary art, a crisis that was exacerbated by the introduction of Western poetry and ideas that accompanied the opening of Japan to the world in the mid-19th c. (in some respects, the debate is still ongoing). By and large, serious haiku poets themselves did not share in this pessimism about the nature of the genre (arising primarily out of its extreme brevity, only 17 syllables in total), but a number of haiku poets felt the need to address the issue.

Masaoka Shiki, the most important haiku poet and reformer of the late 19th c., took up this issue in a series of essays published between 1889 and 1895 and argued not only that the haiku of his time was banal, nothing but doggerel, but that Matsuo Bashō, the saint of haiku himself, wrote mostly rubbish. Shiki took the view that, for haiku to be considered as lit., it needed to be evaluated by literary criteria, not by extraliterary considerations that had elevated Bashō to sainthood and that maintained the moribund schools of traditional haiku of the day.

In the first few decades of the 20th c., Shiki's legacy was split into two schools or factions: one led by Kawahigashi Hekigotō (1873–1937), who advocated haiku written in a mod. free meter format, and the other led by Takahama Kyoshi (1874–1959), who defended the traditional diction of haiku with its fixed syllabic 5-7-5 pattern, season words, and fixed topical themes. Both poets claimed the mantle of Shiki's successor, and for most of the 20th c., the two schools continued to flourish independently. Hekigotō preferred to call his poems *tanshi* (short free verse), following some early tanka poets, rather than haiku. Among Kyoshi's followers, the names of Murakami Kijō (1865–1938) and Iida Dakotsu (1885–1962) are prominent. Both poets composed haiku along traditional, conservative lines, with a strong focus on nature and natural phenomena, incl. animals and insects. Hekigotō's free-verse school included radical poets like Ogiwara Seisensui (1884–1976), who did away with season words, for instance, and also Nakatsuka Ippekirō (1887–1946), whose poetry took haiku to a new depth of experimentation where the verse becomes almost abstract. The traditional school was centered on the magazine *Hototogisu* (Cuckoo) founded by Kyoshi. Kyoshi's preferred aesthetic was *shasei* (sketching from life) advocated by his master Shiki, but Kyoshi interpreted this in a more conservative manner, stressing how haiku should evoke past literary assocs. Although the Cuckoo school dominated prewar haiku circles, by the 1930s a number of poets had turned against its traditional aesthetic in favor of a more modernist style closer to the free-verse school. Mizuhara Shūōshi (1892–1981) and Yamaguchi Seishi (1901–94) led the charge. These two poets stressed musical rhythm and unconventional subjects, respectively. In the late 1920s and 1930s, a school of proletarian haiku emerged, based in Kyoto University, which stressed working-class topics. The poets in the Kyoto school achieved fame by being arrested in 1940 as "spies," presumably because of their left-wing sympathies.

During World War II, in common with tanka poets, haiku poets produced a prodigious quantity of prowar, xenophobic verse mostly devoid of literary merit, and this led to fierce attacks on the genre after the war's end. The Kyoto University philosopher Kuwabara Takeo's famous essay "Dainigeijutsuron—Gendai Haiku ni tsuite" (A Second-Class Art—On Contemporary Haiku), published in November 1946, argued that haiku was a mere craft, not lit. Kuwabara used the technique developed by the Brit. lit. critic I. A. Richards to ask a group of intellectuals to evaluate 15 haiku by various famous haiku poets and a few completely unknown amateurs. The result was that practically none of the intellectuals could tell the difference between the haiku "masterpieces" and the unknown works. Kuwabara's attack plunged the contemp. haiku world into despair and undermined many of the tenets of traditional haiku. Consequently, conventions relating to fixed topics, meter, and so forth were largely abandoned by postwar poets, who composed difficult, abstract verse close to the kind of free verse (*shi*) composed by various mod. poets. Two prominent postwar poets whose poetry can stand for this trend (at times their verse can be very demanding) and who were esp. celebrated for their literary skills are Nakamura Kusatao (1901–83) and Kaneko Tōta (b. 1919).

Contemp. haiku is notable for the large number of women poets now composing verse.

Fujiki Kiyoko is an example of a poet who has become increasingly recognized as an important writer. Fujiki's first book of haiku appeared in 1934, and her wartime verse and erotic poetry have become esp. acclaimed. Her poetic trajectory parallels the practice of many contemp. female tanka poets who also write explicitly erotic verse. Kadokawa Haruki (b. 1942) is another important contemp. haiku poet. The heir to the Kadokawa publishing empire, he has also achieved success as a businessman, film director, and producer. Kadokawa has won many awards for his haiku, which treat a variety of themes in powerful, terse lang., incl. his 2004 collection about life in prison (he was jailed for possessing cocaine). The association between haiku and autobiographical themes seems inescapable given the brevity of the form and the long association of the genre with the life journeys of many famous poets. For this reason, haiku still retains a strong attraction for millions of amateurs who use haiku to record and explore their inner lives in workmanlike lang. with no particular ambition to imitate the austere beauty achieved by haiku masters.

III. Free Verse. Japanese free-verse poetry (shi) originally began from trans. of a group of mostly Eng. poems, which were collected into a single volume (also containing some original poetry), entitled *Shintaishi Shō* (A Collection of Poetry in the New Style, 1882). Three scholars translated these poems into Japanese, none of whom had any reputation as poets. The trans. poetry came from a variety of authors and included extracts from various of Shakespeare's plays and poetry by H. W. Longfellow; Charles Kingsley; Alfred, Lord Tennyson; and Thomas Gray. Many of the poems were translated into a 7-5 syllabic sequence based on the traditional meter of waka. Other influences helped shape the devel. of Japanese "new-style" verse: trans. of hymns, poetry composed in Chinese by Japanese poets (called *kanshi* in Japanese—the word for free verse, *shi*, arises from this; see CHINESE POETRY IN JAPAN), trans. of Brit. military ballads, and songs for children written in simple colloquial Japanese. The chief difference between "new-style" verse and traditional genres of poetry like tanka and haiku was the length and structure of the poems: new-style verse could continue for many stanzas, unlike the exceedingly brief verse of trad. poetry, and did not necessarily follow the metrical structure of traditional genres of poetry. Shimazaki Tōson (1872–1943) was the first major poet to compose verse using the new style. He wrote four volumes of poetry between 1897 and 1904 (when his collected poetry appeared) before he abandoned poetry for fiction and subsequently achieved fame as a novelist. Tōson's musical, romantic verse used the diction of cl. Japanese to achieve a fresh yet elegant tone. He borrowed themes and imagery from cl. lit. as well as phrases from trans. of Western verse and hymns. His success spawned numerous imitators who followed their master in blending elements from cl. waka with themes taken from trans. of Western verse to produce new-style poetry that was pleasing to the ear but still managed to suggest something of the novelty of Western verse. A number of leading new-style poets like Yosano Akiko, Ishikawa Takuboku and Kitahara Hakushū (1885–1942) also wrote tanka, confirming that new-style verse was an intermediate or hybrid form bridging the gap between cl. poetry and free verse.

The first collection to be written entirely in free verse, defined here as poetry composed not in the 7-5 meter and using colloquial rather than cl. grammar, was Kawai Suimei's (1874–1965) volume *Kiri* (Mist), which was published in May 1910. However, another poet called Kawaji Ryūkō (1888–1959), who belonged to Kawai's circle, also wrote a celebrated volume of free verse, titled *Robō no Hana* (Wayside Flowers) that came out a mere three months later and is often cited as the first volume of free verse to appear in Japan. Kawai's poems are mostly prose poems, and Kawaji's collection contains poetry first published in 1907, so this may explain the reason for Kawaji's prominence. Various manifestos arguing for free verse rather than new-style verse or traditional genres of poetry had already appeared, the earliest being Toyama Masakazu's (1848–1900) 1895 essay advocating a movement to write poetry using contemp. Japanese. Also, in 1892, the famous novelist Natsume Sōseki (1867–1916) issued a call for poetry to follow the example of Walt Whitman's free verse. The movement toward free verse had several consequences. A number of outstanding collections of free verse soon resulted, incl. Takamura Kōtarō's (1883–1956) *Dōtei* (The Journey, 1914); Hagiwara Sakutarō's (1886–1942) *Tsuki ni Hoeru* (Howling at the Moon, 1917); and Miyazawa Kenji's (1896–1933) *Haru to Shura* (Spring and Ashura, 1924). Many poets were reluctant to abandon the elegant beauty of cl. diction and continued to compose verse in a mixture of cl. and colloquial syntax or composed verse in both modes. E.g., Hagiwara's last collection *Hyōtō* (The Iceland, 1934) was written entirely in cl. Japanese, unlike the bulk of his earlier collections. Inspired by trans. of Paul Verlaine, Charles Baudelaire, and like-minded Fr. and Ger. symbolist poets, poets belonging to the Japanese symbolist school were esp. noteworthy for their mixture of cl. and colloquial. The two most prominent such poets were Susukida Kyūkin (1877–1945) and Kambara Ariake (1875–1952). Later poets inherited their mantle, most notably Murō Saisei (1889–1962) and Miyoshi Tatsuji (1900–64). Japanese modernist poetry also embraced free verse enthusiastically—avant-garde poets like the Dadaist Takahashi Shinkichi (1901–87) and the surrealist poet Nishiwaki Junzaburō (1894–1982) produced powerful dislocatory collections. Takahashi's self-proclaimed Dadaist collection published in 1923 and Nishiwaki's 1933 collection *Ambarvalia*, which explored the landscape of Tokyo devastated by the 1922 earthquake using techniques developed during his stay in Europe, are both landmark works of poetry.

The advent of World War II inspired a vast outpouring of patriotic and xenophobic verse. After the war, many poets sought to conceal their wartime verse (generally marked by its lack of literary merit) by deleting such poetry from their later collections. In the 1950s and 1960s, the poet and critic Yoshimoto Takaaki (1924–2012) led the charge to expose the wartime writings of these poets as part of the resurgence of the Left (Yoshimoto was widely acknowledged as the leader of the Japanese New Left) in intellectual circles. Yoshimoto did have some sympathy for those poets who underwent a mea culpa and renounced their wartime writings, esp. the poet Takamura Kōtarō, whose verse he championed. The school of poets obsessed with the war and its aftermath has become known as the "postwar" school, although originally they were called the Arechi (Wasteland) group, after the name of the jour. in which their poetry was published. These poets and their successors wrote only free verse, thus assuring the victory of this form over hybrid varieties of poetry incorporating cl. diction. Prominent among this group were Tamura Ryūichi (1923–98), Ayukawa Nobuo (1920–86), Kuroda Saburō (1918–80), and, later, Yoshimoto Takaaki. Their premise was that postwar Japan was a wasteland, virtually a colony of the U.S., so in order to write poetry it was necessary to take up issues such as the war and the suffering it entailed, as well as the legacy of the U.S. occupation. Women poets like Ibaragi Noriko (1926–2006) and Ishigaki Rin (1920–2004) who achieved prominence from the 1950s onward wrote verse with similar concerns but with a stronger focus on the role of women in daily life and society at large.

Opposing the "ideology" of this school, which dominated postwar poetry for a decade or more, was an eclectic group of poets united in very little save their concern with poetic lang. and its limits. Inheriting Nishiwaki's surrealist bent, Yoshioka Minoru (1919–90) dominated poetry circles in the 1950s and 1960s; his powerful style used the ambiguity and indeterminacy of lang. in a masterful way and captured the allegiance of many contemp. poets. His 1958 collection *Sōryo* (Monks) successfully imported the older, prewar modernist trad. into the postwar era. Other poets who were obsessed with lang.—so much so that later critics have called them the "language school"—include Suzuki Shiroyasu (b. 1935) and his successor Nejime Shōichi (b. 1948) who used poetry to transgress the accepted boundaries of decorum concerning sexuality and violence. Like Nejime, Tomioka Taeko (b. 1935) has gone on to a successful career as a novelist, but her poetry of the 1960s established a powerful precedent for women poets to follow, with her long, trademark *monogatari* (tale) poems—seemingly endless dialogues defamiliarizing gender, among much else. One of her successors, Isaka Yōko (b. 1949) has extended this technique to everyday life and achieved a solid reputation from the 1970s onward. Irisawa Yasuo (b. 1931) also explored the long "tale" poem, concentrating on Japanese trad. in his celebrated 1968 collection *Waga Izumo Waga Chinkon* (My Izumo, My Requiem), which could also be read as a parodic homage to T. S. Eliot's *The Waste Land.* Yoshimasu Gōzō (b. 1939) also works in this vein, reading his saga-style poetry aloud to receptive audiences who come to hear his famous oral performances. Shiraishi Kazuko (b. 1931) writes long poetry that seems as much utterances of a seer as anything else and has also been acclaimed by her peers for her achievements.

Tanikawa Shuntarō (b. 1931) has often been mentioned as a possible candidate for the Nobel Prize in Literature, a tribute to his extraordinary gifts as a poet. From his first collection *Nijū Oku Kōnen no Kodoku* (20 Billion Light Years of Loneliness, 1952) to his famous 1968 collection *Tabi* (Journeys) and his award-winning 1993 collection *Seken Shirazu* (The Naïf), his journey as a poet has traversed the entire half-century since the war. A master of verse form, Tanikawa has often experimented with rhymes and other complex metrical devices, exploring the beauty and pathos of everyday life in lang. as fresh as it is readable.

Poets since the 1970s have generally acknowledged Tanikawa's preeminence as a poet but often dispute his emphasis on audience-oriented performance poetry, instead emphasizing poetry as conceptual art, a kind of abstract art marked by difficulty and indeterminancy. "Language" poets of the 1970s and 1980s like Arakawa Yōji (b. 1949) and Iijima Kōichi (1930–2013) have been succeeded by like-minded poets of a younger generation, most notably Inagawa Masato (b. 1949) and Hiraide Takashi (b. 1950). Itō Hiromi (b. 1955), now resident in the U.S. and active also as a novelist, was the quintessential feminist poet of the 1980s and 1990s, with volumes like *Teritorii Ron II* (On Territory 2, 1985) establishing her mastery of disruptive, collage-style verse questioning gender and the self itself. Since the dawning of the 21st c., Japanese poets have moved more in the direction of performance than abstract art, but the challenge of poetry competing in the crowded space of print publication, whether printed paper or cybertext, continually stimulates poets to go beyond recognized boundaries of lang. and convention to stake a claim for poetry as significant art.

■ M. Ueda, *Modern Japanese Haiku* (1976); J. Beichmann, *Masaoka Shiki* (1982); A. Heinrich, *Fragments of Rainbows* (1983); D. Keene, *Dawn to the West: Japanese Literature in the Modern Era,* v. 2 (1984); M. Saitō, *Red Lights,* trans. S. Shinoda and S. Goldstein (1989); *An Anthology of Contemporary Japanese Poetry*, ed. and trans. L. Morton (1993); *Modern Japanese Tanka*, trans. Makoto Ueda (1996); S. Shimaoka, *Shi to wa Nanika* (What Is Poetry?, 1998); J. Beichman, *Embracing the Firebird* (2002)—on Yosano Akiko; H. Kawana, *Modan Toshi to Gendai Haiku* (The Modern City and Contemporary Haiku, 2002); L. Morton, *Modern Japanese Culture* (2003); L. Morton, *Modernism in Practice: An Introduction to Postwar Japanese Poetry* (2004); *Columbia Anthology of Modern Japanese Literature*, ed. J. Rimer and V. Gessel, 2 v. (2005–7); T. Saigusa, *Shōwa Tanka no Seishinshi* (A Spiritual History of Shōwa Tanka, 2005); N. Ōta, *Nihon Kindai Tankashi no Kōchiku* (The Construction of Modern Tanka History in Japanese, 2006).

L. Morton

JAPAN, POETRY OF. Japanese poetry has a recorded hist. of approximately 1,500 years, and the art has occupied a central position in the nation's cultural life. While the term *Japanese poetry* generally applies to verses in the vernacular, i.e., poetry *in* Japanese, it also refers in its most inclusive sense to poetry *by* Japanese, incl. that written in Chinese, which until mod. times was the lingua franca of East Asian literati. Vernacular poetry is called *waka* (or *yamato uta*, Japanese poem or Japanese song) or simply *uta* (poem or song); poetry in Chinese by Japanese poets is called *kanshi* (see CHINESE POETRY IN JAPAN), though that term is also used in Japan for Chinese poetry composed by Chinese. Many Japanese poets composed in both langs. When considered in the context of the geographical boundaries of the Japanese archipelago, the term *poetry of Japan* also includes other poetic trads., incl. those of the Ryūkyū Islands and the Ainu, which are beyond the scope of the discussion below.

The evolution of premod. Japanese vernacular poetry is characterized by shifting ratios of oral versus written expression, native inspiration versus foreign assimilation, public versus personal subject matter, "high" versus "low" topics, court versus plebeian poetic practice, ritual or political versus belletristic purpose, and conventionality versus originality. And yet it maintains certain consistencies throughout, the predominant one being the lyric voice—the ostensibly personal expression of emotion. The premod. Japanese poet generally reserved more discursive or philosophical matters for poetry in Chinese (which, to be sure, also employed the lyric approach). The emotions expressed in vernacular poetry, furthermore, were inspired most importantly by the four seasons and by love, the latter often conveyed through metaphors drawn from nature. Other important topics were lamentation, travel, and congratulation. Though early song included various other topics, such as warfare, those considered appropriate for orthodox vernacular poetry generally came to be fixed early in the written hist. of the medium, as did acceptable treatments, images, and vocabulary. Although Japanese poetic practice could encompass original inspiration, it also placed great store on the conventional, esp. in public, multipoet settings where it might be more desirable to fit in than to stand out. After standardized poetic forms and meter coalesced from irregular preliterate songs, they too remained constant, nearly always being based on alternating segments of five and seven morae. Hypermetric or hypometric segments sometimes occurred. Both short and long segments have an underlying four-beat rhythm, with the last beat of a short segment being a rest. Early Japanese poetry, most of which dates from the 7th and 8th cs. CE, includes the *chōka* (long poem) of an unfixed number (usually a few dozen) of alternating five- and seven-morae segments and two final segments of seven morae; the *sedōka* (head repeating poem) of 5-7-7-5-7-7 morae segments; the *katauta* (half poem) of 5-7-7 morae segments; the *bussokusekika* (Buddha's footstone poem) of 5-7-5-7-7-7 morae segments; and most notably the *tanka* (short poem) of 5-7-5-7-7 morae segments. The last of these became so popular in the ensuing Heian period (794–1185) that the term *waka* grew to be generally synonymous with it, and that is how it will be used below. The chōka came to be employed only infrequently, and the sedōka, katauta, and bussokusekika disappeared entirely. The 31-morae waka retained its creative vitality through the med. era (1185–1600), though as that era progressed, many of the finest poetic minds increasingly turned to linked verse (*renga*), in which a group of poets alternately linked 17- and 14-morae poems into hundred-verse chains. But even linked-verse poets also composed waka. After the turn of the 17th c., orthodox waka was eclipsed in popularity by other poetic forms such as comic waka (*kyōka*), *haikai* linked verse (*haikai* [*no*] *renga* or *renku*), and haiku (see below), though it continued to be widely composed.

The visual layout of a Japanese poem on the page is variable and not necessarily reflective of the 5-7 morae structure. It may be written in one or several lines or artfully arranged on a page decorated with colored underpainting. But no matter how it is recorded on paper, the oral qualities of vernacular Japanese poetry remain vital. These include alliteration and assonance, but generally not end rhyme, since the fact that nearly all morae in Japanese end with one of a small number of vowels makes rhyme altogether too facile.

Waka poetry also figured prominently in other literary genres, e.g., poem tales (*utamonogatari*, short narratives that hinge on a poem or poems), diaries and travel lit. (see JAPANESE POETIC DIARIES), prose fiction (*monogatari*, such as *Genji monogatari* [The Tale of Genji], ca. 1008 CE, which contains hundreds of waka poems), and drama (such as *nō* plays). While poetic composition in Chinese was generally the domain of certain highly literate courtiers and clerics, mostly male, the ability to compose waka was for centuries a necessary polite accomplishment of all court men and women, being central to their education, social interaction, and self-definition. Therefore, unlike other Japanese literary arts such as the nō drama or monogatari recitation, Japanese court poetry was practitioner-oriented, its makers constituting its audience. This resulted in a very sophisticated level of reception and crit., and there remains an enormous body of theoretical and commentarial work (*karon*, literally, "treatise on Japanese poetry"; see JAPANESE POETICS). As the med. period progressed, Japanese poetry became an object of study and enjoyment among warriors and commoners, who likewise began to contribute to the corpus of anthols. and commentaries.

The hist. of Japanese poetry began before the advent of a Japanese writing system, with anonymous bards composing orally on concerns commonly held by the communities they served. These early vernacular songs were simple and declarative, and some of their basic topics, such as love, death, and travel, remained central to the vernacular poetic trad. thereafter, as did the tendency to express those topics against a backdrop of nature. They also dealt frequently with relations between gods and the human world, the border between poetry and religious ritual being porous. With the gradual acquisition of the Chinese writing system, the Japanese began to read Chinese poetry and prose, and the continental example thereafter provided an ever-growing resource through which—and against which—Japanese poetry developed. The 8th c. saw the compilation of the oldest extant anthols. of poetry by Japanese in Chinese (*Kaifūsō* [Florilegium of Cherished Airs], 751 CE) and in the vernacular (*Man'yōshū*, Anthology of Ten Thousand Leaves; last dated poem, 759), both of which include verses of earlier origin. The approximately 4,500 poems in *Man'yōshū* bear witness to the transition during the 7th and 8th c. from early oral vernacular song to a rich and complex written vernacular poetic trad., in which anonymous and communal expression gave way to highly wrought works by named individuals who possessed a sense of historical poetic devel. Increasing courtly sinophilia produced three anthols. of kanshi in the early 9th c., but thereafter the vernacular voice resurfaced publicly in the first imperially sponsored collection of Japanese verse, *Kokin wakashū* (Anthology of Ancient and Recent Japanese Poetry [abbreviated *Kokinshū*], 905), which established the basic orthodox lexicon, topics, and treatments for the subsequent 20 imperially commissioned anthols. (the last being *Shinshoku kokin wakashū* [New Continued Anthology of Ancient and Recent Japanese Poetry, 1439]), as well as the vast number of anthols. that poets privately compiled. The preface to *Kokinshū* is important for its expression of the character and desiderata of the native poetic idiom, notably the idea (itself borrowed from China) that poetry is essentially lyrical, that it "takes the human heart as seed, which burgeons forth in myriad words as leaves." This affective-expressive nexus characterizes the essence of the Japanese poetic medium. But even as it exploited certain approaches from Chinese verse of the Six Dynasties (222–589 CE), *Kokinshū* poetry rigorously excluded Sino-Japanese vocabulary and natural imagery not found in the archipelago. Orthodox waka retained this unadulterated native lexicon throughout the premod. era.

In the late Heian and med. periods, Japanese poetry became increasingly intertextual, expanding the boundaries of the 31-morae form through quotations from earlier waka. The eighth imperial poetic anthol., *Shinkokin wakashū* (or *Shinkokinshū*, New Anthology of Ancient and Recent Japanese Poetry, 1217), is emblematic of this shift. At this time as well, hereditary poetic houses developed, as did secret trads. that were handed down within those houses to buttress their authority. The tone of waka poetry became more melancholic and the Buddhist sense of evanescence more pronounced. This med. aesthetic of bittersweet beauty in perishability is also seen in the nō drama and tea culture, as well as in formal linked verse. Vast numbers of kanshi also continued to be composed, however, notably within the Zen establishment, and later among literati of the early mod. (Tokugawa or Edo) period (1600–1868).

But orthodox Japanese poetic composition was always paralleled by unconventional haikai forms that flouted the topical, thematic, and lexical strictures of formal work. During the social upheaval of the late med. period, such poetry came increasingly to be seen as its own legitimate poetic way, wherein Sino-Japanese vocabulary and aspects of daily life or bawdy humor could be celebrated, just as *kyōgen* comic plays came to coexist with the classic nō theater. Though the term *haikai* was also used in reference to unconventional waka, it was more frequently employed in the context of linked verse, and eventually the first verse of such sequences, the *hokku*, came to stand alone and later be termed *haiku*. Matsuo Bashō (1644–94), who became Japan's most famous premod. poet, participated in numerous haikai linked-verse sessions, and some *hokku* originally composed to initiate 36-verse sequences were later used alone in other contexts. But even as the short 17-morae form was coming into its own, the poet and fiction writer Ihara Saikaku (1642–93) was working in the other direction, single-handedly creating sequences of linked haikai that reached many hundreds of verses in length. Bashō also introduced poetic meter and techniques from haikai into his prose writing, creating a genre known as *haibun*.

With the collapse of the Tokugawa shogunate and the restoration of ostensibly direct imperial rule under Emperor Meiji in 1868, the predominant foreign literary influences no longer entered from China but from Europe and the United States, and Japanese poets began experimenting with new forms (*shintaishi*) and new approaches such as surrealism (see JAPAN, MODERN POETRY OF). While orthodox waka and composition in Chinese gradually declined in popularity, haiku remains widely practiced. Contemp. Japanese poets have also experimented with modernizing the waka through the use of new vocabulary and topics. Japanese poetry, which during the premod. period was almost entirely contained within the boundaries of the archipelago, has also begun to exert an influence outward, evidenced notably by the composition of haiku and linked verse in other langs.

■ **Criticism and History**: R. H. Brower and E. Miner, *Japanese Court Poetry* (1961); E. Miner, *An Introduction to Japanese Court Poetry* (1968); J. T. Rimer and R. E. Morrell, *Guide to Japanese Poetry* (1975); D. Keene, *World within Walls: Japanese Literature of the Pre-Modern Era, 1600–1867* (1976); J. Konishi, *A History of Japanese Literature,* v. 1, trans. A. Gatten and N. Teele (1984), *A History of Japanese Literature,* v. 2, trans. A. Gatten (1986), *A History of Japanese Literature,* v. 3, trans. A. Gatten and

M. Harbison (1991); H. C. McCullough, *Brocade by Night: "Kokin Wakashu" and the Court Style in Japanese Classical Poetry* (1985); Miner et al; M. Morris, "Waka in Form, Waka in History," *HJAS* 46.2 (1986); D. Keene, *Seeds in the Heart: Japanese Literature from Earliest Times to the Late Sixteenth Century* (1993); D. Keene, *Dawn to the West: Japanese Literature of the Modern Era* (1999); *Medieval Japanese Writers*, ed. S. D. Carter, v. 203 of *Dictionary of Literary Biography* (1999); K. Kawamoto, *The Poetics of Japanese Verse*, trans. S. Collington, K. Collins, and G. Heldt (2000).

■ **Translations**: *Japanese Literature in Chinese*, trans. B. Watson, 2 v. (1975–76); *Songs of Gods, Songs of Humans: The Epic Tradition of the Ainu*, trans. D. L. Philippi (1979); *From the Country of Eight Islands: An Anthology of Japanese Poetry*, trans. H. Sato and B. Watson (1981); *Waiting for the Wind: Thirty-Six Poets of Japan's Late Medieval Age*, trans. S. D. Carter (1989); C. Drake, "A Separate Perspective: Shamanic Songs of the Ryukyu Kingdom," *HJAS* 50:1 (1990); *Classical Japanese Prose*, trans. H. C. McCullough (1990); *Classical Japanese Poetry*, trans. S. D. Carter (1991); *A Waka Anthology, Volume One*, trans. E. A. Cranston (1993); *Early Modern Japanese Literature: An Anthology, 1600–1900*, ed. H. Shirane (2002); *Dance of the Butterflies: Chinese Poetry from the Japanese Court Tradition*, trans. J. N. Rabinovitch and T. R. Bradstock (2005); *A Waka Anthology, Volume Two*, trans. E. A. Cranston (2006); *Traditional Japanese Literature*, ed. H. Shirane (2007).

H. M. Horton

JAPANESE POETIC DIARIES. The Eng. term *Japanese poetic diaries* translates no single term used with consistency across the hist. of "diaries" (*niki, nikki; ki, kikō*) in Japanese trad. The practice of keeping more or less dated or dateable records, in either cl. Japanese or Chinese, that include poetry texts of one or more genres was practiced among imperial court officials and the aristocratic elite of the Heian period (794–1185). It continued to flourish and evolve as a mode of cultural production that marries writing in prose with the collection and contextualization of poetry in many different forms serving various purposes throughout Japan's premod. hist. While the practice has never completely died out—examples can be found for Meiji (1868–1912) and later years as well—it no longer forms a main current of Japanese cultural production.

Poetic diaries that have survived from the early 10th c. point to the function of poetry—both native *tanka* or *waka* (short verse in Japanese) and *kanshi* (verse in Chinese; see CHINESE POETRY IN JAPAN)—as an important form of cultural capital in the shifting rivalries between members of the Fujiwara regental house and the imperial family (reigning sovereigns as well as still-active abdicated or "retired" ones). Diaries, as well as poetic collections (*kashū* or *ie no shū*) with more or less extended headnotes, were produced by members of all three groups: the regents' households as well as the entourages of sitting and abdicated emperors. The 10th-c. practice of diary keeping by writers associated with the Fujiwara and other aristocratic families provided a patrimony of precedents for future clan heads to consult. As Heldt has argued in *The Pursuit of Harmony*, it also may have implied—because it mimicked the practice of diary keeping that had been carried on by court officials historically within the imperial palace—a symbolic equivalence between the regental and the imperial households. Heldt reads Ki no Tsurayuki's *Tosa nikki* (The Tosa Diary, 935) within this context as the attempt of a middle-ranking courtier to engage or maintain patronage ties with the high aristocracy via the display of his own talents as a desirable member of the entourage of proxy poets, scribes, and calligraphers surrounding the regent's and its rivals' households. Others have called attention to the impact of male-authored "poetic diaries" (also sometimes labeled "poetic tales" [*uta monogatari*]) composed by writers associated with the Fujiwara regents throughout the 10th c., culminating in the well-known *Kagerō nikki* (The Gossamer Diary, after 974), a poetic diary by a secondary wife of Regent Fujiwara Kaneie (see Mostow).

The *Kagerō nikki* fits easily within a genealogy of Fujiwara cultural production. It narrates its author's 21 years of marriage to Fujiwara Kaneie, highlighting in part the amorous and poetic talents of Kaneie. Just as important, it displays the poetic skills of the diarist herself, a valuable member of Kaneie's extended household. Yet the complexity of the *Kagerō nikki*'s prose and its apparent influence on poetic diaries by later aristocratic wives and ladies-in-waiting suggest the devel. of a differently configured set of motives, forms, and implied readers in the 11th c.

At the outset of her diary, the *Kagerō* author explicitly signals her engagement with the genre of fictional tales. She writes in opposition to the "empty words" of the old tales, she claims, "in the form of a memoir" for those who might ask about "the lives of the well-born." But in fact the rhetorical density of the *Kagerō*'s narrative portions heralds the sophisticated intertexual play between diary and tale genres that will characterize a number of subsequent poetic diaries, most notably the *Sarashina nikki* (The Sarashina Diary, after 1058), and the *Izumi Shikibu nikki* (The Diary of Izumi Shikibu, late 11th c.?; see Sarra). Deliberate blurring of generic boundaries between poetic diaries and fictional narratives (*tsukuri monogatari*) by women from middle-ranking families is visible as late as *Towazugatari* (An Unrequested Tale, after 1306), the memoir of a lady-in-waiting who drew self-consciously on episodes from *The Tale of Genji* (ca. 1008) to craft a record of her life at court and her wanderings as a Buddhist nun. Poetic diaries by mid-Heian and Kamakura period women (1185–1336) often call attention to the diarist's talent in both poetry and prose narrative, with the increased emphasis on narrative implying perhaps the importance of imperial and high-aristocratic women as the diarists' primary audience.

With the establishment of the military government at Kamakura and the increased physical mobility of the literate elite throughout the Kamakura and Muromachi periods (1336–1573), the practice of writing poetic travel diaries (kikō) proliferated. These diaries include not only the traditional courtly waka but the med. genre of *renga* (linked verse), and finally in the Tokugawa period (1600–1867) *haikai* (comic linked verse) and *haibun* (poetic prose), which the poet Matsuo Bashō (1644–94) brought to ripeness. Med. and early mod. poetic diaries bespeak their authors' involvement in establishing or perpetuating their reputations as heads of poetic schools. Their intended readers were other poets and aspiring practitioners of poetry.

One rhetorical feature linking med. poetic travel diaries to each other as well as to earlier and later diaries is the trad. of *utamakura* (poetic toponyms) that informs many of them. An itinerary of actual sites conventionally associated with specific poetic images as far back as the Heian period or earlier provides a structural framework for many poetic travel diaries. Thus, when the poet-nun Abutsu visited Yatsuhashi on her journey to Kamakura, recorded in *Izayoi nikki* (Diary of the Waning Moon, ca. 1283), the poem she composed on the place/place-name deliberately echoes earlier poets' compositions on the same site. Each poem memorializing such sites records the moment at which the diarist's composition joins a poetic dialogue about the place that had been ongoing for centuries. Such poems were also understood to function as ritualized forms of greeting to the resident spirit or deity of the place. The early 17th c. saw the rise of print culture and the spread of literacy beyond the courtly and warrior elites. Along with these profound sociohistorical shifts, a new spirit of parody and linguistic play informs the practice of poetic diaries, as it does so many other early mod. cultural practices. Bashō's poetic diaries sometimes self-ironically record the bouts of performance anxiety that encounters with utamakura inspired in him. He famously laments his failure to produce a poem at Yoshino in *Oi no kobumi* (Rucksack Notebook, 1687). Although poems by Bashō are conspicuously absent in his account of his visit to Matsushima in *Oku no hosomichi* (*Narrow Road to the Interior*, 1689), with its rich Chinese-influenced parallel constructions and allusions, his prose description of the place is a tour de force of the new form of haibun he pioneered in this, his most famous poetic diary.

Bashō's poetry and poetic diaries ultimately found readers beyond Japan, becoming central texts in the 20th-c. cross-cultural trad. of haiku poetry first promoted by the *imagistes*, a group of Anglo-Am. modernist poets publishing under the leadership of Ezra Pound immediately before World War I. The influence of poetic diaries by Heian and early med. women writers has been similarly far-reaching. Canonized by mod. scholars of "national literature" in Japan, early Japanese "women's memoir literature" became a vital source of inspiration for Japanese women writers throughout the 20th c.

See JAPAN, POETRY OF.

■ *The Izumi Shikibu Diary*, trans. E. Cranston (1969); *Lady Daibu's Poetic Memoirs*, trans. P. Harries (1980); L. Miyake, "The Tosa Diary," *The Woman's Hand*, ed. P. Schalow and J. Walker (1996); H. Shirane, *Traces of Dreams* (1998); E. Sarra, *Fictions of Femininity* (1999); T. Suzuki, "Gender and Genre," *Inventing the Classics*, ed. H. Shirane and T. Suzuki (2000); M. Horton, *Song in an Age of Discord* (2002); *The Journal of Sōchō*, trans. M. Horton (2002); *At the House of Gathered Leaves*, trans. J. Mostow (2004);

T. Yoda, *Gender and National Literature* (2004); J. Wallace, *Objects of Discourse* (2005); R. Kubukihara, "Aspects of Classical Japanese Travel Writing," spec. iss. of *Review of Japanese Culture and Society* 19 (2007); G. Heldt, *The Pursuit of Harmony* (2008).

E. SARRA

JAPANESE POETICS. Japanese poetics was shaped by the nature of poetic composition as a social practice among the Heian (794–1185) court aristocracy. The practice spread among the warriors and monks in the castle towns and temples of the med. age (1186–1600) and came to include merchants and commoners of the Edo period (1600–1868). *Waka* or *tanka*, the five-line poem of 5-7-5-7-7 syllables, recorded since the early 8th c., remained the cl. genre, with earlier forms like the long poem (*chōka*) and later genres like *renga* and *haikai* (linked poetry) and *hokku* (or haiku) being variations of it. This means that, apart from subtle historical changes, poetic lang. and themes remained largely the same, with the only revolutionary change occurring when the formerly barred Chinese loan words and daily-life vocabulary came to be included in the Edo period. The authors of poetic treatises were practicing poets themselves, and their readers were students or disciples who needed to acquire the art as a social skill, proof of their qualification as civilized persons. Many of the treatises were like textbooks devised for pedagogical purposes. They invariably included a brief hist. of the practice, usually tracing its primordial origins in the age of the gods as recorded in the first hist. books (*Kojiki*, 712; *Nihongi*, 720) or citing earliest examples from the first poetry anthol., the *Man'yōshū* (ca. 759), and from the 21 imperial anthols. commissioned by successive emperors until 1433. Other sections would consist of long passages of citation of exemplary poems, often with critical comments; equally numerous were stories or anecdotes (*utamonogatari*, *setsuwa*) about the circumstances in which a poem was composed or about particular poets and their deep devotion to the art. A significant portion was devoted to practical instruction about poetic diction and techniques, such as the use of "pillow words" (*makura kotoba*), conventional epithets associated with particular words—e.g., "Izumo, of the rising eight-fold clouds" or "Nara, of the good blue earth"; the use of *joshi* or preface, a metaphorical intro. to the main statement of the poem; the technique of punning or double meaning (*kakekotoba*); and the deploying of word pairs linked by association (*engo*). There was from early on a penchant for numerical categories and classifications such as "the nine grades of waka" (*waka kuhon*) or "the six types of poetry" (*rikugi*)—they were useful for distinguishing among the countless riches of the accumulated archives—and always, in the endeavor to define the appeal of specific poems and styles, a nurturing of the aesthetic sensibility.

There were also treatises, however, that dealt with first-order questions such as the essential nature and function of poetry. The *Kokinshū* Preface (905), written by Ki no Tsurayuki at the beginning of Japanese poetics, is a case in point:

> Japanese poetry has its seed in the human heart-mind [*kokoro*], which sprouts into a myriad leaves of words [*koto no ha*]. The person who lives in this world, faced with life's teeming events and circumstance, expresses what he feels in his heart through the medium of things visible and audible. Listen to the warbler crying among the flowers, the croaking of the frog dwelling in the waters—is there any among creatures vital and alive that does not break out in song? It is poetry that moves heaven and earth without the use of force, stirs to compassion the demons and deities invisible to the eye, harmonizes relations between men and women, and pacifies the heart of raging warriors.

As is often observed, this opening passage comprehends all the elements of a poetic performance: the world, the poet's inner response to it, the lang. he or she uses to communicate it, and the natural imagery that is its embodiment or figure. This is essentially a lyrical poetics: a poem is an effluence of the heart in response to being moved by experience; it comes into being as a natural process. Further, its primary method is imagistic figuration. Finally, the Preface defines the social aspect of poetic function as persuasion without physical force, the pacific containment of violence, be it political or sexual. In sum, poetry is the quintessential art of civility, as confirmed by its social usages, whether in ritual ceremonies, banquets, or quotidian communication, or as the lang. for negotiating the complications of a private relationship.

The *Kokinshū* preface established the parameters of poetics on the twin concepts of the heart-mind and lang., or content and form, requiring a judicious balance between them. Its understanding of poetry as lyric was modified crucially by the leading *Shinkokinshū* (1201) poets in the early med. period. Shunzei, in particular, redefined the poem as an impersonal symbolic construct of the true nature of reality as apprehended in the Tendai Buddhist philosophy of the three truths, i.e., phenomena apprehended according to three orders of understanding as (1) empty in lacking an inner unchanging core; (2) provisionally real in arising and disappearing according to mutable circumstance; and (3) middle or ambiguous in being beyond the dualism of the first two orders while encompassing them. In this new poetics, the process of composition is likened to meditation (*shikan*, literally, stillness and insight), and the poem is seen as the figuration of that deep and concentrated state of mind. Shunzei writes in *Korai fūteishō* (Poetic Styles from Antiquity to the Present, 1197, rev. 1201):

> In the opening passage of the work called *Tendai shikan*, there are these words written by Shōan Daishi: "The luminous tranquility of stillness and insight was yet unheard of in ages past." The very sound of these words, evoking limitless depths, fathoming a remotely inward significance, awesome and splendid, is like the good and bad in poetry, the endeavor to know its deep mind, difficult to convey in words; and yet it is precisely this analogy that enables us to comprehend it in the same way. . . .
>
> It is true that the one are golden words of Buddhist scripture, full of a deep truth, while the other seems to be but an idle game of empty words and fine phrases. And yet it manifests a profound significance in things and can be the circumstance which leads one to the Buddhist way. Moreover, because delusion is of itself wisdom, the *Lotus Sutra* says, "Properly explained, the secular classics . . . and the actions of mundane existence are all following the True Dharma." And the *Fugenkan* teaches, "What is the thing that is designated sinful, what designated fortunate? Neither sin nor fortune possesses a subject; the mind is of itself empty." Consequently, here also in speaking of the deep way of poetry, I draw upon its similarity to the three truths of the empty, the contingent, and the middle [*kū.ke.chū no sandai*] and write of it in the same terms.

The med. theory of a symbolic poetry produced an aesthetics of evocation manifest in the pursuit of such qualities as aura or overtones (*omokage, yojō*) and ineffable depth (*yūgen*), and the eschewing of clarity of meaning as banal.

In the treatise *Sasamegoto* (*Murmured Conversations*, 1463–64), the renga poet-monk Shinkei would found poetic process on discipline in the mind-ground (*shinji shugyō*) and describe the highest poetry as one that is "constituted solely of nuance," with no specific meaning to convey but with the power to evoke an experience of ultimate reality. Similarly, while maintaining impartiality as a general principle, he drew attention to the marvelous effects produced by *soku* (the distant link), as distinct from *shinku* (the close link), in the structure of waka and renga. *Distant* and *close* name the perceived space between the upper and lower parts of a waka or between any two contiguous verses in a linked poetry sequence. This mediate space will seem close when the poem's lines, being closely connected phonologically, syntactically, and semantically, constitute an integral unity, but distant when a caesura divides the poem into two disparate parts and there is no overt semantic connection between them. Instead, the silent link demands to be intuited or interpreted by the audience.

The use of hidden or subtle linkages between verses in Bashō-school haikai of the Edo period, called variously *nioi*, fragrance, or *hibiki*, resonance, manifests the same preference and is similarly motivated by a desire to evoke the interpenetrability of all phenomena or the boundlessness of the mundane when seen through enlightened eyes. Haikai began as a rebellion against the extreme refinement of cl. renga and the proliferation of minute rules of composition in its late stages. Haikai reveled in the low and vulgar aspects of ordinary life, eschewed the pure Japanese of cl. poetic diction, and favored harsh-sounding Chinese compounds and nonsensical colloquial expressions. Edo poetics was divided between high and low, the refined and the vulgar (*ga* and *zoku*), and derived great amusement in the incongruous mixing of the two orders of social reality. But Bashō later tired of amusement for its own sake and succeeded, after much struggle, in elevating the mundane by giving it a sheen of numinosity learned from Taoism, Zen, and med. aesthetics, such that, to the poet, there is nothing that does not own its own unique beauty in the larger scheme of things. As he writes in *Oi no kobumi* (Rucksack Notebook, 1687):

> All art is one in nature, whether in Saigyō's waka, Sōgi's renga, Sesshū's painting, or Rikyū's tea. In matters of art, one follows the dynamic creativity of nature and makes a friend of the four seasons. The man of art sees nothing that is not a flower, longs for nothing but is a moon. Those who do not see flowers are like barbarians, those who do not long for the moon are akin to the birds and beasts. One must leave the barbarians and leave the company of beasts, constantly pursuing nature, always returning to the four seasons.

■ J. Konishi, "Association and Progression," *HJAS* 21 (1958); *Fujiwara Teika's Superior Poems of Our Time*, ed. and trans. R. H. Brower and E. Miner (1967); "The *Mumyōshō* of Kamo no Chōmei and Its Significance in Japanese Literature," trans. H. Katō, *Monumenta Nipponica* 23 (1968); E. Cranston, "Water Plant Imagery in *Man'yōshū*," *HJAS* 31 (1971); "Ex-Emperor Go-Toba's Secret Teachings," ed. and trans. R. H. Brower, *HJAS* 32 (1972); E. Cranston, "The River Valley as *Locus Amoenus* in Man'yō Poetry," *Studies in Japanese Culture*, ed. Japan P.E.N. Club (1973); W. LaFleur, "Saigyō and the Buddhist Value of Nature," *History of Religions* 13 (1973–74); E. Cranston, "The Dark Path: Images of Longing in Japanese Love Poetry," *HJAS* 35 (1975); J. Konishi, "The Art of Renga," *Journal of Japanese Studies* 21 (1975); "Rules for Poetic Elegance," trans. N. Teele, *Monumenta Nipponica* 31 (1976); E. Ramirez-Christensen, "The Essential Parameters of Linked Poetry," *HJAS* 41 (1981); S. Carter, "Rules, Rules, and More Rules: Shōhaku's *Renga* Rulebook of 1501," *HJAS* 43 (1983); W. LaFleur, *The Karma of Words* (1983); J. Wixted, "The *Kokinshū* Prefaces: Another Perspective," *HJAS* 43 (1983); *On the Art of the Nō Drama: The Major Treatises of Zeami*, trans. J. Rimer and M. Yamazaki (1984); "Fujiwara Teika's *Maigetsushō*," ed. and trans. R. H. Brower, *Monumenta Nipponica* 40 (1985); "*Tamekanekyō Wakashō*," trans. R. Huey and S. Matisoff, *Monumenta Nipponica* 40 (1985); M. Morris, "Waka and Form, Waka and History," *HJAS* 46 (1986); "The Foremost Style of Poetic Composition: Fujiwara Tameie's *Eiga no Ittei*," ed. and trans. R. H. Brower, *Monumenta Nipponica* 42 (1987); T. Ikeda, "Continuity and Discontinuity in Renga," *Acta Asiatica* 56 (1989); E. Miner, "Waka: Features of Its Constitution and Development," *HJAS* 50 (1990); J. Rabinovitch, "Wasp Waists and Monkey Tails," *HJAS* 51 (1991); I. Smits, "The Poem as a Painting: Landscape Poetry in Late Heian Japan," *Transactions of the Asiatic Society of Japan*, 4th series, 6 (1991); M. Ueda, *Literary and Art Theories in Japan* (1991); C. Drake, "The Collision of Traditions in Saikaku's Haikai," *HJAS* 52 (1992); M. Horton, "Renga Unbound," *HJAS* 53 (1993); D. Bialock, "Voice, Text, and the Question of Poetic Borrowing in Late Classical Japanese Poetry," *HJAS* 54 (1994); R. Bundy, "*Santai Waka*: Six Poems in Three Modes," *Monumenta Nipponica* 49 (1994); *Conversations with Shōtetsu*, ed. S. Carter, trans. R. Brower (1994); R. Raud, *The Role of Poetry in Classical Japanese Literature* (1994); C. Crowley, "Putting *Makoto* into Practice: Onitsura's *Hitorigoto*," *Monumenta Nipponica* 50 (1995); *The Distant Isle*, ed. T. Hare et al. (1996); E. Kamens, *Utamakura, Allusion, and Intertextuality in Traditional Japanese Poetry* (1997); K. Kawamoto, *The Poetics of Japanese Verse* (2000); S. Carter, "Chats with the Master: Selections from *Kensai zōdan*," *Monumenta Nipponica* 56 (2001); M. Meli, "'Aware' as a Critical Term in Classical Japanese Poetics," *Japan Review* 13 (2001); P. Qiu, "Aesthetic of Uncoventionality: *Fūryū* in Ikkyū's Poetry," *Japanese Language and Literature* 35 (2001); R. Huey, *The Making of the Shinkokinshū* (2002); S. Klein, *Allegories of Desire* (2002); P. Atkins, "The Demon-Quelling Style in Medieval Japanese Poetic and Dramatic Theory," *Monumenta Nipponica* 58 (2003); *Japanese Poeticity and Narrativity Revisited*, ed. E. Sekine (2003); R. Raud, "The Heian Literary System: A Tentative Model," *Reading East Asian Writing*, ed. M. Hockx and I. Smits (2003); *Hermeneutical Strategies: Methods of Interpretation in the Study of Japanese Literature*, ed. M. Marra (2004); K. Kimbrough, "Reading the Miraculous Powers of Japanese Poetry," *Japanese Journal of Religious Studies* 32 (2005); R. Bundy, "Solo Poetry Contest as Poetic Self-Portrait," *Monumenta Nipponica* 61 (2006); *Matsuo Bashō's Poetic Spaces: Exploring Haikai Intersections*, ed. E. Kerkham (2006); W. Denecke, "'Topic poetry is all ours': Poetic Composition on Chinese Lines in Early Heian Japan," *HJAS* 67 (2007); G. Heldt, *The Pursuit of Harmony* (2008); *Literature and Literary Theory*, ed. A. Ueda and R. Okada (2008); E. Ramirez-Christensen, *Emptiness and Temporality* (2008); Shinkei, *Murmured Conversations*, ed. and trans. E. Ramirez-Christensen (2008); R. Thomas, *The Way of Shikishima* (2008).

E. Ramirez-Christensen

JAVA, POETRY OF. *See* INDONESIAN POETRY

JUDEO-SPANISH POETRY. Poetry sung, recited, or written in the Judeo-Sp. (Judezmo, Ladino) dialect, in the various postdiasporic communities of the Sephardic Jews—North Africa (Morocco, Algeria) and the Eastern Mediterranean (the Balkans, Greece, Turkey, Israel)—after their exile from Spain in 1492. By contrast, in Western Eur. centers such as Amsterdam, Bayonne, and Leghorn, there were Jewish authors who did not write in the Judeo-Sp. dialect but continued to form part of the Hispanic (Sp. or Port.) literary trads. Judeo-Sp. poetry may be organized into the following generic categories: *complas* (popular religious or didactic songs), *cantigas* (lyric songs), *romansas* (traditional ballads), *endevinas* (riddles), and *refranes* (proverbs). Complas can be considered essentially written lit.; the other genres are oral. Following World War II, a special subgenre of Sephardic poetry, written in Judeo-Sp. and in Fr., commemorated the tragic events of the Holocaust. In recent decades, poets and singers working both within and without the Sephardic trad. have adopted Judeo-Sp. as a poetic lang. According to Balbuena, this late wave of poetic production in Judeo-Sp. shows how the lang. is used as a tool for creating Sephardic identity in the diaspora. Traditional Sephardic romansas and cantigas have been increasingly recorded by contemp. artists whose musical reconstructions of traditional settings have been studied by Cohen and by Gutwirth.

Complas (Sp. *coplas*) are strophic poems usually of paraliturgical content, by both known and anonymous authors, and are the most characteristic Sephardic genre. Typically, they are sung and often are acrostic poems presenting the letters of the Heb. alphabet or of the author's name. Since they are essentially part of a written trad., they are generally sung by men, unlike the romansas, which are usually performed by women. Among the most traditional complas are those for the festivity of Purim, composed in the 18th and 19th cs., that relate the biblical story of Esther or evoke the joys of the holiday in strophes of varying lengths, with short or long verses in zéjelesque rhyme (*aaab*), often incl. a refrain (cf. It. *ballata*; see ITALIAN PROSODY). Other complas celebrate the festivities of Hanukkah, Passover, Pentecost, the Sabbath, the Rejoicing of the Torah, and Arbor Day. There are also dirgelike complas (*Kinot*) that commemorate the destruction of the Temple (70 CE) and other tragic events in ancient Jewish hist. Other complas of a moralizing, admonitory bent (*complas de castiguerio*) preach the glories of God and warn against the illusory nature of worldly attractions. *Complas del felek* (destiny) present the life and customs of late 19th- and early 20th-c. Sephardic Jewry from a satirical or humorous perspective. In *complas de Tebariá* are celebrated the praises of the city of Tiberias, of venerable sages who lived there, and of miracles concerning its Jewish population. Attias and Peretz published another group of poems, *Complas de 'Aliyá* (Songs of Return to Zion, 1996), which give voice to the Jews' longing for redemption and return to Jerusalem in all its glory. Those complas by Abraham Toledo, devoted to the life of Joseph and first published in 1732—part of a subgenre designated as *complas hagiográficas*—constitute for Hassán (1982) perhaps the single greatest poem in Judeo-Sp. In reworking the biblical account of Joseph's life (Gen. 37: 39–45), Toledo used numerous elements from folklore, rabbinical commentaries, and traditional life, presented with lyrical verve, lexical versatility, and rhetorical strength. In comparison to such genres as ballads and proverbs, which have strong Hispanic connections, the study of complas has, until recently, been gravely neglected.

Cantigas are traditional lyric songs, frequently of Hispanic origin in form and content, but, in the Eastern trad., with significant Gr. and Turkish lexical, structural, and thematic influences. Although love in all its vicissitudes is the predominant theme, there are also lyric songs devoted to various functions in the traditional life cycle: *cantigas de boda* (wedding songs), *de parida* (birth songs), and *endechas* (dirges). Romero (2009) has published a collection of mod. Balkan cantigas on the subject of women's liberation. Many Sephardic lyric songs, esp. in the Eastern communities, are of relatively recent origin (late 19th and early 20th c.) and often consist of quatrains in couplets with assonance; some are modeled on Gr. originals, while others are imported from Spain or Sp. America. But other lyric songs attest to a venerable Sephardic trad. going back to med. Hispanic origins. The parallelistic rhymes of some Eastern poems and of many Moroccan wedding songs—similar to that of the primitive Sp. and Port. lyric—confirm the med. character of the Judeo-Sp. cantiga trad. Some of these songs, given esoteric kabbalistic interpretations, eventually formed part of the liturgy of the Sabbatean *donmeh* sect of Islamized Jews in Turkey and have been ed. and trans. by Peretz.

Romansas (Sp. *romances*) are traditional ballads in assonant octosyllabic verse. In content, they are essentially similar—in some cases, genetically related—to narrative poetry current in other Eur. communities. No other Sephardic genre is so closely linked to its med. Hispanic origins, and none has received as much scholarly attention. Judeo-Sp. ballads can be documented from as early as 1525 through verses used as tune indicators in Heb. hymnals. Several 18th-c. mss. are known, and numerous Eastern ballads were collected and printed in popular Heb.-letter chapbooks in the late 19th and early 20th cs., most recently anthologized by Weich-Shahak (1997, 2010). There are Sephardic ballads derived from med. Sp. and Fr. epics; others concern events in Sp. and Port. hist. or tell stories from the Bible, cl. antiquity, or med. adventure romances; still others concern a variety of topoi (prisoners and captives, the husband's return, faithful or tragic love, the unfortunate wife, the adulteress, amorous adventures, tricks and deceptions). Some ballads function as epithalamia (wedding songs), others as dirges, still others as lullabies. Though a majority of Sephardic ballads have med. or 16th-c. Sp. counterparts, others can be shown to derive from mod. Gr. narrative poetry; some were undoubtedly created in the exile communities by the Sephardim themselves. Bénichou's studies of oral trad. as a creative artistic process are essential to ballad crit.

Endevinas (riddles) are often rhymed and, like proverbs, should count as a part of Sephardic traditional poetry. Of all genres, the riddle has been the most gravely neglected by scholarship. Little fieldwork has been done to collect riddles, and the known Eastern repertoire is still radically limited. Nothing is presently known of the Moroccan Sephardic riddle trad. As far as origins are concerned, a preliminary assessment indicates that Eastern Judeo-Sp. riddles are about evenly divided between texts of med. Hispanic origin and adaptations from Turkish and Gr. In many cases, however, it is impossible to point to a specific origin.

Refranes (proverbs) have been abundantly collected in Heb.-letter chapbooks since the late 19th c. by the Sephardim themselves and also by Western scholars such as Foulché-Delbosc and more recently by the Israeli scholar Alexander-Frizer. Some Sephardic proverbs agree exactly with their Sp. counterparts, while others have obviously been taken over from Gr., Turkish, or biblical Heb. sources.

See HEBREW POETRY; PORTUGAL, POETRY OF; SPAIN, POETRY OF.

■ M. Attias, "Shelôshah shîrê Tsîyôn," *Shevet va-'Am* 4 (1959); P. Bénichou, *Creación poética en al romancero tradicional* (1968); M. Alvar, *Endechas judeo-españolas* (1969), and *Cantos de boda judeo-españolas* (1971); S. Armistead, J. Silverman, I. Katz, *Folk Literature of the Sephardic Jews* (1971–94); M. Attias, *Cancionero judeo-español* (1972); E. Romero, "Complas de Tu-Bishbat," *Poesía: Reunión de Málaga*, ed. M. Alvar (1976); L. Carracedo and E. Romero, "Poesía admonitiva," *Sefarad* 37 (1977); S. Armistead et al., *El romancero en el Archivo Menéndez Pidal* (1978); I. Hassán and E. Romero, "Quinot paralitúrgicos," *Estudios Sefardíes* 1 (1978); S. Armistead and J. Silverman, "El antiguo romancero," *Nueva revista de filología Hispánica* 30 (1981); L. Carracedo and E. Romero, "Refranes," *Sefarad* 41 (1981); P. Díaz-Mas, "Romances de endechar," and E. Romero, "Las coplas sefardíes," *Jornadas*, ed. A. Viudas Camarasa (1981); S. Armistead and J. Silverman, *En torno al romancero* (1982); I. Hassán, "Visión panorámica," *Hispania Judaica*, ed. J. M. Solà-Solé (1982); S. Armistead and J. Silverman, "Adivinanzas," *Philologica Hispaniensia in Honorem Manuel Alvar*, ed. M. Alvar (1983); *And the World Stood Silent: Sephardic Poetry of the Holocaust*, trans. I. J. Lévy (1989); M. Attias and A. Peretz, *Shire ʿaliyah* (1996); S. Armistead, "Nueve adivinanzas de Estambul," *Sefarad* 58 (1998); J. Cohen, "Review of Judeo-Spanish ('Ladino') Recordings," *Journal of American Folklore* 112 (1999); M. Balbuena, *Diasporic Sephardic Identities* (2003); H. Pomeroy, *An Edition and Study of the Secular Ballads in the Sephardic Ballad Notebook of Halia Isaac Cohen* (2005); R. Foulché-Delbosc, *1313 proverbios judeo-españoles* (2006); *Las coplas de Yosef*, ed. L. Girón-Negrón and L. Minervini (2006); A. Peretz, *Mayim, esh ṿe-ahavah* (2006); M. Ha-'Elion, *En los kampos de lah muerte* (2008); T. Alexander-Frizer, *La palabra en su hora es oro* (2008); E. Romero, "Textos poéticos," *Sefarad* 69 (2009); S. Weich-Shahak, *Romancero sefardí de Oriente* (2010); E. Gutwirth, "Archival Poetics," *Bulletin of Spanish Studies* 88 (2011).

S. G. ARMISTEAD; J. H. SILVERMAN;
D. A. WACKS

K

KANNADA POETRY. Kannada, belonging to the Dravidian family of langs., has the second oldest lit. among all the living langs. of South Asia. The earliest specimen of Kannada writing, the Halmiḍi inscription (ca. 450 CE), shows that Kannada must have been in use as a medium of poetry for some time already. The earliest complete extant text, the *Kavirājamārga* (9th c., the oldest work in Kannada on poetics, largely following the theories of the Sanskrit author Daṇḍin), gives the names of many older poets of whose works only the fragments that are quoted in this text remain. The meters of this earliest Kannada poetry resemble those of Old Tamil to some extent but are a clearly independent devel. of Dravidian prosody. In 2008, the government of India granted Kannada the official status of "classical language."

Jainism was the dominant religion in the Kannada-speaking part of India until the 12th c. CE, and correspondingly the oldest period of Kannada lit. hist. is dominated by Jaina authors. The oldest independent poetic works that have been preserved in their entirety are the two writings of Paṃpa (10th c.), whom still today some critics consider the greatest Kannada poet. His *Ādipurāṇa* (completed 942), containing the hagiographical account of the life of the first Tīrthaṅkara, one of the holiest persons in Jainism, and his *Vikramārjunavijayam* (959), based on the *Mahābhārata*, are considered the greatest masterpieces of Old Kannada poetry. Paṃpa and his contemps. Ranna and Ponna are commonly referred to as the *ratnatraya* or "three jewels" of Kannada lit. Other Jaina *purāṇas* in the same *caṃpu* style (a mixture of poetry and prose) continued to be written for several centuries.

The best known works of Kannada poetry in and out of India are the *vacanas*, which are among the most influential literary works in the lang. The vacana (saying) is a particular genre that originated in Kannada in the 11th c. and rose to immense popularity in the 12th c. because of its use as a medium of religious communication in Vīraśaivism, a Śaivite Hindu reform movement. A vacana is a prose poem, usually a few dozen words in length; it lacks audible rhythmical structural elements but as a rule does have a rhythmic structure in its syntax, with syntactic structures being repeated as a device for underlining parallel metaphorical expressions. Thousands of vacanas from the 12th c. have been preserved. The most prominent *vacanakāras* (vacana poets) are Basava, who was the main organizer of the Vīraśaiva movement; his spiritual teacher Allama Prabhu; his nephew, the theologian Cennabasava; and the female mystic Mahādēviyakka. The vacana lit. also marks an important turning point in Kannada ling. hist., and a Kannada speaker today can read and understand the majority of 12th-c. vacanas more or less without the help of special aids. Several excerpts from vacanas have become popular sayings far beyond the Vīraśaiva community. Vacanas are still written today.

Another high point in Kannada lit. hist. was reached in the writings of the *haridāsas* or "servants of Hari," i.e., devotees of the god Viṣṇu. This devotional lit. is associated with the Vaiṣṇava (Viṣṇuite) Hindu reform movement initiated by the philosopher Madhva (1238–1317). The highly lyrical compositions of the haridāsas were in part inspired by earlier Vaiṣṇava devotional poetry by the Āḻvārs in Tamil, esp. by the writings of the aforementioned Kannada *vacanakāras*. Puraṃdaradāsa (1485–1565) is generally considered the foremost among the haridāsa poets, for his poetic imagery and the musicality of his writings; he is also considered the father of Carnatic [South Indian cl.] music. Comparable in fame is his contemp. Kanakadāsa (1491–1580), who wrote not only short lyrical pieces but longer narrative and allegorical poems.

The high quality of mod. poetry in Kannada has been recognized on an Indian national level: the most prestigious national literary award, the Jnanpith Award, has been awarded to seven Kannada writers, among them the three poets Kuvempu (pseud. of K. V. Puṭṭappa, 1904–94, known mainly for his rewriting of the *Rāmāyaṇa* epic in Kannada) in 1967; Aṃbikātanayadatta (pseud. of D. R. Bendre [Dattātreya Rāmacaṃdra Bēṃdre], 1896–1981, linguistically the most virtuosic poet in mod. Kannada) in 1973; and Vināyaka (pseud. of V. K. Gokak [V. K. Gōkāka], 1909–92, epic poet) in 1990. Other leading poets of the 20th c. were Gopalakrishna Adiga [Gōpālakṛṣṇa Aḍiga] (1918–92), who is considered the most important representative of the *navya* or modernist movement, and the highly popular romantic lyricist K. S. Narasimhaswamy [K. S. Narasiṃhasvāmi] (1915–2003), famous esp. for his collection *Maisūru mallige*, (1942). In most recent devels., the socially critical *dalita* movement has produced one noteworthy poet, Siddalingaiah [Siddhaliṃgayya] (b. 1954).

See INDIA, POETRY OF; TAMIL POETRY AND POETICS.

■ R. Narasimhacharya, *Karṇāṭaka kavicarite*, 2d ed. 3 v. (1972); A. K. Ramanujan, *Speaking of Śiva* (1973)—selected vacanas; R. S. Mugali, *History of Kannada Literature* (1975); *Modern Kannada Poetry*, ed. C. Kanavi and K. Raghavendra Rao (1976)—bilingual Kannada-Eng. anthol.; *60 Years of Kannada Poetry*, ed. G. S. Sivarudrappa and L. S. Seshagiri Rao (1977); K. V. Zvelebil, *The Lord of the Meeting Rivers* (1984)—selected vacanas of Basava; *A String of Pearls*, ed. H. S. Shivaprakash and K. S. Radhakrishna (1990); W. J. Jackson, *Songs of Three Great South Indian Saints* (1998)—incl. sections on Puraṃdaradāsa and Kanakadāsa; *The Epic of Nēmi (Nēminātha-purāṇa) of Karṇapārya*, trans. S. Anacker (2002).

R. ZYDENBOS

KASHMIRI POETRY. *Kashmiri poetry* is a multiply referential term: geographically, signifying poetry written from the Kashmir Valley or from the wider region of Jammu and Kashmir that has been territorially disputed between India and Pakistan since 1947; linguistically, signifying poetry written in Koshur, the lang. indigenous to the valley or poetry written in the other langs. in use in Jammu and Kashmir, incl. Persian, Urdu, Hindi, and Eng. Arising from a threshold region between Central and South Asia, the term *Kashmiri poetry* in all senses testifies to a multiethnic *ecumene* defined by cultural diversity and political instability. Iconic within this rich poetic corpus are the med. Sufi philosopher-poets writing in Koshur: Lalleshwari or Lal Ded (b. ca. 1335; she is known by both her Sanskritized name Lalleshwari and its more affectionate, vernacularized version Lal Ded [grandmother Lal] in Koshur), who used the gnomic quatrain form *vakh*; Noor-ud-Din or Nund Rishi (1377–1438), composing in another quatrain form, *shrukh*; and Habba Khatoon (fl. late 16th c.), who perfected the lyrical *lol* form. On this vernacular Sufi trad. was erected a literary modernism, from the foundational Ghulam Husain Mahjoor (1885–1952) to the contemp. poet Abdul Rahman Rahi (b. 1925), creators of a poetry that laments in and exalts the Kashmiri mother tongue within a competitive multilingualism. Since the 1990s, a Hindi poetry of exile has been developed by Agni Shekhar (b. 1956), among others, testifying to a specific Kashmiri Hindu subjectivity. The Kashmiri-Am. poet Agha Shahid Ali (1949–2001) transformed these affective complexities by expressing them in a finely wrought Eng.-lang. idiom that united Eur. (e.g., *canzone*) and Urdu (e.g., *ghazal*) poetic forms, paid homage to poets of exile worldwide, from the Palestinian Maḥmūd Darwīsh (1941–2008) to the Rus. Osip Mandelstam (1892–1938), and infused Islamic sacred hist. with a sharp awareness of the politics of nationalism. Ali's anthols. *The Country without a Post Office* (2000) and *Rooms Are Never Finished* (2002) constitute an exquisitely refined, poignant, and haunting lyrical record of the Kashmir conflict, its roots and its emotional consequences.

See HINDI POETRY; INDIA, ENGLISH POETRY OF; INDIA, POETRY OF; PERSIAN POETRY; SANSKRIT POETICS; SANSKRIT POETRY; URDU POETRY.

■ G. Grierson, *Lalla-Vakyani or The Wise Sayings of Lal-Ded—A Mystic Poetess of Ancient Kashmir* (1920); G. M. Sufi, *Kashir* (1948); N. C. Cook, *The Way of the Swan: Poems from Kashmir* (1958); T. Raina, *An Anthology of Modern Kashmiri Verse, 1930–1960* (1972); B. B. Kachru, *Kashmiri Literature* (1981); C. Zutshi, *Languages of Belonging: Islam, Regional Identity and the Making of Kashmir* (2004); A. J. Kabir, *Territory of Desire: Representing the Valley of Kashmir* (2009).

A. J. KABIR

KOREA, POETRY OF

I. Classical Period
II. Modern Period

I. Classical Period. Cl. Korean poetry pre-20th c. is divided into two categories according to medium: one written in Korean and the other, *hansi*, written in cl. Chinese. Prior to the creation of *han'gŭl*, the Korean alphabet, in the mid-15th c., Korean-lang. poetry was transcribed in Chinese characters, sometimes with variations in the system, borrowing sounds and meaning to signify the original Korean. Even after the promulgation of the Korean alphabet, however, cl. Chinese maintained its prestige as the official written lang. of the ruling class until 1894, the year of the Kabo Reform, when Korea officially adopted han'gŭl as the national alphabet.

A. ***Silla Dynasty.*** Historical records witness singing and dancing as significant aspects of ancient Korean life. Koreans believed in the power of singing, music, and dance as ways to communicate with humans or the heavenly spirits. There are, however, few direct literary records from before the establishment of the Unified Silla kingdom (668–918).

The first Korean literary genre is Silla's most noteworthy, the songs called *hyangga* or "native songs." Fourteen hyangga are included in the monk Iryŏn's book *Samguk yusa* (Remnants of the Three Kingdoms, late 13th c.). The songs range in style and subject matter, from playful folk songs such as the "Sŏdongyo" (Song of Sŏdong) and "Hŏnhwaga" (Flower Offering Song), which suggest that folk songs were absorbed into the hyangga repertoire, to Buddhist devotional hymns and songs dedicated to exemplary *hwarang* (young knights). These hyangga were recorded in *hyangch'al*, a method using Chinese characters to represent sounds and meanings of the Korean lang. rather than as Chinese trans.

Folk songs ascribed to the Koguryŏ (37 BCE–668 CE) and the Paekche kingdoms (18 BCE–663 CE), with titles only, are included in the 15th-c. *Koryŏ sa* (History of Koryŏ); the text of one Paekche song is found in the *Akhak kwebŏm* (Primer for Music Studies, 1492). *Quan Tang shi* (Complete Tang Poetry), a Chinese compilation, includes works by several Silla poets such as Ch'oe Ch'i-wŏn (b. 857) and Kim Ka-gi (d. 859), while the 8th-c. *Nihon shoki* (Chronicles of Japan) refers to a Paekche man who taught Chinese-style *gigaku*, or Buddhist ceremonial dance, in Japan.

B. ***Koryŏ Dynasty.*** The Koryŏ dynasty (918–1392) instituted a state civil-service examination in 958, patterned on the Chinese system, which used Chinese literary, philosophical, and historical sources and materials. One result of this official centering of Chinese materials was the importance of *hansi* (the Chinese *shi* and *fu*, poetry and rhyme prose) in Korean literary compositions. A multiplication of individual works and anthols. and the emergence of writers like Yi Kyu-bo (1168–1241), Ch'oe Ch'ung (984–1068), Kim Hwang-wŏn (1045–1117), and Chŏng Chi-sang (d. 1135), as well as the *Chungnim kohoe* (Bamboo Grove Assembly), a group of seven highly regarded poets of the late 12th c., are a few examples of Koryŏ interest in hansi genres.

The hyangga trad. continued into Koryŏ, the best-known example being the series of 11 devotional hymns composed by the Buddhist monk Kyunyŏ (923–73). The monk Chinul's (1128–1210) disciple Hyesim (1178–1234) wrote hansi poems on *sŏn* (Zen) subjects and collected Buddhist tales, meditation puzzles, allegories, and poems in a 30-v. anthol. *Sŏnmun yŏmsong* (1226) or "Praise and Puzzle in Sŏn Literature." The monk Ch'ungji (1226–93) focused in his poetry on the plight of the Korean people during the late 13th-c. Mongol campaign against Japan, when they were forced to build and man an invasion fleet. References to other Buddhist monks are included in the *Haedong kosŭng chŏn* (Lives of Eminent Korean Monks, 1215).

Notable among Koryŏ writings and lit. were the mostly Chinese-lang. (with Korean-lang. refrains) *kyŏnggi*-style songs, or *kyŏnggich'e ka*, of which the "Hallim pyŏlgok" (Song of the Capital, 13th c.) is exemplary. Koryŏ-era popular songs in Korean, *sogyo*, mostly about love, collected in the *Akchang kasa* (Lyrics for Akchang, 16th c.), include "Kasiri" (Would You Go?) and "Ch'ŏngsanpyŏlgok" (Song of the Green Hills). Kim Pu-sik's (1075–1151) *Samguk sagi* (History of the Three Kingdoms) and Iryŏn's (1206–89) *Samguk yusa*, a compilation from many sources of Korean legends, myths, hists., biographies, songs, and spells, are major landmarks in Korea's political, cultural, and lit. hist.

C. ***Early Chosŏn.*** The first two hundred years of the Chosŏn dynasty, from its founding in 1392 until the invasions by the Japanese armies of Hideyoshi in 1598, was a period of great artistic creativity and accomplishments, both cultural and scientific. The new dynasty was only 50 years old when its fourth king, Sejong (r. 1418–50), promulgated a new phonetic alphabet, now known as han'gŭl, for the Korean lang. Composition in the Korean vernacular flourished, esp. in two verse forms, the three-line *sijo* and the longer *kasa*. Many anthols. of these works were assembled and published later, in the 18th and 19th cs.; various groups coalesced around schools of literary thought, preferences for Chinese or Korean forms of expression, and not infrequently, political-philosophical outlooks.

Akchang was a verse form written for performance at state ceremonies with a distinct political purpose to praise the founding of the dynasty. The two best-known examples are associated with King Sejong. The first, *Yongbi ŏch'ŏn ka* (Song of the Dragons Flying to Heaven), was composed at Sejong's order, to praise the dynasty's founders while presenting a ceremonial alternative to resentments still lingering at the overthrow of the preceding Koryŏ dynasty. It was completed in 1445 as hansi, then translated into Korean, annotated, and finally published two years later in an ed. of 550 copies, distributed at court. Sejong himself is said to have written the other notable akchang, *Wŏrin ch'ŏn'gang chi kok* (The Song of Moonlight on One Thousand Waters, 1449) a remembrance of Queen Sohŏn, who had died in 1446.

The *sijo* is a three-line verse form, originally composed for musical performance. There are several ways of singing, characterized by a deliberate slowness. In singing 40 to 50 syllables, the popular *sijo ch'ang* (sijo song) style takes three to four minutes, while *kagok*, the style performed by professional singers, takes as much as ten. The deliberate slowness of a sijo performance is said to bring the performer and audience into a state of tranquility and profound concentration. While syllable count is not fixed, it does play a role in patterns of syllable distribution among the four phrases that constitute the sijo lines. For the first two lines, the usual syllable count is 3-4-3 (or 4)-4. The third line, with a regular sequence of 3-5-4-3 syllables coupled with a "twist" or "turn" at the beginning of the line, brings the poem to a conclusion. Though sijo is widely believed to date back to the late Koryŏ period, its historical origins are obscured by the relatively late creation of the Korean alphabet. The *yangban* gentry class provided its main authors at least until the 19th c., while most of the sijo anthols. date from the 18th c. or later.

Even though many sijo and vernacular Korean poems are about the enjoyment of life, one characteristic feature of Korean lit. is a seriousness of literary expression, esp. in the works of the ruling class. One of the most famous examples is the exchange between the Koryŏ loyalist Chŏng Mong-ju (1337–92) and Yi Pangwŏn (1367–1422), son of the founding Chosŏn king Yi Sŏng-gye. The story associated with Chŏng's famous sijo relates that the king's son organized a banquet and invited Chŏng, then offered a somewhat mocking, metaphorical toast couched in a sijo, urging Chŏng to stop his resistance to the changing times. Chŏng's reply has become known as the "Tansim ka" or "Song of a Loyal Heart":

Though this body die
and die a hundred times again,
White bones become but dust,
a soul exist, then not,
Still, this heart wholly for my lord:
How could it ever change?

(trans. D. McCann)

In 1416, in the aftermath of Sejo's (r. 1455–68) usurpation of the throne and assassination of its occupant, his own nephew Tanjong (r. 1452–55), Sŏng Sam-mun (1418–56), one of the "Six Martyred Ministers" put to death for a plan to return Tanjong to the throne, composed on the eve of his execution a sijo that echoes Chŏng's:

Once this body is dead and gone
you ask, what will it be?
On the highest peak of Pongnae Mountain
a towering, spreading pine tree.
When sky and earth are filled with white snow,
alone and green, green I shall be.

(trans. D. McCann)

Yi Hwang (1501–70), one of the great neo-Confucian philosophers of Chosŏn Korea, loved the song aspect of sijo and the positive effect that singing and listening could have on both the performer/composer and the audience. The woodblocks carved from Yi's own calligraphy for his *Tosan sibigok* (Twelve Songs of Tosan, 1565) are the oldest of all sijo source materials. Another prominent neo-Confucian scholar Yi I's (1536–84) "Kosan kugok ka" (Nine Songs from Kosan), which echoed a similar work by the Chinese philosopher Zhu Xi, also connotes the popularity of sijo among yangban elites. Chŏng Ch'ŏl (1536–93) composed dozens of sijo, in addition to four famous kasa poems. Some reflect his difficult political circumstances, others a more general philosophical outlook, and still others a directly didactic intent, as in the series written to instruct the people of the province where he had been sent as governor.

It is noteworthy that many sijo were ascribed to the *kisaeng*, the female entertainers, some of whom must have been professional sijo performers. The most famous of all is Hwang Chini, the legendary author—in the absence of contemp. documentation, it is impossible to establish her authorship—of a half dozen truly remarkable sijo and a number of poems in cl. Chinese, a woman with a reputation for beauty, artistic accomplishments, as well as a singularly independent mind and will. One of her sijo reads,

> Alas! What have I done?
> Didn't I know how I would yearn?
> If only I'd said, *Just stay*,
> how could he have gone? But stubborn
> I sent him away, and know now
> I never knew what it is to yearn.
>
> (trans. D. McCann)

The kasa is the other major Korean vernacular verse form. It too uses a four-part line. Narrative and discursive, without stanza divisions, it was often used for travelogues, while upper-class women used the form to express their thoughts at the restraints of social norms. Some went on for hundreds of lines; in 16th- and 17th-c. practice, the final line would be marked by the sijo-like 3-5-4-3 syllable count. The first example of kasa is Chŏng Kŭg-in's (1401–81) "Sangch'un kok" (Song to Spring), praising life in the countryside. Chŏng Ch'ŏl's two famous travelogue kasa, "Sŏngsan pyŏlgok" (Song of Sŏng Mountain) and "Kwandong pyŏlgok" (Song of Kwandong), offer an exuberant view of the Korean landscape, while Chŏng's other two kasa, "Samiin kok" (Longing for the Beautiful One) and "Sok miin kok" (Again, Beautiful One), written in the dramatic persona of a woman abandoned, are read as expressions of Chŏng's own feelings at being dismissed from office and sent into exile. The "Samiin kok" is esp. noteworthy for its dramatic structure, built around the contrast between the natural passing of the seasons and the unnatural human tendency to let warm feelings turn and then stay cold.

Hŏ Ch'o-hŭi (1563–89), better known in Korea by her pseud. Nansŏrhŏn, wrote many highly regarded hansi, as well as two kasa, "Kyuwŏn ka" (Married Sorrow) and "Pongsŏnhwa" (The Touch-Me-Not).

D. ***Later Chosŏn.*** In the 17th c., after the Japanese invasion of Korea, the change of the East Asian political map—most prominently in the demise of the Ming dynasty, which had a strong bond with Korea and the rise of the Qing—led Korea to assert its own cultural identity. Kim Man-jung (1637–92), author of two novels in Korean, declared, "Only Korean vernacular can express genuine Koreanness." Sijo, with changes in form and vernacular subjects, and kasa, as a longer form, became more widely practiced by yangban literati moving away from strictly Chinese models and by women who, confined to the house, nevertheless encouraged the circulation of vernacular Korean works.

The life of the poet Pak Il-lo (1561–1643) marks a high point in the devel. of Korean vernacular poetry. His "T'aep'yŏngsa" (Song of Peace) marked the close of the 16th c.'s final devastating decade. While many of his sijo verse compositions are unimaginative restatements of Confucian precepts, his kasa are another matter entirely. The "Sŏnsangt'an" (Lament on the Waters, 1601) returns to the theme of the naval campaign against the Japanese. "Saje kok" (The Sedge Bank, 1611) is a portrait of a rural retreat. "Nuhang sa" or "Song of a Humble Life" (1611) combines realistic plot, vividly observed setting, and strikingly mod. vernacular dialogue in a unique expression of the traditional theme of rustic retirement.

Yun Sŏn-do (1587–1671) was a brilliant innovator in the sijo form and wrote numerous individual works and sijo sequences. The most famous of the latter is his *Ŏbu sasi sa* (Fisherman's Calendar, 1651), a four-part, four-season sequence on the pleasures of the fisherman's tranquil existence. These poems are notable for their clear and flowing vernacular diction, use of an onomatopoeic refrain, and controlled easing of the usual structural patterns of the sijo.

In the 18th and 19th cs., as Chosŏn society saw significant social changes and economic growth, the new *sirhak*, or practical learning group, produced localized, realist hansi. Chŏng Yag-yong (1762–1836), a famous encyclopedic scholar who produced almost 3,000 poems, declared, "I am a Korean; I compose Korean poetry." He meant Korean poetry written in cl. Chinese. While the circulation of vernacular Korean book narratives significantly increased, poetry in the vernacular also saw diversification in form and subject matter. Perhaps most obvious was the move toward freer expression of desire and emotion, which had been tightly controlled by neo-Confucian attitudes. Some yangban scholars composed *sasŏl sijo*, a longer version of sijo and kasa, depicting blatantly erotic scenes. These devels. coincided with the emergence of *p'ansori*, a performative art of singing and narrating stories, which negotiated a controversial position between kasa and the p'ansori-novel.

The 19th c. brought fundamental transformations to the whole of Korean society. Mid-century saw the defeat of China by Eur. powers, a seismographic change in the Asian cultural sphere. Sijo and kasa continued to be performed and composed, though without notable accomplishment. The practice of hansi faded, prompted by the abolition of the state examination system with the Kabo Reform of 1894, yet it continued through the 20th c. and into the present as a practice suitable for formal occasions. Sijo and kasa, often with rhythmic patterns fitted to Western music, were written and published to accommodate the changing world.

II. Modern Period. Beginning in the late 19th c., rapid social change was accompanied by a fundamental transformation of the cultural system. Most revolutionary was the replacement of cl. Chinese with han'gŭl as the official script. The pursuit of a high art in vernacular Korean defined the ensuing 20th c. In the age of imperialism, many Korean literati were also national leaders, and their literary jours. functioned as instruments for cultural change. A hist. of colonial rule, liberation, and subsequent national division directed Korean lit. toward a sociopolitical agenda that lasted into the final decade of the 20th c.

A. *Japanese Colonial Period (1910–45).* Liberation from conventional poetic form began with the free verse imported from the West through Japan, where many Korean intellectuals studied. The beginning of a "new poetry" was announced in "Hae egesŏ Sonyŏn ege" (From the Sea to Youth, 1908) by Ch'oe Namsŏn, a poem that deploys the repeated refrain of the sea's voice urging change. Ch'oe had studied in Japan and brought back printing equipment to publish *Sonyŏn* (Youth), the first literary magazine devoted to the movement for a new Korean culture. *Onoe ŭi mudo* (Dance of Anguish), was published in 1921, an anthol. of trans. by Kim Ŏk (1895–1950) of Fr., Ir., and other poets. In 1923, Kim published the first mod. Korean poetry collection, *Haep'ari ŭi norae* (Song of Jellyfish). The trans. and poems presented a completely new voice in vernacular Korean. In 1925, one of Kim Ŏk's students, Kim Sowŏl (1902–34), published *Azaleas,* the most favored poetry book of the entire 20th c. Kim Sowŏl's poetry, imbued with the sense of sorrowful loss, brought folk-song rhythm to mod. poetry. The title poem remains his best-known work:

When you leave, weary
of seeing me,
silently I shall send you on your way.

From Mt. Yak in Yŏngbyŏn,
an armful of azaleas
I shall gather and scatter on your way.

Step by step
on the flowers lying before you
tread softly, deeply, and go.

When you go, weary
of seeing me,
though I die I shall not shed one tear.

(trans. D. McCann)

Han Yong-un (1879–1944), a reformist Buddhist monk and a national leader in opposing Japan's colonial rule, also published a canonical poetry book, *Nim ŭi ch'immuk* (Silence of Love, 1926), evoking the absence of love as political metaphor. Many poems of the 1920s mix a nationalistic anger with sentimental tears. Yi Sang-hwa's (1901–43) "Ppaeakkin tŭl edo pom ŭn onŭka" (Will Spring Return to Stolen Fields?) and Yi Yuk-sa's (1904–44) "Chŏlchŏng" (The Summit) more directly lament the lost sovereignty.

The Korean Artists Proletarian Federation (KAPF), organized by Marxist writers in 1925 and led by the poet and critic Im Hwa (1908–53), came to exert strong influence on the literary field. Yet political or ideological differences were accommodated in those days. Im Hwa, e.g., published his critique of Sowŏl's poems in the same jour., *Kaebyŏk* (Dawn), that had published Sowŏl's poems in the first place. Paek Sŏk (1912–95), a poet who with many others was classified in South Korea as having "gone North" after 1945, though in fact he merely stayed at his home following liberation, like So Wŏl used northern dialect and rural themes. Two poets from the modernist group *Kuinhoe* (Nine- Person Group), Chŏng Chi-yong (1902–50) and Yi Sang (1910–37), brought additional changes to Korean poetry in the 1930s. Chŏng, informed by modernism, worked toward refining the mod. Korean lang. Yi Sang's surrealistic wit was a challenge to his contemporaries and remains so today. Yun Tong-ju (1918–45) reflected the turbulent colonial period; his works became widely popular following his death during imprisonment in Tokyo.

In 1938, Japan banned the Korean lang. in schools and, in 1941, the publication of Korean-lang. books. Writers either used the Japanese lang. or hid their works and waited.

B. *After the Liberation.* After liberation in 1945, accompanied by the North-South division of the country, writers occupied two positions in the political spectrum, Left or Right; but for an interval, during the two years or so known as the Liberation Space, they managed to write, publish, and engage in debate. Eventually, many of the leftists went to the communist North, the Democratic People's Republic of Korea (DPRK), while the nationalists remained in the Republic of Korea. Both states were established in 1948 and were at war with one another in 1950. Little remains known about the literary realm of the DPRK beyond its state-mandated ideology of *Juche* (self-reliance). In the South, following the Korean War's end in 1953, a new curriculum was established, built around the Korean lang., which had been banned in the late colonial period, while nationalism emerged as a guiding counterpart to the North's Juche state philosophy. Eager for work in vernacular Korean, the new generation of students welcomed the republication of books by such writers as Kim Sowŏl, Han Yong-un, and Yun Tong-ju.

During this period, Korean poetry also witnessed the arrival of two major poets, Sŏ Chŏng-ju (1915–2000) and Kim Su-yŏng (1921–68). Sŏ created an oeuvre impressive—in addition to its supple use of the Korean lang.—for its imagery, prosody, and vivid voice. One of his poems, "Tongch'ŏn" (Winter Sky), recaptures Kim Sowŏl's use of poetic gesture:

With a thousand nights' dream
I have rinsed clear the gentle brow
of my heart's love,
to transplant it into the heavens.
A fierce bird knows, and in mimicry
arcs through the midwinter sky.

(trans. D. McCann)

Kim Su-yŏng, widely known as a political radical, opened a new imaginary space in Korean lang., urging readers to participate directly in the improvement of society. His poem "P'ul" (Grasses), published after his death, remains an emblematic statement of that democratic ideal:

Grasses lie down
Blown by the wind driving rain from the
east
grasses lie,
at last cried
As the day is overcast, they cried more,
and lay again

Grasses lie
Faster than the wind they lie
Faster than the wind they cry
Earlier than the wind they rise

The day is overcast, and grasses lie
to the ankle
to the sole they lie
Later than the wind they lie
Earlier than the wind they rise
Later than the wind they cry
Earlier than the wind they smile
The day is overcast, and the grass roots lie.

(trans. Y.-J. Lee)

Sŏ Chŏng-ju was presented as a major poet in Korean school textbooks, while Kim Su-yŏng, whose poetry was full of images of revolution mixed with Korean-lang. expression that readers found difficult, was included only after the democratizing changes of the 1980s.

During the latter half of the 20th c., South Korea experienced rapid industrialization and economic growth, accompanied by a series of repressive military dictatorships. Like their predecessors at the beginning of the century, many Korean poets committed their energies to the democratization movement, giving the 1980s the name *si ŭi sidae* (the age of poetry). The works of poets like Chŏng Chi-yong, Paek Sŏk, and others who had "gone North," banned until 1987, met with enthusiastic interest. While many poets were arrested and imprisoned, their works still managed to produce sales of several million volumes, an exceptional sales record. In this period, two major poets, both victims of repeated imprisonments, became recognized in the outer world: Ko Un (b. 1933), esp. for his *Maninbo*, (Record of Ten Thousand People), completed in 30 books over 25 years (1986–2010), and Kim Chi Ha (b. 1941) for his revival of the p'ansori form and rhythm in dissident poetry. Ko Un's *Maninbo* project started while he was imprisoned in solitary confinement, overturned the traditional idea of the elite family genealogical records known as *chokpo.* Kim Chi Ha's long, p'ansori-style poems such as *Ojŏk* (The Five Bandits), received substantial international acclaim during the 1970s when he too was being held in prison.

The 1990s in Korea saw the rise of women's poetry, which had been long neglected. A few women poets such as No Ch'ŏn-myŏng (1912–57) and Kim Nam-jo (b. 1927) had achieved some reputation earlier. Kim Hyesoon's (b. 1955) poems depicted a woman's interiority amid everyday life. Her unabashedly confessional works at times took a dramatic narrative form borrowed from shamanistic trad.

With the Korean economy flourishing in the 1980s, the poetry of Hwang Chi-u (b. 1952), Yi Sŏng-bok (b. 1952), and Chang Chŏng-il (b. 1963) brought pop culture themes laced with everyday trivia into their poetic subject matter. Their focus on the present and explicit commitment to colloquial expression are to be seen and heard among new poetic voices in the 21st c., among whom are a number of women poets grappling with issues of womanhood in 21st-c. Korea.

■ **Anthologies and Translations**: *The Middle Hour: Selected Poems of Kim Chi Ha*, trans. D. McCann (1980); *Anthology of Korean Literature: From Early Times to the Nineteenth Century*, ed. P. Lee (1981); *Selected Poems of Sŏ Chŏngju*, trans. D. McCann (1989); *Modern Korean Literature*, ed. P. Lee (1990); *Sŏ Chŏngju: The Early Lyrics, 1941–1960*, trans. B. Anthony (1991); *Pine River and Lone Peak: An Anthology of Three Chosŏn Dynasty Poets*, ed. and trans. P. Lee (1991); *Selected Poems by Kim Namjo*, trans. D. McCann and H. Y. Sallee (1993); R. Rutt, *The Bamboo Grove: An Introduction to Sijo* (1998); *The Book of Korean Shijo*, trans. K. O'Rourke (2002); *The Columbia Anthology of Traditional Korean Poetry*, ed. P. Lee (2002); *The Columbia Anthology of Modern Korean Poetry*, ed. D. McCann (2004); *Everything Yearned For: Manhae's Poems of Love and Longing*, trans. F. Cho (2005); Ko Un, *Ten Thousand Lives*, trans. Y. M. Kim, B. Anthony, and G. Gach (2005); *Echoing Song: Contemporary Korean Women Poets*, ed. P. Lee (2005); D. Choi, *Anxiety of Words: Contemporary Poetry by Korean Women* (2006); S. Kim, *Azaleas: A Book of Poems*, trans. D. McCann (2007); Ko Un, *What?: 108 Korean Zen Poems*, trans. B. Anthony, G. Gach, Y. M. Kim (2008).

■ **Criticism and History**: P. Lee, *Songs of Flying Dragons: A Critical Reading* (1975); D. McCann, *Form and Freedom in Korean Poetry* (1988); B. Myers, *Han Sŏrya and North Korean Literature* (1994); *Early Korean Literature: Selections and Introductions*, ed. and trans. D. McCann (2000); *The Record of the Black Dragon Year*, trans. P. Lee (2000); P. Lee, *A History of Korean Literature* (2003); M. Pihl, *The Korean Singer of Tales* (2003); D. Seo and P. Lee, *Oral Literature of Korea* (2005).

Y.-J. Lee; D. R. McCann

LADINO POETRY. *See* JUDEO-SPANISH POETRY

LATIN AMERICA, POETRY OF. *See* ARGENTINA, POETRY OF; BOLIVIA, POETRY OF; BRAZIL, POETRY OF; CHILE, POETRY OF; COLOMBIA, POETRY OF; ECUADOR, POETRY OF; EL SALVADOR, POETRY OF; GUARANÍ POETRY; GUATEMALA, POETRY OF; INDIGENOUS AMERICAS, POETRY OF THE; MAPUCHE POETRY; MEXICO, POETRY OF; NICARAGUA, POETRY OF; PERU, POETRY OF; SPANISH AMERICA, POETRY OF; URUGUAY, POETRY OF; VENEZUELA, POETRY OF

LATIN POETRY

I. Classical
II. Medieval
III. Renaissance and After

I. Classical

A. *Preservation and Transmission.* Key to the understanding of ancient Lat. poetry is the issue of transmission. Most of what we have depends for its survival on mss. written in the late antique and med. (sometimes even early mod.) period in western Europe. A very modest contribution comes from ancient written texts (Roman papyri, unlike Gr. papyri, are few, and rarely preserve poetry; epigraphy offers a substantial body of texts but often by marginal or nonprofessional composers).

When compared to the remains of other ancient cultures, however, the amount of accompanying evidence is staggering: archaeology, ling., numismatics, epigraphy, prose sources, and material culture in general offer a great deal (just as for cl. *Greek poetry, while, e.g., the other great premod. corpus of written poems, Vedic poetry, offers the fascinating problem of a rich corpus of mythology and religion in a well-documented lang. being accompanied by very tenuous material evidence; see SANSKRIT POETRY).

Because of the fragility of papyrus and pergamene, only texts that have been copied at least once since the 4th c. CE had a chance to survive, i.e., to reach an age (the 14th–15th cs. in Western Europe) when the recuperation and circulation of antique texts was a major industry. The cl. Lat. texts have been sifted through a triple process of filtering:

—ancient canonization (the school system of the Roman Empire being the key, as it will be again in the mod. age when Eur. state-sponsored education is fundamental in the spread of cl. Lat. culture);
—a more occasional selection guided by med. agendas; and
—the impact of random destruction and material damage.

This has important implications: educational value was crucial to survival. Authors without an obvious support in schooling, like Petronius (ca. 27–66 CE), Catullus (ca. 84–54 BCE), and Lucretius (ca. 99–55 BCE), have been close to disappearing. On the other hand, many of the canonical works have been preserved, and there is a family atmosphere: the authors tend to create a pattern of intertextual relationship based on the practice of imitation. Our first impression of Lat. poetry is frequently related to the striking amount of self-consciousness: the individual poet has a constant awareness of his place in the tradition and a subtle and supple strategy for rewriting past lit. hist. and inserting himself into it. The art of writing poetry in Roman society is a form of networking. The maximum density of this approach to poetic composition and self-promotion is found in the Augustan Age (a concept explicitly used by Horace), with Virgil's (70–19 BCE) pastoral poems, the *Bucolics* (or *Eclogues*), as a first manifesto, and Virgil's *Aeneid* and Ovid's (43 BCE–ca. 18 CE) *Metamorphoses* as the *summae.* Not by chance, the Augustan Age has been canonized and accepted as the climax and the cl. age of Roman lit. hist.

Considering the much that survives, it is easy to forget the losses. Numerous fragments exist of crucial works that were often quoted in prose texts (through so-called indirect transmission), for instance, Ennius's (ca. 239–169 BCE) epic on Roman hist., the *Annales*; but other masterpieces such as Cornelius Gallus's (ca. 70–26 BCE) love elegies (except for a tiny papyrus fragment) and Ovid's tragedy *Medea* have been lost. Then, of course, not all the poetry recovered has been available continuously since late antiquity. It is important to study Eur. culture with an awareness of changes related to successive rediscoveries of Roman texts in the age on humanism. At the end of the first commentary made on Lucretius's Epicurean poem in the early 16th c., a postscript by an It. scholar says, "I submit everything to orthodox belief," to which a different hand has added, "Everything, then, needs revising now."

B. ***Origins and Evolution.*** During the central part of the 3d c. BCE, Rome, a mid-sized republican state in western central Italy, begins to grow at an impressive rate as a "conquest state." During the same period, inscriptions in Lat., some of them in poetic meter, begin to rise in number and complexity (alphabetic writing already had a trad. of many centuries in Italy), and verse in Lat. appears and develops quickly into something that to us looks like a national poetry or lit. (a double anachronism because both "literature" and "nationhood" have been shaped, in their current value, by Eur. modernity and bourgeois ideology). A local, autonomous, native Roman lit. never had a chance to surface.

Later on, the Romans—a community and an empire with a Lat.-speaking as well as a Gr.-speaking elite culture—view the generations between (roughly) the mid-3d c. and mid-2d c. BCE as "the origins." They imagined lit. hist., a concept and practice in which they were pioneers, as a process of increasingly adequate Hellenization—a far cry from romantic ideas of national lit.

The meters are all based on adaptations of Gr. originals. The "primitive" Saturnian looks like an outlier, but it may be the result of an older process of appropriation. As a rule, the most popular genres have a lot of metrical adaptation and "freedom," while elite verse displays a "pure Greek" metrical style. Cicero (106–43 BCE) thought that the lines of verse in comic drama were so low-key that they were not recognizable as something different from prose; Horace (65–8 BCE) avoids this style when he writes iambic poetry, and he regulates and moderates the "freedom" of comic verse. Seneca (ca. 3 BCE–65 CE) creates a sophisticated but overcontrolled template for his tragic verse, not deterred by the effect of monotony that is being imparted to the end of the lines.

The metrical forms are all quantitative and presuppose a melodic word accent: intensive accent is not relevant. The importance of patterns of alliteration, linking the initial parts of adjacent words, however, points to Germanic-Celtic areas more than to Hellenism as a parallel. After the unique explosion of creativity in Plautus's (ca. 254–184 BCE) comedies, the style tends to be regulated by ascetic elitism and separated from colloquial expression, avoiding both low-life speech and "crude" Gr. loan words: the main later exception, the mysterious and transgressive Petronius, is not by chance also the only major artist who dares to combine poetry and prose.

C. ***Roman Hellenism.*** Being oriented on Gr. models, Roman poetry has two dominant states of mind, not mutually exclusive: submission and competition. Most of the surviving texts already belong to a stage when Rome is master of the Gr. world, so there is a constant tension and interplay between Roman domination of Greece and Hellenic intellectual colonization of Roman minds.

Between Gr. and Roman poetry, there is one main difference: Roman poetry is monocentered, centripetal, obsessed with Rome, and works on a center-periphery model (evident, e.g., in Catullus, Virgil, and Horace and in elegy). The lang. often has an artificial feel to it, as if the writers were lifting themselves up by the bootstraps, and lit. is strongly supported and invoked by existing political unity—while Greece is a ling. community where lang., education, and culture overcome a permanent state of political fragmentation and (often) confusion and instability.

Mythology and narrative are by default Gr.-oriented, while Rome tends to supply historical examples or alternatively produces daily life, waiting to be aestheticized or criticized according to the standards of the author. The author arbitrates between the poles of Hellenization and Romanness and capitalizes on this function, drawing power from it. Most genres of Roman poetry, in narrative and theater, are based on the assumption that the poet will not create entirely new characters: the individuals are taken from mythology (in epic and tragedy) or from hist. recorded in prose (in historical epic and historical tragedy or *praetexta*) or from a limited repertory in stock characters (in Gr.-style comedy), and, of course, poetic skill will be evident from innovations and adaptations. In satire, epigram, and other less-than-elevated poetry, the assumption is that characters will be taken from daily life, although often with adaptations or pseuds.: those genres often programmatically decline "seriousness" and ambition, as if to justify their realism and direct intervention into social practice.

Other main differences are as follows: (1) Roman production is multigeneric from the start (a phenomenon rare in Gr. poetry, at least before Callimachus), so we have early Roman poets who already divide themselves among epic, theater, and other genres. (2) The Romans had prose from very early on, and there had been only a very brief time when poetry was not sharing the system with prose. (3) Thus, the Romans inherit a Gr. literary system that was already mature and ramified, the system that was in place in the 3d c. BCE, although they always have the option of going back to previous epochs and layers. (4) Roman poets are often very politicized, sometimes masters of invective and political discourse, but they almost never inhabit a space of communal openness: there is very strong political pressure against freedom of speech of the kind practiced (and revived in Roman historical imagination) in Gr. archaic poetry or in Athenian Old Comedy. This situation favors the devel. of a rhet. of innuendo and of a tension between political control and authorial voice. Seneca addresses Nero and the opposition to Nero obliquely through a dark mythological theater; Ovid absorbs Augustan rhet. of urbanism and world domination and also criticizes Augustan bigotry and repression; Juvenal (ca. 55–127 CE) attacks the corruption of the previous regime; Horace sings about the impossibility of retelling the civil wars. (5) While early Gr. poetry is driven by a performance culture and shows traces of oral composition, Roman poetry is from the beginning onward based on a ripe alphabetic culture: the poets show a recurring concern for "live" performance, but most of their work is oriented toward producing well-wrought scripts or scriptures. Horace's lyric poems have an indirect and belated relationship to the issue of performance and voice, and every single poem stands, or better, oscillates between its vocalized occasion and its inscription in the book.

What happened in Rome was not unavoidable, as we can see by contrasting the very different options of Etruscan civilization: the Etruscans invested in spectacles, like the Romans, and reveled in appropriations of Gr. images and lifestyles, but their appropriations are much less careful and respectful; moreover, they do not link the complex of leisure, art, and spectacle with the production of a systematic body of lit. in Etruscan. In Rome, the theater is a driving force during the first generations of Lat. poetry, but during the middle republic, aggressive "modernist" poets such as Lucilius (ca. 180–103 BCE) and Catullus begin to focus entirely on first-person poetry in textual format. Only one thing is clear about the origins: the initial impulse must have had to do not so much with interactions between Rome and Greece, but more with inter-Italic competition. Rome was surrounded by Italic communities that spoke incompatible langs. (Etruscan, Oscan), and "going Greek" was highly desirable to all of the emerging Italic elites. Only slightly later the phenomenon of Roman Hellenicity became entangled with the pace of conquest, first in the Gr.-speaking communities of the It. south and later all over the eastern Mediterranean. In this new phase, Lat. poems derived from Gr. models are competing not only with the Gr. models but with the furious acquisition of Gr. art, knowledge, and status symbols fueled by conquest, the slave trade, and plunder. Later, in the age of Caesar and Augustus, the Romans begin exporting a complex package of acculturation to the western Mediterranean, centered on urbanism and incl. Lat. lang. and lit. and Gr. educational values and aesthetics.

The position of Rome in relation to Gr. culture is crucial for the hist. of mod. Eur. classicism. Roman appropriation and exploitation of Greece lives on in mod. ideas of the classics as a harmonious sum of Gr. and Lat. The primacy of Greece over Rome in the romantic imagination results in a compromise, where the Greeks are leaders in poetry and philosophy and the Romans, while lacking in the necessary originality and communal atmosphere, are role models of "mediation" and (often) imperial control. The Romans are the ones who absorb and transmit Gr. classics—as well as the Judaeo-Christian trad.—to western and northern Europe, and so ultimately to the superpowers of the 18th, 19th, and early 20th cs. *Classics* is, therefore, based on a double exceptionalism: while the miracle of Greece is self-evident and consists in absolute originality and creativity, the Roman miracle is about imitation, belatedness, and imperial opportunism. (The contingent nature of historical transmission blinded the Europeans to the fact that most of those "exceptions" were already present in Near Eastern cultures before the rise of Greeks and Romans.)

D. *Genres and Authors.* In ancient Rome, the canon is initially formed by authors who impersonate and continue Gr. authors: only in the generation of Tibullus (ca. 55–19 BCE) and later Ovid do we begin to find authors who do not identify themselves as "new X," X being a canonical Gr. poet (e.g., Menander, Homer, Callimachus, Theocritus, Alcaeus). Ovid is also, not coincidentally, the first author who dispenses with the convention of patronage (claiming a powerful figure as friend, protector, and, in some cases, sponsor of the work) and spreads the impression of a wide, anonymous circle of readers as a condition for his success. In a society without licensed products, copyright, and authentic mass media, this means pushing the idea of authorial independence as far as it will go until the early mod. period. Among Ovid's successors, only Martial (ca. 40–103 CE) operates on a similar scale and foregrounds the book as his decisive medium. Before Ovid, Catullus and Horace had offered interesting combinations of a "face-to-face" approach, addressing individual poems to recognizable persons on specific occasions, and of a "generalist" approach, where the same poems are being shifted away from the occasion in the direction of a general public and hedge their bets on universal fame and circulation, while still bearing traces of their primary occasion.

The Roman poets who identify themselves as "new X" are masters of ambiguity: the new work can be perceived as surrogate or continuation in another lang. but also as substitute, stand-in, and direct competitor. The poets writing in Lat. have been learning those strategies from Gr. poetry itself, esp. from the rampant intertextuality in authors who had become "poets for poets," such as Aristophanes, Aratus, Callimachus, Theocritus, and the epigram writers.

The poets use all the resources of tact, irony, and self-fashioning in this kind of self-conscious discourse, more or less the same resources that are necessary to cultivating patronage. In the generations after Ovid, for the first time we see Roman poets who more or less implicitly declare themselves "new versions" of a *Roman,* not a Gr., model. The most famous example (esp. in the med. reception) is Statius (45–96 CE), who uses his main models—Virgil, Ovid, Seneca, and Lucan (39–65 CE)—according to the sophisticated strategies developed by the Augustan authors on their own chosen Gr. forerunners. The closure of the Lat. canon after Juvenal is a decision of great importance, and it contributes, together with the Christian revolution, to the typically introverted nature of late antique poetry: its main hero is the talented but isolated court poet Claudian (ca. 370–404 CE), while Christian poetry will slowly develop its own classicism.

Ubiquitous in Roman poetry is the relationship with prose and with rhet., often too easily deplored and criticized. Important too is the strand of didactic poetry, again nourished by Gr. prose; the genre is influenced by the gigantic and isolated Lucretius and continued by Cicero, Virgil, Ovid, Manilius (fl. 1st c. CE), and less famous poets: in this trad., still active in the Ren., the formal resources of rhythm and beauty are intertwined with more or less strong claims to science and truth. Again, the idea of Roman Hellenism is crucial here, since the acquisition of science and information was inseparable from access to definitive Gr. sources in philosophy, biology, mathematics, and cosmology. Those issues play a fundamental role in the specific ideology of Roman epic (also in narrative and heroic guise) and in its claims to encompass the world and reveal its breadth and secrets. In fact, a didactic element was never absent in any given genre of Roman poetry because every Roman poet, from the erotic Propertius (ca. 50–after 16 BCE) to the fabulist Phaedrus (15 BCE–50 CE), is more or less implicitly "teaching" his audience about the cultural capital of Hellenism, as well as realizing his own vision.

A typical breakthrough, if we focus on the later Western trad., is the reinvention of first-person poetry. Taking some cues from Gr. trads. such as epigram and other nonpublic genres, the Roman poets develop a style related to private life and individual sentiment: hence, the many innovations in lyric, elegy, satire, and epigram, and the rise of personal voice even in the epics of Lucretius, Virgil, and Lucan. This expansion of subjectivity is combined with severe restrictions in formulating political address to the public in communal situations. The strong presence of writing throughout the Roman era and the growth of a reading public (increasingly also of women readers) created the atmosphere for the devel. of love elegy, Horatian lyric, and satire, the main contributions to the literary system initiated by the Greeks with their institutionalization of textual production in the 4th c. BCE.

The poets of ancient Rome have a fundamental role in the idea of the author and of the poetic career, as it will develop in late med.

Europe and beyond. Authors such as Virgil, Ovid, Propertius, Seneca, Lucretius, and Horace are present not only with their texts but in their complex of persona, personal voice, and biography. Some of them, like Virgil, acquire a definitive status as the ideal of the artist. In one respect, however, the "premodern" Romans do not anticipate later devels. From the origins to late antiquity, Roman canonical verse is dominated by male authors: women poets are attested but never claim a public role or rise to the prominence of Sappho or to the almost professional status of other Gr. poetesses. Appropriating and impersonating women's voices, therefore, is a constant preoccupation of the Roman authors: this trend is celebrated in one of the Roman texts that claim maximum influence in the Middle Ages, Ovid's *Heroides*.

II. Medieval. Early evidence of Christian Lat. poetry is sparse and random. If Commodian (prob. fl. mid-3d c. CE), who offers doctrine and exhortation in an accentual approximation of the cl. hexameter, was indeed a 3d-c. African, he is an isolated phenomenon. Indicative of things to come are two short narratives, written in skillful hexameters, on Jonah and on the destruction of Sodom (ca. 300), and the beautiful *Phoenix* (ca. 310), attributed to Lactantius (240–ca. 320), wholly pagan in detail but, to the early Middle Ages, plainly a celebration of the Resurrection—a fact recognized by the later Anglo-Saxon poet who produced a vernacular adaptation of this text.

A coherent Christian Lat. trad. emerges in the 4th c., deliberately conceived as an alternative to the pagan classics on which all learned Christians had been reared but drawing principally on the metrical, stylistic, and narrative conventions of Virgilian epic. The cento of the poetess Proba (mid-4th c.) is a mere pastiche of tags from Virgil, carefully arranged into a biblical narrative. What is innovative in Juvencus's (4th c.) hexameter rendering of the Gospels (ca. 330) and the freer version in Sedulius's (fl. 5th c.) *Carmen paschale* (ca. 430) is their ingenuity in adapting Virgilian style to Christian purposes; and Paulinus of Nola (353–431) expresses his resolve to repudiate pagan models and write a new kind of poetry in verse richly evocative of Virgil, Ovid, and Horace. Prudentius (ca. 348–405), master of many cl. styles and genres, was a brilliant original whose complex attitude toward both Christian and pagan culture we are only beginning to fathom. Alongside his two sequences of hymns (the *Cathemerinon* and the *Peristephanon*), he produced a number of didactic poems on theological subjects. The *Apotheosis*, which opens with a hymn on the Trinity, considers the nature of Christ, while the *Hamartigenia* deals with the question of sin. His *Psychomachia*, a short epic on the conflict of virtue and vice in the human soul, greatly influenced med. iconography and offers one of the earliest and most enduring examples of Christian allegory.

The Christian Lat. poets were to coexist with, and even displace, the great pagans in the school curriculum of the early Middle Ages, but they had few imitators. More significant for med. Lat. poetry was the hymnody that appeared as Lat. replaced Gr. as the lang. of the liturgy. The cumbersome, dogmatic verse of Hilary of Poitiers (310–66) can hardly have had a liturgical function, and the rhythmical prose of the great *Te Deum*, despite its early and abiding popularity, was not imitated; med. Lat. hymnody begins with Ambrose (ca. 340–97), who provided his Milanese congregation with meditations appropriate to the liturgical hours and calendar couched in four-line strophes of iambic dimeter. Psychologically profound and written in beautiful and surprisingly cl. Lat., the Ambrosian hymns were widely imitated (most famously by Prudentius and Venantius Fortunatus [ca. 530–605]) and came to form the nucleus of the med. hymnaries; and their form, four-stress lines in quatrains, has been preserved with only minor variations down to the present day, as may be seen in the metrical index of any hymnal.

The upheavals of the later 5th c. left their mark on the Christian Lat. trad. The bookish verse of Sidonius Apollinaris (d. 480) reflects its survival in an attenuated form in Gaul; the "epic" trad. of Prudentius and Sedulius enjoys a late flowering in the *De laudibus Dei* of Dracontius (ca. 450–500); and the verse in Boethius's *De consolatione philosophiae* (early 6th c.), a prosimetrum including a range of meters imitated from Horace and Seneca, is a last manifestation of inherited familiarity with cl. culture. The verse epistles and occasional poems of Fortunatus, charming and often brilliantly innovative, show a marked loss of syntactic and metrical fluency, though his passion hymns *Vexilla regis* and *Pange, lingua* are among the greatest of Christian hymns. The cl. trad. is still alive in the poems of Eugenius of Toledo (fl. ca. 650) and resurfaces with the Carolingian court poets, but new devels. were also taking place. Rhyme and accentual meters begin to appear, most notably in Ir. hymnody, evidently influenced by native Celtic verse forms and the rules of rhythmical prose formulated by the Lat. grammarians, culminating in the *Altus prosator* of Columbanus (d. 597). Correct Lat. verse in quantitative meters continued to be taught in schools and written by the learned past the 16th c., but accentually measured Lat. verse is the rule after the 4th c., paving the way for the accentually based prosodies of the vernaculars (Beare). The riddles of Aldhelm (d. 709), which inaugurated a popular genre, imitate the African Lat. poet Symphosius (4th or 5th c.), and the metrical life of Cuthbert by Bede (673–736) is couched in a fluent hexameter shaped by 4th-c. Christian models; but the high points of 8th-c. It. Lat. poetry are a rhythmical poem in praise of the city of Milan (ca. 738) and the accentual verse experiments of Paulinus of Aquileia (d. 802). Paulinus's somber lament on the death of Eric of Friuli (799) is an early and influential example of the *planctus*, which became a popular form and may reflect the influence of vernacular trad.

The poets who came to the court of Charlemagne brought their culture with them; much of the poetry of Paul the Deacon (d. 802) was written before he left Italy, and Theodulf (d. 821) and Alcuin (d. 804) were products of thriving schools in Spain and England. But Charles and his court inspired new poetry. Panegyric epistles by Alcuin and Theodulf, and the *Karolus Magnus et Leo Papa* (ca. 800) attributed to Einhard (ca. 770–840) celebrate Charles as the champion of political and cultural renewal and Aachen as a new Rome. The poetry of the court includes charming occasional poems by Paul the Deacon and Theodulf's satire on the courts of law, but its finest product is the Christian Lat. pastoral, best illustrated by Alcuin's nightingale poems, his *O mea cella*, a celebration of the scholarly life at Aachen, and "Conflictus veris et hiemis," probably his, which is both a pastoral and perhaps the first example of the debate poem or *Streitgedicht*. This form is imitated in Sedulius Scottus's (9th c.) "Certamen Rosae Liliique" (ca. 850) and in the "Eclogue" of the pseudonymous Theodulus (9th–10th c.), and was widely popular in later periods, e.g., *The Owl and the Nightingale* in ME.

The later 9th and 10th cs. produced further new departures. The hexameter narrative of an anonymous "Poeta Saxo" (ca. 890) celebrates the deeds of Charlemagne as an example for the Emperor Arnulf, and Abbo of St. Germain (9th c.) combines war poetry with moral reflections on the state of France in a poem on the Norman siege of Paris (ca. 897). The remarkable epic *Waltharius*, commonly attributed to Ekkehard of St. Gall (900–73) but possibly earlier, balances the impulsive and bombastic heroism of Attila against the less heroic but more sophisticated behavior of Walter of Aquitaine and his companions, providing a perspective at once sympathetic and detached on the trad. of Germanic heroism and heroic poetry that it evokes. Vernacular culture is probably reflected also in the *Ecbasis cuiusdam captivi* (ca. 950), a rambling beast fable in leonine hexameters apparently written for the edification of young monks; in the mid-11th-c. *Ruodlieb*, the adventures of a wandering knight, based partly on an oriental tale, provide an early foretaste of chivalric romance.

This period was also a time of innovation in religious music, its most significant form being the sequence, sung at Mass between the Epistle and the Gospel, in which the emotional and dramatic scope of religious lyric is greatly expanded. The origins of the sequence are much debated, though the impulse it reflects is present in emotionally expressive poems like the *Versus de Lazaro* of Paulinus of Aqueliea or the *O mi custos* (ca. 825) of Gottschalk of Orbais (d. ca. 867). A shaping influence (formerly thought to be the originator of the sequence) was Notker of St. Gall (d. 912), whose *Liber hymnorum* expresses a range of spiritual feeling, often in striking dramatic monologues and set forth in rhythmically parallel phrases designed for antiphonal singing. The later scholar of St. Gall, Ekkehard, produced a number of sequences in the same style as Notker but with few original features. Notker's work anticipates the religious poetry of Peter Damian (1007–72) and Peter Abelard (1079–1142) and the great achievements of Franciscan hymnody.

The devel. of the secular lyric is even harder to trace, but as early as the mid-10th c. the lang. of the Song of Songs was being used to celebrate an idealized beloved in a way that clearly anticipates the courtly lyric of the 12th c. The mid-11th-c. *Carmina Cantabrigiensia* (Cambridge Songs) ms. includes the sophisticated "O admirabile Veneris idolum," addressed to a beautiful boy; "Levis exsurgit Zephirus," which dwells on the interplay of emotion and natural setting in the manner of high med. lyric; and the magnificent "Iam dulcis amica venito," here a passionate love song but found elsewhere in a form adapted to religious use. The 12th c. saw a great flowering of secular love lyric, ranging from imitations of popular song to elaborate essays in love psychology and *courtoisie* by poets such as Walter of Châtillon (b. 1135) and Peter of Blois (ca. 1135–1212). Many of the best of these are gathered in collections such as the early 13th-c. *Carmina Burana*, which also includes drinking songs, narrative love visions like *Phyllis and Flora* and *Si linguis angelicis* (which anticipate the *Roman de la Rose*), and satire in the trad. of Goliardic verse, in which poets such as Hugh Primas (fl. ca. 1150) and the anonymous Archpoet of Cologne (fl. 1160s) make their own misfortunes and dissipations, real or imagined, an occasion for discussing the ills of the world.

Religious poetry, too, appears in new forms in this period. The sequence form, now evolved into accentual verse with a regular rhyme scheme, provided a model for the powerful series of planctus in which Abelard dramatizes the sufferings of such OT figures as Samson, Dinah, and the daughter of Jepthah. In the sequences of Adam of St. Victor (d. 1177–92), subtle allegorical and theological arguments appear in forms as intricate as any lyric poetry of the period, and the sonorous rhyming hexameters of the *De contemptu mundi* (ca. 1140) of Bernard of Cluny (fl. 2nd c.) give a new force to religious satire.

Side by side with these new departures is a steadily evolving trad. of "learned" Lat. poetry based on cl. models. Already in the late 11th c., Marbod of Rennes (1035–1123), Hildebert of Le Mans (1056–1133), and Baudri of Bourgueil (1046–1130) had produced a new, urbane poetry, Ovidian in form and manner and devoted to such topics as friendship and the cultivation of relations with noble patrons. The broadly Virgilian biblical epic of the pseudonymous Ger. poet Eupolemius (probably 11th c.) marked a new departure in the poetic treatment of scriptural material. Though this text belongs most clearly to the trad. initiated by Prudentius, Juvencus, and Sedulius centuries earlier, Eupolemius shows little respect for convention. The topic of his lengthy hexameter poem is a battle between good and evil; but fidelity to biblical narrative is not a priority, and biblical names are used sparingly. The renewal of cl. studies in the 12th-c. cathedral schools led to more ambitious exercises. Bernardus Silvestris's (ca. 1085–1178) *Cosmographia* (ca. 1147) and the *De planctu naturae* (ca. 1170) of Alan of Lille (ca. 1128–1202), philosophical allegories in the trad. of Boethius and Martianus Capella, exhibit a new assurance vis-à-vis the great authors of antiquity. Alan's *Anticlaudianus* (1182–83), on the creation of the perfect human, announces itself as a new kind of epic; and the *Alexandreis* (1182) of Walter of Châtillon, Joseph of Exeter's (12th c.) *Ilias* (1188–90), and John of Hauville's (d. ca. 1210) virtually all-encompassing Juvenalian satire *Architrenius* (1184) reflect similar ambition, while Geoffrey of Vinsauf provided a latter-day counterpart to Horace's *Ars poetica* in his *Poetria nova* (ca. 1210). Later critics such as John of Garland (d. 1258) and Hugh of Trimberg (fl. ca. 1280) could claim these writers as mod. *auctores* worthy of the respect and study accorded the ancients. In addition, the 12th and early 13th cs. produced a range of school poetry in less ambitious but widely popular forms: topical satires like the mock-visionary *Apocalypse of Golias*, aimed at ecclesiastical corruption, and the *Speculum stultorum* of Nigel of Longchamps (fl. ca. 1190), an elaborate beast fable allegorizing monastic ambition; narrative imitations of ancient comedy such as the *Pamphilus*, which had a lasting influence on love narrative in several langs.; and a body of pseudo-Ovidian poetry, incl. the mock-autobiographical *De vetula*, which was long considered an authentic Ovidian work.

A number of the greatest examples of med. religious poetry date from the later 13th c., notably the *Philomena* of John Howden (d. 1275), a meditation on the power of love as exemplified in the lives of Christ and the Virgin; the hymns and sequence for the feast of Corpus Christi traditionally attributed to Thomas Aquinas (1229–74), the highest achievement of theological poetry in the trad. of Adam of St. Victor; and the work of a number of Franciscan poets, above all the "Dies irae" and "Stabat mater dolorosa" associated with the names of Thomas of Celano (d. 1255) and Jacopone da Todi (1230–1306). But in other areas, the great proliferation of vernacular lit. led to a decline in the production of Lat. poetry, and the typical 13th-c. works are didactic treatises, designed to systematize and compress the materials of the traditional curriculum, secular and religious, in accordance with the needs of a newly compartmentalized system of education. Examples include the *De laudibus divinae sapientiae* of Alexander Nequam (d. 1217), an encyclopedic review of Creation as a manifestation of divine wisdom; the *Aurora*, a versified biblical commentary by Peter Riga (d. 1209); and the *Integumenta Ovidii* of John of Garland. The 14th c. produces such late flowerings as the devotional verse of the Eng. mystic Richard Rolle (d. 1349) and the powerful anatomy of the social ills of England in the *Vox clamantis* (1380–86) of John Gower (ca. 1330–1408); but the most significant work of this period, the Lat. verse of Dante, Petrarch, and Boccaccio, arguably belongs to the hist. of the Ren.

III. Renaissance and After. Rejecting med. varieties of Lat. poetry, Ren. humanists promoted a closer study of versification and forms from cl. antiquity. The result, from the 14th to the early 17th c., was an immense output of Lat. verse in cl. meters. Petrarch (1304–74) showed the way with hundreds of hexameters on various themes in his versified *Epystole* (1333–64); a hexameter epic on the Punic Wars, *Africa* (1338–41, left incomplete after much revision); and twelve eclogues, *Bucolicum carmen* (1346–68), on poetry, politics, and contemp. hist. Further incursions into epic and pastoral marked the hist. of Lat. poetry in the 15th c., e.g., the incomplete *Sforzias* by Francesco Filelfo (1398–1481) about the rise to power of the poet's Milanese patron; a supplementary 13th book of the *Aeneid* by the humanist Maffeo Veggio (1406–58); and ten widely admired eclogues by Mantuan (Battista Spagnoli, 1447–1516) that recall cl. models while displaying a distinctive piety, humor, and satire.

Some of the best Ren. Lat. poetry appeared in cl. forms that Petrarch did not use, such as epigram, elegy, and ode. Panormita (pseud. of Antonio Beccadelli, 1394–1471) initiated the Neapolitan Ren. with his *Hermaphroditus* (1425), two books of ribald epigrams that out-Martial Martial. His protégé, Giovanni Pontano (1429–1503), wrote lullabies for his son (*Neniae*); Ovidian elegies for his mistresses (*Parthenopeus* and *Eridanus*), his wife (*De amore coniugali*), and deceased loved ones (*De tumulis*); and racy poems in hendecasyllables for his male friends and their courtesans (*Baiae*). At the Florentine *studium*, Cristoforo Landino (1424–98) compiled three books of *Xandra* (1443–60) in various meters about love, friendship, patriotism, and praise of the Medici. The posthumously published *Carminum libellus* of the Venetian humanist Pietro Bembo (1470–1547) offers tribute to friends and lovers in various meters.

Supremely conscious of its imitative debt to cl. texts, the finest Ren. Lat. poetry resonates with explicit echoes from ancient poetry. In Florence, Angelo Poliziano (1454–94) in five verse essays, *Silvae* (1475–86), urged poets to cultivate a cl. style. Poliziano wrought classically inspired epigrams (*Epigrammata*, 1498), as did his friend Michele Marullo (ca. 1453–1500) in poems about his exile from Constantinople and his love for his mistress Neaera. Marullo's four books of *Hymni naturales* illustrate tenets of Neoplatonic philosophy in various meters—hexameter, alcaic, sapphic, iambic. The Neapolitan Jacopo Sannazaro (1458–1530) brought forth a steady flow of elegies and epigrams. His *Piscatoriae* (1526) adapts Virgilian pastoral to a seaside setting, while his short epic on Christ's nativity, *De partu virginis* (1526), appropriates formulas, expressions, and even entire lines from the epics of Virgil, Ovid, Claudian, and others.

The more Ren. humanists sought to recover the cl. past, the greater they realized their distance from it. One consequence was their effort to develop new forms and expand the repertory of Lat. poetry. The Venetian historian Andrea Navagero (1483–1529), e.g., destroyed his didactic verse but salvaged a lively experiment in pastoral epigrams, *Lusus pastoralis* (1530), which exerted great influence on later vernacular poetry. Girolamo Fracastoro (1483–1553), a professor of medicine at Padua, wrote *Syphilis* (1530), three books of hexameter verse attributing the origins of venereal disease to the New World and proposing a cure.

Amid early Reformation turmoil, a Benedictine monk at Mantua, Teofilo Folengo (1491–1544), wrote *Baldus* (1517–21), a rowdy hexameter epic in a macaronic hybrid of Lat. and It. about an outlandish hero who hunts down witches, demons, and religious superstition. Presaging the Counter-Reformation in Rome, Marco Girolamo Vida (1485–1566) applied the principles of his versified *De arte poetica* (1527) to a six-book hexameter epic on the life of Jesus, *Christiad* (1535), and a collection of Christian *Hymni* (1550). Another associate of the papal court, Marcantonio Flaminio (1498–1550), devoted himself to paraphrasing Psalms in cl. meters, *Davidis psalmi* (1546) and *Carmina sacra* (1551).

The devel. of Ren. Lat. poetry beyond the Alps followed similar patterns, confirming the stature of Lat. as a truly international lang. The Hungarian poet Janus Pannonius (1437–72) and the Ger. poet Conrad Celtis (1459–1508) wrote elegies, epigrams, hexameters, and hendecasyllables about their education in Italy and their efforts to bring humanist teachings to the North. The Dutch poet Joannes Secundus (1511–36) earned fame throughout Europe for his *Basia*, 19 erotic songs for his voluptuous mistress. The Fr. poet Salmon Macrin (1490–1557) graced the courts of Francis I and Henry II with a vast output of elegies, epithalamia, political verse, and Christian hymns. The Scotsman George Buchanan (1506–82) issued a vast output of Lat. poetry that encompasses satire, tragedy, versified science, and trans. of the Psalms.

With the devel. of the vernaculars and the prestige of their lits. throughout Europe in the 16th c., many poets who wrote superb Lat. lyrics turned decisively to their native langs. for important projects. Ludovico Ariosto (1474–1533) in Italy, Joachim du Bellay (ca. 1522–60) in France, and John Milton (1608–74) in England exemplify the trend. Some who wrote entirely in Lat. include two 17th-c. Jesuit poets, Maciej Kazimierz Sarbiewski (1595–1640) in Poland and Jacob Balde (1604–68) in Germany, whose religious lyrics accommodate scriptural themes to cl. meters. Though vernacular lit. gained complete ascendance, the composition of Lat. poetry survived in schools and universities well past the Ren. as an accomplishment proper to a cl. scholar.

See BYZANTINE POETRY; GREEK POETRY.

■ **I. Classical.** ***Bibliographies and Histories***: *L'Année philologique* 1—(1927–), http://www.annee-philologique.com/aph/; M. Schanz and C. Hosius, *Geschichte der romischen Literatur*, 4th ed. (1927–35); *CHCL*, v. 2; *Handbuch der lateinichen Literatur der Antike*, ed. R. Herzog and P. L. Schmidt (1989–2002); G. B. Conte, *Latin Literature: A History* (1999); *The Oxford Handbook of Roman Studies*, ed. A. Barchiesi and W. Scheidel (2010). ***Hellenization***: G. Williams, *Tradition and Originality in Roman Poetry* (1968); E. Gruen, *Studies in Greek Culture and Roman Policy* (1990); D. Feeney, *Literature and Religion at Rome* (1998); R. Hunter, *The Shadow of Callimachus* (2006); A. Wallace-Hadrill, *Rome's Cultural Revolution* (2008). ***Language***: J. Farrell, *Latin Language and Latin Culture* (2001); J. N. Adams, *Bilingualism and the Latin Language* (2003); *La lingua poetica latina*, ed. A. Lunelli (2011). ***Poetics, Intertextuality, and Genre***: C. O. Brink, *Horace on Poetry*, 3 v. (1963–82); G. N. Knauer, *Die Aeneis und Homer* (1964); G. B. Conte. *The Rhetoric of Imitation* (1986); P. Veyne, *Roman Erotic Elegy*, trans. D. Pellauer (1988); D. C. Feeney, *The Gods in Epic* (1991); S. Hinds, *The Dynamics of Appropriation* (1998); T. Hubbard, *The Pipes of Pan* (1998); D. P. Fowler, *Roman Constructions* (2000); M. Wyke, *The Roman Mistress* (2002); F. Cairns, *Generic Composition in Greek and Roman Poetry*, 2d ed. (2007). ***Primary Texts and Authors***: R. Heinze, *Virgil's Epic Technique* (1903); E. Fraenkel, *Plautine Elements in Plautus* (1922), and *Horace* (1957); W. S. Anderson, *Essays on Roman Satire* (1982); O. Skutsch, *The Annals of Quintus Ennius* (1985); M. Roberts, *The Jeweled Style* (1989); E. Courtney, *The Fragmentary Latin Poets* (1993); P. Hardie, *The Epic Successors of Virgil* (1993); D. Kennedy, *The Arts of Love* (1993); W. Fitzgerald, *Catullan Provocations* (1995); S. Braund, *Juvenal: Satires Book I* (1996); E. Gowers, *The Loaded Table* (1996); A. J. Boyle, *Roman Tragedy* (1997); M. Leigh, *Lucan: Spectacle and Engagement* (1997); C. Connors, *Petronius the Poet* (1998); E. Oliensis, *Horace and the Rhetoric of Authority* (1998); D. Sedley, *Lucretius and the Transformation of Greek Wisdom* (1998); K. McCarthy, *Slaves, Masters, and the Art of Authority in Plautine Comedy* (2000); K. Freudenburg, *Satires of Rome* (2001); P. Hardie, *Ovid's Poetics of Illusion* (2002); *Ovid: Ars amatoria*, book 3, ed. R. K. Gibson (2003); A. S. Hollis, *Fragments of Roman Poetry, c. 60 BC–AD 20* (2007); S. J. Heyworth, *Cynthia* (2009); A. Feldherr, *Playing Gods* (2010). ***Roman Stage***: *The Tragedies of Ennius*, ed. H. D. Jocelyn (1967); Seneca, *Agamemnon*, ed. R. J. Tarrant (1976); R. L. Hunter, *The New Comedy of Greece and Rome* (1985); A. J. Boyle, *Roman Tragedy* (1997); F. Dupont, *The Invention of Literature* (1999); Seneca, *Thyestes*, ed. R. J. Tarrant (2000); C. Marshall, *The Stagecraft and Performance of Roman Comedy* (2006). ***Social Background***: A. Richlin, *The Garden of Priapus* (1992); P. White, *Promised Verse* (1993); T. N. Habinek, *The Politics of Latin Literature* (1998); J. Henderson, *Writing Down Rome* (1999); W. Fitzgerald, *Slavery and the Roman Literary Imagination* (2000); A. Keith, *Engendering Rome: Women in Roman Epic* (2000); S. Goldberg, *Constructing Literature in the Roman Republic* (2005); M. Lowrie, *Writing, Performance, and Authority in Augustan Rome* (2009). ***Studies of Reception***: T. M. Greene, *The Light in Troy: Imitation and Discovery in Renaissance Poetry* (1982); L. Barkan, *The Gods Made Flesh* (1986); C. Martindale, *Redeeming* *the Text* (1992); D. Quint, *Epic and Empire* (1993); C. Burrow, *Epic Romance* (1993); *Classical Literary Careers and Their Reception*, ed. P. Hardie and H. Moore (2010); P. Hardie, *Rumour and Renown* (2012). ***Style, Meter, and Other Formal Aspects***: L. P. Wilkinson, *Golden Latin Artistry* (1963); R.G.M. Nisbet and M. Hubbard, *A Commentary on Horace: Odes, Book 1* (1970), *A Commentary on Horace: Odes, Book 2* (1978); J. Wills, *Repetition in Latin Poetry* (1996); C. Questa, *La metrica di Plauto e Terenzio* (2007); L. Morgan, *Musa pedestris* (2010).

■ **II. Medieval**. ***Anthologies and Texts***: *MGH*; Migne, *PG* and *PL*—the fullest collection of texts; *Analecta hymnica*—the fullest collections of hymns; *Carmina Burana*, ed. J. A. Schmeller, 4th ed. (1907)—the only complete text, later ed. by A. Hilka and O. Schumann, though only v. 1 (parts 1–2), v. 2 (part 1), and v. 3 (part 1) have appeared (1931–71); *Early Latin Hymns*, ed. A. S. Walpole (1922); *Medieval Latin Lyrics*, ed. and trans. H. Waddell, 5th ed. (1948); *The Goliard Poets*, ed. and trans. G. F. Whicher (1949); F. Brittain, *The Medieval Latin and Romance Lyric*, 2d ed. (1951); *Oxford Book of Medieval Latin Verse*, ed. F.J.E. Raby (1959); *Hymni latini antiquissimi xxv*, ed. W. Bulst (1975); *More Latin Lyrics from Virgil to Milton*, ed. and trans. H. Waddell (1977); *Seven Versions of Carolingian Pastoral*, ed. R.P.H. Green (1980); *Poetry of the Carolingian Renaissance*, ed. P. Godman (1985)—long intro. ***Criticism, History, and Prosody***: Keil—collects the principal med. Lat. grammarians and prosodists; Manitius—the standard lit. hist.; Meyer; H. Walther, *Das Streitgedicht in der lateinische Literatur des Mittelalters* (1920); Faral; "Mittellateinische Dichtung in Deutschen," *Reallexikon I*; Lote; Curtius; Raby, *Christian* and *Secular*; D. Norberg, *Poésie latine rythmique* (1954); Beare—good survey; M. Burger, *Recherches sur la structure et l'origine des vers romans* (1957); K. Strecker, *Introduction to Medieval Latin*, trans. and rev. R. B. Palmer (1957)—excellent intro. and bibl.; Norberg—best account of prosody; M.R.P. McGuire, *Introduction to Medieval Latin Studies* (1964); J. Szövérffy, *Annalen der lateinische Hymnendichtung*, 2 v. (1964–65); A. C. Friend, "Medieval Latin Literature," Fisher; Dronke; J. Szövérffy, *Weltliche Dichtungen des lateinische Mittelalters*, v. 1 (1970); C. Witke, *Numen litterarum* (1971); P. Klopsch, *Einführung in die mittellateinische Verslehre* (1972); Murphy—med. rhet.; F. Brunhölzl, *Geschichte der lateinischen Literatur des Mittelalters*, 3 v. (1975–2003); P. Dronke, *The Medieval Lyric*, 2d ed. (1978); *The Interpretation of Medieval Latin Poetry*, ed. W.T.H. Jackson (1980); J. Stevens, *Words and Music in the Middle Ages* (1980); Brogan, 720 ff.; Norden—art prose; P. Dronke, *The Medieval Poet and His World* (1985); P. Godman, *Poets and Emperors* (1987); O. B. Hardison Jr., *Prosody and Purpose in the English Renaissance* (1989)—incl. med. Lat.; J. Szövérffy, *Latin Hymns* (1989); F. Mantello and A. Rigg, *Medieval Latin: An Introduction and Bibliographical Guide* (1996)—authoritative essays and bibls.; Lausberg—rhet.; *The Oxford Handbook of Medieval Latin Literature*, ed. R. Hexter and D. Townsend (2012).

■ **III. Renaissance and After**. ***Anthologies***: *Poeti latini del quattrocento*, ed. F. Arnaldi et al. (1964)—with It. trans.; *Musae reduces*, ed. P. Laurens, 2 v. (1975)—with Fr. trans.; *An Anthology of Neo-Latin Poetry*, ed. F. J. Nichols (1979)—with Eng. trans., *Renaissance Latin Verse*, ed. A. Perosa and J. Sparrow (1979); *Renaissance Latin Poetry*, ed. and trans. I. D. McFarlane (1980). ***Criticism and History***: L. Spitzer, "The Problem of Latin Renaissance Poetry," *SP* 2 (1955); J. Sparrow, "Latin Verse of the High Renaissance," *Italian Renaissance Studies*, ed. E. F. Jacob (1960); W. L. Grant, *Neo-Latin Literature and the Pastoral* (1965); J. Ijsewijn, *Companion to Neo-Latin Studies* (1977); W. J. Kennedy, *Jacopo Sannazaro and the Uses of Pastoral* (1983); D. Robin, *Filelfo in Milan* (1991); S. Murphy, *The Gift of Immortality* (1997); L. Piepho, *Holofernes' Mantuan* (2001); W. Ludwig, *Miscella Neolatina* (2004); J. C. Warner, *The Augustinian Epic* (2005); *Petrarch: A Critical Guide*, ed. V. Kirkham and A. Maggi (2009). ***Editions and Translations***: G. Fracastoro, *Syphilis*, ed. and trans. H. Wynne-Finch (1935); C. Celtis, *Selections*, ed. and trans. L. Forster (1948); J. Milton, *Variorum: Latin and Greek Poems*, ed. and trans. D. Bush et al. (1970); A. Navagero, *Lusus*, ed. and trans. A. E. Wilson (1973); Petrarch, *Bucolicum carmen*, ed. and trans. T. G. Bergin (1974); M. G. Vida, *De arte poetica*, ed. and trans. R. G. Williams (1976); Petrarch, *Africa*, trans. T. G. Bergin (1977); J. Secundus, *The Latin Love Elegy*, ed. and trans. C. Endres (1981); A. Poliziano, *Silvae*, ed. and trans. C. Fantazzi (2004); M. Vegio, *Short Epics*, ed. and trans. M. Putnam (2004); P. Bembo, *Lyric Poetry*, ed. and trans. B. Radice (2005); G. Pontano, *Baiae*, ed. and trans. R. G. Dennis (2006); T. Folengo,

Baldo, ed. and trans. A. E. Mullaney (2007); C. Landino, *Poems*, ed. and trans. M. P. Chatfield (2008); M. G. Vida, *Christiad*, ed. and trans. J. Gardner (2009).

A. Barchiesi (cl.); W. Wetherbee, T.V.F. Brogan, S. Penn (med.); W. J. Kennedy (ren.)

LATVIA, POETRY OF. The roots of Latvian poetry are found in Latvian folk songs called *dainas*. A single folk meter is characteristic across the territory of Latvia: eight trochaic syllables per line, four unrhymed lines per stanza, the first two lines proposing a general situation, the last two adding a specific comment:

Viena meita Rīgā dzied,
Otra dzied Valmierā;
Abas dzied vienu dziesmu,
Vai bij vienas mātes meitas?

(One girl sings in Riga,
Another sings in Valmiera;
They both sing the same song,
Are they the same mother's daughters?)

Dainas were first celebrated by the Ger. philosophers Johann Georg Hamann and J. G. Herder, who noted that the basic form was sung, not written. Written poetic trads. began with Lutheran hymns, most notably by Christopher Fürecker (ca. 1615–85). From the Reformation to the 19th c., Lutheran pastors and the grassroots Moravian Brethren unsuccessfully urged Latvians to reject dainas in favor of Christian songs.

A 19th-c. movement of Latvian intellectuals sought subject matter in national hist., folklore, and mythology. Juris Alunāns (1832–64) inaugurated Latvian poetry with *Dziesmiņas* (Songs) in 1856. Poems by Auseklis (pseud. of Miķelis Krogzems, 1850–79) became popular in choral performances at the National Song Festivals, established in 1873; his poem "Beverīnas dziedonis" (Singer of Beverina) retells a 13th-c. chronicle account of a singer who halted a war, establishing "the power of song," as a popular theme in Latvian poetry. Andrejs Pumpurs (1841–1902) created the national epic *Lāčplēsis* (*Bearslayer*), based on folktales and dainas.

In the 1880s, Marxism precipitated a deep ideological schism in Latvian lit.; Rainis (pseud. of Jānis Pliekšāns, 1865–1929), however, synthesized national hist. and mythology with a secular love of all humanity. Aspazija (pseud. of Elza Rozenberga-Pliekšāne, 1868–1943) combined neoromantic nationalism with social conscience and feminism in her flamboyant, sensual poetry. A group led by Kārlis Skalbe (1879–1945), Jānis Akurāters (1876–1937), and Kārlis Krūza (1884–1960) published an "art-for-art's-sake" manifesto in the 1906 literary jour. *Dzelme*. Edvarts Virza (pseud. of Jēkabs Liekna, 1883–1940) dropped a bombshell of passionately erotic poetry with *Biķeris* (1907).

After Latvian national independence in 1918, Rainis and Aspazija were greeted as national heroes when they returned from exile in Switzerland. Publications of a new artistic association, *Zaļā vārna* (Green Crow), catalyzed creative energy. Diverse content and style reflected many political and social currents. Expressionism left an impact on Pēteris Ērmanis (1893–1969), the first Latvian poet to experiment with free verse. Urban poet Ēriks Ādamsons (1907–46) was introspective and complex, ironic and refined, scornful of rural simplicities. The opium-laced poems of Jānis Ziemeļnieks (pseud. of J. Krauklis, 1897–1930) are hallmarks of melodic beauty. Aleksandrs Čaks (pseud. of A. Čadarainis, 1902–50) is the most original modernist, carrying a tangible legacy to subsequent generations. Forceful and iconoclastic, mocking and ironic, stressing rhythm over rhyme, he shocked the traditionalists and fascinated the young.

During World War II, many emerging poets such as patriotic bard Andrejs Eglītis (1912–2006) and Velta Toma (1912–99) went into exile in the West. Other émigrés found their voice later, among them urban poet Linards Tauns (pseud. of Arnolds Bērzs, 1922–63), jazz-inspired Gunars Salinš (1924–2010), nuanced master of lang. Astrīde Ivaska (1926–2015), and witty existentialist Olafs Stumbrs (1931–96). The poetry of rock music inspired Juris Kronbergs (b. 1946).

In Latvia, Stalinism and World War II left cultural life in ruins. Soviet Latvian poet Linards Laicens (1883–1938), trans. of the Finnish epic *Kalevala*, was executed during Stalin's purges in Russia. The Soviets deported Leonīds Breikšs (1908–42) from Latvia, his gravesite unknown; he is remembered for his "Prayer," sung during the Singing Revolution of 1988–91. Knuts Skujenieks (b. 1936) was arrested for political activities in 1962 and sentenced to seven years' hard labor. In the final years of Soviet rule, poet of conscience Klāvs Elsbergs

(1959–87) was killed when he fell from a high-rise window under suspicious circumstances.

In Soviet Latvia, socialist realism was required. Among the best-known Stalinist praise poets were Arvīds Grigulis (1906–89) and Jānis Sudrabkalns (1894–1975). Mirdza Ķempe's (1907–74) loud political poems garnered official status, but her love poetry carried the power of truth, drawing young poets to her for mercilessly honest mentoring. Ojārs Vācietis (1933–83) was publicly ostracized for "ideological ambiguity" in his 1962 poem "Einšteiniana"; his first-person poem about Stalin's resurrection remained in ms. until 1987. Immensely popular Imants Ziedonis (1933–2013) expanded Vācietis's stylistic innovations, shaping conversational registers into musical free verse, addressing the reader directly and personally. Vizma Belševica (1931–2005) was first hailed, then silenced for eight years after her 1969 poem about a med. scribe who wrote secret notes in the margins of an official chronicle. Ārija Elksne (1928–84) likewise created islands of non-Soviet truth with her poems of gentle, feminine spirituality and love.

Most of these 20th-c. authors are also well represented in choral and pop songs; composer Imants Kalniņš (b. 1941) forged a particularly powerful combination of genres when he set to music poems by Māris Čaklais (1940–2003), multiplying political meanings hidden between the lines.

The 1970s and 1980s saw a rich influx of styles and themes through trans. by a generation of polyglot poets, among them Uldis Bērziņš (b. 1944), Leons Briedis (b. 1949), Dagnija Dreika (b. 1951), and the abovementioned Skujenieks; their poetry's transnational intertextual relations may never be fully unraveled. Others looked to native folklore. Ziedonis rediscovered the dainas' style and mythological content, while urban singing group Skandinieki revived authentic performance styles and melodies of oral poetry. Māra Zālīte's (b. 1952) simplicity and clarity echoed the powerful, grounded women's voices of folk song trad. Her librettos for musicals and rock operas resonated among the masses during and after the Singing Revolution.

Tension between censorship and honesty meant popularity for those who broke through barriers. The quirky poetry of Aivars Neibarts (1939–2001), e.g., juxtaposed words with phonetic similarities, producing playfully paradoxical, truthful statements. The loud, sometimes aggressive bravura of Māris Melgalvs (1957–2005) was a cover for sincere, vulnerable humanity; his poems were popularized by the underground rock group Pērkons. Poet Jānis Peters (b. 1939) entered politics proper as leader of the 1988 Latvian Writers' Union meeting, a public forum for free political discourse; he was later appointed independent Latvia's ambassador to Russia.

After freedom of speech was ensured by political independence, poetry was no longer needed to veil political statements; literary critic Berelis calls the 1990s a "post-prophetic era" when poets descended back to mortal life. Some lamented the sudden lack of interest in their experiments, but others such as religious poets Broņislava Martuževa (1924–2012) and Anna Rancāne (b. 1959) found broad resonance. Kornēlija Apšukrūma (b. 1937) publishes large print runs of books popular as a source of handwritten inscriptions in greeting cards.

Poets and literary critics Māris Salējs (b. 1971) and Kārlis Vērdiņš (b. 1979) observe that poets nowadays are acutely aware of their social role. A 2005 manifesto by Gaiķu Māris (pseud. of M. Rozentāls, b. 1973) and Kikōne (pseud. of Edgars Mednis, 1984–2006) stressed respect for literary apprenticeship and the author's responsibility: "If the reader feels that the writer has wasted his time, then he reserves the right to kick, or pelt the author with rotten tomatoes."

The sense of social responsibility fosters epic, not lyrical expression, focusing on everyday experience in a larger, nonmaterial reality. Pēters Brūveris (1957–2011) sharpens perceptions through historical memory, reconstructing humanity out of the garbage of civilization. An awareness of lang. is ever present: Rūta Mežavilka's (b. 1971) grammatically crippled lines evoke deformities in life perceptions; the folksy Latgallian speech of Valentīns Lukaševičs (b. 1968) vibrates between witty rural identity and dark existentialism. For Inga Gaile (b. 1976) and Liāna Langa (pseud. of L. Bokša, b. 1960), fluid, organic images and a physical awareness of the body elicit a world of senses, not words. Latvian-Rus. poets Sergejs Timofejevs (b. 1970), Artūrs Punte (b. 1977), and Semjons Haņins (pseud. of Aleksandrs Zapoļs, b. 1970), leaders in the *Orbīta* group, publish bilingually and explore multimedia poetry.

Latvian poetry in the early 21st c. reached its largest audiences through musical performance. Heavy-metal group Skyforger and the rapper Ozols (pseud. of Ģirts Rozentāls, b.

1979) won acclaim abroad, but their success at home depended on effective poetry. Lyrics by Renārs Kaupers (b. 1974) and the popular Latvian band Brainstorm set the tone of the 2005 Youth Song Festival in Riga:

Tie ir vārdi no manas tautas, un dziesma
man arī no tās,
un es zinu, neviens manā vietā to
nedziedās.

(These are words that come from my people, and the song is also from them,
and I know that nobody else can sing it in
my place.)

In contrast to images of civilization's decline and alienation that predominate in print, Kaupers projected an optimistic sense of responsibility for lang. and poetic trads., hinting at a richly multifaceted, resonant future for Latvian poetry.

■ **Anthologies**: *Latvju modernās dzejas antoloģija*, ed. A. Čaks and P. Ķikuts (1930); *Latvju sonets 100 gados 1856–1956*, ed. K. Dziļleja (1956); *Lettische Lyrik*, ed. E. Eckard-Skalberg (1960); *Contemporary Latvian Poetry*, ed. I. Cedriņš (1984); *All Birds Know This*, ed. K. Sadovska (2001); *Citā gaismā*, ed. M. Lasmanis (2005)—Latvian poetry in the West; A. Pumpurs, *Bearslayer, the Latvian Legend*, trans. A. Cropley (2007); *The Baltic Quintet*, ed. E. Page (2008); *Latvian Literature*, 7 v. (2002–), http://www.literature.lv/; *Krišjāņa Barona dainu skapis*, http://www.dainuskapis.lv.

■ **Criticism and History**: E. Virza, *La Littérature lettonne depuis l'époque de réveil national* (1926); R. Ekmanis, *Latvian Literature under the Soviets: 1940–1975* (1978); *Linguistics and Poetics of Latvian Folksongs*, ed. V. Vīķis-Freibergs (1989); *Latviešu literatūras vēsture*, ed. V. Hausmanis et al., 3 v. (1998–2001); G. Berelis, *Latviešu literatūras vēsture* (1999); A. Cimdiņa, *Introduction to Modern Latvian Literature* (2001); J. Kursīte, *Dzejas vārdnīca* (2002); M. Salējs et al., *Latviešu literatūra 2000–2006* (2007).

J. Silenieks; G. Šmidchens

LITHUANIA, POETRY OF. Written lit. arose in Lithuania during the Reformation and Counter-Reformation. Before that, the poetic heritage of the nation was sustained by folk songs (*dainos*), of which about 200,000 have now been recorded and which are best represented by lyrical love songs. The lyrical nature of poetic expression is characteristic of dainos in general, and it is strongly evident even in the war songs and ballads, while mythological songs are rare and epic narratives are altogether lacking. The most typical of the dainos exhibit numerous diminutives and employ highly developed parallelism and a rather intricate, sometimes erotic, symbolism. Because the text and melody are integrally connected in the dainos, rhythm is of great importance; as a result of the free stress in Lithuanian, it is variable and often mixed. Rhyme, however, is not essential. The stanzas have mostly two, three, or four lines, either with or without a refrain. Some older songs have no stanzas at all. The earliest collection of songs, *Dainos* (1825), was by Liudvikas Rėza (Rhesa, 1776–1840), the largest (4 v., 1880–83) by A. Juškevičius (1819–80); much more extensive collections have now been assembled by the Lithuanian Academy of Science. The trad. of folk poetry became a strong factor in the formation of the distinctly national character of Lithuanian poetry.

Written Lithuanian poetry begins in the 16th c. with versions of canticles and hymns, incl. those of Martynas Mažvydas (Mosvidius, d. 1563), who also prepared, in Königsberg, the first printed Lithuanian book, *Catechismusa Prasty Szadei* (The Plain Words of the Catechism, 1547), a trad. of the Lutheran catechism, and prefaced it with a rhymed foreword. The most outstanding 18th-c. work was Kristijonas Donelaitis's (Donalitius, 1714–80) poem *Metai* (The Seasons, 1765–75, pub. 1818), a 3,000-line poem in hexameters that exhibits in forceful lang. a keen love and observation of nature and depicts vividly the life and character of the common people. Imbued with the Pietist spirit, the poem transmits a moving sense of the sacredness of life and of the earth.

A more active literary movement appeared at the beginning of the 19th c., marked first by pseudoclassicism and sentimentalism and later by romanticism and a growing interest in Lithuanian folklore. The latter trend was particularly evident in the poetry of Antanas Strazdas (1760–1833), who was one of the first to merge the folk song trad. with personal expression. The next peak in the devel. of Lithuanian poetry was Antanas Baranauskas (1835–1902), whose picturesque poem *Anykščių šilelis* (The Grove of Anyksciai, 1858–59) is a veiled lament for Lithuania under the tsarist Rus. regime. Baranauskas was esp. successful in creating a melodious flow of lang. using a traditional syllabic versification that is not very well suited to Lithuanian. The pre-20th c. devel. of Lithuanian poetry was concluded by Maironis (pseud. of Jonas Mačiulis, 1862–1932), the creative embodiment of the ideals of the national awakening and a foremost lyric poet (see his collection *Pavasario balsai* [Voices of Spring], 1895). His formal and structural innovations, particularly the introduction of syllabotonic versification, exerted great influence on the growth of the new Lithuanian poetry. Two other poets writing in a lyrical mode in some respects similar to that of Maironis were Antanas Vienažindys (1841–92) and Pranas Vaičaitis (1876–1901).

At the beginning of the 20th c., the general relaxation of Rus. political pressure and an ever-growing cultural consciousness increased literary production and widened its horizon. New approaches were inspired by literary movements abroad. Already evident before World War I, these trends were fulfilled during the period of independence (1918–40) when Lithuanian poetry reached high standards of creative art. Symbolism left a strong imprint on the early period, best represented by Balys Sruoga (1896–1947), also an outstanding dramatist; Vincas Mykolaitis-Putinas (1893–1967), later a leading novelist as well; and Jurgis Baltrušaitis (1873–1944) who, after achieving distinction among Rus. symbolists, began to publish verse in his native Lithuanian. In the 1920s, the more conservative trends were countered by futurist poets who, led by Kazys Binkis (1893–1942), formed the group *Keturi vėjai* (Four Winds). Somewhat later, neoromanticism, neosymbolism, aestheticism, and expressionism appeared on the scene, while the group *Trečias frontas* (Third Front) advocated poetry with a leftist orientation.

These trends were transcended, however, by the achievement of the four leading poets of the second generation: Jonas Aistis (1904–73), a highly intimate poet and a master of subtle and refined expression; Bernardas Brazdžionis (1907–2002), whose poetry, sometimes stylistically innovative, sometimes rhetorical with prophetic overtones, is a synthesis of national trads.; Antanas Miškinis (1905–83); and Salomėja Nėris (pseud. of S. Bačinskaitė-Bučienė, 1904–45), both of whom transformed the best qualities of the dainos into their own personal expression. The traditional features leading to the poetry of the next generation were best reflected in the verse of Vytautas Mačernis (1920–44).

The annexation of the country by the USSR during World War II broke the natural flow of Lithuanian poetry by imposing the paralyzing specter of socialist realism; poets exiled in the West learned to use modes of Western culture to speak, above all, of the pain and virtues of exile. While some poets became eulogists of the Soviet system in Lithuania and others retreated into long silence, new authors came forth to claim the favors of the Muses. Eduardas Mieželaitis (1919–97), paradoxically a loyal communist of philosophical bent, did much to help Soviet Lithuanian poetry break through to a more mod. idiom. Justinas Marcinkevičius (1930–2011), also important as a playwright, was perhaps the most popular poet of that period, speaking with great devotion of love for his country and people. Judita Vaičiūnaitė (1937–2001) sings of love in an intimate urban setting and of myth in dreams of the past. Sigitas Geda (1943–2008) transforms both nature and myth into a single magical presence, his vision of the country and its soul. Marcelijus Martinaitis (1936–2013) mostly converses with his own and the nation's conscience about hist., myth, and the responsibility of being human. Janina Degutytė (1928–90) is an intensely personal, lyrical poet of great integrity and noble dedication to humanity.

The culturally saturated poetry of the dissident poet Tomas Venclova (b. 1937) is committed to philosophical meditations. His poetic lang. may appear direct and simple at times. It contains, though, many implicit intertextual associations with the body of world lit., political views on the life of the Soviet dictatorship, and personal experience of an emotional or intellectual nature. The bleak landscape of Europe's moribund postwar culture shaped Venclova's imagination; he began his career under Soviet occupation and was immediately confronted with its realities and art. In exile, he became the most widely known Lithuanian poet and critic, whose works and critiques of society and culture in the Eastern Bloc hold a longstanding association with the works of Czesław Miłosz and Joseph Brodsky.

A number of prominent poets belong to the second generation of writers who debuted in the 1970s. With their avant-garde orientation, they attempted to broaden literary horizons during the Soviet occupation and looked for ways of self-expression. For Nijolė Miliauskaitė (1950–2002), wife of the outstanding poet Vytautas Bložė (b. 1930), everyday reality itself is a highly poetic and leads to the revelation of metaphysical mystery. Rich in cultural allusions and inventive use of myth, the poetry of Kornelijus Platelis (b. 1951) is a medium for harmony. The meditative and compressed thoughtfulness of Donaldas Kajokas (b. 1953) evokes Eastern poetic trads. through pursuit of an ideal nirvana. Antanas A. Jonynas's (b. 1953) melodious poetry spans a range of emotions, from sentimentality to anxiety to irony.

The generation of poets who matured during the years of independence share a postmod. worldview. Their rebellious despair and psychological distress are conveyed through polemics with traditional values, an ironic voice, and surrealistic images. Aidas Marčėnas (b. 1960) is a master of classic form, whose writings combine contexts of various cultures and lits., poetic visions and dreams that are surrealistically fused with a present reality. Related to the Eur. trad., the aesthetic works of Kęstutis Navakas (b. 1964) can best be described as a play of various combinations of time and space in search of lost time. Sigitas Parulskis's (b. 1965) attachment to the painful existential experiences during the Soviet regime is evident in his poetry.

In the West, the foremost poet was Henrikas Radauskas (1910–70). He spoke in lucid, calmly measured cl. verse of the beauty of the world seen as a carnival of love and death. His loyalty, however, is not with that world but with enchanting mysteries of poetic speech that it engenders. Kazys Bradūnas (1917–2009) looks inward and into the past to awaken the ancient spirits of his native land and engage them in an ongoing dialogue with Christianity and hist. in Lithuania. Jonas Mekas (b. 1922), one of the moving spirits of the "underground cinema" in New York, also writes nostalgic and pensive verse full of self-questioning and yearning for the truthful life. Algimantas Mackus (1932–64) found his own truth in a radical confrontation with the fact of exile that required him to transform all the images of hope and faith from the traditional cultural heritage into grim totems of death. Liūnė Sutema (pseud. of Zinaida Katiliškienė, 1927–2013) chooses the opposite task of allowing the alien world to grow into the very tissue of her soul to rejuvenate both her and the land of remembrance she carries within. Her brother Henrikas Nagys (1920–96) embraces both emotional expressionism and neoromanticism. Alfonsas Nyka-Niliūnas (pseud. of Alfonsas Čipkus, 1919–2015), a cosmopolitan existentialist of a deeply philosophical bent, contemplates the large and bleak presence of the cosmos through the window of Western civilization.

■ **Anthologies**: *The Daina*, ed. U. Katzenelenbogen (1935); *Aus litauischer Dichtung*, ed. and trans. H. Engert, 2d ed. (1938); *Litauischer Liederschrein*, ed. and trans. V. Jungfer (1948); *The Green Oak*, ed. A. Landsbergis and C. Mills (1962); *Lithuanian Writers in the West*, ed. A. Skrupskelis (1979); *Selected Post-war Poetry*, trans. J. Zdanys (1979); *Sigitas Geda: Songs of Autumn*, trans. J. Zdanys (1979); *The Amber Lyre: 18th–20th Century Lithuanian Poetry*, ed. J. Marcinkevičius and V. Kubilius (1983); *Four Poets of Lithuania: Vytautas P. Bložė, Sigitas Geda, Nijolė Miliauskaitė, Kornelijus Platelis*, trans. J. Zdanys (1995); *Lithuania: In Her Own Words*, ed. L. Sruoginis (1997); *Breathing Free/Gyvas atodūsis*, trans. V. Bakaitis (2001); *Voices of Lithuanian Poetry*, trans. L. Pažūsis (2001); *Five Lithuanian Women Poets*, trans. J. Zdanys (2002); *Inclusions in Time: Selected Poems by Antanas A. Jonynas*, trans. J. Zdanys (2002); *Raw Amber: An Anthology of Contemporary Lithuanian Poetry*, ed. and trans. L. Sruoginis (2002).

■ **Criticism and History**: B. Sruoga, "Lithuanian Folksongs," *Folk-Lore* 43 (1932); J. Mauclere, *Panorama de la littérature lithuanienne contemporaine* (1938); J. Balys, *Lithuanian Narrative Folksongs* (1954); A. Senn, "Storia della letterature lituana," *Storia della letterature baltiche*, ed. G. Devoto (1957); A. Rubulis, *Baltic Literature* (1970); R. Šilbajoris, *Perfection of Exile* (1970); *Baltic Drama*, ed. A. Straumanis (1981); *Lithuanian Literature*, ed. V. Kubilius (1997); T. Venclova, *Forms of Hope: Essays* (1999); *Lietuvių literatūros enciklopedija* (2001); R. Šilbajoris, *A Short History of Lithuanian Literature* (2002); *Naujausioji lietuvių literatūra*, ed. G. Viliūnas (2003).

R. Šilbajoris; D. Litvinskaitė

LOW COUNTRIES, POETRY OF THE. Dutch, which is today the native lang. of about 23 million people, originated from Germanic dialects in the delta of the Rhine river, a region in western Europe historically named the Low Countries. An uprising against Sp. sovereignty in the late 16th c. led to the independence of the Dutch- and Frisian-speaking northern provinces, which formed a new country called the Netherlands. The Dutch-, Fr.-, and Ger.-speaking southern provinces remained under Sp. rule and, with the exception of the southeastern part that became Fr. territory, they later formed Belgium (in 1830) and Luxembourg (in 1839). The term *Poetry of the Low Countries* refers to poetry written in Dutch, combining Dutch-speaking people both from the Netherlands and from Belgium. The Dutch-speaking part of Belgium is also called Flanders, and its inhabitants are called Flemish. At some points in its hist., lits. from the Netherlands and from Flanders manifest considerable differences, yet they are considered by most scholars as belonging to the same overall ling. and cultural system. Dutch is also one of the langs. in former Dutch colonies; for Surinamese and Antillean poetry in Dutch, see CARIBBEAN, POETRY OF THE. In South Africa, the descendants of Dutch colonists speak Afrikaans, a lang. similar to Dutch. For Afrikaans poetry, see SOUTH AFRICA, POETRY OF.

The oldest example of Dutch poetic production, three verses of love poetry written in the late 11th c. to test out a new quill pen, are the most famous lines in Old Dutch. The doubts about the geographical origin of the poem's author illustrate the difficulty in distinguishing Dutch from other Germanic and Anglo-Saxon dialects in that period.

During the Middle Ages, esp. the southern part of the Low Countries witnessed the successful production of courtly love poetry in the vernacular. In this respect, the lyrics of Hendrik van Veldeke (ca. 1150–1210), a poet who wrote in a lang. still hesitating between Dutch and Ger., remain important. His influence on Ger. poets such as Wolfram von Eschenbach (ca. 1170–1220), Hartmann von Aue (ca. 1170–1210), and Gottfried von Strassburg (ca. 1165–1210) is widely acknowledged. The poems of Veldeke and of Duke Jan I of Brabant (ca. 1253–94) deal with courtly love in a traditional, rather formulaic manner: the beloved woman is idealized yet remains untouchable; hence, the feelings of the lover hover between ecstatic joy and depression. An original religious version of this ideal of courtly love is to be found in the mystical poetry by Hadewych (ca. 1210–60), a female mystic who evoked the adoration of God (whom she addresses as Love) along similar lines. Her *Liederen* (songs) and *Visioenen* (visions) correspond to attempts by the Beguine movement to develop an authentic female expression of divine love. Next to this lyrical poetry—preserved in the Gruuthuse M.—there was also an important trad. of epic stories in verse. Particularly popular among these were the *chansons de geste*, epic poems about heroic knights, such as the anonymous 13th-c. *Karel ende Elegast* (Charlemagne and Elegast) and the satiric beast epic *Vanden Vos Reynaerde* (Reynard the Fox, ca. 1250), an original version of some branches from the Fr. *Roman de Renart* that mocks the courtly trad. Didactic texts were also written in verse form. Works in Lat. that had traditionally been restricted to the religious world were made available to the lay elite because of Jacob van Maerlant (ca. 1230–90), who wrote the *Spiegel historiael* (Mirror of History), a popular rhymed chronicle of world hist. based on Vincent de Beauvais's *Speculum historiale*; and Jan van Boendale (1280–1351), who presented *Der leken spiegel* (The Layman's Mirror), a moralizing encyclopedic work that compiled all knowledge a layman needed for a virtuous life.

The economic prosperity of cities such as Bruges, Ghent, and Ypres led to an increase in self-awareness among the bourgeois elite. These cities used their influence to acquire special rights—"liberties"—from their sovereigns. The Chambers of Rhetoric represent a typical reflection of this urban pride in the 15th-c. Low Countries, mainly in the county of Flanders and duchy of Brabant. These associations of literary amateurs organized all kinds of festivities and had their own poetic contests. By the end of the Middle Ages, poetry was thus no longer written exclusively for and by the nobility but became an integral component of the literary culture in cities and within the social class of citizens. Poetry was sponsored by city authorities as a way to transmit authority, pride, and moral guidance. Popular lyrical forms were the refrain, a strophic poem that ended with an invocation of the Prince; the ballad; the song; and the rondeau. The most important rhetoricians were Anthonis de Roovere (ca. 1430–82), the first official poet of the city of Bruges, and Matthijs de Castelein (1485–1550). The poet Anna Bijns (1493–1575) also wrote in the trad. of the rhetoricians, but her verses were best known for their explicitly Catholic and vehement polemics against rising Lutheranism. Several of these texts were exported in trans. through the city of Antwerp in Brabant, which in the 16th c. became a Eur. center of book printing. The Low Countries were then ruled by the mighty Hapsburg dynasty, which had extended its power from the Ger. empire over southern Italy and Spain to the Sp. colonies in the Americas and Asia. The cosmopolitan spirit of Antwerp is reflected in the *Antwerps liedboek*

(Antwerp Songbook, 1544), a collection of Dutch lyrical texts that includes several adaptations of foreign songs.

By the end of the 16th c., an increasing number of poets became fascinated by the humanist thinking and artistic ideas of the Ren. The lyrical work of Petrarch and the poets of the Fr. Pléiade (Joachim du Bellay, Pierre de Ronsard) became esp. influential and were imitated in various ways, resulting in the successful introduction of the sonnet in Dutch lit. by Lucas d'Heere (1534–84) and most notably by Jan van der Noot (ca. 1539–1600) in his volume *Het bosken* (The Forest, 1570), which combines the established trad. with Petrarchism and Ronsardian motives, making use of alexandrines and iambic pentameter. Of equal importance is Justus de Harduwijn's (1582–1636) later love poetry.

The combination of discontent with the increasingly centralistic policy of Hapsburg Spain that threatened old "liberties" and anger over the persecution of Protestants led to an anti-Sp. uprising in 1566 under the leadership of William of Orange. Thousands of pamphlets, lampoons, and songs functioned as war propaganda. In 1574, an anonymously edited selection of these songs was printed. Its name, *Geuzenliedboek* (Beggar Song Books), is a reference to a disparaging expression used by the Sp. authorities in reference to the Dutch rebels. The collection included the "Wilhelmus," a call of support for William's uprising, a song considered the world's oldest national anthem.

The war against Spain ended in a stalemate. While the northern provinces gained independence in the late 16th c., the southern provinces remained under Sp. authority. As a result, the center of cultural and literary life shifted toward the north. In the 17th c., the so-called Golden Age, the Netherlands displayed enormous wealth, economically as well as culturally. Besides painting, lit. played an essential role in the cultural construction of a national identity. Poets were eager to raise the Dutch lang. to a prestige that could rival cl. Lat.; they celebrated the greatness of the Netherlands and its capital Amsterdam as the new Rome. Pieter Corneliszoon Hooft (1581–1647), who successfully applied the metrical innovations of the Ren. to his own dramas and sonnets, became one of the leading poets of the new country. In his castle Muiderslot, near Amsterdam, Hooft hosted regular meetings of writers, which included the sister poets Maria Tesselschade Visscher (1594–1649) and Anna Visscher (1584–1651). Another prestigious member of the Muider circle was the influential diplomat Constantijn Huygens (1596–1687). From erudite Neo-Lat. poetry and hermetic Dutch sonnets to vulgar farces, Huygens demonstrated remarkable literary mastery.

The relatively tolerant and economically prosperous Netherlands attracted tens of thousands of immigrants from all over Europe, incl. many religious and political refugees from the southern Low Countries, Sephardic Jews from Portugal, Ashkenazi Jews from Germany and eastern Europe, as well as Fr. Huguenots. Joost van de Vondel (1587–1679), a child of immigrants from the southern Low Countries, established himself as one of the greatest writers of his time; he is famous first and foremost for his theatrical works, but some of his poems have become classics as well. Of importance is Vondel's critical involvement with the religious and political intolerance of his time. While Vondel's work often dealt with complex theological issues, the Calvinist moral teachings of Jacob Cats (1577–1660) were intended for the common people. His poems and emblem books became popular in Eng. and Ger. trans. The genre of the profane and religious love emblem, which may be considered a Dutch invention, became famous all over Europe.

With the creation of the East India Company (in 1602) and the West India Company (in 1621), the Netherlands became a major participant in Europe's colonial expansion. Colonial lit. was written mostly in prose, however, and the occasional poems rarely went beyond habitual clichés about the exotic Other. Jacob Steendam (1615–72), a resident in New Netherland, is interesting insofar as he was the first to write poetry about what would later become the United States.

In the southern Low Countries, much didactic religious poetry was produced, mainly in Jesuit circles. The Catholic emblems by the Jesuit Adriaen Poirters (1605–74), who was much influenced by Jacob Cats, gained lasting success.

During the 18th c., the cosmopolitan spirit of the Enlightenment stimulated growing scientific curiosity and the analysis of humans as rational beings. This led to the elaboration of the first Dutch grammars and numerous Dutch literary spectator magazines, which combined an encyclopedic vision on the world with strong moral principles. The philanthropic side of the

Enlightenment was reflected in the educational poetry for children by Hieronymus van Alphen (1746–1803).

In the winter of 1794–95, a Fr. army, aided by a Dutch contingent of pro-Fr. "patriots," conquered the Netherlands. Pasquinades, lampoons, and songs played an important role in popular protest against Fr. rule, which lasted until 1813. In verses full of pathos, poets such as Jan Frederik Helmers (1767–1813) and Hendrik Tollens (1780–1856) expressed a mixture of pessimism about the apathy of the present generation and hope that the fervor of times past might reawaken. The most significant poetic figure in the Netherlands in the early 19th c. was Willem Bilderdijk (1756–1813). Although he continued to use traditional alexandrines, his conviction that it is the poet's task to achieve a personal voice brings him in line with nascent romanticism. Bilderdijk's Christian fervor corresponded to that of Isaac da Costa (1798–1860), a Jewish convert who was involved in *Het Réveil*, a Christian revival movement with significant influence in Dutch cultural and political life. An exceptional voice among the many clerical poets, who tended to give preference to the (Christian) message over aesthetic quality, was François Haverschmidt (1835–94). Under the pseud. Piet Paaltjens, he wrote poems in which irony, sentimentality, and cynicism alternate.

In 1830, Belgium became independent. Most Dutch-speaking writers in Belgium opposed the fact that the young Belgian state promoted its communication almost exclusively in the Fr. lang. Rather than choosing the (predominantly Protestant) Netherlands as a model, these (predominantly Catholic) writers tried to construct an authentic Dutch-speaking identity. Strongly influenced by the romantic tendency to glorify the Middle Ages, they called themselves *Flemish* after the once-powerful med. county. At first, the objectives of the members of this emancipatory Flemish movement were almost exclusively cultural and scientific. Scholars such as Jan Frans Willems (1793–1846) and F. A. Snellaert (1809–72) collected and edited old folk songs, stories, and poetry in Dutch. Complementary to this preoccupation with the past, attempts were undertaken to establish a new, genuine "Flemish literature" within the political context of a bilingual Belgium. This resulted in a large number of poems that were destined for specific occasions: odes, heroic and historical verses, and didactic poems. Yet, in the same period, poets became increasingly aware of their "literary" status, of the fact that lit. could no longer be reduced simply to a ready-made ethical, religious, or political message.

The greatest genius of Flemish poetry in the 19th c. was Guido Gezelle (1830–99), professionally both a Catholic priest and a teacher. His work manifests brilliantly the ongoing process of literary autonomization. On the one hand, Gezelle was preoccupied with the didactic function of his poetry. Numerous poems were written originally for specific religious occasions: baptisms, communions, ordinations, funerals. In this respect, his work can be characterized as ideological, preoccupied with values and norms. Yet, on the other hand, Gezelle explored the possibilities of poetic lang., combining romantic themes such as religious experiences and nature with fascinating formal experiments in rhythm and sound, verse form, even typography. This latter dimension has been decisive in Gezelle's canonization as a major poet, even in modernist and postmodernist circles. However, poets such as Albrecht Rodenbach (1856–80) or Hugo Verriest (1840–1922), who wrote in Gezelle's trad., never managed to achieve similar fame.

Around 1880, a major event in this shift toward autonomous poetry—in contrast to the worn-out idea that lit. is a mere vehicle for the transfer of extraliterary ideas and norms—occurred in the Netherlands with the emergence of the *Beweging van Tachtig* (Movement of the Eighties). A group of young writers incl. Willem Kloos (1859–1938), Albert Verwey (1865–1937), Frederik van Eeden (1860–1932), and Herman Gorter (1864–1927) rebelled against predominantly didactic and edifying lit. Influenced by the work of John Keats and P. B. Shelley, they rejected putting literary work at the service of any ethical, religious, or social ideal. This radical worship of beauty and of subjective experience in lit. was famously summarized by Kloos in his often-quoted adage: "Art is the most individual expression of the most individual emotion." They called their new jour. *De Nieuwe Gids* (The New Guide), copying part of the name of the most prominent literary jour. of their time. This provocation proved to have a prophetic character; in short time, *De Nieuwe Gids* outshone *De Gids* (The Guide) as the guiding voice in the Dutch literary scene.

The cult of individualism and subjectivism and the plea for an autonomous lit. by the Movement of the Eighties influenced younger generations profoundly. Yet the movement's poets themselves soon abandoned their own radical poetics. Van Eeden became a world-reformer à la H. D. Thoreau and established a communal cooperative. Gorter, who had become famous for his impressionist and sensitive verse in the epic *Mei* (May, 1889) and in his *Liedjes* (Songs), distanced himself from the "bourgeois individualism" of the movement. His later work reveals the influence of the philosopher Baruch Spinoza and the political ideas of Karl Marx. In his poems as well as in his essays, he started to glorify socialism. In this respect, he found a prominent supporter in the socialist poet Henriëtte Roland Holst (1869–1952).

Verwey founded a new jour. in 1905, *De Beweging* (The Movement, 1905–19). Influenced by the Ger. poet Stefan George and by Dutch symbolist painters such as Jan Toorop and Floris Verster, Verwey focused on the deepening of sensual experiences and spontaneous feelings in order to combine life and art. These ideas became prominent in the transformation of impressionist into symbolist poetry. Verwey influenced many poets of a younger generation, incl. P. C. Boutens (1870–1943), Adriaan Roland Holst (1888–1976), J. H. Leopold (1865–1925), and J. C. Bloem (1887–1966), who shared a sense of unfulfilled desire. Their poetry was characterized by an archaic lang., elaborate structure, and solemn tone. Although rooted in neoclassical trads, the emotional basis of their work was more romantic, and the influence of Charles Baudelaire is undeniable. The poetry of Leopold and Bloem is intimate, transforming sensory impressions into general emotions or a sudden revelation of harmony. Holst, on the other hand, sought his inspiration in Gr. and Celtic mythology (notably in the work of W. B. Yeats). The main representative of symbolism in Flanders was Karel van de Woestijne (1878–1928). He started out with hypersensitive and individualist texts, in which meticulous self-analysis was formulated in periodic sentences, using many stylistic devices and ingenious symbolism. In his later work, the style is more sober and the themes are more universal: the "lyric I" considers itself a *Modderen man* (Muddy Man, 1920), a creature torn desperately between the sensuous earth and transcendental spirituality.

At the beginning of the 20th c., this long-established trad. of cl. poetry and poetics was fundamentally threatened by the sudden appearance of avant-garde lit. Although traces of futurism and Dadaism may be found occasionally, expressionism constituted the most important source of innovation. In Flanders, a group of young poets, published in the periodical *Ruimte* (Space, 1920–21), opted resolutely for free verse and nonliterary diction. Thematically, they incorporated explicit elements from mod. times, while advocating a general utopian solidarity among all humans. This strongly ethical "humanitarian expressionism" was put into practice by poets such as Wies Moens (1898–1982) and Marnix Gijsen (1899–1984) and for some time by Paul van Ostaijen (1896–1928), a major writer in Dutch lit. In *Het Sienjaal* (The Signal, 1918), van Ostaijen advocated a quasi-Franciscan idea of personal suffering and a social utopia in which the artist functioned as a major prophet of the ideal future. However, during World War I, he moved to Berlin and wrote *Bezette Stad* (Occupied City, 1921), which testifies to a resolutely Dadaistic and nihilistic stance. This chaotic experience of world and humankind was reflected in a fragmented style, reinforced by avant-garde typography. In his final years, van Ostaijen dismissed this "typographical expressionism" and began to write depersonalized, almost mystical verse, which demonstrated a strong musical and rhythmic awareness. This evolution toward pure poetry or "organic expressionism," which he articulated in a number of theoretical and critical essays, was imitated by numerous younger writers, of whom Gaston Burssens (1896–1965) became van Ostaijen's main follower.

In the Netherlands, the leading Dutch poet in the 1920s was Hendrik Marsman (1899–1940), who was also thoroughly influenced by Ger. expressionism and the ideas of Friedrich Nietzsche. Marsman saw instinctive vitality, the unlimited celebration of life, as the best possible answer to desperation and degeneration. To evoke this new limitless subjectivity, he used hyperbolic lang. and cosmic imagery. However, this vital creativity concealed a strong fear of death or even a longing for destruction and an explicit death wish. In his later poetry, Marsman tried to expand this perspective of humankind into a vision of culture and the need to reconquer a natural paradise. With its prophetic message of a "vitalistic turn" and its desire for a compelling life, Marsman's *Verzen* (Verses, 1923) had an enormous impact on the younger generation.

Next to these avant-garde tendencies, however, cl. poetry remained a prominent trad. in Dutch poetry. Among the numerous adherents of this poetics, some authors gained lasting significance with their oeuvre. Richard Minne (1891–1965) opted for the observation of daily life in an ironic tone, Simon Vestdijk (1898–1971) for an elevated lang. and the principles of an established poetic trad. Gerrit Achterberg (1905–62) achieved an almost mythical status with his passionate neoromantic poems about the search for the deceased beloved and the perfect poem; his integration of nonliterary elements, from journalism as well as from various sciences, became exemplary for a new lang. of lit., in which precision prevailed over aesthetic principles. The most influential figure in this respect is Martinus Nijhoff (1894–1953). His combination of trad. with elements from modernism reinforced the idea of common speech as a genuine lang. of poetry. The influence of T. S. Eliot is crucial for Nijhoff's view of poetry, as expressed in his essays and literary reviews. Nijhoff opted for a poetry in which contemp. reality was integrated as a topic. Yet he also made abundant use of mythology and symbols from cl. lit. His epic poem *Awater* (1934) illustrates the changing literary climate due to growing political tensions in the 1930s; he refuses to continue a certain type of poetry, in which, despite "seeing the ruins," poets would still "sing about the nice weather." Whether the dream of a new human in a new society will eventually be realized remains doubtful. His modernist belief in lit. as the last resource in a decaying world has often been discussed by later Dutch poets.

During World War II, literary life became much more difficult, esp. in the Netherlands where the Ger. occupiers installed a so-called Chamber of Culture in order to push along the Nazification of Dutch lit. As a result, most writers took their work to clandestine publications. Anthols. of resistance poetry, incl. the famous *De achttien dooden* (The Eighteen Dead, 1941) by Jan Campert (1902–43), were called *Geuzenliedboeken* (Beggar Song Books) in remembrance of the rebellious 16th-c. poetry during the war against Spain. Several authors—among them Marsman and Campert—died as a result of the war, while others emigrated.

After World War II, many poets considered the restoration and a revival of the literary trad. the best way to overcome the all-encompassing political, ideological, and cultural crisis in society. Hence, they continued to write neoclassicist verses, in which formal virtuosity and the personal expression of the inner self, combined with the sensory experience of the outer world and the use of symbols, still dominated. Within this traditional poetics, many writers managed to combine public success with lasting literary prestige: Maria Vasalis (1909–98), Ida Gerhardt (1905–97), Bertus Aafjes (1914–93), Ed. Hoornik (1910–70), Jan Greshoff (1888–1971), Karel Jonckheere (1906–93), Maurice Gilliams (1900–82), Hubert van Herreweghen (b. 1920), Anton van Wilderode (1918–98), and Christine D'haen (1923–2009).

In the 1950s, however, Dutch poetry was invaded by a movement of "experimental" poetry that in an aesthetic way anticipated the profound social and political changes that would disrupt Dutch society a decade later. A group of young poets, called the *Vijftigers* (Movement of the Fifties), engaged in vehement polemics with the neoclassicist tendency to ignore traumatic historical events. Instead, they sought their inspiration in surrealism and, above all, in the view of artistic materiality propounded by painters such as Karel Appel, Pierre Alechinsky, and Christian Dotremont linked to the CoBrA Movement. They propagated an "experimental" and "corporeal" poetics, stressing irrationality and imagery instead of rational thought, pregiven schemata and forms. They abandoned elevated literary lang. and wanted to provoke and to challenge readers, rather than providing them with familiar themes and anecdotes.

The views of the Movement of the Fifties were formulated in a number of small periodicals such as *Reflex*, *Braak*, and *Blurb*. Later, *Podium* and its Flemish counterpart *Tijd en Mens* (Time and Man, 1949–55) were particularly influential in promoting experimental poetry. The first generation of experimental poets included Hans Lodeizen (1924–50), Bert Schierbeek (1918–96), Jan Elburg (1919–92), Simon Vinkenoog (1928–2009), Leo Vroman (1915–2014)—who emigrated to the United States and became an Am. citizen—and Remco Campert (b. 1929). They were later joined by H. C. Pernath (1931–75), Paul Snoek (1933–81), and Gust Gils (1924–2002).

The main representatives of the Movement of the Fifties were Lucebert (pseud. of L. J. Swaanswijk, 1924–94), Gerrit Kouwenaar (1923–2014), and Hugo Claus (1929–2008), who dominated Dutch poetry for several decades. Lucebert wrote rhetorical and associative poetry, using abundant imagery. His ambition was to express "the space of the entire life" in his own words. However, since human beings and the world are by no means one-dimensional entities, ambiguity and paradoxes abound in Lucebert's poetry. His work is theatrical, often inspired by his own drawings. In this respect, Lucebert may be regarded as the most radical representative of the Movement of the Fifties. In contrast, Kouwenaar transformed the poem into a "thing" of its own. To this end, the personal tone of the poet disappears in favor of a more abstract and general diction, thus creating an autonomous ling. construct. Gradually, Kouwenaar's hermetic lyrical work opened up to anecdotal and more subjective elements, resulting in a more comprehensible poetry. Claus depicts in his famous volume *De Oostakkerse gedichten* (The Oostakker Poems, 1955) a "vitalistic" world dominated by the senses and by instinctive erotic passion. However, since this primitive ideal is constantly threatened by the consciousness of the human being, Claus's later poetry integrated hist., society, and culture. Although the struggle between historical awareness and the desire for an unconscious life remains central, his later poems are characterized by the many references to Gr. mythology, the Bible, and J. G. Frazer's anthropological collection *The Golden Bough* (1890).

In the 1960s, a younger generation criticized experimental poetry for its excessively esoteric lang. and its contempt for the reading public. Instead, these writers advocated a "new realist" poetics, which took its inspiration from Beat poets and pop art and which promoted a democratic art aimed at broad audience and explicitly related to daily life. Periodicals such as *Barbarber* and *De Nieuwe Stijl* (The New Style, a polemical reference to the modernist *The Style*) advocated this new realist view by introducing the idea of ready-mades: existing texts that were isolated and transformed into poetry. *Barbarber*-poets such as J. Bernlef (1937–2012) and K. Schippers (b. 1936) displayed a relativistic tone and humor in poetry that was influenced by Am. modernist poets such as e.e. cummings and Marianne Moore. New Style poets such as Armando (pseud. of H. D. van Dodeweerd, b. 1929), on the other hand, were more aggressive; they selected material about controversial themes such as sex and violence and banned any subjective interpretation. In Flanders, the poet's subjective view remained decisive in poetic diction. Whereas Roland Jooris (b. 1936) moved toward a more abstract lang., the bestselling Herman de Coninck (1944–97) adopted a melancholic tone. Myriam Van hee (b. 1952) and Luuk Gruwez (b. 1953) became known as "neoromantic" poets because of their personal and emotional involvement. Other prominent poets combine romantic motives with a profound self-analysis: Kees Ouwens (1944–2004) and Leonard Nolens (b. 1947) in a serious manner, Gerrit Komrij (1944–2012) more ironically and theatrically.

Generally speaking, Dutch poetry was dominated by two opposite trends in the 1970s. On the one hand, a number of writers opted for an autonomous, lang.-oriented poetry, taking Kouwenaar as a major example. This focus on the creative power of lang. characterized the work of Hans Faverey (1933–90) and the poets around the literary magazine *Raster*. On the other hand, many poets wrote anecdotal poems in an accessible *parlando* style. Famous representatives are Rutger Kopland (1934–2012), who later turned toward a more suggestive and abstract poetry; Jan Eijkelboom (1926–2008), Ed Leeflang (1929–2008), Judith Herzberg (b. 1934), and Eva Gerlach (b. 1948).

From the 1980s onward, Dutch poetry has been dominated by postmodernism. Two orientations of postmod. poetry may be distinguished. Most poets opt for a rather intuitive, playful, and ironic variant of postmodernism. They articulate the problematic status of lang., world, and subject. Instead of merely expressing a fixed personality, the poet stages the "lyric I," often in a theatrical tone. The borders between high and popular culture are breached, and the fetishes of hectic mod. life become an intriguing theme. This view of lit. was promoted by a group of Dutch artists who called themselves the *Maximalen* (Maximals) as a critique of minimalism. Although the Maximal group as such lasted only for a short period, its main representatives established a major trend in contemp. Dutch poetry. Joost Zwagerman (1963–2015) may be considered a spokesman of this generation: next to his numerous essays and novels, he wrote poems that display an eagerness to show reality in a colorful and exuberant manner. The same can be said about Tom Lanoye (b. 1958), who is also praised for his novels and plays. Pieter Boskma (b. 1956) and K. Michel (pseud. of Michael Kuijpers, b. 1958) have gradually evolved toward a more abstract and philosophical poetry. A similar abundance of images dominates the poetry of Ilja Leonard Pfeijffer (b. 1968).

Next to this popular branch of postmodernism, other poets explore postmodernism more theoretically. Taking their inspiration from Jacques Derrida, Jacques Lacan, Slavoj Žižek,

J.-F. Lyotard, and Paul de Man, they deconstruct the ultimate belief in lang. as an effective means of communication and a way to gain insight into the world and humanity. Instead, they propagate rupture and discontinuity, fragmentation and polyphony. Intertextuality is used to dispel the illusion of coherence and a fixed meaning. Huub Beurskens (b. 1950), Marc Reugebrink (b. 1960), Dirk van Bastelaere (b. 1960), Erik Spinoy (b. 1960), Peter Verhelst (b. 1962), and Stefan Hertmans (b. 1951) are marked by the heritage of modernism. This is less the case for Arjan Duinker (b. 1956), Tonnus Oosterhoff (b. 1953), Nachoem M. Wijnberg (b. 1961), Peter Holvoet-Hanssen (b. 1960), and Jan Lauwereyns (b. 1969), who developed their own poetics, regardless of complex theoretical discussions. Postmodern influences can also be found in the eclectic poetry of H. H. ter Balkt (1938–2015) and Jacques Hamelink (b. 1939), who rewrite Dutch hist. in poetic cantos.

In the early 21st c., Dutch poetry witnessed a boom of performance poetry. Performing poets like Jules Deelder (b. 1944) and Bart Chabot (b. 1954), together with the 1960s legend Johnny van Doorn (1944–91), nicknamed the Selfkicker, influenced the slam poetry of the youngest generation around Erik Jan Harmens (b. 1970), Ingmar Heytze (b. 1970), and Tjitske Jansen (b. 1971). Phenomena like the City Poet and the Poet of the Fatherland—the Dutch variant of the poet laureate—proved to be successful strategies to reach a broad audience.

The growing importance of the work of first- or second-generation immigrants and colonial repatriates—such as the Dutch-Indonesian Marion Bloem (b. 1952), the Dutch-Surinamese Edgar Cairo (1948–2000) and Astrid Roemer (b. 1947), the Dutch-Antillean Alfred Schaffer (b. 1973), the Dutch-Moroccan Mustafa Stitou (b. 1974), the Dutch-Iraqi Al Galidi (b. 1971), and most notably the Dutch-Palestinian poet Ramsey Nasr (b. 1974)—reflects the steady transformation of the Netherlands and Flanders into multicultural societies.

See BELGIUM, POETRY OF; FRANCE, POETRY OF; FRISIAN POETRY; GERMAN POETRY; INDONESIAN POETRY.

■ **Anthologies**: *Harvest of the Lowlands*, ed. J. Greshoff (1945); *Medieval Netherlands Religious Literature*, ed. E. Colledge (1965); *Reynard the Fox and Other Medieval Netherlands Secular Literature* ed. E. Colledge, trans. A. J. Barnouw (1967); *Living Spaces: Poems of the Dutch Fiftiers*, ed. P. Glassgold (1979); *Light of the World: An Anthology of Seventeenth-Century Dutch Religious and Occasional Poetry*, ed. C. Levenson (1982); *Fugitive Dreams: An Anthology of Dutch Colonial Literature*, ed. E. M. Beekman (1988); *Dutch Poetry in Translation: Kaleidoscope from Medieval Times to the Present*, ed. M. Zwart (1989); *From the Low Countries: Poetry from The Netherlands, Belgium, and Luxembourg*, ed. B. R. Strahan and S. G. Sullivan (1990); *Contemporary Poetry of the Low Countries*, ed. H. Brems and A. Zuiderent (1995); *Dutch and Flemish Feminist Poetry from the Middle Ages to the Present*, ed. M. Meijer (1998); *Modern Poetry in Translation 12: Dutch and Flemish*, ed. T. Hermans (1998); *In a Different Light*, ed. P. C. Evans and L. Haft (2002); *Landscape with Rowers*, ed. J. M. Coetzee (2005).

■ **Criticism and History**: T. Weevers, *Poetry of the Netherlands in its European Context* (1960); J. Snapper, *Post-War Dutch Literature* (1972); R. P. Meijer, *Literature of the Low Countries* (1978); R. Nieuwenhuys, *Mirror of the Indies: A History of Dutch Colonial Literature*, trans. F. van Rosevelt (1982); S. Schama, *The Embarrassment of Riches: An Interpretation of Dutch Culture in the Golden Age* (1987); M. A. Schenkeveld-van der Dussen, *Dutch Literature in the Age of Rembrandt* (1991); F. P. van Oostrom, *Court and Culture: Dutch Literature 1350–1450*, trans. A. J. Pomerans (1992); *Medieval Dutch Literature in Its European Context*, ed. E. Kooper (1994); M. Spies, *Rhetoric, Rhetoricians and Poets: Studies in Renaissance Poetry and Poetics* (1999); *A Literary History of the Low Countries*, ed. T. Hermans (2009); J. Dewulf, *Spirit of Resistance: Dutch Clandestine Literature during the Nazi Occupation* (2010).

D. De Geest; J. Dewulf

M

MACEDONIAN POETRY. The hist. of poetry in what is now the Republic of Macedonia includes poetry composed in the Macedonian lang. and poetic trads. of other ling. groups. The focus here will be on poetry in Macedonian, with reference to other trads.

Macedonian poetry emerges from a rich heritage of folk song and folklore; the word *pesna* means both "poem" and "song." But the written trad. remained intermittent before the codification of standard Macedonian in 1945. Years of Turkish domination, followed by regional unrest and the partition of Macedonian territory in 1913, delayed the devel. of Macedonian as a literary lang. Publication in Macedonian was restricted or banned, and the lang. was dismissed as a dialect.

The lyric poem *T'ga za jug* (Longing for the South) by Konstantin Miladinov (1830–62), written in dialect and exploiting folk motifs, is recognized as foundational to mod. Macedonian poetry. Its impact is celebrated by its annual recitation at the opening of the acclaimed international festival, Struga Poetry Evenings.

The next major figure was Koĉo Racin (1908–43). Considered the father of mod. Macedonian poetry, Racin expanded his ling. resources by creating a supradialect; his cycle of poems *Beli mugri* (White Dawns), written in this medium, explores the fate of impoverished Macedonians. Other poets who published in Macedonian during this period include Venko Markovski (1915–88) and Kole Nedelkovski (1912–41). Macedonia's archives contain much poetry written in Macedonian during the interwar years by writers who were unable to publish their work.

The immediate postwar period saw three outstanding writers—Blaže Koneski (1921–93), Aco Šopov (1923–83), and Slavko Janevski (1920–2000)—shape the emerging lit. of standard Macedonian. These central figures enriched the formal and generic variety of Macedonian poetry, as they ranged from the socialist realism of Koneski's lyric poetry cycle *Mostot* (The Bridge) to folkloric ballads, narrative poems, sonnets, and intimate lyrics.

The so-called second-generation poets, incl. Gane Todorovski (1929–2010) and Mateja Matevski (b. 1929), wrote lyrics rich in metaphor and imagery. This group, together with younger contemporaries like Radovan Pavlovski (b. 1937), Ante Popovski (1931–2003), Vlada Urošević (b. 1934), and the internationally recognized Bogomil Gjuzel (b. 1939), devised new modes of expression enriched by contact with other poetic trads., notably Eur. modernism.

The era of postmodernism brought increased access to international currents. Katica Kulavkova (b. 1951) has written intimate and erotic poems pervaded by allusions to folklore, lit., and hist. Lidija Dimkovska (b. 1971) represents a new urbanism, employing lyric, narrative, and prose poetry to explore themes of science, technology, and cultural displacement. The haiku and *haibun* of Nikola Madzirov (b. 1972) and Vladimir Martinovski (b. 1974) have further expanded Macedonian poetry's formal repertoire.

Macedonia's multicultural, multiethnic society has produced acclaimed writers in Albanian, such as Salajdin Salihu (b. 1970) and Lindita Ahmeti (b. 1973); and Turkish, such as Ilhami Emin (b. 1931), Fahri Ali (b. 1948), and Meral Kain (b. 1976). Poetry in Romani and Aromanian is also published in Macedonia.

As this brief survey shows, Macedonian poets have participated in a wide array of literary movements, incl. symbolism, modernism, and postmodernism. They have experimented with lang., refashioned conventional forms, and fused their rich religious and folkloric past with a variety of mod. and transnational themes.

■ **Anthologies**: *Reading the Ashes: An Anthology of the Poetry of Modern Macedonia*, ed. M. Holton and G. W. Reid (1977); *Longing for the South/Contemporary Macedonian Poetry*, ed. S. Mahapatra and J. T. Boškovski (1981); *Contemporary Macedonian Poetry*, ed. E. Osers (1991); *The Song beyond Songs: Anthology of Contemporary Macedonian Poetry*, ed. V. Andonovski (1997); *The End of the Century: Macedonian Poetry in the Last Decade of the Twentieth Century*, ed. D. Kocevski (1999); *An Island on Land: Anthology of Contemporary Macedonian Poetry*, ed. I. Čašule and T. Shapcott (1999); *20. mladi.m@k.poeti.00*, ed. L. Dimkovska (2000); *Unidentified Celestial Bosom: Anthology of Young Macedonian Poets*, ed. T. Eternijan-Jovica and

Z. Ancevski (2001); *Makedonskata poezija vo svetot*, ed. V. Smilevski (2002); *Tisinata megu dva zbora: ars poetica: tematski izbor od sovremenata makedonska poezija,* ed. K. Nikolovska and D. Ahmeti (2005); *Ut pictura poesis: poezijata vo dijalog so likovnite umetnosti*, ed. V. Martinovski, N. Vinca, and D. Ahmeti (2006); *New European Poets,* ed. W. Miller and K. Prufer (2008).

■ **Criticism and History**: B. Mikasinovich, D. Milivojević, M. Dragan, *Introduction to Yugoslav Literature* (1973); *Dictionary of Literary Biography*, v. 181: *South Slavic Writers since World War II*, ed. V. D. Mihailovich (1984); M. Szporer, "Postmodernist Yugoslav Poetry in Macedonia," *World Literature Today* 62 (1988); M. Drugovac, *Istorija na makedonskata književnost XX vek* (1990); *Pregled na ponovata makedonska poezija*, ed. T. Jovčevski (1996); *Orpheus and Jesus: An Overview of Biblical Motifs in Contemporary Macedonian Poetry*, ed. A. Popovski (2000); J. Koteska, *Makedonsko žensko pismo: teorija, istorija i opis* (2002); E. Šeleva, *Otvoreno pismo studii za makedonskata literatura i kultura* (2003); M. Gjurĉinov, *Nova makedonska književnost: 1945–1980* (2008); G. Stardelov, *Osnovopoložnici na sovrementa makedonska poezija: Kočo Racin, Kole Nedelkovski, Venko Markovski, Slavko Janevski, Blaže Koneski, Aco Šopov, Gogo Ivanovski*, ed. G. Stardelov (2008).

C. Kramer

MAGYAR POETRY. *See* HUNGARY, POETRY OF

MALAYALAM POETRY. It is very difficult to date the earliest Malayalam poetry with precision, since there is vast disagreement among scholars on when and how to distinguish Malayalam as a separate ling. entity, different from early Tamil or emerging from a common Proto-South-Dravidian root lang. There seems to have been a variety of coexisting local langs. in the region of today's Kerala, southwestern India, all loosely labeled as *bhāṣa* (Sanskrit, "language"). Early Malayalam has also occasionally been incorrectly subsumed under the category of Tamil (sometimes being called *Kerala Tamil*), the lang. of the larger, culturally dominant neighboring state of Tamil Nadu. The complex mod. Malayalam script developed from *Vaṭṭeḻuttŭ* (round script), a descendant of the *Brahmī* script, but has incorporated *Grantha* script elements to render non-Dravidian, Sanskritic lexicon and morphology. This fusion of Tamil and Sanskritic elements is characteristic of both the ling. and literary devel. of what is today called *Malayalam*. Almost the entire extant corpus of premod. Malayalam lit., i.e., the works composed between the 12th and 18th cs., is poetry, but the categorization of these works according to genres, schools, or literary trads. is still very much contested.

The 14th-c. Sanskrit grammatical treatise *Līlātilakam* distinguishes between various forms of regional langs.: the local bhāṣa; then *maṇipravāḷam*, which mixes bhāṣa with either Tamil or Sanskrit lexical and morphological elements, creating a blend of the two; and finally *pāṭṭŭ*, which does not conform to the Sanskritized style of maṇipravāḷam but seems rather influenced by Dravidian style and meter. Many Malayalam scholars have subsequently read maṇipravāḷam and pāṭṭŭ as a dichotomy of genres or schools, i.e., a more Sanskritized, possibly Brahminical fusion form of bhāṣa vs. a more Dravidian, Tamilized, non-Brahminical, and possibly lower-caste folk style (*nāṭan pāṭṭŭ*). However, it is not possible to distinguish clearly the existing works into either one of these categories. From a mod. critical viewpoint, the two categories of maṇipravāḷam and pāṭṭŭ might stand for a genre as much as for a distinct ling. devel., since they are both lexically and metrically different. The generic difference is important insofar as premod. Malayalam texts, esp. pāṭṭŭ, are deeply tied to various performance trads., as Freeman argues, thus participating in a different kind of literary culture from, e.g., print poetry.

The earliest maṇipravāḷam works known today are *Vaiśikatantram*, *Uṇṇiyaccīcaritam*, *Uṇṇiccirutēvīcaritam* (all ca. 13th c.), and *Uṇṇiyāṭicaritam* (ca. 14th c.). These works are mainly concerned with courtesan culture, prostitution, the beauty of female physicality, and sexuality. The three latter works belong to the literary genre of *campu*, which blends poetry and prose. Another work named *Anantapuravarṇṇanam* (ca. 14th c.) describes the Viṣṇu temple in what is today the state capital of Thiruvananthapuram. *Candrōtsavam* (ca. 15th c.) is a love poem worshipping the moonlight in a female form. *Sandēśa kāvyas* (messenger poems), transmitting a message of love and inspired by the Sanskrit poet Kālidāsa's *Meghadūta*, were also produced during this period; some of the surviving poems are *Śukasandēśa, Uṇṇunīlisandēśam*, and *Kōkasandēśam* (all ca. 13th–15th c.). Prominent examples of pāṭṭŭ are the *Rāmacaritam*, a ca.

12th-c. rendition of the Sanskrit epic *Rāmāyaṇa*, and the *Tiruniḻalmāla* (rediscovered only in 1980), which describes the social life of a temple using Dravidian meter and orthography.

A later phase in the Malayalam pāṭṭŭ trad. (14th–15th cs.) has been strongly shaped by the three so-called *Niraṇam* poets whose work is referred to as *Kaṇṇaśśan pāṭṭukaḷ* (Kanassan poetry). A blend of Sanskrit and Dravidian meters, scripts, and lexicons is characteristic of their work. Ceṟuśśēri's *Kṛṣṇagātha* (ca. 15th c.) is a well-known example of pāṭṭŭ that has found its way into mod. culture by being sung as a lullaby. The 16th-c. poet Eḻuttacchan is often referred to as the founding father of mod. Malayalam. His major works include retellings of the great Sanskrit epics *Rāmāyaṇa* and *Mahābhārata* (*Adhyātma Rāmāyaṇam, Śrīmahābhāratam*) in a lang. that combines characteristics of pāṭṭŭ, maṇipravāḷam, and folk lang. The Malayalam generic term for these stories told by a parrot narrator is *kiḷippāṭṭŭ* (parrot poem). It has found many subsequent imitators.

The interwoven relations between literary and performance art in Kerala are reflected in the devel. of *āṭṭakkatha* (dance story), a type of script for the dance drama *kathakaḷi*. Between the 17th and 18th cs., we find numerous āṭṭakkatha poems, some written by local rulers such as Kōṭṭayam Tamburān (ca. 17th c.), which were enacted in courts and temples. Thematically, they are often renditions of Sanskrit mythological stories (the well-known *Naḷacaritam* by Uṇṇāyivāryar, *Kalyāṇasaugandhikam*, and *Gītagōvindam*). Another 18th-c. example of the performance of lit. is the *Kucēlavṛttam* by Rāmapurattŭ Vāryar, a song to be recited on a boat and written in the *Vañcippāṭṭŭ* (boat song) meter. *Tuḷḷalpāṭṭŭ*, most prominently advanced by Kuñcan Nambiyār in the 18th c., is another poetic type of dance performance that still prevails in contemp. Kerala.

During the course of the 19th c., the lang. gradually developed toward what is mod. Malayalam today. The so-called Kēraḷa Varmma and Veṇmaṇi schools of poetry were characterized by their usage of more Malayalam words as opposed to Sanskrit loans. The *pacca malayāḷam* (pure Malayalam) movement attempted to reform the lang. by avoiding Sanskrit words but did not gain wider acceptance. The 19th c. witnessed a large number of trans. from Sanskrit, Eng., and other langs. into what is now "Malayalam." Koṭuṅṅallūr Kuññikkuṭṭan Tamburān's *Mahābhāratam* dates from this period. The early 20th c. saw a new rise of *mahākāvya* (epic poems), again following Sanskrit models, as well as devotional *Bhakti* poetry with a new take on mythological subjects. The most famous modernists and poetic innovators were Uḷḷūr S. Paramēśvarayyar (1877–1949), Vaḷḷattōḷ Nārāyaṇa Mēnōn (1878–1958), and Kumāran Āśan (1873–1924). Vaḷḷattōḷ and Āśan were also outspoken patriots and critics of social structures and the caste system. Increasing printing and publishing activities contributed to the wider circulation and reception of these literary works at the brink of modernity, while poets began to seek inspiration in indigenous as well as Western literary trads. (e.g., Eng. romanticism).

The mod. and contemp. periods have been immensely prolific with regard to poetry. G. Śaṅkarakkuṟuppŭ (1901–78), Iṭaśśēri Gōvindan Nāyar (1906–74), Caṅṅampuḻa Kṛṣṇapiḷḷa (1913–47), M. Gōvindan (1919–89), P. Bhāskaran (1924–2007), Ayyappappaṇikkar (1930–2006), O.N.V. Kuṟuppŭ (1931–2016), K. Saccidānandan (b. 1946), Bālacandran Cullikkāṭŭ (b. 1957), and V. M. Girija (b. 1961) are a few of the writers shaping this era. Beginning with Bālāmaṇiyamma (1909–2004) and Laḷitāmbika Antarjanam (1909–87) at the turn of the 20th c., women found their way into an otherwise male-dominated literary sphere. Sugatakumāri (b. 1934) and Kamala Das (alias Mādhavikkuṭṭi or K. Surayya, 1934–2009) are among the best-known mod. women poets of Kerala. Twentieth-c. poetry took up virtually every aspect of mod. life, ranging from social and political issues to women's emancipation, and 21st-c. writing continues to find an engaged audience in Kerala's vibrant literary scene.

See INDIA, POETRY OF; RĀMĀYAṆA POETRY; SANSKRIT POETICS; SANSKRIT POETRY; TAMIL POETRY AND POETICS.

■ **Anthologies and Translations**: *Malayalam Poetry Today*, ed. K. M. Tharakan (1984); "Malayalam," *Medieval Indian Literature*, ed. K. Ayyappa Paniker, v. 3 (1999); *Unnayi Varier's Nalacaritam*, trans. S. Gopalakrishnan (2001).

■ **Criticism and History**: C. A. Menon, *Ezuttaccan and His Age* (1940); K. M. George, *Rāmacaritam and the Study of Early Malayalam* (1956); K. Chaitanya, *A History of Malayalam Literature* (1971); K. Ramachandran Nair, *Early Manipravalam* (1971); N. V. Krishna Warrior, *A History of Malayalam Metre* (1977); M. Līlāvati, *Malayāḷakavitāsāhitya caritram* (1980); E. Paramēśvaran Piḷḷa, *Malayāḷasāhityam kālaghaṭṭaṅṅaḷilūṭe* (1998); R. Freeman, "Genre and Society: The Literary Culture of Premodern Kerala," *Literary Cultures in History*, ed. S. Pollock (2003); *Sampūrṇṇa Malayāḷasāhityacaritram*, ed. P. Rāmacandran Nāyar (2008).

N. Kommattam

MALAY POETRY

I. Traditional
II. Modern

The earliest records of the Malay lang. date from South Sumatra, ca 680 CE. Over the next thousand years, Malay spread to the Malay peninsula, Singapore, East Sumatra, coastal Borneo, and the South Celebes, as well as to parts of southern Thailand and the Philippines. It was both a court lang. and a commercial lingua franca and continues in Malaysia and Indonesia to be the lang. of the state, education, and mass communications. Traditional Malay poetry was composed in the regions named above. Mod. Malay poetry comes from Malaysia, Singapore, and Brunei. The lang. is now called "Indonesian" in the Republic of Indonesia and has developed its own mod. poetry (see INDONESIAN POETRY).

I. Traditional. This includes both oral and written genres. The best known oral form is the *pantun*, a four-line verse, with four words to a line, each verse rhyming *abab*. Each stanza consists of two couplets: the first two lines present a sound pattern and an image, usually drawn from nature, that foreshadow the sound patterns and the explicit meaning to be found in the second couplet:

> Where have you gone to, where were you
> from?
> Weeds grow taller than grain.
> What year, what month, will time have
> spun
> Around to when we meet again?
> (trans. B. Raffel)

Although each stanza is self-contained, it is also possible to build "chains," in which the second and fourth lines of the first pantun become the first and third lines of the next pantun, and so on (*pantun berkait*). In this extended form, the Malay pantun has influenced Fr. and Eng. verse (*pantoum*).

The best known written form is the *syair*, a term deriving from the Ar. *syi'r*, although the Malay form is purely indigenous and has no actual connection with any Ar. or Persian form. Syair consist of long series of four-line stanzas recited to an audience, each stanza utilizing the same end rhyme. There are both narrative and nonnarrative syair. Nonnarrative syair deal with religious doctrines and practices, ethics, and such miscellaneous topics as the interpretation of dreams, astronomy, riddles, and the praise of particular people and places. The earliest extant syair are the works of the late 16th-c. religious scholar Hamzah Fansuri. Hamzah developed a mystical theology in short, terse verses, filled with Ar. and Persian words; his works were condemned and burned by antagonistic scholars in the court of Acheh. Narrative syair include romantic tales, accounts of historical events, the lives of religious figures, and moral allegories. One of the most popular romantic tales is the *Syair Ken Tambuhan*, a quest story drawn from Javanese mythology. The same motif of a prince's leaving the court and searching throughout the known world for his true love occurs in *Syair Bidasari* and many other texts as well. The syair form reached its greatest popularity in Indonesia in the late 19th c., when even contemp. murder mysteries were written in verse, thus laying the foundations for the emergence of a mod. prose fiction.

Other traditional Malay poetic forms include riddles, proverbs, spells, the prose lyrics found in narrative tales, and the indefinite structures of the *nazam*, *seloka*, and *gurindam*.

II. Modern. This is considered to have begun in 1934 with publication of a new style of poetry by Muhammad Yasin Ma'mor, in *Majallah Guru*, a magazine for village elementary-school teachers. Possibly influenced by Indonesian poetry, Yasin wrote personal works of melancholy longing provoked by the beauty of nature. Most of his poems used a four-line verse form; a few were written completely in free verse. A more decisive break with traditional Malay verse came after World War II, with the rise of the Generation of the Fifties in Singapore. Members of the generation included teachers but also police officers and journalists. They sought a wide Malay audience and wrote in a simple, easy-to-understand style, which was particularly critical of the social breakdown they attributed to the war and the lingering effects of Brit. colonialism. A typical example is "Kami Anak Zaman Ini" (We Are the Children of This Age) by Masuri S. N., which praises past cultural glory, laments present widespread poverty, and looks forward to a time in which "full sovereignty" will be restored. Another is Usman Awang's "Pak Utih" (Father Utih). The poem falls into two sections: in the first, Usman describes Utih, "the meritorious peasant," and his life of grinding rural poverty and disease; in the second, Utih looks at the emerging nationalist politicians, with their luxury cars and rich banquets, wondering as he "still waits in prayer, Where are the leaders going in their limousines?"

A very different movement that appeared at this same time was labeled the Obscure Poetry movement. The movement emphasized symbolism and sound patterns in a way that was sometimes reminiscent of the first two lines of the pantun. Important poets in this trad. included A. S. Amin, Noor S. I., M. Ghazali, and, occasionally, A. Samad Said, better known as a novelist.

During the 1970s, a number of younger poets reached maturity and continued to dominate Malay poetry throughout the rest of the century. They were less interested in social themes, more concerned with personal emotion, and eager to experiment with new forms. Latiff Mohidin, a painter, wrote heavily imagistic poems, extending the "obscure" trad. Baha Zain used a graphic and harsh contemp. lang. as a way of addressing current social issues.

A. Ghafar Ibrahim moved beyond meaning to pure sound in some of his work: "Tak Tun" captures the rhythm of the village tambourine, "Tak Tun / taktak Tun Taktak Tak Tun Taktak Tak Tun . . ."; "Dundun cakcak" holds the beat of the drum, "dundun / chak-chak / dun / chak / dundun / chakchak . . ."; while his poem "Gagak" (Crows) is shaped like an open beak and filled with the repetitious cry "gak, gak, gak . . .".

An ongoing exploration of mystical Islamic themes has marked the work of Kemala (pseud. of Ahmad Kamal Abdullah). His poetry contains references to prayer and the scriptures; to theological ideas of God, creation, the world as a system of signs, the religious community; to historical figures, incl. the Prophet Muhammad, but also his companions, other prophets and major Middle Eastern poets; and to claims of personal religious illumination. His lang. is rich and evocative, often existing for its own sake but as a way of evoking deep resonances in the heart of the Malay reader. The long poem "Ayn" (Signs), e.g., moves effortlessly across descriptions of the early life of Muhammad, his midnight ascent to Jerusalem, the Prophet's wife Aisyah, the 8th-c. Iraqi poet Rābiʿah al-ʿAdawīyah, the seven sleepers of Ephesus, and various Semitic prophets.

The work of State Literary Laureate Muhammad Haji Salleh is almost the complete opposite of that of Kemala. Muhammad is a major literary scholar. Educated first in Eng. and holding a doctorate in comparative literature from the University of Michigan, he has had to struggle to gain his own Malay identity. His verse is intellectual and absolutely understated. In the poem "Intektuil" (The Intellectual), he describes himself as "the victim of the question," caught between "the pain of emotion / and the thoughts born in his head," and this theme is extensively explored throughout his work.

As in Indonesia, there are fewer women poets writing in Malay than men poets. The two most prominent are Zurinah Hassan and Siti Zainon Ismail. Zurinah's work gently explores the mysteries and uncertainties of human relationships, esp. as these are expressed (or, more often, fail to be expressed) through ordinary speech. Siti Zainon's exploration of human and religious love is more sensuous than Zurinah's work.

Although Malay is the national lang. of Malaysia and the government has provided major publishing opportunities and rewards to encourage a national lit., there are few significant poets writing in Malay from other ethnic communities. The important exception is Lim Swee Tin. Of Chinese-Thai parentage, Lim speaks Hokkien, Mandarin, and Thai but feels that he expresses himself best in Malay. However, he avoids communal references in his work, in favor of a quiet introversion and a gentle nostalgia for a culturally unspecific past.

The support of the government has perhaps ensured the steady devel. of mod. Malay poetry along a path that has maintained quality but provided few radical challenges or different directions for the past 50 years. As Salleh insists in his contemp. rewriting of the cl. hist. *Sejarah Melayu* (*Malay Annals*, composed 1535–1612)—described by Winstedt as "the most famous, distinctive and best of all Malay literary works"—the contemp. author must write "so that from the past may rise greatness, / from our history we may learn the truth" (trans. Muhammad Haji Salleh).

■ **Anthologies and Translations**: *Pantun Melayu*, ed. R. J. Wilkinson and R. O. Winstedt, 2d ed. (1955); *Modern Malay Verse, 1946–61*, ed. O. Rice and A. Majid (1963); *Selections from Contemporary Malaysian Poetry*, ed. M. H. Salleh (1978); *The Poems of Hamzah Fansuri*, ed. G.W.J. Drewes and L. F. Brakel (1986); *Malaysian Poetry 1975–1985*, ed. A. K. Abdullah, trans. H. Aveling (1987); *The Puppeteer's Wayang* (1992), and *Emas Tempawan* (2004), both ed. M. H. Salleh; *Bidasari*, ed. J. Millie (2004). ■ **Criticism and History**: R. O. Winstedt, *A History of Classical Malay Literature*, 2d ed. (1961); B. Raffel, *The Development of Modern Indonesian Poetry* (1967); M. H. Salleh, *Tradition and Change in Contemporary Malay-Indonesian Poetry* (1977); H. M. Piah et al., *Traditional Malay Literature*, trans. H. Aveling, 2d ed. (2002).

H. Aveling

MAORI POETRY. *See* NEW ZEALAND, POETRY OF

MAPUCHE POETRY. The historical territory of the Mapuche people coincides with large tracts of southern Chile and Argentina. The Mapuche lang., *Mapuzungun*, cultivated an oral poetry in pre-Columbian times. During the early colonial period, missionaries of the Catholic Church, who were granted permission to travel through Mapuche territory, made frequent reference to the beauty and significance of the trad. of indigenous poetic song. In some cases, they studied and transcribed it in the original Mapuzungun. Shortly after Mapuche territory was colonized by the Chilean state in the late 19th c., well-known linguists, such as Rodolfo Lenz and Felix José de Augusta, collected and translated hundreds of Mapuche poems as part of a broader anthropological endeavor to salvage what they presumed to be the last remains of a doomed culture.

In the early 20th c., educated bilingual Mapuche began to write and publish in Sp. Most notable were the works of Manuel Manquilef in the 1910s and of Guillermo Igayman, Teodoberta Neculmán, and Anselmo Quilaqueo in the 1930s. The latter published *Cancionero Araucano* (Araucanian Verses) in 1939. In it, he invoked a glorious past when his people had bravely defended their homeland against the Sp. conquistadors: "Oh Arauco! / Remember how one day you spilt /your beautiful blood upon this beloved land / refusing time and again to give in." It was not only the past he wrote of, however. "You took revenge for the way you were punished, / and for that reason you rise up again [today]." In 1966, Sebastián Queupul published the first self-authored, bilingual collection of Mapuche poetry, *Poemas mapuches en castellano* (Mapuche Poems in Spanish). A small, low-cost production, it nevertheless marked an important milestone in Mapuche literary creation. The most widely cited poem of the book was "Arado de palo" (Wooden Plough), which wistfully recalled life in the rural community before the author moved to the more hostile environment of Santiago: "I want to turn over the earth with my wooden plough / And plant my simple words in the wilderness." And yet it was also a story of the survival of indigenous culture in the capital city.

Mapuche poetry experienced a boom in the context of redemocratization (after 17 years of military dictatorship) and the newly elected Concertación government's decision to embrace the rhet. of multiculturalism. In 1989, Leonel Lienlaf published *Se ha despertado el ave en mi corazón* (The Bird Has Awakened within My Heart), the first book by a Mapuche author to be taken on by a major publishing house in Chile. Lienlaf was also the first Mapuche writer to win a national literary award, the Santiago Municipal Literature Prize of 1990. Elicura Chihuailaf was awarded the same prize in 1997 for a collection of poems titled *De sueños azules y contrasueños* (Of Blue Dreams and Counter-dreams, 1995).

Born in rural southern Chile, both Chihuailaf and Lienlaf move between the rural and urban environments. They write in Mapuzungun and Sp. The rural world infuses their verses, but, like Queupul, they address the problems of urban life, emphasizing the alienation and solitude felt by Mapuche migrants in Chile's urban centers. In the poem "Leyendas, visiones" (Legends, Visions, 1991), Chihuailaf writes, "in the city I am barely a rivulet / shrunken and in silence dying." Chihuailaf describes his poetry as *oralitura*: his incorporation of multiple voices, in particular, is inspired by the collective, oral trad. of his ancestors. Much of Lienlaf's poetic production is oral (recorded music, documentary film), and he addresses the limitations of the written word in one of his best-known poems "Rebelión" (1989): "My hand / told me the world / would not be written down." But his verses do not so much reject writing (after all, he has achieved a great deal by writing) as highlight the tension between the spoken and written word.

Lienlaf and Chihuailaf are the most renowned of Chile's Mapuche poets: they attend public conferences at home and abroad, and their verses—which are the subject of numerous scholarly studies—have been included in textbooks and museum exhibitions. But they are by no means the only ones to have achieved academic and popular recognition. At least 20 Mapuche writers have carved a place for themselves in national (and often international) literary circles. They are a highly diverse group, both in themselves—male and female, of different generations and territories, bilingual and monolingual, rural and urban based—and with regard to the poetry they produce. However, there are also strong links between them. They all assert their indigenous origins (making it either an explicit or implicit theme of their writings) and support the Mapuche political movement in its struggles against the Chilean state.

Since the late 1990s, the gritty, urban poetry of two Santiago-based writers—César Millahueique and David Aniñir—has attracted increasing attention. In *Profecía en blanco y negro* (Prophecy in Black and White, 1998), the former plays with a mixture of langs. and communication systems to represent the transcultural experience of the urban Mapuche population: "My codes jump from one program to another, from Word Perfect to Lotus, from Lotus to Windows; I feel the re-heated chips and the shadows staking everything to be a reality and a pacman eating the security codes." He also depicts harrowing scenes of a city dominated by the fear and repression of Augusto Pinochet's military regime. One of Aniñir's most paradigmatic poems is "María Juana la mapunky de la Pintana" (Maria Juna the Mapuche punk girl of la Pintana), in which he underscores the social exclusion of so many Mapuche in Santiago: "you are the Mapuche 'girl' of an unregistered brand / of the cold solitary corner addicted to 'that' bad habit / your dark skin is the network of SuperHyperArchi veins / that boil over with a revenge that condemns." It is a tragic story that Aniñir tells but with a strong sense of the potential for resistance.

Another recent devel. is the publication of the two-volume anthol. of Mapuche women writers: *Hilando en la memoria* (Spinning Memory, 2006–9), ed. by the Chilean scholar Soledad Falabella. These bring together 21 poets, incl. Graciela Huinao, María Isabel Millapan, Maribel Curriao, and Roxana Miranda Rupailaf. The poetry deals with recurrent themes such as orality and historic memory, but also points to the intersections between gender and race in 21st-c. Chile.

See ARGENTINA, POETRY OF; CHILE, POETRY OF; INDIGENOUS AMERICAS, POETRY OF THE.

■ I. Carrasco Muñoz, "Las voces étnicas en la poesía chilena actual," *Revista chilena de literatura* 47 (1995); *Ül: Four Mapuche Poets*, ed. C. Vicuña, trans. J. Bierhorst (1998); J. Park, "Ethnogenesis or Neoindigenous Intelligentsia: Contemporary Mapuche-Huilliche Poetry," *Latin American Research Review* 42 (2007); J. Crow, "Mapuche Poetry in Post-Dictatorship Chile: Confronting the Dilemmas of Neoliberal Multiculturalism," *Journal of Latin American Cultural Studies* 17 (2008); M. E. Góngora and D. Picón, "Poesía mapuche: Actualidad y permanencias. Entrevista a Jaime Huenún," *Revista Chilena de la Literatura* 76 (2010): http://www.revistas.uchile.cl/index.php/RCL/article/viewFile/9141/9142.

J. Crow

MARATHI POETRY. Dnyaneshwar's (1271–96) decision to compose the *Bhavarthdeepika*, a poetic commentary on the *Bhagavad-Gītā*, in Marathi, the common lang. of Maharashtra, instead of Sanskrit, the lang. of priests and scholars, was a radical gesture that inaugurated a powerful trad. of poetry in Marathi. Although Dnyaneshwar is the first major poet in Marathi, he was not the first poet; the poetry of the Mahanubhava, an esoteric sect, was preserved in a coded script that was discovered in the 20th c. and probably predated Dnyaneshwar.

Dnyaneshwar belonged to the pan-Indian *Bhakti* movement (see INDIA, POETRY OF), a spiritual movement that allowed the most marginal segments of feudal, casteist, and patriarchal Indian society to articulate their identities. The Bhakti movement fueled the evolution of mod. Indian langs. and cultures. The bulk of poetry composed in Maharashtra from the 13th to the 18th c. is Bhakti poetry and mostly oral-performative in nature. Dnyaneshwar's compositions are integral to the canon of the Varkari movement, the Marathi branch of the Bhakti movement.

Other major poets in the Varkari canon are Namdev (1270–1350), Eknāth (1533–99), and Tukaram (1608–49). These poets employed folk literary forms like *abhanga*, *ovis*, and *bharud*. Even if the poetry of Ramdas (1606–82) does not belong to the Varkari movement, it can still be located in the Bhakti trad. It is notable for its nationalistic and pragmatic vision. Another trad., more elitist and influenced by Sanskrit *kāvya*, is of poets like Waman

Pandit (1608–95), Mukteshwar (1574–1645), and Moropant (1729–94) in the 17th and 18th cs. They continued the trad. of *akhyana kāvya* (narrative poetry), which was popularized earlier by Eknāth. The consolidation of the Maratha Empire during this period also made *powadas* (heroic ballads) and *lavanis* (romantic songs) composed by *Shahirs* (troubadours) like Honaji Bala (1754–1844) very popular.

Nineteenth-c. Brit. colonialism brought modernity to Maharashtra, and print capitalism and Western education caused a lasting shift in poetic practice. Once primarily oral and performative, poetry now appeared predominantly in print form and bore the distinct influence of the Western intellectual and poetic trads., incl. romanticism, social reformism, and nationalism. The major poet of this period is Keshavsut (pseud. of Krishnaji Keshav Damle, 1866–1905). Other prominent poets of the period are Balkavi (pseud. of T. B. Thombre, 1890–1918), and Bahinabai Choudhary (1880–1951), an outstanding poet whose works were unavailable in her time as they were orally composed.

In the 1920s, a group of poets called Ravikiran Mandal, led by Madhav Julian (1894–1939), rose to prominence in Pune city. The group reacted against the social reformist tone and mystical effusions of the poets like Keshavsut and wrote soft and sentimental lyrics. They cultivated poetic forms like the *ghazal* and the sonnet. In the 1930s, Anil (pseud. of Atmaram Ravji Deshpande, 1901–82) introduced free verse in Marathi. Other notable poets of the period are B. B. Borkar (1910–84) and Kusumagraj (pseud. of V. V. Shirwadkar, 1912–99).

B. S. Mardhekar's (1909–56) *Kahi Kavita* (1947) brought about another shift in Marathi poetry. These avant-garde poems express despair resulting from World War II, growing industrialization, urbanization, and the erosion of traditional values. Mardhekar's attempt to integrate the nonconformist aspects of Bhakti poetics with international modernist aesthetics is a significant characteristic of postcolonial cultural tendencies. Important contemporaries of Mardhekar, whose modernism avoided avant-garde excesses, are Purushottam Shivaram Rege (1910–78), Indira Sant (1914–2000), and Vinda Karandikar (1918–2010).

From 1955 to 1975, avant-garde poetics found its expression in the "little magazine" movement. The little magazines like *Shabda*, *Vacha*, and literary periodicals like *Asmitadarsha* had a distinct antiestablishment outlook, as in the complex, experimental, and challenging poetry by Arun Kolatkar (1932–2004), Dilip Chitre (1938–2009), Vasant Dahake (b. 1942), and Namdeo Dhasal (1949–2014). Their works bear the influence of international modernist and postmodernist poetry. The Dalit poetry, or "the poetry of the oppressed," influenced by the radically reformist philosophy of Babasaheb Ambedkar (1891–1956) and Jyotiba Phule (1827–90), exploded on the scene in the same period. Poets like Dhasal straddled both avant-garde and Dalit poetics. Feminism also began to emerge in this period. Malika Amar Sheikh (b. 1957) writes vigorous poetry that combines feminism with other dissenting political ideologies. In the 1980s, tribal poets like Bhujang Meshram (1958–2007) started writing poetry that combined their quest for tribal identity with protest against the exploitative social system, while poets like Arun Kale (1954–2008) continued the trad. of Dalit poetry.

Poetic idiom was transformed in the 1990s because of the social and cultural crises caused by the processes of globalization, technological revolution, and economic reforms. New little magazines like *Shabadvedh* (1989–2009) and *Abhidhanantar* (1992–2009) played an important role by providing a platform for new voices. New poetry engages with contemp. cultural crises and shows a shift in sensibility and lang. Some of the significant voices to emerge since the 1990s are Sanjeev Khandekar (b. 1958), Mangesh Narayanrao Kale (b. 1966), Saleel Wagh (b. 1967), Hemant Divate (b. 1967), Kavita Mahajan (b. 1967), Manya Joshi (b. 1972), Santosh P. Pawar (b. 1972), and Sachin Ketkar (b. 1972).

■ *An Anthology of Marathi Poetry 1945–1965*, ed. D. Chitre (1968); S. Deo, "Twentieth-Century Marathi Literature," *Handbook of Twentieth-Century Literatures in India,* ed. N. Natarajan (1996); *Live Update: An Anthology of Recent Marathi Poetry,* ed. S. C. Ketkar (2005); D. Chitre, "The Practice of Marathi Poetry: A Survey of Seven Centuries of Interruptions," *New Quest* 175–76 (2009).

S. C. KETKAR

MAYAN POETRY. *See* GUATEMALA, POETRY OF; INDIGENOUS AMERICAS, POETRY OF THE; MEXICO, POETRY OF

MESOAMERICA, POETRY OF. *See* INDIGENOUS AMERICAS, POETRY OF THE

MEXICO, POETRY OF. A first problem: should an article on Mexican poetry consider only the lit. written after the country became independent, in 1821? Should it include colonial times or even the pre-Columbian period? Most anthols. and critical studies on the subject have elected to trace the lit. back to the indigenous past, since that trad. has survived in art and scholarship and still has an influence on present-day authors. The lit. of Mexico is always a mixture of a multiracial (*mestizo*) society with dominant Eur. influences and suppressed indigenous elements that nonetheless arise, sometimes surreptitiously. This entry, thus, envisions the poetry of Mexico as inclusively as possible.

As with all ancient lit., poetry in Mexico before the Sp. conquest was associated with music, dance, and rituals. Although Mesoamerican societies (in the region that roughly comprehends Mexico and northern Central America) developed "books" (known as *amoxtli*), they were used mostly to record hist., genealogies, astronomical charts, divinatory tables, calendars, and religious ceremonies. Transmitted by oral trad., poetry was captured in print by Sp. priests during the colonial period. Even if there were many spoken langs. in Mesoamerica, most of the materials available today come from Nahuatl and Maya, the two langs. that dominated in the region. Two of the major sources on culture at the time of the conquest are Bernardino de Sahagún's *Florentine Codex* (written 1547–69, and after 1575 partially trans. into Sp., as *Historia general de las cosas de la Nueva España* [General History of the Things of New Spain]), a major source on Aztec life and hist., in Nahuatl with illustrations; and Diego de Landa's *Relación de las cosas de Yucatán* (Yucatan before and after the Conquest, written ca. 1566), an important reference for Mayan life and cosmogony, written in Sp. A number of texts would become "poems" that detail the origins of life, according to Mesoamerican beliefs.

For Nahuatl poetry, the discovery at the end of the 19th c. of two mss., the *Cantares mexicanos* (*Songs of the Aztecs*, written in the 16th c.) and the *Romances de los Señores de la Nueva España* (*Ballads of the Lords of New Spain*, written 1582), was key to its later success, thanks to the work of two prominent scholars in this field: Ángel María Garibay and Miguel León-Portilla. Garibay published three volumes studying and translating Nahuatl poetry (from the above-mentioned sources) in the 1950s and 1960s. León-Portilla continued this work, identifying 13 poets in *Trece poetas del mundo azteca* (1967; in a later ed., he adds two more). The most important poet-philosopher known from the pre-Hispanic period was Nezahualcoyotl (1402–72), also king of Texcoco in the eastern part of the Valley of Mexico. After a war against the Tepanecs of Azcapotzalco in 1428 (in alliance with the Aztecs), Nezahualcoyotl governed Texcoco until his death. According to Martínez (1972), 36 poems can be attributed to him. A number of themes appear in the poems: the brevity or fugacity of life, the nature of poetry, philosophical disquisitions about the creator of the world, celebrations of flowers and spring, praise of warriors, prophecies, and the afterlife. Instead of dedicating poems to known Mesoamerican gods (e.g., Quetzalcoatl, Coatlicue, Huitzilopochtli), Nezahualcoyotl addressed his poems to a god with the epithets *Ipalnemoani* (Giver of Life), *Moyocoyatzin* (Inventor of Himself), or *In Tloque in Nahuaque* (Lord of the Close Vicinity), arguably a Toltec influence pertaining to the cl. Mesoamerican period, before the 10th c. The conceit of the world as the creation of a book of paintings (Mesoamericans wrote books using pictograms and ideograms) is strikingly mod. in a Borgesian way: "Like a painting, we will be erased." Nezahualcoyotl was the first major poet of Mexico.

After the conquest, Sp. institutions were established, and most known writers followed literary currents from Spain. Although a significant number of the writings, esp. in the 16th c., were chronicles of the conquest and compilations of oral indigenous lits., poetry was much more elaborate, pertaining mainly to the court. Three Sp. poets (Gutierre de Cetina, 1519–54; Eugenio de Salazar, 1530–1602; and Juan de la Cueva, 1543–1612) traveled to New Spain, bringing the techniques, styles, and worldviews that dominated poetry of the Iberian Peninsula during the 16th c. Cetina lived his last ten years in Mexico. Like Garcilaso de la Vega before him, he practiced Petrarchism. Although his best-known poem, "Ojos claros, serenos" (Bright and Serene Eyes), may not have been written in New Spain, it is frequently quoted in anthols. for bringing Eur. poetic style to the Sp. colonies. Francisco de Terrazas (1525–1600), born in Mexico, continued in the same Petrarchan vein as those who brought it from Spain. Parallel to love sonnets in the 16th c., a common motif is the eulogy to Mexico. The jurist and colonial administrator Salazar wrote an epideictic poem ("Descripción de la laguna") in *ottava rima* about Tenochtitlan or Mexico City, the conquerors, and the viceroyalty of New Spain. The conquistador Bernal Díaz del Castillo's *Historia verdadera de la conquista de la Nueva España* (*True History of the Conquest of New Spain*, written after 1568) includes several passages of description that belong to this motif, notably that relating Cortés's entry into Tenochtitlan in terms of a *locus amoenus*. This trend continued with Mateo Rosas de Oquendo (b. 1559?) in "Indiano volcán famoso" (Famous Indian Volcano), a descriptive poem about Popocatepetl, a volcano near Mexico City. And it culminates with a long poem by Bernardo de Balbuena (1561–1627), "Grandeza mexicana" (The Magnificence of Mexico, 1604), where the author describes with great detail and elaborate lang. all aspects of Mexico City, incl. its vegetation, climate, and architecture, emphasizing the splendor of what he believes is one of the greatest cities in the world. With Balbuena, Mexican poetry also moves toward the baroque under the influence of the Sp. poets Francisco de Quevedo, Lope de Vega, Luis de Góngora, and others. Poetic contests abounded in the 17th c. in New Spain, and many poets, often clerics, wrote elaborate and sophisticated poems for ceremonies at the court or for the church. Luis de Sandoval y Zapata (1620?–71), an honored poet of the time, was, according to some critics, a key figure who was influenced by the Sp. poets. But doubtless the most important writer of this period—and perhaps the greatest baroque poet in any lang.—was the nun Sor Juana Inés de la Cruz (ca. 1648–95), a towering intellectual to whom the convent provided an institutional setting for her poetic and philosophical work. Sor Juana's greatest poetry can be found in her sonnets and in the long poem of ideas called *Primero sueño* (*First Dream*). She uses a battery of logical, poetic, and rhetorical devices (antithesis, parallelism, acrostics, alliteration, paronomasia, hyperbaton, hyperbole), employs satire and wit, and incorporates Lat. and Nahuatl. Fully immersed in her poetic milieu, Sor Juana responded to literary challenges, wrote poems of petition, and addressed ceremonies and special occasions. Although she adapted the rhet. of the Sp. baroque, she was able subtly to alter the male perspective. E.g., in alluding to the last line of Góngora's sonnet "Mientras por competir con tu cabello" (While to compete with your hair) with the motif of carpe diem, she reframed the preceding lines into an *ekphrasis* of a portrait representing not fleeting beauty but deceit: "This that you gaze on, colorful deceit . . . is but cadaver, ashes, shadow, void." Many mod. readers, notably Octavio Paz, see in Sor Juana a poetic program that goes beyond the baroque to anticipate modernism.

During the wars of independence (1810–21), poets participated actively in politics. A first generation of poets celebrated Mexico with "nationalistic" poems, such as Andrés Quintana Roo's (1787–1851) ode "16 de Septiembre" (the date commemorates Independence Day in Mexico). But Quintana Roo and others were still absorbed in neoclassical forms, and their poetry is heavily rhetorical. A little later, two subsequent groups emerged, the Academia de Letrán and the Liceo Hidalgo. With them, romanticism (linked to liberalism) arrived in Mexico, e.g., with the idealized version of the indigenous past, as in "La profecia de Guatimoc" (The Prophecy of Guatimoc, written 1839, pub. 1851) by Ignacio Rodríguez Galván (1816–42). Although better known for his novels, the jurist and politician Ignacio Manuel Altamirano (1834–93), a central figure of the 19th c., also wrote poems. An important poet of the period is Manuel Acuña (1849–73), best known for the "Nocturno (a Rosario)" and also for the melancholic tendency that ended in his suicide. The transition from romanticism to *modernismo* (the Sp. Am. version of Fr. Parnassianism and symbolism) went through Manuel Gutiérrez Nájera (1859–95), a dandy who chronicled the city in many ways, esp. in "La duquesa Job" (Duchess Job), which mocks the lifestyle of the period. He also wrote somber poems, such as "Para entonces" (When My Time Comes). Other *modernista* poets are the highly popular Amado Nervo (1870–1919), Salvador Díaz Mirón (1853–1928), Manuel José Othón (1858–1906), and Efrén Rebolledo (1877–1929; his sonnets, under the title *Caro Victrix*, use explicit sexual imagery influenced by Charles Baudelaire).

Although Enrique González Martínez (1871–1952) wrote a sonnet in 1911 about the killing of the swan (to figure the end of modernismo) in favor of the owl, real poetic change in the 20th c. was introduced by Ramón López Velarde (1888–1921) and José Juan Tablada (1871–1945), both of whom started as *modernistas* but persisted to write a more critical poetry. Unlike the art of the murals or the novel, a poetry of the Mexican Revolution (1910–20) was not developed as such, perhaps because many of the prevailing poets of the time looked on angrily at the violent changes in the country. There was a popular and anonymous poetry associated with the movement, through the *corridos* or ballads that celebrated various heroes and battles. In his first phase, Tablada had been one of the key poets of modernismo; his poem "Misa negra" (Black Mass) used symbolist imagery. As his work evolved, he introduced the Japanese haiku into Sp. (*Un día* [One Day], 1919; and *Jarro de flores* [A Vase of Flowers], 1921) and his poetry moved toward ideographic forms in the avant-garde style of Guillaume Apollinaire's *Calligrammes* (*Li-Po y otros poemas* [Li-Po and Other Poems], 1920). In *La feria* (The Fair, 1928), written in exile, he returned to Mexican folklore, with attention to food, drinks, and typical symbols of the country. López Velarde was called the poet of the province, for having written texts reflecting the ambience of the towns of the Mexican interior. He was also a poet of eroticism fused with humor, irony, and colloquial lang. Similar to that of the Argentine Leopoldo Lugones, his poetry became more self-critical. He is also known for "La suave patria" (The Gentle Homeland, 1921), a poem that commemorates the first centenary of Mexican independence, seeking a more tender and reflective motherland after the armed struggle of the preceding decade. Even though Alfonso Reyes (1889–1959) was arguably the most important Mexican writer of the first half of the 20th c., he is known more for his essays, crit., and trans. than for his poetry.

Even though they were trans. of the lit. of the Eur. avant-garde, the poets who belong to the group called *Contemporáneos* (its name comes from the literary magazine they edited between 1928 and 1931) were reticent about excessive experimentation; for instance, euphony and rhythm were still important elements for them. Their poetry explores topics apart from the political and social issues of the revolution; they are more interested in intimacy, solitude, death, dreams, and love (incl., for Xavier Villaurrutia and Salvador Novo, homoeroticism). Villaurrutia (1903–50) is remembered by the nocturnes of *Nostalgia de la muerte* (*Nostalgia for Death*): reflective, insomniac texts, influenced by the dreamlike imagery of surrealism, but without arriving at automatic writing; poems that explore the space between saying and not saying and forbidden pleasures. *Muerte sin fin* (Death without End) by José Gorostiza (1901–73) is thought to be one of the most significant poems of the 20th c. Inspired by Sor Juana's *Primero sueño*, Góngora's *Soledades*, and T. S. Eliot's *The Waste Land*, it is a philosophical poem concerning the search for intangible forms—God, time, spirit, silence—and the transformation of matter, like water, lang., plants, animals, and the body. All this metamorphosis is an expression of the death that flows as a constant in life. Very different is Carlos Pellicer (1897–1977), who explores the tropics in the Lat. Am. landscape. If the poetry of Villaurrutia and Gorostiza is implosive, Pellicer's is explosive. From his first book of 1921 (contemporaneous with the debut of the young Chilean Pablo Neruda), he had already demonstrated his astonishment with nature through innovative metaphors. Salvador Novo (1904–74) is perhaps the most experimental member of the Contemporáneos group, or at least the most impudent. His humor and irony play with the icons of Mexicanness: "¿Quién quiere jugar tenis con nopales y tunas / sobre la red de los telégrafos?" (Who wants to play tennis with *nopales* and prickly pears / on the network of the telegraphs? [*XX poemas*, 1925]). Later, he will explore "sexual and moral dissent" (according to Monsiváis 1979) in *Nuevo amor* (New Love, 1933), namely, the taboo of homosexuality in the Mexico of the 1930s.

Estridentismo was an explicit avant-garde movement in Mexico, with manifestos and proclamations in the style of futurism, influenced by Sp. *ultraísmo*. The most important poet of the group, Manuel Maples Arce (1898–1981), wrote *Urbe, Super-poema bolchevique* (Urbe: Super-Bolshevik Poem, 1924), a work that links the Mexican and the Rus. revolutions and that attempts to defy poetic conventions, concentrating on movements in the streets of Mexico City. But estridentismo did not have a major impact on future generations, compared to how the Contemporáneos influenced Mexican poets throughout the century.

In the following generation, there are two important poets who at first share a mistrust toward the group of Contemporáneos but eventually delineate two routes for Mexican writers: the poetry of lang. of Octavio Paz (1914–98), and the colloquial and political tones of Efraín Huerta (1914–82). In Paz's *Libertad bajo palabra* (*Freedom on Parole*, 1960) two of the tenets of surrealistic ethics, freedom and poetry, are a point of reference—liberty thanks to poetry,

poetry thanks to liberty. "Piedra de sol" ("Sunstone," 1957), one of the most famous poems of the second half of the century, is circular: it ends with the same lines that begin it. The title is taken from the circular Aztec stone that reveals the cosmogony of the world. In the first part of the poem, analogy helps converge nature and love: "I go among your body as among the world . . . / I go among your eyes as I swim water . . ." But soon the poetic persona is alone, in search of a feminine subject who eludes him. In the middle of the poem, a place and a date seem to break with poetic fluency: "Madrid, 1937." Although this line in Sp. is a perfect hendecasyllable, the numbers cut the poem in two: it is the split of the atrocities of the war that places its mark and interrupts the harmony of the beginning. But opposed to it, a couple makes love in the middle of bombs, defying everything. For Paz, historical time is the conscience that provokes anxiety. Hence, he is constantly looking for the circular time of ancient civilizations, for the paradise of the beginning (before the expulsion from the Garden of Eden), the mystical silence in which everything is annulled to enter a sacred space, where pronouns and differences are obliterated, where the lost unity is found. "Sunstone" presupposes that love, liberty, and poetry (the famous surrealist triad) can transform the world. Several of the poems of *Ladera Este* (*East Slope*, 1969) concentrate on coitus as a way of denying differences through the rites of Tantrism. The culmination of this poetical model is "Blanco" (1967), a poem that combines readings of Stéphane Mallarmé, the theories of silence in the music of John Cage, and the ritual practice of Tantrism brought to the space of the poem. In *Pasado en claro* (*A Draft of Shadows*, 1974), an autobiographical long poem, Paz reflects on the effects of time, the role of lang., and (by the poet's standards) a more visceral tone. His childhood is seen both as troubled and as foundational to his later obsessions. In *Árbol adentro* (*A Tree Within*, 1987), poems in dialogue with painters, and the poem of love (his constant topic) "Carta de creencia" ("Letter of Testimony"), are central to the book.

Huerta is a more political and irreverent poet who uses colloquial idioms and offers paeans and diatribes to Mexico City. Late in his career, he wrote many *poemínimos*, very short sardonic poems that use any topic to make poignant observations. Alí Chumacero (1918–2010) belongs to the same generation as Paz and Huerta. His poetry (e.g., *Palabras en reposo*, [Words at Rest], 1956) uses sophisticated lang. and metaphors, sometimes with biblical and liturgical tones, to evoke people who are lonely, such as a widower, a suicidal person, or a pilgrim.

The next generation continued Huerta's use of colloquialisms and direct discourse. Jaime Sabines (1926–1998) became the most popular poet of Mexico. His use of profanity, blasphemy, and jargon in clear, intelligible verse, and other elements ordinarily excluded from Mexican poetry, made him a celebrated poet known for poems such as "Algo de la muerte del mayor Sabines" (Something of the Death of the Elder Sabines) and "Los amorosos" (The Lovers). His readings attracted thousands of people. Rosario Castellanos (1925–74), also from the southern state of Chiapas, belongs to the same generation, although she focuses on women's role in society. After Sor Juana, she is the first poet to raise her voice against the dominant male culture in Mexican society. Tomás Segovia (1927–2011) is known for his erotic poetry in the surrealist vein, and for *Anagnórisis* (1967), a long poem (incl., in turn, other poems invoked through a phrase or verbal image) that explores the ambience of the exile from different perspectives: memory, travel, and orphanhood. Homero Aridjis (b. 1940) follows this line of continuity in relation to surrealism. Informed by his ecological activism, his poems make constant reference to nature. José Emilio Pacheco (1939–2014) is a poet of daily life who observes with acuteness and pessimism the transience and the innovations of the moment. In his denunciation of the student massacre of 1968, he composed his poems using phrases and words taken from Garibay's trans. of the indigenous voices of the conquest, arranged in such a way that they become a condemnation of the events of the present. His poetry also explores the neglect and devastation of Mexico City. Gerardo Deniz's (pseud. of Juan Almela, 1934–2014) poetry is cryptic, with erudite and mundane references that escape even the most avid readers. For him, every poem is an opportunity to challenge his readers and to amuse himself, sometimes with superficial themes. If the Chilean Nicanor Parra is the transparent antipoet (see CHILE, POETRY OF), Deniz is the baroque and obscure antipoet, combining multiple registers, deliberately confusing his readers. Heir of Dada, he puts in doubt the concept of art itself. In Gloria Gervitz's (b. 1943) *Migraciones* (*Migrations*; a long poem that has grown over the years and in new eds.), a dialogue (or monologue?) devoted to Jewish women who migrated from Eastern Europe to Mexico serves as a reinvention of the past, a reconstruction of the loss. As with Paz, Elsa Cross (b. 1946) is interested in Eastern philosophies, particularly of India. Her poetry explores the sacred as it relates to ancient cultures. David Huerta (b. 1949) has tried several different techniques. His *Incurable* (1987) is a memorable baroque poem, which combines the long verses of the Cuban poet José Lezama Lima and poststructuralist theory. Coral Bracho (b. 1951) is perhaps the most admired poet of her generation. Her first two books, intimately associated with Gilles Deleuze and Félix Guattari's concept of *rhizome*, have had a lasting influence on many younger writers. In *Tierra nativa* (Native Land, 1980), José Luis Rivas (b. 1951) recreates the tropics and his childhood in Veracruz, using long and sophisticated lines, reminiscent of the Fr. modernist Saint-John Perse. With *Ojo de jaguar* (Jaguar's Eye, 1982), Efraín Bartolomé (b. 1950) depicts the rain forest of Chiapas, in association with Mayan mythology, in a defense of nature. Although it may be difficult to point to a general characteristic of Alberto Blanco's (b. 1951) poetry, perhaps his tendency is to see the sacred in mundane situations. Myriam Moscona (b. 1955) is a Sephardic poet who employs Judeo-Sp. Her *Negro marfil* (Black Ivory, 2000) is a cubist poem of sorts, employing space, simultaneity, multiple readings, and images that resemble illegible graffiti or encoded messages. María Baranda (b. 1962) combines epic dimensions with intimate feelings. Her dialogue with Dylan Thomas (*Dylan y las ballenas* [Dylan and the Whales], 2001) was enthusiastically received by the critics.

The number of contemp. poets in Mexico is very large (some would argue as many as 1,000); a diversity of themes, techniques, and poetics has been the norm since the 1970s. But despite the range, a few generalizations about its character are possible. Most Mexican poets inherited from Paz (and also from the Contemporáneos, López Velarde, Sor Juana, and others) the rigorous control of composition, sound, and words. There has tended to be a focus on craft and balance at the expense of spontaneity, even among poets who write in the idiom of the street. Ideology, politics, sentimentality, openly expressed passion, and confessionalism tend to be avoided. The idea of balance also impedes radical experimentation. Mexico lacks the unevenness—the deliberate aim of imperfection—of a poet such as the Peruvian César Vallejo or the frantic tone of the Beat generation such as Allen Ginsberg's *Howl*. In the first decade of the 21st c., a new trend appeared: lit., incl. poetry, in indigenous langs. Mexico is returning to its roots, but with a contemp. edge. An example would be Natalia Toledo (b. 1968), a bilingual poet from Oaxaca, who writes in Zapotec and translates her work into Sp. Some of these poems reveal a world on the brink of obliteration.

See INDIGENOUS AMERICAS, POETRY OF THE; SPAIN, POETRY OF; SPANISH AMERICA, POETRY OF.

■ **Anthologies**: *Antología de la poesía mexicana moderna*, ed. J. Cuesta (1928); *Poetas novohispanos*, ed. A. Méndez Plancarte (1964); *La poesía mexicana del siglo XIX*, ed. J. E. Pacheco (1965); *Poesía en movimiento*, ed. O. Paz et al. (1966; also as *New Poetry of Mexico*, ed. and trans. M. Strand, 1970); *Trece poetas del mundo azteca*, ed. M. León Portilla (1967); *Ómnibus de poesía mexicana*, ed. G. Zaid (1971); *Antología del Modernismo, 1884–1921*, ed. J. E. Pacheco (1978); *Poesía mexicana, 1915–1979*, ed. C. Monsiváis (1979); *Asamblea de poetas jóvenes de México*, ed. G. Zaid (1980); *Palabra nueva*, ed. S. Cohen (1981); *Mouth to Mouth: Poems by Twelve Contemporary Mexican Women*, ed. F. Gander, trans. Z. Anglesey (1993); *De la vigilia fértil: Antología de poetas mexicanas contemporáneas*, ed. J. Palley (1996); *El manantial latent*, ed. E. Lumbreras and H. Bravo Varela (2002); *Reversible Monuments: Contemporary Mexican Poetry*, ed. M. de la Torre and M. Wiegers (2002); *Sin Puertas Visibles: An Anthology of Contemporary Poetry by Mexican Women*, ed. and trans. J. Hofer (2003); *Words of the True Peoples: Anthology of Contemporary Mexican Indigenous-Language Writers*, ed. and trans. C. Montemayor and D. Frischmann, v. 2 (2005); *Connecting Lines: New Poetry from Mexico*, ed. L. Cortés Bargalló, trans. and ed. F. Gander (2006).

■ **Criticism and History**: See prologues from anthols. above; A. M. Garibay, *Historia de la literatura náhuatl* (1953); R. Leiva, *Imagen de la poesía mexicana contemporánea* (1957); J. L. Martínez, *Nezahualcóyotl* (1972); J. J. Blanco, *Crónica de poesía mexicana* (1977); G. Sheridan, *Los Contemporáneos ayer* (1985); F. Dauster, *The Double Strand: Five Contemporary Mexican Poets* (1987); *Lugar de encuentro: Ensayos críticos sobre poesía mexicana actual*, ed. J. Fernández and N. Klahn (1987); O. Paz, *Sor Juana, or the Traps of Faith*, trans. M. Sayers Peden (1988); V. Quitarte, *Peces del aire altísino: Poesía y poetas* *en México* (1993); *Los Contemporáneos en el laberinto de la crítica*, ed. O. Paz, R. Olea Franco, A. Stanton (1994); O. Paz, *Obras completas*, v. 4 (1994); A. Stanton, *Inventores de tradición: Ensayos sobre poesía mexicana moderna* (1998); A. Paredes, *Haz de palabras: Ocho poetas mexicanos recientes* (1999); C. Monsiváis, *Las tradiciones de la imagen: Notas sobre poesía mexicana* (2001); E. Escalante, *Elevación y caída del estridentismo* (2002); E. Cross, *Los dos jardines: Mística y erotismo en algunos poetas mexicanos* (2003); *Poesía mexicana reciente: Aproximaciones críticas*, ed. S. Gordon (2005).

J. Sefamí

MONGOLIA, POETRY OF

I. History. The origins of Mongolian poetic expression lie in shamanic incantation and in epic. The oral culture, which prevailed up until the 1921 revolution and which still exerts a profound influence on the literary arts, was one in which the landscape, the gods, and ancestors were celebrated, propitiated, and invoked. Our principal example of early Mongolian poetry is the 13th-c. *Mongol Nuuts Tuuh*, an uneven collection of passages with lines of varying lengths and meters, presumably fashioned from different sources. Over the following centuries, poets came to write in a more sophisticated style, such as in the chronicle *Erdeniyin Tobchi*, in which regular verse forms were employed and more sophisticated devices developed. Mongolia's epic (*üliger*) trad. contains texts of up to 20,000 verses, centered around heroes such as Chinggis Haan, Erintsen Mergen, and Gesar. These are transmitted orally and are an excellent example of the standard structural form, *tolgoi süül* (see below). Despite the influence of Tibetan Buddhism, and thereby Tibetan culture, from the mid-19th c., poets such as the controversial monk Danzanravjaa (1803–56) began to fashion a specifically Mongolian style of poetry, addressing themes common to nomadic and steppe-dwelling people—livestock (esp. horses), seasonal movement, traditional culture, and ancestral lineage. Danzanravjaa's verses range from love lyrics to lengthy, although witty and entertaining, Buddhist religious instruction. The poetry scene of the 19th c. is also characterized by the preeminence of the family of the poet Vanchingbal, whose four sons (Gularansa, Sunveidanzan, Günchig, and Injinashi) each made his own significant contributions to the devel. of poetic form.

Following the revolution of 1921, Mongolian lit. was severely censored, and Mongolian writers repressed, by the government of Marshal H. Choibalsan. D. Natsagdorj (1906–37), who is generally credited with opening Mongolian lit. (esp. the short-story form) to the West, was educated during the 1920s in Leipzig, and, following his return, became one of the most influential poets and cultural figures in Mongolia. His death, from a stress-induced heart attack, together with that of another poet, S. Buyannemeh (1902–36), in the same year, came at the height of Choibalsan's cultural and political purges. Despite being regarded as a catalyst for postrevolutionary poetry in Mongolia, Natsagdorj's style and imagery are not esp. different from those of his contemporaries. Indeed, the Group of Revolutionary Writers (*Huvsgalin Uran Zohiolchnarin Bülgem*, founded in 1929) consisted of many of Natsagdorj's contemporaries, whose aim was to propagandize and develop revolutionary theory as it applied to lit. and its relationship to the people. Among these, poets such as B. Rinchen (1905–77), C. Chimed (1904–32), Buyannemeh, and Ts. Damdinsüren (1908–86) also made considerable contributions to the poetry from both the literary and the political point of view.

From the 1930s until Nikita Khrushchev's denunciation of Josef Stalin in 1956, Mongolian poetry was very much in a state of ideological repression, with poets writing revolutionary verse to order, while prevented to some degree by their level of personal safety from writing their own poetry. In the late 1950s, B. Yavuuhulan (1929–82) started to revive the traditional poetry, that of Danzanravjaa, Vanchingbal, and his sons, and the earlier writers of epic poetry, under the general title of the New Tendency (*Shine Handlaga*). Yavuuhulan was committed to teaching and developing a poetry that brought the best of foreign lit. (he is famous for his trans. of Sergei Esenin and of Japanese haiku) together with the Mongolian trads. His students included possibly the three most important poets of the late 20th c., D. Nyamsüren (1949–2002), O. Dashbalbar (1957–99), and G. Mend-Ooyo (b. 1952). These three can be credited for the vibrant state of Mongolian poetry at the present time, and Mend-Ooyo's Academy of Culture and Poetry (*Soyol, Yaruu Nairgin Akademi*) publishes Eng. trans. of

Mongolian poetry, as well as original texts by contemp. writers. Of the younger generation, the majority is following Yavuuhulan's trad. T. Bavuudorj (b. 1969) and T- Ö. Erdenetsogt (b. 1974) use Buddhist imagery alongside the ideas of landscape and hist. to develop new ways of working with ancient ideas and forms. Although there are very few writers actively involved with formal experimentation, there is some interest in postmodernism and the Rus. OBERIU movement among poets such as B. Odgerel (b. 1967), G-A. Ayurzana (b. 1970) and B. Galsansuh (b. 1972).

II. Form. There is one standard form of Mongolian poetry, which goes back to the epic and which was clearly a mnemonic device for recitation. This is the head/tail (*tolgoi/süül*) form, where the first letter (occasionally syllable) of every line (whether of a poem, a couplet, or a verse) is the same and where (now less frequently) the last word of every line is the same.

■ W. Heissig, *Geschichte der Mongolische Literatur* (1972); Danzanravjaa, *Perfect Qualities*, trans. S. Wickham-Smith (2006); O. Dashbalbar, *The River Flows Gently*, trans. S. Wickham-Smith (2008); *Anthology of Mongolian Literature*, ed. S. Wickham-Smith and Sh Tsog (2008); B. Yavuuhulan, *Mongolian Verse*, trans. S. Wickham-Smith (2009).

S. Wickham-Smith

MOZARABIC POETRY. *See* AL-ANDALUS, POETRY OF; SPAIN, POETRY OF

N

NAHUATL, POETRY OF. *See* INDIGENOUS AMERICAS, POETRY OF THE; MEXICO, POETRY OF

NATIVE AMERICAN POETRY. *See* INDIGENOUS AMERICAS, POETRY OF THE; INUIT POETRY; MAPUCHE POETRY; NAVAJO POETRY

NAVAJO POETRY. In the late 1890s, Dr. Washington Matthews, an army surgeon who had an interest in Navajo ceremonial ways, described Navajo oral storytellers and singers as "poets" and their songs as "poems." He argued that, if the Navajo lang. (*Diné bizaad*) were written, one would find that Navajo poets had as many poetic devices as their Eng. counterparts, if not more. Written poetry by Navajos, however, began not in the Navajo lang. but in Eng., and, indeed, the impetus for writing poetry came from the Bureau of Indian Affairs (BIA) and the school system of the time. E.g., in 1933, a short, eight-line poem was published in *Indians at Work*, a U.S. government publication (Hirschfelder and Singer). The poem was composed by Navajo students at Tohatchi School in New Mexico, on the Navajo Nation. This poem, "If I Were a Pony," is one of the first published poems by a Navajo; it is written entirely in Eng.

The BIA schools, through their Creative Writing project, encouraged the writing of poetry by young Navajos as a way to teach them Eng., which led to the publication of the annual jour. *Arrow* from 1968 to 1974, a venue for many young Native American poets, incl. Navajos. Some published poetry included Navajo vocabulary such as *mą'ii* (coyote) and *shicheii* (my grandfather), here written in the current orthography of the Navajo Nation. Poems often addressed contemp. issues facing Navajos, such as siblings at war in Vietnam or the poverty in the Navajo Nation. The poet and artist Gloria Emerson published politically engaged poetry in the overtly political *The Indian Historian* out of San Francisco. In 1977, as Eng.-lang. Navajo poetry became more visible, Nia Francisco published a poem in Navajo in the jour. *College English*. In the 1980s, even more poetry would be published by Navajos. By the mid- to late 1980s, individually authored books of Navajo poetry were appearing more frequently. In 1989 and 1995, Rex Lee Jim published two collections of poetry through the Princeton University Library, *Áhí Ni' Nikisheegiizh* and *saad*, that were written entirely in Navajo; and in 1998, Jim published *Dúchas Táá Kóó Diné*, a trilingual collection of poetry in Navajo, Gaelic, and Eng. Alyse Neundorf, a poet and linguist, published poetry in both Navajo and Eng. during the 1990s. In 1993, the Navajo Community College Press published *Storm Patterns*, a collection of poetry by two Navajo women, Della Frank and Roberta Joe—one of the only examples of a book of Navajo poetry published by the Navajo Nation. Most Navajo poetry is published either by university presses in the southwestern U.S. or by independent poetry publishers off the reservation.

Recognized Navajo poets in addition to the figures mentioned above include Tacey Atsitty, Rutherford Ashley, Shonto Begay, Esther Belin, Sherwin Bitsui, Norla Chee, Hershman John, Blackhorse Mitchell, Luci Tapahonso, Laura Tohe, Orlando White, and Venaya Yazzie. Some, like Jim, Tapahonso, and Tohe, are recognized both on and off the Navajo Nation, while others, like Belin, are better known outside the Nation.

Contemp. Navajo poetry is primarily written in Eng. While Navajo is spoken by many residents on the Navajo Nation, literacy in Navajo is not widespread (McLaughlin). Indeed, poets such as Tohe—whose Navajo was almost entirely oral—have actively begun to learn the written lang.

Navajo poets often write about topics and themes connected with home and history. Most Navajo poets have written about the Long Walk (1864–68), when many Navajo were forcibly relocated from their homeland for four years, and connected it with contemp. concerns about identity and homeland. Poets have also written about such topics as the loss of the lang., what it means to be a Navajo in a Western world, and economic and environmental inequalities. Some Navajo poets employ poetry as a way to educate non-Navajos about important cultural, spiritual, and philosophical issues. The themes of growing up on the Navajo Nation and experiencing government-operated boarding schools continue to be central in Navajo poetry. In these examples, Navajo poets present their writing as a historical and cultural supplement to the Westernized education received by young Navajos. The awareness and confirmation of Eng. as a tribal (*Diné*) lang. emerge as intriguing themes in the writing of contemp. Navajo poets.

Sound symbolism (and iconicity more broadly), parallelism, quoted speech, and a variety of poetic devices found in traditional Navajo oral poetry have been actively incorporated into some contemp. written poetry as well. Navajo poets have also experimented with free verse, sestinas, limericks, concrete poetry, haiku, and other poetic trads.

Contemp. poets in performance have taken on the roles of tribal storyteller and *hataali* (traditional Navajo chanter who performs healing through singing). Narrative remains very popular. In many Navajo narrative genres—Coyote stories, e.g.—there can be a sung portion within the narrative (Webster), and two poets in particular, Mitchell and Tapahonso, have incorporated song into their poetry readings. While the strong influence of Eng. literacy and education has thwarted many traditional Navajo practices, the visibility of poets in cultural celebrations indicates the transformation of poetry into an essential factor for Navajo cultural survival.

See INDIGENOUS AMERICAS, POETRY OF THE.

■ **Anthologies and Primary Texts**: W. Matthews, *Navaho Legends* (1897)—reissued 1994; T. D. Allen, "Please Read Loose," in B. Mitchell, *Miracle Hill*, (1967)—2d ed. (2004) omits Allen's intro.; J. Milton, *The American Indian Speaks* (1969); G. Emerson, "The Poetry of Gloria Emerson," *The Indian Historian* 4 (1971); and "Slayers of the Children," *The Indian Historian* 5 (1972); S. Allen, *Yei* (1972); *The Whispering Wind*, ed. T. Allen (1972); J. Milton, *Four Indian Poets* (1974); N. Francisco, "táchééh," *CE* 39 (1977); *The South Corner of Time*, ed. L. Evers (1980); L. Tapahonso, *Seasonal Woman* (1982); L. Tohe, *Making Friends with Water* (1986); L. Tapahonso, *A Breeze Swept Through* (1987); N. Francisco, *Blue Horses for Navajo Women* (1988); R. L. Jim, *Áhí Ni' Nikisheegiizh* (1989); D. McLaughlin, *When Literacy Empowers: Navajo Language in Print* (1992); *Rising Voices: Writings of Young Native Americans*, ed. A. Hirschfelder and B. Singer (1992); D. Frank and R. Joe, *Storm Patterns: Poems from Two Navajo Women* (1993); L. Tapahonso, *Sáanii Dahataał: The Women are Singing* (1993); N. Francisco, *Carried Away by the Black River* (1994); S. Begay, *Navajo Visions and Voices across the Mesa* (1995); R. L. Jim, *saad* (1995); L. Tapahonso, *Blue Horses Rush In* (1997); R. L. Jim, *Dúchas Táá Kóó Diné* (1998); E. Belin, *From the Belly of My Beauty* (1999); A. Neundorf, "Dííjį Nánísdzá, I come home today," "Diné Hosiidlį́į́'gi," "Hayííłką́, At Dawn," "Hóyéé," *Red Mesa Review* 6 (1999); L. Tohe, *No Parole Today* (1999); V. Browne, *Ravens Dancing* (2000); R. Ashley, *Heart Vision 2000* (2001); N. Chee, *Cedar Smoke on Abalone Mountain* (2001); *Sister Nations*, ed. H. Erdrich and L. Tohe (2002); S. Bitsui, *Shapeshift* (2003); G. Emerson, *At the Hems of the Lowest Clouds* (2003); L. Tohe, *Tséyi': Deep in the Rock* (2005); V. Yazzie, *Livin Matriarchal: Chapbook I* (2006); H. John, *I Swallow Turquoise for Courage* (2007); L. Tapahonso, *a radiant curve* (2008); T. Atsitty, *amenorrhea* (2009); S. Bitsui, *Floodsong* (2009); O. White, *Bone Light* (2009).

■ **Criticism and History**: E. G. Belin, "Contemporary Navajo Writers' Relevance to Navajo Society," *Wicazo Sa Review* 22 (2007); All by A. K. Webster—"Coyote Poems: Navajo Poetry, Intertextuality, and Language Choice," *American Indian Culture and Research Journal* 28 (2004); "The Mouse That Sucked: On 'Translating' a Navajo Poem," *Studies in American Indian Literature* 18 (2006); *Explorations in Navajo Poetry and Poetics* (2009); "Imagining Navajo in the Boarding School," *Journal of Linguistic Anthropology* 20 (2010)—ling. analysis of Tohe's *No Parole Today*; "Towards a History of Navajo English in Navajo Poetry," *World Englishes* 29 (2010); "'Please Read Loose': Intimate Grammars and Unexpected Languages in Contemporary Navajo Literature," *American Indian Culture and Research Journal* 35 (2011).

E. G. BELIN; A. K. WEBSTER

NEPĀL BHĀṢA. *See* NEWAR POETRY

NEPALI AND PAHARI POETRY. The Pahari langs. form a band along the Himalayan range from Kashmir through Nepal. By the early 19th c., the entire region was divided among small principalities in the west, territory under the control of the Brit. Empire in the center, and the newly consolidated kingdom of Nepal in the east. Of the various langs., Nepali came to serve as the vehicle of a national lit. of the mod. type, while Dogri has been named one of the official langs. of the Indian state of Jammu and Kashmir. Between these extremes, the territory now forming the Indian states of Himachal Pradesh and Uttarakhand adopted Hindi as the official lang., with Pahari langs. persisting as the tongues of household and of oral lit. and ritual.

One of the striking characteristics of all Pahari-speaking territories is the richness of oral poetic trads. Noteworthy are ballad singing (cf. the Gaine of central Nepal), humorous and satiric poetry and song, and the role of mythic narrative as part of rituals, sometimes of shamanic healing. Throughout, poets have maintained what is probably an ancient office of praising kings. In particular, the Central Himalayan region, incl. Uttarakhand and far western Nepal, shows a distinctive devel. of narrative poetry performed by singer-drummers. These bards perform epics, heroic ballads, vernacular renditions of Hindu epics and myths, and narrative hymns to the regional gods, in a variety of styles.

Throughout the Himalayas, the last centuries have also seen the devel. of vernacular written lits. inspired both by Sanskritic and North Indian models and by local trads.

Western Pahari courtly langs. served for the trans. of religious poetry, while Dogri has had an established literary trad. since the 18th c. In the Central Himalayas, poetry has been written in the two main langs., Garhwali and Kumaoni, since the early 19th c. Lok Ratna Pant "Gumāni" (1791–1846) is said to have established Kumaoni as a literary lang., while Gaurī Datt Pāṇḍe "Gaurdā" (1872–1939) is remembered for sensitive and sometimes satirical poetry, often in the cause of social reform and Indian independence. In the Indian Himalayas, efforts to valorize regional langs. have continued, and there has been a renaissance of topical and popular song, often with a political edge.

In Nepal, the earliest written poetry, dating from the late 18th c., consists of martial epics praising the king. But the foundational text of Nepali lit. is usually considered Bhānubhakta's (1814–68) rendition of the *Rāmāyaṇa*, composed in something close to spoken Nepali. This work was rediscovered by Motīrām Bhaṭṭa (1866–96), another major poet. Three great names dominated the 20th c.: the master craftsman Lekhnāth Pauḍyāl (1884–1965), who was influenced by oral poetic forms; Bālkṛṣṇa Sama (1902–81), known primarily for his dramas; and the neoromantic Lakṣmīprasād Devkoṭa (1909–59; see Rubin), who composed his ballad *Munā Madan*, still sung today, in folk meters. From the 1940s, traditional verse forms were challenged, and from the 1960s, with the *Tesro Āyām* (Third Dimension) poets, there was an opening to personal expression. Since then, Nepali poetry has gone through a series of movements, all related, as elsewhere in the Pahari-speaking region, to political struggles. The tension here is among poetry as a self-referential craft of lang., as a vehicle of sometimes subtle self-expression, and as a tool for social transformation.

See HINDI POETRY; INDIA, POETRY OF; KASHMIRI POETRY; RĀMĀYAṆA POETRY; SANSKRIT POETICS; SANSKRIT POETRY.

■ D. Rubin, *Nepali Visions, Nepali Dreams: The Poetry of Laxmiprasad Devkota* (1980); K. Pradhan, *A History of Nepali Literature* (1984); K. Meissner, *Malushahi and Rajula: A Ballad from Kumaun* (1985); M. Hutt, *Himalayan Voices: An Introduction to Modern Nepali Literature* (1991); C. C. Pande, *Echoes from the Hills: Poems of Gaurda* (1997); G. Maskarinec, *Nepalese Shaman Oral Texts* (1998).

J. LEAVITT

NETHERLANDS, POETRY OF THE. *See* LOW COUNTRIES, POETRY OF THE

NEWAR POETRY. Nepāl Bhāṣā (Kathmandu Newar), the lang. of the Newars, is a Tibeto-Burman lang. spoken primarily in the Kathmandu Valley. The term *Nepāl Bhāṣā* is the traditional and preferred term, although *Newar* and *Newari* are often used. Written sources from the med. period date back as early as 1114 CE. Of the approximately 350 Tibeto-Burman langs., only three others have literary trads. of comparable historical depth.

In the Malla era (1400–1769), the cl. literary lang. was highly Sanskritized, with much of the vocabulary from Indic sources. Verse forms imitating Sanskrit models appeared in the 15th c., sometimes authored by royalty, often anonymous. These sung verse forms (*mye*) were primarily religious, with the exception of the *bākhā mye* (ballad songs) and *sinhājyā mye* (rice-planting songs). Characteristically, in Newar, the sinhājyā mye invoke the spring passions of men and women working together during planting season. Many continue to be sung in the mod. period.

With the Gorkha conquest of the Kathmandu Valley in 1769 and the promotion of Nepāli, an Indic lang., under the Shah regime (1769–1847), Newar cultural institutions began to suffer. During the Rana period (1905–51), Newar-lang. publications were banned outright, writers and activists jailed. Shaped by this oppression, the mod. era also contains the seeds of resistance and a literary renaissance. Among the poets of this period, Siddhi Dās Āmātya (1867–1930) and Yogbir Singh Kansākār (1885–1941) were foundational influences.

The iconic poet of the 20th c. Nepāl Bhāṣā movement is Chittadhar Hṛdaya (1906–82). Jailed five years for literary activism, Chittadhar withstood confinement by writing his masterpiece *Sugata Saurabha* and having the chapters smuggled out of prison. The epic poem (19 chs.) is a deeply erudite Nepāl Bhāṣā redaction of the Buddha's life in rhymed couplets, employing Sanskrit meters and allusions to canonical Buddhist biographical and philosophical trads. More significant where the canonical sources lacked narrative detail, the poet localizes the Buddha's story, weaving in details unique to Newar culture: food, domestic life, clothing and jewelry, music, rites of passages, marriage customs, rituals, festivals, even local architecture. The chapters teem with allusions to contemp. social concerns. Similarly, the vocabulary ranges from esoteric religious terms to colloquial, onomatopoeic expressions ubiquitous in Newar conversation. This complex intertextuality brings Nepāl Bhāṣā poetry into the mod. period. Others of Chittadhar's poems reflect contemp. themes and greater formal flexibility. In *TB*, a recovering wife in a sanitarium finds her husband has taken a second wife. *Pragati* is an allegorical critique of the mod. concept of progress.

With the onset of a fragile democracy in 1951, contemp. poets exhibit increased formal freedoms, political awareness, and secularization. Durga Lāl Śhresta (b. 1937), a prolific composer of songs, plays, and poems, writes richly melodic lines: imagistic, deeply personal and political. Purna Vaidya (b. 1941) brings introspective free-verse sensibilities to contemp. Newar poetry. With the increasing influence of Eng. and the educational system's emphasis on Nepali as a national lang., today's poets face the challenge of sustaining the Nepāl Bhāṣā literary community.

See INDIA, POETRY OF; NEPALI AND PAHARI POETRY; SANSKRIT POETICS; SANSKRIT POETRY.

■ K. P. Malla, *Classical Newari Literature* (1982); *Songs of Nepal*, ed. S. Lienhard (1984); C. Hṛdaya, *Dega* (Pagoda), trans. V. P. Lācoul, M. Karmācārya, U. Malla (1996); *A Representative Collection of Nepal Bhasa Poems*, ed. K. C. Pradhan, trans. T. L. Tulādhar and W. Amtis (1997); D. L. Śhresta, *Twists and Turns*, trans. T. T. Tulādhar (2000); *Contemporary Writing in Nepāl Bhāṣā*, ed. B. P. Śhresta and P. S. Tulādhar (2000); C. Hṛdaya, *Sugata Surabha*, trans. T. T. Lewis and S. M. Tulādhar (2007).

D. HARGREAVES

NEW NORSE (NYNORSK) POETRY. One of the two official written langs. of Norway, Nynorsk was reconstructed in the mid-19th c. by the philologist Ivar Aasen (1813–96) from rural dialects that were directly descended from ON. Aasen wanted to give his country a literary lang. less influenced by Danish, and he demonstrated the viability of *landsmaal*, as it was called at the time, by translating foreign poetry and writing his own literary works of national romanticism in various genres. The first important poet to write in Nynorsk was Aasmund Vinje (1818–70), who established the combination of cosmopolitan intellectual engagement and regional consciousness that can be seen in many later Nynorsk writers. Around the turn of the 20th c., Arne Garborg (1851–1924) and Olav Aukrust (1883–1929) demonstrated the remarkable power and rich melody of the new medium. Since then, many of Norway's most innovative literary figures have used Nynorsk, incl. the expressionist Kristofer Uppdal (1878–1961), the novelist and poet Tarjei Vesaas (1897–1970), and the revered poet Olav H. Hauge (1908–94), who translated many key 20th-c. writings to the lang. Contemp. lit. in Nynorsk boasts some artistically brilliant figures, such as the novelist Kjartan Fløgstad (b. 1944) and the widely acclaimed dramatist and poet Jon Fosse (b. 1959).

See NORWAY, POETRY OF.

■ O. J. Falnes, *National Romanticism in Norway* (1933); L. S. Vikør, *The New Norse Language Movement* (1976); *Twenty Contemporary Norwegian Poets*, ed. T. Johanssen (1984); S. Walton, *Farewell the Spirit Craven: Ivar Aasen and National Romanticism* (1987); T. Vesaas, *Through Naked Branches*, ed. and trans. R. Greenwald (2000); O. H. Hauge, *The Dream We Carry*, trans. R. Bly and R. Hedin (2008).

S. LYNGSTAD; D. KROUK

NEW ZEALAND, POETRY OF

I. Maori Poetry
II. Maori Poetry in English
III. Poetry in English

I. Maori Poetry. Maori poetry is a song and chant trad. beginning more than 800 years ago with the Polynesian settlement of Aotearoa, now

New Zealand; it retains many of its oral features such as adept manipulation of lang., repetition, and patterning accompanied by illustrative gestures by performers. Poetry was recited or sung during everyday activities and group occasions. An orator was supported at the end of a speech by a relevantly themed song or *waiata*. Highly structured musically and thematically, some of the many song types include *waiata aroha* or love lyrics often addressing loss and longing; *pao* or topical, linked epigrams (McLean and Orbell 1979); *poi* or performance art incl. swinging poi-ball actions; *oriori* or educational compositions sung at the birth of children; *waiata tangi* or laments concerning the dead or misfortunes; and *karanga* or ceremonial calls of welcome, encouragement, or farewells to the departed.

Recited types include the *haka* (assertive posture-dance with or without weapons, with vocals akin to "stylized shouting" [McLean and Orbell 1979], "hair-raising blood-curdling shouts" [Ngata] designed "to stiffen the sinews, to summon up the blood" [Kāretu]). *Kaioraora* (cursing chants) are noted for their fury in venting past wrongs. *Karakia* are incantations, charms, and invocations; because of their sacerdotal function, they are rarely recorded. *Whakaaraara pā* were cried by sentinels as they watched fortresses.

Nationally known composers of the past included tribal and pan-Maori nobility, community leaders, and educators. The famed Rihi Puhiwahine's (1816?–1906) lyrics are colorful and deeply felt. In "Kāore Hoki Koia Te Rangi Nei" ("Oh What a Day"; Orbell), she wittily catalogs her aristocratic lovers while making reassuring asides to their spouses and incorporates the symbolic landmarks of her adventures with them. Noted compositions by others include the 19th-c. haka "Ka mate ka mate" (I Die, I Die) by the chief Te Rauparaha (ca. 1760–1849); "Poia atu taku poi" (Swing Out My Poi) by Erenora Taratoa (fl. 1850s), which was composed in response to Puhiwahine's disapproval of Taratoa's affair with Puhiwahine's brother (Royal); and the early 20th-c. songs "Po Atarau" (Moonlit Night) by Maewa Kaihau (1879–1941), popularized overseas as "Now Is the Hour" by Gracie Fields and later by Bing Crosby, and "Pokarekare ana" ([The Waves] Are Breaking) by Paraire Tomoana (1874?–1946). In the 20th c., composers adapted lyrics to popular tunes; for instance, Tuini Ngāwai's (1910–65) Maori battalion farewell "Arohaina Mai" (Bestow Your Love) was set to George Gershwin's "Love Walked In." These well-known tunes aided the recall of concert groups who performed on occasions such as the opening of meeting houses, anniversaries, and welcomes (*Dictionary of New Zealand Biography*, Spittle). Ngāwai wrote many popular songs. Ngoi Pēwhairangi (1922–85) composed the lyrics for the very popular "Poi E" (Swing) which was turned into a music video featuring break dancers with the Pātea Maori Club; the Prince Tui Teka hit song "E Ipo" (Beloved); and the waiata "Whakarongo" (Listen), exhorting listeners to retain and speak the Maori lang. Non-traditional Maori lang. poetry is continually evolving, while traditional forms are relatively fixed vocally and musically in performance.

With the continuing revival of Maori culture and lang., there are many performances of both contemp. and traditional waiata and haka in concert parties; tribal, regional, and national events and competitions; televised performances; and musical albums. The most prominent published collections are by George Grey (1802–98), who compiled *Ko nga moteatea me nga hakirara o nga Maori* (Poems, Chants and Traditions of the Maoris, 1853), and Apirana Ngata (1874–1950), whose four-volume collection *Ngā Moteatea* (The Sung Poems) was completed posthumously by other scholars. There are numerous other book, audiovisual, and ms. collections as well as contemp. composers and performers. Hirini Melbourne (1950–2003) did much to popularize the waiata and traditional Maori music within wider contemp. culture.

II. Maori Poetry in English. The critically and popularly acclaimed Hone Tuwhare (1922–2008) was the first Maori to publish a single-authored literary collection. His oeuvre of 13 books began in 1964 with *No Ordinary Sun*. His poetry is imbued with affective significance, a term coined by the Marxist aesthetician Christopher Caudwell, whose work influenced Tuwhare, and code switching (Manhire) from hieratic to demotic modes. Mitcalfe's term *hotu* (heart notes), used to describe sung feelings in Puhiwahine's Maori-lang. poems, is apt for Tuwhare's complete oeuvre. Naturalistic and sensual, Tuwhare also wrote political verse centered on Maori land-rights struggles from the mid-1970s. Many scholars (Keown, DeLoughrey, Battista, Sullivan) note Tuwhare's mythological symbolism, such as the tree-deity Tāne Mahuta appealing to humanity, in his antinuclear poem "No Ordinary Sun": "O tree / in the shadowless mountains/ the white sea plains and /the drab sea floor / your end at last is written." Tuwhare's animation of natural elements perhaps extends from Maori-lang. poetics, as do repetition of words and musical and incantatory phrasing. His appetitive poetry enjoys sexual themes and humor. Tuwhare was a national icon and influenced many New Zealand poets.

The Booker Prize–winning author Keri Hulme (b. 1947) refers to place names, close observations of the natural environment, "living time" rather than "calendar time," and Maori female deities to indicate indigenous alterities and worldview. Like Tuwhare, Hulme is a connoisseur of land and sea who brings the natural world into the body of her writing ("pink flesh of smoked eels, then tiny succulence of oysters . . ." [*Strands*, 1992]) and delivers a feminist poetics that easily aligns with the earth-mother. Identity is a key issue for the writer in her collection *The Silences Between Moeraki Conversations* (1982).

The pioneer author J. C. Sturm (1927–2009) began publishing poems in 1947. In *Dedications* (1996) and *Postscripts* (2000), Sturm writes on intimate and larger scales about family, death, public occasions, race relations, the contemp. and historical effects of colonization, and life's vicissitudes. Her lines favor a three- or four-stress meter, reminiscent of Maori-lang. poetry. Sturm was married to the eminent New Zealand poet James K. Baxter (1926–72), who was esp. influenced by Maori poetics in his later work.

Robert Sullivan's (b. 1967) collections *Star Waka* (1999), *Captain Cook in the Underworld* (2002), and *Voice Carried My Family* (2005) traverse Eur., Polynesian, and Maori historical figures, as well as personal, family, and tribal narratives. Roma Potiki's (b. 1958) collection, *Oriori: A Maori Child Is Born* (1999), a collaboration with the painter Robyn Kahukiwa, is a series of meditations on birth centered on the traditional book-title form. In *Stones in Her Mouth* (1993), she confronts and negotiates the masculine workings of power within Maori society. Many poems focus on motherhood, its joys and challenges. Apirana Taylor (b. 1955) emerged in the late 1970s as a playwright and poet. His work emphasizes sound qualities and is often performed with musical accompaniment such as with the *koauau* or bone flute and the guitar. Taylor's 1996 poem "Te Ihi" (The Essential Force or Awe) explores the multidimensionality of a Maori word within a repetitive soundscape that directly evokes the haka form. Rangi Faith's (b. 1949) two collections show a concern for the environment within traditional and recreational contexts, excavations of tribal memories, and the impact of war on friends and families. The poet and musician Hinemoana Baker's (b. 1968) opening title poem in her collection *Mātuhi/Needle* (2004) alludes to an oratorical chant used at the beginning of speeches and interlaces Maori phrases throughout that collection while song elements such as the nose-flute also feature. Trixie Te Arama Menzies (b. 1936) belongs to the collective of women writers and artists Waiata Koa. She draws on traditional arts such as weaving by master craftswomen for inspiration. Vernice Wineera Pere (b. ca. 1940), domiciled in Hawai'i, writes from a Maori and Polynesian perspective in nuanced and lyrically adept poems that explore mixed-race identity and spirituality, among other issues. The pioneer playwright Rore Hapipi (1933–2016) composed many poems often sung in dramatic performance, as does Brian Potiki (b. 1953), whose collection *Aotearoa* (2003) is a mixture of songs and poetry influenced by the Beat movement, the hist. of 19th-c. Maori pacifist resistance, and fellow writers and artists. Arapera Blank (1932–2002) deploys rich cultural symbolism in both langs., such as a garden of sweet potatoes representing the abundance of families and flax representing womankind. Michael O'Leary (b. 1950) writes on a wide range of Irish-Maori, personal, literary, satirical, and historical themes. Phil Kawana's (b. 1965) first poetry collection, *The Devil in My Shoes* (2005), ranges from ostensibly cultural to urban themes. Many poets have yet to achieve book publication.

III. Poetry in English

A. *The Nationalist Era.* To understand the hist. of New Zealand poetry in Eng., it is best to begin in the middle. In 1945, Allen Curnow (1911–2001) published the single most influential anthol. of New Zealand poetry, *A Book of New Zealand Verse, 1923–1945*. In a trenchant introduction, Curnow declared his own generation to be the first to see the true purpose of a distinctly New Zealand poetry: "a real expression of what the New Zealander is and a part of what he may become." He was withering in his crit. of the poetry of the first quarter of the 20th c., which he saw as marked by a "lack of any vital relation to experience [and] a fanciful aimlessness." *Kowhai Gold*, the unfortunately twee title of Quentin Pope's 1930 anthol. (referring to the beautiful yellow flowers of the native kowhai tree), became the generic term for these self-consciously "exoticizing" approaches to the New Zealand landscape, and the reputation of the poets from this period has never really recovered from Curnow's attack.

Curnow's unifying account of a generation of poets dedicated to "forms as immediate in experience as the island soil under [their] feet" both relied on and helped foster a certain selectivity of focus. When R.A.K. Mason (1905–71) wrote in "Sonnet of Brotherhood" of "this far-pitched perilous hostile place," he was referring to the planet earth "fixed at the friendless outer edge of space," but the nationalist paradigm made it difficult not to read this alongside Charles Brasch's (1909–73) "Remindingly beside the quays, the white / Ships lie smoking . . . distance looks our way" ("The Islands"); Curnow's own "In your atlas two islands not in narrow seas / Like a child's kite anchored in the indifferent blue" ("Statement from *Not in Narrow Seas*"); or A.R.D. Fairburn's (1904–57) vision of the colonists "sprouting like bulbs in warm darkness, putting out / white shoots under the wet sack of Empire" ("Dominion").

The title of Ursula Bethell's (1874–1945) first England-published collection, *From a Garden in the Antipodes* (1929), suggested an anglocentric approach to her New Zealand experience; but in Curnow's anthol., her universally comprehensible lament for the transience of "our small fond human enclosures" and prayer that her garden "become established quickly, quickly . . . For I am fugitive, I am very fugitive" ("Pause") seemed of a piece with Robin Hyde's (1906–39) account of a "young crude country" forging a new identity and Denis Glover's (1912–80) iconic story of the magpies indifferently singing "Quardle oodle ardle wardle doodle" as a local farm fails and falls to "the mortgage-man" ("The Magpies").

Curnow's own poetry in the anthol. adopts a less confident stance than his introduction. New Zealand's hist. appears marred by violence—"The stain of blood that writes an island story"—and radically ungraspable:

> It is something different, something
> Nobody counted on.
> ("The Unhistoric Story")

In a much-quoted meditation on the skeleton of an extinct native bird, Curnow declared that it would not be him or his generation, but rather "some child, born in a marvelous year" who "will learn the trick of standing upright here" ("The Skeleton of the Great Moa in the Canterbury Museum, Christchurch").

B. ***The Wet Sack of Empire.*** This sense of a hist. evolving too rapidly to be understood would have been familiar to the colonial forebears of the nationalist poets. Eng.-lang. poetry first finds New Zealand as a remote and none-too-welcoming coast; in the brief precolonial period of Eur. contact, Brit., Australian, and Am. seamen, sealers, and whalers work their hard-won New Zealand experience into their shanties and work-songs:

> We cured ten thousand skins for the fur, for
> the fur,
> Yes we cured ten thousand skins for the fur.
> Brackish water, putrid seal,
> We did all of us fall ill,
> For to die, for to die, for to die.
> (Anonymous, "David Lowston,"
> ca. 1810–15)

After the Treaty of Waitangi in 1840 ceded sovereignty from the Maori chiefs to the Brit. Crown, a steady stream of Brit. colonists, the usual mixture of the adventurous and the desperate, began to arrive (and, often, depart again), with many using poetry to make sense of their experience. The prototype of the colonial poet is Alfred Domett (1811–87), the model for Robert Browning's "Waring," who, aged 20, "gave us all the slip . . . With no work done, but great works undone" to build a life "where whole new thousands are." Domett, briefly New Zealand's premier, produced a bloated epic, *Ranolf and Amohia: A South-Sea Day-Dream* (1872), designed to present an exotic world that is readily legible in familiar conceptual frames. Whether as edenic rebuke to our supercivilized world or savage reminder of a primitive past, Domett's poem works to cast the New Zealand landscape and the Maori inhabitants into familiar conceptual templates.

Nonetheless, the poem also registers the "unhistoric" drift that is making a nation "nobody counted on." At the end of the poem, Ranolph, a white adventurer, returns to Britain with Amohia, his Maori princess bride, fully conscious of the shock such a union will create in Brit. drawing rooms but determined "from the ebon-ivory range / Of chequered days and chance and change, / [to] Draw symphonies serene and strange." This same utopian sense of the possibility of a radical reconfiguration of national and racial identity in the fluid colonial environment can be found in David McKee Wright's (1868–1928) "Our Cities Face the Sea" (1900):

> Cousin Jack and Cockney, Irishman and Scot,
> And the native is a brother to the whole blooming lot.
> Pulling, pulling on the one rope strong
> Bringing up the future with a shout and a song.

Colonial plasticity could also offer the possibility of deliberate reinvention. William Pember Reeves (1857–1932), another colonial politician, proclaimed himself "rooted. Firm and fast" in a New Zealand whose apparent crudity masked a vital creative opportunity ("A Colonist in His Garden," 1904):

> "No art?" Who serve an art more great
> Than we, rough architects of State
> With the old Earth at strife?

In "The Passing of the Forest" (1898), though, Reeves acknowledged the "bitter price" of "beauty swept away" that the art of nation building exacted. The "Burnt bush" appeared as a rebuke in Blanche Baughan's (1870–1958) "A Bush Section" (1908), too. Of the Maori inhabitants of that bush and the bloody price they paid for New Zealand's transformation, few Eng.-lang. poets made explicit mention. Jessie Mackay (1864–1938), however, the ardent proponent of Ir. and Scottish Home Rule, universal suffrage, and temperance, wrote scathing satires on the settler government's belligerent and self-serving approach to the Maori.

C. ***The Maori Renaissance.*** The emergence of a Maori voice in New Zealand poetry in Eng. was one of the principal devels. of the post–World War II years. Beginning in the 1950s with the Cook Islands Maori writer Alistair (later Alistair Te Ariki) Campbell (1925–2009), whose first, intensely lyrical, collections made no mention of the ethnic origins that would later become an abiding concern, continuing in the 1960s with Hapipi (also known as Rowley Habib) and with Tuwhare, whose "No Ordinary Sun" drew on a deep Maori reverence for the forests to voice a moving lament for the effects of nuclear testing, and flourishing in the later work of poets such as Taylor, Hulme, Sturm, and Sullivan, Maori poets have in one sense fulfilled the utopian hopes of Wright, while forcing a radical reexamination of the outright racism and blithely paternalistic ethnocentrism that New Zealand's official myth of racial harmony too often belied.

D. ***Marvelous Children.*** Elsewhere, the synthetic power of Curnow's nationalist thesis was challenged almost immediately in the 1950s. The so-called Wellington Group, a loosely affiliated group of poets incl. James K. Baxter (1926–72), W. H. Oliver (1925–2015), Alistair Campbell, and Louis Johnson (1924–88), attacked Curnow's localism as a historical dead end and declared themselves to be internationalists. By the 1960s, both sides in this once heated debate had come to seem old hat. Charles Doyle's 1965 anthol., *Recent Poetry in New Zealand*, features self-descriptions from poets such as Doyle (b. 1928), Fleur Adcock (b. 1934), Kendrick Smithyman (1922–95), and C. K. Stead (b. 1932) that proclaim a rigorously decontextualized commitment to "craft" as their highest ideal.

The 1970s saw an explosion of new voices in New Zealand poetry. The jour. *The Word Is Freed* (1969–72) was the epicenter of the new poetry, and its title gestured toward the formal experimentation that would become the rallying cry of the new generation, incl. poets such as Ian Wedde (b. 1946), Alan Brunton (1946–2002), Jan Kemp (b. 1949), and Murray Edmond (b. 1949). Open form was the shibboleth of the movement, and the championing of Am. models such as Charles Olson and Robert Creeley seemed to mark a turn away both from any last holdovers of colonial fealty to Britain and from the old obsession with "what the New Zealander is."

In the ensuing decades, New Zealand poetry has become at once more popular and widespread than it ever was before (a vibrant culture of poetry performance—owing much to the tireless troubadouring of Sam Hunt [b. 1946]—helps see to that) and far less bold in its claims to public significance. The dominant figure in New Zealand poetry from the late 1970s to the present day is Bill Manhire (b. 1946), a poet of cool ironies and oblique wit. His wry take on Curnow's nationalist isolationism neatly punctures the idea of "New Zealandness" as special burden or heroic challenge: "I live at the edge of the universe, / like everybody else" ("Milky Way Bar").

The work of the best poets of this period—Manhire, Elizabeth Smither (b. 1941), Andrew

Johnston (b. 1963), Jenny Bornholdt (b. 1960), Brian Turner (b. 1944), Michele Leggott (b. 1956), Lauris Edmond (1924–2000), and Fiona Farrell (b. 1947), to name a few—tends to be small-scaled, often domestic or autobiographical and, if formally sophisticated, not overtly experimental. Whether that is "a real expression of what the New Zealander is" is a question for a later, more marvelous, year.

See POLYNESIAN POETRY.

■ **Maori.** ***Anthologies***: *Te Ao Marama: Contemporary Maori Writing*, ed. W. Ihimaera, v. 1 (1993); *Kāti Au i Konei: A Collection of Songs from Ngāti Toarangatira and Ngāti Raukawa*, ed. T.A.C. Royal (1994); H. Melbourne and R. Nunns, *Te Kū Te Whē* (1994)—music CD; *Whetu Moana: Contemporary Polynesian Poems in English*, ed. A. Wendt, R. Whaitiri, and R. Sullivan (2003); *Ngā Moteatea: The Songs*, ed. A. T. Ngata, et al., rev. ed., 4 v. (2004–7); ***Criticism and History***: P.T.H. Jones, "Puhiwahine: Maori Poetess," *Te Ao Hou* 28–33, 6 parts (1959–61), http://www.teaohou.natlib.govt.nz/; B. Mitcalfe, *Maori Poetry: The Singing Word* (1974); A. Salmond, *Hui: a Study of Maori Ceremonial Gatherings*, 2d ed. (1976); *Traditional Songs of the Maori*, ed. M. McLean, trans. M. Orbell (1979); R. Oppenheim, "Internal Exile: Continuity and Community in Maori Poetry," *Journal of the Polynesian Society* 92 (1983); *Dictionary of New Zealand Biography* (1990–), http://www.dnzb.govt.nz/; B. Manhire, "Dirty Silence: Impure Sounds in New Zealand Poetry," *Dirty Silence: Aspects of Language and Literature in New Zealand*, ed. G. McGregor and M. Williams (1991); M. Orbell, *Waiata: Maori Songs in History* (1991); T. Kāretu, *Haka! The Dance of a Noble People* (1993); M. McLean, *Maori Music* (1996); G. Spittle, *Counting the Beat: A History of New Zealand Song* (1997); J. Hunt, *Hone Tuwhare: A Biography* (1998); A.T.P. Somerville, "Nau Te Rourou, Nau Te Rakau: The Oceanic, Indigenous and Postcolonial and New Zealand Comparative Contexts of Maori Writing in English," diss., Cornell University (2006); M. Keown, *Pacific Islands Writing: The Postcolonial Literatures of Aotearoa/New Zealand and Oceania* (2007); E. DeLoughrey, "Solar Metaphors: *No Ordinary Sun*," *Ka Mate Ka Ora* 6 (2009).

■ **English.** ***Anthologies***: *New Zealand Verse*, ed. W. Alexander and A. Currie (1906)—for colonial verse; *An Anthology of New Zealand Poetry in English*, ed. J. Bornholdt, G. O'Brien, M. Williams (1997); A. Curnow, *Early Days Yet: New and Collected Poems, 1941–1997* (1997); *Big Smoke: New Zealand Poems, 1960–1975*, ed. A. Brunton, M. Edmond, M. Leggott (2000); *Twenty Contemporary New Zealand Poets: An Anthology*, ed. R. Marsack and A. Johnston (2009). ***Criticism and History***: E. H. McCormick, *Letters and Art in New Zealand* (1940); K. Smithyman, *A Way of Saying: A Study of New Zealand Poetry* (1965); C. K. Stead, *In the Glass Case: Essays on New Zealand Literature* (1981); H. Ricketts, *Talking about Ourselves: Twelve New Zealand Poets in Conversation with Harry Ricketts* (1986); A. Curnow, *Look Back Harder: Critical Writings, 1935–1984*, ed. P. Simpson (1987); P. Evans, *The Penguin History of New Zealand Literature* (1990); S. Murray, *Never a Soul at Home: New Zealand Literary Nationalism and the 1930s* (1998); *Oxford History of New Zealand Literature in English*, ed. T. Sturm (1998).

R. SULLIVAN (MAORI); H. ROBERTS (ENG.)

NICARAGUA, POETRY OF

I. Rubén Darío and Modernismo
II. Post-modernistas
III. The Vanguard Movement
IV. Generation of the 1940s
V. The Frente Ventana and the Betrayed Generation, New Voices
VI. Women Poets of the 1970s to the Present
VII. Caribbean Coast Writers

I. Rubén Darío and Modernismo. Although Nicaragua is a poor country of only five million inhabitants with scarce resources for education, poetry is important to its cultural identity. This condition is due in large part to the internationally renowned Nicaraguan poet Rubén Darío (1867–1916). Much as Simón Bolívar is associated with Hispanic America's political independence from Spain, Darío initiated—via poetry—the cultural freedom of Sp. America. He championed *modernismo*, a late 19th-c. Hispanic Am. literary movement involving poets of several nationalities, incl. the Cuban nationalist José Martí. Darío transformed the Sp. lang. by creating new rhythmic patterns based on the poetry of Victor Hugo and Walt Whitman, esp. in the extravagant musicality of his poem "Marcha triunfal." He enriched his mother tongue by incorporating a vocabulary and a thematic panorama from indigenous America. Darío's poem to the volcano Momotombo in Nicaragua is a geographical rebellion against Spain, an assertion of identity that contains the ancient force of toponymy. Darío encountered supremacist, racist thinking in Spain during his first visit there in 1892 but insisted on asserting with pride his heritage as a *mestizo*. In *Prosas profanas*, he famously declares, "If there is poetry in our America, it can be found in the old things: in Palenque and Utatlán, in the legendary Indian and the sensual, refined Inca, and in the great Moctezuma on his throne of gold." The indigenous figures in Darío's poems "Caupolicán" and "Tutecotzimí" are a source of liberating and audacious originality that deeply influenced future generations of his literary compatriots.

The magnitude of Darío's major works of poetry, which include *Azul . . .* (1888), *Prosas profanas y otros poemas* (1896 and 1901), *Cantos de vida y esperanza, los cisnes y otros poemas* (1905), *El canto errante* (1907), *El viaje a Nicaragua e intermezzo tropical* (1908), *El poema del otoño y otros poemas* (1910), and *Canto a la Argentina y otros poemas* (1914), gave the country a respected place on the world's literary map. The cosmopolitan Darío spent most of his life outside his homeland, preferring Europe and Europeanized cities such as Buenos Aires, though he traveled constantly, sometimes to far-flung places such as North Africa, to produce the articles for the Argentine newspaper *La Nación* that allowed him to eke out a living.

As a *modernista*, Darío is a poet of conflicting ideals. E.g., in his famous poem "A Roosevelt" ("To Roosevelt"), he portrays the United States as a future invader of Nicaragua, while in "Salutación al águila" ("Saluting the Eagle"), he praises the work ethic and entrepreneurial spirit of his country's northern neighbor. Darío wrote escapist poems, such as the often-recited "A Margarita Debayle," celebrating journeys to exotic places inhabited by mythological creatures. But he is also the author of "Lo fatal" ("Destined to Die"), one of the most famous poems in the lang., revered for its existential anguish and fatalistic pessimism. Each generation of readers has found something new and provocative in the modernismo of Darío.

II. Post-modernistas. Nicaragua's three exemplary postmodernista writers, Azarías H. Pallais (1885–1954), Alfonso Cortés (1893–1969), and Salomón de la Selva (1893–1959), maintain a literary dialogue with their great predecessor but also forge a new poetics. While they shared Darío's passion for cl. lit. and mythology, they grew tired of the legions of his superficial imitators. A rebellious, impoverished priest guided by the teachings of the Gospel, Pallais sided with the poor in his poetry; his volumes include *A la sombra del agua* (1917), *Espumas y estrellas* (1918), *Caminos* (1921), *Bello tono menor* (1928), *Epístola católica a Rafael Arévalo Martínez* (1947), and *Piraterías* (1951). Cortés, a metaphysical poet concerned with the relativity of time and the preeminence of space, used his severe mental illness to create a therapeutic art to assuage his isolation and lack of intimate human contact. Some of Cortés's best poetry (such as the deeply enigmatic "Yo," "La gran plegaria," "Pasos," and "La canción del espacio") was anthologized by the poet Ernesto Cardenal and translated into Eng. by the Catholic writer Thomas Merton at the Trappist monastery in Gethsemani, Kentucky, in the late 1950s. Cortés's most accomplished collections of poetry are *Poesías* (1931), *Tardes de oro* (1934), and *Poemas eleusinos* (1935). De la Selva's *Tropical Town and Other Poems* (1918) appeared in Eng. in the U.S., where the poet lived and worked, publishing his poems in important jours., corresponding with noted poets such as Edna St.Vincent Millay, and teaching at Williams College. His second book, *El soldado desconocido* (1922), is a testimonial work about his experiences as a soldier in World War I. By this time, for ideological reasons that had to do with the interventionist policies of the U.S. in Lat. Am., the bilingual poet had made the decision to publish his work almost exclusively in Sp. His books, which draw on a deep knowledge of Greco-Roman myth and hist. (occasionally mixed with themes from the Aztec world), include *Evocación de Horacio* (1949), *La ilustre familia* (1954), *Canto a la independencia nacional de México* (1956), *Evocación de Píndaro* (1957), and *Acolmixtli Netzahualcóyotl* (1958).

III. The Vanguard Movement. The writers associated with Nicaragua's Vanguard Movement, notably José Coronel Urtecho (1906–94), Pablo Antonio Cuadra (1912–2002), and Joaquín Pasos (1914–47), were young provocateurs who burst onto the literary scene in the city of Granada in the late 1920s by challenging upper-class values and attacking the derivative followers of Darío. The nationalistic, conservative stance of the *vanguardistas* and their fervent belief in *Hispanidad* (Hispanicity) as a bulwark against Communism led them to give moral support to dictators such as Anastasio Somoza García in Nicaragua and Francisco Franco in Spain.

Much of the material they used to renovate Nicaraguan lit. was based on new poetry of the U.S. and France that the vanguardistas translated and incorporated in their own work, as well as Nicaraguan folklore and traditional culture.

Coronel Urtecho's poetry (as well as his Sp. versions of poems by Marianne Moore and T. S. Eliot) is collected in a volume with a title taken from the Greek of the *Odyssey: Pol-la d'ananta katanta paranta* (1970, rev. 1993). This book contains Coronel Urtecho's classic narrative poem "Pequeña biografía de mi mujer," a homage to his wife María Kautz. His *Paneles del infierno* (*Panels of Hell*, 1981) is an extensive historical poem that takes its rhetorical point of departure in support of the 1979 Sandinista revolution from the opening poem of Edgar Lee Masters's *Spoon River Anthology*.

Taken as a whole, the poetry of Cuadra provides deep insights into Nicaraguan culture, esp. when it is collated with his essential book-length essays *El nicaragüense* and *Muestrario del folklore nicaragüense*. In addition, no writer has more vividly portrayed Nicaragua's geographical and biological diversity. Cuadra's major works include *Poemas nicaragüenses* (Nicaraguan Poems), first published in 1934, but revised extensively throughout the poet's life; *El jaguar y la luna* (The Jaguar and the Moon, 1959), poems based on ancient designs of Nahuatl ceramics; *Cantos de Cifar* (*Songs of Cifar*, 1971), narrative verse in clipped lyrical lines about the people who navigate the dangerous Homeric waters of Lake Nicaragua; *Siete árboles contra el atardecer* (*Seven Trees against the Dying Light*, 1980), in which seven different species of Nicaraguan trees store a country's myths, hist. and collective memory; and *La ronda del año* (written primarily between 1984 and 1986), twelve poems that reflect a year's natural cycle in Nicaragua.

Pasos, who died prematurely in 1947, is nearly unknown outside Nicaragua. His collected poetry, *Poemas de un joven* (1962), ed. by Cardenal, contains the apocalyptic long poem "Canto de guerra de las cosas" (War Song of the Things), perhaps the most important overlooked masterpiece in 20th-c. Lat. Am. poetry.

IV. Generation of the 1940s. Ernesto Mejía Sánchez (1923–85), Carlos Martínez Rivas (1924–98), and Ernesto Cardenal (b. 1925), the three most noted writers who followed the Vanguard Movement, looked toward Nicaraguan vanguardistas as mentors, not figures whose work needed to be openly questioned as Coronel Urtecho had done in his iconoclastic "Oda a Rubén Darío" in the late 1920s—a continuation rather than a rupture in the dialogue between literary generations.

Mejía Sánchez was educated in Mexico and is widely recognized as the most gifted scholar of Darío's poetry. His own verse is collected in the anthol. *Recolección al mediodía* (1972). One of his lasting contributions is *prosemas*, short prose poems.

Martínez Rivas produced the single most influential book of poetry in Nicaraguan lit. for several generations, *La insurrección solitaria*, first published in Mexico in a limited ed. in 1953 after his formative years in Madrid and Paris in the late 1940s that enabled him to work with Octavio Paz and Julio Cortázar. Conceived in the French tradition of the *poète maudit*, his poetry creates new, almost impossible, standards for verbal perfection.

Cardenal is Nicaragua's most internationally recognized poet of recent decades. He served as minister of culture during the 1980s; as both a poet and a government official, he has traveled the globe, giving readings to enthusiastic audiences. With Coronel Urtecho, Cardenal translated an influential anthol. of U.S. poetry (which included a selection of Native Am. texts) and formulated what has come to be known as *Exteriorismo*, emphasizing a collage of factual data in prosaic free verse stripped of metaphor and the incorporation of original historical sources. Exteriorista poetry was a defining, albeit controversial, characteristic of Nicaraguan poetry from the 1970s through the mid-1990s.

Cardenal's poetry has a pronounced political trajectory that corresponds in part to his own life. E.g., his peripheral involvement in the 1954 April Rebellion against the government of Somoza García resulted in his poem *Hora cero* (*Zero-Hour and Other Documentary Poems*, 1960). His religious vocation led him to a spiritual friendship with Merton as well as an exploration of the tenets of liberation theology. Merton encouraged Cardenal to become ordained as a priest and, later, to establish a contemplative community called Solentiname on an island in Lake Nicaragua in the mid-1970s. When the repression of Anastasio Somoza Debayle's National Guard destroyed the community, Cardenal went into exile in Costa Rica, where he became a voice of the revolution that finally toppled the dictatorship in July of 1979.

Other works by Cardenal include *Epigramas* (1961), which imitates the cl. style of Martial and Catullus; *Salmos* (Psalms, 1964), modeled on the Psalms of the OT in their poetic indictment of wars, capitalism, and repressive governments; the long historical narrative poem *El estrecho dudoso* (*The Doubtful Strait*, 1967); *Canto nacional* (1972); *Oráculo sobre Managua* (1973), published the year after the earthquake that destroyed Nicaragua's capital; and *Vuelos de victoria* (*Flights of Victory*, 1985), a collection of poems that praise the Sandinista Revolution. In *Homenaje a los indios americanos* (*Homage to the American Indians*, 1969) and *Los ovnis de oro* (*Golden UFOs*, 1985), Cardenal proposes models for contemp. ethical behavior based on ancient civilizations. In his more recent poetry, he has been looking into the far reaches of the universe, exploring the big-bang theory and quantum physics in *Cántico cósmico* (*Cosmic Canticle*, 1989) and, in a more streamlined style in keeping with his monastic poems, *Telescopio en la noche oscura* (Telescope in the Dark Night, 1993).

V. The Frente Ventana and the Betrayed Generation, New Voices. Although there are important Nicaraguan writers of the 1950s such as Guillermo Rothschuh Tablada (b. 1926), Raúl Elvir (1927–98), Ernesto Gutiérrez (1929–88), Mario Cajina-Vega (1929–95), Eduardo Zepeda-Henríquez (b. 1930), Octavio Robleto (1935–2009), Horacio Peña (b. 1936), and esp. Fernando Silva (b. 1927), it was during the 1960s that two divergent literary groups engaged in a debate on poetics that changed the course of Nicaraguan lit. hist. The Frente Ventana (Window Front), based at the university in León and headed by Fernando Gordillo (1940–67) and Sergio Ramírez (b. 1942—now Nicaragua's most prominent novelist), sought ways to link art with a revolutionary struggle in keeping with the idealism, commitment, and sacrifice that attended the birth of the Frente Sandinista de Liberación Nacional (FSLN) in 1963, in conjunction with the influential political writings of Carlos Fonseca Amador (1936–76). One highly promising writer martyred in the armed political struggle of that era was Leonel Rugama (1949–70), whose poetry was published posthumously in the volume *La tierra es un satélite de la luna* (*The Earth Is a Satellite of the Moon*, 1983). The other main literary group from the 1960s, *La Generación Traicionada* (The Betrayed Generation), was based in Managua and founded by Roberto Cuadra (b. 1940), Edwin Yllescas (1941–2016), Iván Uriarte (b. 1942), and Beltrán Morales (1944–86). They tended to identify themselves more with the freewheeling Beat poets of the U.S. than with Marxist struggles for social equality in their own country.

New voices that constitute the Nicaraguan literary scene in recent decades include those of Luis Rocha (b. 1942), former ed. of the literary supplement *El Nuevo Amanecer Cultural*; the surrealist poet Francisco Valle (b. 1942), author of the collection of prose poems *Laberinto de espadas* (1974 and 1996); and Francisco de Asís Fernández (b. 1945), co-organizer with the poet Gloria Gabuardi of the International Poetry Festival in Granada. Three contemp. poet-critics are worthy of mention: Álvaro Urtecho (1951–2007), whose works of poetry include *Cantata estupefacta* (1986), *Esplendor de Caín* (1994), *Tumba y residencia* (2000), and *Tierra sin tiempo* (2007); Julio Valle-Castillo (b. 1952), one of Nicaragua's premier literary scholars and art historians and the author of *Materia jubilosa* (1986) as well as *Lienzo del pajaritero* (2003), a series of poems that document the myths and folk dances of Masaya; and Nicasio Urbina (b. 1958), recently the author of *Viajemas* (2009).

VI. Women Poets of the 1970s to the Present. Perhaps the most important literary phenomenon of the 1970s was the emergence of a new generation of women authors, transforming a literary world that had been dominated by men. Two poets who began publishing in the 1970s are esp. accomplished: Ana Ilce Gómez (b. 1945), author of *Las ceremonias del silencio* (1975) and *Poemas de lo humano cotidiano* (2004), and Gioconda Belli (b. 1948), who published *Sobre la grama* (1973); *Línea de fuego* (1978), which explores themes of sexual and political liberation and won Cuba's Casa de las Américas prize; *Truenos y arco iris* (1982); *Amor insurrecto* (1985); *De la costilla de Eva* (1987); *El ojo de la mujer* (1991); *Apogeo* (1997); and *Fuego soy apartado y espada puesta lejos* (2007).

There were some important precursors to these writers, such as María Teresa Sánchez (1918–94), Mariana Sansón Argüello (1918–2002), and the internationally recognized Claribel Alegría, who was born in Nicaragua in 1924, lived for most of her life in El Salvador and Europe, then returned to Nicaragua, where she currently resides. Alegría's work was translated into Eng. by the U.S. poet Carolyn Forché as *Flowers from the Volcano* (1982).

Other notable women poets who remain active in Nicaragua's literary life include Vidaluz Meneses (b. 1944), Gloria Gabuardi (b. 1945), Michéle Najlis (b. 1946), Daisy Zamora (b. 1950), and Rosario Murillo (b. 1951), author of *Las esperanzas misteriosas* (1990), founder of the group *Gradas*, director in the 1980s of the Sandinista Association of Cultural Workers, and the wife of President Daniel Ortega.

Additional recent women's voices in Nicaraguan poetry include Yolanda Blanco (b. 1954); Isolda Hurtado (b. 1957); Blanca Castellón (b. 1958); Carola Brantome (b. 1961); Esthela Calderón (b. 1970), who published *Soledad* (2002), *Amor y conciencia* (2004) and *Soplo de corriente vital* (2008), a remarkable collection of ethnobotanical poems that recovers traditional knowledge about plants indigenous to Nicaragua's Occidental region; and Marta Leonor González (b. 1972), ed. of *La Prensa Literaria*, cofounder of Nicaragua's most important new literary group *400 Elefantes*, and author of *Huérfana embravecida* (1999) and *Casa de fuego* (2008).

VII. Caribbean Coast Writers. Given the Pacific Coast literary establishment's refusal to recognize multilingual Atlantic Coast writers, one esp. welcome recent develop. is the attention that the Nicaraguan Association of Women Writers (ANIDE) has paid to the country's Caribbean women authors. In the jour. *Anide*, ed. Vilma de la Rocha has published the work of such poets as June Beer (1935–86), the Atlantic Coast's first woman poet, who wrote her work in both Eng.-Creole and Sp.; Gloriantonia Henríquez (b. 1948), author of *Primera vigilia* (2004); Andira Watson (b. 1977), who published the collection *Más excelsa que Eva* (2002) and won the Mariana Sansón National Poetry Prize in 2009; Brígida Zacarías Watson, whose poetry written in the Miskitu lang. appears in *Miskitu tasbaia (Tierra miskita,* 1997); Erna Narcisso Walters, who writes in both Eng. and Sp, and whose work was anthologized in *Antología poética de la Costa Caribe de Nicaragua*; Isabel Estrada Colindres, a Garífuna woman who lives in Bluefields and writes in Eng., Sp., and Creole; and Ana Rosa Fagot Müller (b. 1944), who writes in Miskitu and coedits the jour. *Tininiska*. Some of the work included in this selection published in *Anide* was translated into Sp. by Carlos Rigby, who was born in Laguna de Perlas in 1945 and has been a peripheral part of Nicaraguan poetry for decades. Rigby is the most prominent Nicaraguan Caribbean Coast poet, together with David MacField, who was born in Ciudad Rama in 1936 and who published *Dios es negro* (1967), *En la calle de enmedio* (1969), *Poemas para el año de elefante* (1970), *Poemas populares* (1972), and *Los veinticuatro: poemas y canciones* (1975). Given the lang. barriers, the extreme poverty, and the general isolation of the Atlantic Coast in relation to the western side of Nicaragua, more work is needed to establish greater understanding and cultural respect between the two regions.

See INDIGENOUS AMERICAS, POETRY OF THE; SPANISH AMERICA, POETRY OF.

■ E. Torres, *La dramática vida de Rubén Darío* (1966); E. Mejía Sánchez, *Estudios sobre Rubén Darío* (1968); K. Ellis, *Critical Approaches to Rubén Darío* (1974); J. Concha, *Rubén Darío* (1975); *Poets of Nicaragua: 1918–1979*, ed. S. White (1982); C. L. Jrade, *Rubén Darío and the Romantic Search for Unity* (1983); S. White, *Culture and Politics in Nicaragua: Testimonies of Poets and Writers* (1986); *Modern Nicaraguan Poetry: Dialogues with France and the United States*, ed. S. White (1993); J. E. Arellano, *"Azul . . ." de Rubén Darío: Nuevas perspectivas* (1993); J. E. Arellano, *Literatura nicaragüense* (1997); S. White, *La poesía más que humana de Pablo Antonio Cuadra: un estudio ecocrítico* (2002); *El siglo de la poesía en Nicaragua*, ed. J. Valle Castillo, 3 v. (2005); P. A. Cuadra, *Seven Trees against the Dying Light*, trans. G. Simon and S. F. White (2007); S. White, *Arando el aire: la ecología en la poesía y la música de Nicaragua* (2011).

S. F. White

NORSE POETRY. The vernacular poetry of the Viking Age and med. West Scandinavia. Norse poetry is related to the poetic trads. of OE, Old Saxon, and OHG and is, therefore, based on a structural principle of alliteration, although features such as internal rhyme and the counting of syllables were also important. Norse poetry differs from alliterative poetry in other Germanic langs. in that it is stanzaic rather than stichic. A handful of Viking Age (ca. 800–1100) runic inscriptions contain verse, and scholars believe that poets whose work has survived lived as long ago as the end of the 9th c. and that some anonymous verse may have had an oral prehist. However, virtually all the evidence for Norse poetry is found in mss. from the 13th c. and later. There is ample med. evidence of the analysis of poetics from the Middle Ages: the poem *Háttalykill* (apparently a loan trans. of *clavis rhythmica*) of the Icelander Hallr Þórarinsson and the Orkney Jarl Rǫgnvaldr in the 1140s; four grammatical treatises; and, most important, the *Edda* (composed ca. 1178–1241) of the poet and chieftain Snorri Sturluson. *Edda* probably means "poetics," and the work contains, besides a prologue, sections devoted to the mythology (*Gylfaginning*, "Deluding of Gylfi"), poetic vocabulary (*Skáldskaparmál*, "Poetic Diction"), and *Háttatal* ("Enumeration of Meters"), a poem exhibiting 100 metrical or lexical variations, equipped with a metrical commentary.

Snorri named the most commonly used form *dróttkvæðr háttr* (meter recited before the retinue) or *dróttkvætt* (recited before the retinue). In the beginning of *Háttatal*, he presented this verse to exemplify the use of alliteration, rhyme, and syllable-counting:

> Lætr, sás Hákun heitir
> (hann rekkir lið) bannat,
> jǫrð kan frelsa fyrðum
> friðrofs konungr ofsa;
> sjálfr ræðr alt ok Elfar,
> ungr stillir sá, milli
> (gramr á gipt at fremri)
> Gandvíkr jǫfurr landi.

Snorri explains that there are 12 "staves" (alliterating sounds) in the verse, two in odd lines and one in even lines, and that they link "quarter-stanzas," i.e., pairs of lines. The staves that appear initially in the even lines he calls "head-staves," and, he says, they control the alliteration. The other staves, in the odd lines, are "props." Thus, in the above verse, the head staves are the initial sounds of the syllables *hann*, *frið-*, *ungr*, and *Gand-*, and the alliterations require either identical consonants (e.g., *Hák-* and *heit-* in the first pair of lines) or, when a vowel begins the "head-stave," any other vowel (*ungr*, *alt*, *Elf-*). Besides this principle of alliteration, each line is to contain six syllables (a sequence like *Lætr* or *ungr* is one syllable). In addition, there is a requirement for half rhymes in odd lines (*Lætr/heit-*, *jǫrð/fyrð*, *sjálfr/Elf-*, *gramr/frem-*) and full rhyme in even lines (e.g., *hann/bann-*). Finally, although Snorri does not articulate it here, every line ends in a trochee, and the basic poetic unit is actually the half-stanza (Norse *helmingr*, "half").

Word order is very free. A literal trans. following the word order of the above verse would look something like this: "Causes, the one who is named Hákun (he emboldens an army) to be banned, earth can free for men breaking of the peace the king arrogance; himself rules all Elfr [the Göta River] young prince that between (the prince has fortune the greater) Gandvík [the White Sea] the land." There are three clauses in the first helmingr: Hákun causes the arrogance of war to be banned for men; he emboldens an army; the king can free the earth. The second has only two, but, in characteristic skaldic complexity, the object of the verb in the fifth line is found only in the eighth, and a prepositional phrase has parts in three of the four lines: "That young prince himself rules the land between Elfr and Gandvík; the prince has fortune the greater." Because Norse was a far more inflected lang. than Eng., unraveling the strands is easier than it appears in trans., but it is still tricky enough that many eds. routinely recast verses into normal prose word order, if only to make clear their interpretations.

Later in *Háttatal*, Snorri discusses variations within this 24-syllable scheme with its alternating alliterative staves and alternating half and full rhymes for the helmingr; these concern primarily the syntax and arrangement of the clauses. He also discusses variations from the scheme: changing the syllable count, changing or moving the alliterations, changing or moving the rhymes. To most of these variations, he assigns a name; these terms are still used in the discussion and analysis of Norse poetry.

Snorri used the verse cited above to exemplify the poetic structure. His next order of business, begun in the very next stanza he presented and discussed, was to explain poetic vocabulary. Although he distinguished between a number of concepts, later scholarship names them all kennings: substitution for a single noun of some other term that is "made known" (*kennd*) by another noun. Thus, e.g., *battle* may be expressed with "spear-din." Kennings may, however, be extended: the "fire of battle" is a sword, as is, therefore, "fire of spear-din."

Here is a helmingr from the second stanza of *Háttatal*, with the alliterating staves in bold and rhymes italicized:

> ***H****olt* felr ***h***ildig*elt*i
> ***h****eil*a bœs ok d*eil*ir
> ***g****ull*s í ***g***elmis st*all*i
> ***g***unns*eið* skǫrungr r*eið*ir.

The helmingr contains two clauses, whose verbs are *felr* (covers) in line 1 and *reiðir* (brandishes) in line 4. The subjects are *deilir gulls* (distributor of gold), a kenning for a king based upon his supposed generosity (such references are common; poets may have wished to remind kings of their obligation to reward them) and *skǫrungr* (prominent man) in line 4, also referring to the king. What he covers and brandishes are his head and his sword. "Head" is rendered here with *holt bœs heila* (forest of the inhabited place of the brain): the brain lives in the skull, and its forest is hair, which here functions as a metonym for the head. "Sword" is *gunnseið[r]* (battle fish), a kenning that sounds unlikely to our ears but is based on the similarity in shape. Technically, a *seiðr* is a pollack, but any fish will do for the kenning, and *seið[r]* enables the required full rhyme. The king covers his head with a *hildigǫltr*—the form in line 1 is a dative instrumental—(battle-boar). Although this kenning might conceivably have originated in pagan-cult practice suggested by the archaeological record, it is most easily explained by reference to a helmet with this name in heroic trad. This explanation demonstrates that some kennings required knowledge of traditional narratives from heroic legend and myth.

For nearly all the hist. of Norse poetry, kennings were as important a poetic feature as the strict requirements for alliteration, rhyme, and number of syllables. However, in the high Middle Ages, some Christian poets objected to kennings as obscuring their message and turned away from using them; the most famous manifestation of this objection is the Icelandic monk Eysteinn's mid-14th-c. *Lílja* (Lily), a hist. of Christian salvation. He composed it in a meter called *hrynhent* ("falling" or "floating meter"), which varies from *dróttkvætt* in that it adds another trochee to each line; the result is quite stately.

A poet was called a *skáld*. If, as some scholars argue, the word is etymologically related to verbs like the Ger. *schelten* (reproach) or was the source of the Eng. verb *scold*, we have some indication of the power of poetry in Old Scandinavian society. Further indication of such power is found in narratives about the impact of insult poetry and laws prohibiting insult poetry and certain kinds of erotic verse. We know that skalds were active in the retinues of powerful men and the courts of kings; one text, *Skáldatal* (enumeration of skalds), links known skalds to known kings of the Viking Age. Throughout the Viking Age, at least, skalds functioned as eyewitnesses to kings' deeds, mostly perhaps in battle, but we also have an old trad. of ekphrastic poetry, as well as a large collection of individual occasional verses. Later commentators distinguished a poem equipped with a refrain and other structural features, which they called a *drápa* (etymology unknown), from a more simple grouping, a *flokkr* (flock). Occasional stanzas are called *lausavísur* (unbound verses).

Trad. names the first skald Bragi Boddason, who was probably active in Norway in the late 9th c. Some scholars have imagined that Bragi himself created dróttkvætt, and although no evidence can be brought to bear, it is undeniable that the first skalds use the form with great facility. The mythology also has a Bragi, god of poetry, and it is not difficult to link the two. But the form adapted easily to Christian subjects as well, and there are poems on all manner of Christian themes. The first great Christian drápa was *Geisli* (Sunbeam) by the Icelander Einarr Skulason, an encomium to St. Olaf recited more than a century after his death, when the see of Niðaróss in western Norway was elevated to an archdiocese in 1153–54. By then, skaldic poetry already was an Icelandic monopoly, and in Iceland, the form lived on throughout the Middle Ages. Its metrical complexities were taken up in a new form of long narrative poem, the *rímur* (from OF *rime*).

One ms. contains a collection of poems on mythological and heroic topics in the far simpler alliterative form of other Germanic trads. (but still stanzaic), and the type of poems in it were named "eddic" following an Enlightenment surmise. Other such poems are known as well, many in Icelandic sagas set in the heroic age. Unlike dróttkvætt poetry, these poems are transmitted without the name of a composer, perhaps because they are set in a prehist. about which Icelanders had no information. Because of its Germanic context, eddic poetry has received a great deal of scholarly attention, but it represents only a tiny portion of Norse poetry.

■ L. M. Hollander, *A Bibliography of Skaldic Studies* (1958).

■ **Editions**: *Eddica Minora*, ed. A. Heusler and W. Ranisch (1903); *Den norsk-islandske skjaldedigtning*, ed. F. Jónsson, 4 v. (1912–15); *Íslenzkar miðaldarímur*, ed. Ó. Halldórsson, 4 v. (1973–75); *Snorri Sturluson, Edda*, ed. A. Faulkes (1982–98); *Skaldic Poetry of the Scandinavian Middle Ages*, ed. M. Clunies

Ross et al. (2007–)—in print as of 2009 are v. 2, *Poetry from the Kings' Sagas*, ed. K. E. Gade (2009); and v. 7, *Poetry on Christian Subjects*, ed. M. Clunies Ross.

■ **Translations and Commentaries**: *Snorri Sturluson, Edda*, trans. A. Faulkes (1987); *The Poetic Edda*, trans. C. Larrington (1996); K. von See et al., *Kommentar zu den Liedern der Edda* (1997–); M. Clunies Ross et al., *Skaldic Poetry of the Scandinavian Middle Ages* (see above).

■ **Critical Studies**: R. Meissner, *Die Kenningar der Skalden* (1921); G. Kreutzer, *Die Dichtungslehre der Skalden*, 2d ed. (1977); R. Frank, *Old Norse Court Poetry* (1978); K. von See, *Skaldendicthung* (1980); E. Marold, *Kenningkunst* (1983); M. Clunies Ross, *Skáldskaparmál* (1986); K. E. Gade, *The Structure of Old Norse Dróttkvætt Poetry* (1995); G. Nordal, *Tools of Literacy* (2001); M. Clunies Ross, *A History of Old Norse Poetry and Poetics* (2005).

J. Lindow

NORWAY, POETRY OF. For a small nation on the fringes of Europe, Norway has an exceptional collection of mod. and contemp. poets. Over large stretches of its hist., however, poetry in Norway has not enjoyed such an auspicious climate, and it was not until the late 18th c. that the national trad. began to distinguish itself from that of Denmark.

The story of Norwegian poetry begins in the late Middle Ages, after the eddic and skaldic verse of ON lit. The first major works were folk ballads, which derived their new style from troubadour verse. Of particular interest is *Draumkvæde* (The Dream Ballad), a remarkable visionary poem that blends elements of pagan and Christian myth. The first significant Norwegian poet was Petter Dass (1647–1707), whose *Nordlands Trompet* (The Trumpet of Nordland, composed ca. 1700, pub. 1739) combines a baroque style with descriptions of the life and landscape of northern Norway. Dass's contemporary and Norway's first recognized female author, Dorothe Engelbretsdatter (1643–1716), expressed powerful religious emotions in her hymns and poems, which were published in *Siælens Sang-offer* (The Soul's Offering of Songs, 1678).

The Norwegian-born dramatist and Enlightenment polymath Ludvig Holberg (1684–1750) was the major figure of the joint lit. of Denmark-Norway, a political entity that lasted over 400 years until it was dissolved in 1814. Before writing his well-known comedies and epistles, Holberg published the verse epic *Peder Paars* in 1720. Another high point in 18th-c. Dano-Norwegian verse is the pastoral description of spring in "Majdagen" (1758) by Christian Braunman Tullin (1728–65), which offers a somewhat Rousseauian critique of the corrupting influence of urban culture. In the late 1700s, a group of writers belonging to *Det norske Selskab* (The Norwegian Society) in Copenhagen sought to create poetic tragedy in the Fr. neoclassical style while cultivating a national identity. Though they produced work in many genres, they are remembered chiefly for the ironic satire *Kierlighed uden Strømper* (Love without Stockings, 1772), written in graceful alexandrines by the most talented among them, Johan Herman Wessel (1742–85).

Romanticism reached Norway in the 1830s, when a cultural debate took place between those who followed Danish models and those who wanted to reject Danish cultural hegemony and build a national lit. Henrik Arnold Wergeland (1808–45), leader of the nationalist Patriots, possessed enormous talents and inexhaustible energy, which he directed to politics and popular education in addition to literary creation. Wergeland's production includes the vast lyric drama *Skabelsen, Mennesket og Messias* (Creation, Man, and Messiah, 1830), and narrative poems such as *Jøden* (The Jew, 1842) and *Den engelske Lods* (The English Pilot, 1844). His inventive lyric poetry reached its apex as he neared death, in poems like "Til min Gyldenlak" (To My Wallflower) and "Til Foraaret" (To Spring), the latter in free verse. Whereas lit. meant rapture and organic form to Wergeland, it meant the opposite to the leader of the Intelligentsia Party, Johan Sebastian Welhaven (1807–73), a poet of quiet reflection and chiseled form who adopted the conservative aesthetic ideology of the influential Danish figure J. L. Heiberg. Welhaven represented a more understated and sober strand of romanticism; he attacked Wergeland's artistic excesses in *Norges Dæmring* (The Dawn of Norway, 1834), a series of epigrammatic sonnets that also mocked the Patriots' nationalism and advocated a broadly Eur. cultural orientation. Wergeland and Welhaven can be seen as establishing two models of influence within Norwegian lit.: one protean, passionate, progressive, and nationalistic; the other modest, melancholy, moderate, and Eur.

The 1840s saw the rise of National Romanticism, when the scholars Peter Christen Asbjørnsen (1812–85), Jørgen Moe (1813–82), and M. B. Landstad (1802–80) collected folk culture and lit. While Asbjørnsen and Moe transformed Norwegian lit. with their folktales, Landstad's *Norske Folkeviser* (Norwegian Folk Ballads, 1853) exerted a broad influence on poetry. Another manifestation of National Romanticism was the work of the philologist Ivar Aasen (1813–96), who created *landsmaal*, the lang. now called Nynorsk. Aasmund Vinje (1818–70) was the first important poet to use this lang. as a medium of literary expression, in works such as the well-known poem "Ved Rundarne" (1861). Since that time, the poetic trad. in Norway has been enriched by the presence of two literary langs.

Before writing his world-famous prose dramas, Henrik Ibsen (1828–1906) demonstrated the strengths of Norwegian as a medium for dramatic poetry in his many verse dramas, such as the National-Romantic *Gildet paa Solhaug* (*The Feast at Solhaug*, 1856), a historical idyll based on a folk ballad. *Kjærlighedens Komedie* (*Love's Comedy*, 1862) marks the beginning of Ibsen's realism; its variously rhymed, skipping iambic pentameters abound in caricature and paradox. In the masterpieces *Brand* (1866) and *Peer Gynt* (1867), Ibsen both exposes the faults of the Norwegian national character and offers a romantic depiction of the mountains and fjords of the country's landscape. The metrical variety of *Peer Gynt*, in contrast to the *Knittelvers* used in *Brand*, produced a vast range of effects, from idle daydreaming to physical abandon, from the lightest banter to funereal solemnity. Ibsen also published a single collection of lyric poetry, *Digte* (*Poems*, 1862), which included the popular narrative poem "Terje Vigen."

While Ibsen's poetry was written in the manner of Welhaven, the 1903 Nobel Prize laureate Bjørnstjerne Bjørnson (1832–1910) saw himself as literary heir to Wergeland, and he was similarly vocal about left-wing political causes. His National-Romantic saga dramas *Kong Sverre* (1861) and *Sigurd Slembe* (1862) were meant to give Norway a gallery of heroes matching those of the other Eur. nations. Bjørnson published the narrative romance cycle *Arnljot Gelline* (1870) and a collection of lyric poems, *Digte og Sange* (Poems and Songs, 1880), and he later became a central figure of socially and politically engaged critical realism during the Modern Breakthrough era of Scandinavian lit.

Poetry in the 1890s acquired a more personal tone, one attuned to nature, mysticism, and fantasy. Friedrich Nietzsche, Edvard Munch, and Fr. symbolism were important sources of inspiration for the fin de siècle poets Vilhelm Krag (1871–1933) and Sigbjørn Obstfelder (1866–1900). Krag expressed a world-weary melancholy, while Obstfelder evoked bizarre moods of angst and wonder in a highly original form marked by pauses, repetitions, abrupt transitions, and incompleteness. Though symbolist in conception, Obstfelder's poetry, with its free verse and urban imagery, anticipates Scandinavian modernism. Arne Garborg (1851–1924) continued the Nynorsk trad. with *Haugtussa* (The Elf Maiden, 1895) and *I Helheim* (In Hel's Home, 1901), which give voice to the dark, uncanny forces in humankind and nature while expressing a profound religious nostalgia. Another important writer, the 1920 Nobel laureate Knut Hamsun (1859–1952), published the exquisite mystical poem "Skjærgaardsø" in his influential collection *Det vilde Kor* (The Wild Chorus, 1904).

Hamsun's verse was a source of inspiration for a lyric revival that occurred around 1910, with the work of Herman Wildenvey (1886–1959) and Olaf Bull (1883–1933). Wildenvey's *Nyinger* (Bonfires, 1907) alternates between seductive love lyrics and pantheistic nature poetry, mixing biblical and ballad idioms with jargon and slang. For Bull, as for fellow symbolists such as R. M. Rilke and Paul Valéry, the purpose of poetry was to transmute fugitive moments of experience into what W. B. Yeats called the "artifice of eternity." Bull's masterpiece "Metope" (1927) is a formally perfect and moving meditation on love and the destructiveness of time. Around this time, the Nynorsk trad. was also enriched with the work of Olav Aukrust (1883–1929) and Tore Ørjasæter (1886–1968), who treated religious and philosophical themes in a national spirit using forms derived from the edda and the ballad. Aukrust's main work, *Himmelvarden* (The Cairn against the Sky, 1916), is a visionary poem based on a quasi-mystical experience.

The interwar period brought new themes and original voices, incl. some early signs of modernism, which would become dominant after World War II. The work of Emil Boyson (1897–1979) was influenced by the poetics and preoccupations of Fr. symbolism, while Claes Gill (1910–73) followed the Anglo-Am. modernists to create ecstatic imagist verse that disregards ordinary syntax and logic. Apart from the captivating expressionist poets Kristofer Uppdal (1878–1961) and Åsmund Sveen (1910–63),

Nynorsk poetry in the early 20th c. was formally traditional. One of the major Scandinavian poets of the century, Rolf Jacobsen (1907–94), debuted in the 1930s with *Jord og jern* (*Earth and Iron*, 1933) and *Vrimmel* (*Swarm*, 1935). In these collections, he used free verse and technological imagery in an ambivalent encounter with industrial modernity. In the postwar period, Jacobsen began to see technology as an unstable and sinister force, and he adopted an ecological stance that was highly critical of consumerist culture, for instance, in *Hemmelig liv* (*Secret Life*, 1954) and *Headlines* (1969). Jacobsen's poetry presents a kaleidoscope of contrasting moods, effects, and angles of vision—pathos and humor, the commonplace and the cosmic, sensory vividness and symbolic resonance. The love poems to his deceased wife in Jacobsen's final collection, *Nattåpent* (*Night Open*, 1985), are some of the best in Norwegian lit.

Politically and socially oriented poetry in traditional form was also quite significant in the decades before World War II. The two leading leftist poets were Arnulf Øverland (1889–1968) and Nordahl Grieg (1902–43), both of whom became active in the resistance movement during the Nazi occupation. Øverland survived imprisonment in the Sachsenhausen concentration camp, but Grieg died as a war correspondent in Germany. Much of Øverland's work springs from a religiously conceived socialist ideal, often presented in biblical symbols. *Den røde front* (The Red Front, 1937) is devoted to proletarian songs and other texts with a political message. Notable monuments to the 1930s are the poems "Guernica," inspired by Picasso's famous painting, and the antifascist "Du må ikke sove" (You Must Not Sleep). Øverland's laconic form and austere diction place him decidedly in the formal trad. of Welhaven; he was later a vocal traditionalist opponent of modernist formal experimentation in the poetic debates of the 1950s. Grieg, who was also a novelist and playwright, wrote socially oriented patriotic lyrics in a style of impassioned eloquence. His greatest success was the collection of war poems titled *Friheten* (*Freedom*, 1943). Another mid-century socialist poet, Inger Hagerup (1905–85), wrote condensed love lyrics as well as eloquent war poems (e.g., *Aust-Vågøy*, 1941). Also worthy of mention is Gunnar Reiss-Andersen (1896–1964), who combined a brooding introspection with sensitivity to a world in crisis. During the war he was an important spokesman for his country while in Swedish exile, after which he published *Dikt fra krigstiden* (Wartime Poems, 1945).

The leading postwar modernist was Paal Brekke (1923–93), whose Swedish exile during the war had exposed him to the modernist authors called *Fyrtiotalisterna*. Brekke published his trans. of *The Waste Land* and other poems of T. S. Eliot, as well as his own first collection, *Skyggefektning* (Shadow Boxing), in 1949. Brekke's poetry employs a richly allusive, fractured lang., with abrupt shifts in register, mood, and rhythm—pathos alternates with black humor, personal recollection with glimpses of a world falling apart, quotidian banality with the mythic sublime. His best work, *Roerne fra Itaka* (The Oarsmen from Ithaca, 1960), is a poetic cycle in which Brekke, like Eliot, juxtaposes contemp. actuality with ancient myth. Another distinctive postwar modernist is Gunvor Hofmo (1921–95), whose work deals with the extreme experience of trauma and loss at a personal and historical level; her best friend was murdered at Auschwitz. Hofmo's first collection, *Jeg vil hjem til menneskene* (I Want to Go Home to the People, 1946), contains the starkly powerful poem "Det er ingen hverdag mer" (There Is No Everyday Anymore). Tarjei Vesaas (1897–1970), a key Nynorsk novelist, also adopted a moderate modernism in his poetry, which has been collected in Eng. trans. His wife, Halldis Moren Vesaas (1907–95), was also an accomplished poet whose nonmodernist work explores women's lives and perennial themes of nature, love, life, and death.

By 1960, modernism in poetry was taken for granted, and many new voices were heard. Chief among them were Stein Mehren (b. 1935) and Georg Johannesen (1931–2005). Mehren is a novelist, playwright, and cultural critic as well as poet. His entire oeuvre forms an existential quest for authenticity and an engagement with philosophy of lang. By way of contrast, the work of Johannesen is social and political; he was deeply influenced by Bertolt Brecht, and his style is condensed and elliptical, characterized by bizarre contrasts and mordant irony. *Ars Moriendi eller de syv dødsmåter* (*Ars Moriendi* or the Seven Ways of Death, 1965), his main collection, treats the seven deadly sins within a strict, semischolastic format, a style at odds with the often surrealist imagery.

In the late 1960s, new political and poetic tendencies became evident in the work of Jan Erik Vold (b. 1939), who was associated with the influential left-wing modernist literary magazine *Profil.* Vold began as an experimentalist preoccupied by solipsism, and his early work includes forays into emblematic verse and concrete poetry. *Hekt* (Verge, 1966), framed by a document from the Vietnam War, creates a world poised on nightmare through grotesque imagery that evokes the uncanny. Subsequently, under the influence of W. C. Williams and contemp. Swedish poets, Vold moved toward a "new simplicity," anecdotal and confessional in *Mor Godhjertas glade versjon. Ja* (Mother Goodheart's Glad Version. Yes, 1968), almost purely visual and objective in *spor, snø* (tracks, snow, 1970), where he adapts haiku form. The antisymbolist style of "new simplicity" was also perfected by an important older Nynorsk poet, Olav H. Hauge (1908–94), who progressively simplified his style until, with *Dropar i austavind* (Drops in the East Wind, 1966), he was writing about everyday things in an unadorned idiom akin to his Chinese and Japanese models. Hauge, who lived his whole life in an orchard in western Norway, was also active as a translator of many foreign poets, such as W. B. Yeats, Arthur Rimbaud, Georg Trakl, and Paul Celan. Hauge's sober and minimal style has had an enormous influence on contemp. Norwegian lit., and, with Jacobsen, he is the most revered and most translated 20th-c. Norwegian poet.

In the final decades of the 20th c., after the politicized lit. of the 1970s, Norwegian poetry showed a variety of tendencies, from lyrics influenced by ballads and folk songs to continued late modernist minimalism to new forms of multimedia and genre-crossing experimentalism. Two significant contemp. poets are also celebrated dramatists: Jon Fosse (b. 1959) and Cecilie Løveid (b. 1951). Other figures who may be seen as vital to the landscape of contemp. poetry are Eldrid Lunden (b. 1940) and Paal-Helge Haugen (b. 1945), both of whom emerged from the *Profil* group of 1960s radicals. Like Hauge, Haugen's terse and concrete form of expression was influenced by Chinese and Japanese poetic forms. Perhaps the most fascinating late-20th-c. Norwegian poet is Tor Ulven (1953–95), who crafted a distinctively pessimistic voice with an astonishing use of archaeological motifs, from *Etter Oss, Tegn* (After Us, Signs, 1981) to the prose poems of *Stein og speil* (Stone and Mirror, 1995). In 2004, Øyvind Rimbereid (b. 1966) won the prestigious Kritikerprisen (The Norwegian Critics' Prize for Literature) for *Solaris korrigert* (Solaris Corrected), which contains an epic science-fiction poem written in a futuristic hybrid composed of dialectal Norwegian, Eng., ON, and other langs. Poetic creativity continues to thrive in contemp. Norway, in part because of generous support from the government's Arts Council.

See DENMARK, POETRY OF; ICELAND, POETRY OF; NEW NORSE (NYNORSK) POETRY; NORSE POETRY; SWEDEN, POETRY OF.

■ **Anthologies and Primary Texts:** *Oxford Book of Scandinavian Verse*, ed. E. W. Gosse and W. A. Craigie (1925); H. Wergeland, *Poems*, trans. G. M. Gathorne-Hardy et al. (1929); *Anthology of Norwegian Lyrics*, trans. C. W. Stork (1942); T. Vesaas, *30 Poems*, trans. K. G. Chapman (1971); *Modern Scandinavian Poetry 1900–1975*, ed. M. Allwood (1982); *20 Contemporary Norwegian Poets*, ed. T. Johanssen (1984); H. Ibsen, *Poems*, trans. J. Northram (1987); T. Vesaas, *Through Naked Branches*, ed. and trans. R. Greenwald (2000); R. Jacobsen, *North in the World*, ed. and trans. R. Greenwald (2002); H. Wergeland, *The Army of Truth*, trans. A. Born (2003); O. H. Hauge, *Leaf-Huts and Snow-Houses*, trans. R. Fulton (2004), and *The Dream We Carry*, trans. R. Bly and R. Hedin (2008); *New European Poets*, ed. W. Miller and K. Prufer (2008); H. Wergeland, *Jan van Huysum's Flower Piece*, trans. J. Irons (2009).

■ **Criticism and History:** *Norges litteraturhistorie*, ed. E. Beyer, 6 v. (1974–75); M. K. Norseng, *Sigbjørn Obstfelder* (1982); A. Aarseth, "The Modes of Norwegian Modernism," *Facets of European Modernism*, ed. J. Garton (1985); H. Naess, *A History of Norwegian Literature* (1993); *Etterkrigslitteraturen*, ed. Ø. Rottem, 3 v. (1995–98); L. Bliksrud, *Den smilende makten* (1999); P. T. Andersen, *Norsk litteraturhistorie* (2001); I. Havnevik, *Dikt i Norge* (2002); J. Brumo and S. Furuseth, *Norsk litterære modernisme* (2005); *Lyrikkhåndboken*, ed. J. M. Sejersted and E. Vassenden (2007).

S. LYNGSTAD; D. KROUK

O

OCCITAN POETRY. The root of the term *Occitan* is the word *oc* (yes) in the lang. of med. southern France, in contrast to OF *oïl* (stressed like mod. Fr. *oui*) and It. *sì*; Dante made this triple distinction in his *De vulgari eloquentia* (*On Vernacular Eloquence*, ca. 1304). The Occitan lang. has been called *langue d'oc*, Provençal, and other names since the 12th c. The term *Provençal* was long preferred but has the disadvantage that it seems to refer specifically to Provence (Lat. *Provincia Romana*, the region of Gaul nearest to Rome), which is the area east of the Rhône and home of the 19th-c. poet Frédéric Mistral (1830–1914; see below), but only one part of the larger area from the Atlantic to the Alps where the lang. is or was spoken. As a geographical term, *Languedoc* refers to the territory west of the Rhône. *Occitan* is free from misleading specificity and enjoys increasing acceptance, although it was introduced only recently in both Fr. (1886) and Eng. (1940).

From the time before the troubadours, who appeared ca. 1100, we have a handful of very short poetic texts, most of them fragmentary, that date from the 10th and 11th cs. The oldest one appears to be a birthing charm; another is a fragment of a passion narrative, yet another a religious *alba* in Lat. with a refrain in Occitan. A fragmentary proto-*canso* (see below) evokes the lover as a hawk, while a fragmentary and obscure proto-*sirventes* seems to criticize amorous nuns. Narrative verse begins with the *Boeci*, a longer but incomplete paraphrase of Boethius's *Consolation of Philosophy* that was written about 1000 and continues with the *Chanson de Sainte Foy*, a life of the child saint from about 1050.

In their halcyon days, the troubadours sang of courtly love (which they called *fin'amor* or "true love") and a range of other subjects. Scholars debate whether William IX, Duke of Aquitaine and Count of Poitiers (1071–1126), was the first troubadour who composed or merely the first whose compositions have been transmitted to us. Among William's 11 (or 10) extant poems, some describe the humility and devotion of the courtly lover, but others express explicit eroticism: in one, sometimes called a *fabliau*, the narrator is a sexual athlete and far from humble. In another, William takes leave of earthly power, perhaps because of an imminent departure on crusade or because he believed he soon would die. In the next generation, the moralist Marcabru (fl. 1130–49) scourged the sexual license of married men and women but also retold encounters of a first-person narrator with a young girl. In one of these, the prototypical *pastorela*, the narrator attempts to seduce the girl, but she steadfastly refuses; in another, a girl curses the king who called her lover away on crusade. In the middle years of the 12th c., Peire d'Alvernhe (fl. 1149–68) developed a theory of difficult style, or *trobar clus* (closed composition), which involved elaborate sound patterns, unexpected rhymes, obscure vocabulary, and difficult syntax. Raimbaut d'Aurenga (ca. 1144–73) advocated such an abstruse manner in a debate with Giraut de Bornelh (fl. 1162–99), who defended *trobar leu* or the easy style. Bernart de Ventadorn (fl. 1147–70 or perhaps somewhat later), considered one of the greatest love poets among the troubadours, sang with an air of deceptive simplicity about his adoration for his lady, the joy of love and the grief of yearning, and less frequently about his ecstasy in sexual fulfillment.

By about 1170, the troubadours had developed a set of generic concepts. In terms of this system, their 2,500-odd extant poems comprise about 1,000 cansos or love songs, about 500 sirventes or satires, and about 500 *coblas* or individual stanzas, while those remaining include the pastorela or pastourelle, the alba or dawn poem, debate poems such as the *tenso* and the *partimen*, the *planh* or funeral lament, and minor genres. Bertran de Born (ca. 1150–1215), whose castle of Altafort was besieged and taken by Richard Lionheart, sang sirventes of political passion with the commitment of a lord who regarded warfare as a source of moral stature. The male aristocratic mentality also informs the *chanson de geste* of Giraut de Roussillon (ca. 1150), written in an artificial blend of Occitan and Fr., and the parodic romance *Jaufre* (late 12th c.).

In the early 13th c., the Occitan region was the scene of the Albigensian Crusade, waged at the invitation of the pope by a Fr. leader, Simon de Montfort, against the heretical Cathars who were centered at Albi. According to a long-standing interpretation, the crusade destroyed the courtly society that had nourished the troubadours and so destined Occitan poetry to inevitable decline. However, it is doubtful that this conflict, which was one among many, played so decisive a role. Peire Cardenal (fl. 1205–72) criticized the Church for the failings of unworthy priests, incl. members of the Inquisition, while expressing his own orthodox piety. Perhaps the mid-13th c. saw the composition of the delightful romance of *Flamenca*, whose heroine succeeds, despite the cruelty of her jealous husband, in enjoying the love of a perfect knight. Late in the century, Guiraut Riquier (fl. 1254–92) complained of the insecurity of the courtier's life and lamented that he had come among the last of the troubadours. In the early 14th c., poets of the school of Toulouse turned to increasingly religious themes, esp. the praise of the Virgin. Only one poet of this period, Raimon de Cornet (fl. 1324–40), has left an extensive body of work incl. lyrics, verse letters, didactic texts, and two poems in Lat. Both priest and friar, Raimon de Cornet indulged in a ribald tale of his mistress's revenge for his infidelity, but in another mood, he seriously defended the value of poetry.

Though we have the melodies of only one-tenth of the troubadour poems, it has often been assumed that virtually all of them were set to music. The troubadour wrote both text and melody, which were performed by the *joglar*. Joglars and troubadours traveled widely: William IX on crusade to Syria, Marcabru and Guiraut Riquier to Spain, Bertran de Born to northern France. Peire Vidal (fl. 1183–1204) ventured as far as Hungary. These travels contributed to the diffusion of the art form into other langs. starting at the end of the 12th c. in Fr. and Ger., and continuing in the 13th c. in It. at the court of the Emperor Frederick II, and in Galician-Port. (see GALICIA, POETRY OF). The heritage of the troubadours was acknowledged by Dante and Petrarch, who extended their indirect influence throughout the Europe of the Ren. and beyond. Poets of the 20th c. who returned to the troubadours include Ezra Pound, Paul Blackburn, and W. D. Snodgrass in Eng., Jacques Roubaud in Fr., and Augusto de Campos in Port.

A trad. of commentary on the troubadours and their songs began in the early 13th c. with Raimon Vidal's prose *Razos de trobar* (Principles of Composition) and continued with the *Donatz proensals* (Provençal Grammar) of Uc Faidit. Uc and other writers compiled the *razos*, brief prose commentaries on individual songs, and the *vidas*, or lives of the troubadours. Around 1290, Matfre Ermengau (fl. 1288–1322) attempted to reconcile the love sung by the troubadours with love of God in his encyclopedic verse *Breviari d'amor* (Breviary of Love).

During the 14th and 15th cs., Occitan poetry fell into decline. The trad. was maintained at Toulouse by the *Consistori de la Sobregaia Companhia del Gay Saber* (Consistory of the Merry Band of the Gay Knowledge), which awarded prizes for the best compositions in various troubadour genres. The regulations of these contests were codified in a taxonomy of troubadour practice called *Las Leys d'amors* (ca. 1341), understood as equivalent to a code of poetry. We are still indebted to *Las Leys d'amors* for definitions of the genres and for prosodic distinctions such as those among *coblas unissonans*, in which all the stanzas of a song have the same rhyme sounds; *coblas singulars*, in which the rhyme sounds change with every stanza; *coblas doblas*, in which given rhyme sounds are maintained for two stanzas; *coblas ternas*, in which they are maintained for three stanzas; and *coblas quaternas*, in which they are maintained for four. In *coblas capcaudadas*, the first line of one stanza uses the rhyme sound of the last line of the preceding stanza, whereas in *coblas capfinidas*, the first line of one stanza repeats a key word from the last line of the preceding one. In *coblas retrogradadas*, the rhymes of a stanza repeat those of the preceding one but do so in reverse order. In all these permutations of concrete rhyme sounds, the abstract rhyme scheme remains constant. On the other hand, the authority of the *Leys* has obscured evolutionary devels. in troubadour practice. We are only beginning to realize the implications of the fact that the earliest troubadours used no generic distinctions among types of song, hence that the devel. of the generic system requires explanation. Another fundamental evolution occurred in the practice of metrical imitation, or *contrafacture*, which gradually became characteristic of the sirventes but was adopted in the *Leys* as its timeless defining trait. The elaborate rhyme patterns of the troubadours analyzed by the *Leys* are only a few of the endless variations of their technique.

The fate of Occitan may be illustrated in the career of Gaston Fébus, the powerful Count of Foix (1331–91). Although he requested that the

Lat. encyclopedia by Bartholomaeus Anglicus, *De Proprietatibus Rerum* (On the Properties of Things), be translated into Occitan, in which it became the *Elucidari de las proprietatz de totas res naturals* (Elucidarium of the Properties of All Natural Things), Gaston Fébus chose to use Fr. for his own treatise on hunting and Fr. and Lat. for his collection of prayers. In Occitan, he composed only a single love song. The 14th-c. *Jeu de Sainte Agnès* shows verve in its elaboration of the traditional story and in its use of music, but two cycles of mystery plays from the 15th and 16th cs. are less successful. When, in the edict of Villers-Cotterêts (1539), Francis I decreed that Fr. (and not Lat.) must be the lang. of administration throughout his kingdom, he laid royal claim on the practice of law, against the claim of the Church. Occitan was gradually excluded from usage in law and in other areas.

Historians of Occitan poetry speak of a first Ren. in the 16th c., illustrated by the Gascon Protestant Pey de Garros (ca. 1525–81), the Provençal Bellaud de la Bellaudière (ca. 1543–88), and Pierre Godolin of Toulouse (1580–1649). A second Ren. in the 19th c. was marked by the group of seven poets called the *Félibrige*, led by Mistral. Despite continuing factional disputes, Occitan poetry grew broader in appeal during the 20th c. with the work of poets such as Max Rouquette (1908–2005) and Bernat Manciet (1923–2005). A number of figures such as René Nelli (1906–82), Charles Camproux (1908–94), Pierre Bec (1921–2014), and Robert Lafont (1923–2009) are both troubadour scholars and practicing poets. The composer and singer Claudi Martí (b. 1940), who recorded troubadour songs, allied Occitan poetry with the regionalist movement during the 1970s.

See AL-ANDALUS, POETRY OF; CATALAN POETRY; FRANCE, POETRY OF.

■ **Anthologies**: *Trouvères et Minnesänger*, ed. I. Frank (1952); *Les Troubadours*, ed. R. Lavaud and R. Nelli, 2 v. (1960–66); *Anthologie de la poésie occitane 1900–1960*, ed. A. Lafont (1962); *Anthology of Troubadour Lyric Poetry*, ed. A. Press (1971); *La lírica religiosa en la literatura provenzal antigua*, ed. F. J. Oroz Arizcuren (1972); *Anthology of the Provençal Troubadours*, ed. R. Hill and T. Bergin, 2d ed., 2 v. (1973); *Lyrics of the Troubadours and Trouvères*, ed. F. Goldin (1973); *Los Trovadores*, ed. M. de Riquer, 3 v. (1975); *Anthologie des troubadours*, ed. P. Bec (1979); F. Hamlin et al., *Introduction à l'étude de l'ancien provençal*, 2d ed. (1985); M. Switten et al., *The Medieval Lyric*, 3 v. (1987–88); *Trobairitz*, ed. A. Rieger (1991); *Chants d'amour des femmes-troubadours*, ed. P. Bec (1995); R. Lafont and P. Gardy, *Histoire et anthologie de la littérature occitane*, 2 v. (1997)—to 1789; W. D. Paden, *An Introduction to Old Occitan* (1998); *Songs of the Troubadours and Trouvères*, ed. S. N. Rosenberg et al. (1998); *Songs of the Women Troubadours*, ed. M. Bruckner et al. (2000).

■ **Bibliographies**: A. Pillet and H. Carstens, *Bibliographie der Troubadours* (1933); C. A. Knudson and J. Misrahi in Fisher; F. Pic, *Bibliographie des sources bibliographiques du domaine occitan* (1977); R. Taylor, *La Littérature occitane du moyen âge* (1977); F. Zufferey, *Bibliographie des poètes provençaux des XIVe et XVe siècles* (1981); M. L. Switten, *Music and Poetry in the Middle Ages: A Guide to Research on French and Occitan Song, 1100–1400* (1995); P. Ricketts, *Concordance de l'Occitan Médiéval: COM2, Les troubadours, Les textes narratifs en vers* (2005)—electronic resource with complete texts, bibl., and concordance program.

■ **Criticism and History**: Jeanroy; Patterson; C. Camproux, *Histoire de la littérature occitane* (1953); H.-I. Marrou (pseud. of H. Davenson), *Les Troubadours* (1961); M. Lazar, *Amour courtois et "fin'amors" dans la litt. du XIIe siècle* (1964); R. Lafont and C. Anatole, *Nouvelle Histoire de la littérature occitane*, 2 v. (1970); J. J. Wilhelm, *Seven Troubadours* (1970); L. M. Paterson, *Troubadours and Eloquence* (1975); L. Topsfield, *Troubadours and Love* (1975); R. Boase, *The Origin and Meaning of Courtly Love* (1976); D. Rieger, *Gattungen und Gattungsbezeichnungen der Trobadorlyrik* (1976); N. B. Smith, *Figures of Repetition in the Old Provençal Lyric* (1976); P. Makin, *Provence and Pound* (1978); *GRLMA* v. 2.1 (1979–90); U. Mölk, *Trobadorlyrik* (1982); J. J. Wilhelm, *Il Miglior Fabbro: The Cult of the Difficult in Daniel, Dante, and Pound* (1982); J. Gruber, *Die Dialektik des Trobar* (1983); J. Roubaud, *La fleur inverse: essai sur l'art formel des troubadours* (1986); M. R. Menocal, *The Arabic Role in Medieval Literary History* (1987); L. Kendrick, *The Game of Love* (1988); C. Di Girolamo, *I Trovatori* (1989); S. Gaunt, *Troubadours and Irony* (1989); Hollier; S. Kay, *Subjectivity in Troubadour Poetry* (1990); A. E. van Vleck, *Memory and Re-Creation in Troubadour Lyric* (1991); L. M. Paterson, *The World of the Troubadours* (1993); P. Cherchi, *Andreas and the Ambiguity of Courtly Love* (1994); *Handbook of the Troubadours*, ed. F.R.P. Akehurst and J. M.

Davis (1995); G. A. Bond, *The Loving Subject* (1995)—troubadours and med. Lat.; S. Gaunt, *Gender and Genre in Medieval French Literature* (1995); W. D. Paden, "The Troubadours and the Albigensian Crusade: A Long View," *RPh* 49 (1995); P. Dronke, *The Medieval Lyric*, 3d ed. (1996); G. Brunel-Lobrichon and C. Duhamel-Amado, *Au temps des troubadours* (1997)—external hist.; M. Winter-Hosman, "Domna et dame: Images différentes?" *Le Rayonnement des troubadours* (1998); *Troubadours*, ed. S. Gaunt and S. Kay (1999); W. Calin, *Minority Literatures and Modernism: Scots, Breton, and Occitan, 1920–1990* (2000); O. Holmes, *Assembling the Lyric Self* (2000)—authorship from troubadours to It. poets; D. Vitaglione, *The Literature of Provence* (2000), and *A Literary Guide to Provence* (2001)—east of the Rhône; A. Callahan, *Writing the Voice of Pleasure* (2001); F. L. Cheyette, *Ermengard of Narbonne and the World of the Troubadours* (2001); L. Lazzerini, *Letteratura medievale in lingua d'oc* (2001); D. P. Bec, *Per un païs . . . : Écrits sur la langue et la littérature occitanes modernes* (2002) and "Prétroubadouresque ou paratroubadouresque? Un Antécédent médiéval d'un motif de chanson folklorique Si j'étais une hirondelle," *Cahiers de civilisation médiévale* 47 (2004); W. D. Paden, "Before the Troubadours: The Archaic Occitan Texts and the Shape of Literary History," *De Sens Rassis*, ed. K. Busby et al. (2005); S. Gaunt, *Love and Death in Medieval French and Occitan Courtly Literature* (2006); W. D. Paden, "Provençal and the Troubadours," *Ezra Pound in Context*, ed. I. B. Nadel (2010); W. D. Paden and F. F. Paden, "Swollen Woman, Shifting Canon: A Midwife's Charm and the Birth of Occitan Poetry," *PMLA* 125 (2010).

■ **Translations**: *Personae*, trans. E. Pound (1926); *Songs of the Troubadours*, trans. A. Bonner (1972); *Six Troubadour Songs*, trans. W. D. Snodgrass (1976); *Proensa*, trans. P. Blackburn (1978); *Mais provençais: Raimbaut e Arnaut*, trans. A. de Campos, 2d ed. (1987); *Lark in the Morning*, trans. R. Kehew et al. (2005); *Troubadour Poems from the South of France*, trans. W. D. Paden and F. F. Paden (2007).

■ **Versification and Music**: Patterson, v. 1.1.2; Lote; F. M. Chambers, "Imitation of Form in the Old Provençal Lyric," *RPh* 6 (1952–53); I. Frank, *Répertoire métrique de la poésie des troubadours*, 2 v. (1953–57); F. Gennrich, *Das musikalische Nachlass der Troubadours*, 3 v. (1958–65); F. Gennrich, "Troubadours, trouvères," *MGG*, v. 13 (1966); H. van der Werf, *The Chansons of the Troubadours and Trouvères* (1972); *Las cançons dels trobadors*, ed. I. Fernandez de la Cuesta (1979); U. Mölk, "Zur Metrik der Trobadors," *GRLMA*, v. 2.1 (1979–90); P. Bec, "Le problème des genres chez les premiers troubadours," *Cahiers de civilisation médiévale* 25 (1982); *The Extant Troubadour Melodies*, ed. H. van der Werf and G. Bond (1984); Chambers; F. A. Gallo, *Music in the Castle* (1995)—Occitan troubadours in Italy; E. Aubrey, *The Music of the Troubadours* (1996), and "Genre as a Determinant of Melody in the Songs of the Troubadours and the Trouvères," *Medieval Lyric*, ed. W. D. Paden (2000); J. Haines, *Eight Centuries of Troubadours and Trouvères* (2004); W. D. Paden, "What Singing Does to Words: Reflections on the Art of the Troubadours," *Exemplaria* 17 (2005).

W. D. Paden

ORIYA POETRY. The Oriya-speaking area of India, now called Odisha—a state on the country's eastern coast, between Bengal and Andhra Pradesh—was known as Udra, Kalinga, Kangod, Koshala, and Utkala during different historical periods since the composition of the *Mahābhārata*, ca. 2500 BCE. The ancient form of the lang., now the mother tongue of more than 30 million people, incl. 62 different tribes (which speak various dialects) and the diasporic population, is mentioned in the Sanskrit grammarian Panini's *Astādhyāyi* (5th c. BCE), where he refers to it as "Udra Bibhasha." However, written lit. in Oriya began only in the 10th c. CE. The major poets of that era—such as Sabaripa, Kanhupa, and Luipa—were Buddhist Sahajayana mystics. Their poems, called *Charyapada*, are artistic records of the lives of disciplined spiritual practitioners. They can be read at different levels: they simultaneously evoke the terrestrial and transcendent realms; they also cloak the sublime under a seemingly erotic surface. Poetry seems for them to be the locus in which the natural world and intimations from beyond come together.

This foundational notion that a poet's consciousness is intimately in touch with a subtle, unseen, and all-controlling force, even as the poet remains firmly planted in the visible world of objects, seems to permeate the entire oeuvre of Oriya poetry. Although between the 12th and 19th cs. Sahajayana Buddhism gave way to spiritual practices such as Shakti worship, Shaivism, the Jagannath cult, and Vaishnavism as the dominant belief systems informing poetic art, poetry in Oriya was always seen as an intermediate space between the immanent and the transcendent, an inevitable part of the spiritual practice leading to *Moksha* or liberation. Depending on the methods adopted for such liberation, poet-seekers can be divided mainly into two categories: *Yogis*, who perceive the sensory world as *Maya* or illusion and seek to withdraw from it, and *Bhaktas*, or poets of devotion, who represent the world of objects as a legitimate means by which to transcend it. The poets Achyutananda Das (early 17th c.), Yasobanta Das, and Ananta Das (both later 17th c.) belong to the first category, while Banamali (1729–90), Baladeva Ratha (1789–1845), Gopalakrishna Patnaik (1785–1862), and Gourahari (1814–90) represent the latter. Bhimabhoi (1845–95) dares to embrace hell eternally so that the rest of the world can obtain deliverance. From the margins of society, this poet-activist challenged all forms of the status quo and created a political and poetic idiom that pleaded for an egalitarian social order. He represents the acme of Oriya poetic genius.

The 1,000-year span between the beginnings of Oriya written lit. and the 19th-c. poets includes a number of humanistic poems in various subgenres, such as *bhajans* (devotional songs), *jananas* (songs of supplication), *chaupadis* (rhyming quartrains), *chitaus* (epistolary poems), *chautishas* (poems in 34 couplets, each beginning with a consonant), *koilis* (odes addressed to a cuckoo), *samhitas* and *patalas* (two forms of discursive poetry), and *champus* (chaupadis in chautisha form). In these, poets translate their particular experiences into a universal idiom.

A parallel trad. of *puranas*, epics, and *kavyas* existed as well during this period, originating with Sarala Das's 15th-c. trans. of the *Mahābhārata*, *Saptasati Chandi*, *Devi Māhātmya*, and *Bichitra Rāmāyana* and bolstered by 16th-c. trans. of the *Rāmāyana* and the *Bhāgabata* by Balaram Das (1465–1546) and Jagannath Das (1470–1542), respectively. These trans. were radical attempts at vernacularization and coincided with the founding of a powerful Oriya empire by Kapilendra Dev and its subsequent consolidation by his inheritors. The aesthetic evident in these works can be said to mirror the sociopolitical by subverting the dominant pan-Indian Sanskritic-Brahminical hegemony. The trans. violated the hitherto inviolable purity of the so-called holy texts, producing syncretic works that brought 1,000 years of local hist. and quotidian concerns into confrontation and reconciliation with what was perceived to be universal. These pioneers mediated elite ideas in plebeian lang., humanized the epic characters, and set a model for the subsequent 200 noniconic trans. that constitute the bulk of med. Oriya poetry.

After securely establishing its identity, Oriya poetry began in the 18th c. to compete directly with the Sanskrit master texts. In the isolation and elegance of the royal courts, an ornate poetic trad. was developed by the court poets, who dared to surpass the stylization, verbal artistry, technical elegance, and erudition hitherto available only in Sanskrit poetics. This attempt to valorize Oriya over Sanskrit, at least in the limited and arid realm of stylized expression, by poets like Arjuna Das (16th c.), Dhananjaya Bhanja (1611–1701), Dinakrishna Das (ca. 1670–1740), Upendra Bhanja (ca. 1685–1750), and Abhimanyu Samantasinghar (1757–1806), can be considered an aesthetic recompense in the face of a larger sociopolitical malady. The Gajapati empire, which had held the Oriya people and their pride together, had collapsed. First under the Muslims and then under the Marathas, the Oriyas suffered greatly. The artistic poise that Oriya ornate poetry achieved was absolutely disconnected from the turmoil and uncertainty experienced by the population.

A semblance of order seems to have been restored with the advent of the British in the early 19th c. Oriya poetry now rarely considered Sanskrit to be a competing discourse but rather looked westward for inspiration. The impact of Europe created a Janus-faced poetic consciousness that demonstrated alternately subservience and hostility toward colonial cultural structures. On the one hand, the poets searched for their roots so as to reinvent themselves authentically; on the other, they eagerly appropriated the innovations available in the hegemonic culture. The contributions of Radhanath Ray (1848–1908), Madhusudan Rao (1853–1912), Fakirmohan Senapati (1843–1918), and their 20th-c. inheritors reflect this divided allegiance.

Western contact transformed Oriya poetry in many other ways. Eur. romanticism, democratic ideals, and liberal thought galvanized nationalist consciousness. Quotidian social, economic, political, cultural, and epistemic issues found expression and legitimacy. Major intellectual currents as well as thematic and stylistic innovations tried out in the West found an echo in Oriya poetry. It can be argued that

Oriya poetry in the 20th c. once again became dependent, as ornate poetry in the 18th and 19th cs. had been, through its replication of *Sanskrit poetics. But there is an important difference. While the earlier mode had been more inward and exclusive, cutting itself off from the life of ordinary people, contemp. poetry has been more outward and inclusive, truly global in its aspirations, even as it tries to represent the local faithfully.

The journey of Oriya poetry seems to have come full circle. The genre used by Sarala Das, Balaram Das, and others to shake off intellectual dependence on the elite Sanskrit *epistemē* and assert Oriya regional identity and by the saint-poets of the *Bhakti* movement to articulate indigenous philosophical ideas could not maintain its distinct identity. Sociopolitical conditions created new dependencies in the 18th c. and after. Since literary trends are not immune to economic and political pressure, such dependencies were in a way inevitable. What is significant, however, is that Oriya poetry has profitably negotiated changing conditions. It remains to be seen how Oriya poetry responds to the facts of today's global world, with its threats of monolingualism and monoculturalism.

See INDIA, POETRY OF.

■ S. Dash, *Odia Sahityara Itihasha* (History of Oriya Literature, 4 v., 1963–68); G. Nandasharma, *Sribharata Darpana* (The Mirror of the Mahābhārata, 1964); N. Samantaraya, *Odia Sahityara Itihasha* (History of Oriya Literature, 1964); K. Kar, *Ascharya Charyachaya* (Wonderful Art of Charya Poetry, 1969); S. Acharya, *Odia Kavyakaushala* (Oriya Aesthetics and Stylistics, 1983); S. Mishra, *Atitara Barnabodha* (The Primer of the Past, 2002).

D. R. PATTANAIK

P

PERSIAN POETRY

I. Scope. Evidence for poetic practice in Old and Middle Persian is scanty and reveals little of its prosody, forms, or themes. The substantive hist. of Persian poetry begins in the 9th c. with the emergence of New Persian written in modified Ar. script. Three dialects of Persian now serve as the national lang. of Iran (Fārsī), Afghanistan (Darī), and Tajikistan (Tājīk). Using Farsi to refer to Persian in Eng. sows confusion and obscures two important features of the trad. First is its continuity: the earliest works of Persian poetry from the 10th c. are probably more readily comprehensible to mod. speakers of the lang. than Shakespeare's works are to mod. speakers of Eng. Second is the geographical extent of the trad. Farsi is spoken only in Iran (and the Iranian diaspora), but for centuries Persian poetry was written and read throughout much of Asia. Literary centers in regions that are now part of the nations of not only Iran, Afghanistan, and Tajikistan but of Turkey, Azerbaijan, Georgia, Pakistan, India, Turkmenistan, and Uzbekistan were in constant communication and unified by common poetic practices and values.

II. Prosody, Forms, and Rhetoric. Traditional verse forms employ quantitative metrics. The system of meters was conceptualized according to models laid down for the *ʿarūḍ* system of *Arabic prosody. But because of phonetic differences and perhaps Middle Persian prosody, Persian metrics diverges significantly in practice from its Ar. counterpart. Some of the most frequently used meters in Persian are rare in Ar. Persian does not permit the substitution of long and short syllables found in most Ar. meters and adds a third category of "overlong" syllables (long vowel-consonant) to the Ar. system. Several common words and particles may be counted either short or long, and word-initial vowels may be elided with the final consonants of preceding words. In Persian, repeated, refrain-like syllables, known as the *radīf,* often follow the rhyme, a feature rarely found in Ar. Persian also adopted formal genres of Ar. poetry such as the *qaṣīda*, *ghazal*, and *qiṭʿa* but added new forms, such as the *rubāʿī*, the *masnavī*, and the strophic *tarkīb-band*. The rhymed couplets of the masnavī enable the composition of long narrative poems, which have significantly shaped the hist. of Persian poetry.

Drawing again on Ar. models, Persian writers have cataloged an extensive array of rhetorical devices, from types of puns and verbal figures to varieties of similes, allusions, and metaphors. Traditional lit. crit. in Persian is generally limited to prosody, form, and rhet., but incidental critical comments found in biographies of poets, historical writing, and metapoetic reflections can tell us much about how poetry was read, utilized, and evaluated.

III. Historical Overview. Until the mod. period, poetic novelty was rarely prized for its own sake. Apprentice poets were expected to memorize thousands of verses by their predecessors and contemporaries. Poets drew on a well-established stock of themes, settings, images, and similes; certain poetic metaphors even came to be lexicalized, like the word *laʿl* (ruby), which acquired the definition "beloved's lips." Innovation took place against the background of authoritative models, and poets would often write responses to the work of earlier masters, using the same meter and rhyme scheme or rewriting the same story. Poetic practice, however, changed gradually over the course of generations. Since the early 20th c., the hist. of Persian poetry has been loosely divided into four broad period styles or *sabk*. New Persian poetry emerged in the region of Khorasan (now divided among Iran, Afghanistan, and Uzbekistan), whence the name of the *sabk-i Khurāsānī* to characterize Persian poetry from the 10th to the middle of the 12th c. It is marked by a number of archaic grammatical features; diction tends to be simple and measured, and metaphors and similes are usually explicit and concrete. During the 12th c., Persian poetry began to expand south toward the subcontinent and west across the Iranian plateau, and an esp.

significant school of poetry emerged in Azerbaijan. As populations and poets scattered before the Mongol invasions of the early 13th c., Persian poetry spread past the Hindu Kush into India, to the Persian Gulf in southwestern Iran, and westward into Anatolia. This movement marks the emergence of the *sabk-i ʿIrāqī* (*Iraq* here referring to western Persia). Poetic lang. was standardized and greater use made of words borrowed from Ar. Rhetorical figures of speech are deployed with more frequency and sophistication, as poetic conventions and genres (esp. the ghazal) are crystallized. At the end of this period, the trad. is consolidated and codified in the literary school of Herat, and the end of the 15th c. it has sometimes been considered the end of the high cl. period of Persian poetry. But with the foundation of the centralizing dynasties of the Safavids in Persia and the Mughals in India in the early 16th c., Persian became the authoritative lang. of administration and high culture across western, south, and central Asia and served as a cl. reference point for poets writing in Ottoman Turkish. This innovative period first witnessed the emergence of the relatively short-lived *maktab-i vuqūʿ* (phenomenalist school), which used a plain diction to explore the psychology of amorous encounters. Of much more lasting significance was a style known to its practitioners as the Fresh Style, but later called the *sabk-i Hindī* or Indian style. Despite its name, this style was transregional in its devel. and practice, and poets traveled freely between major literary centers in Persia, India, and central Asia. Emphasis on the fresh is manifest particularly in the use of colloquial idioms and the cultivation of conceptual metaphors, subtle conceits, and other figures of thought. While this style held sway in India and central Asia until the early 20th c. and helped shape emerging vernacular lits. in these areas, in Persia proper, a reaction to the perceived obscurities of this baroque-like style took shape as the Literary Return movement (*sabk-i bāz-gasht-i adabī*), which sought to return to the norms of the Khurāsānī and Iʿrāqī styles. Though poetry in the traditional forms continues to be written today, the economic and cultural impact of the West had far-reaching effects on Persian poetry in the 20th c., weakening the authority of the trad. and leading to wholesale changes in poetic norms.

IV. Genres. There is no strict correlation between theme and form in Persian poetry. Panegyric, e.g., is most commonly associated with the qaṣīda but can also be found in the masnavī, rubāʿī, and even ghazal forms; conversely, the qaṣīda often contains lyrical elements and can be used for didactic purposes or for the praise of religious figures, either living or dead. The discussion below is thus organized around four broad thematic categories: (1) didactic, homiletic, and gnomic, (2) epic and romance, (3) panegyric and eulogy, and (4) lyric.

Poetry is traditionally the privileged form of verbal discourse and the preferred vehicle for the transmission of wisdom and knowledge. Poetry can teach subjects from the mundane to the esoteric. Two early masnavīs indicate the range of possible didactic topics: the *Dānishnāma* (Book of Knowledge, completed in 980) by Ḥakīm Maysarī presents a compendium of medical science, while the *Ḥadīqat al-ḥaqīqa* (Garden of Truth) by Sanāʾī (d. ca. 1131) uses short anecdotes to preach on a wide range of ethical and religious issues. Sanāʾī's model acquires a more distinctively mystical or Sufi content in the masnavīs of Farīd al-Dīn ʿAṭṭār (d. ca. 1221), such as *Manṭiq al-ṭayr* (*Conference of the Birds*), and the *Masnavī-yi Maʿnavī* (Spiritual Couplets) by Jalāl al-Dīn Rūmī (d. 1273). Even in the 20th c., the Indo-Persian poet Muḥammad Iqbāl (d. 1938) used the masnavī to present his revision of Islamic philosophy. Works like these can consist of several thousand verses and contain dozens of anecdotes and exempla, but homiletic themes also appear in gnomic, aphoristic form, as in the rubāʿī or quatrains of ʿUmar Khayyām (d. 1122), which draw on the ancient Near Eastern trad. of wisdom lit. Didactic passages also occur frequently in epic and romance, and panegyrics often include injunctions to the patron to adhere to rules of proper conduct and rule. Even the ghazal, the preeminent lyrical form, may be used as the medium for reflections on theosophy, human nature, and ethics. Throughout Persian poetry, nature and hist. tend to be viewed as *ʿibrat*, as instructive or admonitory manifestations of general laws of existence and behavior, and the wisdom of poetry is to teach its audience to interpret these phenomena. Objects, persons, and events are typically represented as exemplars of ideal, transcendental forms; the particular is of interest insofar as it represents the type. This principle helps explain why mystical Sufism found such a congenial home in Persian poetry, but it holds true for secular as well as explicitly religious lit.

A preexisting oral and written trad. on the pre-Islamic kings of Persia formed the basis for the first great work of New Persian poetry, the *Shāhnāma* (*Book of Kings*) by Abū al-Qāsim Firdawsī (d. 1025). This vast epic tells the story of Persia from the creation of the world and dawn of civilization to the collapse of the Sasanian dynasty and the coming of Islam. The epic is built around the reigns of 50 kings from the legendary Jamshīd to the historical Yazdigird, but some of its most famous stories deal with noble paladins like Rustam, who play major roles in the battles between Īrān and the rival kingdoms of Tūrān and Rūm. Stories of feasting and fighting often give the narrator cause to reflect on the tragic nature of hist. and problems of loyalty, authority, and proper rule. Following on Firdawsī's example, other figures from Persian heroic lore became subjects of a subsidiary epic lit., such as Asadī Ṭūsī's *Garshāspnāma* (Book of Garshāsp, composed 1066). Episodes from the *Shāhnāma* also served as the basis for the devel. of romance narratives focusing on the adventures and loves of noble heroes, most notably *Khusraw va Shīrīn* (Khusraw and Shirin) and *Haft Paykar* (The Seven Beauties) by Niẓāmī of Ganja (d. 1209). But Niẓāmī also drew on the legends of neighboring cultures. His two-part work on Alexander the Great (*Iskandarnāma*) follows Firdawsī in integrating this Gr. hero into the Persian trad., and for his story of the star-crossed lovers Majnūn and Laylā, Niẓāmī turned to the tribal lore of Arabia. These works, together with his collection of didactic tales *Makhzan al-asrār*, would serve as models for poets as late as the 19th c. The first poet to attempt to match Niẓāmī's achievement, Amīr Khusraw of Delhi (d. 1325), initiated two trends that would shape the hist. of the genre. First, he turned to Indian legend and fable for some of his stories, providing a precedent for later poets of the Mughal period to look to Sanskrit sources for their stories; Fayẓī (d. 1596), e.g., adapted his story of Nal and Daman from a tale in the *Mahābhārata*. Second, Amīr Khusraw composed epic-like narrative poems based on contemp. events. Masnavīs modeled on the *Shāhnāma* celebrating the deeds of living monarchs and patrons served to legitimize their rule by integrating it with the epic trad., and an imperial office for the writers of such Persian-lang. *Shāhnāma*s existed for a time even in the Ottoman Empire.

In such poems, the epic masnavī merges with courtly panegyric, but the principal form for eulogistic poetry was the qaṣīda. This genre drew heavily on the long trad. of Ar. court poetry and was the most prestigious literary form in the first period of Persian poetry. From Farrukhī (d. 1038) and Anvarī (d. 1189) in Khorasan to Qaṭrān (d. 1072) and Khāqānī (d. 1199) in Azerbaijan, the most accomplished poets throughout the Persian world earned their living by singing the praises of rulers, soldiers, viziers, and government officials. Qaṣīdas often opened with lyrical descriptions of gardens, the beauties of the season, festival celebrations, or the speaker's experiences in love before turning to ritualistic praise of the patron's victories, prowess in battle, justice in civic administration, or building projects. Generosity was paramount among the noble virtues, and the praise poem served as a social contract among the patron, the poet, and society: the patron was expected to live up to the idealized portrait presented in the poem and to reward the poet for his labors. Failure to do so could unleash the panegyric's dark opposite, the invective or lampoon (*hajv*), in which the object of the speaker's wrath was subjected to public vilification and abuse. Though praise poetry was a product of cultural, economic, and political interests, it was informed by a system of social, ethical, and religious ideals. These come to the fore in the poetry of Nāṣir Khusraw (ca. 1004–72), whose praise for the distant Fatamid rulers of Egypt and North Africa is sometimes overwhelmed by his critique of the society in which he lived in Badakhshan. Panegyric themes are also often found in elegies, as the deceased is praised for virtues and accomplishments that his successor will be expected to preserve. Esp. after the rise of the Shiʾite Safavid dynasty, eulogistic elegies are also composed for the Prophet Muhammad and his descendants, in which the responsibility for preserving their heritage falls to the current temporal rulers and the larger community of believers.

After the Mongol invasions of the 13th c., the qaṣīda lost much of its prestige, and literary patronage spread from the royal court to local lords and landholders, wealthy merchants, and Sufi lodges. The ghazal, which began as amatory lyric for courtly song and entertainment, gradually emerged as the preeminent short poetic form. It occupied an increasingly prominent place in the oeuvre of 12th-c. poets, such as Sanāʾī, ʿAṭṭār, Anvarī, and Khāqānī, and it became the genre of choice of the major 13th-c. poets Rūmī and Saʿdī (ca. 1184–1292), in whose hands it achieved its cl. form. The ghazal is defined by the first-person voice of the lover who describes, praises, cajoles, or complains of his aloof and idealized beloved. Persian pronouns give no indication of the gender, and the beloved was frequently a young male *ephebe*. The ghazal was composed for and performed in a wide range of contexts, and the beloved could take on various identities. While often an object of amorous passion, the beloved could also merge with the patron and the poem serve as a veiled courtly negotiation. In religious and mystical circles, the beloved could stand as a witness to divine grace or a symbol of God. Deciding on the most apt interpretation of this richly polysemous object of desire can be difficult, and the acknowledged master of the genre, Ḥāfiẓ (ca. 1325–89) took full advantage of this ambiguity, his poems sometimes allowing readings in all three registers at once. While it never lost its grounding in the experience of love, the ghazal in the works of fresh-style masters such as Sāʿib (ca. 1601–76) and Bīdil (d. 1725) could serve as a vehicle for wide-ranging existential, theosophical, and ethical ruminations, as conventional lyrical images of flowers, wine, gardens, music, and the beloved's physical features took on increasingly subtle, far-ranging metaphorical and symbolic meanings.

Genres in Persian poetry are frequently mixed. Ghazals and first-person lyrical passages, e.g., are often integrated into the romance, as lovers write to one another or lament their disappointments. Elegies on friends or family members praise the deceased but also explore the speaker's feelings of loss and bereavement and meditate on the transitoriness of human life. The 16th c. witnessed the emergence of the genre *sāqīnāma* (cupbearer's song) in rhymed couplets, in which the lyrical repertoire of wine and intoxication is used to represent a psychological crisis that is often resolved by an affirmation of religious belief or political affiliation. Khāqānī composed the masnavī *Tuḥfat al-ʿIrāqayn* (Gift of the Two Iraqs) in 1157 as an account of his pilgrimage to Mecca, and poets of the 16th and 17th cs. revived this model in versified travelogues and other topographic poetry that cover the vast geographical expanse of the Persian cultural sphere in the early mod. period. The autobiographical narrator describes the natural and manmade environment in terms drawn from epic, romance, and panegyric poetry; praises those who offer sustenance and guidance; censures those who do not; and often pauses to reflect on the lessons of his experience.

V. Modern Developments. Western economic power, political thought, and cultural dominance have had a profound impact on Persian poetry. The transregional cultural continuum of Persian poetry was divided along new national boundaries, and local vernaculars came to replace Persian as a lang. of administration and culture across much of its former range. Economic and political changes destroyed old systems of patronage, and the quest for modernization called into question authoritative trads. and well-established poetic conventions. Proponents of new and free verse challenged the rules of prosody, but the flexible forms and genres of traditional Persian poetry have nevertheless proven remarkably resilient. Questions of political order and authority had long been a concern of epic and panegyric poetry, and this trad. helped inform a new lit. of nationalism and constitutional rule in the poetry of Adīb al-Mamālik (1860–1917) and Muḥammad Taqī Bahār (1884–1951). After World War II, new and free verse forms served as the vehicle for a politically engaged, oppositional poetry in the work of poets such as Nīmā Yūshīj (1896–1960), Siyāvush Kasrāʾī (1927–96), and Aḥmad Shāmlū (1925–2000). The painter and poet Suhrāb Sipihrī (1928–80) dispensed with formal prosody altogether but drew inspiration from the mystical strain of traditional Persian poetry. Even a form as weighted with trad. as the ghazal has found a mod. relevance in the poetry of Sīmīn Bihbihānī (1927–2014), even if her drive for inner authenticity and sexual frankness do not match those of mod. Iran's foremost woman poet, Furūgh Farrukhzād (1935–67). The dust has largely settled on the debate between proponents of free verse and traditional forms, and it is not unusual to find poets today producing work in both idioms.

VI. Poetry and Other Arts. As the most prestigious form of verbal discourse and artistic expression in Persian culture, poetry has exerted a tremendous influence on other art forms. Histories, philosophical and theosophical treatises, and other prose writings are often studded with verses that summarize, elaborate, or comment on their message. Even today, quoting apropos verses of cl. poetry enlivens daily conversation. The highly regarded art of calligraphy has often employed poetry as its subject matter.

Miniature painting evolved as the art of illustrating poetic texts, most notably the *Shāhnāma* and the works of Niẓāmī and presents the same idealized vision of the world as poetry itself. Verses of poetry also decorate metalwork and ceramics, and public buildings are often embellished with poetry, sometimes composed esp. for its placement on the structure.

■ E. G. Browne, *Literary History of Persia*, 4 v. (1902–24); Z. Ṣafā, *Tārikh-i adabiyāt dar Īrān*, 8 v. (1956–90); A. J. Arberry, *Classical Persian Literature* (1958); A. Pagliaro and A. Bausani, *Storia della letteratura persiana* (1960); J. Bečka, "Tajik Literature from the Sixteenth Century to the Present," and J. Rypka, "History of Persian Literature up to the Beginning of the Twentieth Century," *History of Iranian Literature*, ed. K. Jahn (1968); C.-H. de Fouchécour, *Moralia: Les notions morales dans la littérature persane du 3e/9e au 7e/13e siècle* (1968); J. Meisami, *Medieval Persian Court Poetry* (1987); R. Zipoli, *Encoding and Decoding Neopersian Poetry* (1988); D. Davis, *Epic and Sedition: The Case of Ferdowsi's "Shahnameh"* (1992); A. Schimmel, *A Two-Colored Brocade: The Imagery of Persian Poetry* (1992); A. Karimi-Hakkak, *Recasting Persian Poetry: Scenarios of Poetic Modernity in Iran* (1995); F. Lewis, "Reading, Writing and Recitation: Sanā'ī and the Origins of the Persian Ghazal," diss., Univ. of Chicago (1995); J.T.P. de Bruijn, *Persian Sufi Poetry: An Introduction to the Mystical Use of Classical Persian Poems* (1997); G. Doerfer, "The Influence of Persian Language and Literature among the Turks," *The Persian Presence in the Islamic World*, ed. R. Hovannisian and G. Sabagh (1998); P. Losensky, *Welcoming Fighānī: Imitation and Poetic Individuality in the Safavid-Mughal Ghazal* (1998); J. Meisami, *Structure and Meaning in Medieval Arabic and Persian Poetry* (2003); *A History of Persian Literature*, ed. E. Yarshater, v. 1: *General Introduction to Persian Literature*, ed. J.T.P. de Bruijn (2006).

P. Losensky

PERU, POETRY OF. Peru can claim one of the richest and most complex poetic trads. of any Sp. Am. nation. With César Vallejo (1892–1938), it can also take pride in a major 20th-c. poet. Even though there are many splendid anthols. of Peruvian poetry, the sheer volume of Peruvian poetry makes its synthesis a daunting task. Most monographs, like Higgins's *The Poet in Peru*, limit themselves to a handful of poets. In 1964, when the Argentine literary jour. *Sur*, whose editorial board included Victoria Ocampo and Jorge Luis Borges, asked José Miguel Oviedo to prepare a representative anthol. of contemp. Peruvian poetry, the distinguished literary critic found himself in a challenging situation. He regretted the exclusion of many poets, even as he limited his selection to those whose ages ranged from 25 to 40 and who were active as poets in the 1950s and the 1960s. Since the 1950s, it has been customary in Peru to discuss and organize the poetic production of national poets with the convenient and yet anachronistic criterion of generations; and since the late 19th c., a significant share of critical discussion of Peruvian poetry has focused on the tensions between aesthetic and political imperatives informed by the social and historical dilemmas of the moment.

After the seminal *Antología General de la Poesía Peruana* (General Anthology of Peruvian Poetry, 1957) by Alejandro Romualdo (1926–2008) and Sebastián Salazar Bondy (1924–65)—major Peruvian poets in their own right—comprehensive accounts of Peruvian poetry cannot neglect the poetic trads. of the indigenous peoples of Peru. Aboriginal Peruvian peoples did not have a written lang., and their rich and variegated oral trads. came to the attention of most literary critics through transcriptions and trans. Some of the most important sources of the old lits. were unearthed in the 20th c., such as the poetry transcribed from the Quechua by Felipe Guamán Poma de Ayala (ca. 1535–1616) in *El primer nueva corónica y buen gobierno* (*The First New Chronicle and Good Government*, ca. 1615), a fundamental book of Andean culture. These poems include love poetry of seduction and of parental obstacles to the union of star-crossed lovers, which resonate with the concerns of early mod. Eur. lit.

The recognition of indigenous poetry as lit., as opposed to folklore, was made possible by the pioneering work of 20th-c. anthropologists and writers, in particular by José María Arguedas (1911–69), who argued that the belated acknowledgment of this literary corpus was due to the willful repression of indigenous cultures by the descendants of Eur. colonizers. Arguedas was also the ed. and translator of influential anthols. of ancient Peruvian poetry and one of the first Peruvians whose own Quechua poetry was drafted in writing. One of the high points of Arguedas's literary career, his trans. of the anonymous 18th-c. elegy "Apu Inca Atawallpaman" (To the Inca Atahuallpa), expresses "the collective vulnerability of a people suddenly stripped of a destiny," as Ortega has underscored.

The interest in indigenous Quechua poetry also sparked curiosity about the poetry of indigenous peoples from the Andes who spoke Aymara and of the peoples of the Peruvian Amazonian region. It emboldened some to celebrate popular and refined trads. by other neglected groups. Nicomedes Santa Cruz (1925–92) wrote poetry evoking the Af. rhythms of his own Peruvian speech and made considerable efforts to disseminate Afro-Peruvian trads., showing how some of them had synthesized popular improvisation and venerable Sp. forms. No literary critic made a more ardent plea in favor of inclusiveness than Antonio Cornejo Polar, yet he painfully acknowledged, in his own hist. of Peruvian lit., that he could not "offer an alternative to the traditional typologies of our literary hists. because we lack the critical and historical groundwork to introduce Indigenous and popular contributions into an overview of this kind."

The acknowledgment of Andean pre-Columbian langs. in Peru's literary heritage would have felt extraneous to Peruvian poets in the first few decades following the independence of 1821. Not even the Sp.-lang. poetry written during the times of the conquistadors and the Sp. viceroyalty was considered germane to Peruvian lit. until the second half of the 19th c., in a process Cornejo Polar aptly labeled the "nationalization" of the colonial past. Today, no one would exclude the satirical poetry of Juan del Valle y Caviedes (1652–97), who invented a first-person poetic persona to expose the shortcomings of Peruvian colonial society; the epic poetry of Pedro de Peralta Barnuevo (1664–1743); or the baroque poetry of Juan de Espinosa Medrano (1632–88) from the canon of Peruvian lit.; and acute scholarship in the first decade of the 21st c., by Lasarte and others, has shown the extent to which these writers are central to understanding the gestation of a distinctly Peruvian ethos that precedes the creation of the mod. state. Refined poetry in the Petrarchan style was also cultivated in the viceregal court of Peru, and the "Epistola a Belardo" (Letter to Belardo, 1621) by the mysterious Amarilis (an exquisite local poet or a Sp. invention, perhaps by Félix Lope de Vega) stands out as a captivating poetic evocation in the voice of a female descendant of Sp. conquistadors.

To understand the hist. of Peruvian poetry, it is necessary to keep in mind that the late 19th c. laid a claim to the legacy of poetry written in Sp. by Spaniards in the geographical region that today encompasses the Peruvian state and that the legacy of the indigenous world (and of other non-Western cultures, incl. those of Asian immigrants) was claimed in the 20th c. The earliest poets of the Andean region considered themselves to be people of Sp. descent who had made a political break with Spain, and in the case of Peru, the majority of its representative poets had sympathized with the Sp. crown until after the Peruvian nation was established. An exception is Mariano Melgar (b. in Arequipa, 1790–1815), best known for his *yaravíes*, which draw on indigenous forms and themes in his Sp.-lang. poetry of melancholy longing.

Sp. royal forces executed Melgar during the wars of independence. The case of José Joaquín de Olmedo (1780–1847) is more representative of the nationalistic ethos of poets who, until the independence period, were fully committed to Spain. Born in Guayaquil and educated in Lima, Olmedo had written poems deploring the Napoleonic invasion of Spain. Years later he was a member of the constitutional assembly as the nation of Peru was being established; but when Ecuador came into being, he actively participated in its political life and became one of its first heads of state. Peruvians and Ecuadorians both claim him as a national poet, and his "La victoria de Junín: Canto a Bolívar" (The Victory of Junin, Ode to Bolívar, 1825), is the single most important poem about the Sp. Am. wars of independence.

Most hists. of Peruvian poetry stress the significance of the liberal Manuel Ascencio Segura (1805–71) and the conservative Felipe Pardo y Aliaga (1806–68). Inspired by the Sp. trad. of *costumbrismo* (the depiction of local manners and customs), they wrote satirical poems about Peruvian life. These foundational poets of the Republican period, like Olmedo before them, had been previously aligned with Spain during the wars of independence. Ricardo Palma (1833–1919), the greatest Peruvian literary figure of the 19th c., created a hybrid literary genre, the *tradición peruana*, which combined poetry, fiction, local color, and historical anecdotes, presupposing the fluid continuity of a Peruvian culture since pre-Columbian times. The most celebrated Peruvian romantic poet, Carlos Augusto Salaverry (1830–91), expressed intense feelings of sexual longing matched by misogynistic anger and an uneasy relationship with the Christian god.

A positivist and the premier Peruvian political essayist of the 19th c., Manuel González Prada (1848–1918) was also a poet whose clear, sober, and atheist poetry was an affront to the prevailing Christian sensibility of the epoch. González Prada's work was contemporaneous with the rise of *modernismo*, but his poetic search was more in line with a sober romantic sensibility, as he worked with discrete meters, some of his own invention. Restraint was not the hallmark of José Santos Chocano (1875–1934), Peru's most famous and colorful literary figure in his own lifetime. Within the *modernista* idiom of the Nicaraguan poet Rubén Darío, Chocano attempted a sweeping lyrical vision aiming to transcend the Andean world and to encompass all of Sp. America.

A contemporary of Chocano, José María Eguren (1874–1942) emerged out of the modernista trad. but was understated where Chocano was loud. Some dismissed him for his apparent simplicity and for themes evocative of childhood songs and adolescent concerns, but Eguren is one of the Peruvian poets most revered by other Peruvian poets. Ricardo Silva-Santisteban (b. 1941), e.g., considers him to be Peru's first mod. poet. Eguren produced a pristine poetic lang. with a wide but carefully chosen vocabulary, attentive to the emotional resonances of words, with which he creates an alternative reality based on visions and dreams. Abraham Valdelomar (1888–1919) moved away from the mellifluous style of Darío, into dignified meditations about the Peruvian provinces and the family home, with a sense of rueful melancholy. He empowered poets throughout Peru to express regional pride. He also established and edited *Colónida* (1916). The bohemian and groundbreaking literary jour. paved the way for the reception of *Amauta* (1926–30), a jour. founded by José Carlos Mariátegui (1894–1930) that promoted the socialist vindication of the indigenous populations and the reception of a decided avant-garde aesthetic.

This is the context in which Vallejo, one of the greatest poets of the Sp. lang., came into his own. González Prada, Valdelomar, Eguren, and Mariátegui recognized Vallejo's talent from the outset and warmly encouraged his literary career. The emotional rawness of Vallejo's poetry stretched the Sp. lang. beyond grammar and lexicon into compelling dissonances and asymmetries, unprecedented and unsurpassed in the hist. of Hispanic poetry. His affecting directness makes him immediately accessible, even while his poems can defy interpretation. Like Paul Celan, Vallejo has presented daunting perplexities to his readers and translators: his lang., fraught with inner tensions, generates fragmentations, silences, and paradoxes. His poetry cannot be analyzed within a single register because he writes in multiple ones and can shift from one to another or operate simultaneously within several in the same poem. In Vallejo, oral expression and the conventions of written lang. are often in conflict, but his distortions can be moving, and his visual configurations are often emotionally arresting, as are his auditory effects. His ambiguities and ambivalences, made up of embers and auras of meaning, constitute an affront to reductive paraphrase. He managed to reorient the local and cosmopolitan literary trads. on which he drew. His poetry is imbued with feelings of guilt, uncertainty, and intimations that the satisfaction of one's own needs can feel shameful when confronted with the suffering of others. In *Los heraldos negros* (*The Black Heralds*, 1919), his first book of poems, Vallejo faces his theological demons, expressing a tragic vision in which sexuality and sin are one and the same. With *Trilce* (1922), he still longs for attachment and is nostalgic for family bonds but no longer relies on the rhet. of religion to address his angst, reaching his most persuasive experimental heights. In his posthumous books *España, aparta de mí este cáliz* (*Spain, Take This Cup from Me*, 1937), and *Poemas humanos* (*Human Poems*, 1939), his poetry of collective anguish and compassion is expressed with a keener historical awareness and a nettled attentiveness to cosmopolitan concerns. While some have branded Vallejo's most difficult poetry as densely hermetic or as a challenge to the logos of Western culture, others have argued that his difficulties are an aperture into the indigenous soul of the Andean peoples. Vallejo's complete poetry exists in a trans. that the Am. poet Clayton Eshleman took five decades to complete.

As with the poetry of Vallejo, the Peruvian avant-garde made serious attempts to engage with the indigenous. The tensions and contradictions between modernity and trad. informed urgent intellectual discussions of the time. In addition to *Amauta*, the most influential jour. in Peruvian lit. hist., it is important to cite the *Boletín Titikaka* (1926–30), ed. by the brothers Arturo (1897–1969) and Alejandro Peralta (1899–1973). Both jours. made efforts to engage the integration of popular culture and avant-garde cosmopolitanism, giving way to the poetic impulses that were to follow in authors such as César A. Rodríguez (1889–1972), Alberto Hidalgo (1897–1967), Guillermo Mercado (1906–83), Xavier Abril (1905–90), Alejandro Peralta (1899–1973), and most notably Arguedas. There was also an avant-garde current oriented to the populist Alianza Popular Revolucionaria Americana or APRA, the most enduring of all political parties in 20th-c. Peru, which produced important poets such as Magda Portal (1900–89).

In a period concerned with the impact of new information technologies, the star of Carlos Oquendo de Amat (1905–36) has been rising. His *5 metros de poemas* (5 Meters of Poems, 1927) is considered the first Peruvian multimedia poem in which the written word plays with the conventions of x-ray photography, cinema, and advertising. Its 28 pages unfold into a single continuous sheet over four meters long, and some of its pointed effects depend on the visual disposition of the type. Two major poets brought surrealism to Peru, César Moro (1903–55) and Emilio Adolfo Westphalen (1911–2001). Moro, who signed one of the surrealist manifestos, wrote poetry of unbound desire, unrestrained transgression, and pain. *La tortuga ecuestre* (The Equestrian Turtle, 1938–39) is his most important book in Sp. He also wrote poetry in Fr. now included in Eur. anthols. of surrealistic poetry. Westphalen has summarized the gist of his poetic appeal: "After reading Moro one feels trampled under foot and crushed by the beasts of love—inconsolable from the infernal breath that spews out of love and beauty. These demented extremes unleash the lightning that unites, destroys and regenerates." Westphalen's best known books are *Las ínsulas extrañas* (Strange Islands, 1933) and *Abolición de la muerte* (Abolition of Death, 1935). More measured than Moro's, his poetry is concerned with death as it delves into the painful obscurities of love, silence, and the unconscious. Another major figure, Martín Adán (1908–85), was a master of traditional poetic forms as well as free verse. A hermetic poet with mystical urges, he was skeptical that lang. could give relief to the quiet anguish of an introverted poetic persona who struggles with mundane desires against the deterioration of the body and the fragility of the mind.

In the second half of the 20th c., one of the great figures of Peruvian poetry is Carlos Germán Belli (b. 1927), best known for his remarkable mastery of the traditional forms of Sp. and It. poetry, as he addresses the anguish and alienation of contemp. urban life. Jorge Eduardo Eielson (1924–2006) began his career as a poet deconstructing Western myths and Christian images, but he purified his poetry, divesting it of its engagements with trad., in a dialogue with his activities as a visual artist. In the 1960s, Eielson became intrigued with the *quipu*, a pre-Columbian object made of strings and knots whose purpose is the stuff of speculation. Eielson reduced the quipu to a single knot, which became the central object of his most important paintings, installations, and final poems. As Padilla has pointed out, Eielson aimed to deconstruct lang. in order to reconnect with matter, and the knot suggests his lingering attachments to Peru.

Blanca Varela (1926–2009) was a major literary figure. In meticulous poems, her secure lyrical voice explores intense emotions without a hint of sentimentalism but with a tone that can sometimes be playful and even parodic. Her poetry converses with sights and sounds, music and the visual arts, and is often set in a nondescript urban context; but she has also created a lyrical geography that loosely evokes the coast of Lima as it is situated between the sky and the sand, near the sea. Her lyrical world abounds with homes and gardens populated by flowers, animals, insects, and ghosts. Varela transgresses the semantic conventions of the lang., and to some commentators, these transgressions have suggested the disjointedness of surrealism. Her images, however, are neither surrealistic nor impenetrable. Her poetry is not hermetic. She fashioned distinct patterns of signification. Images like "hacer la luz aunque cueste la noche" (to make light even if it costs the night) are paradoxes that reflect one of the central themes of her poetry: the relationship between the light of perception and the dark force of memory. Among Varela's contemporaries one could cite Javier Sologuren (1921–2004), Raúl Destua (1921–2005), José Ruiz Rosas (b. 1928), Pablo Guevara (1930–2006), Juan Gonzalo Rose (1928–83), and Washington Delgado (1927–2003).

Javier Heraud (1942–63) is the legendary poet killed as a guerrilla fighter before he could fulfill the promise of his flowing, seductive lyrical style. With a post-Whitmanesque ease, the poetry of Antonio Cisneros (1942–2012) addresses social concerns and hist. and brings a sense of presence through the sensual evocation of taste and smells. With the publication of his *El libro de Dios y de los húngaros* (The Book of God and the Hungarians, 1978), Cisneros surprised some readers by his conversion to Catholicism, without renouncing his socialist convictions. Rodolfo Hinostroza (b. 1941) captures the esoteric and occultist bent of Peruvian poetry of the 1960s with a New Age embrace of Eastern cultures and of Sigmund Freud. César Calvo (1940–2000) was admired for his love of beauty, compassion for the bereft, exploration of intense experiences, and idealization of the Amazon region. Other significant poets of this period are Luis Hernández (1941–77), Julio Ortega (b. 1942), Mirko Lauer (b. 1947), and Marco Martos (b. 1941).

Toro Montalvo's anthol. *Poesía Peruana del 70* (Peruvian Poetry of the 70s, 1991) underscores the impact for poetry of the 1968 military coup by General Juan Velasco Alvarado and of a new cultural sensibility informed by pop music, *chicha* (a fusion of the indigenous *huaino* and the *cumbia*), and salsa. An influential group in the 1970s was the *Hora Zero* movement, which brought together Enrique Verástegui (b. 1950), Jorge Pimentel (b. 1944), Jorge Nájar (b. 1946), Carmen Ollé (b. 1947), and Tulio Mora (b. 1948). Other significant poets of that moment are Abelardo Sánchez León (b. 1947), Elqui Burgos (b. 1946), José Watanabe (1946–2007), and Mario Montalbetti (b. 1953).

In the 1980s, the belated feminist movement of Peru made decisive inroads in poetry. Giovanna Pollarolo (b. 1952) and Mariela Dreyfus (b. 1960) confronted Peruvian machismo with a sense of freshness and irony. Patricia Alba (b. 1960), Rosella de Paollo (b. 1960), and Rocío Silva-Santisteban (b. 1963) explored dimensions of female sensuality that Peruvian poetry had previously shunned. It was also a period marked by the impact of the Shining Path terrorist movement and by the dirty war that ensued. Among the most notable poets of this time, one could cite Oswaldo Chanove (b. 1953), Carlos López Degregori (b. 1952), Alonso Ruiz Rosas (b. 1959), Eduardo Chirinos (b. 1960), José Antonio Mazzotti (b. 1961), Roger Santiváñez (b. 1956), and Magdalena Chocano (b. 1957).

The anthol. of Peruvian poetry *Los relojes se han roto* (The Clocks Are Broken, 2005) includes poets who grew up in a climate of terrorism followed by the corruption of President Alberto Fujimori's regime. These poets include José Carlos Yrigoyen (b. 1976), Montserrat Álvarez (b. 1969), and Chrystian Zegarra (b. 1971), who stands out for his renewal of Vallejo's jagged undertones to express the despair of a society unable to process psychological and physical trauma in the uncertain cosmopolitanism of the mod. world.

See INDIGENOUS AMERICAS, POETRY OF THE; SPANISH AMERICA, POETRY OF.

■ **Anthologies and Primary Texts:** *Poesía peruana: Antología general.* v. 1: *Poesía aborigen y tradicional popular*, ed. A. Romualdo; v. 2: *De la conquista al modernismo*, ed. R. Silva-Santisteban; v. 3: *De Vallejo a nuestros días*, ed. R. González Vigil (1984); *Antología general de la poesía peruana*, ed. R. Silva-Santisteban (1994); *El bosque de los huesos: Antología de la poesía peruana (1963–1993)*, ed. M. Zapata and J. A. Mazzotti (1995); *Poesía peruana: Siglo XX*, v. 1, *Del modernismo a los años '50*; v. 2, *De los años '60 a nuestros días*, ed. R. González Vigil (1999); *La poesía del siglo XX en el Perú: Antología esencial*, ed. J. M. Oviedo (2008); *Poesía vanguardista peruana I and II*, ed. L. F. Chueca (2009).

■ **Criticism and History:** J. Higgins, *The Poet in Peru: Alienation and the Quest for a Super-Reality* (1982); E. A. Westphalen, *La poesía los poemas los poetas* (1995); A. Cornejo Polar, *Literatura peruana: Siglo XVI a siglo XX* (2000); *En Nudos Homenaje a J. E. Eielson*, ed. J. I. Padilla (2002); J. Ortega, "Transatlantic Translations," *PMLA* 118 (2003); R. Silva-Santisteban, *Escrito en el agua II* (2004); P. Lasarte, *Lima satirizada (1598–1698): Mateo Rosas de Oquendo y Juan del Valle y Caviedes* (2006).

E. Kristal; M. Ortiz Canseco

PHILIPPINES, POETRY OF THE

I. Tagalog
II. English

I. Tagalog. The lang. of the Tagalogs, the largest ethnic group in the Philippines, is spoken in at least eight countries, but most Tagalog poems were and are written by poets living in the central part of Luzon island, where the lang. is the mother tongue.

The earliest poems were handed down orally. These monorhyming poems were riddles, proverbs, and short lyrics (mostly in quatrains). Although other societies have preserved longer poems in the form of oral heroic epics, no precolonial Tagalog long poem has yet been discovered.

Early poems established the three key features of Tagalog poetry: syllabic meter, rhyme based on identity of vowels and equivalence of consonants, and *talinghaga* (a cross between mod. metaphor and med. anagogy, but without the latter's religious context). The second feature is best known in its formulation by José Rizal (1861–96): for purposes of end rhyme, there are only two consonant "sounds" in Tagalog, that of *b*, *d*, *g*, *k*, *p*, *s*, and *t*; and that of *l*, *m*, *n*, *ng*, *r*, *w*, and *y*. Words ending with the same vowel but different consonants, as long as the consonants belong to the same set, are considered rhyming.

Printing was introduced into the islands in 1593 by Sp. colonizers. The first published poems in Tagalog were written by missionaries who learned the lang. for evangelization or by translators of Sp. texts in the early 17th c.; these poems followed Eur. rather than Tagalog prosody. The first published poem that strictly followed the oral trad. was "May Bagyo Ma't May Rilim" ("Though It Is Stormy and Dark," 1835), a 30-line poem in six monorhyming stanzas.

Their encounter with Sp. lit. led Tagalog poets to adapt Eur. genres such as the metrical romance to the native trad. Considered masterpieces are *Ang Mahal na Pasion* (The Passion [of Jesus], 1704) by Gaspar Aquino de Belen (fl. 17th c.) and *Florante at Laura* (1838) by Francisco Baltazar (1788–1862). Baltazar, writing under the pen name Balagtas, is considered the greatest Tagalog poet, having brought the spoken lang. to a high literary level, much as Chaucer did with Eng. and Dante with It.

Balagtas was such a strong influence on subsequent poets that the modernist movement in the 20th c. was characterized as a battle between his disciples and his detractors. Ranged among his disciples were political poets such as Andres Bonifacio (1863–97), Marcelo H. Del Pilar (1850–95), and Amado V. Hernandez (1903–70); and romantic poets such as José Corazon de Jesus (1896–1932). Among those who consciously moved away from his trad. were experimental poets such as Alejandro G. Abadilla (1906–69) and Rolando S. Tinio (1937–97).

Working with traditional forms such as the *tanaga* (a quatrain of heptasyllabic lines), the *dalit* (a quatrain of octosyllabics), and the folk epic or ethnoepic, as well as with Eur. forms, Virgilio S. Almario (b. 1944), considered the major poet of the 20th c., integrated the best features of the oral trad., the Balagtas trad., and modernism. Twenty-first-c. poems have extended the trad. to include the prose poem and electronic poetry, but traces of syllabic count, consonant equivalence, and talinghaga remain strong.

II. English. On the rocky isle of Corregidor, soon after Commodore George Dewey effectively ended Sp. colonial rule in the Philippines on May 1, 1898, the first makeshift Am. public school was established by U.S. soldiers. In 1901, 600 teachers from the U.S. arrived aboard the transport *Thomas* to serve as principals, superintendents, and teachers in the highly centralized public-school system. Since there are more than 170 Philippine langs., Eng. was employed as the medium of instruction and communication; pupils who dared speak their native langs. in the school premises were punished. The Am. colonial government also began sending Filipino students and professionals to various colleges and universities in the U.S., and in 1908, the Philippine legislature established the University of the Philippines (UP). The Philippine Commonwealth was established by the U.S. in 1935, to be interrupted during World War II by the Japanese occupation from 1942 to 1944, and the independent Republic of the Philippines was founded in 1946.

Through the influence of Am. educators after 1898, Eng. effectively became the country's first national lang. or lingua franca. It became not solely the chief instrument for the acquisition of new learning, not only a favored medium by which to represent the Filipinos to themselves and to the world, but a principal means to employment, social status, prestige, and power. The country's lit. in Eng., like its scholarship, was bred in the university, and UP may justly claim to be the cradle of Philippine letters in Eng. through its literary organs *The College Folio* (1910–13) and *The Literary Apprentice* (since 1928) of the UP Writers' Club and through its national writers' workshop every summer since 1964.

In only half a century after the first Eng.-lang. literary endeavors published in *The Filipino Students' Magazine* in Berkeley, California, in 1905, the country already possessed a significant body of fiction, poetry, drama, and essays in Eng. It may be said that, if at first the writers wrote *in* Eng., later they wrought *from* it because its use in lit. had been chiefly toward affirming, within the adopted lang., a Filipino sense of their world. By the mid-1950s, "Philippine Literature in English" was already offered as a formal course at the UP.

Philippine poetry in Eng. may be regarded as having passed through three overlapping transformative phases: a romantic era during the first 40 years or so since 1905, a New Critical phase from the 1950s to the 1970s, and a poststructuralist period from the 1980s to the present.

Because the country already had accomplished writers in Sp., Tagalog, and other native langs., the literary apprenticeship during the romantic phase was ling. and cultural rather than literary or poetic. The tension that inevitably emerged between poets' creative struggle with the adopted lang. and their responses to the new historical situation cleared the poetic terrain for their own sensibility and perception of their circumstances. Such engagement with their own cultural and social milieu is already signaled in Ponciano Reyes's "The Flood" in 1905, a narrative poem that addresses the plight of the working class during a natural disaster. Among the romantic poets of note are Fernando M. Maramág (1893–1936), Luis G. Dato (1906–83), Angela C. Manalang Gloria (1907–95), Jose Garcia Villa (1908–97; known in the U.S. for his experiments such as reversed consonance and comma poems—he appears in a famous photo taken in the Gotham Book Mart on November 9, 1948), Carlos Bulosan (1913–56; author of the influential, partly autobiographical novel *America Is in the Heart* [1943]), Trinidad L. Tarrosa Subido (1912–94), Amador T. Daguio (1912–66), Rafael Zulueta y da Costa (1915–90), and Nick Joaquin (1917–2004), the latter an esp. prolific poet, historian, and journalist.

In the 1950s, the Am. New Criticism began to hold critical sway: Cleanth Brooks, John T. Purser, and Robert Penn Warren's *Approach to Literature* (1936) was the standard textbook for the collegiate introductory course in lit. from the 1950s to the early 1980s; noteworthy also is the series of formalist studies of Philippine lit. in Eng. by the Am. critic Leonard Casper following his anthol. *Six Filipino Poets* (1954), incl. *The Wayward Horizon* (1961) and *The Wounded Diamond* (1964). Indeed, the New Criticism is to the present still conspicuous in writers' workshops, book reviews, and judgments in poetic contests. Of the six poets in Casper's anthol., three—Dominador I. Ilio (1913–2006), Edith L. Tiempo (1919–2011), and Ricaredo Demetillo (1919–98)—were graduates of the University of Iowa Writers' Workshop. Among other poets during this period are Carlos A. Angeles (1921–2000), Virginia R. Moreno (b. 1925), Alejandrino G. Hufana (1926–2003), Emmanuel Torres (b. 1932), Ophelia Alcantara Dimalanta (1932–2010), and Cirilo F. Bautista (b. 1941).

Yet even among these later poets, the transformation of both lang. and sensibility owes more to the poet's creative toil with lang. in response to his or her historical circumstances than to the influence of New Critical formalism. Political activism in the mid-1960s and the martial-law regime under President Ferdinand Marcos from 1972 to 1986 compelled poets to connect with their social reality, even as they recognized a formalist imperative. There are many more contemp. poets of note, among whom are Alfred A. Yuson (b. 1945), Ricardo M. de Ungria (b. 1951), Marne L. Kilates (b. 1952), Eric T. Gamalinda (b. 1956), Luis Cabalquinto (b. 1935), J. Neil C. Garcia (b. 1969), Merlie M. Alunan (b. 1943), Rowena Tiempo Torrevillas (b. 1951), Marjorie M. Evasco (b. 1953), and Luisa Igloria (b. 1961, formerly Maria Luisa B. Aguilar Cariño). Of these, significantly, four—Gamalinda, Cabalquinto, Torrevillas, and Igloria—now reside in the U.S.

■ **Tagalog.** V. Almario, *Balagtasismo versus Modernismo* (1984); B. Lumbera, *Tagalog Poetry, 1570–1898* (1986); V. Almario, *Taludtod at Talinghaga* (1991); V. Almario, *Poetikang Tagalog* (1996); V. Almario, *Pag-unawa sa Ating Pagtula* (2006); V. Almario, *Sansiglong Mahigit ng Makabagong Tula sa Filipinas* (2006).

■ **English.** ***Anthologies***: *Man of Earth*, ed. G. H. Abad and E. Zapanta-Manlapaz (1989); *A Native Clearing*, ed. G. H. Abad (1993); *Brown River, White Ocean*, ed. L. H. Francia (1993); *Returning a Borrowed Tongue*, ed. N. Carbó (1995); *A Habit of Shores*, ed. G. H. Abad (1999); *At Home in Unhomeliness*, ed. J.N.C. Garcia (2007). ***Criticism and History***: *A Passionate Patience*, ed. R. M. de Ungria (1995); J.N.C. Garcia, *Postcolonialism and Filipino Poetics* (2004); *Pinoy Poetics*, ed. N. Carbó (2004); E. L. Tiempo, *Six Poetry Formats and the Transforming Image* (2007); G. H. Abad, *Our Scene So Fair* (2008).

I. R. Cruz (Tagalog); G. H. Abad (Eng.)

POLAND, POETRY OF

I. The Middle Ages to the Fourteenth Century. Pre-Christian oral poetry in Polish dialects has not been uncovered, but its traces may be found in folk lit. Christianity in Western form was adopted in Poland in 966. The result was sustained literary activity in Lat. until the 17th c. Among the numerous liturgical songs of the med. period, the hymn *Gaude Mater Polonia* devoted to St. Stanislaus was esp. important. The anonymous song "Bogurodzica" (Mother of God) is the oldest poem preserved in the Polish lang. The only two copies date from the beginning of the 15th c., but it was most likely composed in the 13th c. It was sung throughout the country in various versions and was even considered an anthem of the Polish kingdom. Consisting of two stanzas and the refrain "Kyrie eleison," the equivalent of the iconographic theme of deesis (Christ Pantocrator, Mary, and St. John the Baptist) is visible in its sophisticated construction. Only fragments of other Polish poems of the Middle Ages have been preserved, but Christian literary production (both oral and written) was probably much more extensive. The first trans. of the Psalms at the end of the 14th c. (the so-called *Psałterz floriański*) had a lasting impact on the devel. of Polish poetry.

II. The Fifteenth Century. Religious literary activity of this period was very rich; some Christmas carols and Lenten and Easter songs are still sung in Polish churches. The song "Żale Matki Boskiej pod krzyżem" (Lament of the Mother of God at the Foot of the Cross) is the most innovative work of the time. The monologue, expressing Mary's powerful emotions, is likely a part of a missing Passion mystery play. Epic poetry is poorly represented. *Legenda o świętym Aleksym* (The Legend of Saint Alexis) is an example of verse hagiography, drawing on foreign sources. Only a few fragments of secular poems have been preserved. The most impressive is "Rozmowa Mistrza Polikarpa ze Śmiercią" (A Dialogue between Master Polycarpus and Death), a form of med. dialogism or perhaps part of a morality play. Opulent in lang., imagery, black humor, and even grotesque elements, it constitutes a reflection on the topos of the *danse macabre*. The verse structure of Polish poetry at that time was based on a system of relative syllabism with approximate rhymes.

III. The Sixteenth Century. Humanist influences are pronounced in Lat. poetry in the first part of the century. In describing Polish landscapes and recounting Polish hist., Janicíus (pseud. of Klemens Janicki, 1516–43) imitated the forms of ancient poetry. Some poets—among them, Jan Kochanowski (1530–84) and Szymon Szymonowic (1558–1629)—cultivated bilingual (Lat. and Polish) poetry.

Poetry in vernacular came into prominence. Mikołaj Rej (1505–69, called the father of Polish poetry) used Polish exclusively in his didactic or satiric poetry expressing the ideology of the Reformation; his verse structure is close to syllabism.

Jan Kochanowski was the most eminent poet of the Polish Ren. He imported the forms of ancient poetry and established a strictly syllabic system of Polish verse, incl. exact rhyme, stabilized caesura, paroxytonic cadence and enjambment, thus making possible an interplay between syntax and verse structure. His poetry consists of the collections *Psałterz Dawidów* (an adaptation of the Psalms, 1578), *Treny* (Laments, 1580), *Fraszki* (Trifles, written throughout his life, ed. 1584), *Pieśni* (Songs, ed. 1586), some epic poems, and the cl. verse tragedy *Odprawa posłów greckich* (*The Dismissal of the Greek Envoys*, 1578). The anacreontic trifles and Horatian songs he composed from his early years until his death express an enjoyment of everyday life and acceptance of nature: they are inspired by Stoic and Epicurean philosophy. In his laments, written after the death of his four-year-old daughter, the poet expresses a wide range of shifting emotions, from despair to final reconciliation with God's will.

Mikołaj Sęp Szarzyński (1550–81) was a profoundly metaphysical poet whose work expressed impassioned spiritual experience. He converted from Calvinism to Catholicism (as was typical for Polish nobles during the Counter-Reformation). His work foreshadowed the emerging poetics of the early baroque (or mannerism): oxymoronic imagery, abundant inversions, ellipses, and enjambments. Sęp Szarzyński was the author of only one volume of poems, edited posthumously: *Rytmy abo wiersze polskie* (Rhythms or Polish Verses, 1601). Another metaphysical poet of the period was Sebastian Grabowiecki (ca. 1543–1607), who expressed quietism through his refined, sophisticated lyricism.

IV. The Seventeenth Century. Szymon Szymonowic was a poet of the late Ren. who followed Kochanowski in his poetics but also imitated the Alexandrian poet Theocritus in his *Sielanki* (Idylls, 1614). His semirealistic pastorals became the model for the genre in the 17th and 18th cs. Maciej Kazimierz Sarbiewski (1595–1640), known as the Christian Horace, vaulted to Eur. fame as an intellectual poet writing in Lat. and the author of a theory of baroque poetry. The Protestant Daniel Naborowski (1573–1640) continued "the metaphysical line" in Polish poetry. His oxymoronic poetry, full of contradictions, expressed the uncertainty of human existence in the world.

Another kind of Polish baroque poetry, court poetry, was inspired by Giambattista Marino and Luis de Góngora. It was more cosmopolitan, close at times to Fr. libertinism. The premier author in this mode was Jan Andrzej Morsztyn (1621–93); his poetry, full of wit and conceits, constituted a kind of verbal game. Its main theme was love and its paradoxes.

The dominant strain in 17th-c. Polish culture was the Sarmatian baroque. Ancient Sarmatia was a founding myth of the Polish nobility, and many poets subscribed to the ideology this myth embodied. Their poetry employed various forms, both epic and lyric. Wacław Potocki (1621–96) composed the epic poem *Wojna chocimska* (War of Chocim, 1670) and the series of "Moralia" (1688). Wespazjan Kochowski (1633–1700) was the author of the collection of lyrics and epigrams *Niepróżnujące próżnowanie* (Unleisurely Leisure, 1674) and of a long poem in biblical prose *Psalmodia polska* (Polish Psalmody, 1695), a messianic interpretation of Polish hist.

V. The Eighteenth Century. Polish poetry in the 18th c. remained under the strong influence of the Sarmatian baroque. In 1766, an epigone of the style, Józef Baka (1707–80), published his devotional and moralistic poems, full of paradoxes and a very particular black humor. A vast wave of anonymous patriotic and religious poetry appeared after the gentry rebellion called Konfederacja Barska (the Confederacy of Bar, 1768). The 1760s marked a significant turn in Polish poetry, in response to the political changes following the election of the last king of independent Poland, Stanisław August Poniatowski (r. 1764–95). The ideology of the Enlightenment gained currency in intellectual circles surrounding the royal court and other aristocratic courts. Didactic poetry propagating the new philosophy and worldview emerged; and the baroque style was replaced by Fr. classicism, rococo, and preromantic sentimentalism. The new tendencies intermingled with older Sarmatian models in the work of Adam Naruszewicz (1733–96). In his poetry, didactic and rhetorical, he employed cl. genres such as the ode or satire. At the same time his lang. was crude and abounded in antitheses.

Ignacy Krasicki (1735–1801) was the most magnificent poet of the Polish Enlightenment. His poetic production encompassed fables, satires, and a mock epic (*Monachomachia*, 1778). His works were full of irony and sophisticated humor, marked by precise lang., brilliant dialogues, innovative rhymes and cl. forms. Krasicki ridiculed contemp. morals, incl. the life of the clergy; his skepticism about human nature shows his affinities with the philosophy of Voltaire. His poetry was didactic without intrusive rhet. Stanisław Trembecki (1739?–1812) and Tomasz Kajetan Węgierski (1756–87) represented the libertine poetry of the rococo. Trembecki composed both political odes and obscene erotic poems; his highest achievements, however, were his anacreontics and the descriptive poem *Sofiówka* (Sophie's Garden, 1806). Węgierski was far more radical in his libertinism, writing not only erotic poems but antireligious poetic pamphlets and harsh moral satires as well. Another stream of rococo verged on sentimentalism. Franciszek Dionizy Kniaźnin (1750–1807) produced anacreontics, fables, and bucolic verse. Franciszek Karpiński (1741–1825) wrote erotic poems, sentimental rather than libertine, idylls, and religious songs (among them one of the most refined Polish Christmas carols, "Bóg się rodzi" (God Is Born).

After several years of political upheaval (a profound crisis in the government, efforts to rectify it, internal tensions, foreign political interference), Poland was partitioned among its neighbors—Russia, Prussia, and Austria—and disappeared as an independent nation in 1795. In Polish lit. and esp. in poetry, an entirely new situation emerged. From this time on, poetry became a substitute for other means of shaping national ideology and culture.

VI. The Nineteenth Century

A. ***The Classical and Preromantic Period.*** The beginning of the century was marked by the continued domination of cl. poetry, but new tendencies also developed. Apart from Trembecki's work, another significant descriptive poem—influenced by Virgil—was *Ziemiaństwo polskie* (Polish Landed Gentry, 1839), which occupied the poet Kajetan Koźmian (1771–1856) for almost three decades. Kazimierz Brodziński (1791–1835) composed a series of sentimental bucolics. Alojzy Feliński (1771–1820) authored a cl. tragedy in syllabic verse inspired by Polish hist., *Barbara Radziwiłłówna* (1811, staged in 1817). Jan Paweł Woronicz (1757?–1829) was the author of *Hymn do Boga* (Hymn to God, 1805), a messianic explication of Polish hist. (the romantics were later inspired by this vision). The *Śpiewy historyczne* (Historic Songs, 1816) of Julian Ursyn Niemcewicz (1758–1841) were written in the style of James Macpherson's Ossianic songs and told of Poland's heroic past. Aleksander Fredro (1793?–1876) was the author of comedies inspired by cl. forms (Molière, Marivaux) but dealing with the Sarmatian trad. (*Zemsta* [Vengeance], staged 1834) or the new romantic sensibility (*Śluby panieńskie* [Maidens' Vows], staged 1839). Fredro's raillery was rooted in both a libertine outlook and rational common sense. He was inventive in his poetics and lang.; wit and play with various styles were the main sources of his humor.

B. *The Romantic Period.* The period between 1818 and 1822 was marked by "the battle between the Classicists and the Romantics." The dispute was settled by the debut of Adam Mickiewicz (1798–1855), with his volume *Ballady i romanse* (Ballads and Romances, 1822). Mickiewicz, the greatest Polish poet since Kochanowski, was the first Polish romantic. He had read J. W. Goethe, Friedrich Schiller, Lord Byron, and other Eur. romantic authors; but, educated in the spirit of the Enlightenment, he knew cl. lit. as well. In his work, both tendencies are visible. *Oda do młodości* (Ode to Youth, 1820) is an example of combining cl. rhet. with the new romantic ideology of youth as a divine power creating a new world. Mickiewicz was a master of Polish verse. He experimented with forms of rhythm, sought out revealing rhymes, and played with multiple genres. Above all, he took full advantage of the possibilities of the Polish lang., esp. its syntax and vocabulary. Mickiewicz's ballads refer to native folklore, though they are more frequently Belarusian or Lithuanian than ethnically Polish. This helped him maintain distance from the described world, full of fantasy and supernatural phenomena but, at the same time, made it possible to oppose rationalist philosophy and express the heart's "living truth." His poetic drama *Dziady* (Forefather's Eve, two parts, 1823; third part, 1832) has the structure of a mystery play; while it refers to folk commemorative ceremonies, its construction and versification are innovative. The sequence of *Sonety krymskie* (Crimean Sonnets, 1826) linked precise cl. form with a romantic way of describing exotic landscapes. His Byronic tale in verse *Konrad Wallenrod* (1828) introduced the political and ethical topic of a secret struggle against the nation's powerful enemies. After the collapse of the November Insurrection of 1830–31, when many Polish intellectuals went into exile in Western Europe (esp. France), Mickiewicz became far more than an eminent poet; he was considered a *wieszcz* (prophet, bard) and gained moral and political prestige through his metaphysical (messianic) interpretation of Polish hist.

In 1834, Mickiewicz published *Pan Tadeusz*, a long poem recognized as the Polish national epic. From one point of view, it constitutes a Homeric epic on the poet's homeland (a province at the border between Poland, Lithuania, and Belarus) during the time of the Napoleonic wars (1811–12). But one can also find attributes of other genres, e.g., the descriptive poem, bucolic, mock epic, sentimental novel, and *gawęda* (a kind of tale, often oral, peculiar to Sarmatian culture). The work mixes nostalgia with humor and irony. In subsequent years, Mickiewicz grew absorbed in mystical soul-searching and political activity and virtually stopped writing poetry. His last sequence of poems (the so-called Lausanne lyrics, written in 1839) could have opened a completely new path in Mickiewicz's work. Ascetic, concise, focused on the word rather than syntax or syllabic rhythm, they violated the romantic paradigm.

A number of young poets followed Mickiewicz in the 1820s and 1830s, but they were much more typically romantic: Antoni Malczewski (1793–1826), Józef Bohdan Zaleski (1802–86), Seweryn Goszczyński (1801–76). The truly distinctive talent among them was Juliusz Słowacki (1809–49). Inventive in his poetics, esp. in his breathtakingly innovative rhymes, he experimented with many genres: lyric poems, tales in verse, visionary epics, and poetic dramas. He opposed Mickiewicz (his play *Kordian*, 1834, was a polemic against Mickiewicz's play *Dziady*) in his interpretation of Polish hist. and his philosophy of existence. Tragedy intermingled with bitter humor and deep romantic irony in his work. He was masterful in his range of emotional expression. In his dramas, inspired by Shakespeare, he experimented with versification, dramatic construction, and the creation of an inner world—realistic, fantastic, dreamlike, symbolic, and ambivalent (e.g., *Balladyna*, written 1834, pub. 1839). In his poems, Słowacki employed complex stanzaic forms, *ottava rima*, and biblical prose, inter alia. His "poem of digression" *Beniowski* (1841), resembling the narrative poems of Byron or Pushkin, is a recapitulation of the author's poetic path and a reckoning with himself, his enemies, poetry, and the world. It was a turning point in Słowacki's work, initiating a mystical period in his life and work. *Król-Duch* (King-Spirit, 1847), a mythopoetic vision of the incarnation of the nation's spirit in the great personalities of hist., was an expression of the poet's new convictions.

Zygmunt Krasiński (1812–59) was considered the third *wieszcz* or bard (after Mickiewicz and Słowacki). However, his poetics lack the force of the others' work. In contemp. times, he is appreciated not so much for his poems as for his political dramas, which express a conservative vision of the crisis of Christian civilization, and his fascinating letters.

In his lifetime, Cyprian Norwid (1821–83) was isolated from the mainstream of Polish poetry. Forgotten for several decades, he was rediscovered in the 20th c. and is considered a precursor of mod. Polish poetry. In his poetics, he developed and even violated romantic rules. He was a master of the brief lyric (*Vade-mecum*, a collection of poems written before 1866, pub. posthumously), but he also wrote long poems, dramas, and stories. He was a magnificent epistolary writer as well. His works are verbally precise; many phrases—pointed and laconic—sound like aphorisms. A poetics of ellipsis and even of silence plays a crucial role in his work. Subtle irony and ambivalence are his key methods of presenting the world; his use of parable, allegory, and symbolism convey an ambiguous vision of reality. Rhythm and rhyme are subordinate to sense in this intellectual poetry. Norwid called into question central tenets of romanticism; he was a humanist or personalist in a mod. sense.

All four great poets lived in exile in Western Europe. The domestic poetry of the time was less interesting. Kornel Ujejski (1823–97) wrote ardent patriotic poems; Teofil Lenartowicz (1822–93) based his lyric style on the folklore of Mazovia (the region where Warsaw is located), while Władysław Syrokomla (1823–62) gave voice to the worldview of the nobility.

C. *The Postromantic Period.* The epoch following the exhaustion of high romanticism—the collapse of the insurrection of 1863 marked a decisive shift—was programmatically antipoetic; the ideology of positivism dominated intellectuals. Though poetry generally continued under the influence of romanticism, a few poets transcended mere epigonism. Adam Asnyk (1838–97) wrote erotic and intellectual lyrics. Apart from her abundant work in prose, Maria Konopnicka (1842–1910) composed numerous poems inspired by folklore; they described landscapes and often expressed social or metaphysical rebellion.

The last decade of the 19th c. saw new trends in poetry: this period was called Young Poland. Poets were inspired by Fr. symbolism and the philosophy of Arthur Schopenhauer and Friedrich Nietzsche: they rediscovered and reinterpreted high Polish romanticism ("neoromanticism"). This signaled the early beginnings of modernism. The most influential poet of the time was Kazimierz Przerwa Tetmajer (1865–1940). He expressed the decadent mood of the generation through his erotic lyrics and descriptive poems employing impressionist methods.

VII. The Twentieth Century

A. *The Modern Period.* The lyric production of Jan Kasprowicz (1860–1926) opened new horizons for poetry. He began with naturalistic poems depicting peasant poverty, while in the 1890s he focused on symbolist, descriptive works. The publication of a sequence of hymns (1898–1901) marked a turning point in his creation: they convey an expressionistic, deeply pessimistic, almost blasphemous representation of the world in Satan's power. He finds reconciliation with God in the sequence's final hymns. In his late works, he invented "tonism," a system of accentual versification based on an equal number of stresses, not of syllables. The way to *vers libre* was open. Stanisław Wyspiański (1869–1907) was a painter, poet, and author of verse dramas. *Wesele* (Wedding, 1901) is a symbolic play inspired by romantic drama and Richard Wagner's idea of the theater as a synthesis of the arts. Poetic lang. is subordinated to the hypnotic rhythm of folk music. The play, full of symbols and ambiguity, is a kind of psychoanalysis of Polish national and social traumas. Leopold Staff (1878–1957) began his career as a "decadent," but after reinterpreting Nietzsche and finding inspiration in Stoicism and Franciscan Christianity, he became a poet of mental equilibrium, *joie de vivre*, and spiritual power. He was inspired by neoclassicism, Parnassianism, and symbolism, and served as a mentor to young poets in the 1920s. He incorporated avant-garde poetics into his late work, in the 1950s.

Bolesław Leśmian (1878–1937) was the greatest poet of the first half of the century. A symbolist, he explored the impossibility of adequately describing a world in constant motion. Following the philosophy of Henri Bergson, he conveyed the instability of a reality always in *statu nascendi*. In his opinion, only poetry could truly articulate élan vital; hence, rhythm (accentual-syllabic verse) was key to his poetics. He wrote ballads in stylized folk forms, which he turned to intellectual, existential, and metaphysical purposes. He was distinguished by the extraordinarily inventive verbal coinages he developed to convey the nuances of his philosophy. Leśmian's first poetic volume was published only in 1912; three subsequent volumes were edited in the 1920s and 1930s.

After World War I and the rebirth of an independent Poland in 1918, new tendencies in Polish poetry appeared. Reinterpretations of trad. were confronted by avant-garde movements on the one hand and a quest for inspiration in folk culture on the other. Many programs were proclaimed, and a wide range of groups and periodicals (most of them ephemeral) came into being. The group Skamander, established in 1918, played a central role in the literary life of the period. Jan Lechoń (1899–1956) reinterpreted the romantic trad. Antoni Słonimski (1895–1976) linked Parnassianism with expressionism and radical political ideas. Jarosław Iwaszkiewicz (1894–1980) created personal, introspective poetry; he chose aestheticism as his principal attitude and was inspired by expressionism, neoclassical and other, sometimes exotic, trads., such as Persian; sensitive to the musical aspects of verse, he discovered the possibilities of dissonance in poetry. Kazimierz Wierzyński (1894–1969) began as a neoclassicist; in his later works, he was inspired by expressionism, romanticism (esp. during World War II), and even the avant-garde (beginning in the 1950s). Julian Tuwim (1894–1953) was the most inventive poet of the group. He played with lang., discovering a new colloquial idiom. He experimented with the sounds and senses of words and sought inspiration in classicism as well. He also composed popular songs, cabaret songs, and children's poetry. In the 1920s, the poets of Skamander focused on ordinary existence; they expressed joy in daily life and discovered popular culture for poetry (Wierzyński, e.g., dedicated a sequence of poems to sports). In the 1930s, their poetic tone grew increasingly dark. Iwaszkiewicz's poems expressed existential fears; Wierzyński became a harsh judge of mod. civilization; Tuwim grew more and more radical politically.

Skamander marked the more traditional wing in Polish poetry of the time. Other poets were close to their orientation. In her refined poems, Maria Jasnorzewska-Pawlikowska (1891–1945) employed paradoxes, oxymorons, and ellipses to express the experience of the mod. woman, esp. her eroticism. Władysław Broniewski (1897–1962) wrote impressive political poems (he was a fellow traveler of the Communist Party) making the most of the new system of versification (tonism) and appealing to the romantic trad. Jerzy Liebert (1904–31) was a poet of dramatic religious experience (in Blaise Pascal's spirit); influenced by classicism, he pursued lucidity in his poetics. Konstanty Ildefons Gałczyński (1905–53) linked grotesquery and mockery with emotional lyricism in his work.

The experimental wing in Polish poetry was represented by futurism and the avant-garde. The futurists were radical in their views on poetics and politics (Communism); in their practice, they came close to Dada. The most important poets of this movement were Bruno Jasieński (1901–39) and Aleksander Wat (1900–67); in his late poetry, Wat changed his aesthetics, reflecting on the experience of pain. The avant-garde program was announced in the 1920s: its most prominent representatives were Tadeusz Peiper (1891–69) and Julian Przyboś (1901–70). The avant-garde reformed poetics: syntax or even the line constituted a poem's rhythm, not equal numbers of syllables or stresses. They proclaimed and practiced economy in lang., leading to their preference for metaphor and ellipsis as basic figures. The avant-garde affirmed mod. civilization: its poetry exuded dynamism and belief in creative potency. The avant-garde of the 1930s was a different matter. Józef Czechowicz (1903–39) linked his experience of these new tendencies with the trads. of folk poetry; in his poems, the bucolic collides with visions of historical catastrophe.

The most eminent poet of this movement was Czesław Miłosz (1911–2004, winner of the Nobel Prize in Literature, 1980). In his early poems, the poetics of neosymbolism and surrealism conjoined with romantic or biblical ways of constructing visions and a cl. rigor of form: it expressed a sense of the eminent metaphysical catastrophe of civilization. During World War II, Miłosz altered his poetics. In his search for the "proper form," he appealed to various trads., from the Bible to Far Eastern poetry, from the Middle Ages to the avant-garde. His poetry is polyphonic, often ironic. In spite of its intellectual and metaphysical character, the poetry is focused on the concrete particulars of reality. Among themes of the Miłosz's works are ethics, hist., God, nature, and the purpose of existence. It is difficult to overestimate Miłosz's influence on Polish poetry of the 20th c.

B. ***Era of War and Totalitarianism.*** A turning point in Polish hist. and culture came in 1939: World War II, which divided Poland between totalitarian regimes (Nazi and Soviet), led in turn to the Holocaust, mass exterminations, displaced peoples, the destruction of cities (esp. Warsaw), and the installation of a Communist regime following the war. Numerous poets lost their lives during the war, and the wartime and postwar years saw waves of emigration among poets, continuing until the 1980s. Under Nazi occupation, official literary life was virtually nonexistent; important works were produced and published only underground. Under Soviet occupation and later in Communist Poland until Stalin's death, all lit. was subordinated to ideology, in the form of socialist realism. Even after the liberalization of 1956, the harsh state censorship controlled and deformed all poetic production. At the same time, numerous authors played games with their readers, conveying indirect meanings through allusions and special codes. From the mid-1970s until the collapse of Communism in 1989, alternative underground publishing houses published many major volumes of poetry.

Poets of the generation born in the 1920s, who came to maturity during the war, chose a variety of aesthetics. For many of them, the experience of war, evil, fear, pain, and death played a crucial role. Krzysztof Kamil Baczyński (1921–44) followed Miłosz in his neosymbolic poetry of visions. Tadeusz Gajcy (1922–44) drew upon the poetics of the baroque and the avant-garde (esp. surrealism). Tadeusz Różewicz (1921–2014), as a descendant of the avant-garde, invented new forms of ascetic verse. Julia Hartwig (b. 1921) was inspired by early Western avant-garde artists such as Walt Whitman and Guillaume Apollinaire. Miron Białoszewski (1922–83) was extremely inventive in his ling. play and imitation of spoken lang.; he crossed the borders between verse and prose in his "ling. poetry." In her intellectual and conceptual poetry, Wisława Szymborska (1923–2012; winner of the Nobel Prize in Literature, 1996) uses irony and exploits ling. ambiguity (in the meanings of words and even in grammar). Zbigniew Herbert (1924–98) linked the inspiration of the avant-garde (esp. in his use of metaphor and ellipsis) with appealing topoi and a stoic philosophy derived from neoclassicism: irony plays a special role in his poetry. Their poetry articulates a sense of deep cultural crisis as it searches for ways to preserve human values—in ethics, in ordinary life, or in poetry itself.

Some older figures found their original poetic ways during this period. For instance, in her late, ascetic poems, Anna Świrszczyńska (known as Anna Swir, 1909–84) candidly described the specifics of women's lives, esp. during wartime. The current of metaphysical or religious poetry continued in the work of Jan Twardowski (1915–2006), a Catholic priest who wrote Franciscan poems full of humor and paradoxes about the "unfinished" Creation. Karol Wojtyła (Pope John Paul II, 1920–2005) composed mystical and intellectual meditations: the best known of these is his late, long poem *Tryptyk rzymski* (Roman Triptych, 2003).

Younger poets looked for inspiration in various aesthetics. In his poetry inspired by folk culture, Tadeusz Nowak (1930–91) expressed the moral and metaphysical unrest of the individual endangered by mod. civilization. Krystyna Miłobędzka (b. 1932) in her minimalistic poetry searches for the exact words in the world's description. Stanisław Grochowiak (1934–76) used a surreal aesthetic of ugliness to demonstrate the crisis of traditional codes of beauty. Jarosław Marek Rymkiewicz (b. 1935) propounds a program of mod. neoclassicism: he appeals to trad., esp. to the late, Sarmatian Polish baroque.

For poets of the Generation of '68 (also called the New Wave) the crucial problem is finding an adequate lang. for describing the contemp. world. In their early poetry, these poets appealed to the experience of the avant-garde (esp. "linguistic poetry"): later, they began to seek out inspiration in various trads. In his ascetic poetry, Ryszard Krynicki (b. 1943) follows the Asian trad. of playing with a minimal number of words and with silence to express his ethical and metaphysical meditations. Using enumerations and inventive metaphors, Adam Zagajewski (b. 1945) tries to represent the world in its opulence and abundance. Ewa Lipska (b. 1945) links sophisticated metaphors with irony to reveal the paradoxes of existence. Rafał Wojaczek (1945–71) used an expressionistic aesthetic of shock to overcome mental and moral taboos. Bohdan Zadura (b. 1945) in his recent works invents a poetics of paradox in the daily lang. Stanisław Barańczak (1946–2014) exposes the ambiguities of lang., esp. of propaganda; in his later work, he draws inspiration from Eng. metaphysical poetry to ask basic questions about life's meaning. Piotr Sommer (b. 1948) follows mod. Eng.-lang. poetry; he describes reality by using words intended to stick as closely as possible to the things themselves. Bronisław Maj (b. 1953) develops Miłosz's poetics of epiphany, representing the world in its moments of beauty and sense.

C. *Post-Communist (Late Modern) Period.* In 1989, Communism in Poland collapsed, and the situation of lit. consequently changed completely. Censorship disappeared; borders were opened; and a new context was shaped by pop culture, mass media, a free market, and democracy. The 1990s were marked by a poetry in evident flux. Apart from the continued activity of older poets (incl. Miłosz), young poets were expansive in their quest for a new and varied poetics. Andrzej Sosnowski (b. 1959) writes intellectual poems, using complicated metaphors to reveal the glimmerings of equivocal words. Marcin Świetlicki (b. 1961), the icon of his generation, is close to the ideology of counterculture and focuses on the experience of ordinary life: as the leader of a rock band, he revolts against traditional forms of poetry. Eugeniusz Tkaczyszyn-Dycki (b. 1962) uses forms of baroque poetry to express the fears and doubts arising from the mod. world. Krzysztof Koehler (b. 1963) is a representative of the cl. tendency in poetry: inspired by various trads. (esp. the baroque), he focuses on metaphysical problems. Jacek Podsiadło (b. 1964) plays with different poetics, between an aesthetic of paradox and shock and an aesthetic of "classical," refined verse. Miłosz Biedrzycki (b. 1967) is inspired by the poetics of surrealism and the "liberated imagination."

VIII. The Twenty-First Century. The beginning of the century was a time of change. The turning point for traditional poetry was Miłosz's death in 2004. Young poets have chosen a variety of aesthetics. Tomasz Różycki (b. 1970) tries to revive cl. forms that clash with the poetics and consciousness of the contemp. individual and experience of avant-garde. Tadeusz Dąbrowski (b. 1979), describing metaphysics in postmod. life, plays with paradox. A radical appeal to the avant-garde is visible among the "neolinguistic" poets (incl. Maria Cyranowicz, b. 1974; Jarosław Lipszyc, b. 1975; and Joanna Mueller, b. 1979).

■ **Anthologies**: *Od Kochanowskiego do Staffa*, ed. W. Borowy (1930); *Poeci renesansu*, ed. J. Sokołowska (1959); *Zbiór poetów polskich XIX wieku*, ed. P. Hertz, 7 v. (1959–75); *Poeci polskiego baroku*, ed. J. Sokołowska and K. Żukowska (1965); *Poezja Młodej Polski*, ed. M. Jastrun (1967); *Poezja polska*, ed. S. Grochowiak and J. Maciejewski, 2 v. (1973); *Kolumbowie i współcześni*, ed. A. Lam (1976); *Poezja polska XVIII wieku*, ed. Z. Libera, 2d ed. (1976); *Antologia polskiego futuryzmu i Nowej Sztuki*, ed. Z. Jarosiński and H. Zaworska (1978); *Five Centuries of Polish Poetry*, ed. J. Peterkiewicz and B. Singer, 3d ed. (1979); *Średniowieczna pieśń religijna polska*, ed. M. Korolko, 2d ed. (1980); *Ze struny na strunę*, ed. A. Lam (1980); *Postwar Polish Poetry*, ed. C. Miłosz, 3d ed. (1983); *Poeta pamięta*, ed. S. Barańczak (1984); *Poezja polska 1914–1939*, ed. R. Matuszewski and S. Pollak, 3d ed. (1984); *Monumenta Polonica: The First Four Centuries of Polish Poetry: A Bilingual Anthology*, ed. B. Carpenter (1989); *Polish Poetry of the Last Two Decades of Communist Rule*, ed. S. Barańczak and C. Cavanagh (1992); *Antologia polskiej poezji metafizycznej epoki baroku*, ed. K. Mrowcewicz (1993); *Young Poets of a New Poland*, ed. D. Pirie (1993); *Określona epoka—Nowa Fala 1968–1993*, ed. T. Nyczek, 2d ed. (1995); *Polish Renaissance*, ed. M. J. Mikoś (1995); *Ambers Aglow: An Anthology of Polish Women's Poetry*, ed. R. Grol (1996); *Macie swoich poetów: liryka polska urodzona po 1960 roku*, ed. P. Dunin-Wąsowicz, J. Klejnocki, K. Varga (1996); *Międzywojenna poezja polsko-żydowska*, ed. E. Prokop-Janiec (1996); I. Krasicki, *Polish Fables*, trans. G. T. Kapolka (1997); *Poezja polska okresu międzywojennego*, ed. M. Głowiński and

J. Sławiński, 2d ed. (1997); *Współcześni poeci polscy: poezja polska od 1956 roku*, ed. K. Karasek (1997); *Panorama literatury polskiej XX wieku*, ed. K. Dedecius (2001); B. Leśmian, *Magic and Glory of Twentieth-Century Polish Poetry*, trans. J. Langer (2000); *Antologia poezji polskiej na obczyźnie*, ed. B. Czaykowski (2002); *Antologia poezji sarmackiej*, ed. K. Koehler (2002); *Literatura staropolska*, ed. P. Borek and R. Mazurkiewicz (2002); *Polska poezja rokokowa*, ed. R. Dąbrowski (2003); *Świat poprawiać—zuchwałe rzemiosło*, ed. T. Kostkiewiczowa and Z. Goliński, 2d ed. (2004); *Gada !zabić? Pa(n)tologia neolingwizmu*, ed. M. Cyranowicz and P. Kozioł (2005); *Poza słowa: Antologia wierszy 1976–2006*, ed. T. Dąbrowski (2006); Z. Herbert, *The Collected Poems*, trans. A. Valles, C. Miłosz, P. Dale (2007); *Poezja drugiej połowy XIX wieku*, ed. J. Bajda (2007); *Poezja pierwszej połowy XIX wieku*, ed. E. Grzęda (2007); *Selected Masterpieces of Polish Poetry*, trans. J. Zawadzki (2007); *Solistki: Antologia poezji kobiet (1989–2009)*, ed. M. Cyranowicz, J. Mueller, J. Radczyńska, (2009); *Poeci na nowy wiek*, ed. R. Honet (2010).

■ **Criticism and History**: W. Weintraub, *The Poetry of Adam Mickiewicz* (1954); M. Kridl, *A Survey of Polish Literature and Culture* (1956); M. Giergielewicz, *Introduction to Polish Versification* (1970); T. Kostkiewiczowa, *Klasycyzm, sentymentalizm, rokoko* (1975); A. Witkowska, *Adam Mickiewicz* (1975); S. Jaworski, *Między awangardą a nadrealizmem* (1976); J.M.G. Levine, *Contemporary Polish Poetry, 1925–1975* (1981); B. Carpenter, *The Poetic Avant-Garde in Poland, 1918–1939* (1983); C. Miłosz, *The History of Polish Literature*, 2d ed. (1983); M. Zaleski, *Przygoda drugiej Awangardy* (1984); *Poznawanie Miłosza*, ed. J. Kwiatkowski (1985); S. Barańczak, *A Fugitive from Utopia* (1987); G. Gömöri, *Cyprian Norwid* (1988); F. W. Aaron, *Bearing the Unbearable: Yiddish and Polish Poetry in the Ghettos and Concentration Camps* (1990); S. Barańczak, *Breathing under Water and Other East European Essays* (1990); R. Sokoloski, *The Poetry of Mikołaj Sęp Szarzyński* (1990); M. Inglot, *Cyprian Norwid* (1991); A. Kowalczykowa, *Słowacki* (1992); J. Dudek, *Poeci polscy XX wieku* (1994); E. Hurnikowa, *Natura w salonie mody: O międzywojennej liryce Marii Pawlikowskiej-Jasnorzewskiej* (1995); S. Stabro, *Poezja i historia: Od Żagarów do Nowej Fali* (1995); R. Nycz, *Sylwy współczesne*, 2d ed. (1996); *Radość czytania Szymborskiej*, ed. D. Wojda and S. Balbus (1996); T. Venclova, *Aleksander Wat: Life and Art of an Iconoclast* (1996); K. Wyka, *Rzecz wyobraźni* (1997); J. Kwiatkowski, *Magia poezji: O poetach polskich XX wieku* (1997); J. Błoński, *Miłosz jak świat* (1998); W. Bolecki, *Pre-teksty i teksty* (1998); M. Głowiński, *Zaświat przedstawiony: Szkice o poezji Bolesława Leśmiana*, 2d ed. (1998); J. Sławiński, *Koncepcja języka poetyckiego Awangardy Krakowskiej* (1998); *Poznawanie Herberta*, ed. A. Franaszek, 2 v. (1998–2000); P. Czapliński, P. Śliwiński, *Literatura polska 1976–1998* (1999); Z. Jarosiński, *Literatura lat 1945–1975*, 3d ed. (1999); H. Markiewicz, *Pozytywizm*, 4th ed. (1999); G. Gömöri, *Magnetic Poles: Essays on Modern Polish and Comparative Literature* (2000); A. Hutnikiewicz, *Młoda Polska*, 6th ed. (2000); *Poznawanie Miłosza 2*, ed. A. Fiut, 2 v. (2000–2001); J. Błoński, *Mikołaj Sęp Szarzyński a początki polskiego baroku*, 2d ed. (2001); M. Dłuska, *Odmiany i dzieje wiersza polskiego* (2001); R. Nycz, *Literatura jako trop rzeczywistości: Poetyka epifanii w nowoczesnej literaturze polskiej* (2001); J. Pelc, *Kochanowski: Szczyt renesansu w literaturze polskiej*, 3d ed (2001); M. Podraza-Kwiatkowska, *Literatura Młodej Polski*, 4th ed. (2001); J. Prokop and J. Sławiński, *Liryka polska: Interpretacje*, 3d ed. (2001); R. Nycz, *Język modernizmu: Prolegomena historycznoliterackie*, 2d ed. (2002); K. Barry, *Skamander: The Poets and Their Poetry, 1918–1929* (2004); B. Kaniewska, A. Legieżyńska, P. Śliwiński, *Literatura polska XX wieku* (2005); J. Święch, *Literatura polska w latach II wojny światowej*, 6th ed. (2005); T. Michałowska, *Średniowiecze*, 8th ed. (2006); J. Ziomek, *Renesans*, 11th ed. (2006); C. Hernas, *Barok*, 8th ed. (2006); M. Klimowicz, *Oświecenie*, 9th ed. (2006); A. Nasiłowska, *Literatura okresu przejściowego 1975–1996* (2006); M. P. Markowski, *Polska literatura nowoczesna: Leśmian, Schulz, Witkacy* (2007); A. Witkowska, R. Przybylski, *Romantyzm*, 8th ed. (2007); J. Kwiatkowski, *Dwudziestolecie międzywojenne*, 3d ed. (2008); R. Koropeckyj, *Adam Mickiewicz* (2008); S. Barańczak, *Etyka i poetyka*, 2d ed. (2009); C. Cavanagh, *Lyric Poetry and Modern Politics: Russia, Poland, and the West* (2009); *Nowa poezja polska: Twórcy—tematy—motywy*, ed. T. Cieślak (2009); A. Kałuża, *Bumerang: Szkice o poezji polskiej przełomu XX i XXI wieku* (2010); *Nowe dwudziestolecie (1989–2009): Rozpoznania.*

Hierarchie. Perspektywy, ed. H. Gosk (2010); J. Fiedorczuk et al., *Literatura Polska 1989–2009: Przewodnik* (2011).

K. Biedrzycki

POLYNESIAN POETRY

I. Polynesian Languages
II. English

I. Polynesian Languages. Polynesia is a vast triangle of thousands of islands, with apexes at Hawai'i to the north, Easter Island to the southeast, and New Zealand to the southwest; Tuvalu and enclaves are farther west in Melanesia and Micronesia. Each of the archipelagoes has majority populations of Polynesian descent, except for New Zealand and Hawai'i, where Maori and Kanaka Maoli remain substantial groups. Before Eur. contact, knowledge was mainly transmitted by oral presentation and by demonstration, which are both of continuing importance. Polynesia elevated oral art to a high level of beauty and subtlety. Poets use numerous homonyms, puns, and repetitions, along with reduplication and alliteration, as they enjoy frequent reiterations of sound.

Western culture introduced by 19th-c. missionaries, settlers, colonial officials, and voyagers stimulated poetic creativity by adding new concepts and symbols without, however, the traditional art's losing its indigenous identity. Poetry's social function, however, has altered with Westernization. Traditional poetry, integral to personal life from birth to death and to both religion and entertainment, was frequently entwined with ritual, vocalization, and dance to express values, give aesthetic pleasure, transmit knowledge, and affirm the connection of human beings to nature and the supernatural. Poetic strategies across introduced and indigenous langs. include personifying nature with gods and spirits (many regarded as ancestors) and reacting emotionally to changing aspects of landscape with minute observation, vivid description, and extensive naming of places and natural forces.

Since traditional poetry and music are inseparable, each adding power to the other, a poet composed text and melody at the same time. Each category of poetry had its characteristic modes of rhythmic oral delivery, the principal modes being song or recitative, with variations and combinations of each. Hawaiians, e.g., distinguished between an *oli* and a *mele* but adapted a poem to either. An *oli* was a dignified recitative, most often a solo, with limited gestures and occasional percussion accompaniment, for dirges, prayers, eulogies, and genealogies, each class with its special oli style. The basic style was a rapid, guttural, vibrating monotone on a single pitch that required a strong, deep voice trained to hold the breath through long phrases often ending with a trill. Continuity of sound was essential because breath carried the words filled with *mana* (supernatural power), and a break or hesitation, except at appropriate places, was believed unlucky in a secular poem and fatal in a sacred. A *mele* was sung or chanted to the accompaniment of dance (*hula*), pantomime, and instruments (not always the three together); a subtype was performed either with or without dance for love songs, name songs honoring individuals, or genital chants celebrating generative powers. A mele, customarily performed with a chorus whose leader sang solo parts, had marked, repeated rhythmic patterns if danced and a wider range of pitch and freedom than the oli. Missionary hymns brought melody, which Polynesians called *hīmeni* and combined with old styles of delivery for new poems, not necessarily sacred, but not danced. While music changed as Westerners introduced their folk and work songs, texts retained many traditional themes and devices. The same was the case in other archipelagos beside the Hawaiian.

A new poem that met an audience's approval was performed repeatedly and might become a classic passed on for generations. In New Zealand, compositions by Kingi Tahiwi, Te Rauparaha, Paraire Tomoana, Sir Apirana Ngata, Te Ari Pitama, Te Arikinui Te Atairangikaahu, Kingi Tawhiao, Ngoi Pewhairangi, Tuini Ngawai and many others are still sung and performed. Their genius lay in fresh and innovative rearrangement or reinterpretation of recurrent themes, images, phrases, and lines.

Samoan chiefs (but not commoners) could sing a *solo* (the Samoan term for a recitative epitomizing a myth or legend) of the subcategory *fa'ali'i*, meaning "royal" and concerning a royal lineage. A politically important trad., e.g., centered on Sanalālā: when his canoe was swept to sea from Tonga to Samoa, his father's land, his Tongan mother, Chieftess Fitimaupaloga, composed a 21-line *solo fa'ali'i* considered "exceedingly beautiful." A chief was much admired when he sang it with a plaintive cadence while accompanying himself on a type of drum only certain chiefly families could use (Freeman).

The *solo* uses common Polynesian poetic devices of inspiration from nature and place; irregular but rhythmic lines; repetition of sounds, words, and syllables; and (peculiarly western Polynesian) deliberate rhyming and termination of sets of lines with a certain sound. Many traditional Maori song poems (*waiata*) follow a quantitative meter where eight or 12 vowels are contained in each half line of text corresponding to a musical phrase. A whole line corresponds to a musical strophe.

Sacred creation and genealogical chants were intoned by senior males and high priests in consecrating a chief's primary wife's first-born son and on other occasions. Numerous resemblances with other chants elsewhere prove the chants share the same Polynesian heritage. Their fundamental function concerned pro-creation and the continuity of life through the chief, on whom, as the closest link to the gods, the fertility of nature and people depended. Starting with creation, a chanter connected the infant to his divine and earthly kin and thereby confirmed his rank, privileges, taboos, territory, and power. Because words had power to produce action, an error or hesitation negated a sacred chant.

An example is the Hawaiian *Kumulipo* (Origin in Deepest Darkness), a 2,102-line masterpiece of the type called *ku'auhau* (pathway lineage), property of the family of Kalākaua and his sister Lili'uokalani, the last rulers in the 19th c. of the monarchy established by Kamehameha I in 1795. When priests ca. 1700 CE chanted the *Kumulipo*, each name activated the latent *mana* of High Chief Keawe's son and heir, named Lono-i-ka-makahiki because he was born during the annual Makahiki festival for Lono, god of peace and prosperity. It may have been recited in 1779 over Captain James Cook as the returned god Lono. It also establishes linkages to pan-Polynesian deities such as Maui.

Eastern Polynesian chiefs and priests, who were educated in sacred houses of learning, excelled in technical skill at composition and erudition. Marquesan and Mangarevan masters served rulers as organizers and directors of ceremonies, determined official versions of sacred chants and hist., and recited the most sacred parts of chants. A Marquesan tribal master of chants, outranked only by the ruler and the inspirational priest, might be deified at death. Nonetheless, if another tribe's master challenged him, he had to compete successfully before an audience, exhibiting his learning, quickness in composition, and ability in other oral arts at the risk of losing his title or even his life. Many Polynesian islands had such contests of wit and learning.

A Samoan chief's talking chief, also a master of ceremony and subject to challenges from a rival, upheld his chief's and village's prestige, esp. on official visits to other villages, by his command of the complex art of oratory, learning, composition, and knowledge of procedure and etiquette due each titled man present. Tonga, by contrast, had a class of professional poets, generally untitled but with status roughly equivalent to a ruler's ceremonial attendants. A poet, though honored, was entirely dependent on his patron chief and usually insecure even as to his life. At one time, contests between poets became so bitter they had to be discontinued. Like other members of ruling families of Polynesia, Queen Salote of Tonga was famed for her compositions.

In New Zealand, Maori women, who as a group predominated as composers, were more likely than men to compose songs about frustrated love or *waiata aroha* ("Would I were a broken canoe that might be mended") and short, informally arranged, intensely personal laments (*waiata tangi*) often for those slain in tribal or anticolonial wars, coupling frank emotion and natural imagery ("Like the tides within Tirau forever rising and falling / Is my wild lamentation within Houhangapa"). Maori men were more likely to compose longer, more formally structured laments, filled with elaborate metaphors to emphasize that the whole tribe had lost a great man ("like a star shining apart in the Milky Way" or "a sheltering rata tree from the north wind"). There are many thematic categories of Maori song poem, or *waiata*, and oratorical chant, or *tauparapara*. The *haka* is a form of assertive or war dance poetry in New Zealand, widely popularized by the national rugby team who perform and chant a haka before international matches. Experts of the form have criticized the team's bowdlerized versions, while there has been a general resurgence in the variety and quality of haka performed by many Maori groups (Karetu, Ngata, Mead).

II. English. Many of the contemp. Eng.-lang. poets are resident in New Zealand and Hawai'i, while Eng.-lang. poets of Melanesia (e.g., John Kasaipwalova, Steven Winduo, Jully Makini, Grace Molisa) and Micronesia (Teresia Teaiwa, Emelihter Kihleng, Craig Santos Perez) highlight the porosity of cultural boundaries as they are influential in the region. The following selected poets have books published.

A. *Cook Islands. Mine Eyes Dazzle* (1950), by the New Zealand-based Cook Islands (Tongareva) poet Alistair Te Ariki Campbell (1925–2009), was the first book of poetry by a Polynesian to be published in Eng. Campbell's early work referenced New Zealand and Eng. romantic modes, while his work from the 1960s on is infused by his Tongarevan and broader Polynesian heritage, incl. *Sanctuary of Spirits*, *The Dark Lord of Savaiki*, *Soul Traps*, and *Maori Battalion*. His lyric poetry, incl. the littoral and the oceanic, fuses a personal desire to belong to a familial collective in dialogue with personae from the historical and mythological past, and always has an elegiac edge. It includes direct trans. of Tongarevan chant and genealogy. Campbell's prolific Cook Islands compatriot Kauraka Kauraka (1951–1997) wrote *tateni* style poetry in praise of persons in Eng. and Cook Islands Maori.

B. *New Zealand (Maori).* Former New Zealand poet laureate Hone Tuwhare (1922–2008) was an arts icon and the first Maori poet in Eng. to be published. His *No Ordinary Sun* (1964) has been reprinted ten times (he published 13 poetry books in all); the title poem was a protest at nuclear testing in the Pacific, reflecting his socialist ideology and environmentalism. His work codeshifted between multiple vernacular and chiefly oratorical registers and featured a strong relationship between myth and nature, romance, a panegyric sensibility, and a cultural relationship to the land. Many Maori poets have followed in Tuwhare's wake, incl. multigenre author Apirana Taylor, who combines the qualities of orature with text—namely, repetition, Maori names and words, short lines composed for the breath, and music in live performance. Roma Potiki employs traditional forms such as the *oriori* or instructional lullaby, while Trixie Te Arama Menzies directly borrows from famous *waiata tangi* (laments), such as *E pā tō hau*. Arapera Blank composed in Maori and Eng., relying on such chiefly symbolism as the *kokako* (a cousin of the highly prized and extinct *huia* wattlebird). J. C. Sturm, a poet of Tuwhare's generation like Blank and Menzies, imbues her poetry with *karanga* (initial call of welcome in greeting ceremonies) and *tangi* (lament). Keri Hulme's poetry is infused with humor, mythological shapes, natural and spiritual omens, gods, and songs. Robert Sullivan's six books of short poems and extended sequences range from personal to cultural subjects, incl. oceanic exploration in *Star Waka*. Rangi Faith also incorporates Maori symbolism in his collections. Hinemoana Baker's first collection draws on traditional models such as the *waiata tangi*, Michael O'Leary is influenced by Pakeha (Eur.) poet James K. Baxter, who borrowed from Maori trads., and Brian Potiki's collection *Aotearoa* studs his texts with praise for artist-heroes such as Tuwhare.

C. *Samoa.* Albert Wendt, the influential and prolific Samoan author and poet, anthologized wider Oceanic (Melanesia, Micronesia, Polynesia) lit. in *Lali*, and *Nuanua* and Polynesian poetry in *Whetu Moana* with Reina Whaitiri and Robert Sullivan. His early elegiac sequence "Inside Us the Dead" incorporates high rhetorical flourishes grounded in immediate referents, as well as elements of genealogical recitations (*gafa*) and formal oratorical codes (*fa'alupega*), while providing a family and social hist. as he recounts the death of his brother. A verse novel, *The Adventures of Vela*, is a contemp. myth-saga featuring a contest between poets. *The Book of the Black Star* merges images with text ranging from relaxed to heightened modes. Tusiata Avia's *Wild Dogs under My Skirt* underscores her work by referring to the Mau Samoan resistance movement and myths, and uses Samoan words. Her contemporary, Sia Figiel, also richly weaves Western with Samoan concepts of the self. Momoe Malietoa Von Reiche uses her relationship with the land as a refuge and source of nourishment (Marsh). Selina Tusitala Marsh's first book, *Fast-talking PI*, pays homage to many poets of the region. Tutuila (Am. Samoan) poet Caroline Sinavaiana negotiates Am. colonialism and indigeneity through the lens of the warrior goddess Nafanua and the power of *tagi* (lament).

D. *Tonga.* Tongan poet Konai Helu Thaman draws on traditional symbolism in her popular work, such as the association of the sun with monarchs, the contrast of *langakali* flowers (symbolizing fertility and regeneration) against corrupting Westernization, as well as other botanical references significant within Tongan-lang. compositions. She composes in Tongan and translates her compositions into Eng.

(Marsh). Karlo Mila's *Dream Fish Floating* summons her family genealogy to rationalize first-generation Tongan-Samoan-Palagi (Eur.) life in New Zealand and adeptly pays homage to poets of the older generation (*tuakana*).

E. *Hawai'i.* Political leader and scholar Haunani-Kay Trask's minimalist free-verse strophes are focused on sovereign justice, dignity in the face of cultural denigration, and recovery. She draws on places, figures, and protocols important to the volcanic goddess Pele, who represents overwhelming indigenous power and who features in traditional poetry cycles. Wayne Kamuali'i Westlake, whose poetry included Dadaist and Confucian ideas, wrote concrete poems using Hawaiian words to inflect his anger at Am. colonialism, such as *pupule* (Hawaiian for "crazy"). The scattered letters in pupule also form words for prayer (*pule*), guns (*pu*), appetizers (*pupu*), and a letter-jumble similar to the litter on the sidewalks of Waikiki (the subject of a sequence), forming random words in multiple langs. Mahealani Perez-Wendt references the last monarch, Queen Lili'uokalani, in the title of her collection *Uluhaimalama,* which was the queen's garden. The hidden meaning of that name refers to growth into the light, both for the plants in the garden and the Hawaiian nation. Imaikalani Kalahele juxtaposes illustrations and poems, using the rhythms of jazz and Hawaiian lang. Joseph Balaz is one of the most accomplished Hawaiian poets, who writes in standard and pidgin Eng. He produced the first spoken-word album, *Electric Laulau*, in 1998. Sage U'ilani Takehiro's *Honua* was published with the assistance of indigenous publisher Kuleana 'Ōiwi Press, also the publisher of skilled lyric poet Brandy Nālani McDougall. Takehiro passionately braids natural elements into a literary shelter (or *honua*).

F. *Rotuma and Niue.* David Eggleton, of Rotuman descent, is one of the most successful New Zealand performance poets of his generation, preceding the spoken-word poets who most obviously link to techniques of orature. When in contemplative mode, he occasionally explores Maori and colonial history. John Puhiatau Pule, who was born in Niue but spent most of his life in New Zealand, incorporates hist., mythology, nature, and love poetry in his novel *The Shark That Ate the Sun* in a 30-poem reconstructed sequence by a fictional 19th-c. poet.

G. *French Polynesia / Te Ao Mā'ohi.* The anthol. *Varua Tupu* has made an extensive selection of Fr. Polynesian writing available in Eng. Notable poets include cultural leader Henri Hiro, Flora Devatine, Patrick Arai Amaru, and Rai a Mai (Michou Chaze). These poets compose in Tahitian and Fr.

See NEW ZEALAND, POETRY OF

■ **Special Publications:** Bishop Museum *Bulletin* 8, 9, 17, 29, 34, 46, 48, 95, 109, 127, 148, 158, 183; Bishop Museum *Memoirs* 4, 5, 6; Bishop Museum *Special Publications* 2, 51, 61; Polynesian Society *Memoirs* 3, 4, 5, 41; *Maori Texts*: A. T. Ngata, ed., trans., and comp., *Nga Moteatea*, part 1 (1959), and A. T. Ngata and P. Te Hurinui, ed., trans., and comp., part 2 (1961); *MANA*, South Pacific Creative Arts Society (1973–1977).

■ **Studies:** W. W. Gill, *Myths and Songs from the South Pacific* (1876), and *Historical Sketches of Savage Life in Polynesia* (1880); N. B. Emerson, *Unwritten Literature of Hawaii: Sacred Songs of the Hula* (1909; rpt. 1977), and *Pele and Hiiaka, a Myth from Hawaii* (c. 1915; rpt. 1978); M. W. Beckwith, "Introduction," *The Hawaiian Romance of Laieikawai* (1919); S. H. Elbert, "Chants and Love Songs of the Marquesas, Fr. Oceania," *Jour. P. Society* 56 (1947); J. D. Freeman, "The Tradition of Sanalāla," *Jour. P. Society* 56 (1947); M. K. Pukui, "Songs (Meles) of Old Ka'u, Hawaii," *JAF* 62 (1948); M. W. Beckwith, *The Kumulipo, a Hawaiian Creation Chant* (1951; rpt. 1972); S. H. Elbert, "Hawaiian Literary Style and Culture," *American Anthropologist* 53 (1951); D. Christensen and G. Koch, *Die Musik der Ellice-Inseln* (1964); S. M. Mead, "Imagery, Symbolism, and Social Values in Maori Chants," *Jour. P. Society* 78 (1969); M. Pukui and A. Korn, *The Echo of Our Song: Chants & Poems of the Hawaiians* (1973); M. McLean and M. Orbell, *Traditional Songs of the Maori* (1975); M. McLean, "Text and Music in 'Rule of Eight' Waiata," *Studies in Pacific Languages & Cultures*, ed. J. Hollyman et al. (1981); K. Luomala, *Voices on the Wind: Polynesian Myths and Chants*, rev. ed. (1986); T. Karetu, *Haka: The Dance of a Noble People* (1993); *Te Ao Marama: Contemporary Maori Writing*, 5 v., ed. W. Ihimaera (1993–96); *Whetu Moana: Contemporary Polynesian Poems in English*, ed. A. Wendt, R. Whaitiri, R. Sullivan (2003); S. T. Marsh, "'Ancient Banyans, Flying Foxes and White Ginger': Five Pacific Women Writers," diss., Univ. of Auckland (2004); K. Ho'omanawanui, "He Lei Ho'oheno no nā

Kau a Kau: Language, Performance, and Form in Hawaiian Poetry," *Contemporary Pacific* 17, (2005); F. Stewart, K. Mateatea-Allain, A. Dale Mawyer, *Vārua Tupu: New Writing from French Polynesia* (2006); R. Sullivan, "Hone Tuwhare Memorial Issue," *Ka Mate Ka Ora* 6 (2008), http://www.nzepc.auckland.ac.nz/kmko/.

R. Sullivan; K. Luomala

PORTUGAL, POETRY OF. Port. poetry originates in the med. (12th–14th cs.) Galician-Port. *cantiga*. The cantigas are generally divided into three major genres: *cantigas de amigo* (songs in the voice of women), *cantigas de amor* (courtly love songs in the voice of men), and *cantigas de escarnho e mal dizer* (joke and insult poetry). Galician-Port. poetry circulated orally and through performance. The cantigas de amigo are unique to Portugal and Iberia and constitute the largest corpus of woman-voiced poetry in Europe, although all extant compositions are attributed to male poets. The cantigas de amor tend to follow the model of *Occitan poetry and in that regard are more conventional. The joke poetry is accomplished in polysemy, revels in transgressive imagery and bawdy humor, and presents ludic constructions of sexuality, gender, and cultural and religious orthodoxies. Many of the cantigas, esp. the cantigas de amigo, invoke the sea and ships as motifs in amatory complaint and yearning and thus establish a trad. of maritime poetry in Portugal. Some salient poets are Pero da Ponte (fl. 1235–60), who composed in all three major genres; Johan Zorro (fl. late 13th c.); Martim Codax (fl. mid-13th c.); Pai Gomez Charinho (ca. 1225–95); and Pero Meogo, whose sea-inspired love songs stand as examples of med. poetic virtuosity. The work of over 150 poets represents the Galician-Port. lyric school.

Following the cantigas, the poetic record is silent for a century until 1516 when Garcia de Resende (ca. 1470–1536) published the bilingual (Port.-Castilian) *Cancioneiro Geral* (General Songbook), a collection of erudite, courtly verse that testifies to the shift from oral to written poetic culture. These poems were intended as palace entertainments. Resende, himself one of the *Cancioneiro* poets, assembled compositions on aristocratic themes (such as the formalities of love and courtship) that are usually structured as the popular *redondilha maior* or line of seven syllables. A common format is an initial refrain (*mote*) that is then glossed (*glosa*). Petrarchan ideas on love first appear here (e.g., love that delights in suffering and contradiction), but some poems take on humorous and satirical topics or reveal the social realities of 15th- and 16th-c. Portugal with personages such as the sorceress, the Jew, and the Moor. Resende's stanzas on the tragic death of Inês de Castro, João Rodrigues de Castelo Branco's "Cantiga sua partindo-se" (Song of Parting), and Jorge da Silveira's contemplation on love are notable examples. The verses of the first known woman poet, Filipa de Almada, appear in this *Cancioneiro*. Other poets include Jorge de Aguiar, Duarte de Brito, Francisco Sá de Miranda, Anrique da Mota (d. after 1544), Francisco de Sousa, and Gil Vicente (ca. 1465–1536), the first major figure of Port. theater who composed his plays in verse and included lyrical passages and interludes in them. Much of his poetry is inspired by traditional forms and subject matter that were reworked to theatrical ends. In this, Vicente's plays are a repository of Port. poetry but one that rewrites and reformulates the trad. through the playwright's acute literary sensibilities. Vicente's command of poetry is apparent across the genres he cultivated, namely, religious plays, comedy, and farce. Later in the 16th c., Joana da Gama (d. 1586) employed the popular verse forms characteristic of Resende's collection to express an anguished vision of life in *Ditos da freyra* (Sayings of the Nun).

After a sojourn in Italy, Sá de Miranda (1481–1558) brought It. Ren. genres to Portugal, incl. the Petrarchan sonnet that would dominate Port. poetry from then on. He would, however, continue to cultivate the old style of poetry even after the introduction of Italianate forms. His *Trovas à maneira antiga* (Stanzas in the Old Style), e.g., are largely composed in the traditional redondilha and explore their topics in learned and erudite lang. and conceits. Alongside his friend Bernardim Ribeiro (1490?–1536?), Sá de Miranda is credited as the first to compose eclogues in Port. following Virgil's example. Sá de Miranda's moralistic poetry is technically proficient and often conceptually difficult, and its Port.-Castilian bilingualism bears evidence, as does other poetry of the time, of the interconnected literary cultures of Portugal and Spain. Ribeiro is the author of five eclogues, and some of his poetry first appears in Resende's *Cancioneiro*. Ribeiro develops a sentimental vein in his work turning on love and its psychological contours that is also reflected in Cristóvão Falcão's *Écloga Crisfal* (Crisfal Eclogue, first pub. anonymously then reprinted together with Ribeiro's works in 1554). Ribeiro's sentimental pastoral fiction *História de Menina e Moça* (Story of a Young Girl, 1554, 1557), which is interspersed with verse, elaborates a psychology of love, nostalgic yearning (*saudade*), and a fatalistic sense of life. Saudade is a cornerstone of Port. literary and cultural identity, beginning with the med. cantigas, and is the basis of the 19th- and early 20th-c. poetic movement known as *saudosismo*. *Menina e Moça* includes literary motifs on the dimensions and characteristics of amorous sentiment and consciousness that will be further elaborated and explored in the widely influential verses of Luís de Camões.

The poetry of António Ferreira (1528–69) and Luís de Camões (1524?–80) stands out as representative of lyric verse in Ren. Portugal, with Camões as the culminating figure now at the heart of the Port. literary canon. Ferreira, an admirer of Sá de Miranda, wrote poems based on It., Lat., and Gr. models and eschewed the Port.-Castilian bilingual practice in favor of Port. alone. His poems were published under the title *Poemas Lusitanos* (Lusitanian Poems, 1598) and rehearse topics important to humanism. (Neo-Lat. humanist poets, such as André de Resende [1500?–73], revived Lat. as a poetic lang.; see LATIN POETRY.) Camões's poetry earned him international renown. He wrote in the Ren. genres of the sonnet, eclogue, song, ode, elegy, and epic. The lyrics were published posthumously under the generic title of *Rimas* (Rhymes, 1595, 1598); they often express their topics through the prevailing lens of Petrarchism. But they also characteristically inflect intense, personal experience with a melancholic tone and perspective and address such universal themes as love, hope, happiness, and death. Maritime expansion and travel, the historical backdrop of 16th-c. Portugal, exercise an influence on the metaphors and the real and imagined experiences of the Camonian poetic subject. As a virtuoso sonneteer, Camões shapes a philosophy of existence informed by the contradictory nature of love, melancholy, sadness, and the "desconcerto do mundo" (disorder of the world) or the dissonance between the world as it should be and as it actually is. He charts the workings of affect in all its contradictions. His epic *Os Lusíadas* (*The Lusiads*, 1572), modeled in large part on Virgil and Ludovico Ariosto, takes as its story the 1497–99 voyage of Vasco da Gama to India. While *The Lusiads* is, on one level, an expression of Christian imperialist ideology, it is also fraught with contradiction and failure and expressed in a rhet. that frequently enters the realm of the lyrical. The poem is an exploration of the Port. Ren. imagination and joins hist., myth, and literary culture into a vibrant cohesiveness. Camões is one of the Ren.'s most influential mythographers and psychologists of love. *The Lusiads* quickly achieved international currency and, along with the *Rimas*, establishes connections to other poets of early modernity writing in the contexts of (maritime) exploration, literary creation, and subjectivity.

Camões's epic initiative was continued and imitated in the 16th and 17th cs. by poems based on other imperial figures or events in Africa, Asia, and Brazil. Jerónimo Corte-Real (1533–88) wrote the *Naufrágio e lastimoso sucesso da perdiçam de Sepúlveda* (Shipwreck and Sorrowful Loss of Sepúlveda, 1594), based on the famous shipwreck off the coast of East Africa in 1552. Bento Teixeira's *Prosopopéia* (1601) tells of Jorge de Albuquerque Coelho's shipwreck off Recife, Brazil, in 1565. Other epic poems in this trad. are Francisco de Andrada, *O primeiro cerco de Diu* (The First Siege of Diu, 1589), Vasco Mouzinho de Quevedo Castel-Branco, *Affonso africano* (Afonso the African, 1611), Francisco de Sá de Meneses, *Malaca conquistada* (Malacca Conquered, 1634), and João Franco Barreto, *Eneida portuguesa* (Portuguese *Aeneid*, 1664), a Port. trans. of the *Aeneid* that often incorporates verses taken directly from *The Lusiads*.

Francisco Rodrigues Lobo (1574?–1621), probably best known for his dialogues on court life (*Corte na Aldeia*, 1619), is an important voice in late Ren. bucolic poetry on the eve of the baroque. In 1596, Rodrigues Lobo imported the genre of the *romance* into Portugal from Spain with his *Romanceiro*. The *Éclogas* (1605) are polished examples of bucolic verse in which the motifs of *desengano* (disillusion) and melancholy are present; the poems also display Sá de Miranda's moralizing influence. Camões and Spain's Luis de Góngora will remain the two major poetic influences throughout the century. Góngora's *conceptismo* and *cultismo* are evident in Sóror Violante do Céu (1601–93), a Dominican nun whose religious and accomplished *Rimas Várias* (Diverse Rhymes, 1646) establishes devotional poetry as a terrain for women poets. Another nun, Sóror Maria do Céu (1658–1753), also composed religious poetry. The multilingual Bernarda Ferreira de Lacerda (d. 1645?) wrote verse on epic (*España libertada*) and bucolic (*Soledades de Buçaco*) themes.

Francisco Manuel de Melo (1608–66), while known more for his prose works, typifies in his poetry the aristocratic and learned peninsular culture in the final years of the Sp. annexation of the Port. crown (1580–1640). His *Obras Métricas* (Metrical Works, 1665) encompass all poetic genres cultivated at the time. They are arranged according to the nine Muses. Satirical poetry flourishes at the end of the century and is to some extent a reaction against Gongorism. This satirical poetry is collected in anthols. of the early 18th c., such as *Fénix Renascida* (Phoenix Reborn, 1715–28), and includes Tomás de Noronha (d. 1651), the Coimbra-educated Brazilian Gregório de Matos (1636–96), and Tomás Pinto Brandão (1664–1743).

The 18th c. witnessed a continuation of baroque practices in its first decades and a neoclassical period beginning roughly in mid-century with the renovation of Port. culture and society under the enlightened despotism or rationalism of the Marquis of Pombal. The distinction between these two periods is approximate, since, despite rationalist arguments against the excesses of the baroque and Gongorism, some aspects of the baroque (such as the reliance on cl. mythology) continued throughout the century. Academic neoclassicism was initiated with the creation of the Arcádia Lusitana or Olissiponense (Lusitanian or Lisbon Arcadia) in 1756 and reaffirmed in 1790 with the Nova Arcádia (New Arcadia). Neoclassical Port. intellectuals (e.g., Luís António Verney [1713–92] and Cândido Lusitano [1719–73]) debated the didactic and learned status of poetry and its social functions and developed dogmatic precepts of lang., grammar, and phonetics guided by the motto "inutilia truncat" (eliminate that which is useless). Unrhymed (blank) verse was widely adopted as appropriate for the imitation of Greco-Roman poets and their numerous genres and subgenres. Arcadian poets, inspired by Fr. authors, adopted literary pseuds. under which they wrote and published, a gesture meant to erase social distinctions and promote a literary form of aristocracy. The realities of daily bourgeois life were a favorite theme. The best-known lyrics on love and the domestic life were the collection titled *Marília de Dirceu* (1792, 1799) by Tomás António Gonzaga (1744–1810). Born in Portugal but sent to Minas Gerais in Brazil and eventually exiled to Mozambique, Gonzaga composed this poetry to his lover Marília under the Arcadian pseud. Dirceu. Like some of the poetry of António Diniz da Cruz e Silva (1731–99), he brought Brazilian nature and landscapes into Port. poetry, and *Marília de Dirceu* was one of the most popular books in Portugal and Brazil at the time. Other lyric poets include Pedro António Correia Garção (1724–72), Domingos dos Reis Quita (1728–70), and Cruz e Silva, who also wrote a comic epic *O Hissope* [The Hyssop]). Nicolau Tolentino de Almeida (1740–1811) was a major figure of the century whose satires target the sordid and vice-laden aspects of Port. society and class structure, while also treating general themes such as war. Social types and manners also frequently appear in his poetry. Tolentino characteristically employs a prosaic idiom in his poems. Manuel Maria Barbosa du Bocage (1765–1805, Elmano Sadino of the Nova Arcádia), like Tolentino, wrote of bohemian life and composed sonnets of considerable accomplishment, many of them engaging motifs that became mainstays of romanticism such as the obsession with death and the tenebrous. António Lobo de Carvalho (ca. 1730–87) was a satirist noted for his scabrous and obscene poems in the spirit of med. joke poetry. Bocage's contemporary, José Agostinho de Macedo (1761–1831), was a lyric poet but is better known for his pamphleteering and virulent crit. of Camões who, in Macedo's opinion, grossly contravened verisimilitude in *The Lusiads*. Macedo countered *The Lusiads* with his poem *O Oriente* (The Orient) and wrote a heroic-comic poem titled *Os Burros* (The Asses). Leonor de Almeida (1750–1839), later the Marquesa de Alorna, also heralds romanticism; her lyrics oscillate between religious devotion and an acute sense of melancholy and, like the work of Reis Quita, present a poetic voice that often turns on saudade. Two friends of the marquesa participate in moving Port. poetry toward the early romantic sensibility: Catarina de Lencastre (1749–1824) expresses a conflict between reason and sentiment, and Francisca de Paula Possolo (1783–1838), the Arcadian "Francília," rejects reason and acknowledges the irrational powers of the imagination.

Romanticism is rooted in the poetry of the later Arcadians but became solidified as a movement with the sociopolitical changes of the liberal revolution of 1832–34 and the new, secular society formed after the abolition of the religious orders in Portugal. Almeida Garrett (b. João Baptista da Silva Leitão, 1799–1854) is credited with introducing romanticism in Portugal after a stay in England and exposure to the works of Walter Scott and Lord Byron with the narrative poem *Camões* (1825). A novelist and playwright, Garrett fueled the Port. romantic desire for a national theater. Garrett's contemporary Alexandre Herculano (1810–77), mostly a prose writer, inaugurates religious-themed romantic poetry. Herculano, who believed that social and political revolution should find literary expression, expounds a theory of romantic lit. as anti-Arcadian, popular, and of the masses but in alignment with current philosophical currents and in which a return to med. roots would displace classicism and absolutism. Garrett, an admirer of the Arcadian Filinto Elísio, first composed neoclassically inspired poetry but moved definitively into the romantic mode with *Adosinda* (1828) and the publication of his *Romanceiro* (1851), a collection of *romances* or popular poetry with med. themes inspired by Madame de Staël and the Ger. interest in folkloric lit. Garrett's best-known book of poetry is *Folhas Caídas* (Fallen Leaves, 1853), which directly expresses states of passion; his belief that lit. should manifest a national character, based on folklore and trad. as the most authentic expressions of *lusitanidade* (Lusitanianness), is adopted by late 19th-c. writers and is known as *neogarrettismo* (neo-Garrettism). António Feliciano de Castilho (1800–75) adheres to a conservative, neoclassical mindset in terms of ling. discipline, though his poetry is regarded as romantic. Poets whose work appeared around 1838 are called the *ultraromantics* (notionally the representatives of the final phase of romanticism, though ultraromantic themes and lang. are present earlier, such as in the poetry of Castilho) and include Maria Browne (1797–1861), António Augusto Soares de Passos (1826–60), and Tomás Ribeiro (1831–1910).

In 1865, a group of students at the University of Coimbra rebelled against romanticism and called for social, political, and scientific reforms that, in the domain of lit., led to realism. This ideological polemic came to be known as the Questão Coimbrã and its adherents as the Generation of 1870, headed by the poet Antero de Quental (1842–91). Antero's poetry culminated in a collection of masterful *Sonetos* (1886), which are, at turns, pessimistic, religious, and philosophical, and borrow concepts from thinkers such as G.W.F. Hegel. Guerra Junqueiro (1850–1923) wrote political poetry and at the time was considered a major exponent of contemporary reality. Toward the end of the century, Port. Parnassianism was briefly practiced by poets such as Gonçalves Crespo (1846–83) and António Feijó (1859–1917). Realist poetry is most accomplished in the work of Cesário Verde (1855–86), whose posthumously published *O Livro de Cesário Verde* (The Book of Cesário Verde, 1901) depicts the concrete realities of Lisbon and the oppressive life of the working class. As one of the most remarkable poets of city life and its sensorial aspects, Verde rejected romantic rhet. with a vividness of description that includes market stalls, the sounds and rhythms of daily living, the squalor of the streets, and yellow fever.

Apart from Verde, Port. symbolism, with its emphasis on the impalpable, autumnal, nostalgic, and distance from the real, characterizes fin de siècle poetry. Eugénio de Castro's (1869–1944) *Oaristos* (1890) formally initiated Port. symbolism, which lasted until 1915. Though not published until 1920, Camilo Pessanha's (1867–1926) *Clepsidra* (Water Clock) constitutes an important moment in symbolist poetry. Other poets of the time are António Nobre (1867–1900) and Teixeira de Pascoaes (1877–1952). Pascoaes is the main proponent of saudade or nostalgia as the basis of the pantheistic, messianic philosophy and literary movement known as *saudosismo*. Saudosismo promoted a certain neoromantic lexicon and sensibility that appear in the early work of some modernist poets.

At the end of the first decade of the 20th c., a group of artists and writers who came together in Lisbon, would usher in modernism, a movement that broke with the past with iconoclastic force, often incorporating ideas on lit. and art brought to Portugal from Paris and expressed through a variety of print and other artistic media. It included movements such as *paulismo*, *interseccionismo*, *sensacionismo*, and *futurismo*. The first group of modernists include Fernando Pessoa (1888–1935), Mário de Sá-Carneiro (1890–1915), and José Sobral de Almada-Negreiros (1893–1970), the latter known more for his paintings and designs but whose *Manifesto Anti-Dantas* stands out as a main text of the new movement. This group published several literary magazines; its first publication, *Orpheu* (1915), provided the name to this first wave of the new, revolutionary aesthetic. A divided, fragmented self, frequently the result of the irreconcilability of thought and emotion, achieves lasting expression in the poetry of Pessoa, by far Port. modernism's preeminent representative and perhaps the greatest mod. poet in any lang. The nature of the (lyric) self in its many textual and philosophical aspects is also evident in Sá-Carneiro (*Dispersão* [Dispersion, 1914], and *Indícios de ouro* [Traces of Gold, 1937]). Pessoa created literary personae or heteronyms—discrete personalities with distinctive styles and poetic attitudes often antithetical to one another. The heteronyms testify to the fluctuation between plurality and unity consistently found as a sort of existential statement in Pessoa's work. Pessoa's three main heteronyms are the pantheistic Alberto Caeiro, the neoclassical Ricardo Reis, and the modernist/futurist Álvaro de Campos. Pessoa also signed poetry under his own name, work that uses the meters and phrasings of traditional verse. Other poets of the first wave of modernism include Ronald de Carvalho (1893–1935), Ângelo de Lima (1872–1921), Luís de Montalvor (1891–1947), Alfredo Pedro Guisado (1891–1975), and Mário Saa (1893–1971). Port. modernism's second moment centers on the magazine *Presença* (1927–40) whose collaborators include Branquinho da Fonseca (1905–74), Adolfo Casais Monteiro (1908–72), José Régio (1901–69), João Gaspar Simões (1903–87), and Miguel Torga (1907–95). While not as subversive as the Orpheu group, *presença* capped the modernist movement as a whole. It validated the Orpheu poets while also seeking to promote pure aesthetic values and extract artistic creation from political concerns as much as possible. It includes a significant amount of prose writing and lit. crit., and the members of the *presença* group (or *presencistas*) experienced moments of ideological dissidence among themselves.

The experimentation with subjectivity, poetic sincerity, and plurality of being typical of the first moment of modernism and the heteronyms extend to the realm of gender and sexual orientation. One of the Orpheu poets, Armando Côrtes-Rodrigues (1891–1971), composed a series of poems under the female identity of Violante de Cysneiros. Poems or parts of poems in Pessoa's work express homoerotic desire, feminized passivity, or masochistic tendencies. António Botto (1897–1959) and Judith Teixeira (1873–1959) were gay and lesbian poets whose work appeared during the first moment of modernism. Pessoa was a friend and literary collaborator of Botto and translated his *Canções* (1920 and subsequent eds.) into Eng. as *Songs*. Unlike Botto's candid homoeroticism, Teixeira's poetry tends toward the ambiguous and the symbolic and often employs a decadent idiom. Other important women poets emerged in the 20th c., such as Irene Lisboa (1892–1958), who published under the male pseud. João Falco, and Florbela Espanca (1895–1930). Espanca's sonnets, with their emphasis on female eroticism and an awareness of a patriarchal literary trad., are precursors to the fully developed feminist consciousness later in the century.

Following the publication of *Presença*, a series of *Cadernos de Poesia* (Poetry Notebooks) were published beginning in the 1940s, a period in which the socially and politically committed agendas of neorealism had already appeared in the 1930s and lasted to the 1950s. Mostly a prose fiction movement, neorealism included the poets Manuel da Fonseca (1911–93) and Fernando Namora (1919–89). After World War II, Port. surrealist poetry emerged, characterized by the automatic workings of the subconscious, black humor, and verbal associations. António Pedro (1909–66) ranks as a major surrealist artist and poet and was a founding member of the first surrealist group in Portugal. Pedro was also a prose writer and cultivated a multimedia oeuvre, incl. ceramics, and exalted the plastic arts. Mário Cesariny de Vasconcelos (1923–2006) became Port. surrealism's best-known figure with poetry that is sarcastic, explosive, and often erotic. It employs the technique of the surrealist inventory, as does the poetry of another of the surrealist writers, Alexandre O'Neill (1924–86).

Jorge de Sena (1919–78), who pursued a career as a professor in the U.S., claims a place among mid-20th c. poets. Eugénio de Andrade (1923–2005) wrote verses of a lyrical musicality that exist outside of movements and schools. Andrade is associated with the Generation of 1927 in Spain, since he admired and translated Federico García Lorca as a young man. Sophia de Mello Breyner (Andresen, 1919–2004) is an important voice of the 20th c.; her prolific work roots itself in limpid lang. and metaphors that extol the Port. maritime landscape and human habitation in it, expressed in a refined poetic diction. Later 20th-c. experimental and concretist poets, who bring visual aspects to poetry and reimagine the poetic or textual sign, include Ana Hatherly (1929–2015), Herberto Hélder (1930–2015), E. M. de Melo e Castro (b. 1932), and Gastão Cruz (b. 1941).

Port. lit. in general was brought definitively in line with feminist concerns with *Novas Cartas*

Portuguesas (New Portuguese Letters, 1972) by Maria Isabel Barreno (b. 1939), Maria Teresa Horta (b. 1937), and Maria Velho da Costa (b. 1938). This book intersperses prose with poetry and further solidifies a female literary subjectivity announced earlier with poets like the Marquesa de Alorna and Espanca. The work of Natália Correia (1923–93) participates in the movement represented by the *Cartas*. (Correia also edited an important anthol. of satiric and erotic poetry in Port.) Other contemp. women poets of note are Luísa Neto Jorge (1939–89), Ana Luísa Amaral (b. 1956), and Adília Lopes (b. 1960).

See SPAIN, POETRY OF.

■ **Anthologies and Translations**: *Poems from the Portuguese*, trans. A.F.G. Bell (1913); *Antologia da poesia feminina portuguesa*, ed. A. Salvado (1973); *Contemporary Portuguese Poetry*, ed. H. Macedo and E. M. de Melo e Castro (1978); *Líricas portuguesas*, ed. J. de Sena, 2 v. (1984); *Songs of a Friend*, trans. B. H. Fowler (1996); S. de M. Breyner, *Log Book*, trans. R. Zenith (1997); *The Lusíads*, trans. L. White (1997); *Antologia de poesia portuguesa erótica e satírica*, ed. N. Correia, 3d ed. (2005); *Luís de Camões*, trans. W. Baer (2005); F. Pessoa, *A Little Larger Than the Entire Universe*, trans. R. Zenith (2006); *Poets of Portugal*, trans. F. G. Williams (2007); *The Songs of António Botto*, trans. F. Pessoa (2010).

■ **Criticism and History**: T. Braga, *História da litteratura portugueza* (1896)—includes summaries of poetic schools and periods; A.F.G. Bell, *Studies in Portuguese Literature* (1914); J. G. Simões, *História da poesia portuguesa das origens aos nossos dias* (1955); *Presença da literatura portuguesa*, ed. A. Soares Amora, 5 v. (1971–74); *Dicionário de literatura: brasileira, portuguesa, galega, estilística literária*, ed. J. P. Coelho, 3d ed. (1985); T. F. Earle, *The Muse Reborn* (1988); A. J. Saraiva and O. Lopes, *História da literatura portuguesa*, 17th ed. (1996); S. Reckert, *From the Resende Songbook* (1998); M. Sousa Santos, "Re-inventing Orpheus: Women and Poetry Today," *Portuguese Studies* 14 (1998); *A Revisionary History of Portuguese Literature*, ed. M. Tamen and H. C. Buescu (1999); K. D. Jackson, *As primeiras vanguardas em Portugal* (2003)—biblios. of poets and critical studies; A. J. Saraiva, *Initiation into Portuguese Literature* (2006); *Embodying Pessoa*, ed. A. Klobucka and M. Sabine (2007); C. C. Stathatos, *A Gil Vicente Bibliography, 2000–2005* (2007); V. Aguiar e Silva, *A lira dourada e a tuba canora* (2008); *A Companion to Portuguese Literature*, ed. S. Parkinson, C. Pazos Alonso, T. F. Earle (2009).

J. BLACKMORE

PRAKRIT POETRY. The term *Prakrit* refers in its broadest sense to a wide range of Middle Indo-Aryan langs., related to but different from Sanskrit. Although the name is drawn from a Sanskrit word referring to these langs. as "original" or "natural" in contrast to the "refined" status of codified Sanskrit, a description pointing to a recognition of their status as vernaculars, several of the Prakrit langs. had standardized forms of their own and enjoyed a long hist. of use both as court langs. in South Asia and by groups such as the Buddhists and Jains, who opposed the claims of authority made by Brahmanical users of Sanskrit. The oldest surviving written examples of Middle Indo-Aryan langs. are from the 3d c. BCE, in the inscriptions of the Buddhist emperor Aśoka, and a very large corpus of Buddhist texts survives both in the Pali lang. and in various Prakrit langs. An unknown portion of Prakrit lit. has been lost; in only the last 15 years, e.g., excavations in Central Asia have increased the numbers of known mss. in Gāndhārī Prakrit from one example to hundreds. In addition to the Buddhist texts, Jain canonical works are preserved in Prakrit langs. such as Ārdhamāgadhī and Jain Māhārāṣṭrī. Alongside these uses, several Prakrit langs. were used for literary purposes by Brahmanical authors as well. In mod. usage (continuing the practice of Sanskrit authors) the term *Prakrit* generally excludes the Pali lang. as well as the later stages of Middle Indo-Aryan known as Apabhraṃśa, despite the literary uses of these langs.

Sanskrit writers on poetics treat Prakrit as a ling. option for poetic purposes alongside Sanskrit and Apabhraṃśa, sometimes incl. as well the "goblin language" or Paiśācī, in which was composed a famous collection of stories called *Bṛhatkathā* (The Great Story), now lost in the original but surviving in several versions in Sanskrit dating from the 6th c. onward. In addition to the use of Prakrit as the lang. in which entire works are composed, in Sanskrit dramaturgy the use of several Prakrit langs. is assigned by rule to characters of certain classes: in the plays, it is generally only educated upperclass men who speak Sanskrit, while women speak in Śaurasenī Prakrit and sing in Māhārāṣṭrī Prakrit, and less refined men speak other forms of Prakrit such as

Māgadhī. Prakrit grammars written in Sanskrit described these langs. largely by giving rules for converting Sanskrit into Prakrit, and from early med. times onward, it became increasingly clear that most Sanskrit playwrights were thinking in Sanskrit and employing such conversions to produce their Prakrit sentences. It is perhaps for this reason that the great poet Bhavabhūti, author of three plays in the 8th c., wrote prose in both Sanskrit and Prakrit but composed verses only in Sanskrit. It is also clear that readers as well were less able over time to understand Prakrit directly, as shown in the fact that commentaries on the plays regularly provide Sanskrit trans. of the Prakrit passages and in the widespread corruption of Prakrit passages in mss.

Māhārāṣṭrī Prakrit, associated with the region in which mod. Marathi is spoken (see MARATHI POETRY), played an esp. important role in poetry and is treated as the fundamental Prakrit in written grammars. The oldest collection of verses is the anthol. named *Sattasaī* (Seven Hundred), attributed to the 1st-c. king Hāla but containing couplets mostly from the 3d to 5th c. and from as late as the 7th c. The verses, called *gāthā*s, are couplets, syntactically independent like Sanskrit couplets but composed in freer meters of the *āryā* pattern, a type apparently related to regional folk songs, not allowed in the most prestigious form of Sanskrit poetry but adopted with enthusiasm in other forms of Sanskrit composition. The verses deal esp. with the psychological aspects of love and were influential in providing the model for similar collections in Sanskrit such as the *Amaruśataka* (The Hundred Verses of Amaru, ca. 7th c.), an anthol. of verses offering psychological vignettes of life in an aristocratic polygamous society, using techniques of poetic suggestion similar to those found in many of the Prakrit gāthās. Such poetry was the impetus for the devel. of the theory of poetic suggestion that looms large in Sanskrit poetics beginning with the 9th-c. *Dhvanyāloka* (Light on Suggestion) treatise of Ānandavardhana, which uses as examples not only Sanskrit verses from Amaru's collection but many Prakrit verses from the *Sattasaī*. Later Sanskrit poetic works such as the 12th-c. *Āryāsaptaśatī* (Seven Hundred Āryā Verses) imitate the *Sattasaī* not only in flavor but in meter as well. Commentaries in Sanskrit were written on many of the Prakrit poems.

In addition to the gāthā lit., Prakrit poets also composed in most of the standard genres of Sanskrit poetry or in related Prakrit genres. Examples are the 7th-c. *sargabandha* (composition in cantos, the ornate epic also called *mahākāvya* or great poem in Sanskrit) of Pravarasena titled *Setubandha* (The Forming of the Bridge), the 8th-c. *campu* (poem in mixed prose and verse) of Uddyotana Sūri titled *Kuvalayamālā* (The Garland of Water Lilies), and the long 8th-c. poem *Gaüḍavaha* (The Slaying of the Gauda) of Vākpatirāja, who was also among the latest of the authors included in Hāla's collection. Several distinctive Prakrit genres are defined in early Sanskrit treatises on poetics, but examples have survived only sporadically. Other authors used Sanskrit and Prakrit together, as in works with Sanskrit verses and Prakrit prose, in macaronic verses with one half in Sanskrit and the other in Prakrit, and even in verses designed to sound the same in both langs.

A considerable portion of these poetic works in Māhārāṣṭrī Prakrit was composed by Jain authors, many of whom continued to use distinctively Jain forms of Prakrit for literary as well as expository and philosophical uses.

Extensive treatment of the differences in effect between Sanskrit and Prakrit, of the distribution of Prakrit langs. geographically and socially, and of the social milieu of the Prakrit court poets is provided in the 9th-c. *Kāvyamīmāṃsā* (Exegesis of Poetry), an encyclopedic work on lit. by Rājaśekhara, who was the most prolific of Sanskrit court poets and prided himself on his abilities in Prakrit, as evidenced in his play titled *Karpūramañjarī* (Camphor Cluster), which is composed entirely in Prakrit langs.

See INDIA, POETRY OF; SANSKRIT POETICS; SANSKRIT POETRY.

■ A. C. Woolner, *Introduction to Prakrit*, 2d ed. (1928); M. A. Selby, *Grow Long, Blessed Night: Love Poems from Classical India* (2000); S. Pollock, *The Language of the Gods in the World of Men* (2006); *Poems on Life and Love in Ancient India: Hāla's "Sattasaī,"* trans. P. Khoroche and H. Tieken (2009).

G. TUBB

PROVENÇAL POETRY. *See* OCCITAN POETRY

PUERTO RICO, POETRY OF. *See* CARIBBEAN, POETRY OF THE

PUNJABI POETRY. Poetry has been written in the Punjabi lang. since around the 12th c. CE. The literary devel. can be divided into roughly three overlapping periods: med. to early mod. Sufi and Sikh devotional writing (12th–18th cs.), epic romantic verse (17th–19th cs.), and the mod. period (1890–present). As Punjabi was historically a demotic rather than a literary lang., Punjabi poetry has been influenced by verse forms from Hindi, Urdu, and Persian, with heavy use of the *sloka*, a couplet-based form common in cl. Sanskrit, in med. and early mod. Punjabi, and forms such as the *ghazal* since the 18th c.

Poets historically have used two scripts when writing in Punjabi, Gurmukhi and Shahmukhi. Though the grammar and diction in the two scripts are identical, Shahmukhi script derives from Persian, while Gurmukhi bears some resemblance to the standard script used in Hindi, Devanagri, though Sekhon and Duggal suggest resemblances to Takri and Sharda scripts as well. Gurmukhi is also associated with the Sikh trad. since it is the script of the Sikh holy book, the *Gurū Granth Sāhib*, while Shahmukhi traditionally has been used by Muslim Punjabi speakers, a division intensified since the partition of the Indian subcontinent in 1947.

Scholars agree that the first major poetry written in Punjabi was composed by Faridud-din Ganj-i-shakar, commonly known as Sheikh Farid (ca. 1173–1265). Sheikh Farid was a Sufi mystic of the Chishti order, whose writings have had a deep and lasting impact on Punjabi speakers from the Muslim, Hindu, and Sikh communities (Chopra). Farid's *slokas* reflect Sufi philosophical precepts, esp. focused on the critique of institutional religious authority as well as material attachments: "Farīdā pankh parāhunī ḍunī suhāvā bāg / Naubat vajī subah sio chalaṇ kā kar sāj" (Farid says, the bird is a guest in the beautiful garden. / Morning bells are ringing, get ready to go).

The Sikh gurus wrote a considerable body of devotional poetry in Punjabi from the 16th to the 18th cs. In his verses, Gurū Nānak (1469–1539) asserted an iconoclastic ethos under the influence of Sufis such as Farid as well as the Hindu *Bhakti* trad. Nanak worked with a variety of elements in his verses, many of them originating in Hindi poetry, incl. *padas* (stanzas) and *ashtapadis* (eight-stanza compositions), as well as *chhants*, *paharas*, *savayyas*, and slokas. The Sikh gurus also set their compositions in 31 different ragas, indicating how the verses were to be recited melodically. Beginning with Guru Arjan (1563–1606) and his contemporary Bhai Gurdas (1551–1636), Sikh devotional poets came to prefer Braj Bhasha (a historical literary lang. closer to Hindi) over demotic Punjabi, opening a window for further devel. of Sufi Punjabi poetry beginning in the 17th c. (Singh 1988).

The themes of Punjabi Sufi poetry from the early mod. period echo that of Sheikh Farid and Gurū Nānak, though the form preferred by these writers is called the *Kāfi*, a monorhyme stanzaic verse form usually set to music. One poet of particular note is Bulleh Shah (ca. 1680–1757), whose iconoclastic verses have been revived in Indian popular music, as in "Bulla ki jāna": "Nā mei momin vich masīt ān / Nā mei vich kufar diyan rīt ān / Nā mei pākān vich palīt ān / Nā mei mūsa nā pharaun" (Not I, a believer inside a mosque / Not I, an infidel doing rituals / Not I, pure amongst the wicked / Neither Moses nor Pharoah, am I). Other important Sufi Punjabi poets include Madhulal Hussain (also referred to as Shah Hussain, 1538–99), Sultan Bahu (1628–91), and Shah Sharaf (1640–1724).

Waris Shah (ca. 1722–98) is the most influential writer in the extended romantic lyric form known in Punjabi as the *qissa* (also spelled *kissa*), derived from the Ar. *qaṣīda*. Shah's most influential contribution is his version of the verse narrative *Heer-Ranjha* (1766), an archetypal tale of doomed lovers. The intense imagery and natural-sounding voices in *Heer* have made it a key text in the Punjabi trad. Related to the qissa is the epic heroic poem, known in Punjabi as the *vār*, which recounted wars and other historical events. The vār form was also used by Sikh gurus in the *Gurū Granth Sāhib* (see HINDI POETRY).

Punjabi poetry was marginalized under Brit. colonialism in India, as educational policies in the 19th c. favored national langs. such as Urdu over regional langs. However, a new phase of Punjabi poetry arose with the reformist Singh Sabha movement in the latter half of the 19th c. Bhai Vir Singh (1872–1957), a leading literary figure in the movement, was an active novelist and publisher, as well as a major poet. He is widely cited by critics (incl. the authors of the major reference works cited below) as the father of modern Punjabi poetry, perhaps because he instantiated the independent short poem in Punjabi; he was also likely one of the first Punjabi poets to distribute his poetry commercially in the form of printed books. Singh's influence on contemporaries is readily evident in the writing of Puran Singh (1881–1931), the latter being a poet also deeply influenced by both Japanese aesthetics and the Am. Walt Whitman. Puran Singh is likely the first Punjabi poet to use free verse, though thematically his writing retains a lyric and devotional focus.

Self-consciously secular poetry in Punjabi emerges as part of the Progressive Writers' movement in South Asian lit. in the 1930s. While the movement is known for works in Hindi, Urdu, and Eng., it had a substantial influence on Punjabi writers such as Mohan Singh (1906–78), Sharif Kunjahi (1915–2007), Amrita Pritam (1919–2005), Prabhjot Kaur (b. 1924), and, slightly later, Shiv Kumar Batalvi (1936–73). As with the Progressive movement more broadly, a significant number of Punjabi Progressive writers were women, incl. Kaur and Pritam. Evidence of the continuing influence of writing from the qissa period is seen in Pritam's "Aj Ākhan Waris Shah Nū," a reflection on the partition of the subcontinent addressed apostrophically to Shah: "Aj ākhan Waris Shah nū kito qabra vicho bol / te aj kitāb-e-ishq da koi aglā varka phol" ("I say to Waris Shah today, speak from your grave / And add a new page to your book of love," trans. D. S. Maini).

Modernism in Punjabi Indian poetry emerged roughly in tandem with modernism in Hindi, where it is referred to as the *Nayī Kavitā* (New Poetry). An experimental, modernist sensibility can be seen in the work of Jasbir Singh Ahluwalia (b. 1935), who published an anthol. of "experimental" (*Prayogashīl*) Punjabi poetry in 1962, which included his own verses as well as those of established poets, such as Pritam and Mohan Singh, associated with the previous generation. Despite the presence of self-conscious experimentalism since the 1960s and free verse since the 1920s, the dominant voices in Punjabi poetry after 1947 have continued to emphasize traditional rhyme (generally monorhyme) associated with the ghazal and Kāfi forms, as well as traditional meters.

Crit. related to 20th-c. Punjabi poetry has been heavily constrained by the partition of 1947, which fractured literary communities in Punjabi along religious lines. Studies by Indian scholars tend to focus exclusively on mod. writers from Hindu and Sikh backgrounds (works by Sekhon and Duggal and by Malhotra and Arora are cases in point), while, in Pakistan, Javeid's study is framed as an explicitly nationalist project and exclusively invokes writers of a Muslim background. Rammah has explored the status of West Punjabi poetry, focusing on Kunjahi, Najm Hosain Syed (b. 1936), Munir Niazi (1928–2006), and Ahmed Rahi (ca. 1923–2002) as the leading voices in postpartition Punjabi poetry from Pakistan.

Finally, the growing body of Punjabi-lang. poetry by writers outside the Indian subcontinent should be noted. The best-known figure is Sadhu Binning (b. 1947, Canada), whose bilingual ed. of *No More Watno Dur* (No More Distant Homeland, 1994) has been widely influential. Other frequently cited Punjabi poets in the diaspora include Ajmer Rode (b. 1940, Canada) and Amarjit Chandan (b. 1946, Kenya). Diasporic writing uses elements from traditional Punjabi poetry but adds themes associated with the diasporic experience, often with an infusion of transliterated Eng. vocabulary.

See INDIA, ENGLISH POETRY OF; INDIA, POETRY OF; INDIAN PROSODY; PERSIAN POETRY; RĀMĀYAṆA POETRY; URDU POETRY.

■ J. S. Ahluwalia, *Prayogashil Punjabi Kavita* (1962); N. H. Syed, *Recurrent Patterns in Punjabi Poetry* (1968); D. S. Maini, *Studies in Punjabi Poetry* (1979); J. Bedi, *Modern Punjabi Poets and Their Vision* (1987); A. Singh, *Secularization of Modern Punjabi Poetry* (1988); S. S. Sekhon and K. S. Duggal, *A History of Punjabi Literature* (1992); I. H. Javeid, *Pakistan in Punjabi Literature* (1993); M. Singh, *Glimpses of Modern Punjabi Literature* (1994); T. Rahman, *Language and Politics in Pakistan* (1996); S. Mukherjee, *A Dictionary of Indian Literature*, v. 1, *Beginnings–1850* (1998); P. M. Chopra, *Great Sufi Poets of the Punjab* (1999); P. K. Singh, *Representing Women: Tradition, Legend and Panjabi Drama* (2000); *Encyclopaedic Dictionary of Punjabi Literature*, ed. R. P. Malhotra and K. Arora (2003); L. Sakata, "Kafi," *South Asian Folklore: An Encyclopedia: Afghanistan, Bangladesh, India, Nepal, Pakistan, Sri Lanka*, ed. P. Claus, S. Diamond, M. A. Mills (2003); P. Gopal, *Literary Radicalism in India: Gender, Nation, and the Transition to Independence* (2005); *Journal of Punjab Studies* 13.1–2 (2006)—Z. Ahmad, "Najm Hosain Syed: A Literary Profile"; T. S. Gill, "Reading Modern Punjabi Poetry from Bhai Vir Singh to Surjit Patar"; S. Rammah, "West Punjabi Poetry: From Ustad Daman to Najm Hosain Syed."

A. SINGH

R

RĀMĀYAṆA POETRY. Few if any works of world lit. have had as great an impact on the theorization and production of poetry as the monumental ancient Indian epic poem the *Rāmāyaṇa*, composed in Sanskrit, according to trad., by the legendary poet-seer Vālmīki sometime in the middle of the 1st millennium BCE.

First and foremost, the ancient and copious Indian lit. on poetry and poetics generally agrees that the epic is the original example of the poetic genre in hist. The poem itself, as it has been transmitted, contains a prologue in the form of a celebrated metapoetical narrative that tells how the sage Vālmīki, moving through a sequence of transformative personal experiences, the first edifying, the second emotive, and the third inspirational, is able to fuse them into the production of a new medium of expression, the poetic. The incident is referred to many times in later poetic works and theoretical treatises on the nature of poetry. Thus, the work is often referred to as the *ādikāvya* (first poem), while its author is celebrated as the *ādikavi* (first poet).

Equally noteworthy is how the epic has served as the inspiration for countless poetic retellings of its central narrative in virtually all of the langs. of South and Southeast Asia and several langs. of West, Central, and East Asia as well. According to some traditional works, there are no fewer than one *crore* (10 million) extant in the world. Many langs. have more (sometimes many more) than one *Rāmāyaṇa* to their credit, and in many instances, like Vālmīki's influential work, these regional versions are regarded as standing at the head of their lit. trads. Several of these are among the most important and influential literary works in their respective langs.

In Sanskrit alone, the *Rāmāyaṇa* has inspired dozens, perhaps hundreds, of major poems and poetic dramas that highlight different aspects of the epic tale. Important literary examples, to name but a few, are Kālidāsa's major narrative poem, the *Raghuvaṃśa,* and Bhavabhūti's powerful poetic dramas, the *Mahāvīracarita* and the *Uttararāmacarita*. Many Jain versions in Prakrit, such as Vimalasūri's *Paumacariya*, were central to that religion's lit. hist. Important and highly influential med. and early mod. poetic *Rāmāyaṇas* in major regional langs. continue to be read and performed and exert tremendous cultural influence. Important examples are the Tamil poet Kamban's *Irāmāvatāram* (early 13th c.), Kṛttibās's Bengali version (early 15th c.), and the incomparably influential devotional poem the *Rāmcaritmānas* of the Avadhi (Old Hindi) poet-saint Tulsīdās (late 16th c.).

See ASSAMESE POETRY; BENGALI POETRY; GUJARATI POETRY; HINDI POETRY; INDIA, ENGLISH POETRY OF; KANNADA POETRY; KASHMIRI POETRY; MALAYALAM POETRY; MARATHI POETRY; NEPALI AND PAHARI POETRY; NEWAR POETRY; ORIYA POETRY; PUNJABI POETRY; SANSKRIT POETICS; SANSKRIT POETRY; TAMIL POETRY AND POETICS; TELUGU POETRY.

■ B. S. Miller, "The Original Poem: Vālmīki-Rāmāyaṇa and Indian Literary Values," *Literature East and West* 17 (1973); J. Brockington, *The Sanskrit Epics* (1998); *The Rāmāyaṇa of Vālmīki: An Epic of Ancient India*, ed. R. P. Goldman, 6 v. (1984–2009); R. P. Goldman, "The Ghost from the Anthill: Vālmīki and the Destiny of the *Rāmakathā* in South and Southeast Asia," *A Varied Optic: Contemporary Studies in the Rāmāyaṇa*, ed. M. Bose (2000); R. P. Goldman and S. J. Sutherland Goldman, "The Ramayana," *The Hindu World*, ed. S. Mittal and G. Thursby (2004).

R. P. GOLDMAN

ROMANIA, POETRY OF. Poetry is one of the few areas of Romanian culture in which one notices a kind of organic continuity over the centuries. The earliest surviving texts of Romanian poetry date from the 17th c. In the 17th and 18th cs., Romanian poetry is chiefly of three kinds. The first is religious poetry, esp. verse trans. of biblical books. Thus, Dosoftei, a learned Moldavian clergyman, translated the Psalms (1673) in rhymed couplets of variable length that indicate equally the influence of Romanian oral folk verse and of classicist Polish poetry (see POLAND, POETRY OF). The second is occasional verse following Western models—elegies, odes, pattern poetry, and epigrams. The most prominent example is by the historian and statesman Miron Costin (1633–91), whose *Viața lumii* (The World's Life, ca. 1672) is a meditation on the vanity of life and the mutability of fortune, written in rhymed couplets of 12 or 13 syllables in irregular meter. The third kind is represented by a wide variety of historical chronicles in verse that flourished in the 18th c. in the southern principality of Wallachia. These are often polemical, always picturesque, and undoubtedly circulated orally.

The 18th c. also witnessed the culmination of oral folk verse, references to and quotations from which are found already in the 15th and 16th cs. They express in a variety of genres the existential horizon and emotional universe of a stable agrarian society. While steeped in a religiosity that combines a simplified Christianity and a broad pantheistic sacrality, this poetry also preserves some traces of a pre-Roman pagan mythology. Heroic trads. are rendered not in epics but rather in short ballads. The bulk of folk poetry consists of *doinas*, lyrical expressions of love, loneliness, grief, and yearning, or, less often, glee, carousal, or revolt. Broader visions are provided by the myth of the master-builder Manole, who sacrificed his and his wife's lives to the achievement of a unique building, and particularly by *Miorița*, which is often said to embody a Romanian folk philosophy. It tells the story of a migrant shepherd who, on hearing his companions' plot to murder him, does not defend himself but rather turns the occasion into a grand reconciliation with nature, the stars, and the animals. The popularity of folk poetry declined toward the end of the 19th c., and it had virtually disappeared by the middle of the 20th.

The end of early Romanian lit. was marked by Anton Pann (1796?–1854), who synthesized the oral, didactic, and mythical-historical modes in a mock-naïve style. The decisive turn of Romanian poetry toward Western values and forms occurred in the last two decades of the 18th c. The Wallachian nobleman Ienache Văcărescu (1740?–93) and his two sons wrote gracious and erotic anacreontic verse on Gr., It., and Fr. models. At almost the same time, in Transylvania, Ion Budai-Deleanu (1760?–1820) wrote a satirical mock epic of the medieval struggle against the Ottoman Empire.

The first half of the 19th c. in Romanian poetry is characterized by the simultaneous assimilation of Enlightenment, neoclassical, romantic, and Biedermeier forms and ideas, which led to a number of interesting combinations. Dimitrie Bolintineanu (1819–72) and Grigore Alexandrescu (1814–85) wrote historical ballads, satires, fables, and elegies much influenced by Alphonse de Lamartine and Lord Byron. Vasile Alecsandri (1821–90) combined the fervent struggle for democratic reform and national unity common to the generation inspired by the ideals of 1848 radicalism with poetic serenity, a smiling Epicureanism, and a search for cl. balance. He excelled in patriotic verse, natural description, poetic drama, and adaptations of the newly recovered oral trad.

The greatest 19th-c. Romanian poet was Mihai Eminescu (1850–89), who was influenced by the Ger. romantics and by the philosophies of Immanuel Kant and Arthur Schopenhauer. Unfortunate love, social marginality, intense nationalism, mental illness, and early death no less than his towering poetic achievement soon turned Eminescu into a mythic figure. He gave to Romanian poetry the mod. form of its poetic lang. Eminescu's poetry (melancholy meditations on hist., society, sentimental love, and allegory) is founded on a deeper level of mythical cosmology, irrational vision, and subjective pantheism. Eminescu's unpublished work contains huge fragmentary epics that describe the universe as emerging out of the lamentations of universal or divine self-consciousness; he also evoked the pre-Roman society of the Dacians as a pristine, luxuriant, and crystalline world of which later hist. is but a series of deformed copies. Eminescu's radical conservatism was the wellspring for all later forms of nationalism in Romania.

For three decades after Eminescu's death, two poetic schools vied for primacy. One was symbolism, which appeared largely under Fr. influence; its most important representative was Alexandru Macedonski (1854–1920), a flamboyant artist who believed fervently in aesthetic perfection; his poetry abounds in images of precious stones, fabulous mirages, and morbid obsessions. Ion Minulescu (1881–1944), an able manipulator of grandiloquent images and sentimental intimations, continued the movement. The other school was the populist and idyllic movement mainly advocated by the jour. *Semănătorul*. Its proponents emphasized the use of simple lang. and drew their inspiration from national trads. and local themes. The best poets in this trad. were George Coşbuc (1866–1918), who also produced a superb trans. of Dante's *Divine Comedy*; Octavian Goga (1881–1938), whose best verse expresses a kind of primeval suffering; and Stefan O. Iosif (1875–1913).

The unification of all Romanian provinces following World War I and the beginnings of capitalist democracy favored an unparalleled growth of poetic diversity and power. The Romanian high modernists strove to combine trad. and innovation; the influence of Ger. expressionism and of Fr. modernists such as Stéphane Mallarmé and Paul Valéry can often be recognized in them. George Bacovia (1881–1957) expressed a universal hopelessness through his austere and obsessive verse, full of images of rain, mud, illness, and provincial dreariness. His poems, inspired by Moldavian towns, evoked a symbolic universe of humidity and putrefaction. Ion Barbu (1895–1961), a mathematician, wrote obscure, semantically packed, tightly structured verse exploring philosophical propositions; for him, the formal order of poetry outlined "a purer, secondary game." In other poems, Barbu indulged his voluptuous pleasure in the verbal thickness of a lush and lurid Balkan world, with its jesters, whores, and sages. Lucian Blaga (1895–1961), philosopher, diplomat, and professor, inquired poetically into the connections between natural reality and transcendent mystery; he evolved from Dionysian rhapsodic tones to praise of the agrarian order as a suggestion of cosmic harmony. Tudor Arghezi (1880–1967) renewed the discourse of Romanian poetry by mixing metaphysics and realism. He is particularly impressive for his astounding thematic range, from pamphleteering virulence, coarse violence, and sexuality to the worlds of children and of wrestling with religious faith and doubt.

In the same generation, there were able traditionalists such as the cultivated neoclassicist Ion Pillat (1891–1945); the natural mystic Vasile Voiculescu (1884–1963); Adrian Maniu (1891–1968), who clothed a decadent weariness in the mock simplicity of folk iconography; and the late neoromantic Alexandru Philippide (1900–79), whose poems abound in cosmic visions and historical nightmares. Among the many nationalist poets of the age, the most prominent was Aron Cotruş (1891–1957), whose messianic thunderings were couched in rolling free verse and a racy, sonorous vocabulary.

At least as vital and effective was the group of experimentalists, surrealists, and avant-garde radicals who eventually came to influence even Western Eur. poetry. Best known among them was the founder of Dada, Tristan Tzara (1896–1963), but of comparable distinction were Benjamin Fondane (1898–1944), Ilarie Voronca (1903–46), and Gherasim Luca (1913–1994), all of whom emigrated to France. Gellu Naum (1915–2001) and Saşa Pană (1902–81) were among the chief animators of poetic anarchism, which they aligned with leftist political attitudes. Camil Baltazar (1902–77), with his fluid and melodious verse and his morbid yearning for paradisal innocence, as well as Ion Vinea (1895–1964), with his jazzy rhythms and strident prose inserts, strove to bring experimental poetry closer to the mainstream and to endow it with more finished forms.

The poets who emerged in the later 1930s and 1940s had to suffer the trauma of war and of repeated political upheavals. Some chose exile. Others had to accept long periods of silence. They can be roughly grouped into the Bucharest and the Sibiu schools. The former is exemplified by Ion Caraion (1923–86), Geo Dumitrescu (1920–2004), Dimitrie Stelaru (1917–71), and Constant Tonegaru (1919–52), all ironic pessimists who clamored for adventurous vitality and the demolition of philistine prejudices. Among them Caraion is remarkable for the unrelenting and ferocious darkness of his images. The Sibiu group, exemplified by Radu Stanca (1920–62), the abstractionist Ion Negoiţescu (1921–1993), and above all Stefan Aug Doinaş (1922–2002), eloquently pleaded for the autonomy of culture and the humanizing role of aesthetic production. Doinaş is a consummate craftsman in a wide range of genres and forms, an admirable translator of poetry (e.g., *Faust*), a poet of intense metaphoric creativity, and the author of ethical satire and Neoplatonic visionary evocations.

The establishment of a communist regime in 1947 that suppressed artistic freedoms led to more than a decade of poetic barrenness. Only the more liberal 1960s brought a revival of poetry. Nichita Stănescu (1933–83) became the standard-bearer of a generation devoted to experiment and to a metaphorical version of reality free from ideological interference. Ioan Alexandru's (1941–2000) best verse moved from the cruelty of tragic naturalism toward a kind of religious harmony. Ion Gheorghe (b. 1935) manages to alternate crass primitivism and oracular obscurities with sophisticated lang. games. Mircea Ivănescu (1931–2011) wrote self-analytic elegies in which stream-of-consciousness techniques are applied with lucid irony. Marin Sorescu (1936–1997) dealt in parody and in the jocular debunking of habit. Leonid Dimov (1926–1987) inaugurated an "oneiric" movement based on dream imagery and associations of verbal music. Despite adverse political pressures, the feeling that the maintenance of high aesthetic standards is crucial for national survival encouraged the continuation of these efforts, either in the direction of lyrical purity, as in the poems of Sorin Mărculescu (b. 1936) and Ana Blandiana (b. 1942), or in the more open discontent and ethical rage of Ileana Mălăncioiu (b. 1940), Mircea Dinescu (b. 1950), and the dissident Dorin Tudoran (b. 1945). Many of these poets were in the forefront of the 1989 anti-Communist revolution. A new generation emerged soon thereafter, led by the postmodernist Mircea Cărtărescu (b. 1955); the cynical, street-wise Florin Iaru (b. 1955); the elegant religious poet Eugen Dorcescu (b. 1942); and Ion Stratan (1955–2005).

Two things should be added. One is that poetic and aesthetic values occupied a much more prominent place in Romanian culture than in the West: lit. was a respected mode of conveying wisdom and social values. The greater poets and movements were flanked for two centuries by hundreds of minor authors, and only an awareness of these can suggest the thick texture of Romanian poetry. The other is that the Romanian territory was hospitable to lit. written by numerous ethnic groups—Hungarian, Serbian, Saxon Ger., Bukowina Jewish, and others. Important literary figures such as Nikolaus Lenau (1802–50) and Paul Celan (1920–70), besides others mentioned above, originated here and can thus round off our understanding of the landscape of Romanian poetry.

■ **Anthologies**: *Rumanian Prose and Verse*, ed. E. D. Tappe (1956); *Anthology of Contemporary Romanian Poetry*, ed. R. McGregor-Hastie (1969); *46 Romanian Poets in English*, ed. and trans. S. Avădanei and D. Eulert (1973); *Antologia poeziei româneşti*, ed. Z. D. Buşulenga (1974); *Petite anthologie de poésie roumaine moderne*, ed. V. Rusu (1975); *Poezia româna clasică*, ed. A. Piru, 3 v. (1976); *Modern Romanian Poetry*, ed. N. Catanoy (1977); *Poezia romena d'avanguardia: Testi e manifesti da Urmuz a Ion Caraion*, ed. M. Cugno and M. Mincu (1980); *An Anthology of Contemporary Romanian Poetry*, ed. B. Walker and A. Deletant (1984); *Born in Utopia: An Anthology of Modern and Contemporary Romanian Poetry*, ed. C. Firan (2006).

■ **Criticism and History:** E. Lovinescu, *Istoria literaturii române moderne* (1937); B. Munteano, *Modern Romanian Literature* (1939); G. Calinĕscu, *Istoria literaturii române* (1940); G. Lupi, *Storia della letteratura romena* (1955); V. Ierunca, "Littérature roumaine," *Histoire des littératures*, ed. R. Queneau, v. 2 (1956); K. H. Schroeder, *Einführung in das Studium des Rumänischen* (1967); C. Ciopraga, *La Personnalité de le littérature roumaine* (1975); *Scriitori romăni*, ed. M. Zaciu (1978); V. Nemoianu, "The Real Romanian Revolution," *The World and I* 6 (1991); I. Negoiţescu, *Istoria literaturii române, 1800–1945* (1991), *Scriitori contemporani* (1994); M. Popa, *Istoria literaturii române de azi pe mîine* (2001); A. Stefănescu, *Istoria literaturii române contemporane, 1941–2000* (2005); I. Rotaru, *O istorie a literaturii române de la origini pîna în prezent* (2006); N. Manolescu, *Istoria critică a literaturii române* (2008).

V. P. Nemoianu

ROMANI POETRY. The ancestors of today's Roma (Gypsies) left northern India ca. 1000 CE and migrated to Europe and later to other parts of the world. Although traditionally regarded as nomadic, many Roma have been sedentary for generations. Persecution, exclusion, injustice, and poverty have characterized much of Romani hist. and find expression in Romani poetry. Romani, a lang. of Indo-Aryan origin, is spoken by numerous Roma, although many also or only speak the dominant tongue of their surroundings. There is no standard literary form of Romani, but there are many spoken dialects. Romani is the vehicle of both oral and written lit., but Roma also compose poetry in non-Romani langs.

Oral traditional poetry, both ritual and lyric, was the only Romani poetry until the mid-20th c. Ritual wedding songs express joy and bittersweet sorrow, while funeral laments articulate the grief of separation. In this Hungarian-Romani lament, the voice of the deceased cries out in the first two stanzas, while the mourner speaks in the third; a tragic sense of the Romani plight is pervasive:

To die, to die, one has to die.
I have to leave my family behind.
Unfortunate as I am,
I must perish this way.

I am wandering and cannot find a place
Where I can put my head down.
I put my head on the soil
Look how much I am suffering!

I live, I live, but for what?
When I do not have a single happy day?
Oh, my God, it is so bad for me.
My life is full of mourning.

(Kertész-Wilkinson)

Oral lyric songs at times celebrate the pleasures of family life, but many more tell of hardship, sorrow, and heartache. Roma proverbially claim that a "Gypsy song is a song that expresses pain and suffering."

In the late 1920s and 1930s, with the founding of Romani jours. in the USSR, Romania, and Yugoslavia, Roma began to voice their concerns in written lit. Literary poetry emerged after World War II. It is primarily lyric, inspired by oral poetry in both form and content; like Romani song, it overwhelmingly expresses pain. The collective anguish of being Romani in a cruel world permeates the poetry, as do metaphors of traveling and forced migration. The Romani soul is often portrayed as finding solace and shelter in nature.

Bronisława Wajs (1910–87) from Poland, known as Papusza (doll), is considered the mother of Romani poetry. She was discovered in the late 1940s by the poet Jerzy Ficowski, who translated her verse for publication from Romani to Polish. Papusza's "Tears of Blood" is a moving account of how she and fellow Roma suffered in hiding under Ger. occupation in the 1940s. Her most famous poem, "O Land, I am Your Daughter," also autobiographical, evokes nostalgia and her own sense of being Romani and connecting with nature:

> Oh land, mine and afforested,
> I am she, your daughter.
> The woodlands and plains are singing.
> The river and I combine our notes
> into one Gypsy hymn.
> I will go into the mountains
> in a beautiful swinging skirt
> made of flower petals.
> I shall cry out with all my strength . . .
> (Hancock et al.)

Because of her association with Ficowski, who became linked to the Polish government's program to settle Roma after the war, Papusza was ostracized in the mid-1950s by the local Romani community and pressured to lay down her pen. A contemporary of Papusza (known primarily for his prose), Mateo Maximoff (1917–99), was a well-known Rus.-Romani author living in France who wrote poetry in both Fr. and Romani.

A new generation of Romani poets emerged in the 1960s and 1970s. In Western Europe, Sandra Jayat (b. 1938) published Fr. verse starting in 1961. José Heredia Maya (1947–2010) was a prominent Romani poet, essayist, and playwright, whose poems in Sp. appeared since the 1970s. Romani has developed as a written lang.—although with numerous dialects—and is employed esp. by poets from Eastern Europe. One of the best-known cultural figures of this generation was Leksa Manuš (1942–97) of Latvia. He viewed the migrations and constant struggles of his people with wearied, longing eyes, as in his "Roads of the Roma":

> Each night, my God, as I close my eyes,
> I see before me the roads of the Roma.
> But where, my God, is the long-lost road,
> the one true road, the one first-traveled?
> (Hancock et al.)

Dezider Banga (b. 1939), from Slovakia, published his first volume of lyric poetry in 1964 in Slovak; he has also written in Romani. Rajko Djurić (b. 1947), from Serbia, is a poet and journalist. Writing in Serbian and Romani, he focuses on the hist. and culture of the Roma and depicts the Holocaust and injustices meted out to Roma, often conveying anger and futility in his poems. Originally from Slovakia but presently residing in Belgium, Margita Reiznerová (b. 1945) evokes the burden of persecution in her Romani verse. From Belarus, Valdemar Kalinin (b. 1946) now dwells in England where he writes poetry in Romani and advocates its standardization to unify Roma globally. In Macedonia, where radio and periodicals foster Romani lang. and culture, a circle of poets developed. Šaban Iljaz (b. 1955), from Skopje, is one of the best known of this group; his verse includes bitter meditations on Romani suffering and forced migration.

Romani authors of the 1980s and 1990s were increasingly involved in social causes, e.g., Béla Osztojkán, from Hungary (1948–2008), a prolific poet (and prose writer) who began publishing verse in 1981. Djura Makhotin (b. 1951), a poet, journalist, and musician from Russia, is also a Romani activist. From Romania, Luminița Cioabă (b. 1957) writes in both Romani and Romanian as she embraces the ethnic communities of her world. Among a more recent generation of bards, Alexian Santino Spinelli (b. 1964), a poet, essayist, and musician from Italy, is involved in advancing Romani lang., lit., and music worldwide. Nicolás Jiménes González (b. 1968), from Spain, writes poetry (in Sp.) to promote Romani culture.

While hampered by the lack of a standardized written lang., Romani poets are at the same time part of the wider Eur. trad. and vital agents in the devel. of genuine Romani culture.

■ **Anthologies**: *Stimme des Romani PEN*, ed. R. Djurić and R. Gilsenbach (1996–); *Littérature*, spec. iss. of *Études Tsiganes* n.s. 9 (1997); *The Roads of the Roma*, ed. I. Hancock, S. Dowd, R. Djurić (1998).

■ **Criticism and History**: J. Ficowski, *Gypsies in Poland* (1989); N. B. Tomašević et al., *Gypsies of the World* (1990); I. Kertész-Wilkinson, "Song Performance: A Model for Social Interaction among Vlach Gypsies in South-eastern Hungary," *Romani Culture and Gypsy Identity*, ed. T. Acton and G. Mundy (1997); *What Is the Romani Language?*, ed. P. Bakker and H. Kyuchukov (2001); G. Kurth, *Identitäten zwischen Ethnos und Kosmos* (2008).

■ **Journals**: *Romani Studies* (*Journal of the Gypsy Lore Society*): http://www.gypsyloresociety.org/journal.htm; *Études Tsiganes:* http://www.etudestsiganes.asso.fr/; *Lacio Drom*; *Patrin*: http://reocities.com/Paris/5121/; *Roma*.

■ **Poetry**: B. Osztojkán, *Halak a fekete citeràban* (1981); J. Heredia Maya, *Charol* (1983); S. Jayat, *Nomad Moons*, trans. R. Partington (1995); D. Banga, *Slnečný vánok* (1999).

M. H. Beissinger

ROMANSH POETRY. *See* SWITZERLAND, POETRY OF

RUSSIA, POETRY OF

I. Seventeenth and Eighteenth Centuries
II. Nineteenth Century
III. Twentieth Century and Beyond

Four interrelated tendencies characterize the hist. of Rus. poetry from its origins in the 17th c. until the early 21st c. The first concerns the incremental growth of the versification system. While writers and readers have valued strict-form verse, every period has produced innovation in the prosodic resources of Rus. verse in response to movements such as classicism, romanticism, and modernism. The second direction relates to openness to foreign poets, trads., and aesthetic movements through adaptation, imitation, and trans. The third pattern concerns the pervasive intra- and intergenerational affiliations that poetic texts express through subtextual and intertextual allusion. Rus. poets acquire with their education almost complete access to the entire trad., with the result that poets and readers are highly attuned to the connotative and associative connections triggered by the poetic, as opposed to prosaic, word. The fourth characteristic is the continuous regulation of Rus. poetry by political authorities. While the severity of censorship varied under both the imperial and Soviet regimes (as did the self-censorship practiced by writers), periods of complete freedom of expression were curtailed, leading on occasion to poetry of outright dissidence, as well as encouraging subtle techniques of satire and ironic suggestion.

I. Seventeenth and Eighteenth Centuries. From the mid-17th c. until the early 1760s, poetry was restricted to centers of learning, the bureaucracy, and court. The roots of early mod. Rus. literary culture lie in the Lat. and Scholastic orientation of 17th-c. Kyivan literary culture and its transfer to Moscow. The earliest writers to produce a corpus of poems were the literate functionaries collectively known as the Chancery school (*Prikaznaya shkola*). Their activity in the mid-17th c. demonstrates the relation between lit. and the court, personal ideals and state service as expressed in verse dedications, epistolary petitions, acrostic dedications, and rebus poems. At court, the major figure was the erudite Simeon Polotsky (1629–80), who displayed his mastery of the baroque poetics of Polish, Ukrainian, and Neo-Lat. lit. in two massive collections of verse, the *Rifmologion* (Rhymology) and the *Vertograd mnogotsvetnyi* (Variegated Vine). Backed by Tsar Aleksei Mikhailovich, whose policies of secular enlightenment anticipated those of his son, Peter the Great, Polotsky and his followers Silvester Medvedev (1641–91) and Karion Istomin (1650–1717) introduced the idea that poetry has an autonomous role in culture. Cast in the baroque form of the allegorical garden, Polotsky's two enormous poetic cycles, which contain a verbal labyrinth and emblem poem in the shape of a heart, invite the reader into a morally pure world of Christian virtue. Polotsky is the first in a long series of Horatian imitators in Russia, extending all the way to Joseph Brodsky in the 20th c., who maintain that the purpose of poetry, as Polotsky thought, "is to teach, please and move by means of connected speech."

In this respect, his successor, and the great innovator of the next generation, is Prince Antiokh Kantemir (1709–44). A diplomat posted in Paris and London, Kantemir defined his ambitions for poetry and Rus. culture by adopting Fr. neoclassicism as a progressive model. Kantemir saw satire as an efficient didactic mode in which to take a stand on cultural politics in support of Peter's reforms. Based on contemp. speeches of Peter's chief propagandist Feofan Prokopovich, the *Petriada*, Kantemir's epic fragment, celebrates the physical splendor of the city (more illusion than reality before the 1740s) and the speed of its creation. Kantemir's juxtaposition of civilization and nature anticipates a recurrent theme in the Petersburg myth. His *Satires* drew on the techniques of irony and caricature from a wide range of Eur. exemplary satirists, from Horace to Nicolas Boileau to Voltaire to Jonathan Swift. The poems project a Eur. sophistication well beyond the competence of all but the smallest readership in Russia at the time. Kantemir, whose work was published first in London and circulated in ms. in Russia before printed Rus. eds. appeared from the 1740s, received due recognition only after 1762, when Catherine the Great espoused Peter the Great's more secular vision of culture.

Debates about genre, imitation, innovation, and ling. and prosodic norms engaged with neoclassical theory and progressed by trial and error from the late 1730s into the first decades of the 19th c. There were no official court poets during the reigns of Peter the Great or his successors, and a culture of literary patronage is more notional than material during Catherine's reign. The prominent poets and theoreticians were Vasily Trediakovsky (1703–69), Mikhail Lomonosov (1711–65), and Alexander Sumarokov (1717–77). Despite personal rivalry, their common purpose was to prescribe the ling., syntactic, and prosodic system that would enable Rus. poets to domesticate Western genres and create a native trad. Trediakovsky and Lomonosov argued in their treatises (respectively, "New and Brief Method for Composing Russian Verse," 1735; "Epistle on the Rules of Russian Versification," 1739) that the syllabotonic system was the appropriate basis for mod. Rus. versification. Lomonosov applied his rules with panache in his "Ode on the Capture of Chocim" (1739). This spelled the end for syllabic verse as the basis of versification. Sensitive to the relation between form and affect, each theorist attributed to the selection of feet a fundamental role in the creation of poetry's emotional capacity. Trediakovsky advocated the trochee as the basic metrical foot, whereas Lomonosov promoted the iamb. In the event, Lomonosov prevailed. Trediakovsky had devised such complex rules of syntax for verse that his system became unworkable (though it is displayed with great ingenuity in *Tilemakhida* [1766], his transposition into verse of François Fénelon's *Télémaque*). The transition to the syllabotonic system has been attributed to numerous factors: statistical analysis of syllabic verse, in fact, suggests that tonicization was under way and that these theoretical pronouncements reflected a transition rather than a dislocation. These discussions yielded a new repertory of varied stanza forms and modes, incl. epic, song, epitaph, verse epistle and elegy, from which two subsequent generations drew heavily.

In the newly secular culture of the mid-18th c., dozens of poets, some dilettantish nobles, some translators, and some figures of lasting achievement created a substantial poetic canon. The composition of poetry among the educated elite, who absorbed the lessons of native and foreign handbooks and enthusiastically formed literary associations, enjoyed prestige as a demonstration of civility and cultivation. The most important poets were the scientist Lomonosov and the statesman Gavrila Derzhavin (1743–1816), who enjoyed early acclaim and earned lasting renown. Their biographies—each was from a remote part of Russia and reached a high rank at court—conferred an aura of genius, lending stature when they addressed the monarch. Both Lomonosov and Derzhavin took the notion of a poetic persona to new heights. The ode is the definitive high genre of 18th-c. Rus. poetry, a showcase for ling. experimentation as well as a mirror to the image of the monarch. Lomonosov's solemn odes, relentlessly paced by iambic tetrameter and alternating masculine and feminine rhyme, reveled in Pindaric chains of metaphors contained by the signature ten-line stanza. Rhetorically, these occasional poems restored poetry to its ceremonial place at court in the trad. of Polotsky. The turgidity of the Lomonosovian ode derives from a propensity to create semantic clusters, usually through etymologic play or tropes, such as zeugma. Lomonosov made Enlightenment progress (from the uses of glass to the advantages of Western dress) the subject of his verse. He evoked cl. allegory in celebration of Russia's triumphs of the 1750s and 1760s, advised on cultural policy, declared the arrival of a utopian age, encouraged imperial expansion, and promoted the political economy of a mercantile nation. The authority of the poet derives less from vatic inspiration, which turns out to be rational rather than visionary in the display of loyalty and practical wisdom.

Lomonosov speculates in verse on the nature of the universe, but in the famous evening and morning meditations written in 1743, he becomes the first Rus. poet to capture a sublime appreciation of nature.

This view of poetry as a mode of inquiry into the universe, society, and man finds its most eloquent spokesman in Derzhavin at his peak in the 1780s. Famed as a rule-breaker in both his poetic style—his idiosyncratic attitude to rhyme would look particularly clumsy to later generations—and subject matter, Derzhavin is a philosophical poet imbued with an Enlightenment belief in self-examination, rational skepticism, and empiricism. A spirit of cosmic enquiry inspires Derzhavin's remarkable meditation "God" (1784), a text that employs the discourse of natural philosophy (with some debt to G. W. Leibniz) as well as contemp. optics. Derzhavin is, above all, an eloquent poet who experiences metaphysical problems with pictorial vividness.

Derzhavin's poems often proceed by counterpointing reason and emotion and abstraction with realistic detail. His aim in mixing high and low, elevated diction and colloquialism, is to show that the genre system, with its rules about form and diction, is subordinate to the style of the poet's mind. Thanks to this force of personality and stylistic liberty, poems fold the sheer matter of everyday life into their argumentative structure. As a statesman, Derzhavin, like Horace, wrote in a civic mode with a view to instructing the ruler on the theory of natural law, good governance, and progress, all mainline Enlightenment topics. Whereas Lomonosov remained the respectful courtier, the senatorial Derzhavin in the late 1770s and 1780s showed greater boldness in mixing flattery with irony and dressing up topical discussion in thinly veiled allegory. In poems of statecraft, read and sometimes appreciated by Catherine the Great, he put the ruler and poet on virtually equal footing. He is the first Rus. poet to use the lang. of natural law in reminding the ruler of limits to autocracy. Derzhavin's choice of philosophical and political subjects conferred gravitas on the figure of the poet.

Yet not all is high seriousness in the period. Numerous poets from the 1730s to the 1770s were adept at song as well as verse tragedy and comedy. Light verse of an ephemeral nature enjoyed a vogue. Alexander Sumarokov, the director of the Imperial Theatre (and dubbed the Rus. Boileau), preferred pastoral themes. Parody and burlesque reached sparkling heights in the mock epic *Dushen'ka* (a transposition into poetry of Jean de La Fontaine's *Les Amours de Psyche et Cupidon* [1669]), which brought Ippolit Bogdanovich (1744–1803) admirers well into the 1820s.

II. Nineteenth Century. This rapid experimentation with styles and genres laid the ground for the first generation of classic Rus. poets of the 1810s. In the roughly 25 years before Alexander Pushkin published his first poem in 1815, the poetic norms established during Catherine's reign persisted. Most lyric poetry earlier in the period continued to circulate among a small coterie of amateur men of letters. Before the mid-1820s, public and private readerships were identical, since national literacy rates remained low and there was no system of distribution to bookshops. No one could aspire to be a professional poet much before the early 1820s. Lomonosov's poems had been published at court in tiny print-runs. Derzhavin's poetry circulated mostly in handsome ms. copies, but he lived long enough to see the transition toward printed eds., overseeing the publication of his own collected verse in 1814.

The devel. of smaller lyric forms proved to be a boon when sentimentalism reached Russia in the 1780s. Much more than prose in the period, which tended to emulate archaic models, Rus. poetry remained up to date in its openness to other national trends and movements, esp. from France. The lang. of sensibility developed in the 1790s by Nikolai Karamzin (1766–1826) and his acolytes Mikhail Muravev (1757–1807) and Ivan Dmitriev (1760–1837), all accomplished writers of *poèsie fugitive*, attracted the poets of early romanticism. Vasily Zhukovsky (1783–1852), a writer and translator of ballads, opened new conduits to Eur. currents as a smooth and idiomatic translator. His 1802 version of Thomas Gray's "Elegy Written in a Country Churchyard" (1750) was considered a masterpiece of the art of trans. in Russia and marked the inception of early romanticism. Older-generation canonical figures include the classicists Alexei Merzliakov, a translator of Virgil and professor of rhet.; Nikolai Gnedich (1784–1833), famed for his 1831 trans. of the *Iliad* into heroic hexameter; and Konstantin Batiushkov (1787–1855), an imitator of the musicality and sensibility of Tibullus and Torquato Tasso. Batiushkov exercised a formative influence on Pushkin and his contemporaries.

The elegiac speakers of the 18th c., drawn from tragedy, proved archaic after sentimentalism, which cultivated the expression of feeling. From the 1800s, the lyric landscape utilized manifold props and techniques of preromanticism, incl. ruins, pathetic fallacy, epigraphs, and wanderers. Poets employed a wider repertory of verse forms, turning out epistles in iambic trimeter, narratives in trochaic tetrameter with dactylic rhyme, and verse fables in mixed iambs, with notable success, e.g., in the fables of Ivan Krylov (1769–1844). For the next generation, working in the 1820s and 1830s, versification roughly adhered to the norms developed at this time: the default narrative meter was the iambic tetrameter (in more than 40% of works written in the 1820s), blank verse rather than alexandrines or iambic hexameter was employed in tragedy with Shakespearean overtones, and exact rhyme gradually became the norm. However, stanza boundaries, which a generation earlier had adhered to strophic forms like the eight- and ten-line ode, were relaxed as the romantics preferred openness and continuity in their lyric forms.

The greatest poet of the 19th c. is Alexander Pushkin, whose body of lyric and narrative verse was unprecedented in its variety and standard of accomplishment. From the 20th c. on, he has also been widely considered Russia's national poet. A discussion of Pushkin's unparalleled standing in the Rus. poetic trad. necessarily has three components: his intrinsic creative qualities, his contribution to the growth of the professional status of the writer in Russia, and finally the symbolic position he occupies in aesthetic debates, literary politics, and national identity from the time of his death through the Soviet period up to the present day. His idiom flows from the lang. that Karamzin and others refined, and he deploys it with unfailing elegance and deeper psychological nuance. His command of the genres is impeccable, yet his mastery of parody and pastiche are one source of delight, most esp. in *Evgenij Onegin*, his novel in verse that appeared in installments from 1825–32. Dubbed by the influential critic Vissarion Belinsky an "encyclopedia of Rus. life," it is also an encyclopedia of Rus. lit., packed with quotation and allusion. It is highly sophisticated in its narrative voice, creation of time frames, deconstruction of realism, and metatextual play. If Pushkin's metrical profile tends to the standard iambic tetrameter and his stanza forms are traditional, numerous examples demonstrate his aptitude for verse forms that match the mobility of his thought. Emotional transparency, conveyed in cultivated and conversational diction, characterizes his lyric corpus of nearly 700 poems in which he sloughs off poetic cliché—or uses it to devastating effect. The publication of his lyric poetry as a collection in 1826 was a landmark, following on the critical and financial success of early romantic narratives on Byronic themes. Lyric poetry had been the preserve of the amateur elite; few poets previously had courted a readership for their verse. The step was decisive in establishing the preeminence of lyric poetry in the 1820s and Pushkin's superiority among practitioners. He took a conservative approach to organizing the poems chronologically and according to genre, as was the custom among Fr. poets. By contrast, his highly esteemed contemporary Evgenii Baratynsky (1800–44) would later arrange the poems of his landmark collection *Sumerki* (*Twilight*, 1842) thematically, creating an impression of psychological coherence and implied linkages. This approach anticipated the thematic structure of the poetic book that many later poets, esp. the symbolists in the 1890s, would develop. Lapidary diction and pace characterize Pushkin's eight narrative poems, which move from Byronic themes to the greatest Rus. poetic meditation on hist., *The Bronze Horseman* (1834), while his fairytales have the vitality of folk idiom and considerable humor. His famed clarity does not negate a capacity to use polyphony, intertextual allusion, and form to suggest depth and dialogue with the trad. In his hands, for instance, blank verse rather than the alexandrine becomes an ideal medium for dramatic soliloquy in the Shakespearean historical tragedy *Boris Godunov*.

Poetry for Pushkin was certainly a calling, but he also called it "my trade, a branch of honest industry, which provides me with food and domestic independence." Bedeviled by censorship and goaded by his precarious critical reception, Pushkin was acutely aware that financial independence was a risk for aristocratic writers unable to live on revenues from their estates and reluctant to serve in the bureaucracy. Yet Pushkin braved different types of self-assertion in promulgating the authority of the poet. In "The Prophet" (1826), which may well be the most famous of all Rus. poems, he asserted the twin principles of the divine basis for the poet's genius and a duty of public enlightenment. The first claim grew out of Pushkin's appropriation of the romantic discourse of genius, rather than from any clear belief in a divine mission, and the second reflected his hopes that a poet of his talent, intelligence, and noble ancestry could advise the tsar. It is doubtful whether Pushkin subscribed to P. B. Shelley's view that poets were the legislators of humankind, but his exalted image of the poet fit in well with the younger generation of Moscow-based Schellingians like Dmitrii Venevitinov (1805–27) and found favor among the intelligentsia in the late 19th c., esp. symbolist writers, who adopted a hieratic notion of the poet.

The slump in Pushkin's critical reputation and his death in a duel created the perception that he was the victim of a repressive government and society hostile to poetic genius—suppositions in which there is some grain of truth, although these were not the immediate causes of the debacle. In "The Death of the Poet" (1837), the younger Mikhail Lermontov (1814–41) railed against an unworthy society, positioning the martyred poet as the upholder of cultural and moral values. Read as an attack on the government, it earned Lermontov a term of exile that bolstered his pose as a "Pushkin" to the younger generation. In his final years, Lermontov, who was also the victim of a duel, extended Pushkin's theme of the poet's aloofness from the debased crowd. His mature verse—and virtually all the poems written in 1841 are anthologized masterpieces—embraces a persona of alienation and despair, partly as a romantic reflex of Rus. Byronism, partly as a response to the constraints of life in Russia under Nicholas I. His narrative poetry explored topics such as the interrelation of consciousness and nature, jealousy and love, while his lyrics project a poet-figure afflicted by a sense of solitude and fate. His view of the poetic calling as a lonely destiny reverberated in the work of later poets facing hostile imperial and Soviet regimes.

Alongside Pushkin and Lermontov, the two outstanding poets of the period were Baratynsky and Fyodor Tiutchev (1803–73). They are often paired because of their philosophical themes and their common debt to Ger. idealist thought on hist. and nature. Baratynsky's gift is for compressing material of different logical kinds—observation, meditation, simile, satire—into a syntactically varied but metrically stable pattern that proves adaptable for the searching tones of his voice, which slips suddenly into bitter regret, then rises in metaphysical exaltation; and in his last poetry, achieves a distance from the world that is sublime. Both are poets of nature, the first imbued with a sense of awe and reason akin to J. W. Goethe, the second informed by F.W.J. Schelling and later Arthur Schopenhauer's pessimism. Both are among the most powerful love poets in Rus., expert at portraying an unrequited longing that corrodes hope and breeds disillusion. Baratynsky treated the relationship of poetry to hist. in one of the greatest lyrics of the century, "Poslednii poet" ("The Last Poet," 1835). Inspired by Viconian theories about the evolutionary cycles of culture, Baratynsky surveyed the progress of poetry from Homer to Pushkin, which for him marked the beginning of an Iron Age pitting prose against poetry, industrialization against creativity, capital against intangible genius. Like Lermontov's theme of the wanderer poet, this vision of an age governed by commercialism, positivist intellectual values, and mechanization would strike a chord with later poets.

The generation following Pushkin and his younger contemporaries, which includes now-forgotten but then-celebrated poets like Alexander Polezhaev (ca. 1805–38), saw itself as the possessor of a ready-made poetic lang. and a substantial trad. Nonetheless, there is a widespread perception that, from the 1840s to the 1890s, the rise of the novel eclipsed Rus. poetry. This judgment, which reflects some critical distaste for the breakdown of thematic boundaries between prose and poetry, is simplistic. Even in the supposedly fallow decades leading up to the rise of the next major movement, symbolism, poetry was highly productive and widely printed from the 1850s. If anything, the cultural status of poetry became increasingly an issue for debate, polarizing factions according to their position on an ideological spectrum between, at one end, Afanasy Fet (1820–92), Tiutchev, and others, who combined conservative nationalism with a commitment to Pushkinian values of art and craft; and, at the other extreme, the gifted democratic and radical Nikolai Nekrasov (1821–78). Along with lesser writers like Aleksei Khomiakov (1804–60) who used verse as a vehicle for a Slavophile ideology, it was Fet and Tiutchev who perfected the capacity of the Rus. lyric to create speakers of psychological depth and to distill entire areas of thought about nationalism, politics, and, above all, nature as a pantheistic force.

From the 1840s, the literary field was transformed by the rapid growth in literacy, demographic shifts toward cities, the improvement in print technology and the publishing infrastructure, and the crumbling of both class and gender barriers. Few notable women poets were active during Rus. classicism, although the early 19th-c. poets Anna Bunina (1774–1829) and Anna Volkova (1781–1834) were treated respectfully by literary societies. Over the next decades, Bunina, an amateur, would be followed by female poets like the formidable Evdokiia Rostpochina (1811–58), Elizaveta Shakhova (1822–99) and, above all, Karolina Pavlova (1807–93), who published substantial collections to positive critical and public response. Pavlova is a pioneer of poetry as a type of emotional diary and devoted lyric cycles to her affairs with Adam Mickiewicz and Boris Utin, while also departing from ostensibly "feminine" themes in more polemical verse about Russia and the mission of the poet.

The growth of an educated nongentry class, from which teachers, university professors, translators, and writers emerged, led to an expansion of the number of jours. in which poetry was featured. While the Rus. reading public consumed prose fiction above all, poetry sold and circulated in quantities that would have struck Pushkin as fabulous. Aesthetic debates current in Western Europe about the social function of lit. and "art for art's sake" reached Russia in the 1860s and 1870s. Yet in the "thick journals" that treated the famous "accursed questions" of Rus. politics and hist., the radical critics contested the worth of Pushkin and "pure" poets to a country experiencing severe social tensions because of agrarian reform and industrialization. Poets declaimed with prosaic explicitness in defense of the downtrodden and urban poor.

Pushkin's status as an object of attack from the Left, veneration from the Right, and adoration from the nonpolitical middle classes in itself gives evidence of the unusual importance accorded to poetry in ideological debates about the purpose of art. Some regarded him as irrelevant because he had failed to produce a positive hero who would be a model of political activism: *Onegin for Our Times* (1865) by Dmitrii Minaev (1835–89) fought fire with fire by parodying Pushkin's novel-in-verse. For the so-called radical critics, Pushkin's name was largely a byword for effete aestheticism. The vehement critic Dmitrii Pisarev (1840–68) derided Pushkin and Zhukovsky as "parodies of poets" and Lermontov as the author of "absurdities." In fact, Pushkin's reputation was a moving target since the true nature of his legacy was only then becoming known in Russia through radical émigré publications. There is an irony that attacks from radicals on Pushkin coincided with the first publication in the émigré press of some of his most radical poetry, which had been banned in Russia, incl. the pornographic burlesque *Gabrieliad* (1821), which mocked church dogma, and the lyric "Sower of the seed in the desert" (1823). By the time Fyodor Dostoevsky, in his famous speech on the opening of the Pushkin monument in Moscow (1880), elevated him as the embodiment of the Rus. soul, Pushkin had been claimed by all camps from radicals to pan-Slavists.

Readers continued to respond personally to Pushkin's lyric poetry. A large (and predominantly female) section of the now-substantial readership turned to poets as soul mates who intuited reader's private feelings. These included second-tier masters like A. K. Tolstoy (1817–75) and Konstantin Sluchevsky (1837–1904). Apollon Grigoriev (1822–64), Yakov Polonsky (1819–98), and Aleksei Apukhtin (1840–93) enjoyed particular favor thanks to their autumnal landscapes, moonlit-night settings, and emotional vagueness, often adapted in song.

Nonetheless, these melodists were out of step with an age gripped by questions of political and social change. The best of the "naturalists" is Nekrasov, ed. of the leading liberal jour. *The Contemporary*, who believed that all the prose of life could be made the subject of poetry. To the service of this credo, Nekrasov, nicknamed the Poet-Citizen, applied a formal mastery and an acute ear for popular idiom and dialect. The characters of his narrative poems are drawn from the world of the peasantry and new urban underclass.

The publication of *Poems* (1856) was a historic populist call. It unites the virtues of craft and irony that Nekrasov esteemed in Pushkin and Baratynsky with a forthrightness and cynicism seen earlier only in Derzhavin and Krylov. If any poem speaks for Nekrasov's generation, and for his aspirations for poetry, it is that collection's explicitly anti-Pushkinian and programmatic "Muse," which begins by repudiating "a Muse who sings gently and beautifully," but whose inspiration is imbued with a spirit of revenge that will sustain the poet across the "dark abysses of despair and evil." Nekrasov further expressed this ethos with verse portraits of radical critics such as Nikolai Chernyshevsky

(1828–89), whose views on lit. would later become precepts of Marxist-Leninist aesthetics in Soviet lit. crit.

The culmination of Nekrasov's career was the cycle of lyric and narrative poems united under the title *Komu na Rusi zhit' khorosho'* (*Who Lives Well in Russia?*, 1863–78), which applies a satirical eye to all facets of the Rus. empire. Nekrasov's ability to orchestrate polyphony and different modes makes him the true contemporary of Dostoevsky, while his eye for detail owes much to populist movements in the visual arts. Like Pushkin's lyric hero who spoke in the tones and manner of his social class, Nekrasov fashioned a speaker in the social image of his reader, thereby creating an intense emotional bond between him and a larger, socially engaged readership of urban professionals, incl. writers, students, and doctors, who made up the "mixed estates." Nekrasov's funeral became a mass demonstration at which Dostoevsky (in the company of the young Marxist philosopher Georgii Plekhanov) proclaimed him the legitimate heir of Pushkin and Lermontov.

Poets of Nekrasov's generation had engaged intensely with the so-called accursed questions, adding women's rights, poverty, and political freedoms. The assassination of Alexander II in 1881 and a period of reaction led to a gradual national subsidence into relative torpor until the first Rus. Revolution of 1905. The most popular poets of the 1870s were hackneyed imitators of Nekrasov, their politics expressed in often crudely sloganizing verse. By the late 1880s, Rus. poetry regained some measure of sophistication, deploying longer verse lines and ternary meters and, as in the poetry of the highly popular Semen Nadson (1862–87), even altering the rhythmic balance of iambic tetrameter. In the 1880s, Fet broke his 20-year silence with his final collection, *Vechernie ogni* (*Evening Flames*, 1891). His exquisite mastery of short forms combined subtle shifts in rhythm, verbal inventiveness, and sound play to mirror the febrile moods of his subjects. It came as a timely reminder of the lyric trad.'s marvelous fusion of music and psychology, inspiring the next two generations of poets to concentrate on smaller forms and personal subjects.

III. Twentieth Century and Beyond. These tentative stirrings in the 1880s anticipated the burst of formal daring shown by both generations of symbolist poets who were great enlargers of the tonal and rhythmic palette of Rus. verse. From the start, the Europeanness of Rus. symbolism is reflected in its culture of trans. Trans. and imitations of numerous other authors, incl. Arthur Rimbaud, Stéphane Mallarmé, Maurice Maeterlinck, E. A. Poe, as well as Pre-Raphaelite critics such as Walter Pater and John Ruskin, steered the symbolists away from civic topics toward personal themes expressed for an intimate circle of readers. Cross-currents in the aesthetic affiliations and philosophies of poets made the entire period highly dynamic and rich. First-generation symbolists, incl. Dmitrii Merezhkovsky (1865–1941), the febrile Zinaida Gippius (1869–1945), and the hugely popular Konstantin Bal'mont, shared the decadent preoccupation with death together with a yearning for an unattainable fullness of life, the belief in art for art's sake, self-obsession, and a tendency to conflate art and life. With hypnotic musicality, Fyodor Sologub (1863–1927) created a poetic dream-world of secret gardens and imagined realms in which symbolist hopes for cosmic renewal vied with Schopenhauerian pessimism about a decadent world. We are back in the world of coterie poetry. Valerii Briusov (1873–1924) and Georgy Ivanov (1894–1958), for instance, indicated their exclusivity by assigning Lat. titles to their collections, e.g., Briusov's *Me eum esse* (1898) and *Tertia Vigilia* (1901). Lyric, rather than narrative, was the dominant form. Poetic collections presented complex cycles. The degree to which poets become known to readers through the book of poems rather than miscellaneous publications is striking. It would be possible to write a hist. of Rus. poetry starting at this juncture by following a series of such titles. Some poets arranged their collections according to hidden feelings that obscurely moved the reader like a musical impulse. Others viewed the collection as a lyric diary, attaching dates to create a chronological progression. The first poetic collection to represent his spirit of pessimism and despair is Bal'mont's *Pod severnym nebom* (Under a Northern Sky, 1894). Unlike Bal'mont, who emphasized the musical expressivity of the word over its sense, Innokenty Annenskii (1856–1909), an older symbolist whose first collection was not published until 1908, conveyed a sense of existential unease and ennui through oblique images and periphrastic diction, the music of his verse stored up in the intonation of its questioning phrases rather than in sound orchestration.

The poetry of Annenskii has a hypnotic musicality. Briusov occupied a unique position as critic, scholar, and publisher and was a leading arbiter of taste until after the revolution. While his eclecticism may now look more affected than genuine, younger writers respected his formal virtuosity, fell under the spell of his versatile poetic persona, and were dazzled by his aptitude in adapting mod. Fr. verse, whether Charles Baudelaire's misanthropic brilliance or the coldness and exoticism of the Parnassians.

Both Alexander Blok (1880–1921) and Andrei Bely (1880–1934) conveyed the symbolist belief that the concrete world is only a damaged reflection of the world of eternal essences and that poetry captures the movement of the spirit from *realia ad realiora*. Blok's poetry, which shares Fet's plangent sound structure, mesmerized contemporaries with the new rhythmic capacities he revealed by using the *dol'nik*, rather than the iamb, to give his lines an accentual (and more speech-like) beat. This flexibility of rhythm, adapted to the intonation and changing mood of each line, and exemplified in the *Verses on the Beautiful Woman* (*Stikhi o prekrasnoi dame*, 1903), became widely imitated over the 20th c. Blok's *Collected Verse* (1911–1912) united his first five collections and reordered the poems according to chronology, thereby creating an autobiographical narrative about the growth of the poet from a Baudelairean *poète maudit* under the spell of the Eternal Feminine into a visionary attuned to the elemental music of hist. Blok was a phenomenon because the individual personality and voice of his lyric speaker was patently autobiographical to a greater degree than any other poet since Baratynsky. The interrelation of life and art and the symbolist project of perfecting life through art inform the poet's spiritual presentation throughout his collections. In the heady aestheticism of the prerevolutionary period, writers from the next generation like Anna Akhmatova (1889–1966) and Marina Tsvetaeva (1892–1941) fell under Blok's spell, dedicated youthful cycles to him, and emulated him by giving biographical detail and psychological continuity to their lyric cycles. Arguably, Blok did more than any previous writer to give thematic cohesion and a sense of psychological devel. to the unitary poetic collection, and while he enjoys much less popularity in the post-Soviet period, his status and influence were once towering.

Blok felt that the poet possessed an acute sense of hist. that came with an obligation, in the trad. of Pushkin's Prophet, to teach the nation. Clearly, some members of the intelligentsia, esp. in St. Petersburg, subscribed to these pretensions, but it is hard to substantiate the persistent claim that the mass of readers generally endowed their poets with mystical charisma. Even before the revolution of 1917 elevated proletarian art, a host of factors had already enlarged the popular base for poetry. There is clear evidence that, like the cinema, poetry readings were enjoyed as a type of elevated entertainment and a conduit for popular expression. Both Blok and Bely caught the turbulence of their revolutionary age at an early stage. In his 1905 collection *Pepel'* (Ashes), Bely shed his learned style and assumed a more popular persona under the inspiration of Nekrasov. Anxiety about Russia's future pervades Blok's prose in which he warned his readers about the "music of history"—and perhaps for the last time in the hist. of Rus. poetry, he invoked the authority of the poet in making such national pronouncements. When the October Revolution occurred, Blok captured the actual violence of the revolution in *Dvenadtsat'* (*The Twelve*, 1918), which tells the story of a marauding band of soldiers let loose on Petrograd. This cycle fuses the symbolic lang. of Blok's philosophy of hist. with a polyphonic narrative of upheaval at street level. Blok punctuates whole sections with onomatopoeic, nonverbal explosions of sound effects to convey rifle fire. Class distinctions mark the speech of characters, and Blok makes extensive use of accentual verse to characterize peasant speech. All the great 20th-c. narrative poems, incl. Tsvetaeva's *Krysolov* (*Ratcatcher*, 1925), Mikhail Kuzmin's *Forel' razbivaet led'* (*The Trout Breaks the Ice*, 1929) and Akhmatova's *Rekviem* (*Requiem*, written 1935, pub. 1963) follow his example in forging a sequence out of highly varied metrical structures.

In the years between the revolutions of 1905 and 1917, symbolism made way for the most remarkable concentration of great poets since the Pushkin period. Poetic groups across a spectrum of artistic philosophies came together and by dint of sometimes marginal differences splintered into numerous subgroups. One common denominator across the Silver Age (as it was retrospectively called) was the cult of Pushkin, who appears in many guises as a ghostly interlocutor for Annenskii, a haunting friend for Akhmatova, a poetic sun for Osip Mandelstam (1892–1938), and a dandy for Mikhail Kuzmin (1872–1936). In her prerevolutionary collections, Akhmatova, whose understatement and irony communicated this poetic kinship, freed erotic psychology from the frenzy and melodrama of the decadents. Voiced in cl. binary meters, these short lyrics present subdued dramas of emotional reckoning. The very different characterizations of Pushkin in the work of Akhmatova and Tsvetaeva show how malleable his reception and image continued to be and help crystallize the differences in their poetics (Akhmatova was clearly cl., while Tsvetaeva was an iconoclast in idiom and sentiment). Tsvetaeva, one of the great formal innovators of Rus. poetry, celebrated Pushkin as the "scourge of tsars," a poet of Af. ancestry whose protean genius and aptitude set the standard in many genres. If Akhmatova's attention to the emotions finds its natural form of expression in short poems, Tsvetaeva required the expansiveness of confessional, autobiographical modes practiced with devastating candor in poems written after her emigration in 1922 such as the "Poema gory" ("Poem of the Mountain," 1924) and at a metaphysical level in her ethereal *Novogodnee* (*New Year Letter*, 1927) to R. M. Rilke, works that blur generic boundaries by expanding the introspection and dense imagery associated with the lyric on a narrative scale.

Literary futurism was officially inaugurated in 1913 when Vladimir Mayakovsky (1893–1930) displayed its antiestablishment credentials by repudiating Pushkin as an aesthetic standard. Certain slogans ("A slap in the face of public taste," "Throw Pushkin overboard") together with deliberate outrageousness in public displaced the listless symbolist persona with the bad-boy image cultivated by Mayakovsky. The graphic appearance of futurist poetry, with its jagged lines and use of the verse ladder (*lesenka*), gives a visceral sense of the distance it puts between itself and cl. poetry. While futurism is best known by representatives such as Mayakovsky, the term is a portmanteau word for a range of subgroups responsible for the doctrine of cubo-futurism, and the imaginists (made up of thirteen poets incl. Anatoly Mariengof [1897–1962] and Vladimir Shershenevich [1893–1942]), as well as the later Left Front in Art (LEF). Individual poets and factions were heavily implicated in producing and applying the lessons of post-Saussurean ling. theory elaborated across a wide spectrum of thinkers from A. A. Potebnya to members of the formalist movement whose theories of the literary device, the literary system, and the dynamic literary word galvanized poets to exploit poetic lang. in all its semantic, phonetic, and even visual complexity and to assume that the poetic word has a special density of expressivity that exceeds its denotative function as a signifier. The poetic avant-garde experimented with form and lang. as the means to defamiliarize reality for new readers in a mod. age. This common impulse, shared by all groups, animates some of the most daring formal innovation in Rus. poetry, whether expressed in the trans-sense lang. that the imagist-futurist poet Velimir Khlebnikov (1885–1922) coined or in Mayakovsky's attention to poetic lang. as a nearly material substance (*faktura stikha*) that delivers the shock of the new through neologism, unusual rhymes, explosive intonation, rapid syntax, and unusual verse forms.

Mayakovsky remains one of the great iconoclasts of Rus. verse, a magnetic civic poet, and in the cycle *Pro eto* (*About That*, 1923) a moving writer of love poetry. By setting out his revolutionary rhet. in lines of unprecedented metrical variety over extensive monologues, he maximized intonational variety and rhythmic flexibility. But Mayakovsky is hardly alone in taking metrical sophistication to new lengths. Readers appreciated the skillful amphibrach in Boris Pasternak's second collection, just as they esteemed the dexterity with which Tsvetaeva (in the trad. of Bal'mont) mastered Gr.-style logoaedic meters in her verse tragedies. Boris Pasternak (1890–1960) initially participated in futurist groups before going his own way. Like Tsvetaeva, he refracted the observation of contemp. historical events, such as the Kronstadt rebellion and the October Revolution, through a lyric optic. His second book *Sestra moia zhizn'* (*My Sister Life*, 1917), a lyric diary of emotional upheaval during a year of revolution, remains one of the great collections of Rus. poetry, remarkable as a phenomenological transcription of consciousness. The subject is the poet's emotional and intellectual hist. when his ardent openness to the sensual experience of life merges with utopian excitement. Like Tiutchev and Fet, Pasternak presents nature as a Schellingian force, imbued with subjectivity and spirit. His landscapes, defamiliarized through metonymy and metaphor, reflect his common heritage with the futurists.

Like the imagists, the acmeist poet—and here Mandelstam excelled in his first collection *Kamen'* (*Stone*, 1913)—creates out of the verbal texture of the poem an image of an object that seems real in material terms (thus, opposing the Platonic ideal of symbolist poetry). Many of the poems in *Stone* weave together a tissue of allusions to Eur. poets and themes, creating a concentrated sense of culture in a manner similar to T. S. Eliot's high modernism. Great buildings like Notre Dame and Hagia Sophia are emblems of the syncretism of religions and civilizations and communicate a modernist conviction that culture can be remade from its own past. The collections Mandelstam published in his lifetime are touchstones of Rus. poetry, not least because they seem to sum up their historical moment. In their focus on memory and beauty, strategies of poetic identity and the interrelation of painting, poetry, and music, *Stone* managed to be a timeless example of lyric perfection while also being steeped in the mood and idioms of fin de siècle Europe.

Mandelstam's next collections, *Tristia* (1923) and *New Verse* (1928), have a formal inventiveness and a range of reference and allusion that consciously distance them from the proletariat poetry sanctioned by the regime. Haunted by Lermontov's image of the poet as an outcast, Mandelstam reacted to the historical turmoil of "War Communism," the emergency economic measures Lenin imposed between 1918 and 1921, by introducing a new type of complexity into Rus. poetry characterized by layered allusion, metaphorical density, and the trans. of the contemporary into mythic archetypes. Poetic composition for Mandelstam (as well as for Mayakovsky) was an exercise in multiplying the self and describing its tension points within a tumultuous political and literary context. His later poems, most of which were written from exile in Voronezh in the 1930s, have a Mallarmé-like poise in considering the relation between music and silence and explore consciousness and an intersubjective perception of time and space.

As the Bolsheviks established state-run literary organizations and publishing houses, poets of all schools were mobilized for propagandistic purposes in building the "dictatorship of the proletariat." The poetic landscape changed in direct measure as the new Soviet state progressed in the 1920s through the next stages of civil war and War Communism to the establishment of the New Economic Policy and finally its demise in 1929. Much ephemeral poetry (now collected in historical anthols.), often expressed in the form of versified slogans or songs, captured public jubilation during the October Revolution. Poems by the thousand were written in a utilitarian style to mark technological achievements of the new state, to celebrate workers, and to vilify counterrevolutionaries. Professional writers were not immune to such propaganda. Numerous poetic narratives sympathetic to the Bolsheviks, like *Glavnaia ulitsa* (Main Street, 1922) by the proletarian poet Demian Bednyi (1883–1945), depicted—and approved—the violence inflicted on the peasantry.

A qualitative difference, however, surely marks out masterpieces of Communist poetry from hackwork. Like the constructivists who sought to move art out into the public realm by applying it to mass-produced textiles and household goods, poets of the stature of Mayakovsky, Nikolai Aseev (1889–1963), and the young Nikolai Tikhonov (1896–1979) tried to create a new revolutionary art by joining poetry and agitprop. Nothing was too prosaic to be turned into easily memorizable verse, incl. the endless decrees produced in the new jargon of the regime. The same poets also projected their utopian vision of revolutionary reality by mythologizing the new state and its leaders. Just as he rallied workers to the socialist cause, so did Mayakovsky (whose style was far too modernist for the conservative Vladimir Lenin) in his narrative poems cast the revolution in cosmic terms.

Meanwhile, poets of the so-called neo-peasant school, which included the wildly popular Sergei Esenin (1895–1925) and the Old Believer Nikolai Kliuev (1887–1937), were focused on the countryside: their writings during War Communism caught the hardship of the times in popular folk idiom. Contrary to the image of official propaganda, the neo-peasants frankly depicted the devastated landscapes of Russia during its civil war. Even as the Bolsheviks purged institutions of perceived enemies, the restored free-market economy of the 1920s led to wild bursts of prosperity. The cityscape that Nikolai Zabolotsky (1903–1958) created in *Stolbtsy* (Columns, 1929) combines cinematic montage with Gogolian grotesque, presenting an expressionist portrait of city life. The poets grouped as OBERIU, incl. Daniil Kharms (1905–42), Nikolai Oleinikov (1898–1942), and Konstantin Vaginov (1899–1934), in the years before their arrest and suppression in the early

1930s, created a new style of absurdist poetry that expressed their alienation from a menacing Soviet context by contrasting the grammatical logic of propositions with their sometimes violent content.

By the end of the 1920s, the regime's strong preference for conservative form and lang. in poetry had forcefully curtailed proletarian groups, demoralized the futurists (Mayakovsky committed suicide in 1930), hounded Akhmatova into silence, and marginalized Mandelstam (in whose fate Stalin took a personal interest). Literary institutions, under instruction from Stalin, began to orchestrate the cult of Pushkin as a national poet, culminating in a series of mass events and publications that made this elite poet into a household name, a proverbial byword, and a comrade. The Soviet literary establishment systematically inculcated respect for poetry by pedagogical means, by cultivating a rich children's lit. written in verse and, perhaps above all, by publishing in large print-runs the Soviet equivalent of the Fr. Pléiade eds., the Biblioteka Poeta series founded by Maksim Gor'ky (1868–1936). The 250-plus titles published over the entire lifetime of the Soviet Union signified official acceptance and canonical status for individual poets and poetic movements.

The official requirement that writers adhere to socialist realism, together with Josef Stalin's terror, created a sorry record for Rus. poetry as published from the 1930s until the 1960s. Socialist realism required lit. to deliver a positive message confirming the achievement of socialism and the party's ideals. Form and lang. were to be simple, and all traces of irony and ambivalence were expunged by the censors or preempted through self-censorship. Poetic anthols. devoted to national anniversaries show how quickly poetry fossilized into fixed tropes and ideological clichés; unsurprisingly, the formal blandness and thematic repetitiveness blighted poetry during the Stalinist period.

While the official picture was superficially one of monolithic conformity, unofficial channels led poetry in more creative directions from the end of the 1950s. In the post-Stalin period, and esp. the thaw of the early 1960s, innumerable talented poets were associated with dozens of separate, and often ephemeral, poetic groups that tested official limits. Three misleading perceptions about Soviet lit. in the post-Stalin thaw and subsequent stagnation under the regime of Leonid Brezhnev have arisen: first, that Joseph Brodsky (1940–1996) was the only significant poet at this time; second, that the gulf between official and unofficial lit. was unbridgeable; and finally, that the description "practitioner of unofficial lit." during these years is coterminous with "political dissident." The truer picture is one of interrelated backgrounds and artistic formations joining many major and minor Leningrad poets of the time with officially sanctioned literary groups.

While censorship persisted, the state's efforts to turn out talented poets unwittingly encouraged new directions. Poets trained in a quasi-official literary group like Gleb Semenov's famous LITO (Literary Society) also broadened their horizons by meeting other young poets and sharing unorthodox views and copies of both foreign and Rus. poetry that had been smuggled from abroad. A whole new generation of poets came of age in the 1960s. Akhmatova, who survived official denunciation in the 1940s, was a beacon to younger poets like Brodsky, Evgenii Rein (b. 1935), Dmitrii Bobyshev (b. 1936), and Viktor Sosnora (b. 1937), known after Akhmatova's death as her "orphans." Similarly, another survivor of a legendary era, Pasternak inspired a younger generation in Moscow, and his Zhivago poems remain one of the high points of his oeuvre. Both older writers treated the moral standing of the poet in works that could only be published abroad, such as *Requiem,* published in Munich in 1963, the cycle in which Akhmatova reacted to the Stalinist terror by articulating her grief as a victim and mother and as spokesman for the traumatized people of Leningrad.

For every poet like Evgenii Evtushenko (b. 1933), who moderated his political message for advantage, numerous others followed an anti-Soviet direction. This is the case with Alexander Galich (1918–1977), a master of dissident song, and the subtle strict-form lyric poet Vladimir Ufliand (1937–2007). Many other poets in both metropolitan Russia and provincial cities ignored the transparency and prosaic sense demanded by socialist realism. In this diversity and wealth of talent, we might cite the minimalism of Aleksei Khvostenko (1940–2004); the delightful illogic of the Muscovite Evgenii Kharitonov (1941–1981), which harks back to the techniques and absurdist outlook of Kharms; Igor Holin (1920–1999), who in the mid-1960s applied the jingle-type rhymes of the *chastushka* to questions about identity and ontology; and

Genrikh Sapgir (1928–1999), a member of the Lianosovo group of painters and poets, whose ironical vignettes and epigrammatic brilliance have a moral force. Much poetry circulated unofficially in ms., in samizdat publication in Russia and abroad in "tamizdat" anthols. like *The Blue Lagoon* (1980–86).

In the 1960s, the "guitar poets" or bards Vladimir Vysotsky (1938–1980) and Bulat Okudzhava (1924–1997) achieved popularity as lyric poets and balladeers; their poetic songs eschewed official lang. and were much closer to people's daily lives and concerns, while also expressing subversive countercultural and sometimes implicitly anti-Soviet views. Brodsky's first collection, *Ostanovka v pustyne* (*A Halt in the Wilderness*, 1970), which contained a formally startling tribute to John Donne and a poignant elegy for T. S. Eliot, caused a sensation when published abroad and galvanized the literary underground in Leningrad. Mannerisms and innovations that would become unmistakable appear, incl. his extensive relaxation of verse line through enjambment, intricate stanza forms (a striking contrast with the iambic tetrameter quatrain sanctioned by Soviet practice), aphorism and paradox, religious themes (again, a provocation), and his obsession with time and space. Brodsky voiced a degree of self-irony shared by many if not all his contemporaries, an irony that stripped away the residual mystical status of the poet as spiritual guide and prophet that was a legacy of the trad. from the romantics to Blok. The generation of the 1960s sought wit, novelty, and individuality of voice. A lack of explicit interest in Pushkin is a striking feature among poets from both Leningrad/St. Petersburg and Moscow, reflecting fatigue with his Soviet-sponsored familiarity.

The hist. of 20th-c. Rus. poetry contains many chronological displacements due to censorship. Much poetry written from the 1930s until the 1960s would not officially see the light in Russia before perestroika. Poets who had fallen into disfavor were rarely granted posthumous publication. Tsvetaeva was at the height of her creative powers after leaving Russia, and her unique body of metrically startling narrative and vivid autobiographical lyrics were known clandestinely in Russia to a small readership. During the thaw, while noteworthy eds. were published abroad, the Soviet rehabilitation of figures like Mandelstam and Tsvetaeva was uneven; their work was subject to distortion through censorship and unreliable editing. Their legacy remained more legendary than real until the 1980s.

The same period also saw significant geographical displacement. We should not leave 20th-c. poetry without mentioning the possibly unique phenomenon of Rus. poetry abroad, a stunning and essential chapter in its hist. The degree to which poetry written in Rus. from the diaspora is separate from and even in counterpoint to devels. in Soviet Russia is hard to assess. The poets of the first wave of emigration in the 1920s who achieved lasting distinction had already started writing in imperial Russia or the Soviet Union. The experience of revolution and emigration deeply marked Vladislav Khodasevich (1886–1939), author of two exquisite collections full of bitter self-irony and truculence about the immediate past who sought refuge in nostalgia for the Pushkinian trad. By contrast, Georgy Ivanov (1894–1958), whose Rus. collections had taken up fashionable decadent themes, became increasingly experimentalist and surreal in emigration, while Boris Poplavsky (1903–35) quickly assimilated the program of André Breton and his followers. Despite the large numbers of poets in the diaspora from the 1930s (incl. Vladimir Nabokov [1899–1977], who was a prolific writer of lyric poems), it is not until the third wave of emigration in the 1970s that a generation of truly significant poets, incl. Brodsky, Lev Loseff (1937–2009), and Rein emerges. All came of age in Soviet Russia and took up residence either in the U.S. or Europe. Their poetry was often first appreciated in the West before becoming known to readers in Russia through underground distribution and subsequently in print from the inception of perestroika.

In post-Soviet Russia, poetry quickly regained formal innovativeness, acquired an edge of political unorthodoxy, and reveled in the shock of the new. While many gifted poets born in the 1930s no longer lived in Russia, a generation of young poets born in the late 1940s and 1950s included outstanding lyric talents, among them Oleg Chukhontsev (b. 1938), Elena Shvarts (1948–2010), Ol'ga Sedakova (b. 1949), and Yunna Morits (b. 1937), whose individual voices spoke with uncommon interiority and religious feeling long before the collapse of the Soviet Union. In the post-Soviet period, their poetry continues to develop in familiar directions. Among Moscow poets who bridged the Soviet and post-Soviet division, Aleksei Tsvetkov (b. 1947) and Sergei Gandlevskii (b. 1952) write in the elegiac trad. about core existential questions. While their poems evoke great reaches of the Rus. trad., their grandeur is offset by irony, mordant humor, and highly inventive rhyme. The experience of unfettered freedom in the Boris Yeltsin years lent rampant experimental exuberance to the poet's task in the 1990s. Avant-garde poetic movements reflected the outlook and methods of deconstruction and postmodernism. The act of writing, which in recent memory had carried extreme personal risk, became an act of ling. and philosophical daring for many poets. This is nowhere better seen than in the work of the "metametaphorist" Alexei Parshchikov (1954–2009), as well as the "conceptualists" Lev Rubinshtein (b. 1947) and Dmitrii Prigov (1940–2007) and the "postconceptualists," incl. Timur Kibirov (b. 1955), all of whom were originally based in Moscow. Like the futurists, these poets flaunted their colorful personalities and exploited ling. resources to the full, reconnecting with the trad. of Khlebnikov and Dada while also displaying the assimilative powers of Rus. verse by domesticating foreign writers like the Beat poets. Each in his highly individual fashion combines verbal energy with sarcasm and affected innocence. For many readers, the cleverness with which these writers dismantled the Soviet experience and its made-to-order art remains the most memorable feature of their works. Interestingly, Pushkin's stock rose once again in the 1990s, as post-Soviet avant-garde groups claimed him as a fellow postmodernist.

■ **Anthologies**: *Na Zapade*, ed. J. P. Ivask (1953); *Anthologie de la poésie russe*, ed. K. Granoff (1961); *Poety 1820–1930-kh godov*, ed. L. Ia. Ginzburg (1961); *The Heritage of Russian Verse*, ed. D. Obolensky (1965); *Modern Russian Poetry*, ed. V. Markov and M. Sparks (1966); *The New Russian Poets 1953–1968*, ed. G. Reavey (1968); *Fifty Soviet Poets*, ed. V. Ognev and D. Rottenberg (1969); *Russkaia sillabicheskaia poeziia XVII–XVIII vv.*, ed. A. Panchenko (1970); *The Silver Age of Russian Culture*, ed. C. and E. Proffer (1971); *Poety XVIII veka*, ed. G. Makognenko and I. Z. Serman (1972); *Russkaia poeziia XVIII-ogo veka*, ed. G. Makogonenko (1972); *Poeziia 1917–1920 godov*, ed. A. Mikhailov (1975); *The Blue Lagoon*, ed. K. K. Kuzminsky and G. L. Kovalev, 5 v. (1980–86); *Third Wave*, ed. K. Johnson and S. M. Ashby (1992); *Contemporary Russian Poetry*, ed. G. S. Smith (1993); *Russkaia poeziia serebrianogo veka, 1890–1917*, ed. M. L. Gasparov (1993); *In the Grip of Strange Thoughts*, ed. J. Kates (1999); *The Garnett Book of Russian Verse*, ed. D. Rayfield (2000); *Sto odna poetessa serebrianogo veka*, ed. M. L. Gasparov, O. B. Kushlina, T. L. Nikol'saia (2000); *Contemporary Russian Poetry*, ed. E. Bunimovich and J. Kates (2008).

■ **Criticism and History**: A. Sinyavsky and A. Menshutin, *Poeziia pervykh let revoliutsii, 1917–1920* (1964); *Istoriia russkoi poezii*, ed. B. P. Gorodeckii, 2 v. (1968–69); R. Silbajoris, *Russian Versification* (1968); V. Zhirmunskii, *Teoriia stixa* (1968); B. Eikhenbaum, *O poezii* (1969); V. Markov, *Russian Futurism* (1969); A. M. Panchenko, *Russkaia stikhotvornaia kul'tura XVII-ogo veka* (1973); L. Ginzburg, *O lirike*, 2d ed. (1974); J. M. Lotman, *Analysis of the Poetic Text*, ed. and trans. D. B. Johnson (1976); *Modern Russian Poets on Poetry*, ed. C. R. Proffer (1976); J. M. Lotman, *The Structure of the Artistic Text*, trans. G. Lenhoff and R. Vroon (1977); P. France, *Poets of Modern Russia* (1983); G. Struve, *Russkaia literatura v. izgnanii*, 2d ed. (1984); G. S. Smith, *Songs to Seven Strings* (1984); P. Steiner, *Russian Formalism* (1984); S. Pratt, *Russian Metaphysical Romanticism* (1984); M. Altshuller and E. Dryzhakova, *Put' otreniia: Russkaia literatura 1953–68* (1985); Terras—see "Bylina," "Poema," "Versification, Historical Survey"; W. M. Todd III, *Fiction and Society in the Age of Pushkin* (1986); Scherr; D. Lowe, *Russian Writing since 1953* (1987); E. Beaujour, *Alien Tongues* (1989)—writers of the first emigration; R. Jakobson, *Language in Literature* (1990; includes "On the Generation That Squandered Its Poets"); J. Doherty, *The Acmeist Movement in Russian Poetry* (1995); M. Epshtein, *After the Future* (1995); M. L. Gasparov, *Izbrannye stat'i* (1995); K. Hodgson, *Written with Bayonet* (1996)—Soviet poetry of WWII; M. L. Gasparov, *Izbrannye trudy* (1997); D. S. Mirsky, *Stikhotvoreniia; Stat'i o russkoi poezii*, ed. G. K. Perkins and G. S. Smith (1997); R. Polonsky, *English Literature and the Russian Aesthetic Renaissance* (1998); M. Wachtel, *The Development of Russian Verse* (1998); M. L. Gasparov, *Metr i smysl* (1999); *Rereading Russian Poetry*, ed. S. Sandler (1999); S. Küpper, *Autostrategien im Moskauer Konzeptualismus* (2000); G. S. Smith, *Vzgliad izvne* (2002); E. Lygo, *Leningrad Poetry 1953–1975: The Thaw Generation* (2010).

■ **Web Sites**: Russkaia poeziia 1960-kh godov, http://ruthenia.ru/60s/poets/index.htm; Vavilon, Sovremennaia russkaia literature, http//www.vavilon.ru/.

■ **Works on Individual Writers**: L. Ginzburg, *Tvorcheskii put' Lermontova* (1940); R. A. Gregg, *Fedor Tiutchev* (1965); R. F. Gustafson, *Imagination of Spring* (1966)—on Afanasy Fet; I. Z. Serman, *Derzhavin* (1967); S. S. Birkenmeyer, *Nikolai Nekrasov* (1968); C. Brown, *Mandelstam* (1973); E. Brown, *Mayakovsky* (1973); G. Khetso, *Evgenii Baratynskii* (1973); S. Hackel, *The Poet and the Revolution* (1975)—on Blok's *The Twelve*; G. McVay, *Esenin* (1976); A. Pyman, *The Life of Aleksandr Blok*, 2 v. (1979–80); B. M. Eikhenbaum, *Lermontov* (1981); D. M. Bethea, *Khodasevich* (1983); V. Terras, *Vladimir Mayakovsky* (1983); R. Vroon, *Velimir Xlebnikov's Shorter Poems* (1983); J. D. Clayton, *Ice and Flame* (1985)—on *Eugene Onegin*; J. D. Grossman, *Valery Bryusov and the Riddle of Russian Decadence* (1985); S. Karlinsky, *Marina Tsvetaeva* (1985); G. Freidin, *A Coat of Many Colors* (1987)—on Osip Mandelstam; K. O'Connor, *Boris Pasternak's "My Sister-Life"* (1988); I. Z. Serman, *Mikhail Lomonosov* (1988); D. A. Sloane, *Alexander Blok and the Dynamics of the Lyric Cycle* (1988); S. Sandler, *Distant Pleasures* (1989)—on Pushkin; L. Fleishman, *Boris Pasternak* (1990); S. Amert, *In a Shattered Mirror: The Later Poetry of Anna Akhmatova* (1992); M. Makin, *Marina Tsvetaeva* (1993); C. Cavanagh, *Osip Mandelstam and the Modernist Creation of Tradition* (1995); A. Kahn, *Pushkin's "Bronze Horseman"* (1998); *Joseph Brodsky*, ed. L. Loseff and V. Polukhina (1999); J. E. Malmstad, *Mikhail Kuzmin* (1999); O. Proskurin, *Poeziia Pushkina, ili Podvizhnyi palimpsest* (1999); S. Sandler, *Commemorating Pushkin* (2004); N. Skatov, *Nekrasov* (2004); C. Ciepiela, *The Same Solitude: Boris Pasternak and Marina Tsvetaeva* (2006); L. Losev, *Iosif Brodskii* (2006); A. Kahn, *Pushkin's Lyric Intelligence* (2008).

A. Kahn

S

SANSKRIT POETICS

I. Early History
II. Middle Period: Sanskrit Poetics in Kashmir and Beyond
III. New Poetics in Early Modernity

Sanskrit poetics is an intellectual discipline that accompanied literary production in the highly prestigious medium of Sanskrit for nearly two millennia. The discipline had its roots in the early centuries of the 1st millennium CE and continued uninterrupted into the early mod. era. It formed an important component of the education of Sanskrit literati and of writers, scholars, and artists in other langs. and media.

Indeed, while Sanskrit poetics tended to ignore local langs. in the vast area stretching from present-day Afghanistan in the west to the Indonesian archipelago in the east, it had a profound impact on lit. and culture in these regions. Works on Sanskrit poetics traveled throughout this world and were trans. into many of its langs. A prominent example is Daṇḍin's *Kāvyādarśa* (Mirror of Poetry, ca. 700 CE), a work that was transmitted to southeast Asia, if not to China, and translated into Tamil and Kannada in the south of the Indian peninsula, Pali and Sinhalese in Sri Lanka, and Tibetan (see TIBET, TRADITIONAL POETRY AND POETICS OF) far to the north. Poets, intellectuals, and artists in the Indian subcontinent proper constantly kept up to date with Sanskrit poetics. A case in point is Bhānudatta (fl. ca. 1500), whose treatises on aesthetics inspired early mod. literati in Telugu and Hindi, as well as miniature painters in various Indian locations in the 17th and 18th cs.

The achievements of this long-standing and sophisticated discipline include an unparalleled analysis of figurative lang., as in the investigation of the formal, logical, semantic, and pragmatic aspects of simile and its numerous sister tropes; a complex and overarching theory of readers' emotional response to lit.; and a highly complex semantic-cognitive analysis of denotation, metaphor, and suggestion, ling. capacities identified as enabling the readers' emotional and aesthetic responses.

We can divide the hist. of Sanskrit poetics into three phases: first, an early stage, from the discipline's mostly lost origins in the first centuries of the Common Era to about the 8th c., during which it was primarily concerned with imparting the prescriptions of poetry. A second stage, from the 9th c. to the 15th c., was marked by repeated attempts to turn the early discussion into a respectable, coherent theory, on a par with Sanskrit's other branches of thought, and by an increasing focus on reading rather than writing poetry. During a third phase, which lasted until the early colonial era, Sanskrit poetics reinvented itself as a prestigious theory that attracted thinkers from other disciplines and provided space and tools for philosophical and theological issues outside poetics proper. While this tripartite division is crude and while earlier disciplinary strands continued to thrive concurrently with the new ones, it may help to frame the important voices, topics, and tensions in the long hist. of Sanskrit poetics.

I. Early History. Sanskrit poetics must have evolved late relative to the poetry itself. The first extant works of this discipline are Bhāmaha's *Kāvyālaṃkāra* (Ornamenting Poetry), written in the 6th or 7th c. CE, and Daṇḍin's *Kāvyādarśa*. These works lag behind Sanskrit's first surviving narrative poems and plays by Aśvaghoṣa (fl. 2d c. CE) and Kālidāsa (fl. 4th c.), even though the poetry assumes some codified knowledge about it. It is also clear that Bhāmaha and Daṇḍin follow predecessors whom they occasionally name, and fragments of this earlier discussion are traceable. But it is telling that later authors hardly ever refer to ancient sources: in the eyes of posterity, Bhāmaha and Daṇḍin are the discipline's founding fathers.

Indeed, Bhāmaha and Daṇḍin were deeply influenced by ideas and analytical tools that were first formulated in separate, more established knowledge systems. These include the authoritative Veda-related trads. of grammar, which devised a highly complex descriptive tool kit and a metalinguistic idiom for the analysis of vast ling. phenomena; *Mīmāṃsā* (Vedic hermeneutics), which developed a sophisticated philosophy of lang. for the purpose of clarifying Vedic statements and countering the Buddhist critique of the Veda; and *Nyāya* (logic), which produced, among other things, a comprehensive theory of inference, oral testimony, and verbal debate with the aim of examining the validity of Vedic utterances. Another corollary of Vedic scripture worth mentioning here is the separate science of prosody, which Daṇḍin dubs a "raft for those who sail the sea of poetry." Common to all these disciplines was their focus on lang., a trajectory shared by the nascent poetics. A major question of Sanskrit poetics was what distinguishes the lang. of poetry from other "things made of language," as Daṇḍin put it. In a way, Bhāmaha's and Daṇḍin's works are generative grammars for poetic lang.; Bhāmaha's even has a chapter dedicated to grammatical issues per se.

In addition to the Veda-related knowledge systems, Sanskrit poetics was also influenced by practical and artistic discourses that had a ling. dimension to them. Particularly important in this connection is dramaturgy (*Nāṭyaśāstra*), where aspects of stage plays, incl. plot construction, character types, and various poetic qualities of the script have already been theorized. Although Sanskrit did not develop an independent discipline of rhet., practical knowledge regarding eloquent and persuasive speech, accumulated in South Asian courts and chanceries and preserved in inscriptional panegyrics, also influenced Sanskrit poetics. The latter strand of knowledge, like the poetry it accompanied, was closely associated with the royal court.

These varied influences are apparent in the discipline's early phase, when theoreticians were busy documenting the charming elements of poetry, whether euphonic, syntactic, or semantic, in an approach reminiscent of grammar's description of all elements of the lang. from the level of phonemes on. The key category in this investigation was the *alaṃkāra* or ornament (to the body of a poem), a highly flexible concept allowing for a wide variety of aesthetic effects and analyses. Under this heading, the quintessential literary devices of simile (*upamā*) and metaphor (*rūpaka*) were defined and analyzed according to their propositional structure (A is like B; A is B) and the logical relationship they entail (semblance, identity). The method and lang. for analyzing such figures were borrowed originally from grammar, where both figures were described as occurring in normal nominal compounds (as in *snow-white* or *moon-face*). A second group of alaṃkāras allowed for the intimation of similarity through propositions of "doubt" (*saṃśaya*: "is this a lotus, or is it your face?") and its "resolution" (*nirṇaya*: "The luster of the lotus simply cannot shame the moon. / For, after all, the moon has it soundly defeated. / This therefore must be nothing but your face."). These were modeled after steps in the logicians' syllogism. A third group of ornaments, defined by their emotional content (e.g., *rasavat*, "flavorful"), reflected the insights of theorists of drama, who analyzed a play's ability to evoke certain emotional "flavors" or *rasas*. Other ornaments mimicked courtly speech behaviors, such as the elegant pretext (*paryāyokta*), veiled critique (*aprastutapraśaṃsā*), and artful praise (*vyājastuti*); and still others involved auditory effects, such as alliteration (*anuprāsa*) and twinning (*yamaka*).

In addition to ornaments, two other early categories need mention here: Bhāmaha and Daṇḍin defined a set of literary qualities (*guṇa*s) such as lucidity (*prasāda*) and intensity (*ojas*), and explained how these combine in regional poetic dialects (although these were ideal-type dialects that poets could adopt regardless of their region), and flaws (*doṣa*s) that hinder the success of poetry (anything from nongrammaticality and loose construction to obscenity). The early works also include a cursory mapping of literary genres (both in verse and prose) and of literary langs. of the cosmopolitan variety (which, in addition to Sanskrit, included a few Middle Indic langs. collectively known as *Prakrits*). But there is no attempt to present anything like a rigorous conceptual framework that incorporates all the different elements of analysis. The early trad. was not invested in developing a universal theory of poetics or aesthetics, but rather in cataloging, defining, and illustrating the various figurative and ornamental devices, typically exemplified on the level of single verses created ad hoc for the purpose of discussion and primarily under the catchall category of alaṃkāra.

Nonetheless, the discussion was not entirely particularistic or atheoretical. General aesthetic (and socioaesthetic) criteria were occasionally invoked in debating the value of certain devices. E.g., Bhāmaha did not endorse factuality (*svabhāvokti*) in the description of (typically natural) entities, whereas Daṇḍin believed that such portrayals, although more typical of scientific idiom, are welcome in poetry as well, if the entities in question are pretty in and of themselves. Still, both agreed that a certain type of "crookedness" or indirection (*vakrokti*) is the defining characteristic of poetic expressivity. Precious little is said about this crookedness.

Bhāmaha mentions it in the context of poetic intensification or hyperbole (*atiśayokti*). His example concerns the dita tree: so white is its blossom that it becomes entirely invisible in moonlight, when its presence can only be inferred by the humming of bees. This is not the most straightforward way of describing the tree, but it is precisely the circuitous highlighting of its ties with moonlight, which replicates the hue of its flowers, and with the melodious bees, which call to mind its fragrance, that, according to Bhāmaha, allows the poet to capture its unworldly beauty. For Daṇḍin, a key to poetic crookedness is the poet's exploitation of polysemy and other ling. accidents to create additional layers of signification. This "embrace" (*śleṣa*) of extra signification into the text, a phenomenon far wider in scope than paronomasia and allegory combined, emerged as a serious theoretical problem in Sanskrit poetics, partly because of its capacity to inhabit and replicate the entire spectrum of tropes. Bhāmaha was at pains to contain śleṣa and present it as an encapsulated form of figuration, but for Daṇḍin, it is coterminous with crooked expressivity.

Indeed, Daṇḍin's work offers a subtle but holistic framework, wherein a self-reflexive interplay exists between a host of ornamental devices that liken, intentionally confuse, or blatantly identify entities from the poem's here and now (say, a woman's face) and those of a figurative realm (the moon), and those that playfully question or sever the ties between the two realms: from "distinction" (*vyatireka*), where the face is said to excel the moon; to "dissimilarity" (*viṣama*), where the two are said to be worlds apart; and "incongruity" (*ananvaya*), where the very notion that the beloved's face can have a parallel is effectively denied by comparing it to itself. Daṇḍin's inventory of ornamental devices hints at the relations between such unions and separations and indicates how ling. doubling can heighten the coexistence of these contradictory trajectories every step of the way.

II. Middle Period: Sanskrit Poetics in Kashmir and Beyond. Starting in the last decades of the 8th c., the Himalayan kingdom of Kashmir strove to turn itself into the center of Sanskrit learning and arts. Here, thinkers first ventured to make Sanskrit poetics an independent and respectable science (*śāstra*). Several tendencies typify the long-standing and highly influential discussion on poetics in Kashmir. First was the push for systematization: this trend is first illustrated by Vāmana, who worked at the court of Kashmir's King Jayāpīḍa (r. 779–813) and whose treatise on poetics deliberately mimics Pāṇini's aphorisms on grammar. Among his theoretical innovations, Vāmana demonstrated that the highly heterogeneous alaṃkāras are analyzable within a single and coherent paradigm, as variations on the basic formula of the simile. But while many later thinkers agreed that simile was the core of Sanskrit's figuration, the subjecting of all tropes to a single analysis acquired little following. This failure indicates the danger in oversystematization, when the discipline's multifaceted conceptual insights are put in a formal straitjacket.

A second dominant trend was the large-scale incorporation of semantic theories. An early example is in the work of Udbhaṭa, Vāmana's colleague at the same court. Udbhaṭa sought to move from a formal/logical analysis of tropes to grounding them in specific semantic capacities and cognitive scenarios. Consider Udbhaṭa's own illustration of metaphor: "Pouring moonlight-spray / from their lunar jars, / the night-maidens watered the heavens, / that garden whose blossoms are stars." Earlier writers dubbed the metaphorical identification at play here "forming" (rūpaka), since of the two entities, one—namely, gardeners—lends its form (*rūpa*) to the other—namely, moonrise. Udbhaṭa, however, explained this process not by the proposition of identification or the notion of form lending but by a secondary ling. capacity (*guṇavṛtti*) it necessitates: the primary denotative function of a word such as "spray," as soon as it is equated with "moonlight," is blocked and gets replaced by qualities that are only metaphorically associated with "spray," such as purity and coolness. Rudraṭa, who followed Udbhaṭa by several decades, showed similar tendencies in his innovative analysis of "embrace" or manufactured polysemy (śleṣa). Whereas earlier writers dealt with the tendency of polysemy to inhabit the propositional structures of simile, metaphor, and other tropes, Rudraṭa was interested in exploring the cognitive interplays between the two sets of meaning (supplanting, supplementing, etc.) in a śleṣa and their charms.

A third important tendency was the gradual assimilation of a separate discussion, much of which was also taking place in Kashmir, concerning theatrical performance and the spectators' response to it. Unlike Aristotle's notions of mimesis and catharsis, this debate highlighted a fixed set of eight or nine emotional states on the part of the depicted character and/or actor and the dramatic conditions that allowed the spectator to experience, or "taste," them in a special aesthetic form. Kashmiri theorists were increasingly drawn to discussing such emotional "flavors" (rasas) in poetry as well. Thus, in addition to writing on tropology, Udbhaṭa composed a (now lost) commentary on the ancient treatise on dramaturgy, and Rudraṭa divided his work on poetics proper between alaṃkāras and rasas, although still without a theoretical framework combining the two types of concepts.

All these trends are combined masterfully in the *Dhvanyāloka* (Light on Suggestion) of Ānandavardhana, one of the trad.'s seminal figures, who worked at the court of Kashmir's King Avantivarman (r. 855–83). Ānandavardhana merged the aesthetic theory of drama, which highlights the evocation of rasas, with a teleological hermeneutic model derived from the discipline of scriptural analysis (*Mīmāṃsā*), according to which all the elements of a text are seen as subordinate to the production of a single overriding import (a dictum, in the case of the Veda). For him, the overriding telos of poetry is inducing rasa. This goal cannot, of course, in lit., be achieved by means of artistic performance, as on stage. It comes about instead through suggestion, a semantic capacity beyond denotation and metaphor that, as he points out, none of his predecessors had recognized. This newly discovered ling. power is potentially informative (*vastu-dhvani*) when facts are intimated, or figurative (*alaṃkāra-dhvani*), when tropes are implied; but, in poetry, these analytically separable types of insinuation ultimately culminate in the suggestion of an emotional flavor (*rasa-dhvani*). Indeed, Ānandavardhana subordinated all the other elements his predecessors had identified—and in particular the poetic ornaments—to emotive suggestion, which he identified as poetry's "soul." Ānandavardhana, thus, cleverly inverted his discipline's old root metaphor to support his new theory: literary ornaments, he said, just like bracelets and necklaces, can embellish an already beautiful body, but they cannot explain its intrinsic charm.

Consider a verse by Kālidāsa (fl. 4th c.) describing the god Śiva when awakened from deep meditation by the beautiful Umā: "Śiva, his calm somewhat disturbed, / like the ocean when the moon begins to rise, / cast his eyes on Umā's face / with its balsam pear of a lip" (trans. adapted from McCrea). Umā's lip is identified here with the red balsam pear, and Śiva's disturbed composure is likened to the ocean's turbulence during moonrise, implying that Umā's face *is* the moon. Earlier theorists would have analyzed this verse using the categories of metaphor and simile. But for Ānandavardhana, its poetic effect rests on its emotional content, namely, Śiva's budding love for Umā, which these literary ornaments serve only to enhance. Śiva's falling in love, argues Ānandavardhana, is neither denoted nor brought about through metaphorical usage. Rather, it is suggested by the poet's depiction of Śiva's loss of composure and gazing at Umā's beautiful face. Actors on stage evoke emotional states through bodily gestures, and sensitive spectators can "taste" the flavor of the depicted love. But Ānandavardhana argued that responsive readers too can enjoy the same flavor, thanks to Kālidāsa's skilful use of suggestion. Indeed, he demonstrated that his new semantic-aesthetic theory empowered Sanskrit literati to engage, perhaps for the first time, in serious lit. crit.: he identified the chief emotional components in the great epics, judged some classics by their success in producing a good balance among the different "flavors," and maintained that it is only *dhvani* that explains both the genius of masters such as Kālidāsa and the possibility of meaningful innovation in poetry.

Initially stirring a heated debate, Ānandavardhana's thesis was adopted by all Kashmiri thinkers after 1100 CE. With dhvani as its centerpiece, the Kashmiri strand of Sanskrit poetics emerged as a unified, hierarchical, and powerful theory. The highly influential *Kāvyaprakāśa* (Light on Poetry, ca. 1100) by Mammaṭa, yet another illustrious Kashmiri thinker, provided a definitive synthesis of Kashmiri poetics following Ānandavardhana's intellectual revolution. Mammaṭa used the different capacities of lang. as described by Ānandavardhana—denotation, metaphorical usage, and suggestion—to explain the existence of different grades of poetry. It is at its best when dominated by suggestion that leads to the tasting of emotions (dhvani); ranking second is "ancillary suggestion" (*guṇībhūtavyaṅgya*), poetry whose suggested content is subordinate, aesthetically or otherwise, to what is directly or metaphorically expressed; finally, "flashy" (*citra*) poetry is devoid of suggestion and based only on other ling. capacities. Within this gradation, the discipline's different analytical categories were put to use: suggestive processes and emotional flavors were crucial for the analysis of dhvani, while the charm of "flashy" poetry was analyzed using the alaṃkāra tool kit, which Mammaṭa revisited at length. If Ānandavardhana led a "paradigm shift" in Sanskrit poetics, Mammaṭa signaled the resumption of "normal science." The overall framework he provided invited new studies on alaṃkāras, rasa-related matters (in poetry or dramaturgy), semantics, and cognition, either in independent treatises or commentaries on older works (Mammaṭa's own work in particular). "Normal science" also meant that the new theory was now used in the analyses of poems by leading literati and commentators such as Arjunavarmadeva (fl. 13th c.) and Mallinātha (fl. 14th c.), both of whom lived outside Kashmir.

And yet the discipline's paradigm shift was never complete, as the new paradigm was ridden by several irresolvable tensions. The subsequent discussion was, thus, never entirely "normal" and was primarily driven by these frictions. One important friction was between the new theoretical framework with dhvani at its center and the earlier conceptual apparatus, in particular the alaṃkāras. Note that, despite the rather marginal role Ānandavardhana assigned these devices, he was unwilling to dispose of them altogether. At the same time, his theory, for all its universality, did not really explain the aesthetic effects of individual alaṃkāras, esp. in poetry that was not oriented toward the suggestion of emotional flavors, and this problem found no real solution in Mammaṭa's synthesis. After Mammaṭa, the discipline increasingly regravitated toward the analysis of the expressivity, structure of, and interrelations among the many "ornaments" of poetry. This analysis was carried out outside the dhvani framework and often resisted any overriding scheme. A clear indication of this tension is that Sanskrit poetics, now claiming dhvani as its greatest theoretical achievement, nonetheless came to be called the Science of Literary Ornaments (alaṃkāras), or *Alaṃkāraśāstra*.

Another problem was the location of rasa and how readers accessed it. Ānandavardhana left out of his discussion the mysterious process by which readers "savor" the emotions of depicted characters while avoiding the complications of sharing the love of others or the potential unsavoriness of emotions such as grief or fear. Another pair of seminal Kashmiri thinkers, Bhaṭṭa Nāyaka (fl. ca. 900) and Abhinavagupta (fl. ca. 1000), tried to fill this lacuna by producing yet another semantic theory of literary lang. modeled after Mīmāṃsā, one that came with a groundbreaking aesthetic psychology. Both argued that, just as a Vedic passage that describes a sacrificial act has the *pragmatic* effect of producing a desire to take similar action in the faithful, so lit. has a special kind of "illocutionary" power (*bhāvanā*) to produce an aesthetic experience in readers. This experience, they argued, is necessarily pleasurable because lit. abstracts characters of their individuality, precisely by identifying Umā's face with the moon and similar "alienating" features of literary lang.; it thus enables readers to "taste" love for no one in particular or to experience fear that is stripped of any frightening cause. Rasa is, thus, the experience of emotions in the pure state, outside the boundaries of subject and object, self and other, an experience that leads to a rapturous state that both Bhaṭṭa Nāyaka and Abhinavagupta compared to the religious ecstasy of self-transcendence. In the case of Abhinavagupta, this comparison was further colored by his nondualist metaphysics, according to which the rasa experience resulted from the temporary removal of a veil covering the ultimate self (*ātman*). But whereas Ānandavardhana's theory became a consensus, those of Bhaṭṭa Nāyaka and Abhinavagupta were not: the location and experience of rasa remained an unresolved question. There were even those who postulated that rasa was overrated. As early as the late 10th c., a Kashmiri thinker named Kuntaka cataloged a large variety of aesthetically pleasing elements. These included both "ornaments" and "flavors" but also many other aspects of poetry—from the name of a work to its strategies of intertextuality—all of which he viewed as part of an expanded but very loosely defined catalog of poetry's "crooked" nature. Many of the items on Kuntaka's vast catalog could not find a place in a rasa-dominated theory.

This rasa-centered tension is related to another friction, between Kashmir and the rest of the subcontinent. The centuries-long intellectual hegemony of the small northern vale notwithstanding, work of literary thinkers elsewhere was not suspended. These thinkers paid close attention to the discussion in Kashmir but often had their own ideas about where the discipline should go. Particularly worthy of mention here are King Bhoja of Dhār (r. 1011–55) and the Jain mendicant Hemacandra (fl. 11th c., Gujarat). Both these highly prolific writers composed encyclopedic texts on poetics, and both attempted their own syntheses of the field. Like Kuntaka, both combined the theories coming from Kashmir with a vast variety of other materials, incl., in the case of Hemacandra, ideas about how poets should work and lead their lives. While the syntheses of Bhoja and Hemacandra never proved as influential as Mammaṭa's, they did produce innovative arguments and followers, esp. with respect to the question of rasa. Bhoja saw the Kashmiri discussion as obsessed with the reader, where in fact, he believed, rasa was located in the depicted character. This character-centered model of rasa is crucial to the socially normative function of lit. as understood by Bhoja, for whom the emotional experience of characters such as Rāma functions *didactically* as a model for emulation. As for Hemacandra, two of his direct students, Rāmacandra and Guṇacandra, boldly challenged the Kashmiri theory that the experience of rasa is necessarily pleasant, even when the underlying emotions are not. Rather, they believed, the aesthetic flavor of the emotion is not very different from the emotion itself (i.e., grief is the "flavor" of grief), even if the spectator/reader can intellectually appreciate, and thus enjoy, the skill involved in evoking it. These views reflect an undying resentment against the powerful rasa theory of Abhinavagupta and also, in the case of these Jain thinkers, to its specific theological inflection.

Another noteworthy tension pertains to Sanskrit poetics' constant borrowing from older and prestigious knowledge systems while attempting to establish itself as an independent discipline. A clear manifestation of this tension is in Ānandavardhana's crowning of the hierarchical semantic model, which he borrowed wholesale from Mīmāṃsā, with a ling. capacity not recognized in the discipline of Mīmāṃsā or, for that matter, in any South Asian philosophical school. Indeed, most of Ānandavardhana's immediate critics attacked his postulating the ling. capacity of suggestion for the evocation of rasa. Even after this argument subsided, the need for respectability for Sanskrit poetics and independence as a branch of thought continued to be felt in the subsequent discussion.

III. New Poetics in Early Modernity. The clearest indication that something fresh was happening in Sanskrit poetics starting around the 1500s is that the literary theorists themselves began to label in profusion particular views and viewers as new. Researchers have only started to explore this trend, found across Sanskrit knowledge systems around this time, and identify what, in fact, was novel in the last active period of Sanskrit poetics. Here we will mention several areas of innovation, using two of the discipline's last towering figures as our primary reference point: Appayya Dīkṣita (1520–93), who was associated with several minor courts in South India, and Jagannātha Paṇḍitarāja, so-called King of Pundits at the Mughal court of Shāh Jahān (r. 1628–58) in the north.

Newness in this era consists, first, of a new engagement with the old topics. Early mod. writers approached the received categories with an acute historical awareness of a sort the discipline had never before seen. They tended to write in a pioneering essay style, where the product, in the form of refined answers to older, unresolved questions, was often subjugated to the process: an exercise in the hist. of ideas. An example is Appayya Dīkṣita's essay on simile in his incomplete magnum opus *Citramīmāṃsā* (Investigation of Figuration). While the essay does provide a new definition for one of the discipline's quintessential tropes, it focuses more on previous formulations and the difficulties facing any attempt to capture simile accurately.

Historical awareness is tied to a new methodology, partly related to the procedures and jargon of Sanskrit's Navyanyāya (New School of Logic), of applying unprecedentedly demanding standards of intellectual rigor, consistency, parsimony, and clarity in dealing with the disciplinary issues. This methodology emboldened explorations about which earlier generations had seemed hesitant. Appayya Dīkṣita, e.g., described *suggestion* as a process involving attention to subtle clues and the systematic elimination of alternative conclusions that is not unlike *deduction*. This rather subversive view of dhvani forced Sanskrit literati to revisit a position that had been emphatically rejected many centuries before, namely, Mahimabhaṭṭa's (ca. 1050) critique of Ānandavardhana's "suggestion" as another name for *inference*.

Jagannātha, who wholeheartedly opposed Appayya's views on dhvani, was nonetheless receptive to other bold suggestions inspired by the same rigorous method. Consider, e.g., his breathtaking survey of the views on rasa in his encyclopedic *Rasagaṅgādhara* (Ocean of Rasa), another example of the discipline's new historicity. Here Jagannātha reports not unfavorably that the new view on the rasa experience is that it is based on a temporary identification with a fictive character, made possible by the reader's sensitivity, which is theoretically analyzed as a form of a cognitive defect. It is this "defect" that allows the reader to feel, while the illusion lasts, the character's emotion, such as Rāma's love for Sītā. This novel view, as presented by Jagannātha, audaciously inverts Abhinvagupta's cl. metaphor. For Abhinavagupta, the rasa experience results from the temporary removal of a veil covering the self, but, for Jagannātha's contemporaries, it results from the imposition of a veil. Thus, in this case, the new position moves away from mysticism and metaphysics to a logical stance and a mundanely oriented psychology. The same is true with respect to the joyousness of the experience. For Abhinavagupta, the question receives an automatic and extreme answer in the mystical doctrine of the inherently blissful nature of the self, which needs only to be unveiled to shine forth. But the new position allows for the possibility that the identification with a suffering character may produce a mixture of pleasure and pain, even if pleasure is more dominant.

Another novelty is in the status of Sanskrit poetics, which finally comes to enjoy considerable cross-disciplinary prestige and asserts its autonomy from other branches of learning. Several trends are indicative of this change. First, poetics suddenly began to attract scholars in the authoritative fields of grammar, logic, Mīmāṃsā, and Vedānta, who composed in profusion treatises or commentaries in poetics (Appayya himself is a writer on Mīmāṃsā and Vedānta who took to poetics). Second, reversing the pattern characterizing the previous millennium, concepts and terminology from Sanskrit poetics were now widely applied to other philosophical, theological, and sectarian discussions. The most famous example of this is in the works of Rūpa Goswamin and his followers, who made a new "devotional" (*Bhakti*) rasa the centerpiece of a soteriology, wherein acting in Kṛṣṇa's cosmic play led to tasting his essence. Both Appayya and Jagannātha reject the "devotional rasa," but Appayya himself applies the poetical toolkit to a sectarian debate concerning the theological message of the *Rāmāyaṇa*. Arguing against attempts by followers of Viṣṇu to appropriate this epic poem (and also against Ānandavardhana's claim that its main suggested content is the flavor of compassion), Appayya used his subversive notion of dhvani to assert that the *Rāmāyaṇa* is scattered with subtle clues about the power of the god Śiva and is, therefore, carefully designed to suggest his supremacy. Third, late thinkers such as Jagannātha constantly maintain that the stances of poetics are independent of those of all other knowledge systems. Indeed, at the heart of this "new poetics" is an appeal to the taste and sensibilities of the expert reader as the only authority in a discipline that had a rather turbulent hist. and never possessed a core (*sūtra*) treatise of unchallenged command. This stance is both the source of a new confidence in early mod. poetics and a cause of anxiety when, as in the case of Jagannātha's critique of Appayya, the reader's judgment is thoroughly contested.

Anxiety may also be understood in the context of new external challenges. For centuries, Sanskrit literary culture maintained a largely stable set of conventions, characters, and scenarios; and the basic tool kit of Sanskrit poetics did not significantly change since the introduction of dhvani. But in the second half of the 2nd millennium CE, this long-standing trad. found itself in a radically new political context and facing increasing competition from a series of fully formed and confident literary cultures: regional lits. in Telugu, Hindi, and a host of other South Asian literary langs.; Persian, the prestige lang. of India's Muslim courts, incl. the mighty Mughals; and finally Eng., the lang. of colonial power. The extent to which Sanskrit literary culture reacted to these new challenges is still open to debate. In poetics, to be sure, one can detect the presence of new realities. Appayya Dīkṣita invents a pair of poetic ornaments for the reworking of proverbs, and one of his examples is explicitly presented as translating a popular Telugu saying. Then, there is the "new" position famously reported by Jagannātha, namely, that out of Mammaṭa's three "conditions" for composing poetry—talent, learning, and training—only the first was essential. It has been argued that this stance reflects the new ideal of spontaneity claimed by Hindi's devotional poets. It has also been suggested that Jagannātha's ideas and poetry bear traces of Persian lit., in which he was well versed. These traces, however, are peripheral to the main current of Sanskrit poetics in early modernity. Despite the fact that every writer on alaṃkāra and rasa was fluent in at least one regional lang. and although the regional literary cultures constantly engaged with Sanskrit's cosmopolitan model, Sanskrit poetics remained largely oblivious to devels. in the vernaculars. The discipline likewise ignored Persian, even as many literati received patronage from Muslim rulers and even though some Sanskrit poets undertook daring experiments of incorporation and trans. In the 19th c., when Eng. gradually became the lang. of power, education, and lit. in South Asia, the discipline of Sanskrit poetics, not unlike other Sanskrit knowledge systems, dwindled and came to be studied more as an object of mod. intellectual and cultural hist. than practiced as the living and ever-innovative trad. that it once was.

See HINDI POETRY; INDIA, POETRY OF; KANNADA POETRY; PERSIAN POETRY; RĀMĀYAṆA POETRY; SANSKRIT POETRY; TAMIL POETRY AND POETICS; TELUGU POETRY.

■ **Introduction and Early History:** E. Gerow, *A Glossary of Indian Figures of Speech* (1971), and *History of Indian Poetics* (1977)—the former for looking up the different tropes, the latter for a historical overview; V. Raghavan, *Bhoja's Śṛṅgāra* Prakāśa (1978)—excellent overview of *guṇas*; I. Peterson, "Playing with Universes," *Shastric Tradition in the Indian Arts*, ed. A. L. Dallapiccola (1989)—interplay between objective and figurative; S. Pollock, *The Language of the Gods in the World of Men* (2006)—Sanskrit's cosmopolitan space and vision; H. Tieken, "Aśoka's Fourteenth Rock Edict and the Guṇa *mādhurya* of the Kāvya Poetical Tradition," *Zeitschrift der Deutschen Morgenländischen Gesellschaft* 156 (2006)—poetics and chanceries; S. Pollock, *Bouquet of Rasa and River of Rasa* (2009)—on Bhānudatta; Y. Bronner, *Extreme Poetry* (2010)—esp. ch. 7 on Daṇḍin.

■ **Middle Period**: R. Gnoli, *The Aesthetic Experience according to Abhinavagupta* (1968); K. K. Raja, *Indian Theories of Meaning* (1969); D.H.H. Ingalls, J. M. Masson, M. V. Patwardhan, *The Dhvanyāloka of Ānandavardhana with the Locana of Abhinavagupta* (1990)—annotated trans. of Ānandavardhana's treatise and Abhinavagupta's commentary; S. Pollock, "Bhoja's Śṛṅgāraprakāśa and the Problem of *Rasa*," *Asiatische Studien/Études asiatiques* 70 (1998); G. Tubb, "Hemacandra and Sanskrit Poetics," *Open Boundaries*, ed. J. Court (1998); D. Mellins, "Unraveling the *Kāvyaprakāśa*," *Journal of Indian Philosophy* 35 (2007)—discusses Mammaṭa; Y. Bronner and G. Tubb, "Blaming the Messenger," *Bulletin of the School of Oriental and African Studies* 71 (2008)—frictions in Sanskrit poetics; L. McCrea, *The Teleology of Poetics in Medieval Kashmir* (2008)—main source for this section; S. Pollock, "What Was Bhaṭṭa Nāyaka Saying?," *Epic and Argument in Sanskrit Literary History*, ed. S. Pollock (2010).

■ **Early Modernity**: D. Haberman, *Acting as a Way of Salvation* (1988)—devotional rasa; S. Pollock, "The New Intellectuals in Seventeenth-Century India," *Indian Economic and Social History Review* 38 (2001); Y. Bronner, "What Is New and What Is Navya?," *Journal of Indian Philosophy* 30 (2002); and "Back to the Future," *Weiner Zeitschrift für die Kunde des Südasiens* 48 (2004); S. Pollock, *The Ends of Men at the End of Premodernity* (2005)—influence of vernacular literary culture and Persian on Sanskrit poetics; D. Shulman, "Illumination, Imagination, Creativity," *Journal of Indian Philosophy* 36 (2008); G. Tubb and Y. Bronner, "Vastutas tu," *Journal of Indian Philosophy* 36 (2008)—methodology of new poetics.

Y. BRONNER

SANSKRIT POETRY

I. The Origins of Kāvya
II. Elements of Sanskrit Poetry
III. The Production and Appreciation of Sanskrit Poetry
IV. A Summary History of Sanskrit Poems and Poets

I. The Origins of Kāvya. Lit. in India—and in particular poetry in an early form of the Sanskrit (*Saṃskṛtam*) lang.—has a hist. of least 3,500 years, from roughly the 2nd millennium BCE to the present. An IE (Indo-Aryan) lang. spoken and used primarily by social and cultural elites in early and med. India, Sanskrit continues to serve as a medium of creative expression in mod. India as well. At some point in the early centuries of the Common Era, the descriptive designation *Sanskrit* becomes synonymous with what was previously conceived of as only a sophisticated register of lang. (*bhāṣa*) itself. The word *Sanskrit* connotes sophistication, a lang. that has been "processed," "crafted," and "refined." While ordinarily it is the notion of lang. processed by grammar that is intended in the appellation *Sanskrit*, poetry in Sanskrit—esp. "classical" belles lettres—also bears the qualities of refinement, sophistication, and high levels of craftsmanship.

In the interest of precision and concision, the focus of this entry is on Sanskrit poetry understood as belles lettres *(kāvya, vānmaya, sāhitya)*, whose origins may be fixed around the several centuries prior to the beginning of the Common Era and whose cl. period culminates around the 12th c. CE; Sanskrit poetry more or less in the cl. style, however, continues to be written and received to the present day. The existing corpus from these centuries alone is, at a conservative estimate, at least 1,000 times larger than what has survived in cl. Gr. While certainly relevant to a broader discussion of Sanskrit lit., this entry excludes any elaboration on the multiple genres of Sanskrit poetic lit. that precede, prefigure, and inform what ultimately comes to be called kāvya—lit. (largely in verse and written, though with a strong emphasis on recitation and oral transmission) consciously crafted as an art form that is predominantly secular and humanist in scope. While kāvya can be written in numerous langs.—at least 40, incl. the various regional langs. of premod. South Asia (Prakrit) and the several Jain langs. called the *Apabhraṃśa*—the preponderance of extant poems are in Sanskrit. Kāvya subsumes most poetic forms (lyric, narrative, dramatic, panegyric, etc.), but its significance as "imaginative literature" excludes (for the Sanskrit intellectual trad.) sacred scripture (*āgama*), such as the versified collection of ancient hymns to Vedic gods and poems of Vedic life (*Rig Veda*), e.g., or the flashes of poetry in the early Buddhist Pali canon known as the *Tripiṭaka* (Three Baskets). While often regarded as the "longest poem in the world" (seven times the length of the *Iliad* and the *Odyssey* together) and replete with elements of kāvya, the great epic *Māhabhārata* (The Great Story of Bharata's Descendants) technically falls out of the purview of kāvya since it is regarded as a work of received "history" or "tradition" (*itihāsa*) and also a discourse on ethics and morality (*dharmaśāstra*), likewise the store of versified myths and legends known as *purāṇa*.

Since the *Mahābhārata* sometimes refers to itself as a kāvya, however, and contains within it the widely trans. *Bhagavad-Gītā* (The Song of the Lord)—a lyrically charged philosophical poem regarded both as lit. and scripture—many plausibly consider it as among the earliest Sanskrit poems. The other "historical" epic of the ancient period that complements the *Mahābhārata* certainly fits the category of kāvya by all emic estimations: in fact, the *Rāmāyaṇa* (Rāma's Journey) is considered to be the first poem (*ādi-kāvya*) in Sanskrit and its author Vālmīki the first poet (*ādi-kavi*). Both epics (assuming some semblance of a final form sometime around the beginning of the Common Era) take in a wide scope, subsuming Vedic India's social, political, moral, spiritual, and aesthetic imagination. The *Mahābhārata* creatively details the dynastic struggles and ultimate destruction of early Indian royalty (the self-styled lunar dynasty) centered on Yamuna river settlements north of mod. Delhi. A dramatically tragic and gloomy work—punctuated with moments of romance, comedy, riddles, and hymns, prosaic moralizing, and the epiphanic grandeur of divine revelation (Kṛṣṇa as God)—the *Mahābhārata* has been the single greatest source for later Sanskrit poetry's narrative themes. The poetry of the *Mahābhārata* is often described as a rough diamond, with frequent irregularities in terms of standard grammatical practice (magnificently described and codified sometime in the 4th or 5th c. BCE by the grammarian Pāṇini) and loaded with oral formulas of stock epithets and similes; in contrast are the later *mahākāvya*s (great courtly epic poems) and *muktaka*s (loose stanzas and epigrams), written in pristine cl. Sanskrit and fancied as chiseled diamonds with favored angles and cuts. Unlike the confused status of the *Mahābhārata* as kāvya, the *Rāmāyaṇa* prefigures the major elements (through a narrative of poetry's origins embedded in the story itself) that will come to define Sanskrit kāvya for at least two millennia: a self-conscious literariness that contains complex tropes (of sound and sense) and is composed in the most popular Sanskrit meter (that can be sung, recited, with or without musical instrumentation); a consistent narrative trajectory with choice interludes; and the devel. of the all-important aesthetic concept of *rasa*, or taste (treated below). The structure of the *Rāmāyaṇa* is akin to a classic fairy tale with important culture-specific twists and turns (prince meets princess, evil demon abducts princess, prince defeats demon and saves princess, prince and princess live happily ever after) or of a picaresque novel (hero-prince is initiated into manhood through a series of adventures and misfortunes while exiled from his kingdom). The *Rāmāyaṇa*, reflecting a seminal moment in the dynastic hist. of the kings of the "solar dynasty" clustered around a tributary of the great river Gaṇgā, simultaneously functions as a great devotional text, with the hero Rāma as an avatar of Lord Viṣṇu. Like the *Mahābhārata*, the *Rāmāyaṇa* has been an immensely important source text for later Sanskrit poets.

II. Elements of Sanskrit Poetry. While, according to many proverbial formulations in Sanskrit, the poet is not beholden to any rules, literary theorists over the centuries have observed and marked essential presuppositions for the production and appreciation of Sanskrit poetry. Recent commentators on Sanskrit poetry have emphasized its "impersonal" stamp, its oscillation between explicit frankness and understated sublimity, and its occasionally impassioned or disturbing lyricism. Another aspect of much of Sanskrit poetry is its frequent didactic, proverbial, but generally nonmoralizing tone. Med. literary critics continually emphasize that kāvya teaches softly and indirectly like a lover, whereas other genres teach like a master (*śāstra*) or a friend (*itihāsa-purāṇa*). Ubiquitous also is the notion that the purpose of kāvya is to delight and to create an uplifting (*maṅgala*) atmosphere; to bring pleasure, solace, scholarly and worldly erudition, as well as indirect moral instruction to the audience; and to shower the poet with fame and wealth.

Kāvya is characterized by a polished and self-conscious use of poetic lang. that crosses seamlessly over such generic formulations as lyric or epigram (*padya*), epic (*itihāsa*), drama (*nāṭya*), lyrical prose (*gadya*), extended hymn (*stotra*), and prose narrative (*ākhyāna*, *ākhyāyikā*, *kathā*). Whereas the practice of lit. crit. on individual poems (as well as on prose, drama, etc.) is scanty before mod. times, analysis of the lang. of poetry and the study of its effects have been given ample attention in Sanskrit poetics. Some argue that kāvya presupposes "kāvya theory" and, in essence, they are mutually constitutive, the full appreciation of which (like cl. music) requires some measure of theoretical familiarity and training. The great masters of Sanskrit poetics (from the 6th c. CE onward) draw many of their ideas from earlier texts like the *Nāṭyaśāstra* (A Treatise on Drama), the foundational text on dramaturgy, and the encyclopedic *Agnipurāṇa* (Ancient Lore of Agni, Lord of Fire). For nearly a thousand years, they debate a variety of definitions for *kāvya* and its broader significance. Kāvya can be recited and visualized in performance (*dṛśya*) as in drama, or it can be solely recited and aurally received (*śravya*). Kāvya can be further divided along three formal and three evaluative axes. Formally, it can be prose (gadya), verse (padya), or a mixture of prose and verse (*miśra*) known as *campu-kāvya*. It can be judged as either a superior composition (*uttama*), a mediocre one (*madhyama*), or an inferior composition (*adhama*). The values on which to judge superiority, mediocrity, or inferiority are themselves multiple, one of the most common being the extent to which a poem suggests meaning rather than explicitly delivering it.

The unique creations of Sanskrit poetry are ultimately informed by the lang. Sanskrit's particular ling. characteristics (case inflection, variable syntax and word order, euphonic coalescence of sound sequences, limitless potential to compound words to create specific meaning, etc.) render a body of poetry that is at once flexible and restrained: flexible in that poets are free to create complex syntax patterns and inscribe within them hosts of simultaneous literary effects, incl. extremely complex and subtle rhythms of assonance and alliteration alongside expressions within the same word or compound unit carrying multiple meanings. Even double narrative poems are possible and common in Sanskrit, where entire texts are read in two or more senses. A long parade of more or less interchangeable synonyms for commonly occurring entities goes a long way in providing Sanskrit poets with the freedom to match the sonic with the semantic in ways that are unique, e.g., from what is available to poets of other cl. or mod. Indian langs.

Synonyms also enable the Sanskrit poet to function within the extraordinary restraints placed on him or her by metrical considerations. Since the metered hymns of the earliest Vedic poets, Sanskrit poetry has marked itself—like poetry in other cl. langs.—by strict adherence to metrical principles. Thus, the most common meters consist of four feet with a defined number of syllables (or syllabic instants) allowed within each foot. These meters are governed by certain defined principles (a short or long syllable preceding a conjunct consonant or a diphthong, e.g., is considered metrically long). Caesuras are present, though optional or variable for many meters. Sanskrit poets also work within a circumscribed world of signifying conventions (*kavi-samaya*), although they frequently reinvent these conceits in the service of creating novel images and meanings. Nevertheless, unlike other literary trads. in South Asia, Sanskrit poetry reveals a consistent conformity to the notion that inspiration and imagination flow free so long as they violate neither convention nor a factual precision within that conventionalized world that could stand the test of critical analysis.

While all genres of imaginative lit. fall more or less under the scope of kāvya, the two major divisions of Sanskrit poetry are mahākāvya and *laghukāvya*. The mahākāvya are grand, multicantoed entertainments employing multiple meters and telling a story or a part of a story from one of the great epics or narrative cycles. Laghukāvya, on the other hand, take various forms that reflect such genres as the epigram, short lyrics about seasons, love poetry and erotica, extended devotional poems to gods and goddesses, hymns to nature, reflective philosophical poems, and loose collections of verses on all of the above topics and also such common themes as adolescence and old age, eulogies to kings and patrons, emotional states such as greed and anger, scenes of village and field, and works about all the social groups that comprise the Sanskrit *imaginaire*. These poems may be in any one of multiple meters (or combinations thereof)—easily recitable and memorizable in a variety of tunes and bearing names such as the *vasanta-tilaka* (mark of spring) and *śārdūlavikrīḍitam* (tiger's play). Many Sanskrit poets place as much effort on producing dazzling sound effects as they do on producing profound sense. Often Sanskrit verses are at once compact of form and broad in expression. Imagery is refined, exacting, and concrete, assuming visceral and emotional semiotic codes whose suggestive qualities need to be elucidated by a trained reader. Frequently, Sanskrit poets compose playful verse, fully taking advantage of the extensive punning available to them in the lang. Sometimes, however, kāvya verses can be dreamy or impassioned.

III. The Production and Appreciation of Sanskrit Poetry. According to literary critics, the competent Sanskrit poet must possess, in addition to inborn imaginative power (*śakti*, *pratibhā*), a broad cultural education about the world and its ways (*vyutpatti*). Once the poet has married these two qualities and embarked on his profession as a poet, he must then uninterruptedly practice (*abhyāsa*) his art. Being the creator in the "boundless world of poetry," as the 9th-c. literary theorist Ānandavardhana puts it, the Sanskrit poet could in principle treat any subject he desires. Sanskrit poetry reveals the breadth of the Sanskrit poet's erudition and training. Part of the standard curricula of a Sanskrit poet included such subjects as erotics and scripture, logic and the arts, political science and the natural world, and, of course, Pāṇinian grammar. The able poet could describe with equal facility scenes of city and forest, things royal and rustic, the psychic world of lovers and ascetics, the abstruse details of philosophy and the earthy charms of drunken revelry. In essence, all four of the traditionally formulated Vedic "ends of human life" (*puruśārtha*) were open to the poet's explorations: virtue (*dharma*), power (*artha*), pleasure (*kāma*), and spiritual freedom (*mokṣa*). While the poet is rarely a moralist (in the way authors of philosophical, religious, or legal treatises could be), Sanskrit poetry is filled with moral aphorisms (*subhāṣita*) that often encapsulate in pithy form the spirit of entire passages composed in prose.

According to Sanskrit literary critics throughout hist., one who would appreciate Sanskrit poetry essentially has to have a modicum of the cultural training, sensibility, and experience of the poet in order to be one who can "be of one mind and heart" (*sahṛdaya*) with the poetry. Another way theorists understand the appreciator of Sanskrit poetry is as a *rasika*—one who can "taste" in aesthetic terms the flavors of poetic composition (rasa). The "theory of rasa" stands as the most important discourse of Indian poetics and essentially comprises an entire knowledge system of the modes, mechanics, and psychology of art production and art reception. The eight rasas roughly correspond to the major genres of popular cinema: the romantic comedy (*śṛṅgāra*), the sad story evoking pity (*karuṇā*), the uplifting heroic drama (*vīra*), the action film (*raudra*), gore (*bibhatsā*), horror (*bhayānaka*), the slapstick comedy (*hāsya*), and science-fiction fantasy (*adbhuta*). A more subtle, not universally accepted, and heavily theorized "ninth rasa" is known as *śānta*, or the rasa of contemplative peace that one associates with meditation practice. Alongside these eight (or nine) chief rasas are differently numbered sets of transient aesthetic experiences, such as envy, anxious tension, shame, pride, excitement, depression, confusion, and indignation. Any short or long Sanskrit poem, according to theorists who observe poetry in practice, should have one predominant rasa and perhaps other secondary ones. These same theorists variously characterize the rasa experience of drama and of poetry as either utterly similar, utterly different, or somewhere in between.

IV. A Summary History of Sanskrit Poems and Poets. The early hist. of cl. Sanskrit poetry (distinct from the epic poetry of the *Mahābhārata* and the *Rāmāyaṇa*) ranges from kāvya royal panegyrics (*praśasti*) on stone inscriptions (the earliest one in Sanskrit being the famous Junāgaḍh inscription of Rudradāman from the 2nd c. CE) to free-floating, Indian miniature paintinglike stanzas (*muktaka*) collected later into anthols. (*kośa*) such as the 10th-c. *Subhāṣitaratnakośa* (Treasury of Well-Spoken Verse), collected by a Buddhist monk named Vidyākara, or the 12th-c. *Saduktikarṇāmṛta* (Nectar for the Ears in the Form of Good Verse). Many aphorisms in these collections also come from fable and literary-folkloric texts such as the *Panchatantra* (Five Strategies for Worldly Success), *Hitopadeśa* (Fables Offering Good Advice), and *Kathāsaritsāgara* (The Ocean of Rivers of Stories). In terms of Sanskrit poetry understood as kāvya, however, most commented upon are the lengthy, canto-bound court poems (mahākāvya, *sargabandha*) of Aśvaghoṣa and Kālidāsa, both flourishing one after the other sometime (dates are debated) between the last century before the Common Era and the early centuries of the Common Era. Aśvaghoṣa's two poems describe the early life and awakening of Prince Siddhartha Gautama (*Buddhacarita*) and the Buddha's leading his half-brother Nanda from worldly society to the monastery (*Saundarānanda*).

Kālidāsa—hailed as the greatest of all Sanskrit poets—left two surviving mahākāvya in addition to two dramas and two laghukāvya. The two mahākāvyas treat the regal dynastic hist. of the Raghu clan (*Raghuvaṃśa*), of which Rāmā is the best-known king, and the lyrical retelling of the courtship and marriage of Lord Śiva and goddess Pārvatī, culminating in the birth of their son, the god of war Kumāra (*Kumārasambhava*). Kālidāsa's plays include *Mālavikāgnimitra* (The Story of Mālavikā and Agnimitra), a "middle-class" love story; the *Vikramorvaśiya* (The Story of Urvaśī Won through Valor), whose theme is drawn from the legendary romance of Pururavas and Urvaśī; and the world-famous *Abhijñānaśākuntala* (Recognition of Śakuntalā), about the romance and tribulations of lovers Śakuntalā and King Duṣyanta. Kālidāsa's *Meghadūta* (The Cloud Messenger), a long lyric poem of about 100 connected verses composed in the same meter (*khaṇḍakāvya*), is celebrated as one of the most refined pieces of poetry ever composed in Sanskrit. Most well-known of the "messenger" genre (*sandeśakāvya*), the poem personifies a cloud bringing a comforting message between separated lovers across a vast span of natural and urban landscape, perceptively commenting on the scenes of life below along the way. Another poem attributed to Kālidāsa is the short "Ṛtusaṃhāra" (On the Various Seasons).

After Kālidāsa, there are at least 300 surviving specimens of mahākāvya and numerous laghukāvya. Although there are multiple canons of Sanskrit poetry within which traditional Sanskrit audiences have immortalized significant works, the five model poems of the mahākāvya genre are composed by Kālidāsa, Bhāravi (early 7th c. CE), Māgha (late 7th c. CE), and Śrīharṣa (mid-to-late 12th c. CE). Kālidāsa's two mahākāvya works have already been discussed above. The other three draw the subject matter of their plots strictly from the *Mahābhārata*: Bhāravi's *Kirātārjunīya* (Arjuna and the Kirāṭa), Māgha's *Śiśupālavadha* (Śiśupāla's Slaying), and Śrīharṣa's *Naiṣadhīyacarita* (The Life of Nala). The *Kirātārjunīya* inaugurates a poetic trad. that proudly incorporates the considerable weight of a Sanskrit intellectual's learning with the delicate craftsmanship of a wordsmith skilled in shaping meter, trope, and thought into refined stanzas. The other two poems, by Māgha and Śrīharṣa, have for centuries been studied, commented on, and emulated by Sanskrit intellectuals and poets. Other well-received poems include works by 7th-c. mahākavis Kumāradāsa (*Jānakīharaṇa* [The Abduction of Sītā]) and Bhaṭṭi (*Rāvaṇavadha* [Rāvaṇa's Slaying], aka *Bhaṭṭikāvya*). This latter work artfully tells the story of the *Rāmāyaṇa* while simultaneously exemplifying the aphorisms of Pāṇini's *Aṣṭādhyāyi*, a masterpiece of descriptive grammar from the 4th c. BCE. The *Bhaṭṭikāvya* eventually becomes the major source for the devel. of both an indigenous Javanese *Rāmāyaṇa* trad. and a broader interest in kāvya culture. From the 9th and 10th cs., important works include the *Haravijaya* (Victory of Śiva) by Ratnākara and *Kapphinābhyudaya* (The Rise of Kapphina) by Śivasvāmin. The 11th c. produced several notable mahākāvyas, incl. Bilhaṇa's *Vikramāṅkadevacarita* (The Life of His Majesty King Vikramāṅka) and Padmagupta's *Navasāhasāṅkacarita* (The Life of King Navasāhasāṅka).

Many of the great prose and short poems of Sanskrit lit. were written in the 7th c. Among works of epigrammatic poetry, the most famous is Bhartṛhari's *Śatakatrayi* (Three Sets of One Hundred Verses) on love, life, and world-weariness. Bāṇa's (or Bāṇabhaṭṭa's) romance narrative *Kādambarī* (named after the heroine), Subandhu's *Vāsavadattā* (also named after the heroine), and Daṇḍin's *Daśa-kumāra-carita* (The Tale of Ten Young Princes) rank among the great prose works of Sanskrit lit. Bāṇa's *Caṇḍīśataka* (One Hundred Verses to the Goddess Caṇḍī) and

Mayūra's *Sūryaśataka* (One Hundred Verses to the Sun) represent two of the finest examples of intricate kāvya panegyrics structured around a "century" of verses. The most famous lyric on love's various forms also appears around this time in the oft-anthologized collection of verses known as the *Amaruśataka* (One Hundred Verses of King Amaru), a work that treats the entire spectrum of moods associated with courtship, romance, and consummation in specific social contexts—from the longing for love, its loss and recovery, to specific reactions of elation and depression experienced by lovers at different stages of a passionate relationship. Also from this period are well-known literary dramas, incl. Bāṇa's historical play *Harṣacarita* (The Story of King Harṣa), Harṣa's *Ratnāvali* (Princess Ratnāvali), and Bhaṭṭanārāyaṇa's *Veṇisaṃhāra* (The Tying Up of the Braid). The 8th c. produced one of the great literary dramatists of Sanskrit lit. in Bhavabhūti, whose three plays *Mahāvīracarita* (The Life of the Great Hero Rāma), *Mālatīmādhava* (The Romance of Mālatī and Mādhava), and *Uttararāmacarita* (The Later Life of Rāma) have drawn much comment over the centuries. The last work, a sensitive exploration of the inner conflicts and psychic trauma that torment the characters of the *Rāmāyaṇa*, has been hailed by many over the centuries as the finest specimen of Sanskrit drama. A notable laghukāvya from the 11th c. includes Bilhaṇa's *Caurasuratapañcāsika* or *Caurapañcāsika* (Fifty Verses on Secret Love or Fifty Verses of the Love Thief). From the 12th c., there is the unique and much-trans. work *Gītagovinda* (*Love Songs of Rādhā and Kṛṣṇa*) by the poet Jayadeva; this poem, about Kṛṣṇa and Rādhā's love, has the structure of a mahākāvya but is essentially a collection of lyrics that fuses devotional passion and erotic love in ways much emulated and explored by succeeding trads. of lit., music, dance, and painting.

In a hist. so varied and long, many other kāvya works bear mentioning, not the least of which are the difficult-to-date dramas of the very early playwright Bhāsa, incl. *Svapnavāsavadatta* (The Vision of Princess Vāsavadatta) and the vastly popular *Mṛcchakaṭika* (Little Clay Cart) by Śūdraka. Essentially an offbeat romantic comedy—at the center of which is a financially strapped hero, an intelligent courtesan as his romantic interest, and a sociopathic villain and his entourage—this latter play has been adapted numerous times over the centuries on the stage, in books, and in film. Also important to mention are influential works in Māhārāṣṭrī Prakrit such as Hāla's *Sattasaī* (Seven Hundred Poems)—the oldest collection of lyric poetry in any Indian lang.—and Pravarasena's *Setubandha* (Building the Bridge), both of which preceded and served often as intertexts with kāvya composed in Sanskrit. Govardhana's 12th-c. *Āryasaptaśati* is an especially well-known collection of erotically charged lyric stanzas, modeled on Hāla's Prakrit work and, in turn, profoundly influential for similarly themed works that emerge later in regional langs. like Bihāri's *Sattsai* in Hindi. Prior to but esp. after the 12th c., in the form of genres of Sanskrit poetry already detailed and in newer creative formats, there are hosts of poems and poets that deserve attention. These poems range from the cl. mahākāvya to the historical mahākāvya; messenger poems in the style of the *Meghadūta*; Sanskrit collections of similar works earlier produced in Prakrit; adaptations of popular works; and hosts of erotic, hagiographic, and religious poems (covering the vast spectrum of India's religions, incl. Hindu, Buddhist, Jain, Islamic, and Christian themes). The reader is directed to the 20th-c. lit. hists. of Sanskrit lit. cited at the end of this entry for detailed information about the numerous Sanskrit poems composed between the 13th and 20th cs.

Since the first centuries of the Common Era, kāvya and poetry in the style of Sanskrit kāvya have also been composed and chiseled in the archaeological record of what today are the nation-states of Myanmar, Thailand, Cambodia, Indonesia, Malaysia, and Singapore. Though deserving, Sanskrit poetry from the 19th to 21st cs. has thus far received little sustained scholarly attention. However, poets, scholars, and Indian governmental bodies such as the Rashtriya Sanskrit Sansthan (National Institute of Sanskrit) are promoting the continuing production and study of mod. Sanskrit lit. through various scholarly projects and programs. In contemp. India, Sanskrit poetry continues to be written, performed, and published alongside lit. in the 20 or so other Indian langs. Numerous magazines and jours. (such as *Saṃskṛta Vimarśaḥ* and *Saṃskṛta Sāhitya Pariṣat*) publish the work of Sanskrit poets working in contemp. India, and "gatherings of poets" (*kavi-sammelana*) continue to recite and share their work in centers of Sanskrit learning and diverse public spaces. Since the 1970s, a biannual gathering of international scholars of

Sanskrit known as the World Sanskrit Conference has also provided a forum for poets from all over the world to share their literary compositions with each other.

See INDIA, POETRY OF; PRAKRIT POETRY: RĀMĀYAṆA POETRY; SANSKRIT POETICS.

■ D.H.H. Ingalls, "Introduction," *Sanskrit Poetry from Vidyakara's Treasury*, trans. D.H.H. Ingalls (1968); A. K. Warder, *Indian Kāvya Literature*, 6 v. (1972–92); S. Lienhard, *A History of Classical Poetry: Sanskrit, Pali, Prakrit* (1984).

D. M. PATEL

SCOTLAND, POETRY OF

I. Scots and English
II. Gaelic

I. Scots and English. Scottish poetry has been written in Welsh, Lat., Gaelic, Lallans (Scots), and Eng.; in this section, the concern is for the last two and their admixture. Because Lallans from Northumbrian Anglian is undeveloped, it has steadily lost ground to Eng. (of the 1,200 separate poems submitted to *New Writing Scotland* 5 [1987], e.g., "a bare sprinkling" is in Lallans); nevertheless, just how much freshness, range, color, and memorability it can still command is clear in *Sterts & Stobies*, the Scots poems of Crawford and Herbert, as well as in the poetic prose of W. Lorimer's brilliant trans. of *The New Testament in Scots*.

The main sources of early Scottish poetry are three 16th-c. mss.: Asloan, Bannatyne, and Maitland Folio; however, Andrew of Wyntoun's (ca. 1350–ca. 1423) rhymed *Cronykil* (1424) is the source for what is possibly the oldest surviving fragment (ca. 1286)—eight octosyllabic lines rhyming *abababab*, of which the last three have now epitomized Scotland's hist. for 700 years: "Crist, borne in virgynyte, / Succoure Scotland, and ramede, / That is stade in perplexitie." Several unskilled romances such as *Sir Tristrem* followed these verses before 1374–75, when John Barbour (ca. 1320–95) composed *The Bruce,* Scotland's first literary achievement. A superb story of freedom, this "factional" romance, based on the med. Fr. romance, introduces a new subject matter: Scotland. Barbour, the poet-chronicler, seldom slackens his pace through 20 books of octosyllabic couplets; when he does, it is often to show that he is remembered in Scotland because he himself remembers his countrymen's "hardyment," with such lines as "And led thair lyff in gret trawaill, / And oft, in hard stour of bataill, / Wan eycht gret price off chewalry, / And was woydyt off cowardy."

In 1424, Scotland crowned James Stewart after his 18-year imprisonment in London. As James I (1394–1437), he described Chaucer and John Gower to his court as "Superlative poetis laureate" and under their influence composed "The Kingis Quair." Here rhyme royal, conventional allegory of lover and rose, matter from Boethius, and ME all suggest that this James is the first and last Scottish Chaucerian. The mid-15th c. claims Sir Richard Holland's (ca. 1415–82) *The Buke of the Howlat*, an ingenious beast epic examining Scotland's court life. The late 15th c. claims Blind Harry's (ca. 1440–92) extravagant *The Wallace*, an epic romance in heroic couplets extending Barbour's nationalism; *Cockelbie's Sow*, an anonymous country tale with alliterative play in irregular three- and five-beat couplets; and the anonymous, amusing *Rauf Coilyear*, a satiric antiromance on the theme of a king (Charlemagne) among unaware rustics. The 13-line stanza of *Rauf* (nine long and four short lines of black letter) parodies the old alliterative stanza of *Sir Gawain and the Green Knight*. Last, the anonymous descriptive pieces "Christ's Kirk on the Green" and "Peblis to the Play" start a trad. of rustic brawl that finds new life in the 20th-c. merrymaking of Robert Garioch's "Embro to the Ploy." Other poems in this trad., like Robert Fergusson's "Leith Races" and Robert Burns's "Holy Fair," adapt the "Christ's Kirk" stanza of ten lines, 4-3-4-3-4-3-4-3-1-3 rhyming *ababababcd*, the last as refrain.

Nowhere are the post–World War II advances in Scottish studies more apparent than with respect to Scottish poetry of the 15th c., the Aureate Age, the high creativity of the Scottish Chaucerians or *makars*. Influences on these superior poets are today known to have been not only Eng. but directly Fr. and It., as well as native. At the forefront were Robert Henryson and William Dunbar.

Robert Henryson (ca. 1425–1505?) drew on several med. literary forms (lyric, ballad, pastoral) for his delightful "Robene and Makyne," arguing "The man that will nocht quhen he may, / Sall haif nocht quhen he wald." "The Annunciation" is unusual as religious verse of the Middle Ages in that its appeal is to intellect through paradox; "Orpheus and Eurydice," the most famous of the shorter love poems, masterfully illustrates cl. narration of romance material under Fr. and It. influences. The 13 beast fables after Aesop and Pierre de Saint Cloud are uncompromisingly Scottish. Skillfully, Henryson reveals personality by gesture and remark; delicately, he controls narrative rhythm in a blend of entertaining story and central moral. Political questions within the allegory (e.g., "The Tale of the Lion and the Mouse") present the poet as a democrat in the line of David Lindsay, Fergusson, and Burns. The fable "The Preiching of the Swallow" and *The Testament of Cresseid*, both in rhyme royal, are Henryson's two finest poems, full of charity, humanity, and high-mindedness. Central to the *Testament* is the question of why men made in the image of God become "beistis Irrational."

William Dunbar (ca. 1460–1513) was priest and poet at the court of James IV. Strong Fr. and Occitan influences on a variety of lyric forms are apparent in his 80-odd poems, never long. The temperament is Eur.; the craftsmanship superb in its intricacies, ling. virtuosity, and harmony of sound and sense; the tone variously personal, witty, exuberant, eccentric, blasphemous, and manic-depressive: "Now dansand mery, now like to dee." Dunbar's favorite subjects are himself, his milieu, woman (dame, widow, Madonna), and Catholic Christianity. Some poems, like "The Goldyn Targe," a dream allegory, and "Ane Ballat of Our Lady," belong to the poetry of rhet. and the court; thus, they are replete with the favorite phrase "me thocht," internal rhyme, and aureate diction. Other poems, such as "The Flyting of Dunbar and Kennedie" and "The Tretis of the Twa Mariit Wemen and the Wedo" (the first blank verse in Scots, strongly alliterative), belong to the poetry of ribald speech.

Bishop Gavin Douglas (1475?–1522) and Sir David Lindsay (1490?–1555?) complete the makars' roll. More learned than either Henryson or Dunbar, Douglas focused his dream vision *The Palice of Honour* on the nature of virtue and honor in educating a young poet and, therewith, acknowledged indebtedness to such It. humanists as Gian Francesco Poggio Bracciolini and Petrarch. Douglas's magnum opus is his trans. of the *Aeneid*, also in heroic couplets, the first trans. of a classic into Scots and a major source for Henry Howard, the Earl of Surrey's *Aeneid*, the first Eng. blank verse. Its prologues, notably that to book 7, reveal an individual voice, a wealth of lang., and the typical Scots poet's eye for nature and weather. Sir David, Lyon King-at-Arms, promoter of John Knox, intellectual revolutionary, and early defender of writing for "Iok" and "Thome"—i.e., the common people—in the maternal lang., made his reputation as the most popular Scots poet before Burns primarily on *Ane Pleasant Satire of the Thrie Estaitis*, a morality play or propaganda drama with Lady Sensuality and Flattery as the leads. Blending comedy and common sense, Lindsay gives answer to "What is good government?" in sophisticated verse forms: bob and wheel, eight-line stanzas of iambic pentameter in linking rhyme for formal speeches, and exchange of single lines in couplets of stichomythia.

With Robert Wedderburns's (ca. 1510–57) *Gude and Godlie Ballatis* (assisted by his brothers John and James) and the songs of Alexander Scott (1520?–1583?), national Scotland approached the death of the Eng. queen, Elizabeth I (d. 1603), the Union of the Crowns (James VI of Scotland crowned James I of England), and the loss of court and courtly lang. Such loss, together with the King James Bible, the splendor of Edmund Spenser and Shakespeare, and the victories of Covenanting Puritans, makes it impossible to name one Scots poet of high distinction during the entire 17th c., not excluding Alexander Montgomerie (1555?–97?), poet of *The Cherrie and the Slae*, dream vision and allegory; any other member of King James's "Castalian band"; or William Drummond of Hawthornden (1585–1649), who showed with some success what a Scotsman could compose in Eng. No longer a court lang., Scots lived on as the vernacular of folk lit.: ballad and song.

Scottish ballads represent an oral trad. (see Buchan 1972) of anonymous narrative songs arising in the late Middle Ages to flourish in the 16th and 17th cs. and to be collected in the later 19th c. by F. J. Child. Chief subjects are violent hist. ("Oterborne"), tragic romance ("Clerk Saunders"), and the supernatural ("Tam Lin"). The vernacular is simple and stark, grimly realistic and fatalistic. The vividly dramatic story unfolds through unity of action, characterization, and the relentless pace of the ballad meter. Formula, epithet, incremental repetition, refrain, alliteration, and question and answer also advance the plot. Colors are primary; images are violent ("The curse of hell frae me sall ye beir / Mither, mither"), tender ("O waly, waly! but love be bony / A little time, while it is new"), eerie ("The channerin worm doth chide"), and beautiful ("And she has snooded her yellow hair / A little aboon her bree").

The period from 1603 to World War I produced many poets who began to choose literary Eng. as their medium because they thought it was impossible to use Lallans and be taken seriously. So, James Thomson (1700–48), poet of *The Seasons*; Robert Blair (1699–1746); and James Beattie (1735–1803) used standard Eng. for their remembered works. Sir Walter Scott (1771–1832) retained the vernacular of the ballads he collected and improved for his *Minstrelsy* but chose Eng. for his long poems (*The Lady of the Lake*) and for the excellent songs in his novels ("Proud Maisie"). Lord Byron (1728–1824) and Thomas Campbell (1777–1844) used Eng. and later poets such as Bysshe Vanolis (pseud. of James Thomson, 1834–82) and Robert Louis Stevenson (1850–94) again chose Eng. for *City of Dreadful Night* and *A Child's Garden of Verses*, respectively. Published poetry in Lallans, however, had been kept alive—just barely—until it experienced a significant revival when the 1707 Union of Parliaments had seemed to reduce Scotland to a "region" of Great Britain.

James Watson's *Choice Collection* in two vols. (1706–9) includes Robert Sempill the Younger's (ca. 1595–1663) mock elegy "The Life and Death of Habbie Simpson" (ca. 1650) in a stanza that gives name to the "standard Habbie," better known as the Burns stanza; William Hamilton of Gilbertfield's (?1665–1751) "Bonny Heck" has the same stanza for the last words of a dying greyhound, anticipating Burns's "Poor Mailie's Elegy." These poems are in Lallans. So, too, are such works of Allan Ramsay (1685–1758) as are his invention of the verse epistle (usually in tetrameters), his burlesque elegy on a church treasurer who could smell out a bawd, his poetic drama *The Gentle Shepherd*, many of the songs in his *The Tea Table Miscellany*, and all of the older Scots poems published in his *The Ever Green*. Ramsay's prosody becomes Robert Fergusson's (1750–74); Fergusson's becomes Burns's. Within the vernacular revival, these three poets compose their satires, genre poems, epistles, and comic narratives, principally in six verse forms: ballad meter, octosyllabic couplets, heroic couplets, the standard Habbie, "Christ's Kirk," and "The Cherrie and the Slae." Among Fergusson's poems in Lallans is his masterpiece "Auld Reekie," realistically describing everyday life in Edinburgh, "Whare couthy chiels at e'ening meet / Their bizzin craigs and mou's to weet."

More and more, the measure of Robert Burns's (1759–96) high accomplishment has become the satires like "Holy Willie's Prayer," *The Jolly Beggars*, the narrative "Tam o' Shanter," and the hundreds of songs. The cantata *The Jolly Beggars* has his characteristic merits of description, narration, dramatic effect, metrical diversity, energy, and sensitivity to the beauties inherent in Scottish words and music. Otherwise, hearing a song like "Scots wha hae" or "Ca' the Yowes," each showing masterful skill at uniting words and music, will unforgettably illustrate this genius. To Burns under the Scottish Enlightenment we owe the perpetuation of Scottish folk song. How rich this heritage is has been the further study of those like Cecil Sharp, James Bruce Duncan, and Gavin Greig in the 19th c. and Hamish Henderson and others at the School of Scottish Studies in the 20th. By contrast, literary songs from the 18th c. to the 20th c. tend toward sentimentalism, such as Jean Elliot's (1727–1805) "Flowers o' the Forest" or Carolina Oliphant, Lady Nairne's (1766–1845) "Caller Herrin."

Seldom does 19th-c. Scottish poetry better James Hogg's (1770–1835) idiosyncratic verse. Slavish imitations of Burns strike low, nor rise by the *Whistle-Binkie* (fiddler's seat at merrymakings) anthol. or the couthy (sociable) sentimentality of Kailyard, a type of fiction from about 1880 of rural life, dialect, and sentiment; see James M. Barrie's (1860–1937) *A Window in Thrums* or Ian Maclaren's (pseud. of Rev. John Watson [1850–1907]) verse epigraph. Industrialization and the Calvinist ethic of profitability and genteel respectability bring poets to their knees. At century's close, however, Stevenson composes poems like "The Spaewife" in a literary Scots, the precision of which opposes the Kailyard; "blood and guts" John Davidson (1857–1909) experiments in Eng. with new myths, symbols of science's dethroning religion; and the founder of the Scottish renaissance grows as a lad in Langholm.

Christopher Murray Grieve (1892–1978) initiates the revival of cultural and creative confidence in the 1920s, throwing off Victorian sentimentalism with the war cry "Back to Dunbar!" Abandoning his early Eng. verse, he took the pseud. Hugh MacDiarmid to produce two collections of lyrics in a revived form of lowland Scots (Lallans). The audacious images of love and death in these poems combine expressionist intensity with a fine melodic power and balladlike structures in settings that are both domestic and cosmic:

> Mars is braw in crammasy,
> Venus in a green silk goun,
> The auld mune shak's her gowden feathers,
> Their starry talk's a wheen o' blethers,
> Nane for thee a thochtie sparin',
> Earth, thou bonnie broukit bairn!
> —*But greet, an' in your tears ye'll droun*
> *The haill clanjamfrie!*
> ("The Bonnie Broukit Bairn")

Such verses recall and indeed surpass the lyrical concentration and estrangement of early imagism. MacDiarmid coined another slogan, "Not Traditions—Precedents!," to catch the energy of his masterpiece *A Drunk Man Looks at the Thistle* (1926). This long poem sequence in different verse forms is Whitmanesque in scale, and as a romantic celebration of ever-changing and contradictory modes and moods, it is also modernist, invoking flux and crisis to match what the poet took to be the glorious instability of life itself, not to mention the parlous condition of mod. Scotland.

Taking their cue from MacDiarmid, poets (and poetry) play a leading part in the early years of the Scottish literary renaissance, with William Soutar (1898–1943) aiming to revive Lallans by way of "whigmaleeries" and "bairn rhymes" to capture a young audience. Soutar looked back to the ballad trad., as did Violet Jacob (1863–1946) and Marion Angus (1866–1946), whose eerie Scots lyrics (not without sentiment) anticipated and supported MacDiarmid's early work. In the 1930s, MacDiarmid returns to Eng. for an overtly socialist verse, followed by the free verse and intermittent rhymes of "On a Raised Beach" (1934), one of the finest long philosophical poems in mod. lit. His late work seeks a unifying vision of scientific materialism and world lang. in a densely prosaic "poetry of fact," epic in scale and (rather like Ezra Pound's *Cantos*) finally unfinished or unfinishable. The Eng. lyrics of Edwin Muir (1887–1959) are the antithesis of MacDiarmid's materialistic optimism, as Muir is haunted by a sense of loss, going back to his idyllic childhood in Orkney and the family's traumatic move to Glasgow in 1901. Muir did not support MacDiarmid's program for the revival of Scots lang. and culture ("Burns and Scott, sham bards of a sham nation": "Scotland 1941"), and the two leading poets of the day fell out with each other. Images of frozen time and Edenic expulsion characterize Muir's often symbolic and melancholy verse ("Childhood," "One Foot in Eden," "The Labyrinth"). He and his wife, Willa, were the first to translate Franz Kafka into Eng. ("The Interrogation").

Notable work was done in Scots by Sydney Goodsir Smith (1915–75), whose poetic persona harks back to the rambunctious Edinburgh of Fergusson. *Under the Eildon Tree* (1948) is his masterpiece, as 24 elegies on legendary lovers lead him to confront mortality and desire. The Scots poems of Robert Garioch (1909–81) are closer to contemp. urban speech, whether he is translating the 19th-c. Roman dialect sonnets of Giuseppe Belli or casting a wry and often humorously satirical eye on the pretensions of his fellow citizens in the "Edinburgh Sonnets" or striking a more personal note on the constraints of everyday living in "The Percipient Swan." The verses of Tom Scott (1918–95) and Alexander Scott (1920–89) have a forceful and combative wit, and their commitment to the medium of Scots was taken up in later years by William Neill (1922–2010), who also wrote in Gaelic, and by the tender and understated plainness that is the characteristic Scottish voice of Alastair Mackie (1925–95) and his publisher, the ed. and poet Duncan Glen (1933–2008).

Some of the best poetry of World War II was produced in Eng. by Hamish Henderson (1919–2002), most notably his sequence *Elegies for the Dead in Cyrenaica* (1948); by G. S. Fraser (1915–80); and by the Gaelic poets Sorley MacLean (1911–96) and George Campbell Hay (1915–84). A founder member of the School of Scottish Studies, Henderson wrote his own ballads and was an influential scholar of the folksong revival in the 1950s and 1960s.

The leading lyric poets of what has been called the second generation of the literary renaissance are Norman MacCaig (1910–96) and George Mackay Brown (1921–96), who wrote only in Eng.; Iain Crichton Smith (1928–98), who also wrote in Gaelic; and MacLean, who wrote exclusively in Gaelic. The urbane poet and broadcaster Maurice Lindsay (1918–2009) was a tireless proponent of the cultural revival, editing its first anthol., *Modern Scottish Poetry*, in 1946. MacCaig's first poems were in the syntactically dense and quasi-surreal mode of the New Apocalypse group, two of whose leading members, J. F. Hendry (1912–86) and Fraser, were also Scottish; but the hundreds of short lyrics he went on to write, first in formal verse and later in a succinct free verse, are characterized by clarity, compassion, and an unsentimental delight in the natural world.

These factors, along with his gift for memorable and witty images and a dryly humorous reading style, made him Scotland's most popular poet for over 30 years. Brought up in Lewis and indelibly marked by his Free Kirk background, Crichton Smith's poetry can achieve a piercing lyrical beauty ("Old Woman") with an undercurrent of loneliness and existential unease. Never quite "confessional," his later work was influenced nevertheless by Robert Lowell, with elliptical poems that reflect on exile and on the concept of the island as both a literal and metaphysical place ("Australia").

The "island" for Brown was undoubtedly his native Orkney. Unlike Muir, Brown spent almost all his life in Orkney, creating an impersonally spare free verse modeled on the sagas and the cryptic understatement of OE and ON verse. In collections such as *Fishermen with Ploughs* (1971), the cyclic patterns of farming and fishing are merged with the rituals of Catholic faith and carried across time to invoke archetypes of meaning and value that he could not find in the mod. world. George Bruce (1909–2002) had his own roots in the fishing communities of the northeast of Scotland. His Eng. verse also takes spareness as a virtue, but his vision is extravert and enthusiastic. After an early flirtation with the New Apocalypse and *The Nightfishing* (1955), a long poem that linked net fishing with the creative struggle, W. S. Graham (1918–86) spent most of his life in Cornwall reflecting on the nature of lang. and meaning. Poems such as "What Is the Language Using Us For" and "Malcolm Mooney's Land" show his finely nuanced, meditative, and subtly cerebral lines at their best.

Ian Hamilton Finlay (1925–2006) was also haunted by boats and nets, and the early poems of *The Dancers Inherit the Party* (1960) were influenced by the prosody of Robert Creeley. They offer minimalism, gentle humor, and a Zen-like inconsequence as an antidote to what he saw as MacDiarmid's nationalist stridency and the grandiose ambitions of Anglo-Am. modernism. Finlay matured to become an internationally recognized exponent of concrete poetry, though he was less well appreciated in his home country. The 1960s and 1970s see what might be termed a third generation of poets, such as Finlay, who looked to America or Europe and were less interested in, or even hostile to, the cultural nationalism of the original renaissance. As a correspondent for *The New Yorker* and a major verse translator of Jorge Luis Borges and Pablo Neruda, Alastair Reid (1926–2014) stands outside to reflect on both lang. and place in a poetry that stems from his life in Scotland, Spain, and the U.S. The poetry of Kenneth White (b. 1936) is marked by the Black Mountain school; his long engagement with Fr. academic culture marks the discipline he has called "geopoetics" and his interest in the value of marginal and in-between states. In the 1970s, D. M. Black (b. 1941) created surreal narratives with echoes of Kafkaesque absurdity, while the hip Blakean rage of Alan Jackson (b. 1938) caught the youth culture of the times with street-wise, protopunk performance poems satirizing consumerism, bourgeois hypocrisy—and Scottishness.

The year 1968 saw the publication of *The Second Life* by Edwin Morgan (1920–2010). Although Morgan had published poems (and a verse trans. of *Beowulf*) beginning in the 1950s, *The Second Life*, followed by *From Glasgow to Saturn* (1973), marked his arrival as Scotland's most innovative, influential, and popular poet for decades to come, writing concrete poetry, sound poetry, and "science fiction" poetry, as well as stark reflections on urban deprivation in his native Glasgow ("Glasgow Green"). Looking to Europe, America, and the cosmos rather than to England, experimental and eclectic, Morgan sees Scotland in even wider perspectives of space and time than MacDiarmid ever envisaged (*Sonnets from Scotland*, 1984), and not least in the discreet and finely tender love poems that speak for the poet's homosexuality ("One Cigarette," "Absence," the late sequence "Love and a Life"). Equally adept as a playwright, essayist, and translator, Morgan was appointed Scotland's first national makar in 2004, the year he composed a poem for the opening of the new parliament building.

Scottish writing gained renewed energy in the last 30 years of the 20th c., and poetry was no exception. The finely measured work of Douglas Dunn (b. 1942) comes to terms with class and national identity ("Washing the Coins") in formally structured poems, offering reflective commentaries on the world around him (*Barbarians*, 1979; *St Kilda's Parliament*, 1981; *Northlight*, 1988). The collection *Elegies* (1985) offers an almost unbearably powerful set of poems on the death by cancer of his first wife. At odds with Dunn's almost Georgian decorum, the poetry of Tom Leonard (b. 1944) uses the demotic Scots accent of the Glasgow streets to challenge all preconceptions of what poetry is or can be, along with the conventions of spelling and every social discrimination against those whose voices do not "fit": "if / a toktaboot / thi truth / lik wanna yoo / scruff yi / widny thingk / it wuz troo" (*Intimate Voices*, 1984). Less concerned with MacDiarmid's case for Lallans and the nation, these younger writers are much more engaged with issues of class, identity, and gender. Liz Lochhead (b. 1947) draws on the demotic energy of common lives and voices, in poems infused with subtle speech dynamics, colored by an ironic ear for rhyme, clichés, and puns, and marked by a sharp eye for the female condition in the masculinist culture of her native Glasgow. Lochhead is only the first of the women to have transformed contemp. Scottish writing in prose and poetry. Kathleen Jamie (b. 1962) came to interrogate her Scottish roots starting with the title poem of *The Queen of Sheba* (1994), which throws a wry and energizing light on the stifling of female aspiration in her home village and Scotland at large. Jackie Kay (b. 1961) draws on her own experience as an adopted black child in a working-class Glasgow family, to write beautiful poems transfused with compassion and energy, even as they recognize the pains of sexual and racial difference. Carol Ann Duffy (b. 1955) and Kate Clanchy (b. 1965) found themselves living in England from their early years, but their first sense of transition and ling. difference informs their work and their reflections on sexism in all its forms. Tessa Ransford (1938–2015) is more conventionally lyrical, while the poems of Valerie Gillies (b. 1948) are deeply engaged with ecology and the landscape. Sheena Blackhall (b. 1947) writes in broad northeastern Scots, while Magi Gibson (b. 1953), Dilys Rose (b. 1954), and Angela McSeveney (b. 1964) use Eng.

Lang. and identity are still an issue in the witty Eng. poems of Robert Crawford (b. 1959) who fondly reimagines Scotland's past and present through every kind of eclectic metaphor. He is joined in this by W. N. Herbert (b. 1961). They shared a volume (*Sterts & Stobies*) that revisited and supercharged the "artificial Scots" of MacDiarmid's lyrics to hilarious effect, but Herbert's muse is wilder still, simultaneously intellectual and playful, dense with arcane information and popular culture. Fellow Dundonian Don Paterson (b. 1963) shares something of this esoteric breadth. His work is self-aware, rooted in the real but ironically alert to literature, contingency, and mortality (*God's Gift to Women*, 1997). David Kinloch (b. 1959) reflects tellingly on sexuality and identity, while the long free-verse sequences of Frank Kuppner (b. 1951) generate a unique voice that is formal, even pedantically distanced, low-key, and ultimately strangely moving. The poetry of John Burnside (b. 1955) is much more conventionally lyrical, nuanced by his own Catholic faith, his fine landscapes, and interiors that often seem existentially numinous. The humane verse of Stewart Conn (b. 1936) has been steadily engaged with the interface between personal hist. and culture over many years, while Ron Butlin (b. 1949), Tom Pow (b. 1950), Brian McCabe (b. 1951), Andrew Greig (b. 1951), Donny O' Rourke (b. 1959), Gerry Cambridge (b. 1959), Richard Price (b. 1966), and Robin Robertson (b. 1955) have all made significant contributions to the richness that is the contemp. scene.

II. Gaelic

A. ***The "Classical" Tradition.*** The origins of written Scottish Gaelic poetry are closely entwined with those of the poetry of Ireland, a commonality evidenced in the shared "classical" trad. of the professional court poets, formalized in Ireland in the 12th c. and sustained by a hereditary caste of learned males who had undergone arduous training in established bardic schools (see IRELAND, POETRY OF). Cl. poetry in its strictest form continued to be composed without significant regional variation across Ireland and Gaelic Scotland into the early mod. period (as late as the 18th c. in Scotland), written in a shared literary supradialect, using identical heroic diction and identical meters (based on syllable count rather than the stress patterns of Gaelic speech), with an identical attention to complex rules of ornamentation. Poems of identifiably Scottish provenance are preserved in mss. of the 16th to 18th c. but are many fewer in number than their Ir. counterparts.

The excellence of bardic verse lies in its highly developed lang., its sophisticated allusive style, and above all in the elaborate, subtly modulated music of its intricate metrical patterns. Its limitations inhere neither in subject matter nor technique, but rather in a formalism of conventions inseparable from the office of the professional poet, that of public panegyrist to the great men of his society. Syllabic verse that uses an easier, modified technique and makes concessions to vernacular speech is fairly common too, whether written by professionals or by aristocrats—male and female—who had at least some facility for composing competent verse. All these features of style are displayed in the earliest and principal collection of cl. verse surviving in Scotland: the book of the Dean of Lismore, compiled 1512–42, with the bulk of the Scottish poetic content composed from 1400 to ca. 1520. This ms. provides a surprisingly eclectic sample of the range and thematic variety of syllabic verse: as well as the predictable encomia of court poets for their patrons, we find satire, religious poetry, heroic "ballads" of Fionn and Oisein, moral and didactic verse, and poetry in the Eur. courtly love trad., much of this occasional verse composed by nonprofessionals. A prominent interest in the "argument about women" and the morals of the clergy further links the compilation to Lowland-Scots, Eng., and continental literary cultures. While much of the impetus and early leadership for cl. Gaelic culture came from Ireland, it is clear from the dean's book and other sources that, by the later med. and early Ren. period, some of the Scottish Gaelic literati were as engaged with their multilingual Scottish environment as with the pan-Gaelic world, not least in their preference for a Lowland-Scots-based orthography in "secretary hand" over the *corra litir* script of the bardic schools.

B. ***Vernacular Panegyric.*** The culture of the cl. poets was by definition literate, but oral song trads. (equally old or, conceivably, older) existed alongside the high-prestige bardic productions. The late survival of heroic clan society and the siege mentality brought about by the balkanization of the Gaelic polity in early mod. Scotland stimulated the devel. of a vernacular court panegyric praising the caste of aristocratic warrior-hunters who protected and rewarded their people. Panegyric—organized in sets of conventional images or formulas that work as a semiotic code—is a pervasive style, particularly in the period ca. 1600–1800, with its workings and reflexes traceable even in contemp. poetry. The vernacular bards were not, on the whole, literate, and their work was captured in writing only by 18th-c. or later collectors. Yet, too much can be made of the literacy-orality disjunction, since vernacular poetry continued to express many of the attitudes of cl. poetry and employ many of its tropes, and irregularly stressed meters derived from syllabic versification survived demotically.

Among regularly stressed meters, one of the most distinctive is the so-called strophic meter, closely associated with vernacular panegyric—minimally, an asymetrical verse of two short lines and a longer line, to which musical symmetry is restored through repetition either of the unit or of the final line. A particularly interesting variant, deployed for occasions of high solemnity, allows the poet to stretch the run of short lines from anything between 4 and 14 lines within the same song, creating dramatic crescendos of musical and lyrical tension. The two great early practitioners of strophic forms whose work has survived, Mairi Nighean Alasdair Ruaidh (Mary Macleod, ca. 1615–1707) and Iain Lom (John MacDonald, ca. 1620–1710), are not, as was once claimed, innovators: although MacDonald is exercised by national issues, both are clan poets composing in a strong panegyric trad., and both clearly have the security of established practice behind them—perhaps even extending to before the introduction of Lat. learning.

C. ***The Female Tradition.*** Both Macleod and MacDonald also used meters associated with the subliterary trad. of generally anonymous female composition (typically marked by short verses and more complex refrains and often used for laments). Largely ignored by 18th- and 19th-c. collectors, this "folk-song" corpus has been hailed in more recent times as one of the glories of Gaelic lit., exceptional in its emotional intensity, its rhythmic subtleties, and its apparent lack of artifice. It ceased as an active creative trad. in the course of the 18th c. (in tandem with the demise of clan society), but a large static repertoire was preserved and transmitted well into the 20th c.

D. ***The Eighteenth to Twenty-first Centuries.*** In the dominant male canon, fresh dimensions were added in the 18th c. to the scope and expressiveness of Gaelic poetry, particularly by Alastair mac Mhaighstir Alastair (Alexander MacDonald, 1700–70), the nationalist bard of the 1745 Jacobite uprising, and by the hunter-poet Donnchadh Bàn (Duncan Ban Macintyre, 1724–1812). A highly educated and daringly innovative poet who drew on all the resources of Gaelic, MacDonald is the outstanding literary figure of his age. Along with the controlled, detailed naturalism of Macintyre's "Praise of Ben Dorain," much of MacDonald's work embodies an audacious movement away from clan poetry and aristocratic panegyric. Rob Donn (Robert Mackay, 1714–78), like Macintyre a completely oral poet, is the most subtle satirist in Gaelic lit., while the poetry of Uilleam Ros (William Ross, 1762–90) manifests a wider sensibility—particularly in his anguished love songs—which certainly owes something to his learning in Eng. and the cl. langs.

In contrast to the innovative glories of the 18th c., 19th-c. verse has tended to be judged harshly as the nadir of Gaelic lit., the weak and sentimental expression of a trad. debilitated by the social upheaval of land clearance and mass emigration, the encroachment of Eng., and the nostalgic conservatism of émigré Gaelic communities. But more recent scholarship has highlighted the thematic breadth of songs of the period and their engagement with the technological and sociopolitical changes of their era. Certainly, while the devel. of a mod. Gaelic prose will continue to be seen as the period's greatest literary achievement, an appreciable body of vigorous oral poetry continued to be composed, notably against the background of land politics. The best work of Màiri Mhòr nan Òran (Mary Macpherson, 1821–98) is memorable for its delicate lyricism and its political commitment, while from the university-educated Seonaidh Phàdraig Iarsiadair (John Smith, 1848–81) came powerful, radical indictments of an immoral social order.

After World War I, the oral poetic trad. entered an era of terminal decline: it suffered irremediably from the ling.-cultural shift toward Eng. (in the wake of the 1872 Education Act) and from the loss of its organic context (communal orality centered around the *cèilidh* house) as mod. media and population change fundamentally altered Gaelic society. It showed astonishing resilience in its decline, however, its practice skillfully upheld into the later 20th c. by aging and increasingly isolated song makers. The most formidable of these was the stonemason Dòmhnall Ruadh Phàislig (Donald Macintyre, 1889–1964), who displayed the technical range and mastery of the best 18th-c. practitioners while addressing the issues of his own era. But the dependence of the oral bardic trad. on high-level ling. dexterity and density of diction and its attachment to traditional modes of thought and transmission placed it beyond the reach or tastes of most younger poets following World War II, so that the dominant devels. in poetic practice since the 1940s have been in written mod. poetry, typically by university graduates, and increasingly composed in freer metrics, though with not infrequent reference to the sung oral trad. (Songwriters, meanwhile, increasingly gravitated towards folk, country, and rock idioms.) The poetry of Somhairle MacGill-Eain (1911–96) in particular marked a point of no return, in its extraordinary fusion of traditional and modernist, Gaelic and non-Gaelic sensibilities; George Campbell Hay (1915–84) rehabilitated the subtle movement of older meters and opened up a vast creative space through his multilingual, multicultural adventurism; Ruaraidh MacThòmais (Derick S. Thomson, 1921–2012) decisively developed *vers libre*, a departure of great interest in Gaelic metrics and of irreversible impact in Gaelic poetic practice. Iain Mac a' Ghobhainn (Iain Crichton Smith, 1928–98) and Dòmhnall MacAmhlaigh (1926–89) gave the modernist push further impetus.

The influence of MacGill-Eain and MacThòmais on younger poets has been liberating rather than shackling, and interestingly varied voices came to prominence in the last decades of the 20th c. (incl. those of nonnative Gaelic speakers), some of them startling in their detachment from Gaelic trad. Of these, a good number have gone on to develop an important body of work, e.g., Aonghas MacNeacail (b. 1942), Maoilios Caimbeul (b. 1944), Crìsdean Whyte (b. 1952), Meg Bateman (b. 1959), and Rody Gorman (b. 1960). In the 21st c., new voices have been sparser, with few signs of a wave of poets to rival the exuberant creativity of the 1980s and 1990s, a lull perhaps attributable to the remarkable florescence in fiction writing (supported by substantial public funding) in the first decade of the new millennium.

■ **Anthologies and Primary Texts.** *Scots and English: The Scots Musical Museum*, ed. J. Johnson, 6 v. (1786–1803); *Bishop Percy's Folio Manuscript*, ed. J. Hales and F. Furnivall, 3 v. (1867–68); *English and Scottish Popular Ballads*, ed. F. J. Child, 5 v. (1883–98); *The Bruce*, ed. W. W. Skeat, 2 v. (1894); *Scott's Minstrelsy of the Scottish Border*, ed. T. Henderson, 4 v. (1902); *Traditional Tunes of the Child Ballads*, ed. B. Bronson, 4 v. (1959–72); *Oxford Book of Scottish Verse*, ed. J. MacQueen and T. Scott (1966); *Contemporary Scottish Verse*, ed. N. MacCaig and A. Scott (1970); *A Scottish Ballad Book*, ed. D. Buchan (1973); *Made in Scotland*, ed. R. Garioch (1974); *Collected Poems of S. G. Smith* (1975); *Voices of Our Kind: An Anthology of Modern Scottish Poetry*, ed. A. Scott, 3d. ed.

(1975); *Poetry of Northeast Scotland*, ed. J. Alison (1976); *Modern Scottish Verse, 1922–77*, ed. A. Scott (1978); *Choice of Scottish Verse, 1560–1660*, ed. R.D.S. Jack (1978); *Akros Verse, 1965–82*, ed. D. Glen (1982); *Twelve More Modern Scottish Poets*, ed. C. King and I. C. Smith (1986); A. Mackie, *Ingaitherins: Selected Poems* (1987); D. Dunn, *Northlight* (1988); *The Best of Scottish Poetry: Contemporary Scottish Verse*, ed. R. Bell (1989); D. Lindsay, *Ane Satyre of the Thrie Estaitis*, ed. R. Lyall (1989); *Radical Renfrew: Poetry from the French Revolution to the First World War*, ed. T. Leonard (1990); *An Anthology of Scottish Women Poets*, ed. C. Kerrigan (1991); *The New Makars: Contemporary Poetry in Scots*, ed. T. Hubbard (1991); *The Faber Book of Twentieth-Century Scottish Poetry*, ed. D. Dunn (1993); *Scottish Ballads*, ed. E. Lyle (1994); *The Poetry of Scotland, Gaelic Scots and English, 1380–1980*, ed. R. Watson (1995); *The Christis Kirk Tradition: Scots Poems of Folk Festivity*, ed. A. MacLaine (1996); *Scottish Literature: An Anthology*, ed. D. McCordick, 3 v. (1996); J. Barbour, *The Bruce*, ed. A. Duncan (1997); *The Mercat Anthology of Early Scottish Literature, 1375–1707*, ed. R.D.S. Jack and P.A.T. Rozendaal (1998); *The Triumph Tree: Scotland's Earliest Poetry, AD 530–1350*, ed. T. Clancy (1998); *The Makars: The Poetry of Henryson, Dunbar and Douglas*, ed. J. A. Tasioulas (1999); *The New Penguin Book of Scottish Verse*, ed. R. Crawford and M. Imlah (2000); *Scottish Religious Poetry: An Anthology*, ed. M. Bateman and R. Crawford (2000); *Before Burns: Eighteenth-Century Scottish Poetry*, ed. C. MacLachlan (2002); *Dream State: The New Scottish Poets*, ed. D. O'Rourke, 2d ed. (2002); *Scottish Literature in the Twentieth Century: An Anthology*, ed. D. McCordick (2002); Blind Harry, *The Wallace*, ed. A. McKim (2003); *The Canongate Burns*, ed. A. Noble and P. S. Hogg, rev. ed. (2003); *Modern Scottish Women Poets*, ed. D. McMillan (2003). ***Gaelic***: *Gàir nan Clàrsach / The Harps' Cry*, ed. C. Ó Baoill, trans. M. Bateman (1994)—17th-c. verse; *An Tuil*, ed. R. Black (1999)—20th-c. verse; *An Lasair*, ed. R. Black (2001)—18th-c. verse; *Caran an t-Saoghail / The Wiles of the World*, ed. D. E. Meek (2003)—19th-c. verse; *Duanaire na Sracaire / Songbook of the Pillagers*, ed M. Bateman and W. McLeod (2007)—verse to 1600.

■ **Criticism and History.** ***Scots and English***: T. F. Henderson, *Scottish Vernacular Literature* (1900); J. H. Millar, *A Literary History of Scotland* (1903); G. G. Smith, *Scottish Literature, Character and Influence* (1919); A. Mackenzie, *Historical Survey of Scottish Literature to 1714* (1933); J. Speirs, *The Scots Literary Tradition* (1940); *Scottish Poetry*, ed. J. Kingsley (1955); K. Wittig, *The Scottish Tradition in Literature* (1958); T. Crawford, *Burns: A Study of the Poems and Songs* (1960); D. Craig, *Scottish Literature and the Scottish People* (1961); K. Buthlay, *Hugh MacDiarmid* (1964); D. Daiches, *The Paradox of Scottish Culture* (1964); D. Glen, *Hugh MacDiarmid and the Scottish Renaissance* (1964); F. Collinson, *Tradition and National Music of Scotland* (1966); T. Scott, *Dunbar* (1966); J. MacQueen, *Robert Henryson: A Study of the Major Narrative Poems* (1967); T. C. Smout, *A History of the Scottish People, 1560–1830* (1969); H. M. Shire, *Song, Dance and Poetry of the Court of Scotland under King James VI* (1969); A. M. Kinghorn, *Middle Scots Poets* (1970); D. Buchan, *The Ballad and the Folk* (1972); *Hugh MacDiarmid: A Critical Survey*, ed. D. Glen (1972); R.D.S. Jack, *The Italian Influence in Scottish Literature* (1972); *Robert Burns*, ed. D. Low (1974); R. Fulton, *Contemporary Scottish Poetry* (1974); A. Bold, *The Ballad (Critical Idiom)* (1979); R. Knight, *Edwin Muir* (1980)—best study; G. Kratzmann, *Anglo-Scottish Literary Relations, 1430–1550* (1980); W. R. Aitken, *Scottish Literature in English and Scots* (1982)—excellent bibl.; D. Daiches, *Literature and Gentility in Scotland* (1982); C. Kerrigan, *Whaur Extremes Meet* (1983)—study of MacDiarmid's work; J. MacQueen, *Progress and Poetry, 1650–1800* (1982); *Scotch Passion*, ed. A. Scott (1982)—erotic poetry; *The New Testament in Scots*, trans. W. L. Lorimer (1983); *Concise Scots Dictionary*, ed. M. Robinson (1985)—intro. is Aitkin's excellent "History of Scots"; R.D.S. Jack, *Scottish Literature's Debt to Italy* (1986); W. Scheps and J. A. Looney, *The Middle Scots Poets: A Reference Guide* (1986); T. C. Smout, *A Century of the Scottish People, 1830–1950* (1986); *The History of Scottish Literature*, ed. C. Craig, 4 v. (1987–88); A. Bold, *MacDiarmid: A Critical Biography* (1988); T. Lopez, *The Poetry of W. S. Graham* (1989); F. Stafford, *The Sublime Savage: James Macpherson and the Poems of Ossian* (1989); *About Edwin Morgan*, ed. R. Crawford and H. Whyte (1990); E. Morgan, *Nothing Not Giving Messages: Reflections on His Life and Work*, ed. H. Whyte (1990); *N. MacCaig: Critical Essays*, ed. J. Hendry and R. Ross (1990); P. Bawcutt, *Dunbar the Makar* (1992); *Iain Crichton Smith: Critical Essays*, ed. C. Nicholson (1992); M. Lindsay, *History of Scottish Literature*, 2d ed. (1992); C. Nicholson, *Poem, Purpose, Place: Shaping Identity in Modern Scottish Verse* (1992); *Hugh MacDiarmid: Man and Poet*, ed. N. K. Gish (1993); *Liz Lochhead's Voices*, ed. R. Crawford and A. Varty (1993); T. Royle, *The Mainstream Companion to Scottish Literature* (1993); *Wood Notes Wild, Essays on the Poetry and Art of Ian Hamilton Finlay*, ed. A. Finlay (1995); M. Walker, *Scottish Literature since 1707* (1996); J. Corbett, *Language and Scottish Literature* (1997); *A History of Scottish Women's Writing*, ed. D. Gifford and D. McMillan (1997); *Contemporary Scottish Women Writers*, ed. A. Christianson and A. Lumsden (2000); J. D. McClure, *Language, Poetry and Nationhood: 1887 to the Present* (2000); L. McIlvanney, *Burns the Radical: Politics and Poetry in Late Eighteenth-Century Scotland* (2002); *Scottish Literature in English and Scots*, ed. D. Gifford, S. Dunnigan, A. MacGillivray (2002); J. Sheeler and A. Lawson, *Little Sparta: The Garden of Ian Hamilton Finlay* (2003); *Modernism and Nationalism: Source Documents for the Scottish Renaissance*, ed. M. McCulloch (2004); C. White, *Modern Scottish Poetry* (2004); M. Fergusson, *George Mackay Brown: The Life* (2006); B. Kay, *Scots: The Mither Tongue* (2006); R. Crawford, *Scotland's Books* (2007); *The Edinburgh History of Scottish Literature*, ed. I. Brown, 3 v. (2007); R. Watson, *Literature of Scotland*, 2d ed., 2 v. (2007); *The Edinburgh Companion to Contemporary Scottish Poetry*, ed. M. McGuire and C. Nicholson (2009); *The Edinburgh Companion to Twentieth-Century Scottish Literature*, ed. I. Brown and A. Riach (2009). ***Gaelic:*** See the intros. to the anthols. above; J. MacInnes, "The Panegyric Code in Gaelic Poetry and Its Historical Background," *Transactions of the Gaelic Society of Inverness* 50 (1979); D. S. Thomson, "Gaelic Poetry in the Eighteenth Century: The Breaking of the Mould," *The History of Scottish Literature*, v. 2, ed. A. Hook (1987); W. Gillies, "Gaelic: The Classical Tradition," *The History of Scottish Literature*, v. 1, ed. R.D.S. Jack (1988); J. MacInnes, "Gaelic Poetry in the Nineteenth Century," *The History of Scottish Literature*, v. 3, ed. D. Gifford (1988); D. Thomson, *An Introduction to Gaelic Poetry*, 2d ed. (1989); W. Gillies, "Traditional Gaelic Women's Songs," *Alba Literaria*, ed. M. Fazzini (2005), and "Gaelic Literature in the Later Middle Ages: *The Book of the Dean* and Beyond," *The Edinburgh History of Scottish Literature*, v. 1, ed. T. O. Clancy et al. (2007); T. A. McKean, "Tradition and Modernity: Gaelic Bards in the Twentieth Century," *The Edinburgh History of Scottish Literature*, v. 3, ed. I. Brown et al. (2007); D. E. Meek, "Gaelic Literature in the Nineteenth Century," *The Edinburgh History of Scottish Literature*, v. 2, ed. S. Manning et al. (2007).

R. D. Thornton, R. Watson (Scots and Eng.); J. MacInnes, M. Byrne (Gaelic)

SCOTTISH GAELIC POETRY. *See* SCOTLAND, POETRY OF

SEPHARDIC POETRY. *See* JUDEO-SPANISH POETRY

SERBIAN POETRY. The earliest Serbian poetry dates from the period of the Nemanjići dynasty (12th–14th c.) and is of an ecclesiastical nature influenced by the Byzantine trad. The liturgical verse mostly originated from Gr. sources and was rendered in the Serbian recension of Old Church Slavonic, written in the Cyrillic alphabet. From the 14th c. comes a laudatory poem by Siluan (dates unknown) in honor of St. Sava, who established the Serbian monastery Hilandar on Mt. Athos and was a pivotal figure in reinforcing the Christian Orthodox faith among the Serbs. A prose poem by Stefan Lazarević (1377–1427), *Slovo ljubve* (Of Love, 1404 or 1409), is among the most lyrical texts of the period, as are two elegies by the nun Jefimija (ca. 1349–after 1405), wife of the despot Uglješa Mrnjavčević, one on the loss of her infant, the other in praise of Prince Lazar. The vibrant med. culture of the powerful Serbian state was brought to its knees by the invasion of the Ottomans, who ruled the region until the 19th c. Owing to these politically unfavorable conditions, the Serbian literary scene returned to life only during the Enlightenment. Even during the Ottoman period, however, traditional folk poetry continued to flourish, commemorating important historical events and preserving an awareness of national identity. Although lyric and ballad genres prospered as well, the most famous works are decasyllabic epic songs, in particular one cycle dealing with Kraljević Marko and another with the battle of Kosovo, an event that marked the decline of the med. Serbian state.

Reduced literary activity led to closer ties with Russia and the introduction of the Rus. version of Church Slavonic. The two principal authors of the 18th c. were Jovan Rajić

(1726–1801), who composed an allegorical-historical epic *Boj zmaja s orlovi* (The Battle of the Dragon with the Eagles, 1791), and Zaharije Orfelin (1726–85; *Plač Serbii* [Serbia's Lament, 1761]). Both wrote in the archaic lang. of the intellectual elite, which differed significantly from the vernacular. The Enlightenment introduced a note of individualism, as in the poetry of Lukijan Mušicki (1777–1837), which is dominated by a didactic orientation and cl. motifs.

While the romantic period saw folk poetry used throughout Europe as a way of encouraging greater national awareness, this was particularly true of Serbia. Vuk S. Karadžić (1787–1864) not only systematically collected a vast body of oral songs but proposed the lang. reform based on the vernacular lang. of folk songs and tales that became the foundation of contemp. Serbian. One of the most prominent singers in his collections is Filip Višnjić (1767–1834). Also influenced by both the romantic spirit and folk trad. is Sima Milutinović (1791–1847), best known for his long epic *Serbijanka* (1826), a chronicle of the Serbian uprising against the Turks. His student, the Prince-Bishop of Montenegro Petar Petrović Njegoš (1813–51), wrote work resembling oral epic poetry but using clearer, more refined lang. His most famous works are *Luča mikrokozma* (The Torch of the Microcosm, 1845), a philosophical epic poem in the manner of John Milton; and *Gorski vijenac* (Mountain Wreath, 1847), an epic that offers a vivid picture of Montenegrin life and hist.

A new orientation in Serbian poetry was introduced by Branko Radičević (1824–53), who built on the more diverse rhythms of folk lyric songs but also gradually departed from the folk idiom in favor of the more mod. expression typical of the Eur. scene. Lyric poetry and the romantic spirit remained staples of literary life for decades to come and produced some of the most important Serbian writers of the 19th c.: Jovan Jovanović Zmaj (1833–1904), known for his moving personal lyrics as well as his commentaries on contemp. society; Đura Jakšić (1832–78), who oscillated between elegiac personal verses (e.g., *Na Liparu* [In the Linden-Grove, 1866]) and patriotic poems; and Laza Kostić (1841–1910), a trans. of Shakespeare and author of numerous lyric poems.

The epoch of realism is reflected in the descriptive poetry of Vojislav Illić (1862–94), who also raised the formal and aesthetic bar for later modernist authors. Aleksa Šantić (1868–1924) and Jovan Dučić (1874–1943), two poets from Herzegovina, both continued the legacy of Ilić, the former remaining more of a traditionalist with a focus on a range of themes from love to patriotism and social justice, and the latter very much a follower of Parnassianism with an exceptional feel for the nuances of lang. and form. Milan Rakić (1876–1938) was an intellectually minded poet whose formally impeccable verses, influenced by Fr. poetic schools, are imbued with pessimism and irony. Dark motifs dominate the poetry of another symbolist, Sima Pandurović (1883–1960), for whom love is inevitably tied to the theme of dying. The collection *Utopljene duše* (The Drowned Souls, 1911) by Vladislav Petković-Dis (1880–1917) not only announced a new modernist era but eerily foreshadowed the author's tragic death by drowning. Unlike the more measured poets of his time, Dis often embarked on a journey in his verses, capturing the irrational quality of dreamlike states. Veljko Petrović (1884–1967) was a poet from Pannonia whose poems are filled with mythical motifs of fertile soil.

Although modernism brought with it a number of different orientations, it was expressionism—with its quest for vital immediacy, its merging of the unexpected and irrational, and its pursuit of cosmic heights—that left the deepest imprint. Poetry was liberated from formal requirements, and free verse became predominant. Stanislav Vinaver (1891–1955) took this approach to an extreme by placing exclusive emphasis on sound while rejecting the importance of the semantic level.

Although better known for his prose works, Miloš Crnjanski's (1893–1977) elegiac verses about love and his homeland (*Stražilovo*, 1921) are some of the finest from this period. Other important authors include Momčilo Nastasijević (1894–1938), a poet of folkloric impressionism and conciseness; Rastko Petrović (1898–1949), who oscillates between Slavic paganism and dark expressionist moods; and the pacifist Dušan Vasiljev (1900–1924). The poems of Rade Drainac (1899–1943), a neo-romantic who soon showed a kinship with the surrealist school, reflect in their imagery the technological advancement of his time but also provide powerful emotional landscapes. The prolific surrealist Oskar Davičo (1909–89) is best known for his early poetry bursting with emotion and unusual metaphors. One of a limited number of women poets, Desanka

Maksimović (1898–1993), marked a whole era with her lyrical poetry of exceptional clarity and fluidity. Vasko Popa (1922–91), one of the finest Serbian authors, abandoned the surrealist model and treated poetry as a rational process in which one has to be cognizant of the form. His poems typically form part of a larger cycle. Miodrag Pavlović (1928–2014) is a contemplative poet who often employs images from Serbia's mythical past, while Stevan Raičković (1928–2007) was a melancholic nature-oriented lyricist.

Despite Branko Miljković's (1934–61) premature death, he left a deep mark on the Serbian poetic scene, particularly with his first collection, *Uzalud je budim* (I Am Waking Her in Vain, 1957), a symbiosis of mod. imagery and a heightened sensitivity for lang. Ivan V. Lalić (1931–96) was a neoclassicist of refined expression whose works include a vivid visual component, while Ljubomir Simović (b. 1935) turns toward rustic Serbia for his inspiration. Aleksandar Ristović (1933–94) was a neosymbolist poet of the quotidian, while Jovan Hristić (1933–2002) captured in his measured expression both the elegiac and resilient aspects of life. Belonging to the same generation but representing a host of poetic styles are Borislav Radović (b. 1935), Aleksandar Petrov (b. 1938), Matija Bećković (b. 1939), Rajko Petrov Nogo (b. 1945), Stevan Tontić (b. 1946), Novica Tadić (1949–2011), and Radmila Lazić (b. 1949).

■ **Anthologies**: *Srpske narodne pjesme*, ed. V. Karadžić, 4 v. (1958–64); *Antologija srpskog pesništva*, ed. M. Pavlović (1964); *Antologija novije srpske lirike*, ed. B. Popović, 12th ed. (1968); *Srpske pesnikinje od Jefimije do danas*, ed. S. Radovanović and S. Radaković (1972); *Marko the Prince: Serbo-Croat Heroic Songs*, ed. and trans. A. Pennington and P. Levi (1984); *Anthology of Serbian Poetry: The Golden Age*, ed. M. Dordevic (1984); *Mediaeval and Renaissance Serbian Poetry*, ed. P. R. Dragić Kijuk (1987); *Serbian Poetry from the Beginnings to the Present*, ed. M. Holton and V. D. Mihailovich (1988); *Staro srpsko pesništvo: IX–XVIII vek*, ed. Đ. S. Radojičić (1988); *The Horse Has Six Legs: An Anthology of Serbian Poetry*, ed. and trans. C. Simic (1992); *Songs of the Serbian People: From the Collections of Vuk Karadžić*, ed. and trans. M. Holton and V. D. Mihailovich (1997); *Antologija moderne srpske lirike (1920–1995)*, ed. M. Šutić (2002); *The Serbian Epic Ballads: An Anthology*, trans. G.N.W. Locke (2002); *Places We Love: An Anthology of Contemporary Serbian Poetry*, ed. G. Božović (2006); *An Anthology of Serbian Literature*, ed. V. D. Mihailovich and B. Mikasinovich (2007); *Jutro misleno: Nemanjićsko doba: Zbornik srednjovekovne srpske poezije*, ed. V. Popa (2008).

■ **Criticism and History**: A. Kadić, *Contemporary Serbian Literature* (1964); M. P. Coote and M. Kašanin, *Srpska književnost u srednjem veku* (1975); M. P. Coote, "Serbocroatian Heroic Songs," *Heroic Epic and Saga*, ed. F. J. Oinas (1978); S. Koljević, *The Epic in the Making* (1980); C. Hawkesworth, *Voices in the Shadows: Women and Verbal Art in Serbia and Bosnia* (2000); J. Deretić, *Istorija srpske književnosti*, rev. ed. (2002); D. Andrejević, *Srpska poezija XX veka* (2005).

A. Vidan

SIAMESE POETRY. *See* THAILAND, POETRY OF

SINDHI POETRY. *See* INDIA, POETRY OF

SINHALESE POETRY. *See* SRI LANKA, POETRY OF

SLAVIC POETICS. *See* BOSNIAN POETRY; CROATIAN POETRY; CZECH POETRY; POLAND, POETRY OF; RUSSIA, POETRY OF; SERBIAN POETRY; SLOVENIAN POETRY

SLOVAKIA, POETRY OF. Poetry in Slovakia has evolved amid overlapping lang. trads., incl. Lat., Hungarian, Czech, and Ger. Since the reign of St. Stephen (977–1038), Upper Hungary—today's Slovakia—has been within the orbit of the Western Church. Czech and Slovak speech forms are very closely related, and earlier Slovak writing adhered in general to broadly Czech-derived ling. norms.

Earlier surviving compositions include Lat. humanist works, vernacular ballads of love and war, and much devotional poetry. From 1526 until the later 17th c., the Turks occupied much of Hungary. Some anonymous Slovak love poetry recorded in 1604 is linked by affinity to the Hungarian poet Bálint Balassi (1554–94). Vernacular hymnography is represented esp. by *Tranoscius* (1636), named for its Lutheran Czech compiler, Jiří Třanovský (1592–1637). Love poems include "Obraz pani krásnej, perem malovaný" (Picture of a Beautiful Lady, Painted by the Pen, 1701), by a law student, Štefan Selecký (fl. 1700). A long moralizing cycle of 17,000 lines, *Valašská škola—mravov stodola* (Wallachian School—Garner of

Morals, 1755) was composed by the Franciscan Hugolín Gavlovič (1712–87). Traditional song and balladry abounded, and the story of Juraj Jánošík, a Robin Hood-like bandit figure in 1711–13, captured, and hung from one of his ribs, became a favorite national theme.

A standardized West Slovak produced under the modernizing Hapsburg emperor Joseph II (1780–90) by the Catholic priest Anton Bernolák (1762–1813) was short lived. Its outstanding poet, the father of mod. Slovak poetry, was another priest, Ján Hollý (1785–1849), who translated Virgil's *Aeneid* (1828) and composed, in quantitative hexameters, some cl.-style historical epics, most notably *Svatopluk* (1833). His Theocritan pastoral verse produces a fresh fusion of cl. and vernacular idiom. As a writer in Czech, Jan Kollár (1793–1852), a Protestant pastor and proponent of pan-Slavism, produced a celebrated and monumental sonnet cycle *Slávy dcera* (Daughter of Slavia, 1824, 1832), with a sonorous prologue in quantitative elegiac couplets, lamenting past oppression. The poet's beloved Mína metamorphoses into a Slav goddess's daughter; a pilgrimage traverses the Slav lands, then goes, Dante-style, into a Slavic Lethe and Acheron. Kollár's sonnets (and most later Slovak poetry) use stress-based meters. (Slovak has first-syllable word stress, like Czech, though premod. verse was generally syllabic.)

In the 1840s, Lutherans led by Ľudovít Štúr (1815–56) derived a new standard Slovak from central dialects, fundamentally today's variety (Kollár was antagonistic). Like Herder, Štúr stressed native originality. Poetry, the highest product of the spirit, should take folk song as a starting point, not its goal. Štúr's group energized Slovak poetry. In the revolutionary year of 1848, Janko Kráľ (1822–76) exhorted the villagers to overthrow their landowners. Incarcerated briefly, he then involved himself with pro-Hapsburg volunteers, entered government service after 1849, and virtually ceased writing. In his best work (sharply analyzed by Jakobson), folk idiom combined with a solitary central figure, *divný* Janko (weird Janko)—aspiring eagle-like to soar to freedom but relapsing into suicidal melancholy. Pastor Andrej Sládkovič (1820–72) wrote his lyrical-narrative masterpiece *Marína* (1846) in ten-line, sonnet-like stanzas, inspired by unhappy love. Where, for Kollár, erotic and patriotic love are divided, here they harmonize. Love is no mere sensual adventure of youth: it is a divine gift, enabling Hegelian transcendence, harmonizing body and mind, embracing truth through beauty. Ján Botto (1827–76) is most celebrated for his balladic *Smrť Jánošíkova* (Jánošík's Death, 1862). Tension between fairy-tale-like, messianic visions, and gloomy near-realism places freedom's ideals apart from the human world—where a chasm divides the bandit's dream world from the impassive peasantry.

Post-1867 Hungarian autonomy closed some Slovak high schools, giving the Hungarian lang. preference in education. Pavol Országh Hviezdoslav (1849–1921), a lawyer, became a prolific, preeminent poet. In *Hájnikova žena* (The Gamekeeper's Wife, 1884–86), Hanka kills her would-be rapist, a corrupted aristocrat. The life of the seasons blends with the life of the forest—fetching water, felling trees, picking raspberries, hunting deer, looking at the night stars, the woodland torrent crashing like chains, "which however does not bind, does not fetter legs, or spirit, does not confine in its circle the spirit which flew like an eagle in between the hills, to sate itself with freedom, and feel that it is spirit." Hviezdoslav's Parnassian diction pursues dense textures. His *Krvavé sonety* (Sonnets of Blood, 1919) laments the madness of war, doubting divine justice, ending with hope. Svetozár Hurban-Vajanský (1847–1916), another lawyer and twice-imprisoned newspaper ed., combines realistic and nationalistic notes in his collection *Tatry a more* (The Tatras and the Sea, 1879). The pre-1914 *Moderna* group, close to symbolism, had, as its major poet, Ivan Krasko (1876–1958), with two collections, *Nox et solitudo* (1909) and *Verše* (1912), of musically refined, often ostensibly simple (but enigmatic) lyricism, evoking landscapes of loneliness, melancholy, pessimism, hesitation, in mistily defined (often erotic) situations; Christianity functions here nostalgically, evoking trad. or collapsed values.

The Slovak lang. dominated after Czechoslovakia's creation in 1918. Emil Boleslav Lukáč (1900–79), pastor and parliamentary deputy, evolved from home-and-abroad meditations into tersely agonized erotic and reflective verse and castigatory treatment of social themes. Ján Smrek (1898–1982) established himself as a vitalist and deftly lyrical eroticist. Valentin Beniak (1894–1973) was a more enigmatic word spinner. His topics involve rural hardship, trad. and beauty, existential disharmony, artistic themes of France and Italy, apocalyptic war, with stimuli from symbolism, Czech poetism, surrealism, and folklore. Ladislav Novomeský

(1904–76), a communist of the DAV (Throng) group, although skeptical about poetry's public role, wrote associative, playful, gently melancholy, reminiscing, social, and personal avant-garde verses, loosely related to Czech poetism. Later, he recalled his 1952 incarceration as a "bourgeois nationalist" (rehabilitated 1962) but reaffirmed his socialism. Surrealism's chief voice was Rudolf Fabry (1915–82), with arresting imagery and phrases, e.g., in *Vodné hodiny piesočné* (Water Sandglass, 1938). Slovak *Nadrealismus* (suprarealism) also espoused antifascism.

Leading post-1945 and post-Stalinist names include Miroslav Válek (1927–91) and Milan Rúfus (1928–2009). Women have now become more prominent: Maša Hal'amová (1908–95), the intimate Viera Prokešová (1957–2008), the sexually provocative Taťjana Lehenová (b. 1961), and the complex, psychologically probing Mila Haugová (b. 1942). In the bilingual volume *Six Slovak Poets* (2010), Haugová is placed alongside Ján Buzássy (b. 1935), Ivan Štrpka (b. 1941), Peter Repka (b. 1944), and Kamil Peteraj (b. 1945)—poets all variously meditative, inward, complex, elusive, or cryptic—as well as the younger Daniel Hevier (b. 1955), representing a more humorous poetic streak.

See CZECH POETRY; HUNGARY, POETRY OF.

■ **Anthologies and Translations**: J. Botto, *The Death of Jánošík*, trans. I. J. Kramoris (1944); *Anthology of Slovak Poetry*, trans. I. J. Kramoris (1947); *The Linden Tree*, ed. M. Otruba and Z. Pešat (1963); P. O. Hviezdoslav, *A Song of Blood: Krvavé sonety*, trans. J. Vajda (1972); *Janko Kráľ 1822–1972*, trans. J. Vajda (1972); *Anthology of Slovak Literature*, ed. A. Cincura (1976); *Not Waiting for Miracles: Seventeen Contemporary Slovak Poets*, trans. J. Sutherland-Smith, V. Sutherland-Smith, Š. Allen (1993); M. Válek, *The Ground beneath Our Feet*, trans. E. Osers (1996); J. Buzássy, *Melancholy Hunter*, trans. J. Sutherland-Smith and V. Sutherland-Smith (2001); M. Haugová, *Scent of the Unseen*, trans. J. Sutherland-Smith and V. Sutherland-Smith (2003); *In Search of Beauty: An Anthology of Contemporary Slovak Poetry in English*, trans. J. Sutherland-Smith and J. Bajánek (2003); L. Novomeský, *Slovak Spring*, trans. J. Minahane (2004); M. Rúfus, *And That's the Truth*, trans. E. Osers, J. Sutherland-Smith, V. Sutherland-Smith (2006); *Six Slovak Poets*, trans. J. Minahane (2010).

■ **Criticism and History**: R. Jakobson, "The Grammatical Structure of Janko Kráľ's Verses," *Sborník filozofickej fakulty Univerzity Komenského* 16 (1964); S. Šmatlák, *Hviezdoslav: A National and World Poet* (1969); P. Brock, *The Slovak National Awakening* (1976); G. J. Kovtun, *Czech and Slovak Literature in English: A Bibliography*, 2d ed. (1988); *The Everyman Companion to East European Literature*, ed. R. Pynsent and S. Kanikova (1993); *Traveller's Literary Companion to Eastern and Central Europe*, ed. J. Naughton (1995); P. Petro, *History of Slovak Literature* (1996); V. Petrík, *Slovakia and Its Literature* (2001).

J. NAUGHTON

SLOVENIAN POETRY. *Brižinski spomeniki* (Monuments of Freising, ca. 10th c.), a semi-poetic trans. of three religious texts into Slovenian, are the oldest recorded documents in the Lat. alphabet in any mod. Slavic lang. Not until the Protestant era many centuries later was the first poem proper written in Slovenian. Primož Trubar (1508–86) paved the way for the Slovene literary lang. with his composition of several original religious poems.

The first to write poetry of artistic value was the Franciscan friar Valentin Vodnik (1758–1819). But during the romantic period, France Prežeren (1800–49) developed Slovenian to as yet unequalled artistic heights. He is still considered the greatest Slovenian poet; he played an important role in establishing the Slovenian nation and is the author of the Slovene anthem.

The poetry of Simon Jenko (1835–69) marks the transition from late romantic poetry to the work of four modernist poets of the late 19th c.: Oton Župančič (1878–1949), Josip Murn (1879–1901), Dragottin Kette (1876–99), and Ivan Cankar (1876–1918), who later become the leading Slovenian writer.

Expressionism became the leading influence in the early 20th c., giving rise to revolutionary poetry during World War II. Numerous poets, incl. the apocalyptic Miran Jarc (1900–42), Edvard Kocbek (1904–81), Božo Vodušek (1905–78), and Lojze Krakar (1926–95), later joined by the revolutionary poets Matej Bor (1913–93) and Karel Destovnik Kajuh (1922–44), became strong social critics, while France Balantič (1921–43), a devout Catholic, died battling the partisan resistance.

The two leading 20th-c. Slovenian poets are Srečko Kosovel (1904–26) and Edvard Kocbek. Kosovel reached the peak of his short but creative life in his avant-garde constructivist poetry, published over 40 years after his death in 1926. Kocbek suffered under the post-World

War II regime because of his dissident views, but his poetry of cosmic energy and vision never voiced complaints.

Postwar poets faced the political suppression of free speech. The work of such poets as Jože Udovič (1912–86), Dane Zajc (1929–2008), Gregor Strniša (1930–70), Kajetan Kovič (1931–2014), Veno Taufer (b. 1933), Saša Vegri (1934–2010), Niko Grafenauer (b. 1940), and Svetlana Makarovič (b. 1939) became intimate, full of double meanings, and surrealistic imagery.

The next generation of poets—incl. Franci Zagoričnik (1933–97), Tomaž Šalamun (1941–2014), Iztok Geister (b. 1945), Andrej Brvar (b. 1945), Aleš Kernmauner (1946–66), Andrej Medved (b. 1947), Matjaž Hanžek (b. 1949), and Ivo Volarič-Feo (1948–2010)—deconstructed the semantic use of the word and turned it into a graphic or textual element. This poetic transformation paralleled political changes that allowed poets to explore their newly discovered freedom of expression. The new formalists Milan Dekleva (b. 1946), Ivo Svetina (b. 1948), Milan Jesih (b. 1950), and Boris A. Novak (b. 1953) went back to cl. poetic forms, while the generation of Vojko Gorjan (1949–75), Marjan Strojan (b. 1949), Jure Detela (1951–92), Iztok Osojnik (b. 1951), and Vladimir Memon (1953–80) clung to free verse, insisting rather on a radical ethical stance.

Since the 1980s, there have been two poetic trends: the postmodernists Tone Škrjanec (b. 1953), Aldo Žerjal (b. 1957), Brane Mozetič (b. 1958), Aleš Debeljak (1961–2016), Alojz Ihan (b. 1961), Uroš Zupan (b. 1963), Peter Semolič (b. 1967), Primož Čučnik (b. 1971), Miklavž Komelj (b. 1973), Aleš Šteger (b. 1973), and Gregor Podlogar (b. 1974); and a group of women poets representing the strongest creative force in contemp. Slovene poetry, incl. Meta Kušar (b. 1952), Maja Vidmar (b. 1961), Tatjana Soldo (1962–92), Barbara Korun (b. 1963), Taja Kramberger (b. 1970), and Lucija Stupica (b. 1971).

■ **Anthologies**: *Iz roda v rod duh išče pot*, ed. J. Menart (1962); *Afterwards Slovenian Writing, 1945–1995*, ed. A. Zawacki (1999); *The Imagination of Terra Incognita*, ed. A. Debeljak (1999); *Nova slovenska lirika*, ed. R. Dabo (2002); "Unlocking the Aquarium: Contemporary Writing from Slovenia," ed. F. Sampson, A. Jelnikar, I. Osojnik, *Orient Express* 5 (2004)—spec. iss.; *Nevihta sladkih rož, Antologija slovenske poezije 20. stoletja*, ed. P. Kolšek (2006).

■ **Criticism and History**: B. Paternu, *Od ekspresionizma do postmoderne* (1965); *Slovenska književnost, Leksikon Cankarjeve založbe*, ed. K. Dolinar et al. (1982); J. Pogačnik, *Twentieth-Century Slovene Literature*, trans. A. Čeh (1989); B. A. Novak, "Poetry in the Slovene Language," trans. A. McDonell Duf, *Left Curve* 22 (1997), http://www.leftcurve.org/LC22WebPages/slovene.html; *Slovenska književnost I, II, III*, ed. J. Pogačnik and F. Zadravec (1998–2000); M. Mitrovič, *Geschichte der slowenischen Literatur* (2001); D. Poniž, *Beseda se vzdiguje v dim, stoletje slovenske lirike 1900–2000* (2000); I. Popov Novak, *Sprehodi po slovenski književnosti* (2003).

■ **Web Sites**: *Slovenia, Poetry International Web*, http://slovenia.poetryinternationalweb.org/piw_cms/cms/cms_module/index.php?obj_id=23.

I. Osojnik

SOMALI POETRY. Poetry is at the core of Somali expressive culture and, until relatively recently, was composed, memorized, and disseminated in purely oral form. There are many genres, some folkloric in nature, such as work songs that accompany rural activities like watering camels, weaving mats, or loading camels. These songs may be widespread, but the original composer is no longer known. They are short and are often performed in sequence; furthermore, they may be changed by anyone who wishes to do so. They may also be composed to convey messages allusively to people within earshot to whom the performer might not be able to present his or her thoughts directly. Of the dance-song genres, such as *dhaanto* and *wiglo*, some are specific to certain areas of the Somali-speaking territories. These may be composed during the performance of a dance, and traditionally light-hearted competition in poetry between young men and women in such dances may occur. The generic term used for the work and dance songs is *hees*, although this term is now mostly used for mod. songs performed to musical accompaniment. Other genres, which are regarded as more prestigious, are those belonging to the classification sometimes referred to in Somali as *maanso*. These are poetic works of which the composer is known and of which, following the original recitation by the poet, the goal is to memorize them verbatim, which means that for each such poem there is a definitive text. Traditionally, all forms were performed to a particular type of tune (*luuq*), although this is much less common for maanso genres such as *gabay* and *geeraar*. One genre known as *buraambur* is used exclusively by women in a variety of contexts.

The earliest known Somali poems date from the middle of the 19th c. Some of the most famous are those of Raage Ugaas Warfaa, who is regarded as one of the greatest Somali poets and who composed on a range of subjects, such as the famous "Alleyl Dumay" (Night Has Fallen), a lament after the poet's fiancée married another. In the early 20th c., Sayid Maxamed Cabdille Xasan, the leader of the Dervish movement that fought the imperial powers in the northern areas, used poetry as a powerful tool for influence and propaganda. The use of poetry in the sociopolitical domain remained important. Some time after the defeat of the Sayid in 1921, a poet named Cali Dhuux composed an invective poem addressing a particular lineage, which was replied to by a poet from that lineage, Qammaan Bulxan. Others then also joined in, and a poetic chain (*silsila*) ensued known as *Guba*, which became widely known. Such chains still occur every so often; some have been conducted via the Internet.

During the 1940s, a new form, the *heello*, developed out of another form known as *belwo*. Initially these were predominantly love poems and were also the first to be performed to musical accompaniment after Cabdullaahi Qarshe introduced the oud, a stringed instrument, to Somali culture and became one of the most important composers, not just of the music but of the poems. The heello subsequently developed into an important vehicle for nationalist poetry as part of the Somali struggle for independence, which was assisted by the introduction of radio as a further means of dissemination to a wider audience. It was at this time that theater began in Somalia. Plays were based on poetic texts composed by the playwright and then memorized by the actors, who would improvise the connecting parts in prose. Some parts of plays were sung to musical accompaniment as songs and became popular in their own right. After Somalia became independent in 1960, the heello developed into the mod. hees, which became the dominant form during the 1970s, a time when a number of famous young poets pioneered further devels., such as the use of traditional work song and children's song metrical patterns in serious poetry. Poetry became important politically both in support of and in opposition to the military regime that came to power in a coup in 1969.

All Somali poetry conforms to two stylistic requirements: meter and alliteration. The pattern of alliteration is such that every line in a poem, or every half line in certain genres, must contain a word beginning with the same sound, as in this extract from "Beledweyne" by Maxamed Ibraahim Warsame 'Hadraawi' (nicknames are widely used in Somali and are given throughout this entry in single quotation marks), in which the alliterative sounds are in italics: "webigoo *b*utaacoo / *b*eeraha waraabshoo / dhulka *b*aadku jiifshoo / dhirta ubaxu *b*uuxshoo" (as the river overflowed / watering the farms / the pasture lay on the ground / the flowers filled the trees). The alliterative sound is always the word's initial, and just the one sound is used throughout the poem. A poem may also alliterate in *alif*, which means that there must be a word beginning with a vowel in each line; any vowel may be used, in the short or long pronunciation. Alliteration is so important that it is used in naming characters in plays, in proverbs, even occasionally in naming children. In chain poems, mentioned above, the alliteration of each poem within the chain is most often the same; the *Siinley* chain of the early 1970s and *Deelley* of 1979–80 (both important chains of political poems) were named after the alliterative sound used in the poems. Certain sounds are considered more difficult than others depending on the number of words that begin with that sound; *alif*, *b*, or *d* are regarded as easier to compose in than *n* or *j*, with *y* probably the most difficult and recognized as such.

Meter in Somali poetry is quantitative and based on the patterning of long and short vowel syllables and syllable final consonants, which was first written about by the poet and scholar Maxamed Xaashi Dhamac 'Gaarriye' in 1976. The *jiifto* meter is the one most commonly used in mod. hees poetry, and its metrical patterning is presented here as an example of how the system works. In the basic pattern, ⏖ is a metrical position in which either one long or two short vowel syllables may occur, and ⏑ indicates an obligatory short vowel syllable:

(⏑) ⏖ (⏑) ⏖ ⏑ ⏖ ⏖

A short optional vowel syllable might be found at the beginning of the line or after the first metrical position when the following syllable has a long vowel (only one optional syllable is allowed). Syllable final consonants can occur at the end of metrical positions; but when a position of the type ⏖ is realized as two short vowel syllables, then the first of these syllables may contain a final consonant only in the first metrical position. E.g., the word *dhulka* (the earth, ground) may be found in the first metrical position, as in *dhulka baad ku jiifshoo*, but not in the other three positions of the shape ◡◡. The position in which a syllable final consonant may occur is also the only position in which a word break may occur and, hence, where the alliteration also occurs. Geminate or doubled consonants are always analyzed as heterosyllabic, so these also may only occur in these positions as do the consonants *sh*, *s*, *f*, *t*, *k*, *j*, *w*, and *y*, which behave in the meter as geminate consonants. A large number of metrical patterns are associated with particular genres of poetry. Free verse never emerged in Somali, although some Somali poetry, particularly that of Cabdi Muxumed Aamiin, seems to use patterning that does not follow the accepted meters; this poetry was composed to be sung to musical accompaniment, however. The demands of meter and alliteration are used artistically by good poets as extra raw material with which to enhance their poems aesthetically, a characteristic that brings value to poetry in the mind of the audience.

■ B. W. Andrzejewski and I. M. Lewis, *Somali Poetry: An Introduction* (1964); J. C. Ciise, *Diwaanka Gabayadii Sayid Maxamed Cabdulle Xasan* (1974); J. W. Johnson, *Heellooy Heelleellooy: The Development of the Genre Heello in Modern Somali Poetry* (1974); S. S. Samatar, *Oral Poetry and Somali Nationalism* (1982); *Literature in African Languages*, ed. B. W. Andrzejewski et al. (1985); *Poesia orale somala: storia di una nazione*, ed. F. Antinucci and A. F. Cali 'Idaajaa' (1986); A. C. Abokor, *Somali Pastoral Work Songs* (1993); *An Anthology of Somali Poetry*, trans. B. W. Andrzejewski with S. Andrzejewski (1993); G. Banti and F. Giannattasio, "Music and Metre in Somali Poetry," and J. Johnson, "Musico-Moro-Syllabic Relationships in the Scansion of Somali Oral Poetry," *Voice and Power: The Culture of Language in North East Africa*, ed. R. J. Hayward and I. M. Lewis (1996); M. Orwin, "On Consonants in Somali Metrics," *Afrikanistische Arbeitspapiere* 65 (2001), and "On the Concept of 'Definitive Text' in Somali Poetry," *Bulletin of the School of Oriental and African Studies* 63 (2003); *War and Peace: An Anthology of Somali Literature*, ed. R. S. Cabdillaahi 'Gadhweyne' (2009); "Night Has Fallen," trans. M. Orwin, http://pacoarts.com/PoetLangSite/flashpaper/raagel.swf.

M. Orwin

SOUTH AFRICA, POETRY OF

I. Afrikaans
II. English

I. Afrikaans. The first examples of poetry in Afrikaans date from the late 19th c. and formed part of efforts to raise the political consciousness of Afrikaner people by elevating the status of the spoken lang. Afrikaans—derived from the 17th-c. Dutch spoken by the first colonizers of the Cape of Good Hope and influenced by Malay, Creole-Port., Ger., Fr., southern Nguni langs., and Eng.—to the status of a written lang. with its own lit. Because of the racially divided nature of South Af. society, this process partly excluded Afrikaans speakers of mixed racial descent who played a significant role in the devel. of the lang. The primary aims of the early Afrikaans poets were to inspire readers to fight for the official recognition of their lang., to educate, and to entertain. To do this, they focused on the lives of ordinary burghers, their folklore, South Africa as fatherland, religion, and topical events, also using humor in poems that contained elements of the surreal or absurd. The style was mostly rhetorical rather than original, naïve rather than sophisticated.

After the Anglo-Boer War (1899–1902), attempts to standardize Afrikaans and produce a body of lit. in that lang. gathered renewed impetus; Afrikaans gained official status only in 1925. This process gained credibility through the greater sophistication and literary sensibility displayed by poets of the "first generation": Jan F. E. Celliers (1865–1940), Totius (pseud. of J. D. du Toit, 1877–1953), and C. Louis Leipoldt (1880–1947). Their early volumes show the effects of the war, but their work included other subjects (the landscape, religion, historical themes, political matters), as well as a variety of poetic techniques and styles, incl. free verse and the dramatic monologue.

The following generation added new elements to the repertoire of Afrikaans poetry, such as greater individualism, eroticism, and cl. allusions; but it did not make the same impact as its predecessors. Toon van den Heever (1894–1956) can be regarded as the most important of the new poets, while older poets like Eugène Marais (1871–1936) and A. G. Visser (1878–1929) also published distinctive work in the 1920s. Marais explored new terrain in the volume *Dwaalstories en ander vertellings* (*Rain Bull and Other Tales from the San*, 1927), a small collection of stories and poems based on the oral trad. of the San tribe.

The early 1930s brought an important renewal in Afrikaans poetry with the emergence of a group of poets (N. P. van Wyk Louw [1906–70], W.E.G. Louw [1913–80], Uys Krige [1910–87], Elisabeth Eybers [1915–2007]) who consciously reflected on their vocation as artists. They argued for a lit. that would adhere to the highest possible aesthetic and artistic standards, taking the best in Dutch, Ger., Eng., Fr., and Sp. lit. as their benchmark. Their poetry was known for its confessional nature and explorations of inner life but also turned to topics such as hist., religion, philosophy, and politics. All these poets built important oeuvres in the subsequent decades; van Wyk Louw achieved the highest status with works such as the epic poem *Raka* (1942) and the volume *Tristia* (1962). Eybers dealt with female experience in poems of great sobriety and technical refinement in an oeuvre that spanned nearly 60 years.

The poets who made their debut in the late 1940s (D. J. Opperman [1914–85], Ernst van Heerden [1916–97], S. V. Petersen [1914–87], Olga Kirsch [1924–97], G. A. Watermeyer [1917-72]) reflected the reality of a modernizing, urban, postwar world in the themes, imagery, and formal attributes of their work. The most important poet of this generation was Opperman, whose poetry distinguished itself through its concrete imagery, symbolic layering, and verbal economy as well as its portrayal of racial tension in South Af. society. High points are the epic poem *Joernaal van Jorik* (Jorik's Journal, 1949) and the volume *Blom en baaierd* (Flower and Chaos, 1956).

The 1960s brought revolutionary change to Afrikaans lit., signaling the beginning of a strong antihegemonic strain in Afrikaans. This was preceded by the work of certain poets in the late 1950s. The immigrant Peter Blum (1925–90) published only two volumes before leaving South Africa in the early 1960s but remains acclaimed for the sophisticated, satirical, and challenging nature of his work. Ingrid Jonker's (1933–65) poetry is known for its surreal imagery and spontaneous musicality. She became an iconic figure after her early suicide and is esp. remembered for her poem "Die kind" (The Child) about the shooting of a child during political unrest in 1960. In this period, political verse was also written by Barend Toerien (1921–2009) and Adam Small (1936–2016), who used the Cape vernacular in his volume *Kitaar my kruis* (Guitar My Cross, 1961). The most radical departure from the existing trad. came with the work of Breyten Breytenbach (b. 1939), who made his debut in 1964. Under the influence of the Fr. surrealists and the Dutch experimental poets of the 1950s (see LOW COUNTRIES, POETRY OF THE), Breytenbach wrote powerfully original free verse that transgressed boundaries through its use of every available register of lang. and the inclusion of startling imagery, explicit erotic content, and political commentary. Breytenbach's poetry also introduced Zen Buddhism to the largely Protestant Afrikaans trad.

The 1970s saw the emergence of several strong women poets. The most important of these were Sheila Cussons (1922–2004), who brought Catholic mysticism to Afrikaans poetry; Wilma Stockenström (b. 1933), who probed human insignificance within the vast theater of the Af. landscape; and Antjie Krog (b. 1952), who explored the compromised position of the creative woman in a patriarchal and racist society.

Although there were a number of new poets in the 1970s and 1980s who addressed existential issues in the traditional mode (Lina Spies [b. 1939], I. L. de Villiers [1936–2009], Petra Müller [b. 1935], T. T. Cloete [1924–2015]), this period also brought the introduction of poetry that openly explored gay sexuality (Lucas Malan [1946–2010], Johann de Lange [b. 1959], Joan Hambidge [b. 1956]), as well as "struggle poetry," written by mixed-race poets (Peter Snyders [b. 1939], Clinton V. du Plessis [b. 1963], Patrick Petersen [1951–97], Marius Titus [b. 1946]) in protest against the apartheid regime.

After the first democratic election in South Africa in 1994, new themes emerged under the pressure of the changing political and social landscape. Apart from exploring existing themes, poets focused on identity issues (Krog, Ronelda Kamfer [b. 1981]), ownership of the land (Krog, Bernard Odendaal [b. 1955]), ecological questions (Johann Lodewyk Marais [b. 1956], Martjie Bosman [b. 1954]), the position of Afrikaans in a multilingual society (Breytenbach, Diana Ferrus [b. 1953], Spies), and the new South Africa as a dystopia plagued by poverty, crime, and corruption (Toerien, Louis Esterhuizen [b. 1955]). In recent years Afrikaans poetry has seen a narrative turn, with poets using narrative elements, a parlando style, and a more accessible manner of writing in reaction to the existing trad. of hermetic poetry.

Although doubts were expressed about the sustainability of Afrikaans poetry around the change of the millennium, it regained its vigor and vitality by the end of the new century's first decade, showing an increase in the number of volumes published since 2005, as well as a lively interest in the *Versindaba* Web site (http://versindaba.co.za/) established to promote Afrikaans poetry.

II. English. South Africa first appears in Eng. poetry in the work of John Donne, John Milton, and John Dryden, in the wake of the Port. Luís de Camões, who creates in his epic The *Lusiads* (1572) the vivid mythological character Adamastor to stand for the dangers of the Cape of Good Hope. Anonymous Brit. visitors to South Africa, wintering from service in India, brought poetry to its shores, which, in 1820, became substantially colonized by Eng. speakers. The first South Af. Eng. poet as such, Thomas Pringle (1789–1834), emigrated from Scotland to the Eastern Frontier and adapted Scottish border ballads and the Wordsworthian reverie for lyrics such as the widely anthologized "Afar in the Desert." Pringle also established *The South African Literary Journal* in 1824.

In 19th-c. South Africa, the violent conflict among Dutch speakers, indigenous blacks, and the Brit. gave rise to an alternate popular trad. of antiemancipationist verse in the person of Andrew Geddes Bain (1797–1863), who in the Victorian era used his polyglot resources for humorous purposes. His successor, Albert Brodrick (1830–1908), wrote of the diamond fields, the goldfields, and the early process of industrialization.

The Anglo-Boer War, which became a media event (incl. the first newsreels), was the first major occasion of 20th-c. war poetry that extended into World War I. Rudyard Kipling on the jingo side advocated imperial progress; Thomas Hardy mourned the losses due to the imperial war in poems such as "Drummer Hodge" and "The Man He Killed." Meanwhile, Beatrice Hastings (1879–1943), born in London and raised in South Africa, defended home rule through her writings for the jour. *New Age* (1909–14). Black poets, particularly in multilingual newspapers, began a trad. of protest against deprivation of human rights, which persists to the present day.

After the Union of South Africa was established in 1910, Natal produced two major poets whose careers developed around the cultural magazine *Voorslag* in the 1920s: Roy Campbell (1901–57) and William Plomer (1903–73). Both eventually settled in Europe to pursue right-wing and left-wing politics, respectively. Campbell's early *The Flaming Terrapin* (1924) combined influences from imagism and symbolism to assert a futuristic Af. life force, while Plomer's successive volumes of 1927 maintained a democratic, satirical view of the segregated south.

After World War II, many returning soldier-poets, such as Anthony Delius (1916–89) and Guy Butler (1918–2001), asserted a "stranger-to-Europe" view of their local culture with a white Af. sense of belonging in the subcontinent. This, in turn, produced the jours., societies, and academic disciplines that constructed South Af. Eng. poetry as at least somewhat independent of the Brit. mainstream.

With the accession to power of the Afrikaner apartheid government in 1948, Eng. as a cultural medium moved into an oppositional role that has produced a lit. of resistance written by blacks and whites alike. The banning or forcing into exile of many poets in the 1960s, such as Dennis Brutus (1924–2009) and Mazisi Kunene (1930–2006), further fragmented the poetry into an international diaspora whose links to the internal scene were sometimes tenuous. But in 1971, with *Sounds of a Cowhide Drum* by Oswald Mtshali (b. 1940), a period of intense internal publication commenced and gave rise to the Black Consciousness movement, notably in the work of Sipho Sepamla (1932–2007), Keroapetse Kgositsile (b. 1938), and Mongane Serote (b. 1944), sometimes known (after the June 1976 uprising) as "Soweto poets."

The struggle over the end of apartheid, from the 1980s to the 1990s, led poets to question the role and importance of poetry in resisting continuing effects of colonialism and reimagining the newly democratic nation after 1994. Important poets of the 1980s include Douglas Livingstone (1932–96), Lionel Abrahams (1928–2004), Stephen Gray (b. 1941), Jeni Couzyn (b. 1942), Christopher Hope (b. 1944), and Jeremy Cronin (b. 1949). With the transition to democracy, South Af. poetry—like other postcolonial poetries in Eng.—has become increasingly transnational and global in thematic content and cross-cultural formal experimentation. Writing in traditional Eng. forms, Ingrid de Kok (b. 1951) borrows from Brit., Ir., Am., and Caribbean poetic trads. Born in South Africa but living in New York, Yvette

Christiansë (b. 1954) writes of overlapping Af. Am. and South Af. hists. of racism and diaspora. Although many South Africans vigorously promoted the antiapartheid struggle, they have also been sharply critical of the ineffectiveness of South Africa's postapartheid governments in transforming the social order. Performance poetry by Gcina Mhlophe (b. 1959), Lesego Rampolokeng (b. 1965), and Vonani Bila (b. 1972), among others, has been a powerful venue for making black South Af. experiences seen and heard, both at home and abroad. A younger generation of poets includes Seitlhamo Motsapi (b. 1966), Rustum Kozain (b. 1966), Mxolisi Nyezwa (b. 1967), Gabeba Baderoon (b. 1969), and Isobel Dixon (b. 1969). Jours. as diverse as *Botsotso*, *Carapace*, *New Coin*, and *Timbila*; the publishing houses Snail Press and Deep South; and online resources such as *Poetry International* have published an abundance of South Af. poems. South Af. poetry is marked by its ling. and ethnic hybridity: poets of many ethnic backgrounds borrow from indigenous and foreign cultural resources to embody the diversity of South Africa, whether their work concerns violence and poverty, HIV/AIDS and economic globalization, race and sexuality, the domestic and the everyday, or poetry itself.

See AFRICA, POETRY OF; XHOSA POETRY; ZULU POETRY.

■ **Afrikaans**. ***Anthologies***: *Afrikaans Poems with English Translations*, ed. A. P. Grové and C.J.D. Harvey (1962); *The New Century of South African Poetry*, ed. M. Chapman (2002); *Groot verseboek Deel 1–3*, ed. A. Brink (2008). ***Criticism and History***: *Perspektief en Profiel Deel 1–3*, ed. H. P. van Coller (1998, 1999, 2006); J. C. Kannemeyer, *Geskiedenis van die Afrikaanse literatuur 1652–2004* (2005).

■ **English**. ***Anthologies***: *Centenary Book of South African Verse*, ed. F. C. Slater, 2d ed. (1945); *A Book of South African Verse*, ed. G. Butler (1959); *Penguin Book of South African Verse*, ed. J. Cope and U. Krige (1968); *Return of the Amasi Bird: Black South African Poetry* (1891–1981), ed. T. Couzens and E. Patel (1982); *Soweto Poetry*, ed. M. Chapman (1982); *Modern South African Poetry*, ed. S. Gray (1984); *Paperbook of South African English Poetry*, ed. M. Chapman (1986); *Penguin Book of Southern African Verse*, ed. S. Gray (1988); *Breaking the Silence: A Century of South African Women's Poetry*, ed. C. Lockett (1990); *Essential Things: An Anthology of New South African Poetry*, ed. A. W. Oliphant (1992); *The Heart in Exile: South African Poetry in English*, 1990–95, ed. L. de Kock and I. Tromp (1996); *The Lava of This Land: South African Poetry, 1960–1996*, ed. D. Hirson (1997); *Ten South African Poets*, ed. A. Schwartzman (1999); *The New Century of South African Poetry*, ed. M. Chapman (2002); *It All Begins: Poems from Postliberation South Africa*, ed. R. Berold and K. Sole (2003); *Botsotso: An Anthology of Contemporary South African Poetry*, ed. A. K. Horwitz and K. Edwards (2009).***Criticism and History***: G. M. Miller and H. Sergeant, *A Critical Survey of South African Poetry in English* (1957); M. van Wyk Smith, *Drummer Hodge: The Poetry of the Anglo-Boer War* (1978); M. Chapman, *South African English Poetry* (1984); *Companion to South African English Literature*, ed. D. Adey et al. (1986); M. Van Wyk Smith, *Grounds of Contest: A Survey of South African English Literature* (1989); *Writing South Africa: Literature, Apartheid, Democracy, 1970–1995*, ed. D. Attridge and R. Jolly (1998); S. Nuttall, *Entanglement: Literary and Cultural Reflections on Post-Apartheid* (2000); A. O'Brien, *Against Normalization: Writing Radical Democracy in South Africa* (2001); D. Attwell, *Rewriting Modernity: Studies in Black South African Literary History* (2006); S. Graham, *South African Literature after the Truth Commission* (2009).

L. Viljoen (Afrikaans);
S. Gray, O. Hena (Eng.)

SOUTH AMERICA, POETRY OF.

See ARGENTINA, POETRY OF; BOLIVIA, POETRY OF; BRAZIL, POETRY OF; CHILE, POETRY OF; COLOMBIA, POETRY OF; ECUADOR, POETRY OF; GUARANÍ POETRY; INDIGENOUS AMERICAS, POETRY OF THE; MAPUCHE POETRY; PERU, POETRY OF, URUGUAY, POETRY OF; VENEZUELA, POETRY OF

SPAIN, POETRY OF

I. To 1700
II. 1700 to the Present

I. To 1700

A. ***Early Romance Orality***. The origins of poetry in Spain are neither national nor exclusively Sp. Poetry flourished with many arts and sciences in med. Iberia under Muslim rule (711–1492). Thriving poetic communities in Ar. and Heb. antedate the earliest record (ca. 1042) of verse in Sp. (then called *romance* or Romance), in turn a century later than the first extant prose example. First recovered in 1948 by S. M. Stern, the *kharjas*, fragments in Mozarabic Romance (the lang. spoken by Christians living in Muslim territory) or vernacular Ar., serve as lyric codas to panegyric and erotic poems written in cl. Ar. and Heb. Used in *Al-Andalus (Muslim Spain) during the cultural flowering of the 10th and 11th cs., these brief single-rhymed refrains stand in marked contrast to the longer *muwashshaḥ*. Yet the separate parts are yoked in perfect symbiosis: the young girl's love-longing serves as a figure for a male speaker's formal expressions of humility, gratitude, or expectation to a political superior. Kharjas and muwashshaḥāt were invented and cultivated by leading Andalusian poets of the 11th–13th cs., incl. King al-Mutamid, Ibn Quzmān (1078–1160), Jehudah Halevi (ca. 1074–1141), Moses Ibn Ezra (1055–1135), and Todros Abulafia (1247–after 1300). Both forms speak eloquently of med. cultural interaction among Arabs, Christians, and Jews.

The vernacular refrains point to the existence of an oral Romance trad. of love lyrics in the feminine voice. The Galician-Port. *cantiga de amigo* (a girl's song for her beloved), dating to the late 12th c., launches the collaborative poetic trad. known as *lírica de tipo popular* (lyric of the popular type). Its earliest forms, refrain-based, are the *zéjel* or *zajal* (another peninsular innovation in Ar.), *villancico*, and *cossante*. Codified, colloquial female-voiced poetry forms one of the strongest strands of Sp. lyric. Its direct eroticism, set in the natural fertility of agrarian life, is heard in contrast with the tortured male-voiced codes of Occitan and Sp. courtly poetry and the tendentious voices of epic and philosophical and didactic verse.

Cantiga forms, intermingled with Occitan themes and song types, are also found in male-voiced lyric, most famously in the *Cantigas de Santa María* of Alfonso X *el Sábio* (the Wise; 13th c.), who offers himself as Mary's "troubadour," promising to abandon objects of idolatrous devotion. The 420 cantigas fuse praise and petitions with testimonials to Mary's intervention on behalf of efforts to return southern Spain to Christian control. Its text and musical notation, preserved in a ms. richly illuminated with scenes from the Toledan court and the frontier with Islam, constitute an invaluable resource for studying the intertwining of art and life in 13th-c. Spain.

It is telling that the first instances of Iberian Romance lyric should perform poetic crossings of lines of gender, race, lang., and class. In kharjas, muwashshaḥāt, and cantigas is foreshadowed the complex coexistence of multiple codes and compositional forms, each bearing traces of different national and ling. origins, that is a hallmark of Sp. poetry. In the later med. and early mod. periods, the interweaving of motifs and langs. shapes voices, works, genres, movements, and literary polemics. The strength of early oral lyric also works to extend poetry's ties with music well into the early mod. period.

B. ***Medieval Epic and Religious Verse.*** Epic trads. germinated in the conflicted political and social world of the so-called *Reconquista* (Reconquest). The *Poema del Cid*, saga of the life and deeds of Rodrigo Díaz de Vivar, is the most complete *cantar de gesta*, composed in the 12th c. and extant in a 1207 copy by the cleric Per Abat (Peter Abbott). Like other poems of the minstrel school (*mester de juglaría*) lost and only partially reconstructed (*Poema de Fernán González*, *Los siete Infantes de Lara*), Abbott's version of the *Poema del Cid* draws on hist. and legend for its two plots, the hero's exile and his daughters' unfortunate marriages, stories connected through King Alfonso VI and his vassal's shared quest to restore Rodrigo's honor. The rise of Castile to political leadership and the emergence of Castilian as the dominant Iberian vernacular are both reflected and enabled by this remarkable poem, laced with appeals to a communal audience to endorse standards of vassalage, Christian soldiery, familial devotion, and personal honor. Among the poem's vividly rendered voices are Rodrigo weeping as he goes into exile, his men and wife Ximena, the young girl who defies the king's order to shun Rodrigo, hoodwinked Jewish moneylenders, and Moors calling on a Christian to rescue them from their rulers.

The broad popularity of minstrel sagas becomes clear in succeeding centuries with the emergence of the *romance* (ballad), the most uniquely Sp. of poetic forms. Early ballads adapt epic into octosyllabic verses with a single assonant rhyme on even lines and no strophic division, creating a model still standard in the 21st c. Like the cantares de gesta, the anonymous ballads of the *Romancero Viejo* (Old Balladry) were performance art, acted and sung for audiences before being transcribed and provided with musical scores beginning in the 14th c. Ballad families include tales from national hist. and legend (King Rodrigo, blamed for Muslim dominance, and celebrated in epic episodes), frontier encounters (Reconquest sieges, intrigues involving Christians, Moors, and half-castes), Carolingian chivalric material, and "novelesque" songs about faithful wives, adulterers, incest, prisoners, and sentimental treason (as in the famous "Fontefrida" [Cooling Fount]). As a group, according to Gilman, ballads speak a distinct poetic lang., used to conjure a shared past and a communal present. Ballad speeches often become proverbial, repeatedly cited by figures like Don Quixote and in colloquial usage. The trad. has offered poets of many centuries the lang. of conservatism on the one hand and of protest and popular empowerment on the other. Med. Sp. balladry has enjoyed a long life in peninsular orality and in Sephardic and other Sp.-speaking communities around the world, giving rise to later ballad genres such as the Mexican *corrido*.

Med. religious poetry reflects the larger contexts of two strikingly different centuries. The 13th c., under Fernando III *el Santo* (the Holy) and Alfonso X *el Sábio*, saw unification of Castile and León and dramatic Christian advances into southern Andalusia, while Aragon conquered Mallorca. With these successes, Castilian monasteries expanded their local influence and royal courts enjoyed a cultural flowering of the arts reflecting Alfonso's cosmopolitan cultural vision. Early works like *Vida de Santa María Egipcíaca* (Life of St. Mary the Egyptian) and the Catalan *Libre dels tres reys d'Orient* (Book of the Three Kings of the Orient) reflect Fr. influence. As the clerical style (*mester de clerecía*) coalesces in the form known as *cuaderna vía* (monorhyme quatrains of 14-syllable lines divided at the hemistich), poems such as the *Libro de Aleixandre* on the life of Alexander the Great and the *Libro de Apolonio* on Apollonius of Tyre, anticipate the work of the century's most important poet, the Rioja native Gonzalo de Berceo (ca. 1196–ca. 1264). Berceo wrote four saints' lives in verse (two associated with local Benedictine monasteries: Santo Domingo de Silos and San Millán de la Cogolla) and a number of devotional poems to the Virgin Mary (*Duelo de la Virgen* [The Virgin's Lament], *Loores de Nuestra Señora* [A Eulogy on Our Lady], *Milagros de Nuestra Señora* [Miracles of Our Lady]), all preserved in 14th-c. copies. His poetic lang.—learned, yet intimate and gracefully colloquial—reveals ties to the mester de juglaría, the cantiga trad., and troubadour lyric. His *Milagros* show Berceo's familiarity with Marian lore popularized by Gautier de Coincy (1177–1236). The 13th c. also nurtured a lively trad. of poetic debates on religious and philosophical issues, notably *Disputa del alma y el cuerpo* (Debate between the Body and the Soul) and *Elena y María*. Another remarkable debate poem, made famous by the 20th-c. poet Pedro Salinas, is *Razón de amor con los Denuestos del Agua y el Vino* (Poem of Love with the Dispute between Water and Wine), which frames its debate with the dream of a young scholar whose beloved appears to him, speaking the lang. of female desire of the cantigas.

Three major figures and a pair of works reflect the 14th c.'s dynastic struggles, growing cities, and intellectual and religious ferment. Little is known of Juan Ruiz (ca. 1284–1351) other than what he reports in the celebrated *Libro de buen amor* (*Book of Good Love*, 1330–43), where he styles himself simultaneously as a wayward priest in search of erotic fulfillment and a penitent sinner bent on teaching "Good Love" to his fellow men. Framed with prayers to Christ and the Virgin, Aristotelian discourses on natural sexuality, and Ovidian lessons in lovemaking, his sentimental adventures move through social and literary worlds of unprecedented variety, evoked in multiple prosodic forms (cuaderna vía, traditional lyric, *serranilla*) and narrative types (notably the Oriental *alcahueta* or procuress motif). Ruiz's mirror of cultural diversity, the piquancy and freshness of his lang., and his own ironic and ambivalent authorial figure ensure the book's enduring popularity and influence. More recognized in his own day was the great Heb. poet Sem Tob ibn Ardutiel ben Isaac (ca. 1290–1369), known as Santob de Carrión. The dark vision of his only work in Sp., *Proverbios morales* (ca. 1350), whose text also circulated in Heb. characters, spoke powerfully from trads. of Jewish scripture and thought, using Ar., Lat., and Castilian sources, to communities in impending religious crisis. Two other texts at the intersection of three cultures are cuaderna vía poems about Joseph in Egypt: the early 14th-c. *Coplas de Yosef*, composed in Sp. in Heb. script, and the later Aragonese *Poema de Yúçuf*, in *aljamiado* or Sp. in Ar. script. A third figure from the public sphere, the chancellor of Castile Pero López de Ayala (1332–1407), anthologized his religious, moral, and didactic poems, with some Marian lyrics, in the *Rimado de Palacio*.

C. *Poetry of Fourteenth- and Fifteenth-Century Courts.* The reigns of Castilian monarchs Juan I (1379–90), Enrique III (1390–1406), and Juan II (1406–54) witnessed factional strife over royal succession, eventually resolved in favor of the Catholic Queen Isabel I (1479–1504), whose marriage in 1469 to Fernando of Aragon ultimately brought political unity with the taking of Granada in 1492. The period also saw widespread anti-Jewish riots in 1391 and a subsequent wave of conversions, ominous signs of the high human and cultural price that would be paid for national unification. But thriving courts, urban centers, and increased trade prompted a cultural renewal that Lida de Malkiel called a "Spanish pre-Renaissance."

Poetry of the 15th c. boasts its share of giants. Juan de Mena (1411–56) studied in his native Córdoba and in Salamanca and Rome before entering the service of Juan II as royal chronicler and Lat. secretary. Author of short love lyrics and political and moral verses, Mena owes his exalted place in lit. hist. to the long poem titled *Laberinto de Fortuna* (1444). Merging the goddess Fortune with the figure of the labyrinth, the poet creates an allegory for his time that is at once political, philosophical, theological, and aesthetic. Alternating examples contrast Fortune's followers with those of a personified Providence, who ultimately points the way out of the maze. Politically, the *Laberinto* puts forward Juan II and the controversial constable of Castile Álvaro de Luna as instruments of Providence. Composed in *arte mayor* (regularly accented 12-syllable lines), the poem itself constitutes a maze of Latinate lexicon and syntax, cl. allusions, and imitations that earned the scholar-poet the admiration of 16th- and 17th-c. apostles of learned poetry.

Another giant is Mena's friend, Íñigo López de Mendoza, the Marqués de Santillana (1398–1458), author of allegorical *decires*, a poetic tribute to a Catalan poet contemporary (*Coronación de Mossén Jordi di Sant Jordi*), a *Triumphete de Amor* inspired by Petrarch, and the political poems *Comedieta de Ponza* and *Bías contra Fortuna*. Noted for his 42 *Sonetos fechos al Itálico modo* (Sonnets in the Italian Style), which anticipate the 16th-c. Italianate mode, and a *Carta-Prohemio* (Letter-Preface) on the aristocratic practice of poetry, Santillana is perhaps most admired for his eight serranillas, light-hearted, rustically erotic *pastorelas*. A third singular voice is that of the soldier-courtier Jorge Manrique (1440–79), known for fine courtly love lyrics and a celebrated elegiac poem dedicated to his father, Rodrigo Manrique. In these *Coplas por la muerte de su padre* (Verses on the Death of His Father, ca. 1476–79) Manrique meditates on the transitory nature of mortal existence, celebrates his father's devotion to family and society, and imagines Death knocking at Don Rodrigo's door, received with "free and cheerful will" as a messenger of God's omniscience. The poem musters literary devices such as the *ubi sunt* (where are they?) topos and cl. heroic examples, biblical lang., and the med. trad. of the *danza de la muerte* (dance of death), intertwining them with simple imagery (the soul waking from mortal sleep, life as a delta of rivers flowing to the sea), simple axioms, and direct, intimate address of the ethical and metaphysical dimensions of life and death. Unique in med. poetry, this elegant fusion of elevated and colloquial registers, of popular and learned discourses, has earned the *Coplas* their firm place in the memory of Sp. speakers. A fourth figure deserving of special mention is the great Catalan lyric poet Ausiàs March (1397–1459), inheritor of Fr. and It. lyric trads., whose arresting psychological portrayals inspired numerous 16th-c. Castilian poets.

The *arte menor* (short Castilian meters) production of the late 14th and 15th cs. is found in the period's numerous *cancioneros*, which anthologize compositions representing decades of poetic activity. Chief among these are the Castilian and Aragonese *Cancionero de Palacio* (ca. 1400), the *Cancionero de Baena* (1445–54), the Navarrese *Cancionero de Herberay des Essarts* and contemp. Neapolitan *Cancionero de Stúñiga* (ca. 1460–63), Hernando del Castillo's *Cancionero general* (1511), and the *Cancionero Musical de Palacio* (1505–20). The cancioneros' aristocratic and chivalric conception of poetry as science, lettered ally of arms, suasory discourse, sister art of music—formulated in the poetics of Juan Alfonso de Baena (1406–54), Santillana, and Juan del Encina (ca. 1468–1529 or 30)—grows out of a courtly and urban context. Among cancionero poets and their audiences, there was considerable diversity of region, class, education, occupation, religion, and ethnic identity. Eclectic in content, anthols. embraced many poetic kinds (political poems and panegyrics, satires, religious verse, love poetry) and verse and compositional types.

Whether sacred or profane, elevated or colloquial, cancioneros favor the code known as *conceptismo*, which features a tightly controlled lexicon, witty wordplay, and a taste for antithesis, paradox, and contradiction. Their figurative lang. draws on social and bodily experience (wars, castles, prisons, cathedrals, servitude, wounds, plagues, death) rather than on nature. Courtly love poems represent the psychic anguish of individual subjects in the mirror (often inverted) of social and political order. Paradigms of frustration, defeat, and morbidity enact rhetorically willed subjection of the (usually male) body and soul. Like med. balladry, cancionero poetry and its *conceptista* lang. have a long afterlife in the polyphonic world of Ren. and baroque poetry.

D. ***Renaissance Reinvention of the Lyric.*** The hist. of Sp. poetry took a striking turn early in the reign of the Hapsburg king and Holy Roman emperor Charles V (1516–58), as It. prosodic and compositional types brought the themes and practices of Ren. humanism fully into courtly verse, revising the traditional hierarchy of poetic codes. Spearheading the Italianizing movement were the Catalan Juan Boscán (ca. 1490–1542) and the Toledan Garcilaso de la Vega (1503–36). Italianate modes held understandable appeal for these well-placed courtiers and imperial soldiers, who collaborated (Boscán as trans., Garcilaso as prologuist) in bringing out Baldassare Castiglione's *Book of the Courtier* in Sp. (1534). The two friends' works were published together (1543) following Boscán's death. The latter's poems feature Petrarchan sonnets of frustrated love, a striking verse epistle on the joys of married life, and a version of the fable of Hero and Leander.

Strictly speaking, the Italianate revolution had begun a century or more earlier, with Santillana's experimental sonnets and with imitations of Petrarch by Mossén Jordi di Sant Jordi (ca. 1400–24) and March. But it was with Garcilaso's works that It. forms and the imitation of cl. authors were naturalized into the Castilian lang., altering it permanently. Running to a handful of villancicos, 40 sonnets, two elegies, a verse epistle, and three eclogues, the slim corpus won the young poet, killed in battle in Provence at 33, instant recognition; a host of imitators; a series of learned commentaries of the sort devoted to Virgil, Dante, and Petrarch; and the title Prince of Spanish Poets. Eclectic by contrast with the It. giants and dispensing with their Christian itinerary of sin, guilty penance, and the journey toward salvation, the Toledan chooses entirely secular subjects set against the competing backdrops of pastoral's *locus amoenus* and the military campaigns and the imperial geography of his aristocratic experience. New to Sp. vernacular verse is his attention to idealized nature, human beauty, Neoplatonic love, and unchristianized cl. mythology. While continuing to draw on 15th-c. poets such as March and Garci Sánchez de Badajoz (ca. 1460–1526), particularly in sonnets and *canciones*, Garcilaso demonstrates familiarity with Lat. authors and It. models encountered during imperial service.

Most of his sonnets are love sonnets. Although often startling in their movement between the stark conceits and insistent redundancy of cancionero codes and the copious sensuous imagery of Lat. and Italianate material, they nonetheless achieve unprecedented collaboration among these trads. Garcilaso experiments with the flexible structure of the *canción*, inventing a new type, subsequently much used, the *lira*, in the "Oda ad florem Gnidi" ("Ode to the Flower of Gnido [Naples]"). The solitary deserts and allegorical dramas of *Canciones* 1, 2, and 4 stand in dramatic contrast to the verdant island setting and political subtext of the third song and to the discursive coyness and mythological figures of the fifth.

Their choice of subject anticipated in turn-of-the-century pastoral dramas of Encina, Garcilaso's eclogues display the poet's extraordinary range. The three poems share themes, characters (Salicio, Nemoroso, Elisa), and the device of *ekphrasis*. The first prefaces two freestanding, symmetrical monologues of shepherds with a dedication to the viceroy of Naples, whom Garcilaso served from 1532 to 1536. The second, longest and most challenging, is divided into two parts, posing a pastoral drama about the shepherd Albanio's love madness against the river spirit Severo, whose ekphrastic description of an urn depicting exploits of the House of Alba is offered as a cure for lovesickness. In the third, an invisible poet describes four nymphs who spin from the sands of the Tagus river tapestries representing tragic love stories. Three of their stories come from ancient fable (Orpheus and Eurydice, Daphne and Apollo, Venus and Adonis); the last and most elaborate creates the mod. myth of Elisa and Nemoroso. The poem, whose Orphic dedication gave Pedro Salinas the title for his volume *La voz a ti debida*, also features an eclogue within an eclogue, as the poet catches strains of the exchanged songs of living shepherds, whose approach sends the weaver nymphs back into the waves.

In the *Eclogues,* the poet's figure occupies the center of Garcilaso's self-mirroring and self-monumentalizing creation, acting as protagonist, in parallel with military and political figures such as the emperor or the Duke of Alba, in campaigns of cultural conquest acted out not on a placeless allegorical landscape but on real geography (the rivers Tagus and Tormes, the Mediterranean, North Af. outposts, and shores of the Danube) as the poetic project of emulative imitation of ancient Rome coincides with Hapsburg imperialism. Garcilaso's use of Virgil's homoerotic shepherds and the *Aeneid's* Dido as prototypes for tragic subjectivity, projected against ancient and mod. contexts, opens new avenues of expression for male lyric subjects.

Firmly established for succeeding generations of poets is the Ren. aesthetic of imitation and the practice of syncretic appropriation from multiple models. Garcilaso borrows not only from Petrarch but from Dante, Jacopo Sannazaro, Pietro Bembo, and Luigi Tansillo; not only from Virgil, Ovid, and Horace but from Lucretius, Seneca, Tibullus, and more. In the area of style, Garcilaso embraces the hendecasyllable (11-syllable line—impossible to divide into hemistichs), melodious cadences, subtle enjambments, cultivated (though not obscure) Latinate lexicon and allusion, luxurious near-synonyms, narrative pathos, and plastic idealization of human and natural beauty. Key to the success of Italianization was Garcilaso's demonstration that rich conceits and melodic syntax could be fused, elegantly and seamlessly, with the stark imagery, terse wit, emphatic rhythms, and insistent repetition of Castilian codes.

Success in courtly circles did not guarantee the Italianate coup universal acceptance. Cristóbal de Castillejo (ca. 1490–1550) called the new poetry and its jarringly new lang. to account in mock-inquisitorial proceedings against the suspect foreigners and heretics, charges that would resonate throughout 16th- and 17th-c. polemics. If some traditionalists rejected alien forms and diction, most 16th-c. poets opted for ambidextrous alternation between native and imported styles. Period anthols. and prosimetric pastoral *romances* like the Port. Jorge de Montemayor's *Diana* collect diverse examples of both kinds. The new poetics spread through educated, cosmopolitan circles, where humanistic imitation of It. and Roman culture was an article of personal pride and Sp. imperial ambition, refashioning cultivated Sp. to a degree comparable with Petrarch's reinvention of Tuscan It.

Among the first to adopt Italianate poetics were three other soldier-poets: Diego Hurtado de Mendoza (1503–75), historian, satirist, imperial ambassador to Rome and Venice, and author of sonnets on paradoxes of sentiment and *Fábula de Adonis*; Gutierre de Cetina (ca. 1510–54), native of Seville, soldier in Europe and Mexico, best known for the sweetness of his verse and for his madrigal "Ojos claros, serenos" (Bright and Serene Eyes), who (like Garcilaso) uses the ruins of empire as a figure for erotic anguish; and Hernando de Acuña (ca. 1520–80), friend of the emperor, author of sonnets and *Fábula de Narciso,* best known as author of the emblematic imperial sonnet, "Ya se acerca, señor, o es ya llegada" (Now approaches, sire, or has already arrived). In the next generation, a Castilian school of soldier-poets, incl. Francisco de la Torre (1534?–94?), Francisco de Figueroa (1536–1617), and Francisco de Aldana (1537–75), who died with King Sebastian of Portugal in Africa, contributed to the growing body of Sp. sonnets, canciones, eclogues, elegies, and epistles. A Salamanca school of contemplative, Christian humanist poets took shape around the figure of the university professor, biblical scholar, and Inquisition target Luis de León (1527–91), who translated into Sp. the Song of Songs and the Book of Job, as well as Virgil and Horace. The Augustinian's Neoplatonic odes—notably "Vida retirada," "A Francisco de Salinas" (organist at Salamanca's cathedral), and "Noche serena"—set the standard for elegant clarity favored by Francisco de Quevedo (1580–1645), who published León's poems with those of Torre in 1631 as a poetic manifesto against Gongorism.

To the south, a Sevillian school of Andalusian poets headed by Fernando de Herrera (1534–97) included Baltasar del Alcázar (1534–78), Juan de Arguijo (1567–1623), Andrés Fernández de Andrada (1575–1648, probable author of "Epístola moral a Fabio"), Rodrigo Caro (1573–1647, known for his "Canción a las ruinas de Itálica"), and Pedro Espinosa (1578–1650), who published an influential anthol., *Flor de poetas ilustres* (Flower of Illustrious Poets, 1605), and *Fábula de Genil.* The densely figured diction of Herrera's Pindaric odes (commemorating the Christian naval victory at Lepanto and King Sebastian's ill-fated Af. campaign), Petrarchan sonnets dedicated to the Countess of Gelves ("Luz"), canciones, and eclogues, representing the height of Sp. mannerism, earned him the epithet *El Divino* and the role of ling. innovator, forerunner of Luis de Góngora. Fittingly, the schools of Salamanca and Seville produced the first erudite commentaries on Garcilaso's verse: the restrained notes to the ed. (1574) of Francisco Sánchez de las Brozas (1523–1600), known as *El Brocense*, and Herrera's encyclopedic *Anotaciones* (1580), which offer lengthy treatment of imitation, metaphor, vernaculars, the passions, and Sp. national character. Enunciating a heroic poetics of Sp. cultural supremacy, the Andalusian scholar-poet champions learned difficulty and figurative abundance but pronounces against obscurity, thereby standing both as a forerunner of the baroque and a rhetorical conservative who will be invoked in the battle over Góngora.

Throughout the 16th c., religious themes attract poets like Montemayor (1520?–1561), much of whose verse uses traditional Sp. meters. In 1575, Sebastián de Córdoba's (1545–1604) Christian adaptation "*a lo divino*" of love poems by Boscán and Garcilaso ushers in a vogue of Petrarchan sonnets addressed to Jesus and Mary. Partly prompted by these forgettable verses come the extraordinary mystical poems of Juan of Yepes or St. John of the Cross (1542–91), the Carmelite friar tied to Salamanca and, like Luis de León, imprisoned by the Inquisition. Using Garcilaso's five-line lira stanza, John's three most celebrated poems—*Cántico espiritual* (*Spiritual Canticle*, ca. 1584), *Noche oscura del alma* (*Dark Night of the Soul*, ca. 1578) and "Llama de amor viva" ("Living Flame of Love," ca. 1584)—draw deeply on León's trans. of the Song of Songs, traditional feminine-voiced lyric, cancionero conceits, and Garcilaso's own verses to evoke the erotic torment and rapture of the Bride (Soul) searching for union with God. The poet and his fellow Carmelite Teresa of Ávila (1515–82) use Castilian meters and the cancionero code to ponder the mystical paradoxes of learned ignorance and death in life.

E. *Imperial Epic and the New Balladry.* The Italianate turn also led to the reinvention of epic, from mid-century on composed mainly in tercets and octaves, dressed in diction elevated by Latinate vocabulary and cl. learning. Imitators of Homer, Virgil, Lucan, Ludovico Ariosto, Luís de Camões, Torquato Tasso, and others could draw on a wave of prose and verse trans. into Sp., widely disseminated by printing. There they found Virgilian similes, heroic orations, sea battles and shipwrecks, dramas of exile and discovery, fables of dynastic foundation, and philosophical and ideological lessons germane to national and imperial projects. Publication statistics put their broad appeal beyond dispute: Pierce finds some 150 Sp. epic poems in print from 1550 to 1700, often reprinted and extended. The largest number treat Christian themes (lives of Mary, Jesus, OT figures; saints' lives, crusades, miracles, and conversions). Notable among these are Félix Lope de Vega's (1562–1635) *El Isidro* (1599), a life of Madrid's farmer patron composed in Castilian *quintillas*; his voluminous Tasso imitation *La Jerusalén conquistada* (1609); Cristóbal de Virués's (1550–1614) *El Montserrate* (1587); and Diego de Hojeda's (1570–1615) *La Christiada* (1611). Luis Barahona de Soto (ca. 1548–95) and Lope, among others, produce Ariosto spinoffs featuring the elusive Angelica. Celebrating Sp. hist. and legend are works such as Juan de la Cueva's (ca. 1550–1610) *Conquista de la Bética* (1603), Juan Rufo Gutiérrez's (1547–1620) *La Austríada* (1584, about the emperor's son and Lepanto commander Juan de Austria), and Bernardo de Balbuena's (1561–1627) *El Bernardo* (1624). Among New World verse epics are Alonso de Ercilla's (1533–94) influential *La Araucana* (1569–89), Gabriel Lobo Lasso de la Vega's (1555–1615) *Mexicana* (1594), Juan de Castellanos's (1522–1607) *Elegías de Varones Ilustres de Indias* (Eulogies of Illustrious Men of the Indies, 1589), the Chilean Pedro de Oña's (ca. 1570–1643) *Arauco domado* (Arauco Tamed, 1596), and Lope's saga of Francis Drake, *La Dragontea* (1598). The 17th c. sees the creation of burlesque epics such as Miguel de Cervantes's (1547–1616) *Viaje del Parnaso* (Journey to Parnassus, 1614) on the mock-heroic quest of Sp. poets and Lope's feline epic *La Gatomaquia* (War of the Cats, 1634).

The popularity of the cultivated epic is matched by a new vogue of balladry, visible in the proliferation of anthols. of med. ballads such as the 1547–48 *Cancionero de romances*, the 1561 *Silva de varios romances*, and the 1600 *Romancero general*. This most accessible and easily improvised form is pressed into the service of news making, self-promotion, scandal-mongering, political manipulation, and mockery. Seventeenth-c. poetic giants gravitated toward the ballad. Lope de Vega, who styled himself in pastoral and Moorish ballads as the rustic Belardo and the sentimental Moor

Zaide, also published a *Romancero espiritual* (1619). Luis de Góngora (1561–1627), who launches the captive's ballad, uses the form to appropriate Ariosto's Angelica and Medoro in intensely erotic verses and to subject cl. myths (Hero and Leander, Pyramus and Thisbe) to parodic deformation. Quevedo's caustic ballads send up cl., chivalric, and national myths; his most original contribution are picaresque ballads called *jácaras*, whose protagonists, the convict Escarramán and his concubine La Méndez, trade missives about their low-life adventures.

Bardic narrative, dialogue, and performative lyric are among the resources that make ballads the bedrock of poetic dramatization in the theater, where they play the leading prosodic role in the polymetric *Comedia Nueva* (New Comedy). Many plays spin out stories from traditional *romances viejos*. As ballads came to be written in a vast range of poetic and rhetorical codes, from the religious and aesthetic sublime to the obscene, they serve as sites for the intermingling of learned and popular (*culto* and *popular*), native and foreign, that spills over into other forms.

F. ***Horizons of Baroque Poetry.*** The mannerist transition toward baroque poetics begins to appear in the last decades of the 16th c., in the poetry of figures such as Herrera and the equally learned Aragonese brothers Lupercio and Bartolomé Leonardo de Argensola (1559–1613 and 1562–1631, respectively), in anthols. like Espinosa's, and in early compositions by Cervantes, Góngora, Lope de Vega, and Quevedo. The overwhelming majority of 17th-c. poets are literary polyglots, fluent in a variety of poetic idioms, rhetorical registers, and tones, and increasingly inclined to mix them. Heirs to Petrarch, Garcilaso, and earlier generations of their imitators, most poets were from the start avid sonneteers, though not—or not long—to the exclusion of other types. Many, as we have just seen, wrote ballads, along with other traditional Sp. forms like the villancico and the *letrilla*. Italianate canción varieties continued in frequent use; tercets were a popular choice for verse epistles, solemn and satiric, and other long poems. In addition to heroic octaves, poets gravitated toward the more open, irregular patterning of the *silva*, famously used by Góngora in his meandering *Soledades* (Solitudes, 1613) and by Lope de Vega in his feline epic.

New thematic and formal preferences emerge. One is the long mythological poem, whose larger-than-life protagonists provide allegorical mirrors for dramas of affect (love, jealousy, melancholy) and art. Among poems of this kind, Góngora's sensational *Fábula de Polifemo and Galatea* (1613), which adopts Polyphemus as a prototype of erotic frustration and his tortured song as the standard-bearer for the Cordoban's controversial new poetics, enjoys pride of place as the period's most original mythography. Along with Góngora's fable and Lope's *Filomena* (1621) and *Circe* (1624) came others: an earlier *Polifemo* by Luis Carrillo de Sotomayor (1585–1616), *Phaetons* and an *Adonis* by Juan de Tassis y Peralta, Count of Villamediana (1582–1622) and Pedro Soto de Rojas (1584–1658), a *Hero and Leander* by Gabriel Bocángel (1603–58), and many mythological dramas by Pedro Calderón de la Barca (1601–81) and others, incl. the Mexican nun Sor Juana Inés de la Cruz (ca. 1648–95).

The choice of outsized allegorical personifications of the poet went along with flamboyant self-fashioning and complex poetic personas made up of contradictory extremes. Two cases in point are Lope de Vega, whose Petrarchan *Rimas* (1602) are transmuted *a lo divino* into histrionic confessionals and penance in his *Rimas sacras* (1614) and later subjected to a festive send-up in the *Rimas humanas y divinas* (1634) of his alter ego, the Licenciado Tomé de Burguillos. Quevedo's verse spans perhaps the most extreme range of moods and tastes, running from the spiritual sublime of *Un Heráclito cristiano* (1613) and the erotic sublime of love lyrics to biting satire sonnets and taste for the grotesque, obscene, and scatological. Affinity for extreme contrasts generates ubiquitous antitheses and the baroque *coincidentia oppositorum* of the conceit.

Publication hist. in this period tells its own story. Many poets did not gather their own work in published volumes but instead circulated it in ms., recited it in poetic contests and meetings of literary academies, or contributed it to collections. Many published discrete works separately, as Lope de Vega did often. Cervantes left his lyrics scattered throughout his prose works; Góngora circulated his major poems in ms. only; and Quevedo, like his Andalusian rival, left most of his poetry to be collected after his death. In this age of inflated opulence and class-enforced leisure, poetry was a social practice and a widespread one at that. Many complained that there were far too many aspiring poets; others could rejoice that practicing poets included women like María de Zayas y Sotomayor (1590–1669?) and Catalina Clara Ramírez de Guzmán (1611–70?).

Poetry's popularity meant that its form and matter could become burning questions for society. The central issue for early 17th-c. Spain was the proper nature of poetic lang. and the purpose (moral, social, epistemological) of poetry itself. Tensions over competition between Sp. and Italianate styles boiled over in reaction to the ms. circulation (1613–14) of Góngora's *Polifemo* and the unfinished *Soledades*. Enthusiasts of the poems' layered artifice seized on this new New Poetry, which would earn the poet posthumous epithets such as the Sp. Homer and the Andalusian Pindar, as heroic cultural triumph. But critics including Juan de Jáuregui (1583–1641) and Francisco Cascales (1564–1642) decried their prohibitive difficulty as the mask of heresy (the pejorative term *culteranismo*, used to caricature Góngora's style, is modeled on *Luteranismo* or Lutheranism) or atheistic nihilism, designed to bring down the edifice of Poetry and Culture. The poet, once hailed as Prince of Light, became a Luciferine Prince of Darkness. Lope and Quevedo joined the traditionalist assault claiming that Góngora's multiple metaphors, Latinate lang., and cl. allusions were anti-Sp. They proposed native conceptismo, based on *agudeza* or wit—which Baltasar Gracián (1601–58) would honor as the quintessential Sp. attribute in his *Agudeza y arte de ingenio* (*Cleverness and the Art of Wit*, 1642, rev. ed. 1648)—rather than on ornament, as the intellectually and politically respectable choice. Over critics' objections, many poets imitated Góngora eagerly; most were influenced by his verse. Indeed, while partisan rhet. made culteranismo and conceptismo appear to be worlds apart, it is not easy to find clear examples of one or the other. Superficially imitated in the 18th c. and discredited in the 19th, this baroque giant would be resurrected by the Generation of 1927 as artistic patron of a poetics centered on the image and on ling. freedom.

Debts to Counter-Reformation theology are implicit in the contradictory baroque aesthetic, which embraces corporeal beauty, opulence, and artifice, only—or the better—to represent their disintegration, disappearance, and annihilation. Among the period's most exquisite poems are sonnets by Góngora ("Mientras por competir con tu cabello" [As long as, to compete with your hair], "Ilustre y hermosísima María" [Illustrious and Beautiful Maria], "Menos solicitó veloz saeta" [Less swiftly did the arrow seek]) and Quevedo ("Cerrar podrá mis ojos" [My eyes may be closed], "¡Ah de la vida!" [Is any life home?], "Miré los muros de la patria mía" [I gazed upon my walls]) that reflect acute consciousness of the imminence of death. Frequent effects of ling. and sensory trickery (hyperbaton, paronomasia, catachresis, paradox, *trompe-l'oeil*, dreams) set up dramas in which illusion is ritually succeeded by disillusion, the baroque *desengaño*. These interests give poetry strong ties to comedies of trickery such as Tirso de Molina's (1584–1648) *El burlador de Sevilla* (*The Trickster of Seville*, 1630), philosophical plays such as Calderón's *La vida es sueño* (*Life Is a Dream*, 1635–36), allegorical and liturgical drama, painting, architecture, ekphrasis, emblems, and public ceremonials.

The relevance of Spain's trans-Atlantic experience to the evolution of baroque poetry is generally acknowledged, though the nature of that relation remains unclear. It is often said that the peninsular baroque was exported to *Spanish America, where it did some of its most exuberant flowering. But there is considerable evidence to suggest that the baroque style may be as much a response to awareness of that New World as a cultural gift to it. Words, proper names, and poetic rhythms in Lope; Góngora's gold, silver, and gems; Quevedo's obsession with Sp. greed, alchemy, the perils of navigation, and nouveau riche intruders—such references work to make the New World the invisible backdrop against which dramas of desire, identity, and cultural values are played out.

II. 1700 to the Present

A. *The Eighteenth Century.* The death in 1681 of Calderón, the last major author of the Sp. baroque, marked the end of an epoch. The 1737 *Poética* of Ignacio de Luzán (1702–54)—heavily indebted to It. sources and somewhat less to Nicolas Boileau—denounced the excesses of baroque poetry, esp. Góngora and his followers, but did not lead immediately to a vital Sp. neoclassicism. The canonical poets of the 18th c., in fact, are clustered in the last third of the century. Sp. lit. of this period is still the object of a great deal of condescension. In the standard view, the turn away from the achievements of the Sp. baroque, together with the emulation of Fr. neoclassical poetics, led to an epoch of dutifully mediocre verse. Not coincidentally, other genres of imaginative writing suffered a similar fate during this period. The theater fared better than prose fiction, but provided little that might be compared to the achievements of the *siglo de oro* (Golden Age) of Lope de Vega and Calderón.

Some critics continue to value the poetry of the 18th c. only to the extent that it is preromantic—as though the neoclassical aesthetic itself were inherently devoid of interest. From the perspective of intellectual hist., however, we can see this period as one in which prominent Enlightenment figures, *ilustrados*, used the medium of verse along with that of prose, and for similar ends. Eighteenth-c. writers held a Horatian idea of verse as a medium suited to a wide variety of purposes, incl. satire, epistle, and moral instruction. Many significant intellectuals of the Sp. Enlightenment left behind a significant body of verse along with their prose writings. The result is a healthy diversity of genres, metrical forms, and poetic subjects.

The most prominent poet of the century was Juan Meléndez Valdés (1754–1817), who imitated Alexander Pope's *Essay on Man* and participated in the vogue for anacreontic odes. This genre, practiced by many other poets of the period, incl. others in Meléndez Valdés's circle such as José Cadalso (1741–82), was devoted to the celebration of the pleasures of life. The animal fables in verse of Tomás de Iriarte (1750–91) and Félix María de Samaniego (1745–1801) are also worthy of note, although Iriarte is now better regarded than Samaniego. Neither is as significant as Jean de La Fontaine is for Fr. lit. Nicolás Fernández de Moratín (1737–80) practiced a Horatian aesthetic of instructing and delighting, devoting poems to bullfighting and prostitution. Gaspar Melchor de Jovellanos (1744–1811), the most prominent thinker of his time, also left behind a significant number of poems. He is perhaps the best model of the *ilustrado* whose works of literary creation form part of a larger intellectual project but who does not conform to the postromantic ideal of the literary creator.

Cadalso's preromantic anguish is more in tune with later taste, although, in this case, the poetic prose of *Noches lúgubres* (*Lugubrious Nights*, 1798) remains somewhat better known than the verse of *Ocios de mi juventud* (Leisures of my Youth, 1781).

B. *The Nineteenth Century.* Sp. romanticism has been disparaged, in much the same way Sp. neoclassicism was, as belated, lacking in first-rate poets, and overly derivative of foreign models. The failure of neoclassical poetics, in this conventional view, derives from a weak and imitative Sp. Enlightenment, whereas the weakness of Sp. romanticism parallels the political failure of liberalism, repressed by the regime of Fernando VII (1813–33).

The historical *romances* of Ángel de Saavedra, Duke of Rivas (1791–1865) are of interest mostly to specialists, though they kept alive the ballad trad. that had always been a part of Sp. popular culture. This trad. had persisted in the anonymous *romances de ciego* (blind man's ballads) of the 17th and 18th cs.—a genre often disparaged by Enlightenment intellectuals. José Zorrilla (1817–93), whose most famous work was the play *Don Juan Tenorio* (1844), originally made his name with a funeral oration in verse read at the funeral of José de Larra, the prominent essayist who committed suicide in 1837. Like Larra, the Byronic José de Espronceda (1808–42) died young. His long poem, *El estudiante de Salamanca* (1840), reprises the Don Juan myth. He wrote two other long poems, *El diablo mundo* (1841) and *Canto a Teresa* (1837), preserving some of the generic diversity of the neoclassical period.

The Sevillian Gustavo Adolfo Bécquer (1836–70) wrote romantic poetry long after the heyday of Eur. romanticism. His adaptation of some features of the oral trad., such as assonant rhyme, makes him a favorite of 20th-c. poet Luis Cernuda. Most other 19th-c. Sp. poets, in contrast, are given to overblown rhet. Rosalía de Castro (1837–85), one of the most interesting figures of the period, wrote poetry both in Sp. and in Galician and is often compared to Bécquer. Her major work in Sp. was *En las orillas del Sar* (On the Banks of the Sar, 1884). Castro was not the only female poet of the century: Carolina Coronado (1821–1911) and Gertrudis Gómez de Avellaneda (1814–73) were more or less conventional romantic poets who enjoyed some popularity.

While not a poet himself, the Sp. folklorist Antonio Machado y Álvarez (1848–93) collected the lyrics of the *cante jondo* in two major anthols., anticipating the neopopularist movement of the early 20th c. and the work of his own sons, Antonio and Manuel Machado. The latter part of the century also saw the satirical *Humoradas* of Ramón del Campoamor (1817–1901) and the patriotic verse of Gaspar Núñez de Arce (1834–1903). Something of the 18th-c. impulse toward generic diversity and moral edification persists in the work of these poets, who otherwise have little to offer. The residence in Spain of the Nicaraguan poet Rubén Darío, beginning in 1898, introduced *modernismo* to the peninsula, a welcome antidote to the prosaic poetic realism of Campoamor.

C. ***The Twentieth Century and Beyond.*** Two influential poets stand at the beginning of the 20th c.: Antonio Machado (1875–1939) and Juan Ramón Jiménez (1881–1958). Both come to reject the perceived excesses of modernismo, with its ornamental conception of verse. Machado, following Bécquer, purified his style in the neosymbolist *Soledades, Galerías y otros poemas* (Solitudes, Passageways, and Other Poems, 1907). *Campos de Castilla* (Fields of Castile, 1912) is another emblematic book, bringing the consciousness of Sp. decadence characteristic of other writers of the so-called Generation of 1898. Machado famously defined himself as "good, in the good sense of the word" and denounced the decadence of a Castilian culture that "despises all that it does not know." Such phrases have become touchstones for subsequent Sp. poets and intellectuals.

Jiménez, like Machado, rejected modernismo but did so in order to pursue an even more rigorous stylistic perfection. In so doing, he became the sponsor of high modernist projects like those of José Ángel Valente. He has often been disparaged for developing a kind of narcissistic poetics, even as he was admired for his devotion to his craft. Jorge Guillén (1893–1984) and Pedro Salinas (1891–1951) began as neosymbolist poets influenced by Jiménez's pure poetry. Salinas is known mostly for the rather abstract love poetry of *La voz a ti debida* (*My Voice Because of You*, 1936). Guillén, while a close friend of Salinas, is ultimately a different sort of poet: he devised a formally elaborate discourse to express a jubilant vision of a reality subjected to the poet's ordering imagination. The second ed. of *Cántico*, published in 1936, collected his most enduring poetry.

The most celebrated poet of the 1920s and 1930s is Federico García Lorca (1898–1936). In Spain, Lorca is known mostly as a neopopularist poet, somewhat akin to the virtuosic Rafael Alberti (1902–99). Internationally, he is the sponsor of the *duende* and the quasi-surrealist author of *Poeta en Nueva York* (*Poet in New York*), which was not published until 1940. His most popular work in his own lifetime was the 1928 *Primer romancero gitano* (First Gypsy Ballad Book). His most significant influence has been on the poetry of the U.S., where Af. Am. and gay poets took up his cause. Lorca is known in the Eng.-speaking world primarily as a "Spanish surrealist," but he was not, in fact, affiliated with surrealism. The surrealist-influenced poetry of Vicente Aleixandre (1898–1984) and Luis Cernuda (1902–63), along with analogous works by the Chilean poet Pablo Neruda (who resided in Spain in the 1930s), has had an enthusiastic reception in the Eng.-speaking world; but, in reality, most Sp. poetry of this period was not surrealist.

The period from about 1918 to 1936 is a fertile one, with a profusion of styles arising in rapid succession: the pure poetry of Jiménez, Guillén, and Salinas; ultraism, an avant-garde movement derived from Vicente Huidobro's Chilean creationism; neopopularism; some short-lived experiments in a neobaroque aesthetic (Alberti's *Cal y canto* [1929], e.g.); neoclassicism; and the quasi-surrealist mode seen in some books of Aleixandre and Cernuda. In many cases, a single poet might experiment with two or three of these styles with no sense of contradiction. Alberti and Gerardo Diego (1896–1987) were poets of great flexibility and virtuosity.

During the Sp. Civil War (1936–39), poets affiliated with both sides wrote ballads to be sung on the front lines. Miguel Hernández (1910–42), who died of tuberculosis in a Francoist prison, composed the heart-wrenching "Nanas de la cebolla" (Lullaby of the Onion) lamenting that his young son had only onions to eat. His *Romancero y cancionero de ausencias* (Ballads and Songs of Absence, 1958), to which this poem belongs, turns away from the neobaroque style of his prewar work as well as from the propagandistic rhet. of his war poetry. Poets on the right included Luis Rosales (1910–92), Luis Felipe Vivanco (1907–75), and Manuel Machado (1874–1947), the latter an erstwhile follower of Darío's modernismo. Many poets who initially supported the military rebellion became dissidents during the ensuing Franco dictatorship, experiencing a kind of "inner exile."

The assassination of Lorca at the beginning of the war, the death of Antonio Machado in 1939 as he was fleeing to France, and the exile of numerous other significant figures (Salinas, Guillén, Cernuda, Alberti) left a void in Sp. poetry of the postwar period. Prominent poets who remained behind in Spain included Diego, Dámaso Alonso (1898–1990), and Aleixandre.

Aleixandre became a mentor to young poets of successive generations within Spain and would go on to win the Nobel Prize in 1984. Major works written by exile poets include Salinas's *El contemplado* (The Contemplated One, 1946), a set of formally virtuosic variations on a single theme, the contemplation of the sea, and Jiménez's densely metaphysical *Dios deseado y deseante* (God Desired and Desiring, 1949). Jiménez won the Nobel Prize in 1956. Cernuda's dramatic monologues, collected in successive eds. of *La realidad y el deseo* (Reality and Desire, 1936) were more influential on subsequent Sp. poets than any other comparable figure. His final work, *Desolación de la quimera* (Desolation of the Chimera, 1962), contains vitriolic attacks on figures of his own generation such as Salinas and Alonso.

The *Garcilasismo* of José García Nieto (1914–2001), emphasizing traditional forms and patriotic content, enjoyed a brief vogue in the 1940s. This movement was a carryover from the neoclassical trend of the years immediately before the war. The major movement in postwar poetry, however, was the social poetry of Blas de Otero (1916–79) and José Hierro (1922–2002). These poets are both masters of traditional verse. Otero began with the existentialist anguish typical of the 1950s and moved toward a more sharply defined political stance. Hierro's groundbreaking *Libro de las alucinaciones* (Book of Hallucinations, 1964) presented a phantasmagoric vision of reality. Gabriel Celaya (1911–91) wrote poetry of social protest in a more bombastic and verbose mode. At the margins of major trends was a belated avant-garde movement: *postismo*, led by Carlos Edmundo de Ory (1923–2010). The use of the label *postismo* for this avant-garde movement indicates its anachronism, but, in some respects, Ory was ahead of his time, anticipating the neo-avant garde of the 1970s and 1980s.

Claudio Rodríguez (1934–99), a visionary poet, inaugurated a new era with *Don de la ebriedad* (Gift of Drunkenness, 1954), heralding the decline of social poetry in the following decade. Rodríguez, the most naturally gifted Sp. poet since Lorca, is linked to other contemporaries in the so-called Generation of the 1950s. These poets practiced a more ironic mode of social poetry or, like Francisco Brines (b. 1932), wrote in a meditative mode at the margins of political engagement. Jaime Gil de Biedma (1929–90), influenced by W. H. Auden, founded the School of Barcelona along with his friends Carlos Barral (1928–89) and José Agustín Goytisolo (1928–99). Some poets of this cohort who lived in neither Madrid nor Barcelona emerged into view somewhat later, in the 1970s and 1980s: María Victoria Atencia (b. 1931) in Málaga, and Antonio Gamoneda (b. 1931) in León. The cultural decentralization of the post-Franco period led to a greater recognition of these peripheral figures.

The anthol. *Nueve novísimos poetas españoles* (Nine Very New Spanish Poets, ed. J. Castellet), published in 1970, brought to the foreground a group of younger poets who rejected what they felt was the drab realism of social poetry, drawing inspiration instead from the poetic modernism of Sp. poetry of Lorca's generation, from the international avant-garde of the period between the two world wars, and from popular culture, esp. the movies. These poets practiced an exuberantly allusive, though sometimes melancholic, "culturalism." Of the nine poets included in the anthol., José María Álvarez (b. 1942), Pere Gimferrer (b. 1945), Guillermo Carnero (b. 1947), and Leopoldo María Panero (1948–2014) best illustrated the prototype of *novísmo* poetry. Gimferrer produced his early work in Sp. before turning to his native Catalan. *La muerte en Beverly Hills* (Death in Beverly Hills, 1968) is a dreamlike collage of images from classic Hollywood movies. Carnero's 1967 *Dibujo de la muerte* (Sketch of Death) reflects the aestheticism of this era, while the hyperrationalism of *Variaciones y figuras sobre un tema de La Bruyère* (Variations and Figures on a Theme by La Bruyère, 1974) connects him to neoclassical lit. The poetry of Panero, the son of the prominent right-wing poet of the 1940s Leopoldo Panero (1909–62), self-consciously reflects on the discourse of schizophrenia. Other poets emerging in this period, like Aníbal Núñez (1944–87), Jenaro Talens (b. 1946), José-Miguel Ullán (1944–2009), and Jaime Siles (b. 1951), who were not included in this anthol., may ultimately turn out to be as significant as the novísimos themselves.

Sp. poetry after 1980 witnesses three major devels.: (1) The emergence of a new movement of women poets, incl. Ana Rossetti (b. 1950), Isla Correyero (b. 1957), Blanca Andreu (b. 1959), and Amalia Iglesias (b. 1962), who use a neo-avant-garde style to write freely about issues of gender identity and sexuality; (2) a neorealist reaction against the perceived excesses of the novísmo aesthetic, spearheaded by a group of mostly Andalusian poets, among them Luis

García Montero (b. 1958), Felipe Benítez Reyes (b. 1960), and Aurora Luque (b. 1962); and (3) the persistence of a "late modernist" aesthetic in the work of two major figures, José Ángel Valente (1929–2000) and Gamoneda, and in the work of many younger poets, incl. Miguel Casado (b. 1954), Chantal Maillard (b. 1951), and Juan Carlos Mestre (b. 1956). Valente was a somewhat imperious presence, championing an austere aesthetic rooted in the trads. of Sp. mysticism. Gamoneda takes inspiration from mod. Fr. poetry (René Char, Saint-John Perse) in *Libro del frío* (Book of the Cold, 1992). In *Libro de los venenos* (Book of Poisons, 1997), a multilayered commentary on a Ren. trans. of an ancient treatise on poisons and their remedies, Gamoneda breaks down the barrier between poetry and prose.

Because proponents of both the neo-avant garde and of Valente's high modernism tend to disparage García Montero's "poetry of experience," and vice versa, there is as yet no universally accepted canon for the poetry of this period. During the 1990s, it seemed as though García Montero's approach, in the trad. of the dramatic monologues of Cernuda and the ironic social poetry of Gil de Biedma and Ángel González (1925–2008), was the most significant tendency in contemp. Sp. poetry. In the first decade of the 21st c., however, Gamoneda has emerged as a significant elder statesman. His mature work, beginning with his 1977 *Descripción de la mentira* (Description of the Lie), strongly resonates with the contemp. concern for the recuperation of the historical memory of the Civil War and the political repression of the Franco regime. Poets who are more or less in Gamoneda's orbit practice a wide variety of styles. They are linked only by a certain seriousness of purpose and by a rejection of facile aesthetic solutions. Olvido García Valdés (b. 1950) writes an extremely subtle poetry of sharp syntactic and prosodic ruptures, working through cinematic montage. Jorge Riechmann (b. 1962), influenced by Char and by the intellectual trad. of Marxism, writes out of a deep social and environmental consciousness.

The dominance of an artificial canon of male poets, perpetuated by institutional sclerosis, by the "generational" method of literary historiography, and by the ghettoization of women's writing, persists even in post-1975, democratic Spain. Two significant anthols. of poetry written by women have made an impact on this situation. The 1985 *Las Diosas Blancas* (The White Goddesses), ed. by Ramón Buenaventura, presented poetry written by women through the anthologist's sexualized filter: while celebrating the genuine novelty of this body of work, Buenaventura tended to highlight its more sensationalistic aspects. *Ellas tienen la palabra* (They Have the Word, ed. Noni Benegas and Jesús Munáriz), published in 1998, presents a more inclusive and measured view. The critical introduction frames the work of women poets born after 1950 in the context of a trad. in women's poetry from the romantic movement to mid-century precursors such as Gloria Fuertes (1917–98) and Ángela Figuera (1902–84). Significant poets represented in this anthol. are too numerous to list by name. Standouts include Julia Otxoa (b. 1953), who experiments with the prose poem and laments the violent hist. of her native Basque country; Concha García (b. 1956), who explores the tedium of everyday life in a neobaroque style; Lola Velasco (b. 1961), who writes long sequences with a subtle interplay among poetic voices; and Luisa Castro (b. 1966), with her unsparing vision of a semisavage childhood.

See AL-ANDALUS, POETRY OF; BASQUE COUNTRY, POETRY OF THE; CATALAN POETRY; GALICIA, POETRY OF; ITALIAN PROSODY; ITALY, POETRY OF; JUDEO-SPANISH POETRY; SPANISH AMERICA, POETRY OF; SPANISH PROSODY.

■ **I. To 1700.** ***Anthologies, Bilingual Editions, and Translations***: *Spanish Poetry of the Golden Age*, ed. B. W. Wardropper (1971); *Garcilaso de la Vega y sus comentaristas*, ed. A. Gallego Morell et al., 2d. ed. (1972); *Renaissance and Baroque Poetry of Spain*, ed. E. L. Rivers (1972)—Sp. texts with Eng. paraphrase; *The Spanish Traditional Lyric*, ed. J. G. Cummins (1977); J. Ruiz, *Libro de Buen Amor/The Book of True Love*, ed. A. N. Zahareas, trans. S. R. Daly (1978); *Poesía de la Edad de Oro*, v. 1, *Renacimiento*, v. 2, *Barroco*, ed. J. M. Blecua (1984); *Corpus de la antigua lírica popular hispánica (siglos XV a XVII)*, ed. M. Frenk (1987); *Poesía de cancionero*, ed. A. Alonso (1995); Alfonso X, el Sabio, *Cantigas de Loor*, ed. by M. G. Cunningham (2000)—Sp. and Eng. texts with musical score; St. John of the Cross, *The Poems*, trans. R. Campbell (2000); *The Golden Age: Poems of the Spanish Renaissance*, trans. E. Grossman (2006); *The Dream of the Poem: Hebrew Poetry from Muslim and Christian Spain*, 950–1492, ed. and trans. P. Cole (2007); *Selected Poems of Góngora*, trans. J. Dent-Young (2007); *Spanish Ballads*, trans. W. S. Merwin (2008); *Selected Poems of Garcilaso de la Vega*, trans. J. Dent-Young (2009); *Selected*

Poems of Francisco de Quevedo, trans. C. D. Johnson (2009). ***Criticism and History***: P. Salinas, *Reality and the Poet in Spanish Poetry* (1940); M. R. Lida de Malkiel, *Juan de Mena, poeta del Prerrenacimiento español* (1950); R. Menéndez Pidal, D. Catalán, J. Galmés, *Cómo vive un romance* (1954); T. Navarro Tomás, *Métrica española* (1956); R. *Lapesa, La obra literaria del Marqués de Santillana* (1957); B. W. Wardropper, *Historia de la poesía lírica a lo divino en la cristiandad occidental* (1958); D. Alonso, *Estudios y ensayos gongorinos* (1960); O. H. Green, *Spain and the Western Tradition*, 4 v. (1963–66); R. Menéndez Pidal, *En torno al Poema del Cid* (1963); C. F. Fraker, *Studies on the "Cancionero de Baena"* (1966); A. Collard, *Nueva poesía: conceptismo, culteranismo en la crítica española* (1967); P. Bénichou, *Creación poética en el romancero tradicional* (1968); F. Pierce, *Poesía épica del Siglo de Oro*, 2d. ed. (1968); R. Lapesa, *La trayectoria poética de Garcilaso*, enlarged ed. (1968); S. Reckert, *Style and Symbol in Iberian Traditional Verse* (1970); A. D. Deyermond, *A Literary History of Spain: The Middle Ages* (1971); M. Frenk, *Entre folklore y literatura: lírica hispánica antigua* (1971); R. O. Jones, *A Literary History of Spain. The Golden Age: Prose and Poetry* (1971); S. A. Gilman, "On *Romancero* as a Poetic Language," *Homenaje a Casalduero*, ed. R. Pincus Sigele et al. (1972); F. Márquez Villanueva, *Investigaciones sobre Juan Álvarez Gato*, 2d ed. (1974); E. de Chasca, *The Poem of the Cid* (1976); M. Molho, *Semántica y poética: Góngora, Quevedo* (1977); A. Martínez Arancón, *La batalla en torno a Góngora* (1978); E. L. Bergmann, *Art Inscribed: Essays on "Ekphrasis" in Spanish Golden Age Poetry* (1979); J. Beverley, *Aspects of Góngora's "Soledades"* (1980); *Quevedo in Perspective*, ed. J. Iffland (1982); C. Smith, *The Making of the "Poema de Mío Cid"* (1983); L. S. Lerner, *Metáfora y sátira en la obra de Quevedo* (1984); F. López Estrada, *Las poéticas castellanas de la Edad Media* (1984); L. López Baralt, *San Juan de la Cruz y el Islam* (1985); J. A. Maravall, *Culture of the Baroque*, trans. T. Cochran (1986); M. E. Barnard, *The Myth of Apollo and Daphne from Ovid to Quevedo* (1987); M. P. Manero Sorolla, *Introducción al estudio del Petrarquismo en España* (1987); F. Márquez Villanueva, *Lope: vida y valores* (1988); P. J. Smith, *Writing in the Margin* (1988); A. Egido, *Fronteras de la poesía en el Barroco*. B. López-Bueno, *Templada lira: Estudios sobre la poesía del Siglo de Oro* (1990); A. L. Martin, *Cervantes and the Burlesque Sonnet* (1991); A. Terry, *Seventeenth-Century Spanish Poetry: The Power of Artifice* (1993); I. E. Navarrete, *Orphans of Petrarch: Poetry and Theory in the Spanish Renaissance* (1994); R. Greene, *Unrequited Conquests* (1999); E. B. Davis, *Myth and Identity in the Epic of Early Modern Spain* (2000); "Poetry of Medieval Spain," "Renaissance Poetry," "Making of Baroque Poetry," *The Cambridge History of Spanish Literature*, ed. D. T. Gies (2004); L. M. Girón-Negrón, "El laberinto y sus 'reveses' en Juan de Mena, *Medioevo Romano* 28 (2004); R. Padrón, *The Spacious Word* (2004); R. Helgerson, *A Sonnet from Carthage: Garcilaso de la Vega and the New Poetry of Sixteenth-Century Europe* (2007); C. Chemris, *Góngora's "Soledades" and the Problem of Modernity* (2008); J. Dodds, M. R. Menocal, A. K. Balbale, *Arts of Intimacy: Christians, Jews, and Muslims in the Making of Castilian Culture* (2008); L. Middlebrook, *Imperial Lyric: New Poetry and New Subjects in Early Modern Spain* (2009); *Studies on Women's Poetry of the Golden Age*, ed. J. Olivares (2009); C. D. Johnson, *Hyperboles: The Rhetoric of Excess in Baroque Literature and Thought* (2010).

■ **II. 1700 to the Present.** ***Anthologies***: *Poesía española*, ed. G. Diego (1932); *Veinte años de poesía española*, ed. J. M. Castellet (1962); *Nueve novísimos poetas españoles*, ed. J. M. Castellet (1970); *Roots and Wings*, ed. H. St. Martin (1976); *Las diosas blancas*, ed. R. Buenaventura (1985); *Ellas tienen la palabra*, ed. N. Benegas and J. Munáriz (1998); *Feroces*, ed. I. Correyero (1998). ***Criticism and History***: D. Alonso, *Poetas españoles contemporáneos* (1952); J. Guillén, *Language and Poetry* (1961); J. A. Valente, *Las palabras de la tribu* (1971); C. B. Morris, *Surrealism and Spain* (1972); G. Siebenmann, *Los estilos poéticos en España desde 1900* (1973); A. P. Debicki, *Poetry of Discovery* (1982); S. Daydí-Tolson, *The Post–Civil War Spanish Social Poets* (1983); G. Carnero, *La cara oscura del siglo de las luces* (1983); P. Silver, *La casa de Anteo* (1985); C. Soufas, *Conflict of Light and Wind* (1989); S. Kirkpatrick, *Las románticas* (1989); C. Soufas, *Conflict of Light and Wind* (1989); *Novísimos, postnovísimos, clásicos*, ed. B. Ciplijauskaité (1990); J. Mayhew, *The Poetics of Self-Consciousness* (1994); A. P. Debicki, *Twentieth-Century Spanish Poetry* (1994); J. Wilcox, *Women Poets of Spain* (1997); M. Persin, *Getting the Picture* (1997); P. Silver, *Ruin and Restitution* (1997); J. Mayhew, *Apocryphal Lorca* (2008), and *The Twilight of the Avant-Garde* (2008).

M. M. Gaylord (to 1700);
J. Mayhew (1700 to present)

SPANISH AMERICA, POETRY OF. At the time of the first Sp. conquests in the Americas (notably Mexico in 1519–21 and Peru in 1532), the poetry of Castilian-speaking Spain was being transformed by Italianate and Petrarchan forms, Greco-Roman mythology, and cl. models. Spain's first viceroyalties, New Spain and then Peru, established court societies and monasteries in which poetry played a significant role. While the *romance* (ballad), based on the octosyllable, continued to flourish as the basis of popular poetry (Rio Plate gauchesque, Chilean *lira*, Mexican *corrido*), the hendecasyllable became the standard for lettered verse, two strands that continued until the 20th c., when free verse became dominant. Poetry's strength was perhaps enhanced by the fact that prose romances and, later, novels were nominally banned in the colonies from 1531.

Naturally, the first Sp. Am. poets were Spaniards who had settled in the New World. Alonso de Ercilla y Zúñiga (1533–94) is the author of *La Araucana* (1569, 1578, and 1589), a verse epic in *ottava rima* that both celebrates the Sp. conquest in Chile and praises the enemy. Particularly moving are the scenes of Araucanian women seeking to bury their dead and of vivid battle. Recognized as the best epic poem in Sp., it was followed by Pedro de Oña's (1570–1643?) *Arauco domado* (1596).

Baroque practice took hold in Sp. America toward the end of the 16th c. Conventions of cl. mythology, strange and wonderful phenomena, and a highly wrought lang. are signs of the *Barroco de Indias* (Baroque of the Indies). Just as architecture adapted elements from indigenous cultures, so lit. recorded Am. wonders and marvels. Bernardo de Balbuena's (Spain, 1561–1627) *Grandeza Mexicana* (1604) extols Mexico City's riches. Later, Rafael Landívar (Guatemala, 1731–93) wrote an extensive poem in Lat. celebrating Am. landscapes, *Rusticatio Americana* (1781). This celebration of America's distinctive bounty will recur throughout 18th- and 20th-c. poetry, from Andrés Bello's *silvas* to Pablo Neruda's *Canto general.*

Satire was prominent in colonial poetry, inevitable where fortunes were quickly made and lost, circumstances of birth were reinvented, and viceregal courts dazzled in stark contrast to surrounding native realities. Juan del Valle Caviedes's (Peru, 1652–97) *Diente del Parnaso* (The Tooth of Parnassus, 1689) attacks doctors; its coarse lang. and physical emphasis present a counterpoint to religious or courtly verse. Also in Lima, Mateo Rosas de Oquendo (b. 1559?) published a scatological romance of over 2,000 lines, "Sátira . . . a las cosas que pasan en el Perú" (Satire of Events in Peru) in 1598.

The place of honor in colonial letters is occupied by a poet at the close of the baroque period, the Mexican nun Sor Juana Inés de la Cruz (ca. 1648–95), who exhibited a genius for all forms of poetry and theater, as well as her famous epistle in defense of her intellectual ambitions. Showing the cultural fluidity of the times, she wrote *villancicos* in Nahuatl, the Aztec lang., as well as in Sp. Her masterwork is the *Primero sueño* (*First Dream*, 1692), an exploration of the mind's coming into consciousness.

Like Sor Juana, poets wrote in other langs. and translated from native langs. to Sp. In Perú, the Andean chronicler Felipe Guamán Poma de Ayala (ca. 1535–1616) includes poems in Quechua in his *El primer nueva corónica y buen gobierno* (*First New Chronicle and Good Government*, ca. 1615). The Peruvian mestizo historian known as El Inca Garcilaso de la Vega (1539–1616), a cousin of the Sp. poet of the same name, dedicated a chapter of the *Comentarios reales de los Incas* (*Royal Commentaries of the Incas*, 1609, 1617)—book 2, ch. 27—to a description of Incan poetry.

Enlightenment ideals came late to Sp. America, brought in part by scientists such as Alexander von Humboldt. These intellectual values had to struggle against the vestiges of the Counter-Reformation, which had attempted to silence Sor Juana and frustrated ideals of liberty and scientific experiment. The Jesuits, teachers of cl. langs. and scholars of native langs., were expelled in 1767. The ideal of liberty, important for 18th-c. revolutions and for the Haitian Revolution of 1802, was seen as dangerous by both church and crown.

In the 18th and 19th cs., periodical publications took on greater importance, and the long poem (whether narrative, dramatic, or lyric), unwieldly for the aims of journalism and popular debate, ceded importance to shorter forms. The introduction of photography in the 19th c. shifted the notion of representation itself, just as the introduction of film at the turn of the 20th c. was to change the dynamics of represented movement.

Early 19th-c. poetry was involved in the revolutionary struggles, with countless odes to military heroes and statesmen. Anthols. collected these poems and distributed them throughout the Americas, helping to establish national literary trads. in the nascent republics (except for Cuba and Puerto Rico, which remained colonies of Spain until the Sp.-Am. War of 1898). The period witnessed an intense interest in the space of Sp. America—its landscape, its indigenous civilizations (particularly ruins), and patriotic fervor. Mariano Melgar (Peru, 1790–1815) adapted the Quechua song form, the *yaraví,* to Sp. poetry.

Andrés Bello (Venezuela, 1781–1865) was an architect of Lat. Am. independence. Sent to England in 1810 by the revolutionaries, he had been exposed to Eng. and Continental philosophy and poetics, as well as to the Industrial Revolution. His "Alocución a la poesía" (Discourse to Poetry, 1823) proclaimed the future to be Am., not Eur. His *Silvas americanas* (1823), which include "A la agricultura de la zona tórrida" (The Agriculture of the Torrid Zone), set forth an ideal, bucolic society to heal the ravages of the revolutionary wars. Bello replaces cl. allusions with Am. ones; he is important as a translator of Lord Byron, Alphonse de Lamartine, and Victor Hugo. (Neruda will return to the *Silvas* as one of his primary sources for *Canto general.*)

The Cuban José María Heredia (1803–39) presents, contemporaneously with Bello's neoclassical stance, a romanticism tinged with melancholy, evoking his exile from Cuba. "En el teocalli de Cholula" (On the Pyramid of Cholula, 1820), a meditation on the Aztec past, and "A Niágara" (To Niagara, 1824) embody romanticism's divided self and the sublime. His focus on exile will be repeated by other poets.

Gertrudis Gómez de Avellaneda (Cuba, 1814–73) was a poet, dramatist, and novelist tutored by Heredia. While she lived most of her adult life in Spain, America, esp. Cuba, is a central topic of her poetry, which involved experimentation with metrics. "Al partir" (On Leaving, 1836), dedicated to Cuba, is her most famous sonnet.

José Joaquín de Olmedo (Ecuador, 1780–1847) contributed the best-known ode to the wars of independence. His "Victoria de Junín: Canto a Bolívar" (1825), modeled on Virgil, incorporated the Incan past as a ghost who prophesies Simón Bolívar's victory and acclaims the revolutionaries as scourges of the Sp. Although Bolívar himself noted the paradox of an Indian figure applauding the Spaniards' descendants, the Indian in 19th-c. poetry often appears as a prophetic muse or a doomed hero.

Esteban Echeverría (Argentina, 1805–51) was sent to Paris, where he was initiated into romantic doctrines. Because of his publications, he was forced into exile in Uruguay in 1840. His masterwork in poetry is the long narrative poem "La cautiva" (The Captive, 1837), which relates the story of a white woman captured by Indians, a common topic in 19th-c. lit.

Bartolomé Hidalgo (Uruguay, 1788–1823) brought to print culture the oral trad. of the *gauchos,* whose singing contests had roots in the med. romance. Hidalgo, with the *cielito* (little heaven) and the *diálogo,* initiates a lettered trad. that reaches its height with the Argentinian epic *Martín Fierro* (1872) by José Hernández (1834–86). *Martín Fierro* recounts the story of the outcast gaucho as deserter soldier in the eyes of the government, an enemy as seen by the Indians. The *Vuelta de Martín Fierro* (The Return of Martín Fierro, 1879) reconciles the gaucho with his past and with the law. As shown by Ludmer, the passage to print culture parallels the government's militarization of the gaucho (wanderer, delinquent) during the wars of independence; thus, his body is used by the army and his voice by print culture. Comic and parodic possibilities of the gauchesque are exploited in Estanislao del Campo's (Argentina, 1834–80) *Fausto.*

The rise of *modernismo* begins with the publication of Rubén Darío's (1867–1916) *Azul . . .* (1888); the movement is often thought to end with his death in 1916. Yet by the 1880s, there was already poetry in the new spirit. Manuel Gutiérrez Nájera (Mexico, 1859–95), José Martí (Cuba, 1853–95), Julián del Casal (Cuba, 1863–93), and José Asunción Silva (Colombia, 1865–96) were innovative poets who explored outside Sp. trad. Unquestionably the poet of his century, Darío transformed poetry in Spain as well as in Sp. America. For the first time, the leadership of an influential literary movement in a Eur. lang. emerged from the New World, not from Europe.

Modernismo appeared in a Sp. America on the threshold of modernity, esp. in its largest cities. The central premise of the *modernistas* was innovation, and they reacted against emergent capitalism, positivism, and 19th-c. canons of propriety. Their models were Charles Baudelaire, Paul Verlaine, Walt Whitman, and E. A. Poe, as well as visual sources such as the Pre-Raphaelite Brotherhood and art nouveau. The modernistas introduced to poetry a new technical vigor, a cosmopolitanism (their orientalism is notable), and a new syntax. Modernismo rediscovered the musical harmonies of poetry, and Darío himself reached back into med. Sp. trad., Fr. Parnassianism, and symbolism for his inspiration. He reintroduced the alexandrine into Sp. and experimented rhythmically as well as metrically. Besides *Azul*. . . , his central volumes are *Prosas profanas* (1896) and *Cantos de vida y esperanza* (1905), where he addresses political themes, particularly the domination by the U.S. after the Sp.-Am. War.

Born of mixed ancestry in Nicaragua, Darío ventured first to Chile, where he published *Azul*. . . , and then to Buenos Aires. Like many modernistas, he supported himself through journalism. Darío's taste for the exotic, his explicit eroticism, and his direct, often intimate tone shocked many who disparaged him and his followers as modernistas, a title they soon embraced.

Martí was very different from Darío but is important as an innovator. His *Ismaelillo* (1886) and *Versos sencillos* (Simple Verses, 1891, in *redondillas* based on the octosyllable) reintroduced into lettered culture traditional and popular rhythms. His posthumous *Versos libres* (Free Verse, 1913) are more hermetic, with reflections on exile, mod. urban life (he spent a great deal of his life in New York), and internal strife.

Gutiérrez Nájera was known for his natural scenes and lively verse such as the poem "La Duquesa Job" (Duchess Job, 1884). A journalist, he specialized in short, contemp. accounts called *crónicas* (chronicles). In Mexico, the modernistas grouped around the *Revista Moderna* (1894–96) and the *Revista Azul* (1892–1915), whose art and poetry emphasized decadence and eroticism. Del Casal produced a series of sonnets based on paintings by Gustave Moreau. His "impure love of the city" shifts the scene from the natural world to an urban one. His younger compatriot and friend Juana Borrero (1877–96) excelled at both painting and poetry until her early death.

In Argentina, the primary modernist was Leopoldo Lugones (1874–1938). His *Lunario sentimental* (Sentimental Moon Calendar, 1909) introduced verse free of conventional meter, and its parody of the moon and introduction of the colloquial signaled a fissure in the aesthetics of modernismo. Jorge Luis Borges acknowledged Lugones as an antecedent to ultraism. The careers of Lugones and Julio Herrera y Reissig (Uruguay, 1875–1910) converge in their early works, since both were influenced by the Fr. symbolist Albert Samain. They are also counterparts in pushing poetic systems to the limit, as in Herrera y Reissig's "Tertulia lunática" (Lunatic Gathering, 1911) where shocking wordplay presaged vanguardist energies.

One of the most striking voices of modernismo was the Uruguayan Delmira Agustini (1886–1914). She is the most sexually explicit, introducing female sexuality into modernista currents, and was the starting point for a new generation of female poets, incl. the Argentinian Alfonsina Storni (1892–1938) and the Chilean Gabriela Mistral (1889–1957).

Other modernistas include Ricardo Jaimes Freyre (Bolivia, 1868–1933), who explored Nordic mythology, and Enrique González Martínez (Mexico, 1871–1952), whose 1912 poem on wringing the neck of the swan complains about striving for eloquence. José Santos Chocano (Peru, 1875–1934) introduced a new thematics into modernista poetry called *mundonovismo* (New Worldism) that exalted America's indigenous past. Amado Nervo (Mexico, 1870–1919) was the most read poet of his generation. José Juan Tablada (Mexico, 1871–1945) experimented with haiku and ideographic forms incl. the calligramme. Ramón López Velarde's (Mexico, 1888–1921) poetry has gained increased critical attention. His "Suave patria" (The Gentle Homeland, 1921) is a tribute to a gentler Mexico of the provinces. His work (e.g., "Mi prima Agueda" [My Cousin Agueda], 1916) wrestles with eroticism but also the speech of daily life.

Octavio Paz writes that, after modernismo, there are two directions in Sp. Am. poetry: that of Lugones in *Lunario sentimental* and that of Darío; and that mod. poetry follows the path of Lugones. This is true in the sense of poetic form, since vanguardist poets and their followers will largely dispense with rhyme and meter, while another trad. will employ the forms of previous centuries. This second trad. is also tied to the declamation of poetry, a performance practice important in public events in Latin America until the mid-20th c.

Closely following the modernistas was a new generation eager to clear the way for a different kind of lit. Vanguardist movements sprang up in all Lat. Am.—e.g., *estridentismo* in Mexico, *ultraísmo* in Argentina, *indigenismo* in Peru, *diepalismo* in Puerto Rico, *antropofagia* in Brazil—as did little magazines such as *Prisma* (Argentina 1921–22), *Martín Fierro* (1924), *Proa* (1922–25), *Elipse* (Chile, 1922), *Irradiador* (Mexico, 1923), *Vórtice* (Puerto Rico,

1922), *Revista de Avance* (Cuba, 1927–30), and *Contemporáneos* (Mexico, 1928–31). In Peru, the vanguard is often linked to the indigenous question, most famously in José Carlos Mariátegui's jour. *Amauta* (1926–30), but also in *Boletín Titikaka* (based in Puno) with poets such as Gamaliel Churata (1897–1969).

The vanguard sought to strip poetry of its excess, to reduce it to essentials. They dispensed with meter, rhyme, and extended patterns of imagery in favor of free verse of high visual and aural impact. With film now widespread, poets sought ways to incorporate new techniques of perception. In the *estridentistas*, the influence of It. futurism and the fascination with technology was strong; the *ultraísta* movement in Buenos Aires, led by Borges (Argentina, 1899–1986), sought to reduce poetry to its basic element, the metaphor. Borges adopted the orthography of colloquial speech in his books dedicated to Buenos Aires: *Fervor de Buenos Aires* (1923), *Luna de enfrente* (Moon across the Way, 1925), and *Cuaderno San Martín* (San Martín Notebook, 1929). Over time, he returned to conventional forms, disavowing his vanguardist past.

What distinguishes the vanguards of Sp. America from those of Europe and the U.S. are the political and ethnic issues involved. Yet this presented a dilemma: how is vanguard poetry to be meaningful socially? Many believed, like Vicente Huidobro (Chile, 1893–1948), that changing lang. was itself revolutionary. Huidobro called his aesthetic *creacionismo* (creationism) and was, with César Vallejo, the most radical innovator of his generation. Interested in cubism, he collaborated with artists such as Juan Gris in poem-paintings. His *Altazor* (1931) is a verse epic of a journey through the spheres in the aftermath of destruction. As the poem evolves, lang. loses its representational character, becoming only dispersed sounds.

In Peru, César Vallejo (1892–1938), from a provincial background, became, with Neruda, the most influential Sp. Am. poet of the 20th c. His *Heraldos negros* (*The Black Heralds*, 1919) has echoes of modernismo but shows the earthiness of his stripped down lang. and a loss of faith in overarching systems, esp. Christianity. *Trilce* (1922) is hermetic and baffling, destroying syntax and confounding meaning. Its visceral appeal has inspired generations of poets, as has the posthumous political poetry collected in *Poemas humanos* (1939).

In Chile, Pablo Neruda (pseud. of Ricardo Neftalí Reyes Basoalto) (1904–73) gained notice first as the author of *Veinte poemas de amor y una canción desesperada* (*Twenty Love Poems and a Song of Despair*, 1924). As a diplomat in Asia, he continued work on the *Residencia en la tierra* (*Residence on Earth*, 1933–47), which expressed inner turmoil in relation to the natural and material world. In 1937, he published *España en el corazón* (*Spain in Our Hearts*) in solidarity with the Republicans in the Sp. Civil War. *Canto general* (*General Song*, 1950) is a vast epic of the Americas. Originally inspired by Bello's *Silvas americanas* (1823), Neruda traces Am. origins from prehistoric vegetal and animal states to the cold-war realities of the 1940s. He recounts hist.—esp. conquest and independence heroes, along with sections devoted to rivers, birds, the common man and woman ("La tierra se llama Juan"). The most famous section is "Alturas de Macchu Picchu," which evokes the Incan past out of its slumber within the stones of the ruined city. Neruda went on to break new ground in his *Odas elementales* (*Elemental Odes*, 1954), celebrating the natural and the everyday in short verses, with odes to artichokes, socks, and dictionaries.

Nicolás Guillén's (Cuba, 1902–89) long writing career gave voice to Afro-Cuban aesthetics and a new political urgency. His early publications, *Motivos de son* (Son Motifs, 1930) and *Songoro cosongo* (1931), develop the possibilities of an Afro-Cuban music and dance in the form of the *son*, a rhythmic pattern with roots in African slave culture of the colonial period. Guillén reproduces vernacular diction and dialect in these works, asserting the legitimacy of Afro-Cuban speech and affirming the beauty of the black woman, taking her from racist cliché to personhood. Guillén joined Fidel Castro's revolution and became a cultural symbol and the head of the writers' union in Cuba.

Not all poets cast off formal restraints. Mistral and Storni, both teachers of modest origins, were traditionalists in form. Mistral, who favored the nine-syllable line, paid special attention to themes of motherhood, children, and the natural world, and generations of children in Sp. America have learned to recite her poems. *Desolación* (1922), *Tala* (Clearcut, 1938), and *Lagar* (Winepress, 1954) are her principal poetic works; the latter volume introduces a new hermeticism, and *Poema de Chile* (1967) presents a puzzling antiepic of a journey through the homeland. Mistral received the Nobel Prize in 1945, the first Lat. Am. to be so honored. Storni presents a sharper edge to the female voice in poetry. She is faithful to poetic form until her final works but shatters convention by expressing rage and sorrow at the female condition in a male-dominated society as in her most anthologized poems, "Tú me quieres blanca" (You Want Me White, 1918) and "Hombre pequeñito" (Little Man, 1919). Her urban poems capture the dislocations brought about by immigration. After a prolonged illness, she committed suicide in 1938 in a dramatic and self-publicized way. Her contemp. Juana de Ibarbourou (Uruguay, 1895–1979) was extremely well known in her time, fitting more easily into the conventions for women. Her lyric poetry includes themes of nature and of love.

The Mexican Revolution (1910–20) brought visibility to indigenous and mestizo issues in a range of arts, incl. the murals of Diego Rivera, David Alfaro Siqueiros, and José Clemente Orozco and the later paintings of Frida Kahlo. Nonetheless, a group of poets, *Los Contemporáneos* (named for their magazine), ignored post-revolutionary politics and devoted themselves to interiority, as in Xavier Villaurrutia's (1903–50) beautiful and sometimes homoerotic *Nocturnos* (1933), José Gorostiza's (1901–73) *Muerte sin fin* (Death without End, 1939), and Carlos Pellicer's (1897–1977) tropical landscapes. Salvador Novo (1904–74) is also associated with this group.

The impact of surrealism continued well into the century, esp. with Octavio Paz (Mexico, 1914–98). In addition to being the leading poet of his era (he won the Nobel Prize in 1990), Paz was a commanding voice on poetics and lit. hist. The books of criticism *El arco y la lira* (*The Bow and the Lyre*, 1956) and *Los hijos del limo* (*Children of the Mire*, 1974) have shaped our understanding of poetry in theory and act. His poetic work ranges widely, with roots in pre-Columbian and Asian cosmologies, eroticism, and Mexican realities.

Conversational style became increasingly important around mid-c. with Nicanor Parra's (Chile, b. 1914) "anti-poetry" (*Poemas y antipoemas*, 1954) and the work of Roque Dalton (El Salvador, 1935–75). Dalton's colloquial style became associated with Central Am. liberation movements and the poetry of political denunciation throughout Lat. Am. A special mention should be made of Violeta Parra (Chile, 1917–67) and her incorporation of oral culture into written poetry. Basing her work on the octosyllable, she wrote and performed her *décimas* throughout Chile and in Europe, bringing full circle a trad. as old as the conquest.

Military conflicts and dictatorships of the 1970s and 1980s provided poets such as Juan Gelman (Argentina, 1930–2014), Ernesto Cardenal (Nicaragua, b. 1925), Claribel Alegría (El Salvador, b. 1924), Juan Luis Martínez (Chile, 1942–93), and Raúl Zurita (Chile, b. 1950) material for some of their most notable poetry.

Gonzalo Rojas (Chile, 1917–2011), Blanca Varela (Peru, 1926–2009), José Emilio Pacheco (Mexico, 1939–2014), and Alejandra Pizarnik (Argentina, 1936–72) are central to recent decades.

Also important is a group of neobaroque poets inspired by the Cuban José Lezama Lima (1910–76), incl. the Argentine Néstor Perlongher (1949–92), the Cuban José Kozer (b. 1940), and the Argentine Diana Bellessi (b. 1946), among others. A renewal of pan-indigenous movements in the Americas has sparked new interest in indigenous langs. and topics.

See ARGENTINA, POETRY OF; BOLIVIA, POETRY OF; CARIBBEAN, POETRY OF THE; CHILE, POETRY OF; EL SALVADOR, POETRY OF; GUATEMALA, POETRY OF; INDIGENOUS AMERICAS, POETRY OF THE; MEXICO, POETRY OF; NICARAGUA, POETRY OF; PERU, POETRY OF; SPAIN, POETRY OF; URUGUAY, POETRY OF; VENEZUELA, POETRY OF.

■ G. Brotherston, *Latin American Poetry: Origins and Presence* (1975); A. Rama, *Las máscaras democráticas del modernismo* (1985); O. Rivera-Rodas, *La poesía hispanoamericana del siglo XIX (Del romanticismo al modernismo)* (1988); *Las vanguardias latinoamericanas: textos programáticos y críticos*, ed. J. Schwartz (1991); O. Paz, *Children of the Mire: Modern Poetry from Romanticism to the Avant-Garde*, trans. R. Phillips (1991); V. Unruh, *Latin American Vanguards: The Art of Contentious Encounters* (1994); *The Cambridge History of Latin American Literature*, ed. R. González-Echeverarría and E. Pupo-Walker, 2 v. (1996); C. Jrade, *Modernismo, Modernity, and the Development of Spanish American Literature* (1998); W. Rowe, *Poets of Contemporary Latin America: History and Inner Life* (2000); A. Bush, *The Routes of Modernity: Spanish American Poetry from the Early Eighteenth to the Mid-Nineteenth Century* (2002); M. González and D. Treece, *The Gathering of Voices: The Twentieth-Century Poetry of Latin America* (2002); J. Ludmer, *The Gaucho Genre: A Treatise on the Motherland*, trans. M. Weigel (2002); S. Yurkiévich, *Fundadores de la nueva poesía latinoamericana: Vallejo, Huidobro, Borges, Girondo, Neruda, Paz, Lezama Lima* (2002); *Encyclopedia of Twentieth-Century Latin American and Caribbean Literature, 1900–2003*, ed. D. Balderston and M. González (2004); J. Kuhnheim, *Spanish American Poetry at the End of the Twentieth Century: Textual Disruptions* (2004); *Literary Cultures of Latin America: A Comparative History*, ed. M. J. Valdés and D. Kadir, 3 v. (2004); *Compromiso e hibridez: Aproximaciones a la poesía hispánica escrita por mujeres*, ed. T. Escaja (2007); A. González, *A Companion to Spanish American "Modernismo"* (2007).

G. Kirkpatrick

SPANISH PROSODY. Until the advent of free verse and aside from time-measured song form (*verso lírico medieval*) and the chanted epic verse (*verso épico, mester de juglaría*), Sp. verse measure was based on syllable count, involving the principles of hiatus, synaloepha, synaeresis, and diaeresis. Syllables per line are counted to the last stressed syllable, plus one count. In the earliest period, hiatus was obligatory in syllable counting, but by the late 14th c., synaloepha in court poetry prevailed. Hemistichs are metrically independent.

One of the earliest and most durable of Sp. verse forms is the octosyllable or *romance* (Sp. ballad) meter. The earliest strophe is probably the couplet (*pareado*). Med. two-part verse of the mester de juglaría (minstrel verse) dating from or before the 12th c. is the earliest known long-form measure, found primarily in the *cantar de gesta* (popular epic). The hemistichic lines vary in length from about 10 to 20 syllables. The more sophisticated *mester de clerecía* (clerical verse) poems composed in *cuaderna vía* stanzas, whose seven + seven syllable *alejandrino* lines were probably in imitation of the Fr. alexandrine, date from ca. 1200. The all-purpose *copla de arte menor*, a stanza of any moderate length in octosyllabic or shorter verse, and its variation, the *copla de pie quebrado*, became popular. In verse, the favored long lines, all with caesuras creating metrically independent hemistichs, were 12, 14, or 16 syllables in length, each with its optional *quebrado*.

While these forms, along with other less prominent strophic arrangements (e.g., *villancico*), were being developed for both didactic purpose and popular entertainment, the courtly and learned poets of the 14th and 15th cs. were often composing in Galician-Port., which had been used in the 13th c. by King Alfonso X *el Sábio* (the Wise), e.g., in his *Cantigas de Santa María*, and was still lingering in the early 15th c., when most poets were favoring Castilian. The couplet (*pareado, pareja*), the tercet (*terceto*) in any rhyme scheme, various types of *eco*, and some experimental forms are found. Poetic license was tolerated, e.g., accent shift in a word, syncope, haplology, disregard of the penult of a proparoxytone, and acoustic equivalence for true rhyme.

The 16th and 17th cs. in Spain firmly established Italianate verse and stanza forms. The *sáfico* soon appeared. Old forms were regularized (e.g., the alejandrino, the *seguidilla*). The *pentasílabo* (pentasyllable) served occasionally as hemistich of the hendecasyllable and was also used with the *adónico* (pentasyllabic paroxytonic verse) to form the sáfico adónico strophe (three sáficos plus one adónico), also known as the *oda sáfica*. Italianate importations incl. the *soneto, terza rima, octava rima*, or *heroico* or *real* octave, *verso suelto* (unrhymed verse, usually hendecasyllabic, sometimes combined with seven- or five-syllable verse). The hendecasyllabic *romance heroico* (or *endecasilábico* or *real*), the *lira* variations, and the *silva* are among the new. The *redondilla, quintilla*, seguidilla, and their relatives became popular, as did irregular meters and such minor stanza forms as the *ensalada, espinela*, and *folia*.

Publication of Ignacio de Luzán's *Poética* (1737) coincides approximately with the beginning of Sp. neoclassicism, when poets resurrected, restored, and regularized the old and borrowed (mainly from Fr.) or created new variations on old verse and stanza forms. Experimentation was common. From the alejandrino and *verso de arte mayor* to the *trisílabo* (three-syllable verse), every verse length, often with set rhythmic pattern, can be found. Decasyllabic patterns included (1) ◡ ◡ – ◡ ◡ – ◡ ◡ – (◡); (2) – ◡ ◡ – ◡ | – ◡ ◡ – (◡); (3) ◡ – ◡ – ◡ | ◡ – ◡ – (◡); (4) the double adonic (*adónico doblado* or *asclepiadeo*); and (5) the *libre*, without fixed pattern. The nine-syllable line includes the *eneasílabo iriartino* (predominantly ◡ ◡ – ◡ ◡ – ◡ – [◡]), the *esproncedaico* (◡ – ◡ ◡ – ◡ ◡ – [◡]), the *eneasílabo de canción* (◡ ◡ ◡ – ◡ ◡ ◡ – [◡]), the *eneasílabo laverdaico* or *brachycatalecto* (◡ – ◡ ◡ ◡ – ◡ – [◡]), and the *eneasílabo libre* or *polirrítmico* (no set pattern). Occasionally, an octosyllabic poem has stress consistently on the third syllable, simulating pie quebrado. A fixed rhythm, esp. iambic, sometimes appears in heptasyllabic compositions; the *hexasílabo*, usually with fluctuating inner stress patterns, is occasionally trochaic. The seldom independent pentasyllabic adónico, generally in combination with the hendecasyllabic sáfico, may have fluctuating inner stress.

Romantic nostalgia was reflected in the use of the verso de arte mayor, the alejandrino, and their quebrados but did not slow the process of innovation: the *alcaico* (five + five syllable line), the nine-syllable *laverdaico*, and the anapestic 13-syllable were added to the repertory. Within a poem, random assonance could replace true rhyme, and rhythm mixing served a purpose. Essentially ad hoc strophes were common; free verse was in the offing. In the mod. period, poets continued reaching for the new while clinging to the old, further loosening the rules without releasing them completely. The major advance was the full acceptance of *verso libre*, a natural outgrowth of centuries of change. Metrical structure no longer dominates or restricts verse but serves it flexibly as the background instrumental accompaniment to the words.

See CATALAN POETRY; GALICIA, POETRY OF; SPAIN, POETRY OF.

■ J. Vicuña Cifuentes, *Estudios de métrica española* (1929); P. Henríquez Ureña, *Versificación irregular en la poesía castellana*, 2d ed. (1933); D. C. Clarke, *Una bibliografía de versificación española* (1937); E. Díez Echarri, *Teorías métricas del siglo de oro* (1949); D. C. Clarke, *Chronological Sketch of Castilian Versification* (1952); Navarro; J. Domínguez Caparrós, *Diccionario de métrica española* (1985); A. Quilis, *Métrica española*, 3d ed. (1986); *Issues in the Phonology and Morphology of the Major Iberian Languages*, ed. F. Martínez-Gil and A. Morales-Front (1997); G. A. Toledo, "Jerarquías prosódicas en español," *Revista Española de Lingüística* 29 (1999); J. Domínguez Caparrós, *Métrica española*, 2d ed. (2000).

D. C. Clarke

SRI LANKA, POETRY OF

I. Sinhala
II. Tamil
III. English

Sri Lankan poetry covers work in three langs.: Sinhala, which dates to the 1st c. CE; Tamil, which developed a distinctly Sri Lankan identity in the 20th c.; and Eng., of which a small but significant body of work now exists, dating mainly from the mid-20th c.

I. Sinhala. The Sinhala lang. has been used almost exclusively in Sri Lanka, but the contours of Sinhala's poetic heritage resonate with those generally found elsewhere in South Asia. These contours include two key features of literary cultures in premod. South Asia: the restriction of the production of poetry to a limited number of langs., such as Sanskrit and various literary Prakrits, and the recourse to multiple langs. by authors within a single literary culture. These two features have left a profound imprint on Sinhala poetry writing across the centuries, first, in terms of a continuing sense of Sinhala's intrinsic exceptionalism in poetry and, second, in terms of how Sinhala poetry was often inflected by values and conventions that originated in poetry written in other langs.

The most striking feature of exceptionalism in Sinhala literary cultures is in the very fact of the use of Sinhala as a vehicle for poetry. Along with Tamil, Sinhala was among the first local langs. used for poetry in South Asia, with significant examples of poetry and poetic crit. surviving from at least the 7th c. CE. Sinhala poets seem remarkably early to have considered the Sinhala lang. as equal to Sanskrit in its capacity to be a vehicle for poetry, and, ironically, they displayed this confidence in their poems at about the same time that theorization about poetry in Sanskrit explicitly denied that local langs. like Sinhala were capable of poetry. If Sinhala provides some of the earliest evidence for a literary culture in South Asia using a local lang. for poetry, it also provides evidence that this choice must have involved self-consciousness on the part of poets about not being bound by at least some of the conventions that defined literary works and persons in Sanskrit literary culture, even though it was generally normative in premod. South Asia.

Sinhala also provides evidence that the transformation of a lang. used for everyday interaction into one capable of poetry occurred through a standardization and theorization of lang. in grammar and poetics. The processes that transformed Sinhala into a lang. of poetry, however, were often the result of interaction with thinking about poetry found in other langs. The 9th-c. *Siyabaslakara* (Poetics of One's Own Language), one of the earliest extant scholarly works in Sinhala, is a handbook on poetics that turned to Sanskrit texts such as Daṇḍin's

Kāvyādarśa for models of thinking about poetics, while the cl. *Sidatsangarava* (Compilation of Methods), a work of both grammar and poetics, seems related to a similar text in Tamil, the 11th-c. *Viracoliyam.* Moreover, in view of this exceptionalism, Sinhala poets were quite self-conscious about their literary heritage, and they took a variety of steps to ensure the continuity of the lang. used in Sinhala poetry. Their success in this is evident in the gulf between the lang. commonly used in poetry and that used in other written expressions and in speech.

The generative interaction between Sinhala literary cultures and the poetry and poetics produced in other langs. has resulted in a composite Sinhala poetic heritage, one with distinct strands that display their origin in the interaction of Sinhala poets with other literary langs., esp. with Sanskrit, Tamil, and Eng. Another distinct strand within the Sinhala poetic heritage comes from interaction with various forms of folk poetry in Sri Lanka, whether in the form that shades into secular songs or in the form that shades into religious rituals. Folk poetry, whether closer to song or to ritual expression, is marked by the absence of identifiable poets. A case could be made that the trads. of folk poetry continually nourished and sustained the poetic heritage of Sinhala literary cultures but that, in a stricter sense, those cultures were concerned with the production of poets, as identifiable figures, as much as with the production of poems.

The earliest extant examples of poetry in Sinhala are found at Sigiriya, a ruined palace complex in central Sri Lanka. A body of poems about representations of women in paintings found at these ruins was inscribed by visitors at Sigiriya between the 7th and 9th cs., and the poetic conventions found in these graffiti are clearly continuous with the lang. and form of Sinhala poetry written between the 10th and 15th cs. While there are meters used in the poems that seem to be unique to Sinhala poetry, there also seems to be a sophisticated awareness of *Sanskrit poetry and poetics.

Beginning around the 11th or 12th c., Sinhala poets began to adapt more of the conventions of Sanskrit poetry, esp. in ornate poems (*mahākāvya*) that recounted the stories of the previous lives of the Buddha. The content of these poems often seems subordinate to the conventions of the genre in Sanskrit, such as the descriptions of a set number of topics, but they also preserved the formal qualities of Sinhala poetry in meter and style. The greatest of these poems perhaps is *Kavsilumina* (The Crest Gem of Poetry), which continues to occupy a central place in the canon of Sinhala poetry.

This adaptation of models from Sanskrit for Sinhala poetry continued throughout the med. period, esp. in the genre of messenger poems (*sandēśa*), which took Kālidāsa's *Meghadhūta* as a model. The Sinhala poems produced in this genre, such as the *Sälalihini sandēśa*, share distinctive features with poems composed on the same model across southern South Asia—in Sanskrit, *Malayalam, and *Tamil—in the same period.

In the early mod. period, Sinhala poets adapted more from Tamil poetry than seems to have been the case earlier, as can be seen in internal rhyming patterns and literary allusions, but at the same time, Sinhala poets of this era expanded the scope of appropriate subjects for poetry writing beyond the set topics that had characterized earlier poetry. As a result, these poets, writing in the colonized southern coastal regions of the island, introduced a greater sense of personal emotion into the heritage of Sinhala poetry. New forms of adaptation from other poetic models occurred in the 20th c., when nationalist movements stimulated literary activity, much of it Buddhist, classicist, revivalist, and didactic. The 20th c. also saw the growth of a secular poetry, nationalist in theme and traditional in form. By the 1930s, Munidasa Kumaranatunge (1887–1944) had begun a movement for lang. reform termed *Hela*, to rid Sinhala of Sanskrit influences. Kumaranatunge's critical writings had considerable impact, and his poems for children introduced a new simplicity into Sinhala poetry.

The major breakthrough came with the introduction of *nisandäs kavi* (free verse). G. B. Senanayake (1913–85) had experimented with unrhymed verse forms as early as 1945 in his poems in *Paligänima* (Revenge). However, it was Siri Gunasinghe (b. 1925) in *Mas Le Näti Äta* (Bones without Flesh or Blood, 1956), *Abhinikmana* (Renunciation, 1958), and *Ratu Käkulu* (Red Buds, 1962) who established and popularized the form. Gunasinghe together with others such as Gunadasa Amerasekera (b. 1929) and Wimal Dissanayake, who were part of the literary world of the University of Peradeniya in the 1950s, became known as the Peradeniya poets. Influenced by the literary theories of Am. New Criticism, they were at first criticized as Westernized ivory-tower aesthetes, but their work soon gained acceptance. Their writings gave a new vitality and flexibility to the lang. Ediriweera Sarachchandra (1914–96), the foremost critic and theorist of the group, also revolutionized the theater with his poetic dramas *Maname* (1956) and *Simhabahu* (1958).

The 1970s saw a fresh burst of poetic activity by writers whose works reflected a strong social concern. However, their evocative use of lang. and the confidence with which they drew on cl. and folk as well as foreign lits. gave their work an energy that overrode the didacticism. Mahagama Sekera's (1929–76) *Heta Irak Payayi* (Tomorrow a Sun Will Rise, 1971), *Nomiyami* (I Will Not Die, 1973), and *Prabuddha* (1976); Parakrama Kodituwakku's *Akikaru Putrayakuge Lokayak* (The World of a Disobedient Son, 1974) and *Alut Minihesk Ävit* (A New Man Has Come, 1976); and Monica Ruwanpathirana's (1945–2004) *Tahanam Desayakin* (From a Forbidden World, 1972) and *Obe Yeheliya Äya Gähäniya* (Your Friend, She Is Woman, 1975) are some of the important works of this group.

The dynamic energy of the 1970s slackens perceptibly by the 1980s. The civil war, disturbing and demoralizing but strangely distant because it was fought in the north, left hardly any mark on the poetry. The creative impetus seems to shift away from poetry to drama. However, the 21st c. has seen the resurgence of a vibrant poetic idiom in the work of Liyanage Amarakeerthi. He draws from life in rural Sri Lanka in conflict with political and social change in his collection *Ekamatha Eka Pita Rataka* (2005).

II. Tamil. While the Tamil presence in Sri Lanka goes back to very early times, Tamil lit. gained a distinct Sri Lankan identity only much later. The earliest reference to a Sri Lankan Tamil poet is in the Sangam lit. of the 3d c. CE, where verses attributed to Putatevanar with the prefix *Elathu* (Lanka) appear. In 1310 CE, *Caracotimalai* by Pocaraca Panditar was presented in the court of the Sinhala king Parakramabahu III at Dambadeniya. These are the only references for the early period.

The flourishing Tamil kingdom in the Jaffna peninsula (14th–17th c.) gave rise to several poetical works. The best known was *Rakuvamcam* by Aracakecari, the poet laureate. Under colonial rule, the proselytizing activities of Christian missionaries spawned a genre of religious poetry that was given further impetus by the introduction of printing.

Early Sri Lankan Tamil poetry had traditionally been seen merely as an extension of Indian Tamil writing; but by the 1940s, a renaissance occurred, when many young poets began to emphasize their Sri Lankan identity. A distinctly different Tamil poetry soon evolved. Nantaran, Kantacami, and Mahakavi are important poets of this period. Simplicity, colloquial meters, and concrete visual images are the hallmarks of this Lankan Tamil poetry.

When Sinhala was made the official lang. in 1956, a new political consciousness evolved among the Tamils. Three schools of poetry emerged. The first was nationalist, in support of a Tamil federal state. The second group called themselves *Progressives*, was influenced by left-wing ideologies, and advocated a radical transformation of Sri Lankan society, both Sinhala and Tamil. The third refused to be identified with either group and wrote a very individualized poetry. Mod. forms such as free verse were introduced, and poets and poetry proliferated.

By the 1970s, Tamil political aspirations for a separate state led to guerrilla war. Thereafter, the experience for Sri Lankan Tamil poets was blood, tears, violence, battle, exile, death, and life amid death. The new war poetry reflected these realities. Sri Lankan Tamil poetry now charts its own course and is entirely different from Indian Tamil writing unexposed to such experiences. During the second half of the war, from the mid-1990s, poetry became the foremost choice as the medium of literary expression. The major poets of the time are Jayapalan, Ceran, Ceyan, Yecuraca, Vicayentran, Puthuvai Rathnadurai, and Vilvaratnam.

Love and war had been the basic themes of early Sangam lit. Once Tamil military exploits ceased after colonial conquest, war poetry died out. It is notable that Tamil-speaking writers of different regions in Sri Lanka have used the medium of poetry to express their lives in time of war and interethnic conflict. The Muslim writers in Tamil from the eastern region, such as Vedanti, Natchathiran Sevvinthiyan, N. Atma, Deva Abira, and Aswagosh have written about their distinct experience of displacement during the Tamil-Muslim conflict in the north and their experience as a Tamil-speaking community separate from the ethnically Tamil community of Sri Lanka. There are also the writers of the Tamil diaspora based in countries such as Canada, the U.K., France, and Germany who are using the poetic medium to express their experience of the Sri Lankan conflict and their private experience within the context of exile. Jayapalan, Vijayendran, and Aravinthan use imagery at times that is a part of their migrant lives but new to *Tamil poetry.

III. English. English poetry in Sri Lanka developed its own identity in the mid-20th c. Lakkdasa Wickremasinghe in his pioneering work boldly experimented with the rhythms of Lankan Eng. *Lustre Poems* (1965) has a dynamic energy, while later works such as *The Grasshopper Gleaming* (1976) show his growing control of his medium. Yasmine Gooneratne's (b. 1935) *Word, Bird and Motif* (1971) and *Lizard's Cry* (1972) reveal her flair for the satiric mode, where her control of tone and sensitivity to the nuances of words have full play. Anne Ranasinghe's (b. 1925) *Poems* (1971) and *Plead Mercy* (1975) provide sharp insights into a range of personal experiences that bridge two worlds. Ranasinghe's works draw from her experiences as a Holocaust survivor and a child growing up in Europe during World War II and later as a resident in Sri Lanka by marriage. In works such as *July 1983* (1983), she comments from the inside with the perspective of the outsider, drawing parallels between historic events of extreme violence and cruelty in Europe and South Asia. Basil Fernando (b. 1944) in *A New Era to Emerge* (1973) and Jean Arasanayagam (b. 1931) in *Apocalypse* (1983) and *A Colonial Inheritance* (1985) write movingly of the realities of Sri Lankan life. Several new voices emerged at the beginning of the 21st c.: Vivimarie VanderPoorten (b. 1967), *Nothing Prepares You* (2007) and *Stitch Your Eyelids Shut* (2010); Ramya Chamalie Jirasinghe (b. 1971), *There's an Island in the Bone* (2010); and Malinda Seneviratne (b. 1965), *Threads* (2007). VanderPoorten uses sparse lang. to capture the experiences of violence, war, and exclusion, while Jirasinghe employs local metaphor and vivid imagery to write about personal narratives of identity and belonging against larger political and social structures. There are also a few of poets and writers of Sri Lankan origin who reside overseas, such as Rienzi Crusz (b. 1925) in Canada. They have appropriated a poetic lang. heavy with desire and longing to write about the experience of displacement, as Crusz does in *Love Where the Nights Are Green* (2008). The readership for Eng. poetry in Sri Lanka is small but influential, with the potential of international importance.

See SANSKRIT POETICS.

■ **Anthologies**: *Poetry from the Sinhalese*, trans. G. Keyt (1939); *Sigiri Graffiti*, ed. and trans. S. Paranavitarne (1955); *An Anthology of Classical Sinhalese Literature*, ed. C. Reynolds (1970); "Poetry of Sri Lanka," *Journal of South Asian Literature* 12.1 (1976)—spec. iss.; *Modern Writing in Sinhala*, ed. R. Obeyesekere and C. Fernando (1978); "Sinhala and Tamil Writing from Sri Lanka," *Journal of South Asian Literature* 22.2 (1987)—spec. iss.; *Twelve Centuries of Sinhala Poetry*, trans. L. de Silva (2004); *The Penguin Book of Tamil Poetry: The Rapids of a Great River*, ed. and trans. L. Holstrom (2009); *Kaleidoscope 2: An Anthology of Sri Lankan English Literature*, ed. D.C.R.A. Goonetilleke (2010).
■ **Criticism and History**: C. E. Godakumbura, *Sinhalese Literature* (1955); K. S. Sivakumaran, *Tamil Writing in Sri Lanka* (1964); R. Obeyesekere, *Sinhalese Writing and the New Critics* (1974); K. Sivathamby, *Tamil Literature in Eelam* (1978); *The Sri Lanka Reader: History, Culture and Poetics*, ed. J. C. Holt (2011).

C. Hallisey, R. Obeyesekere (Sinhalese); D.B.S. Jeyaraj (Tamil); R. Obeyesekere, R. C. Jirasinghe (Eng.)

SUMERIAN POETRY. A corpus of more than 100 compositions in the Sumerian lang. written out on clay tablets in verse form, ranging from short lyric pieces to narrative epics of over 700 lines. Uncertainty about Sumerian phonetics hinders appreciation of how Sumerian poetry sounded. The earliest Sumerian poetry dates to the mid-3d millennium BCE. Most manuscripts date approximately to the 18th c. BCE, when Sumerian was a cultural rather than a spoken lang.; the latest date to the Achaemenid and Hellenistic periods. Native rubrics suggest that Sumerian poetry was closely associated with performance, by singers individually or in chorus, accompanied by drums, winds, and harps.

Although lines of Sumerian poetry often show a loose rhythm of syllables or words, no strict meter has been detected. Simile, metaphor, wordplay, and chiasmus are highly cultivated. Some genres, such as laments, make extensive use of refrains, repetition, and simple replacive parallelism. More complex parallelism is developed in love poetry and epic narratives. Assonance and alliteration are rare but striking when they occur, as in magic spells, which also use concatenation and chain rhyme. Political and historical allegory have been alleged but disputed.

Religious poetry includes hymns of praise to deities and temples and laments. Frequently compared to mountains, temples are described as linking heaven and earth, their glory radiating throughout the land. Hymns to major deities, such as Enlil, Utu, Nanna, and Inanna, praise their transcendent powers, support of justice and order, beauty, and valor. Some of the earliest known religious hymns of praise were written cryptographically, but this practice disappeared thereafter. Laments over the destruction of cities and the land of Sumer range from 300 to 500 lines, divided into units called *kirugus*. These depict social disorder, violence, invasion, famine, and destruction, followed by restoration at the command of the gods. Although they contain historical references, their lang. tends to be stereotypical. Ritual laments to appease the anger of the gods are known as late as the Hellenistic period. They were performed in a special Sumerian dialect called "thin," characterized by major phonetic changes (e.g., *zeb* for *dug*, sweet).

Mythological narratives relate the deeds of deities, among them creation stories and etiologies. They include a group about the hero-god Ninurta, in one of which he defeats a volcano and assigns destiny to stones; a group about the chief god on earth, Enlil, and his sanctuary at Nippur; a group about Enki, god of wisdom, in one of which he organizes the world; and a group about Inanna, goddess of love and procreation.

Court poetry includes epic tales of kings of the remote past, praises of living kings, and poetic contests. Four epics celebrate the victories of two legendary kings of Uruk—Enmerkar and Lugalbanda—over the lord of the city of Aratta in Iran. These trials of valor, rhet., and ingenuity provide vehicles for fanciful and entertaining narratives. A cycle of poems about the hero-king Gilgamesh includes episodes incorporated into the later Mesopotamian *Epic of Gilgamesh*, such as an expedition to cut cedar trees and a battle with the bull of heaven; but others not in the later epic, notably the death and burial of Gilgamesh, in the later epic are transformed into the death and burial of Gilgamesh's companion Enkidu.

Hymns in praise of kings of the dynasty of Ur (late 3d millennium BCE), in the case of Shulgi redolent of a personality cult, praise their bravery, athleticism, musical and linguistic skills, and other courtly attainments, and in some cases refer to important events of their reigns. These were imitated in the successor state of Isin, the best known focusing on the king's role in the *hieros gamos*, or ritual wedding with a goddess, but disappear thereafter.

Poetic contests pit against each other elements of Sumerian civilization, such as sheep and grain; tools, such as plow and pickaxe; seasons, such as summer and winter; animals, such as bird and fish; and materials, such as silver and gold and tree and reed, disputing their relative usefulness to the human race. At the end, a winner is declared. Like the court epics, these are witty, elegant, and amusing, but they offer penetrating analyses of Sumerian culture. Other poetic dialogues include literary abuse and school debates between masters and students.

More than 25 love songs deal with the courtship and marriage of the deities Inanna and Dumuzi (Tammuz), portrayed as young lovers. These too have been associated with the hieros gamos. Related to these are mythological narratives dealing with Dumuzi's death, such as *Dumuzi's Dream* and *The Descent of Inanna to the Netherworld*, and laments about Dumuzi's death.

Miscellaneous Sumerian poetry includes short drinking, work, and love songs; elegies; and even a royal lullaby.

Much Sumerian poetry was copied and composed in an Akkadian-speaking environment (see ASSYRIA AND BABYLONIA, POETRY OF) and some was transmitted in bilingual versions, but mutual literary influences have not yet been explored in depth.

The native term *sher* (song) comes closest to the mod. term *poetry*. There is no word for "poet" but only for performers of poetry (*nar*, singer; *gala*, singer of ritual laments). There are no native treatises or remarks on poetics. Most Sumerian poetry is anonymous, with the major exception of a group of compositions ascribed in antiquity and mod. times to Enheduanna, daughter of King Sargon of Akkad (ca. 2300 BCE). These are noteworthy for their original style and subject matter, difficult diction, autobiographical content, remarks on the creative process, and intense feeling, so invite consideration as the first identifiable oeuvre of an individual poet in world lit.

■ **Anthologies**: *The Harps That Once*, trans. T. Jacobsen (1987); *The Literature of Ancient Sumer*, trans. J. Black (2009); *Love Songs in Sumerian Literature*, ed. Y. Sefati (1998).

■ **Criticism**: C. Wilcke, "Formale Gesichtspunkte," *Assyriological Studies* 20 (1976); W. Heimpel, "Mythologie" [in Eng.], *Reallexikon der Assyriologie* (1993, 1997); A. Zgoll, *Rechtsfall der En-hedu-Ana* (1997); G. Rubio, "Sumerian

Literature," *From an Antique Land*, ed. C. Ehrlich (2009).

B. Foster

SWAHILI POETRY

I. Swahili Prosody
II. History of Swahili Poetry

Swahili lit. occupies a distinctive place among lits. in Af. langs., having a trad. that dates to the 18th or even the 17th c. All the old mss., written in Ar. script, were of poetic texts, composed predominantly in the dialects of the islands of Pate (Kipate) and Lamu (Kiamu), and from the 19th c. onward also in the dialect of Mombasa (Kimvita); mss. in prose appear only in the 19th c. (chronicles of the coastal Swahili towns).

I. Swahili Prosody. Most Swahili poetry is metrical and meant to be sung or chanted. Swahili prosody is based on counting syllables (sing. and pl. *mizani*) and involves a monosyllabic rhyme (*kina*, pl. *vina*) at the end of metrical units. The shortest independent metrical unit is called *kipande* (pl. *vipande*), of three, four, five, six, or eight mizani. The arrangement of vipande in a stanza (*ubeti*, pl. *beti*) characterizes the individual poetic forms. Vipande are written down in lines (*mstari*, pl. *mistari*, or *mshororo*, pl. *mishororo*).

The most common poetic forms are *utenzi* and *shairi*. Utenzi (or *utendi*, pl. *tenzi*/*tendi*) is the form used for long epic descriptions (tenzi frequently have hundreds, even thousands of stanzas), but also for religious instruction. It has four vipande per stanza, and each kipande has eight (rarely six) mizani. The three first vipande rhyme with one another, and the last kipande has a rhyme that goes throughout the entire poem (*aaax*).

Shairi (pl. *mashairi*) is a form used for witty elaborations of moral and philosophical concepts. Typically, it has four lines with two eight-syllable vipande per line. The first vipande of the first three lines rhyme, as do the second vipande of these lines. The last line may only consist of one kipande, rhyming with the last vipande of the first lines, or a second kipande rhyming with the first vipande of the first lines (*ab*/*ab*/*ab*/*ba*); sometimes this last kipande does not rhyme with anything, or it has a rhyme going through the whole poem (*ab*/*ab*/*ab*/*bx*). The last line may also be the same in every stanza in the shairi, making a refrain (*ab*/*ab*/*ab*/*xy*).

Other forms include *wimbo* (three 12-syllable lines per stanza), *kisarambe* (four 11-syllable lines per stanza), or *ukawafi* (two, four, or five 15-syllable lines per stanza).

II. History of Swahili Poetry. The dating of Swahili mss. or the compositions themselves is often controversial. It relies on available historical sources (e.g., information known about the events or the poets), coupled with a relative chronology based on ling. criteria. Although some of the poems include a poetic colophon—the last stanza or stanzas naming the poet and the year of composition—it does not always provide reliable information to date the ms. The dates may contain unclear words or illegible figures and, depending on the interpretation of these, the dating can differ by as much as a century.

Ancient Swahili compositions were mostly religious in content, such as *qaṣīda* (praise poems to the Prophet Muhammad and his family) and *maghazi* (descriptions of fights between the early Muslims and their enemies). A famous example of the former is *Hamziya* (literally, "a poem rhyming in [the Ar. character of] *hamza*"; the Swahili poem is a trans. from the Ar.; in Swahili, the poem rhymes in *-ma*), composed by Sayyid Aidarus bin Athman. The ms. is dated by Knappert (1968) to 1062 AH (1651/52 CE), but Hichens (1934) dates it to 1162 AH (1748/49 CE), a discrepancy derived from different readings of one word in the colophon. The poem, an ukawafi in two-line stanzas, describes the extraordinary qualities of the Prophet Muhammad. An example of early maghazi lit. is *Utendi wa Tambuka* (Utenzi of [the battle of] Tabuk), also called *Chuo cha Herkali* (Book of Herakleios), by Mwengo bin Athuman. It is dated to 1141 AH (1728/29 CE) by Knappert (1979), but 1241 AH (1825/26 CE) by Zhukov. This utenzi describes the miraculous victory of Muslims led by Muhammad over the army of the Byzantine emperor Herakleios.

A secular trad. in old Swahili poetry is represented by the half-legendary hero Fumo Liyongo. While the lifetime of the warrior and poet is disputed, the dates suggested by researchers range from the 9th c. (Ahmed Nabhany, Joseph Mbele, cited in Mulokozi 1999) to the 1700s (Neville Chittick, cited in Knappert 1983). Fumo Liyongo is the possible author of the ancient *Takhmis ya Liyongo*, a praise poem to himself. The composition is usually attributed to Sayyid Abdallah bin Ali bin Nasir, who lived in Pate sometime between 1720 and 1820 and who is also the author of the renowned *Al-Inkishafi* (see below), but convincing arguments have been presented by Carl Meinhof that the poem may have double authorship: the last two lines of this five-line ukawafi appear to be more ancient (the lang. is older and contains fewer Arabisms, and the imagery is more vivid), and the first three lines may have been added by a later poet.

The early 19th c. produced some of the most remarkable compositions in Swahili. *Al-Inkishafi* (literally "it is revealed," also translated as "the soul's awakening" or "self-examination") describes the fall of the once powerful and rich Pate sultanate. Built on the commonplaces of the vanity of earthly delights and the illusory nature of worldly fame and riches and presenting plastic descriptions of downfall and decay, the poem admonishes the soul to turn to religion, the way to avoid the punishment for sins in hell and a source of true happiness.

The secular trad. continues in the poems of the Mombasan poet Muyaka bin Haji bin Ghassaniy (ca. 1776–1840) and his contemporaries in Lamu, who employed the shairi form in dialogic political poetry. Muyaka's poems are characterized by great wit and ingenious use of lang., typically playing with the many meanings of homonymous words.

A famous composition from the second half of the 19th c. is *Utendi wa Mwana Kupona*, composed by Mwana Kupona binti Mshamu (ca. 1810–1860) in 1858 for her 17-year-old daughter. Within the framework of Islam, the poet tells her child how a Swahili woman is expected to behave in society and in the domestic sphere, how to treat her husband, how to keep herself and her home clean and appealing for the husband, and how to observe religious duties.

The period of the early colonization of the Swahili territory by the Brit. and the Germans (ca. 1890–1930) has produced a vast historiographic lit., mostly in utenzi or shairi form. The most notable poets of this era came from the family of poets from Tanga, el Buhriy. In 1930, the Inter-Territorial Language Committee of the East African Dependencies decided the standard form of Swahili (*Kiswahili Sanifu*), based on the dialect of Zanzibar Town (Kiunguja). Among the ardent devotees of Standard Swahili was Shaaban Robert (1909–62), who introduced new genres (such as the novel) and topics into Swahili lit. while remaining true to the existing trad. of Swahili poetry in form and spirit.

In the first decades after independence, poetry developed in different ways in Tanzania and Kenya. Kenyan poets, who mostly originated from the coastal area, often rejected Standard Swahili and continued writing in their native dialects (Kimvita, Kiamu, etc.). The most prominent among them are the Mombasan half-brothers Ahmad Nassir Juma Bhalo (b. 1936), the prolific author of several poetry collections and innumerable lyrics for *taarab* songs, and Abdilatif Abdalla (b. 1946), who became famous for poetry he wrote during his imprisonment for opposing the Kenyatta regime (1969–72), *Sauti ya Dhiki* (The Voice of Agony, 1973).

Tanzanian poetry after independence was much less traditionalist, possibly because of revolutionary spirit of the policy of *ujamaa* (Tanzanian socialism). Standard Swahili, used in all areas of life, became the medium of expression of many authors whose ethnic background was not Swahili. Poetry was often used for the propagation of ujamaa. Mathias Mnyampala (1917–69) revived a type of dialogic poetry called *ngonjera* and employed it for political education of the masses. A true revolution in Swahili poetry took place at the University of Dar es Salaam in the late 1960s and early 1970s. A group of students rejected the traditional prosodic rules and started writing poetry in free verse, inspired both by oral poetry in their native langs. and by Eng. poetry. Euphrase Kezilahabi (b. 1944), one of the best Swahili novelists, is the author of three collections: *Kichomi* (Sharp Pain, 1974), *Karibu ndani* (Welcome Inside, 1988), and *Dhifa* (Banquet, 2008). As in his novels, Kezilahabi uses a simple, everyday lang. in his poems to elaborate highly complex philosophical topics.

Since the 1990s, the literary devels. of Tanzania and Kenya have converged, with Kenya gradually gaining the upper hand in publishing and on the book market. In both countries, metrical poetry continues to be highly popular (daily newspapers have a poetry page with circumstantial commentaries in verse). A number of young poets are convinced "traditionalists," producing poetry that is metrical in form and conservative in tone, such as the poet and novelist Omar Babu (1967–2015). On the other hand, many authors do not feel obliged to subscribe to either metrical or free-verse poetry and write in both ways or in a mixture of styles.

This is the case of the nestor of Swahili lit., Said Ahmed Mohamed (b. 1947) from Zanzibar, and the versatile Kenyan poet, novelist, and literary theorist Kyallo Wadi Wamitila (b. 1965).

■ **Anthologies:** "Das Lied des Liongo" (Liongo's Song), ed. and trans. C. Meinhof, *Zeitschrift für Eingeborenen-Sprachen* 15 (1924–25); *The Advice of Mwana Kupona upon the Wifely Duty*, ed. and trans. A. Werner and W. Hichens (1934); *Al-Inkishafi: The Soul's Awakening*, ed. and trans. W. Hichens (1939); *Swahili Poetry*, ed. and trans. L. Harries (1962); *Poems from Kenya: Gnomic Verses in Swahili by Ahmad Nassir bin Juma Bhalo*, ed. and trans. L. Harries (1966); *Traditional Swahili Poetry*, ed. and trans. J. Knappert (1967); "The Hamziya Deciphered," ed. and trans. J. Knappert, *African Language Studies* 9 (1968); *Swahili Islamic Poetry*, ed. and trans. J. Knappert, 3 v. (1971); *Tendi*, ed. and trans. J.W.T. Allen (1971); *Al-Inkishafi: Catechism of a Soul*, ed. and trans. J. de V. Allen (1977); *Muyaka: Nineteenth-Century Swahili Popular Poetry*, ed. and trans. M. H. Abdulaziz (1979); *Four Centuries of Swahili Verse*, ed. and trans. J. Knappert (1979); *Epic Poetry in Swahili and Other African Languages*, ed. and trans. J. Knappert (1983); *Tenzi Tatu za Kale* (*Fumo Liyongo, Al-Inkishafi, Mwanakupona*) (Three Ancient Tenzi; Fumo Liyongo, Al-Inkishafi, Mwanakupona), ed. M. M. Mulokozi (1999); *Kala Shairi: German East Africa in Swahili Poems*, ed. and trans. G. Miehe, K. Bromber, S. Khamis, R. Grosserhode (2002); *Liyongo Songs: Poems Attributed to Fumo Liyongo*, ed. and trans. G. Miehe et al. (2004).

■ **Criticism and History:** F. Topan, "Modern Swahili Poetry," *Bulletin of the School of Oriental and African Studies* 37 (1974); G. Miehe, "Die Perioden der Swahililiteratur und ihre sprachliche Form," *Paideuma* 36 (1990); A. A. Zhukov, "The Dating of Old Swahili Manuscripts: Towards Swahili Paleography," *Swahili Language and Society. Notes and News* 9 (1992); M. M. Mulokozi and T.S.Y. Sengo, *History of Kiswahili Poetry (AD 1000–2000)* (1995); A. Biersteker, *Kujibizana: Questions of Language and Power in Nineteenth- and Twentieth-Century Poetry in Kiswahili* (1996).

■ **Swahili Prosody:** K. A. Abedi, *Sheria za Kutunga Mashairi na Diwani ya Amri* (Rules of Composing Poetry and Amri's Collection, 1954); J. Knappert, "Swahili Metre," *African Language Studies* 12 (1971); I. N. Shariff, *Tungo Zetu* (Our Compositions, 1988).

A. Rettová

SWEDEN, POETRY OF. While runic inscriptions show the existence of a lost heroic poetry, the oldest preserved poems in Sweden date from the beginning of the 14th c., in the form of trans. of three Fr. verse novels. The anonymous versified chronicle *Erikskrönikan* was written a few decades later. The many folk ballads are a significant feature of the poetry of the Swedish Middle Ages. They exist only in late records from the end of the 16th c. and onward. Most likely, the majority of them were created in the 14th and 15th cs. and then transmitted orally until they were written down.

All the ballads are anonymous. With a few exceptions, it is not until the 17th c. that we find poets identified, most important, Georg Stiernhielm (1598–1672). His *Hercules* (1658) is a long allegorical and didactic poem written in hexameters where the quantity of cl. poetry was replaced by accentuation. Ascending rhythm, however, soon became the rule, and the most common verse form is the alexandrine. This is the case both in the pseudonymous Skogekär Bergbo's collection of sonnets (1680) and in Gunno Dahlstierna's (1661–1709) long poem in *ottava rima* written for the funeral of King Karl XI. More appreciated by mod. readers are the poems of Lars Wivallius (1605–69), Lars Johansson Lucidor (1638–74), and Johan Runius (1679–1713).

In the 18th c., the strong Ger. influence on Swedish poetry was replaced by Fr. and, later, Eng. models. Olof von Dalin (1708–63) was most important as a prose writer, but he also developed most genres of poetry. His writing was a step away from the baroque style of the previous century and a step closer to Fr. neoclassicists like Nicolas Boileau and Voltaire.

An even more crucial contribution was made around 1760, when Hedvig Charlotta Nordenflycht (1718–63), Gustaf Fredrik Gyllenborg (1731–1808), and Gustaf Philip Creutz (1731–85) published their best poems. Nordenflycht stood out as early as the 1740s as a pioneer for a subjective, emotional poetry, which has been compared to Eng. preromanticism, and Creutz is the author of a minor classic, the long pastoral poem *Atis och Camilla* (1761).

The breakthrough of Fr. neoclassical taste came during the reign of Gustav III (1771–92), a time that saw a great rise in cultural life. In 1786, the Swedish Academy was established, and over the following hundred years, the academy would influence literary life in various ways. The most important author and critic during this period was Johan Henrik Kellgren (1751–95), who wrote both satires in Voltaire's spirit and lyrical poems influenced by Eng. and Ger. preromantics. The leading Swedish preromantics, however, were Thomas Thorild (1759–1808) and Bengt Lidner (1757–93), while Fr. neoclassicism was represented by Johan Gabriel Oxenstierna (1750–1818) and Carl Gustaf Leopold (1756–1829). Anna-Maria Lenngren's (1754–1817) witty satires, written in a simple, informal style and with a keen eye for realistic details, still have their dedicated readers.

The most important Swedish poet of the 18th c. is Carl Michael Bellman (1740–95). His poetry is deeply original but indebted nonetheless to the songs of Lucidor, Runius, and Dalin. Most of his poems are songs, which is one explanation for their enormous success. *Fredmans epistlar* (Fredman's Epistles, 1790), published with an enthusiastic foreword by Kellgren, is regarded by many as the most important of all Swedish poetry collections. Fredman is an apostle of Bacchus, and the songs are letters to his faithful group of followers, worshipers of the gods of wine and love.

The poetry collection most read in the 18th and 19th c. was the hymnbook, legalized by the state and the Lutheran Church. The ed. of 1695, where the most important poets were Jesper Svedberg (1653–1735) and Haquin Spegel (1645–1714), was used until 1819, when a new ed. was published, in which Johan Olof Wallin (1779–1839) and Frans Michael Franzén (1772–1847) made the greatest contributions.

In the 1810s and 1820s, Swedish poetry moved toward romanticism. The Fr. influence became weaker, and the models now were Eng. and Ger. Fr. Enlightenment ideas made room for Ger. romanticism and philosophical idealism. Med. material—mainly from ON—was often used. The interest in the Vikings had its center in Götiska Förbundet (The Gothic Society), whose leading poet was Erik Gustaf Geijer (1783–1847).

The greatest poet of the period was Esaias Tegnér (1782–1846). His poems connect to Ger. neoclassicism in both form and ideas. Tegnér is the author of some of the greatest occasional poems in Swedish lit. but also of subjective lyrical poems. His best-known work is *Frithiofs saga* (1824), a formally brilliant cycle of 24 romances in different meters, with a story based on an Old Icelandic saga. This work with its synthesis of cl., ON, and romantic motifs and forms became the foremost Swedish poetic classic for the following hundred years.

The central figure in Swedish romanticism, both as a poet and a critic, was Per Daniel Amadeus Atterbom (1790–1855). Several of his shorter poems have worn well, but his largest poetical work *Lycksalighetens ö* (The Isle of Bliss, 1824–27), an extensive drama, formally and ideologically highly interesting, has not been much read by posterity. The case of Erik Johan Stagnelius (1793–1823) is quite different. He was little noticed by his contemporaries but has been more appreciated by succeeding generations. His formally perfect poems, cl. in form but romantic in motifs, are influenced by Neoplatonic ideas. Thematically, they often express the opposition between mysticism and erotic passion.

Tegnér's metaphor-laden, rhetorical style was infectious for his many imitators over the 19th c., and the reaction was not late in coming. Carl Jonas Love Almqvist's (1793–1866) poems *Songes,* written in the 1830s and 1840s, are distinguished by a simplicity free from both metaphors and rhetorical patterns, which must have been seen as a powerful deviation from Tegnér's poetry. And as early as 1830, Johan Ludvig Runeberg (1804–77) made his debut with a collection of poems that, with a simple style and few metaphors, also strongly contrasted to Tegnér's poetry. Runeberg lived in Finland but was hailed by many contemporaries as the greatest poet in the Swedish lang. He was a master both in lyric poetry and in narratives in hexameter, in which he portrays the life of the Finnish people. In other poems, he uses ancient Nordic and cl. motifs. The most important of his works is *Fänrik Ståls sägner* (The Tales of Ensign Stål, 1848), a series of poems portraying characters from the war with Russia (1808–9), in which Sweden lost Finland and thereby its position as a great political power. A second part of the tales was published in 1860.

Among the poets from the 1860s and 1870s, Carl Snoilsky (1841–1903) stands out with his formal virtuosity. His *Svenska bilder* (Swedish Pictures, 1894), a series of poems with motifs from Swedish hist., was for a long time a classic reader in Swedish schools. Viktor Rydberg (1828–95) continued the idealistic line from the romantics and from Tegnér. Many of his poems were written as early as the 1870s, but his two collections of poems were published relatively late, in 1882 and 1891.

The most important genres in the 1880s were the drama and the novel, with August Strindberg (1849–1912) as the main representative of both. He was, however, important as a poet as well. *Dikter* (Poems, 1883) and *Sömngångarnätter på vakna dagar* (*Sleepwalking Nights on Wide-Awake Days*, 1884) are both connected to Strindberg's general critique of society and to his programmatic anti-idealism. In *Ordalek och småkonst* (*Word Play and Minor Art*, 1905), which includes some of his best poems, Strindberg is not far from Fr. and Ger. symbolism.

The poets from the end of the 19th c. who are closest to symbolism are Ola Hansson (1860–1926) and Oscar Levertin (1862–1906). Verner von Heidenstam (1859–1940) stood for a more romantic, national—if not provincial—direction. His mix of orientalism, decadence, the cult of beauty, and national activism were features typical of the end of the century, but they have led to a diminished interest in his poems by posterity. He is at his best in the short format. His last collection, *Nya dikter* (New Poems, 1915), is marked by simplicity and a strong expression.

Erik Axel Karlfeldt (1864–1931) and Gustaf Fröding (1860–1911) both derived motifs from their native provinces, Karlfeldt from Dalarna and Fröding from Värmland. Karlfeldt is formally masterful but impersonal in his poetry, whereas Fröding does not shy away from depicting his broodings and his loneliness in deeply personal poems. With Fröding's five collections of poems from the 1890s, traditional verse reaches its culmination in Swedish poetry. He is probably the most popular of all Swedish poets. Formally, he has never been surpassed. After him, Swedish poetry would be forced to find new ways.

A new direction was pointed out by Vilhelm Ekelund (1880–1949). In the first decade of the 20th c., he published seven collections of poems, in which he gradually approaches a free verse without rhyme, mainly built on rhythm. The starting point is Fr. symbolism, but gradually patterns from antiquity and Ger. neoclassicism emerge. His poems became important both formally and thematically for a growing modernist poetry over the following decades.

The first attempts at modernism came in the 1910s. In 1916, Pär Lagerkvist (1891–1974) published a collection of poems with a title typical of its time: *Ångest* (Anguish). In the same year, Edith Södergran (1892–1923) made her debut with a volume *Dikter* (Poems). Södergran belonged to the Swedish-speaking minority in Finland. She had studied in St. Petersburg and had read both Rus. and Ger. contemp. poetry. Her four collections of poems are among the highlights in Swedish 20th c. lit., and they constitute the prelude to Finland-Swedish modernism in the interwar period. During this time, Elmer Diktonius (1896–1961), Gunnar Björling (1887–1960), and Rabbe Enckell (1903–1974) would become leading names.

Both Södergran and Lagerkvist could be called expressionists. Birger Sjöberg (1885–1929) started his writing with very popular songs—*Fridas bok* (Frida's Book, 1922)—that he also performed. A few years later, he surprised his audience with the expressionistic *Kriser och kransar* (Crises and Wreaths, 1926), the most remarkable of all Swedish collections of poems in the 1920s. It would gradually gain great importance, esp. for poets during the 1940s and 1950s.

Bo Bergman (1869–1967), Anders Österling (1884–1981), and Hjalmar Gullberg (1898–1961) are more traditional. Gullberg was the most praised poet of the 1930s. He was a virtuoso with a simple, often ironic style of expression. In his last collections of poems from the 1950s, he approached modernism without ever neglecting formal demands. Johannes Edfelt (1904–97), who was close to Gullberg stylistically and thematically, positioned himself between traditional verse and modernism, as did Karin Boye (1900–41) and Nils Ferlin (1898–1961), who was one of the most original and popular poets of the period.

Three writers most prominently represented poetic modernism in the 1930s: Artur Lundkvist (1906–91), Harry Martinson (1904–78), and Gunnar Ekelöf (1907–68). For four decades, Lundkvist was the most influential Swede in introducing foreign modernist poetry, primarily as a critic but also as a translator. While Lundkvist's poems are expansive, a never-ending torrent of images, many of Martinson's best poems are highly compressed. He is a master of form, creating exquisite nature poems with precise observations of reality. But he is also a committed poet of ideas, strongly critical of mod. technical civilization. The various themes in his poetry join together in his most famous work, the space epic *Aniara* (1956), published at the beginning of the space age.

Ekelöf occupies the main position in Swedish 20th-c. poetry. In his first two collections of poetry (from 1932 and 1934), he introduces surrealism—in style, in theme, and in the ideas presented. In *Färjesång* (Ferry Song, 1941), the influence of T. S. Eliot can be detected. These three collections of poetry would have considerable influence in the 1940s. *Non serviam* (I will not serve, 1945) and *Om hösten* (In Autumn, 1951) include several of Ekelöf's best-known poems. *Strountes* (Trifles, 1955) marked a new phase in his career, one that would have great significance for Swedish poetry in the 1960s. His three last collections of poems from 1965 to 1967 form a trilogy distinguished by formal simplicity, Byzantine motifs, and an attitude to life close to mysticism. Its intensity is unmatched in 20th-c. Swedish lit.

The real breakthrough for lyric modernism came in the 1940s. Erik Lindegren's (1910–68) *mannen utan väg* (the man without a way, 1942) is the most important collection of poems of that decade, both formally and thematically. More accessible are the poems in his two subsequent collections, *Sviter* (Suites, 1947) and *Vinteroffer* (Winter Rites, 1954).

While Lindegren is linked with symbolism and surrealism, Karl Vennberg (1910–95) was most influenced by Eliot. For decades, Vennberg would be a leading critic and poet; he personified better than anyone the lyric modernism of the 1940s with its demand for a poetry that is ideologically aware, covers essential and preferably universal themes, and is written in a trad. of experimentation.

Werner Aspenström's (1918–97) style is clear and simple, and his motifs are often concrete and close to reality. His nature miniatures sometimes resemble the poetry of Martinson. Ragnar Thoursie (1919–2010) has a place of his own. His poetic technique was of great importance for the poets of the 1950s and 1960s. Elsa Grave (1918–2003) and Rut Hillarp (1914–2003) have motherhood and love as their leading themes.

The 1950s was a harvest time for Swedish poetry, a decade when many poets from the 1930s and 1940s published their best works. The lyrical modernism in Swedish lit. would reach its peak with Lindegren's and Ekelöf's late poems. Among the new poets that would appear in the 1950s, Lars Forssell (1928–2008) is of special interest. In his poetry, the links to the modernism of the 1940s are quite clear. Formally, he is a virtuoso in several genres, high and low, serious and humorous. However, the Nobel laureate Tomas Tranströmer (1931–2015) is the key figure continuing the modernist legacy and the most important Swedish poet of the latter half of the 20th c. His works are not extensive, however. The poems are often short, strongly compressed, and rich in ingenious and innovative metaphors. More than any other Swedish poet, he has reached an international audience. Among the other poets of the 1950s, Östen Sjöstrand (1925–2006), Göran Printz-Påhlson (1931–2006), Majken Johansson (1930–93), Lennart Sjögren (b. 1930), and Kjell Espmark (b. 1930) should be mentioned.

A reaction against lyrical modernism, or perhaps rather against its symbolist variant, came in the early 1960s. The reaction was twofold, through a poetic lang. that approached spoken lang. and dealt with everyday motifs (the so-called neosimplicity) and through a sort of neo-avant-gardism (the so-called concrete poetry). Concrete poetry would prove to be a poetic cul-de-sac. The most important of the movement's representatives, Bengt Emil Johnson (1936–2010), would soon abandon it and develop into a tranquil poet of nature.

Neosimplicity was more successful, at least when it came to its most prominent representatives. Sonja Åkesson (1926–77) is one of the truly important poets of the period. Her style is often ironic, and the poems deal with everyday experiences and women's lives. She has a successor in Kristina Lugn (b. 1948), whose poems are not formalistically innovative but use a subtle self-irony. Göran Palm (1931–2016), in his capacity as both critic and writer, led the attack on symbolism. Consequently, he turns his back on the whole of modernism in his main work *Sverige En vintersaga* (Sweden: A Winter Tale, 1984–2005), an extensive and genre-transcending poem written in blank verse.

Göran Sonnevi (b. 1939), on the other hand, would remain faithful to modernism. He was one of the first in the 1960s to write poetry with political themes. His collections of poems are often extensive, filled with what could be described as torrents of images and reflections. Because of this, he is in many ways the opposite of Tranströmer. The same can be said about Lars Norén (b. 1944), who in the beginning of the 21st c. was the most celebrated playwright in Sweden but who from his debut in 1963 and in the following two decades published poetry almost exclusively (15 collections of poems in various styles over 18 years).

Lars Gustafsson (1936–2016) has since the early 1960s established a place of his own. His poems have a distinctly intellectual mark. They often have philosophical content and use images and motifs from technical and scientific hist.

This intellectual line in poetry is continued by, among others, Jesper Svenbro (b. 1944) and Ulf Eriksson (b. 1958).

Among the poets who had their breakthrough in the 1970s, Tobias Berggren (b. 1940), Gunnar Harding (b. 1940), and Bruno K. Öijer (b. 1951) attracted the most attention. In the last decades of the 20th c., female dominance was striking in Swedish poetry. Eva Ström (b. 1947), Eva Runefelt (b. 1953), and Birgitta Lillpers (b. 1958) have all been noticed for their personal style and their existential themes.

In the 1980s, modernism returned, now as postmodernism, and with Stig Larsson (b. 1955) as its leading poet. The most important poets at the end of the 20th c. were Katarina Frostenson (b. 1953), who works with a fragmented poetical lang. with great power of suggestion, and Ann Jäderlund (b. 1955), whose poetry is based on rhythmic patterns and merges simplicity with complexity. At the beginning of the 21st c., Swedish poetry shows great variation, both formally and thematically.

See FINLAND, POETRY OF.

■ **Anthologies**: *Svensk dikt från trollformler till Lars Norén*, ed. L. Gustafsson (1987); *Svensk lyrik från medeltid till nutid*, ed. G. Lindström et al. (1993); *De bästa svenska dikterna: från Stiernhielm till Aspenström*, ed. J.-O. Ullén (2007).

■ **Criticism and History**: A. Gustafson, *A History of Swedish Literature* (1961); E. H. Linder, *Fem decennier av 1900-talet*, 2 v. (1965–66); *Ny illustrerad svensk litteraturhistoria*, ed. E. N. Tigerstedt, 2d ed., 4 v. (1967); G. Brandell and J. Stenkvist, *Svensk litteratur 1870–1970*, 3 v. (1974–75); I. Algulin, *A History of Swedish Literature*, trans. J. Weinstock (1989); I. Algulin and B. Olsson, *Litteraturens historia i Sverige* (1995); *A History of Swedish Literature*, ed. L. G. Warme (1996); *Aspects of Modern Swedish Literature*, ed. I. Scobbie (1999); *Den svenska litteraturen*, ed. L. Lönnroth et al., 2d ed., 3 v. (1999); *Finlands svenska litteraturhistoria*, ed. J. Wrede and C. Zilliacus, 2 v. (1999–2000); S. Bergsten, *Den svenska poesins historia* (2007).

S. Göransson

SWITZERLAND, POETRY OF

I. German
II. French
III. Italian
IV. Romansh

Although Switzerland officially defines itself as a multilingual country, each lang. group forms a geographically separate and—with few exceptions—monolingual area. Ger. is the dominant lang.; with approximately 64% of the speakers in 2002, it largely outnumbers Fr. (20%), It. (6.5%), and Romansh-speaking (0.5%) Swiss. The question of whether lit. from Switzerland should be considered a single entity constitutes a matter of debate. Official cultural institutions such as Pro Helvetia uphold a national perspective by supporting interaction among the four lang. groups. Attempts by Swiss intellectuals to promote a truly national lit., linked to a privileged role for Switzerland as mediator between Latin and Germanic cultures in Europe—the *Helvetia Mediatrix* idea—proved to be utopian. In reality, each lang. group forms a separate literary entity. For this reason, they are presented here discretely.

In a country with only 7.8 million inhabitants, writers largely depend on sales outside Switzerland. Most authors reject the label "Swiss writer" because of the fear of appearing provincial and choose instead to be grouped with writers from other countries who write in the same lang. A constitutive element in all Swiss lits. is the perception of belonging to a minority. Even Ger.-Swiss writers, who form the majority in Switzerland, constitute a small minority within Ger. lit. Another important characteristic of Swiss intellectual life is the tension between internationalism and localism in the definition of identity. Migration is a recurrent topic; several of the most important Swiss authors lived abroad and incorporated this foreign experience in their work. In addition, the influx of refugees during times of international crisis made neutral Switzerland a temporary intellectual center of Eur. importance. Examples include the foundation of the Dada movement in Zurich during World War I and the Zurich *Schauspielhaus*, the major anti-Fascist theater in Ger.-speaking Europe during World War II. However, Switzerland's multilingual conception of national identity and its international orientation stand in sharp contrast to its tendency toward political isolation and intellectual "narrowness." *Heidi*, the country's famous literary creation by Johanna Spyri (1827–1901), symbolizes the glorification of alpine, "typically Swiss" virtues in combination with a strong distrust of potentially dangerous urban and foreign influences. This tendency was reinforced in the late 1930s with the promotion of Swiss patriotism in order to combat aggressive Fascist and Nazi propaganda from neighboring countries. Lit. played a key role in this "spiritual defense" of Switzerland.

I. German. During the Middle Ages, present-day Switzerland was officially part of the Holy Roman Empire of the Ger. nation. Lat. was the written lang. in Ger.-speaking Europe, but religious centers such as the abbey of Saint Gall aided the devel. of med. poetry in the Ger. vernacular. In the mid-14th c., a rich collection of songs by *Minnesingers*, the Codex Manesse, was compiled in Zurich. The military victories against Hapsburg in the 14th c. and the expansion of the Swiss Confederacy until 1515 created an awareness of cultural singularity within Ger.-speaking Europe. This perception reflected itself in the production of heroic verse about battles and mythical figures such as William Tell. Switzerland's separate evolution from Germany was reinforced by the Reformation, which stimulated the use of the vernacular in militantly Protestant religious poetry.

The birth of a consciously distinctive Swiss lit. is traditionally linked to the publication, in 1732, of *Die Alpen* (The Alps), a long poem by the famous naturalist Albrecht von Haller (1708–77). Haller idealized the alpine people as the true successors of the heroic Confederates who had guaranteed Swiss freedom against foreign aggressors. Haller himself lived in the city of Berne and used the Alps as a contrast to the decadent lifestyle of the Bernese upper class. With his poems, he created the basis of the alpine myth that strongly influenced both the national and international image of Switzerland. A similar utopian vision of harmony and purity characterized the internationally famous *Idyllen* (Idylls, 1756) by Salomon Gessner (1730–88). The trad. of patriotic lit. was continued by the physiognomist Johann Caspar Lavater (1741–1801) in his collection of *Schweizerlieder* (Swiss Songs) in 1767.

In the 19th c., lit. from Switzerland achieved a prominent position in Ger.-speaking lit. with the novelists Jeremias Gotthelf (1797–1854), Gottfried Keller (1819–90), and Conrad Ferdinand Meyer (1825–98). Keller and Meyer also wrote poetry. Many of Keller's poems reflect his commitment to the foundation of the liberal Swiss Federal State in 1848. The words of his poem *O mein Heimatland!* (Oh My Fatherland) acquired the popularity of a national anthem. Meyer's poetic work is apolitical and characterized by an aesthetic symbolism. He excels in the evocation of landscapes and city life, most famously those of Venice and Rome. His description of a Roman fountain in *Der Römische Brunnen* is considered a perfect *Dinggedicht*. Heinrich Leuthold (1827–79) is one of the few Swiss authors who dedicated himself almost exclusively to poetry. His work is strongly aesthetic, though considerably less expressive than that of Meyer.

The work of Nobel Prize winner Carl Spitteler (1845–1924) has almost completely fallen into obscurity, incl. his allegoric-epic poem *Olympischer Frühling* (Olympic Spring, 1905). The opposite can be said about his contemp. Robert Walser (1878–1956), whose short stories, novels, and poems were rediscovered in the 1970s as important writings of literary modernism. Hans Morgenthaler (1890–1928) also made his reputation posthumously. He worked as a geologist in Asia and attempted to transcend exoticism in his literary work, incl. poems. The poetic work of the Ger. Nobel laureate Hermann Hesse (1877–1962), who in 1923 became a naturalized Swiss, is characterized by its introspection and Buddhist influence. Despite the presence in Zurich of prominent Ger. Dadaists such as Hugo Ball (1886–1927), Emmy Hennings (1885–1948), and Hans (Jean) Arp (1887–1966), the impact of expressionism and the avant garde was weak among Swiss poets. These new currents did, nevertheless, influence the work of the graphologist Max Pulver (1889–1952), the melancholic poetry of Albin Zollinger (1895–1941), the politically committed, urbane work of Albert Ehrismann (1908–98), and the surrealistic poems of the famous artist Meret Oppenheim (1913–85).

As Switzerland had remained neutral during World War II, there was no immediate need for a break with the past. The division of Berlin and consequent loss of a dominant Ger. cultural center increased the importance of Swiss cities such as Zurich and Basel that could compete as equals with Frankfurt, Munich, Hamburg, Cologne, and Vienna. The Swiss novelists and playwrights Max Frisch (1911–91) and Friedrich Dürrenmatt (1921–90) achieved leading positions in Ger.-speaking lit. In postwar poetry, traditional forms continued with the aesthetic work of Werner Zemp (1906–59), the melancholic poems of the gardener Rainer Brambach (1917–83), and most prominently with Gerhard Meier (1917–2008) and Erika Burkart (1922–2010), whose poems on the splendor of nature, the discovery of beauty in small things, and the lost innocence of childhood transcend nostalgic romanticizing.

A different path was chosen by Alexander Xaver Gwerder (1923–52), who vehemently opposed the bourgeois mentality in his cynical poetry. Gwerder's lifelong search for a poetic form that suited his rebellious character ended in resignation and suicide. An important formal innovation was achieved by Eugen Gomringer (b. 1925), the father of concrete poetry. Gomringer originally worked as secretary of the architect and designer Max Bill (1908–94), whose ideas on concrete art he applied to poetry.

The poetic work of Kurt Marti (b. 1921) combines the ideas of two leading Swiss intellectuals: formally, Marti was influenced by Gomringer, and intellectually, he followed the trad. of political commitment set out by the theologian Karl Barth. Commitment is also a key word in Dürrenmatt's (few) poems as well as in the protest poetry of investigative journalist Niklaus Meienberg (1940–93).

While poetry in the 1950s and 1960s was a hotbed of literary innovation, this has changed since the 1970s. Poets such as Herbert Meier (b. 1928) and Jörg Steiner (1930–2013) turned to prose, and younger writers such as Klaus Merz (b. 1945), who started with poetry, favored prose as soon as their talent was discovered. Prominent authors such as Hugo Loetscher (1929–2009), Jürg Federspiel (1931–2007), Franz Hohler (b. 1943), and Thomas Hürlimann (b. 1950) published important poetic work but remained primarily focused on prose. Poetry has become a niche market for devotees yet continues to surprise with the beautifully illustrated broadsheets of Beat Brechbühl (b. 1939), for instance, or the musical poetry of Raphael Urweider (b. 1974), influenced by the lively Swiss hip-hop scene.

Although local dialects can be found all over Ger.-speaking Europe, nowhere do they have a higher social standing and a greater common usage than in Switzerland. There exists an important Swiss dialect poetry. The trad. began at the end of the 18th c., when Switzerland's autonomy was threatened by France. For a long time, patriotism was an important characteristic of this poetry. With Josef Reinhart (1875–1957) and Meinrad Lienert (1865–1933), dialect poetry achieved a status almost comparable to standard Ger. During the "spiritual defense" in the 1930s, the use of dialect was encouraged in order to distinguish the Swiss from their Ger. neighbors. In protest against this overly patriotic policy, the famous dialect writer Carl Albert Loosli (1877–1959) provocatively switched to standard Ger. and restricted his use of dialect to poetry. In the 1960s, dialect poetry went through a revival with singer-songwriter Mani Matter (1936–72), who had a great influence on the lively Swiss dialect music scene. Prominent authors have also used colloquial dialect for their poetry, as was the case with Gomringer, Marti, and Kuno Raeber (1922–92), who developed his unique poetic lang. on the basis of the Lucerne dialect.

II. French. The unique identity of lit. from Fr.-speaking Switzerland (Romandy) is primarily the result of the Reformation (in opposition to Catholic France). The teachings of John Calvin stimulated the use of the vernacular in poetry supporting the Protestant cause. Fr. refugees, driven by religious persecution, stimulated intellectual life in Romandy. In the mid-18th c., Geneva temporarily became a Eur. intellectual center with the presence of the philosophers Voltaire (1694–1778) and Jean-Jacques Rousseau (1712–78), whose introspection and celebration of natural purity had a long-lasting influence on Romand lit.

For centuries, poetry in Romandy remained moralizing and didactic. Although the general mood was patriotic, poets such as Juste Olivier (1807–76) slavishly imitated Fr. patterns. With Charles Ferdinand Ramuz (1878–1947), a radical break took place. On his return from Paris in 1914, Ramuz rejected all moralization and provocatively identified himself no longer with France, Switzerland, or Romandy, but only with his rural canton Vaud. He abandoned the artificial Fr. he had been using and invented his own syntax in combination with an expressive, polyphonic lang. that he applied in lyrical novels and poems. In *Le Petit Village* (The Little Village, 1903), he experimented with free verse. Ramuz's literary jour. *Cahiers vaudois* (Journal from Vaud) generated new talents, among them the deeply solitary poet Gustave Roud (1897–1976) and Pierre-Louis Matthey (1893–1970), whose strongly musical and baroque poetry achieved mythological dimensions. The journalist and poet Edmond-Henri Crisinel (1897–1948) represents a singular case. Crisinel's poetry, in cl. prosodic forms, reflects his paranoia, which resulted in long periods of institutionalization.

Whereas Ramuz was a confirmed regionalist, albeit in a metaphysical, tragic, and cosmic dimension, Blaise Cendrars (1887–1961) was a quintessential cosmopolite. In 1904, he left Switzerland and later became a naturalized Fr. citizen. Inspired by the modernity of New York, Cendrars wrote *Les Pâques à New York* (Easter in New York, 1912), which became a landmark in the devel. of mod. poetry. His strongly rhythmic, utterly mod. and wholly unconventional style in free verse had a strong influence on the surrealist Guillaume Apollinaire and Brazilian modernism.

The dominant figure in postwar Romand poetry is Philippe Jaccottet (b. 1925), who analyzes poetry from different angles: in his theoretical works, his literary trans., and his own poetic production. Jaccottet, who left Switzerland at young age and has lived in France ever since, writes introspective poetry in which light and darkness, nature and the trauma of war play an essential role. Introspection also characterizes the work of Anne Perrier (b. 1922), Pierre Chappuis (b. 1930), and Pierre-Alain Tâche (b. 1940). Alexandre Voisard (b. 1930) placed much of his poetry at the service of the secessionist movement in the (Fr.-speaking and Catholic) Jura in opposition to the (primarily Ger.-speaking and Protestant) canton Bern. The work of Maurice Chappaz (1916–2009) and Jacques Chessex (1934–2009) combines regionalism with baroque magniloquence. Chappaz's poetry reveals concern about the environment in his canton Valais. His struggle with Calvinist morality led to an unrestrained celebration of sensuality. In 1973, he was the first Swiss to win the prestigious Fr. Prix Goncourt award. Ágota Kristóf (1935–2011), who came to Switzerland as a refugee from Hungary, made her literary debut in Fr. with poetry. Her later prose work on topics such as war and destruction, love and loneliness, remained characterized by a strongly lyrical lang.

Romand poets of a younger generation such as Pierre Voélin (b. 1949), Frédéric Wandelère (b. 1949), and José-Flore Tappy (b. 1954) found themselves confronted by the cultural centralism of Paris. In the wake of trends toward regionalization, however, Romandy has undoubtedly gained a sharper profile against Fr. cultural domination.

III. Italian. Theoretically, It.-speaking Switzerland is limited to some 300,000 people in the (traditionally Catholic) canton Ticino and some valleys in the (traditionally Protestant) canton Grisons. Because of immigration from Italy, however, there are some 200,000 It.-speaking Swiss in other parts of the country. Nevertheless, It. remains a tiny minority lang. in Switzerland, and the cultural attraction of Italy and its nearby metropolis Milan is immense.

The first Swiss-It. writer of Eur. importance is Francesco Chiesa (1871–1973), who, because of his long life, remained the dominant literary personality in Ticino for almost a century. Chiesa was a traditionalist, who celebrated an idyllic and slightly moralistic, though not humorless, vision of his region in poems and novels.

After the war, a new generation of writers took over Chiesa's dominant position. Among them was Giorgio Orelli (1921–2013), whose strongly rhythmical poetry, characterized by an ironic ambiguity, made him famous beyond the borders of Switzerland. With Remo Fasani (1922–2011), whose poetry reflects a deep concern about the environment, the It.-speaking Grisons transcended its literary provincialism. Alberto Nessi (b. 1940) writes poetry primarily about outsiders: people stricken by illness, poverty, and physical decay.

The youngest generation of Swiss-It. poets increasingly manifests itself in close collaboration with colleagues from the northern It. Lombardy region. Many of them combine their literary activities with teaching, journalism, and trans. work. One example is Fabio Pusterla (b. 1957), who played an essential role in the dissemination of Jaccottet's poetry in Italy.

IV. Romansh. With approximately 40,000 speakers, Romansh is one of the smallest langs. in the world. Its official status, achieved in 1938, should be seen in the context of Switzerland's "spiritual defense" and emphasis on a multilingual, democratic Swiss identity in opposition to Nazi Germany and Fascist Italy. Romansh is a generic term for several langs. that were only (artificially) standardized in 1982. Despite considerable government support, its chances of survival in the predominantly Ger.-speaking canton Grisons are uncertain.

The emergence of Romansh as a literary lang. is generally dated to the mid-16th c. when the Reformation stimulated the use of the local vernacular. Cultural awareness became stronger in the 19th c. in opposition to both an attempted Germanization of the region and to It. irredentism that considered Romansh an It. dialect. Much of the poetry by Gion Antoni Huonder (1824–67), Giacun Hasper Muoth (1844–1906), and Peider Lansel (1863–1943) reflects this concern about a proper Romansh identity.

After World War II, poetry became less political and more concerned with aesthetics, most notably in the case of Andri Peer (1921–85), Hendri Spescha (1928–82), and Luisa Famos (1930–74). The youngest generation of poets increasingly publishes bilingual (Romansh-Ger.) work, in which both langs. appear separately or in a mixed form.

See AUSTRIA, POETRY OF; FRANCE, POETRY OF; GERMAN POETRY; ITALY, POETRY OF.

■ **Swiss Poetry, General:** M. Gsteiger, "Comparative Literature in Switzerland," *Yearbook of Comparative and General Literature* 30 (1981); H. Loetscher, *How Many Languages Does Man Need?* (1982); *Anthology of Modern Swiss Literature*, ed. H. M. Waidson (1984); *Modern Swiss Literature*, ed. J. L. Flood (1985); *The Four Literatures of Switzerland*, ed. B. Stocker et al. (1996); *Images of Switzerland*, ed. J. Charnley and M. Pender (1998); H. Loetscher, *Lesen statt klettern* (2003); *Nationale Literaturen heute*, ed. C. Caduff and R. Sorg (2004); *Schweizer Literaturgeschichte*, ed. P. Rusterholz and A. Solbach (2007); *From the Margins to the Centre*, ed. P. Studer and S. Egger (2007).

■ **In German**: *Geschichte der deutschsprachigen Schweizer Literatur im 20. Jahrhundert*, ed. K. Pezold (1991); P. von Matt, *Die tintenblauen Eidgenossen* (2001); P. von Matt and D. Vaihinger, *Die schönsten Gedichte der Schweiz* (2002); "Young Swiss Writers," *Dimension 2*, ed. R. Sabalius and M. Wutz (2007).

■ **In French**: J. Monnier, *Contemporary French-Swiss Literature* (1975); D. Maggetti, *L'Invention de la littérature romande* (1995); *Histoire de la littérature en Suisse romande*, ed. R. Francillon, 3 v. (1996–99); *Dictionnaire de poésie*, ed. M. Jarrety (2001); *La poésie en Suisse Romande depuis Blaise Cendrars*, ed. M. Graf and J.-F. Tappy (2005); *L'anthologie de la poésie romande hier et aujourd'hui*, ed. J. Küpfer and C. Delafontaine-Küpfer (2007).

■ **In Italian**: G. Calgari, *Storia delle quattro letterature della Svizzera* (1959); *Svizzera italiana*, ed. G. Orelli (1986); *Lingua e letterature italiana in Svizzera*, ed. A. Stäuble (1989); A. Stäuble and M. Stäuble, *Scrittori del Grigioni Italiano* (1998).

■ **In Romansh**: *The Curly-Horned Cow*, ed. R. R. Bezzola (1971); I. Camartin, *Rätoromanische Gegenwartsliteratur in Graubünden* (1976); D. B. Gregor, *Romontsch Language and Literature* (1982); C. Riatsch, *Mehrsprachigkeit und Sprachmischung in der neueren bündnerromanischen Literatur* (1998).

J. DEWULF

T

TAMIL POETRY AND POETICS. The Tamil lang., the earliest attested member of the Dravidian lang. family, is India's only mod., living lang. with a lit. trad. reaching back over 2,000 years. Tamil is spoken by about 65 million people in the South Indian state of Tamil Nadu but also in Sri Lanka, Malaysia, Singapore, Mauritius, and diasporic communities around the world, notably in Europe, Canada, and the United States. Premod. or cl. Tamil lit., i.e., the lit. composed before roughly the second half of the 19th c., is almost entirely written in verse. Narrative prose lit. (such as novels and short stories) did not emerge before the colonial period. Tamil developed its own prosody based on different combinations of various elements: letters/syllables (*eḻuttu*), metrical syllables (*acai*), feet (*cīr*), linkage between feet (*taḷai*), metrical lines (*aṭi*), and ornamentation or tropes (*toṭai*) such as alliteration (*mōṉai*), initial rhyme (*etukai*), and others. The earliest extant Tamil texts, datable to the beginning of the Common Era, are known today collectively as *Caṅkam* lit., since a legend tells us that they were composed by academies of poets (*caṅkams*). This lit. consists of approximately 2,400 poems ranging in length from four to about 800 lines that are collected in two books, each containing several anthols. of poems: the *Eṭṭuttokai* (Eight Anthologies), which includes the famous collections *Kuṟuntokai* (Anthology of Short [Poems]) and *Puṟanāṉūṟu* (Four Hundred [Poems on] *Puṟam*), and the *Pattuppāṭṭu* (Ten Poems). The theoretical framework required to understand the highly refined and sophisticated poetics underlying Caṅkam lit. is detailed in the *Tolkāppiyam*, the oldest known treatise on Tamil grammar and poetics (considered to be contemporaneous with the Caṅkam poems but probably altered variously until perhaps the 5th c. CE). The *Tolkāppiyam* divides the poems into two distinct genres: *akam* (interior), love poetry, and *puṟam* (exterior), poems on war, kings, or social and historical circumstances. Both akam and puṟam poems derive much of their beauty from a complex system of nature imagery that draws on a taxonomy of five poetic Tamil landscapes (hill, seashore, forest and pasture, countryside, wasteland), providing repertoires of flora, fauna, and other elements deployed to evoke specific feelings. In the akam poems, these landscapes are linked metaphorically to different phases of love, the times of day, and the seasons appropriate for these phases. Thus, the hillside is the landscape of (first) union, at night, during the cool season; forest and pasture provide the landscape of the woman's patient waiting for her lover and of domestic togetherness, late in the evening and during the rainy season, and so on.

Between ca. 400 and 900 CE, there developed a trad. of epic poetry, notably with the two thematically interlinked poems *Cilappatikāram* (Tale of an Anklet, 5th c.?) and *Maṇimēkalai* (The Jewel Belt, ca. 500). The *Cilappatikāram*, combining great poetic beauty with a gripping narrative, tells the story of a young merchant who is unjustly executed by the king of Madurai for a crime he did not commit and of his faithful wife who takes revenge, destroys the city of Madurai, and turns into a goddess of chastity. While the *Maṇimēkalai*, which continues the story of the *Cilappatikāram*, is clearly influenced by Buddhism, the *Cīvakacintāmaṇi* (9th c.?), which describes the many love conquests of prince Cīvakaṉ, is considered a Jain text. Jain influence is also found in the *Tirukkuṟaḷ* (ca. 5th c.), a comprehensive manual on ethics, polity, and love in 1,330 pithy couplets and a book that remained highly popular through the ages as a repository of ancient Tamil wisdom and a symbol of Tamil culture.

After about the 6th c., some of the poetic strategies of Caṅkam poetry were absorbed by a corpus of religious hymns extolling the Hindu gods Śiva and Viṣṇu through the expression of intense personal devotion (*Bhakti*). The earliest Tamil Bhakti poets were devotees of Śiva known as *nāyaṉmār* (lords). This group included the female poet Kāraikkāl Ammaiyār and the three poets whose verses are collected in the *Tēvāram*, Appar and Campantar (both 7th c.) and Cuntarar (8th c.), known as the "harsh devotee." The 9th-c. Śaivite poet-saint Māṇikkavācakar is known for his collection of hymns *Tiruvācakam* and his poem *Tirukkōvaiyār*. The latter explicitly redeploys akam amatory poetics for religious purposes and weaves the discrete vignettes of the Caṅkam poems into a narrative. Among the devotees of

Viṣṇu, known as Āḻvār, were the female poet Āṇṭāḷ (8th c.) and Nammāḻvār (9th c.). Their works and the works of the other Vaiṣṇava saint-poets were collected during the 10th or 11th c. as the *Nālāyirativviyappirapantam* (Four Thousand Divine Works), the Vaiṣṇava canon.

The period between the 11th and 14th cs. saw the flourishing of the great courtly culture of the med. Cōḻa (Chola) dynasty that led to the production of new literary texts, such as the most famous Tamil version of the pan-Indian *Rāmāyaṇa* story, the *Kamparāmāyaṇam*, and the authoritative hagiography of Śaivite *nāyaṉmār* saints, the *Periyapurāṇam* (Great History [of the Holy Servants of Lord Śiva]). At the same time, a process of "philologization" led to new perspectives on Tamil grammar and poetics, crystallizing in the heavily Sanskrit-influenced treatises *Vīracōḻiyam* and *Taṇṭiyalaṅkāram*, and later the *Naṉṉūl*, which remained the standard Tamil grammar for several centuries. Iḷampūraṇār's commentary on the *Tolkāppiyam*, written during this period, may have been part of this new surge of interest in and revision of Tamil lit. and grammar, as were the works of the other three great commentators on the *Tolkāppiyam*, Cēṉāvaraiyar, Pērāciriyar, and Nacciṉārkkiṉiyar, all of which belong to the period between the 11th and 14th cs. and which are some of the few examples of premod. Tamil prose. The extant Chola court poems stand out as tokens of refined literary sensibilities and courtly culture, e.g., the court poet Oṭṭakkūttar's *Mūvarulā* (Procession Poems on the Three [Kings]), which portray how women of various ages are entranced by seeing the Chola king, a paragon of virtue and beauty, ride by in his glamorous royal procession (*ulā*); or Cayaṅkoṇṭār's panegyric *Kaliṅkattupparaṇi* (1113–18), which not only celebrates the victory of the Cholas in the second Kaliṅga war but is a masterful satire with terrifying and macabre imagery in its descriptions of the fierce goddess Kāḷi and her demons feasting on corpses on the battlefield. The ulā and the *paraṇi* were new poetic genres that, together with a number of others, became known as *pirapantam*s (compositions). The term *pirapantam* (from Sanskrit *prabandha-*) subsumes a motley group of traditionally 96 different genres in verse form as described in the so-called *pāṭṭiyal* grammars (the nature [*iyal*] of poetry [*pāṭṭu*]), which were written from about the 10th c. until the end of the 19th c. with a view toward theorizing the characteristics of pirapantam poems. Some of these genres may be defined by their form (especially stanzaic structure), e.g., *antāti* or *iraṭṭaimaṇimālai*, some by their content, e.g., ulā (poems about the king in procession), *kātal* (courtly love poems), or paraṇi (poems on war and the battlefield); and some by a combination of both content and form, e.g., *piḷḷaittamiḻ* (poems in praise of the childhoods of gods or human characters), *tūtu* (messenger poems), *kōvai* (narrative "garlands" of love or devotional poems), or *kuṟavañci* (fortune-teller dramas). Their length varies, and some of them are older than others. This relative diversity, however, has not prevented Tamil poetological trad. from grouping all of them together under the single term *pirapantam* or under the term *ciṟṟilakkiyam* (small or minor lit.).

Despite its name, this "minor literature" came to play an increasingly important part in the literary production from the late med. period on. The two most important locales of literary production and circulation were the courts of local kings and princes and religious institutions, such as monasteries and temples. Many poets depended entirely on the patronage of kings and religious authorities and wrote all their verses as commissioned works. Some of the better-known poetic works during this period include the religious poetry of Aruṇakirinātar (15th c.) and Tāyumāṉavar (17th c.); the 16th-c. epic *Naiṭatam*, which elaborates the love story between prince Nala and princess Damayantī from the *Mahābhārata*; and the *Tirukkuṟṟālakkuṟa-vañci* (ca. 1718), a play on Lord Śiva in Kuṟṟālam. This period also saw the rise of the great Tamil temple myths (*talapurāṇams*), verse narratives relating the myths and legends around the foundation of a Śiva temple, as well as the oldest fully extant Muslim poem in Tamil, Vaṇṇapparimaḷap Pulavar's *Āyiramacalā* (One Thousand Questions, 1572). The widespread system of late med. literary patronage gradually fell apart during the latter half of the 19th c., when the many transformations of a colonial society also affected literary production and reception. While the advances of the printing press meant that more texts reached more people than ever before, prose became valued over poetry as the vehicle of mod. thought and expression.

Mod. Tamil poetry begins for many critics with the works of the famous patriot-poet and social reformer C. Cuppiramaṇiya Pārati (1882–1921), better known simply as Bharati and perhaps the most important voice of 20th-c. Tamil lit. But while Bharati certainly is much better known, a case can also be made for Māyūram Vētanāyakam Piḷḷai (1826–89), remembered chiefly as the first Tamil novelist, to have been the first mod. poet, since his *Nītinūl* (Book of Moral Conduct), published in 1859, purposely deviated from the traditional learned poetics of his time in order to create something that was both formally and thematically new. Though Bharati died young, his more than 250 poems cover a wide range of themes, such as love, nature, mythology, philosophical and religious speculation, and political ideas. His candid patriotism is important, as is his experimentation with what he called prose poetry, an ancestor of Tamil free verse or what was later referred to as *putukkavitai* (new poetry). Bharati's poetic innovations and experimentations were continued in the 1930s and 1940s by a number of writers associated with the avant-garde literary magazine *Maṇikkoṭi* (The Jewel Banner), notably N. Pitchamurthy (1900–77), who was inspired by Walt Whitman's *Leaves of Grass* (1855), and K. P. Rajagopalan (1902–44), who wrote about love and village life. Kanaka Subburatnam (1891–1964) called himself Bharatidasan (Bharati's slave) and continued to write patriotic and nature poetry following but also modifying Bharati's style. Another literary magazine, C. S. Chellappa's *Eḻuttu* (Writing) founded in 1959, gave further impetus to the develop. of mod. poetry or putukkavitai. In 1962, ed. Chellappa published his milestone anthol. *Putukkuralkaḷ* (New Voices), featuring some of the now canonical mod. poets: Nakulan (pseud. of T. K. Doraiswamy, 1922–2007), Sundara Ramaswamy (1931–2005), S. Vaidheeswaran (b. 1935), S. Mani (1936–2009), and Pramil (pseud. of Dharmu Sivaram, 1939–97).

In the 21st c., Tamil poetry is a multifaceted global phenomenon, with Tamil poets and their audiences living in many different countries. Some of the most exciting contemp. poetry is written by South Indian Dalit poets, such as Ravikumar (b. 1960), Vizhi. Pa. Idayavendhan (b. 1962), Adhavan Deetchanya (b. 1964), and N. T. Rajkumar (b. 1968), calling for a renegotiation of the role of Dalits in society, as well as by female, often feminist, poets. Candid poems about women's roles in society and the female body by poets such as Salma (b. 1968), Kutti Revathi (b. 1974), Malathi Maitri (b. 1968), and Sukirtharani (b. 1973) have caused considerable controversy. Poets of Sri Lanka such as S. Sivasegaram (b. 1942), M. A. Nuhman (b. 1944), V.I.S. Jayapalan (b. 1944), S. Vilvaratnam (1950–2006), Solaikkili (b. 1957), R. Cheran (b. 1960), and S. Sivaramani (1968–1991) have focused—among other themes—on the atrocities of the Sri Lankan civil war and the new modes of life found in the diaspora. Malaysian hip-hop artists, such as Yogi B. (b. 1974) and Dr. Burn (b. 1981), continue to explore new poetic modes and possibilities of doing things with Tamil words.

See INDIA, POETRY OF; SRI LANKA, POETRY OF.

■ **Anthologies and Translations**: *The Interior Landscape*, trans. A. K. Ramanujan (1967); *Hymns for the Drowning: Poems for Viṣṇu by Nammāḻvār,* trans. A. K. Ramanujan (1981); *Poems of Love and War,* trans. A. K. Ramanujan (1985); *Modern Tamil Poetry,* trans. M. S. Ramaswami (1988); *Bharathi Patalkal,* ed. T. N. Ramachandran (1989); *Songs of the Harsh Devotee: The Tēvāram of Cuntaramūrttināyaṉār,* trans. D. Shulman (1990); *Tiruvalluvar: The Kural,* trans. P. S. Sundaram (1990); *The Tale of an Anklet,* trans. R. Parthasarathy (1993); *The Four Hundred Songs of War and Wisdom (Puṟanāṉūṟu),* trans. G. L. Hart and H. Heifetz (1999); "Ancient Tamil Literature," *Ancient Indian Literature,* ed. T.R.S. Sharma (2000); "Tamil," *Medieval Indian Literature,* ed. K. Ayyappa Paniker (2000); *Lutesong and Lament: Tamil Writing from Sri Lanka,* ed. C. Kanaganayakam (2001); *The Kamba Ramayana,* trans. P. S. Sundaram (2002); *Cīvakacintāmaṇi: The Hero Cīvakaṉ, the Gem That Fulfills All Wishes,* v. 1, trans. J. D. Ryan (2005); *Tamil New Poetry,* trans. K. S. Subramanian (2005); *The History of the Holy Servants of the Lord Siva: A Translation of the Periya Purāṇam of Cēkkiḻār,* trans. A. McGlashan (2006); *The Rapids of a Great River: The Penguin Book of Tamil Poetry,* ed. L. Holmström, S. Krishnaswamy, K. Srilata (2009).

■ **Criticism and History**: K. Zvelebil, *The Smile of Murugan* (1973); K. Zvelebil, *Tamil Literature* (1974); G. L. Hart, *The Poems of Ancient Tamil* (1975); K. Zvelebil, *Tamil Literature* (1975); D. Shulman, *Tamil Temple Myths* (1980); Vallikkaṇṇaṉ, *Putukavitaiyiṉ tōṟṟamum vaḷarcciyum* (The Emergence and Development of New Poetry), 2d ed. (1980); F. Hardy, *Viraha Bhakti: The Early History of Kṛṣṇa Devotion in South India* (1983); U. Niklas, "Introduction to Tamil Prosody," *Bulletin de l'École Française d'Extrême-Orient* 77 (1988); I. V. Peterson, *Poems to Śiva: The Hymns of the Tamil Saints* (1989); K. Zvelebil,

Lexicon of Tamil Literature (1995); M. Muilwijk, *The Divine Kuṟa Tribe: Kuṟavañci and Other Prabandhams* (1996); I. Manuel, *Literary Theories in Tamil* (1997); P. Richman, *Extraordinary Child* (1997)—on the piḷḷaittamiḻ genre; E. Wilden, *Literary Techniques in Old Tamil Caṅkam Poetry* (2006); S. Ebeling, *Colonizing the Realm of Words: The Transformation of Tamil Literature in Nineteenth-Century South India* (2010).

S. Ebeling

TELUGU POETRY. Telugu, a Dravidian lang. spoken by about 70 million people who live mostly in the south Indian state of Andhra Pradesh, has a thousand years of continuous literary production in various separate but interrelated trads.

The earliest extant text in Telugu is the first two and a half volumes of a Telugu rendering of the Sanskrit *Mahābhārata*, by the 11th-c. Nannaya, who is called the *ādi kavi*, the first poet. Nannaya was associated with the court of the Calukya king Rājarāja, who ruled from Rājamahendri, the present day Rajahmundry, on the banks of the river Godavari. Though Rājarāja's kingdom was short-lived, he commissioned a poem that survived to create lasting conventions of courtly poetry in Telugu. The poem begins with a prayer to the gods; goes on to describe its royal patron; describes in some detail the court scene where the king praises the poet, his scholarship, and his literary skills; expresses his interest in the particular book he wants composed; and commissions the poet to write it. The poet reverently accepts the commission and prepares to compose the poem, wishing continued good luck to his patron. The chapters are addressed to the patron as they open and end with eulogizing vocatives. The colophon includes the poet's name and titles.

This template, which Nannaya established, lasted for almost a thousand years with minor changes to the end of the 19th c. Nannaya's choice of meters selected from Sanskritic and Dravidian sources, along with a judicious combination of verses with heightened prose, also lasted as long. However, Nannaya's storytelling style, his economy of words with deep meaning that make the character come alive in the narrative, and his talent of combining words to create controlled and balanced sonic effects were never replicated in a thousand years. Nannaya's narrative requires a trained performer to present it for an educated audience, the performer adding his own commentary to make it immediately accessible. Nannaya's discrete verses captivate the attention of listeners, who memorize them for their mantric quality of sound. Such qualities make Nannaya the "first poet" for Telugu in a sense other than the chronological accident of his being the earliest. He mapped the literary path for all later generations. His followers, Tikkana (13th c.) and Errāpragaḍa (14th c.), who completed the Telugu rendering of the *Mahābhārata* Nannaya had begun, firmly established the path Nannaya had created.

The trad. Nannaya created does not, however, indicate a singularity of literary production. In less than two centuries after Nannaya's achievement, Pālkuriki Somanātha voices a protest calling for a countertrad. in a meter not derived from Sanskrit. This meter, called *dvipada* (a unit of two lines that can be combined to narrate a long story or a series of stories) and amenable to being sung collectively, closes the distance between the reader and the listener, which Nannaya's work requires, and promotes instead absorption into a collective identity. Pālkuriki Somanātha wrote two major works in dvipada—*Basavapurāṇa* and *Paṇḍitārādhya caritra*—to celebrate the two 12th-c. leaders of the *Vāra Śaivas*, militant worshippers of the god Śiva—Basaveśvara and Mallikārjuna Paṇḍitārādhya—who propagated an antiestablishment religion that demanded that its adherents reject their caste in favor of an egalitarian ethic and treat all members of their cult equally, even if they were untouchables and other low castes. In time, this movement gave way to its own caste hierarchy. The literary trad. of this group gradually waned for lack of patronage.

Meanwhile, the dominant literary trad. continued to flourish with poets such as Nācana Somanātha and Śrīnātha of the 14th and 15th cs., respectively. Śrīnātha, who was called *kavisārvabhauma* (the emperor of poets), was a prolific author who traveled across the length and breadth of the Telugu-speaking area. His legendary biography speaks of his conquest of a certain Diṇḍima Bhaṭṭu in the court of the Karṇāṭa king Devarāya II. Diṇḍima, the legend says, carried a bronze drum to exhibit his superiority over other poets. Śrīnātha, who defeated him in a literary debate, had the drum smashed in public and was, in the end, rewarded by the emperor with a shower of gold. Śrīnātha's works include *Sṛṅgāranaiṣadhamu,* a Telugu rendering of Srīharsha's *Naiṣadhīyacarita*, which tells the love story of Nala and Damayanti and which is celebrated as the most erudite poem in Sanskrit. Śrīnātha was the first poet to imagine an Andhra land and a Telugu literary empire of which he was the unchallenged ruler.

The 16th c. is generally called the golden age of Telugu poetry. During this period, court poets of the Vijayanagara emperor Krishnadevarāya (r. 1509–29) wrote superbly imagined and exquisitely descriptive poems called *mahā-prabandha*. Among them, Peddana excels with his justly famous *Svārocișamanusambhavamu*, popularly called *Manucaritramu*. This is ostensibly the story of the birth of the first man Manu but famously includes the celebrated love story of the heavenly Gandharva woman Varūdhini, who falls in love with a brahmin man called Pravara.

The poets of the mahā-prabandha broadly follow the narrative structure Nannaya initiated but entirely transform the quality of the poetic lang. with descriptions of events and things in minute detail—a richly imagined world. Characters in their psychological nature are exquisitely presented, and extensive, detailed descriptions intensify the narrative. The ornate diction deliberately maintains a ling. distance but surprisingly brings the poem's evocative quality closer to real-life experience. The mahā-prabandhas of this period, at least the best of them, can be classed among the classics of any great lit. produced by the world's great civilizations.

The emperor Krishnadevarāya himself wrote one of the masterworks of this period, *Āmukatamālyada* (The Girl Who Gave the Garland She Had Worn to God), perhaps the most remarkable poem in Telugu. A long narrative of human-divine love loosely combined with several other narratives, descriptions of seasons and lives of common people and kings, and an argument concerning the policy a king should adopt in ruling his kingdom, in verses that range from lyrical to ornate, realistic to fantastic, in simple Telugu words and jaw-breaking Sanskrit compounds, this long poem remains a high literary achievement.

This period includes another great poet, Bhaṭṭumūrti, also known as Ramarājabhūṣaṇuḍu, who wrote *Vasucaritramu* (The Story of Vasu). This is an artful poem of semantically dense verses that are nonetheless lyrical and musical, creating inexhaustible new worlds in every reading.

During the late 16th and early 17th cs., Telugu poetry underwent a significant shift in the works of Piṅgaḷi Sūranna, who flourished in the second half of the 16th c. His two verse narratives, *Kaḷāpūrṇodayamu* (Birth of Kaḷāpūrṇa) and *Prabhāvatī Pradyumnamu* (The Story of Prabhāvatī and Pradyumna), might be called the earliest novels in Telugu. These poems follow the psychological devel. of the characters through their inner conflicts, with unpredictable surprises.

While the mahā-prabandha genre continued in a courtly style, an entirely different line of poetry flourished, composed by poets who were devoted to a deity associated with temples. Potana (14th c.) wrote the *Bhāgavatamu*, which told stories of Viṣṇu and his avatars, chiefly Kṛṣṇa, and of his devotees. Prahlāda, the demon king Bali, the elephant Gajendra, Rukmiṇi who eloped with Kṛṣṇa, and the *gopi* cowherd girls who fell in love with him became household names in Telugu primarily because of Potana.

Among the temple poets, Annamayya or Annamācārya (15th c.), who served the god Venkaṭeśvara in Tirupati, a temple town in southern Andhra Pradesh, stands out as a composer of songs. His songs, known as *padams*, number into the several thousands—Annamayya's grandson gives a symbolic number, 32,000. The songs, editorially classified into two groups, *śṛṅgāra* (erotic) and *adhyātma* (metaphysical), were inscribed on copper plates even during the life of Annamayya and are now preserved in the temple museum.

Later padam writers who followed Annamayya include Kṣetrayya and Sāraṅgapāni. The erotic lyrics that Kṣetrayya wrote were objectionable to Eng.-educated, Victorianized new literati but came to be preserved when new interpretations of the songs emerged, reading spiritual meanings into them. Earlier, these songs had been sung by courtesans to their customers. The practice ended when, in the mid-20th c., the occupation of the courtesan was prohibited as immoral.

During the 17th and 18th cs., Telugu poets moved south to Tanjavur and Madurai (presently in Tamil Nadu), under the patronage of Nayaka kings and later Maratha kings who ruled the area. During this period, women who were courtesans flourished as poets, such as Rangājamma and Muddupaḷaṇi. Muddupaḷaṇi's *Rādhikāsvāntanamu* was condemned by 20th-c. male critics as obscene in that a female poet wrote explicitly about Kṛṣṇa and his beloved Rādhā making love; however, the poem received better treatment among feminist critics. The 17th c. is also the period in which new classes of literati, who mostly served as scribes and accountants for landowners but acquired a social status of their own, composed poems that they attributed to famous poets and kings of the past such as Peddana and Krishnadevarāya. Stories told about Tenāli Rāmalingaḍu, a fictitious poet said to be in the court of Krishnadevarāya, belong in this trad. These verses and stories were and continue to be quoted orally in conversations among literate communities. Such verses, known as *cāṭus*, number in the hundreds and suggest a public literary culture unrelated to any king or his court. Themes in these verses represent a subtle social crit. of irresponsible kings and bad poets and demonstrate a community with a good taste for poetry.

A genre called *śataka*, comprising about 100 independent verses loosely connected with one vocative addressing a deity in a local temple, became popular in the late 16th c. and after. Several of these śatakas are known for their social crit. and protest, and were written by poets frustrated by the behavior of degenerate kings or those who could not accept the many radical changes occurring in society around them. Among such śatakas, Dhūrjaṭi's *Kāḷahastīśvara śatakamu* is noteworthy for the quality of poetry and for the courage of the poet. It is partly confessional in nature, and its agonizing subjectivity and emotional intensity appeal to any reader who recognizes the pain of living in a troubled world.

By and large, the period of the 17th and 18th cs. ushers in what might be called an indigenous modernity in Telugu poetry, with its depiction of a new subjectivity, a cultivation of interiority, a psychologized personhood, and a representation of personal privacy and social mobility.

The 19th and 20th cs. bring about yet another radical shift in Telugu lit. with the opening of new ideas and sensibilities from the introduction of Eng. into colonial schools and colleges. Gurajada Apparao is often credited as the leading figure of modernity during this period, and his play *Kanyāśulkam* is regarded as the first mod. play in Telugu. A movement called *Bhāvakavitvam* (Poetry of Feeling) follows Apparao. Poets of Bhāvakavitvam sing of romantic love and celebrate nature. They depict woman not as an object of desire but as a person to be loved and adored. Poets such as Devulapalli Krishna Sastri and Rayaprolu Subbarao set the tone for the poetry of this period, with their delicate and carefully chiseled verses speaking of the meeting of hearts and dreamlike images of the beloved. Poets of this period rebelled against the excessively eroticized descriptions of women in the prabandha poetry, rejecting conventional pundits who tried to control poetry with their outdated grammar and fossilized poetics.

Within decades, Bhavākavitvam was rejected by a group of poets influenced by an international wave of Marxism. Led by Srirangam Srinivasa Rao, better known as Sri Sri, a large number of young poets, who called themselves *abhyudaya* (progressive) poets, wrote about the poor and the downtrodden working class, calling for them to reject the dominance of the wealthy. Rapid changes in Telugu poetry such as these brought about a rejection of what was considered to be the misguided and derivative modernity of the colonial period in favor of the imported revolutionary fervor of the progressive poets, with an invitation to celebrate India's indigenous literary and cultural strength, which had suffered under colonialism. Viswanatha Satyanarayana led this move with his six-volume *Rāmāyaṇa Kalpavṛkṣamu* (Ramayana, the Wish-Giving Tree) and his magnum opus *Veyipaḍagalu* (Thousand Hoods).

More recent devels. include feminist poems by women against male dominance, by Dalits (former untouchables) against the injustices done to them by the upper castes, and by Muslims about their oppression as minorities. Muslim women and Dalit women write about the double injustice done to them by men of upper castes, as well as their own community. Telangana writers also demand recognition of their identity separate from Andhra.

The hist. of Telugu poetry of the past thousand years presents a conspectus of the historical and cultural devels. in Andhra. At the same time, the corpus transcends time and place to appeal to literary connoisseurs across langs.

See ASSAMESE POETRY; BENGALI POETRY; GUJARATI POETRY; HINDI POETRY; INDIA, POETRY OF; INDIA, ENGLISH POETRY OF; RĀMĀYAṆA POETRY; SANSKRIT POETICS; SANSKRIT POETRY.

■ *Siva's Warriors: Basava Purāna of Pālkuriki Somanātha*, trans. V. Narayana Rao (1990); *When God Is a Customer: Telugu Courtesan Songs by Ksetrayya and Others*, ed. A. K. Ramanujan, V. Narayana Rao, D. Shulman (1994); *A Poem at the Right Moment: Remembered Verses from Premodern South India* (1998), and *Classical Telugu Poetry: An Anthology* (2002), both ed. V. Narayana Rao and D. Shulman; V. Vallabharaya, *A Lover's Guide to Warrangal: Vallabharaya's Kridabhiramamu*, trans. V. Narayana Rao and D. Shulman (2002); *Hibiscus on the Lake: Twentieth-Century Telugu Poetry from India*, ed. and trans. V. Narayana Rao (2003); P. Sūranna, *Sound of the Kiss, or the Story That Must Never Be Told*, trans. V. Narayana Rao and D. Shulman (2003); Annamayya, *God on the Hill: Temple Songs from Tirupati*, trans. V. Narayana Rao and D. Shulman (2005); P. Sūranna, *The Demon's Daughter: A Love Story*, trans. V. Narayana Rao and D. Shulman (2006); G. Apparao, *Girls for Sale: Kanyasulkam. A Play from Colonial India*, trans. V. Narayana Rao (2007).

V. Narayana Rao

THAILAND, POETRY OF. Poetry dominated Thai lit. until the early 20th c., when prose also became widespread. Noted for rhyme and sound play, Thai poetry is written in syllabic meters in five major verse forms: *rāī*, *khlōng*, *kāp*, *chan*, and *klọn*. The Thai (Siamese) lang. presently has five tones that also form part of the metrical requirements. The king and court poets used these forms nearly exclusively until 1932, though in many cases the works are anonymous.

The earliest verse appeared during the Sukhothai period (ca. 1240–1438). Sukhothai reached a high level of civilization, but extant poems are few; the only significant extant text is *Suphāsit phra ruang*, a series of moral maxims written in rāī and credited to King Ramkhamhaeng (ca. 1279–98). These stanzas have an indefinite number of five-syllable lines linked by rhyme. Melodious and concise phrases, suggestive of poetry, also appear in inscriptions from the period.

The Ayutthaya period (1351–1767) saw the rise of classics in rāī, khlōng, kāp, and chan. Khlōng, like rāī, originally appeared when Thai had only three tones. Khlōng consists of five-syllable lines grouped into stanzas of two lines (*khlōng sọng*), three (*khlōng sām*), and four (*khlōng sī*). The kāp stanzas, probably borrowed from Khmer, include *yānī* with two 11-syllable lines, *surāngkhanāng* with seven four-syllable lines, and *chabang* with one four-syllable line between two six-syllable lines. Indic in origin, the chan meters were adapted from meters found in *Sanskrit and Pali poetry during this period.

One of the earliest and most difficult Ayutthayan works is *ōngkān chāēng nam* (the Water Oath), a composition used by officials to reaffirm their loyalty to the king. Throughout the era, Buddhist themes dominate many compositions. In 1482, King Traylokkhanat (1448–88) commissioned a royal version of the *Vessantara Jataka*, the Buddha's life prior to his last birth on earth. This version, the *Mahāchāt kham luang*, consists of passages in Pali followed by Thai trans. into rāī, khlōng, and chan. Important compositions with historical themes began with *Lilit yuan phāī* (ca. 1475). Written anonymously in *lilit*, a combination of rāī and khlōng, this poem describes the victories of King Traylokkhanat. The popular *nirāt* genre, in which the poet compares his lover's features to the beauties of nature, also developed about this time. During the reign of King Narai (1656–88), the court became a major center of poetry production, and the era came to be known as the Golden Age of Thai lit. Probably the most famous of Narai's court poets was Sri Prat. In and out of favor with the king because of his sharp wit, he composed the famous *Kamsuan sī prāt*, a nirāt describing his journey into exile. The chan meters gained prominence with the adaptation of Buddhist birth stories into verse such as the *Samutthakhōt kham chan* and *Sụa khō kham chan*. The most famous work from this period, although some scholars date it in the reign of King Traylokkhanat, is the lilit classic *Phra lọ*, the tragic romance of Prince Phra Lọ and two princesses from a neighboring kingdom. Literary output declined after Narai, however, because of war and internal strife. Notable works from the end of the Ayutthaya period include a collection of boating songs in kāp, *Kāp hāē rụa*, and a description in chan of the king's journey to a Buddhist shrine, *Bunnōwāt kham chan*. In 1767 the Burmese destroyed Ayutthaya.

The establishment of the new capital at Bangkok in 1782 revived literary production at court, this time primarily in *klọn*, which probably first appeared during the Thonburi period (1767–82). Since then it has been the favored Thai verse form, with two types used regularly: *klọn hok* with six syllables per line and *klọn pāēt* with eight. The four-line klọn stanzas are famous for rhyme schemes and rhyme links that often continue for thousands of stanzas. Hoping to recreate lost works, Rama I, Phra Phutthayotfa (1782–1809), the first king at Bangkok, organized a royal composition committee that produced the *Rāmakian* (the Thai version of the Indian classic, the *Rāmāyaṇa*) and parts of *Inau* and *Dālang* (romances based on the Javanese Panji cycle introduced through Malaysia). Rama II, Phra Phutthaloetla (1809–24), continued the literary revival with another version of the *Rāmakian* and a complete version of *Inau*, which, it is thought, he composed much of himself. Sunthorn Phu (1786–1856), arguably Thailand's greatest poet, used klọn for many nirāt poems and for the long imaginative romance *Phra aphaimanī*. Probably written down as a complete poem after the founding of Bangkok with parts attributed to Rama II and Sunthorn Phu, *Khun Chāng Khun Phāēn* relates the lifelong competition between two friends for the love of a village beauty, who also happens to be their childhood friend. Originally composed by wandering poets in the late Ayutthaya period, the poem is famous for its depiction of customs, trads., and lifeways of ordinary people. Prince Paramanuchit (1790–1853), monk, poet, and Indic classicist, contributed textbooks on the chan meters, the final part of *Samutthakhōt kham chan*, and *Lilit talēng phāī*, a glorification of the battles of King Naresuan. Khun Phum (1815–80), the leading woman poet of the 19th c., produced satirical poems of biting wit in her famous literary salons. Traditional narrative poetry continued into the 20th c. in compositions by Prince Bidyalongkarana (1876–1945): one of his most noted works is *Sām krung*, a hist. of the three Thai capital cities, Ayutthaya, Thonburi, and Bangkok.

The 1932 revolution gave Thailand a constitutional monarchy, and court-dominated poetry thereafter ceased. Post-1932 poetry differed from cl. works in its brevity, its lyricism, and its emphasis upon crit. and instruction in the ongoing social world. Many of these changes resulted from the efforts of Chao Phraya Thammasakdimontri, known as Khru Thep (1876–1943), a journalist-poet. Later, in the 1940s and 1950s, Assani Phonlachan (1918–1987) sought to deemphasize the importance of rhyme and sound in Thai poetry. At the same time, Chit Phumisak (1932–66), a left-wing political idealist, helped launch the Art for Life's Sake movement, which attacked individuals and even whole political systems; Phumisak criticized cl. Thai poetry for not meeting the needs of the people. Other poets such as Prakin Xumsai, writing as Ujjeni (b. 1919), and later Naowarat Pongpaiboon (b. 1940) emphasized nature, love, and emotion along with social crit. The 1960s saw much experimentation with verse forms, incl. free verse (*klọn plāū*). During this time, the poet-painter Angkarn Kalayanapong (1926–2012), probably the most respected of contemp. poets, developed his themes and style. Often described as a nature poet, he finds expressions of universal messages in Buddhism, nature, art, and the past. The fluid political climate of the early 1970s revived protest and socialist themes. The student uprising of October 14, 1973; the return to democracy; and the subsequent suppression on October 6, 1976, have provided the themes for much of Thai poetry up to the present. Naowarat Pongpaiboon has emerged as the most eloquent chronicler of these events. Women's issues, along with moral, political, and social concerns, remain major themes in contemp. poetry. Paramount among these themes is the lament for the loss of the environment and traditional Thai culture and values because of Western influences and globalization. Important poets working with these themes include Sujit Wongthet (b. 1945), Saksiri Meesomsueb (Krittisak, b. 1957), Chiranan Pitpreecha (b. 1955), Rewat Phanpipat (b. 1966), and Montri Sriyong (b. 1968). The emergence of regional lit., esp. from northeastern Thailand, can be found in the poetry of Paiwarin Khaongam (b. 1961) and in Tossa's 1990 study of a northeastern folk epic. Political and social crit. provides major themes of Thai poetry today, and poets continue to use both cl. and a variety of experimental verse forms.

■ **Anthologies and Translations**: P. na Nakhọn, *Prawat wannakhadī Thai* (History of Thai Literature [1964]); R. Jones and R. Mendiones, *Introduction to Thai Literature* (1970); *Sang Thong*, trans. F. S. Ingersoll (1973); *Ramakien*, trans. J. M. Cadet (1982); *Mere Movement*, trans. N. Pongpaiboon (1984); *Thai P.E.N. Anthology*, ed. N. Masavisut and F. S. Jose (1984); *A Premier Book of Contemporary Thai Verse*, ed. M. Umavijani et al. (1985); *Phādāēng Nāng Ai: A Thai-Isan Folk Epic in Verse*, trans. W. Tossa (1990); *Sunthorn Phu*, ed. M. Umavijani (1990); T. J. Hudak, *The Tale of Samuttakote* (1993); P. Khaongam, *Banana Tree Horse and Other Poems*, trans. B. Kasemsri (1995); *The S.E.A. Write Anthology of Thai Short Stories and Poems*, ed. N. Masavisut and M. Grose (1996); S. Chongstitvatana, "Love Poems in Modern Thai Nirat," *Journal of the Siam Society* 88 (2000); *ASEAN Short Stories and Poems by S.E.A. Write Awardees, 1999*, ed. S. Poolthupya (2001); C. Baker and P. Phongpaichit, "Phlai Kaeo Ordains as a Novice: A Chapter from *Khun Chang Khun Phaen*," *Journal of the Siam Society* 95 (2007); C. Baker and P. Phongpaichit, "The Career of *Khun Chang Khun Phaen*," *Journal of the Siam Society* 97 (2009).

■ **Criticism and History**: H. H. Prince Bidyalankarana, "The Pastime of Rhyme-making and Singing in Rural Siam," *Journal of the Siam Society* 20 (1926); P. Schweisguth, *Étude sur la littérature siamoise* (1951); J. N. Mosel, *A Survey of Classical Thai Poetry* (1959), and *Trends and Structure in Contemporary Thai Poetry* (1961); M. Chitakasem, "The Emergence and Development of the Nirat Genre in Thai Poetry," *Journal of the Siam Society* 60 (1972); T. H. Bofman, *The Poetics of the* Ramakian (1984); K. Wenk, *Sunthǫn Phū—ein Thai Literat* (1985); C. Nagavajara, "Literary Historiography and Socio-cultural Transformation: The Case of Thailand," *Journal of the Siam Society* 73 (1985); H. P. Phillips, *Modern Thai Literature with an Ethnographic Interpretation* (1987); W. J. Gedney, "Siamese Verse Forms in Historical Perspective," *Selected Papers on Comparative Tai Studies*, ed. W. J. Gedney and R. J. Bickner (1989); T. J. Hudak, *The Indigenization of Pali Meters in Thai Poetry* (1990); R. J. Bickner, *An Introduction to the Thai Poem "Lilit Phra Law"* (1991); *Thai Literary Traditions*, ed. M. Chitakasem (1995); N. Eoseewong, *Pen & Sail*, ed. C. Baker and B. Anderson (2005); T. J. Hudak, "Tai Aesthetics," *The Tai-Kadai Languages*, ed. A.V.N. Diller et al. (2008).

T. J. Hudak

TIBET, CONTEMPORARY POETRY OF. From the adoption of Indian *kāvya* poetic codes in the 13th c. until the 1950s, Tibetan poetic production was tremendous, but poets demonstrated limited interest for innovation. One late exception was the iconoclastic genius Gendun Choephel (1903–51), who brought in a new tone and contemp. themes, while in some pieces rehabilitating pre-kāvya versification (mainly hexameters) and ancient historical themes. He may be considered a key figure in the transition from the Indian-inspired cl. Tibetan poetry to the new Tibetan poetry.

With the Chinese occupation starting in 1950, the Tibetan literary scene saw the emergence of a "monastic vanguard" (Hartley 2008), consisting of traditionally trained Buddhist clerics co-opted by the Chinese Communist Party, to eulogize the new regime and its platforms, as well as material progress. The clerics' poetic works, communist in content, remained strongly reminiscent of their traditional, Indian-influenced literary training. From the mid-1950s onward, strong resistance to radical communist reforms led to a virtual halt in original Tibetan literary production, as many intellectuals and educated people were excluded from official circles, imprisoned, or even killed. The Cultural Revolution (1966–76) further ostracized the intellectual elite. As a consequence, between the late 1950s and the late 1970s, hardly any poetic innovation, or even writing, is to be noted in the Tibetan lang.

Within a few years of Mao Zedong's death in 1976, a new era dawned: Tibetan-lang. literary and cultural jours., supported and controlled by the Chinese state, started to appear. A turning point in contemp. Tibetan lit. occurred in 1983 when the poem *Lang-tsho'i rbab-chu* (Waterfall of Youth) was published. This long poem, written by the short-lived prodigy Dondrupgyal (1953–85), is considered the very first free-verse work in Tibetan, although rare instances of verse irregularity can be found in earlier writings. The irregular structure of *Lang-tsho'i rbab-chu* encouraged people not trained in the cl. Tibetan canon to compose poetry according to their own terms, without restraint or arduous training in the subtleties of traditional poetics. The result was a sudden and long-lasting surge in poetic composition among Tibetan lay youth, whereas poetic composition had been for centuries a quasi-monopoly of clerics.

The next evolution came with Jangbu (pseud. of Dorje Tsering, b. 1963), who was inspired both by Dondrupgyal and by Chinese "obscure poetry" (Chinese *menglong shi*, Tibetan *rab-rib kyi snyan-ngag*). An obscurity of meaning, a chaotic flow of clauses, and total irregularity in form became marks of this new genre. A small coterie of Tibetan authors, trained in the mod. educational system, familiar with Chinese, and possessing a strong connection to Tibetan folk culture, led this movement. Like Dondrupgyal, they were frowned upon by traditionalists, who despaired at finding neither meaning nor Tibetan flavor in these enigmatic and personal works. But the new, lay intellectual elite, eager to be in tune with literary modernity in the rest of the world, was enthusiastic.

The year 2005 marked the latest turning point, with the first privately organized poetry festival in Tibet, also titled "Waterfall of Youth." The festival has since been held in 2007, 2009, and 2011. Under Jangbu's leadership, it has brought together eminent poets to discuss and recite their poetry and to meet students in local schools. Also in 2005, led by Kyabchen Dedröl (b. 1977), the poetic circle *mi-rabs gsum-pa* (Third Generation, a name inspired by Chinese artistic circles) was formed, a group of about 20 poets and intellectuals in their 30s and 40s who write either in Tibetan or Chinese, who are free from any trend or current, and whose generation follows that of Dondrupgyal and Ju Kälzang (b. 1960). Members of the group do not profess a particular style, nor any political stance. Their specificity lies not so much in their style or content as in their close friendship and openness to world lit.

Although it is difficult to summarize the wealth of themes that inform Tibetan poems today, religion is no longer the dominant theme. Instead, frequent themes include individual moods, with an emphasis on sadness and solitude; a sense of commonality among Tibetans; and dismay toward an uncertain future, with nature offering convenient and discreet parallels to political concerns too sensitive to be expressed openly. Social concerns and everyday life also have become prominent topics.

A common feature of Tibetan poets is their relatively young age: very few manage to develop a literary career in the long term. Only a handful have become lasting and prolific: Jangbu, Ju Kälzang, and, in the younger generation, Kyabchen Dedröl, Chän Metak (b. 1968), and Gangzhün (pseud. of Sangye Gyatso, b. 1969). Among them, only Jangbu has achieved international fame and is published in Eng. Women poets also lack visibility, with the exception of Palmo (b. 1968) and Dekyi Drolma (b. 1966), who have earned well-deserved recognition in the otherwise male-dominated Tibetan poetic scene.

While there are six million Tibetans, only half of whom are literate, about 100 Tibetan-lang. magazines are currently being published in China, half of them state sponsored. Most are either literary or cultural, and they always include poems, sometimes to the exclusion of other literary genres, as is the case for *Ganggyän Metok* (Snow Flower). In addition, websites in the Tibetan lang. have gradually begun to appear since 2005, and many offer a daily delivery of online poems.

With the occupation of Tibet, a number of highly educated Tibetans have gained mastery in the Chinese lang. and have begun writing poetry in Chinese. First came Yidam Tsering (1933–2004), whose poetry is informed by a good knowledge of Chinese and Tibetan culture. His often nationalistic tone endeared him to Tibetans, and a selection of his works has been trans. into Tibetan. Tsering Woeser (b. 1966) has also published a number of poetic works, some of which have been trans. into Eng. Tsobu Gade, born in the late 1980s and a member of the third-generation group, won two all-China literary prizes in 2009.

Regarding the exiled Tibetans after the Chinese occupation, poetic creation temporarily came to a halt in the first years after the settlement in India (1959), although some poems did appear in *Shecha* (Knowledge), the first magazine founded by the Tibetan government-in-exile. The new generation educated in India started *Young Tibet* (later changed to *Lotus Fields*) in 1977, the first exile Tibetan literary magazine, which published only poems written in Eng. Poetic writing in the Tibetan lang. gained vitality and renewal only after the second wave of refugees, fleeing Tibet from the mid-1980s onward, brought with them the concept of literary magazines written in Tibetan and free-verse poetry. The launching of *Jangshön* (Young Shoot) in December 1990, a magazine dedicated to old and new Tibetan-lang. poetry and fiction, heralded a new era. From then onward, more and more magazines began to be published, usually at the initiative of recently arrived exiles with a poor knowledge of Eng. but good mastery of Tibetan script. There are currently over 30 jours. and magazines in Tibetan published in exile, most of which include poetry. A Guild of Tibetan Writers was created in India in 1999 and joined the PEN Club in 2003, becoming the Tibetan Writers Abroad PEN Center. It is headed by the acclaimed writer and Tibetan lit. expert Chabdak Lhamokyab (b. 1963).

Finally, a number of exiled Tibetans now write poetry in Eng., such as Tenzin Tsundue (living in India, b. ca. 1975) and Bhuchung Sonam (India, b. 1972). Their work is often political, with a strong presence of Tibet- and exile-related themes. Tsering Wangmo Dhompa (U.S., b. 1969) stands out as an acclaimed award-winning woman poet whose work is highly personal and creative.

See CHINA, MODERN POETRY OF; TIBET, TRADITIONAL POETRY AND POETICS OF.

■ **Anthologies and Primary Texts**: *The Blighted Flower and Other Stories*, ed. R. Virtanen (2000); *Song of the Snow Lion*, ed. F. Stewart, H. J. Batt, T. Shakya (2000); *Muses in Exile: An Anthology of Tibetan Poetry*, ed. B. D. Sonam (2005); T. Woeser, *Tibet's True Heart: Selected Poems*, trans. A. E. Clarke (2009); Jangbu, *The Nine-eyed Agate: Stories and Poems*, trans. H. Stoddard (2010).

■ **Criticism and History**: L. R. Hartley, "Themes of Tradition and Change in Modern

Tibetan Literature," *Lungta* 12 (1999); *Contemporary Tibetan Literary Studies. PIATS 2003: Proceedings of the Tenth Seminar of the International Association for Tibetan Studies, Oxford, 2003,* ed. S. J. Venturino (2007); *Modern Tibetan Literature and Social Change*, ed. L. R. Hartley and P. Schiaffini-Vedani (2008)—esp. L. R. Hartley, "Heterodox Views and the New Orthodox Poems: Tibetan Writers in the Early and Mid-Twentieth Century"; Y. Dhondup, "Roar of the Snow Lion: Tibetan Poetry in Chinese"; P. Bhum, "'Heartbeat of a New Generation': A Discussion of the New Poetry," and "'Heartbeat of a New Generation' Revisited"; S. Gyatso (Gangzhün), "Modern Tibetan Literature and the Rise of Writer Coteries"; H. Jigme, "Tibetan Literature in the Diaspora."
■ **Electronic Sources**: The Lamp (in Tibetan), www.tibetcm.com; *Where Tibetans Write* (in Eng.), www.tibetwrites.org.

F. Robin

TIBET, TRADITIONAL POETRY AND POETICS OF. The Tibetan formal term for poetry is *snyan-ngag* (Sanskrit, *kāvya*), "ornamental language," and its author is the *snyan-ngag-mkhan* (Sanskrit, *kavi*). Snyan-ngag is characterized by the use of rhetorical ornament (*don-rgyan*, Sanskrit, *arthālaṃkāra*) and phonetic ornament (*sgra-rgyan*, Sanskrit, *śabdālaṃkāra*). It may be either verse or prose, and there is little deliberate use of rhyme. Colloquially, however, Tibetans speak of *rtsom*, literally "composition," to refer to poetic verse in particular. Tibetan verse typically consists of quatrains, with lines of 5, 6, 7, 8, 9, 11, 13, or 15 syllables, and sometimes more in very ornate verse. The use of shorter lines is characteristic of archaic and folk poetry, while trans. of Sanskrit verse and poetry influenced by Sanskrit models use lines of seven or more syllables. The lines forming a single verse most often are metrically regular, generally in trochaic feet, with the addition of a final stressed syllable when the line consists of an odd number of syllables, though meters not according with this scheme are also known. Parallel syntax is often employed, one or more syllables being repeated at the beginning, middle, or end of each line, or with repetitions of the same syllable within a single line. Tropes include various sorts of simile (*dpe-rgyan*) and metaphor (*gzugs-rgyan*), and the use of elegant literary synonyms (*mngon-brjod*).

The indigenous Tibetan poetic genres, little influenced by trans. lit., include folk songs (*glu*, songs of varied meter, and *gzhas*, dance songs of four six-syllable lines), epic and bardic verse (*sgrung-glu*), and versified folk oratory (*tshig-dpe/mol-ba*). Traditionally, these were generally unwritten but have informed Tibetan lit. in many respects, beginning with the earliest known Tibetan poetic works, dating to the early 9th c. and discovered at Dunhuang. In later times, the inspiration of folk song permeates the poems of the Sixth Dalai Lama (1683–1706), as in this example, in the characteristic trochaic trimeter of the dance song (using accents to mark the stressed syllables):

Mdzángs ma'i thúgs dang bstún na
Tshé 'di chós skal chád 'gro
Dbén pa'i rí khrod 'gríms na
bú mo'i thúgs dang 'gál 'gro.

(If I follow my girl friend's heart,
Life's religious wealth will run out;
If I adhere to single retreat,
I'll be running against my girl's heart.)

The subject matter of Tibetan folk song may include love and courtship; politics; grief; nature; or activities such as grazing, sowing, and harvesting; construction work; or picnicking. Literary redactions of Tibet's epic and bardic trads. are represented by ms. and printed versions of the popular tales of King Gesar (*ge-sar sgrung*). Folk oratory, on the other hand, was seldom recorded before recent times, though its colorful rhet. occasionally punctuates Tibetan yogic songs and biographical lit., particularly in the writings of authors from the nomadic regions of Tibet's far eastern provinces, Khams and Amdo.

The Tibetan script and literary lang. developed in the 7th c. CE, an early literary effort incl. very extensive trans., particularly of Indian Buddhist lit. During the 13th c., this trans. lit. was canonized in the form of two great collections: the Kanjur (literally "translated pronouncements") in roughly 100 volumes, consisting of the discourses attributed to the Buddha, and the Tanjur (literally "translated treatises") in roughly 200 volumes, consisting mostly of the writings of later Indian scholars and sages. These include much verse, providing enduring examples for Tibetan writers. The latter collection also includes trans. of Sanskrit treatises on the "language sciences" (*sgra-rig*, Sanskrit *śabdavidyā*)—grammar, synonymics, poetics (above all the *Kāvyādarśa* [Mirror of Poetry], by the Indian poet Daṇḍin, ca. 700), metrics, dramaturgy—the basis for all later Tibetan literary education. Following are notes on some of the major genres of Indian-influenced Tibetan poetic composition, with the names of a few prominent authors and works in each field. (For reasons of space, a given author is mentioned only once, even though he may have contributed to several of the genres mentioned.)

As in India, verse was often the vehicle for works on philosophy and dogmatics (*lta-ba/grub-mtha'*). While highly technical works were versified for mnemonic reasons, poetic elaboration of Buddhist doctrine employed scriptural figures of speech, as in this example from the work of Klong-chen Rab-'byams-pa (1308–64):

> Life is impermanent like clouds of autumn,
> Youth is impermanent like flowers of spring,
> The body is impermanent like borrowed property,
> Wealth is impermanent like dew on the grass.

Many of Tibet's major religious writers, incl. Karma-pa III Rang-byung-rdo-rje (1287–1339), Tsong-kha-pa (1357–1419), and 'Jigs-med Gling-pa (1729–98), composed outstanding doctrinal verse.

Gnomic poetry (*legs-bshad*, Sanskrit *subhāṣita*) modeled on aphorisms from Indian books of polity (*nītiśāstra*) found its greatest exponent in Sa-skya Paṇḍita (1181–1252), whose *Legs-bshad rin-po-che'i gter* (*Treasury of Aphoristic Gems*) is cited proverbially. Other famed aphoristic collections are those of Paṇ-chen Bsod-nams grags-pa (1478–1554), Gung-thang Bstan-pa'i sgron-me (1762–1823), and Mi-pham rnam-rgyal (1846–1912). Ethical and spiritual instructions (*zhal-gdams*) may closely adhere to doctrinal models or to the conventions of gnomic verse, but they may also make powerful use of colloquialisms and elements of folk song, as do the *Ding-ri brgya-rtsa* (Hundred Admonitions to the People of Ding-ri) attributed to Pha-dam-pa Sangs-rgyas (12th c.), by origins an Indian yogin, and the *Rgyal-sras lag-len so-bdun-ma* (Thirty-Seven Skills of the Bodhisattva) by Rgyal-sras Thogs-med bzang-po (1295–1369).

The intricate ritualization of Tibetan religion encouraged the devel. of ritual and devotional verse (*cho-ga, gsol-'debs*). Accomplished academic poets, such as Paṇ-chen Blo-bzang chos-rgyan (1570–1662), author of a popular *Bla-ma mchod-pa* (Worship of the Guru), have contributed here, as have inspired "treasure-discoverers" (*gter-ston*), whose visionary verses are chanted daily by devout Buddhists throughout Tibet.

Drama (*zlos-gar*) often included vivid poetic passages and was represented above all by the popular "Tibetan opera" (*lha-mo*), usually based on religious legends. Indian dramaturgy also inspired some Tibetan poems, though these were not, despite their titles, actually plays. An example is the much admired *Lha-chos-dang mthun-pa'i gtam Padma'i tshal-gyi zlos-gar* (Drama of Padma-tshal: A Divine Discourse) by O-rgyan 'Jigs-med chos-kyi dbang-po (1808–87).

Verse narratives (*rtogs-brjod*) embrace fables and legends, as well as hists. and biographies (*rnam-thar*), incl. autobiographies. Among them are works that are sometimes reminiscient of Indian Puranic texts, as is the *Padma bka'-thang* (Testament of Padmasambhava), redacted by O-rgyan Gling-pa (b. 1323), or ornate poems modeled on refined Sanskrit kāvya, as are the *Mi-dbang rtogs-brjod* (Narrative of the Lord of Men) and other writings by Mdo-mkhar Tshe-ring dbang-rgyal (1697–1763).

Drawing thematic inspiration from the Apabhraṃśa songs of the Indian Buddhist tantric masters and imagistic and metrical resources from indigenous bardic and popular verse, the Buddhist yogins of Tibet created an entirely distinctive family of verse forms, collectively known as *mgur* (yogic songs). The greatest author of mgur was the inspired sage Mi-la-ras-pa (1040–1123), who is famed as Tibet's national poet. Here he sings of his foremost disciple, Ras-chung (1085–1161):

> He's gone off riding a fine steed:
> Others' steeds are skittish,
> But Ras-chung's steed doesn't shy.
> On the stallion of thought's vital wind,
> My son Ras-chung, he's gone riding off.

The poetry anthol. was not a well-developed form in Tibet, perhaps owing to the emphasis placed on the collected works (*gsung-'bum*) of single authors and the collected songs (*mgur-'bum*) of individual yogins, above all. Commentarial treatises on Buddhist doctrine often make such extensive use of quotations that they amount to anthols. in any case. Nonetheless, mention must be made of the extraordinary

Bka'-brgyud mgur-mtsho (Ocean of Songs of the Bka'-brgyud School), originally compiled by the eighth Karma-pa hierarch, Mi-bskyod rdo-rje (1507–54), an anthol. of masterpieces of the mgur genre.

Indian erotic lore was known primarily through tantric Buddhist lit., and frankly erotic imagery is often used symbolically in religious verse, less frequently in secular verse. A mod. author, Dge-'dun chos-'phel (1894–1951), composed an original and highly amusing *'dod-pa'i bstan-bcos* (Treatise on Love), inspired primarily by the *Kāma Sūtra* but in some respects reminiscent of Ovid's *Ars amatoria*.

Owing to the stability of the Tibetan cl. literary lang., the form and lexicon of Tibetan poetic composition until very recently differed little from models dating back a millennium. The secularizing and colloquializing tendencies of contemp. Tibetan writing in general have influenced recent Tibetan poetry, however, as has exposure to contemp. poetry from outside of Tibet. These devels. are addressed in the entry TIBET, CONTEMPORARY POETRY OF.

■ **Criticism and History**: P. Poucha, "Le vers tibetain," *Archiv Orientalni* 18 (1950) and 22 (1954); J. Vekerdi, "Some Remarks on Tibetan Prosody," *Acta Orientalia* 2 (1952); K. Chang, "On Tibetan Poetry," *Central Asiatic Journal* 2 (1956); R. Stein, *Tibetan Civilization* (1972); *Tibetan Literature: Studies in Genre*, ed. J. Cabezón and R. Jackson (1995); M. Kapstein, "The Indian Literary Identity in Tibet," *Literary Cultures in History: Perspectives from South Asia*, ed. S. Pollock (2003).

■ **Folk Verse and Bardic Traditions**: R. Stein, *L'épopée tibétaine de Gesar dans sa version lamaïque de Ling* (1955), and *Recherches sur l'épopée et le barde au Tibet* (1959); G. Tucci, *Tibetan Folk Songs*, 2d ed. (1966); N. N. Dewang, "Musical Tradition of the Tibetan People: Songs in Dance Measure," *Orientalia Romana: Essays and Lectures, II*, ed. V. S. Agrawala (1967); M. Helffer, *Les chants dans l'épopée tibétaine de Ge-sar d'après le livre de la Course de cheval* (1978); B. Aziz, "On Translating Oral Traditions: Ceremonial Wedding Poetry from Dingri," *Soundings in Tibetan Civilization*, ed. B. N. Aziz and M. T. Kapstein (1982).

■ **Translations**: *Three Tibetan Mysteries*, trans. J. Bacot (1924); *Le Dict de Padma*, trans. G. Toussaint (1933); *The Buddha's Law among the Birds*, trans. E. Conze (1955); *The Hundred Thousand Songs of Milarepa*, trans. G. Chang (1962); *A Treasury of Aphoristic Jewels*, trans. J. Bosson (1969); *Vie et Chants de 'Brug-pa Kun-legs le Yogin*, trans. R. Stein (1972); *The Rain of Wisdom*, trans. Nalanda Translation Committee (1980); *Songs of the Sixth Dalai Lama*, trans. K. Dhondup (1981); *Visionary Journey: The Story of Wildwood Delights and the Story of Mount Potala Delights*, trans. H. Guenther (1989); *The Life of Shabkar: The Autobiography of a Tibetan Yogin*, trans. M. Ricard et al. (1994); *The Tale of the Incomparable Prince*, trans. B. Newman (1996); *Songs of Spiritual Experience*, trans. T. Jinpa and J. Elsner, (2000); *In the Forest of Faded Wisdom: 104 Poems by Gendun Chopel*, trans. D. Lopez Jr. (2009).

T. T. RINPOCHE; M. T. KAPSTEIN

TURKIC POETRY

I. Oral Poets in Central Asian Nomadic Turkic Society
II. Pre-Islamic Poetry
III. Islamic Poetry
IV. The Modern Period

I. Oral Poets in Central Asian Nomadic Turkic Society. The term *Central Asia* is here understood as the region of the newly independent Turkic republics of Kazakhstan, Kyrgyzstan, Uzbekistan, and Turkmenistan. After Russia had concluded its conquest of the region (1864–89), it became known as Rus. Turkistan, which also included Tajikistan. Under Soviet rule (1917–91), the territory was referred to as Kazakhstan and Central Asia. The following is an overview of common devels. in Kazakh, Kyrgyz, Uzbek, and Turkmen poetry and prosody.

The Kazakhs, Kyrgyz, Turkmens, and the so-called Kypchak Uzbeks led a nomadic or semi-nomadic life until the beginning of the 1930s, when Soviet policies forced them to become sedentary. Nomads in general honored oral poets called *aqïn, jïrchï/ïrchï* (Kaz., Kyr.), *jïrau* (Kaz.), *bagshï/baxshi* (Trkm., Uzb.), or *doston-chi, shoir* (Uzb.) who were the historians of their tribes and tribal groups, accompanying themselves on the *dombïra* (Kaz.) or the *dutar/dutor* (Trkm., Uzb.), a two-stringed lute, or the *qobïz/komuz* (Kaz., Kyr.), *qopuz* (Trkm.), a two- or three-stringed fiddle. These poets sang heroic and romantic-lyrical epic songs and competed in singing contests of improvised poetry in which women too participated.

The oral poets enjoyed a high status in Turkic nomadic society. Well-known Kazakh aqïn/jïrau would serve as advisors to khans, as, e.g., Bûxar jïrau (ca. 1693–1787) served

Khan Ablay (1711–81), himself a gifted singer and *küychi* (composer of melodies). Kazakh singer/poets were also known as leaders of the many uprisings the Kazakhs staged against the Rus. conquerors. Famous is the aqïn Maxambet Ütemisûlï (1804–46), who together with his friend Isatay Taymanûlï led an uprising in 1837–38. He composed several fiery songs against some of the khans who had collaborated with the Russians. In one of them, he sings,

Xan emessiñ—qasqïrsiñ.
Qara albastï basqïrsïñ.
Dostarïñ kelip tabalap,
Dûspanïñ seni basqa ursïn!

(You are not a khan—you are a wolf.
You are an evil spirit, an oppressor.
May your friends scorn you,
May your enemy hit you on the head!)

Maxambet's outspokenness was much admired. He inspired generations of Kazakh poets before and after the establishment of Soviet colonial rule in 1917. His continuing influence can be seen in a collection of poems about him written by 98 Kazakh poets between 1963 and 2003 (*Jïr arqauï—Maxambet* [The Power of the Song—Maxambet], 2003).

II. Pre-Islamic Poetry

A. ***Orkhon Turkic Poetry.*** All Turkic peoples consider the funeral inscriptions of the 8th c., written in the Turkic runic alphabet and known as the Orkhon Inscriptions, their common heritage. Although the texts were written in prose, certain lines have always stood out as lines of poetry. A good example is the Kül Tegin Inscription, inscribed on a stele erected in 732 for Prince (Tegin) Kül, the younger brother of Bilgä Kaghan, "the Wise Kaghan" (d. 734). Bilgä Kaghan himself eloquently commemorates in the second part of the inscription the life story of his brother Kül, relating his accomplishments and campaigns until his death: *inim kül tegin kärgäk boltï* (My younger brother Kül passed away). At this point, Bilgä Kaghan is overcome by grief:

Özim saqïntïm.
Körir közim körmäz täg boltï
Bilir bilgim bilmäz täg boltï
Özim saqïntïm.

(I mourned deeply.
My eyes, always seeing, became like
not-seeing.
My mind, always knowing, became like
not-knowing.
So much I mourned.)

By arranging the above lines, written as prose in the original text, into consecutive lines, we have before us the original, pre-Islamic metrical scheme of Turkic poetry characterized by a fixed number of syllables in each line expressing one complete idea. The internal alliteration in the second and third verse lines is remarkable. The end rhyme occurs as the result of repetition and parallelism. By repeating the same sentence structure, the same one-syllabic suffix will appear at the end of each verse line, creating a simple grammatical end rhyme.

Poetical lines like those cited above prompted Stebleva (1965) and Joldasbekov (1986) to rearrange the prose texts, particularly those of the Kül Tegin and the Tonyuquq Inscriptions into verses and to translate them into Rus. and Kazakh, respectively. In doing so, both scholars paid attention to the close connection between the poetic style of the inscriptions and the memorial songs and laments recorded much later, considered to be the foundation of the Turkic heroic epic (Joldasbekov, Winner). The Orkhon Inscriptions present the first written examples of Turkic oral poetry.

B. ***Old Uighur Poetry and the Syllabic Meter/Initial Alliteration.*** Written Old Uighur poetry that has come down to us dating from the 8th to the 13th c. can be considered a continuation of the Orkhon Turkic poetry with one additional distinctive feature: initial alliteration. The written Manichaean and Buddhist Old Uighur poetry (Arat) displays the fully developed features of the syllabic meter that became known as *barmak* (finger) meter (ttü. *parmak hesabi*, finger counting). On the basis of the examples given by Arat, one can characterize the barmak as follows: (1) restricted number of syllables in each verse line, the preferred number being seven or eight, but extension to 11 or 14 syllables is also possible; (2) initial alliteration, whereby the initial word of two or more consecutive verse lines must start with the same syllable, consisting either of a vowel or a consonant and a vowel (the vowels *u* and *o* and *ö* and *ü* are equivalent in alliteration).

The syllabic meter with mostly seven or eight syllables, combined with initial alliteration, has been considered the traditional meter of Central Asian Turkic oral lit., particularly of the epic songs such as the Kyrgyz heroic epic *Manas*. Most likely because of the influence of the singers of *Manas*, many of today's Kyrgyz poets continue to use initial alliteration with the barmak meter. The situation is different in Kazakhstan. Texts of heroic epic songs recorded in the second half of the 19th c. rarely show lines with initial alliteration, although they use syllabic meter. However, some Kazakh oral poets like Maxambet employed initial alliteration in their songs, as in the example above. Kazakh-writing poets of the crucial period before and after the establishment of Soviet rule, like Mağjan Jumabayûlï (1893–1938), seemed to have revived the initial alliteration in some of their patriotic songs. In Uzbek, as in Ottoman Turkish poetry, initial alliteration seems to be less known, though the barmak meter is widely employed in oral as well as written poetry (Andrews). The strongest use of initial alliteration in combination with the seven- or eight-syllable meter is to be found in Mongolian oral poetry, notably in epic songs (Poppe). It survived in mod. Mongolian written poetry (Wickham-Smith and Shagdarsüren). The prevalence of initial alliteration in conjunction with the syllabic seven or eight meter among the Altai Turks and the Tuvans (Taube) is probably due to Mongolian influence (Doerfer).

III. Islamic Poetry

A. *Arabo-Persian ʿAruz Meter*. With the acceptance of Islam, the knowledge of Ar. and Persian became fashionable among the intellectuals of the sedentary and later the nomadic groups of the Turkic world. Soon Arabo-Persian rules and trads. were introduced, regardless of the fact that they did not fit the Turkic lang. The prosodic system of the Arabo-Persian *ʿaruz* distinguishes between short and long vowels, a distinction that does not exist in Turkic (Andrews).

B. *Karluk-Karakhanid Poetry*. The first Turkic poetical work displaying the influence of Arabo-Persian prosody is the *Qutadgu Bilig* (The Knowledge of How to Become Happy, 1069–70) by Yusuf Hass Hajib, who wrote the work in Karakhanid Turkic or Middle Turkic, based on Old Turkic, i.e., Orkhon Turkic and Old Uighur. In his choice of verse pattern, the poet was influenced by Firdawsī's (940–1025) use of the Arabo-Persian *mutaqārib* in the *Shahnameh* (Dankoff).

C. *Chagatay Turkic Poetry*. Like in the *Qutadgu Bilig*, a sense of urgency of writing down one's life experiences as a lesson for future generations can also be detected in Mir Ali-Shir Navāʾī's (1441–1501) last work *Mahbub-ul-qulub* (The Beloved of the Hearts, composed in 1500). The work consists of three parts. The first two present a crit. of society, whereas the third part, *Tanbihlar* (Admonitions), consists of authoritative advice in the oral style of proverbs. Indeed, Navāʾī's words were soon accepted as proverbs, cited by Uzbek elders even today, as, e.g., *tilga ihtiyorsiz, elga eʾtiborsiz* (Disrespect for one's language is disregard for one's people). Navāʾī wrote mostly in Chagatay Turkic and has been revered as the promoter of the Chagatay Turkic literary lang. However, his extensive use of Persian and Ar. words cannot be overlooked. He also favored exclusively the Arabo-Persian meter and poetical forms, as, e.g., the *ghazal*. The 15th c., esp. the second half, has been called the golden period of Chagatay Turkic poetry. Because of Navāʾī's *Majālis un-nafāʾis* (Meeting of the Finest, 1492), a collection of short biographies of over 400 poets with citations of their works, we are well informed about the poets of that time.

IV. The Modern Period

A. *From Oral to Written Poetry*. Among the forerunners of the mod. period was the much revered Turkmen poet Makhtumqulï (Trkm. Magtïmgulï, 1733–98). Like Navāʾī, Makhtumqulï was a Sufi. His poems express mystical-religious messages, wisdom, and advice like those of the Sufi saint Ahmad Yasawï (d. 1166). Concerned with the political situation of the Turkmen tribes, he also composed patriotic songs calling on the Turkmens to unite in the face of attempts by Persia, Chiwa, and Bukhara to occupy their territory. Makhtumqulï is considered the first Turkmen poet to write his verses; his counterparts in the other Turkic regions are the Kazakh oral poet Abay (1845–1904) and the Kyrgyz Moldo Kilich (1868–1917). Like Makhtumqulï, Abay received his first education in Muslim schools (*maktab, madrasa*), learned Persian and Ar., and became acquainted with cl. Persian-Ar. lit. Later, he studied Rus. and translated many Rus. poets into Kazakh. His greatest concern was the survival of the Kazakh trads., lang., and culture after the Rus. conquest of the Kazakh steppe. Kilich composed his poetry in such a pure Kyrgyz that it was suggested that his lang. be made a model for a common literary lang. for all Turkic people, one of the goals of the reformer Ismail Gaspirali/Gasprinskiy (1851–1914). Kyrgyz scholars termed his poems ghazals (Kyr. kazal) without commenting on his frequent initial alliteration, short lines of seven or eight syllables, and the lack of strophic arrangements. In 1910, he composed a long poem, *Zilzala*, about an earthquake which had occurred in the same year in northern Kyrgyzstan. He describes in this poem the earthquake itself and predicts that in five or six years more calamities will strike the Kyrgyz. These lines have been interpreted as a forecast of the great uprising of 1916, when the Central Asian Turkic people revolted against Rus. colonialism.

B. *Poetry of the Jadids/Reformers, 1905–38.* Meanwhile in the region of the Kazakhs, Abay's concern about the future of his people was soon taken up by other Kazakh intellectuals. Their voices were echoed in the neighboring Turkic regions as well, becoming stronger and stronger after 1905, the year of Russia's defeat in its war against Japan, demonstrating to the Central Asians that Russia was not invincible. In all Central Asian Turkic regions intellectuals (*Jadids*) established schools according to the methods (*usul-i jadid*) of the Crimean Tatar Gaspirali/Gasprinskiy. While they cared about their native langs. and the education and status of girls and women, their ultimate concern was freedom from Rus. and Soviet colonial oppression. The Jadids' preferred medium for reaching out to the public was poetry. The Kazakh Jadids, by some called *enlighteners*, Baytursïnûlï (1873–1937), Älixan Bökeyxanûlï (1870–1937), and others, though originally not known for their poetry, trained themselves as poets. Writing or composing poetry was expected of any educated Central Asian, and only poetry was considered lit. Moreover, the high regard for the oral poet as a leader and teacher had been transferred to the writing poet. In the Central Asian Turkic regions, written poems, if well received, would become songs (Kaz. *öleñ*), thus reaching a wider audience.

The voices from Uzbekistan were equally powerful, reminding the people of their hist. and invoking the spirits of their ancestors. Abdurauf Fitrat (1886–1938), a scholar and educator who had spent several years in Istanbul, appealed in his poems to the spirit of Amir Temur (1336–1405) to help the Turkic people gain their freedom. His poetry is written in a free style or in the *barmak* (Uzbek *barmoq*) meter. He was against the use of the ʿaruz meter and urged his contemporaries to write in the syllabic barmoq, which he called "our national meter." Next to Fitrat, the most influential and courageous poet of the period was Abdulhamid Sulayman (1898–1938), known as Cholpon (the Morning Star). Like Fitrat and other Jadids, he felt obligated as a poet to be a spokesperson for his people, disregarding any dangers. His poetic style shows many variations, with no preference for Arabo-Persian prosody. To some of his poems, he would give the title *qo'shiq* (folk song), or he would even indicate the melody for a given poem, as if he were striving to become an oral poet through the combined power of word and sound. A few lines from one of his most frequently sung and cited poems will show the intensity of his words:

Men va Boshqalar
Kulgan boshqalar, yig'lagan menman
O'ynagan boshqalar, yigragan menman,
Erk ertaklarini eshitgan boshqa.
Qulluq qo'shig'ini tinglagan menman. . .
Erkin boshqalardir, kamalgan menman,
Hayvon qatorida sanalgan menman. (1921)

(I and the Others
Others are laughing, but I am weeping,
Others are playing, but I am wailing,
Others are hearing tales of freedom,
Only I listen to words of slavery.
Others are free, only I am a prisoner,
Only I am treated like an animal.)

As a subtitle to this poem, Cholpon added the words "From the Mouth of an Uzbek Girl," prompting many readers to interpret it as a reflection of the restricted life of women living behind the walls of the traditional homes in Uzbekistan. It is more likely, however, that Cholpon is describing here life in general and his own life under Soviet rule. He voices similar sentiments in other poems published in 1922 in a collection titled *Uyg'onish* (Awakening), e.g., in *Vijdon erki* (Freedom of Conscience), where he concludes "faqat, erkin vijdonlarga / ege bo'lmoq munkin emes" ([Tyrants] can never control free consciences).

In 1937–38, all Jadids mentioned above and countless more were shot on the orders of Josef Stalin. During these years, Kazakhstan alone lost about 60,000 intellectuals. The Uzbek losses may have been even higher.

Stalin's purges affected not only individuals but their families, who were also sent to concentration camps. Generally, poets and writers could be grouped in two: the silent or silenced ones and those who carried out the directives of the Communist Party. All this changed with the death of Stalin in March 1953, when the terror was lifted.

C. ***The Generation of the 1960s: Heralds of Independence.*** With the new Soviet leader Nikita Khrushchev's denouncement of Stalin's crimes in 1956, a period of relaxation began, called the Thaw. Censorship became less strict, and Stalin's victims who were still alive were released from the gulags. Those who had perished were posthumously acquitted. A young generation of poets and writers, who were between 20 and 30 years of age at the beginning of the 1960s, became known as the Generation of the 1960s. Their first task was to challenge the restrictive Soviet doctrine of socialist realism. Next, they took up the question the Jadids had asked: "Who were we, who are we now?" Like the much admired Kyrgyz writer Chingiz Aitmatov (1928–2008), who raised this question in all his works, poets reminded their compatriots to honor the spirits of their ancestors and to respect their traditions and values. Some wrote patriotic poems about their own motherland and their own people. Others wrote about historical personalities. The Uzbek poet Muhammad Ali (b. 1942), e.g., composed a lengthy poem (*doston*) about Amir Temur in 1967 and in 1979 a doston centered on Dukchi Eshon, the leader of the 1898 uprising against the Russian colonizers. During the years of Gorbachev's glasnost and perestroika (1985–91), Central Asian Turkic poets and writers of the generation of the 1960s became fully engaged in the struggle for independence, which they helped to achieve in 1991.

See ARABIC POETRY; PERSIAN POETRY.

■ **General Introductions**: B. Hayit, "Die Sowjetisierung Turkistans," *Turkestan im XX. Jahrhundert* (1956); A. Adamovich, "The Non-Russians," *Soviet Literature in the Sixties*, ed. M. Hayward and E. I. Crowley (1964); E. Allworth, "The Changing Intellectual and Literary Community" and "The Focus on Literature," *Central Asia: 130 Years of Russian Dominance, A Historical Overview*, ed. E. Allworth (1994).

■ **Pre-Islamic Literature**: R. R. Arat, *Eski Türk Şiiri* (1965); A. Bombaci, "The Turkic Literatures: Introductory Notes on the History and Style"; and G. Doerfer, "Die Literatur der Türken Südsibiriens," *Philologiae Turcicae Fundamenta*, ed. J. Deny and L. Bazin, v. 2 (1965); I. V. Stebleva, *Poetika Drevnetyurkskoy Literatury i ee Transformatsiya v Ranne-Klassiceskiy Period* (1976); N. Poppe, *The Heroic Epic of the Khalkha Mongols*, trans. J. Krueger, D. Montgomery, M. Walter (1979); A. von Gabain, "Zentralasiatische türkische Literaturen I: Nichtislamische alt-türkische Literatur," *Handbuch der Orientalistik*, ed. H. Altenmüller et al. (1982); M. Joldasbekov, *Asïl Arnalar* (1986); K. Reichl, *Turkic Oral Epic Poetry: Tradition, Form, Poetic Structure* (1992).

■ **Islamic Period**: J. Eckmann, "Die Tschagataische Literatur"; and M. F. Köprülü, "La Metrique ʿAruz Dans la Poesie Turque, *Philologiae Turcicae Fundamenta*, ed. J. Deny and L. Bazin, v. 2 (1965); Z. V. Togan, "Zentralasiatische Türkische Literaturen II: Die Islamische Zeit," *Handbuch der Orientalistik, Turkologie*, ed. H. Altenmüller et al. (1982); W. G. Andrews, *Poetry's Voice, Society's Song* (1985); O. Nosirov, "Aruz va O'zbek xalq og'zaki ijodi," *Xalq ijodi xazinasi*, ed. O. Nosirov and O. Sobirov (1986).

■ **Regions.** ***Kazakh***: T. G. Winner, *The Oral Art and Literature of the Kazakhs of Russian Central Asia* (1958); *Qazaq Poeziyasïndağï Dästür Ûlasuï*, ed. A. Narïmbetov et al. (1981)—trad. in Kazakh poetry; *XV–XVIII Ġasïrdağï Qazaq Poeziyasï*, ed. A. Derbiselin et al. (1982); *XIX: Ġasïrdağï Qazaq Poeziyasï*, ed. A. Derbiselin, B. Aqmuqanova et al. (1985)—anthol. of 19th-c. lit; *BesĠasïr jïrlaydï. 15. Gasïrdan 20. ġasïrdïñ bas kezine deyingi qazaq aqïn-jïraularnïñ shïgarmalarï*, ed. M. Maġauïn and M. Baydildaev (1989); M. Dulatûlï, *Oyan Qazaq* (1991); *Qazaqtïñ XVIII–XIX Ġasïrdağï ädebiyetiniñ tarixïnan oçerkter*, ed. S. Muqanov (2002)—hist. of 18th and 19th-c. lit. ***Kyrgyz***: M. Kïlïç, *Kazaldar*, ed. Sooronov (1991)—ghazals; Z. Bektenov and T. Bayjiev, *Kïrgïz adabiyatï* (1993); *Manas: Kïrgiz elinin baatïrdïk eposu. Sagïmbay Orozbakovdun variantï boyuncha akademiyalïk basïlïshï*, 3 v. (1995)—*Manas*, Kyrgyz national epic; "Kïrgïz Ruxu—*Manas*," *Ala-Too* (1995)—spec. iss. on *Manas*. ***Turkmen***: *Türkmen Poeziyasïnïñ Antologiyasï* (1958)—anthol.; J. Benzing, "Die Türkmenische Literatur," *Philologiae Turcicae Fundamenta*, ed. J. Deny and L. Bazin, v. 2 (1965); *Mahtumkulu Divani*, ed. H. Biray (1992)—divan of Makhtumquli; W. Feldman, "Interpreting the Poetry of Makhtumquli," *Muslims in Central Asia: Expressions of Identity* *and Change*, ed. J.-A. Gross (1992); *Songs from the Steppes of Central Asia: The Collected Poems of Makhtumkuli, Eighteenth Century Poet-Hero of Turkmenistan*, ed. B. Aldiss, trans. Y. Azemoun (1995); S. Zeranska-Kominek and A. Lebeuf, *The Tale of Crazy Harman*, trans. J. Ossowski (1997). *Uzbek*: E. Vohidov, *Muhabbat: Saylanma*, 2 v. (1986)—poetry; E. Allworth, *The Modern Uzbeks: From the Fourteenth Century to the Present: A Cultural History* (1990); T. Kocaoglu, "Özbekler ve Özbek Edebiyati," *Türk Dili ve Edebiyati Ansiklopedisi* 7 (1990); B. Orak, "Modern Özbek Edebiyati va Erkin Vohidov," *Erkin Vohidov*: *Seçme Şiirler*, ed. B. Orak (1991); M. Ali, *Saylanma* (1997)—poetry; A. Oripov, *Tanlangan Asarlar*, 4 v. (2000).

■ **Translations**: T. Tekin, *A Grammar of Orkhon Turkic* (1968); *Tuwinische Lieder: Volksdichtungen aus der Westmongolei*, ed. and trans. E. Taube (1980)—oral poetry from western Mongolia; Y. K. Hajib, *Wisdom of Royal Glory (Kutadgu Bilig): A Turko-Islamic Mirror of Princes*, trans. R. Dankoff (1983); *Rawshan: Ein Usbekisches Mündliches Epos*, trans. K. Reichl (1985)—oral epic *Ravshan*; S. Cabbar, *Kurtulush Yolĭnda: A Work on Central Asian Literature in a Turkish-Uzbek Mixed Language* (2000)—Jadid period poetry; *Das usbekische Heldenepos Alpomish: Einführung, Text, Übersetzung*, trans. K. Reichl (2001)—epic *Alpomish*; *Ancient Splendor: The Best of Mongolian Poetry*, ed. and trans. S. Wickham-Smith and T. Shagdarsüren (2006); *The Semetey of Kenja Kara: A Kirghiz Epic Performance on Phonograph with Musical Score and AC*, ed. and trans. D. Prior (2006).

I. LAUDE-CIRTAUTAS

TURKISH POETRY

I. Early Poetry: Prosody, Form, Content
II. The History of Ottoman/Azeri Poetry
III. The Tanzimat and the Dawn of Modernism
IV. Modern Turkish and Azeri Poetry
V. Modern Azeri Poetry

The poetry of the major western Turkic dialects, Azeri, and Ottoman Turkish are the heirs of two quite different trads.: that of Turkic peoples with roots in Central Asia and an adopted Perso-Ar. Islamicate high-culture trad. (Here and below, *Islamicate* and *Persianate* refer to the fact that not all "Islamic" style poetry was written by Muslims and not all "Persian" poetry was written by Persians.) When Turkic peoples began to enter the central Middle East in large numbers as invaders or settlers in the 11th c., they encountered a highly developed Persian literary trad. dominated by poetry. At the courts of Turkic rulers and among the intellectual and literary elites in Asia Minor, the early tendency was to adopt Persian as the lang. of poetry, together with its verse forms, style, and poetic sensibility. At the same time, village and nomadic Turks generally retained their native forms and lang., which had gradually absorbed themes and some vocabulary from the Islamicate trad. since as early as the 9th c. in Central Asia. The tensions, divisions, and junctions between these two distinct formal and ling. trads. and their reflections of class and status ground nearly all general discussions of Turkish poetry of all periods.

I. Early Poetry: Prosody, Form, Content. The Turkish lang. does not recognize vowel qualities (vowel length and brevity, or accent) as rhythmic elements, so the traditional prosody of the Turkic dialects—called *parmak hesabı* (finger counting) or *hece vezni* (syllable meter)—was based on the number of syllables in a line and on repeated groups of syllables separated by caesuras (+). E.g., an 11-syllable line might scan as 11 unbroken syllables and repeat itself in that form throughout a poem. However, each 11-syllable line in another poem might be broken by caesuras into groups of 4+4+3 syllables or, in yet another poem, 5+6 syllables. There are many possible syllable counts for a poetic line and many possible groupings, and each verse form has its own preferred line lengths and groupings. E.g., the following is one 4+3 stanza of a verse form called *mani*, in which the four-line stanzas rhyme *aaba ccda*:

Kız saçların + örmezler
Seni bana + vermezler
Sen bu gece + bana kaç
Ay karanlık + görmezler

(Girl they'll never + braid thy hair
Let us live as + wedded pair
So tonight run + off to me
Moonless dark will + hide us there)

Turkish poetry—written, oral, and sung—in this trad. has continued to be popular from the earliest days of the Turkish presence in the western Middle East to the present. Although the popular trad. is generally oral and anonymous, even the devel. of a high-culture Turkish poetry in the Persian style was strongly influenced by mystical love (*aşk, ışk*) poetry in popular Turkish forms with which Sufi missionaries began to spread Muslim mysticism among Turkish and non-Turkish villagers and nomads at least as early as the 12th c. Perhaps the most widely known poet from this period is Yunus Emre (late 13th, early 14th cs.), whose nondoctrinal mystical verses hover between Persianate and Turkic forms as in the following excerpt in four-line stanzas with a refrain and eight-syllable lines (4+ 4×2) rhyming *aaab cccb*:

> Ben yürürem + yana yana // aşk boyadı + beni kana
> Ne âkilem + ne divane // gel gör beni + aşk neyledi
>
> Geh eserim yiller gibi geh tozarım yollar gibi
> Geh akarım seller gibi gel gör beni aşk neyledi
>
> (I go and as + I go I cry // love's painted me + with bloody dye
> Nor wise nor wit + less now am I // come see what love + has made of me
>
> Now just like the winds do I blow, then like the roads all dusty grow
> Now like the torrents do I flow, come see what love has made of me)

Following the Mongol invasions of the mid-13th c., the Seljuk dynasty of Rum (Asia Minor) lost control of large areas that were dominated culturally and intellectually by Persian and Ar. This, combined with the need to express the Islamic cultural heritage in a lang. that they and their supporters could understand, inclined Turkic rulers to begin demanding and patronizing Turkish poetry in the Persian style.

The Turkish version of the Perso-Ar. trad. employs the traditional Islamic verse forms: the *gazel* (Ar. *ghazal)*, a more or less sonnet-length lyric love poem; the *kaside* (Ar. *qaṣīda*), a longer panegyric or occasional poem; the *mesnevi* (Ar. *masnavī* or *mathnavī*), an extended narrative poem in rhyming couplets, *rubāʿī* (quatrain), and an assortment of stanzaic forms incl. some (*şarkı*, *türkü*, *tuyug*) that closely resemble popular Turkic forms. The basic building block of these forms is the couplet (*beyt*) and all, except the mesnevi and some stanzaic forms, are monorhyming, most often with a rhyming first couplet. Serious poets collected their poems in volumes called *divans* and this type of Ottoman-Azeri poetry is often referred to as *divan poetry*.

The prosodic system, which the Turks called *aruz*, is a further adaptation of the Persian adaptation of the formal rhythms of Ar. In all three cases, rhythm is created by the alternation of "long" syllables (cV: consonant + long vowel) or cvc (consonant + short vowel + consonant) and "short" syllables (cv) grouped into "feet" of various lengths (e. g., short [u] + long [–] + long [u– –] or long + short + long + long [–u– –]), which are combined in standardized rhythmic lines (*mişraʿ*). In Ar., the feet have some syllables that can be lengthened or shortened. In Persian, the feet are fixed, with a few minor exceptions, and flexibility is achieved by permitting certain vowels (e.g., the vowel of the *izafet* [the adjectival/genitive connector] and the "vocalic h = a/e") to be read as either long or short and by using "shortened" versions of some common words (e. g., *māh* = > *meh* [moon]). Ottoman Turkish poets, who copiously adopted Persian and Ar. vocabulary and even some syntax, created their own adaptation of Persian prosody and its flexibility, much as the Persians had adapted Ar. Because there are no long vowels in Turkish, only "closed" (cvc), syllables are naturally long according to Perso-Ar. prosody, and words with extended strings of short (cv) syllables are quite common. However, unlike Ar. and Persian, there was no fixed spelling of Turkish words in the Ar.-Ottoman script, so it was always possible, although frowned on to some extent, to spell Turkish words using some Ar.-Ottoman script long vowels and at times to consider such vowels as long for purposes of rhythm. The following is the initial couplet, with an indication of scansion and rhyme, of a five-couplet gazel by Zātā (1471–1546), an elite Ottoman poet of the early 16th c.:

> u– – – /u– – – /u– – –/ u– – –
> Garībem gur/bete düşdüm/ gönül āvā/ re yār*um yok*
> Benüm āh etdügüm ʿayb etmen kim ihtiyār*um yok*
>
> (I'm a stranger, plunged into exile, my heart a vagabond, no beloved do I have
> Do not find fault with me, when I go around sighing, for no choice do I have)

In these lines, the rhyme is in *ār* (underlined) with a repeated postrhyme element called *redif* (originally the name for a warrior who rides on the back of another's saddle).

Poetry that adapted the Perso-Ar. trad. was hugely popular among western Turkish speakers during the Ottoman period, from the 14th c. through the early 20th. Hundreds upon hundreds of recognized poets from rulers, high officials, and courtiers to soldiers, shopkeepers, and mendicant dervishes are recorded in the collections of biographies of poets of every era and were said to be only the visible members of a vast poetic population. Although poems were written about almost everything, the core of Ottoman and Azeri elite poetry, whether lyric, narrative, or panegyric, was the emotional content of a love, most commonly homoerotic love, which often carried with it a burden, large or small, of mystical passion. In a context where public expressions of heterosexual love were disapproved, love poetry commonly had as its object young men, some of whom became quite famous. The presumed occasion of this poetry was a gathering of friends (often transmuted into mystical [dervish] ceremonial gatherings) that in many ways resembled the Gr. *symposion*, in which food, drink (often alcoholic), witty conversation, love, music, and, above all, poetry were the primary ingredients. Its setting was an idealized garden—reflected everywhere in Ottoman art and decoration—wherein every natural phenomenon was a potential metaphor for some feature of the lover, the beloved, and the gathering.

II. The History of Ottoman-Azeri Poetry. The periodization of Ottoman-Azeri poetry is a controversial topic. However, it is possible to sketch some broad tendencies and trends. The rise of the Ottomans as the dominant power in western Anatolia and Eastern Europe, which began in the second quarter of the 14th c., initiated a gradual consolidation of literary patronage affirmed by an Ottoman literary historical view that adopted, as Ottoman precursors, famous early poets such as Şeyhi (d. ca. 1431), a court poet whose primary patron was the prince of the independent province of Germiyan, and Nesimi (d. ca. 1404), an Eastern Anatolian-Syrian Azeri mystical poet.

The centralization of Ottoman Islamic poetic production escalated with the conquest of Constantinople in 1453. The patronage of poetry burgeoned in the court of Mehmet the Conqueror. His grand vizier and court poet Ahmet Pasha (d. 1469) is said to have raised the level of Ottoman poetry to compete with Persian, in part by translating some Chagatai (Eastern Turkic) gazels by Mir Ali-Shir Navā'ī (1441–1501) sent from the court of the Timurid ruler Huseyn Baykara in Herat. At much the same time, the other acknowledged foundational poet, known by the pseud. Necati (1451?–1509), rose from slave status to wealth and fame with verses such as the following that reflect his skill at combining folk wisdom with the most refined themes:

> The whole world is ignited by your beauty
> from the tip of your locks
> When they happen by night, fires cause the
> populace great loss
>
> Is it any wonder that my heart moans as
> you give me advice
> You should know, if they sprinkle water on
> it, the fire cries out

By the late 15th c., the stage had been set for the great Ottoman renaissance of Islamic culture that would take place in the 16th c. At the cultural pinnacle, Turkish incorporated the vocabularies of Persian and Ar. to create a ling. tool capable of astounding flights of rhetorical fancy, which adorned expressions of intense emotional power. From the Anatolian courts of Ottoman princes and cultural centers in Eastern Europe, poets flocked to the capital, competing to join the literary salons of the rich and powerful. The princely court of Amasya in the east produced Mihri Hatun (d. ca. 1512), the most famous Ottoman woman poet. The courtly-mystical poet Hayali (d. 1557) came from Vardar Yeniçesi in Bosnia, Zātī from the town of Balıkesir. From the time of Mehmet the Conqueror to the mid-16th c., hundreds of poets received annual stipends from the royal treasury.

During this time, Lami'i (1472–1532) adapted several masterpieces of Persian narrative verse to Turkish, and Ca'fer Chelebi (ca. 1463–1515), a powerful official, composed a unique narrative describing a love affair with a married woman during a spring camping trip to a popular park. Zātī made a living solely on gifts given in exchange for panegyrics and love poems. Even the rulers of the age participated in poetry. Shah Ismail Safavi (1487–1524), founder of the Safavid dynasty of Persia, composed Azeri mystical love poetry in both the Islamicate and popular Turkic trads., which helped rally the Turkmen tribes to his Sufi vision of Shi'ite Islam:

Go now, go now, go . . . let Him be yours
Let a fully committed beloved be yours

If you launch yourself into the air and fly
high
Let the sky reaching up from all the earth
be yours

Suleyman the Magnificent (r. 1520–66) too was an avid poet and patron of poets. He writes of his beloved wife Hurrem:

My solitude, my everything, my beloved,
my gleaming moon
My companion, intimate, my all, lord of
beauties, my sultan

My life's essence and span, my sip from the
river of Paradise, my Eden
My springtime, my bright joy, my secret,
my idol, my laughing rose

In Suleyman's intimate circle was the master poet of the century, Baki (1526–1600), who rose to the second highest canon-law position in the empire and dominated the period with verses, such as the first and last couplets of his famed meditation on old age:

The time of spring has suffered
loss of fame and loss of face
The leaves of trees have fallen
in the meadow far from grace
. . .
On this meadow-earth, the leaves
of books and trees are torn, Baki
It seems they have a true complaint
against the winds of time and fate

The Iraqi poet Fuzuli (d. 1556), who compiled divans in Ar., Persian, and Azeri Turkish, is much beloved by the Turks and is considered an Ottoman poet, which has more to do with the conquest of Iraq in 1534 than his actual lang. and culture. He composed exquisite love poetry often in a mystical mode and produced a retelling of the mystical love story of Leyla and Mecnun in Azeri Turkish. The following is an example of his passionate mystical verses:

My heart blooms joyous when it sees your
tousled locks
I lose the power to speak, when I see your
rosebud laughing

I look at you, blood spatters from my eyes
When our glances meet, eyelash arrows
pierce my heart

By the 17th c., the regularization of bureaucratic and intellectual institutions combined with a decline in patronage reduced opportunities for aspiring poets, many of whom then found their inspiration in dervish lodges rather than in the gatherings of the powerful. Nonetheless, one of the most brilliant poets of the age, Nef'i (d. 1635), was best known as a court panegyrist (and lampooner of rivals and stingy patrons). His most famous panegyric begins with a paean to spring initiated by the following couplet (with a supererogatory internal rhyme reminiscent of popular quatrains):

As the springtime breezes blew, at morn the
roses bloomed anew
Oh let our hearts be blooming too, please,
saki, pass the cup of Djem

Perhaps the most striking elite poetic movement during this period was the introduction of an adaptation of the Persian "Indian Style" (named for the style perfected in the Mughal courts of India). Complex and often formidably obscure, this style was esp. suitable for mystical verse, as the following by Na'ili (d. 1666) exemplifies:

Who thirsts with dry lips for the stream of
desire, slips onto paths of rejection
Who rushes in haste after his desire, ever
wanders the waste of distraction

The 17th-c. decline in opportunity for poets at the elite level is balanced by the burgeoning of more popular poetry. The *saz* (long lute) poets and wandering *aşıks* (lovers) like the famed Aşık Ömer (d. ca. 1707), who also dabbled in elite-style verses, provided a link between elite and common, village and city with their verses most often set to music. E.g., from Aşık Ömer,

I'm a lover, alas, alack
Bewitched by you, don't burn me black
Keep that dog of a rival back
One soul has tight embraced another

In the early 18th c., an era of peace and the rise of a prosperous merchant class led to a period of exuberant cultural production called the Tulip Period (1718–30) after the tulip craze that swept the Ottoman Empire and Europe. In an atmosphere of lavish spending on parties, pleasure gardens, and parks, poetry flourished, typified by the poems of Nedim (d. 1730), many of which echoed the lang., forms, and topical themes of popular verse, as in this example:

> Saki, let my soul rejoin my body, come to the gathering
> To that goblet sacrifice all promises and all repenting
> Have a care where you set your foot, my monarch and my king
> There may be wine spilt here and too the broken bottles of the drunks

The latter years of the century were marked by the poetic genius of Şeyh Galip (1757–99), who while still young became the master of a prestigious Mevlevi dervish lodge, the confidant of a reformist sultan, and the author of an original narrative poem entitled "Beauty and Love" that represents an allegorical summing up in the Indian style of the mystical trad. descended from Rūmī and the last great masterpiece of Ottoman narrative poetry.

III. The Tanzimat and the Dawn of Modernism. By the 19th c., the impetus for political, social, and even cultural reform gradually became overwhelming. The reformers were energized, but adherents of the old cultural order despaired, as is poignantly expressed in the following couplet by ʿİzzet Molla (1786–1829):

> We have reached a season of spring in this world
> When the bulbul is silent, the pool empty and the rose-bed is in ruins

The bulbul, one of the central metaphors of cl. poetry, would soon be relegated to the footnotes of lit. hist. by advocates of literary modernization. Namık Kemal (1840–88), one of the major proponents of constitutionalist reform, subverted the mystical subtext of the ageless topos and evoked an encaged nightingale crying out for freedom, a direct reference to the liberal inclinations of the Young Ottomans. The new focus of poetry was on the here and now. In the wake of the westernizing *Tanzimat* reforms of 1839, reformist intellectuals, paying little heed to the high levels of illiteracy, domesticated Fr. literary models and focused on the need to develop an engaged lit. that would enlighten the people and support even more wide-ranging changes. They argued that the metaphorical nature of cl. lit. was unsuited to that purpose. The lang. issue became central. Writers explored ways to bridge the gap between the learned literary lang. and ordinary speech. Though poets, such as İbrahim Şinasi (1826–71), Ziya Paşa (1825–80), and Kemal explored a great variety of new themes, poetry was the least affected by change. Traditional high-culture poetry, its prosody, and its major genres were maintained. This relative conservatism was not surprising since the reformists' main endeavor was the appropriation of new literary genres such as the novel, short story, and drama. Nonetheless, huge controversies raged over the origins, sources of inspiration, and role of poetry.

IV. Modern Turkish and Azeri Poetry. In the light of conflicting influences ranging from Fr. romanticism to Parnassianism, poets such as Abdülhak Hamit (1852–1937) and Recaizade Mahmud Ekrem (1847–1914) questioned the instrumentalization of poetry and introduced new aesthetic concerns together with a more confessional dimension. In particular, Ekrem's theoretical writings had a lasting impact on the neo-Parnassian poets of the *Edebiyat-ı Cedide* (New Literature) group who advocated an elitist art-for-art's-sake approach. Muallim Naci (1850–93) defended ideas that were quite close to those of Ekrem, his nemesis; but as he was closer to intellectual circles linked to the authoritarian regime of Sultan Abdülhamid II, he is unjustly seen as an advocate of literary conservatism by historians. The neo-Parnassian poets' elaborate and sometimes artificial lang. was the source of much crit. by the nationalist proponents of neofolk poetry, who supported the use of the syllabic folk meter and the Istanbul vernacular. The publication of *Türkçe Şiirler* (Poems in Turkish) in 1899 by Mehmed Emin (1869–1944) was the starting point of a long-lasting and often ruthless battle of words between elitist neo-Parnassians and populists. After the relative liberalization following the promulgation of the second constitution in 1908, the ephemeral jour. *Genç Kalemler* (1911) played a major role in the promotion of the neofolk movement. With the blessings of the Union and Progress government and later the early republican authorities, nationalist versifiers, such as the Five Syllabists, influenced by the writings of Ziya Gökalp (1867–1915), the father of Turkish nationalism, developed a discourse on the supposed foreignness of the traditional aruz prosody and its inappropriateness for the Turkish lang. Nonetheless, four late masters of the aruz had a major impact on the devel. of Turkish poetry even after the foundation of the republic in 1923: Tevfik Fikret's (1867–1915) engaged humanism, Mehmet Akif's (1873–1936) mod. Islamicist verse, Ahmet Haşim's (1884–1933) Ottoman symbolism, and Yahya Kemal's (1884–1958) neoclassicism. Fikret's, Akif's and Haşim's experiments with free verse (*şiʿr-i müstezad*) that broke up the traditional couplet into lines with changing numbers of aruz rhythmic feet were a precursor of truly mod. free verse. This devel. took place partly under the influence of Fr. *vers libre*, but it was also partly in response to a perceived need to integrate the spoken lang. into poetry. A new generation of syllabists emerged, marrying the symbolist quest for musical perfection with nationalist endeavors. Among them, Fazıl Hüsnü Dağlarca (1914–2008) deserves particular notice as he lived through the century, unaffected by changing fashions, and left behind works that delved into themes ranging from mysticism to anticolonialism and remained popular for generations.

Syllabism, however, was outflanked by younger poets such as Ercüment Behzad Lav (1903–84), who discovered Ger. expressionism, and Nazım Hikmet (1901–63), who explored Rus. futurism. A new divide appeared between the mainly left-wing advocates of free verse and the mostly conservative and nationalist proponents of folk prosody.

Relentlessly hounded by the Kemalist state, Hikmet nonetheless revolutionized Turkish poetry. After a short-lived futurist period, he worked, while imprisoned in Bursa in the 1930s, toward a fusion of futurist, folk, and cl. elements while developing a novel form of subjective realism. Heavy censorship made it difficult for socialist poets to explore Hikmet's new endeavors, which explains why they, with some exceptions, espoused a rather rigid interpretation of socialist realism. Only after the military coup of 1960 and the ensuing democratic reforms did Hikmet's poetry become easily available and hugely influential for a new generation of socialist poets, such as Ataol Behramoğlu (b. 1942).

Toward the end of the 1930s, a group of young poets, Orhan Veli (1914–50), Melih Cevdet Anday (1915–2002), and Oktay Rifat (1914–88) launched the *Garip* movement. They combined subjective realism and surrealism and finally published a groundbreaking manifesto in 1941. The movement caused a huge upheaval during the 1940s, even though its perceived apolitical stance was often the subject of reproach. Influenced by independent poets, such as Asaf Halet Çelebi (1907–58) and Behçet Necatigil (1916–79), who explored correspondences between modernist verse and the cl. trad., a new generation of poets who were later to be known as the *İkinci Yeni* (Second Renewal) questioned the downgrading of poetry by the prolific offspring of the Garip generation and developed a more individualist, and to a certain extent opaque, poetry that explored even the darkest realms of human experience and consciousness. Some of the original advocates of this new trend, among them Turgut Uyar (1927–85), Edip Cansever (1928–96), Cemal Süreya (1931–90), Gülten Akın (1933–2015), and Hilmi Yavuz (b. 1936), proved to have a profound influence on a new generation of poets who rediscovered their works in the 1990s, in the context of wide-ranging debates about the role of the Ottoman trad. in mod. Turkish poetry.

Reclaiming and subverting the heritage of Akif and Necip Fazıl Kısakürek (1905–83), a modernist Islamicist poetry movement surfaced. It was championed by Sezai Karakoç (b. 1933) and Cahit Zarifoğlu (1940–87) and gained strength during the 1970s. Though political, in particular socialist, poetry was much in vogue during that decade, the years following the 1980 military coup were characterized by the depoliticization of the literary field and saw the devel. of elitist concerns ranging from neoimagism to modernist appropriations of Ottoman elite lit. Nonetheless, two major new devels. testified to the transformations affecting Turkish society and poetry. One was the growing number of women poets published during the 1980s. Some of them, such as Gülseli İnal (b. 1947), Lale Müldür (b. 1956), and Nilgün Marmara (1958–87), were hugely influential. Though their works bore the marks of post-1980 poetry, they consciously subverted the male-dominated poetry trad. with a novel lang. and daring images. The other was a group of young Kurdish poets who published both in niche magazines and mainstream literary jours. They introduced original features such as proclaiming their Kurdishness in Turkish through a deconstruction of Turkish syntax and the transposition of Kurdish expressions into Turkish, as well as by focusing on the Kurdish experience.

V. Modern Azeri Poetry. In Azeri-speaking regions during the 18th and 19th cs., cl. trends survived. The Rus.-Iranian wars of 1813–28 and subsequent treaties dividing Azeri-speaking populations on both sides of the Araxes River did not impede cultural and social interactions. Poets such as Molla Panah Vagif (1717–97), Mirza Shafi Vazeh (1792–1852), Seyyid Azim Shirvani (1835–88), and Ali Agha Vahid (1896–1965) continued to write love poems, many glorifying earthly love in cl. aruz meters, and achieved fame throughout the area with poems often set to music. The 20th c. saw the rise of a realistic trend that became more pronounced after the workers' uprising in Russia (1905) and the Iranian constitutional revolution (1906). Ali Akbar Sabir (1862–1911) and Mo'juz of Shabustar (1872–1932), e.g., devoted themselves to poetic socialist realism, condemning illiteracy, injustice, and the plight of women. In the second half of the century, poets wrote a wide variety of poetry in both aruz and free-verse forms, among them Shahriyar (pseud. of Mohammad-Hoseyn Behjat-Tabrizi, 1907–86), Suleyman Rustam (1906–89), and Bakhtiyar Vahabzada (1925–2009).

■ **Anthologies**: ***English***: *Ottoman Literature: The Poets and Poetry of Turkey*, trans. E.J.W. Gibb (1901); *The Penguin Book of Turkish Verse*, ed. N. Menemencioğlu (1978); *Modern Turkish Poetry*, ed. F. Kayacan Fergar (1982); *An Anthology of Turkish Literature*, ed. K. Silay (1996); *Eda: An Anthology of Contemporary Turkish Literature*, ed. M. Nemet-Nejat (2004); *Translation Review: Turkish Literature and Its Translation* 68 (2004)—trans., biblio., articles; *A Brave New Quest: 100 Modern Turkish Poets*, ed. T. S. Halman (2006); *Ottoman Lyric Poetry: An Anthology*, ed. and trans. W. G. Andrews, N. Black, M. Kalpakli, rev. ed. (2006). ***French***: *Anthologie de la Poésie Turque Contemporaine*, ed. J. Pinquié and Y. Levent (1991); *Anthologie de la poésie turque XVIIIè–XXè siècle*, ed. N. Arzik (1994). ***German***: *Aus dem Goldenen Becher: Türkische Gedichte aus Sieben Jahrhunderten*, ed. A. Schimmel (1993).

■ **Criticism and History**: ***Modern Azeri Poetry***: *Azerbaijan Poetry: Classic, Modern, Traditional*, ed. M. Ibrahimov (1976); S. Berengian, *Azeri and Persian Literary Works in the Twentieth Century Iranian Azerbaijan* (1988); H. Sultan-Qurraie, *Modern Azeri Literature: Identity, Gender and Politics in the Poetry of Mo'juz* (2003). ***Ottoman Poetry***: E.J.W. Gibb, *A History of Ottoman Poetry*, 6 v. (1900–09)—copious information, but unacceptable racist and orientalist critique; W. G. Andrews, *Introduction to Ottoman Poetry* (1976), and *Poetry's Voice, Society's Song* (1985); V. Holbrook, *The Unreadable Shores of Love* (1994); W. G. Andrews and M. Kalpakli, *The Age of Beloveds* (2005). ***Post-Tanzimat Poetry***: T. S. Halman, "Poetry and Society: The Turkish Experience" *Modern Near East: Literature and Society*, ed. C. M. Kortepeter (1971); M. Fuat, "Giriş," *Çağdaş Türk Şiiri Antolojisi* (1985); G. Turan, "The Adventure of Modernism in Turkish Poetry," *Agenda* 38.3–4 (2002).

W. G. Andrews; L. Mignon

U

UKRAINE, POETRY OF. The hist. of Ukrainian poetry can be divided into three major periods, made all the more distinct by sharp discontinuities among them. Underlying and producing these discontinuities are profound shifts in Ukrainian society; not only do basic political and social structures disappear, to be replaced by entirely new ones, but, at least until the mod. period, Ukrainian literary and historical consciousness does not succeed in bridging these changes.

The first period, from the 10th–11th cs. to roughly the 14th c., coincides largely with the lit. of Kyivan Rus', which is taken as the common patrimony of the East Slavs—the Ukrainians, Belarusians, and Russians. The second, middle period, late 16th to the late 18th cs., reflects primarily the poetics of the baroque; and the third period, beginning 19th c. to the present, coincides with the birth of the mod. Ukrainian nation and the emergence of literary Ukrainian based on the vernacular.

One can speak of poetry in Old Ukrainian (Kyivan) lit. in terms of (1) the oral trad., (2) trans. and "borrowed" lit., and (3) verse elements in the original lit. Old Ukrainian oral lit. is often identified with folklore, but this lit., while oral, was probably a product of a court or "high" trad., which over the centuries "sank" into the repertoire of folklore. Whether the epic cycle of *byliny* (in Ukrainian *staryny*) that depict the Kyivan context but were preserved in the northern Rus. territories or the gamut of ritual poetry related to the agricultural cycle and pagan rites, the actual texts date only from the 18th–19th cs., and conclusions about the range and function of oral lit. in this earliest period remain speculative.

Verse as such is found in the various trans. and adaptations of Byzantine liturgical lit., particularly hymnography (see BYZANTINE POETRY). These hymns influenced contemp. Kyivan texts and had an impact on the bookish versification of the 16th to 18th cs. The major poetic work of this period is the *Slovo o polku Ihorevi* (Tale of Igor's Campaign) describing an unsuccessful military campaign of 1185. Written in the early 13th c., it was discovered and published at the turn of the 19th c. Its sonorous, vivid lang. and imagery, its deft narrative of rhythmic prose, have made the *Slovo* for all the mod. East Slavic lits. the quintessential poetic correlative of Kyivan Rus'.

In the middle period, sometime in the 16th c., a new form of oral poetry emerged, the *duma* (pl. *dumy*), which supplanted the older staryny and was to have a strong impact on much of subsequent Ukrainian poetry. The dumy, sung by wandering, often blind singers, were not a narrowly folkloric genre—its perspective encompassed all Ukrainian society. These "sacred songs," conveying profound social and historical experiences like wars with the Turks and Tatars or wars of liberation from Poland, reflected elements of heroic epic, ballad, and elegy.

At the end of the 16th c., Ukrainian society and culture underwent a remarkable revitalization, which culminated in the mid-17th c. with an autonomous Cossack state that was to last more than a century. A characteristic feature of Middle Ukrainian lit. is its bilingualism: in the 17th and early 18th cs., it is Ukrainian or Polish, depending on theme, genre, or projected audience; by the mid-18th c., it is Ukrainian-Rus. In both cases, the choice of the other lang. reflects not a hedging of the writer's Ukrainian identity but rather the conventions of the literary system.

The earliest poetry of this period, beginning from the 1580s and 1590s, is syllabic in meter; in genre, emblematic and heraldic. Throughout the first part of the 17th c., Ukrainian poetry is represented mainly by panegyric, historical, and didactic poetry; by the second half of the 17th c., it shows a relatively broad range of forms and a differentiation into "high" genres (reflecting baroque poetics) and popular genres. In the former, such important poets as Lazar Baranovych (1616–93) and esp. Ioan Velychkovs'ky (ca. 1640–1701), writing in both bookish Ukrainian and Polish and reflecting religious themes, give a new depth to national self-expression. The popular genres—fables, satires, and Christmas and Easter verse—are mostly anonymous and close to the vernacular.

The early 18th c. witnesses the maturation of Ukrainian school drama. Feofan Prokopovich's (1681–1736) tragicomedy *Vladymir* (1705) exemplifies the didactic poetics of this genre, as the historical theme—the Christianization of Kyivan Rus'—becomes a vehicle for political satire and for the apotheosis of the Ukrainian *hetman* (leader) Ivan Mazepa. At the end of the 18th c., there appears the most significant talent of premod. Ukrainian lit.: the peripatetic philosopher and poet Hryhorii Skovoroda (1722–94). His book of devotional poetry, *The Garden of Divine Songs*, synthesizing cl. and biblical, mystical and folk elements, remains the high point of 18th-c. Ukrainian poetry.

Mod. Ukrainian poetry is traditionally dated with the appearance of Ivan Kotliarevs'ky's *Eneida* of 1798, a travesty of Virgil's *Aeneid*. Finding its analogue to the fall of Troy in the destruction of the last Cossack stronghold (the Zaporozhian Sich), marking the end of Ukrainian autonomy in the 18th c., *Eneida* focuses on the wanderings of a band of Cossacks and provides an encyclopedic and loving account of Ukrainian provincial life and customs. Mixing an energetic optimism, satire, and nostalgia for the past with broad humor, the poem became a rallying point for a new Ukrainian lit. in the vernacular. Kotliarevs'ky (1769–1838) drew on a wide range of comic and burlesque devices characteristic of 18th-c. Ukrainian poetry, and this burlesque mode was adopted by other poets, Petro Hulak-Artemovs'ky (1790–1865) among them.

Beginning with the 1820s, Ukrainian romanticism introduced an entirely new poetics: the focus of this poetry fell on the turbulent Cossack past and on the wealth of Ukrainian folklore. Early romantic poets, like Levko Borovykovys'ky (1806–89), Amvrosii Metlyns'ky (1814–70), and esp. Mykola Kostomarov (1817–85), and clergymen-poets in western Ukraine, then under Austria-Hungary, the so-called Ruthenian Trinity (Markiian Shashkevych [1811–43], Ivan Vahylevych [1811–66], and Yakiv Holovats'ky [1814–88]), sought to legitimize the vernacular lang., to rediscover historical and ethnic roots, and to advance cultural and national autonomy.

Taras Shevchenko (1814–61), born a serf and freed at the age of 24, came to be lionized by both Ukrainian and Rus. society as a uniquely powerful and inspired romantic poet. Arrested in 1847 in connection with the secret society the Brotherhood of Saints Cyril and Methodius and exiled for ten years, he returned in ill health but with poetic powers unimpaired. Seen as a martyr and bard even in his lifetime, Shevchenko became on his death the animating spirit of the Ukrainian national movement and remains a popular cult figure to this day. Shevchenko's poetry, traditionally called *Kobzar* (the Minstrel) after his first collection of 1840, divides along the lines of intimate lyric poetry; political poetry, with powerful excoriations of social and national oppression, particularly by tsarist authority; and narrative poems, incl. historical poems and ballads. All these modes are unified and guided by structures of mythical thought, which project a movement from the present state of victimization to a redeemed and purified humanity.

Panteleimon Kulish (1819–97)—friend, critic, and rival of Shevchenko—significantly broadened the range of Ukrainian poetry by new historical themes and expanded formal concerns and by renderings of the Bible, Shakespeare, Lord Byron, and other Western poets. Shevchenko's successors tended either to emulate him, like the western Ukrainian poet Yuri Fed'kovych (1834–88), or to resist the pull of the bard's model, like Stepan Rudans'ky (1834–73) and Yakiv Shchoholiv (1823–98), two poets on the borderline of romanticism and realism.

Ukrainian poetry in the second half of the 19th c. was strained by the weight of perceived realist obligations and by official Rus. edicts of 1863 and 1876 banning the publication and importation of Ukrainian books. A poet who exemplifies both the call of national civic duty and the thrust of an authentic personal poetry is the western Ukrainian Ivan Franko (1856–1916). A renaissance man of indefatigable energy, Franko covers a broad gamut of genre and styles—historical, satiric, lyrical, and confessional, the last by far the most successful.

Throughout much of the 20th c., Ukrainian lit. was dominated by two competing aesthetic views: modernism with its call for innovation and artistic freedom and its Eur. orientation vs. the populism that morphed into socialist realism under Soviet rule. Another important classification of Ukrainian literary production that resulted from the failure to establish a Ukrainian state after World War I and that remained valid until independence is the split of lit. into Soviet and émigré. This political divergence influenced aesthetic approaches and resulted in different literary models.

The period of early modernism, generally from the 1890s to World War I, witnessed the differentiation of the Ukrainian literary marketplace and the emergence of poetry for a more select public. One of the first to turn to

Eur. and universal historical and philosophical themes was Lesia Ukrainka (1872–1913); her poetic drama also presents a powerful vehicle for gender concerns. A call for modernization and a rejection of utilitarian obligations were at the heart of the *Moloda muza* (The Young Muse) poetic group's activity, whose oeuvre betrays decadent and neoromantic inclinations.

On the eve of World War I, there appeared the symbolist poetry of Mykola Vorony (1871–1942), Mykola Filians'ky (1873–1938), and Oleksandr Oles' (1878–1944), anticipating the outstanding poet of the 20th c.: Pavlo Tychyna (1891–1967). At first a symbolist and spirited supporter of the Ukrainian national revolution and at the end of his life an orthodox spokesman for the Soviet system, Tychyna underwent a complex evolution; but in his early and mature poetry, he remains the most innovative and influential poetic voice of his time.

In the 1920s, with the establishment of Soviet rule in Ukraine and the official policy of "Ukrainization," Ukrainian lit. experienced a spectacular revival, as manifested in the proliferation of separate modernist and avant-garde movements, mainly neoclassicism, with such outstanding poets as Maksym Ryl's'ky (1895–1969) and Mykola Zerov (1890–1937); and futurism, with Mykhail Semenko (1892–1937) and Mykola Bazhan (1904–83), who began as a futurist but quickly shifted to become the second most important Ukrainian Soviet poet of the century. Other notable poets from this period include Yevhen Pluzhnyk (1898–1936) and Volodymyr Svidzins'ky (1885–1941).

By the 1930s, the Stalinist terror had crushed the national and cultural revival, and hundreds of writers perished in camps. The poetic scene shifted to western Ukraine, then under Poland, and farther abroad. The most significant émigré poetic group that emerged in the interwar period was the so-called Prague school. Such poets as Yevhen Malaniuk (1897–1968), Oleksa Stefanovych (1899–1970), and Oksana Liaturyns'ka (1902–70) evinced patriotic fervor without sacrificing high standards of poetic craft. But the greatest poet of that period in western Ukraine was Bohdan Ihor Antonych (1909–37), known for his novel imagery and formal experimentation. In his mature poetry, he attained an expressive power and metaphysical and symbolic complexity that put him in the forefront of 20th-c. Eur. poetry.

In the postwar period, the high point of Ukrainian émigré poetry was the New York Group that originated in the mid-1950s and continued its activity into the 1990s. Such poets as Bohdan Boychuk (b. 1927), Yuriy Tarnawsky (b. 1934), Bohdan Rubchak (b. 1935), and Emma Andijewska (b. 1931), all born in the interwar period, eagerly experimented with poetic forms privileging *vers libre* and metaphor and embraced such fashionable artistic and philosophical trends as surrealism and existentialism. Gravitating toward the group were two poets of a slightly older generation, Oleh Zuievs'ky (1920–96) and Vasyl Barka (1908–2003), whose oeuvre manifested hermetic difficulty in its search for purity.

Soviet Ukrainian poetry experienced a major revival in the early 1960s with the appearance of such poets as Lina Kostenko (b. 1930), Mykola Vinhranovs'ky (1936–2004), and Ivan Drach (b. 1936). Known as the Generation of the Sixties, they strove for authenticity and liberalization. Their works, imbued with lyric intensity, centered on ethical and historical concerns but did not overtly experiment with poetic forms. More innovative and experimental were the poets of the Kyiv school who had their literary debuts also in the 1960s, though they were not encouraged by the state. Nonconformists and aesthetes, Vasyl Holoborod'ko (b. 1945), Mykola Vorobiov (b. 1941), Viktor Kordun (1946–2005), and Mykhailo Hryhoriv (b. 1947) published most of their oeuvre in the 1980s and 1990s, having a limited impact on the literary process of the 1960s. This is also true of such cerebral dissident poets as Vasyl Stus (1938–85) and Ihor Kalynets' (b. 1939). Their contribution was fully acknowledged only after 1991.

Beginning with the 1980s, a new generation of poets emerged. With the advent of Mikhail Gorbachev's perestroika, this generation no longer faced the prospects of harsh censorship. They focused on aesthetic freedom and on constructing a new cultural identity. The poetry of Ihor Rymaruk (1958–2008) and Vasyl Herasym'iuk (b. 1956) offers a dense, metaphoric language, biblical and regional motifs, and contemplates creativity as such. Other poets of the same generation reacted differently to the Soviet legacy. The period immediately preceding independence in 1991 witnessed the formation of many poetic groupings in Lviv, Kyiv, Kharkiv, and other cities, all finding distinctive ways to resist the symptoms of Sovietization. The most prominent among them, the Bu-Ba-Bu group, founded in the mid-1980s by Yuri Andrukhovych (b. 1960), Viktor Neborak

(b. 1961), and Oleksandr Irvanets' (b. 1961), professed poetry as performance and employed postmodernist devices such as parody, pastiche, and self-reference. Mocking the seriousness of their predecessors and debunking Soviet and nationalistic taboos became Bu-Ba-Bu's favorite pastime.

Ukrainian poetry of the postindependence period is dynamic and stylistically diverse. There is a strong undercurrent of female poetic voices, from the fiercely feminist and intellectual oeuvre of Oksana Zabuzhko (b. 1960) to more gender-balanced approaches of the younger Mar'iana Savka (b. 1973) and Marianna Kiianovs'ka (b. 1973). While the performative and playful manner of the Bu-Ba-Bu poetics appealed to some younger poets, with Serhii Zhadan (b. 1974) as the most talented, others rejected the group's carnivalesque spirit in favor of a more intellectual, ironic, and even metaphysical approach. Among the latter, Kostiantyn Moskalets' (b. 1963) and esp. Vasyl Makhno (b. 1964) deserve recognition. The youngest generation of Ukrainian poets, entering the poetic scene in the 2000s, displays a wide range of attitudes, from an offhand colloquiality to existential reflection. Unlike the poets of the 1980s, this generation does not need to assert its artistic freedom: these young poets just live it.

■ **Anthologies**: *The Ukrainian Poets*, ed. and trans. C. H. Andrusyshen and W. Kirkconnell (1963); *Khrestomatiia davn'oi ukrains'koi literatury*, ed. O. I. Bilets'kyi (1967); *Koordynaty*, ed. B. Boychuk and B. T. Rubchak (1969); *Antolohiia ukrains'koi liryky*, ed. O. Zilyns'kyi (1978); *Ukrains'ka literatura XVIII st.*, ed. O. V. Myshanych; (1983); *Antolohiia ukrains'koi poezii*, ed. M. P. Bazhan et al. (1984); *Visimdesiatnyky*, ed. I. Rymaruk (1990); *Poza tradytsii*, ed. B. Boychuk et al. (1993); *From Three Worlds: New Ukrainian Writing*, ed. E. Hogan et al. (1996); *A Hundred Years of Youth: A Bilingual Anthology of Twentieth-Century Ukrainian Poetry*, ed. O. Luchuk and M. M. Naydan (2000); *Pivstolittia napivtyshi*, ed. M. G. Rewakowicz (2005); *Dvi tonny naikrashchoi molodoi poezii*, ed. B.-O. Horobchuk and O. Romanenko (2007); *Dyvoovyd*, ed. I. Luchuk (2007); *In a Different Light: A Bilingual Anthology of Ukrainian Literature*, ed. O. Luchuk (2008); *Ukrains'ki literaturni shkoly ta hrupy 60–90 rr. XX st.*, ed. V. Gabor (2009).

■ **Criticism and History**: G. Luckyj, *Literary Politics in the Soviet Ukraine 1917–1933* (1956); *Istoriia ukrains'koi literatury*, ed. IE. P. Kyryliuk et al. (1967–71); D. Čyževs'kyj, *A History of Ukrainian Literature* (1975); G. Grabowicz, *Toward a History of Ukrainian Literature* (1981); G. Grabowicz, *The Poet as Mythmaker* (1982); O. S. Ilnytzkyj, *Ukrainian Futurism* (1997).

G. G. Grabowicz; M. G. Rewakowicz

UNITED STATES, POETRY OF THE

I. English

A. *Beginnings to 1900*. A hist. of poetry in the U.S. "from the beginning" must begin by acknowledging that "the beginning" has always been a matter of debate. "Where to begin?" is the critical question, and the common answer has been to begin again in the present. The earliest anthol. to use *American poetry* as an organizing concept was Elihu Hubbard Smith's (1771–98) *American Poetry, Selected and Original* (1793), which heavily emphasized the poems of Smith's fellow Connecticut Wits (1770s–90s) while ignoring the poetry of the 17th c. Later canonmakers followed the same strategy by excising the 18th c. to endorse the 19th. Rufus Wilmot Griswold's (1815–57) anthols. of the 1840s, *The Poets and Poetry of America* (1842) and *Female Poets of America* (1848), centered on the work of New York poets affiliated with the Young America movement (1840s); and Edmund Clarence Stedman's (1833–1908) *Poets of America* (1885), an influential collection of essays, grounded Am. poetry in the work of the Fireside poets (1870s–80s). All these efforts were overturned in the 20th c., which reinvented two minor poets of the previous century, Walt Whitman (1819–92) and Emily Dickinson (1830–86), as the only legitimate claimants to the beginnings of a poetic trad. that could genuinely be called *American*. Thus, the poetic hist. of the U.S. has often been conditioned by the effort to find a usable beginning that leads to the present.

Perhaps the major problem is that Am. poetry seems always to have begun somewhere else. The Am. hemisphere, depicted as an Edenic paradise of noble savages and natural abundance or as a howling wilderness of pagan devilry, was a rich source of imagery and inspiration for a number of Eur. poets who wrote from a distance, such as Shakespeare, Luís de Camões, or Joost van den Vondel, as well as others who envisioned and settled North Am. colonies, including George Sandys (1577–1644), Walter Ralegh (1552–1618), and George Berkeley (1685–1753), whose "Verses on the

Prospect of Planting Arts and Learning in America" (written 1726, pub. 1752), prompted by a sojourn in Rhode Island, coined the line "Westward the Course of Empire takes its Way," which encapsulated a key motif for New World poetics.

Early poetry on America was generally published in Europe and tended to adopt cl. themes, meters, and styles. It also participated overtly in the imperial contests between Eur. powers. While elite authors took from New World materials to furnish poems for a Eur. readership, the process also worked in reverse: Port., Dutch, Sp., Fr., and Eng. settlers in New World plantations brought songs with them. These popular ballads, sea chanteys, work songs, and bawdy lyrics often adapted the Native Am. and Af. song trads. with which Eur. settlers came into contact. While primarily oral and improvisational, such songs were also based on established trads. of versification mediated by cheap print. New words could readily be fitted to old tunes, making it easy for songs to comment on current, local events in modes familiar to audiences that need not have been literate to enjoy them.

Like such popular lyrics, religious hymns and psalms also circulated widely, usually with the consent of colonial authorities. *The Bay Psalm Book* (1640, known in its day as *The New England Psalter*), a metrical trans. of the Psalms, is considered the first book of poems printed in colonial North America. The Puritan apostle John Eliot (ca. 1604–90) also published verse trans. of the Psalms in the Massachusett lang., to aid in converting the Native Am. peoples in the New England colonies.

Although these song and hymn trads. ranged across North America, the earliest printing press was licensed in Cambridge, in the Massachusetts Bay colony, in 1638, and printing penetrated most deeply in New England (no other press was licensed until 1686, in Philadelphia); thus, the Eng. Puritans have tended to dominate the hist. of 17th-c. colonial poetry. Anne Bradstreet (1612?–72) is perhaps the best-known Puritan poet; her volume *The Tenth Muse Lately Sprung Up in America* (1650) employed the conceits and elaborate similes of the metaphysical poets on religious, political, and domestic subjects. Other popular New England poets included Michael Wigglesworth (1631–1705), whose best-selling poem on the Last Judgment, *The Day of Doom* (1662), popularized a style of quatrain with internal rhymes on the first and third lines; and Benjamin Tompson (1642–1714), author of *New England's Crisis* (1676), a providential epic recounting King Philip's War. This sort of text was both poetry and also information about the conflict for highly interested audiences around the Atlantic. Such work indicates the multiple functions poetry served in early Am. culture.

It is important to note that, with the exception of the rhyming abecedarius *The New England Primer* (1690), possibly the best-selling book of the 18th c., books of poems were published in London (as were most books for the Am. market) and remained unavailable to all but the wealthiest colonial readers. Aside from psalters and primers, the most common type of poetry printed in North America was the elegy, which was typically written by one minister for another (or a person of wealth and standing), as illustrated by Urian Oakes's (1631–81) elaborately titled "An Elegie Upon that Reverend, Learned, Eminently Pious, and Singularly Accomplished Divine, my ever Honoured Brother, Mr. Thomas Shepard" (1677). While they circulated freely, usually as broadsides, such texts also extolled the ministry as the proper guardians of public discourse. Elegies were performed as part of Puritan mourning rituals and were reproduced in commonplace books, weavings, and tombstones, among other locations, underwriting a culture of mourning that would be satirized by Benjamin Franklin and Mark Twain.

Like the Puritan elegy, almost every early Am. poem printed in North America appeared in the cheapest possible formats: single-sheet broadsides, stitched pamphlets, almanacs, newspapers (after 1720 or so), and magazines (after 1760 or so); typical genres included ballads, satires, squibs, pasquinades, execution songs, tavern songs, and versified sermons, which were usually anonymous, set to a familiar tune (such as "Chevy Chace") and sold for a penny or two. "The Poor Unhappy Transported Felon's Sorrowful Account of His Fourteen Years Transportation at Virginia" (ca. 1670s), by the possibly apocryphal author James Revel (1659–80), is an example of a broadside narrative derived from a long trad. of scaffold verse. Its opening stanza indicates the mixed mediation characteristic of so much 17th-c. verse:

> My loving countrymen pray lend an ear,
> To this relation that I bring you here,
> My present sufferings at large I will unfold,
> Altho' its strange, 'tis true as e'er was told.

We can imagine a ballad monger singing these lines in a London street, gathering an audience that would indeed lend an ear to the story and possibly buy a sheet to take home. This poem about the hardships of Virginia was published in London for an Eng. audience; it is hard to overstate the degree to which colonial poetry was oriented toward London, the cosmopolitan metropole of the anglophone world. Only from the retrospective vantage point of U.S. nationalism does such an orientation seem a problem; early Americans located themselves within the world system of Eur. colonialism. Colonial literary rivalries, such as that between the Tory wits Joseph Green (1706–80) and Mather Byles (1707–88), were triangulated through Brit. periodicals like the *London Magazine*, where Green placed two poems in 1733. Metropolitan jours. carried greater weight in Boston than the local *New-England Weekly Journal*, where Byles's popular "Proteus Echo" series had appeared, and colonial authors often wrote with a trans-Atlantic audience in mind.

Yet despite the prestige that certain publications offered, the vast majority of early Am. poets did not publish in print but circulated their works in ms., often to a small coterie of friends, but sometimes to a much more extended audience. The circulation of ms. poems through competing coffeehouses fueled most of the conflict between Byles and Green. The now-famous works of the Massachusetts minister Edward Taylor (1642–1729), *Preparatory Meditations* and *Gods Determinations* (1680s–1720s), known only to a few contemporaries, were not published until 1939. Unlike the worldly wit of Byles and Green, which was meant to dazzle and win prestige, Taylor used complex syntax and elaborate metaphysical conceits to make his poems a form of spiritual exercise, as in a meditation on 1 Cor. 3.22:

> Thy Grace, Dear Lord's my golden Wrack,
> I finde
> Screwing my Phancy into ragged Rhimes,
> Tuning thy Praises in my feeble minde
> Untill I come to strike them on my
> Chimes.

While Taylor intended his poems for private devotional use, many colonial poets chose ms. circulation as the polite alternative to print. Literary circles like the Annapolis-based Tuesday Club (1745–56) sprang up across the colonies in emulation of London counterparts. Their purpose was to cultivate members' sentiments and sensibilities through belles lettres and polite conversation. Epigrams, acrostics, riddles, anagrams, and dialogues were some of the favored poetic vehicles for the display of wit and learning among members.

"Publishing" poems through the circulation of mss. was esp. common for early Am. women poets, whose access to print was highly limited. Even an elite woman like Annis Boudinot Stockton (1736–1801), who wrote more than 100 poems, published only about 20, all anonymously. Instead of print publication, most women poets participated in coteries. One prominent circle of elite Quaker women living in the Delaware Valley included poets Milcah Martha Moore (1740–1829), Hannah Griffitts (1727–1817), Susanna Wright (1697–1784), and Elizabeth Graeme Fergusson (1737–1801). They gathered to read and discuss poems, commented on them in letters and diaries, and wrote poems in response to each other on a wide variety of topics. Another circle living around Boston promoted the ms. poetry of Phillis Wheatley (1753–84) before the publication in London of her volume *Poems on Various Subjects, Religious and Moral* (1773). Wheatley, known as the "the sable prodigy" and "the Ethiopian Poetess," had been kidnapped as a child from the Gambian coast and, as a slave, became a literary celebrity in prerevolutionary Boston. These coterie poems tended to adopt neoclassical styles (authors often signed in pastoral pseuds. like "Aminta") and discussed matters of both domestic and political interest. Poetry was a key vehicle for debating gender roles and the place of women in colonial society (a discussion known as the *battle of the sexes*), but such debates mostly occurred within the constraints of politeness—in ms., in parlors, and among fellow elites—rather than in the emerging realm of printed discourse.

That printed discourse was often hurlyburly. The dismantling of Stuart absolutism that followed the Glorious Revolution in England (1688), esp. the end of prepublication state censorship in 1695, created the conditions for a market-oriented print world. The Whig ascendancy after the Hanoverian succession (1714) forced a generation of Tory authors, thrown out of power and with no hope of state patronage, to write for money. Concentrated in an impoverished district surrounding London's Grub Street, these "hacks," as they became known, developed a combative poetic idiom that sought to expose the corruptions of the new social and economic order through scurrilous, personalized attacks on figures of authority. The Grub Street ethic translated easily to 18th-c. colonial entrepôts such as Boston, Philadelphia, and New York City, where perennial conflicts among colonial governors (appointed by the Crown), assemblies (elected by the local population), and various local factions ensured a steady market for political controversy. In these "paper wars," stinging, catchy ballads (passed in song, ms., and print) proved esp. useful. In Philadelphia, Henry Brooke (1678–1736), an Oxford-educated scion, led a riotous campaign against the Quaker authorities, particularly their crackdown on public drinking. Brooke's mastery of impromptu compositions, esp. epigrams, combined the Georgian ideal of belletristic wit with tavern culture's masculine ethos and led to instantly popular satirical portraits of officials such as William Penn. The reign of Jonathan Belcher (1730–41) in Massachusetts provoked another such war, in which anonymous pasquinades against the governor were nailed to doors, copied into commonplace books, and passed around in taverns. In New York, Cadwallader Colden (1688–1776), James Alexander (1691–1756), and Lewis Morris Sr. (1671–1746) used an extensive arsenal of poems to further the political aims of their Country Party in endless machinations against the Merchant Party of Governor William Cosby. Morris's verse fable "The Mock Monarchy; or, the Kingdom of the Apes" (1730) circulated in ms. throughout the colony and in England. Morris also used the press to attack his political enemies, who retaliated by publicly burning two Country Party ballads denouncing Cosby. Meeting fire with fire, Cosby hired Archibald Home (1705–44) to circulate anti-Morris songs and poems. So impressed was Morris by his rival's literary flair that he recruited Home to his side.

Home later moved to New Jersey, where he presided over a polite literary circle in Trenton. His example shows how the rowdy culture of the tavern, the coffeehouse, and the press developed in tandem with the polite realm of the coterie, the parlor, and the tea table. Benjamin Franklin (1706–90) memorably described the masculine culture of the printing houses in Boston, Philadelphia, and London, where hard words, hard work, and hard drinking went together. However, Franklin's rise was driven by his facility with both the vituperative discourse of print and the polite conversation of civility. As a boy, he wrote several successful broadside poems, which he described as "wretched Stuff, in the Grubstreet Ballad Style," as well as an Aesopian fable against Governor Jonathan Belcher, "The Rats and the Cheese" (1730), and throughout his career he capitalized on his mastery of print controversy. But access to the library of his patron Matthew Adams (d. 1753) familiarized Franklin early with key works in the discourse of civility (famously, *The Spectator*), and this familiarity with the rhet. of politeness helped him flourish in the sociable world of 18th-c. mercantilism. Some of Franklin's closest associates were fellow belletrists, such as the poets Aquila Rose (1695–1723) and Joseph Breintnall (1695–1746), an inaugural member of the Junto, the literary circle Franklin founded in 1727.

Breintnall's elegy "To the Memory of Aquila Rose, Deceas'd" (1740) addressed a trans-Atlantic circle of friends in the terms of poetic sociability:

> Ye *Rose's* Friends, that in *Britannia* dwell
> Who knew his Worth, and best the Loss
>   can tell:
> As I transmit such mournful News to you,
> Do you the tuneful sad Account pursue.
> And ye bright Youths, that meet at *Bendall's*
>   Board,
> An Elegy his hov'ring Shade afford:
> Had one of you deceas'd, and he surviv'd,
> His Memory by him had been reliv'd.

The transmission of poetry grounded communities locally (in Boston, Philadelphia, or London) and across long distances, and the spaces opened by death could be filled, at least in part, by the circulation of "tuneful sad Accounts" or elegies, which secured the bonds of fellowship.

While Britain's victory in the Seven Years' War (1756–63) secured Eng. hegemony in North America, it also drove the Crown to seek ever greater control over the economy and governance of the colonies. The resulting imperial crisis was mediated through institutions of oratory (club, tavern, pulpit) and print (broadsides, pamphlets, newspapers), and poetry worked through all the media of debate. Popular songs such as "Yankee Doodle" ostentatiously appropriated well-known Brit. tunes for patriot purposes. Poets such as Wheatley petitioned key figures such as the Earl of Dartmouth and George Washington in verse. A leading circle of revolutionary-era poets, the Connecticut Wits, incl. Joel Barlow (1754–1812), Timothy Dwight (1752–1817), John Trumbull (1750–1831), and David Humphreys (1752–1818), made recourse to poetry in support of the colonies. Trumbull's mock epic *M'Fingal* (1775, 1782), e.g., was a ubiquitous piece of revolutionary rhet. Philip Freneau (1752–1832), Ann Eliza Bleecker (1752–83), Lemuel Haynes (1753–1833), and Mercy Otis Warren (1728–1814) all produced patriotic verse supporting Am. independence. Sung in homes, taverns, and battlefields; recited during sermons and orations; or circulated in mss., broadsides, and newspapers, this poetry underwrote the discourse of liberty that authorized revolution.

After the revolution, however, poetry was circuited into the partisanship of the Federalist era. Humphreys, Barlow, Trumbull, and Lemuel Hopkins (1750–1801) collaborated on *The Anarchiad* (1786–87), a mock epic satirizing social disorder in the wake of Shays's Rebellion; Dwight wrote one epic attacking deism (*The Triumph of Infidelity*, 1788) and another supporting Federalist orthodoxy (*Greenfield Hill*, 1794). Barlow switched sides to Paineite democracy (*The Conspiracy of Kings*, 1792), and Jeffersonian republicanism (*The Columbiad*, 1808). These epics and mock epics featured neoclassical balance, periphrasis, and an immensely complex set of references that can be difficult for mod. readers to parse without extensive footnotes. But their rhet. of satirical declension, ideological unmasking, and civic renewal was well known to contemporaries through the popularity of Augustan authors such as Alexander Pope, Jonathan Swift, and James Thomson.

The Boston wit Robert Treat Paine Jr. (1773–1811) expressed Federalist ambitions for the U.S. amid the welter of Eur. revolutions and Barbary Coast warfare in a 1798 song, "Adams and Liberty":

> In a clime, whose rich vales feed the marts
> of the world,
> Whose shores are unshaken by Europe's
> commotion,
> The trident of Commerce should never be
> hurled,
> To incense the legitimate powers of the
> ocean.
> But should pirates invade,
> Though in thunder arrayed,
> Let your cannon declare the free charter of
> trade.

(Incidentally, Paine's anthem of Federalist pieties borrowed the tune of "To Anacreon in Heaven," a ribald drinking song that Francis Scott Key's (1779–1843) "The Defense of Fort McHenry"—later "The Star-Spangled Banner"—also adopted). In reality, the U.S. population in 1798 was young, rural, agrarian, and poor. Literacy rates were increasing, but the rise was uneven, with the Northeast outpacing the South and the trans-Appalachian West. Limited roads and bridges made transportation and communication between regions difficult. Consequently, there was no national market for books, periodicals, or newspapers; and chronically undercapitalized printers preferred steady sellers to risky new imaginative works. Coastal ports and, later, river and canal boomtowns were distinct literary capitals with a flourishing business reprinting popular Eng. authors. The existence of parallel domestic markets and the absence of an international copyright meant that Am. readers were more likely than Eng. to read books such as William Wordsworth and S. T. Coleridge's *Lyrical Ballads* (1798) or Walter Scott's *The Lay of the Last Minstrel* (1805). The literary nationalist James Kirke Paulding (1778–1860) expressed his frustrations about the Am. scene in an 1818 epic, *The Backwoodsman*:

> Neglected Muse! of this our western clime,
> How long in servile, imitative rhyme,
> Wilt thou thy stifled energies impart,
> And miss the path that leads to every
> heart? . . .
> Thrice happy he who first shall strike the
> lyre,
> With homebred feeling, and with home-
> bred fire.

Paulding's call for "homebred" materials would be echoed by the Young America movement of the 1840s and the International Copyright League of the 1890s. Yet while an Am. poetry did not gain a stable institutional form until after the Civil War, Am. citizens, *pace* Paulding, were writing, reading, singing, circulating, and performing all kinds of poems. The Marylander Francis Scott Key published "The Defense of Fort McHenry" (the first stanza of which became the national anthem in 1916) in a Baltimore newspaper in 1814; William Cullen Bryant (1794–1878), who had written an anti-Jeffersonian satire, "The Embargo," as a 13-year-old, published the instant classic "Thanatopsis"

(1817) in *The North American Review*, a Boston jour. founded in 1815 to foster Am. letters; and "A Visit from St. Nicholas," by Clement Moore (1779–1863), was published anonymously in a Troy, New York, newspaper in 1822. All these poems were wildly popular across the entire country.

However, the most influential poet of early 19th-c. America was Lydia Huntley Sigourney (1791–1865). Sigourney commanded national acclaim and attention in poems on all possible topics, from child elegies ("dead-baby poems") and domestic instruction to Indian removal and slavery. Following the model of the Eng. poet Felicia Hemans, Sigourney deployed the persona of the Poetess, a gendered form of literary authority that spoke in nationalist, even imperialist cadences through the voice of sentimental domesticity. Her best work, like "To a Shred of Linen" (1838), demonstrated the centrality of women's labor to the hist. of the nation. Many, although not all, women poets gained access to public representation through the privatized figure of the Poetess: these included Elizabeth Oakes Smith (1806–93), Sarah Helen Whitman (1803–78), Maria Brooks (Maria del Occidente, 1794–1845), and the Ojibwe poet Jane Johnston Schoolcraft (Bamewawagezhikaquay, 1800–42).

As a figure for popular verse, the Poetess also influenced mid-century male authors. Two of the most prominent, E. A. Poe (1809–49) and H. W. Longfellow (1807–82), followed dramatically opposed trajectories in the literary world. By the 1830s, improved material conditions in the U.S. (a larger reading public, greater economic capitalization, and better internal communication), had made a literary career possible; but economic instability (exemplified by the Panic of 1837) made it a tenuous occupation, at best. Hundreds of newspapers and periodicals were founded in the 1830s, but the average one lasted less than a year before closing. Poe tried unsuccessfully to make his way in this literary climate, editing magazines in Richmond, Baltimore, Philadelphia, and New York, but always seeming to fail on the brink of success. His work was very popular—"The Raven" (1845) was one of the most reprinted and parodied poems in Am. lit.—but it could not earn him a living, and he died in poverty.

Poe's Gothic work cannily adopted many of the Eur. themes and motifs that abounded in antebellum magazine culture. "Lenore" (1843), "Ulalume" (1847), and "Annabel Lee" (1849) evoke a dreamy state of unreality, like the Am. Republic of Letters Poe imagined but could not realize. Poe was eccentric to the circles of literary authority that existed in his lifetime, and he reserved particular wrath for the literary culture of Boston ("Frogpondia" to him): the Transcendentalist circle associated with R. W. Emerson (1803–82); and the group of Harvard-based poets that included O. W. Holmes (1809–94), J. R. Lowell (1819–91), and, esp., Longfellow.

Longfellow was the most successful poet of the mid-19th c. In long poems such as *Evangeline* (1847), "Hiawatha" (1855), and *Tales of a Wayside Inn* (1863), he fused North Am. themes such as Native Am. lore and the Revolution with cl. and Eur. meters and the narrative structures of poems like the *Canterbury Tales* and the *Divine Comedy* (which Longfellow, a scholar of the Romance langs., translated in the 1860s). *Hiawatha* combined Ojibwe stories (based on the ethnography of H. R. Schoolcraft) with the trochaic tetrameter of the Finnish epic the *Kalevala*, while *Evangeline* was one of the most successful (and controversial) experiments with Eng. hexameters:

> This is the forest primeval. The murmuring
> pines and the hemlocks,
> Bearded with moss, and in garments green,
> indistinct in the twilight,
> Stand like Druids of eld, with voices sad
> and prophetic,
> Stand like harpers hoar, with beards that
> rest on their bosoms.

The syncretism of this work (Poe called it "plagiarism") aspired to an ideal of comparative lit. that Longfellow, the Smith Professor of Modern Languages at Harvard, sought to forge in the image of J. W. Goethe's *Weltliteratur*. From his position at Harvard and by way of his close alliances with Boston's publishers, Longfellow enjoyed unprecedented cultural prestige and business success (he became the first author to own the stereotype plates of his work, e.g.). "Hiawatha" was a runaway best seller in 1855, the same year a relatively obscure newspaperman in New York City issued *Leaves of Grass*.

Although its eccentricity to the orbit of antebellum letters was greatly exaggerated in the 20th c., *Leaves of Grass* was an unusual book (mostly because it lacked the organizing structures that mid-c. readers had come to expect: a table of contents, titles for poems, line numbers, and, esp., a named poet). In lieu of a name (which appeared unexpectedly within the poems), the frontispiece showed the image of a typical workingman, with open collar and hand on hip, eyes staring boldly into the reader's. This sort of assertive yet anonymous intimacy also marked the poems. The long lines, mostly lacking a recognizable meter or rhyme pattern, conformed to the space of the page, thus incorporating print materiality into the poems' structure, while the loosely organized strophes encouraged readers to create their own ways of reading the work. "I celebrate myself, / And what I assume you shall assume," it began, and, throughout the long poem later known as "Song of Myself," Walt Whitman pursued a leveling strategy for the reading of poetry: "Have you practiced so long to learn to read? / Have you felt so proud to get at the meaning of poems? / Stop this day and night with me and you shall possess the origin of all poems, / You shall possess the good of the earth and sun." Interpretation was very much subordinated to intimacy in Whitman's poetics: reading, for him, should be like sex.

This project of intimacy thrust *Leaves of Grass* into the fraught and violent politics of the 1850s: not only did Whitman (who 13 years earlier had written a temperance novel) seek to check the growing stigmatization of the body in reform discourses like the temperance movement ("Welcome is every organ and attribute of me, and of any man hearty and clean, / Not an inch nor a particle of an inch is vile"), he sought to establish a poetic basis for collective experience, which the political system of the era had resoundingly failed to provide. Thus, the poems were filled with the daily experiences of ordinary people in lengthy catalogs (the most aesthetically controversial aspects of the poems, then and now). Whitman piled incident atop humdrum incident in an effort to make working life poetic, to extend the circle of democratic belonging further and further outward. We could all find ourselves in these poems, he suggested, and no one would assume priority over anyone else.

Whitman's faith in Am. democracy was shaken by the Civil War and the assassination of Abraham Lincoln (who, incidentally, also wrote poetry). But by way of his elegies to Lincoln, "When Lilacs Last in the Dooryard Bloom'd" (1865) and "O Captain! My Captain!" (1865), his most popular poem, he gradually reached wide appreciation in the 1880s, with devoted readers (known as *Whitmaniacs*) making pilgrimages to his small home in Camden, New Jersey.

Between 1882 and 1894, all the major poets of the mid-19th c. died. The culture felt a palpable sense of loss. Where would poetry go? In the last decade of the century, the first eds. of Emily Dickinson's poems produced an unexpected publishing sensation. Dickinson had died in 1886, but for almost 30 years before her death she had been known to her familiar correspondents as a poet (though no one knew how extensive her collection of ms. poetry had grown until after her death). Some of those correspondents were important in the public sphere, so 11 of Dickinson's poems appeared in print during her lifetime by their hands. But in the elaborately ed. volume *Poems* (1890), her editor's description of Dickinson's verse as "something produced absolutely without the thought of publication, and solely by expression of the writer's own mind" became a model of lyric expression protected from what one review called "the mass of popular print." Somewhat ironically, the poet whose writing life participated intimately and actively in so many of the reading and writing practices we have traced in Am. poetry (hymnal meter, the figure of the Poetess, familiar circulation followed by publication in print) became representative of a poetry held apart from the spirit of its age.

This myth about Dickinson has been so persistent that she and Whitman are still often mischaracterized as the first mod. Am. lyric poets, but it is important to note that, at the end of the 19th c., Dickinson and Whitman were not the only examples of poets produced in expensive print eds. and made to look like exceptions to earlier rules. In 1896, Paul Laurence Dunbar's (1872–1906) *Lyrics of Lowly Life* was introduced as if it were an innocent version of black culture removed from the realities of the last decade of the 19th c. If Dickinson became a lyric representative by being characterized as isolated from the public in which her lyrics would circulate, Dunbar became another representative made to personify a culture imagined as less mod. than the rest of America. The framing of Dickinson and Dunbar as throwbacks, as poets too pure for the modernity that welcomed them, speaks to the ways that the 20th c. would begin to think of poems as expressions of individual alienation and as dramatic versions of fictional speakers. Before 1900, poetry in America was much more often thought of as the expression of a group and, after the late 18th c., as the expression of a nation. The era after 1900 would seek to elevate poetry through an ever-increasing complexity of lyric expression, thus closing a period when all kinds of verse circulated as the most popular genres of literary production in the U.S.

B. *Modernist Poetry, 1900–1945*. The "word of the modern, the word En-Masse" that Whitman celebrates describes the dynamic modernity of an emerging mercantile America—a dynamism that many modernists deplored. Dickinson's formal innovations were effaced by early eds. who limited her canon to more conventional poems on love and nature. The two most important poets of the late 19th c. had to wait for their modernism to be born.

Poetry in the United States entered the 20th c. as a conservative retrenchment. Edwin Arlington Robinson (1869–1935), Edgar Lee Masters (1868–1950), Robert Frost (1874–1963), and John Crowe Ransom (1888–1974) form a transitional group that confronted the period's secularization and materialism by vaunting a rural, regional ethos. Building on the model of Robert Browning, several of these poets developed dramatic monologues and poetic dialogues, often in the voices of rural speakers who epitomized the virtues of small-town values against cosmopolitan malaise.

Masters's *Spoon River Anthology* (1915) offers an example of these tendencies, chronicling the diverse population of his western Illinois small-town heritage. His portraits earned him a wide reputation, even though he often satirized the limits and provincialism of his readers. Perhaps speaking for the limits of poets of his generation, Petit, the poet, ruefully regrets his blindness to the heroic potential of his rural life composing "Triolets, villanelles, rondels, rondeaus, / Seeds in a dry pod, tick, tick, tick . . . what little iambics, / While Homer and Whitman roared in the pines?"

Robinson did write villanelles and rondeaux, chronicling the varied life of rural America based on his native town, Gardiner, Maine. Robinson's preference for complex stanzaic forms, regular rhyme schemes, and conventional meters contrasts with the psychological realism and dramatic voice of his characters. His persistent exploration of the unfulfilled life anticipates T. S. Eliot.

Frost offers the closest bridge between the Emersonian trad. of New England and his modernist peers. Like Masters and Robinson, Frost chronicled rural life through dramatic monologues. Often regarded as a New England moralist, Frost is a considerably more complex figure whose poems present irreconcilable ethical choices for people often ill equipped to confront the implications of their acts. "Mending Wall" (1914) is usually seen as a warning against the building of barriers ("Something there is that doesn't love a wall, / That sends the frozen-ground-swell under it"), yet as its farmer-philosopher speaker demonstrates, the act of seasonal rebuilding of a rustic wall brings neighbors together to cement a taciturn yet resilient community. Frost's repudiation of free verse made him a reluctant modernist, yet his mastery of blank verse offered "a momentary stay against confusion."

Frost's preference for rural life looks back to Wordsworth, and it was perhaps this retrospective quality to much U.S. poetry that prompted the Brit. poet and critic George Barker to observe in his 1948 essay "Fat Lady at the Circus" that "American poetry is a very easy subject to discuss for the simple reason that it does not exist." W. C. Williams (1883–1963) saw this as Am. poetry's great advantage—the possibility of a new, perhaps violent beginning. In *Paterson* (1946–58), Williams posed the question that animated the work of many of his generation:

> How to begin to find a shape—to begin to
>   begin again,
> turning the inside out: . . .

For Williams, son of a Brit. father and a Puerto Rican mother, the question was how "American" was Am. poetry when written by ex-slaves, Rus. Jewish immigrants, Native Americans, and the sons and daughters of Mexican Californios?

Poets responded to the claim that the U.S. lacked a unitary culture in a variety of ways. Some, such as T. S. Eliot (1888–1965), H.D. (1886–1961), Gertrude Stein (1874–1946), and Ezra Pound (1885–1972), expatriated to Europe in order to "make it new" amid older, more established cultural trads. Others, including Frost, Hart Crane (1899–1932), Wallace Stevens (1879–1948), Marianne Moore (1887–1972), and Williams hoped to "find a shape" on native soil and in the Am. idiom. Af. Am. poets who migrated to Harlem following World War I negotiated what it meant to be both black and a bard in Jim Crow America. A number of these writers—Langston Hughes (1902–67), Richard

Wright (1908–60), Claude McKay (1890–1948)—also traveled abroad, living for periods of time in Europe and the Soviet Union.

Of the expatriate group, Pound offered the most sustained diagnosis of what was wrong with contemp. verse. He felt poetry needed to rid itself of sentimentality, platitudes, and "emotional slither" by means outlined in the March 1913 issue of *Poetry*:

1. Direct treatment of the "thing" whether subjective or objective.
2. To use absolutely no word that does not contribute to the presentation.
3. As regarding rhythm: to compose in the sequence of the musical phrase, not in sequence of a metronome.

These axioms, the basis of imagism, provided an alternative to Victorian rhet. and romantic excess by their advocacy of clear, concrete images. Pound's third axiom proposed a more flexible metric tied to emotive and acoustic properties in each line. In defining the image, Pound fused a symbolist poetics of the autonomous aesthetic object with a psychologist's model of integrated consciousness, "an intellectual and emotional complex in an instant of time." His own imagist experiments reflected the influence of Chinese and Japanese precedents. "In a Station of the Metro" (1913) reflects the influence of Japanese haiku:

The apparition of these faces in the crowd,
Petals on a wet, black, bough.

Imagism was only one component in Pound's early attempt to master all forms and idioms of poetry. His early "masks of the self" constituted a poetic apprenticeship on his way to writing an epic poem. The most important transitional poem, in this respect, is *Hugh Selwyn Mauberley* (1920), which provided Pound with a method of collating different voices to mark a historical epoch, a method already being tested in the early sections of *The Cantos*, upon which he worked for the rest of his life.

The Cantos (1925–72) attempted to tell the "tale of the tribe," to create a cultural hieroglyph of values, both Eastern and Western, that would awaken society from its collective sleep. Mythological references, trans. from cl. sources and Romance langs., quotations from historical chronicles, catalogs of historical figures, personal conversations, and moments of great lyrical beauty create a dense, often incomprehensible cultural collage. Rather than link these fragmentary materials via editorial or rhetorical commentary, Pound left them as "luminous details" to constellate a larger cultural edifice. Unfortunately, that edifice increasingly took the form of a totalitarian ethos. Pound's support for Mussolini and the Axis powers during World War II led to his incarceration near Pisa and then in a Washington, D.C., mental hospital for 13 years after the liberation. While he was incarcerated after the war, he published in 1948 *The Pisan Cantos* (Cantos 74–84), which, amid controversy, won the Bollingen Prize sponsored by the Library of Congress. Pound continued to work on *The Cantos* until his death, publishing *Rock Drill* (Cantos 85–95) in 1955 and *Thrones* (Cantos 96–109) in 1959. In the poem's last segments, *Drafts and Fragments* (1969), Pound seemed to feel that his poem would itself resemble one of the ruins depicted in his poem: "Tho' my errors and wrecks lie about me. / And I am not a demigod, / I cannot make it cohere."

In the January 1913 "Imagist" number of *Poetry*, Pound presented as his exemplary case the work of Hilda Doolittle (who took the pen name H.D.), whose early poetry (*Sea Garden* [1916], *Heliodora* [1924]) provided a model of spareness that fused the economy and clarity of the *Greek Anthology* with streamlined modernity, as in her "Oread" (1914):

Whirl up, sea–
whirl your pointed pines,
splash your great pines
on our rocks,
hurl your green over us,
cover us with your pools of fir.

H.D.'s early poetry drew from the cl. lyric and drama (she translated Euripides' *Ion*). Her first books of poetry refined a short, epigrammatic lyric, often spoken from the standpoint of a nymph or nature god. The poems in *Sea Garden* contested the usual romantic association of women with flowers by creating poems about violent natural forces, gods of the harvest, and tough, resilient plants that survive against the elements. In her later, longer poems, she expanded her critique of patriarchal authority by rewriting masculine stories—stories of war and violence often legitimated by reference to deceptive female figures such as Helen of Troy or Eve or Pandora. In place of masculinist stories of deceptive or dangerous women, H.D. posited priestesses and worshippers of Isis. Much of her work was indebted to readings in hermetic trads., Neoplatonic philosophy, and pre-Christian myth. *Helen in Egypt* (1961) has been seen as a pointed riposte to many of her male colleagues who see the Trojan War from the standpoint of its putative cause.

T. S. Eliot also benefited from Pound's support and tutelage, most famously through the latter's editing of *The Waste Land* (1922), which turned a pastiche of Popean satire, Browningesque monologues, and Pre-Raphaelite imitations into one of the most important poems of the era. Born in St. Louis, Missouri, Eliot completed most of his Ph.D. in philosophy at Harvard, then moved to London, where he lived for the rest of his life. His early poems, collected in *Prufrock and Other Observations* (1917), were influenced by the Fr. symbolists as well as Browning's dramatic monologues. "The Love Song of J. Alfred Prufrock" (1915) summarizes a mood of claustrophobia and solipsism that typified his early verse, and other poems—"Preludes" (1910–11), "Portrait of a Lady" (1917), and "Gerontion" (1920)—provided psychological portraits of the era.

Eliot's "impersonal theory of art," as he developed it in the essays "Tradition and the Individual Talent" (1919), "Hamlet and His Problems" (1919), and "The Metaphysical Poets" (1921), constitutes one of the most important components of modernist poetics, providing much of the theoretical armature for the New Criticism of the 1940s and 1950s. At the core of his poetics is an abiding desire to recover what he calls "the historical sense," which can be achieved only if the poet transcends his or her particular psychological state and creates a "general emotion" to which all readers throughout time could respond. Eliot's advocacy of impersonality was by no means strictly literary; it bespoke his own psychological condition, an instability that led to several stays at sanitaria and a disastrous early marriage.

Eliot's most important work, *The Waste Land*, chronicles in five sections the mod. era's malaise and spiritual vacuity through a series of vivid images of sterility:

> April is the cruellest month, breeding
> Lilacs out of the dead land, mixing
> Memory and desire, stirring
> Dull roots with spring rain.

The poem represents a series of disembodied voices that narrate the fall of empires, the despoliation of nature, and the debasement of sexuality and reproduction. Underlying these instances of contemp. violation lie subterranean references to Arthurian legend, pre-Christian vegetation myth, and Eastern religion. Precedent for this layering of cultural materials, past and present, had been provided by the "mythic method" that Eliot saw in James Joyce's novel *Ulysses* (1922). Although Eliot provided no single narrator for his poem, he adapted the cl. figure of the blind Theban prophet Tiresias into a "spectator" to the events of the poem.

Eliot found doctrinal solution to this dehumanized landscape by converting to Anglo-Catholicism in 1927, following which the poems became increasingly concerned with theological questions of faith, incarnation, and belief. *Ash Wednesday* (1930), the inaugural poem of this period, coincided with his new religion and Brit. citizenship. Later poems such as *The Four Quartets* (1936–42) and his plays were attempts to give vertical authority to temporal progress, seeking, as he said, "the still point of the turning world" and a kind of incarnation of the word in silence. This synthesis of religious incarnation with aesthetic perfection is the hallmark of Eliot's contribution to many poets of the 1940s seeking an organic fusion of local particulars and universals in a secular age.

Eliot's impact on subsequent poets was substantial, but not everyone appreciated his example. Williams spent much of his career in a one-way debate with the poet of *The Waste Land*, feeling that, by adopting Eurocentric values and conservative political and religious views, Eliot had turned his back on the possibility of a vibrant U.S. trad. *The Waste Land*, Williams wrote in his *Autobiography* (1951), "set me back twenty years." Eliot's cultural elitism provided Williams with a much-needed foil for his own home-grown avant-garde response. Instead of living the bohemian life in Europe, Williams went to medical school and served as a general practitioner for the rest of his life in Rutherford, New Jersey. He maintained contact with Am. abstract painters such as Marsden Hartley, Charles Sheeler, and Charles Demuth and supported vanguard publications such as *Broom* and *Others* that forged alliances between new poetry and Eur. movements such as Dada and surrealism.

Williams's early poetry in *Al Que Quiere!* (1917), *Sour Grapes* (1921), and *Spring and All* (1923) celebrates the quotidian and the ordinary:

so much depends
upon

a red wheel
barrow

glazed with rain
water

beside the white
chickens

This focus on the unadorned reality of things—what he and others later called *objectivism*—stressed not only the value of the ordinary object but the power of the imagination to bring the object into view. The wheelbarrow upon which "so much depends" is framed in a specific landscape, "glazed with rain / water // beside the white / chickens," and the alternating three- and one-word lines reinforce the material creation of that landscape in words.

Williams's frontal attack on trad., manners, and received opinion are characteristic of his work, culminating in his epic poem *Paterson*. Unlike Pound's *Cantos* with its sources in Eur. and Chinese hist., *Paterson* is based on the author's New Jersey hometown as a metonymy for the possibility of renewal. Like William Blake's archetypal Albion, Paterson is a sleeping giant, waiting to be reborn, while Dr. Paterson, the local poet-doctor tries to piece him together. In this sense, Williams continued Whitman's hope for an epic grounded in his native country and Am. speech. Williams identified his doctor-hero with the city itself, its hist. merging with the poet's own hist. In book 2, he begins to deploy a new kind of lineation, a triadic, stepped stanza that became the model for much of his later verse. In *The Desert Music* (1954) and *Pictures from Breughel* (1962), he experimented further with what he called this *variable foot*, which he linked with the possibilities of a specifically Am. idiom.

Stevens is Williams's counterpart in his desire to ground the poem in a reality that does not exist without the imagination. But whereas Williams stakes everything on the object (incl. the poem), Stevens is interested in the subjective apprehension of the object, the constant oscillation of imaginative self and bare reality. In the absence of sustaining myths and transcendental options, "Poetry / exceeding music must take the place / Of empty heaven and its hymns." This may sound like a latter-day version of symbolist escapism, yet Stevens felt that, through poetry, one would be returned to an earth one had forgotten how to see. Like Williams, Stevens had a professional career, working as an insurance lawyer in the firm of Hartford Accident and Indemnity Company. It was not until he was 44 that he published his first book, *Harmonium* (1923), in whose lyrics and satires Stevens wrote dazzling, often witty monologues on philosophical matters, often in vivid, color-drenched imagery. In subsequent work, he increasingly dramatized the mind in its speculative acts. Later long poems such as "Notes toward a Supreme Fiction" (1942), "Esthetique du Mal" (1945), "The Auroras of Autumn" (1947), and "An Ordinary Evening in New Haven" (1950) are less a departure from his early, symbolist-influenced lyrics than a logical evolution of problems advanced in them. "Notes toward a Supreme Fiction" speculates over 31 sections on how the "first idea" or "supreme fiction" is incarnated in the poem. But the "supreme fiction" must be discovered in the propositional logic of the poem itself; it cannot be imposed, as Stevens's Canon Aspirin supposes: "He imposes orders as he thinks of them, . . . But to impose is not / To discover." Stevens rejects imposition in favor of immanent discovery, marking a crucial link with earlier romantics and looking ahead to the immanent poetics of postmod. poets.

If poetry for Stevens offers a "supreme fiction" for a skeptical age, poetry for Moore offers "sincerity" in a mendacious age, "a magnetism, an ardor, a refusal to be false." Semantic approximations of *sincerity*, such as *authenticity*, *integrity*, and *genuine*, appear throughout her poetry, but one never encounters the kinds of moral imperatives that such terms imply. Sincerity in "Poetry" (1919) is hard won:

I, too, dislike it: there are things that are
important beyond all this fiddle.
Reading it, however, with a perfect contempt for it, one discovers in
it after all, a place for the genuine.

Moore's poetry seeks the genuine in a wild menagerie of flora and fauna—jerboas, steam rollers, pangolins, elephants, and wood weasels. An inveterate fan of the Brooklyn Dodgers and hired for a time to name a new Ford automobile (her suggestions were rejected in favor of the name *Edsel*), Moore was often portrayed as a kind of spinster crank; yet her tightly controlled syllabic lines, extensive allusions to literary and scientific texts, and wry, spare irony show her work to be a good deal more complicated. Moore's longtime affection for mythological beasts, sea creatures, armored animals, and curious insects is more than a naturalist's curiosity but an objective correlative for psychological and affective states. She often begins a poem with a minute description of an animal but then becomes distracted by other associations. In "The Pangolin" (1936), Moore seems to remark in her opening lines on the persistence of these figures and, perhaps, on herself: "Armor seems extra," yet like her tightly controlled syllabics, armor offers a shield that is both decorative and protective at the same time.

If Moore conducted her critique of lang. by quoting works of natural hist. and H.D. by revising cl. myth, Stein conducted hers by a radical deformation of lang. itself. There are no vegetation gods or cl. sources behind her works; nor, in fact, are there symbols attached to them. For Stein, words are returned to their grammatical, phonemic, and morphemic elements, as if to ground writing in the sheer materiality of words on the page. Her early psychological experiments while a student of William James at Radcliffe College convinced her that patterns of verbal repetition are a marker of character or "bottom nature" by which each person could be recognized. Although she applied such theories in her early prose works such as "Melanctha" (1905) or *The Making of Americans* (1911), she deployed repetition extensively in her poems as well, particularly those that she called "portraits" of objects and people. Her theory of repetition was also influenced strongly by Eur. modernist painters, particularly Henri Matisse, Pablo Picasso, and Georges Braque, whom she and her brother Leo befriended in Paris. In her most sustained comment on poetry, "Poetry and Grammar" (1934), she notes that the function of poetry is with "using with abusing, with losing with wanting, with denying with avoiding with adoring with replacing the noun." Nowhere is this practice of uncovering the noun more pronounced than in *Tender Buttons* (1914), a series of prose meditations on ordinary objects, rooms, and food, in discontinuous sentences often generated by paronomasia, verbal associations, and rhymes.

Stein, Moore, Stevens, and Williams all in some way attempted to return, as Stevens said, to the "basic slate" of a given locale, to deal with a godless world and to find immanent potential in ordinary things. For their younger contemporary Hart Crane, the Brooklyn Bridge, which serves as the centerpiece of his epic poem, stands as a complex symbol for Am. potentiality, space, and psychic resonance. The bridge "lends a myth to God" and gives form to a hist. from which we have become alien. Crane, like Eliot, imbibed the spirit of symbolism through Arthur Symons's *The Symbolist Movement in Literature* (1899) and, throughout his short career, attempted to follow what he called a "logic of metaphor" to map unconscious associations between things. The son of a candy manufacturer, Crane worked in his early years for his father's business while imbibing A. C. Swinburne, Ernest Dowson, and Oscar Wilde, the decadent lit. of the fin de siècle. His early poems were modeled on the Victorian poetry of Swinburne and Alfred, Lord Tennyson, and he never quite lost his taste for sensuous, alliterative textures in lang. His first book, *White Buildings* (1926), reflects his reading of other modernist peers via pastiches of Eliot, Pound, Stevens, Williams, and others.

Crane's magnum opus, *The Bridge* (1930), attempts an epic survey of United States hist., from Columbus's first landing through the Civil War, westward expansion, and Indian Wars to mod. technologies (rail, electricity, telephones, subways). *The Bridge* features multiple voices, from its rhapsodic opening ("O Sleepless as the river under thee . . .") to the jazz rhythms of "The River" ("Stick your patent name on a signboard / brother–all over–going west–young man / Tintex–Japalac–Certainteed Overalls ads . . .") to the ecstatic finale of "Atlantis." Throughout, Crane is conscious of prior epic trads.—from Homer to Dante to Whitman—and self-consciously places himself as their Am. heir. As much as *The Bridge* is a celebration of Am. hist. and accomplishment, it is often a poem of the *isolato*, in Crane's case, the homosexual poet whose solitude is flanked by the bustling crowds, tall buildings, and racing conveyances of the mod. metropole.

Crane's optimistic belief in the mythic potential of the Am. city was not shared by Af. Am. poets, who had yet to achieve anything like social or economic equality. The first real flowering of an Af. Am. intellectual and artistic renaissance could be seen in the Harlem Ren. of the 1920s. Alain Locke (1885–1954) provided the seminal call to arms through his anthol. of writings by black intellectuals *The New Negro* (1925), whose introduction observed that the Negro had been more of a formula than an expression of human complexity and that the time had come for a change in black self-expression through music, painting, lit., and debate. Among black poets, this change took the form of a debate over lang. Should Af. Am. poetry be based, as Langston Hughes believed, in the vernacular, oral trad. of black people, influenced by jazz rhythms and speech rhythms—or should it be based, as Countee Cullen (1903–46) and Claude McKay demonstrated, in traditional meters and stanzaic forms? Dunbar, the early James Weldon Johnson (1871–1938), and McKay had written significant black dialect poetry, and among Harlem Ren. poets, a number, incl. Hughes and Sterling Brown (1901–89), drew on the rich heritage of the black vernacular. Writing in reaction to Cullen's tendency to write in traditional sonnets and versification, Hughes argued in "The Negro Artist and the Racial Mountain" (1926) that the use of such models reflected the hegemony of whiteness—the "racial mountain" by which black writers configured their work around white models. In "The Weary Blues" (1926), Hughes quotes a blues lyric within the larger poem, thereby creating a double-voiced representation of the black experience.

Cullen and McKay's ballads and sonnets often asserted race-conscious themes, in a sense "blackening" the white canon just as white poets had attempted, through Uncle Remus tales and popular music, to "whiten" black culture. McKay's "If We Must Die" (1919) is written in the form of an Elizabethan sonnet, yet its content concerns black resistance to racism and lynching:

> If we must die, let it not be like hogs
> Hunted and penned in an inglorious spot,
> . . .

Harlem Ren. women writers such as Georgia Douglas Johnson (1880–1966), Anne Spencer (1882–1975), Angelina Weld Grimké (1880–1958), and Alice Dunbar-Nelson (1875–1935) also wrote in traditional meters and stanzaic patterns yet filled these forms with issues relating directly to the politics of an emerging black community, as well as to matters of gender and domesticity.

The 1930s and the Popular Front produced another version of modernism, galvanized by the Depression and fueled by political activism. Prominent poets of the period—Muriel Rukeyser (1930–80), Edwin Rolfe (1909–54), and Edna St. Vincent Millay (1892–1950)—rejected avant-garde formal strategies of the earlier modernists and subjected poetic form to political ends. "Not Sappho, Sacco," Rukeyser advised other poets, speaking of the need to turn from modernists' appropriation of cl. models to contemp. events such as the trial of accused anarchists Ferdinando Nicola Sacco and Bartolomeo Vanzetti. Rukeyser adapted Eliot's mythic method in her own documentary poem "Book of the Dead" (1938), which chronicles a mining workplace disaster in West Virginia and the congressional hearings into corporate malfeasance that led to the deaths of miners from silicosis. Millay, in "Justice Denied in Massachusetts" (1927), attacked the legal malfeasance surrounding the Sacco and Vanzetti trial in 1920, and in "Say That We Saw Spain Die" (1938) responded to the defeat of the Sp. Republic by Franco's fascists.

One group of poets who came to prominence during the Popular Front era and combined modernist aesthetics and politics were the objectivists: Louis Zukofsky (1904–78), George Oppen (1908–84), Charles Reznikoff (1894–1976), Carl Rakosi (1903–2007), and Lorine Niedecker (1903–70). Although they resisted defining themselves as a movement, they nevertheless built upon the examples of Pound and Williams in creating a poetry of direct presentation and economy. Zukofsky's essay "An Objective" (1930–31) stresses the unity of seeing eye and object: "*An Objective: (Optics)—The lens bringing the rays from an object to a focus. That which is aimed at. (use extended to poetry)—Desire for what is objectively perfect* . . ." Such perfection implies not fidelity to nature but sincerity or honesty in "thinking with the things as they exist." Zukofsky's involvement in Left politics can be felt in his long poem *"A,"* composed throughout the poet's life between 1927 and 1978, where, in several instances, he quotes directly from Karl Marx's *Das Kapital* and relates the labor of writing to other forms of social materiality. Similarly, his colleague Oppen in *Discrete Series* (1934) creates short lyrics that attack capitalism and its excrescences: "Closed car—closed in glass— / At the curb, / Unapplied and empty: / A thing among others: . . ." The bare-bones style of such poems offers lang. unadorned, its surfaces and grammatical structure returning a degree of use value to lang., a quality that would become important to poets of the Black Mountain school and Language poetry movement.

More conservative poets of the period felt that ideological concerns of the Popular Front were irrelevant to art. In the wake of modernist excesses and experimentation, what was needed was a return to the poem as aesthetic artifact, detached from its historical conditions or its author's psychology. Poets and critics who formed around John Crowe Ransom at Vanderbilt University, known as the Fugitives, included Allen Tate (1899–1979) and Robert Penn Warren (1905–89). Their agrarian manifesto *I'll Take My Stand* (1930) endorsed Southern rural values and the cl. curriculum against forms of collectivism and cosmopolitanism. They staked their aesthetics on Eliot's crit., with its emphasis on the impersonality of the poet, the devel. of the objective correlative, and the formally closed text. Their poems used traditional meters and complex metaphors and, in many cases, were based on southern hist. Tate's "Ode to the Confederate Dead" (1928) is an elegy for universal ideals and moral authority that he associates with the defeated South. The subject of the poem is twofold: the crisis of mod. solipsism and the death of heroic possibilities in a secular society. The narrator, speaking on an autumn afternoon in a Confederate military cemetery, muses on his alienation from the heroic dead but also senses his inability to rectify the "fragmentary cosmos," as Tate calls it in an essay on the poem ("Narcissus on Narcissus," 1938), of contemp. reality. To this extent, Tate echoes Eliot's warnings against solipsism in poems like "Prufrock" and *The Waste Land,* except that in his ode, Tate locates the crisis of inaction against a specific U.S. historical moment.

Warren, Tate, and Ransom, along with fellow Fugitive Cleanth Brooks (1906–94), were perhaps better known as literary critics whose New Criticism offered a technical, even scientific alternative to the often impressionistic, biographical crit. of the era. Ransom's crit., esp. "Poetry: A Note in Ontology" (1934), repudiated what he called "Platonic poetry" (the poetry of ideas) and "Physical Poetry" (imagism and the various forms of objectivism) in favor of what he called "Metaphysical Poetry," which created a "miraculist" fusion of universal ideas and concrete particulars. The religious implications of miraculism suggest the ways that the New Critics sought a secular version of Christian incarnation through the aesthetic. Such ideas, when institutionalized in Brooks and Warren's influential teaching anthol. *Understanding Poetry* (1938), exerted an enormous influence on literary pedagogy for generations to come.

C. ***Postwar Poetry, 1945–2010.*** World War II produced its own poetry. Perhaps the most representative poem of the period was Randall Jarrell's (1914–65) "The Death of the Ball Turret Gunner" (1945), written from the standpoint of an Air Force gunner, "hunched" in the belly of an airplane like an animal and who, when killed, is "washed . . . out of the turret with a hose." This bleak vision of the hopelessness of war is matched by the sequence of 12 sonnets by Gwendolyn Brooks (1917–2000), "Gay Chaps at the Bar" (1945), based on letters from black soldiers in the then-segregated army that chronicles the difficult tension between learning "white speech" and knowing black alienation. Finally, there are poems by those who opposed the war, incl. Pound, William Everson (1912–94), Robert Lowell (1917–77), William Stafford (1914–93), and Robert Duncan (1919–88), who, whether as conscientious objectors or, in the case of Pound, war criminals, were incarcerated for periods during the war. One might add to this list many poets and intellectuals on the Left who were disaffected by the pact between Hitler and Stalin at the war's outset.

Poets who came of age in the period immediately after World War II found themselves in a difficult relation to their modernist predecessors. On the one hand, the work of Eliot, Pound, Stevens, Frost, Moore, and Crane had provided younger poets with an extraordinary range of formal and thematic resources; at the same time, this variety also proved a stumbling block to further experimentation. It seemed to Jarrell that modernism, "the most successful and influential body of poetry of this century—is dead." Such an elegiac assessment of the era masked a desire felt by many poets of this generation to have a clean slate. Innovative works such as Williams's *Spring and All,* Pound's *Cantos*, Stein's *Stanzas in Meditation*, or Eliot's *The Waste Land* had challenged the structure of traditional verse, and now it was time for a stock-taking that would seize upon the liberating advantages of Fr. *vers libre* and the derived Anglo-Am. free verse while curbing their excesses.

Writers born in the first two decades of the 20th c.—Theodore Roethke (1908–63), Elizabeth Bishop (1911–79), John Berryman (1914–72), Jarrell, Lowell, Howard Nemerov

(1920–91), and Richard Wilbur (b. 1921)—turned away from free verse and developed a technically complex, rhetorically difficult poetry modeled on the values of the New Critics, esp. the work of metaphysical poets such as John Donne and George Herbert. Where poets of the first generation capped their careers by writing long epic or dramatic poems, postwar poets perfected a kind of reflective, ironic lyric that would become the formal model for the two decades following World War II.

Eliot's lit. crit. provided a major impetus for many of these tendencies, and his cultural crit. introduced a religio-ethical frame within which poetry could be assessed. The characteristic voice in poems written during this period is arch and ironic, cautious of bardic pronouncements yet assured in its mastery of complexity and contradiction. Irony now implies more than saying one thing while meaning another; it signals that the artist is in control, able to moderate feeling by transforming it into rhet. In a paradox that seemed quite normal to the age, Wilbur spoke of irony as being the "source . . . of what richness and honesty we may sense in a poem," as illustrated by his own example from *The Beautiful Changes* (1947):

> Does sense so stale that it must needs
> derange
> The world to know it?

Wilbur's "Praise in Summer" (1947), with its careful management of ironic tension, richly embroidered figuration, and steady iambic meters, seems destined less for sensual appreciation than for explication. As Jarrell conceded, it was an "age of criticism" in which the techniques of close reading and scientific analysis were perfected in ways that ultimately affected how poems were written. The postwar years saw colleges and universities expanding their enrollments with students on the G.I. Bill, and the curriculum needed practical critical methodologies to accommodate this influx. For the first time in hist., poets in increasing numbers became teachers, and creative writing became part of the literary curriculum. Whereas for the first generation of modernists, poetry emerged within bohemian enclaves and expatriate communities, it now became a province of the university quarterly and the English Department classroom.

Arguably, the three poets who most typify—but at the same time challenge—the conservative tenor of the times were Lowell, Berryman, and Bishop. Lowell's first two books, *Land of Unlikeness* (1944) and *Lord Weary's Castle* (1946), exhibit the effects of his close relationship to his New Critical mentors, Ransom and Tate. In these works, Lowell takes the metaphysical mode to an extreme, employing a gnarled, convoluted syntax and alliteration to represent issues of incarnation and existential doubt. With *Life Studies* (1959), Lowell shocked his teachers and friends by dropping his metaphysical style and speaking in a more personal voice about his ambivalent relationship to his patrician New England family, troubled marriages, mental breakdowns, and theological anxieties. Despite Lowell's new personalism, he still maintained the formal diction and iambic cadences of his earlier work:

> These are the tranquilized *Fifties*,
> and I am forty. Ought I to regret my
> seedtime?

Lowell's rather archaic diction and heavy alliterations temper his confessional poetry with a need to contain feeling within definite formal boundaries. In later volumes (*History*, *For Lizzie and Harriet*, and *The Dolphin*, all 1973) he returned to a more traditional verse, working extensively in unrhymed, blank-verse sonnets.

Berryman began by writing in the style of W. H. Auden and W. B. Yeats, but with "Homage to Mistress Bradstreet" (1956) and even more powerfully in *77 Dream Songs* (1964), he developed an idiosyncratic use of persona that permitted him a wide range of voices to dramatize various sides of his rather volatile personality. In the former poem, he collapses his own voice into that of America's first poet, speaking of his own existential malaise through Anne Bradstreet's confessions of spiritual doubt. His major work, *The Dream Songs* (1969), confronts the poet's own biography in a long sequence of lyrics, each built on three six-line stanzas, written from 1955 until the time of his death in 1972. Despite its autobiographical content, *The Dream Songs* offers a complex series of personae in which mocking accusation merges with ironic self-deprecation:

> Life, friends, is boring. We must not say so.
> After all, the sky flashes, the great sea yearns.
> ("Dream Song 14")

Bishop, though less rhetorically explosive than either Lowell or Berryman, combined flexible meters with microscopically sharp observations to achieve a broken, tense lyricism, reminiscent of Moore. She describes the skin of a fish as

> . . . like wallpaper:
> shapes like full-blown roses
> stained and lost through age.
>
> ("The Fish")

In such lines, lang. isolates and refines the image until it loses its conventional associations and becomes something exotic and even heroic. Without moralizing commentary, Bishop sees a world of vivid particulars that gain luster by her patient, at times obsessive, enumerations. In Bishop, as in her two poetic peers, formal mastery implies less the creation of seamless artifice than it does a charged ling. and rhetorical field in which cognitive acts may be tested. Lowell's and Berryman's harsh, crabbed lang. and Bishop's enjambed, condensed lines represent a formalism impatient with its own limits, dramatizing by sheer verbal energy areas of psychological intensity that cannot yet be expressed.

Lowell's poetry after *Life Studies* made an indelible mark on a number of writers, incl. Sylvia Plath (1932–63), Anne Sexton (1928–75), W. D. Snodgrass (1926–2009), and, to a lesser extent, Berryman. Despite their emphasis on charged psychic materials, these poets reflect a much more carefully modulated response to their personal content. The strength of Plath's vehement attack in "Daddy" (1962) comes not from its specific address to her actual father, Otto Plath, who died when she was a child, but from its conscious and careful manipulation of conflicting discursive modes (childhood rhymes, holocaust imagery, obsessive repetitions) that form an objective correlative to her psychological condition. Confessional poetry, as M. L. Rosenthal pointed out in his inaugural essay on that movement ("Poetry as Confession," 1959), should be considered not as a prescriptive formula held by any one group but as a general permission felt by most poets of the period to treat personal experience, even in its most intimate and painful aspects.

If Eliot, Auden, and Frost exerted a pervasive influence on the dominant trad. of the 1950s, Pound and Williams began to exert a like effect on an emerging experimental trad. Pound's *Cantos* had provided a model for a historical, "open" poetry, and Williams's hard, objectivist lyrics had encouraged a poetics of visual clarity and metrical experimentation. Charles Olson's (1910–70) essay on "projective verse" (1950) extended their ideas with a special emphasis on the poetic line as a register of physiological and emotional contours. He sought to reinvigorate poetic lang. by what he called *composition by field*, in which poetic form extends directly from subject matter and in which the line is a register of momentary perceptions. He explored this stance in his *Maximus Poems* (written 1950–70, pub. 1960–75), which dwells on the separation of the individual from his or her locale because of the ill effects of entrepreneurial capitalism. Early portions of *The Maximus Poems* engage the hist. of Olson's hometown, Gloucester, Massachusetts; but in later sections, his interests extend outward to Asia, Africa, and the Americas and back to the Pleistocene period.

Although "projective verse" had few adherents when it first appeared, it was a harbinger of things to come, as poets sought a loosening of poetic forms and an alternative to New Critical strictures. The most public announcement of a change came from Allen Ginsberg (1926–97), whose long poem *Howl* (1956) revived romanticism in its most vatic form and with Whitmanesque enthusiasm made the poet's specific, personal voice the center of concern:

> I saw the best minds of my generation de-
> stroyed by madness, starving hysterical
> naked, dragging themselves through the
> negro streets at dawn, looking for an
> angry fix

Ginsberg's protest against institutional mind control and McCarthy-era paranoia was made in what he called his "Hebraic-Melvillian bardic breath" and in a lang. as direct and explicit as Wilbur's or Lowell's was oblique. The carefully nuanced ironies of the period were jettisoned in favor of a tone alternately funny, frank, and self-protective. *Howl* received its first major critical forum in the San Francisco Municipal Court when its publisher, City Lights Books, went on trial for pornography, adding new meaning to the poem's social indictment and bringing a mass readership to the work of other Beat generation writers. Many of Ginsberg's colleagues—Jack Kerouac (1922–69), Lawrence Ferlinghetti (b. 1920), LeRoi Jones (1934–2014, later known as Amiri Baraka), Gregory Corso (1930–2001), Michael McClure (b. 1932)—provided their own critique of the era, reviving a demotic, populist poetics inspired by Whitman and Williams as well as the romantic, visionary work of William Blake and P. B.

Shelley. Performing their poetry in jazz clubs or coffeehouses, occasionally accompanied by jazz, the Beat poets made the poetry reading a primary fact of postwar literary life.

The Beat movement is the most public face of a general romantic revival during the late 1950s and 1960s. Whether through Olson's notion of composition by field, Robert Bly's (b. 1926) ideas of the psychological deep image, or Frank O'Hara's (1926–66) personism, poets began to think of the poem not as an imitation of experience but as an experience itself, a map of moment-to-moment perceptions whose value is measured by immediacy and sincerity rather than artistic unity. As Duncan said, "[T]he order man may contrive upon the things about him . . . is trivial beside the divine order or natural order he may discover in them." Duncan's remark reinvests John Keats's negative capability with sacramental implications: the poet relinquishes order that he may discover an order prior to and immanent within experience.

In the late 1950s, these general tendencies could be seen in little magazines such as *Origin*, *The Black Mountain Review*, *Yugen*, *The Fifties*, *Evergreen Review*, and, most important, in Donald Allen's 1960 anthol. *The New American Poetry 1945–1960*, which first divided the experimental tendencies of Am. poetry into five groups. One group consisted of the poets associated with Black Mountain College in North Carolina, incl. Olson, Robert Creeley (1926–2005), Duncan, Denise Levertov (1923–1997), and Edward Dorn (1929–99). Another group, the New York school, incl. O'Hara, John Ashbery (b. 1927), Kenneth Koch (1925–2002), and James Schuyler (1923–91), was closely associated with painters and musicians. The San Francisco Ren. was represented by poets such as Jack Spicer (1925–65), Robin Blaser (1925–2009), Brother Antoninus (the aforementioned William Everson), and Philip Lamantia (1927–2005). A fourth category included other West Coast writers such as Gary Snyder (b. 1930), Philip Whalen (1923–2002), and David Meltzer (b. 1937). Along with the Beats, these groups shared less a common aesthetic than a spirit of bohemian exuberance and antiestablishment camaraderie.

In a similar vein but coming from different sources, Bly, James Wright (1927–80), W. S. Merwin (b. 1927), Galway Kinnell (1927–2014), Mark Strand (1934–2014), and others were developing a poetics of the "deep image." Using Sp. and Fr. surrealism as a source, they experimented with associative techniques that would circumvent discursive thought and tap into unconscious realms. Among Deep Image poets, one can draw a distinction between those who create discontinuous "leaps" within a minimal, denuded landscape and those for whom the "leap" implies access to a world of numinous presence. Strand and Merwin would be examples of the first sort, creating poems in which lang. has been reduced to a bare minimum. In Wright's or Bly's poetry, conversely, the deep image serves to join quotidian, unreflective experience with realms of spiritual or natural value. Taking a walk, mailing a letter, or wasting time becomes an initiatory rite of passage into archetypal experiences. In Bly's "Snowfall in the Afternoon," (1962), a snowstorm transforms a barn into a "hulk blown toward us in a storm at sea; / All the sailors on deck have been blind for many years." Waking in the morning "is like a harbor at dawn; / We know that our master has left us for the day" ("Waking from Sleep," 1962).

The Eur. avant-garde provided a common ground for another group that was initially associated with Bly and Wright but ultimately moved in a very different direction. David Antin (b. 1932), Jackson Mac Low (1922–2004), Jerome Rothenberg (b. 1931), and Armand Schwerner (1927–99) merged a strong interest in Dada and surrealism with the poetics of Stein, the aesthetic theories of Marcel Duchamp and John Cage, and the theatrical "happenings" movement. In a desire to find aesthetic models that exist outside of Western trad. (or marginalized within it), many of these poets turned to oral and nonliterate cultures, creating along the way an ethnopoetics that stresses cultural and social sources of poetry.

The identity politics of the 1960s brought new constituencies into the poetry world, assisted by access to cheap, offset printing technologies and art venues. Af. Am., gay and lesbian, Asian Am., Native Am., and Chicana/o poets drew on alternative cultural models to challenge the canon of anglocentric, male models. Poet and playwright LeRoi Jones threw off his previous Black Mountain and Beat affiliations and adopted the name Imamu Amiri Baraka to signal his alliance with the Black Nationalist movement. The Black Arts movement with which Baraka was associated created an angry, frontal poetry that addressed racism, drawing on Afrocentric cultural trads., free jazz improvisation, and street vernacular. Other poets not directly tied to the Black Arts movement—David Henderson (b. 1942), Audre Lorde (1934–92), June Jordan (1936–2002), and Michael S. Harper (1938–2016)—also worked to foreground black cultural experience and lang. Although alternate cultural sources became important allies in this endeavor (the use of jazz rhythms in black writing, the use of oral chant in Native Am. poetry, bilingualism in Chicana/o poetry), the primary formal imperatives came from the more populist, oral styles of the Beats and other new poetry movements.

Coinciding with the growth of literary communities among ethnic minorities, women writers began to write out of the social and political context of the feminist movement. Presses, reading spaces, distribution services, and anthols. provided a range of new resources for women writers, many of whom—like Adrienne Rich (1929–2012)—began their careers within the predominantly male literary community. Although "women's poetry" defines less a set of stylistic features than a spectrum of gendered concerns, many women writers agreed with the necessity for revision as defined by Rich: "the act of looking back, of seeing with fresh eyes, of entering an old text from a new critical direction." Many of Rich's poems are just such revisions of previous texts as she sorts through the "book of myths" ("Diving into the Wreck," 1972) to find moments in which women have been marginalized—or ignored outright. Although she began by writing poems very much in the formalist mode of the 1950s, Rich's style gradually loosened to admit her own changing awareness of women's oppression and to express her anger at patriarchal authority.

The proliferation of poetic styles during the 1970s and 1980s repeated many of the tendencies of the modernist period, with subtle refinements. Poets rejected the more bardic and expressive gestures—what Stanley Plumly (b. 1939) calls "experience in capital letters"—of the 1960s in favor of a discursive, even chatty surface that belies more complex social and psychological issues. The dominant mode of the 1970s and 1980s is a reflective lyricism in which technical skill is everywhere evident but nowhere obtrusive. The overtly romantic stance of 1960s poetry, with its emphasis on participation, orality, and energy, gave way to quiet speculation.

One can identify three general areas of practice among mainstream writers of the 1970s and 1980s linked by a shared concern with voice and tone. Among the first group, A. R. Ammons (1926–2001), Ashbery, Robert Pinsky (b. 1940), Louise Glück (b. 1943), Sandra McPherson (b. 1943), and Robert Hass (b. 1941) merge the philosophical skepticism of Stevens with the ethical, cultural concerns of Yvor Winters (1900–68) or Warren. Ashbery's poetry, perhaps the most sophisticated and complex of the group, manifests what he calls "the swarm effect" of lang., vacillating between opposing lures of what he calls "leaving out" or "putting in." His long, desultory lyrics such as "The Skaters" (1966), *Self-Portrait in a Convex Mirror* (1975), and the prose trilogy *Three Poems* (1972) record the fluctuating patterns of a disjunct consciousness. Unable to believe either in a supreme fiction or in a self-sufficient ego, Ashbery leaves "the bitter impression of absence" in lines that are often hilariously funny even as they are self-deprecating. Ammons's poetry, while similar to that of Stevens in its treatment of philosophical issues, builds upon Frost's naturalism and his concern for the morality of "place." For Ammons, "small branches can / loosen heavy postures" ("Essay on Poetics," 1970), and he conducted a quiet campaign for the restorative effects of weather, seasonal change, animal life, and horticulture as they interact with the speculative intellect. Hass's poetry continues Ammons's naturalist concerns—Frost and Kenneth Rexroth (1905–82) are important sources as well—but builds upon subtle shifts of voice and tone. Philosophical speculation alternates with epiphanic moments.

A second group, closely aligned with the first but extending more directly out of the deep-image aesthetic of Bly and Merwin, would include poets such as C. K. Williams (1936–2015), Marvin Bell (b. 1937), Philip Levine (1928–2015), Tess Gallagher (b. 1943), Charles Wright (b. 1935), Plumly, and Carolyn Forché (b. 1950). In their work surrealist juxtaposition combines with a spare, sometimes minimalist style to expose unconscious or atavistic resonances in everyday events. Less inclined toward the ecstatic "leaps" of Bly and JamesWright, these poets prefer a more narrative progression and an elaborate use of analogy that allows the poet to achieve some kind of transcendence or political clarity amid mundane particulars.

A third variation on the dominant mode, what von Hallberg characterizes as "the Cosmopolitan Style," is represented by John Hollander (1929–2013), Richard Howard (b. 1929), James Merrill (1926–95), and Anthony Hecht

(1923–2004). In this work, discursiveness becomes a foil for strategies of self-preservation and effacement. At the same time, a tendency toward conversation conflicts with the use of formal meters and complex internal and terminal rhymes. This tension can be felt in the work of Merrill, which often uses its own aesthetic virtuosity to mock aesthetic solutions. His poems are willfully bookish, his tone, derived to some extent from Auden, arch and urbane. Merrill's reticence and detachment are calculated frames for viewing a conflicted personal hist., a condition given fullest treatment in his trilogy, *The Changing Light at Sandover* (1980). In this long poem, the poet's personal ardors, his "divine comedies," are subjected to an extraordinary anthol. of literary forms, from sonnets and verse dramas to blank-verse paragraphs, all subsumed under the pose of having been received during Ouija board séances. Like many of his earlier poems, *The Changing Light at Sandover* is a poem about writing, a celebration of the "surprise and pleasure [of] its working-out," that offers an elaborate allegory about erotic and spiritual love in an increasingly secularized society.

Merrill is usually regarded as a principal influence on a movement known as the New Formalism, which would include Alfred Corn (b. 1943), Marilyn Hacker (b. 1942), Brad Leithauser (b. 1953), Katha Pollitt (b. 1949), and Gjertrud Schnackenberg (b. 1953). Their renewed interest in traditional forms (as well as the possibilities of narrative poetry) has been undertaken less as a rear-guard attack on debased culture than as a recovery of the liberating potential of limits. New Formalists stress that writing in traditional forms aims to rebalance scales that had tipped too strongly in the direction of free verse since the 1960s, leading, as a result, to a rather amorphous autobiographical lyricism in which open form became an excuse for sloppy practice. The challenge for New Formalists has been to hide or at least diminish pattern through the use of slant rhyme, nonce forms, syllabic rhythms, and expressive variants on repeated meters. At the same time, poets attempt to combine their use of regular meters and rhyme with diction drawn from contemp. life, using the idiom of urban experience, technology, and advertising to blur the usual association of traditional forms with "high" or nonstandard diction.

All these tendencies could be linked by their resistance to the more autobiographical and vatic modes of the 1960s. The most frontal critique of such tendencies has come from writers associated with Language poetry. The work of Lyn Hejinian (b. 1941), Bruce Andrews (b. 1948), Rae Armantrout (b. 1947), Carla Harryman (b. 1952), Charles Bernstein (b. 1950), Ron Silliman (b. 1946), Bob Perelman (b. 1947), and Barrett Watten (b. 1948) explores the degree to which the "self" and "experience" are constructs, enmeshed in social discourse. Deriving from Black Mountain, futurism, and objectivism, these writers foreground lang. as signifying system. Fragmentation and non sequitur open up new realms of play and semantic complexity that invite (or cajole) the reader into cocreation of the poem. Language poets' interest in the prose poem and nonlinear sentencing challenges the generic boundaries of lined verse. That interest can be taken as a marker of a certain *crise de vers* that haunts recent poetry in general. If "a word is a bottomless pit" (Hejinian), a lang.-oriented poetry joins poet and reader in an agency by which that pit shall be explored, and postmod. poets have taken this realization as a generative fact.

By the end of the 20th c., many of the techniques associated with Language writing (non sequitur, collage, decentered point of view) became standard features of much mainstream verse, leading the Marxist critic Fredric Jameson to feel that avant-garde innovation was the cultural dominant, as evident in advertising or fashion as in experimental art. At the same time, the increased importance of creative-writing programs and the MFA in college curricula has produced a generic "workshop poem" that, as Altieri explains, "appears spoken in a natural voice [with] a sense of urgency and immediacy to this 'affected naturalness' so as to make it appear that one is re-experiencing the original event." Such "studied artlessness" has itself become a kind of formula, leading some academic critics to wonder if poetry can survive its own institutionalization. Books and articles with titles like *After the Death of Poetry* (V. L. Shetley, 1993) and *Can Poetry Matter?* (D. Gioia, 1992) bemoan the domestication of poetry through creative writing programs and the detachment of poetry from public life. This elegiac response to an increasing professionalization on the one hand and to the increasing fragmentation of traditional poetic values on the other is premised on the illusion that there was an earlier, more vibrant moment in which poetry mattered in public life.

These elegiac remarks conflict with the historic upsurge of performance poetry in coffeehouses, art spaces, and bars. Often distant from academic venues, slams, stand-up, and spoken-word events have brought poetry back to the public arena, merging formal rhymes and patterned rhythm with hip-hop and rap music. The Nuyorican Poets Café, founded by Miguel Algarín (b. 1941) in 1973 in New York, featured a multicultural mix of spoken-word poetry, open mike, and performance events. Poetry slams involve poets competing for the best improvised poem on a given theme. Although the spirit of spoken-word poetry has precedents in Dada performance as well as Beat poetry readings, its strongly community-based, democratic ethos contrasts with coterie or school-based poetry movements.

If the "little magazine" revolution of the 1960s was a poetry of the page in which typography and lineation represented expressive intent, the digital revolution of the 1990s and after inaugurated new forms of digital poetry in which the word is released to cyberspace. In some cases, poets adapted the computer to aleatory (chance-generated) composition. In other cases such as Flarf, poems are created out of Web searches and databases. This new media also made poetry available in ways unimaginable in an era of tape recorders and offset printing. Sites such as the Buffalo Electronic Poetry Center (EPC), Ubuweb, Pennsound, and online magazines such as *Jacket* and *Big Bridge* allow readers around the world to hear live poetry readings and interviews and even to participate in the composition of new work.

The collaborative potential of digital poetry problematizes the expressivist basis of much previous poetry. The natures of presence, voice, orality, and identity are rendered esp. complex in hypertext, where different links may provide multiple narrative roads for the reader to follow or where multiple readers may interact with the text. Issues of beginnings and closure, the page and scoring no longer have the same relevance in the age of the scrolling screen. Claims for the democratization of poetry through digital media have led to a renewed consideration of new forms of public address. Flarf practitioners use open-source software principles to access free information on the Web that is then modified, redistributed, and deformed.

It seems clear that the emergent poetry of the 21st c. no longer can be described by binaries such as "raw and cooked" (Robert Lowell's description of his contemporaries in 1960), experimental and formalist, symbolist and immanent, speech-based and text-based. In a digital and postidentity age, collective labels (Black Mountain, Deep Image) and categories of identity seem both limiting and beside the point. The strong lyric tendency of poetry of the 1970s and 1980s is now matched by an equally strong commitment to narrative, prose poetry, performance, and satiric verse. To adapt the title of a recent anthol., we live in an age of the Am. hybrid, linking formalists and experimentalists, proceduralists and stand-up poets. The outlines of a 21st-c. U.S. poetry are still difficult to see, but the resilient spirit of Emerson's "metre-making argument" endures.

II. Spanish. See CARIBBEAN, POETRY OF THE (SPANISH).

III. Indigenous Language. See INDIGENOUS AMERICAS, POETRY OF THE; INUIT POETRY; NAVAJO POETRY.

■ **To 1900.** ***Anthologies***: *African-American Poetry of the Nineteenth Century*, ed. J. R. Sherman (1992); *American Poetry: The Nineteenth Century*, ed. J. Hollander, 2 v. (1993); *American Women Poets of the Nineteenth Century*, ed. C. Walker (1995); *American Poetry: The Seventeenth and Eighteenth Centuries*, ed. D. S. Shields (2007). ***Criticism and History***: F. O. Matthiessen, *American Renaissance* (1941); R. H. Pearce, *The Continuity of American Poetry* (1961); A. Gelpi, *The Tenth Muse: The Psyche of the American Poet* (1975); S. Cameron, *Lyric Time: Dickinson and the Limits of Genre* (1979); W. Dowling, *Poetry and Ideology in Revolutionary Connecticut* (1990); D. S. Shields, *Oracles of Empire: Poetry, Politics, and Commerce in British America* (1990); S. Cameron, *Choosing Not Choosing: Dickinson's Fascicles* (1992); *Breaking Bounds: Whitman and American Cultural Studies*, ed. B. Erkkila and J. Grossman (1996); D. S. Shields, *Civil Tongues and Polite Letters in British America* (1997); M. P. Brown, "'BOSTON/SOB NOT': Elegiac Performance in Early New England and Materialist Studies of the Book," *American Quarterly* 50 (1998); M. L. Kete, *Sentimental Collabo-rations: Mourning and Middle-Class Identity in Nineteenth-Century America* (2000); C. Wells, *The Devil and Doctor Dwight: Satire and Theology in the Early American Republic* (2002); P. B. Bennett, *Poets in the Public Sphere: The Emancipatory*

Project of American Women's Poetry, 1800–1900 (2003); C. C. Calhoun, *Longfellow: A Rediscovered Life* (2004); M. Loeffelholz, *From School to Salon: Reading Nineteenth-Century American Women's Poetry* (2004); E. Richards, *Gender and the Poetics of Reception in Poe's Circle* (2004); M. Warner, "Introduction," *The Portable Walt Whitman* (2004); V. Jackson, *Dickinson's Misery: A Theory of Lyric Reading* (2005); M. Cavitch, *American Elegy: The Poetry of Mourning from the Puritans to Whitman* (2007); *The Traffic in Poems: Nineteenth-Century Poetry and Transatlantic Exchange*, ed. M. McGill (2008); M. C. Cohen, "Contraband Singing: Poems and Songs in Circulation during the Civil War," *AL* 82 (2010); J. van der Woude, "The Migration of the Muses: Translation and the Origins of American Poetry," *Early American Literature* 45 (2010).

■ **1900–2010.** ***Anthologies***: *The Book of American Negro Poetry*, ed. J. W. Johnson (1931); *An "Objectivists" Anthology*, ed. L. Zukofsky (1932); *The Morrow Anthology of Younger American Poets*, ed. D. Smith and D. Bottoms (1985); *Shadowed Dreams: Women's Poetry of the Harlem Renaissance*, ed. M. Honey (1989); *The Oxford Anthology of Modern American Poetry*, ed. C. Nelson (2000); *In the American Tree*, ed. R. Silliman (2002); *American Hybrid: A Norton Anthology of New Poetry*, ed. C. Swensen and D. St. John (2009); *Against Expression: An Anthology of Conceptual Writing*, ed. C. Dworkin and K. Goldsmith (2011). ***Criticism and History***: J. H. Miller, *Poets of Reality: Six Twentieth-Century Writers* (1965); H. Kenner, *The Pound Era* (1971); C. Altieri, *Enlarging the Temple: New Directions in American Poetry during the 1960s* (1979), and *Self and Sensibility in Contemporary American Poetry* (1984); M. Perloff, *The Dance of the Intellect: Studies in the Poetry of the Pound Tradition* (1985); R. von Hallberg, *American Poetry and Culture, 1945–1980* (1985); H. A. Baker Jr., *Afro-American Poetics: Revisions of Harlem and the Black Aesthetic* (1988); M. Levenson, *A Genealogy of Modernism: A Study of English Literary Doctrine, 1908–1922* (1989); C. Nelson, *Repression and Recovery: Modern American Poetry and the Poetics of Cultural Memory, 1910–1945* (1989); R. Pérez-Torres, *Movements in Chicano Poetry: Against Myths, Against Margins* (1995); A. Nielsen, *Black Chant: Languages of African-American Postmodernism* (1997); *The Objectivist Nexus: Essays in Cultural Poetics*, ed. R. B. DuPlessis and P. Quartermain (1999); R. B. DuPlessis, *Genders, Races and Religious Cultures in Modern American Poetry* (2001); *New Media Poetics: Contexts, Technotexts, and Theories*, ed. A. Morris and T. Swiss (2006); T. Yu, *Race and the Avant-Garde: Experimental and Asian American Poetry since 1965* (2009); M. Davidson, *On the Outskirts of Form: Practicing Cultural Poetics* (2011).

M. Cohen (to 1900); M. Davidson (modernist, postwar)

URDU POETRY. Urdu, the mother tongue of more than 60 million people in India and Pakistan, is read or understood by many more millions across South Asia and around the world. In the past, most Urdu poets were better known by their *takhallus*, pen names either derived from the poet's actual name or words reflective of the poet's sense of himself. The practice is much less common now. (Below, takhallus are given within quotation marks at the end of a name.)

Urdu's earliest poetic texts appeared chiefly at two Muslim courts in South India, Bijapur and Golconda, where rulers of the Adil Shahi (1490–1685) and Qutub Shahi (1518–1687) dynasties patronized major poets and often practiced the art. Much of that sizable poetry—now linguistically remote—consists of *ghazals* (lyrics) and substantially long *masnawī* (or *masnavī* in Ar., narrative poetry). The latter are either historical accounts or indigenous and foreign love stories, enjoyable both as secular romances and tales of Sufi quests.

When in the second half of the 17th c. the Mughals destroyed the two courts, the center of patronage for Urdu poetry moved northward, eventually to Delhi. A shift in literary taste also occurred. While the ghazal remained greatly popular, the masnawī seemingly lost appeal. Two other significant devels. took place at Delhi. First, poetry became an art that one learned by becoming the pupil (*shāgird*) of some master poet (*ustād*). The master explained the intricacies of poetics to the pupil, corrected his verse for grammar and idiom, and defended him if the pupils of another master criticized him at frequently held assemblies of poets called *mushā'ira*. Second, more poets began to compile books, called *tazkira*, containing very brief biographies of their peers and earlier poets, together with a selection of their verses, frequently interspersed with evaluative comments—commonly regarded as the first examples of lit. crit. in Urdu.

As the Mughals grew weaker in the 18th c., various invaders plundered Delhi, and the city's ability to provide patronage rapidly declined.

By the 1780s, Delhi was steadily losing its best poets to such regional courts as Lucknow and Hyderabad. At Lucknow, Shi'a rulers and nobility provided particular patronage to the poets who excelled at writing religious elegies known as *marsiya*. Also at Lucknow, some poets popularized a kind of verse called *rekhtī*. Written exclusively by men, it used vocabulary, idioms, and themes that were intimately feminine. Originally merely entertaining, rekhtī is now invaluable for its unusual lexical richness.

After the Brit. took Delhi from the Marathas and the Fr. in 1803, peace and prosperity gradually returned to the city. Talented people stopped emigrating, and before long Delhi again had its share of notable poets. Meanwhile, Urdu poetry continued to flourish at Lucknow, Patna, Hyderabad, and other places, leading to much rivalry among poets on the basis of their affiliation to an ustād or a place. The introduction of lithography in the 1840s revolutionized book production in Urdu and made possible newspapers and literary jours. that enabled poets to gain readership far beyond local audiences.

After the failed rebellion of 1857, Brit. control over North India became absolute. Earlier, in 1837, the Brit. had replaced Persian with Urdu in official use, and now they gave the lang. further prominence by making it a part of school curricula. Through their tight control of public education, colonial authorities encouraged lit. that would, in their view, be "useful" and "moral." Their ideas found immediate favor with the emerging Muslim middle class and its reform-oriented leaders, who scorned traditional poetry for its elaborate conceits, hyperbole, and frank descriptions of love. Invoking the prestige of poetry in Urdu culture, the reformists called for a new poetry that could lift Muslim youth into worldly success. Two influential poet-critics, Muhammad Husain "Āzād" (1830–1910) and Altāf Husain "Hālī" (1837–1914), set out to create an Urdu poetry that was "simple" and "natural," thus also "moral" and "useful." They quickly found many followers. These ideas remained dominant until the 1920s, when a rehabilitation of Urdu's poetic heritage began, partly as a generational reaction but mostly inspired by a better understanding of Western, Persian, and Indian poetries. Though the Nationalist movement and Marxist Progressivism briefly reinforced the notion that poetry must serve some good cause, a more balanced literary view has prevailed since the 1950s.

Until the 1880s, Urdu poetics was fundamentally what Urdu poets had adopted from Persian and Ar. The primary unit of expression in that poetics was *bait*—two metrically identical lines, each line generally a syntactic whole. The bait was then used as the chief building block to construct poems in various genres. Even a quatrain, e.g., used a binary logic. Previously, the most significant genres had been *qaṣīda*, masnawī, marsiya, and ghazal; in the 20th c., a fifth—*nazm*—became equally important.

A qaṣīda is a poem of substantial length in high diction, consisting of couplets, with the rhyme scheme *aa ba ca da ea*. In Urdu, it is usually a panegyric, praising some religious figure or the poet's actual or prospective patron and seeking some spiritual or worldly gain. The opening section of a qaṣīda, called *tashbīb*, can itself be an ode-like poem on any theme, in which the poet can display his prowess with words and thought. Some powerful satires and literary polemics also exist in this form. The famous names in qaṣīda are Muhammad Nusrat "Nusratī" (d. 1674), Muhammad Rafiʿ "Saudā" (1713–80)—he is also Urdu's fiercest satirist—Insha'allah Khan "Inshā" (1756–1817), Shāh Nasīr "Nasīr" (d. 1838), Muhammad Ibrāhīm "Zauq" (1788–1854), and Asadullah Khan "Ghālib" (1797–1869).

In a masnawī, both lines of every couplet rhyme, but the rhyme itself changes from couplet to couplet. Its relative freedom makes masnawī the preferred genre for narratives that demand linear progression, such as romances, hists., ethical discourses, and topical or anecdotal verse. It flourished more in South India, where several poems of epic length were composed. While those poets mostly treated popular romances as narratives of mystical passion, the practice became rare at Delhi and disappeared completely at Lucknow. The best masnawī writers in Urdu were Nusratī, Asadullah "Wajahī" (d. 1659), and Sirājuddin "Sirāj" (1714–63) in the Deccan; Muhammad Taqī "Mīr" (1722–1810) at Delhi; and Mīr Hasan "Hasan" (1727–86), Dayāshankar "Nasīm" (1811–43), and Nawāb Mirzā "Shauq" (1773–1871) at Lucknow.

Marsiya literally means "elegy," but in Urdu lit. hist. it chiefly refers to poems that honor the martyrdom of Imam Husain—a grandson of the Prophet Muhammad—and his companions in the battle of Karbala (680 CE). These elegies form an integral part of the ritual of public mourning during certain months for the

Shi'a Muslims of South Asia. Initially, a marsiya could be written in any form. But in the early 19th c., both the writing of a marsiya and its public declamation—often accompanied with hand gestures and facial expressions—became profound arts at the hands of several masters, who exclusively used the six-line stanza form called *musaddas* (*aaaabb*). A marisya ultimately seeks to produce a cathartic effect in its listeners. It is never exclusively lachrymose; it makes an effort to exhilarate the devout by presenting, at various moments, descriptions of natural beauty, amusing details of familial relationships, and awe-inspiring battle scenes. Two outstanding practitioners of this genre at Lucknow were Babar Alī "Anīs" (1802–74) and Salāmat Alī "Dabīr" (1803–75), whose family members and pupils further enriched the trad. The religious elegies of Anīs and Dabīr elevated musaddas to such high esteem that several later poets chose the form for their own secular poems on social and political themes. Hālī's *Madd-o-Jazr-i-Islām* (The Tide and Ebb of Islam)—a poem of unique significance in the cultural hist. of South Asian Muslims—is a musaddas, as are "Shikwa" (Complaint) and "Jawāb-i-Shikwa" (Reply to the Complaint)—an exchange with God—by Muhammad Iqbāl "Iqbāl" (1877–1938).

Formally identical to the qaṣīda, the ghazal is shorter in length but more discursive thematically. Also, in almost every ghazal, each couplet demands that it be experienced as a discrete little poem in itself. That perhaps came about because Urdu poetry was more heard than read, and two lines were easier to hold in attention and savor than five or six. Even now, as in the past, Urdu speakers regularly experience poetry at gatherings called *mushā'ira*, where poets present their verses—predominantly ghazals—to large audiences over several hours. The audience, in turn, interacts with the poets, responding to each couplet as it is presented, praising or criticizing it. Further, ghazal couplets are quite casually quoted in common discourse in Urdu—from ordinary conversations to newspaper columns—and deemed to possess the same quality of truth or wisdom as a proverb or an epigram.

The ghazal, in essence, is poetry of relationships, be they cosmic, human, elemental, verbal, or graphic. Images in a ghazal couplet come bundled with other images, and metaphors open into other metaphors—if the rose reminds the poet of his beloved and makes him think of himself as a nightingale, it also recalls for him the garden that bloomed in spring but was ravaged in autumn, and where a hunter lurked to catch the nightingale, or lightning crashed down from a gladdening rain cloud and destroyed the bird's meager nest. So it is also with the words: they link up with each other on the basis of phonetics, etymology, or calligraphic features; through conventional binary oppositions; or in some other manner. At its best, a traditional ghazal couplet lays down a "net of awareness," woven out of different strands, that grabs the reader's attention with tantalizing multiple readings. The list of great ghazal poets is long, but two names tower above everyone: Mīr and Ghālib—the first for a simplicity of diction that belies perceptive explorations of human emotions and the second for a deliberate intellectuality that is rich with wit while profound in thought. Other major names are Sirāj, Saudā, Ghulām Hamdānī "Mushafī" (1750–1824), and Khwaja Haidar Alī "Ātish" (1778–1846) among the elders. Iqbāl and Wājid Ali "Yagāna" (1822–87) dominated the 20th c. in ghazal, followed by Shād Arifī (1900–64), Faiz Ahmed "Faiz" (1911–84), and Asrārul Hasan Khan "Majrūh" (1919–2000) in setting the trends for other poets. In the 1950s, there began a new phase in the Urdu ghazal's hist. when poets such as Nāsir Kāzmī (1925–72), Munīr Niyāzī (1928–2006), Ahmed Mushtāq (b. 1929), Zafar Iqbāl (b. 1933), and Parvīn Shākir (1952–94) further pushed the possibilities in the form.

Nazm first meant "poetry" but in the late 19th c. also came to indicate "poem." From then through the 1930s, the word identified any poem that carried a title or had a single definable topic. Ever since blank verse and free verse took firm hold in Urdu in the 1930s, *nazm* has come to mean a poem that is constructed with lines, not couplets, and has an irrevocable linear progression that gives the poem completeness and is itself not bound to some traditional genre convention. Topical poems were always popular in Urdu. Walī Muhammad "Nazīr" of Agra (1735–1830) excelled at the nazm, and his poems on festivals and market scenes are still read with pleasure. But nazm gained much greater currency under the impetus of the sociopolitical movements mentioned above. Earlier poets had used various traditional forms; those who followed employed stanzaic poems of several kinds. Now blank and free verse are the preferred forms.

In popularity with Urdu poets, nazm is second only to the ghazal. Iqbāl's profound explorations of myriad issues—philosophical, political, and existential—were done in nazm. Shabbīr Hasan Khān "Josh" (1898–1982) wrote on nature and politics in this genre. Faiz and two of his contemporaries, Nūn Mīm Rāshid (1910–75) and Sanā'ullah Dār "Mīrājī" (1912–49), created separate distinct contours of thought and diction that still attract imitators. Other major poets of that generation were Asrārul Haq Majāz (1909–55), Majīd Amjad (1914–74), and Akhtarul Īmān (1915–96). Since the 1960s, many more distinct voices have established themselves, the most noteworthy being Wazīr Āghā (1922–2010), Shafīq Fātima Shi'rā (b. 1937), Muhammad Alvī (b. 1927), Munīr Niyāzī, Sāqī Fārūqī (b. 1936), Kishwar Nāhīd (b. 1940), Fahmīda Riyāz (b. 1946), Afzāl Ahmad Sayyad (b. 1946), and Azrā Abbās (b. 1950).

See ARABIC PROSODY; INDIA, POETRY OF; PERSIAN POETRY.

■ **Anthologies**: *The Golden Tradition*, ed. and trans. A. Ali (1973)—premod. poetry; *We Sinful Women*, ed. and trans. R. Ahmad (1990)—feminist poets; *An Evening of Caged Birds*, ed. and trans. F. Pritchett and A. Farrukhi (1999)—postmodernist poets; *An Anthology of Modern Urdu Poetry*, ed. and trans. R. Habib (2003); *The Oxford Anthology of Modern Urdu Literature*, ed. M. A. Farooqi, 2 v. (2008); *Pakistani Urdu Verse: An Anthology*, ed. and trans. Y. Hameed (2010).

■ **Criticism and History**: R. Russell and K. Islam, *Three Mughal Poets* (1968); *Studies in the Urdu Ghazal and Prose Fiction*, ed. M. U. Memon (1979); M. Sadiq, *A History of Urdu Literature* (1984); R. Russell, *The Pursuit of Urdu Literature* (1992); A. J. Zaidi, *A History of Urdu Literature* (1993); F. Pritchett, *Nets of Awareness* (1994)—premod. poetry and its critics; C. M. Naim, *Urdu Texts and Contexts* (2004); S. R. Faruqi, *The Flower-Lit Road* (2005)—premod. and mod. poetics; S. A. Hyder, *Reliving Karbala* (2006)—the marsiya; A. H. Mir and R. Mir, *Anthems of Resistance* (2006)—Marxist "progressive" poetry.

C. M. NAIM

URUGUAY, POETRY OF. There is no documentary evidence of an indigenous oral poetic trad. within the territory now called Uruguay, whose genesis is the product of imperialist disputes among the Sp., Port., and Brit. empires and among the centralist aspirations of Montevideo and Buenos Aires. Generally speaking, in the 18th and 19th cs., poets were either Hispanic or descendants of Sp. families settled in the River Plate region. Literary tendencies were, thus, mostly rooted in Hispanic foundations. Poetic production attests to the conflict between the city, as an image of cosmopolitanism but also of dependence, and the countryside as an image of freedom and telluric nationality. This conflict is evidenced in the works of Bartolomé Hidalgo (1788–1822) and Francisco Acuña de Figueroa (1791–1862), whose extensive oeuvre encompassed all poetic trends and tendencies manifest in Sp.-Am. cultural centers until the advent of romanticism. The latter movement was considered as a national project by the epic poem *Tabaré* (1886) by Juan Zorrilla de San Martín (1855–1931). In the 20th c., the dialectic between urban and rural life resurfaced in diverse quarrels among different poetic schools and found a synthesis in the works of Juan Cunha (1919–85) and Washington Benavídes (b. 1930).

The hist. of Uruguayan poetry in the 20th c. is often considered by starting with the works of Julio Herrera y Reissig (1875–1910) and Delmira Agustini (1886–1914), two poets who contributed in a fundamental way to the devel. of Latin Am. and Sp. *modernismo*. Among the late flourishing of avant-garde movements, the work of Alfredo Mario Ferreiro (1899–1959), a response to It. futurism, is the most important. The poets who subverted and undermined that trad. include Álvaro Figueredo (1907–66), who developed a highly personal and critical use of received forms—esp. the sonnet—that stood out against the more conventional formalist approach of the established Uruguayan poetic writing in the first half of the century. After 1945, the Generation of '45 or Critical Generation—as the critic Angel Rama named it—showed a new appraisal of everyday reality and the poet's social and political commitment to the problems of his or her times. One of the foremost figures of this period was the poet and translator Idea Vilariño (1929–2009), for decades a highly visible intellectual presence; the most complex counterfigure of the era was Juana de Ibarbourou (1895–1979), whose work is often strongly telluric and erotic.

The military dictatorship (1973–85) favored silence and exile for poets; therefore, poetry arose from the countercultural margins, whether it was overtly opposed to the values of the established culture (as was the group that formed around the publishing house Ediciones de Uno) or symbolically so, as expressed in the brief and intense work of Julio Inverso (1963–99). It also brought about a reapprochement among poets of the Southern Cone, such as the hermeneutic project of the *Neobarroso*, a southern reaction of the 1980s—partly mediated through Brazilian *antropofagia*—to the Lat. Am. *Neobarroco* or neobaroque, the name first applied by critics of Caribbean origins. (Since *barroso* is a neologism, the term *Neobarroso* is untranslatable into Eng.) Exile as a poetic trope also inspired new readings of the works of Uruguayan poets writing in Fr., such as Isidore Ducasse (1846–70; pub. as the Comte de Lautréamont) and Jules Supervielle (1884–1960). Among the poets who work in exile, Eduardo Milán (b. 1952) is worthy of mention, while among those who did so in *insile*, Marosa Di Giorgio (1932–2004) was one of the most original and influential. Two of the foremost names of the 20th c. are Melisa Machado (b. 1966) and Aldo Mazzucchelli (b. 1961).

At the beginning of the 21st c., Uruguayan poetic production is highly dispersed. Revisionist currents producing different readings of social and gendered poetic trads. and readings of postmodernism coexist—more or less aligned with the poetic productions of Argentina and Chile. In addition, there is also strong evidence of attempts to revitalize traditional verse forms and hybridized versions of popular song and refined poetry forged in performative spaces and visual poetry, whose most important local exponents are Clemente Padín (b. 1939) and Jorge Caraballo (b. 1941).

See SPANISH AMERICA, POETRY OF.

■ **Anthologies and Primary Texts**: *Poesía uruguaya siglo XX*, ed. W. Rela (1994); *Antología Plural de la poesía uruguaya siglo XX*, ed. W. Benavides, S. Lago, R. Courtoisie—20th-c. poetry (1996); *Medusario*, ed. R. Echavarren et al. (1996)—Neobarroso poems; *Orientales*, ed. A. Hamed (1996)—20th-c. poetry.

■ **Criticism and History**: A. Zum Felde, *Proceso Intelectual del Uruguay y Crítica de su Literatura* (1930); Á. Rama, *180 años de literatura: Enciclopedia uruguaya II* (1968); C. Maggi, C. Martínez Moreno, C. Real de Azúa, *Capítulo oriental*: (1968–69); *Nuevo Diccionario de Literatura Uruguaya*, ed. A. Oreggioni and P. Rocca (2001).

F. TOMSICH

V

VEDIC POETRY. *See* INDIA, POETRY OF

VENEZUELA, POETRY OF. Venezuela first acquired geopolitical status in 1777, when the Sp. colonial power issued a *real cédula* (royal decree) by which seven provinces were united in the Capitanía General (General Captaincy) of Venezuela. Its politically independent status, however, was reached in a series of steps: first, the Declaration of the Republic in 1811; then, the War of Independence, which ended in 1821; and, finally, the definitive secession from Gran Colombia in 1830. Venezuelan poetry is considered to begin in the early stages of the republic, from the 1820s on.

Nineteenth-c. poetry in Venezuela is conventionally organized by the same categories as Fr. lit.: neoclassicism, romanticism, and Parnassianism. The founding figure of Venezuelan poetry is Andrés Bello (1781–1865), whose voluminous oeuvre spanned philological and literary studies, speeches, political essays, trans., and poetry. His best-known poems are the *silvas* "Alocución a la poesía" (Address to Poetry, 1823) and "A la agricultura de la zona tórrida" (Agriculture of the Torrid Zone, 1826). Both texts, neoclassical in style and intention, undertake a distinctly Americanist project: to create poetry inspired by the themes and the landscape of the New World. This neoclassical Americanism inspired the poetry of the humanist *bellistas*, incl. Fermín Toro (1806–65), Rafael María Baralt (1810–60), and Cecilio Acosta (1818–81).

Perhaps because he translated Victor Hugo's poetry, Bello's diction demonstrated recognizable romantic influence, heralding a new generation of romantic Venezuelan poets: José Antonio Maitín (1804–74), Abigaíl Lozano (1821–66), José Ramón Yepes (1822–81), José Antonio Calcaño (1827–97), and Juan Antonio Pérez Bonalde (1846–92). Although Maitín and Lozano were no doubt consequential, the most prominent figure of the group is Pérez Bonalde, whose writing evokes a life besieged by loss and haunted by existential doubts. His two most significant poems are "Vuelta a la patria" (Return to the Homeland), included in his first book of poems, *Estrofas* (Stanzas, 1876), and "Poema del Niágara" (Poem on Niagara Falls), published in his second book of poems, *Ritmos* (Rhythms, 1880).

The *poetas parnasianos* were inspired by the precepts and rhet. of the Fr. Parnassian movement. The group included, among others, Jacinto Gutiérrez Coll (1845–1901), Miguel Sánchez Pesquera (1851–1920), Gabriel E. Muñoz (1863–1908), and Andrés Mata (1870–1931). They adopted without reserve the characteristic traits of Parnassian poetry: exotic and cl. subject matter along with highly crafted composition. Nowadays, however, they are considered rather marginal or transitional figures.

At the end of the century, Venezuelan literary historiography began to deviate from the Fr. model. The Sp.-Am. literary movement *modernismo*, which evolved from Eur. symbolism, had a small following in Venezuela; however, few of its adherents achieved international renown. Rufino Blanco Fombona (1874–1944), Alfredo Arvelo Larriva (1883–1934), José Tadeo Arreaza Calatrava (1882–1970), and Ismael Urdaneta (1885–1928), among others, influenced by the Nicaraguan *modernista* Rubén Darío, opened the spectrum of lyric subject matter and diction: the politics of contemp. Venezuela, eroticism, military life, mining, and the emergence of modernity appear in their poetry presented in a variety of forms.

In 1901, Francisco Lazo Martí (1869–1909) published his "Silva criolla" (Creole Silva), a poem that revived the regionalist trend inaugurated by Bello. This interest in regionalism, labeled *criollismo* (creolism) or *nativismo* (nativism), emphasized the themes and motifs of Venezuelan rural life and landscape.

Perhaps because of the ironclad dictatorship (1908–36) of Juan Vicente Gómez, the avant-garde movement was almost unsubstantial in Venezuela, although Salustio González Rincones (1886–1933) is sometimes considered an early adherent. His "Carta de Salustio para su mamá que estaba en Nueva York" (Letter from Salustio to his mother, who was in New York [1907]), which combines colloquialism, humor, and self-referentiality, has no precedent in Venezuelan poetry. José Antonio Ramos Sucre (1890–1930) and Antonio Arráiz (1903–62) are also counted as defining authors of Venezuelan avant-garde poetry. Arráiz's book *Áspero* (Rough, 1924), which explored native Venezuelan themes, is usually considered the point of inception of the avant-garde; Ramos Sucre, on the other hand, wrote prose poems of an extreme verbal austerity and precision.

Twentieth-c. Venezuelan lit. is typically organized either in terms of generations or by the literary magazines that gave cohesion to groups of writers. Two generations emerged during Gómez's dictatorship: the Generation of 1918 and the Generation of 1928, although only the first one was distinctly artistic and literary. The *Semana del estudiante* (Week of the Student) of February 6–12, 1928, characterized by a series of student protests and political editorials, gave name to the second, but it is unclear what produced the first appellation. The Generación del 18 was made up by the poets Enrique Planchart (1894–1953), Fernando Paz Castillo (1893–1981), Andrés Eloy Blanco (1897–1955), Luis Enrique Mármol (1897–1926), and Jacinto Fombona Pachano (1901–51). Paz Castillo wrote highly reflective, metaphysical poetry; Planchart, Mármol, and Fombona Pachano explored sober forms of expression, interiorizing the landscape, while Blanco wrote poetry with a decidedly popular slant.

In 1936, a collective of writers founded the literary group *Viernes* (Friday), which would later become a literary magazine and press of the same name. This magazine responded to the new political aperture with a cosmopolitan agenda, publishing trans. and reviews of world lit. alongside texts by contemporaneous Venezuelan writers. The group included Luis Fernando Álvarez (1901–52), Vicente Gerbasi (1913–91), Otto de Sola (1908–75), José Ramón Heredia (1900–87), Ángel Miguel Queremel (1899–1939), Miguel Ramón Utrera (1909–93), and Pablo Rojas Guardia (1909–78). Álvarez adopted the prose poem and a kind of surrealist lang. to explore the inner anxiety of urban life. Gerbasi's work, on the other hand, exhibited a balanced mixture of surrealism, metaphysics, magical transfiguration of landscape, and exuberant versification. His book-length poem *Mi padre, el inmigrante* (My Father, the Immigrant, 1945) is considered his masterpiece, along with his next book, *Los espacios cálidos* (Balmy Spaces, 1952).

Not all poets, however, can be categorized by generations or literary magazines. While the poets of *Viernes* were publishing their first books, three women poets published theirs independently: Enriqueta Arvelo Larriva (1886–1962), Luisa del Valle Silva (1902–62), and María Calcaño (1906–56). These three poets were the founders of a women's literary movement that would not consciously develop until the late 20th c. In their works, they explored motifs of immediacy, intimacy, and reflection, sometimes in a gender-defined, body-conscious erotic poetry.

In the 1940s, a heterogeneous group of poets reacted against the cosmopolitanism of *Viernes* and proposed a return to conservative aspects of the Sp. poetic trad. This reactionary movement is mostly identifiable in isolated figures rather than a single group. Ida Gramcko (1924–94), Luz Machado (1916–99), and Ana Enriqueta Terán (b. 1918) rigorously explored complex rhythmic and rhyme patterns in a thematically idiosyncratic poetry, while reinforcing the growing trad. of women's poetry in the country. Juan Liscano (1915–2001), a markedly productive and versatile poet who explored a variety of subjects (eroticism, metaphysics, Americanism, etc.), was to become as well a prolific essayist and one of the most dedicated critics and promoters of Venezuelan lit.

José Ramón Medina (1921–2010) was the most relevant figure of the literary magazine *Contrapunto* (Counterpoint, 1948–50). He was not only one of Venezuela's main poets but a devoted historian and anthologist of its lit. Among the founders of the literary magazine *Cantaclaro* (Chanticleer, one issue in 1950) were Rafael José Muñoz (1928–81), Jesús Sanoja Hernández (1930–2007), and Miguel García Mackle (b. 1927). Muñoz was the first avant-garde Venezuelan poet in the strict sense of the term, and his book *El círculo de los tres soles* (The Three-Sun Circle, 1968) displayed a gamut of invented langs., nonsense, neologisms, and mathematical speculations.

A herald of the *Generación de los 60* (Generation of the 1960s), Juan Sánchez Peláez (1922–2003) is considered the most revolutionary, complex, and stimulating Venezuelan poet of the 20th c. His poetry bore some thematic resemblance to previous poets (Ramos Sucre, Gerbasi) but distinguished itself by a revolutionary lang. that combined the grammatical transgressions of the avant-garde with a singular and tender intimacy, recognizable even in his first book *Elena y los elementos* (Elena and the Elements, 1952). The publication of his *Animal de costumbre* (The Usual Animal, 1958)—notably, in the same year as the downfall of dictator Marcos Pérez Jiménez—marked the beginning of a new era of poetic experimentation. The Generación de los 60 enjoyed the newfound creative liberty enabled by Sánchez Peláez. Arnaldo Acosta Bello (1927–96), Rafael Cadenas (b. 1930), Francisco Pérez Perdomo (1930–2013), Juan Calzadilla (b. 1931), Alfredo Silva Estrada (1933–2009), Guillermo Sucre (b. 1933), and Ramón Palomares (1935–2016) constituted the most remarkable series of poets in the hist. of Venezuelan poetry. Each of these writers created highly idiosyncratic forms of poetry; Palomares renewed and complicated the *nativista* trad. by infusing it with a new lang. simultaneously regional and surrealistic; Silva Estrada adopted a constructivist poetics (a unique case in Venezuelan poetry) marked by rigorous experiment with classic forms applied in the trad. of abstract poetry; Calzadilla explored short forms (epigrams, aphorisms) to make a resolutely urban poetry; and Cadenas created a multifarious oeuvre—beginning with existential and hallucinatory situations à la Rimbaud, and (influenced by Ramos Sucre), he later wrote a concentrated, reflexive, almost aphoristic poetry with a philosophical slant.

The subsequent group of authors is sometimes classified with the Generación de los 60, although they are usually considered a transitional group because of their attempts to undermine the tenets of that generation. This group included Victor Valera Mora (1935–84), Caupolicán Ovalles (1936–2001), Ludovico Silva (1937–88), Miyó Vestrini (1938–91), Gustavo Pereira (b. 1940), Eugenio Montejo (1938–2008), Luis Alberto Crespo (b. 1941), José Barroeta (1942–2006), Reinaldo Pérez So (b. 1945), Julio Miranda (1945–98), Hanni Ossott (1946–2002), Márgara Russotto (b. 1946), William Osuna (b. 1948), Ramón Ordaz (b. 1949), and Alejandro Oliveros (b. 1949). Vestrini and Russotto reinforced the women's poetry movement with new forms of verbal exploration; Crespo and Barroeta revitalized the movement of regional poetry through their oneiric and even abstract perspective; Valera Mora and Ovalles, in the trad. of avant-garde poetry, combined lang. experimentation and political positioning; Ossott created an intensely personal and hermetic poetry in which abstract elements were supplemented with motifs from the philosophical trad.; Osuna inscribed himself in the trad. of urban poetry; Oliveros adopted an objectivist form of poetry; and, finally, Montejo—along with Cadenas, the most internationally renowned Venezuelan poet—left behind a complex oeuvre, published under several heteronyms. His verbal explorations ranged from quasi-vanguardist experimentation to playful engagement with cl. formality, sometimes with a whiff of irony. Under the name Montejo (also a pseud.) he wrote poetry in which remembrance and presence are woven through an artisanal attention to lang.

The last discernible cohort is the *Generación de los 80*. These poets were divided into two literary groups: *Tráfico* (Traffic) and *Guaire*, the name of the river that runs through Caracas. Both groups reacted bitterly against what they considered the deviations of previous poetry. Theirs was to be the poetry of reality—a poetry that would put an end to the outdated metaphysical, hermetic, escapist writing of the recent past, with Caracas (the "real" city) as its background. This generation included, among others, Armando Rojas Guardia (b. 1949), Igor Barreto (b. 1952), Yolanda Pantin (b. 1954), Miguel Márquez (b. 1955), Rafael Arráiz Lucca (b. 1959), Rafael Castillo Zapata (b. 1959), and Luis Pérez Oramas (b. 1960). After their early confrontational phase, most of these poets would go on to produce personal works that would become integrated into the poetic trad. they originally challenged.

The poets of the last decade of the 20th c. generally assembled in groups with no explicit creative agendas. However, a strongly growing trend is that of women's poetry, led by María Auxiliadora Álvarez (b. 1956), Laura Cracco (b. 1959), Martha Kornblith (1959–97), María Antonieta Flores (b. 1960), Patricia Guzmán (b. 1960), Claudia Sierich (b. 1963), Gabriela Kizer (b. 1964), Jacqueline Goldberg (b. 1966), Carmen Verde Arocha (b. 1967), and Eleonora Requena (b. 1968). Three poets—Arturo Gutiérrez (b. 1963), Luis Moreno Villamediana (b. 1966), and Luis Enrique Belmonte (b. 1971)—won international awards at the turn of the century and, along with Alexis Romero (b. 1966), already have a consolidated oeuvre. Each of these figures exhibits a heightened awareness of the trad. of Venezuelan poetry. They renew and rewrite it, combining a reflexive attention to the details of the surrounding world with the complex use of a number of verbal registers. The future, therefore, seems open to a widening spectrum of possibilities.

See INDIGENOUS AMERICAS, POETRY OF THE; SPAIN, POETRY OF; SPANISH AMERICA, POETRY OF.

■ **Anthologies**: *Las cien mejores poesías líricas venezolanas*, ed. P. P. Barnola (1935); *Las mejores poesías venezolanas*, ed. G. Sucre (1958); *La nueva poesía venezolana*, ed. J. R. Medina

(1959); *Antología venezolana. Verso*, ed. J. R. Medina (1962); *La antigua y la moderna literatura venezolana*, ed. P. Díaz Seijas (1966); *Antología general de la poesía venezolana*, ed. J. A. Escalona-Escalona (1966); *Poesía de Venezuela: Románticos y modernistas*, ed. J. R. Medina (1966); *Orígenes de la poesía colonial venezolana*, ed. M. Páez Pumar (1979); *Antología actual de la poesía venezolana*, ed. J. A. Escalona-Escalona, 2 v. (1981); *Antología dispersa de la poesía venezolana*, ed. E. R. Pérez (1981); *Poetas parnasianos de Venezuela*, ed. P. A. Vásquez (1982); *Contemporary Venezuelan Poetry*, ed. J.Tello (1983); *Antología de la moderna poesía venezolana*, ed. O. D'Sola, 2 v., 2d ed. (1984); *Antología de la poesía venezolana*, ed. D. Palma (1987); *Los poetas de 1942*, ed. L. Pastori (1988); *Poetas parnasianos y modernistas*, ed. L. León, 2d ed. (1988); *Antología comentada de la poesía venezolana*, ed. A. Salas (1989); *Cuarenta poetas se balancean*, ed. J. Lasarte (1990); *Poesía en el espejo*, ed. J. Miranda (1995); *Antología de la poesía venezolana*, ed. R. Arráiz Lucca (1997); *Veinte poetas venezolanos del siglo XX*, ed. R. Arráiz Lucca (1998); *Diez poetas venezolanos del siglo XIX*, ed. R. Arráiz Lucca (2001); *Antología histórica de la poesía venezolana del siglo XX (1907–1996)*, ed. J. Miranda (2001); *Navegación de tres siglos (antología básica de la poesía venezolana 1826/2002)*, ed. J. Marta Sosa (2003); *Antología. La poesía del siglo XX en Venezuela*, ed. R. Arráiz Lucca (2005); *Conversación con la intemperie*, ed. G. Guerrero (2008); *Enobra*, ed. G. Saraceni (2008).

■ **Criticism and History**: P. Venegas Filardo, *Estudios sobre poetas venezolanos* (1941); E. Crema, *Interpretaciones críticas de la literatura venezolana* (1955); F. Paz Castillo, *Reflexiones de atardecer*, 3 v. (1964); P. Díaz Seijas, *La antigua y la moderna literatura venezolana* (1966); D. Miliani, *Vísperas del modernismo en la poesía venezolana* (1968); F. Paz Castillo, *De la época modernista* (1968); R. Agudo Freites, *Pio Tamayo y la vanguardia* (1969); P. P. Barnola, *Estudios crítico-literarios* (1971); U. Leo, *Interpretaciones estilísticas* (1972); G. Picón Febres, *La literatura venezolana en el siglo XIX*, 3d ed. (1972); V. Vargas, *El devenir de la palabra poética* (1980); J. Liscano, *Panorama de la literatura venezolana actual*, 2d ed. (1984); and *Lectura de poetas y poesía* (1985); N. Osorio, *La formación de la vanguardia literaria en Venezuela* (1985); M. Picón Salas, *Formación y proceso de la literatura venezolana*, 5th ed. (1984); G. Sucre, *La máscara, la transparencia*, rev. ed. (1985); E. Vera, *Flor y canto: 25 años de poesía venezolana* (1985); *Diccionario general de la literatura venezolana*, ed. L. Cardozo and J. Pintó, 2. v. (1987); P. Venegas Filardo, *53 nombres de poetas venezolanos* (1990); J. R. Medina, *Noventa años de literatura venezolana* (1992); J. Miranda, *Poesía, paisaje y política* (1992); G. Zambrano, *Los verbos plurales* (1993); J. Miranda, "Generaciones, movimientos, grupos, tendencias, manifiestos y postulados de la poesía venezolana del siglo XX," *Antología histórica de la poesía venezolana del siglo XX* (1907–1996), ed. J. Miranda (2001); E. Nichols, *Rediscovering the Language of the Tribe in Modern Venezuelan Poetry* (2002); Jorge Romero, *La sociedad de los poemas muertos* (2002); R. Arráiz Lucca, *El coro de las voces solitarias* (2003); *Nación y literatura*, ed. L. Barrera, C. Pacheco, B. González (2006).

■ **Electronic Resources**: Poetas Venezolanos (in Sp.), http://poetasvenezolanos.blogspot.com; Veneopoetics (in Eng.), http://venepoetics.blogspot.com/; El Salmon, http://revistadepoesiaelsalmon.blogspot.com.

L. M. Isava

VIETNAM, POETRY OF. Poetry permeates all aspects of Vietnamese life and became the most important medium of expression in Vietnamese society. Vietnamese lyric poetry is indebted to both the poetic and cultural trads. and vernacular, or the spoken lang. At the same time, the cl. or formal trad. was modeled on poetic trads. from China (see CHINA, POETRY OF). The commitment to Confucian orthodoxy affixed poetry as a principal mode of literary production using Chinese script among the scholar gentry. Because of the tonal lang., the folk poetic trad.—meant to be sung—gave birth to a variety of verse forms and poetic genres.

Vietnamese independence, established in 939 CE, combined with nation-building, provided the textual trad. of different poetic forms. By the late 15th c., the canonical poetic trad. in Vietnam developed in ways that differed significantly from the folk trads. both in content and form. From the time of Vietnamese independence, *thơ Đườg luật* (*lüshi*) became the ideal literary form within the intelligentsia's textual trad. and was required as part of civil-service exams. The *thất ngôn bát cú,* seven syllables and eight lines styled after the lüshi form, became the preferred poetic pattern until the *thơ mới* period at the beginning of the 20th c. Borrowed from 9th-c. Tang Dynasty poetry, this form was modified by poets to fit Vietnamese ling. features and taste. There were also the *song thất lục bát*, a hybrid form combining the seven-syllable Tang lüshi form and the indigenous Vietnamese *lục bát* or six-eight couplet, with a structure of the two seven-syllable lines and six eight-syllable lines; *ngũ ngôn* (five-syllable), and *tứ tuyệt* (a four-line poem with either four, five, or seven syllables per line). Cl. poetry dealt with the Confucian view of the world and the relationship between the individual and society; topics included moral cultivation, filial piety, neo-Confucian ideologies, heaven and earth, humanity and nature, love, fate, leisure, and beauty.

Poet-scholars adopted both the more formal lüshi as well as *lục bát* (six-eight), a more open, freer, indigenous Vietnamese form originally propagated orally. Most folk poems are written in lục bát. A lục bát poem in its smallest unit consists of a six-eight couplet. There is no limit to the number of couplets in a lục bát poem, though it must end in an even number. The Vietnamese lang. uses six tones divided into two main groups: low and high. The letter *S* (sharp or *trắc*) indicates an accented syllable, and the letter *F* (flat or *bằng*) indicates an unaccented syllable or tone. The odd numbered positions in a line can either be flat (bằng) or sharp (trắc) and is symbolized as *O*. The second, sixth, and eighth syllables are flat (F), while the fourth syllable is sharp (S). As a rule, the last syllable of the first line (FR1) rhymes with the sixth syllable of the second line (the eight-syllable line, FR1). If a poem has four lines (two couplets), the eighth syllable of the second line (FR2) rhymes with the sixth syllable of the third line (FR2). The rhyme scheme continues with the same pattern—i.e., the sixth syllable of the third line (FR2) rhymes with the sixth syllable (FR2) of the fourth line:

	1	2	3	4	5	6	7	8
1st line	O	F	O	S	O	FR1		
2d line	O	F	O	S	O	FR1	O	FR2
3d line	O	F	O	S	O	FR2		
4th line	O	F	O	S	O	FR2	O	FR3
5th line	O	F	O	S	O	FR3		
6th line	O	F	O	S	O	FR3	O	FR4

From the 11th to the 16th cs., the Buddhist trad. predominated under the Lý and Trần kings. Poets became more familiar with Buddhist concepts during this period. *Thơ Văn Lý Trần* (A Collection of the Poetry of Lý and Trần Dynasties), esp. the *Thiền Uyển Tập Anh* in Chinese script, provided reputable matter (Nguyen 1997). Buddhist notions of delusion, temporality, enlightenment, nirvana, and Buddha nature are distinctive characteristics of Lý Trần Zen poetry. Most of the poems are composed using the five-syllable quatrain characteristic of Tang style.

The vernacular lang. played a significant role in the emergence of nationalism and modernity in Vietnam. During the Trần Dynasty (13th c.), the devel. and standardization of the *nôm* script, modified Chinese characters used to record Vietnamese phonetics and vernacular lang., transformed and demarcated a distinctive Vietnamese literary trad. With the devel. of the nôm script, Vietnamese poetry arose as the preferred form to express the Vietnamese psyche, experience, and identity. Nôm script also prepared the way for the creation of the romanized writing system in the 17th c. The great Vietnamese poet Nguyễn Trãi (1380–1442) is noted for his *Quốc Âm Thi Tập* (Anthology of Verse in the National Language). The *Hồng Đức Quốc Âm Thi Tập* (Hồng Đức's Anthology of Verse in the National Language), a collection of cl. Vietnamese poetry composed by King Lê Thánh Tông (1442–97) and members of his Tao Đàn Academy, was also compiled in the 16th c.

The reestablishment of national unity, expansion, and order under the Nguyễn Dynasty (1802–1945) ushered in social and political conditions conducive to the formulation of a new literati aesthetic. Bà Huyện Thanh Quan (b. 1800?), often writing in nôm script in the lüshi form and thất ngôn bát cú, skillfully captured natural images and sceneries with the intention of conveying the psychological states of the individual. Her poems can be read as autobiographical narratives. Hồ Xuân Hương (1772–1822) championed an indigenous and feminine perspective by using poetry as a critique of Confucian morality, esp. attitudes toward sexuality. She skillfully used the vernacular lang. and lüshi forms, as well as Confucian philosophical tropes. She often masterfully used wordplay, esp. a form of Vietnamese secret lang. called *nói lái* (inverted speech). Many of her poems are designed to be read in two wholly different manners; thus, a reader may find her poems beautiful while remaining oblivious to the hidden meaning. Using inverted speech, her poems are also playful and full of sexual innuendoes alluding to and depicting sexually obscene images and sex acts. She frequently challenged the unconditional acceptance of norms—namely, the rights and privileges bestowed on male scholars—and ridiculed the oppression of women.

During this period, scholars became disillusioned and apathetic toward sociopolitical affairs and more focused on personal expression. New poet-scholars emerged, most notably Nguyễn Du (1765–1820), the author of *Truyện Kiều* or *The Tale of Kieu*. This novel in verse, considered to be the masterpiece of Vietnamese poetry, is composed in both verse and the vernacular using the lục bát form in 1,627 couplets. Nguyễn Du used romantic love as an allegory for political affiliation and suffering, simultaneously negotiating loyalty and its multiple obligations. Less concerned with the sociopolitical realm, 19th-c. poets such as Nguyễn Công Trứ, Cao Bá Quát, and Nguyễn Khuyến composed poems focused on personal experiences.

It took more than 300 years for the Vietnamese to embrace and adopt *chữ Quốc ngữ*, or the Roman alphabet writing system, after it was introduced to Vietnam by Eur. missionaries, specifically Alexander de Rhode (1591–1660). Poet Tản Đà Nguyễn Khắc Hiếu (1889–1939) delineated the sharp transition from the cl. trad. to the thơ mới movement, allowing countless others to follow suit. Phan Khôi experimented with the new form in "Tình Già" (Old Love) and was credited with using the first free verse in romanized Vietnamese writing. As the Western writing system became more readily accepted, significant transformations in the aesthetic and content of poetry occurred, and a new crop of poets burgeoned: Thế Lữ, Lưu Trọng Lư, Huy Cận, Tố Hữu, Nguyễn Bính, Chế Lan Viên, Hàn Mạc Tử (who died of leprosy), and Xuân Diệu (who advocated art for art's sake). The form of the new poetry movement preserved many aspects of the lüshi form but was freer in rhyme patterns. These prewar poets (*thi nhân tiền chiến*) sought to cut Vietnamese poetry off from past conventions by incorporating Fr. poetic styles and metaphors.

Poetry at the second half of the 20th c. was profoundly influenced by war. Leading prewar poets like Huy Cận, Xuân Diệu, Chế Lan Viên, and esp. Tố Hữu (who later served as minister of culture under the Social Democratic government of Vietnam) chose to join the Việt Minh and were committed to writing political poetry. Other poets of the thơ mới movement either emigrated to the South or remained invisible in the North throughout the war. On the emergence of a relatively free land in the South, a new poetic movement in the Republic of South Vietnam (RSVN) evolved. Vũ Hoàng Chương, Tô Thùy Yên, Tương Phố, Nguyên Sa, Đông Hồ, and Bùi Giáng, to name a few, brought the movement to new heights. Bùi Giáng used poetic tropes to play with meaning. He often used the lục bát style and is considered the most prolific poet for his ability to create poetry extemporaneously; he is famous for having written a hundred couplets in a day. While the war in the North generated a more radical tendency, poets such as Trần Dần, Phùng Quán, Hoàng Cầm, Lê Đạt, and others distanced themselves from political involvement and used free verse to experiment with form. Poetry in the postwar period followed a number of paths. Young female poets such as Vi Thùy Linh and Ly Hoàng Ly defied poetic conventions and male-dominant sexual politics by exploring female sexualities. However, their works were subject to censure and unfavorable crit.

■ **Criticism and History**: M. Durand and T. Nguyen, *An Introduction to Vietnamese Literature* (1985); D. H. Nguyen, *Vietnamese Literature: A Brief Survey* (1994); C. T. Nguyen, *Zen in Medieval Vietnam: A Study and Translation of Thiền Uyển Tập Anh* (1997); E. Pastreich, "Reception of Chinese Literature in Vietnam," *Columbia History of Chinese Literature*, ed. V. H. Mair (2001).

■ **Translations**: N. B. Nguyen et al., *A Thousand Years of Vietnamese Poetry* (1975); *The Heritage of Vietnamese Poetry*, trans. S. T. Huynh (1979); D. Nguyễn, *The Tale of Kieu*, trans. S. T. Huynh (1983); *An Anthology of Vietnamese Poems*, trans. S. T. Huynh (1996); X. H. Ho, *Spring Essence*, ed. and trans. J. Balaban (2000); *Black Dog, Black Night: Contemporary Vietnamese Poetry*, trans. D. Nguyen and P. Hoover (2008).

Q. Phu Van

W

WELSH POETRY has a hist. spanning 15 centuries, from the odes of Taliesin and Aneirin to the odes of the poets who now compete for the chair every year at the Royal National Eisteddfod of Wales. From Gildas's diatribe on the bards of Maelgwn, king of Gwynedd (d. ca. 547 CE), who used their gift to glorify their king rather than God, we can deduce that theirs was a trad., derived through the Celts from IE peoples, that accorded bards a special role in relation to their rulers because of the magical powers attributed to them. They were expected to call into being and to praise in those rulers the qualities most needed to fulfill their functions, esp. prowess and valor in battle. In short, bards were assigned a sacral role in the life of their people.

While the earliest known Welsh poetry is attributed to poets who flourished in the 6th c., the oldest surviving texts of these poems date from the 13th c., and these necessarily reflect a long hist. of oral transmission and adaptation by generations of reciters and scribes. Poetry composed from the beginning of the Welsh lang. to the end of the 11th c. is usually called *Yr Hengerdd* (the Old Song), and its composers are called *Y Cynfeirdd* (the Early Bards). Nennius's *Historia Brittonum* (9th c.) records the names of five 6th-c. Cynfeirdd: Talhaearn (known as *Tad Awen*, "Father of the Muse"), Neirin (or Aneirin), Taliesin, Blwchfardd, and Cian (known as *Gwenith Gwawd*, "Wheat of Song"). Of these, only two—Taliesin and Aneirin—have left works that survive to the present day. Most of the extant poetry written before the death of the last Welsh princes in 1282–83 is preserved in the *Black Book of Carmarthen*, *The Book of Aneirin*, *The Book of Taliesin*, *The Hendregadredd Manuscript*, and the *Red Book of Hergest*, ms. v. written between ca. 1250 and ca. 1400.

The Book of Taliesin, written in the first half of the 14th c., purports to contain the poems of Taliesin, but it is obvious from linguistic and thematic features that several of these works are of later date and relate to a different Taliesin: a legendary figure loosely connected with the 6th-c. poet, who, like Myrddin (Merlin), was credited with magical and prophetic powers by med. Welsh writers. While this mystical and mythological poetry represents a later accretion to the Taliesin corpus, there remains a core of twelve poems, mainly panegyrics, that have been accepted by scholars as the work of the historical Taliesin. Most of these poems are addressed to Urien, who ruled ca. 575 over Rheged, a realm incl. parts of mod. Galloway and Cumbria.

The Book of Aneirin (ca. 1265) opens with the statement in Welsh, "This is the *Gododdin*. Aneirin sang it." The *Gododdin*, originally the name of a people in northeast England and southeast Scotland, is a long poem celebrating the bravery of a war band sent to recapture a stronghold from the English about the year 600 CE, although the date lacks any archaeological backing. The warriors fought and died almost to a man, gloriously but unsuccessfully. Aneirin eulogizes them for the most part individually, so that the poem comprises a series of elegies. The *Book of Aneirin* contains two versions of the *Gododdin*, one (the A text) roughly contemporaneous in lang. with the date of the ms., and the other (the B text) datable on ling. grounds to the 9th or 10th c.; both presumably derive from an older oral trad. that may extend back to the 7th c.

While these earliest works of the Cynfeirdd may have been composed outside Wales, there is a considerable degree of continuity between the poetic trad. of the Britons of southern Scotland and the Britons of Wales, which enabled the Welsh in later centuries to appropriate the poetry of Taliesin and Aneirin as their own. Like later Welsh verse, this poetry was sung to exalt the rulers on whose heroic qualities the survival of the people depended, and it used the same types of poetic embellishments: end rhyme to link lines and, within the line, the repetition of consonant or vowel sounds, a kind of incipient *cynghanedd*. In any case, there is very little linguistically to distinguish the earliest poetry produced in Wales from that of ancient northern England and southern Scotland, since at such an early date the differences between the various Brit. dialects were not great.

By the middle of the 9th c., Powys, the kingdom adjoining Gwynedd in north Wales, was hard pressed by the Eng. Its struggle is reflected in the work of a bard or school of bards who composed series of linked *englynion* woven round the 6th-c. figure of Llywarch Hen (Llywarch the Old) and the 7th-c. princess Heledd, sister of Cynddylan, prince of Powys. While the narrative voices in these poems are those of Llywarch and Heledd and the events recounted are set in the 6th and 7th cs., the works themselves date from a later period and reflect the emotions aroused by contemp. events on the borders of Powys. These poems are often referred to as the *saga englynion*, since it has been theorized that they represent verse passages extracted from longer prose epics—now lost—that told the tales of Llywarch and Heledd. Such examples of prosimetra (prose tales with verse inserted at moments of strong emotion or heightened tension) are typical of early Ir. lit., but there is no clear evidence for the existence of comparable sagas in early Welsh lit., and the figures described in these englynion would likely have been familiar to 9th-c. poets and their audiences even if the poems were presented without an epic narrative framework.

The med. Welsh kingdoms found themselves in a state of endemic warfare not only against the Eng. but among themselves. Since they were slow to accept primogeniture inheritance, internecine dynastic feuds were frequent, and in their function as praise poets for the princes, Welsh bards could not fail to be propagandists. Some of them claimed powers of vision and prognostication; in times of dire distress, these took on the role of prophesying victory against the Eng. foe. The most remarkable Welsh prophetic poem, *Armes Prydain* (The Prophecy of Britain), composed about 930 CE, foretold that the Welsh would be joined by the Cornishmen, the Bretons, the Britons of Strathclyde, and the Irish, incl. the men of Dublin (the Danes), to overthrow the Eng. and banish them across the sea whence they had come. Although in the Welsh trad. the legendary Taliesin and the equally legendary Myrddin were the seers par excellence and as such were credited with many anonymous prophecies, internal evidence suggests that *Armes Prydain* was composed by a monk in one of the religious houses of south Wales. Vaticinatory poems appear throughout the Middle Ages and were esp. numerous in the form of *cywyddau* (pl. of *cywydd*; sometimes referred to as *cywyddau brud*, prophetic cywyddau) during the Wars of the Roses.

At one time, it appeared that the Normans would conquer Wales as easily as they had conquered England, but the Welsh rallied and preserved their independence more or less intact until 1282–83. The national revival that secured the survival of the Welsh under their princes manifested itself also in a fresh flowering of poetry. The *Beirdd y Tywysogion* (the Poets of the Princes), sometimes called the *Gogynfeirdd* (the "not-so-early" bards, to distinguish them from their predecessors the Cynfeirdd) sang in much the same way Taliesin had sung, but they were not content simply to imitate their predecessors; they developed a much more complex poetic style and a more sophisticated system of cynghanedd, sometimes called *cynghanedd rydd* ("free" cynghanedd, to distinguish it from the codified *cynghanedd gaeth* or "strict" cynghanedd that the bards of the nobility later evolved). The meters of the traditional Welsh verse forms also became more fixed and regularly syllabic during this period. The increased attention paid to structure and ornament in the poetry of the Gogynfeirdd reflects the likelihood that they formed a kind of order in which the *pencerdd*, the master craftsman who had won his position in competition, taught one or more apprentices in a school of *ars poetica*. According to some accounts, the function of the pencerdd was to sing the praise of God and the king. Next in order of rank stood the *bardd teulu*, originally the bard of the king's household troops; apparently he was expected to sing to these troops before they set off for battle, but he could also be called to sing to the queen in her chamber. At the bottom of the scale and not accepted as full members of the poetic class were the *cerddorion* or "minstrels," also known as the *clêr*: low-class performers who lacked the bards' professional training and were sometimes criticized for their ribald or satirical verses.

Among the foremost of these Gogynfeirdd were Gwalchmai (ca. 1140–80), Cynddelw (ca. 1155–1200), Llywarch ap Llywelyn (ca. 1173–1220), and Dafydd Benfras (ca. 1220–57). Their range of themes was not large, and their poetry dazzles by the intricacies of its cynghanedd, the superb command of lang., and by the wealth of literary and historical references rather than by any great individuality of thought. If the Gogynfeirdd borrowed their themes and much of their technique from the Cynfeirdd, they succeeded by their ingenuity in elaborating the former and refining the latter, producing poems remarkable for their subtlety of expression. After the defeat of the Welsh princes who were their patrons, they were saved from extinction partly by the resilience of their guild, though mostly by patronage from the newly emergent nobility. It is thus appropriate that the Welsh poets after 1282 are known as the Poets of the Nobility, *Beirdd yr Uchelwyr*.

In the reorganization following 1282, Welsh society finally had to shed its heroic-age features: no wars were allowed, and martial prowess and valor ceased to have their old value. The poets as well as the nobility had to reassess their function, the former becoming more of a craft guild than an order. The *cywydd deuair hirion* superseded the various forms of *awdl* (ode; pl. *awdlau*) as the favorite meter, "strict" cynghanedd took the place of "free" cynghanedd, and entertaining the nobility became more important than exalting it. The effects of foreign influences were mediated mainly by the new religious orders and by a few *clerici curiales*, esp. Einion Offeiriad, whose "bardic grammar" sought not only to impose order on the practice of the poets but to give it a new intellectual framework. Einion's is the earliest extant attempt at a metrical analysis of Welsh poetry. His division of "meters" into the three categories of awdl, cywydd, and englyn—subject to the modifications by Dafydd ab Edmwnd, who in 1450 arranged the traditional "24 meters" of Welsh poetry into these three classes—remains a fundamental feature of "strict-meter" poetry to this day.

Dafydd ap Gwilym (fl. 1320–50) perhaps owes a great deal of his indisputable brilliance as a poet to the fact that he had inherited the poetic craft of the Gogynfeirdd and was able to adapt it to popularize the new poetic forms of the 14th c. He wrote awdlau in the old style, but by grafting the embellishments associated with them, the system of cynghanedd, on a lower-order verse form, the *traethodl*, he made the resulting cywydd deuair hirion into a meter that the new poets of the nobility took pride and delight in using and that won the favor and patronage of the nobility. Because of the popularity of the cywydd form in the 14th to 16th cs., Dafydd and his followers are collectively referred to as the *Cywyddwyr* (cywydd poets). Dafydd addressed cywyddau to his patron Ifor ap Llywelyn (fl. 1340–60), celebrating Ifor's generosity so much that he became renowned as Ifor *Hael* (the generous), henceforth the exemplar of all bardic patrons. But Dafydd's fame rests ultimately on his cywyddau to women and his masterly expression in them of his love of women and of nature.

Dafydd must have recited or sung these cywyddau to small audiences for their entertainment. One of his favorite strategies is to picture himself in a false or undignified situation, making himself the butt of his audience's laughter. Thus, he describes in a cywydd how one night in an inn he tried to make his way in the dark to the bed of a girl whose favor he had obtained by wining and dining her, only to strike his leg against a stool and his head against a trestle table, knocking over a huge brass pan in the process, and creating such a din that the household woke up and began to search for him as an intruder. It was only through the grace of the Lord Jesus and the intercession of the saints, he tells us, presumably with tongue in cheek, that he escaped detection, and he begs God for forgiveness. But Dafydd describes such situations with such wit, invention, verbal dexterity, and technical skill that one must conclude that the audience's enjoyment of the theme was secondary to its enjoyment of the expression and that the poet's extensive use of *dyfalu* (hyperbolic metaphor), *sangiadau* (poetic asides), and other complex ornamentation presumes a high degree of literary appreciation on the part of his listeners.

It was inevitable that Dafydd ap Gwilym should set the stamp of his poetry on that of his younger contemporaries and immediate successors and that, once the shock of his originality and exuberance had been absorbed, the trad. should reassert itself, albeit in modified form. The poets retained their guild organization, their way of transmitting knowledge of the poetic craft, and sundry privileges. But they and their patrons had become aware of the world outside Wales—the influences of the Hundred Years' War must not be underestimated—and some at least had become conscious that the eulogies that Welsh poets produced for their patrons could be interpreted as sycophancy. A poet of strong conscience, such as Siôn Cent in the first quarter of the 15th c., could not fail to feel this tension, and his vivid pessimism and gloomy *Weltanschauung* made him condemn the traditional Welsh muse as deceitful and proclaim his own as the "true" or Christian muse. But Siôn Cent had few followers. The bardic institution was strong enough to withstand his influence, as well as the disastrous effects of the Owain Glyndŵr Rebellion and the Black Death.

Indeed, there is evidence that, contrary to expectation, Wales shared, albeit to a lesser extent, the prosperity that England enjoyed in the 15th c. The Black Death seems to have put greater wealth in the hands of fewer people, and the poets shared in the new prosperity of their patrons. The result is that the century 1435–1535, the *grand siècle* of Welsh poetry, is remarkable not only for its large number of poets but for the very high standard achieved by many of them. The poets were sufficiently self-confident to assemble in *eisteddfodau*—first in Carmarthen (about 1450) and then in Caerwys (1523)—to make improvements in the rules of meter and cynghanedd. Dafydd ab Edmwnd is the poet esp. associated with the first eisteddfod, and Tudur Aled with the second, but other great names are not lacking: Dafydd Nanmor, Guto'r Glyn, Lewis Glyn Cothi, and Gutun Owain. Such poets (and the work of many has survived) broadened the themes of praise to include the more domestic and civilized: dynastic marriages, well-built mansions with gardens, excellent table fare, and material as well as cultural wealth. Although Middle Welsh strict-meter poetry was almost exclusively a male domain, at least one female poet, Gwerful Mechain (fl. 1462–ca. 1500), left a significant corpus of verse and participated in *ymrysonau* (poetic debates, conducted in verse) with her male colleagues.

After 1282, perhaps the most important date for Welsh poetry is 1485, the year Henry VII acceded to the throne of England, though the implications of that event became apparent only gradually. Under the Tudor dynasty, the Welsh nobility found greater opportunities for advancement in England, so that many of them abandoned their role as patrons of the Welsh muse. And there were a number of others whose contact with the Reformation and the Ren. made them eager to bring their native culture into line with that of England and the continent. This meant that Welsh poets should abandon their guild organization, make the secrets of their craft accessible to the general public, and, more important still, assimilate the new learning proffered by the recently invented printing press, esp. knowledge of the art of rhet. Above all, a purpose other than praise, particularly unwarranted praise, had to be found for the Welsh muse.

Most of these points were raised in the famous *ymryson farddol* (poetic debate) of 1580–87 between Archdeacon Edmwnd Prys and the poet Wiliam Cynwal and in an open letter that Siôn Dafydd Rhys addressed to the poets in 1597. Some efforts were indeed made to help the Welsh poets adjust to the new circumstances: descriptions of the Welsh poetic art and handbooks of rhet. were published. Of special interest is the description of the poetic art published by Dr. Gruffydd Robert of Milan, a Roman Catholic in exile: he advocated a relaxing of the rules of "strict" cynghanedd and the adoption of the "free" accentual meters for epic poetry. But it was extremely difficult to abandon a poetic trad. and practice that had endured for a thousand years, and very few Welsh poets found it possible to take up the new learning. Deprived of patrons, the poets found themselves devoid of incentive either to teach or to learn the art that hitherto had been handed down from generation to generation. Gruffydd Phylip of Ardudwy, who died in 1666, was the last of the "old" or professional poets. Henceforth their art was to be kept alive by amateurs drawn from the clergy or the ranks of the gentry. By the end of the first quarter of the 18th c., the old poetic trad. seemed dead.

In some mss. written after 1550, poems in free accentual meters began to appear side by side with poems in the strict (syllabic) meters. There is no reason to suppose that the free accentual meters had not previously been used; however, it would seem that they were not at first considered worthy enough to be copied into ms. collections with the more professional strict-meter poems. Their presence in increasing numbers implies that they were becoming more esteemed. It is usual to distinguish two kinds of free accentual meters, one old and native, the other new and borrowed, although some of the embellishments of the strict meters were added to both. The newly borrowed accentual meters were based on those of Eng. songs set to popular airs. There is, for instance, a Welsh ballad dated 1571 to be sung to the tune "Adew my Pretie Pussie." The practice of composing Welsh lyrics to musical airs, native and borrowed, continued throughout the 18th and 19th cs. and persists to this day.

In the quatrains of the *hen benillion* (literally, "old verses" or "old stanzas") that have been preserved orally and are sung to the accompaniment of the harp, we may find traces of a more indigenous trad. of Welsh verse in free meters. Sometimes several stanzas are strung together and deal with one theme, but generally the hen benillion consist of single verses. Some are strongly didactic, functioning as verse proverbs; most give expression to familiar feelings with varying degrees of literary artifice. Of anonymous authorship, they have been kept alive for their didactic and entertainment value and have been collected and preserved since the 16th c. The best-known collection is T. H. Parry-Williams's *Hen Benillion* (1940), and Glyn Jones has produced many fine Eng. trans. Dafydd Johnston notes that many of the hen benillion "project a female point of view" and suggests that this verse form may have provided an outlet for women poets excluded from the "male-dominated" world of Welsh strict-meter poetry.

Wales experienced two revivals in the 18th c.: one religious, the other literary. The religious or Methodist revival is important in the hist. of Welsh poetry, indirectly because it helped to extend literacy among the people by encouraging Bible reading and directly because it gave an impetus to the composition of hymns and hence to other kinds of poetry as well. William Williams, "Pantycelyn" (1717–91), wrote a long poem, *Theomemphus*, in which he describes the spiritual experiences of a soul caught up in the Methodist revival, as well as hundreds of hymns. Pantycelyn has every right to be regarded as the father of the mod. Welsh lyric. A later hymn-writer, Ann Griffiths (1776–1805), rivals him in the emotional intensity of her expression, if not in the extent of her poetic output. Unlike Pantycelyn, Griffiths never published any of her hymns during her lifetime, and most of her surviving work consists of verses reconstructed from memory by Ruth Evans, a maidservant who heard Ann sing them.

The literary revival is associated with the "Morrisian" circle, whose leading members—Lewis Morris (1701–65), Goronwy Owen (1723–69), and Evan Evans ("Ieuan Fardd," 1731–88)—were not only poets but scholars and, as such, drew much of their inspiration from the contemp. Eng. literary scene. The Ossianic productions of the Scot James Macpherson had stimulated general interest in the ancient popular lits., and the Morrisian circle was eager to demonstrate the antiquity of the Welsh poetic trad. Evans, their finest scholar, searched for material in the libraries of the landed gentry. Though most of the material he collected remained unpublished, his *Specimens of the Poetry of the Antient Welsh Bards* (1764) marked an important milestone in the rediscovery of the Welsh poetic trad. It also anticipated the publication of the *Myvyrian Archaiology of Wales* in three volumes, of which volume 1 (1801) was until mod. times the only printed source for the texts of the work of the Cynfeirdd and the Gogynfeirdd.

Goronwy Owen, the Morrisian circle's most accomplished poet, was so enamored with the Welsh strict-meter trad. that he could not bring himself to call anything else poetry. He was prepared to accord every praise to John Milton's compositions, but since they were not written in cynghanedd, he could not call them poetry. Yet at the same time he was too much of a cl. scholar not to accept that the most significant poetic genre was the heroic epic. Much to his disappointment, the Welsh poetic trad. could not boast a heroic epic in strict meter. This deficiency he attempted to supply by writing *Cywydd y Farn Fawr* (The Cywydd of the Great Judgment); he also left a legacy of critical ideas, esp. the principles that poetry should follow strict rules of composition and that it could be judged according to criteria derived therefrom.

Edward Williams (1747–1826), a stonemason from the *Morgannwg* (Glamorgan) region in southern Wales, better known by his bardic name "Iolo Morgannwg," was another of the chief architects of the Welsh revival of the 18th and early 19th cs. Although today he is largely remembered as a forger and a laudanum addict, Iolo was also a prolific writer and an autodidact who had gained an encyclopedic knowledge of the bardic trad. and Welsh strict-meter poetry from studying the great ms. collections of 18th-c. Wales. He contributed to the production of the first published ed. of Dafydd ap Gwilym's poetry, *Barddoniaeth Dafydd ap Gwilym* (1789), and was one of the eds. of the *Myvyrian Archaiology*. Unfortunately—much like Macpherson with his Ossian cycle—Iolo was unable to resist inventing material to fill in the gaps in the Welsh bardic trad.: both *Bardd. Dafydd ap Gwilym* and the *M. Arch.* contain numerous forgeries fabricated by Iolo. Determined to prove the primacy of his native Glamorgan in the hist. of Welsh versification, he even concocted an entire system of *mesurau Morgannwg* (Glamorgan measures), which he claimed were older than the 24 cl. meters standardized by the eisteddfod of 1450. Iolo's mastery of Welsh literary forms enabled some of his forgeries to remain undetected for many years after his death, and some 19th-c. Welsh poets even composed verse in his "Glamorgan measures," believing them to be authentic.

The eisteddfodau of the early 19th c. were meetings at which small groups of poets delivered themselves of impromptu verses to test their skill and to entertain a few bystanders.

The eisteddfod has since developed in several ways, but even as the range of the competitions held has been extended to include music and the other arts, one feature has remained constant: the highest honor (the "chair") is still awarded to the poet who can produce the best long poem in strict meters. When Goronwy Owen's view that poetry without strict meters was impossible could no longer be maintained, the second highest honor (the "crown") was added to reward the poet who could produce the best *pryddest*, a long poem in the free accentual meters or even in free verse. However, the presupposition for all these poetic competitions remained Owen's tenet that poetry is composed according to certain rules, so that success in following these rules can be measured and judged. On the whole, poems in the strict meters lent themselves better than those in the free accentual meters to this kind of competition: indeed, the two categories invited different kinds of crit. Still, both sorts of poems tend to have common characteristics: they are predominantly objective, impersonal, descriptive, formal in structure, and stylized in diction.

Although Welsh literary culture in the 19th c. had remarkable achievements to its credit, incl. the work of Evan Evans ("Ieuan Glan Geirionydd," 1795–1855), John Blackwell ("Alun," 1707–1840), and Robert Williams ("Robert ap Gwilym Ddu," 1766–1850), it had no firm base in a well established educational system. Schooling did not become compulsory until the end of the century, and even then only scant attention was paid to the Welsh lang. One of the results was a curious lack of self-confidence shown even by the most talented poets: an inability to recognize what they could do best and a failure to persevere and develop it when they achieved success. This is true of Ebenezer Thomas ("Eben Fardd," 1802–63), who wrote the best eisteddfodic awdl of the century in strict meter, *Dinystr Jerusalem* (The Fall of Jerusalem) for the Welshpool Eisteddfod of 1824 and then, dissatisfied with his success in the strict meters, wrote a long mediocre poem on the Resurrection (*Yr Adgyfodiad*) in the free accentual meters.

As a poet, critic, and ed., William Thomas ("Islwyn," 1832–78) concentrated in his mature years on poetry in the strict meters, but his major contribution to Welsh poetry was made as a young man, when he wrote two long poems entitled *Y Storm* (The Storm). They show a young poet struggling to express thoughts and emotions vaguely understood in words only rarely adequate, but they leave the reader with a feeling that, in better circumstances and with more persistence, he could have developed into a finer poet. Islwyn was claimed as the "father" of a group of poets who called themselves the New Poets. They believed that they were breathing new life into the Welsh poetic trad. by eschewing the strict meters in favor of the free accentual meters for long philosophical poems. But the nebulous nature of their thought is betrayed in their equally nebulous lang., which is often extremely bombastic.

John Morris-Jones (1864–1929) had a clearer vision than the "New Poets" of what was needed and undertook the task of restoring the literary standards of cl. Welsh. By emphasizing the entire span of the Welsh poetic trad. from its beginnings, he was able to reveal its greatness and to uncover some of the forgotten secrets of the prosody underlying that greatness. As a professor and author of both the standard grammar of the lang. and the definitive description of its prosody, his authority was unassailable; but he was also a successful poet in both strict and free meters and, hence, a constant adjudicator at the national eisteddfodau of his time. He took the Welsh nation to school. And he was fortunate in his brilliant disciples, some even more generously gifted at poetry than he. His influence is most obvious in the work of T. Gwynn Jones, W. J. Gruffydd, and R. Williams Parry. The next generation of poets—T. H. Parry-Williams, D. Gwenallt Jones, Waldo Williams, and Saunders Lewis—also benefited from his work on the lang. but developed their own ideas of poetic diction and form. Although many mastered the art of the strict meters, their most outstanding contributions have been in the free accentual meters. Some, notably Euros Bowen, have developed vers libre in which a form of cynghanedd is almost essential. Euros Bowen, Bobi Jones (R. M. Jones), and Gwyn Thomas are among the most prolific, most diverse, and most significant poets of their generation.

Under the leadership of strict-meter poets like Alan Llwyd, Dic Jones, T. Arfon Williams, and Gerallt Lloyd Owen, the period since 1970 has witnessed a remarkable increase in the popularity of traditional verse forms among the younger generation of Welsh poets. This is perhaps because television and radio have provided a platform for poetry as entertainment. Teams drawn from the Welsh counties compete with each other in composing poems in the strict meters, the cywydd, the englyn, as well as lyrics in the free accentual meters; their meetings are recorded for broadcast, and successful teams compete again at the National Eisteddfod in *Y Babell Lên*, the Literary Pavilion. Such has been the success of these meetings that a Strict Meter Society (*Cymdeithas Cerdd Dafod*) has been established with more than a thousand members, publishing a periodical called *Barddas* as well as volumes of poetry and lit. crit. As a revitalized strict-meter poetry reaches a growing and receptive audience in Wales, poets like Menna Elfyn and Einir Jones continue to expand the horizons of Welsh lit. with innovative works in free meters and vers libre, while other writers like Iwan Llwyd successfully cross back and forth between the two trads.

See BRETON POETRY; CELTIC PROSODY; IRELAND, POETRY OF.

■ **General:** C. Donahue, "Medieval Celtic Literature" in Fisher; R. Bromwich, *Medieval Celtic Literature* (1974); *Llyfryddiaeth Llenyddiaeth Gymraeg*, ed. T. Parry and M. Morgan (1976); G. O. Watts, "Llyfryddiaeth Llenyddiaeth Gymraeg," *Bulletin of the Board of Celtic Studies* 30 (1983).

■ **Anthologies:** *Poems from the Welsh* (1913), *Welsh Poems of the 20th Century* (1925), both ed. H. I. Bell and C. C. Bell; *The Burning Tree* (1956), *Presenting Welsh Poetry* (1959), both ed. G. Williams; *Oxford Book of Welsh Poetry*, ed. T. Parry (1962); *Medieval Welsh Lyrics* (1965), ed. J. P. Clancy; *The Gododdin*, ed. K. H. Jackson (1969); *The Earliest Welsh Poetry*, ed. J. P. Clancy (1970); *The Poetry of Llywarch Hen*, trans. P. K. Ford (1974); *Dafydd ap Gwilym: A Selection of Poems*, ed. R. Bromwich (1982); *Dafydd ap Gwilym*, trans. R. M. Loomis (1982); *20th-Century Welsh Poems*, ed. J. P. Clancy (1983); *Welsh Verse*, ed. T. Conran, 2d ed. (1986)—long intro. and useful appendices; *Cyfres Beirdd y Tywysogion*, 7 vols., ed. R. G. Gruffudd et al. (1989–96); *Early Welsh Saga Poetry*, ed. J. Rowland (1990); *Cyfres Beirdd yr Uchelwyr*, 36 v., ed. A. P. Owen et al. (1994–2007); *A People's Poetry: Hen Benillion*, trans. G. Jones (1997); *The Bloodaxe Book of Modern Welsh Poetry*, ed. M. Elfyn and J. Rowland (2003); *Welsh Women's Poetry 1460–2001*, ed. K. Gramich and C. Brennan (2003); *Legendary Poems from the Book of Taliesin*, ed. and trans. M. Haycock (2007).

■ **Criticism and History:** H. I. Bell, *The Development of Welsh Poetry* (1936); G. Williams, *An Introduction to Welsh Poetry* (1953); Parry, *History*; R. Bromwich, *Aspects of the Poetry of Dafydd ap Gwilym* (1986); B. Jones and G. Thomas, *The Dragon's Pen* (1986); H. Fulton, *Dafydd ap Gwilym and the European Context* (1989); *The New Companion to the Literature of Wales*, ed. M. Stephens (1998); *A Guide to Welsh Literature*, 7 v., ed. O. H. Jarman, G. R. Hughes, R. G. Gruffydd et al. (1992–2003).

■ **Prosody:** J. Loth, *La métrique galloise*, 2 v., (1900–2), but see the rev. by Morris-Jones in *ZCP* 4 (1903), 106–42; Morris-Jones—still useful, indexed by G. Bowen, *Mynegai i Cerdd Dafod* (1947); E. I. Rowlands, "Introduction" to *Poems of the Cywyddwyr* (1976); R. M. Jones, "Mesurau'r canu rhydd cynnar," *Bulletin of the Board of Celtic Studies* 28 (1979); A.T.E. Matonis, "The Welsh Bardic Grammars and the Western Grammatical Tradition," *MP* 79 (1981); "Appendix on Metres," *Welsh Verse*, 2d ed. (1986); *The New Companion to the Literature of Wales*, ed. M. Stephens (1998); M. ap Dafydd, *Clywed Cynghanedd* (2003); A. Llwyd, *Anghenion y Gynghanedd* (2007).

J.E.C. WILLIAMS; B. BRUCH

WELSH PROSODY. *See* CELTIC PROSODY

WEST INDIAN POETRY. *See* CARIBBEAN, POETRY OF THE

X

XHOSA POETRY. Xhosa is the lang. spoken by a group of peoples who settled along the southeastern coast of South Africa. It is a member of the Bantu family of langs. widely distributed throughout the southern continent and is closely related to neighboring Nguni langs. such as Zulu, Swazi, and Ndebele. Poetry in Xhosa is principally transmitted through the spoken word and the printed word in books and newspapers.

Xhosa oral poetry (*izibongo*) is of one kind: it is praise poetry, commonly found in Africa in forms such as the Yoruba *oríkì*, Bahima *ekyevugo*, or Shona *nhétémbo*. It consists essentially of a set of names that can be expanded into a line or a variable number of lines. The names that form the core of these verses and stanzas can be metaphors (often drawn from the animal kingdom) or compound names such as Stamps while Fighting (*Lwaganda*) or Watch the Red Dawn (*Jongumsobomvu*) or the names of relatives or ancestors. Nelson Mandela, e.g., is known by the praise name of one of his royal forebears, Madiba, a name that is expanded into the praise verse *uMadiba owadib' iindonga* (Filler who filled gullies), because the original Madiba united the estranged factions of his people. The core praise names, which may be used as alternative names in ordinary discourse, commemorate poetically physical features, actions, or attributes. These units—praise names, verses, and stanzas—are the "praises" that constitute a "praise poem."

Praises may be composed about domestic animals such as dogs, cattle, or horses or about inanimate objects such as motor cars; traditional praise poems about birds once formed a common stock. At various times, praises may be composed by any member of the community about him- or herself or by his or her associates and assembled to form a personal praise poem; there are also traditional poems about clans, which consist of the names and praises of the clan ancestors. Izibongo may be uttered to encourage animals or people, to express pride or gratitude. The clan praises, or the praises of ancestors, may be cited as invocations in ritual contexts. The order of the praises varies from one performance to the next: izibongo are not linear in structure, but are unified in presenting facets, not always flattering, of the subject of the poem. Nor are izibongo explicitly narrative. The elliptical allusions, often cryptic in their compression, may be clarified by narrative if explanations are sought, but not in the poetry itself: izibongo are a set of shorthand references that encapsulate a person's evolving career or defining qualities or establish his or her relation to others. They are expressions of individual and communal identity.

Izibongo of members of the royal family are performed by men who present themselves as praise poets (*iimbongi*, sing. *imbongi*). They undergo no formal training in poetry, any more than ordinary members of the public do: they appear on ceremonial occasions and are tacitly absorbed into the royal entourage. They are poets of the chiefdom, not appointees of the chief. They wear hats and cloaks of animal skin and carry two spears or clubs. Through their poetry they mold social cohesion, uphold social norms, criticize excess or injustice, and mediate between ruler and ruled. The presence of iimbongi at royal courts is attested by visiting missionaries as early as 1825 and can be documented throughout the 19th and early 20th cs. The greatest of all iimbongi is widely acknowledged to be Samuel Edward Krune Mqhayi (1875–1945), who produced an izibongo in honor of the Prince of Wales on his visit to South Africa in May 1925. During the apartheid period, when many chiefs were co-opted under the government's homeland policy, many iimbongi declined to celebrate illegitimate rulers; but since 1994, the trad. has undergone a resurgence and national recognition, with iimbongi performing at the inauguration of Nelson Mandela as president and appearing in television commercials. Women, formerly barred as iimbongi, now perform poetry in public. An ed. and trans. of the oral poetry of the imbongi Bongani Sitole (1937–2003) was published in 1996, and a biography of the imbongi D.L.P. Yali-Manisi (1926–99), with trans. of his poetry, was published in 2005.

Christian missionaries transcribed and printed the Xhosa lang. for the first time in 1823. In the first decade of the 20th c., they began publishing original works of creative lit., but these books were mainly designed for use in schools.

Submissions to mission presses that did not conform to Christian ideology or were considered too political were rejected or bowdlerized. Later commercial publishers were also constrained to satisfy the requirements of government departments, since there was a limited readership for Xhosa books outside educational institutions. Xhosa authors, obliged to censor themselves, were further disadvantaged when the spelling system was revised in 1936 and submissions that did not conform to the new orthography were rejected; this unpopular orthography was revised yet again in 1955. Xhosa lit. in published books is thus skewed, restricted in content and directed at students. It encouraged Western genres such as drama, which does not exist in Xhosa oral trad., and Western forms of poetry. Lyric poetry was solicited for early anthols. and narrative poetry for junior classes; poetry in Western stanzaic structures and rhyme, alien to Xhosa trad., was favored.

The earliest volumes of poetry published under such restrictions were John Solilo's *Izala* (A rubbish heap, 1925) and Mqhayi's *Imihobe nemibongo* (Songs and lullabies, 1927). To bypass the ideological control of the press, eds. and poets occasionally paid for the printing of their own books: W. B. Rubusana (1858–1936) paid for the printing and distribution of his pioneering anthol. *Zemk'inkomo magwalandini* (There go your cattle, you cowards!, 1911), which included the earliest collection of traditional izibongo, now long out of print and available only in an abridged ed. that excludes the poetry; D.L.P Yali-Manisi paid for the printing of his second volume of poetry, *Inguqu* (A return to the attack, 1954), which includes the earliest poem in praise of Nelson Mandela, then under banning orders.

Perhaps the most successful early poet who wrote in a Western mode was J.J.R. Jolobe (1902–76), who published two volumes of poetry, *Umyezo* (The orchard, 1936) and *Ilitha* (The sunbeam, 1959), as well as a volume of poetry for younger children (1952). The dominant poet who wrote largely in the style of traditional izibongo remains Mqhayi. In addition to *Imihobe nemibongo*, he wrote a set of poems about the king Hintsa (1937) and *Inzuzo* (Reward, 1942); his novel *Ityala lamawele* (The trial of the twins, 1914) includes more of his poetry. Michael S. Huna published two epic poems, on the cattle sickness (1966) and on the prophet Ntsikana (1973), while in recent years Peter T. Mtuze has been prominent as an ed. and poet. Poets are now free to adopt Western or traditional style.

Newspapers and jours. in Xhosa were issued by mission presses as of 1837. They sought to encourage contributions from readers but initially accepted poetry only in Western form. This restriction lapsed after 1884, with the appearance of secular newspapers under black editorial control, which served as major vehicles for lit. until the middle of the 20th c. A large proportion of this literary output was in poetry, written by adults for adult readers, free of ideological restrictions. Many poets who contributed to newspapers never subsequently published books; some of the poetry that appeared in newspapers was later included in published books; the vast majority of the newspaper poetry awaits collecting and publication. But it is to this medium that one must turn to find the unrestricted voice of the Xhosa poet in print.

The first generation of poets whose reputations were made in newspapers included M. K. Mtakati (fl. 1880s); Isaac Williams Wauchope (1852–1917); Jonas Ntsiko (d. 1918), who wrote under the pseud. Uhadi waseluhlangeni (Harp of the Nation); and William Wellington Gqoba (1840–88), all of whom adopted Western form. As ed. of the newspaper *Isigidimi samaXosa* (The Xhosa messenger), Gqoba published obituary poems, as well as two long serial poems that for many years remained the most sustained poetic achievements in Xhosa. Presented in octosyllabics as formal debates on education and on Christianity, they included strong expressions of social crit.

As of 1897, Mqhayi began contributing poetry to newspapers, mostly in traditional form, under a variety of pseuds. He is the most prolific Xhosa poet in this medium, publishing poetry regularly until 1944, the year before his death. Hundreds of his poems await republication, though a start has been made with an ed. and trans. of his historical and biographical articles (2009), many of which include poems about people. From 1920 to 1929, Nontsizi Mgqwetho published nearly a hundred poems in a Johannesburg newspaper, the first woman to write Xhosa poetry on a considerable scale. Her poetry is highly critical of ineffective black political leadership and immoral behavior among urban blacks; of white territorial dispossession, political control, and economic exploitation; and of male dominance over women. As a woman, she could not function as an imbongi, nor would her poetry have been suitable for publication in book form; but the medium of the newspaper empowered her and gave her access to her public. Her poetry was collected, trans., and republished in 2007.

■ *Zemk'inkomo magwalandini*, 2d ed., ed. W. B. Rubusana (1911); J. Opland, *Xhosa Oral Poetry* (1983); *Qhiwu-u-u-la!! Return to the Fold!! A Collection of Bongani Sitole's Xhosa Oral Poetry*, ed. and trans. R. H. Kaschula and M. C. Matyumza (1996); J. Opland, *Xhosa Poets and Poetry* (1998); R. H. Kaschula, *The Bones of the Ancestors Are Shaking: Xhosa Oral Poetry in Context* (2002); J. Opland, *The Dassie and the Hunter* (2005); N. Mgqwetho, *The Nation's Bounty*, ed. and trans. J. Opland (2007); S.E.K. Mqhayi, *Abantu besizwe* (People of the country), ed. and trans. J. Opland (2009).

J. Opland

Y

YIDDISH POETRY

I. Pre-nineteenth-century Verse
II. The Nineteenth Century
III. The Twentieth Century

Yiddish is the lang. of Eastern Eur. Jewry and that culture's offshoots the world over. It is commonly believed to date back at least a thousand years, with its roots in Western Europe. Mod. Yiddish poetry exhibits every subject and technique known in the lits. of Europe and America and derives an extra measure of cosmopolitanism from a readership distributed over five continents. But out of its combined prehist. and hist. of nearly a millennium, only two or three generations have witnessed this unrestricted flourishing. In traditional Ashkenazic culture, it was rather study—the continuous interpretation of basic Talmudic law in the light of changing conditions of life—that absorbed the creative passions of the society. Literary expression in the Western sense was unimportant, and Jewish poetry of the premod. period (both Yiddish and Heb.) is marked, for all its diversity, by a generally ancillary character.

Then, with the revolutionary upheavals in Eastern Eur. Jewry in the late 19th and 20th cs.—urbanization, industrialization, internal migration and emigration, political organization, and eventual civic emancipation, attended by widespread secularization and "Europeanization" of Jewish culture—Jewish poetry in both langs. was lifted to the very top of the cultural values of Jewish culture. It attracted a body of talent that, in previous centuries, would have been otherwise engaged; and, in accordance with the increased receptivity of its writers and readers to outside influences, it quickly managed to catch up with common Eur. accomplishments. Yiddish poetry "in one grand leap landed in the general 20th century" (Harshav and Harshav 1986). Even in its treatment of specifically Jewish themes in an imagery full of traditional allusions, Yiddish poetry became avowedly and factually part and parcel of mod. Eur. and Am. poetic culture.

I. Pre-nineteenth-century Verse. The origins of Yiddish lit. have been lost, but early contemp. references to it, as well as the developed poetic technique of the oldest dated works so far discovered (1382), indicate a prehist. antedating the extant evidence. Prior to the 19th c., Yiddish lit., the bulk of which is in verse, was written in an idiom based predominantly on Western Yiddish dialects, a standardized lang. that functioned without interruption until it fell into disuse in Western Europe about 1800 and was superseded by a rapidly evolving new standard based on Eastern Eur. Yiddish dialects. In the premod. period, the influence of med. Ger., its poetic trads., and a stylistic irradiation from intentionally literal Bible trans. caused the literary Yiddish to be highly stylized, thereby offering only a weak reflection of contemp. colloquial speech.

Epic poems both of the general Eur. repertoire (King Arthur, Gudrun, etc., with specifically Christian references deleted) and OT themes (e.g., Samuel or the sacrifice of Isaac) are extant in 14th- and 15th-c. recensions that show relatively strict meters and, generally, "long-line" stanza structure of the type *xaxa xbxb*. Scholars originally theorized that much of this verse was meant for oral performance by professional minstrels or laymen, esp. since, even after the intro. of printing, the tune was often specified at the beginning or end of a work. More recently, however, strong arguments have been advanced against the so-called *shpilman* theory, positing that the Eur. epics are transcriptions or trans. of Ger. originals, while the works based on Jewish themes (Bible and Midrash) were authored by scribes or other well-educated writers (Shmeruk 1988). This critical revision, however, still awaits further research. In the "post-epic" period (at least since the 17th c.), there is a case to be made for the direct association of Yiddish poetic creativity with contemporaneous modes of public entertainment and performances at weddings or on holy days.

Two 16th-c. verse novels, *Bove Bukh* (1541) and *Pariz un Viene* (1556), strikingly bridge the gap between original Jewish works and borrowed secular ones. The first was composed by Elye Bokher (Elia Levita, 1469–1549) in 1507, and the second either by him or his unidentified disciple. Using It. sources, these works created novels in ostensibly superior versions in which the primary material has been reworked and

Jewish elements freely integrated. In addition, Elye Bokher introduced ottava rima into Yiddish well over a century before it was attempted in Ger. poetry, and he seems to have been the first to use accentual iambs in any Eur. poetry.

The metrical structures of epic poetry were not carried forth elsewhere in Yiddish verse. This is evident in collections of 16th- and 17th-c. popular songs (which reflect a convergence of traditional with current Ger. models), in religious lyrics, in the many verse chronicles and dirges describing historical events, and in satirical or moralizing occasional verse, where the meters decrease in regularity until the number of syllables per measure of music varies widely and sometimes grows quite high. Yiddish poetry of early mod. times thus corresponds in its free-accentual basis to most contemp. Ger. verse. Drawing on the Heb. liturgical trad., Yiddish verse sometimes made use of the acrostic and ornamental extravagances such as making all lines of a reasonably long poem end in the same syllable.

II. The Nineteenth Century. Through most of the 19th c., the folk song flourished, and the recitative improvisation, the narrative (on biblical subjects), and the moralizing poem remained productive genres. Meanwhile, Yiddish lit. made a new beginning, centered this time in Eastern Europe and carried by the emigrations toward the end of the century to England, the U. S., and the far corners of the globe. The new writers were stimulated mostly by the *Haskalah* (Enlightenment) movement, which encouraged familiarity with Eur. (esp. Ger. and Rus.) lit. and made Jewish writers increasingly self-conscious about the underdeveloped state of their langs., Yiddish and Heb., for the purposes of social crit., philosophy, and secular education.

While Heb. lit. toyed with a biblical manner, Yiddish writers explored the cultural framework offered by the folk song, which was noticed at last after a "submerged" existence spanning centuries, during which it was neither recorded nor reflected in lit. The Yiddish folk song favored an *xaxa* stanza and a free-accentual meter (usually four stresses per line) in which, compared with Ger. folk song, the use of unstressed syllables to fill the musical measures was increased, probably as a result of the Slavicized prosodic structure of the lang. However, more Eur. standards of song construction and phrasing introduced more elaborate rhyme schemes (*abab* and *aabccb* became widespread), and strict syllabotonic meters became de rigueur in the theater and in quasi-theatrical songs. The rising labor movement furnished a new public for song verse but also for declamatory verse—an additional factor conducive to regular syllabotonic meters.

In the 1890s, Yiddish poetry hit its stride at last. Though it lagged noticeably behind the devel. of prose—particularly the shorter forms—it now became the vehicle of truly lyrical expression, as exemplified by Shimen Frug (1860–1916, widely credited with introducing syllabotonic prosody into mod. Yiddish poetry), I. L. Peretz (1852–1915), and Morris Rosenfeld (1862–1923). These authors, who had all complained about the lexical and stylistic inadequacy of Yiddish, now laid the foundations of mod. Yiddish poetry by efforts to master a lyrical viewpoint and experiments with a variety of imagery and structural patterns.

III. The Twentieth Century. The existence of a new intelligentsia with secular education, some of it acquired in Yiddish-lang. schools, cast Yiddish poetry in this period of its culmination into the mainstream of contemp. world trends. Yiddish lit. now showed itself more sensitive than ever to devels. in other lits. with which it was in contact. Writers had the interest and the formal means to attempt modernism along Am., Ger., and Rus. lines. At the same time, in the Yiddish poetic culture, there appeared genuine internal responses to innovation. In Russia, Dovid Hofshteyn (1889–1952) introduced some decisive innovations in meter and strophic structures. In America, the group *Di Yunge* (Young Ones, e.g., M.-L. Halpern [1886–1932], Mani Leib [1883–1953], and Zisha Landau [1889–1937]) early in the century reacted to the political tendentiousness and rhet. of the labor poets by trying to write poetry that would be "more poetic" in diction and subject matter and more individuated in its sentiments.

Dedicated to art for art's sake, the poets of Di Yunge emphasized the expression of aesthetic experience even while supporting themselves as laborers: "Thank goodness I'm not a cobbler who writes poems, / But a poet who makes shoes" (Mani Leib). Di Yunge cherished a vision of Yiddish lit. in which a monolingual reader could be a well-educated world citizen. To this end, they turned some of their energies to trans. and to introducing "exotic" themes, such as Christianity and sexuality, into Yiddish poetry.

Di Yunge called forth the protest of *In zikh* (the Introspectivists), a group (Aaron Leyeles [1889–1966], Jacob Glatstein [1896–1971], and N. B. Minkoff [1893–1958], among others) which, avowedly inspired by Yehoyosh (1872–1927), and influenced by contemp. Eng. and Am. poetry, denied in principle a distinction between the intellectual and the emotional and opened wide the door of its poetry to all themes, all words, all rhythms, no matter how free or regular, so long as they embodied the personal experience of the poet. As expressed in its manifesto of 1920, the In zikh poets saw no theoretical reason to identify themselves as Jewish artists other than that they were Jews and wrote Yiddish. Moreover, although they accepted syllabotonic meters as a possibility, they were, in fact, convinced that free rhythms were the surest vehicle for achieving poetic truth. Finally, they had no fear of exposing their deepest psychic realities, embracing free association as their chief poetic method.

As the cumulative effect of a growing corpus of poetry made itself felt, the demands for originality pushed Yiddish poets onto new paths. Assonance as a substitute for rhyme was explored (e.g., by Alter Katzizne [1885–1941] and Peretz Markish [1895–1952]). Sonnet sequences and works in the more difficult Romance fixed forms were successfully created (e.g., by Mani Leib). Syntactic parallelism, etymological figures, and consonance were mobilized to recreate biblical Heb. effects in a new Jewish medium. Epic poems, verse novels, and verse drama (esp. by H. Leivick [1888–1962]) were produced and acclaimed. Interest in Old Yiddish poetry was awakened, and several writers attempted new works in 16th-c. lang. The poems of Solomon Etinger (1800–56), a forgotten modernist, were published posthumously. The folk song reappeared, but this time in subtly stylized forms (e.g., by Halpern and Itzik Manger [1901–69]).

Post-World War I regional constellations such as the expressionist group *Di Khalyastre* (the Gang) in Warsaw (U. Z. Greenberg [1896–1981], Melech Ravitch [1893–1976], and others) and *Yung-Vilne* (Young Vilna) in Vilna (notably Chaim Grade [1910–82] and Abraham Sutzkever [1913–2010]) set themselves specialized tasks against a common literary background. The sweet awareness of a poetic trad. being formed was reflected in poetic allusions to well-known poems. A standardized literary lang. came into use in which dialectal rhymes became often restricted for conspicuously emotive mood.

In this period, the "discovery of the mother tongue," now emancipated in its functions, was completed. Poets by the scores, following the major writers of the late 19th c., learned to use the Yiddish lang. to its full extent. Yiddish prosodic structure, Germanic but largely reconfigured along Slavic lines (concomitant with mod. Rus. poetry), was employed to create easy triple and even paeonic meters. The refreshing syntax of conversational folk Yiddish was channeled into poetry (notably by Eliezer Shteynbarg, 1880–1932). The pernicious etymologizing approach of the past was dead: words were used according to their precise Yiddish phonology and semantics, without reference to—and sometimes in defiance of—their form and meaning in the stock langs. Sound frequencies typical of a particular component of Yiddish were forged into a new poetic device, making it possible, for instance, to suggest "Slavicness," and hence village earthiness, by an accumulation of *z* and *c* sounds (thus, Moshe Kulbak, 1896–1940), or "Germanness" by emphasizing *a* and final *e* sounds (e.g., Glatstein).

At the same time, the idiom of traditional Jewish study was annexed to the mod. literary lang.; it found use not only when required by the subject (as in the poetry of Menahem Boreisho [1888–1949], Aaron Zeitlin [1899–1974], or Grade), but in thematically unspecialized writing, where it functions simply as a flexible abstract vocabulary. Above all, the many derivational patterns of Yiddish grammar were exploited for the enrichment of the lang. New coinages abounded, and some, like *umkum* (violent death) and *vogl* (restless wandering), have become common elements of the lang. The poetry of Glatstein and Sutzkever is particularly rich in novel derivations.

With the genocide of six million Jews by Germany and her Axis collaborators, Jewish cultural life in most of Eastern Europe was virtually destroyed; what was left received a second devastating blow through Stalin's ban of Yiddish culture and the elimination of Yiddish writers in the USSR after 1949, culminating in the August 12, 1952, murder of the Yiddish poets Peretz Markish, Dovid Hofshteyn, Leib Kvitko (b. ca. 1890), and Itzik Fefer (b. 1900), among others. The Holocaust of the war years naturally became the central theme of Yiddish lit., not only in the Nazi-made ghettos but globally. After 1948, however, the rebirth of a Jewish state in Israel opened new vistas, descriptive, psychological, existential, and ethical, to Yiddish poetry. Soon, an active Yiddish cultural life rapidly developed in Israel, incl. publication of *Di goldene keyt* (The Golden Chain), the premier Yiddish literary jour. (1949–95), and the establishment of a few Yiddish publishing houses in the late 1950s. Major postwar centers of Yiddish poetry were also in North America, Europe (esp. in France and, until the late 1960s, Poland), and post-Stalin Soviet Union (since the 1960s).

The technical brilliance of Yiddish poetry did not diminish in the postwar period. In its rhythmic features, however, postwar writing seems to have retreated from the experimentation of the previous period. As Leyeles put it, "When there are no bounds to suffering, create, through pain, a ritual fence [i.e., a preventive measure] of rigorously restrained patterning."

What might be called the second generation since the catastrophic events of the Holocaust and Stalinism reveals a shift in the balance of Yiddish verse. Whereas actual poetic production is shrinking, scholarship has reached new levels of sophistication and intensity. This phenomenon is directly related to the decline of the Yiddish-speaking community and, hence, the number of native speakers of Yiddish. Those poets who remained in the final decades of the 20th c., such as Yonia Fain (1914–2013), Rivka Basman Ben-Haim (b. 1925), and Alexander Spiegelblatt (b. 1927) had to contend with the problem of creating in a lang. whose future as a vibrant medium of mod. poetry was at best uncertain: "During daytime a funeral, at night a concert / And inevitably, I go to both" (Sutzkever). Scholarly research, by contrast, became increasingly active and undertaken more and more by those who are not native speakers of Yiddish. Their work, encompassing a wide variety of perspectives, e.g., historical, social, feminist, psychoanalytic, and comparative, highlights the tremendous vitality of the poetic corpus, even if the number of living poets is small. Among the major outcomes of late 20th-c. studies and anthols. were the greater recognition and appreciation of Yiddish women poets, as well as poets whose work had been ignored out of earlier political considerations.

The turn of the 21st c. witnessed the steep decline of secular Yiddish lit. Since the 1990s, however, a new postwar generation has begun to make its mark, albeit on a substantially reduced scale and often in estranged surroundings. It consists of a drastically smaller and geographically dispersed group of poets born between the 1950s and the 1980s. Their work continues to be published in contemp. Yiddish periodicals, e.g., *Di tsukunft* (New York), *Gilgulim* (Paris), and *Yerusholaymer Almanakh* (Jerusalem).

See HEBREW POETRY.

■ **Anthologies**: *Di yidishe muze*, ed. J. Fichman (1911); *Antologye: finf hundert yor yidishe poezye*, ed. M. Bassin, 2 v. (1917); *Yidishe dikhterins*, ed. E. Korman (1928); *Naye yidishe dikhtung*, ed. Y. Paner and E. Frenkl (1946); *Dos lid iz geblibn*, ed. B. Heller (1951); *Mivhar shirat yidish*, trans. M. Basuk (1963)—Hebrew; *A shpigl af a shteyn*, ed. K. Shmeruk (1964)—works of murdered Soviet Yiddish writers; *A Treasury of Yiddish Poetry*, ed. I. Howe and E. Greenberg (1969); *Selected Poems of Jacob Glatstein*, trans. R. Whitman (1972); *Perl fun der yidisher poezye*, ed. J. Mlotek and E. Mlotek (1974); M.-L. Halpern, *In New York: A Selection*, ed. and trans. K. Hellerstein (1982); *American Yiddish Poetry: A Bilingual Anthology*, ed. B. Harshav and B. Harshav (1986); *Penguin Book of Modern Yiddish Verse*, ed. I. Howe et al. (1987)—Yiddish and Eng.; *Early Yiddish Texts, 1100–1750, with Introduction and Commentary*, ed. J. Frakes (2004)—Yiddish; *Proletpen: America's Rebel Yiddish Poets*, ed. A. Glaser and D. Weintraub, trans. A. Glasser (2005)—Yiddish and Eng.; *Sing, Stranger: A Century of American Yiddish Poetry: A Historical Anthology*, ed. B. Harshav and B. Harshav (2006); *Step by Step: Contemporary Yiddish Poetry*, ed. E. Bemporad and M. Pascucci (2009)—Yiddish and Eng.; *With Everything We've Got: A Personal Anthology of Yiddish Poetry*, ed. and trans. R. Fein (2009)—Yiddish and Eng.

■ **Criticism and History**: L. Wiener, *History of Yiddish Literature in the Nineteenth Century* (1899); M. Erik, *Di geshikhte fun der yidisher literatur* (1928); D. Hofshteyn and F. Shames, *Literatur-kentenish (poetik)*, 2 v. (1928); and *Teorye fun literatur: Poetik* (1930); Z. Reyzen, *Leksikon fun der yidisher literatur*, 4 v. (1928); M. Weinreich, *Bilder fun der yidisher literatur-geshikhte* (1928); Y. Tsinberg, *Di geshikhte fun der literatur bay yidn*, v. 6 (1935); N. B. Minkoff, *Yidishe klasiker poetn*, 2d ed. (1939); Y. Mark, "Yiddish Literature," *The Jews*, ed. L. Finkelstein, v. 2 (1949); N. B. Minkoff and J. A. Joffe, "Old Yiddish Literature," and S. Niger, "Yiddish

Literature of the Past 200 Years," *The Jewish People Past and Present*, v. 3 (1952); B. Hrushovski [Harshav], "On Free Rhythms in Modern Yiddish Poetry," *The Field of Yiddish*, ed. U. Weinreich, v. 1 (1954); *Leksikon fun der nayer yidisher literatur*, 8 v. (1956–81); Y. Tsinberg, *Pyonern fun yidisher poezye in amerike*, 3 v. (1956); U. Weinreich, "On the Cultural History of Yiddish Rime," *Essays on Jewish Life and Thought*, ed. J. L. Blau (1959); B. Hrushovski, "The Creation of Accentual Iambs," *For Max Weinreich on his Seventieth Birthday* (1964); S. Liptzin, *The Flowering of Yiddish Literature* (1964); and *The Maturing of Yiddish Literature* (1970); I. Howe, *World of Our Fathers* (1976), ch. 13; J. Hadda, *Yankev Glatshteyn* (1980); D. Goldberg, "The Juncture of Dialect and Rhyme in Yiddish Poetry," *Ha-Sifrut* (1986)—in Heb.; K. Shmeruk, *Prokim fun der yidisher literatur-geshikhte* (1988); R. Wisse, *A Little Love in Big Manhattan* (1988); F. W. Aaron, *Bearing the Unbearable: Yiddish and Polish Poetry in the Ghettos and Concentration Camps* (1990); B. Hrushovski, *The Meaning of Yiddish* (1990); A. Spiegelblatt, *Bloe vinklen, Itsik Manger—lebn, lid un balade* (2002); K. Hellerstein, "Gender and the Anthological Tradition in Modern Yiddish Poetry," and J. Shandler, "Anthologizing the Vernacular: Collections of Yiddish Literature in English Translations," *The Anthology in Jewish Literature*, ed. D. Stern (2004); M. Lev, *Literarishe portretn* (2007).

U. Weinrich; J. Hadda; D.-B. Kerler

YORUBA POETRY. *See* africa, poetry of

Z

ZULU POETRY

I. Verse Structure
II. Early Zulu Poets
III. Post-Apartheid Era

Zulu (*isiZulu*) poetry has developed from oral to written form. Traditional Zulu poetic genres consist of oral praise poems called *izibongo*, the most important and influential of the traditional forms, which include clan praises (*izithakazelo*), lullabies (*imilolozelo*), and folk songs (*amaculo*).

Characteristics retained in mod. Zulu poetry reflect the influence of the praise poem. Compositional techniques can be divided into external and internal. External characteristics refer to sentences, e.g., oppositions and patterns of repetition; and to stanza construction, e.g., two lines, three lines, or more than three lines. Internal characteristics refer to the content, esp. to the various figures of speech (*izifengqo*) and imagery.

I. Verse Structure. Traditional Zulu poets could not have had any idea of verses. Their poetry knew no structural appearance of poetry as we know it today. The division into verse structure was introduced by the mod. poet when he or she tried to commit the oral poem to paper, and the idea of the length of each line must have been based on formulas. This loose style of the praise poem generally has been referred to as poetry composed in lines without patterns of rhyme and meter.

Zulu traditional poems, esp. praise poems, are composed in lines that are based on the stresses resulting from the meaning of the line and its natural and punctuated pauses. Intonation is important in Zulu praise poems because Zulu is a tonal lang., like most Af. langs., and it is difficult to apply Eng. structural patterns to it. Various types of repetitions are characteristic of Zulu poetry. Rhythm in Zulu results from a particular patterning of the sounds of words in a line that reflects the poet's use of emphasis and tempo as well as stressed and unstressed syllables. Some elements of verse structure are:

(1) *Apostrophe, or honorific address.* E.g., in *UMenzi kaNdaba!* (He is Menzi [the Doer)], son of Ndaba!), King Senzangakhona, father of King Shaka, is praised as a descendant of King Ndaba and also as a member of the royal family. An apostrophe is often formulated in relationship to someone else, esp. important members of the family.

(2) *Simile and Metaphor. Simile* involves using comparative words, such as *njenga* (like), *nganga* (as), *kuna* (than):

UBhid' elimathetha ngezinyembezi
Linjeng' elikaPhik' eBulawini

(Variegation like a multicolored animal
Like that of Phiko at Bulawini)

Metaphors are often poetic exaggerations.

(3) *Description.* Description is often couched in metaphoric lang.:

Ibhicongo elimzimba buthaka
Ozithebe zihle uMjokwane
Ozithebe zihle zidlel' amancasakazi

(Tree with a fragile trunk
Whose eating mats are beautiful
Whose beautiful eating mats are eaten
from by the womenfolk)

This means that King Senzangakhona was popular with women.

(4) *Parallelism* (*Impindamqondo*). In *parallelism*, related (similar or contrasting) ideas are linked by using similar constructions or words in successive lines. The following lines from the praises of King Ndaba show perfect parallelism:

Obeyalala wangangemifula,
Obeyavuka wangangezintaba.

(Who when he lay down was the size
of rivers,
Who when he got up was the size of
mountains.)

Normally, parallelism by final linking involves repetition of a noun, as in King

Shaka's praises, where the term *uhlanya* joins the following two lines:

UMahlom'ehlathini onjengohlanya,
Uhlanya olusemehlwen' amadoda.

(He who armed in the forest, who is like a madman,
The madman who is in full view of the men.)

II. Early Zulu Poets. B. W. Vilakazi is the pioneer of Zulu poetry. In his first book, *Inkondlo kaZulu* (Zulu Poems, 1935), Vilakazi experimented with rhyme. According to Nyembezi (1961), Vilakazi's eminence can be attributed to the fact that "he was mainly responsible for developing poetry whose form departed radically from the Izibongo (or praises). Instead of adapting the style and pattern of the Izibongo, he experimented with Eur. form." Ten years later, in 1945, Vilakazi's second book of poems appeared under the title *Amal'Ezulu* (Zulu Horizons); he apparently was not happy with the results of his Eur. experiment because, in *Amal' Ezulu*, he discarded rhyme almost completely.

The most important poet to appear in the 1950s was J. C. Dlamini. His first volume, *Inzululwane* (Dizziness), was published in 1959. Cope remarks, "In his volume of verse he shows a return to the traditional model of the praise poem, with a completely different sort of content. Dlamini uses the technique of the traditional praise-poem to express his philosophical and psychological problems . . . often obscure but constantly strong and deep."

The 1980s can justifiably be regarded as the "decade of poetry" in Zulu. More volumes of poetry in Zulu were published than at any previous time. Poets who published at least four titles include L.B.Z. Buthelezi, L.T.L. Mabuya, and C. T. Msimang. Msimang's *Iziziba Zothukela* (Deep Pools of the Thukela River, 1980) contains both praise poems and mod. poems. Like their predecessors, these poets manage to produce a synthesis of traditional and mod. styles, composing many poems in the style of the typical oral praise poem. The most outstanding book, however, is Z.L.M. Khumalo's voluminous work *Amabhosho* (Bullets, 1989); in this work, Khumalo composed mod. praise poems and used parallelism, linking, refrains, and repetitions that are characteristic of Zulu poetry.

III. Post-Apartheid Era. The beginning of the 1990s saw many political changes in South Africa, particularly the coming of democracy in 1994. The new era brought its own difficulties and challenges, incl. reconciling the various factions formed under apartheid, dealing with the past, building a cohesive nation, and fighting crime, drugs, and HIV/AIDS. These challenges demanded the focus and energy of the Zulu poets to respond to the situation with their poetry.

The 21st c. saw the emergence of many female Zulu poets. An anthol. of women's poetry, *Izimbali Zesizwe* (Flowers of the Nation), was published in 2005; *Ithunga Lenkosazana* (The Lady's Milking Pail) in 2007; *Izintombi Zengcugce* (Maidens of Ingcugce Regiment) in 2008. The poet Lungile Bengani published *Kwenzekeni Bazali Bami?* (What Has Happened, My Parents?) in 2008. These titles do not provide any significant description; the poet chooses any title for his or her book.

Traditional oral Zulu poetry was characterized by simplicity of form. Mod. Zulu poets have since tried their hand at more sophisticated Western forms, with a certain measure of success. In these attempts, they have also realized the necessity of retaining some of the simpler elements found in traditional poetry so that their work may retain a distinct form, a typical Zulu character that cannot be achieved by following Western standards in all respects.

■ C.L.S. Nyembezi, *A Review of Zulu Literature* (1961); *Izibongo, Zulu Praise-Poems*, ed. T. Cope (1968); D.B.Z. Ntuli and C. F. Swanepoel, *South African Literature in African Languages* (1993); N. Canonici, *Zulu Oral Poetry* (1994); C.L.S. Nyembezi, *A Catalogue of Literature* (2007).

A. M. Maphumulo

Index

Page numbers in **boldface** indicate article titles.

Guarino, Guido, 321
Guatemala, poetry of, **243–46**; indigenous, 243, 245
Guðbrandur Þorláksson, 276
Gueguënce, The (anon.), 298
Guerau de Cabrera, 106
Guesa, O (Sousa Andrade), 62, 290, 291
Guevara, Pablo, 426
Guido y Spano, Carlos, 31
Guilhem IX, 192
Guillaume de Lorris, 191
Guillem de Bergiedà, 106
Guillén, Jorge, 104, 512
Guillén, Nicolás, 93, 101, 103, 104, 519
Guillet, Pernette du, 194
Guillevic, Eugène, 201
Guimaraens, Alphonsus de, 63
Guinizzelli, Guido, 318
Guirao, Ramón, 101
Guiraut Riquier, 414
Guisado, Alfredo Pedro, 446
Guittone d'Arezzo, 315, 318
Gujarati poetry, **246–47**
Gullar, Ferreira, 65
Gullberg, Hjalmar, 531
Gumāni (Lok Ratna Pant), 396
Guṇacandra, 475
Gunasinghe, Siri, 523
Gunderrode, Karoline von, 227
Gundulić, Ivan, 136
Gung-thang Bstan-pa'I sgron-me, 549
Gunn, Thom, 174
Günther, Johann Christian, 219
"Guo feng" (*Shijing* section), 125
Guo Moruo, 116
Guramishvili, David, 212
Gurdas, 449
Guri, Haim, 257
Gustafsson, Lars, 532–33
"Guthlac" (OE poem), 213
Gutiérrez, Arturo, 592
Gutiérrez, Ernesto, 405
Gutiérrez Coll, Jacinto, 590
Gutiérrez Nájera, Manuel, 98, 388, 517, 518
Guto'r Glyn, 599
Gutt, Tom, 55
Gutun Owain, 599
Guzmán, Patricia, 592
Gwala, Mafika Pascal, 3
Gwalchmai, 597
Gwaram, Hauwa, 248
Gwerder, Alexander Xaver, 535
Gwerful Mechain, 599
Gwernig, Youenn, 67
Gwilhom, Joakim, 67
Gwreans an Bys (anon.), 135
Gyllenborg, Gustaf Fredrik, 529
Gyöngyösi, István, 272
Gypsy poetry. *See* Romani poetry

Haan, Josse de, 207
Haavikko, Paavo, 188
Habask, Padrig an, 67
Habba Khatoon, 350
Habib, Rowley, 401
Habibe, Henry, 87
Habspurgische Ottobert, Der (Hohberg), 46
Hacker, Marilyn, 583
Haddad, Fouad, 152
Hadewych, 372
Hadraawi (Maxamed Ibraahim Warsame), 498
"Hae egesŏ Somyŏn ege" (Ch'oe Namsŏn), 354
Hāfez Ibrāhīm, 151
Ḥāfiẓ, 57, 221, 422
Ḥafsa bint al-Ḥajj al-Rakuniyya, 11
Haft Paykar (Niẓāmī), *421*
Hagedorn, Friedrich von, 220
Hagerup, Inger, 411
hagiography, 57, 66, 68, 134, 155, 156, 190, 213, 216, 347, 349, 430, 504, 539
Hagiwara Sakutarō, 337–38
Hahn, Oscar, 114
haikai, 116, 340, 341, 343, 344, 345
haiku: Japanese, 335–37, 341, 344; Western, 82, 182, 379, 389, 412, 518, 573
Haiti, poetry of, 92, 93–96
Hájnikova žena (Hviezdoslav), 495
Hāla, 448, 482
Hal'amová, Maša, 496
Halas, František, 140
Halbertsma, Eeltsje, 206
Hálek, Vítězslav, 139
Halevi, Jehudah, 254, 503
Hālī (Altāf Husain), 586, 587
Halkin, Simon, 258
Hallam, Arthur, 170
Haller, Albrecht von, 220, 534
Hallgrímur Pétursson, 276
Hallr Þórarinsson, 407
Halpern, Moyshe-Leyb, 607
Halt in the Wilderness, A (Brodsky), 467
Hamann, Johann Georg, 367
Hämärän tanssit (Saarikoski), 188
Hambidge, Joan, 500
Hamelink, Jacques, 378
Hamilton, William, 485
Hamit, Abdülhak, 559
"Hamlet" (Carson), 313
Hamlet (Shakespeare), 163, 179
Hammann, Kirsten, 146
Hamoir, Irène, 53